American History

A SURVEY

Volume II: Since 1865

SEVENTH EDITION

American History

A SURVEY

Volume II: Since 1865

Richard N. Current
*Emeritus, University of North Carolina
at Greensboro*

T. Harry Williams
late of Louisiana State University

Frank Freidel
Emeritus, Harvard University

Alan Brinkley
Harvard University

ALFRED A. KNOPF   NEW YORK

THIS IS A BORZOI BOOK
PUBLISHED BY ALFRED A. KNOPF, INC.

Seventh Edition
98765432

Copyright © 1959, 1961, 1964, 1966, 1971, 1975, 1979 by Richard N. Current,
       T. Harry Williams, Frank Freidel
       © 1983, 1987 by Richard N. Current, T. H. W., Inc., Frank Freidel, Alan
       Brinkley

All rights reserved under International and Pan-American Copyright Conventions. No
part of this book may be reproduced in any form or by any means, electronic or
mechanical, including photocopying, without permission in writing from the publisher.
All inquiries should be addressed to Alfred A. Knopf, Inc., 201 East 50th Street, New
York, N.Y. 10022. Published in the United States by Alfred A. Knopf, Inc., New York,
and simultaneously in Canada by Random House of Canada Limited, Toronto.
Distributed by Random House, Inc., New York.

Library of Congress Cataloging in Publication Data

American history.

   Includes bibliographies and indexes.
   1. United States—History. I. Current, Richard Nelson.
E178.1.A492 1987   973   86-21099
ISBN 0-394-34303-4 (pbk. : v. 2)

Manufactured in the United States of America

Published 1961; reprinted five times
Second edition, 1966; reprinted three times
Third edition, 1971; reprinted four times
Fourth edition, 1975; reprinted four times
Fifth edition, 1979; reprinted three times
Sixth edition, 1983; reprinted six times

Maps and charts by David Lindroth

Cover and text design by Leon Bolognese

Cover photograph: Detail of the Chrysler Building. Kishin Shinoyama/Rikoyo-Sha
Publishing, Inc.

Preface

When the first edition of this book appeared in 1959, historians were in general agreement about what was important in the American past. The story of the United States, most believed, was the story of great public events: of politics and government, of war and peace, of great leaders and great events. Much has changed in the years since.

Historical scholarship in America (and, indeed, throughout much of the world) has experienced something close to a revolution during the last two and a half decades. Aspects of the past that received only slight attention in earlier eras have now emerged as central themes in the writing of American history. Scholars today are interested not just in great events and great leaders, but in the experiences of ordinary men and women. They are concerned not just with politics and government, but with less visible changes in the structure of society. Historians in recent years have begun to reveal whole new realms of the American past about which we previously knew relatively little: the historical experiences of blacks, Hispanics, Asians, Indians, and other minorities; the process by which America was settled by successive waves of immigrants and the process by which those immigrants adapted to their new surroundings; the rise and transformation of the city and the wrenching changes in the nature of agrarian society; the evolution of popular culture and popular values; and, perhaps most prominently in recent years, the experiences of American women and the story of the American family.

No single work can hope to tell the full story of any nation. And in the case of the United States, a country of almost unparalleled diversity, in which change has occurred at such a constant and dizzying speed that historical time seems almost to have accelerated, that task is particularly difficult. Nevertheless, this book attempts to present as full a picture as possible of the extraordinary history of the American nation and its people. This new edition, which is the result of the most significant single revision in the long life of this book, tries to ensure that this picture does justice to the many areas of the past that recent scholarship has revealed. It includes, as previous editions have, a thorough discussion of great public events, of politics and government and diplomacy. But it gives at least equal attention to the other, less familiar aspects of the American past. And, above all, it tries to illuminate the way the nation's public history and its social history have interacted with and shaped one another.

Four broad themes in particular shape the contents of this volume. First, we have told the story of the creation of the nation's political institutions and the way they have evolved in response to changing circumstances, changing popular expectations, and the achievements and failures of individual public figures. Second, we have examined the development of America's role in the world, from its position as a weak dependency of the British and Spanish empires to its rise to international preeminence. Third, we have recounted the story of the development of the American economy from its simple agrarian beginnings through its triumphant rise to industrial greatness to its present uncertain condition. And fourth, we have described the way in which the American people have lived: the cultural and social arrangements they have developed for themselves; the impact of social and economic changes on those arrangements; and the efforts of groups divided by class, race, ethnicity, religion, gender, and region to find ways of living together in a single society.

Those familiar with earlier editions of this book will notice many changes in this edition. The most visible, of course, is our new full-color design and our introduction of a wholly new and much larger program of maps, charts, and illustrations. We have added as well a chronology of significant events at the end of each chapter. We have expanded and reorganized the bibliographical essays, both to bring them up to date and to make them easier to use. We have added a new essay on the Vietnam War to our series entitled "Where Historians Disagree," and we have reworked and expanded many of the existing essays in that series.

But the most important changes are those in the narrative itself. What most distinguishes this edition from its predecessors is its more extensive coverage of social, cultural, and economic history—and above all perhaps, our effort to incorporate into the story the results of the recent explosion of scholarship in the field of women's history. We have reviewed and revised virtually every section of the book in light of new evidence and interpretations. We have substantially reorganized several important sections, and we have added several entirely new ones. We have made a significant stylistic revision, to improve the consistency and flow of the narrative.

Several changes will be particularly noticeable to previous users of this book. Chapter 1 has been radically revised to provide more attention to the history of America before Columbus and to explore more fully the interaction among Europeans, Africans, and Indians that dominated the history of sixteenth- and seventeenth-century America. The chapters on the colonial period in general have been substantially recast to take into account the important and rapidly burgeoning new scholarship in that field. There have also been some significant organizational and substantive changes in the chapters dealing with the twentieth century. Chapters 21 and 22 have been thoroughly recast: Chapter 21 now provides an expanded discussion of the social underpinnings of progressive reform and of reform efforts at the state and local level, while Chapter 22 brings together the material on national reform in the progressive era. Chapter 25 consolidates and expands the discussion of the social and cultural impact of the Great Depression. Chapter 26 focuses on the history of the New Deal in its entirety. Chapter 27 offers a comprehensive picture of diplomatic developments in the period from 1921 to 1945, as well as a full discussion of both the domestic and international repercussions of World War II itself. And Chapter 32 presents new material on the Carter and Reagan presidencies and on the social, economic, and cultural events of the 1970s and 1980s. Finally, major new sections on the history of women and the family can be found throughout the book; some of the most important appear in chapters 3, 5, 9, 11, 14, 15, 18, 21, 24–27,

29, and 31. The result of all these changes, we hope, is a book that provides a fuller and richer view of American history, one that illuminates more clearly how the study of history can enhance our understanding of our own world and our own lives.

The editorial and production staffs at Alfred A. Knopf deserve much of the credit for whatever new strengths the present edition brings to this book. David Follmer helped draw up some of the initial plans for this edition, and Chris Rogers presided expertly over the bulk of the revision. David Lindroth is responsible not only for drafting the elegant new maps and charts, but also for conceptualizing many of them. Leon Bolognese contributed a handsome new design for both the cover and the interior. Despite a very tight schedule, Deborah Bull brought both taste and imagination to the task of researching an attractive and effective new set of illustrations. Kathy Bendo and Stacey Alexander saw to the many details of photo permissions and production follow-through with remarkable competence. Evelyn Katrak, as she has done in previous editions, copy edited this enormous manuscript with her usual elegance and professionalism. Our greatest debt is to Elaine Romano, who supervised the preparation of this new edition from start to finish, coordinated the many different aspects of editing production, repaired uncountable errors and inconsistencies, and made this a much better book than it would otherwise have been —all with unfailing patience, skill, and courtesy.

As always, we appreciate the efforts of the many scholars and teachers who read and commented on the sixth edition of this book and whose suggestions were of incalculable value to us in preparing the seventh. Many of these reviewers have asked not to be identified, and so we have chosen here to thank them all anonymously. We are also grateful to those students and teachers who have used this book over the past several years and who have offered us their unsolicited comments, criticisms, and corrections. We hope they will continue to inform us of their reactions in the future by sending their comments to the authors in care of the College Department, Alfred A. Knopf, Inc., 201 East 50th Street, New York, N.Y. 10022.

ALAN BRINKLEY
Cambridge, Massachusetts
November 1986

Contents

Illustrations

Maps

Charts

A Reconstruction Era Tribute to the Election of Blacks to Congress
From left to right: Sen. Hiram R. Revels, Rep. Benjamin S. Turner, the Reverend Richard Allen, Frederick Douglass, Representative Josiah T. Walls, Representative Joseph H. Rainy, and writer William Wells Brown.   (Library of Congress)

Chapter 15 Reconstructing the Nation

Few periods in the history of the United States have produced as much bitterness or created such enduring controversy as the era of Reconstruction—the years following the Civil War during which Americans attempted to reunite their shattered nation. Those who lived through the experience viewed it in sharply different ways. To white Southerners, Reconstruction was a vicious and destructive experience—a period of low, unscrupulous politics, a time when vindictive Northerners inflicted humiliation and revenge on the prostrate South and unnecessarily delayed a genuine reunion of the sections. Northern defenders of Reconstruction, in contrast, argued that their policies were the only way to prevent unrepentant Confederates from restoring Southern society as it had been before the war; without forceful federal intervention, there would be no way to forestall the reemergence of a backward aristocracy and the continued subjugation of blacks—no way, in other words, to prevent the same sectional problems that had produced the Civil War in the first place.

To most black Americans at the time, and to many people of all races since, Reconstruction was notable for other reasons. Not a vicious tyranny, as white Southerners charged, nor a drastic and necessary reform, as many Northerners claimed, it was, rather, an essentially moderate, even conservative program that fell far short of providing the newly freed slaves with the protection they needed. Reconstruction, in other words, was significant less for what it did than for what it failed to do. And when it came to an end, finally, in 1877—as a result of exhaustion and disillusionment among the white leaders of both sections, and of a series of complex bargains in the aftermath of the election of 1876—black Americans found themselves once again abandoned. Although they had, with the help of federal protection, won some important gains during Reconstruction, those gains were limited; and after 1877 nothing would save black people from being consigned to a system of economic peonage and legal subordination. The nation's racial problem, which had done so much to produce the Civil War, was left unresolved—to arise again and again in future generations.

The Problems of Peacemaking

In 1865, when the Confederacy finally surrendered to the North, no one knew quite what to do in response. Abraham Lincoln could not negotiate a treaty with the defeated government; he continued to insist that that government had no legal right to exist. Yet neither could he simply readmit the Southern states into the Union as if nothing had happened. The South had been devastated by the war—socially, economically, and politically. And there was now an enormous population of freed slaves, many of them wandering bewildered through the shattered land. Clearly the federal government had to act.

The Aftermath of War

In the North, the wartime prosperity continued into the postwar years; but Northerners who visited the South were appalled when they gazed on the desola-

Charleston, 1865
Not until 1864 did substantial fighting and destruction begin to take place in Southern cities and towns. But in the last year of the war, several major cities (and many towns and smaller communities) experienced devastation at the hands of the Northern armies— among them Richmond, Atlanta, and (as seen here) Charleston. (Library of Congress)

tion left in the wake of the war—gutted towns, wrecked plantations, neglected fields, collapsed bridges, and ruined railroads. Much of the personal property of white Southerners had been lost with the lost cause. Confederate bonds and currency were now worthless, and capital that had been invested in them was gone forever. With the emancipation of the slaves, Southern whites were deprived of property worth an estimated $2 billion. Southern blacks were left with no property at all.

Matching the shattered economy of the South was the disorganization of its social system. In the months that followed the end of the war, thousands of soldiers drifted back to their homes; but 258,000 had died in the war, and additional thousands returned wounded or sick. Many families approached the difficult task of rebuilding, therefore, without the help of adult males. Many white Southerners faced the prospect of starvation and homelessness.

If conditions were bad for Southern whites, they were generally far worse for Southern blacks—the 4 million men and women now emerging from the bondage that had held them and their ancestors for up to two and a half centuries. Many of these people, too, had seen service of one kind or another during the war. Some had served as body servants for Confederate officers or as teamsters and laborers for the Confederate armies. Nearly 200,000 had fought as combat troops in the Union ranks, and more than 38,000 had given their lives for the Union cause. Countless other blacks, who had never worn a uniform or drawn army pay, had assisted the Union forces as spies or scouts. Still others had run off from the plantations and flocked to the Union lines in search of freedom and protection, often to be put to work for the Union armies. As soon as the war ended, many thousands more left the plantations in search of a new life in freedom. Old and young, many of them feeble and ill, they trudged to the nearest town or city or roamed the countryside, camping at night on the bare ground. Few had any possessions except the clothes they wore.

In 1865, in short, Southern society was in disarray. Blacks and whites, men and women faced a future of great uncertainty, in which traditional institutions and assumptions no longer seemed suitable. Nevertheless, people of both races had, even in 1865, distinct and very different ideas about how to respond to the new postwar world.

Many white Southerners hoped to restore their society to its antebellum form. Slavery, of course, had already been abolished in much of the South by the Emancipation Proclamation. The Thirteenth Amendment, which declared slavery unconstitutional, passed Congress on February 1, 1865; the amendment became law on December 18, 1865. But many white planters were determined to retain the essence of slavery even if its legal basis was now destroyed. Some planters continued to detain their black workers. In some instances, the former slaves simply did not learn that slavery had been abolished. But in other cases, they fell victim to efforts by white Southerners to re-create slavery in another form. Most planters agreed with a former Confederate leader who was saying (in June 1865) that slavery had been "the best system of labor that could be devised for the Negro race" and that the wise thing to do now would be to "provide a substitute for it."

Blacks, of course, had a very different vision of the postwar South. They wanted, above all, to know and feel their freedom and to be assured that they were not again to lose it. In the short run, they wanted protection from the threat of starvation. Beyond that, they wanted economic independence; and since the vast majority had always worked as farmers, that meant ownership of land. Blacks also longed for schooling—for their children if not for themselves. Finally, many blacks demanded political rights. "The only salvation for us besides the power of the Government is in the *possession of the ballot*," a convention of the black people of Virginia resolved in the summer of 1865. "All we ask is an *equal chance*."

In the immediate aftermath of the war, the federal government made modest efforts to help the emancipated slaves achieve their dreams of freedom. The government kept troops (many of them black) in the South to preserve order and protect the freedmen. In March 1865, Congress established the Bureau of Freedmen, Refugees, and Abandoned Lands (known as the Freedmen's Bureau) as an agency of the army. The bureau was empowered to provide former slaves with food, transportation, assistance in getting jobs and fair wages, and schools, and also to settle them on abandoned or confiscated lands. Under the able

direction of General Oliver O. Howard, the bureau distributed 20 million rations. Missionaries and teachers, who had been sent to the South by Freedmen's Aid Societies and other private and church groups in the North, cooperated with the bureau in setting up schools for the former slaves. There were efforts as well to settle blacks on lands of their own. (The Freedmen's Bureau also offered considerable assistance to poor whites, many of whom were similarly destitute and homeless after the war.) But the Freedmen's Bureau was only a temporary expedient, not a permanent solution. Congress had given it authority to operate for only one year; and it was, in any case, far too small to deal by itself with the enormous problems facing Southern society. The real nature of Reconstruction, therefore, remained to be determined. It would be up to the federal government to determine whether the hopes of Southern whites or those of Southern blacks would prevail.

Issues of Reconstruction

At the time, it was by no means clear how the leaders of the North envisioned the future. The question of what kind of society should exist in the South and what kind of future blacks should enjoy there was tied to questions about the political and economic future of the North. The result was a prolonged debate about the proper course.

The terms by which the Southern states rejoined the Union had important implications for both major political parties. For the Democrats, a rapid readmission of the former Confederate states on easy terms was enormously appealing. To the Republicans, the prospect was alarming. The Republican victories in 1860 and 1864 had been a result, in large part, of the division of the Democratic party and the removal of the South from the electorate. The return of the South would, leaders of both parties believed, reunite the Democrats and reduce the Republicans to minority status—especially since the South's representation in Congress would, ironically, increase as a result of the abolition of slavery and with it the "three-fifths" clause of the Constitution, by which only three-fifths of the slave population had been counted in determining the number of members a state could send to the House of Representatives. The black population of the South would now be counted in full.

These political questions overlapped, of course, with important economic questions. The Republican party had taken advantage of the absence of the South from Congress to pass a program of nationalistic economic legislation—railroad subsidies, protective tariffs, and other measures of benefit to Northern business leaders and industrialists. Should the Democratic party regain power with heavy dependence on Southern support, these programs would be in jeopardy. Complicating these practical questions were emotional concerns of considerable importance: the widespread Northern belief that the South should in some way be punished for its rebellion and for the suffering and sacrifice that rebellion had cost; and the belief among many Northerners that the South should be transformed, made over in the North's image—its backward, feudal, undemocratic society civilized and modernized.

Even among the Republicans in Congress, there was considerable disagreement about the proper approach to Reconstruction—disagreements that reflected the same factional division (between the party's Conservatives and Radicals) that had created disputes during the war over emancipation. The Conservatives advocated a mild peace and the rapid restoration of the defeated states to the Union; they insisted that the South accept the abolition of slavery; but beyond that they did not propose to interfere with race relations or to alter the social system of the region. The Radicals, directed by such leaders as Thaddeus Stevens of Pennsylvania and Charles Sumner of Massachusetts, stood for a harder peace. Their most militant spokesmen urged that the civil and military chieftains of the late Confederacy be subjected to severe punishment, that large numbers of Southern whites be disfranchised, that the legal rights of blacks be protected, and that the property of rich Southerners who had aided the Confederacy be confiscated and distributed among the freedmen. Some Radicals favored granting suffrage to the former slaves, as a matter of right or as a means of creating a Republican electorate in the South. Other Radicals hesitated to state a position for fear of alienating public opinion—few Northern states permitted blacks to vote.

Between the Radicals and the Conservatives stood a faction of uncommitted Republicans, the Moderates. They rejected the punitive goals of the Radicals; but they supported measures to extract at least some concessions from the South on the matter of black rights. It would be this group, ultimately, that would determine the fate of the Reconstruction process.

Lincoln's Plan

Even before the war ended, President Lincoln formulated a Reconstruction plan that reflected his own sympathies for the Moderate and Conservative wings of his party. Lincoln believed there were a considerable number of actual or potential Unionists in the South—most of them former Whigs—who could be encouraged to join the Republican party and thus prevent the readmission of the South from strengthening the Democrats. More immediately, the Southern Unionists could serve as the nucleus for creating new, loyal state governments in the South. Lincoln was not uninterested in the fate of the freedmen; but he wanted to restore the Union as soon as possible and was willing, therefore, to defer considering questions about race relations.

Lincoln announced his plan in December 1863. It offered a general amnesty to all white Southerners——with the temporary exception of high civil and military officials of the Confederacy—who would take an oath pledging future loyalty to the government and acceptance of the wartime measures eliminating slavery. Whenever 10 percent of the number of voters in 1860 took the oath in any state, those loyal voters could proceed to set up a state government. Lincoln also hoped to extend the suffrage to at least a few blacks—to those who were educated, owned property, and had served in the Union army. In three Southern states—Louisiana, Arkansas, and Tennessee, all under Union occupation—loyal governments were reestablished under the Lincoln formula in 1864.

The Radical Republicans were angered and astonished at the mildness of Lincoln's program, and they persuaded Congress to repudiate the new governments. Congress refused to seat representatives from the three "reconstructed" states and refused to count the electoral vote of those states in the election of 1864. But the Radicals could not simply reject Lincoln's plan; they needed an alternative plan of their own. And for the moment, they were uncertain about what form that plan should take.

Their first effort to resolve that question was the Wade-Davis bill, passed by Congress in July 1864. By its provisions, the president would appoint for each conquered state a provisional governor who would take a census of all adult white males. If a majority of that group took an oath of allegiance to the Union, the governor was to call an election for a state constitutional convention. The privilege of voting for delegates to this meeting would be limited to those who would swear that they had never borne arms against the United States, the so-called ironclad oath. The state convention would be required to include provisions in the new constitution abolishing slavery, disfranchising Confederate civil and military leaders, and repudiating debts accumulated by the state governments during the war. After these conditions had been met, Congress would readmit the state to the Union.

The Wade-Davis bill was more drastic in almost every respect than the Lincoln plan. Instead of requiring 10 percent of prior voters to swear loyalty to the Union, the Radical plan called for a majority of all adult white males to do so. Instead of assuming, as Lincoln did, that the Southern states had never left the Union, it insisted that the states had in effect forfeited their rights as members of the republic and were thus subject to the dictates of Congress. Like the president's proposal, however, the Wade-Davis bill left up to the states the question of political rights for blacks.

Congress passed the bill a few days before it adjourned in 1864, and Lincoln disposed of it with a pocket veto. His action enraged the authors of the measure, Benjamin F. Wade and Henry Winter Davis, who issued a blistering denunciation of the veto, the Wade-Davis Manifesto, warning the president not to interfere with the powers of Congress to control Reconstruction. Lincoln could not ignore the bitterness and the strength of the Radical opposition. Practical as always, he realized that he would have to bow to at least some of the Radical demands; and so he began to move toward a new approach to Reconstruction.

The Death of Lincoln

What plan he might have produced no one can say. On the night of April 14, 1865, Lincoln and his wife attended a play at Ford's Theater in Washington. As they sat in the presidential box, John Wilkes Booth, an unsuccessful actor obsessed with aiding the Southern cause, entered the box from the rear and shot Lincoln in the head. Then he leaped to the stage (breaking his leg in the process), shouted "Sic, semper tyrannis!" ("Thus always to tyrants!"—the motto of the state of Virginia), and disappeared into the night. The president was carried unconscious to a house across the street, where early the next morning—surrounded by family, friends, and political associates (including a tearful Charles Sumner)—he died.

The circumstances of Lincoln's death—the heroic war leader, the Great Emancipator, struck down in the hour of victory—earned him immediate martyrdom. It also produced wild fears and antagonisms throughout the North. There were widespread accusations that Booth had acted as part of a great con-

Abraham Lincoln and His Son Tad
During the last difficult months of the Civil War, Lincoln often found relief from the strains of his office in the company of his young son, Thomas (known as "Tad"), shown here with his father in an 1864 photograph by Matthew Brady. Much has been written about Lincoln's turbulent family life. His wife, Mary Todd Lincoln, was apparently a moody and difficult woman; but the marriage seems generally to have been a happy one. The Lincolns did, however, experience a series of heartbreaking bereavements as three of their four sons died in childhood. Their second child, Edward, died in 1850 at the age of three; their third, "Willie," died of fever in 1862 at the age of eleven; Tad outlived his father by only a few years and died in 1871 at the age of eighteen. Robert Todd Lincoln, the president's eldest son, lived a long and successful life during which he served as secretary of war, American minister to England, and president of the Pullman Railroad Car Company. (Library of Congress)

spiracy—accusations that contained at least a grain of truth. Booth did indeed have associates, one of whom shot and wounded Secretary of State Seward the night of the assassination, another of whom set out to murder Vice President Johnson but abandoned the scheme at the last moment. Booth himself escaped on horseback into the Maryland countryside, where, on April 26, he was cornered by Union troops and shot to death in a blazing barn. Eight other conspirators were convicted by a military tribunal of participating in the conspiracy (at least two of them on the basis of virtually no evidence). Four were hanged.

To many Northerners, however, the murder of the president seemed evidence of an even greater conspiracy—one masterminded and directed by the unrepentant leaders of the defeated South. (There was never any conclusive evidence to support this—and many another—theory of the assassination; but questions continued to be raised about the event well into the twentieth century.) Militant Republicans exploited such suspicions relentlessly in the ensuing months, ensuring that Lincoln's death would doom his plans for a relatively generous peace.

Johnson and "Restoration"

The Conservative leadership in the controversy over Reconstruction fell to Lincoln's successor, Andrew Johnson. Of all the men who have accidentally inherited the presidency, Johnson was undoubtedly the most unfortunate. A Southerner and former slaveholder, he became president as a bloody war against the South was drawing to a close. A Democrat before he had been placed on the Union ticket with Lincoln in 1864, he became the head of a Republican administration at a time when partisan passions, held in some restraint during the war, were about to rule the government. As if these handicaps of background were not enough, Johnson himself was an intemperate and tactless man, filled with resentments and insecurities, and plagued by a serious drinking problem.

Johnson revealed his plan of Reconstruction—or "Restoration," as he preferred to call it—soon after he took office, and he proceeded to implement it during the summer of 1865 when Congress was not in session. In some ways Johnson's scheme resembled Lincoln's; in many other respects, it reflected the more drastic demands of the Radicals. Like his predecessor, Johnson assumed that the seceded states had never left the Union; and, also like Lincoln, he offered amnesty for past conduct to all who would take an oath of allegiance. High-ranking Confederate officials and any white Southerner with land worth $20,000 or more would have to apply to the president for individual pardons. (Himself a self-made man, Johnson harbored deep resentments toward the old Southern aristocracy and apparently relished the pros-

pect of these Confederate leaders humbling themselves before him to ask for amnesty.) For each state, the president appointed a provisional governor, who was to invite the qualified voters to elect delegates to a constitutional convention. Johnson did not specify that a minimum number of voters had to take the oath, as had the Lincoln and Wade-Davis proposals, but the implication was plain that he would require a majority. As conditions of readmittance, a state had to revoke the ordinance of secession, abolish slavery and ratify the Thirteenth Amendment, and repudiate the Confederate and state war debts—essentially the same stipulations that had been laid down in the Wade-Davis bill. The final procedure before restoration was for a state to elect a state government and send representatives to Congress.

By the end of 1865, all the states not previously reorganized under Lincoln's plan had complied with Johnson's requirements. All of the seceded states, therefore, had been reconstructed and were ready to resume their places in the Union—if Congress chose to recognize them when it met in December 1865. But the Radicals were determined not to recognize the Johnson governments, just as they had previously refused to recognize the Lincoln regimes. In that determination they had the support of much of the Northern public.

Many Northerners were disturbed by the seeming reluctance of some members of the Southern conventions to abolish slavery and by the refusal of all the conventions to grant suffrage to even a few blacks. They were astounded that states claiming to be "loyal" should elect as state officials and representatives to Congress prominent leaders of the recent Confederacy. Particularly hard to accept was Georgia's choice of Alexander H. Stephens, former vice president of the Confederacy, as a United States senator.

Radical Reconstruction

This initial phase of Reconstruction—often known as "presidential Reconstruction"—lasted only until Congress reconvened in December 1865. At that point, Republican leaders looked over Andrew Johnson's handiwork and expressed their displeasure. Congress immediately refused to seat the senators and representatives of the states the president had "restored." Instead, Radical leaders insisted, Congress needed to learn more about conditions in the postwar South. There must be assurances that the former Confederates had accepted their defeat and that emancipated blacks and loyal whites would be protected. Accordingly, Congress set up the new Joint Committee on Reconstruction to investigate conditions in the South and to advise Congress in laying down a Reconstruction policy of its own. The period of "congressional" or "Radical" Reconstruction had begun.

The Response to the Black Codes

During the next few months, the Radicals advanced toward a more severe program than their first plan— the Wade-Davis bill of 1864, which had left to the states the question of what rights the freed slaves should have. Johnson, unlike Lincoln, refused even to consider compromising; and his intransigence helped the Radicals gain the support of many Moderate Republicans. The president insisted that Congress had no right even to consider a policy for the South until his own plan had been accepted and the Southern congressmen and senators had been admitted.

In the meantime, Northerners were learning more about what was happening in the defeated South; and what they learned persuaded many of them—including most of the important leaders in Congress—that far more drastic measures were necessary than the president had contemplated. For throughout the South in 1865 and early 1866, state legislatures were enacting sets of laws known as the Black Codes. These measures were the white South's solution to the problem of the free black laborer, and they were modeled in many ways on the codes that had regulated free blacks in the prewar South. As such, they created a new set of devices to guarantee white supremacy. Economically, the codes were intended to regulate the labor of a race that, in the opinion of whites, would not work except under some kind of compulsion. Although there were variations from state to state, all codes authorized local officials to apprehend unemployed blacks, fine them for vagrancy, and hire them out to private employers to satisfy the fine. Some of the codes tried to force blacks to work on the plantations by forbidding them to own or lease farms or to take other jobs except as domestic servants. Socially, the codes were designed to invest blacks with a legal status outside slavery, but one that ensured that they would remain clearly

subordinate to whites. To the white South, the Black Codes were a realistic approach to a great social problem. To the North, and to most blacks, they seemed to herald a return to slavery in all but name.

An appropriate agency for offsetting the Black Codes was the Freedmen's Bureau, but its scheduled year of existence was about to expire. In February 1866, Congress passed a bill to prolong the life of the bureau and to widen its powers. For settling labor disputes, it could now establish special courts, which could disallow work agreements forced on freedmen under the Black Codes. Johnson vetoed the bill, denouncing it as unconstitutional. Efforts to override him fell just short of the necessary two-thirds majority.

In April, Congress struck again at the Black Codes by passing the Civil Rights Act, which declared blacks to be U.S. citizens and empowered the federal government to intervene in state affairs when necessary to protect the rights of citizens. Johnson vetoed this bill, too. With Moderates and Radicals acting together, Congress promptly overrode the veto. Then Congress repassed the Freedmen's Bureau Act and overrode a second presidential veto of that law.

The Fourteenth Amendment

Emboldened by their evidently growing support in Congress, the Radicals now struck again. The Joint Committee on Reconstruction submitted to Congress, in April 1866, a proposed amendment to the Constitution, the Fourteenth, which constituted the second Radical plan of Reconstruction. The amendment was adopted by Congress and sent to the states for approval in the early summer. It consisted of three sections. Taken together, they constituted one of the most important additions to the Constitution in American history.

Section 1 of the amendment declared that all persons born or naturalized in the United States were citizens of the United States and of the state of their residence—the first official, national definition of citizenship. Next came a statement that no state could abridge the rights of citizens of the United States or deprive any person of life, liberty, or property without due process of law or deny to any person within its jurisdiction the equal protection of the laws. Section 2 provided that if a state denied the suffrage to any of its adult male inhabitants, its representation in the House of Representatives and the electoral college would suffer a proportionate reduction. Section 3 prohibited persons who had previously taken an oath to support the Constitution and later had aided the Confederacy (in other words, former Southern members of Congress and other former officials) from holding any state or federal office—until Congress by a two-thirds vote of each house should remove their disability.

The Southern legislatures knew that if they ratified the amendment their states would be readmitted and Reconstruction probably would end. But they could not bring themselves to approve the measure, mainly because of Section 3, which put a stigma on their late leaders. Johnson himself advised Southerners to defeat the amendment. Only Tennessee, of the former Confederate states, ratified it, thus winning readmittance. The other ten, joined by Kentucky and Delaware, voted it down. The amendment thus failed to receive the required approval of three-fourths of the states and was defeated—but only temporarily. When the time was more propitious, the Radicals would bring it up again. Meanwhile, its rejection by the South strengthened the Radical cause.

The Northern public gave striking evidence of its support for the Radical program in the elections of 1866. The Radicals could point to recent events in the South—bloody race riots in New Orleans and other Southern cities in which blacks were the victims—as further evidence of the inadequacy of Johnson's policy. Johnson attempted to derail the Radical cause by campaigning for Conservative candidates; but he did his own cause more harm than good by the intemperate, brawling (and, some believed, drunken) speeches he made on a stumping tour (a "swing around the circle," as it was called) from Washington to Chicago and back. The voters returned to Congress an overwhelming majority of Republicans, most of them Radicals. In the Senate, there were to be 42 Republicans to 11 Democrats; in the House, 143 Republicans to 49 Democrats. Now the Republicans could enact any kind of Reconstruction plan they could themselves agree on. Confidently they looked forward to the struggle with Johnson that would ensue when Congress assembled in December 1866—and to their final victory over the president.

The Congressional Plan

After compromising differences among themselves and with the Moderates, the Radicals formulated their third plan of Reconstruction in three bills that passed Congress in the early months of 1867. All three were vetoed by Johnson and repassed. Together, they constituted a single program. Finally, nearly two years after the end of the war, the federal government had established a consistent plan for Reconstruction.

That two-year delay had important effects on the way the South would react to the program. In 1865, with the South reeling from its defeat and nearly prostrate, the federal government could probably have imposed on the region an even more radical plan than it ultimately did, without provoking immediate resistance. But by 1867, the South had begun to recover from the humiliation of defeat and had begun to reconstruct itself under the reasonably generous terms Lincoln and Johnson had extended. By then, therefore, measures that might once have seemed moderate had come to seem radical; and the congressional reconstruction plan created deep resentments and continuing resistance.

The congressional plan was based squarely on the principle that the seceded states had forfeited their political identity. The Lincoln-Johnson governments were declared to have no legal standing, and the ten seceded states (Tennessee was now out of the Reconstruction process) were combined into five military districts. Each district was to have a military commander, supported by troops, who was to prepare his provinces for readmission as states. To this end, he was to institute a registration of voters, which was to include all adult black males and those white males who were not disqualified by participation in rebellion.

After the registration was completed in each province, the commanding general was to call the voters to elect a convention to prepare a new state constitution, which had to include provisions for black suffrage. If this document was ratified by the voters, elections for a state government could be held. Finally, if Congress approved the constitution, if the state legislature ratified the Fourteenth Amendment, and if this amendment was adopted by the required number of states and became a part of the Constitution—then the state was to be restored to the Union.

By 1868, seven of the former Confederate states (Arkansas, North Carolina, South Carolina, Louisiana, Alabama, Georgia, and Florida) had complied with the process of restoration outlined in the Reconstruction Acts—including ratification of the Fourteenth Amendment, which now became part of the Constitution. These states were readmitted to the Union. Delaying tactics by whites held up the return of Virginia and Texas until 1869 and Mississippi until 1870. And by then, Congress had added an additional

Political Reconstruction, 1866–1877

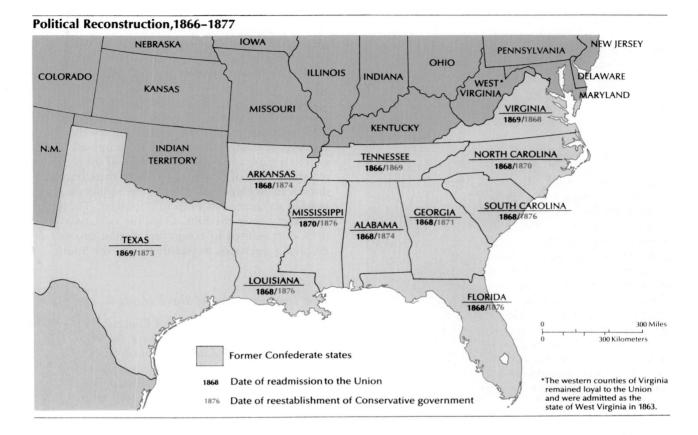

Former Confederate states

1868 Date of readmission to the Union

1876 Date of reestablishment of Conservative government

*The western counties of Virginia remained loyal to the Union and were admitted as the state of West Virginia in 1863.

requirement for readmission, which constituted the fourth and final congressional plan of Reconstruction. They had to ratify another constitutional amendment, the Fifteenth, which forbade the states and the federal government to deny the suffrage to any citizen on account of "race, color, or previous condition of servitude."

Sponsors of the Fifteenth Amendent were motivated by both idealistic and practical considerations. They wished to be consistent in extending to blacks in the North a right they had already given to them elsewhere. The great majority of the Northern states still denied the suffrage to blacks when the Reconstruction Acts granted it to blacks in the Southern states. At the same time the amendment would put into the Constitution, where it would be safe from congressional repeal, a provision that would serve as a basis of Republican strength in the South. Sponsors of the amendment also saw it as a vehicle for protecting the party's precarious future in the North. A warning of trouble ahead had appeared in the state elections of 1867 in Pennsylvania, Ohio, and Indiana,

all of which went Democratic that year. "We must establish the doctrine of national jurisdiction over all the states in state matters of the franchise," the Radical leader Thaddeus Stevens now concluded. "We must thus bridle Pennsylvania, Ohio, Indiana et cetera, or the South *being in*, we shall drift into Democracy." In several of the Northern states the black vote, although proportionally small, would be large enough to decide close elections in favor of the Republicans. A number of Northern and border states refused to approve the Fifteenth Amendment, and it was adopted only with the support of the four Southern states that had to ratify it in order to be readmitted to the Union.

The Radicals saw themselves as architects of a revolution, and they did not intend to let the executive or the judiciary get in their way. They were prepared, if necessary, to establish a kind of congressional dictatorship.

To stop the president from interfering with their designs, Congress in 1867 passed two remarkable laws. One, the Tenure of Office Act, forbade the

Thaddeus Stevens
Stern, uncompromising, and severe, Thaddeus Stevens of Pennsylvania was the incarnation of the North's vindictive designs in the eyes of many Southerners during (and long after) Reconstruction. Others admired him as one of the few white leaders who remained firmly committed to racial equality. He served in the House of Representatives from 1849 to 1853 and again, more prominently, from 1859 until his death in 1868. He spent much of the last year of his life organizing and managing the impeachment trial of Andrew Johnson. (Library of Congress)

president to remove civil officials, including members of his cabinet, without the consent of the Senate. The principal purpose of the law was to protect the job of Secretary of War Edwin M. Stanton, who was cooperating with the Radicals. The other law, the Command of the Army Act, prohibited the president from issuing military orders except through the commanding general of the army (General Grant), whose headquarters were to be in Washington and who could not be relieved or assigned elsewhere without the consent of the Senate.

The congressional Radicals also took action to curb the Supreme Court from interfering with their plans. The Court, under Chief Justice Salmon P. Chase, had in 1866 declared in *Ex parte Milligan* that military tribunals were unconstitutional in places where civil courts were functioning. Although the decision was applied to a case originating in the war, it seemed to threaten the system of military government that the Radicals were planning for the South. Radicals in Congress immediately proposed legislation to require a two-thirds majority of the justices to overrule a law of Congress, to deny the Court jurisdiction in Reconstruction cases, to reduce its membership to three, and even to abolish it. The judges apparently took the hint. Over the next two years, the Court refused to accept jurisdiction in any cases involving questions of jurisdiction in the South.

The Impeachment of the President

The most aggressive move of Congress against another branch of government was the effort of the Radicals to remove Andrew Johnson from office. Although the president had long since ceased to be a serious obstacle to the passage of Radical legislation, he was still the official charged with administering the Reconstruction programs; and as such, the Radicals believed, he was a serious impediment to their plans. Early in 1867, therefore, they began searching for evidence that Johnson had committed crimes or misdemeanors in office, the only legal grounds for impeachment; but they could find nothing on which to base charges. Then he gave them what was, in their view, a plausible reason for action by deliberately violating the Tenure of Office Act—in hopes of bringing a test case of the law before the courts. Johnson suspended Secretary of War Stanton, who had worked with the Radicals against the president, and named General Grant as his successor. When the state refused to concur in the suspension, Grant relinquished the office to Stanton. Johnson then dismissed Stanton.

In the House of Representatives the elated Radicals presented to the Senate eleven charges against the president. The first nine accusations dealt with the violation of the Tenure of Office Act. The tenth and eleventh charged Johnson with making speeches calculated to bring Congress into disrespect and with not faithfully enforcing the various Reconstruction Acts. The trial before the Senate lasted for two months—from March 25 to May 26, 1868. Johnson's lawyers maintained that he was justified in technically violating a law in order to force a test case. And they argued that the measure did not apply to Stanton anyway: It gave tenure to cabinet members for the term of the president by whom they had been appointed, and Stanton had been appointed by Lincoln. The House managers of the impeachment stressed the theme that Johnson had opposed the will of Congress and was thus guilty of high crimes and misdemeanors. They put heavy pressure on all the Republican senators, but seven Republicans joined the twelve Democrats to vote for acquittal. On three of the charges the vote was identical, 35 to 19, one short of the required two-thirds majority. After that, the Radicals dropped the impeachment campaign.

The South in Reconstruction

When white Southerners spoke bitterly in later years of the effects of Reconstruction, they referred most frequently to the governments Congress imposed on them—governments that were, they claimed, both incompetent and corrupt, that saddled the region with enormous debts, and that trampled on the rights of citizens. When black Southerners and their defenders condemned Reconstruction, in contrast, they spoke of its failure to guarantee to freedmen even the most elemental rights of citizenship—a failure that resulted in a new and cruel system of economic subordination. Controversy has raged for more than a century over which viewpoint is more nearly correct. (See "Where Historians Disagree," p. 446.) Most students of Reconstruction tend now to agree, however, that the complaints of Southern whites, although in some respects accurate, greatly exaggerated the real nature of the postwar governments; while the complaints of blacks, although occasionally overstated, were largely justified.

The Reconstruction Governments

In the ten states of the South that were reorganized under the congressional plan, approximately one-fourth of the white males were at first excluded from voting or holding office. The voter registration of 1867 enrolled a total of 703,000 black and 627,000 white voters. The black voters constituted a majority in half of the states—Alabama, Florida, South Carolina, Mississippi, and Louisiana—although only in the last three of these states did the blacks outnumber the whites in the population as a whole. But once new constitutions had been framed and new governments launched, most of them permitted nearly all whites to vote (although for several years the Fourteenth Amendment continued to keep the leading ex-Confederates from holding office). This meant that in most of the Southern states the Republicans could maintain control only with the support of a great many Southern whites.

These Southern white Republicans, whom their

"The First Vote"
This cover illustration from an 1867 issue of *Harper's Weekly* shows freedmen exercising the right recently guaranteed them by the Fifteenth Amendment. Before the development of the technology that permitted the printing of photographs, woodcuts such as this one—usually based on drawings made on the scene by an artist and then transferred to wood blocks by skilled engravers—brought a sense of immediacy to the reporting of the news. (New-York Historical Society)

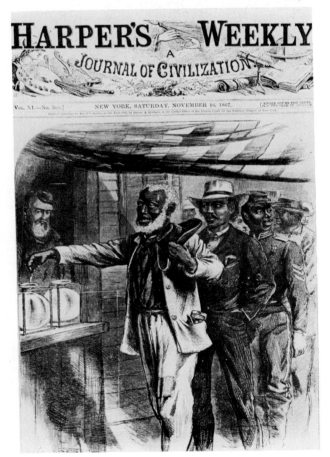

─────WHERE HISTORIANS DISAGREE─────

Reconstruction

Debate over the nature of Reconstruction—not only among historians, but among the public at large—has created so much controversy over the decades that one scholar, writing in 1959, described the issue as a "dark and bloody ground." Among historians, the passions of the debate have to some extent subsided since then; but in the popular mind, Reconstruction continues to raise "dark and bloody" images.

For many years, a relatively uniform and highly critical view of Reconstruction prevailed among historians, a reflection of broad currents in popular thought. By the late nineteenth century, most white Americans in both the North and the South had come to believe that few real differences any longer divided the sections, that the nation should strive for a genuine reconciliation. And most white Americans believed as well in the superiority of their race, in the inherent unfitness of blacks for political or social equality. In this spirit was born the first major historical interpretation of Reconstruction, through the work of William A. Dunning. In his *Reconstruction, Political and Economic* (1907), Dunning portrayed Reconstruction as a corrupt outrage perpetrated on the prostrate South by a vicious and vindictive cabal of Northern Republican Radicals. Reconstruction governments were based on "bayonet rule." Unscrupulous and self-aggrandizing carpetbaggers flooded the South to profit from the misery of the defeated region. Ignorant, illiterate blacks were thrust into positions of power for which they were entirely unfit. The Reconstruction experiment, a moral abomination from its first moments, survived only because of the determination of the Republican party to keep itself in power. (Some later writers, notably Howard K. Beale, added an economic motive—to protect Northern business interests.) Dunning and his many students (who together formed what became known as the "Dunning school") compiled evidence to show that the leg-acy of Reconstruction was corruption, ruinous taxation, and astronomical increases in the public debt.

The Dunning school not only shaped the views of several generations of historians. It also reflected and helped to shape the views of much of the public. Popular depictions of Reconstruction for years to come (as the book and movie *Gone with the Wind* suggested) portrayed the era as one of tragic exploitation of the South by the North. Even today, some white Southerners and many others continue to accept the basic premises of the Dunning interpretation. Among historians, however, the old view of Reconstruction has gradually lost all credibility.

W. E. B. Du Bois, the great black scholar, was among the first to challenge the Dunning view in a 1910 article and, later, in a 1935 book, *Black Reconstruction*. To him, Reconstruction politics in the Southern states had been an effort on the part of the masses, black and white, to create a truly democratic society. The misdeeds of the Reconstruction governments had, he claimed, been greatly exaggerated and their achievements overlooked. The governments had been expensive, he insisted, because they had tried to provide public education and other public services on a scale never before attempted in the South. But Du Bois's use of Marxist theory in his work caused many historians who did not share his philosophy to dismiss his argument; and it remained for a group of less radical white historians to shatter the Dunning image of Reconstruction for good.

In the 1940s, historians such as C. Vann Woodward, David Herbert Donald, Thomas B. Alexander, and others began to reexamine the history of the Reconstruction governments in the South and to suggest that their record was not nearly as bad as had previously been assumed. They looked, too, at the Radical Republicans in Congress and suggested that they had not been

opponents derisively called "scalawags," consisted in part of former Whigs who, after the breakup of the Whig organization in the 1850s, had acted with the Southern Democrats but had never felt completely at home with them. Some of the scalawag leaders were wealthy (or once wealthy) planters or businessmen. Many other Southern whites who supported the Republican party were farmers living in areas where slavery had been unimportant or nonexistent. These men, many of whom had been wartime Unionists,

WHERE HISTORIANS DISAGREE

motivated by vindictiveness and partisanship alone. By the early 1960s, a new view of Reconstruction had emerged from these efforts (and in response to the influence of the "second Reconstruction"—the civil-rights movement). This revisionist approach was summarized finally by John Hope Franklin in *Reconstruction After the Civil War* (1961) and Kenneth Stampp in *The Era of Reconstruction* (1965), which claimed that the postwar Republicans had been engaged in a genuine, if flawed, effort to solve the problem of race in the South by providing much-needed protection to the freedmen. The Reconstruction governments, for all their faults, had been bold experiments in interracial politics; and the congressional Radicals, while far from being saints, had displayed a genuine concern for the rights of former slaves. Andrew Johnson was not a martyred defender of the Constitution but an inept, racist politician who resisted reasonable compromise and brought the government to a crisis. There had been no such thing as "bayonet rule" or "Negro rule" in the South. Blacks had played only a small part in Reconstruction governments and had generally acquitted themselves well. The Reconstruction regimes had, in fact, brought important progress to the South, establishing the region's first public school system and other important social changes. Corruption in the South had been no worse than corruption in the North at that time. What was tragic about Reconstruction, the revisionist view claimed, was not what it did to Southern whites but what it did not do for Southern blacks. By stopping short of the reforms necessary to ensure blacks genuine equality, Reconstruction had consigned them to more than a century of injustice and discrimination.

By the 1970s, then, the Dunning view of Reconstruction had all but disappeared from serious scholarly discussion. Instead, historians seemed to agree that Reconstruction had, in fact, changed the South relatively little; and they began to debate why Reconstruction fell as short as it did of guaranteeing racial justice. Some scholars have claimed that conservative obstacles to change were so great that the Radicals, despite their good intentions, simply could not overcome them. Others have argued that the Radicals themselves were not sufficiently committed to the principle of racial justice, that they abandoned the cause quickly when it became clear to them that the battle would not easily be won.

In recent years, however, scholars have begun to question the revisionist view—not in an effort to revive the old Dunning interpretation but in an attempt to draw attention to those things Reconstruction in fact achieved. Leon Litwack's *Been in the Storm So Long* (1979) reveals that the former slaves used the relative latitude they enjoyed under Reconstruction to build a certain independence for themselves within Southern society. They strengthened their churches; they reunited their families; they refused to work in the "gang labor" system of the plantations and forced the creation of a new labor system in which they had more control over their own lives. Eric Foner, in *Nothing But Freedom* (1983), compares the aftermath of slavery in the United States to similar experiences in the Caribbean and concludes that what is striking about the American experience in this context is not how little was accomplished but how far the former slaves moved toward freedom and independence in a short time. Reconstruction permitted blacks a certain amount of legal and political power in the South. And even though some of that power did not survive, they used it for a time to strengthen their economic and social condition and win a position of limited but genuine independence that brought them, if not equality, something that emancipation alone had not guaranteed: freedom.

favored the Republican program of internal improvements, which would help them get their crops to market.

White men from the North also served as Republican leaders in the South. Opponents of Reconstruction referred to them as "carpetbaggers," thus giving the impression that they were penniless adventurers who had arrived with all their possessions in a carpetbag (then a common kind of suitcase covered with carpeting material) in order to take advantage of the black vote for their own power and profit. In fact, the majority of the so-called carpetbaggers were veterans of the Union army who had looked on the South as a new frontier, more promising than the West, and at the war's end had settled in it as hopeful planters or business or professional men.

The most numerous Republicans in the South were the freedmen, the vast majority of whom had no formal education and no previous experience in public affairs. Among the black leaders, however, were well-educated men, most of whom had never been slaves and many of whom had grown up in the North or abroad. The blacks quickly became politically self-conscious. In various states, they held their own conventions to chart their future course. One such "colored convention," as Southern whites called them, assembled in Alabama in 1867 and announced: "We claim exactly *the same rights, privileges and immunities as are enjoyed by white men*—we ask nothing more and will be content with nothing less." Blacks were also organized, often with the assistance of Freedmen's Bureau agents and other Northern whites, in chapters of the Union League, which had been founded originally as a Republican electioneering agency in the North during the war. In addition, black churches helped give unity and political self-confidence to the former slaves. After emancipation, blacks withdrew from the white churches and formed their own—institutions based on the elaborate religious practices they had developed (occasionally surreptitiously) under slavery. "The colored preachers are *the great power* in controlling and uniting the colored vote," a carpetbagger observed in 1868.

Blacks served as delegates to the conventions that, under the congressional plan, drew up new state constitutions in the South. Then, in the reconstructed states, blacks were elected to public offices of practically every kind. Altogether (between 1869 and 1901) twenty blacks were sent to the House of Representatives in Washington. Two went to the Senate, both of them from Mississippi. In 1870, Hiram R. Revels, an ordained minister and a former North Carolina free black who had been educated at Knox College in Illinois, took the Senate seat that Jefferson Davis once had occupied. In 1874, Blanche K. Bruce, who had escaped from slavery in Virginia and studied in the North, became a senator.

Yet while Southern whites complained loudly (both at the time and for generations to come) about "Negro rule" during Reconstruction, no such thing ever truly existed in any of the states. No black man was ever elected governor of a Southern state, al-

The Burdened South

This Reconstruction era cartoon expresses the South's sense of its oppression at the hands of Northern Republicans. President Grant (whose hat bears Abraham Lincoln's initials) rides in comfort in a giant carpetbag, guarded by bayonet-wielding soldiers, as the South staggers under the burden in chains. More evidence of destruction and military occupation is visible in the background.   (Culver Pictures)

though Lieutenant Governor P. B. S. Pinchback briefly occupied the governor's chair in Louisiana. Blacks never controlled any of the state legislatures, although for a time they held a majority in the lower house of South Carolina. In the South as a whole, the number of black officeholders was less than proportionate to the number of blacks in the population.

The record of the Reconstruction governments is many-sided. The financial programs they instituted were a compound of blatant corruption and well-designed, if sometimes impractical, social legislation. The corruption and extravagance are familiar aspects of the Reconstruction story. Officeholders in many states enriched themselves through graft and other illicit activities. State budgets expanded to hitherto unknown totals, and state debts soared to previously undreamed-of heights. In South Carolina, for example, the public debt increased from $7 million to $29 million in eight years.

But these facts are misleading when considered alone. In large measure, the corruption in the South was part of a national phenomenon, with the same social force—an expanding capitalism eager to secure quick results—acting as the corrupting agent in all sections of the country. Corruption did not decline in Southern state governments once Reconstruction came to an end; in many states, in fact, it increased.

And the state expenditures of the Reconstruction years seem huge only in comparison with the tight budgets of the conservative governments of the pre-war era; they do not appear large when measured against the sums appropriated by later legislatures. The expenditures, moreover, represented an effort to provide the Southern states with services they desperately needed and that no governments had ever attempted to provide in the antebellum period: public education, public works programs, poor relief, and other costly new commitments. There was, to be sure, graft and extravagance in Reconstruction governments; there were also positive and permanent accomplishments.

Education

Perhaps the most important of those accomplishments was a dramatic improvement in Southern education—an improvement that benefited both whites and blacks. In the first years of Reconstruction, much of the impetus for educational reform in the South came from outside groups—from the Freedmen's Bureau and from Northern private philanthropic organizations—and from blacks themselves. Over the opposition of many Southern whites, who feared that education would give blacks "false notions of equality," these reformers established a large network of schools for former slaves—4,000 schools by 1870, staffed by 9,000 teachers (half of them black), and teaching 200,000 students (about 12 percent of the total school-age population of the freedmen). In the course of the 1870s, moreover, the Reconstruction governments of the states assumed the initiative and began to build a comprehensive public school system in the South. By 1876, more than half of all white

children and about 40 percent of all black children were being educated in Southern schools. Several black "academies" were also beginning to operate—institutions that were, perhaps, not yet genuine colleges but that were offering more advanced education to freedmen than the public schools provided. Gradually, these academies grew into an important network of black colleges and universities, which would form the basis of black higher education in the South for many decades. Among the early institutions, for example, were schools that later became Fisk and Atlanta universities and Morehouse College.

Already, however, Southern education was becoming divided into two separate systems—one black and one white. Early efforts to integrate the schools of the region were a dismal failure. The Freedmen's Bureau schools, for example, were open to students of all races, but almost no whites attended them. New Orleans set up an integrated school system under the Reconstruction government; again, whites almost universally stayed away. The one federal effort to mandate school integration—the Civil Rights Act of 1875—had its provisions for educational desegregation removed before it was passed. And as soon as the Republican governments of Reconstruction were replaced, the new Southern Democratic regimes quickly abandoned all efforts to promote integration.

Land Ownership

The most ambitious goal of the Freedmen's Bureau, and of some Republican Radicals in Congress, was to make Reconstruction the occasion for a fundamental reform of land ownership in the South. The effort failed. In the last years of the war and the first years of Reconstruction, the Freedmen's Bureau did oversee the redistribution of substantial amounts of land to freedmen in some areas—notably the Sea Islands off South Carolina and Georgia, and areas of Mississippi that had once belonged to the Davis family. By June 1865, the bureau had settled nearly 10,000 black families on their own land—most of it drawn from abandoned plantations. Blacks throughout the South were growing excited at the prospect of achieving a real economic stake in their region—the vision of "forty acres and a mule." By the end of that year, however, the experiment was already collapsing. Southern plantation owners were returning and demanding the restoration of their property. And Andrew Johnson was supporting their demands. Despite the resistance of General Oliver O. Howard and other officials of the Freedmen's Bureau, most of the confiscated land was eventually returned to the original white owners. Congress, moreover, never exhibited much stomach for the idea of land redistribution. Despite the pleas of such Radicals as Thaddeus Stevens, very few Northern Republicans believed that the federal government had the right to confiscate property. Land reform did not become a part of Reconstruction.

Nevertheless, there was a substantial change in the distribution of land ownership in the South in the postwar years—a result of many factors. Among whites, there was a striking decline in ownership of land. Whereas before the war more than 80 percent of Southern whites had lived on their own land, by the end of Reconstruction that proportion had dropped to about 67 percent. Some whites had fallen into debt and been forced to sell; some had fallen victim to increased taxes; some had chosen to leave the marginal lands they had owned to move to more fertile areas, where they rented. Among blacks, during the same period, the proportion who owned land rose from virtually none to more than 20 percent. Black landowners acquired their property through hard work, through luck, and at times through the assistance of such agencies as the Freedman's Bank, established in 1865 by antislavery whites in an effort to promote land ownership among blacks. (The bank failed in 1874, after a combination of internal corruption and a nationwide financial panic had destroyed its reserves.)

Despite these impressive achievements, however, the vast majority of blacks (and a growing minority of whites) did not own their own land during Reconstruction, and some of those who acquired land in the 1860s lost it in the 1890s. These nonlandowners worked for others, through a great variety of systems. Many black agricultural laborers—perhaps 25 percent of the total—simply worked for wages. Most, however, became tenants of white landowners—that is, they acquired control of their own plots of land, working them on their own and paying their landlord either a fixed rent or a share of their crop (hence the term "sharecropping"). The new system represented a breakdown of the traditional plantation system, in which blacks had lived together and worked together under the direction of a master. As tenants and sharecroppers, blacks enjoyed at least a physical independence from their landlords and had the sense of working their own land, even if in most cases they could never hope to buy it. (See Chapter 16 for a fuller discussion of the new Southern economy.)

Incomes and Credit

The economic effect of Reconstruction on the freedmen, to the extent that it can be gauged, was mixed. In some respects, the postwar years were a period of remarkable economic progress for blacks. If the food, clothing, shelter, and other material benefits they had received under slavery are considered as income, then prewar blacks had earned about a 22 percent share of the profits of the plantation system. By the end of Reconstruction, they were earning 56 percent of the return on investment in Southern agriculture. Measured another way, the per capita income of blacks rose 46 percent between 1857 and 1879, while the per capita income of whites declined 35 percent. This represented one of the most significant redistributions of income in American history.

Nevertheless, the economic status of blacks did not improve as much as these figures suggest. For one thing, while their share of the profits was increasing, the total profits of Southern agriculture were declining—a result of the dislocations of the war and of a reduction in the world market for cotton. For another thing, while blacks were earning a greater return on their labor than they had under slavery, they were working less. Women and children were less likely to labor in the fields than in the past. Adult men tended to work shorter days. In all, the black labor force worked about one-third fewer hours during Reconstruction than it had under slavery—a reduction that brought the working schedule of blacks roughly into accord with that of white farm laborers. The income redistribution of the postwar years raised both the absolute and the relative economic status of blacks in the South substantially. It did not, however, lift many blacks out of poverty. Black per capita income rose from about one quarter of white per capita income to about one-half in the first few years after the war. But after this initial increase, it rose virtually not at all.

For blacks and poor whites alike, whatever gains there might have been as a result of land and income redistribution were often overshadowed by the ravages of another economic burden: the crop lien system. In the postwar South, the traditional credit structure—based on "factors" (see pp. 322–325) and banks—was unable to reassert its former control. In its stead emerged a new system of credit, centered in large part on local country stores—some of them owned by planters, others owned by independent merchants. Blacks and whites, landowners and tenants: all depended on these stores for such necessities as food, clothing, seed, farm implements, and the like. And since the agricultural sector does not enjoy the same steady cash flow as other sectors of the economy, Southern farmers often had to rely on credit from these merchants in order to purchase what they needed. The credit came at high cost. Interest rates were, in effect, as high as 50 or 60 percent. Suppliers held liens (claims) on the crops of debtor farmers as collateral on the loans. If a farmer suffered a few bad years in a row, as often happened in the troubled agricultural markets of the 1870s, he could become trapped in a cycle of debt from which he could never escape.

This burdensome credit system had a number of effects on the South. One was that some blacks who had acquired land during the early years of Reconstruction gradually lost it as they fell into debt. (So, to a lesser extent, did white small landowners.) Another was that Southern farmers became utterly dependent on cash crops—and most of all on cotton—because only such marketable commodities seemed to offer any possibility of escape from debt. Thus Southern agriculture, never sufficiently diversified

even in the best of times, became more one-dimensional than ever. Before the war, the South had grown most of its own food. By the end of Reconstruction, the region was importing a large proportion—in some areas more than 50 percent—of what it needed to feed itself. The relentless planting of cotton, moreover, was contributing to an exhaustion of the soil. The crop lien system, in other words, was not only helping to impoverish small farmers; it was also contributing to a general decline in the Southern agricultural economy.

The Black Family in Freedom

One of the most striking features of the black response to Reconstruction was the concerted effort to build or rebuild family structures and to protect them from the interference they had experienced under slavery. A major reason for the rapid departure of so many blacks from the plantations on which they had spent their lives was the desire to find lost relatives

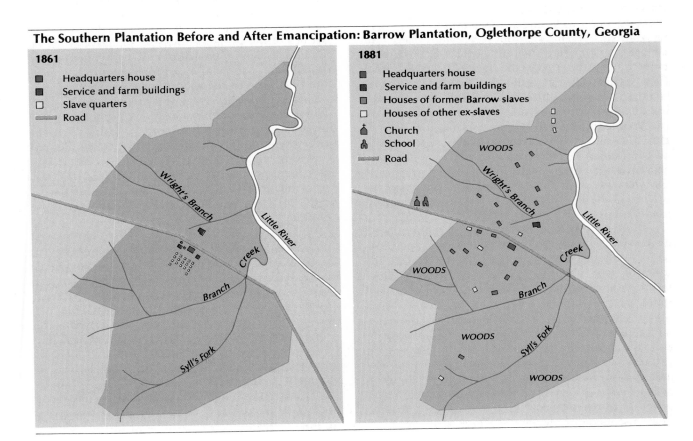

The Southern Plantation Before and After Emancipation: Barrow Plantation, Oglethorpe County, Georgia

1861

- ■ Headquarters house
- ■ Service and farm buildings
- □ Slave quarters
- ⸺ Road

1881

- ■ Headquarters house
- ■ Service and farm buildings
- ▢ Houses of former Barrow slaves
- □ Houses of other ex-slaves
- ⛪ Church
- ♟ School
- ⸺ Road

and reunite families. Thousands of blacks wandered through the South looking for husbands, wives, children, or other relatives from whom they had been separated. Sometimes they found their loved ones, often by relying on an informal information network that quickly grew up in the black community or through advertising in newspapers. Sometimes, the search was in vain.

Former slaves were adamant in insisting that under the new economic system of the South they would acquire control over their own family lives. They rushed to have marriages, previously without legal standing, sanctified by church and law. At times, blacks held mass marriage ceremonies—sixty or seventy couples taking their vows simultaneously. Black families resisted living in the former slave quarters and moved instead to small cabins scattered widely across the countryside, where they could at least enjoy a modest level of privacy. It was often those blacks who had lived in closest proximity to whites—former house servants, for example—who were most determined to separate themselves from white society and create a home in which they would be able to control their own private lives.

Within the black family, the definition of male and female roles quickly came to resemble that within white families. Black men often forbade their wives and children to work in the fields. Such work, they believed, was a badge of slavery. Instead, women were to perform primarily domestic tasks—cooking, cleaning, gardening, raising children, attending to the needs of their husbands. Some black husbands refused to allow their wives to work as servants in white homes. "When I married my wife I married her to wait on me," one freedman told a former master who was attempting to hire his wife as a servant. "She got all she can do right here for me and the children."

But the effort to adapt the ideal of "domesticity" to the black family encountered at least some resistance. Not all black women wished to emulate the roles of their white counterparts—particularly those black women who, as former house servants, had observed the lives of white women closely. More important, however, economic necessity often required black women to engage in income-producing activities: working as domestic servants, taking in laundry, or helping their husbands in the field. By the end of Reconstruction, fully half of all black women over the age of sixteen were engaged in paid labor of some sort. And unlike among the whites, most black female income earners were married.

The Grant Administration

Exhausted by the political turmoil of the Johnson administration, American voters in 1868 yearned for a strong, stable figure to guide them through the troubled years of Reconstruction. They did not find one. Instead, they turned trustingly to General Ulysses S. Grant, the conquering hero of the war and, by 1868, a widely revered national idol. Grant had been an inspired general, but he was a disastrous president. During his two terms in office, he faced problems that would have taxed the abilities of a master of statecraft. Grant, whatever his qualities, was no such leader. He was, rather, a generally dull and unimaginative man with few political skills and little real vision.

The Soldier President

Grant could have had the nomination of either party in 1868. But as he watched the congressional Radicals triumph over President Johnson, he concluded that the Radical Reconstruction policy expressed the real wishes of the people; so he was receptive when the Radical leaders approached him with offers of the Republican nomination. Virtually without opposition, he received the endorsement of the party convention. The Democrats nominated former governor Horace Seymour of New York. The campaign was a bitter one, and Grant's triumph was by no means overwhelming. Grant carried twenty-six states and Seymour only eight. But Grant received only 3,013,000 popular votes to Seymour's 2,703,000, a scant majority of 310,000; and this majority was a result of black votes in the reconstructed states of the South.

Ulysses S. Grant entered the White House with no political experience of any kind. After graduating from West Point with no particular distinction, Grant had entered the regular army, from which after years of service he had resigned under something of a cloud. In civilian life he undertook several dismal ventures that barely yielded him a living. His career before 1861 could be characterized as forty years of failure. Then came the Civil War, and Grant found at last the one setting, the one vocation for which he was supremely equipped—combat.

In choosing his official family, Grant proceeded as if he were creating a military staff. He sent several appointments to the Senate for confirmation without asking the recipients if they would serve; they first heard the news in the papers. Hamilton Fish, whom Grant appointed secretary of state, had been out of politics for twenty years when he heard the news that his name had been submitted to the Senate. He wired Grant that he could not accept, but he ultimately agreed to serve. Fish proved to be one of Grant's few truly distinguished appointees. Most of his later appointments went to men who were at best average and at worst incompetent or corrupt or both. Increasingly, Grant came to rely on the machine leaders in the party—the group most ardently devoted to the spoils system.

Diplomatic Successes

The Grant administration and the Johnson administration achieved their greatest success in foreign affairs. These were the accomplishments not of the presidents themselves, who displayed little aptitude for diplomacy, but of two outstanding secretaries of state: William H. Seward, who had served Lincoln during the Civil War and remained in office until 1869; and Hamilton Fish, who served throughout the two terms of the Grant administration.

An ardent expansionist and advocate of a vigorous foreign policy, Seward acted with as much daring as the demands of Reconstruction politics and the Republican hatred of President Johnson would permit. When Russia let it be known that it would like to sell Alaska to the United States, Seward readily agreed to pay the asking price of $7.2 million. Only by strenuous efforts was he able to induce the Senate to ratify the treaty and the House to appropriate the money (1867–1868). Critics jeered that the secretary had bought a useless frozen wasteland—"Seward's Icebox" some critics called it. But Alaska was an important fishing center in the North Pacific, and it was potentially rich in such resources as gold (and, as the nation would discover much later, oil). Seward was not content with expansion in continental North America. In 1867, he engineered the annexation of the tiny Midway Islands west of Hawaii.

In contrast with its sometimes shambling course in domestic politics, the performance of the Grant administration in the area of foreign affairs was, under the direction of Hamilton Fish, generally decisive and firm. A number of delicate and potentially dangerous situations confronted Fish from the beginning, but the most serious one arose out of a burning American grievance against England that had origi-

"Seward's Folly"
The American purchase of Alaska from Russia (engineereed by Secretary of State William Seward) was ridiculed in this 1867 cartoon. The drawing suggests the widespread belief that Alaska was a useless frozen wasteland unfit for human habitation and populated only by polar bears. (Bettmann Archive)

nated during the Civil War. Many Americans believed that the British government had violated the laws of neutrality by permitting Confederate ships, the *Alabama* and others, to be built and armed in English shipyards and let loose to prey on Northern commerce. American demands that England pay for the damages committed by these vessels became known as the *"Alabama* claims."

Seward tried earnestly to settle the *Alabama* claims before leaving office, but to no avail. The one successful effort to negotiate a settlement—the Johnson-Clarendon Convention of 1869, which would have submitted claims on both sides to arbitration—was rejected by the Senate shortly after Johnson left office because it contained no British apology. The debate featured a speech by Charles Sumner, chairman of the Committee on Foreign Relations, arguing that Britain's conduct had prolonged the war by two years. Therefore, Sumner insisted, England owed the United States for "direct damages" committed by the ships and "indirect damages" for the cost of the war for two years—which would have reached the staggering total of some $2 billion.

England naturally would have nothing to do with any arrangement involving indirect claims, and settlement of the problem was temporarily stalled. Secretary Fish, however, continued to work for a solution, and finally, in 1871, the two countries agreed to the Treaty of Washington, providing for international arbitration of the issue and other pending controversies. In the treaty, Britain expressed regret for the escape of the *Alabama* and agreed to a set of rules governing neutral obligations that in effect conceded the case to the United States. This meant that the arbitrators would have only to fix the sum to be paid by Britain. They awarded $15.5 million to the United States.

The Defection of the Liberals

On both international and domestic matters, a wide breach soon developed between President Grant and a number of prominent Republicans, among them the famous Radical Charles Sumner. Sumner's extravagant demand for damages from Great Britain embarrassed Secretary Fish. Sumner also blocked a treaty for the annexation of Santo Domingo (now the Dominican Republic), a project in which Grant took a deep, even monomaniacal personal interest. The angry president got revenge by inducing his Senate friends to remove Sumner from the chairmanship of the Committee on Foreign Relations.

Among the principal political controversies of these years was the spoils system of presidential appointments, which Grant had used even more blatantly than most of his predecessors to reward party machine politicians. Sumner and other Republican leaders joined with reformers to agitate for a new civil service system to limit the president's appointive powers. Such scholarly journalists as E. L. Godkin of *The Nation* and George William Curtis of *Harper's Weekly* argued that the government should base its appointments not on services to the party but on fitness for office as determined by competitive examinations, as the British government already was doing. Grant reluctantly agreed to establish a civil service commission, which Congress authorized in 1871, to

devise a system of hiring based on merit. This agency, under the direction of Curtis, proposed a set of rules that seemed to meet with Grant's approval. But Grant was not really much interested in reform, and even if he had been he could not have persuaded his followers to accept a new system that would undermine the very basis of party loyalty—patronage. Congress declined to renew the commission's appropriation, and the commission disbanded.

Nevertheless, controversy over civil-service reform remained one of the leading political issues of the next three decades of American life. The debate involved more than simply an argument over patronage and corruption. It reflected, too, basic differences of opinion over who was fit to serve in public life. Middle-class reformers were saying, implicitly, that only educated, middle-class people (the "best men") should be permitted access to government office. Those opposing them—not simply party leaders but immigrant and labor groups, some farmers, and others—argued that the establishment of an elite corps of civil servants would exclude these groups from participation in government and restrict power to the upper classes.

Republican critics of the president also denounced him for his support of Radical Reconstruction. Grant continued to station federal troops in the South, and on many occasions he sent them to support Republican governments that were on the point of collapse. To growing numbers in the North this seemed like dangerous militarism, and they were more and more disgusted by the stories of governmental corruption and extravagance in the South. Some Republicans were beginning to suspect that there was corruption not only in the Southern state governments but also in the federal government. Still others criticized Grant because he had declined to speak out in favor of a reduction of the tariff.

Thus before the end of Grant's first term, members of his own party had begun to oppose him for a variety of reasons, all of which added up to what the critics called "Grantism." In 1872, hoping to prevent Grant's reelection, his opponents bolted the party. Referring to themselves as Liberal Republicans, they nominated their own presidential and vice-presidential candidates. Horace Greeley, veteran editor and publisher of the New York *Tribune*, headed their ticket. The Democratic convention, seeing in Greeley's candidacy (and in the alliance with the Liberals it would achieve) the only chance to unseat Grant and the Republicans, endorsed Greeley with no great enthusiasm. Despite Greeley's recent attacks on Radical Reconstruction, many Southerners, remembering his own Radical past, chose to stay home on election day. Grant polled 286 electoral votes and 3,597,000 popular votes to Greeley's 66 and 2,834,000. Greeley had carried only two Southern and four border states. Three weeks later, apparently crushed by his defeat, Greeley died.

The Grant Scandals

During the campaign, the first of a series of political scandals had come to light. It originated with the Crédit Mobilier construction company, which had helped build the Union Pacific Railroad. The Crédit Mobilier was, in fact, controlled by a few Union Pacific stockholders who had awarded huge and fraudulent contracts to the construction company, thus milking the Union Pacific, a company of which they owned only a minor share, of money that in part came from government subsidies. To avert a congressional inquiry into the deal, the directors in effect gave Crédit Mobilier stock to key members of Congress. A congressional investigation in 1872 revealed that some highly placed Republicans—including Schuyler Colfax, now Grant's vice president—had accepted stock.

One dreary episode followed another in Grant's second term. Benjamin H. Bristow, Grant's third Treasury secretary, discovered that some of his officials and a group of distillers operating as a "whiskey ring" were cheating the government out of taxes by means of false reports. Among those involved was the president's private secretary, Orville E. Babcock. Grant defended Babcock, appointed him to another office, and eased Bristow out of the cabinet. Then a House investigation revealed that William W. Belknap, secretary of war, had accepted bribes to retain an Indian-post trader in office. Belknap resigned with Grant's blessing before the Senate could act on impeachment charges brought by the House. Other, lesser scandals added to the growing impression that "Grantism" had brought rampant corruption to government.

The Greenback Question

Meanwhile, the Grant administration and the nation at large suffered another blow: the Panic of 1873. It began with the failure of a leading investment banking firm, Jay Cooke and Company, which had in-

The Grant Scandals

Grant's last years in office were plagued by revelations of scandals at various levels of the government. Although the president himself was never shown to have been involved, his reputation suffered nevertheless. This cartoon from *Puck* magazine shows Grant providing support for various corrupt members of his administration. (Historical Pictures Service)

vested too heavily in postwar railroad building. Depressions had come before with almost rhythmic regularity—in 1819, 1837, and 1857—but this was the worst one yet. It lasted four years.

Debtors pressured the government to follow an inflationary policy, which would have made it easier for them to pay their debts. But President Grant and most Republicans preferred what they called a "sound" currency—based solidly on gold reserves—

which was to the advantage of the banks, money-lenders, and other creditors. The money question had confronted Grant and the Republicans in Congress from the beginning of his administration. The question was twofold: How should the war bonds be paid? And what should be the permanent place of greenbacks in the national currency? Representatives of the debtor interests argued that the bonds should be redeemed in greenbacks, thus increasing the amount of currency in circulation. The president favored payment in gold, and the Republican Congress moved speedily to promise redemption in "coin or its equivalent"; but refunding of the debt was to stretch out over a number of years.

The question of what to do about the greenbacks, however, remained unresolved. When Grant entered the White House, approximately $356 million of greenbacks were circulating. And in 1873, when the Supreme Court reversed an earlier decision and, in *Knox* v. *Lee*, affirmed the legality of greenbacks, the Treasury moved to increase the amount in circulation in response to the panic. For the same reason Congress, in the following year, voted to raise the total further. Grant, responding to pressures from Eastern financial interests, vetoed the measure—over the loud objections of many members of his own party.

With the greenback issue becoming more and more heated and divisive, and with an election year approaching, Republican leaders in Congress began searching for some way to settle the controversy. Their solution—introduced initially by Senator John Sherman of Ohio—was the Specie Resumption Act of 1875. This law provided that after January 1, 1879, the government would redeem greenback dollars at par with gold; that is, the present greenbacks, whose value constantly fluctuated, could be exchanged for new paper currency, whose value would be firmly pegged to the price of gold. The law protected the interests of the creditor classes, who had worried that debts would be repaid in debased paper currency. In theory, the new law protected the interests of debtor groups as well, by calling for an increase in the amount of specie-backed currency in circulation. In fact, however, "resumption" did not satisfy those who had been clamoring for an increase in greenbacks, because the gold-based money supply was never able to expand as much as they believed was necessary.

Thus the greenback issue survived after 1875, and the question of the proper composition of the currency now emerged as one of the most controversial and enduring issues in American politics. Creditors and established financial interests continued to insist on a sound currency based on gold. Debtor groups—farmers, laborers, and some manufacturers—and debtor regions—the South and the West—continued to clamor for a currency based not on gold reserves but on the productive capacity of the nation. Otherwise, they claimed, they would continue to be strangled by an overvalued dollar circulating in insufficient quantities.

The question of greenbacks and the many other currency controversies that followed also became symbols of much deeper concerns. Agrarian dissidents and others came to see in the maintenance of the gold standard a conspiracy by entrenched financiers to keep farmers in economic bondage. Southerners and Westerners saw in the currency policies evidence of their subordination to the Northeast. Because in accepting the gold standard the United States was following the example of Great Britain and other European nations, many Americans came to view the policy as part of a dire international plot to enslave the American people. The greenbackers, as they were called, expressed their displeasure in 1875 by forming their own political organization: the National Greenback party. Active in the next three presidential elections, it failed to gain widespread support. But it did keep the money issue alive. And in the 1880s, the greenback forces began to merge with another, more powerful group of currency reformers—those who favored silver as the basis of currency—to help produce a political movement that would ultimately attain enormous strength.

The Abandonment of Reconstruction

As the North grew increasingly preoccupied with its own political and economic problems, interest in Reconstruction began to wane. The Grant administration continued to protect Republican governments in the South, but less because of any interest in ensuring the position of freedmen than because of a desire to prevent the reemergence of a strong Democratic party in the region. But even the presence of federal troops was not enough to prevent white Southerners from overturning many of the Republican governments that they believed had been so ruthlessly thrust upon them. In a few states, the Democrats (or Conservatives) returned to power almost as soon as civilian government was restored. In Virginia, North Carolina, and Georgia, Republican rule came to an end before or by 1871. In other states, the Democrats gradually regained control over several years. Texas was "redeemed"—as Southerners liked to call the restoration of Democratic rule—in 1873; Alabama and Arkansas in 1874; and Mississippi in 1876. For three other states—South Carolina, Louisiana, and Florida—the end of Reconstruction had to wait for the withdrawal of the last federal troops in 1876, a withdrawal that was the result of a long process of political bargaining and compromise at the national level.

The Southern States "Redeemed"

In the states where whites constituted a majority—the states of the upper South—overthrow of Republican control was a relatively simple matter. The whites had only to organize and win the elections. Restoration of suffrage to those whites who had been deprived of it helped them in their task. Presidential and congressional pardons returned the vote to numerous individuals; and in 1872, Congress passed the Amnesty Act, which restored political rights to 150,000 ex-Confederates and left only 500 excluded from political life.

In other states, where blacks were in the majority or the populations of the two races were almost equal, the whites resorted to intimidation and violence. Secret societies, complete with hooded robes and elaborate rituals, appeared in many parts of the South: the Ku Klux Klan, the Knights of the White Camellia, and others. They were frankly terroristic and attempted to frighten or physically prevent blacks from voting. Moving quickly to stamp out these societies, Congress passed two bills (1870 and 1871), which white Southerners called "force acts," and the Ku Klux Klan Act (also in 1871). These measures authorized the president to use military force and martial law in areas where the orders were active. Only rarely, however, did the laws have a significant impact.

More potent than the secret orders were open semimilitary organizations in the South that operated as rifle clubs under such names as Red Shirts and White Leagues. The first such society was founded in Mississippi, and the idea soon spread to other states; their tactics were called the Mississippi Plan. The plan called for whites in each community to organize and arm, and to be prepared, if necessary, to use force to win elections. But the heart of the scheme was in the phrase "drawing the color line." By one method or another, legal or illegal, every white man was to be

Klansmen

Two members of the Ku Klux Klan, dressed in their regalia, posed in a studio for this photograph. (The figure on the left has apparently been defaced through the addition of a beard and side whiskers.) Organized at first as a social club, the Klan became a powerful political organization in the early years of Reconstruction. Ex-Confederate General Nathan Bedford Forrest became "Grand Wizard" in 1867 and attempted to make the order a respectable, patriotic organization. But Klansmen increasingly resorted to violence and intimidation in their efforts to suppress their foes, and they suffered as well from crimes committed in their name by outsiders. In 1869 Forrest resigned as leader and ordered the organization to disband. Shortly thereafter, Congress passed legislation restricting Klan activities and ultimately declared the organization illegal. It maintained a covert life, however, until the late nineteenth century. The modern Ku Klux Klan, founded in 1915, has no direct link to the Reconstruction order. (Rutherford B. Hayes Library) forced to join the Democratic party or leave the community. By similar methods, every black male was to be excluded from political activity. In a few states, blacks were to be permitted to vote—if they voted Democratic.

Perhaps an even stronger influence than the techniques practiced by the armed bands was the simple weapon of economic pressure. The war had freed the slaves, but they were still laborers—hired workers or tenants—dependent on whites for their livelihood. Whites quickly discovered ways to use this dependence to increase their power over blacks. Planters refused to rent land to Republican blacks; storekeepers refused to extend them credit; employers refused to give them work. Without a secure economic base of their own—something Reconstruction had done nothing to give them—blacks were powerless to resist these pressures.

Southern blacks were, in the meantime, losing the support of many of their former supporters in the North, even of many humanitarian reformers who had worked for emancipation and equal rights. After the adoption of the Fifteenth Amendment in 1870, most reformers convinced themselves that their long campaign in behalf of black people at last was over; that with the vote, blacks ought to be able to take care of themselves. The party split of 1872, in part a response to the perceived corruption in Southern Reconstruction governments, weakened the Republicans in the South still further. Former Radical leaders such as Charles Sumner and Horace Greeley now began calling themselves Liberals, cooperating with the Democrats and outdoing even the Democrats in denunciations of what they viewed as black-and-carpetbag misgovernment. Within the South itself, many white Republicans joined the Liberals and moved into the Democratic party. Friction between black Republicans and those whites who remained in the party grew because of a well-justified feeling on the part of the blacks that they were not receiving a fair share of the power and the jobs.

The depression that began in 1873 aggravated political discontent in both the North and the South. In the congressional elections of 1874, the Democrats gained a majority of the seats in the House of Representatives, thus denying the Republicans control of the whole Congress for the first time since 1861. And President Grant, in view of the changing temper of the North, no longer was willing to use military force to prop up the Republican regimes that were still standing in the South. In 1875, when the Mississippi governor, Adelbert Ames (originally from Maine),

appealed to Washington for troops to protect blacks from the terrorism of the Democrats, he received in reply a telegram that quoted Grant as saying: "The whole public are tired out with these annual autumnal outbreaks in the South, and the great majority are now ready to condemn any interference on the part of the government."

After the Democrats gained political control of Mississippi, only three states were left in the hands of the Republicans—South Carolina, Louisiana, and Florida. In the elections of 1876, again using terrorist tactics, the Democrats claimed victory in all three. But the Republicans claimed victory as well, and they were able to continue holding office because federal troops happened to be on the scene. If the troops were to be withdrawn, the last of the Republican regimes would fall. Resolution of the conflict would depend on the presidential election of 1876, which was itself in dispute because of the electoral controversies in the South.

The Compromise of 1877

Ulysses S. Grant was eager to run for another term in 1876, but the majority of the Republican leaders refused to consider him. Impressed by the recent upsurge of Democratic strength and fearful that a third-term campaign would create controversy, they searched for a candidate who was not associated with the scandals of the past eight years and could entice the Liberals back into the fold and unite the party until after the election. Senator James G. Blaine of Maine offered himself, but he had recently been involved in an allegedly crooked railroad deal. The Republican convention settled instead on Rutherford B. Hayes, a former Union army officer and congressman, three times governor of Ohio, and a champion of civil-service reform.

No personal rivalries divided the Democrats. Only one aspirant commanded serious attention: Governor Samuel J. Tilden of New York, whose name had become synonymous with governmental reform. A corporation lawyer and a millionaire, Tilden had long been a power in the Democratic organization of his state, but he had not hesitated to turn against the corrupt Tweed Ring of New York City's Tammany Hall and aid in its overthrow. His fight against Tweed brought him national fame and the governorship, in which position he increased his reputation for honest administration.

The campaign was an unusually bitter one, but there were in fact almost no differences of principle between the candidates. Hayes supported withdrawal of troops from the South and civil-service reform, and his record for probity was equal to Tilden's. Tilden vaguely supported a tariff reduction, but on other economic issues he was at least as conservative as his rival. He supported the gold standard—"sound money"—and he believed that government had no business interfering with economic interests. He looked on himself as a modern counterpart of Thomas Jefferson.

The November election produced an apparent Democratic victory. Tilden carried the South and several large Northern states, and his popular vote was 4,301,000 to 4,036,000 for Hayes. But the situation was complicated by the disputed returns from Louisiana, South Carolina, and Florida, whose total electoral vote was 19. Both parties claimed to have won these states, and double sets of returns were presented to Congress. Adding to the confusion was a contested vote in Oregon, where one of the three successful Republican electors was declared ineligible because he held a federal office. The Democrats contended that the place should go to the Democratic elector with the highest number of votes; but the Republicans insisted that according to state law, the remaining electors were to select someone to fill the vacancy. The disputed returns threw the outcome of the election into doubt. As tension and excitement gripped the country, two clear facts emerged from the welter of conflicting claims. Tilden had undisputed claim to 184 electoral votes, only one short of the majority. The 20 votes in controversy would determine who would be president, and Hayes needed all of them to secure the office.

With surprise and consternation, the nation now learned that no method existed to determine the validity of disputed returns. The Constitution stated: "The President of the Senate shall, in the presence of the Senate and House of Representatives, open all the certificates and the votes shall then be counted." The question was, how and by whom? The Senate was Republican and so, of course, was its president; the House was Democratic. Constitutional ambiguity and congressional division rendered a fair and satisfactory solution of the crisis impossible. If the president of the Senate counted the votes, Hayes would be the victor. If the Senate and House judged the returns separately, they would reach opposite decisions and checkmate each other. And if the houses voted jointly, the Democrats, with a numerical ma-

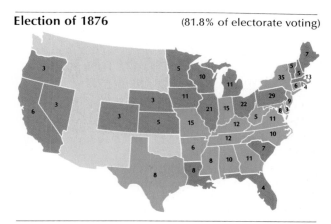

Election of 1876 (81.8% of electorate voting)

	ELECTORAL VOTE	POPULAR VOTE (%)
Rutherford B. Hayes (Republican)	185	4,036,298 (48)
Samuel J. Tilden (Democratic)	184	4,300,590 (51)

jority, would decide the result. Resort to any one of these lines of action promised to divide the country and possibly result in chaos.

Not until the last days of January 1877 did Congress act to break the deadlock by creating a special electoral commission to pass on all the disputed votes. The commission was to be composed of five senators, five representatives, and five justices of the Supreme Court. The congressional delegation would consist of five Republicans and five Democrats. The Court delegation, as established by the legislation creating the commission, would consist of two Republicans, two Democrats, and an independent. But before the commission could meet, the designated independent was elected to the Senate and resigned his seat on the Court. His place on the commission fell to a more partisan Republican. The commission sat throughout February and reached decisions by a straight party vote of 8 to 7, awarding every disputed vote to Hayes. Congress accepted the final verdict of the commission on March 2, only two days before the inauguration of the new president.

Ratification of the commission's findings, however, required a series of elaborate compromises among leaders of both parties. Behind the dealing, and partially directing it, were certain powerful economic forces with a stake in the outcome. Republican leaders, hoping to end a Democratic filibuster in the Senate, met secretly with Southern Democratic leaders to work out terms by which they would support the election of Hayes. According to the traditional account, certain Republicans and Southern Democrats met at Washington's Wormley Hotel, and the Republicans pledged that Hayes, after becoming president, would withdraw the troops from the South. Since withdrawal would mean the downfall of the last carpetbag governments, the Southerners, convinced they were getting as much from Hayes as they could get from Tilden, agreed to abandon the filibuster.

Actually, the story behind the "Compromise of 1877" is somewhat more complex. Hayes was on record before the election as favoring withdrawal of the troops, and in any event the Democrats in the House could have forced withdrawal simply by cutting out appropriations for the army in the Reconstruction process. The real agreement, the one that won the Southern Democrats over, was reached before the Wormley meeting. As the price of their cooperation, the Southern Democrats (among them some old Whigs) exacted from the Republicans the following pledges: the appointment of at least one Southerner to the Hayes cabinet, control of federal patronage in their areas, generous internal improvements, federal aid for the Texas and Pacific Railroad, and, finally, withdrawal of the troops. Many of the Conservatives who controlled the Democratic parties of the redeemed Southern states were interested in industrializing the South, and they believed that the Republican program of federal aid to business would be more beneficial for their region than the archaic states' rights policy of the Democrats.

In his inaugural address, Hayes spoke primarily about the Southern problem. While he was careful to say that the rights of blacks must be preserved, he announced that the most pressing need of the South was the restoration of "wise, honest, and peaceful local self-government"—a signal that he planned to withdraw the troops and let the whites take over control of the state governments. Hayes knew that this would lend weight to charges that he was paying off the South for acquiescing in his election and would strengthen those critics who referred to him as "his Fraudulency." But in fact, the political crisis surrounding the election had already created such bitterness there was probably nothing Hayes could have done to mollify his critics.

The president hoped to build up a "new Republican" party in the South composed of whatever conservative white groups could be weaned away from the Democrats and committed to some acceptance of black rights. But his efforts, which included a tour of

Southern cities and even the decoration of a memorial to the Confederate war dead, failed. Although many Southern leaders sympathized with the economic credo of the Republicans, they could not advise their people to support the party that had imposed Reconstruction. Nor were Southerners pleased by Hayes's bestowal of federal offices on carpetbaggers or by his vetoes of Democratic attempts to repeal the force acts. The "solid South," although not yet fully formed, was beginning to take shape. Neither Hayes nor any other Republican could reverse the trend—particularly since no one was willing to use federal power to protect black voting rights, which alone held promise of giving the Republicans lasting strength in the region. The withdrawal of the troops was a signal that the national government was giving up its attempt to control Southern politics and to determine the place of blacks in Southern society.

The Tragedy of Reconstruction

The record of the Reconstruction years is not one of complete failure, as many have charged. That slavery would be abolished was clear well before the end of the war; but Reconstruction worked other changes upon Southern society as well. There was a significant redistribution of income, from which blacks benefited. There was a more limited but not unimportant redistribution of land ownership, which enabled some former slaves to acquire property for the first time. There was both a relative and an absolute improvement in the economic circumstances of most blacks.

Nor was Reconstruction as disastrous an experience for Southern whites as most believed at the time. The region had emerged from a prolonged and bloody war defeated and devastated; and yet within a decade, the South had regained control of its own institutions and, to a great extent, restored its traditional ruling class to power. No harsh punishments were meted out to former Confederate leaders. No drastic program of economic reform was imposed on the region. Few lasting political changes were forced on the South. Not many conquered nations fare as well.

Yet for all that, Americans of the twentieth century cannot help but look back on Reconstruction as a tragic era. For in those years the United States made its first serious effort to resolve its oldest and deepest social problem—the problem of race. And it failed in the effort. What was more, the experience so disap-

SIGNIFICANT EVENTS

1863   Lincoln announces preliminary Reconstruction plan

1864   Louisiana, Arkansas, Tennessee readmitted to Union under Lincoln plan

Wade-Davis bill passed

1865   Lincoln assassinated; Andrew Johnson becomes president (April 14)

Johnson readmits rest of Confederate states to Union under Lincoln plan

Black Codes enacted in South

Freedmen's Bureau established

Congress reconvenes (December) and refuses to admit Southern representatives; creates Joint Committee on Reconstruction

1866   Freedmen's Bureau renewed over Johnson's veto

Congress approves Fourteenth Amendment; most Southern states reject it

Republicans gain in congressional elections

Ex parte Milligan challenges Radicals' Reconstruction plans

Ku Klux Klan formed in South

1867   Military Reconstruction Act (and two supplementary acts) outlines congressional plan of Reconstruction

Tenure of Office Act and Command of the Army Act restrict presidential power

Southern states establish Reconstruction governments under congressional plan

Alaska purchased

1868   Most Southern states readmitted to Congress under congressional plan

Andrew Johnson impeached but not convicted

Fourteenth Amendment ratified

Ulysses S. Grant elected president

1869   Congress passes Fifteenth Amendment

First "redeemer" governments elected in South

1870   Last Southern states readmitted to Congress

Force Act passed

1871   *Alabama* claims settled

1872   Liberal Republicans defect

Grant reelected president

1873   Commercial and financial panic disrupts economy

1875   Civil Rights Act passed

Specie Resumption Act passed

"Whiskey ring" scandal discredits Grant administration

1877   Rutherford B. Hayes elected president after disputed election

Last federal troops withdrawn from South after Compromise of 1877

Last Southern states "redeemed"

---

pointed, disillusioned, and embittered the nation that it would be many years before an attempt would be made again.

Why did this great assault on racial injustice—an assault that had emerged over a period of more than fifty years—end so badly? In part, of course, it was because of the weaknesses and errors of the people who directed it. But in greater part, it was because the resolution of the racial problem required a far more fundamental reform of society than Americans of the time were willing to make. One after another, attempts to produce solutions ran up against conservative obstacles so deeply embedded in the nation's life that they could not be dislodged. Veneration of the Constitution sharply limited the willingness of

national leaders to infringe on the rights of states and individuals in creating social change. A profound respect for private property and free enterprise prevented any real assault on economic privilege in the South, ensuring that blacks would not win title to the land and wealth they believed they deserved. Above all, perhaps, a pervasive belief among even the most liberal whites that the black race was inherently inferior served as an obstacle to the full equality of the freedmen. Given the context within which Americans of the 1860s and 1870s were working, what is surprising, perhaps, is not that Reconstruction did so little, but that it did even as much as it did. The era was tragic not just because it was a failure—the failure may have been inevitable from the beginning—

but also because it revealed how great the barriers were to racial justice in the United States.

Given the odds confronting them, therefore, black Americans had reason for pride in the limited gains they were able to make during Reconstruction. And the nation at large had reason for gratitude that, if nothing else, the postwar era produced two great charters of freedom—the Fourteenth and Fifteenth amendments to the Constitution—which, although largely ignored at the time, would one day serve as the basis for a "Second Reconstruction," one that would renew the drive to bring freedom and equality to all Americans.

SUGGESTED READINGS

General Studies The studies by McPherson and by Randall and Donald cited in the readings for the previous two chapters are likewise valuable for the Reconstruction period, both for their narratives of the era and for their bibliographies. William A. Dunning, *Reconstruction, Political and Economic, 1865–1977* (1907), long the standard study of Reconstruction, is now widely conceded to be marred by deep prejudices. More recent overviews of the period, better in tune with contemporary values, are Kenneth Stampp, *The Era of Reconstruction* (1965), and John Hope Franklin, *Reconstruction After the Civil War* (1961). W. E. B. Du Bois, *Black Reconstruction* (1935), is an early challenge to the pro-Southern orthodoxy about the period; whereas E. Merton Coulter, *The South During Reconstruction* (1947), adheres strictly to traditional views of the period as a time of Northern vindictiveness and Southern suffering. Rembert Patrick, *The Reconstruction of the Nation* (1967), is a modern overview that provides more detail than the relatively brief studies by Stampp and Franklin.

Presidential Reconstruction Herman Belz, *Reconstructing the Union* (1969), examines the theoretical basis of the Reconstruction problem. William B. Hesseltine, *Lincoln's Plan of Reconstruction* (1960), considers the first presidential plan; and Willie Lee Rose, *Rehearsal for Reconstruction: The Port Royal Experiment* (1964), describes wartime reconstruction policies in an area of South Carolina captured early by the Union. Louis S. Gerteis, *From Contraband to Freedman* (1973), examines federal policy toward blacks during the war itself. Richard H. Abbott, *The First Southern Strategy* (1986), is a study of early Southern efforts to shape postwar politics and society.

Congressional Reconstruction There are several valuable studies of the political battles that accompanied the switch from presidential to congressional Reconstruction. William R. Brock, *An American Crisis* (1963), is a particularly judicious work. Howard K. Beale, *The Critical Year: A Study of Andrew Johnson and Reconstruction* (1930), is a traditional approach to the subject; Eric McKitrick, *Andrew Johnson and Reconstruction* (1960), is far more hostile toward Johnson. Two works by Michael Les Benedict, *A Compromise of Principle: Congressional Republicans and Reconstruction, 1863–1869* (1974) and *The Impeachment and Trial of Andrew Johnson* (1973), consider congressional politics and antagonisms toward the president. Hans L. Trefousse, *The Radical Republicans* (1963), and David Donald, *The Politics of Re-*

construction (1965), also examine congressional Radicals. Hans Trefousse is the author of another study of the impeachment proceedings, *The Impeachment of a President* (1975). La Wanda Cox and John H. Cox, *Politics, Principles, and Prejudice, 1865–1867* (1963), is an early work that was important in revising previous views of Reconstruction politics. Also useful for the politics of the era are biographies of leading Reconstruction figures. Richard N. Current, *Old Thad Stevens* (1942), is a hostile view; Fawn Brodie, *Thaddeus Stevens* (1959), is more sympathetic. David Donald, *Charles Sumner and the Rights of Man* (1970), is also important. Harold Hyman, *A More Perfect Union* (1973), and Stanley Kutler, *The Judicial Power and Reconstruction Politics* (1968), examine the constitutional problems that Reconstruction posed. Mark W. Summers, *Railroads, Reconstruction, and the Gospel of Prosperity* (1984), explores some of the economic factors shaping policy. Charles Fairman, *Reconstruction and Reunion* (1971), considers the Supreme Court in the postwar years. See also Herman Belz, *A New Birth of Freedom* (1976) and *Emancipation and Equal Rights* (1978). William Gillette, *The Right to Vote* (1965), is a study of the framing of the Fifteenth Amendment.

The South in Reconstruction Two works by Michael Perman, *Reunion Without Compromise* (1973) and *The Road to Redemption: Southern Politics, 1869–1879* (1984), examine white Southern resistance to Reconstruction. Valuable works on individual states include Joel G. Taylor, *Louisiana Reconstructed* (1974); Vernon Wharton, *The Negro in Mississippi, 1865–1890* (1965); Peyton McCrary, *Abraham Lincoln and Reconstruction* (1978), on policies toward Louisiana; Joel Williamson, *After Slavery: The Negro in South Carolina During Reconstruction* (1965); Thomas Holt, *Black over White* (1977), also on South Carolina; C. Peter Ripley, *Slaves and Freedmen in Civil War Louisiana* (1976); and Michael Wayne, *The Reshaping of Plantation Society: The Natchez District* (1983), on Mississippi. William Gillette, *Retreat from Reconstruction* (1980), examines the end of Reconstruction in the South. A valuable study of the economic impact of Reconstruction on the South is Roger Ransom and Richard Sutch, *One Kind of Freedom* (1977). Robert Higgs, *Competition and Coercion* (1977), is a controversial economic analysis of the period. Crandall A. Shifflett, *Patronage and Poverty in the Tobacco South: Louisa County, Virginia, 1860–1900* (1982), examines planters during Reconstruction. Leon Litwack, *Been in the Storm So Long* (1979), Eric Foner, *Nothing But Freedom: Emancipation and Its Legacy* (1983), and Peter

Kolchin, *First Freedom* (1972), examine the effects of Reconstruction on blacks. Allen Trelease, *White Terror* (1967), discusses the Ku Klux Klan. William S. McFeely, *Yankee Stepfather: General O. O. Howard and the Freedmen* (1968), portrays the head of the Freedmen's Bureau; and George Bentley, *A History of the Freedmen's Bureau* (1955), examines the institution itself. On carpetbaggers, see Otto Olsen, *Carpetbagger's Crusade: Albion Winegar Tourgée* (1965); L. N. Powell, *New Masters: Northern Planters During the Civil War and Reconstruction* (1980); William C. Harris, *The Day of the Carpetbagger: Republican Reconstruction in Mississippi, 1867–1975* (1979); and Elizabeth Jacoway, *Yankee Missionaries in the South* (1979). Sarah Wiggins, *The Scalawag in Alabama Politics, 1865–1881* (1977), examines Southern "collaborationists." Likewise valuable are Jacqueline Jones, *Soldiers of Light and Love* (1980), and James Sefton, *The United States Army and Reconstruction* (1967).

The Grant Administration   The best biography of the president is William McFeely, *Grant* (1981). Allan Nevins, *Hamilton Fish* (1936), is a biography of the secretary of state that provides a portrait of the administration as a whole. William B. Hesseltine, *U. S. Grant, Politician* (1935), is another study of the Grant presidency. On the scandals of the era, see David Loth, *Public Plunder* (1938). John G. Sproat, *The Best Men* (1968), examines the role of liberal reformers during the period. Specific political controversies of the time are considered in Ari Hoogenboom, *Outlawing the Spoils* (1961), on civil-service reform, and Irwin Unger, *The Greenback Era* (1964), on monetary controversies. Two views of the compromise of 1877 are C. Vann Woodward, *Reunion and Reaction* (1951), and K. I. Polakoff, *The Politics of Inertia* (1973). Edwin C. Rozwenc (ed.), *Reconstruction in the South*, rev. ed. (1952), is a valuable collection of essays on the subject.

Progress and Its Discontents, 1877–1920

America's industrial revolution had begun well before the Civil War, and by the end of Reconstruction it was already far advanced. But it was in the last thirty years of the nineteenth century that the revolution came of age. During these decades, the United States transformed itself from a predominantly rural, agrarian society into a highly industrialized, urbanized one. It moved from a position of relative unimportance in world affairs to that of a major international power. It changed from a fragmented, largely provincial society into an increasingly centralized and consolidated one. It became a modern nation.

It became, too, a nation with a sharply divided view of itself and its future. On the one hand, most Americans took pride in their country's remarkable economic growth, in its great technological advances, in its enhanced world power. They had good reason to do so. The United States by 1900 was the leading industrial nation on earth, and the potential of its economy seemed virtually unlimited. Its natural resources were plentiful. Its labor supply was large and growing. Its technological and administrative capacities were becoming more and more sophisticated. The nation was, its people sensed, on the eve of an era of unbounded prosperity.

P·A·R·T F·I·V·E

But the last years of the nineteenth century also gave Americans reason for alarm. For along with the undoubted benefits of economic growth had come great costs: crowded cities, concentrations of power, disparities of wealth, political corruption, and general instability. Nor had economic growth done very much to solve some of the nation's oldest problems. Large segments of the population—blacks, Indians, many members of the industrial work force, major immigrant groups, most women—were finding themselves excluded from the fruits of industrial progress just as they had often found themselves excluded from the mainstream of national life in the past. Entire regions of the country—the South and much of the West, both of which remained primarily agricultural—similarly did not much share in the nation's prosperity and at times seethed with discontent. These and other problems combined in the 1890s to produce a series of wrenching social and economic crises.

In the course of that turbulent decade, the nation experienced upheavals in one area of society after another. Industrial workers rose up in several notable, and occasionally violent, protests to challenge the labor system that they believed oppressed them. Farmers in the West and the South, both white and black, organized a great political movement—known as populism—in opposition to financial and social institutions that they considered exploitive and dangerous. And Americans of all regions and all classes suffered from the effects of a great economic depression, the worst in the nation's history to that point, which called into question many of the optimistic assumptions that had fueled the industrial growth of the previous two decades.

The crises of the 1890s seemed to confirm what many Americans had been saying for years: that industrialization had brought not only progress but chaos and injustice; that the nation must reshape itself to deal with the problems its new economy had created. Out of this perceived need for reform emerged a wide-ranging effort to produce new institutions and procedures that might bring order and justice to American society—an effort that won for the first years of the twentieth century the label the "progressive era."

Progressivism was perhaps most clearly visible in the dramatic political battles of the period, which produced far-reaching changes in the nature of government at every level and elevated the federal government to a position of new importance. But the reform impulse touched far more than politics. It reached out into virtually every area and every segment of society: business, the professions, the arts, education, racial minorities, women, and others. By the time the nation entered World War I, the effects of progressivism had become so pervasive, many of its impulses so absorbed into the fabric of national life, that it was no longer a movement so much as a description of the social outlook of vast numbers of Americans. And while the war took its toll on some strands of progressive thought, it helped others to survive and grow stronger. In the years following the fighting, the United States would embark on a series of new experiments in reform that would rest in large part on the progressive legacy.

Held Up by Buffalo, by N. H. Trotter, c. 1880   (Smithsonian Institution)

Chapter 16

The New South and the Last West

Much of the United States in the years following Reconstruction was preoccupied with the expansion and development of an already advanced urban-industrial society. In two regions of America, however, the experience was quite different. In the South, the first region of the country to have been settled by Europeans, and in the West, the last such region, the late nineteenth century was a time of new beginnings. It also became a period of decline relative to the rest of the nation—a decline that would ultimately produce in both regions major social and political upheavals.

The South, recovering from a disastrous war and confronting once again the reality of an economy far less developed than that of the North, faced several choices in the years after Reconstruction. It could attempt to transform itself into a modern, industrial region able to compete effectively with its former enemy. Or it could attempt to rebuild its agrarian economy and restore some semblance of the comfortable stability that many white Southerners had so valued in their civilization before the Civil War. In fact, the South attempted to do both. Substantial groups of white Southerners set out to promote the modern economic development of their region, to imitate Northern ways, even occasionally to elevate the status of blacks—to build what they liked to call a New South. Their efforts were not without result. But despite substantial progress in certain areas, the South remained at the end of the century what it had long been: an impoverished, primarily agricultural region, far behind the North in the development of commerce and industry. The failure was a result in part of economic obstacles over which the region had

little control; but it was a result, too, of the determination of the vast majority of white Southerners to protect the supremacy of their race—a determination that often came to overshadow all efforts at reform.

For the new West—the areas beyond the Mississippi River, most of which had remained unsettled or sparsely settled by white Americans in the years before the Civil War—the late nineteenth century was a time of dramatic growth and development. White settlers (and some blacks) now poured into the region—a region larger than all the previously settled area of America combined. And they established there a new civilization of farms, ranches, mining operations, and more. It was a civilization that had much in common with the older regions of the United States, but one that took on a distinctive character of its own. The conquest of the West was in part the story of a courageous struggle against imposing natural obstacles. It was also the story of a brutal assault against the Indian tribes of the region, who were once again disrupted and ultimately displaced by the onward march of white society.

The South in Transition

The Compromise of 1877—the agreement between Southern Democrats and Northern Republicans that helped settle the disputed election of 1876—was supposed to be the first step toward developing a stable, permanent Republican party in the South. In that respect, at least, it failed. In the years following the

469

end of Reconstruction, white Southerners began to establish the Democratic party as the only viable political organization for the region's whites. And they created a social system that, for all its differences from the system of the antebellum period, concentrated most political and economic power in the hands of a powerful white aristocracy. Slowly but systematically, the white leadership excluded black Southerners from any meaningful access to power or influence in the region. The New South was indeed new in some respects; but in others, it was distinctly familiar.

The "Redeemers"

By the end of 1877—after the last withdrawal of federal troops—every Southern state government had been "redeemed." That is, political power had been restored to white Democrats. Many Southerners rejoiced at the restoration of what they liked to call "home rule." In fact, political power in the region was soon more restricted than at any time since the Civil War. Once again, the South fell under the control of a powerful, conservative oligarchy, whose members were known variously as the "Redeemers" or the "Bourbons."

This post-Reconstruction ruling class was in some areas of the South much the same as the ruling class of the antebellum period. In Alabama, for example, the old planter elite—despite challenges from new merchant and industrial forces—retained much of its former power and continued largely to dominate the state for decades. In other areas, however, the Redeemers constituted a genuinely new class. Merchants, industrialists, railroad developers, financiers—some of them former planters, some of them Northern immigrants who had become absorbed into the region's life, some of them ambitious, upwardly mobile white Southerners from the region's lower social tiers—combined a commitment to "home rule" and social conservatism with a commitment to economic development.

Whatever their differences, the various Bourbon governments of the New South behaved in many respects quite similarly. Although one of the most heated conservative criticisms of the Reconstruction governments had been that they had fostered widespread corruption, the Redeemer regimes were, if anything, even more awash in graft, fraud, and waste. (In this, they were little different from governments in every region of the country.) Virtually all the new

Democratic regimes, moreover, adopted policies of lowered taxation, reduced spending, and drastically diminished state services. The carpetbag governments of Reconstruction, they complained, had saddled the South with huge debts. (In fact, some of the debt predated the Civil War.) It was the duty of the new leaders, therefore, to put the region back on a sound financial footing. Many of the most valuable accomplishments of Reconstruction were now dismantled. In one state after another, for example, state support for public school systems was reduced or eliminated. "Schools are not a necessity," commented a governor of Virginia.

The rule of the Bourbon oligarchies was not unchallenged. By the late 1870s, powerful dissenting groups were protesting the cuts in services. Even more, they were denouncing the commitment of their present governments to paying off the prewar and Reconstruction debts in full, at the original (usually high) rates of interest. In Virginia, for example, a vigorous "Readjuster" movement emerged, demanding that the state revise its debt payment procedures so as to make more money available for state services. In 1879, the Readjusters won control of the legislature; and in the next few years they captured the governorship and a U. S. Senate seat. In other states, similar protests emerged. There were demands for greenbacks and for other economic reforms, as well as for debt readjustments. (A few such independent movements included significant numbers of blacks in their ranks, but all consisted primarily of lower-income whites.) For a moment, at least, it seemed as though Southern politics was to become genuinely competitive. But the dissident uprising proved only temporary. By the mid-1880s, conservative Southerners—largely by exploiting racial prejudice—had effectively destroyed the Readjusters and other such movements. It would be several years before a new challenge to the power of the Bourbons would arise.

Whites and the New South

The fondest dream of some Southern leaders in the post-Reconstruction era was to see their region become the home of a vigorous industrial economy. The South had lost the war, many now argued, because its economy had been unable to compete with the modernized manufacturing capacity of the North. The region's task, therefore, must now be to "out-Yankee the Yankees." Influential spokesmen—most prominent among them Henry Grady, editor of the *Atlanta Constitution*—espoused a new Southern "creed," one that preached the virtues of thrift, industry, and progress: the same qualities that prewar Southerners had so often denounced in Northern society. "We have sown towns and cities in the place of theories," Grady boasted to a New England audience in the 1880s, "and put business above politics. . . . We have fallen in love with work."

Such boasts were not without merit. Southern industry expanded dramatically in the years after Reconstruction and became a more important part of the region's economy than ever before. Most visible was the growth in textile manufacturing. In the past, Southern cotton had usually been shipped out of the region to manufacturers in the North or in Europe. Now, textile factories appeared in the South itself. The number of spindles in the region increased 900 percent in the last twenty years of the century. The tobacco processing industry, similarly, established an important foothold in the region—largely through the work of James B. Duke of North Carolina, whose American Tobacco Company became for a time a virtual monopoly in the processing of raw tobacco into marketable smoking materials. In the lower South—and particularly in Alabama—the iron (and, later, steel) industry expanded rapidly. The city of Birmingham grew within a decade from modest beginnings to become a major center of pig iron pro-

cessing. By 1890, the Southern iron and steel industry represented nearly a fifth of the nation's total capacity.

And the South made important progress as well toward remedying one of its greatest economic problems: its obsolete transportation system. Railroad development increased substantially in the post-Reconstruction years—at a rate far greater than that of the nation at large. Between 1880 and 1890, the total miles of track in the region more than doubled. And the South took a giant step toward integrating its transportation system with that of the rest of the country when, in 1886, it changed the gauge (width) of its trackage to correspond with the standards of the North. No longer would it be necessary for cargoes heading into the South to be transferred from one train to another at the borders of the region.

Yet Southern industry developed within strict limits, and its effects on the region were never even remotely comparable to the effects of industrialization on the North. The Southern share of national manufacturing doubled in the last twenty years of the century—to 10 percent of the total. But that percentage was the same the South had claimed in 1860; the region had, in other words, done no more than regain what it had lost during the war and its aftermath. The region's per capita income increased 21 percent in the same period. But at the end of the

Old South, New South

A black farmer drives a crude oxcart past an ironworks in Rockwood, Tennessee. Many Southerners made strenuous efforts in the aftermath of the Civil War to bring industrialization to their overwhelmingly agrarian region; and they pointed to the growth of cotton mills, coal and copper mines, lumbering operations, and iron plants as evidence of their success in creating a "New South." The region remained far less developed and far less affluent, however, than most of the rest of the nation. (Historical Pictures Service)

century, average income in the South was only 40 percent of that in the North; in 1860 it had been more than 60 percent. And even in those areas where development had been most rapid—textiles, iron, railroads—much, if not most, of the capital had come from the North. Once again, the South was developing a colonial economy.

The benefits of Southern industry, moreover, were not widely shared. Southern wages remained far below the Northern equivalent; indeed, one of the greatest attractions of the South to industrialists was that employers were able to pay workers there as little as half of what Northern workers received. Some industries—textiles, for example—offered no opportunities at all to black workers. Others—tobacco, iron, and lumber, among others—did provide some employment for blacks but usually only the least desirable and lowest-paid positions. At times, industrialization proceeded on the basis of no wage-paying employment at all. Through the notorious "convict-lease" system, Southern states leased gangs of con-

victed criminals to private interests as a cheap labor supply. The system not only exposed the convicts to brutal and often fatal mistreatment without pay (the leasing fees went to the states, not the workers); it also denied employment in railroad construction and other projects to the free labor force.

The most important economic reality in the post-Reconstruction South was the impoverished state of agriculture, which continued to dominate the region. The 1870s and 1880s saw an acceleration of the process that had begun in the immediate postwar years: the imposition of systems of tenancy and debt peonage on much of the region; the reliance on a few cash crops, rather than on a diversified agricultural system; and an increasing absentee ownership of valuable farmlands (many of them purchased by merchants and industrialists, who paid little attention to whether the land was being properly used). During Reconstruction, perhaps a third or more of the farmers in the South were tenants; by 1900, the figure had increased to 70 percent. It was remarkable, per-

The Crop Lien System: The South in 1880

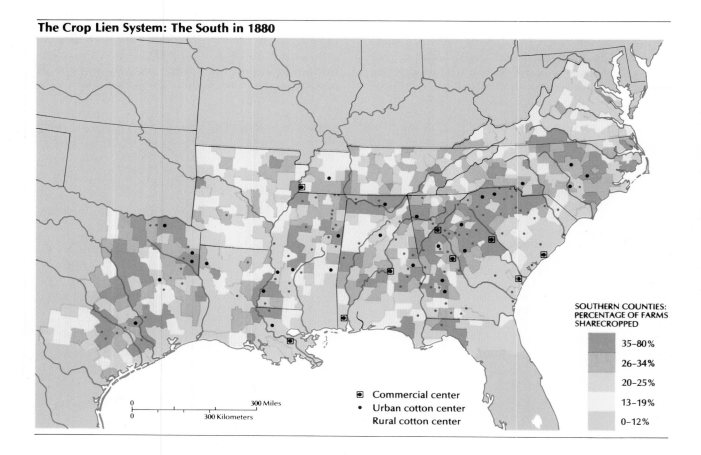

SOUTHERN COUNTIES:
PERCENTAGE OF FARMS
SHARECROPPED

35–80%
26–34%
20–25%
13–19%
0–12%

⊡ Commercial center
• Urban cotton center
   Rural cotton center

0 ___ 300 Miles
0 ___ 300 Kilometers

haps, that despite all this, more than 121,000 blacks owned their own land in 1890. But that figure still represented a tiny percentage of the black population as a whole.

That the white South was not yet entirely willing to break with its past was evident, too, in the popular literature of the region. At the same time that Southern writers were extolling the virtues of industrialization in newspaper editorials and speeches, they were painting nostalgic portraits of the Old South in their literature. Few Southerners advocated a literal return to the old ways; but most whites eagerly embraced romantic talk of the "lost cause." And they responded warmly to the local-color fiction of such writers as Joel Chandler Harris, whose folk tales—the most famous being *Uncle Remus* (1880)—presented the slave society of the antebellum years as a harmonious world, marked by engaging dialect and close emotional bonds between the races. Thomas Nelson Page similarly extolled the old Virginia aristocracy. The whites of the New South, in short, faced their future with one foot still in the past.

Blacks and the New South

The spirit of the New South was not the property of whites alone. Many blacks became enchanted by the vision of progress and self-improvement as well. Some blacks succeeded in elevating themselves into a distinct middle class—one economically far inferior to the white middle class but nevertheless significant. These were former slaves (and, as the decades passed, their offspring) who managed to acquire property, establish small businesses, enter professions. A few blacks accumulated substantial fortunes by establishing banks and insurance companies for their race; most middle-class blacks, however, experienced more modest gains by becoming doctors, lawyers, or teachers serving members of their own race.

A cardinal tenet of this rising group of blacks was that education was vital to the future of their race. With the support of Northern missionary societies and, to a far lesser extent, a few Southern state governments, they expanded the network of black colleges and institutes that had taken root during Reconstruction into an important educational system. The chief spokesman for this commitment to education, and ultimately the major spokesman for his race as a whole, was Booker T. Washington, founder and president of the Tuskegee Institute in Alabama. Born into slavery, Washington had worked his own way out of poverty by virtue of having acquired an education (at Virginia's famous Hampton Institute). Once established, he urged other blacks to follow the same road to self-improvement.

Washington's message was both cautious and hopeful. The "great leap from slavery to freedom," he warned, should not permit blacks to forget how to work with their hands. They should attend school, learn skills, and establish a solid footing in agriculture and the trades. Industrial, not classical, education should be their goal. Blacks should, moreover, refine their speech, improve their dress, and adopt habits of thrift and personal cleanliness; they should, in short, adopt the standards of the white middle class. Only thus, he claimed, could they win the respect of the white population, the prerequisite for any larger social gains. In a famous speech in Georgia in 1895, Washington outlined a philosophy of race relations that became widely known as the Atlanta Compromise. "The wisest among my race understand," he said, "that the agitation of questions of social equality is the extremest folly." Blacks should, rather, engage in "severe and constant struggle" for economic gains; for, as he explained, "no race that has anything to contribute to the markets of the world is long in any degree ostracized." If blacks were ever to win the rights and privileges of citizenship, they must first show that they were "prepared for the exercise of these privileges."

In the context of his time, Washington's message was not as timid and conservative as it would later sound. As the first black leader to acquire a wide audience among members of his race, he offered a powerful challenge to those whites who strove to discourage blacks from acquiring an education or winning any economic gains. He helped to awaken the interest of a new generation to the possibilities for self-advancement.

But Washington's message was comforting to Southern whites as well. For in it was an implicit promise that blacks would not challenge the system of segregation that they were then in the process of erecting.

The Birth of Jim Crow

Most white Southerners had never accepted the idea of blacks as equal citizens of their region. That the former slaves acquired any legal and political rights at all after emancipation was in large part the result of federal support. That support all but vanished after

1877. Federal troops were no longer available to police the polls and prevent whites from excluding black voters. Congress was no longer taking an interest in the condition of the former slaves. And the courts were signaling a retreat as well. In a series of decisions in the 1880s and 1890s, the Supreme Court effectively stripped the Fourteenth and Fifteenth amendments of much of their significance. In deciding the so-called civil-rights cases of 1883, the Court ruled that the Fourteenth Amendment prohibited state governments from discriminating against people because of race but did not restrict private organizations or individuals from doing so. Thus railroads, hotels, theaters, and the like could legally practice segregation. Eventually, the Court also validated state legislation that discriminated against blacks. In *Plessy* v. *Ferguson* (1896), a case involving a law that required separate seating arrangements for the races on railroads, the Court held that separate accommodations did not deprive blacks of equal rights if the accommodations were equal, a decision that survived for years as part of the legal basis of segregated schools. In *Cumming* v. *County Board of Education* (1899), the Court went even further: Laws establishing separate schools for whites, the justices ruled, were valid even if they provided no comparable schools for blacks.

Even before these decisions, white Southerners were at work ensuring their supremacy and, gradually, their separation from contact with the black race to the extent possible. This movement from subordination to segregation was clearly illustrated in the case of black voting rights. In some states—particularly those such as South Carolina and the Deep South cotton states, where blacks constituted close to a majority of the population— disfranchisement began almost as soon as Reconstruction ended. South Carolina, for example, effectively reduced the black vote beginning early in the 1880s by introducing a complicated system of ballot boxes that illiterate voters could not decipher. Georgia required payment of a poll tax, which blacks generally could not afford. In some areas, however, black voting continued for some time after Reconstruction—largely because conservative whites believed they could use the black electorate to maintain their own power. Bourbon leaders often paid or intimidated blacks to vote for their candidates; thus they managed to beat down the attempts of poor white farmers to take control of the Democratic party.

The relative laxness of these franchise restrictions enabled blacks to continue through the 1880s and much of the 1890s to exercise some political influence—far less than that to which their numbers entitled them but more than they would later have. Until the end of the century, Republican candidates in some Southern states continued to receive as much as 40 percent of the vote—most of it from black voters. At least one Southern black served in every session of Congress until 1901. By the late 1890s, however, franchise restrictions were becoming much more rigid. During those years, some small white farmers began to demand complete black disfranchisement—both because of racial animosity and because they objected to the black vote being used against them by the Bourbons. Many members of the conservative elite, at the same time, began to fear that poor whites might unite politically with poor blacks to challenge their hegemony. They too began to support further franchise restrictions. The prospect of whites competing for the black vote—of blacks conceivably becoming the balance of power in the region—frightened whites at all economic levels. The time had come, they believed, to close ranks if white supremacy was to be maintained.

In devising laws to disfranchise blacks, the Southern states had to find ways to evade the intent of the Fifteenth Amendment. That measure had not *guaranteed* suffrage to blacks; it had simply prohibited states from denying anyone the right to vote because of color. The Southern problem, then, was to exclude blacks from the franchise without seeming to base the exclusion on race. Two devices emerged before 1900 to accomplish this goal. One was the poll tax or some form of property qualification; few blacks were prosperous enough to meet such requirements. Another was the "literacy" or "understanding" test, which required voters to demonstrate the ability to read and to interpret the Constitution. The laws permitted local registrars to administer impossibly difficult reading tests to would-be voters or to rule that their interpretation of the Constitution was inadequate.

Such restrictions affected poor white voters as well as blacks. By the late 1890s, the black vote had decreased by 62 percent, the white vote by 26 percent. One result was that some states passed so-called grandfather laws, which permitted men who could not meet the literacy and property qualifications to be enfranchised if their ancestors had voted before Reconstruction began, thus barring the descendants of slaves from the polls while allowing poor whites access to them. In other states, however, the ruling elites were quite content to see poor whites, a potential source of opposition to their power, barred from voting.

The Supreme Court proved as compliant in ruling on the disfranchising laws as it was in dealing with the civil-rights cases. The Court eventually voided the grandfather laws, but it validated the literacy tests (in the 1898 case of *Williams* v. *Mississippi*) and displayed a general willingness to let the Southern states define their own suffrage standards as long as evasions of the Fifteenth Amendment were not too glaring.

Laws restricting the franchise and segregating schools were only part of a network of state statutes—known as the Jim Crow laws—that had by the first years of the twentieth century established an elaborate system of segregation reaching into almost every area of Southern life. Blacks and whites could not ride together in the same railroad cars, sit in the same waiting rooms, use the same washrooms, eat in the same restaurants, or sit in the same theaters. Blacks were denied access to parks, beaches, and picnic areas; they were barred from many hospitals. Much of the new legal structure did no more than confirm what had already been widespread social practice in the South since well before the end of Reconstruction. But the Jim Crow laws also served to strip many blacks of the social, economic, and political gains they had made in the more fluid atmosphere of the late nineteenth century. Segregation was now rigid and unyielding; and it was to survive without serious challenge for decades.

More than legal efforts were involved in this process. The 1890s witnessed a dramatic increase in a phenomenon that had been a part of Southern life for many years: white violence against blacks, which (along with the Jim Crow laws) served to inhibit

A Lynch Mob, 1893
A large, almost festive crowd gathers to watch the lynching of a black man accused of the murder of a three-year-old white girl. Lynchings remained frequent in the South until as late as the 1930s, but they reached their peak in the 1890s and the first years of the twentieth century. (Library of Congress)

black agitation for equal rights. The worst such violence—lynching of blacks by white mobs, either because the victims were accused of crimes or because they had seemed somehow to violate their proper stations—reached appalling levels. In the nation as a whole in the 1890s, there was an average of 187 lynchings each year, more than 80 percent of them in the South and the vast majority of those inflicted on blacks.

Just as in the antebellum period, the shared commitment to white supremacy helped to dilute the class animosities between poorer whites and the Bourbon oligarchies that might otherwise have emerged. Economic issues tended to take a subordinate role to race in Southern politics, distracting the gaze of the region from the glaring social inequalities that afflicted blacks and whites alike. Even when such issues did arise—as they did in the 1890s—the racial question ultimately proved an effective vehicle for dampening their impact. The commitment to racial supremacy, in short, was a burden for poor whites as well as for blacks.

The Origins of Black Protest

Black Americans faced enormous obstacles—legal, economic, social, and political—in challenging their oppressed status. Thus it was not surprising, perhaps, that so many embraced the message of Booker T. Washington in the late nineteenth century: a message that urged them to "put down your bucket where you are," to work for immediate self-improvement rather than long-range social change. Not all blacks, however, were content with this approach. And by the turn of the century a powerful challenge was emerging—to the philosophy of Washington and, more important, to the entire structure of race relations. The chief spokesman for this new approach was W. E. B. Du Bois.

Du Bois, unlike Washington, had never known slavery. Born in Massachusetts and educated at Harvard, he grew to maturity with a far more expansive view than Washington of the goals of his race and the responsibilities of white society to eliminate prejudice and injustice. In *The Souls of Black Folk* (1903), he launched an open attack on the philosophy of the Atlanta Compromise, accusing Washington of encouraging white efforts to impose segregation and of unnecessarily limiting the aspirations of his race. "Is it possible and probable," he asked,

> that nine millions of men can make effective progress in economic lines if they are deprived of political rights, made a servile caste, and allowed only the most meagre

chance for developing their exceptional men? If history and reason give any distinct answer to these questions, it is an emphatic *No.*

Rather than content themselves with education at the trade and agricultural schools, Du Bois advocated, talented blacks should accept nothing less than a full university education. They should aspire to the professions. They should, above all, fight for the immediate restoration of their civil rights, not simply

W. E. B. Du Bois

Although Du Bois, unlike Booker T. Washington, never developed a large popular following, he was the acknowledged leader of the black elite in the late nineteenth and early twentieth centuries. He was the first black man ever to earn a doctorate at Harvard University, and he published a number of distinguished works of history during his long career. He also served for more than twenty years as editor of *The Crisis,* the newspaper of the NAACP. He died in 1963, at the age of ninety-five, having lived long enough to see the emergence of a powerful civil rights movement dedicated to achieving many of the goals for which he had fought throughout his life. The pastel portrait here was drawn around 1925 by Winhold Reiss. (National Portrait Gallery)

wait for them to be granted as a reward for patient striving.

In 1905, Du Bois and a group of his supporters met at Niagara Falls (on the Canadian side of the border; no hotel on the American side of the Falls would have them), and launched what became known as the Niagara Movement. Four years later, after a race riot in Springfield, Illinois, they joined with white progressives sympathetic to their cause to form the National Association for the Advancement of Colored People (NAACP). Whites held most of the offices; but Du Bois, its director of publicity and research, was the guiding spirit. In the ensuing years, the new organization led the drive for equal rights, using as its principal weapon lawsuits in the federal courts.

Within less than a decade, the NAACP had begun to win some important victories. In *Guinn* v. *United States* (1915), the Supreme Court supported their position that the grandfather clause in an Oklahoma law was unconstitutional. (The statute denied the vote to any citizen whose ancestors had not been enfranchised in 1860.) In *Buchanan* v. *Worley* (1917), the Court struck down a Louisville, Kentucky, law requiring residential segregation. Disfranchisement and segregation would survive through other methods for many decades to come, but the NAACP had established a pattern of black resistance that would ultimately bear important fruits. It had also established itself, particularly after Booker T. Washington's death in 1915, as one of the nation's leading black organizations, a position it would maintain for many years.

The NAACP was not a radical, or even an egalitarian, organization. It relied, rather, on the efforts of the most intelligent and educated members of the black race, the "talented tenth" as Du Bois called them. And it stressed not so much the elevation of all blacks from poverty and oppression as the opportunity for exceptional blacks to gain positions of full equality. Ultimately, its members believed, such efforts would redound to the benefit of all blacks. By creating a trained elite, blacks would, in effect, be creating a leadership group capable of fighting for the rights of the race as a whole. In the meantime, however, the NAACP remained largely a force of and for the middle class.

The Conquest of the Far West

By the time of the Civil War, the western rim of English-speaking settlement had already moved far

beyond what it had been even twenty years before. American civilization had crossed the Mississippi and established a permanent foothold in the next tier of states—Minnesota, Iowa, Missouri, and Arkansas—as well as in the eastern parts of Nebraska, Kansas, and Texas. But vast regions remained largely empty of white settlement. Much of the West was the province of nomadic Indian tribes, of wild animals, and of a few scattered immigrants from the East (most of them white, but some—in regions as scattered as Montana, Kansas, and Nebraska—black).

Even in 1860, however, there were clear signs that the United States would not much longer be content to leave these vast Western territories to the Indians. For one thing, important white settlements had already been established on the Pacific coast, in California and Oregon. For another, ambitious men and women continued to press for access to new lands in the West; as one region began to fill up with settlers, such people demanded the right to move on to the next. And so, in the decades following the Civil War, Americans continued their great migration into the interior of their country until the line of European settlement stretched unbroken to the Pacific.

Delayed Settlement

When the westward-pushing pioneers entered the Great Plains, they saw an environment utterly different from the fertile prairies behind them. They saw a land distinguished by its level surface, its lack of timber, and its deficiency in rainfall. Early explorers had dubbed this region "the Great American Desert," and in the 1840s settlers had hastened through it on their way to California and Oregon. Its forbidding reputation was largely responsible for the fact that the edge of white settlement, after crossing the Mississippi, had jumped 1,500 miles to the Pacific coast.

By the 1860s, however, whites had begun to move into the unsettled parts of the West. They were attracted by gold and silver deposits, by the short-grass pasture for cattle and sheep, and finally by the plains' sod and the mountain meadowland that seemed suitable for farming or ranching.

The completion of the great transcontinental railroad lines helped encourage settlement. These roads and their feeders moved settlers and supplies into the vast interior spaces and furnished access to outside markets. The railroad companies themselves had an incentive, of course, to promote migration into the West; settlement of the region would provide markets for the lines they were building. So the companies actively solicited settlers by a number of devices, including selling their lands to migrants at low prices.

The land policy of the federal government also worked to encourage settlement. The Homestead Act of 1862 permitted settlers to buy a plot of 160 acres for a small fee if they occupied and improved it for five years. The Homestead Act had been intended as a democratic measure. It would bestow a free farm on any American who needed one; it would serve as a form of government relief to raise the living standards of the masses. But in practice the act proved a disappointment. Some 400,000 homesteaders became landowners, but a much larger number ultimately abandoned their lands in the face of the bleak life on the windswept plains.

The Homestead Act had rested on a number of false premises. The framers of the act assumed that mere possession of land was enough to sustain farm life; they ignored the increasing mechanization of agriculture and the rising costs of operation. They had made their calculations, moreover, on the basis of Eastern agricultural experiences that were inapplicable to the region west of the Mississippi. A unit of 160 acres was too small for the grazing and grain farming of the Great Plains.

Responding to Western pressures, Congress acted to increase allotments. The Timber Culture Act (1873) permitted homesteaders to receive grants of 160 additional acres if they planted on them 40 acres of trees. The Desert Land Act (1877) provided that claimants could buy 640 acres at $1.25 an acre provided they irrigated part of their holdings within three years. The Timber and Stone Act (1878), presumably applying to nonarable land, authorized sales of quarter sections at $2.50 an acre. These laws ultimately made it possible for individuals to acquire as much as 1,280 acres of land at little cost. And some enterprising settlers got much more. Fraud ran rampant in the administration of the acts. Lumber, mining, and cattle companies, by employing "dummy" registrants and using other illegal devices, seized millions of acres of the public domain.

Political organization followed on the heels of settlement. After the admission of Kansas as a state in 1861, the remaining territories of Washington, New Mexico, Utah, and Nebraska were divided into smaller and more convenient units. By the close of the 1860s, territorial governments were in operation in the new provinces of Nevada, Colorado, Dakota, Arizona, Idaho, Montana, and Wyoming. Statehood rapidly followed. Nevada became a state in 1864, Nebraska in 1867, and Colorado in 1876. In 1889,

North and South Dakota, Montana, and Washington won admission; Wyoming and Idaho entered the next year. Utah was denied statehood until its Mormon leaders convinced the government in 1896 that polygamy (the practice of men taking several wives) had been abandoned. At the turn of the century, only three territories remained outside the fold: Arizona and New Mexico, excluded because of their scanty population, their politics (they were predominantly Democratic), and their refusal to accept admission as a single state; and Oklahoma (formerly Indian Territory), which was opened to white settlement and granted territorial status in 1889–1890.

The Arrival of the Miners

The first economic boom in the Far West came in mining, and the first part of the area to be settled was the mineral-rich region of mountains and plateaus. The life span of the mining frontier was brief. It burst into being around 1860, flourished until the 1890s, and then abruptly declined.

News of a gold or silver strike would start a stampede reminiscent of the California gold rush of 1849. Settlement usually followed a pattern of successive stages. Individual prospectors would exploit the first ores largely by hand, with pan and placer mining. After the shallower deposits had been depleted by these methods, corporations would move in to engage in lode or quartz mining. Then, as those deposits dwindled, commercial mining would either disappear or continue on a restricted basis, and ranchers and farmers would appear on the scene to establish a more permanent economy.

The first great mineral strikes occurred just before the Civil War. In 1858, gold was discovered in the Pike's Peak district of what would soon be the territory of Colorado; and the following year, a mob of 50,000 prospectors stormed in from California and the Mississippi Valley and the East. Denver and other mining camps blossomed into "cities" overnight. Almost as rapidly as it had developed, the boom ended. Eventually, corporations, notably the Guggenheim interests, revived some of the glories and profits of the gold boom, and the discovery of silver near Leadville supplied a new source of mineral wealth.

While the Colorado rush of 1859 was in progress, news of another strike drew miners to Nevada. Gold had been found in the Washoe district, but the most valuable ore in the great Comstock Lode and other veins was silver. The first prospectors to reach the

Mining Towns, 1848–1883

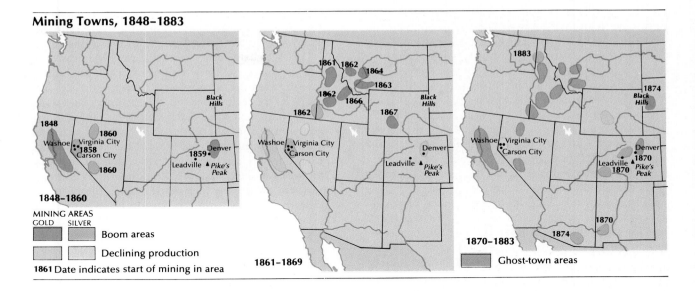

1848–1860

MINING AREAS
GOLD   SILVER

▮ ▮   Boom areas

▮ ▮   Declining production

1861 Date indicates start of mining in area

1861–1869

1870–1883

▮   Ghost-town areas

Colorado Boom Town

After a prospector discovered silver nearby in 1890, miners flocked to the town of Creede, Colorado, at a tremendous rate. For a time in the early 1890s, 150 to 300 people arrived there daily. Although the town was located in a canyon so narrow that there was room for only one street, buildings sprouted rapidly to serve the growing community. Like other such boom towns, however, Creede's prosperity was short-lived. In 1893 the price of silver collapsed; and by the end of the century, Creede was almost deserted.   (Henry Ford Museum)

Washoe fields came from California; and from the beginning, Californians dominated the settlement and development of Nevada. In a remote desert without railroad transportation, the territory produced no supplies of its own, and everything—from food and machinery to whiskey and prostitutes—had to be shipped in from California to Virginia City, Carson City, and other roaring camp towns. When the placer deposits ran out, California capital bought the claims of the pioneer prospectors and installed quartz mining. For a brief span, the outside owners reaped tremendous profits; from 1860 to 1880 the Nevada lodes yielded bullion worth $306 million.

There were no more important mineral discoveries until 1874, when gold was found in the Black Hills of southwestern Dakota Territory. Prospectors swarmed into the area, then (and for years to come) accessible only by stagecoach. For a short time the boom flared, and then came the inevitable fading of resources. Corporations took over from the miners, and one gigantic company, the Homestake, came to dominate the fields. The population declined, and the Dakotas, like other boom areas of the mineral empire, waited for the approach of agricultural settlement.

Life in the camp towns of the mineral empire had a hectic tempo and a gaudy flavor not to be found in any other part of the Far West. A speculative spirit, a mood of heady optimism, gripped everyone and dominated every phase of community activity. The conditions of mine life—the presence of precious minerals, the vagueness of claim boundaries, the cargoes of gold being shipped out—attracted outlaws and "bad men," operating as individuals or gangs, to ply their trade. When the situation became intolerable in a community, those members interested in order set up their own law and enforced it through a vigilance committee, an agency used earlier in California. Sometimes criminals themselves secured control of the committee, and sometimes the vigilantes continued to operate as private "law" enforcers after the creation of regular governments.

The Cattle Kingdom

A second important element of the boom economy in the Far West was cattle ranching. The open range—the unclaimed grasslands of the public domain—provided a huge area on the Great Plains where cattlemen could graze their herds free of charge and unrestricted by the boundaries of private farms. The railroads gave birth to the range-cattle industry by giving it access to markets. Then the same railroads destroyed it by bringing farmers to the plains.

The Western cattle industry was Mexican and Texan by ancestry. Long before citizens of the United States invaded the Southwest, Mexican ranchers had developed the techniques that the cattlemen and cowboys of the Great Plains later employed: branding (a device known in all frontier areas where stock was common), roundups, roping, and the equipment of the herder—his lariat, saddle, leather chaps, and spurs. Americans in Texas adopted these methods and carried them to the northernmost ranges of the cattle kingdom. Texas also had the largest herds of cattle in the country; the animals were descended from imported Spanish stock—the famous wiry, hardy longhorns—and allowed to run wild or semiwild. From Texas, too, came the horses that enabled the caretakers of the herds (the cowboys) to control them—small, muscular broncos or mustangs ideally adapted to the requirements of the cow country.

At the end of the Civil War, an estimated 5 million cattle roamed the Texas ranges, and Northern markets were offering fat prices for steers in any condition. Early in 1866, some Texas cattlemen began driving their combined herds, some 260,000 head, north to Sedalia, Missouri, on the Missouri Pacific Railroad. Traveling over rough country and beset by outlaws, Indians, and property-conscious farmers, the caravan suffered heavy losses, and only a fraction of the animals arrived in Sedalia. But the drive was an important experiment. It proved that cattle could be driven to distant markets and pastured along the trail, and that they would even gain weight during the journey. This first of the "long drives" prepared the way for the cattle kingdom.

With the precedent of the long drive established, the next step was to find an easier route through more accessible country. Special market facilities grew up at Abilene, Kansas, on the Kansas Pacific Railroad, and for years this town reigned as the railhead of the cattle kingdom. Between 1867 and 1871, cattlemen drove 1,460,000 head up the Chisholm Trail to Abilene—a town that, when filled with rampaging cowboys at the end of a drive, rivaled the mining towns in rowdiness. But by the mid-1870s, agricultural development in western Kansas was eating away at the open range land. At the same time, the supply of animals was increasing. Cattlemen therefore had to develop other trails and other market outlets. Dodge City and Wichita in Kansas, Ogallala and Sidney in Nebraska, Cheyenne

The Cattle Kingdom, c. 1866–1887

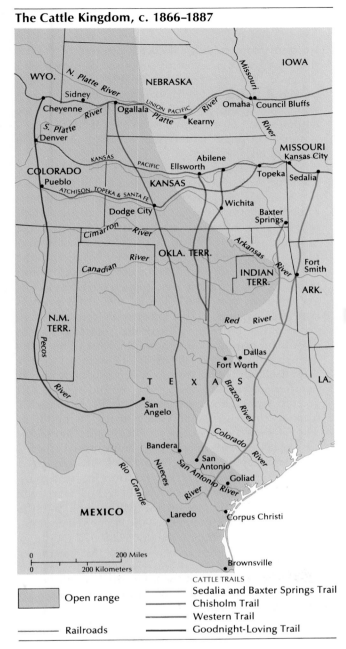

CATTLE TRAILS

▨ Open range	—— Sedalia and Baxter Springs Trail
	—— Chisholm Trail
	—— Western Trail
—— Railroads	—— Goodnight-Loving Trail

calves with no identifying symbols, "mavericks," were divided on a pro-rata basis. Then the cows and calves were turned loose to pasture, while the yearling steers (year-old males) were readied for the drive to the north. The combined herds, usually numbering from 2,000 to 5,000 head, moved out. Cowboys representing each of the major ranchers accompanied them.

Among the cowboys, the majority (in the early years) were veterans of the Confederate army. The next largest group consisted of blacks, who were more numerous than white Northerners or Mexicans and other foreigners. They were usually assigned such jobs as wrangler (herdsman) or cook. (In other contexts, black men played a role in the West not only as cowboys but also as explorers, trappers, miners, outlaws, and cavalrymen.)

Every cattleman had to have a permanent base from which to operate, and so the ranch emerged. A ranch consisted of the employer's dwelling, quarters for employees, and a tract of grazing land. In the early years of the cattle kingdom, most ranches were relatively small, since so much of the grazing occurred in the vast, open areas that cattlemen shared. But as farmers and sheepmen encroached on the open plains, ranches became larger and more clearly defined; cattlemen gradually had to learn to raise their stock on their own land.

There had always been an element of risk and speculation in the open-range cattle business. At any time, "Texas fever"—a disease transmitted to cattle by parasite-carrying ticks—might decimate a herd. Rustlers and Indians frequently seized large numbers of animals. But as settlement of the plains increased, these traditional risks combined with new forms of competition. Sheepmen from California and Oregon brought their flocks onto the range to compete for grass. Farmers ("nesters") from the East threw fences around their claims, blocking trails and breaking up the open range. A series of "range wars"—between sheepmen and cattlemen, between ranchers and farmers—erupted out of the tensions between these competing groups. Some of the wars resulted in significant loss of life and extensive property damage.

Accounts of the lofty profits to be made in the cattle business—it was said that an investment of $5,000 would return $45,000 in four years—tempted Eastern, English, and Scottish capital to the plains. Increasingly, the structure of the cattle economy became corporate in form; in one year, twenty corporations with a combined capital of $12 million were chartered in Wyoming. The inevitable result of this

and Laramie in Wyoming, and Miles City and Glendive in Montana all began to rival Abilene as major centers of stockherding.

A long drive was a spectacular experience. It began with the spring, or calf, roundup. The cattlemen of a district met with their cowboys at a specified place to round up the stock of the owners from the open range. As the cattle were driven in, the calves were branded with the marks of their mothers. Stray frenzied extension was that the ranges, already severed and shrunk by the railroads and the farmers, were becoming overstocked. There was not enough grass to support the competing herds or sustain the long drives. Finally, nature intervened with a destructive finishing blow. Two severe winters, in 1885–1886 and 1886–1887, with a searing summer between them, stung and scorched the plains. Hundreds of thousands of cattle died, streams and grass dried up, princely ranches and costly investments disappeared in a season.

The open-range industry never recovered; the long drive disappeared for good. But the established cattle ranches—with fenced-in grazing land and stocks of hay for winter feed—survived, grew, and prospered, eventually producing more beef than ever.

The Romance of the West

The unsettled West had always occupied a special place in the American imagination. But the vast regions of this "last frontier" had a particularly strong romantic appeal. Some of the reasons were obvious. The Great Plains, the Rocky Mountains, the basin and plateau region beyond the Rockies, and the Sierra Nevada-Cascade ranges beyond that—all constituted a landscape of such brilliant diversity, such spectacular grandeur, so different from anything white Americans had encountered before, it was little wonder that newcomers looked on it with reverence and wonder. Painters of the new "Rocky Mountain School"—of whom the best known was Albert Bierstadt—celebrated the new West in grandiose canvases. They emphasized the ruggedness and dramatic variety of the region, exhibiting the same awe toward the land that earlier regional painters had displayed toward the Hudson River Valley and other areas.

Even more appealing than the landscape, perhaps, was the rugged, free-spirited life style that many Americans associated with the frontier—a life style that stood in sharp contrast to the increasingly stable and ordered world of the East. Particular public interest attached to the figure of the cowboy, who was transformed remarkably quickly into a powerful and enduring figure of myth. Admiring Americans seldom thought about the drearier aspects of the cowboy's life: the tedium, the loneliness, the physical discomforts, the relatively few opportunities for advancement. Instead, in Western novels such as Owen Wister's *The Virginian* (1902), they romanticized his freedom from traditional social constraints, his affinity with nature, even his supposed propensity for violence. The cowboy became the last and most powerful symbol of what had long been an important ideal in the American mind—the ideal of the natural man. That symbol survived for more than a century—in popular literature, in song, and later in film and on television.

Yet it was not simply the particular qualities of the new West that made it so important to the nation's imagination. It was also the fact that Americans considered it the *last* frontier. Since the earliest moments of European settlement in America, the image of uncharted territory to the west had always been a comforting and inspiring one. Now, with the last of that unsettled land being slowly absorbed into the nation's civilization, that image exercised a stronger pull than ever. Mark Twain, one of the greatest American writers of the nineteenth century, gave voice to this romantic vision of the frontier in a series of brilliant novels and memoirs. In some of his writing—notably *Roughing It* (1872)—he wrote of the Far West itself, and of his own experience as a newspaper reporter in Nevada during the mining boom. His greatest works, however, dealt with life on an earlier frontier: the Mississippi Valley of his boyhood. In *The Adventures of Tom Sawyer* (1876) and *The Adventures of Huckleberry Finn* (1885), he produced characters who repudiated the constraints of organized society and attempted to escape from it into a more natural world. For Huck Finn, the vehicle of escape might be a small raft on the Mississippi; but the yearning for freedom reflected the larger vision of the West as the last refuge from civilization.

One of the clearest and most influential statements of this romantic vision of the frontier came not from an artist but from the famous historian Frederick Jackson Turner, of the University of Wisconsin (and later Harvard). In 1893, Turner delivered a memorable paper to a meeting of the American Historical Association entitled "The Significance of the Frontier in American History." In it, he took note of the findings of the 1890 census that the unsettled area of the West had been "so broken into by isolated bodies of settlement" that a continuous frontier line could no longer be drawn. And he argued that the passing of that line ended an era in the nation's history. For, as Turner explained it, "the existence of an area of free land, its continuous recession, and the advance of settlement westward, explain American development." This experience of expansion into the frontier, by stimulating individualism, nationalism, and democracy, had made Americans the distinctive people that they were. "Now," Turner concluded ominously, "four centuries from the discovery of America, at the end of a hundred years of life under the Constitution, the frontier has gone and with its going has closed the first period of American history."

In fact, Turner's forebodings were premature. A vast public domain still existed in the 1890s, and during the forty years thereafter the government was to give away many more acres than it had given as homesteads in the past. But Turner did express a growing and generally accurate sense that much of the best farming and grazing land was now taken, that in the future it would be far more difficult for individuals to acquire land for little or nothing.

In the "passing of the frontier," perhaps the greatest loss to the American people was a psychological one. As long as the country had remained open at one end, there had seemed to be constantly revitalizing opportunities in American life. Now there was a vague and ominous sense of being hemmed in. The psychological loss was all the greater because of what historian Henry Nash Smith, in *Virgin Land* (1950), called the "myth of the garden": the once widely held belief that the West was a kind of potential Garden of Eden where life could be begun anew and the ideals of democracy realized. The setting for utopia, once the New World as a whole, had shrunk to the West of the United States. And now even that West was vanishing as a pristine, unconquered land.

The Dispersal of the Tribes

White Americans liked to think of the Far West as a vast unpeopled land awaiting settlement. In fact, the West already had a large population—of Indians. Some were members of Eastern tribes—Cherokees, Creeks, Winnebagos, and others—who had been forcibly resettled west of the Mississippi before the Civil War. Others were members of tribes indigenous to the West.

The Western tribes had developed a number of patterns of civilization. The Pueblo of the Southwest lived largely as farmers and established permanent settlements. They grew corn; they built adobe houses; they practiced forms of irrigation. Other tribes in that region—the Navajos and Apaches of western Texas and eastern New Mexico—lived more nomadically and combined hunting with farming and sheep herding, moving their settlements from place to place. The most numerous Indian groups in the West, however, consisted of the plains Indians—the Sioux, Blackfoots, Cheyennes, Kiowas, Apaches, Comanches, Crows, and others—who occupied large parts of what became Minnesota, the Dakotas, Nebraska, Idaho, and Montana.

Unlike many of the Eastern tribes—the woods Indians whom white Americans had dispersed in earlier years—the plains Indians were powerful warriors, strong and militant. They fought a prolonged and often successful battle against the encroachments of white settlement, a battle in which, according to some estimates, the Indians inflicted the greater casualties on their enemy. In the end, however, the tribes could not effectively resist the superior numbers and technology of the white invaders. Defeated and broken, they were finally forced to accept what meager lands the whites were willing to give them and to adapt themselves to an approximation of the sedentary, agrarian culture of their conquerors.

The Plains Indians

On the rolling, semiarid, treeless plains, the plains Indians lived a largely nomadic life. Riding their small but powerful horses, which were descendants of Spanish stock, the tribes roamed the spacious expanses of the grasslands. Permanent settlements were rare; when a band halted, it quickly constructed tepees as temporary dwellings.

The magnet that drew the wanderers and guided their routes was the buffalo, or bison. This huge grazing animal provided the economic basis for the plains Indians' way of life. Its flesh was their principal source of food, and the skin supplied materials for clothing, shoes, tepees, blankets, robes, and utensils. "Buffalo chips" (dried manure) served as a fuel source; buffalo bones became knives; buffalo tendons formed the strings of bows. To the Indians, the buffalo was, as someone has said, "a galloping department store." They trailed the herds—estimated to number at least 15 million head in 1865—all over the plains.

The culture of the plains Indians reflected their nomadic life style and their close relationship with nature. Tribes (which sometimes numbered several thousand) were generally subdivided into "bands" of up to 500 men and women, each with its own governing council (which complicated the problems of the United States government in dealing with the tribes). Within each band, tasks were generally divided by sex. Women performed largely domestic and artistic roles. They raised children, cooked, gathered roots and berries, prepared hides, and created many of the impressive artworks of tribal culture. Men worked largely as hunters and traders; and they supervised the religious and military life of the band.

The plains Indians were martial, proud, and aggressive. They learned the arts of warfare in their frequent (and usually brief) skirmishes with rival tribes. Each tribe sustained a distinct warrior class, whose members competed with one another in developing a reputation for fierceness and bravery. These warriors proved to be the most formidable foes white settlers had yet encountered.

White Policies Toward the Tribes

It was the traditional policy of the federal government to regard the tribes simultaneously as independent nations and as wards of the president in Washington, and to negotiate agreements with them in the form of treaties that were solemnly ratified by the Senate (and then ignored or repudiated when their provisions became inconvenient). This concept of Indian sovereignty had been responsible for the attempt of the government before 1860 to erect a permanent frontier between whites and Indians, to reserve the region west of the bend of the Missouri as permanent Indian country.

By the early 1850s, however, the idea of establishing one great territory in which all the tribes could live gave way—in the face of white demands for access to lands on the "One Big Reservation"—to a new policy, known as "concentration." In 1851, each tribe was assigned its own, defined territory, confirmed by a separate treaty. This arrangement had many benefits for whites and few for the Indians. It divided the tribes from one another and made them easier to defeat. It allowed the government to force tribes into scattered locations and to take over the most desirable lands for white settlement. But it did not survive as the basis of Indian policy for long.

In 1867, in the aftermath of a series of bloody conflicts, Congress established an Indian Peace Commission, composed of soldiers and civilians, to recommend a new and presumably permanent Indian policy. The commission decided that the earlier "concentration" policy should be replaced by a new one. All the plains tribes would be relocated in two large reservations—one in "Indian Territory" (Oklahoma), the other in the Dakotas. At a series of meetings with the tribes, government agents cajoled, bribed, and tricked the Arapahos, Cheyennes, Sioux, and others into agreeing to treaties establishing the new reservations.

But this "solution" proved no more satisfactory than the previous ones. Part of the problem was the way in which the government administered the reservations it had established. White management of Indian matters was entrusted to the Bureau of Indian Affairs, located in the Department of the Interior. The bureau was responsible for distributing land, making payments, and supervising the shipment of supplies. Its record was not a distinguished one. The bureau's agents in the West—products of political patronage—were men of varying competence and honesty. But even the most honest and diligent agents were generally ill prepared for the job, had no understanding of tribal ways, and had little chance of success. The poor administration of the reservations was one reason for the constant conflicts between the tribes and the whites who were surrounding them.

But the problem was also a result of what was, in effect, economic warfare by whites: the relentless slaughtering of the buffalo herds that supported the tribes' way of life. After the Civil War, the white demand for buffalo hides became a national phenomenon—partly for economic reasons and partly as a fad. (Everyone east of the Missouri seemed to require a buffalo robe from the romantic West.) Gangs of professional hunters swarmed over the plains to shoot the huge animals. Some hunters killed merely for the sport of the chase, although the lumbering victims did not present much of a challenge. Railroad companies hired riflemen (such as Buffalo Bill Cody) and arranged large shooting expeditions to kill vast numbers of buffalo, hoping to thin the herds, which were an obstruction to railroad traffic. The southern herd was virtually exterminated by 1875, and within a few years the smaller northern herd had met the same fate. Fewer than a thousand of the magnificent beasts survived. The army and the agents of the Bureau of Indian Affairs condoned and even encouraged the killing. By destroying the buffalo herds, whites were destroying the Indians' source of food and supplies and their ability to resist the white advance. They were also, however, contributing to a climate in which Indian warriors felt the need to fight to preserve their way of life.

The Warriors' Last Stand

There was almost incessant Indian fighting on the frontier from the 1860s to the 1880s, as Indians struggled against the growing threats to their civilizations.

Indian Relocation, 1860–1890

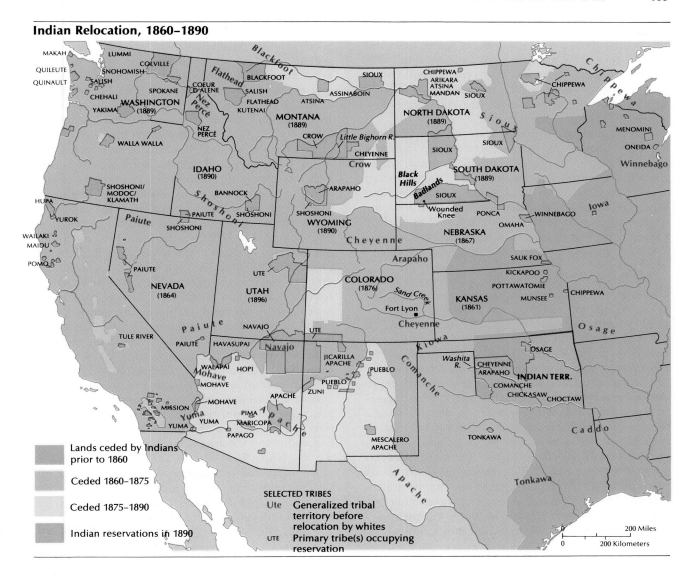

Lands ceded by Indians prior to 1860

Ceded 1860–1875

Ceded 1875–1890

Indian reservations in 1890

SELECTED TRIBES
Ute — Generalized tribal territory before relocation by whites
UTE — Primary tribe(s) occupying reservation

During the Civil War, the eastern Sioux in Minnesota, cramped on an inadequate reservation and exploited by corrupt white agents, suddenly rebelled against the restrictions imposed on them by the government's policies. Led by Little Crow, they killed more than 700 whites before being subdued by a force of regulars and militiamen. Thirty-eight of the Indians were hanged, and the tribe was exiled to the Dakotas.

At the same time, trouble flared in Colorado, where the Arapahos and Cheyennes had been restricted to the Sand Creek reservation. Bands of Indians attacked stagecoach lines and settlements in an effort to regain territory they believed was theirs. In response to these incidents, whites called up a large territorial militia; the army issued dire threats. The governor urged all friendly Indians to congregate at army posts before retribution fell on the hostiles. One Arapaho and Cheyenne band under Black Kettle came into Fort Lyon on Sand Creek and encamped nearby. Although some members of the party were undoubtedly warriors, Black Kettle understood he was under official protection. Nevertheless, Colonel J. M. Chivington, apparently encouraged by the army commander of the district, led a militia force to the unsuspecting camp and massacred a large number of men, women, and children (the precise figure, a subject of dispute). Some of the Arapahos and Cheyennes had another tragic experience before being finally settled on their reserve. Black Kettle, who had escaped the Chivington massacre, and his Cheyenne braves, some of whom had taken the warpath, were caught on the Washita River, near the Texas border, by Colonel George A. Custer; the chief was killed and his people were slaughtered.

At the end of the Civil War, wars against the Western Indians flared up on several fronts. The most serious and sustained conflict was in Montana, where the army attempted to build a road, the Bozeman Trail, from Fort Laramie, Wyoming, to the mining centers. The Sioux resented this intrusion into the heart of their buffalo range, and led by one of their great chiefs, Red Cloud, they so harried the soldiers and the construction party that the road was never completed.

The treaties of 1867 brought a temporary lull in the conflicts. But new forces soon shattered the peace again. In the early 1870s, more waves of white settlers—mostly miners—began to penetrate some of the lands in the Dakotas, territory supposedly guaranteed to the tribes in 1867. At the same time, the federal government, responding to the recommendations of a commission, decided that it would no longer recognize the tribes as independent entities or negotiate with tribal chiefs. It was a step intended to undermine the collective nature of Indian life and to force them to assimilate into white culture.

Indian resistance flared anew, this time with even greater strength. The Sioux in the northern plains rose up in 1875, in response to the entrance of miners into the Black Hills and in anger at the corrupt behavior of white agents. They suddenly left the reservation; and when commanded by white officials to return, they gathered in Montana under Crazy Horse, probably the greatest leader of the plains Indians, and Sitting Bull.

Three army columns were sent to round them up. With the expedition, as colonel of the famous Seventh Cavalry, was the colorful and controversial George A. Custer, golden-haired romantic and glory seeker. At the Battle of the Little Bighorn in 1876, the Indians surprised Custer with part of his regiment and killed every man. Custer has been accused of rashness, but he seems to have ridden into something that no white man would have believed possible at that time. On this occasion, the chiefs had concentrated at least 2,500, but perhaps 4,000, warriors, the largest Indian army ever assembled at one time in the United States.

The Indians did not have the political organiza-

tion or the supplies to keep their troops united, however. Soon the warriors drifted off in bands to elude pursuit or search for food, and the army ran them down singly and returned them to Dakota. The power of the Sioux was now broken. The proud leaders, Crazy Horse and Sitting Bull, accepted defeat and the monotony of life on reservations. Both were later killed by reservation police after being tricked or taunted into a last pathetic show of resistance.

In 1877, one of the most dramatic episodes in Indian history occurred in Idaho. Here the Nez Percé, a small and relatively peaceful and civilized tribe, refused to accept white demands that they move to a smaller reservation. When troops converged on them, their able leader, Chief Joseph, attempted to conduct the band to Canada. A remarkable chase ensued. Joseph moved with 200 men and 350 women, children, and old people. Pursued by four columns, he covered 1,321 miles in seventy-five days, repelling or evading the army time and again. But he was caught just short of the Canadian border. Like so many other crushed tribes, the Nez Percé were shipped to the Indian Territory in Oklahoma, where most of them soon died of disease and malnutrition.

The last Indians to maintain organized resistance against the whites were the Apaches, who fought intermittently from the 1860s to the late 1880s. The two ablest chiefs of this fierce tribe were Mangas Colorados and Cochise. Mangas was murdered during the Civil War, and in 1872 Cochise agreed to peace and a reservation for his followers. But one leader, Geronimo, continued to carry on the fight. His capture in 1886 marked the end of formal warfare between Indians and whites.

A final, tragic encounter occurred in 1890—the result of a religious revival among the tribes that symbolized, in many ways, the catastrophic effects of the white assaults on Indian civilization. As the Indians saw their culture and their glories fading, and as they suffered near starvation when corrupt government agents reduced their food rations, many turned to an emotional religion that emphasized the coming of a messiah and featured a "ghost dance," which inspired mystical visions. Agents on the Sioux reservation, fearing that the dance might be the preliminary to hostilities, called for troops to stop the ceremonies. Some of the Indians fled to the Dakota Badlands, to join other ghost dancers under the leadership of chief Big Foot. The Seventh Cavalry (which had once been Custer's regiment) pursued them and caught up with them at Wounded Knee, in South Dakota. A brief battle ensued in which about 40 sol-

The Battle of Little Big Horn: An Indian View

This 1898 watercolor by one of the Indian participants portrays the aftermath of the Battle of Little Big Horn, June 25–26, 1876, in which an army unit under the command of General George Armstrong Custer was surrounded and wiped out by Sioux and Cheyenne warriors. This grisly painting shows Indians on horseback riding over the corpses of Custer and his men. Custer can be seen lying at left center, dressed in yellow buckskin with his hat beside him. The four standing men at center are Sitting Bull, Rain-in-the-Face, Crazy Horse, and Kicking Bear (the artist). At lower right, Indian women begin preparations for a ceremony to honor the returning warriors. (Southwest Museum, Pasadena, California)

Geronimo

Geronimo (on horseback at left) was not a formal chieftain, but he assumed the leadership of an aggressive band of Apache warriors in 1876, when the United States government attempted to force the tribe onto a reservation in Arizona. Geronimo established a base in the mountains of Mexico and for more than ten years led his warriors on raids across the border, terrorizing the American countryside. (Culver Pictures)

diers and more than 200 of the Indians, including women and children, died. What precipitated the conflict is a matter of dispute; it is likely that an Indian fired the first shot. But the fighting soon turned into a one-sided massacre, as the white soldiers aimed their new machine guns at the Indians and mowed them down in the snow.

In 1887, Congress finally moved to destroy forever the tribal structure that was the cornerstone of Indian culture. Although some supporters of the new policy believed they were acting for the good of the Indians, the action was frankly designed to force the Indians to become landowners and farmers, to abandon their collective society and culture, to become, in short, part of white civilization. The Dawes Severalty Act (usually known simply as the Dawes Act) provided for the gradual elimination of tribal ownership of land and the allotment of tracts to individual owners: 160 acres to the head of a family, 80 acres to a single adult or orphan, 40 acres to each dependent child. Adult owners were accorded the status of citizenship, but unlike other citizens, they could not gain full title to their property for twenty-five years. The act was hardly a success. The Indians were not prepared for the wrenching change from a collective society to individualism. Congress attempted to speed the transition with the Burke Act of 1906. Under its terms, citizenship was deferred until after the completion of the twenty-five-year period contemplated in the Dawes Act, but Indians who proved their adaptability could secure both citizenship and land ownership in a shorter period.

Neither then nor later, however, did legislation provide a satisfactory solution to the problem of the Indians—largely because there was no entirely happy solution to be had. The interests of the Indians were not compatible with those of the expanding white civilization. The conflict between the two peoples was, therefore, never truly resolved. White society simply prevailed.

The Rise and Decline of the Western Farmer

The arrival of the miners, the empire building of the cattle ranchers, the dispersal of the Indian tribes—all served as a prelude to the decisive phase of white settlement of the Far West. Even before the Civil War, farmers had begun moving into the plains region, challenging the dominance of the ranchers and the Indians and occasionally coming into conflict with both. By the 1870s, what had been a trickle had become a deluge. Farmers poured into the plains and beyond, enclosed land that had once been hunting territory for Indians and grazing territory for cattle, and established a new agricultural region.

For a time in the late 1870s and early 1880s, the new Western farmers flourished—enjoying the fruits of an agricultural economic boom comparable in many ways to the booms that Eastern industry periodically enjoyed. Beginning in the mid-1880s, however, the boom turned to bust. American agriculture—not only in the new West but in the older Middle West and the South as well—was producing more than it ever had. But at the same time, farmers were suffering from declining prices for their goods. Both economically and psychologically, the agricultural economy began a long, steady decline—often in absolute terms, almost always in relation to the rest of the nation. Those who tried to improve their lot by moving west found that the frontier no longer provided them with a way out.

Farming on the Plains

Some farmers had drifted into the Great Plains region during its first stages of development, but the great rush of settlement came in the late 1870s. In the course of the next decade, the relentless advance of the farming frontier would gradually convert the plains country to an agricultural economy.

Many factors combined to produce this surge of Western settlement, but the most important was undoubtedly the railroads. Before the Civil War, the Great Plains had been virtually inaccessible to all but the most hardy pioneers, who could reach it only through an arduous journey by wagon. But beginning in the 1860s, a vast new network of railroad lines started to develop that would, by the 1870s, open access to huge new areas of settlement. The first step toward this new access was the construction of the great "transcontinental" lines. An 1862 act of Congress (amended in 1864) chartered two railroad corporations, the Union Pacific and the Central Pacific. The Union Pacific was to build westward from Omaha, Nebraska, the Central Pacific eastward from Sacramento, California, until they met. To provide the new companies with the necessary financial incentive, Congress made use of a practice that would become of vital importance to the future of the West:

Completing the Transcontinental Railroad

Officials of the Union Pacific and Central Pacific companies shook hands and exchanged bottles of champagne at Promontory Point, Utah, on May 10, 1869, after the last spike was driven to join the two lines and complete the nation's first transcontinental railroad. The Union Pacific line began in Nebraska at the end of existing railroad connections to the East; the Central Pacific built its line eastward from California.   (Union Pacific Railroad Museum Collection)

the land grant. For each mile of track a company laid, it would receive—in addition to the right of way for the track bed itself—twenty square miles of land in alternate sections (laid out in a checkerboard pattern) along the right of way.

The building of the transcontinental line was itself a dramatic and monumental achievement. Thousands of immigrant workers—mostly Irish on the eastern route, Chinese on the western—labored in what were at times unimaginably difficult conditions to penetrate mountain ranges, cross deserts, ward off Indians, and—finally—connect the two lines at Promontory Point in Utah in the spring of 1869. But while this first transcontinental line captured the greatest share of the public imagination, it was the construction of the great network of subsidiary lines in the years which followed that proved of greatest importance to the West. By the end of the century, five transcontinental lines were in operation; and from them were springing more and more spurs, penetrating much of the Great Plains. State governments, imitating Washington, induced railroad development by offering direct financial aid, favorable loans, and more than 50 million acres of land (on top of the 130 million acres the federal government had already offered). In some cases, government aid actually exceeded the cost of construction. Although operated by private corporations, the railroads were essentially public projects.

The construction of the railroad lines helped spur agricultural settlement in several ways. For one thing, it made access to the Great Plains easier—first enabling the farmers to reach the new lands, and later enabling them to ship their crops to market and to receive goods and supplies in return. For another, the railroad companies themselves now had great incentive to promote settlement—both to provide themselves with customers for their services and to increase the value of their vast land holdings. Thus the railroads embarked on a great advertising campaign to lure settlers into the new region, distributing posters and brochures throughout the East and Midwest with glowing descriptions of the "great fertility," "nutritious grasses," and "numerous streams" to be found in the plains. More than that, the companies set rates so low for settlers that almost anyone could afford the trip West. And it sold much of its land at very low prices, usually between $2 and $5 an acre (which, since the railroads had gotten the land for nothing, was still a significant profit). Some railroad companies even provided liberal credit to prospective settlers to encourage them to move West.

Contributing further to the great surge of expansion was a temporary change in the climate. For several years in succession, beginning in the 1870s, rainfall in the plains states was well above average. People now rejected the old idea that the region was the Great American Desert. Some even claimed that

The Receding Frontier, 1860–1890

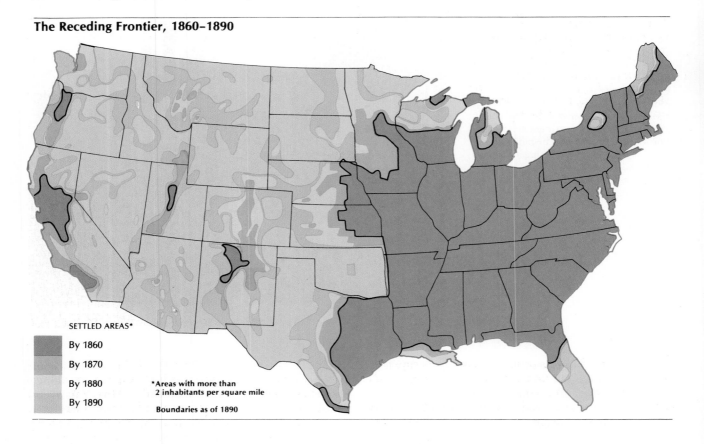

SETTLED AREAS*

By 1860

By 1870

By 1880

By 1890

*Areas with more than
2 inhabitants per square mile

Boundaries as of 1890

cultivation of the plains actually encouraged rainfall. Confident that they faced an era of indefinite prosperity, the new farmers scoffed at those who warned that the climate might change again. They scoffed too at the old cattle ranchers who warned that the light soil of the plains should not be deprived of its protective turf by cultivation.

But even under the most favorable conditions, farming on the plains presented problems not encountered in any previously settled region. First and most critical was the problem of fencing. Farmers had to enclose their land, if for no other reason than to protect it from the herds of the cattlemen. But the traditional wood or stone fences were impossible on the plains; the materials were expensive to import and were, in any case, ineffective as barriers to cattle. In the mid-1870s, however, two Illinois farmers, Joseph H. Glidden and I. L. Ellwood, solved this problem by developing and marketing barbed wire. Produced in large quantities—40,000 tons a year—it sold cheaply, became standard equipment on the plains, and revolutionized fencing practices all over the country.

The second problem, a serious one even when rainfall was above average, was water. That problem became particularly acute after 1887, when a series of dry seasons began. Lands that had come to seem fertile and well watered now began to turn back into semidesert. Farmers attempted to devise one technique after another to deal with the problem, but none was fully satisfactory. One solution was the use of deep wells pumped by steel windmills, which ensured a steady water supply for stock. Another was dry farming—a system of tillage designed to conserve moisture in the soil by covering it with a dust blanket—and the planting of drought-resistant crops. But these techniques were of limited usefulness. In many areas of the plains, commercial agriculture could not continue without large-scale irrigation, which in turn required government assistance. The federal government hoped state governments would take the lead in financing these expensive projects; and in the Carey Act of 1894, it transferred several million acres of public land to various states, on the understanding that the states would reclaim them through irrigation and then sell them. The states,

Threshing Wheat
Oregon farmers stand on stacks of
straw thrown out by their enormous
steam thresher. Farm machinery such
as the thresher helped double the
production of American grain between
1860 and 1880, and helped double it
again by 1900. (Oregon Historical Society)

however, made little progress, largely because the
problems of reclamation cut across state boundaries.
Irrigation, therefore, remained limited through most
of the plains; and the majority of farmers had to deal
with the water shortage as best they could on their
own.

Farming on the plains was always expensive and
often risky. The uncertainty of rainfall and the danger of grasshopper plagues and tornadoes made every
farm year a speculative experiment. Costs of operation were high, partly because many supplies had to
be imported into the region from distant points, but
mainly because of the nature of plains farming. In all
the farm areas of the country, machines were playing
a larger part in the agricultural process, and they were
especially vital on the plains, where grain farming
was conducted on large land units. Farm machinery
made it possible for farmers with limited labor supplies to cultivate expansive landholdings. But machinery required a major capital investment, which
not all prospective farmers could easily afford. The
necessity of making that investment helped to create
one of the central realities of life on Western farms:
debt.

The Great Plains were not, as some have claimed,
a refuge for the urban poor or a safety valve for pro-
letarian unrest. The people who moved into the region were mostly people who had previously been
farmers elsewhere; and they came from agricultural
areas in the Middle West, the East, and Europe. In

the booming years of the early 1880s, with land values rising, the new farmers had no problem obtaining extensive and easy credit and had every reason to
believe they would soon be able to retire their debts.
But the arid years of the late 1880s—years in which
crop prices were falling at the same time as production was becoming more expensive—changed that
prospect with grim suddenness. Thousands of farmers found it impossible any longer to keep up payments on their loans and were forced to abandon
their farms. What followed was a reversal of the
frontier movement—settlers departing the Great
Plains in large numbers, sometimes turning once-
flourishing communities into desolate ghost towns.
Those who remained continued to suffer from falling
prices (wheat, which had sold for $1.60 a bushel at
the end of the Civil War, dropped to 49 cents in the
1890s) and persistent indebtedness.

Changes in Agriculture

Americans had always liked to romanticize farm life.
According to popular myth, the farmer was a sturdy
yeoman—simple, honest, happy, dwelling close to
nature, independent, self-reliant. The myth may once
have had some basis in fact, but by the late nineteenth
century it no longer reflected the reality of agricultural life. The simple, self-sufficient yeoman of myth
had become a commercial farmer—attempting to do

in the agricultural economy what industrialists were doing in the manufacturing economy.

Commercial farmers were not self-sufficient and made no effort to become so. They specialized in cash crops and sold them in national or world markets. They ceased making their own household supplies and growing their own food and bought them instead at town or village stores. This kind of farming, when it was successful, raised the farmers' living standards. But it also made them dependent on other people and on impersonal factors they could not control: bankers and interest rates, railroads and freight rates, national and European markets, world supply and demand. In short, farmers had become businessmen—but with a difference. Unlike the capitalists of the industrial order, they could not regulate their production or influence the prices of what they sold.

The period between 1865 and 1900 witnessed a tremendous expansion of agricultural facilities, not only in the United States but all over the world: in Brazil and Argentina in South America, in Canada, in Australia and New Zealand, and in Russia. World production increased at the same time as modern means of communication and transportation—the telephone, telegraph, cable, steam navigation, railroads—were welding the producing nations into one international market. American commercial farmers, constantly opening new lands, now produced more than the domestic market could absorb and had to depend on the world market to absorb their surplus. Cotton farmers depended on export sales for 70 percent of their annual income, and wheat farmers for 30 to 40 percent; other producers exported smaller proportions of their crops but enough, in most cases, for the exports to make the difference between a year of profit and one of loss.

But world prices were highly unpredictable. Starting in the 1880s, almost every sector of the farm economy began suffering from the effects of worldwide overproduction. And international prices soon declined to a point that made it difficult for even the most efficient farmers to make a profit. Despite the surface similarities between the growth of commercial agriculture and the growth of industry, the results were starkly different. Between 1860 and 1910, the number of farm families rose from 1.5 million to over 6 million. But whereas in 1860 agriculture had represented 50 percent of the total wealth of the country, by the early 1900s it represented only 20 percent. Where farmers had received 30 percent of the national income in 1860, they received only 18 percent by 1910. By the 1890s, 27 percent of the

owned farms in the country were mortgaged, and by 1910, 33 percent. In 1880, 25 percent of all farms had been operated by tenants; by 1910, the proportion had grown to 37 percent. Commercial farming did, it is true, make some people fabulously wealthy. But the farm economy as a whole was suffering a significant decline relative to the rest of the nation.

The Farmers' Grievances

Farmers were painfully aware that something was wrong. Neither they nor anyone else yet understood, however, the full implications of national and world overproduction. Instead, they concentrated their attention and anger on more immediate, more comprehensible—and no less real—problems: inequitable freight rates, high interest charges, and an inadequate currency.

The farmers' first and most burning grievance was against the railroads. In all sections of the country, and especially in the states west of the Mississippi, farmers depended on the railroads to carry crops to the markets. In many cases, the roads charged higher rates for farm than for other shipments, and higher rates in the South and West than in the Northeast. Freight rates sometimes consumed so much of the current price that farmers refused to ship their crops and either let them rot or used them as fuel. Railroads also controlled elevator and warehouse facilities in buying centers and charged arbitrary storage rates.

In the farmers' list of villains, the sources that controlled credit—banks, loan companies, insurance corporations—ranked second only to the railroads. Commercial farming was by its nature expensive, and ambitious producers needed credit to purchase machines or enlarge holdings. Although lenders had been eager to advance loans during the boom period of rising land values, they had insisted on high interest rates. Since sources of credit in the West and South were few, farmers had had to take loans on whatever terms they could get, often at interest rates of from 10 to 25 percent. Farmers who had borrowed in the flush times had to pay their loans back in later years, when prices were dropping and currency was becoming scarce. With good reason, the farmers fought for an increase in the volume of currency.

A third grievance concerned prices: both the prices farmers received for their products and the prices they paid for goods they bought. Farmers disposed of their products in a competitive world market over which they had no control and of which they had no ad-

SIGNIFICANT EVENTS

1851	"Concentration" policy devised for Western tribes
1859	Colorado gold rush launches Western mining bonanza
1864	Nevada admitted to Union
1865–1867	Sioux War
1866	"Long drives" launch Western cattle bonanza
1867	Nebraska admitted to Union Indian Peace Commission establishes "Indian Territory" (later Oklahoma)
1869	Union Pacific, first transcontinental railroad, completed
1873	Barbed wire invented Comstock Lode silver deposits discovered in Nevada Timber Culture Act passed
1874	Gold rush begins in Black Hills, Dakota Territory
1875	Sioux uprising begins
1876	Battle of Little Bighorn Colorado admitted to Union Nez Percé Indians resist relocation
1879	Readjusters win control of Virginia legislature
1880	Joel Chandler Harris publishes *Uncle Remus*
1883	Supreme Court upholds segregation in private institutions
1885–1887	Harsh winters help destroy open-range cattle raising
1885	Mark Twain publishes *Huckleberry Finn*
1886	Geronimo captured
1887	Dawes Act passed Prolonged drought in Great Plains begins
1889	North Dakota, South Dakota, Montana, Washington are admitted to Union Oklahoma (formerly "Indian Territory") opened to white settlement
1890s	"Jim Crow" laws passed throughout South Lynchings increase in South
1890	Battle of Wounded Knee fought Wyoming and Idaho admitted to Union
1891	Hamlin Garland publishes *Main-Traveled Roads*
1893	Frederick Jackson Turner proposes "Turner thesis"
1895	Booker T. Washington outlines Atlanta Compromise
1896	*Plessy* v. *Ferguson* upholds "separate but equal" racial facilities Utah admitted to Union
1898	*Williams* v. *Mississippi* validates literacy tests for voting

vance knowledge. A farmer could plant a large crop at a moment when prices were high and find that by the time of the harvest the price had declined. There were no storage facilities in which farmers could hold their crops and wait for the price to go back up. They had few options, and their fortunes rose and fell in response to unpredictable forces. Naturally, they attempted to find some explanation for their plight; and they tended increasingly to blame their troubles on particular villains: speculators in distant cities, international bankers, regional and local middlemen. Many farmers became convinced (often with some justice) that such people were combining to fix prices so as to benefit themselves at the expense of the growers.

Many farmers also came to believe (again, not without justice) that manufacturers in the East were conspiring to keep the prices of farm goods low and the prices of industrial goods high. Farmers sold their crops in a competitive world market; but they bought manufactured goods in a domestic market protected by tariffs and dominated by trusts and corporations. According to government reports, more than 100 articles purchased by farmers—farm machinery, tools, sewing machines, blankets, staple foods, clothing, plowshares, and others—were protected. On these necessary items, the tariff added from 33 to 60 percent to the purchase price.

The Agrarian Malaise

Adding to these economic grievances, and in many ways a direct result of them, was a less tangible but deeply felt resentment. In part, it was an outgrowth of the isolation of farm life in these days before paved roads, automobiles, telephones, and radios. Farm families in some parts of the country—particularly in the prairie and plains regions, where large farms were scattered over vast areas—were virtually cut off from the outside world and human companionship. During the winter months and spells of bad weather, the loneliness could become nearly unbearable.

In addition to the isolation, there was often a general drabness and dullness to farm existence. Many farmers lacked access to adequate education for their children, to proper medical facilities, to recreational or cultural activities, to virtually anything that might give them a sense of being valued members of a community. Older farmers felt the sting of watching their children leave the farm for the city. They felt the humiliation of being ridiculed as "hayseeds" by the new urban culture that was coming to dominate American life. There was, in short, a general feeling of obsolescence, of being left behind by a society that no longer placed much value on the virtues of rural life.

This emerging agrarian malaise found reflection in the growing discontent of many farmers, a discontent that would help to create a great national polit-ical movement in the 1890s. It found reflection, too, in the literature that emerged from rural America. Writers in the late nineteenth century might romanticize the rugged life of the cowboy and the Western miner. For the farmer, however, the image was different. Hamlin Garland, perhaps the most celebrated writer to deal with the nature of agrarian life in this period, reflected the growing disillusionment in a series of novels and short stories. In the past, Garland wrote in the introduction to *Jason Edwards* (1891), the agrarian frontier had seemed to be "the Golden West, the land of wealth and freedom and happiness. All of the associations called up by the spoken word, the West, were fabulous, mythic, hopeful." Now, however, the bright promise had faded. In this novel and in other works (including his most famous achievement, a collection of stories entitled *Main-Traveled Roads*, also published in 1891), he showed how the trials of rural life were crushing the human spirit. "So this is the reality of the dream!" a character in *Jason Edwards* exclaims. "A shanty on a barren plain, hot and lone as a desert. My God!" Once, sturdy yeoman farmers had viewed themselves as the backbone of American life. Now, they were becoming painfully aware that their position was declining in relation to the rising urban-industrial society to the east.

SUGGESTED READINGS

The New South Many of the studies of the South during Reconstruction cited at the end of Chapter 15 are of relevance to the New South as well. The classic study of the post-Reconstruction South, from which most other efforts stem, is C. Vann Woodward, *Origins of the New South* (1951). Woodward has also authored two collections of essays valuable to the study of this period: *The Burden of Southern History*, rev. ed. (1968) and *American Counterpoint* (1971). In *Thinking Back: The Perils of Writing History* (1986), Woodward reflects on his own earlier work and its critics. Jonathan Wiener, *Social Origins of the New South: Alabama, 1860–1885* (1978), challenges some of Woodward's conclusions. Paul Buck, *The Road to Reunion* (1937), is an older study of Reconstruction and its aftermath in the South. Paul Gaston, *The New South Creed* (1970), is a useful examination of the ideology of progress of the post-Reconstruction years. W. J. Cash, *The Mind of the South* (1941), continues to arouse controversy with its bold interpretation of the Southern psyche. Orville Vernon Burton, *In My Father's House* (1985), is an ambitious examination of family and community in the town of Edgehill, South Carolina. J. Morgan Kousser and James M. McPherson (eds.), *Region, Race, and Reconstruction* (1982), is a collection of essays on Southern history of both the postbellum and antebellum eras.

Politics in the South The impact of national politics on the South is considered in C. Vann Woodward, *Reunion and Reaction* (1951), a study of the Compromise of 1877; Stanley P. Hirshson, *Farewell to the Bloody Shirt: Northern Republicans and the Southern Negro* (1962); Kenneth E. Davison, *The Presidency of Rutherford B. Hayes* (1972); and Vincent P. DeSantis, *Republicans Face the Southern Question: The New Departure Years, 1877–1897* (1959). On politics within the New South, see—in addition to the Woodward works cited above—J. Morgan Kousser, *The Shaping of Southern Politics: Suffrage Restriction and the Establishment of the One-Party South, 1880–1910* (1974); Paul Lewinson, *Race, Class, and Party* (1932); and V. O. Key, Jr., *Southern Politics and the Nation* (1949). Francis B. Simkins, *Pitchfork Ben Tillman* (1944), C. Vann Woodward, *Tom Watson: Agrarian Rebel* (1938), and Joseph F. Wall, *Henry Watterson: Reconstructed Rebel* (1956), are biographies of leading Southern political figures. Sheldon Hackney, *Populism to Progressivism in Alabama* (1959), is a valuable study of late nineteenth-century and early twentieth-century political movements in a single state. David Potter, *The South and the Concurrent Majority* (1972), and Carl Degler, *The Other South: Southern Dissenters in the Nineteenth Century* (1974), are also useful.

Race and Economics in the South Melvin Greenhut and W. Tate Whitman (eds.), *Essays in Southern Economic Development* (1964), examines a number of economic issues. David Carlton, *Mill and Town in South Carolina, 1880–1920*

(1982), and Melton A. McLaurin, *Paternalism and Protest: Southern Cotton Mill Workers and Organized Labor* (1971), describe labor relations in the new industrial towns of the South. Steve Hahn, *The Roots of Southern Populism: Yeoman Farmers and the Transformation of the Georgia Upcountry* (1983), traces the introduction of a market economy into the Georgia interior and its effects on poor whites. John Dittmer, *Black Georgia in the Progressive Era, 1900–1920* (1970), carries the story into this century. Roger Ransom and Richard Sutch, *One Kind of Freedom* (1977), examines the origins of the crop lien system. Gavin Wright, *Old South, New South* (1986), is a sweeping overview of the Southern economy. On race relations, see C. Vann Woodward, *The Strange Career of Jim Crow*, rev. ed. (1974); Howard Rabinowitz, *Race Relations in the Urban South, 1865–1890* (1978); James M. McPherson, *The Abolitionist Legacy: From Reconstruction to the NAACP* (1975); Robert Higgs, *Competition and Coercion: Blacks in the American Economy, 1865–1914* (1977); and two works by Joel Williamson: *After Slavery* (1965), which challenges Woodward's view of the origins of segregation, and *The Crucible of Race: Black-White Relations in the American South Since Emancipation* (1985), a sweeping study. George Frederickson, *The Black Image in the White Mind* (1968), provides another overview of race relations. Louis R. Harlan, *Booker T. Washington*, 2 vols. (1972, 1983), is an excellent study of the preeminent black leader of the New South. Donald Spivey, *Schooling for the New Slavery: Black Industrial Education* (1978), studies the results of Washington's approach to racial uplift. See also August Meier, *Negro Thought in America* (1963). Francis Broderick, *W. E. B. DuBois* (1959), and Elliott M. Rudwick, *W. E. B. DuBois: Propagandist of Negro Protest*, rev. ed. (1969), examine the founder of the NAACP. George F. Kellogg, *NAACP* (1970), discusses the formation of that organization.

Westward Expansion Ray A. Billington, *Westward Expansion* (1967), and Frederick Merk, *History of the Westward Movement* (1978), are general studies. Billington and Merk were both disciples of Frederick Jackson Turner. Thomas D. Clark, *Frontier America*, rev. ed. (1969), offers an alternative interpretation. Howard R. Lamar, *The Far Southwest, 1846–1912* (1966), is a more specialized study of the period discussed in this chapter. Henry Nash Smith, *Virgin Land* (1950), examines the myth of the West in the American literary imagination. Frederick Jackson Turner, *The Frontier in American History* (1920), presents the influential "frontier thesis" of its author. Ray A. Billington, *Frederick Jackson Turner* (1973), is a good biography. Patricia Nelson Limerick, *Desert Passages: Encounters with the American Deserts* (1985), is a study of how various Americans have responded to the Great Plains over time.

Miners and Cattlemen The arrival of the miners is discussed in Rodman W. Paul, *Mining Frontiers of the Far West, 1848-1880* (1963); William S. Greever, *Bonanza West: Western Mining Rushes* (1963); and Duane A. Smith, *Rocky Mountain Mining Camps* (1967). The expansion of ranching is the subject of Lewis Atherton, *The Cattle Kings* (1961);

Ernest E. Osgood, *The Day of the Cattleman* (1929); Edward E. Dale, *The Range Cattle Industry*, rev. ed. (1969); and J. M. Skaggs, *The Cattle Trailing Industry* (1973). Robert K. Dykstra, *The Cattle Towns* (1968), looks at several cattle towns in Kansas. Among books exploring the life of the cowboy, see Andy Adams, *The Log of a Cowboy* (1927); Joe B. Frantz and Julian Choate, *The American Cowboy: The Myth and the Reality* (1955); and L. Steckmesser, *The Western Hero in History and Legend* (1965). Odie B. Faulk, *Tombstone: Myth and Reality* (1972), examines a fabled Western town. Earl Pomeroy, *The Pacific Slope* (1965), is a study of urban growth in the West, and Gunther Barth, *Instant Cities* (1975), explores the sudden rise of San Francisco and Denver.

Indians On the plight of Native Americans, see the general account by Wilcomb E. Washburn, *The Indian in America* (1975), as well as his *Red Man's Land/White Man's Law* (1971). Of more specific interest are Ralph K. Andrist, *The Long Death: The Last Days of the Plains Indians* (1964); Francis Paul Prucha, *American Indian Policy in Crisis* (1976); and Robert M. Utley, *Frontier Regulars: The United States Army and the Indian* (1973), *Last Days of the Sioux Nation* (1963), and *The Indian Frontier of the American West, 1846–1890* (1984). Margaret Coel, *Chief Left Hand: Southern Arapaho* (1981), examines clashes between whites and Indians in Colorado. Loretta Fowler, *Arapahoe Politics, 1851–1978: Symbols in Crisis of Authority* (1982), is a study of symbols and political behavior among the Arapaho. John Powell, *People of the Sacred Mountain: A History of the Northern Cheyenne Chiefs and Warrior Societies, 1830–1879*, 2 vols. (1981), is a large-scale study of the northern and southern Cheyenne. Robert Mardock, *Reformers and the American Indian* (1971), considers white efforts on behalf of the tribes. Robert F. Berkhofer, Jr., *The White Man's Indian* (1978), examines white images of the Native American.

Western Women Julie Jeffrey, *Frontier Women: The Trans-Mississippi West, 1840–1880* (1979), and Sandra L. Myres, *Westering Women and the Frontier Experience, 1880–1915* (1982), examine the experience of woman migrants to the West. Polly Welts Kaufman, *Women Teachers on the Frontier* (1984), examines Eastern women who moved west to teach. Joanna L. Stratton, *Pioneer Women: Voices from the Kansas Frontier* (1981), is an oral history. John Mack Faragher, *Women and Men on the Overland Trail* (1979), is a study of social interaction during the movement west.

Western Agriculture Walter Prescott Webb, *The Great Plains* (1931), is a classic study of the opening of America's last agricultural frontier; Fred A. Shannon, *The Farmer's Last Frontier, 1860–1897* (1945), and Gilbert C. Fite, *The Farmer's Frontier* (1966), are more recent studies. Paul W. Gates, *History of Public Land Development* (1968), examines government policy. Life on the frontier is the subject of Everett Dick, *The Sod-House Frontier* (1937). Allan Bogue, *From Prairie to Corn Belt* (1963), is a broad view of agricultural development. The growth of the agrarian malaise and the emergence of protest are examined in the section on Populism in the readings for Chapter 19.

***The Big Blow,* by Aaron Bohrod** (National Steel Corporation)

Chapter 17 Industrial Supremacy

"With a stride that astonished statisticians, the conquering hosts of business enterprise swept over the continent; twenty-five years after the death of Lincoln, America had become, in the quantity and value of her products, the first manufacturing nation of the world. What England had accomplished in a hundred years, the United States had achieved in half the time." So wrote the historians Charles and Mary Beard in the 1920s, expressing the amazement many Americans felt when they considered the remarkable expansion of their economy in the late nineteenth century.

In fact, America's rise to industrial supremacy was not as sudden as some observers believed. The nation had been building a manufacturing economy since early in the nineteenth century; industry was well established before the Civil War. But Americans were clearly correct in observing that the accomplishments of the last three decades of the nineteenth century overshadowed all the earlier progress. Those years witnessed nothing less than the transformation of the nation.

Many factors contributed to this dramatic industrial growth. The United States had an abundance of basic raw materials and energy sources: coal, iron, timber, petroleum, water power, and more. There was a large and growing supply of labor, the result of two great migrations: the movement of American farmers into the cities and the movement of European peasants across the ocean to the nation's industrial centers. American industry benefited as well from a remarkable technological inventiveness—widely heralded as "Yankee ingenuity"—which created the necessary machinery for industrial growth.

A talented, energetic, and ambitious group of entrepreneurs—known by some as "captains of industry" and by others as "robber barons"—developed new financial and administrative structures capable of organizing large-scale production and distributing manufactured goods to a national market. And the market itself was growing as a result of population growth, the new railroad network, and a host of new marketing techniques. Finally, the federal government worked to promote economic growth. It resisted pressures to interfere with the prerogatives of capitalists, and it worked at the same time to promote corporate growth. It made public resources available for private exploitation on generous terms; it erected protective tariff barriers against foreign competition; it established a new banking and currency system; and it provided direct subsidies of land and money.

The remarkable growth that resulted from these factors did much to increase the wealth and improve the lives of many Americans. But such benefits were far from equally shared. While the industrial titans and a growing middle class were enjoying a prosperity without precedent in the nation's history, workers, farmers, and others were experiencing an often painful ordeal that slowly edged the United States toward a great economic and political crisis.

Sources of Industrial Growth

Virtually all the forces that contributed to American economic growth were in operation in some form before the Civil War. But there were other forces at work in those years to inhibit economic development. Perhaps most important, conservative Southern planters, exercising great political power, had served as an obstacle to governmental policies favoring Northern capitalists. The years of war and Reconstruction removed that obstacle, as well as others. And in the 1870s and 1880s, the forces of economic progress took on renewed strength.

Industrial Technology

No one factor can be called the most important prerequisite of industrial growth. Indeed, industrialization depends above all on the working together of many forces at once. But one of the most important of such forces, certainly, is the emergence of new technologies and the discovery of new materials and productive processes. In the last decades of the nineteenth century, inventions appeared at a dizzying pace. In the entire history of the United States up to 1860, only 36,000 patents had been granted. For the period from 1860 to 1890, the figure was 440,000.

Many of the postwar inventions and discoveries were in the field of communication. In 1866, Cyrus W. Field succeeded in laying a transatlantic telegraph cable to Europe. During the next decade, Alexander Graham Bell developed the first practicable telephone; and by the 1890s, the American Telephone and Telegraph Company, which handled his interests, had installed nearly half a million instruments in American cities. Other inventions that speeded the pace of business organization were the typewriter (by Christopher L. Sholes in 1868), the cash register (by James Ritty in 1879), and the calculating or adding machine (by William S. Burroughs in 1891).

The technological innovation that probably had the most revolutionary effect on industry and on the lives of the urban masses was the introduction in the 1870s of electricity as a source of light and power. Among the several men who pioneered this development were Charles F. Brush, who devised the arc lamp for street illumination, and Thomas A. Edison, who invented, among many other electrical devices, the incandescent lamp (or light bulb), which could be used for both street and home lighting. Edison and others designed improved generators and built large power plants to furnish electricity to whole cities. Before the turn of the century, 2,774 power stations were in operation, and some 2 million electric lights were in use in the country. Electric power was by then becoming commonplace in street railway sys-

tems, in the elevators of urban skyscrapers, and in factories.

Another important technological breakthrough was the development of steel. A process by which iron could be transformed into steel—a much more durable and versatile material—had been discovered simultaneously in the 1850s by an Englishman, Henry Bessemer, and an American, William Kelly. (The process consisted of blowing air through molten iron to burn out the impurities.) After the Civil War, the new process transformed the metal industry; and in 1868, another method of making steel—the open-hearth process, introduced from Europe by the New Jersey ironmaster Abram S. Hewitt—made an appearance as well. Together, these techniques made possible the production of steel in great quantities and in large dimensions, thus facilitating use of the metal for the production of locomotives, steel rails, and ultimately, heavy girders for the construction of tall buildings.

The steel industry emerged first, unsurprisingly, where the iron industry already existed, in western Pennsylvania and eastern Ohio—a region where iron ore and coal were abundant. Pittsburgh quickly became the center of the steel world. But the rapid growth of the industry soon stimulated the development of new sources of ore in other areas. The mines of the upper peninsula of Michigan were furnishing over half of the supply by the 1870s. Beginning in the 1890s, the extensive Mesabi range in Minnesota developed into the greatest ore-producing region in the world. Another rich source was discovered around Birmingham, Alabama. Eventually new centers of production emerged closer to the new sources of ore and coal: Cleveland and Lorain in Ohio; Detroit, Chicago, and Birmingham.

The petroleum industry emerged in the late nineteenth century largely in response to the steel industry's need for lubrication for its machines. (Not until later did oil become important primarily for its potential as a fuel.) Many Americans had been aware for some time of the existence of petroleum reserves in western Pennsylvania, where oil often seeped to the surface of streams and springs. At first, however, no one was quite sure what it was or what to do with it. (Some charlatans bottled it and sold it as a patent medicine.) In 1855, however, the Pennsylvania businessman George H. Bissell sent a sample of oil to Professor Benjamin Silliman of Yale for analysis. Silliman told him that the substance could be used for lighting purposes and that it would also yield such products as paraffin, naphtha, and lubricating oil.

Convinced now that oil had commercial possibilities, Bissell raised money to begin drilling; and in 1859, Edwin L. Drake, one of Bissell's employees, established the first oil well near Titusville, Pennsylvania, which was soon producing 500 barrels of oil a month. Skeptics called the well "Drake's folly," but demand for petroleum grew quickly enough to precipitate an oil rush. Promoters began to develop other fields in Pennsylvania, Ohio, and West Virginia. By the 1870s, nearly 40 million barrels of petroleum had been produced; oil had advanced to fourth place among the nation's exports; and annual production was approaching 20 million barrels.

New technologies and materials similarly transformed other industries. The refrigerated freight car made possible the expansion of the great meat-packing organizations of Gustavus Swift, Philip Armour, and others. New ways of milling flour made possible the emergence of large milling companies in the Midwest (and particularly in Minnesota). New methods of canning foods and condensing milk helped establish the prepared-foods industry under the leadership of Gail Borden and others.

By the beginning of the twentieth century, the new technology was leading to even greater advances. There were early experiments in communication by radio conducted by the Italian inventor Guglielmo Marconi in the 1890s. There were the first steps toward the development of the airplane—the famous flight by the Wright brothers at Kitty Hawk, North Carolina, in 1903. But of more immediate importance was the development of the automobile. In the 1870s, designers in France, Germany, and Austria—inspired by the success of railroad engines—were already beginning to develop engines that might drive independently controlled vehicles. They achieved early successes with an "internal combustion engine," which used the expanding power of burning gas to drive pistons; and with this new engine, they created the first automobiles—essentially traditional carriages fitted with their own source of power to replace the horse.

Meanwhile, in the United States, inventors such as Charles and Frank Duryea, Elwood Haynes, Ransom Olds, and Henry Ford were designing their own automobiles. The Duryeas built and operated the first gasoline-driven motor vehicle in America in 1903. (Earlier American cars had used other, cruder fuels.) Three years later, Ford produced the first of the famous cars that would bear his name. In 1898, the first automobile advertisement appeared in *Scientific American,* under the headline: "Dispense With a Horse." The first automobile showroom opened in New York in 1901. By 1900, automobile companies were turn-

Drake and His Oil Well, c. 1866
Edwin L. Drake became the first American to tap petroleum at its source by drilling when he constructed an oil well (derided by many at the time as "Drake's Folly") at Titusville, Pennsylvania, in 1859. Drake got the idea by watching salt-well drilling operations around Syracuse, New York, and Pittsburgh; using similar techniques, he struck oil at Titusville on August 27, 1859, at a depth of sixty-nine feet. He is shown here, at right, wearing a top hat, in front of his well. (Bettmann Archive)

ing out more than 4,000 cars a year. A decade later—when manufacturers were finally able to streamline operations so as to bring the cost down, and when American roads began to be improved to make extensive automobile traffic possible—the industry had become a major force in the economy, and the automobile was beginning to reshape American social and cultural life. In 1895, there had been only four automobiles on the American highways. By 1917, there were nearly 5 million.

The Science of Production

Central to the growth of the automobile and other industries were advances in the science of production. Convinced that a modern economy required modernization of the manufacturing process, industrialists by the turn of the century were turning in growing numbers to the new principles of "scientific management." The leading force behind the new science was Frederick Winslow Taylor.

Taylor's ideas were controversial during his lifetime, and they have remained controversial ever since. Taylor himself, and his many admirers, argued that scientific management was an essential prerequisite to an efficient, modern economy. It was a way to manage human labor to make it compatible with the demands of the machine age. But scientific management had another purpose as well, which made it far less appealing to many workers. It was a way to increase the employer's control of the workplace, to make working people less independent.

Taylor's first experiments were targeted not at machine operators but at manual laborers. Among other things, he urged employers to reorganize the production process by subdividing tasks. This would be a way to speed up production; it would also make workers more interchangeable and thus diminish a manager's dependence on any particular employee. But Taylor's ideas found their greatest influence in industries where machinery was becoming central to production. The new technology, Taylor argued, would be of little use unless workers could be trained to operate the machinery efficiently and effectively. If properly managed, he argued, fewer and fewer workers could perform simpler tasks at infinitely greater speed, greatly increasing productive efficiency. They would also be easier to control if they could be made part of a scientifically designed process of production rather than left in control of the process themselves. Not until well into the new century—indeed not until the 1920s—did the influence of what became known as "Taylorism" reach its fullest extent. But the impulse behind it—the attempt to bring to the performance of workers the same scientific standards that industrialists were bringing to the creation of new technologies—was affecting industry much earlier than that.

Manufacturers also began placing greater emphasis on industrial research. In part because of the phenomenal success of Thomas Edison's famous industrial laboratory in Menlo Park, New Jersey, dozens of corporations were, by the early years of the twentieth century, establishing laboratories of their own. By 1913, Bell Telephone, Du Pont, General Electric, Eastman Kodak, and about fifty other companies were budgeting hundreds of thousands of dollars each year for research by their own engineers and scientists.

Out of all the new methods and machines emerged the greatest triumph of production technology: mass production and, above all, the moving assembly line, which Henry Ford introduced in his automobile plants in 1914. This revolutionary technique cut the time for assembling a chassis from twelve and a half hours to one and a half hours. It enabled Ford to raise the wages and reduce the hours of his workers while cutting the base price of his Model T from $950 to $290. And it served as an example for many other industries.

Railroad Expansion

The principal agent of industrial development in the late nineteenth century was the expansion of another transportation system: the railroads. Railroads promoted economic growth in many ways. As the nation's principal method of transportation, they made possible the expansion of genuinely national commerce by giving industrialists quick and relatively inexpensive access to distant markets and distant sources of raw materials. As the nation's largest businesses, the railroads created new forms of corporate organization that served as models for other industries. And as America's biggest investors, they stimulated economic growth through their own enormous expenditures on construction and equipment.

Even before the Civil War, railroads had been the most important single economic interest in the United States. In the years that followed, their importance grew still further. Every decade, the total railroad trackage increased dramatically: from 30,000 miles in 1860, to 52,000 miles in 1870, to 93,000 in 1880, to 163,000 in 1890, and to 193,000 at the turn of the century. Along with the extension of lines came improvements in technology that made railroad travel safer and more efficient: steel rails, heavier locomotives and cars, uniform track gauge, wider roadbeds, and perhaps most important, new braking systems

Railroads, 1870–1890

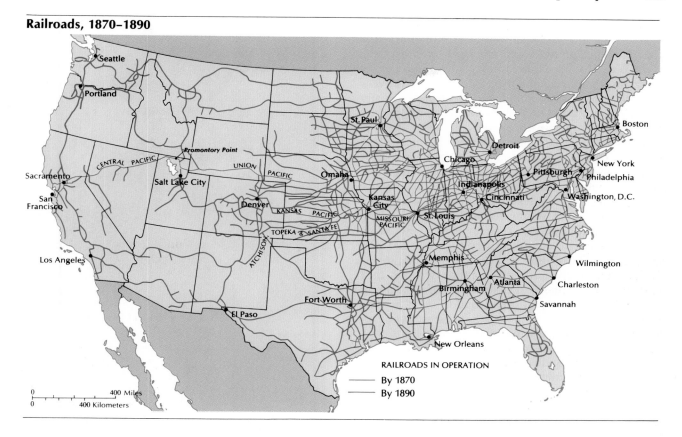

RAILROADS IN OPERATION
—— By 1870
—— By 1890

(first introduced by George Westinghouse) that reduced the danger of derailments and pileups.

Government subsidies—those by the federal government to support the transcontinental lines and those by state and local governments to encourage subsidiary routes—were vital to these vast undertakings, which required far more capital than private entrepreneurs could raise by themselves. Equally important, perhaps, was the emergence of great railroad corporations—the first large economic combinations—which brought a vast proportion of the nation's rails under the control of a very few men. Among the earliest such combinations was the Pennsylvania Railroad. It was one of the first companies to combine a large number of short lines under the direction of a single management. It also introduced a new system of administration—by trained managers who ran the company efficiently. Profits still went to the stockholders; but the actual running of the company was lodged in the hands of people who were not necessarily owners.

Other railroad combinations, however, saw owners continue to play a central role in management through the last decades of the nineteenth century: the vast New York Central empire of Cornelius Vanderbilt (a former steamship owner widely known as "the Commodore"), for example; or the Erie Railroad, controlled by the unscrupulous speculators Daniel Drew, Jay Gould, and James Fisk, whose self-serving exploitation of the company ultimately led to disaster. Indeed, these and other railroad tycoons—James J. Hill, Collis P. Huntington, and others—became symbols to much of the nation of great economic power concentrated in a single individual. But railroad development was less significant for the individual barons it created than for its contribution to the growth of a new institution: the modern corporation.

The Corporation

There had been corporations in America since colonial times: organizations chartered by governments and charged with running such public facilities as bridges, roads, and banks. But the corporation in the modern sense of the word emerged only after the Civil War. By then, railroad magnates and other industrialists were realizing that many of the great ventures they envisioned could not be financed by any single person, no matter how wealthy, nor even by any single group of partners.

Under the laws of incorporation, business organizations could raise money by selling stock to members of the public; and in the decades after the Civil War, one industry after another adopted this practice of financing its undertakings. The phenomenon of people investing in businesses with which they had no direct connection was almost entirely new. What made the practice appealing was the new idea that investors had only "limited liability"—that is, investors risked only the amount of their investments; they were not liable for any debts the corporation might accumulate beyond that point. Suddenly, it became possible for entrepreneurs to gather vast sums of capital and undertake great projects.

The new type of corporation quickly spread beyond the railroad industry to other areas of the economy. In steel, the central figure was Andrew Carnegie, a Scottish immigrant who had worked his way up in the railroad industry. In 1873, he opened his own steelworks in Pittsburgh; and in the following decades, he expanded his company to a place of dominance in the industry. His methods were much like those of other rising industrial titans. From the railroads, he obtained rebates on his shipments so that he could cut his costs and hence his prices. He bought out rival concerns that could not meet his competition. He set up—in collaboration with his able associate Henry Clay Frick—a carefully integrated system that enabled him to control the processing of steel from mine to market. His company bought up coal mines and leased part of the Mesabi range, operated a fleet of ore ships on the Great Lakes, and acquired railroads. He financed his undertakings not only out of his own profits but out of the sale of stock. Then, in 1901, he sold out to the banker J. Pierpont Morgan, who merged the Carnegie interests with others to create the giant United States Steel Corporation—a $1.4 billion enterprise that controlled almost two-thirds of the nation's steel production.

A similar process, although usually on a more modest scale, was at work in other industries. Gustavus Swift developed a relatively small meat-packing company into a great national corporation, in part because of profits earned during the Civil War,

Andrew Carnegie
Carnegie was one of a relatively small number of the great industrialists of the late nineteenth century who genuinely rose "from rags to riches." Born in Scotland, he came to the United States in 1848, at the age of thirteen, and soon found work as a messenger in a Pittsburgh telegraph office. His skill in learning to transcribe telegraphic messages (he became one of the first telegraphers in the country able to take messages by sound) brought him to the attention of a Pennsylvania Railroad official; and before he was twenty, he had begun his ascent to the highest ranks of industry. After the Civil War, he shifted his attention to the growing iron industry; in 1873 he staked all his assets on the development of the first American steel mills. Two decades later he was one of the wealthiest men in the world. In 1901 he abruptly resigned from the industrial world and spent the remaining twenty years of his life as a philanthropist. By the time of his death in 1919, he had given away some $350 million. (Culver Pictures)

in part because of his success in attracting investors in the years after the war. Isaac Singer had patented a sewing machine in 1851 and created—in I. M. Singer and Company—one of the first modern manufacturing corporations.

It was not simply the accumulation of capital that characterized the new organizations. It was also a new approach to management. Large, national business enterprises needed more systematic administrative structures than the limited, local ventures of the past. As a result, corporate leaders introduced a set of managerial techniques—the genesis of modern business administration—that relied on the division of responsibilities, a carefully designed hierarchy of control, modern cost-accounting procedures, and perhaps above all a new breed of business executive: the "middle manager," who formed a layer of command between workers and owners. Beginning in the railroad corporations, these new management techniques moved quickly into virtually every area of large-scale industry.

Efficient administrative capabilities helped make possible another major feature of the modern corporation: consolidation. Railroad companies attempting to create a national network of lines had quickly discovered that combination—the joining of small local enterprises into huge national organizations—enabled them to move more quickly and efficiently toward their goals. Other industries attempting to take advantage of the expanding national markets for manufactured goods did likewise, creating giant industrial organizations.

Businessmen created these organizations through two primary methods. The first was "horizontal integration"—the combining of a number of firms engaged in the same enterprise into a single corporation. The consolidation of many different railroad lines into one company was an example. The second method, which became prevalent in the 1890s, was "vertical integration"—the taking over of the businesses on which a company relied for its primary function. Carnegie Steel, which came to control not only steel mills, but mines, railroads, and other enterprises, was an example of vertical integration.

The most celebrated corporate empire of the late nineteenth century was Standard Oil. The greatest consolidationist of the time, John D. Rockefeller, pieced it together by using both methods. Beginning at the age of nineteen, when he became a partner in a Cleveland produce commission that earned great profits during the Civil War, Rockefeller displayed remarkable talents. Farsighted, acquisitive,

and skilled at organization, he decided that his own economic future lay with the oil industry; and shortly after the Civil War, he launched a refining company in Cleveland (which he believed was destined to become a national center of the industry). From the beginning, he sought to eliminate his competition—especially the many small-scale companies that he believed were ruining the petroleum industry by introducing destabilizing competition. Allying himself with other wealthy capitalists, he proceeded methodically to buy out other refineries. In 1870, he formed the Standard Oil Company of Ohio, which in a few years had acquired twenty of the twenty-five refineries in Cleveland, as well as plants in Pittsburgh, Philadelphia, New York, and Baltimore.

So far, Rockefeller had expanded only horizontally. But soon he began expanding vertically as well. He built his own barrel factories and terminal warehouses and a network of pipelines that gave him control over most of the facilities for transporting petroleum. Standard Oil also owned its own freight cars and developed its own marketing organization, thus avoiding commissions to middlemen. By the 1880s, Rockefeller had established such dominance within the petroleum industry that to much of the nation he served as the leading symbol of monopoly.

Rockefeller and other industrialists saw consolidation as a way to cope with what many believed was the greatest curse of the modern economy: cutthroat competition. Businessmen insisted that they believed fervently in free enterprise and a competitive marketplace—but such beliefs often lasted only until they themselves were exposed to competition. Then they realized that the existence of too many competing firms in a single industry could spell instability and ruin for all, that a successful enterprise was one that could eliminate or absorb its competitors.

As the movement toward combination accelerated, new vehicles emerged to facilitate it. Again it was the railroads that moved first. They began with so-called pool arrangements—informal agreements among various companies to stabilize rates and divide markets (arrangements that would, in later years, be known as cartels). But the pools ultimately proved unworkable, especially after the economic panic of the 1890s began to wreak havoc on the railroads and other corporations. If even a few firms in an industry were unwilling to cooperate (as was almost always the case), the pool arrangements could not survive.

The failure of the pools raised demands for new, more rigorous techniques of consolidation—resting less on cooperation than on centralized control. At first, the most successful such technique was the creation of the "trust"—pioneered by Standard Oil in the early 1880s. Over time, the word *trust* became in popular discourse a term for any great economic combination. But the trust was in fact a particular kind of organization, one that soon became a common vehicle for consolidating railroads and other industries as well. Under a trust agreement, stockholders in individual corporations transferred their stocks to a small group of trustees (in the case of the Standard Oil trust, to men chosen and dominated by Rockefeller) in exchange for shares in the trust itself. Owners of trust certificates often had no direct control over the decisions of the trustees; they simply received a share of the profits of the combination. Thus while John D. Rockefeller officially owned only a few refinery companies, he managed through the mechanism of the trust to extend his reach over a vast range of enterprises.

An even greater master of the trust was J. P. Morgan. In theory, Morgan was simply a bank president. In reality, he dominated scores of industrial organizations. Morgan's bank took control of one after another failing railroad line, reorganized it, and stabilized its operations. In the 1880s, he played a major role in saving the New York Central Railroad from collapse. Other railroads soon looked to Morgan (and such other banking firms as Kuhn Loeb and Company) for assistance. In the decades that followed, a similar system extended into other industries as well.

A third form of consolidation, closely related to the trust, began to emerge in the 1890s. In 1889, the state of New Jersey—followed later by many other states—changed its laws of incorporation to permit companies actually to buy up other companies. That made the cumbersome vehicle of the trust unnecessary and permitted actual mergers. Rockefeller quickly relocated Standard Oil in New Jersey and created there what became known as a "holding company"—a central corporate body that would formally buy up the stock of various members of the Standard Oil trust and establish direct, formal ownership of the corporations in the trust. Many other corporations followed suit.

Corporate organization in the late nineteenth century moved, therefore, through several stages on the way to establishing the modern system of business consolidation. It began with efforts to control competition and reduce instability by creating loose, informal pool arrangements, or *cartels*. It then moved to the more effective, but still awkward, *trust* arrangement. And then, in the 1890s, it took the final step of creating formal corporate structures controlling vast enterprises—*holding companies*. As a result, by the end of the nineteenth century 1 percent of the corporations in America were able to control more than 33 percent of the manufacturing. A congressional investigation disclosed in 1913 that Rockefeller and Morgan controlled between them companies valued at more than $22 billion. What was emerging, in other words, was a system of economic organization that lodged enormous power in the hands of a very few men—the great bankers of New York, industrial titans such as Rockefeller (who himself gained control of a major bank), and others.

Whether or not the ruthless concentration of economic power was the only way (or the best way) to promote industrial expansion became a major source of debate in America in the late nineteenth century and beyond. But it is clear that the industrial giants of the era were reponsible for substantial economic growth. They were integrating operations, cutting costs, creating a great industrial infrastructure, stimulating new markets. They were opening the way to large-scale mass production. Perhaps without realizing it, they were building the foundations of a great economic society. They were also creating the basis for some of the greatest public controversies of their era.

Capitalism and Its Critics

The rise of big business depended not only on technology, transportation, and organization, but on an ideology of growth and progress. Industrialists and financiers in the last decades of the nineteenth century developed a complex and wide-ranging rationale for their methods and power. And while this new set of ideas was in large part meant simply to justify what already existed, it also became a positive force, spurring others to greater efforts.

The new business philosophy was not without its critics. Farmers and workers were the most strident opponents, seeing in the growth of the great new corporate power centers a threat to their traditional notions of a republican society in which wealth and authority were widely distributed. The new economy, they argued, was eroding the opportunities for individuals to advance in society; it was stifling mobility. Middle-class critics pointed to the corruption that the new industrial titans seemed to produce, not only in their own enterprises but in local, state, and national politics as well. Even many businessmen were critical of the system and charged that the large corporations were not yet sufficiently modernized, that their methods were wasteful and inefficient.

The growing criticisms presented the captains of industry with a challenge. They not only had to build the new corporate economy. They had to legitimize it. They had to find a way to convince the public (and themselves) that the new structures they were creating were compatible with the ideology of individualism and equal opportunity that were so central to American life. Their efforts were never entirely successful. Critics continued to assail corporate power and to attract widespread popular support for their positions. But the philosophy of big business had a powerful impact nevertheless—not only among industrialists themselves, but among large groups of the American population.

The "Self-Made Man"

An important part of the emerging philosophy of capitalism rested squarely on the older ideology of individualism. The new industrial economy, its defenders argued, was not shrinking opportunities for individual advancement. It was expanding those opportunities. It was providing every individual with a chance to succeed and attain great wealth.

There was an element of truth in such claims, but only a small element. Before the Civil War there had been few millionaires in America; by 1892 there were more than 4,000 of them. Most of the new business tycoons had begun their careers from comfortable and privileged positions on the economic scale. But some—enough to invest the entire group with the aura of the American success story—had emerged from obscurity to riches. Andrew Carnegie had worked as a bobbin boy in a Pittsburgh cotton mill; James J. Hill had been a frontier clerk; John D. Rockefeller had started out as a clerk in a Cleveland commission house; and E. H. Harriman had begun as a broker's office boy. Some millionaires, in other words, were in fact what nearly all claimed to be: "self-made men."

And yet their rise to power and prominence was not always a result simply of hard work and ingenuity. It was also a result of ruthlessness and, at times, rampant corruption. Cornelius Vanderbilt expressed the attitude of many of his fellow tycoons with the belligerent question: "Can't I do what I want with my own?" So did his son William, in a much-quoted-

"Modern Colossus of (Rail) Roads"
Cornelius Vanderbilt, known as the "Commodore," accumulated one of America's great fortunes by consolidating several large railroad companies under his control in the 1860s. His name became a synonym not only for enormous wealth, but also (in the eyes of many Americans) for excessive corporate power—as suggested in this cartoon, showing him standing astride his empire and manipulating its parts. (Culver Pictures)

statement: "The public be damned." Once, when the elder Vanderbilt's lawyers warned him that a move he contemplated was illegal, he bellowed: "What do I care about the law? Hain't I got the power?" Not all tycoons were as openly contemptuous of the public and the laws as the Vanderbilts at times seemed to be. But many displayed a similar belief that their own activities were somehow exempt from normal restraints.

Industrialists showed little restraint, certainly, in their efforts to get what they wanted from the political system. They made large financial contributions to politicians and to political parties. They presented gifts of stock and cash to public officials in exchange for support. And more often than not, state and local governments responded to these tactics by doing the industrialists' bidding. Cynics said that Standard Oil did everything to the Ohio legislature except refine it. On one occasion a member of the Pennsylvania legislature was reported to have said: "Mr. Speaker, I move we adjourn unless the Pennsylvania Railroad has some more business for us to transact." During the notorious "Erie War" of 1868, in which Cornelius Vanderbilt did battle against Jay Gould and Jim Fisk for control of the Erie Railroad, both sides in the dispute offered lavish bribes to members of the New York State legislature to support measures favorable to their cause. The market price of legislators during the fight was $15,000 a head. One influential and enterprising leader collected $75,000 from Vanderbilt and $100,000 from Gould. The corruption was not all on one side. Politicians were not innocent victims. Many of them openly demanded bribes and in effect blackmailed businessmen.

The average industrialist of the late nineteenth century was not, however, a Rockefeller or a Vanderbilt, but a more modest entrepreneur engaged in highly risky ventures in an unstable economy. For every successful millionaire, there were dozens of aspiring businessmen whose efforts failed in the face of overexpansion or vicious competition. Some industries fell under the control of a single firm or a small group of large firms. But far more industries remained fragmented, with many small companies struggling to carve out a stable position for themselves in an uncertain environment. The annals of business did indeed include real stories of individuals rising from rags to riches. They also included stories of people moving from riches back to rags.

Survival of the Fittest

Most tycoons liked to claim that they had attained their wealth and power through hard work, acquisitiveness, and thrift—the traditional virtues of Protestant America. Those who succeeded, they argued, deserved their success. "God gave me my money," explained John D. Rockefeller, expressing the assumption that riches were a reward for worthiness. On the other hand, those who failed had earned their

failure—through their own laziness, stupidity, or carelessness. "Let us remember," said a prominent Protestant minister, "that there is not a poor person in the United States who was not made poor by his own shortcomings."

Such assumptions became the basis of a social theory popularized by a number of leading intellectuals of the late nineteenth century: Social Darwinism, the application to human society of Charles Darwin's laws of evolution and natural selection among species. Just as only the fittest survived in the process of evolution, so in human society only the fittest individuals survived and flourished in the marketplace.

The English philosopher Herbert Spencer was the first and most important proponent of this theory. Struggle, Spencer argued, was a normal human activity, especially in economic life. The weak failed; the strong endured and became stronger. Society benefited from the elimination of the unfit and the survival of the strong and talented. In the end, the competitive process would lead to what Spencer called "the ultimate and inevitable development of the ideal man."

Spencer's books were enormously popular in America in the 1870s and 1880s. And his teachings found prominent supporters among American intellectuals, most notably William Graham Sumner of Yale, who promoted related ideas in a series of celebrated lectures, in magazine and journal articles, and finally in a famous 1906 book, *Folkways*. Sumner's philosophy did not always accord with Spencer's. But on one crucial point, he agreed fully with the ideas of Social Darwinism. Individuals, he argued, must have absolute freedom to struggle, to compete, to gratify their instinct for self-interest. The struggle for survival should be allowed to work itself out and should not be delimited by laws or the state.

The great financial titans themselves seized on the theories of Spencer and Sumner to justify their positions. "The growth of a large business is merely the survival of the fittest," Rockefeller proclaimed. "This is not an evil tendency in business. It is merely the working out of the law of nature and a law of God." Carnegie, who became the leading exponent of Social Darwinism among American industrialists, later described his reaction on first reading Spencer: "I remember that light came as in flood and all was clear."

Social Darwinism appealed to businessmen because it seemed to legitimize their success and confirm their virtues. It appealed to them because it placed their activities within the context of traditional American ideas of freedom and individualism. Above all, it appealed to them because it justified their tactics. Social Darwinists insisted that all attempts by labor to raise wages by forming unions and all endeavors by government to regulate economic activities would fail, because economic life was controlled by a natural law, the law of competition. And Social Darwinism coincided with another "law" that seemed to justify business practices and business dominance: the law of supply and demand as defined by Adam Smith and the classical economists. The economic system, they argued, was like a great and delicate machine functioning by natural and automatic rules, by the "invisible hand" of market forces. The greatest among these rules, the law of supply and demand, determined all economic values—prices, wages, rents, interest rates—at a level that was just to all concerned. Supply and demand worked because human beings were essentially economic creatures who understood and pursued their own interests, and because they operated in a free market where competition was open to all.

The ideas of Social Darwinism and classical economics provided an appealing ideology to justify business success and business tactics. It was not, however, an ideology that had very much to do with the realities of the corporate economy. At the same time that businessmen were celebrating the virtues of competition and the free market, they were making active efforts to protect themselves from competition and to replace the natural workings of the marketplace with control by great combinations. Vicious competitive battle—the thing that Spencer and Sumner celebrated and called a source of healthy progress—was in fact the very thing that American businessmen most feared and tried to eliminate.

Gospel of Wealth

Some businessmen attempted to temper the harsh philosophy of Social Darwinism with a more gentle, if in some ways equally self-serving idea: the "gospel of wealth." People of great wealth had not only great power but great responsibilities. It was their duty to use their riches to advance social progress. Carnegie himself elaborated on the idea in his 1901 book *The Gospel of Wealth*. People of wealth, he wrote, should consider all revenues in excess of their own needs as "trust funds" that they should administer for the good of the community; the person of wealth was "the

mere trustee and agent for his poorer brethren." Carnegie did not believe in giving aid directly to the poor; he feared that such charity would encourage a sense of dependency. He preferred to contribute to institutions, notably libraries, that presumably would help the poor to help themselves. Carnegie was only one of many great industrialists who devoted large parts of their fortunes to philanthropic works.

The notion of private wealth as a public blessing existed alongside another popular concept: the notion of great wealth as something available to all. Russell H. Conwell, a Baptist minister, became the most prominent spokesman for the idea by delivering one lecture, "Acres of Diamonds," more than 6,000 times between 1880 and 1900. Conwell told a series of stories, which he claimed were true, of individuals who had found opportunities for extraordinary wealth in their own backyards. One such story involved a modest farmer who discovered a vast diamond mine in his own fields in the course of working his land. "I say to you," he told his audiences, "that you have 'acres of diamonds' beneath you right here . . . that the men and women sitting here have within their reach opportunities to get largely wealthy. . . . I say that you ought to get rich, and it is your duty to get rich." Most of the millionaires in the country, Conwell claimed (inaccurately), had begun on the lowest rung of the economic ladder and had worked their way to success. Every industrious individual had the chance to do likewise. Another promoter of the success story was Horatio Alger, a New York minister whose more than 100 novels—under such titles as *Andy Grant's Pluck, Tom the Bootblack,* and *Sink or Swim*—sold over 20 million copies. In every volume a poor boy from a small town went to the big city to seek his fortune. By work, perseverance, and luck, he became rich.

Alternative Visions

Alongside the celebrations of competition, the justifications for great wealth, and the legitimation of the existing order stood a group of alternative philosophies, many of which openly challenged the premises of Social Darwinism and the gospel of wealth.

One such philosophy emerged from the work of Lester Frank Ward, author of a number of notable books, beginning with *Dynamic Sociology,* published in 1883. Ward was just as much a Darwinist as Sumner and Spencer, but he drew very different conclusions about the implications of Darwinism for human society. Civilization, he argued, was not governed by the abstract laws of natural selection. It was controlled by human intelligence, which was capable of shaping society as it wished. The chief goal of modern society, therefore, should not be unrestrained freedom of action for every individual. It should be the pursuit of the general good through cooperative action. The best instrument for the attainment of that goal was government. In contrast to Sumner, who believed that state intervention to remodel the environment was futile, Ward thought that an active government engaged in positive planning was society's best hope. Ward's ideas coincided with those of a growing number of American thinkers who believed that "survival of the fittest" was a ruthless and inefficient system for achieving social progress. He helped promote the idea that institutions should be "functional," that they should work actively to meet social needs, that human welfare should not be left to the impersonal workings of the capitalist economy. The people, through their government, could intervene in the economy and adjust it to serve their needs.

Other Americans skeptical of the laissez-faire ideas of the Social Darwinists adopted more drastic approaches to reform. Relatively few Americans embraced genuinely radical challenges to the existing order; but some dissenters did raise fundamental questions about the viability of capitalism. Some of these dissenters found a home in the Socialist Labor party, founded in the 1870s and led for many years by Daniel De Leon, an immigrant from the West Indies. Other party leaders were recent immigrants from eastern Europe. Although De Leon attracted a modest following in the industrial cities, the party never succeeded in polling more than 82,000 votes. De Leon's theoretical and dogmatic approach appealed to intellectuals more than to workers, and a dissident faction of his party, eager to forge ties with organized labor, broke away and in 1901 formed the more enduring American Socialist party.

Other radicals gained a wider following. One of the most influential was Henry George. His angrily eloquent *Progress and Poverty*, published in 1879, was an immediate success; reprinted in successive editions, it became one of the ten best-selling nonfiction works in American publishing history. George tried to explain why poverty existed amidst the wealth created by modern industry. "This association of poverty with progress is the great enigma of our times," he wrote. "So long as all the increased wealth which modern progress brings goes but to build up great fortunes, to increase luxury and make sharper the contrast between the House of Have and the House

of Want, progress is not real and cannot be permanent."

George blamed these social problems on the ability of a few monopolists to grow wealthy as a result of rising land values. An increase in the value of land, he claimed, was a result not of any effort by the owner, but of the growth of society around the land. This "unearned increment," this increase in the value of land resulting from increased demand rather than active improvement of the property by the owner, was rightfully the property of the community. And so George proposed a "single tax," to replace all other taxes, which would return the increment to the people. The tax, he argued, would destroy monopolies, distribute wealth more equally, and eliminate poverty. Single-tax societies sprang up in many cities; and in 1886, George, with the support of labor and the socialists, narrowly missed being elected mayor of New York.

Rivaling George in popularity was Edward Bellamy, whose utopian novel *Looking Backward,* published in 1888, sold more than 1 million copies. It described the experiences of a young Bostonian who in 1887 went into a hypnotic sleep from which he awakened in the year 2000. He emerged from his trance to find a new social order, based on universal membership in a workers' army, where want, politics, and vice were unknown, and where everyone was happy and fulfilled. The new society had emerged from a peaceful, evolutionary process. The large trusts of the late nineteenth century had continued to grow in size and to combine with one another until ultimately they formed a single, great trust, controlled by the government, which absorbed all the businesses of all the citizens and distributed the abundance of the industrial economy equally among all the people. All aspects of life were organized with military efficiency. Society had become a great machine, "so logical in its principles and direct and simple in its workings" that it almost ran itself. "Fraternal cooperation" had replaced competition. Class divisions had disappeared. He labeled the philosophy motivating this vision "nationalism." *Looking Backward* had a remarkable impact. It inspired the formation of more than 160 Nationalist Clubs to propagate Bellamy's ideas. Bellamy himself devoted the remainder of his life to championing his brand of socialism.

The Problems of Monopoly

Relatively few Americans shared the views of those who questioned the entire structure of modern capitalism. But a growing number of people were by the end of the century becoming deeply concerned about a particular, glaring aspect of capitalism: the growth of monopoly.

From the beginning, large segments of the population had looked on the proliferation of business combinations with mistrust and hostility. The popular description of such men as Rockefeller, Carnegie, and Morgan as "robber barons" suggests the attitude of much of the public. So do the reports of the numerous conferences, commissions, and study groups that pointed with alarm to the effects of consolidation on the marketplace. The United States Industrial Commission reported in 1902 that "in most cases the combination has exerted an appreciable power over prices, and in practically all cases it has increased the margin between raw materials and finished products." Combinations were, in other words, the cause of artificially inflated prices; the influence of the free market was being restricted by the monopolistic practices of a few men. By the end of the century, a wide range of groups had begun to assail monopoly and economic concentration. Laborers, farmers, consumers, small manufacturers, conservative bankers and financiers, advocates of radical change—all joined the attack.

Defenders and opponents of combination alike looked with alarm at another problem of the modern economy: its disturbing pattern of instability. Although industrial output and agricultural production were expanding rapidly, other areas of the economy could not always keep pace. The nation's banks and financial institutions were neither strong enough nor efficient enough to meet adequately the new demands for their services. The increasingly important stock market was riddled with corruption. Above all, the market for goods was not growing as rapidly as the supply.

The result was one of the most troubling and distinctive features of modern industrial economy: a cycle of booms and busts that plagued American life throughout the late nineteenth and early twentieth centuries. Beginning in 1873, the economy fluctuated erratically, with severe recessions creating havoc every five or six years, each recession worse than the previous one, until finally, in 1893, the system seemed on the verge of total collapse.

One reason for the economic instability was that the new industries were not passing on enough of their profits to their workers to create an adequate market for the goods they were producing. This growing disparity in the distribution of wealth was producing not only an imbalance between supply and demand but a deep popular resentment. The standard of living may have been rising for virtually everyone, but the gap between rich and poor was visibly widening into an enormous chasm.

According to one estimate early in the century, 1 percent of the families in America controlled nearly 88 percent of the nation's assets. A small but conspicuous new class had emerged whose wealth almost defied description, whose fortunes were so vast that great feats of imagination were often required to enable them to be spent. Andrew Carnegie earned $23 million from his steel company in 1900 alone, and that was only part of his income (in an era in which there was as yet no income tax). John D. Rockefeller's personal wealth was estimated at one time to exceed $1 billion.

Some of the wealthy—Carnegie, for example—lived relatively modestly and donated large sums to philanthropic causes. Others, however, lived in a conspicuous luxury that earned the resentment of much of the nation. Like a clan of feudal barons, the Vanderbilts maintained, in addition to many country estates, seven garish mansions on seven blocks of New York City's Fifth Avenue. Other wealthy New Yorkers lavished vast sums on parties. The most notorious, a ball on which Mrs. Bradley Martin spent $368,000, created such a furor that she and her husband fled to England to escape public abuse.

Observing these flagrant displays of wealth were the four-fifths of the American people who lived modestly, and the one-eighth of the population (10 million people) who lived below the commonly accepted poverty line. To those in difficult economic circumstances, the sense of relative deprivation could be as frustrating and embittering as the poverty itself.

The Ordeal of the Worker

For the American worker, the experience of industrialization after the Civil War was similar in many ways to the experience before it. It was a mixed blessing. On the one hand, the average standard of living for laborers—in quantitative terms at least—rose significantly during the last decades of the nineteenth century. On the other hand, workers continued to suffer from the wide disparities in distribution of the nation's new wealth; from working conditions that were often arduous and unsafe; and from the intangible problems of adjusting to the impersonal character of work in the factory. Yet for workers, the

The Hatch Family, 1871
This family portrait by Eastman Johnson was commissioned by Alfrederick Smith Hatch, a prominent Wall Street broker. The family is shown gathered in the regal library of their home on Park Avenue. The painting includes portraits of Hatch himself (seated at right), his wife (leaning against the mantle), the couple's ten children, Hatch's father, and Mrs. Hatch's mother. The relatively informal poses of many family members may reflect the influence of group photographs, which were becoming common in the 1870s.   (Metropolitan Museum of Art)

late nineteenth century was also different from any previous era, if for no other reason than that their numbers were now much larger and the dimensions of both the promise and the problems of industrialization far greater.

The Immigrant Work Force

The dramatic expansion in the industrial work force, which was both a cause and a result of economic growth, arose out of a massive migration into industrial cities—immigration of two sorts. The first was the continuing flow of rural Americans into factory towns and cities—people disillusioned with or bankrupted by life on the farm and eager for new economic and social opportunities. The second was the great wave of immigration from abroad (primarily from Europe, but also from Asia, Canada, and other areas) in the decades following the Civil War—an influx that all but overshadowed all previous periods of immigration. The 25 million immigrants who arrived in the United States between 1865 and 1915 were more than four times the number who had arrived in the fifty years before. The greatest wave of new arrivals came after 1890; by the end of the first decade of the new century, immigrants were debarking in America at the rate of more than 1 million each year.

In the 1870s and 1880s, most of the immigrants came from the nation's traditional sources: England, Ireland, and northern Europe. Skilled artisans continued to emigrate from Great Britain to take advantage of the expanding opportunities in America.

Economic troubles in European industry in the 1880s induced factory workers from Sweden, Germany, and England to move to the United States. And the declining agricultural economy of northern Europe (and of Ireland, in particular) pressured still others to journey to America. By the end of the century, however, the major sources of immigrants had shifted, with large numbers of southern and eastern Europeans (Italians, Poles, Russians, Greeks, Slavs, and others) pouring into the country and into the industrial work force.

The new immigrants were coming to America in part to escape the poverty and oppression of their homelands. But they were coming as well because they felt the pull of the United States—a pull based in part on realistic expectations of the opportunities available, and in part on distorted and artificial promises. Railroads, in order to dispose of their Western landholdings, painted an alluring picture of America in advertisements overseas. Industrial employers actively recruited workers under the Labor Contract Law, which—until its repeal in 1885—permitted them to pay for the passage of workers in advance and deduct the amount later from their wages. Even after the repeal of the law, employers continued to encourage the immigration of unskilled laborers, often with the assistance of foreign-born labor brokers, such as the Greek and Italian *padrones* who recruited work gangs of their fellow nationals.

The arrival of these new ethnic groups became a complicating factor in the dynamics of the working class, which were already complicated enough. In addition to the traditional concerns about wages, working conditions, and the declining need for skilled artisans in the face of modern technology, there were now also serious ethnic tensions. Americans of old stock, as well as ethnics who had arrived a decade or so before, often looked on the new immigrants with fear and hostility. Industries that had traditionally been dominated by one national group now began to replace them with members of others—who could be hired at lower wages than the earlier workers. Poles, Greeks, and French Canadians began to displace the British and Irish workers in the textile factories of New England. Italians, Slavs, and Poles began to emerge as a major source of labor for the mining industry, which had traditionally been the province of native workers or northern European immigrants. Within industries, moreover, workers tended to cluster in particular occupations (and thus, often, at particular income levels) by ethnic group. In industry, at least, the idea of the "melting pot"—of Americans of

The Statue of Liberty in Paris
The head of the Statue of Liberty sits in a Paris courtyard in 1883, awaiting shipment to the United States. The idea for the statue originated with the French politician Edouard Laboulaye, who proposed it in 1875 to commemorate the French and American revolutions. Frederic Bartholdi designed the 152-foot-high sculpture (originally known as "Liberty Enlightening the World"). It was presented as a gift to the United States in 1884 and dedicated in 1886. The millions of immigrants who entered the country through New York harbor in the late nineteenth and early twentieth centuries saw the statue as a symbolic promise of fulfillment for the economic and political liberty they sought. (Library of Congress)

different ethnic backgrounds melding together into one common culture—was of limited applicability.

Wages and Working Conditions

The average standard of living for workers may have been rising in the years after the Civil War; but for many laborers, the return for their labor remained pitifully small. It appeared even smaller in relation to the vast fortunes the industrial titans were accumulating—even in comparison with the rising incomes of the middle class. At the turn of the century, the average income of the American worker was $400–$500 a year—below the $600 figure that many believed was the minimum required to maintain a reasonable level of comfort. Nor did most workers enjoy any real job security. The boom-and-bust cycle of the economy made laborers in all industries vulnerable; and in some areas, workers were particularly susceptible to losing their jobs because of technological advances or because of the cyclical or seasonal nature of their work. Even those who were spared unemployment could find their wages suddenly and substantially cut in hard times. Few workers, in other words, were ever very far from the prospect of poverty.

But American laborers faced a wide array of other hardships as well. There was, first, the painful adjustment to the nature of modern industrial labor: the performance of routine, repetitive tasks, often requiring little skill, on a strict and monotonous schedule. In 1900, most workers labored at least ten hours a day (twelve hours a day in the steel industry), six days a week. To rural men and women, accustomed to flexible and changing work patterns, the new routine was harsh and disorienting. To skilled artisans, whose once-valued tasks were now performed by machines, the new system was impersonal and demeaning. Factory workers were employed, moreover, in plants free from effective government regulation or inspection. The result was workplaces that were often appallingly unsafe or unhealthy. Industrial accidents were frequent and severe. Compensation to the victims, either from their employers or from the government, was limited.

Women and Children at Work

The reduction of skilled work in factories induced many employers to increase greatly the use of women and children, whom they could hire for lower wages than adult males. By 1900, 20 percent of all manufacturing workers were women; and 20 percent of all women (well over 5 million) were wage earners. Women worked in all areas of industry, even in some of the most arduous jobs—for example, as machinists, railroad workers, and stokers. Most women, however, worked in a few industries where unskilled and semiskilled machine labor (as opposed to heavy manual labor) prevailed. The textile industry remained the largest single employer of women.

Women worked for wages as low as $6 to $8 a week, well below the minimum necessary for survival (and well below the wages paid to men working the same jobs). Advocates of a minimum wage law for women created a sensation when they brought several women to a hearing in Chicago to testify that low wages and desperate poverty had driven them to prostitution. (It was not, however, sensational enough for the Illinois legislature, which promptly defeated the bill.)

Child labor, which had always existed in the United States, had by 1900 become a national scandal. At least 1.7 million children under sixteen years of age were employed in factories and fields, more

Occupational Distribution, 1880 and 1920

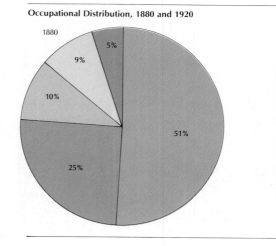

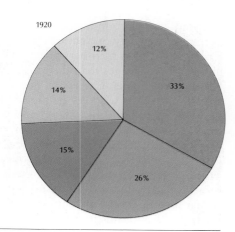

Child Labor and Child Luxury

Many working-class children of the early twentieth century found employment as "breaker boys," picking pieces of slate out of piles of coal at Pennsylvania mines. The coal dust was often so thick that they could hardly see one another, as this Lewis Hine photograph suggests. The children of wealthy industrialists would have found such lives almost unimaginable. Here, the children of American railroad executive George Jay Gould (son of Jay Gould) ride through a Paris park in "voiturettes," miniature automobiles manufactured in France. (Left, International Museum of Photography. George Eastman House; below, Culver Pictures)

than twice the number so employed thirty years before; 10 percent of all girls aged ten to fifteen, and 20 percent of all boys, held jobs. Under the pressure of outraged public opinion, thirty-eight state legislatures passed child labor laws in the late nineteenth century; but these laws were painfully insufficient. Sixty percent of child workers were employed in agriculture, which was typically exempt from the laws; and such children often worked twelve-hour days picking or hoeing in the fields. The laws were hardly more effective for children employed in factories; they set a minimum age of twelve years and a maximum workday of ten hours, but employers often ignored even these minimal standards. In the cotton mills of the South, children working at the looms all night were kept awake by having cold water thrown in their faces. In canneries, little girls cut fruits and vegetables sixteen hours a day. Exhausted children were particularly susceptible to injury while working at dangerous machines, and they were maimed and even killed in industrial accidents at an alarming rate.

Yet as much as the appalling conditions of many woman and child workers troubled the national conscience, conditions for men were at least equally dangerous. In mills and mines, and on the railroads, the American accident rate was higher than that of any industrial nation in the world. As late as 1907, an average of twelve railroad men a week died on the job. In factories, thousands of workers faced such occupational diseases as lead or phosphorus poisoning, against which employers took few precautions.

Emerging Unionization

Labor attempted to fight back against such conditions by adopting some of the same tactics their employers had used so effectively: creating large combinations. In the last three decades of the nineteenth century, American workers engaged in a series of escalating struggles to form and win recognition for labor unions. By the end of the century, however, their efforts had met with little success.

There had been craft unions in America, representing small groups of skilled workers, for many years; and their number increased significantly during and after the Civil War. Alone, however, the unions could not hope to exert significant power in the economy; and in the 1860s some labor leaders began to search for ways to combine the energies of labor organizations. The first attempt to federate separate unions into a single national organization came

in 1866, when William H. Sylvis founded the National Labor Union—a polyglot association, claiming 640,000 members, that included a variety of reform groups having little direct relationship with labor. After the Panic of 1873 the National Labor Union disintegrated and disappeared.

The individual unions experienced stormy times in other ways during the hard years of the 1870s. With their bargaining power weakened by depression conditions, they faced antagonistic employers eager to destroy them and a hostile public unsympathetic to their demand for job security. When labor disputes with employers turned bitter and violent, as they occasionally did, the public instinctively blamed the workers (or the "radicals" and "anarchists" they believed were influencing the workers) for the trouble, rarely the employers. Particularly alarming to middle-class Americans was the emergence of the "Molly Maguires" in the anthracite coal region of Pennsylvania. The Mollies operated within the Ancient Order of Hibernians (an Irish fraternal society) and used terrorist tactics. They attempted to intimidate the coal operators through violence and occasionally murder; and they added to the growing perception that labor activism was motivated by dangerous radicals.

But excitement over the Molly Maguires was nothing compared to the near hysteria that gripped the country during the railroad strike of 1877. The trouble started when the principal Eastern railroads announced a 10 percent slash in wages. Immediately, railroad workers, whether organized or not, went out on strike. Rail service was disrupted from Baltimore to St. Louis, equipment was destroyed, and rioting mobs roamed the streets of Pittsburgh and other cities. As the strike continued, it began to take on many of the features of an open class war. State militias were called out against the strikers; and finally, in July, the president agreed to a request by the governor of West Virginia and ordered federal troops to suppress the disorders there. Clashes between workers and soldiers were frequent and often vicious. In Baltimore, eleven demonstrators died and forty were wounded in a conflict between workers and militiamen. In Philadelphia, state militia opened fire on thousands of workers and their families attempting to block the railroad crossings; twenty died. Similar (if less bloody) encounters occurred throughout the industrial United States (including a general strike in St. Louis). In all, over 100 people died before the strike finally collapsed several weeks after it had begun.

The great railroad strike was America's first major labor conflict and a vivid illustration of a new reality in the American economic system. With business becoming national in its scope, disputes between labor and capital could no longer be localized but could affect the entire nation. It was an illustration as well of the depth of resentment among many American workers and of the lengths to which they were prepared to go to express that resentment. It was an indication, too, of the serious weaknesses afflicting the labor movement, which still lacked an institutional base adequate to sustain its efforts. The failure of the strike seriously weakened the railroad unions and damaged the reputation of labor organizations in other industries as well.

The Knights of Labor

The first major effort to create a genuinely national labor organization was the founding in 1869 of the Noble Order of the Knights of Labor, under the leadership of Uriah S. Stephens. Instead of attempting to create a federation of preexisting unions, as the National Labor Union had done, the Knights recruited individual members directly from the working class. Membership was open to all who "toiled," and the definition of a toiler was extremely broad: The only excluded groups were lawyers, bankers, liquor dealers, and professional gamblers. Members met in local "assemblies"; an assembly might consist of the workers in a particular trade or a local union, or simply all the members of the Knights in a particular city or district. Presiding laxly over the entire order was an agency known as the general assembly. Much of the program of the Knights was as vague as the organization. Although they championed an eight-hour day and the abolition of child labor, the leaders were more interested in long-range reform of the economy than in the immediate objectives of wages and hours that appealed to the trade unions. Indeed, leaders of the Knights hoped to replace the "wage system" with a new "cooperative system," in which workers would themselves control a large part of the economy.

For several years, the Knights remained a secret fraternal organization and engaged in no public activities. But in the 1870s, it moved out into the open. Under the leadership of Terence V. Powderly, who was elected "grand master workman" in 1879, the order entered a spectacular period of expansion. By 1886, it claimed a total membership of over 700,000. Important factors contributing to the increase in numerical strength were a business recession in 1884 that threw many workers out of jobs and a renewal of industrial strife that induced unorganized laborers as well as some trade unions to affiliate with the Knights. Not only did the membership grow, but the order now included many militant elements that the moderate leadership could not always control. Against Powderly's wishes, local unions or assemblies associated with the Knights launched a series of strikes. In 1885, striking railway workers forced the Missouri Pacific, a link in the Gould system, to restore wage cuts and recognize their union. But the victory was a temporary one. In the following year, a strike on another Gould road, the Texas and Pacific, was crushed, and the power of the unions in the Gould system was broken. By 1890, the membership of the Knights had shrunk to 100,000. A few years later, the organization disappeared altogether.

The AFL

Even before the Knights had entered on their period of decline, a rival organization based on an entirely different organizational concept had appeared. In 1881, representatives of a number of craft unions formed the Federation of Organized Trade and Labor Unions of the United States and Canada. Five years later, this body took the name it has borne ever since, the American Federation of Labor (AFL). Under the direction of its president and guiding spirit, Samuel Gompers, the Federation soon became the most important labor group in the country. As its name implies, it was a federation or association of national trade unions, each of which enjoyed essential autonomy within the larger organization. Rejecting the idea of individual membership and the corollary of one big union for everybody, the Federation was built on the principle of the organization of skilled workers into craft unions. Unlike the Knights, the AFL was generally hostile to organizing unskilled workers, who did not fit within the structure of the craft unions. The AFL also resisted organizing women (many of whom, of course, were unskilled workers, but some of whom worked in AFL-represented crafts); the Knights, in their openness to all, had included substantial numbers of woman members.

The program of the Federation differed as markedly from that of the Knights as did its organizational arrangements. Gompers and his associates accepted the basic premises of capitalism; their purpose was simply to secure for labor a greater share of capitalism's material rewards. Repudiating all notions of fundamental alteration of the existing system or long-range reform measures or a separate labor party,

Samuel Gompers
Gompers migrated to the United States from England as a boy and began work at the age of thirteen as a cigar maker, rising to become head of his local union. When the American Federation of Labor was organized in 1886, Gompers became its first president, a position he held (with only a single, one-year interruption) until 1924. Gompers helped the AFL to become the premier labor organization in the United States; he also helped commit the organization to a narrow, craft-oriented view of unionism that excluded an increasing proportion of workers as mass-production industries rose to prominence. He is shown here during a union-organizing drive in West Virginia. (George Meany Memorial Archives)

the AFL concentrated on labor's immediate objectives: wages, hours, and working conditions. While it hoped to attain its ends by collective bargaining, the Federation was ready to employ the strike if necessary.

As one of its first objectives, the Federation called for a national eight-hour day. It set May 1, 1886, as the date by which the goal was to be achieved, and it

determined that the AFL would stage a general strike if that was what was necessary to achieve it. On the target day, strikes and demonstrations for a shorter workday took place all over the country. Although the national officers of the Knights of Labor had refused to cooperate in the movement, some local units joined in the demonstrations. So did a few unions that were dominated by European radicals who wanted to destroy "class government" by terroristic methods and that were affiliated with the so-called Black International. The most sensational demonstrations occurred in Chicago, which was a labor stronghold and a center of radicalism.

A strike was already in progress in Chicago at the time, at the McCormick Harvester Company; and when the police harassed the strikers, labor and radical leaders called a protest meeting at the Haymarket Square. During the meeting, the police appeared and commanded those present to disperse. Someone—the person's identity was never determined—threw a bomb that resulted in the death of seven policemen and injury to sixty-seven others. The police, who on the previous day had killed four strikers, fired into the crowd and killed four more people. News of the Haymarket affair struck cold fear into Chicago and the business community of the nation. Blinded by hysteria, conservative, property-conscious Americans demanded a victim or victims—to demonstrate to labor that it must cease its course of violence. Chicago officials finally rounded up eight anarchists and charged them with the murder of the policemen, on the grounds that they had incited the individual who hurled the bomb. In one of the most injudicious trials in American history, all were found guilty. One was sentenced to prison and seven to death. Of the seven, one cheated his sentence by committing suicide, four were executed, and two had their sentences commuted to life imprisonment.

Neither the AFL nor the Knights of Labor had anything to do with the Haymarket bombing or even with the conflicts leading up to it. Yet both organizations found themselves saddled with much of the blame for the episode. The Knights, in particular, never recovered from the widespread vilification they encountered in the aftermath of the bombing. To most middle-class Americans, however, the significance of Haymarket was larger than the guilt or innocence of particular labor organizations. It was a sign, they believed, of how widespread the chaos of their society had become, a sign of the proliferation of radicalism. "Anarchism," most of whose adherents were relatively peaceful visionaries dreaming of a new social order, became in the public mind a code word for terrorism and violence; and for the next thirty years, the specter of anarchism remained one of the most frightening concepts in the American imagination.

The Homestead Strike

Some of the most violent strikes in American labor history occurred in the economically troubled 1890s. Two of the strikes, the one at the Homestead plant of the Carnegie Steel Company in Pennsylvania and the one against the Pullman Palace Car Company in the Chicago area, took place in companies controlled by men who prided themselves on being among the most advanced of American employers: Andrew Carnegie, who had written magazine articles defending the rights of labor, and George M. Pullman, who had built a "model town" to house his employees.

The Amalgamated Association of Iron and Steel Workers, which was affiliated with the American Federation of Labor, was the most powerful trade union in the country. Its members were skilled workers, in great demand by employers and thus able to exercise significant power in the workplace. Employers sometimes called these skilled workers "little shopfloor autocrats," and in some plants the workers had won substantial control over the conditions under which they labored. The union had a rulebook with 56 pages of what it called "legislation," designed to limit the power of employers.

In the mid-1880s, however, the steel industry was changing in ways that threatened the power of the union. Demand for skilled workers was in decline as new production methods and new, large-scale corporate organizations streamlined the steelmaking process. The union was unable to establish a foothold in most of the Carnegie plants, which were coming to dominate the industry. In only one of the three major steel mills in the Carnegie system—the Homestead plant near Pittsburgh—was the union a force. By 1890, Carnegie and his chief lieutenant, Henry Clay Frick, had decided that the Amalgamated "had to go," even at Homestead. Over the next two years, they worked to undermine the union by announcing a series of wage cuts at Homestead. At first, the union acquiesced, aware that it was not strong enough to wage a successful strike. But in 1892, the company refused even to discuss its decisions with the Amalgamated, in effect denying the union's right to exert any influence at all on corporate policy. Carnegie was in Scotland, and the direction of the company was in the hands of Frick, who was determined to break the union once and for all.

Trouble began when the management announced a new wage scale that would have meant cuts for a small minority of the workers. Frick gave the union two days to accept the proposal; and when the union refused and called instead for a strike, he abruptly shut down the plant and asked the Pinkerton Detective Agency to furnish 300 guards to enable the company to resume operations on its own terms—by hiring nonunion workers. (The Pinkerton Agency was in reality a strikebreaking concern.)

The hated Pinkertons, whose mere presence was often enough to incite workers to violence, approached the plant on barges in an adjacent river. Warned of their coming, the strikers met them at the docks with guns and dynamite, and a pitched battle ensued on July 6, 1892. After several hours of fighting, which brought death to three guards and ten strikers and severe injuries to many participants on both sides, the Pinkertons surrendered and were escorted roughly out of town. The company and local law officials then asked for militia protection. The Pennsylvania governor responded by sending the state's entire National Guard contingent, some 8,000 troops, to Homestead. Public opinion, at first sympathetic to the strikers, turned against them when a radical made an attempt to assassinate Frick. Production resumed, with strikebreakers now protected by troops. Slowly workers drifted back to their jobs; and finally—four months after the strike began—the Amalgamated surrendered. Carnegie, hearing the news in Europe, sent a wire to Frick: "Life is worth living again."

The story of the Amalgamated in the aftermath of the Homestead strike was a dismal one. By 1900, every major steel plant in the Northeast had broken with the union, which now had virtually no power to resist. Its membership shrank from a high of 24,000 in 1891 (two-thirds of all eligible steelworkers) to fewer than 7,000 a decade later.

The Pullman Strike

A dispute of greater magnitude and equal bitterness, although involving less loss of life, was the Pullman strike in 1894. The Pullman Palace Car Company constructed sleeping and parlor cars, which it leased to most of the nation's railroads. It manufactured and repaired the cars at a plant near Chicago. There the company had built the 600-acre town of Pullman and rented dwellings to the employees. George M. Pullman, inventor of the sleeping car and owner of the company, liked to exhibit his town as a model solution of the industrial problem and to refer to the workers as his "children."

Strikers at Homestead
In this photograph, striking steelworkers (one of them holding a rifle) stand guard overlooking the great Carnegie Mills at Homestead, Pennsylvania, during their brief occupation of the town in 1892. (Carnegie Library)

Nearly all of the workers were members of a militant labor organization, the American Railway Union, recently organized by Eugene V. Debs. Debs had once been active in the Railroad Brotherhoods, an older railworkers' union affiliated with the AFL. But he had become impatient with the union's lack of interest in the lot of the unskilled workers and had formed his own union, which soon attained a membership of 150,000, mainly in the Middle West.

The strike at Pullman began during the winter of 1893–1894, when the company slashed wages, through five separate reductions, by an average of 25 percent. With revenues reduced by depression conditions, there was some reason for the company's action; but the cuts were more drastic than the workers could accept. Several of them who served on a committee to protest the cuts were discharged. At the same time, Pullman refused to reduce rents in its model town, even though the charges there were 20 to 25 percent higher than for comparable accommodations in surrounding areas. The strikers appealed to the Railway Union for support, and that organization voted to refuse to handle Pullman cars and equipment.

The General Managers' Association, representing twenty-four Chicago railroads, prepared to fight the boycott. Switchmen who refused to handle Pullman cars were discharged. Whenever this happened, the union instructed its members to quit work. Within a few days thousands of railroad workers in twenty-seven states and territories were on strike, and transportation from Chicago to the Pacific coast was paralyzed.

Ordinarily, state governors responded readily to appeals from strike-threatened business; but the governor of Illinois, John P. Altgeld, was different—a man with demonstrated sympathies for workers and their grievances. Altgeld had pardoned the Haymarket anarchists remaining in prison, and he had made it clear he would not call out the militia to protect employers now. Bypassing Altgeld, the railroad operators asked the federal government to send regular army troops to Illinois. At the same time, federal postal officials and marshals were bombarding Washington with complaints that the strike was preventing the movement of mail on the trains. President Grover Cleveland, a man with a punctilious regard for the letter of the law, responded favorably to such requests. His attorney general, Richard Olney, a former railroad lawyer and a bitter foe of labor, was even more eager to accommodate the employers. Cleveland and Olney decided that the government could employ the army to keep the mails moving; and in July 1894, the president, over Altgeld's objections, ordered 2,000 troops to the Chicago area.

At Olney's suggestion, government lawyers obtained from a federal court an order restraining Debs and other union officials from interfering with the interstate transportation of the mails. This "blanket injunction" was so broad that it practically forbade Debs and his associates to continue the strike. They ignored the injunction and were arrested, tried for contempt of court (without a jury), and sentenced to six months in prison. With federal troops protecting the hiring of new workers and with the union leaders in a federal jail, the strike quickly collapsed.

It left a bitter heritage. It convinced many laborers that the government was not a neutral arbiter representing the common interest but a supporter of one side alone. Debs emerged from prison a martyr in the eyes of workers, a convert to Marxian socialism, and a dedicated enemy of capital.

Sources of Labor Weakness

The last decades of the nineteenth century were years in which labor, despite its organizing efforts, made few real gains. Industrial wages rose, but not enough even to keep up with the rising cost of living. Labor leaders won a few legislative victories—the abolition by Congress in 1885 of the Contract Labor Law; the establishment by Congress in 1868 of an eight-hour day on public works projects and in 1892 of the same workday for government employees; and a host of state laws governing hours of labor and safety standards. But most such laws were not enforced. Labor organizations emerged and staged strikes and protests, but the end of the century found most workers with less political power and less control of the workplace than they had had forty years before. Historians have explained this failure in numerous ways.

One explanation stresses the nature of the labor unions themselves, which never succeeded in organizing more than a small percentage of the industrial work force. Only about 4 percent of all American workers (fewer than 1 million) were union members in 1900. What members there were came largely from a few sectors of the economy where skilled labor

remained important. The great mass of unskilled laborers, who were emerging as the core of the industrial work force, were not represented by any union. The AFL, the most important labor organization in the country, was particularly weak. It excluded many potential members—women, blacks, recent immigrants, and others—who might have contributed to its strength. Women responded in 1903 by forming their own organization, the Women's Trade Union League, but the WTUL agitated primarily for legislation to protect woman workers, not for the organization and mobilization of labor. Divisions within the work force contributed to this weakness. Tensions among different ethnic and racial groups kept laborers divided and frustrated many efforts to mobilize against employers.

A second source of labor weakness was the shifting nature of the work force. Many immigrant workers came to America intending to remain only briefly, to earn some money and return home. Although some of these workers ultimately did stay in the United States permanently, the assumption that they had no long-range future in the country eroded their willingness to organize. Other workers—natives and immigrants alike—were in constant motion, moving from one job to another, one town to another, seldom in one place long enough to establish any sort of stake or exert any real power. A study of Newburyport, Massachusetts, over a thirty-year period shows that 90 percent of the workers there vanished from the town records in those years, many of them presumably because they moved elsewhere.

Even workers who stayed put often did not remain in the same job for long. The rags-to-riches stories of the Horatio Alger novels had few counterparts in reality. But a certain amount of real social mobility did exist, and it served to undercut worker militancy. In the course of a generation, workers or their offspring might advance a step or two up the ladder—from unskilled to semiskilled worker, from skilled worker to foreman. The gains were small, but they were often enough to keep hope alive and to limit discontent.

Above all, perhaps, workers made few gains in the late nineteenth century because of the strength of the forces arrayed against them. They faced corporate organizations of vast wealth and power, which were generally determined to crush any efforts by workers to challenge their prerogatives. Moreover, as the Homestead and Pullman strikes suggest, the corporations had the support of government—local, state, and federal—which was willing to send in

SIGNIFICANT EVENTS

1851   I.M. Singer and Company, one of first modern corporations, founded

1859   First oil well drilled in Pennsylvania

1866   William H. Sylvis founds National Labor Union

        First transatlantic cable laid

1868   Open-hearth steelmaking begins in America

1869   Knights of Labor founded

1870   John D. Rockefeller founds Standard Oil

1873   Carnegie Steel founded

        Commercial and financial panic disrupts economy

1876   Alexander Graham Bell invents telephone

1877   Railroad workers strike nationwide

1879   Thomas A. Edison invents electric light bulb

        Henry George publishes *Progress and Poverty*

1881   American Federation of Labor founded

1882   Rockefeller creates first trust

1886   Haymarket bombing blamed on anarchists

1888   Edward Bellamy publishes *Looking Backward*

1892   Workers strike Homestead plant

1893   Depression begins

1894   Workers strike Pullman Company

1901   J. P. Morgan creates United States Steel Corporation

        American Socialist party founded

1903   Women's Trade Union League founded

        Wright brothers make first successful flight at Kitty Hawk, North Carolina

1906   Henry Ford produces his first automobiles

        William Graham Sumner publishes *Folkways*

1914   Ford introduces assembly line in his factories

troops to "preserve order" and crush labor uprisings on demand. The corporations also managed to control and intimidate their employees through an elaborate system of infiltration and espionage within working-class communities.

Despite the creation of new organizations, despite a wave of strikes and protests that in the 1880s and 1890s reached startling proportions, workers in the late nineteenth century failed on the whole to create successful organizations or to protect their interests in the way the large corporations managed to do. In the battle for power within the emerging industrial economy, the workers steadily lost ground as big business entrenched itself.

SUGGESTED READINGS

General Studies   Several general accounts of the late nineteenth century emphasize industrial development and its consequences. John A. Garraty, *The New Commonwealth* (1968), has a broad focus; Edward C. Kirkland, *Industry Comes of Age: Business, Labor, and Public Policy, 1860–1897* (1961), lays greater emphasis on industry itself. Samuel P. Hays, *The Response to Industrialism, 1885–1914* (1957), offers a challenging interpretation of the period. Other general studies include Ray Ginger, *The Age of Excess* (1963); Carl Degler, *The Age of the Economic Revolution* (1977), a balanced and thorough survey; Daniel Boorstin, *The Americans: The Democratic Experience* (1973), a wide-ranging social and cultural history of the era that combines a controversial interpretive stance with a valuable examination of cultural institutions; and Thomas C. Cochran and William Miller, *The Age of Enterprise* (1942), a basic study with an economic focus. Robert Higgs, *The Transformation of the American Economy, 1865–1914* (1971), is an economist's view. Robert Wiebe, *The Search for Order, 1877–1920* (1968), is a provocative interpretation.

Technology   Roger Burlingame, *Engines of Democracy: Inventions and Society in Mature America* (1940), is a general account; Lewis Mumford, *Technics and Civilization* (1934), is a provocative interpretive work. George Daniels, *Science and Society in America* (1971), and Nathan Rosenberg, *Technology and American Economic Growth* (1972), are more recent studies. Elting E. Morison, *Men, Machines, and Modern Times* (1966), is a broad-ranging study. Robert W. Bruce, *Bell* (1973), examines the invention (and inventor) of the telephone. Frank E. Hill and Allan Nevins are the authors of *Ford*, 3 vols. (1954–1962), a study of the auto pioneer and his company. Peter Temin, *Steel in Nineteenth Century America* (1964), considers one of the largest of the emerging industries. Frederick A. White, *American Industrial Research Laboratories* (1961), illuminates an important component of industrial growth; and Robert Conot, *A Streak of Luck* (1979), is a biography of Thomas Edison, the head of the most famous of such laboratories. Richard N. Current, *The Typewriter and the Men Who Made It* (1954), discusses the invention of a machine that revolutionized business.

Railroads Railroad expansion, the key to industrial growth, is examined in George R. Taylor and I. D. Neu, *The American Railroad Network, 1861–1890* (1956). John F. Stover, *The Life and Decline of the American Railroad* (1970), is another good survey. On specific areas of rail development, see Richard C. Overton, *Burlington West* (1941) and *Gulf to Rockies* (1953), for the West; John F. Stover, *The Railroads of the South, 1865–1900* (1955); and Edward C. Kirkland, *Men, Cities, and Transportation*, 2 vols. (1948), for New England. Railroad management is the subject of Thomas C. Cochran, *Railroad Leaders* (1953); and railroad consolidation is examined in Edward G. Campbell, *The Reorganization of the American Railroad System* (1938). Gabriel Kolko, *Railroads and Regulation, 1877–1916* (1965), challenges traditional views of the reasons for reform. See also Lee Benson, *Merchants, Farmers, and Railroads* (1955), and George H. Miller, *Railroads and the Granger Laws* (1971), for more on the subject of regulation. Robert Fogel, *Railroads and American Economic Growth* (1964), questions the centrality of railroads to economic development.

The Corporation The emergence of the modern corporation is examined in an important book by Alfred P. Chandler, Jr., *The Visible Hand: The Managerial Revolution in American Business* (1977). Other valuable studies include Glenn Porter, *The Rise of Big Business* (1973), a succinct overview; Glenn Porter and H. C. Livesay, *Merchants and Manufacturers* (1971); and Alfred P. Chandler, Jr., *Strategy and Structure: Chapters in the History of American Industrial Enterprise* (1966). Matthew Josephson, *The Robber Barons* (1934), is a classic (and critical) study of the industrial titans. On individual corporate leaders, see Alfred D. Chandler, Jr., *Pierre S. du Pont and the Making of the Modern Corporation* (1971); Harold C. Livesay, *Andrew Carnegie and the Rise of Big Business* (1975); Allan Nevins, *Study in Power: John D. Rockefeller*, 2 vols. (1953); David F. Hawkes, *John D.: The Founding Father of the Rockefellers* (1980); Joseph Wall, *Andrew Carnegie* (1970); and Bernard Weisberger, *The Dream Maker* (1979), on William Durant, the founder of General Motors.

Ideologies The ideology of late nineteenth-century capitalism is described in Edward C. Kirkland, *Dream and Thought in the Business Community, 1860–1900* (1956); Sidney Fine, *Laissez Faire and the General Welfare State: A Study of Conflict in American Thought, 1865–1901* (1956); and Irvin G. Wylie, *The Self-Made Man in America* (1954). An important study of the work ethic is Daniel T. Rodgers, *The Work Ethic in Industrial America, 1850–1920* (1978). Louis Galambos, *The Public Image of Big Business in America, 1880–1940* (1975), is an examination of attitudes toward business as seen in various popular periodicals. Richard Hofstadter, *Social Darwinism in American Thought*, rev. ed. (1955), is the basic work on the subject. Robert G. McCloskey, *American Conservatism in the Age of Enterprise* (1951), is also valuable. Samuel Chugerman, *Lester F. Ward: The American Aristotle* (1939), and Arthur E. Morgan, *Edward Bellamy* (1944), examine two important social critics; Charles A. Barker, *Henry George* (1955), considers another. John L. Thomas, *Alternative America: Henry George, Edward Bellamy, Henry Demarest Lloyd, and the Adversary Tradition* (1983), is a comparative biography of three utopian thinkers of the late nineteenth century. T. J. Jackson Lears, *No Place of Grace: Antimodernism and the Transformation of American Culture, 1880–1920* (1981), is the story of intellectuals rebelling against the industrial-bureaucratic order.

Labor Henry Pelling, *American Labor* (1960), is a useful survey of the subject, with several chapters on this period. A more focused overview is Melvyn Dubofsky, *Industrialism and the American Worker, 1865–1920* (1975). Herbert G. Gutman, *Work, Culture, and Society in Industrializing America* (1976), is a collection of provocative essays about the lives of American workers. David Montgomery, *Beyond Equality* (1975) and *Workers' Control in America: Studies in the History of Work, Technology, and Labor Struggles* (1979), are important social histories. Daniel Nelson, *Managers and Workers: Origins of the New Factory System in the United States, 1880–1920* (1975), examines new forms of interaction. On Gompers and the early AFL, see Stuart Kaufman, *Samuel Gompers and the Origins of the American Federation of Labor* (1978); Philip Taft, *The A.F. of L. in the Time of Gompers*, 2 vols. (1957–1959); and Gompers's autobiography, *Seventy Years of Life and Labor*, 2 vols. (1975). Stanley Buder, *Pullman* (1967), is a study of the town and the strike. Henry David, *The Haymarket Affair* (1936), and Paul Avrich, *The Haymarket Tragedy* (1984), discusses the celebrated incident. P. K. Edwards, *Strikes in the United States, 1881–1974* (1981), examines long-term trends in labor unrest.

Women Susan E. Kennedy, *If All We Did Was to Weep at Home* (1979), and Barbara Wertheimer, *We Were There: The Story of Working Women in America* (1977), examine woman workers. Tamara Hareven, *Family Time and Industrial Time: The Relationship Between the Family and Work in a New England Industrial Community* (1982), examines the effects of the new industrial system on the family. Alice Kessler-Harris, *Out to Work: A History of Wage-Earning Women in the United States* (1982), is an important overview of working women. Susan Levine, *Labor's True Women: Carpet Weavers, Industrialization, and Labor Reform in the Gilded Age* (1984), is a more specialized study.

The Left J. H. M. Laslett, *Labor and the Left* (1970), studies radical influences on the labor movement. Nick Salvatore, *Eugene V. Debs: Citizen and Socialist* (1982), is an important study of the socialist leader. Mari Jo Buhle, *Women and American Socialism, 1870–1920* (1981), examines the tension between native socialists, to whom women's issues were important, and immigrant activists, to whom they were secondary. Melvyn Dubofsky, *We Shall Be All: A History of the Industrial Workers of the World* (1969), is a major study of the "Wobblies." Gerald N. Grob, *Workers and Utopia* (1961), considers labor reform visions.

***Six O'Clock*, by John Sloan, c. 1912** (Phillips Collection, Washington)

Chapter 18 # The Age of the City

The progress of industrialization and the rapid expansion of commerce changed the face of American society in countless ways. Nowhere, however, were the effects of these changes more visible than in the cities. It was there that most of the factories and corporate offices were located, there that the new economic system had its seat. And it was from the city that there emerged a new set of social and cultural values that would ultimately extend to most areas of the country. The United States was becoming an urban nation.

The change did not come easily. The rapid growth of the urban population placed an enormous strain on the capacities of most metropolitan communities. Roads, sewers, transportation facilities, housing, social services—all proved inadequate to the new demands being placed on them. Urban political systems fell victim to corruption and ineptitude. And American sensibilities often rebelled at the new and intimidating pace of urban life. Indeed, the crisis of the cities seemed to many Americans a symbol of all the many problems confronting a society in the throes of rapid and destabilizing change. Sociologist Charles Horton Cooley wrote:"Our cities, especially, are full of the disintegrated material of the old order looking for a place in the new."

Yet for all the problems, the city continued its rise to dominance in American society—in part because of economic developments over which individuals seemed to have little control, in part because the diversity and excitement of urban life proved alluring to increasing numbers of Americans. Traditional rural values changed slowly in response to the influence of the urban environment, but change they did. By

the end of the nineteenth century, the city had clearly emerged as the central focus of American economic, social, and cultural life.

The New Urban Growth

The great folk movement from the countryside to the city was occurring simultaneously throughout much of the Western world, as industrialization and the factory system changed the face of Europe as well as the United States. From countries or regions that were industrializing slowly or not at all, people moved to other countries or other regions that were industrializing rapidly. Rural people from both America and Europe, therefore, made their way to the business and industrial centers of the United States in search of opportunity.

The City's Lure

"We cannot all live in cities, yet nearly all seem determined to do so," Horace Greeley wrote soon after the Civil War. " 'Hot and cold water,' baker's bread, gas, the theatre, and the streetcars . . . indicate the tendency of modern taste." The city attracted people because of the many conveniences it offered years before such things reached the village or the farm. It drew people because of its institutions of entertainment and culture—its theaters and amusements, its libraries and museums, its superior schools and colleges. It attracted people, above all, because it offered

America in 1900

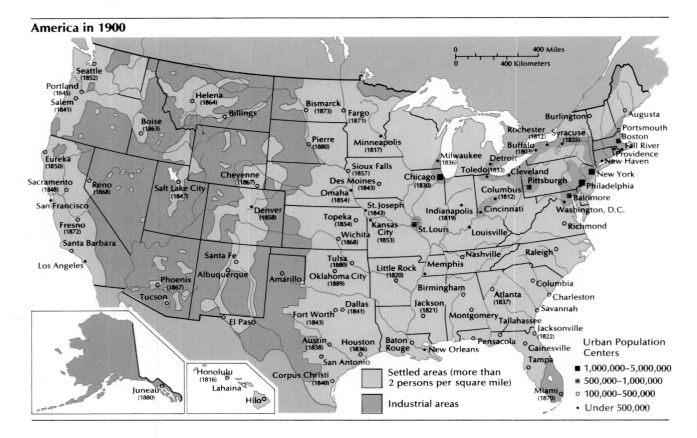

Urban Population Centers

- ■ 1,000,000–5,000,000
- ⊞ 500,000–1,000,000
- ○ 100,000–500,000
- • Under 500,000

Settled areas (more than 2 persons per square mile)

Industrial areas

more opportunities for employment and higher wages than the countryside afforded. The lure of the city persisted despite the disappointments and hardships it presented to those who moved there.

In the half-century from 1860 to 1910, the rural population of the United States almost doubled, but the urban population increased sevenfold. In 1860, approximately one-sixth of the American people had lived in towns of 8,000 or larger; by 1900, one-third of the people lived in such places. The number of cities with more than 50,000 inhabitants was 16 in 1860 and 109 in 1910. And in 1920, the census revealed that for the first time, a majority of the American people lived in "urban" areas—defined as communities of 2,500 people or more. The combined population of New York City and Brooklyn (until 1898 a separate municipality) grew from 1.2 million in 1860 to more than 3 million in 1900. Even more spectacular was the growth of Chicago, which had 100,000 inhabitants in 1860 and more than a million at the end of the century. Towns and cities were

getting bigger and more numerous in all sections of the country.

Natural increase accounted for only a small part of the urban growth. Urban families experienced a high rate of infant mortality, a declining fertility rate, and a high death rate from disease. Without immigration, cities would have grown relatively slowly.

Domestic migration accounted for a substantial portion of city growth, as Americans left declining agricultural regions and moved to more urban areas, where economic opportunities were presumed to be better. During the 1880s, the number of inhabitants was decreasing in two-fifths of Pennsylvania's total area, three-fifths of Connecticut's, more than half of Ohio's and Illinois's, and five-sixths of New York's. The decrease occurred almost entirely in farm areas, while increases were occurring simultaneously in the cities of the region. People did not always move directly from the farm to the city. Many tended to move first to a nearby village, then to a local town, and only then to the city itself. Ultimately, however,

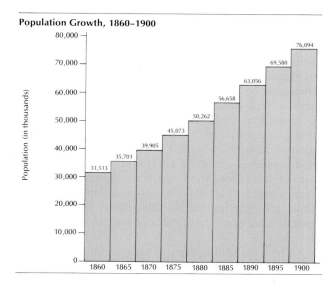

Population Growth, 1860–1900

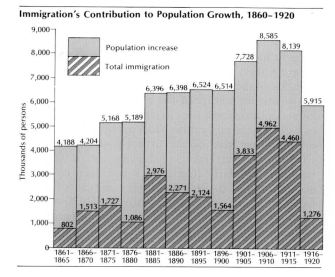

Immigration's Contribution to Population Growth, 1860–1920

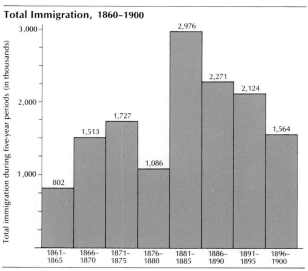

Total Immigration, 1860–1900

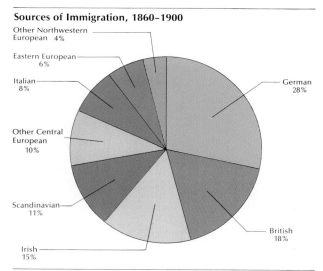

Sources of Immigration, 1860–1900

most migrants from the countryside found their way to the cities.

The 1880s saw as well the beginnings of a population change that would, in the early twentieth century, become one of the most important migrations in American history: the movement of blacks from the rural South to industrial cities. The poverty and oppression of the late-nineteenth-century South accounted for the movement more than did opportunities in the industrial North, for blacks arriving in the cities found relatively few prospects open to them. Factory jobs for blacks were rare and professional

opportunities almost nonexistent. Instead, urban blacks tended to work as cooks, janitors, and domestic servants, and in other service occupations. Since many such jobs were considered women's work, black women often outnumbered black men in the cities. By the end of the nineteenth century, there were substantial black communities in over a dozen cities—many of them in the South but some (Washington, Baltimore, Chicago) in the border states or the North. The movement of blacks out of the South remained limited, however, until what became known as the "Great Migration" began in 1915.

The Ethnic City

The most important source of urban population growth in the late nineteenth century was the arrival of great numbers of new immigrants from Europe and elsewhere. This immigration had done much to transform the nature of the industrial work force. It helped to transform the character of the nation's cities as well. The immigration had a profound effect, first, on the sheer size of the urban population. But it changed the social fabric of the city, too, in countless ways—particularly after 1880, when the flow of new arrivals began to include large numbers of people from southern and eastern Europe. By the 1890s, more than half of all immigrants came from these new regions, as opposed to fewer than 2 percent in the 1860s.

In earlier stages of immigration, the majority of the new arrivals had headed west. Most Germans, for example, had moved to the farming regions of the

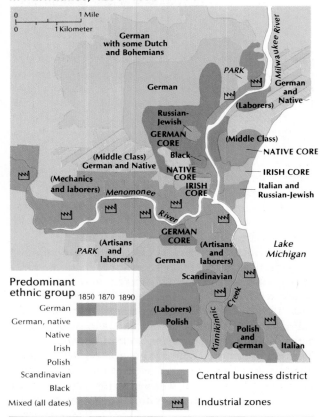

Evolving Ethnic and Class Segregation in Milwaukee, 1850–1890

Midwest. Those who had chosen urban life had generally settled not on the East coast but in such Midwestern cities as St. Louis, Cincinnati, and Milwaukee. Nearly all the Scandinavians had moved to farms in the Middle West or on the Great Plains. Immigrants who had settled in cities were often relatively well-educated and upwardly mobile people: businessmen, professionals, and skilled workers—although significant minorities of many immigrant groups became unskilled urban workers. The Irish had presented a marked exception to the general pattern. Even before the Civil War, they had tended to congregate in Eastern cities as unskilled workers, although by the late nineteenth century many had begun to achieve new and enhanced social and economic levels.

The new immigrants of the late nineteenth century, in contrast, settled almost without exception in industrial cities, where they occupied largely unskilled jobs. They lacked the capital to buy land and begin farming in the West. They needed immediate employment, and only the city—with its factories, stockyards, railroads, and other industries—could provide it. The city had another appeal for them as well. As strangers in an alien land, they could find refuge in the city by living in communities with their fellow nationals.

The result was a radical transformation of life in the nation's large cities. By 1890, the majority of the population of the major urban areas consisted of immigrants: 87 percent in Chicago, 80 percent in New York, 84 percent in Milwaukee and Detroit. (London, the largest industrial city in Europe, had by contrast a population that was 94 percent native.) Equally striking was the diversity of the new immigrant populations. In other countries experiencing heavy immigration in this period, most of the new arrivals were coming from one or two sources. Argentina, for example, was experiencing a great influx of Europeans in this era, but almost all of them were coming from Italy or Spain. In the United States, no single national group dominated the new immigrant population. In the last half of the nineteenth century, 18 percent of the new arrivals came from Italy, 13 percent from the Austro-Hungarian Empire (itself a potpourri of different nationalities), 16 percent from Germany, 10 percent from Russia, 10 percent from Poland, 6 percent from Scandinavia, and 30 percent from Great Britain and Ireland. Other, smaller groups arrived from Greece, Canada, Japan, China, Holland, Mexico, and other nations. In some towns, a dozen different ethnic groups might find themselves living in close proximity to one another. No country had ever gathered its population from so wide a range of sources in so short a period of time.

Most of the new European immigrants were people from rural backgrounds, and the adjustment to city life was often a painful one. To help ease the transition, therefore, national groups usually formed close-knit ethnic communities within the cities: Italian, Polish, Jewish, Slavic, and other neighborhoods (often known as "immigrant ghettoes") that attempted to re-create in the New World many of the features of the Old. It was impossible, of course, to reproduce in the modern city the social fabric of the farm villages from which many immigrants came— the seasonal work patterns, the intimate communal ties passed on from generation to generation, the strength of family life based on common economic activities. But the ethnic neighborhoods did provide immigrants with a sense of belonging to a coherent community. The newcomers could find newspapers and theaters in their native languages, stores selling their native foods, church and fraternal organizations that provided links with their national pasts. And they could move through large areas of the city surrounded by their fellow nationals, an experience that helped cushion them against the loneliness of being in a new land. The immigrants also maintained close ties with their native countries. They kept in contact with relatives who had remained behind. Some (perhaps as many as a third in the early years) returned to Europe after a relatively short time; others attempted to help bring the rest of their families to America.

The cultural cohesiveness of the ethnic communities clearly eased the pain of separation from the immigrants' native lands. Whether it helped immigrants to become absorbed into the economic life of America is a more difficult question to answer. It is clear that some ethnic groups (Jews and Germans in particular) advanced economically more rapidly than others (for example, the Irish). Why that was so is a matter of considerable controversy. But one explanation is that by huddling together in ethnic neighborhoods, immigrant groups tended to reinforce the cultural values of their previous societies. When those values were particularly well suited to American life— as was, for example, the high value that Jews placed on education—then this ethnic identification helped members of a group to advance. When other values predominated—maintenance of community solidarity, strengthening of family ties, preservation of order—progress was often less rapid.

Assimilation and Exclusion

In virtually all immigrant communities, the strength of ethnic ties had to compete against another powerful force: the desire for assimilation. Most of the new arrivals had come to America with romantic visions of the New World. And however disillusioning they might find their first contact with the United States, they usually retained the dream of becoming true "Americans." Even many first-generation immigrants worked hard to rid themselves of all vestiges of their old cultures, to become thoroughly Americanized. Second-generation immigrants were even more likely to attempt to break with the old ways, to assimilate themselves completely into what they believed was a genuinely American culture. Some even looked with contempt on parents and grandparents who continued to value traditional ethnic habits and values. The tension between the desire to become assimilated and the strength of ethnic ties was one that countless immigrants and their children wrestled with for years.

The arrival of these vast numbers of new immigrants, and the conspicuousness with which many of them clung to old ways and created culturally distinctive communities, provoked fear and resentment among many native Americans in much the same way earlier arrivals had done. Some people reacted against the immigrants out of generalized fears and prejudices, seeing in their "foreignness" the source of all the disorder and corruption of the urban world. "These people," a Chicago newspaper wrote shortly after the Haymarket bombing of 1886, "are not American, but the very scum and offal of Europe, . . . Europe's human and inhuman rubbish." Others had economic concerns. Native laborers, fighting to raise their incomes and improve their working conditions, were often incensed by the willingness of the immigrants to accept lower wages and to take over the jobs of strikers.

The rising nativism provoked a series of political responses. Henry Bowers, a self-educated lawyer obsessed with a hatred of Catholics and foreigners, founded in 1887 the American Protective Association, committed to stopping the immigrant tide. By 1894, membership in the organization reportedly reached 500,000, with chapters throughout the Northeast and Midwest. That same year, a more genteel organization—the Immigration Restriction League—was founded in Boston by five Harvard alumni. It was dedicated to the belief that immigrants should be screened, through literacy tests and other

Chinatown, San Francisco
This photo shows a toy stand in San Francisco's Chinese community, the oldest and for many years the largest "Chinatown" in the United States. Although a few immigrants from China appeared in what is now the United States at around the time of the Revolution, there was no large-scale Chinese presence in North America until the second half of the nineteenth century. Political instability and economic hardship in China beginning in the 1840s resulted in the emigration of some 2.4 million people between 1840 and 1900. Only a small proportion of them could afford passage to America. Nevertheless, more than 320,000 Chinese entered the United States between 1850 and 1882, when the Chinese Exclusion Act, halting further immigration, went into effect. (California Historical Society Library)

standards designed to separate the desirable from the undesirable. The League avoided the crude theories of conspiracy and the rabid xenophobia of the American Protective Association; its more sophisticated nativism was ultimately far more effective in winning public support for restriction.

Even before the rise of these new organizations, politicians were struggling to find some answer to the immigration question. Congress acted in 1882 to exclude the Chinese, who had been arriving in large numbers on the West Coast and who, among other things, made up a significant portion of the work force building the Western railroads. In the same year, Congress passed a general immigration law, which denied entry to certain undesirables—convicts, paupers, idiots—and placed a tax of 50 cents on every person admitted. Legislation of the 1890s enlarged the proscriptive list and increased the tax. These measures reflected a rising fear that continuing unlimited immigration would exhaust the resources of the nation and endanger its social institutions. But the laws kept out only a small number of aliens and fell far short of fulfilling the hopes of either the American Protective Association or the Immigration Restriction League. Congress passed a literacy law in 1897, but President Grover Cleveland vetoed it. Powerful business interests, the employers of cheap labor, continued to oppose restrictions.

The Urban Landscape

The city was a place of remarkable contrasts. It had homes of almost unimaginable size and grandeur, and hovels of indescribable squalor. It had conveniences unknown to earlier generations and problems that seemed beyond the capacity of society to solve. Both the attractions and the problems were a result of one central fact: the stunning pace with which cities were growing. The demands of (and the potential for profit from) the urban population helped to spur important new technological and industrial developments. But the rapid expansion also produced misgovernment, poverty, overcrowding, traffic jams, filth, epidemics, and great fires. The pace of growth was simply too fast for planning and building to keep pace. "The problem in America," one municipal reformer said, "has been to make a great city in a few years out of nothing."

One of the greatest problems of this precipitous

growth was that of finding housing for the thousands of new urban residents who were pouring into the cities every day. For the wealthy, housing was seldom a worry. The availability of cheap labor, and the increasing accessibility of tools and materials, reduced the cost of building in the late nineteenth century and permitted anyone with even a moderate income to afford a house. The richest urban residents often lived in palatial mansions in the heart of the city. Others of the rich, and many of the moderately well-to-do, took advantage of the less expensive land on the edges of the city and settled in new suburbs. Chicago, for example, boasted in the 1870s of having nearly one hundred residential suburbs connected with the city by railroad and offering the joys of "pure air, peacefulness, quietude, and natural scenery." Boston, too, saw the development of some of the earliest "streetcar suburbs"—Dorchester, Brookline, and others—which catered to both the wealthy and the middle class. New Yorkers of moderate means settled in the new suburb of Harlem, on the northern fringes of

Manhattan, and commuted downtown by trolley or river boat.

The majority of urban residents, however, could not afford to move to the suburbs or own their own housing. Instead, they stayed in the city centers and rented. And because demand was so high and space so scarce, they had little power with which to exact high standards. Landowners, to maximize their rental incomes, tried to squeeze as many residents as possible into the smallest available space. In Manhattan, for example, the average population density in 1894 was 143 people per acre—a rate higher than that of some of the most crowded cities of Europe (Paris had 127 per acre, Berlin 101) and far higher than any other American city. More than a million poor New Yorkers were jammed into "tenements"—a term that had originally referred simply to multiple-family rental buildings, but that had by the late nineteenth century come to be applied to slum dwellings only. The tenement, which first appeared in 1850, had been hailed as a great improvement in housing for the poor.

Streetcar Suburbs in Nineteenth-Century New Orleans

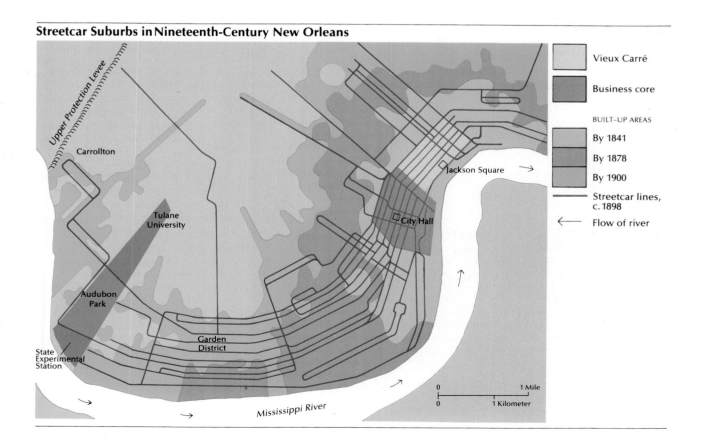

"It is built with the design of supplying the laboring people with cheap lodgings," a local newspaper commented, "and will have many advantages over the cellars and other miserable abodes which too many are forced to inhabit." But tenements themselves became miserable abodes. The typical structure was three to five stories high, with many windowless rooms, little or no plumbing or central heating, and perhaps a row of privies in the basement. A New York state law of 1879 required a window in every bedroom of tenements built thereafter, but developers generally complied by providing openings onto dank and sunless airshafts.

Jacob Riis, a Danish immigrant and New York newspaper reporter, shocked many middle-class Americans with his sensational (and some would say sensationalized) descriptions of tenement life in his 1890 book *How the Other Half Lives*. Slum dwellings, he said, were almost universally sunless, practically airless, and "poisoned" by "summer stenches." "The hall is dark and you might stumble over the children pitching pennies back there."

Urban growth posed monumental challenges to the transportation systems of the nation's cities. Old downtown streets were often too narrow for the heavy traffic that was beginning to move over them. Some were paved with cobblestones, but most lacked a hard surface and were a sea of either mud or dust—depending on the weather. In the last decades of the century, more and more streets were paved, usually with wooden blocks, bricks, or asphalt; but paving could not keep up with the laying out of new thoroughfares. By 1890, Chicago had surfaced only about 600 of its more than 2,000 miles of streets.

It was not simply the conditions of the streets, however, that impeded urban transportation. It was the numbers of people who needed to move every day from one part of the city to another—back and forth between their homes and their workplaces, churches, stores, and schools. Private vehicles could not answer the need; the solution lay in the development of mass transportation. Streetcars drawn on tracks by horses had been introduced into some cities even before the Civil War. New York had sixteen lines by 1866, using 800 cars and nearly 8,000 horses. But the horsecars, while faster than the omnibuses and other smaller vehicles that had served as public transportation in the past, were still not fast enough. As a result, cities embarked on new efforts to improve their mass transit. New York in 1870 opened its first elevated railway, whose steam-powered trains moved rapidly above the city streets on massive iron structures; but the trains inflicted noise, filth, and often dangerously hot embers on the pedestrians be-

Chicago, 1910
The stunning urban growth of the late nineteenth and early twentieth centuries taxed American cities up to, and often beyond, their limits. This view of Dearborn Avenue in Chicago, looking south, illustrates one of the problems of the industrial city: chronic congestion. Horse-drawn vehicles jostle here with electric streetcars and swarms of pedestrians. (Chicago Historical Society)

low. New York, Chicago, San Francisco, and other cities experimented with cable cars, towed by continuously moving underground cables. Richmond, Virginia, introduced the first electric trolley line in 1888, and by 1895 such systems were operating in 850 towns and cities, with a total of 10,000 miles of track. Boston in 1897 opened the first American subway when it put a mile and a half of its trolley lines underground.

Cities were growing upward as well as outward—a result of the convergence of technological discoveries and the need for new space in the increasingly crowded downtown areas. The first modern "skyscraper," constructed in Chicago in 1884—by later standards a relatively modest ten stories high—inaugurated a new era in urban architecture. Once builders perfected the technique of constructing tall buildings with cast-iron and then steel beams, and once inventors produced the electric elevator to make possible quick and safe vertical movement, no obstacle remained to even higher buildings. The greatest figure in the early development of the skyscraper was the Chicago architect Louis Sullivan, who introduced many of the modern, functional elements to the genre—large windows, sheer lines, limited ornamentation—in an attempt to emphasize the soaring height of the building as its most distinctive feature. Sullivan's students—among them Frank Lloyd Wright—expanded the influence of these innovations still further and applied them to low buildings as well as tall ones.

Strains of Urban Life

The increasing congestion of the city, and the slow development of new services to cope with that congestion, produced a number of serious health and safety hazards. One was fires. In one major city after another, major conflagrations in the late nineteenth century swept through downtowns, destroying blocks of buildings (many of them still constructed of wood) and forcing the almost total reconstruction of large areas. Chicago suffered its "great fire" in 1871, and Boston a disastrous fire the same year. Other cities experienced similar disasters—Baltimore, for example, and San Francisco, where a tremendous earthquake produced a catastrophic fire in 1906. The great fires were terrible experiences for those who lived through (or died in) them. But they were also important events in the development of the cities involved. Not only did they induce new strategies to prevent or limit future fires—the construction of fireproof buildings, the development of professional fire departments, and more; they also forced cities to rebuild at a time when new technological and architectural innovations were available. Many of the modern, high-rise downtowns of American cities arose out of the rubble of great fires.

An even greater hazard than fire was disease, especially in poor neighborhoods with inadequate sanitation facilities. But while slums suffered the worst from disease, the entire city was vulnerable. An epidemic that began in a poor neighborhood could (and often did) spread easily into other neighborhoods as well. Even though the germ theory of disease was known to public health experts, few municipal officials recognized the relationship of sewage disposal and water contamination to such epidemic diseases as typhoid fever and cholera. As late as the turn of the century, most city dwellers relied on private vaults and cesspools for the disposal of human wastes. Flush toilets and public sewer systems began to appear in the 1870s; but for many years they failed to solve the problem—largely because such systems emptied their sewage into open ditches within the city limits or into streams nearby, often polluting the city's own water supply in the process.

Urbanization brought more than new conveniences and new insecurities. It also brought a new concept of time and organization. "The complex interrelationship of life in the modern city called for unprecedented precision," wrote Oscar Handlin. "The dictatorship of the clock and the schedule became absolute." Thus the modern city forced the rural people who were increasingly flowing into it to shift their notions of time—which traditionally had been a matter of human whim and of such natural phenomena as the rising and setting of the sun—to reflect the importance of precise scheduling.

Rural Americans and Europeans alike reacted to the city, therefore, with marked ambivalence. It was a place of strong allure and great excitement. Yet it was also a place of alienating impersonality, of a new feeling of anonymity, of a different kind of work, with which the individual could feel only limited identification. To many, moreover, it was a place of poverty and sin. Theodore Dreiser's 1900 novel *Sister Carrie* exposed one troubling aspect of urban life: the plight of single women (such as Dreiser's heroine, Carrie) who moved from the countryside into the city and found themselves without any means of support. Carrie first took an exhausting and ill-paying job in a Chicago shoe factory, then drifted into a "life of sin," exploited by predatory men. The novel was so shocking to contemporary sensibilities that Dreiser's publisher attempted to suppress it for a time. But many women were experiencing in reality the dilemmas Carrie experienced in fiction. Living in conditions of extreme poverty and hardship, some drifted into prostitution.

The apparent sinfulness of the city—with its prostitutes, its foreigners with their strange customs, its saloons, its dance halls—appalled many long-time city dwellers and many recent migrants as well. Yet however ambivalent Americans may have felt about the city, urban influence grew steadily in the late nineteenth century. Not only those who lived in the city but many who remained outside it found themselves affected by urban customs and values. More and more, the city was setting the pattern for American character and culture.

The Machine and the Boss

New arrivals to the cities, and foreign immigrants in particular, faced severe obstacles. Many could not speak English. Few knew how to deal with the laws and customs of the new land. Large numbers found themselves indigent for long periods after their arrival before they could find work. There was, in short, an enormous demand for institutions to help immigrants adjust to American urban life.

Private charitable societies answered part of this need. But generally these organizations were run by middle-class humanitarians who insisted on middle-class standards of morality and had little understanding or appreciation of immigrant cultures. Many such societies operated on the assumption that poverty was more commonly a result of laziness and vice than of misfortune, and they confined their help to what they called the "deserving poor"—those who truly could not help themselves (at least according to the standards of the organizations themselves, which conducted elaborate "investigations" to separate the "deserving" from the "undeserving"). Other charitable societies—for example, the Salvation Army, which began operating in America in 1879, one year after it was founded in London—concentrated more on religious revivalism than on the relief of the homeless and hungry. Tensions often arose between native Protestant philanthropists and Catholic immigrants over religious doctrine and standards of morality.

The limitations of these private charitable organizations forced many immigrants to look elsewhere for assistance. They could not look to the government. It would be many years before government at any level—local, state, or federal—would assume any substantial responsibility for welfare work. Instead, the main welfare agency was often the urban machine—one of America's most distinctive political institutions. The machine owed its existence to the potential voting power of the large immigrant communities. Any politician who could mobilize that power stood to gain enormous influence. And so there emerged a group of urban "bosses"—most themselves of foreign birth or parentage, many of them Irish (who had the advantage of English as a native language). The major function of the boss was to win votes for his organization. And to do so, he engaged in a wide array of activities. To win the loyalty of his constituents, a boss might provide them with occasional relief—a basket of groceries or a bag of coal. He might step in to save from jail those arrested for petty crimes. When he could, he found work for the unemployed. Above all, he rewarded many of his followers with political jobs and with opportunities to rise in the political organization.

Yet machines were not simply mechanisms for maintaining political power. They were also vehicles for making money. Machine politicians enriched themselves and their allies through various forms of graft and corruption. Some of it might be fairly open—what the outspoken New York politician George Washington Plunkitt called "honest graft." For example, a politician might discover in advance where a new road or streetcar line was to be built, buy an interest in the land near it, and profit when the city had to buy the land from him or when property values rose as a result of the construction. But there was also a great deal of covert graft. A politician would award contracts for the construction of streets, sewers, public buildings, and other projects (usually at prices well above the real cost) on condition that he himself receive a portion of the contract money—that is, a "kickback." In addition to awarding contracts, a municipal official could sell franchises for the operation of such public utilities as street railways, waterworks, and electric light and power systems.

Few city bosses were as expansively corrupt as William M. Tweed, boss of New York City's Tammany Hall. Tweed's notorious "ring" once spent over $11 million of city funds to build a modest courthouse originally budgeted at $250,000. And at times, apparently, Tammany officials raided the public treasury in even more direct and blatant ways. Tweed's excesses finally landed him in jail in 1872, but his organization survived his demise to become a prototype of the

"Keeping Tammany's Boots Shined," c. 1887
This lithograph by cartoonist Joseph Keppler shows the heavy foot of New York's Tammany Hall sitting atop City Hall, while Hugh Graham, a Tammany mayor elected in 1886, applies the patronage polish that was the organization's lifeblood. The strap dangling from the boot bears the name of Richard Croker, who emerged as one of Tammany's principal leaders after the fall of Boss Tweed and who served as the undisputed chief of the organization from 1886 until 1901. *(Bettmann Archive)*

Tammany after Tweed was less exuberant in its excesses but more efficiently profitable.

Several factors made the continuation of boss rule possible despite the abuses and corruption. One, of course, was the power of immigrant voters, who were less concerned with political morality than with obtaining desperately needed services. The machine provided services; reformers usually did not. Another was the link between the political organizations and wealthy, prominent citizens who profited from their dealings with bosses and resisted efforts to overthrow them. Still another was the structural weakness of many city governments. Within the municipal government, no single official usually had decisive power or responsibility. Instead, authority was generally divided among many officeholders—the mayor, the aldermen, and others—and was limited by the state legislature, which often had the ultimate authority over municipal affairs. The boss, by virtue of his control over his machine, formed a sort of "invisible government" that seemed to provide an alternative to the inadequacy of the regular government. He might not hold an official position himself. (Leaders of Tammany Hall, for example, seldom held public office.) But through his organization, on which the politicians of his party depended for election, he often controlled a majority of those who were in office.

The urban machine was not without competition. Reform groups frequently mobilized public outrage at the corruption of the bosses and often succeeded in driving machine politicians from office. Tammany, for example, saw its candidates for mayor and other high city offices lose almost as often as they won in the last decades of the nineteenth century. But the reform organizations typically lacked the permanence of the machine; and more often than not, their power faded after a few years. Only basic, permanent, structural change in the institutions of government, many critics of the machine were by 1900 beginning to argue, could effectively rescue the city from "boss rule."

modern urban machine. Tammany leaders after Tweed—John Kelley, Richard Croker, and Charles Francis Murphy—ran organizations less personal in structure than Tweed had done. They created a well-ordered hierarchy, in which district and ward leaders exercised substantial autonomy. Loyalty to the organization itself became the ultimate value, survival of the organization the overriding goal. "A well-organized political club," Richard Croker once remarked, "is made for the purpose of aggressive warfare. It must move, and it must always move forward against its enemies. . . . If it is encumbered by useless baggage or half-hearted or traitorous camp followers, it cuts them off and goes ahead." Machine leaders also forged important economic relationships with local businesses—especially streetcar and utilities companies, dependent on government contracts and franchises.

Society and Culture in Urbanizing America

The rise of industry and the growth of cities had a profound effect on the way most Americans came to live their lives in the late nineteenth century. Americans realized that they were living in an era of rapid and remarkable change. Some welcomed the new ways, others feared them, but few could escape them.

For urban middle-class Americans, who were increasing rapidly in numbers, wealth, and influence, the last decades of the nineteenth century were a time of dramatic advances. Indeed, it was in these years that the United States began to build a distinctive middle-class culture that would eventually exert a powerful influence over the whole of American life. Other groups in society, however, viewed the changes of these years with less enthusiasm. Immigrants, blacks, factory workers, and many others experienced some marginal economic gains in these years; but they also became more aware of the enormous gap separating them from the more affluent middle class. The majority of Americans continued to live on farms or in small communities; as late as 1900, only 40 percent of the population was located in towns or cities of 2,500 inhabitants or more. And to them, the rise of the city—and the growing dominance of urban culture in American life as a whole—often seemed threatening.

Even those who viewed the changes in American society with ambivalence, however, often found themselves drawn to the new culture in various ways. They purchased the new products of the industrial economy; they shopped in the new chain stores or mail-order houses; they observed or participated in organized sports and leisure activities. Whether they liked it or not, Americans were encountering the birth of a new mass culture.

The industrial era also had an important impact on the ideas and activities of intellectuals, artists, and educators. It became a time of greatly expanding educational opportunities, at least for some portions of the population; a time of revolutionary new scientific discoveries; and a time in which traditional spiritual beliefs found themselves severely tested.

The Rise of Mass Consumption

The rise of American industry could not have occurred without the growth of markets for the goods being produced. Although many Americans could not afford to buy the products of their factories, the growing middle class began to form a large mass market for industrial goods.

One important change was the emergence of ready-made clothing as the basis of the American wardrobe. In the early nineteenth century, most Americans had made their own clothing—usually from cloth they bought from merchants, at times from fabrics they spun and wove themselves. The invention of the sewing machine and the spur that the Civil War (and its demand for uniforms) gave to the manufacture of clothing created an enormous industry devoted to producing ready-made garments. By the end of the century, virtually all Americans bought their clothing from stores; and partly as a result, much larger numbers of people were becoming concerned with questions of style.

There were also important changes in the way Americans bought and prepared food. The development of mass-produced tin cans beginning in the 1880s created a large new industry devoted to packaging and selling canned food. Refrigerated railroad cars were making it possible for perishables—meats, vegetables, and other foodstuffs—to be transported over long distances without spoiling. The production of artificially frozen ice made possible the proliferation of iceboxes in homes that in the past had not been able to afford them. For most Americans, the changes meant greatly improved diets, better health, and ultimately longer life expectancy.

Changes in marketing also served to alter the way Americans consumed. Small local stores began to face competition from national chain stores. The Atlantic and Pacific Tea Company (the A&P) began to establish a national network of grocery stores beginning in the 1870s. F. W. Woolworth created a chain of dry goods stores. Sears Roebuck established a vast market for its mail-order merchandise by distributing each year an enormous catalogue from which even people in remote rural areas could order new products.

In larger cities, the emergence of the great department stores helped to transform buying habits and to turn shopping into a more alluring and glamorous activity. Marshall Field in Chicago created one of the first department stores—a place deliberately designed to create a sense of wonder and excitement. Similar emporia emerged in New York, Boston, Philadelphia, and other cities.

Uses of Leisure

Not only was American society becoming more attracted to consuming. It was also becoming more concerned with finding uses for leisure time, which was rapidly increasing for most people. Members of the urban middle and professional classes, in particular, found themselves with large blocks of time in

Baseball in Chicago
The Boston Red Sox play the Chicago White Sox in
August 1904, a year after the Red Sox had won the first
World Series between the American and National League
champions. An interleague squabble led to the cancellation of the World Series in 1904, but it resumed in
1905 and has experienced no interruption since. Professional baseball was already drawing large crowds
in the early 1900s. Over 8,000 attended this game in
Chicago.   (Library of Congress)

the most popular of all the organized sports was baseball, which was by the end of the century well on its
way to becoming the "national pastime." A game
very similar to baseball—known as rounders and derived from cricket—had enjoyed limited popularity
in Great Britain since the early nineteenth century.
Versions of the game began to appear in America in
the early 1830s, well before Abner Doubleday (who
is erroneously believed to have invented the sport)
laid out a diamond-shaped field in West Point, New
York, in 1839 and attempted to standardize the rules.

By the end of the Civil War, interest in the game
had grown rapidly. More than 200 teams or clubs
existed, some of which toured the country playing
rivals; they belonged to a national association of
"baseball players" that had proclaimed a set of standard rules. These were amateur or semiprofessional
teams. But as the game grew in popularity, it offered
opportunities for profit, and the first salaried team,
the Cincinnati Red Stockings, appeared in 1869.
Other cities soon fielded professional teams; and in
1876, the National League (which still exists) was
organized, chiefly by Albert Spalding. Soon a rival
league appeared, the American Association. Competition between the two was intense, and in 1883 they
played a postseason contest, an early ancestor of the
World Series. The American Association eventually
collapsed; but in 1901, the American League was organized. And in 1903, the first modern World Series
was played, in which the Boston Red Sox defeated
the Pittsburgh Pirates. By then, baseball had become
an important business and a great national preoccupation—attracting paying crowds at times as large as
50,000, building substantial ball parks in which to
play the games, and engaging the interest of many
Americans through extensive reports of the contests
in newspapers and magazines.

Baseball was from the beginning a sport that had
great appeal to working-class people: Baseball players tended to be people from modest backgrounds;
baseball crowds consisted to a great degree of urban
laborers. The second most popular game, football,
appealed for a time to a more elite segment of the
population, in part because it arose in the colleges and
universities. At first, football was a game played informally by rival student groups at the same school.
Then, in 1869, the first intercollegiate game in America occurred between Princeton and Rutgers, with
twenty-five men on each team. Soon other Eastern
schools fielded teams, and the game began to become
entrenched as part of collegiate life. Early intercollegiate football bore only an indirect relation to the

which they were not at work—evenings, weekends,
even vacations. Factory workers in many industries
found their hours declining (from an average of nearly
seventy hours a week in 1860 to under sixty in 1900)
and thus also had more time to engage in leisure
activities. Even farmers found that the mechanization
of agriculture gave them more free time to enjoy
nonoccupational pastimes. Many Americans, in other
words, were coming to live lives that were neatly
compartmentalized, with rigid distinctions between
work and leisure that had not existed in the past. The
change produced a search for new forms of recreation
and entertainment.

Among the most important responses to this
search was the rise of organized spectator sports. And

modern game; it was far more similar to what is now known as rugby. By the late 1870s, however, the game was becoming standardized and was taking on the outlines of its modern form.

As college football grew in popularity, it spread to other sections of the country, notably to the state universities of the Midwest, destined soon to replace the Eastern schools as the great powers of the game. It also began to exhibit taints of the professionalism that have marked it ever since. Some schools employed as players "ringers"—tramp athletes who were not even registered as students. In an effort to eliminate such abuses, Amos Alonzo Stagg, athletic director and coach at the University of Chicago, led in forming the Western Conference, or Big Ten, in 1896, which established rules governing eligibility. Football also became known for an appalling level of violence on the field; eighteen college students died of football-related injuries and over a hundred were seriously hurt in 1905. The carnage prompted the formation of a new intercollegiate association (which, in 1910, became known as the National College Athletic Association, the NCAA), which revised the rules of the game to make it safer and more honest.

A wide range of other sports also emerged, both as entertainment for spectators and as recreation for large groups of participants. Basketball was invented in 1891 at Springfield, Massachusetts, by James A. Naismith, a Canadian working as athletic director for a local college. Boxing, which had long been a disreputable activity concentrated primarily among the urban lower classes, became by the 1880s a more popular and in some places more reputable sport—particularly after the adoption of the Marquis of Queensbury rules (by which fighters were required to wear padded gloves and to fight in rounds limited to three minutes) and the emergence of the first modern boxing hero, John L. Sullivan, who became heavyweight champion of the world in 1882. Nevertheless, boxing remained illegal in some states until after World War I.

Participation in the major spectator sports of the era was limited exclusively to men. But a number of nonspectator sports were emerging in which women became important participants. Golf and tennis seldom attracted crowds in the late nineteenth century; but both experienced a rapid increase in popularity among relatively wealthy men and women—usually

Cycling in Massachusetts

A middle-class couple enjoys a popular diversion of the late nineteenth century: touring by cycle. The first cycling club was organized in Boston in the 1870s, and within a few years similar organizations had appeared in many communities. Pictured here are Mr. and Mrs. William Quennell of Chelsea, Massachusetts, who were among the participants in the annual Ladies' North Shore Tricycle outing, a four-day expedition near Boston in October 1887, during which cyclists traveled from Malden to Gloucester, a distance of over seventy miles. Lady cyclists generally traveled on tandem tricycles or quadricycles, accompanied by "wheelmen" (often their husbands), who provided much of the muscle power. Men and women alike used such tours not only to get exercise but to display fashions. (Brown Brothers) the only people who could afford to join the exclusive clubs where facilities for the sports were available. Bicycling and croquet also enjoyed widespread popularity in the 1890s and also engaged women as well as men. Women's colleges were beginning to introduce their students to more strenuous sports as well—track, crew, swimming, and (beginning in the late 1890s) basketball.

Other forms of entertainment emerged in the late nineteenth century to fill the leisure time of Americans. Traveling circuses—such as those run by P. T. Barnum and James Bailey—took advantage of the railroad system to move from town to town and perform under large tents, which they carried with them. Wild West shows, vaudeville troupes, and black minstrel shows also traveled widely.

Mass Communications

The new urban industrial society required new vehicles for transmitting news and information. Consequently, American publishing and journalism experienced an important change in the decades following the Civil War. Between 1870 and 1910, the circulation of daily newspapers increased nearly ninefold (from under 3 million to more than 24 million), a rate three times as great as the rate of population increase. And while standards varied widely from one paper to another, American journalism began to develop the beginnings of a professional identity. Salaries of reporters increased greatly; many newspapers began separating the reporting of news from the expression of opinion; and newspapers themselves became important businesses.

One striking change was the emergence of national press services, which made use of telegraphic communication to supply papers throughout the country with news and features and contributed, as a result, to the standardization of the product. Such services furnished the same news to all their subscribing papers, and syndicates provided their customers with identical features, columns, editorials, and pictures. By the turn of the century important newspaper chains had emerged, of which the most powerful was William Randolph Hearst's. By 1914, Hearst controlled nine newspapers and two magazines.

Another major change occurred in the nature of American magazines. In the past, most weekly and monthly periodicals had been literary journals. Now, beginning in the 1880s, there appeared a new kind of magazine, designed to appeal to the masses and achieve a mass circulation. One of the important pioneers of the popular magazine was Edward W. Bok, who took over the *Ladies' Home Journal* in 1899 and, by employing writers who aimed their material at a mass female audience, built the circulation of the journal to over 700,000. By the end of the century, there was a large array of popular magazines, priced at 5 to 15 cents, some of them with circulations of up to 1 million.

What made these new mass-circulation publications possible was the growing importance of advertising in American commercial life. New industries needed above all to create new markets, and advertising was, many believed, the best way to do so. Not only did the amount of advertising increase in the decades after the Civil War, but the nature of the advertisements changed as well. Instead of small-type announcements listing products and prices, merchants began to use pictures, bold headlines, and enticing slogans. They attempted to make advertising a vehicle not just for alerting the public to the existence of a product but also for stimulating a demand for that product among people who might otherwise not have had any interest in buying it.

Intellectual Life

In addition to the important changes in popular culture that accompanied the rise of cities and industry, there were profound changes in the realm of "high culture"—the ideas and activities of intellectuals. Such changes occurred in many areas, but the single most profound intellectual development in the late nineteenth century was the widespread acceptance of the theory of evolution. The doctrine was associated most prominently with the English scientist Charles Darwin, although it was in fact the culmination of many years of theorizing by many people. It argued that the human species had evolved to its present state from earlier forms of life (and most immediately from apes) through a process of "natural selection."

Darwinism challenged almost every tenet of traditional American faith. If the evolutionists were right, then human beings were not necessarily innately endowed by God with a higher nature. They were only biological organisms, another form (even if the highest form) of animal life. History, Darwinism suggested, was not the working out of a divine plan, as many Americans had believed. It was a random process dominated by the fiercest or luckiest competitors.

The theory of evolution met widespread resistance at first from educators, theologians, and even many scientists. By the end of the century, however, the evolutionists had converted most members of the urban professional and educated classes to their point of view. Even most middle-class Protestant religious leaders had accepted the doctrine, making significant alterations in theology to accommodate it. Evolution had become enshrined as an irrefutable theory in schools and universities; virtually no serious scientist any longer questioned its basic validity.

Most urban Americans at the time failed to see, however, that the rise of Darwinism was contributing to a deep schism between the new, cosmopolitan culture of the city—which was receptive to new ideas such as evolution—and the more traditional, provincial culture of the rural areas—which remained wedded to fundamentalist religious beliefs and older values. Urban Americans smugly assumed that Darwinism had become as basic a scientific truth as the idea that the earth revolved around the sun, that challenges to it were now restricted to only a few superstitious people. In fact, opposition to the theory of evolution remained strong and deep among vast numbers of Americans. Indeed, the late nineteenth century saw not only the rise of a new, liberal Protestantism more in tune with new scientific discoveries. It also saw the beginning of an organized Protestant fundamentalism, which would gain in strength in the ensuing decades and would make its presence felt politically in the 1920s and again in the 1980s.

Out of the controversy over Darwinism emerged a wide range of new intellectual currents. There was the Social Darwinism of William Graham Sumner and others, which industrialists used so enthusiastically to justify their favored position in American life. (See p. 506.) But there were also more sophisticated philosophies—among them the doctrine that became known as "pragmatism" and that seemed to many to be peculiarly the product of Americans and peculiarly suited to the nation's changing material civilization. William James, a Harvard psychologist (and brother of the novelist Henry James), was the most prominent publicist of the new theory, although earlier intellectuals such as Charles S. Peirce and later ones such as John Dewey were at least equally important in its development and dissemination. According to the pragmatists, who accepted the idea of organic evolution, modern society should rely for guidance not on inherited ideals and moral principles but on the test of scientific inquiry. No idea or institution was valid, they claimed, unless it worked. Even religious beliefs, James insisted, were subject to the test of experience. If faith helped an individual understand his or her world, then it was valid for that person; if it did not, then it was not. "The ultimate test for us of what a truth means," James wrote, "is the conduct it dictates or inspires."

An expanding network of social scientists soon brought this same concern for scientific inquiry into areas of thought long dominated by traditional orthodoxies. New economists, such as Richard T. Ely and Simon Patten, challenged old economic assumptions and argued for a more active and pragmatic use of the discipline. Sociologists such as Edward A. Ross and Lester Frank Ward urged the application of scientific method to social and political problems. Historians such as Frederick Jackson Turner and Charles Beard challenged prevailing assumptions by arguing that economic factors more than spiritual ideals had been the governing force in historical development. John Dewey, for many decades one of the most influential of all American intellectuals, proposed a new approach to education that placed less emphasis on the rote learning of traditional knowledge and more on a flexible, democratic approach to schooling, one which enabled students to acquire knowledge that would help them deal with the realities of their society. The scientific method, he believed, would be the governing principle of this new, "instrumental" education.

The Arts in Urban America

Foreign observers and even some American intellectuals in the late nineteenth century often viewed the culture of the United States with contempt. "There is little to nourish and delight the sense of beauty there," wrote the English critic Matthew Arnold in 1888. Mark Twain, a more knowledgeable critic, expressed an equally dismissive view of American culture in 1873, when, in collaboration with Charles Dudley Warner, he published a novel satirizing the new urban-industrial society. The book's title—*The Gilded Age*—suggests its message. To Twain, Warner, and others, American life, despite its glittering surface, was essentially acquisitive and corrupt, with little cultural depth.

Whatever the quality of culture and society in late-nineteenth-century America, it was clear that the growth of industry and the rise of the city were having profound effects on them. Some writers and artists—the local-color writers of the South, for example; even Mark Twain, in such novels as *Huckleberry Finn*—responded to the new civilization by evoking an older, more natural world. But others grappled directly with the modern order, exposing its problems and offering solutions.

One of the strongest impulses in late-nineteenth- and early-twentieth-century American literature was the effort to re-create social reality. There were, of course, many writers who continued to produce novels and poetry of adventure and romance; indeed these books generally attracted the greatest popular audiences. But the nation's most serious writers began to probe more compelling issues: the oppression and suffering that they believed the urban-industrial society had created. The trend toward realism found an early voice in Stephen Crane, who—although best known for his novel of the Civil War, *The Red Badge of Courage* (1895)—was the author of a powerful indictment of the plight of the working class: *Maggie: A Girl of the Streets* (1893). Crane's glum descriptions of urban poverty and slum life created a sensation among the book's many readers. Theodore Dreiser was even more influential in encouraging writers to abandon the genteel traditions of earlier times and turn to the social dislocations of the present, both in *Sister Carrie* and in later novels—*The Financier* (1912), *The Titan* (1914), and others—that explored the injustices of the American economic system.

Many of Dreiser's contemporaries joined him in chronicling the oppression of America's poor. Frank Norris published *The Octopus* in 1901, an account of a struggle between oppressed wheat ranchers and powerful railroad interests in California. Another novel, *The Pit* (1903), attacked exploitation in the grain markets of Chicago. Upton Sinclair's *The Jungle* (1906) exposed abuses in the American meat-packing industry and helped to inspire legislative action to deal with the problem. Kate Chopin, a Southern writer who explored the oppressive features of traditional marriage, encountered widespread public abuse after publication of her shocking novel *The Awakening* in 1899. It described a young wife and mother who abandoned her family in search of personal fulfillment. It was formally banned in some communities.

One of the greatest, and certainly one of the most prolific, of the literary realists was William Dean Howells. Unlike the writers who focused on extremes of poverty and injustice, Howells described the common and the average, exposing the shallowness and corruption in ordinary American life styles. In *The Rise of Silas Lapham* (1884), he offered an unflattering portrait of the self-made businessman. His later novels, written during the more turbulent years of the 1890s and the early twentieth century, dealt more explicitly with social problems and injustices.

Other critics of American society responded to the new civilization not by attacking it but by withdrawing from it. Some, such as Henry Adams, chose intellectual withdrawal. His great autobiography, *The Education of Henry Adams* (1906), portrayed a man disillusioned with and unable to relate to his society, even though he continued to live in it. Others retreated physically from the United States. Henry James, one of the preeminent writers of the era, lived the major part of his adult life in England and Europe and produced a series of complex, coldly realistic novels—*The American* (1877), *Portrait of a Lady* (1881), *The Ambassadors* (1903), and many others—that showed the impact of Europe on Americans and his own ambivalence about the merits of the two civilizations.

American art through most of the nineteenth century had been undernourished and overshadowed by Europe. Most major American artists received their education overseas, painted in a European style (although many chose American subjects), and exhibited—if they exhibited at all—in foreign galleries. By 1900, however, important changes were already well under way. Now, nearly every major American city had a museum or gallery of at least modest proportions in which native artists could display their work and in which European masterpieces—many of them purchased by the great industrial magnates—could be seen. And a number of American artists, although they continued to study and even at times to live in Europe, broke from the Old World traditions and experimented with new styles. John La Farge, for example, made use of light and color in ways that anticipated the French impressionists. Winslow Homer, perhaps the greatest American artist of the era, was vigorously and almost blatantly American in his paintings of New England maritime life and other native subjects. James McNeil Whistler was one of the first Western artists to appreciate the beauty of Japanese color prints and to introduce Oriental concepts into American and European art.

By the first years of the new century, however, some American artists were turning even more decisively from the traditional academic style (a style perhaps best exemplified in America by the brilliant portraitist John Singer Sargent). Instead, younger painters were exploring the same grim aspects of

Hairdresser's Window
This 1907 painting is by John Sloan, an American artist who belonged to the so-called Ashcan School. Sloan and others were in revolt against what they considered the sterile formalism of academic painting and chose instead to portray realistic scenes of ordinary life. In 1913 they stirred the art world with their startling exhibit in New York, known as the Armory Show. In it they displayed not only their own work (which was relatively conventional in technique, even if daring in its choice of subjects) but also the work of innovative European artists, who were already beginning to explore wholly new artistic forms. (Wadsworth Atheneum, Hartford)

modern life that were becoming the subject of American literature. Influenced by the work of the French impressionists, but shaped too by the tenor of American urban life, members of the so-called Ashcan School produced work startling in its naturalism and stark in its portrayal of the social realities of the era. John Sloan, for example, attempted to capture the dreariness of American urban slums in his paintings; George Bellows caught the vigor and violence of his time in paintings and drawings of prize fights; Edward Hopper chose as his theme the grimness (and often the loneliness) of the modern city. Ultimately, some of these young artists would move beyond the Ashcan revolt to explore the fields of expressionism and abstraction; they showed their interest in new forms when, in 1913, they helped stage the famous Armory show in New York City, which displayed the works of the French postimpressionists and some American moderns. For a time, however, their work closely paralleled that of the naturalist writers of the era.

Toward Universal Schooling

A society that was coming to depend increasingly on specialized skills and scientific knowledge was, of course, a society with a fundamental need for effective systems of education. The late nineteenth century was, therefore, a time of rapid expansion and reform of American schools and universities.

Most influential, perhaps, was the spread of universal free public education. That had long been an ideal of American society, but only after the Civil War did it truly begin to become a reality. In 1860, for example, there were only 100 public high schools in the entire United States. By 1900, the number had reached 6,000. And by 1914, that number had doubled—and along with it the number of students attending high school. Even more spectacular was the expansion of elementary education. By 1900, compulsory attendance laws were in effect in thirty-one states and territories. Most of this expansion, however, occurred in urban areas; regions with few major cities—such as the South and parts of the Middle West—trailed far behind the urban-industrial areas in providing public education to their citizens. And in the South in particular, such educational facilities as existed were largely unavailable to blacks.

Although opportunities for education above the high-school level did not expand to nearly the same degree as those below it, colleges and universities were proliferating rapidly in the late nineteenth century. They benefited particularly from vast new resources made available by the national government. The federal government, by the Morrill Land Grant Act of the Civil War era, had donated land to states

Caprice in Purple and Gold, No. 2
James McNeill Whistler painted this formal study in 1864, an example of the academic style against which the Ashcan artists were rebelling. Whistler was one of the few American artists of the late nineteenth century to win serious attention from the artistic establishment of Europe. In this painting, he shows the growing influence of the Far East on European and American art. (Freer Gallery, Smithsonian Institution)

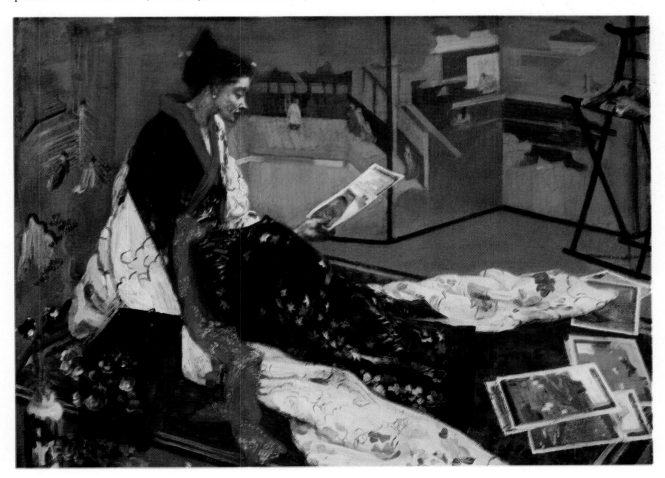

for the establishment of colleges to teach, among other things, agriculture and the mechanical arts. After 1865, particularly in the South and West, states began to take advantage of the law to strengthen existing institutions or to found new ones. In all, sixty-nine land-grant institutions came into existence in the last decades of the century—among them the state university systems of California, Illinois, Minnesota, and Wisconsin.

Supplementing the resources of the government were the millions of dollars contributed by business and financial tycoons, who endowed private institutions. The motives of the magnates were various: They were influenced by the gospel of wealth; they believed that education would ease class tensions; they realized that the demands of an industrial society called for specialized knowledge; or they were simply vain. Men such as Rockefeller and Carnegie gave generously; among the schools that benefited were Harvard, Chicago, Northwestern, Syracuse, Yale, Princeton, and Columbia. Other philanthropists founded new universities and thereby perpetuated their family names—Vanderbilt, Johns Hopkins, Cornell, Duke, Tulane, and Stanford.

Charles W. Eliot, who became president of Harvard in 1869 at the age of thirty-five and remained in that position for forty years, pioneered a break with the traditional curriculum. The usual course of studies at American universities emphasized classical and humanistic courses; and each institution prescribed a rigid program of required courses. Under Eliot's leadership, Harvard dropped most of its required courses in favor of an elective system and increased its course offerings to stress the physical and social sciences, the fine arts, and modern languages. Soon other institutions in all sections of the country were following Harvard's lead.

Eliot also renovated the Harvard medical and law schools, raising the requirements and lengthening the residence period; and again the Harvard model affected other schools. Improved technical training in other professions accompanied the advances in medicine and law. Both state and private universities hastened to establish schools of architecture, engineering, education, journalism, and business. The leading center for graduate study, based on the German system with the Ph.D. degree as its highest award, was Johns Hopkins University (founded in 1876). In 1875, there were only 399 graduate students in the United States; by 1900, the number had risen to more than 5,000.

Education for Women

The post–Civil War era saw, too, an important expansion of educational opportunities for women—although such opportunities continued to lag far behind those available to men (and were almost without exception denied to black women). More than half of all high-school graduates in the late nineteenth century were girls; and some of these students naturally looked for opportunities to extend their education further.

A number were able to do so by attending existing universities. At the end of the Civil War, only three American colleges (one of them Oberlin) had been coeducational. But in the years after the war, many of the land-grant colleges and universities in the Midwest began to admit women along with men—in large part because of their inability to attract enough male students to fill up their space. And some private universities (notably Cornell and Wesleyan) began admitting small numbers of women, in an effort to promote a new sexual egalitarianism.

But the idea of coeducation did not prevail as the foundation of women's education in this era. Instead, most women hoping for schooling beyond the secondary level turned to the growing network of women's colleges—most of them developed as the result of donations from philanthropists. A few women's colleges had struggled to establish themselves early in the century. Mount Holyoke, for example, opened its doors to eighty students in 1836 as a "seminary" for women. It did not become a full-fledged college until the 1880s. By then, however, many new female institutions had emerged: Vassar, Wellesley, Smith, Bryn Mawr, Wells, and Goucher. Some of the larger private universities created on their campuses separate colleges for women (such as Barnard at Columbia and Radcliffe at Harvard). Proponents of women's colleges saw the institutions as places where female students could find the greatest outlet for their own skills and creativity, where they would not be treated as "second-class citizens" by predominantly male student bodies and faculties.

The new women's colleges confronted a complex task. On the one hand, they were committed to providing their students with wide opportunities to expand their intellectual and even professional horizons. On the other hand, they felt the need to defend themselves against charges that higher education was not, as many men and even some women believed, too "arduous" for women's presumed delicate physical capacities. At times, the administrators of women's

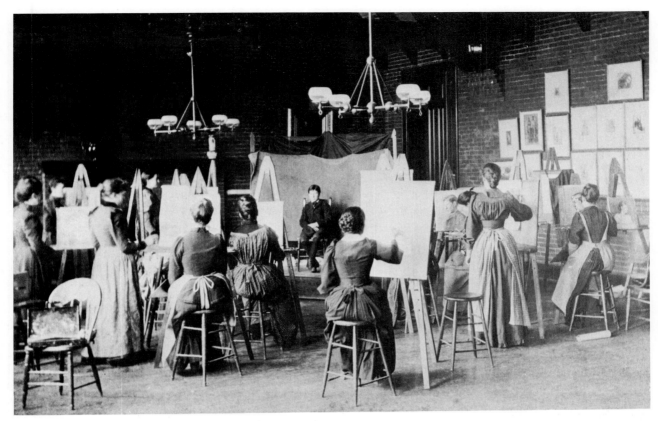

Smith College Students in Art Class

Smith College, in Northampton, Massachusetts, was chartered in 1871 and opened its doors in 1875. It was one of a number of institutions founded shortly after the Civil War to provide young women with access to advanced education. Although most graduates went on to lead conventional lives as wives and mothers, many used college as a way of preparing for careers outside the home. Administrators at Bryn Mawr (outside Philadelphia) used to remark: "Our failures marry." (Smith College Archives)

colleges displayed a firm determination to prove that their students were capable of doing the same demanding work as men. At the same time, however, they often included special programs of physical activity, to strengthen their students for the "ordeal" of education. And many women's colleges included as well training in traditional women's roles.

The female college was among the first examples of an important phenomenon in the history of modern American women: the emergence of a distinctive women's community. Most faculty members and many administrators were women (almost always unmarried). And the life of the college produced a spirit of sorority and commitment among educated women that had important effects in later years, as women came to spearhead many reform activities. Most female college graduates ultimately married, but they married later than their noncollege counterparts. A significant minority, perhaps over 25 percent, did not marry at all but devoted themselves to careers. Leaders of Bryn Mawr remarked at times that "our failures marry." And while that was surely an exaggeration, the growth of female higher education clearly became for some women a liberating experience—persuading them that they had roles to perform in society other than as wives and mothers.

SIGNIFICANT EVENTS

1839   Abner Doubleday establishes standardized rules for baseball

1869   Princeton and Rutgers play first intercollegiate football game

1870   New York City opens elevated railroads

1871   Great fires destroy much of Chicago and Boston

1872   Tammany's Boss Tweed convicted of corruption

1876   Baseball's National League founded

Johns Hopkins University creates first modern graduate school

1879   Salvation Army begins operations in America

1882   Congress restricts Chinese immigration

1884   First "skyscraper" built in Chicago

William Dean Howells publishes *The Rise of Silas Lapham*

1887   American Protective Association founded

1890   Jacob Riis publishes *How the Other Half Lives*

1891   James Naismith invents basketball

1894   Immigration Restriction League founded

1895   Stephen Crane publishes *The Red Badge of Courage*

1897   Boston opens first subway in America

1899   Kate Chopin publishes *The Awakening*

1900   Theodore Dreiser publishes *Sister Carrie*

1901   Baseball's American League founded

1903   Boston Red Sox win first World Series

Henry James publishes *The Ambassadors*

1906   Earthquake and fire destroy much of San Francisco

Upton Sinclair publishes *The Jungle*

1910   National College Athletic Association founded to regulate collegiate football

1913   Ashcan School artists stage Armory show in New York City

SUGGESTED READINGS

General Studies   General accounts of the rise of the city in American life include Blake McKelvey, *The Urbanization of America* (1963); Constance M. Green, *The Rise of Urban America* (1965); Charles N. Glaab and Andrew T. Brown, *A History of Urban America* (1967); and Arthur M. Schlesinger, *The Rise of the City, 1878–1898* (1933). A more recent overview is Howard Chudacoff, *The Evolution of American Urban Society*, rev. ed. (1981). Sam Bass Warner, Jr., *The Urban Wilderness* (1972), examines the physical landscape of the city; his *Streetcar Suburbs* (1962) describes urban expansion. John Teaford, *City and Suburb: The Political Fragmentation of Urban America* (1979), describes some of the consequences of that expansion. Lewis Mumford's *The Culture of the Cities* (1938) and *The City in History* (1961) are broad, historical views of the city. Alan Trachtenberg, *The Incorporation of America: Culture and Society in the Gilded Age* (1982), is a broad interpretive study of the cultural impact of urbanization and industrialization.

Mobility and Race   A number of works examine the issue of social mobility in urban society. Two of the most important are by Stephan Thernstrom: *Poverty and Progress* (1964) and *The Other Bostonians* (1973). Michael Frisch, *Town into City* (1972), Richard Sennett, *Families Against the City* (1970), and Clyde Griffen and Sally Griffen, *Natives and Newcomers* (1977), also examine the issue. Howard

Chudacoff, *Mobile Americans* (1972), considers geographical mobility as well. Stephan Thernstrom and Richard Sennett (eds.), *Nineteenth Century Cities* (1969), is a valuable collection of essays. The formation of urban black communities is the subject of Gilbert Osofsky, *Harlem: The Making of a Ghetto* (1966), Allan H. Spear, *Black Chicago* (1967), and Kenneth L. Kusmer, *A Ghetto Takes Shape* (1976). See also David M. Katzman, *Before the Ghetto* (1966), and Olivier Zunz, *The Changing Face of Inequality: Urbanization, Industrial Development, and Immigrants in Detroit, 1880–1920* (1982).

Immigration   Oscar Handlin, *The Uprooted*, rev. ed. (1973), has long been a standard work on the subject of immigration but has come under criticism from other historians. See, for example, Thomas Kessner, *The Golden Door: Italian and Jewish Immigrant Mobility* (1977); Josef Barton, *Peasants and Strangers: Italians, Rumanians, and Slovaks in an American City* (1975); and Virginia Yans-McLaughlin, *Family and Community: Italian Immigrants in Buffalo, 1880–1930* (1977). Other useful general studies of immigration include John Bodnar, *Immigration and Industrialization* (1977); Philip Taylor, *The Distant Magnet: European Emigration to the U.S.A.* (1971); Marcus Hansen, *The Immigrant in American History* (1940); Maldwyn A. Jones, *American Immigration* (1960); David Ward, *Cities and Immi-*

grants (1965); and Barbara Solomon, *Ancestors and Immigrants* (1965). For specific immigrant groups, see Jack Chen, *The Chinese of America* (1980), and Francis L. K. Hsu, *The Challenge of the American Dream* (1971), on the Chinese; Moses Rischin, *The Promised City: New York's Jews* (1962); Humbert S. Nelli, *The Italians of Chicago* (1970), and John W. Briggs, *An Italian Passage* (1978); John B. Duff, *The Irish in the United States* (1971); Mario T. Garcia, *Desert Immigrants: The Mexicans of El Paso, 1880–1920* (1981), and Matt S. Maier and Feliciano Rivera, *The Chicanos: A History of Mexican-Americans* (1972); Harry Kitano, *Japanese-Americans: The Evolution of a Subculture* (1969); Victor Greene, *For God and Country: The Rise of Polish and Lithuanian Ethnic Consciousness in America* (1975), and Edward R. Kantowicz, *Polish-American Politics in Chicago* (1975). Nathan Glazer and Daniel P. Moynihan, *Beyond the Melting Pot* (1963), is a controversial study of the process of assimilation. Leonard Dinnerstein and David Reimers, *Ethnic Americans: A History of Immigration and Assimilation* (1975), and Milton M. Gordon, *Assimilation in American Life* (1964), offer different perspectives. Thomas Sowell, *Ethnic America* (1981), is a controversial interpretation. Robert D. Cross, *The Church and the City* (1967), examines immigrant religion. John Higham, *Strangers in the Land* (1955), is an important study of nativism; his *Send These to Me* (1975) is a valuable collection of essays on immigration and related issues.

Urban Poverty and Reform Robert H. Bremner, *From the Depths* (1956), is an important study of urban poverty. James T. Patterson, *America's Struggle Against Poverty* (1981), examines poverty (rural as well as urban) in the twentieth century. Thomas L. Philpott, *The Slum and the Ghetto* (1978), examines poor urban neighborhoods. The most prominent contemporary studies of the ghetto are those of Jacob Riis: *How the Other Half Lives* (1890), *Children of the Poor* (1892), and *The Battle with the Slum* (1902). For a general account of reform efforts, see Allen F. Davis, *Spearheads for Reform* (1967). For more specific reform issues, see Marvin Lazerson, *Origins of the Urban School* (1971); Selwyn K. Troen, *The Public and the Schools* (1975); David B. Tyack, *The One Best System: A History of American Urban Education* (1974); Barbara Gutmann Rosencrantz, *Public Health and the State* (1972); James H. Cassedy, *Charles V. Chapin and the Public Health Movement* (1962); and James F. Richardson, *The New York Police* (1970).

Urban Politics John M. Allswang, *Bosses, Machines and Urban Voters* (1977), is a good introduction to the machine. On Tammany Hall in New York, see Alexander B. Callow, *The Tweed Ring* (1966), and Seymour Mandelbaum, *Boss Tweed's New York* (1965). Lyle Dorsett, *The Pendergast Machine* (1968), examines Kansas City's organization. Zane Miller, *Boss Cox's Cincinnati* (1968), is a study of machine rule in that city. On urban political reformers, see John G. Sproat, *The Best Men* (1968).

Social Thought and Urban Culture General studies of social thought in the late nineteenth century include Morton White, *Social Thought in America* (1949); D. W. Marcell, *Progress and Pragmatism* (1974); and Charles Forcey, *The Crossroads of Liberalism* (1961), which traces the origins of early-twentieth-century progressive ideals. Lawrence Cremin, *The Transformation of the School* (1961), is a broad study of changes in education, which should supplement the more specific works on urban schools cited above. Frank Luther Mott, *American Journalism*, rev. ed. (1962), is a standard work. Larzer Ziff, *The American 1890s: Life and Times of a Lost Generation* (1966), examines the literary life of the era. See also Jay Martin, *Harvests of Change* (1967). Gunther Barth, *City People* (1980), examines urban leisure activities; John A. Lucas and Ronald Smith, *Saga of American Sport* (1978), is a general study of the subject; Dale Somers, *The Rise of Sports in New Orleans* (1972), is a local study. Lewis Mumford, *The Brown Decades* (1931), examines art in the late nineteenth century. Architecture is the subject of Christopher Tunnard and H. H. Reed, *American Skyline* (1955).

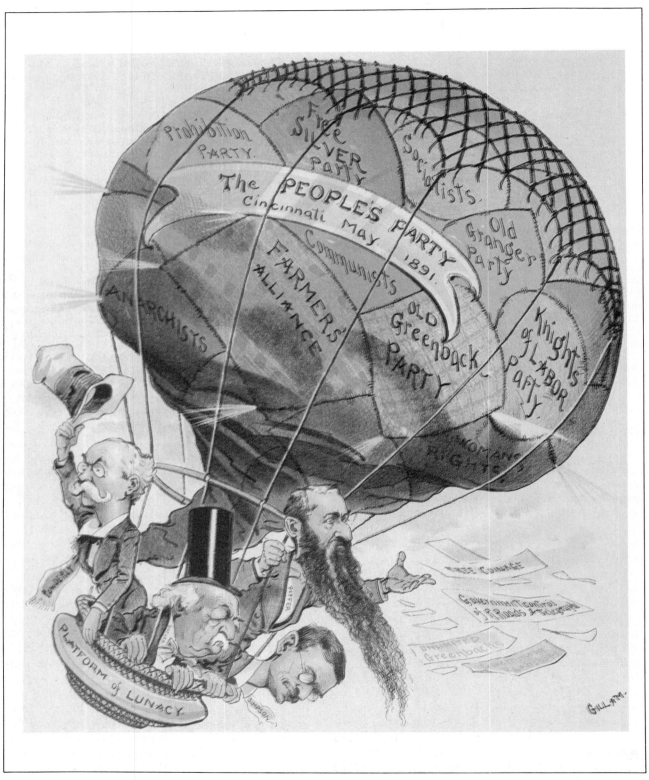

"A Party of Patches," *Judge* magazine, June 6, 1891   (Kansas State Historical Society, Topeka)

Chapter 19 From Stalemate to Crisis

The enormous social, economic, and cultural changes America was experiencing in the late nineteenth century strained not only the nation's traditional social arrangements but its political institutions as well. Growth and change brought both progress and disorder. And it was to government, gradually, that Americans would begin to look for leadership in their search for stability.

Yet American government during much of this period was ill equipped to deal with the new challenges confronting it. In the face of unprecedented dilemmas, it responded with apparent passivity and confusion. Its leaders, for the most part, seemed political mediocrities. The issues with which it was concerned were generally of minor relevance to the problems at hand. Rather than taking active leadership of the nation's dramatic transformation, the American political system for nearly two decades after the end of Reconstruction was locked in a rigid stalemate—watching the remarkable changes that were occurring in the nation and doing little to affect them.

Many observers pointed to the doldrums of the American party system as the major cause of this inaction. For in many respects the two parties had by the 1880s come to seem almost identical. "Tenets and policies, points of political doctrine and points of political practice have all but vanished," wrote the English historian James Bryce in 1888. "All has been lost, except office or the hope of it." And indeed there was much in the behavior of both the Democrats and the Republicans to support that view. Both parties strove to avoid taking positions on the great issues of the day: the rise of monopoly, the conflict between labor and management, the decline of the agrarian economy, and the defects of a financial system that produced a major collapse every twenty years or so. They tried, rather, to obscure such issues. And politicians often did appear more concerned, as Bryce had lamented, with government jobs than governmental principles.

But the torpor of the party system was more a symptom than the cause of the political stalemate of the late nineteenth century. The retreat from ideology may have been more pronounced during this period than usual, but seldom do American parties take sharply defined stands on major issues. The real problem in American politics in the 1880s and 1890s was that social and economic conditions were changing more rapidly than were ideas about public policy. Most people recognized that there were problems; few people had any idea what to do about them. Consequently, there was little in American political life to counteract the influence of conservative assumptions and powerful private interests.

The result was a political system in which problems and grievances could fester and grow without any natural outlet. And it was not surprising, under the circumstances, that by the 1890s the United States was heading into a grave national crisis. Difficulties emerged on all sides. An economic depression, the worst in American history to that point, produced widespread suffering and instability. American labor grew militant and at times violent. Above all, American farmers—building on years of slow, determined political effort—raised a powerful challenge to the established order through what became known as the Populist revolt. By the mid-1890s, many people were beginning to fear that the nation faced revolution or collapse. Virtually everyone was forced to recognize that American society, for all its progress, faced serious maladjustments.

The Politics of Equilibrium

To modern eyes, the nature of the American political system in the late nineteenth century appears in many ways paradoxical. The two political parties enjoyed during those years a strength and stability that neither was ever to know again. And yet the federal government, which the two parties were struggling to control, was doing little of any importance. The enormous popular enthusiasm for party politics seemed to have had little to do with the very modest substantive actions of government.

What explains this apparent paradox is the nature of popular politics in the late nineteenth century. Americans in those years generally engaged in political activity not because of an interest in particular issues but because of broad regional, ethnic, or religious sentiments. Party loyalty had less to do with positions on public policy than with the way Americans defined themselves culturally.

The Party System

The most striking feature of the late-nineteenth-century party system was its remarkable stability. From the end of Reconstruction until the late 1890s, the electorate was divided almost precisely evenly between the Republicans and the Democrats; and loyalties fluctuated almost not at all. Sixteen states were solidly and consistently Republican, and fourteen states (most of them in the South) were solidly and consistently Democratic. Only five states were usually in doubt, and it was in them that national elections were commonly decided. The Republican party captured the presidency in all but two of the elections of the era, but those victories are misleading as an indication of Republican strength. In the five presidential elections beginning in 1876, the average popular vote margin separating the Democratic and Republican candidates was 1.5 percent. In three of those elections, the margin was .5 percent or less; and in two of those three (1876 and 1888) the victorious candidate actually polled fewer popular votes than his opponent but won in the electoral college. The congressional balance was similarly stable. Between 1875 and 1895, the Republicans generally controlled the Senate and the Democrats generally controlled the House; in any given election, the number of seats that shifted from one party to the other was extraordinarily small.

As striking as the balance between the parties was the intensity of public loyalty to them. In most of the country, Americans viewed their party affiliations with a passion and enthusiasm that is difficult for later generations to understand. Voter turnout in presidential elections between 1860 and 1900 averaged over 78 percent of all eligible voters. Even in nonpresidential years, from 60 to 80 percent of the voters turned out to cast ballots for congressional candidates. Large groups of potential voters were disfranchised in these years: women in most states; most blacks and many poor whites in the South. But for adult white males outside the South, there were virtually no franchise restrictions. The remarkable turnout represented a genuinely mass-based politics.

In fact, party politics in the late nineteenth century occupied a central position in American culture, comparable in some ways to the role that spectator sports and mass popular entertainment play today. Political campaigns were often the most important public events in the lives of communities. Political organizations served important social and cultural functions. Political identification was almost as important to most individuals as identification with a church or an ethnic group. Partisanship was an intense, emotional force, widely admired and often identified with patriotism.

What explains this remarkable loyalty to the two political parties? It was not, certainly, that the parties took distinct positions on important public issues; in most respects they were virtually indistinguishable. Both parties were solidly probusiness; and while the Republicans were somewhat more prominently identified with the protective tariff and other policies favored by the corporations, the Democrats often supported such measures as well. Both parties were firmly opposed to economic radicalism. Both were committed to a "sound currency" and to the existing financial system. Neither supported any positive programs to aid such troubled economic groups as farmers and workers.

What determined party loyalties was less concrete issues than cultural factors. Region was perhaps the most important of these factors. To white Southerners, loyalty to the Democratic party was a matter of unquestioned faith. The party had been the vehicle for their victory over the hated Reconstruction policies of the Republicans, and it remained the vehicle for the preservation of white supremacy. To many old-stock Northerners, white and black, Republican loyalties were equally intense for the opposite reason. The Grand Old Party had been the party of Lincoln; it had freed the slaves and preserved the Union; it was a bulwark against the forces of slavery and treason.

Religious and ethnic differences also helped determine party loyalties. The Democratic party attracted most Catholic voters, most recent immigrants, and most of the poorer workers; those three groups were, of course, often the same. The Republican party appealed to Northern Protestants and citizens of old stock. Among the few substantive issues on which the parties took clearly different stands were matters concerning immigrants. The Republicans tended to be more nativist and to support measures restricting immigration. (The American Protective Association was commonly associated with the GOP, a fact the Democrats lost no opportunity to point out—and exaggerate.) Republicans tended as well to favor temperance legislation—laws to restrict the sale of alcoholic beverages. Catholics and immigrants viewed such proposals as an assault on their urban life style and opposed them, and the Democratic party followed their lead.

In the end, then, party identification was usually a reflection of a wide range of vague cultural symbols and prejudices, not of the rational calculation of economic interests. Individuals might choose to affiliate with a particular party because their parents had done so; or because it was the party of their region, their church, or their ethnic group. And they would typically cling to their party loyalties with great persistence and passion.

Presidents and Patronage

One reason the two parties managed to avoid substantive issues was that the federal government (and for the most part state and local governments as well) did very little, and was expected to do very little. Thus, there were very few concrete issues over which people could have disagreed. The leaders of both parties, therefore, were generally less concerned with policy than with office—with winning elections and controlling patronage.

Both parties were dominated by powerful bosses and machines chiefly concerned with controlling and dispensing jobs. The Democrats relied on the important city organizations (such as New York's Tammany Hall), which enabled them to mobilize the voting power of immigrants. The Republicans tended to depend on strong statewide organizations. Roscoe Conkling of New York—tall, handsome, and flamboyant—ruled New York Republicans and exercised considerable power in the United States Senate. To him, politics was a game for professionals, not for amateur "carpet knights." And it was a rough game: "Parties are not built by deportment, or by ladies' magazines, or gush." Matt Quay of Pennsylvania at times all but dominated not only his own state's Republicans but the national party as well. When Benjamin Harrison won the presidency in 1888, the candidate ascribed his victory to providence. Quay knew better. "Providence hadn't a damn thing to do with it," he announced. He wondered if the candidate knew how many men had violated laws to make him president.

The power of party bosses had an important effect on the power of the presidency, which remained an office of great symbolic importance but one whose occupants in these years found themselves without power to do very much of anything except distribute government appointments. Indeed, filling jobs was almost all a president had time to do. He had to make almost 100,000 appointments (most of them in the post office, the only really large government agency); and to do that, he had to rely on a tiny staff working in a few rooms in the White House. James Garfield, who became president in 1881, once complained, "I have heretofore been treating of the fundamental principles of government, and here I am considering all day whether A or B should be appointed to this or that office."

Even in making appointments, however, presidents enjoyed only limited latitude. They generally had to tread carefully to avoid offending the various factions within their own parties. Rutherford B. Hayes, the victor in the disputed election of 1876 and a man who spent his entire four years in office under a cloud, discovered this unhappy state of affairs early in his presidency. While Democrats ridiculed him unmercifully as "His Fraudulency," he encountered formidable difficulties within his own party. By the end of his administration, two groups—the Stalwarts, led by Roscoe Conkling of New York, and the Half-Breeds, captained by James G. Blaine of Maine—were competing for control of the Republican party and threatening to split it.

President and Mrs. Rutherford B. Hayes
Hayes was one of a series of generally undistinguished
late-nineteenth-century presidents whose subordination
to the fiercely competitive party system left them with
little room for independent leadership. This photograph
captures the dignity and sobriety that Hayes and his wife
sought to convey to the public. His wife was a temperance advocate and refused to serve alcoholic beverages in
the White House, thereby earning the nickname "Lem-
onade Lucy." Hayes attracted less whimsical labels.
Because of the disputed 1876 election that elevated him
to the presidency, critics referred to him throughout his
term as "His Fraudulency." (Library of Congress)

The dispute between the Stalwarts and the Half-
Breeds, which consumed so much political energy
and attention, was one of those political battles—
characteristic of the era—that had virtually no substantive foundation. Rhetorically, the Stalwarts favored traditional, professional machine politics while
the Half-Breeds favored reform. In fact, neither group
was much interested in real political change; each
simply wanted a larger share of the patronage pie.
Hayes tried ineffectually to satisfy both groups and
also to award offices on the basis of merit; he succeeded only in antagonizing virtually everyone.

Hayes's fondest dream was the institution of a
civil-service system, which would insulate many
government jobs from the quadrennial patronage
scramble. But he had little luck with Congress, or
even within the executive branch, in promoting his
ideas. He was unable even to win support for a renewal of the weak civil service commission created
under Grant.

The battle over patronage overshadowed all else
during Hayes's unhappy presidency. And his early
announcement that he would not seek reelection only
weakened him further. He had virtually no power in
Congress. The Democrats controlled the House
throughout his presidency, and the Senate during the
last two years of his term. And the Senate Republicans, led by Roscoe Conkling, fervently opposed his
efforts to defy the machines in making appointments.
Hayes's presidency was a study in frustration.

The Republicans managed to retain the presidency
in 1880 despite Hayes's unhappy experience—in part
because of rising prosperity and in part because they
managed to agree on a ticket that made it possible for
the Stalwarts and the Half-Breeds briefly to paper
over their differences. After a long convention deadlock between the Stalwart candidate, former president Grant, and the Half-Breed hopes, James G.
Blaine and John Sherman, the Republicans finally
nominated a "dark horse," James A. Garfield, a veteran congressman from Ohio. Garfield was known
as a Half-Breed; to conciliate the Stalwarts, the convention thus gave the vice-presidential nomination to
Chester A. Arthur, a Conkling henchman who had
become the focus of considerable controversy when
he was dismissed from a post in the New York customs house by Hayes. To oppose Garfield, the Democrats nominated General Winfield Scott Hancock, a
minor Civil War commander with no national following. Hancock's relative anonymity, combined with a
number of serious Democratic blunders during the
campaign, produced a decisive victory for Garfield,
whose electoral majority was 214 to 155. (His popular
vote margin, however, was very thin. He polled only
about 10,000 more votes than his rival.) The Republicans also captured both houses of Congress.

Garfield entered the White House as a seemingly

perfect example of the American success legend. Born in a log cabin in Ohio, he had spent his youth and early manhood as a manual laborer, once working as a mule driver on the Ohio Canal—giving rise to a popular Republican campaign slogan, "from the towpath to the White House." He had worked his way through college, become a teacher, studied law, and been admitted to the bar. In 1863, he was elected to the House of Representatives, where he served with increasing (although never enormous) distinction until he became the Republican standard-bearer.

Garfield began his term in office by provoking some of the same fights that had plagued Hayes—attempting to defy Conkling and the Stalwarts in his appointments and showing support for civil-service reform. He soon found himself embroiled in an ugly public quarrel with both Conkling and Thomas Platt, the other senator from New York and another important Stalwart leader. But before it could be resolved, Garfield found himself victimized by the spoils system in a more terrible sense. On July 2, 1881, only four months after his inauguration, Garfield was shot twice while standing in the Washington railroad station by a gunman who shouted, "I am a Stalwart and Arthur is president now!" The assassin, Charles J. Guiteau, held a grudge because Garfield had refused to give him a government job. (Despite his apparent insanity, Guiteau was ultimately hanged.) Garfield lingered for nearly three months—receiving medical treatment that actually worsened what was originally an only moderately serious condition. At his death, people concerned about the menace of machine politics were doubly grieved. Even some Republicans echoed the sentiment of the man who groaned: "Chet Arthur president of the United States! Good God!"

Chester A. Arthur had spent a political lifetime as a devoted, skilled, and open spoilsman and a close ally of Roscoe Conkling. But on becoming president, he tried—like Hayes and Garfield before him—to follow an independent course and even to promote reform. He was undoubtedly influenced by the horrible circumstances that had brought him to the presidency and by his realization that the Garfield assassination had to some degree discredited the traditional spoils system.

The revelation of the "new" Arthur dismayed most of the party bosses. He kept most of Garfield's appointees in office. He also prodded Congress to pass a civil-service law. An astute politician, he realized that sentiment for reform was running high and that civil-service legislation was likely to pass whether he supported it or not. In 1883, finally, Congress passed the first national civil-service measure, the Pendleton Act. Under its terms, a limited number of federal jobs would be "classified"; applicants for them would be chosen on the basis of competitive written examinations. The law also barred the common practice of forcing officeholders to contribute to political campaigns. A bipartisan Civil Service Commission would administer the act.

At first only about 14,000 of some 100,000 offices were placed on the classified list. But the act gave future presidents the authority to increase the number of civil-service positions by executive order. Every chief executive thereafter extended the list, even if usually to prevent his own appointees from being removed by his successor. By this piecemeal and partisan process, the government finally achieved by the 1940s a system in which the majority of the people working for it were under the merit system.

The Return of the Democrats

The unsavory election of 1884 in many ways epitomized the way in which national political contests in the late nineteenth century focused on personality and factionalism rather than issues. The Republicans refused to nominate Arthur (who was in any case already suffering from an illness that would kill him two years later) and chose instead their most popular and controversial figure, Senator James G. Blaine of Maine—known to his adoring admirers as "the plumed knight" but to thousands of other Americans as a symbol of seamy party politics. To Republican Stalwarts, Blaine was anathema; Conkling, asked if he intended to campaign for Blaine, snapped that he did not engage in criminal activities. An independent reform faction, known derisively by their critics as the "mugwumps," announced they were prepared to bolt the party and support an honest Democrat. Rising to the bait, the Democrats nominated Grover Cleveland, the reform governor of New York. In fact, however, there was virtually no difference between Blaine and Cleveland on any substantive issue.

The campaign became an exercise in personal invective. At torchlit rallies, Democrats chanted: *Blaine! Blaine! James G. Blaine! Continental liar from the state of Maine!* The Republicans, unable to find any evidence of corruption in Cleveland's brief political career as mayor of Buffalo and governor of New York, seized instead on a personal scandal. Cleveland had been accused of fathering an illegitimate child as a young

Campaign Banner for Grover Cleveland, 1884
Cleveland, a New York Democrat, won renown in the early 1880s as an honest reformer in a party widely identified with machine politics and corruption. He served a single term as mayor of Buffalo and another single term as governor of New York before being elected president in 1884. He lost his bid for reelection in 1888, but was returned to the White House in 1892. He remains the only American president to have served two nonconsecutive terms.   (Smithsonian Institution)

man; and although his paternity had never been proved, he had agreed to support the infant. Republicans roared out at their rallies: *Ma! Ma! Where's my pa? Going to the White House. Ha! Ha! Ha!*

What may have decided the election, however, was the last-minute introduction of a religious controversy. In the closing days of the campaign, a delegation of Protestant ministers called on Blaine in New York City; and their spokesman, Dr. Samuel Burchard, referred to the Democrats as the party of "rum, Romanism, and rebellion." Blaine (whose mother was a Catholic) seemed not to notice Burchard's indiscretion; and soon the Democrats were spreading the news through New York and other Eastern cities that Blaine had tolerated a slander on the Catholic church. His denial came too late to counteract the charge. New York (with its large numbers of Catholic voters) was the pivotal state in what turned out to be an extremely close election. Cleveland won 219 electoral votes to Blaine's 182; the popular vote showed 4,875,000 for Cleveland and 4,852,000 for Blaine—a Democratic plurality of only 23,000.

Grover Cleveland—short, corpulent, brusque—was not a particularly appealing figure. He was rigid, self-righteous, and haughty. He did not evoke either public or private affection. He did, however, inspire respect. In his brief public career, he had fought politicians, grafters, pressure groups, and Tammany Hall. He had become famous as the "veto mayor" and the "veto governor," as an official who was not afraid to say no. He was the perfect embodiment of an era in which few Americans believed the federal government could, or should, do very much; in which most believed that the main function of politics was to stay out of the way of the expansion of business.

Cleveland hoped to use his presidency to streamline the federal government, to make it more businesslike. He was essentially uninterested in such issues as the currency and the tariff or the problems of farmers and workers. There was no proper role for government, he believed, in dealing with such problems. And he gave voice to that conviction when he explained his veto of an appropriation of $10,000 for drought-stricken farmers. The lesson must never be forgotten, he explained, that "though the people support the Government, the Government should not support the people." His administration was characterized from beginning to end by an unwavering commitment to economy in government.

Like his predecessors, Cleveland had to spend a large proportion of his time dealing with patronage. After years in the wilderness Democrats were hungry for office, and they expected the president to throw the Republican "rascals" out—immediately and in wholesale lots. Instead, the president compromised in a manner that did not completely satisfy either his own party or his mugwump followers. He placed an additional 12,000 offices on the classified list; but of the jobs not under civil service, he removed two-thirds of the incumbents and replaced them with deserving Democrats.

Cleveland did introduce one major economic issue into the political arena. He had always been mildly dubious about the wisdom of high tariffs. And he concluded finally that the existing high rates were responsible for the annual surplus in federal revenues, which was tempting Congress to pass the "reckless" and "extravagant" legislation he so frequently vetoed. In December 1887, therefore, he asked Congress to reduce the tariff rates. Southern and Western Democrats, who already supported tariff reductions, responded enthusiastically to the president's request and pushed through the House a bill incorporating Cleveland's recommendations and providing for moderate reductions. In the Senate, however, the Republican leaders were defiant. Instead of enacting the House measure, they passed a bill of their own actually raising rates. A deadlock ensued, and the tariff became an issue in the election of 1888.

The Democrats renominated Cleveland and supported tariff reductions in their platform. The Republicans settled on former senator Benjamin Harrison of Indiana, who was relatively obscure but formidably respectable (the grandson of President William Henry Harrison); and in their platform they endorsed protection for American producers and generous pensions for Union veterans. The campaign was the first since the Civil War in which an issue of substance was an important factor, the first to involve a clear question of economic difference between the parties. It was also one of the most viciously corrupt (and one of the closest) elections in American history. Harrison won an electoral majority of 233 to 168, but Cleveland's popular vote exceeded Harrison's by 100,000.

Emerging Issues

Unlike William Henry Harrison, who had died only a month after assuming the presidency forty-eight years earlier, Benjamin Harrison lived out his full term of office. Yet his record as president was little more substantial than his grandfather's.

One reason for Harrison's failure was the intellectual drabness of the members of his administration—beginning with the president himself and extending through his cabinet. Another was Harrison's unwillingness to make any effort to influence the Congress. And yet during Harrison's dreary administration, public opinion was finally beginning to force the government to confront some of the pressing economic issues of the day. Most notably, per-haps, sentiment was rising in favor of legislation to curb the power of trusts.

By the mid-1880s, some fifteen Western and Southern states had adopted laws prohibiting combinations that restrained competition. But corporations found it easy to escape limitations by incorporating in states that offered special privileges. (New Jersey and Delaware were particularly notorious examples.) Any form of state regulation, moreover, was liable to be rejected by the Supreme Court. If antitrust legislation was to be effective, it would have to come from the national government. In 1888, both parties had made vague promises in their platforms to curb monopolies.

With little debate and by almost unanimous votes in both houses of Congress, the Sherman Antitrust Act became law in July 1890. Congress's only basis for national action against the trusts lay in its constitutional power to regulate interstate commerce; and that power determined the provisions of the new law, which declared illegal any "contract, combination in the form of trust or otherwise, or conspiracy in restraint of trade or commerce." The Sherman Act has been the basis for nearly a century of federal antitrust activity. At the time, however, relatively few members of Congress expected (or wanted) the new law to have any real effect on the structure of the economy. As one senator explained, his colleagues merely wanted to get up "some bill headed 'A bill to Punish Trusts'" with which to go to the country" and get themselves reelected.

For over a decade after its passage, the Sherman Act had virtually no impact. Before 1901, the Justice Department instituted only fourteen suits under the law against business combinations, and it obtained almost no convictions. The courts were uniformly hostile to the law and proceeded to emasculate it. In *United States* v. *E. C. Knight Co.* (1895), a case in which the government charged that a single trust controlled 98 percent of the manufacture of refined sugar in the country, the Supreme Court rejected the government's case by drawing a curious distinction between manufacturing and commerce. The sugar trust was engaged in manufacturing, not in interstate commerce, the Court declared; and so, despite its obviously monopolistic characteristics, it was not illegal.

The Republicans were more interested, however, in the issue they believed had won them the 1888 election: the tariff. William McKinley of Ohio, a rising party luminary and chairman of the House Ways and Means Committee, and Senator Nelson W.

"The Jaws of Monopoly Power," c. 1890

The rise of great industrial combinations—evidence of the growing concentration of economic power in national institutions that was coming to characterize the modern American economy—alarmed many Americans in the late nineteenth century, as this lurid cartoon suggests. Congress responded to such concerns in 1890 by passing the Sherman Antitrust Act, which remains one of the cornerstones of national policy toward business; but the new law did little to stop the rise of combinations.   (Bettmann Archive)

Aldrich of Rhode Island framed the highest protective measure yet offered to a Congress. It became law in October 1890 as the McKinley Tariff Act. But Republican leaders apparently misinterpreted public sentiment, as the 1890 congressional elections seemed to prove.

Seldom has a party in power suffered such a stunning reverse as befell the Republicans in 1890. Their once substantial majority in the Senate was slashed to 8, and in the House they retained only 88 seats to 235 for the Democrats. Popular revulsion against the McKinley duties, pictured by the Democrats as raising the living costs of the masses, was an undoubted factor in the Republican debacle; McKinley himself was among those who went down to defeat. Nor were the Republicans able to recover in the course of the next two years. In the presidential election of

1892, Benjamin Harrison was again the Republican nominee and Grover Cleveland the Democratic. Once more the platforms of the two parties were almost identical except for the tariff, with the Republicans upholding protection and the Democrats pledging reduction. Only a new third party, the People's party, with James B. Weaver as its candidate, advocated economic reform.(See below, pp. 558–561.) Cleveland amassed 277 electoral and 5,557,000 popular votes as compared to Harrison's 145 and 5,176,000 votes. Weaver ran far behind. For the first time since 1878, the Democrats won a majority of both houses of Congress.

Despite Cleveland's negative record, a large proportion of the people who had voted for him expected him to devise some original approach to the new problems troubling America. His inaugural address rudely disillusioned them, as he reaffirmed his devotion to laissez faire in words that had become tiresomely familiar: "The lessons of paternalism ought to be unlearned." The policies of Cleveland's second term, therefore, were much like those of his first—devoted to minimal government and hostile to active state measures to deal with social or economic problems. As in his first term, he called on Congress to lower the existing tariff rates. And again, he won passage of a moderate downward revision in the House in 1894, only to see the bill gutted in the Senate. Cleveland denounced the result but allowed it to become law without his signature. The Wilson-Gorman Tariff, as the new law was known, provided a moderate (10 percent) reduction in the general tariff rate. But it offered special protection to sugar refiners and virtually every other important trust.

The bill threw one small crust to reformers: a minuscule tax on incomes (a 2 percent levy on incomes over $4,000), a concession to agrarian interests. But the Supreme Court, in *Pollock* v. *The Farmer's Loan and Trust Co.* (1895), declared the income tax unconstitutional. Only a constitutional amendment would permit the government to levy such a tax. (The nation approved such an amendment—the Sixteenth—in 1913.)

In addition to the questions of trusts and tariffs, the federal government began in the 1880s to encounter public pressure for action on another major issue: railroad regulation. For years, Congress had so studiously ignored all public clamor for regulation that proponents of reform had looked instead to the states. Farm organizations in the Midwest (most notably the Grangers—see below, pp. 556–557) succeeded in persuading several state legislatures to pass regulatory legislation in the early 1870s. The so-called Granger Laws in Illinois, Iowa, Minnesota, and Wisconsin authorized maximum rates for passenger and freight traffic, provided rules and rates for the storing of grain, and prohibited a number of alleged discriminatory practices.

The railroad corporations contested the Granger Laws in court, arguing that the statutes preempted Congress's exclusive power to regulate interstate commerce and that they acted to deprive corporations of their property without the "due process" guaranteed under the Fourteenth Amendment. At first, however, the challenges had no effect. The Supreme Court, in *Munn* v. *Illinois* (1877), rejected such arguments, ruling that a state could under some circumstances regulate interstate commerce affecting it, in the absence of national regulation, and that a cor-

poration was not a "person" within the meaning of the Constitution.

These initial Granger victories, however, proved short-lived once new justices friendly to an expanded notion of property rights were appointed to the Supreme Court. The so-called *Wabash* case of 1886 (*Wabash, St. Louis, and Pacific Railway Co.* v. *Illinois*) was the first indication of the new judicial view of state regulation. The Court held that an Illinois statute regulating freight rates was an unconstitutional attempt to control interstate commerce and infringed on the exclusive power of Congress. Later, the Courts limited the powers of the states to regulate commerce even within their own boundaries (in *Chicago, Milwaukee and St. Paul Railroad* v. *Minnesota*, 1890, and later rulings).

If there was to be any meaningful regulation of the railroads, it was now clear, it could come only from the federal government. And Congress, subjected to increasing pressure, soon grudgingly and inadequately responded. There had been demands both in and out of the government since the 1870s for some kind of supervisory legislation to prevent the unsavory techniques by which the railroads gave preferential rates to favored customers and discriminated against others. Even some railway operators, alarmed by the fierce competition in their industry, were eager for regulation. As a result, Congress responded in 1887 with the Interstate Commerce Act, aptly described by its chief sponsor, Senator Shelby M. Cullom of Illinois, as "conservative legislation."

The Interstate Commerce Act prohibited discrimination in rates between long and short hauls and other unpopular railroad practices. It required railroads to publish their rate schedules and file them with the government. It provided that all fees for interstate rail transportation should be "reasonable and just"—but failed to furnish a standard or method to determine the justness of a rate. A five-person agency, the Interstate Commerce Commission, was to administer the act, although the commissioners did not have clear authority to fix rates. The ICC could demand a rate reduction, but it could enforce its demands only by turning to the courts—a cumbersome procedure that militated against effective regulation.

For almost twenty years after its passage, the Interstate Commerce Act—haphazardly enforced and exceedingly narrowly interpreted by the courts—was without practical effect; it did not accomplish widespread rate reduction or eliminate discrimination. No wonder an attorney general of the United States advised a railroad president not to ask for repeal of the act: "It satisfies the popular clamor for government supervision of the railroads at the same time that that supervision is almost entirely nominal."

The agitation over the tariff, the trusts, and the railroads was a sign that the dramatic growth of the American economy—and the emergence of powerful new institutions as a result—was creating problems that much of the public considered too important and dangerous to ignore. But the federal government's response to that agitation reflected the continuing weakness of the American state. The government still lacked institutions adequate to perform any significant role in American economic life. And American politics still lacked an ideology sufficient to justify any major expansion of government responsibilities. The effort to create such institutions and to produce such an ideology would occupy much of American public life in the coming decades. And it became visible first in a dramatic dissident movement that shattered the twenty years of political equilibrium the nation had experienced.

The Agrarian Revolt

No group watched the dismal performance of the federal government in the 1880s with more dismay than American farmers. Isolated from the urban-industrial society that was beginning to dominate national life, suffering from a long, painful economic decline, afflicted with a sense of obsolescence, rural Americans were keenly aware of the problems of the modern economy and particularly eager for government assistance in dealing with them. The result was the emergence of one of the most powerful movements of political protest in American history: what became known as Populism.

The Grangers

American farmers were, according to popular myth, the most individualistic of citizens, the least likely to join together in a cooperative economic or political movement. In reality, however, farmers had been making efforts to organize for many decades. There had been occasional cooperative movements in the first decades of the nineteenth century; but the first major farm organization appeared in the 1860s, less

as a movement of protest than as a social and self-help association. The depression of 1873 turned it into an agency of political change.

The Grange had its origins shortly after the Civil War in a tour through the South by a minor Agriculture Department official, Oliver H. Kelley. Kelley was appalled by what he considered the isolation and drabness of rural life, and in 1867 he left the government and, with other department employees, founded the National Grange of the Patrons of Husbandry, to which Kelley devoted years of labor as secretary and from which emerged a network of local organizations. At first, the Granges defined their purposes modestly. They attempted to bring farmers together to learn new scientific agricultural techniques—to keep farming "in step with the music of the age." The Granges also hoped to create a feeling of community, to relieve the loneliness of rural life. An elaborate system of initiation and ritual and a strict code of secrecy lent to the organization many of the trappings of urban fraternal organizations.

At first the Grange grew slowly. But when the depression of 1873 caused a major decline in farm prices, membership rapidly increased. By 1875, the Grange claimed over 800,000 members and 20,000 local lodges; it had chapters in almost every state but was strongest, naturally, in the great staple-producing regions of the South and the Midwest.

As membership grew, the lodges in the Midwest began to focus less on the social benefits of organization and more on the economic possibilities. They attempted to organize marketing cooperatives to allow farmers to circumvent the hated middlemen. And they urged cooperative political action to curb the monopolistic practices of the railroads and warehouses. Throughout the midlands on Independence Day 1873, embittered farmers assembled to hear Granger orators read "The Farmers' Declaration of Independence," which proclaimed that the time had come for farmers, "suffering from long continued systems of oppression and abuse, to rouse themselves from an apathetic indifference to their own interests." The declaration also vowed that farmers would use "all lawful and peaceful means to free [themselves] from the tyranny of monopoly."

The Grangers launched the first major cooperative movement in the United States, although successful collective societies had existed earlier in England and other countries. They set up cooperative stores, creameries, elevators, warehouses, insurance companies, and factories that produced machines, stoves, and other items. Some 400 enterprises

The Purposes of the Grange
This 1873 lithograph illustrates the benefits of membership in the National Grange of the Patrons of Husbandry. Each panel portrays a different aspect of farm life, suggesting the variety of Grange goals. The writer Hamlin Garland, who grew up in the agrarian Midwest in the 1870s, later recalled how the organization served as an important social and cultural institution for rural Americans: "Many of our social affairs were now connected with the Grange. . . . Its meetings became very important dates on our calendars. . . . Nothing more picturesque, more delightful, has ever risen out of American rural life. Each of these assemblies was a most grateful relief from the loneliness of the farm." (Library of Congress)

were in operation at the height of the movement, and some of them forged lucrative relationships with existing businesses. One corporation emerged specifically to meet the needs of the Grangers: Montgomery Ward and Company, founded in 1872, the first mail-order business. Eventually, however, most of the Grange enterprises failed, both because of the inexperience of their operators and because of the opposition of the middlemen whose businesses they were challenging.

The Grangers worked as well to elect state legislators pledged to their program. Usually they operated through the existing parties, although occasionally they ran candidates under such independent party labels as "Antimonopoly" and "Reform." At their peak, they managed to gain control of the legislatures in most of the Midwestern states. Their purpose, openly and angrily announced, was to subject the railroads to government controls.

The Granger Laws of the early 1870s, by which many states imposed strict regulations on railroad rates and practices (see above, p. 555), seemed for a time to vindicate the predictions of those farmers who claimed that their new organization foretold a permanent change in the political status of agriculture. But the new regulations were soon destroyed by the courts. That defeat, combined with the political inexperience of many Grange leaders and above all the return of prosperity in the late 1870s, produced a dramatic decline in the power of the association. Some of the Granger cooperatives survived as effective economic vehicles for many years; but the movement as a whole dwindled rapidly. By 1880, its membership had shrunk to 100,000.

The Alliances

The successor to the Granges as the leading vehicle of agrarian protest began to emerge even before the Granger movement had faded. As early as 1875, farmers in parts of the South (most notably in Texas) were banding together in so-called Farmers' Alliances. Under the leadership of the Texan C. W. Macune and others, the Southern Alliance grew rapidly in the 1880s and by the end of the decade could boast more than 4 million members. In the meantime, a comparable movement was under way in the plains states and in the Midwest. This Northwestern Alliance never achieved the size or militancy of its Southern counterpart, but it too became a significant force. As the movement grew, the two Alliances developed an ever closer association with each other.

Like the Granges, the Alliances were in large part a response to local conditions and began by working for primarily local objectives; but they defined those objectives far more broadly. In addition to forming cooperatives and other marketing mechanisms, the Alliances also established stores, banks, processing plants, and other facilities for their members—to free them from dependence on the hated "furnishing merchants" who bound so many farmers into a miserable system of indebtedness. Alliance leaders were concerned, first and foremost, with immediate economic problems and particular local political struggles. Many, however, embraced as well a larger vision of a restored community, in which individuals could once again control their own economic future. Essential to such communities, they argued, was cooperation—not a rigid collectivism that would suppress individuality, but a sense of mutual, neighborly responsibility that would enable farmers to resist the oppressive outside forces that threatened to enslave them. Alliance lecturers traveled throughout rural areas exhorting farmers to a new awareness of their political and economic plight. They lambasted the tendency in modern society for more and more power to be concentrated in the hands of a few great corporations and financial institutions.

Although the Alliances quickly became far more widespread than the Granges had ever been, they suffered from similar problems. Their cooperatives did not always work well, partly because the market forces operating against them were sometimes too strong to be overcome, partly because the cooperatives themselves were occasionally mismanaged. Some came under the control of unscrupulous local entrepreneurs, who made them as exploitive as the old system of reliance on railroads and local stores. The enormous numerical strength and ideological fervor of the Alliance movement, combined with its economic failure, helped push it into a new phase at the end of the 1880s: the creation of a national political organization.

The first step came in 1889, when the Southern and Northwestern Alliances, despite continuing differences between them, agreed to a loose merger. But the decisive moment came in 1890, when the Alliances staged a national convention at Ocala, Florida, and issued the so-called Ocala Demands. Although Alliance members were not yet formally proclaiming the existence of a new party, the demands were nothing less than a party platform.

The Alliances played an active role in the 1890 off-year elections and surprised both conservatives and themselves with their success. The farm forces won partial or complete control of the legislatures in twelve states, eight in the South and four in the West. They elected six governors, three senators, and approximately fifty congressmen. The magnitude of the triumph was not perhaps as great as it seemed at first glance. Over forty of the successful Alliance candidates for Congress were loyal members of the Democratic party, who benefited—often passively—from the Alliance endorsements. Nevertheless, the dissident farmers drew enough encouragement from the results to contemplate further political action and—as it gradually became clear that neither of the two major parties was likely to respond to their demands—to form a party of their own.

Sentiment for a third party was strongest among the members of the Northwestern Alliance. But several Southern leaders—among them Tom Watson of Georgia, the only Southern congressman elected in 1890 openly to identify with the Alliance, and Leonidas L. Polk of North Carolina, perhaps the ablest mind in the movement—were similarly becoming convinced of the need for a new political organization. Plans for a third party were discussed at meetings in Cincinnati in May 1891 and St. Louis in February 1892—meetings attended by many Northern Alliance members, a smaller but still significant number of Southern Alliance leaders, and representatives of the fading Knights of Labor (see above, p. 515), whom some farm leaders hoped to bring into the coalition. Then, in July 1892, 1,300 excited and exultant delegates poured into Omaha, Nebraska, to proclaim formally the creation of the new party, approve an official set of principles, and nominate candidates for the presidency and vice presidency. By common consent, the party already had a name, one first used by the Kansas agrarians: the People's party. The movement was more commonly referred to, however, by the Latin version of that name: Populism.

The election of 1892 dispelled whatever doubts may have remained as to the potential power of the new movement. The Populist presidential candidate—James B. Weaver of Iowa, a former Greenbacker who received the nomination after the sudden death of the early favorite, Leonidas Polk—polled more than 1 million votes, 8.5 percent of the total, and carried six mountain and plains states for 22 electoral votes. Nearly 1,500 Populist candidates won election to seats in state legislatures. The party elected three governors, five senators, and ten congressmen. It could also claim the support of the numerous Republicans and Democrats in Congress who had been elected by appealing to Populist sentiment.

The Populist Constituency

There is no decisive evidence of precisely how many Populists there were, where they came from, or what characteristics they shared. Some generalizations, however, are possible. First, Populism was stronger in some regions than others. Its greatest influence was in an arc of states extending from the Dakotas southward through Nebraska and Kansas; in a string of Southern states stretching from Texas through northern Louisiana, Alabama, and Mississippi, and into Georgia and the Carolinas; and in the Rocky Mountain states. It was weakest in those areas where the Granges had been most successful, because that was where agriculture had managed to achieve its greatest security and stability.

Populism was also more appealing to certain kinds of farmers than to others. Unsurprisingly, it was most often small farmers with little long-range economic security who flocked to the movement—people whose operations were only minimally mechanized, if at all, who relied on one crop, and who had access only to limited and unsatisfactory mechanisms of credit. Large, diversified, efficient producers were not likely to flock to the Populist banner; smaller, imperiled farmers were. The status of such farmers differed, of course, from region to region. In the Midwest, the Populists were usually family farmers struggling to hold onto their land (or to get it back if they had lost it). In the South, there were many modest landowners too, but in addition there were significant numbers of sharecroppers and tenant farmers. Whatever their differences, however, most Populists had at least one thing in common: They were engaged in a type of farming that was becoming less viable in the face of new, mechanized, diversified, and consolidated commercial agriculture.

There is evidence, too, that Populists tended to be not only economically but culturally marginal, that the movement appealed above all to geographically isolated farmers who felt cut off from the mainstream of national life and resented their isolation. Populism gave such people an outlet for their grievances; it also provided them with a social experience, a sense of belonging to a community, that they had previously lacked.

The Populist constituency was as notable for the groups it failed to attract as for those it attracted. There were energetic and continuing efforts to include labor within the coalition. Representatives of the Knights of Labor attended early organizational meetings; the new party added a labor plank to its platform—calling for shorter hours for workers and restrictions on immigration, and denouncing the use of private detective agencies as strikebreakers in labor disputes. Populist spokesmen attempted to generate enthusiasm for the movement within the working class; and Populist publications spoke of the natural connection between oppressed farmers and oppressed industrial workers. But it was all to little avail. One problem was that the labor organizations themselves were too weak to be able to deliver any substantial support. Another problem was a consistent failure to define clearly enough the areas of common interest between the two groups.

In the South in particular, the movement also considered the desirability of attracting blacks, whose numbers and poverty made them possibly valuable allies. And indeed there was an important black component to the movement—a network of "Colored Alliances" that by 1890 numbered over one and a quarter million members. Many Midwestern Alliancemen advocated a full merger of the Colored Alliances with the national movement. Even some white Southern leaders displayed a notable willingness to foster interracial cooperation. But in the end, the influence of white racism proved stronger than the influence of common economic interests. Most white Populists were willing to accept the assistance of blacks only as long as it was clear that whites would remain indisputably in control. When conservatives began to attack the Populists for undermining white supremacy, the interracial character of the movement quickly faded.

Populist leaders, although easier to identify than their constituencies, are nevertheless also difficult to typify. Most were members of the rural middle class: professional people, editors and lawyers, or long-time politicians and agitators. Few were themselves marginal farmers. Almost all leaders were, like their constituents, Protestants. But beyond these basic characteristics, there were wide variations. Some Populist leaders were somber, serious theoreticians; others were semihysterical rabble-rousers. In the South, in particular, Populism produced the first generation of what was to become a distinctive and enduring political breed—the "Southern demagogue." Tom Watson in Georgia, Jeff Davis in Arkansas, and others attracted widespread popular support by arousing the resentment of poor Southerners against the entrenched Bourbon aristocracy. They were the beginning of a line of such figures that stretched well into the twentieth century. There were similarly flamboyant leaders in the Midwest: "Sockless" Jerry Simpson of Kansas, for example, or Ignatius Donnelly of Minnesota. Donnelly, in particular, seemed to exemplify the divided character of the movement: sincere idealism combined with crassness and opportunism. A

Mary Ellen Lease
Although critics insisted that stump speaking was an unsuitable activity for women, Mary Lease was one of the fieriest and most popular of the Populist orators. In 1890 alone, she delivered 160 speeches. Although she is perhaps best remembered for her admonition to Kansas farmers to "raise less corn and more hell," she was outspoken on a wide range of issues, including the troubles in Ireland and women's rights. (Historical Pictures Service)

committed, principled man who spoke eloquently on behalf of Populist ideals and appeared sincerely to believe in them, Donnelly was also at times something of a charlatan. As a member of Congress, he compiled a shabby legislative record marked, among other things, by a series of seamy, secret deals with railroad companies.

The Populist Ideology

The ideology of Populism, like the character of its leadership, was a complex combination of progressive idealism and bewildering rhetorical excess. There were three basic elements of that ideology: a concrete program of reform, a strident and at times almost hysterical denunciation of enemies, and a millennial vision of a just and stable society.

The reform program of the Populists was spelled out first in the Ocala Demands of 1890 and then, even more clearly, in the Omaha platform of 1892. Among the most prominent of the many issues included in these documents was a proposal for a system of "subtreasuries," which would replace and strengthen the cooperatives with which the Grangers and Alliances had been experimenting for years. The government would establish a network of warehouses, where farmers could deposit their crops. Using those crops as collateral, growers could then borrow money from the government at low rates of interest and wait for the price of their goods to go up before selling them. In addition, the Populists called for the abolition of national banks, which they believed were dangerous institutions of concentrated power; the end of absentee ownership of land; the direct election of United States senators (which would weaken the power of conservative state legislatures); and other devices to improve the ability of the people to influence the political process. They called as well for regulation and (after 1892) government ownership of railroads, telephones, and telegraphs. And they demanded a system of government-operated postal savings banks, a graduated income tax, the inflation of the currency, and later, the remonetization of silver. Some of the Populist proposals were clearly unrealistic, but much of the platform was a serious and responsible effort to find solutions to difficult problems.

Less serious and responsible were the Populist denunciations of enemies, which often became so strident and hysterical as to border on the irrational. A few Populists were openly anti-Semitic, pointing to the Jews as leaders of the obscure financial forces attempting to enslave them. Others were anti-intellectual, anti-Eastern, and antiurban. Some of the leading Populists gave an impression of personal failure, brilliant instability, and brooding communion with mystic forces. Ignatius Donnelly, for example, wrote one book locating the lost isle of Atlantis, another claiming that Bacon had written Shakespeare's plays, and still another—*Caesar's Column* (1891)—embodying an almost lunatic vision of bloody revolution and the creation of a Populist utopia. Tom Watson, once a champion of interracial harmony, ended his career baiting blacks and Jews.

Yet the occasional bigotry of the movement should not be allowed to dominate the image of Populism. The hysterical quality of some Populist "scapegoating" can be explained in part by the condition of many of the members of the movement—people whose personal distress was so great that some excesses were all but inevitable. Some of this denunciation of enemies, moreover, was not as irrational as critics often charged. The rhetoric may have been excessive, but the most frequent targets—banks, railroads, monopolies—were far from guiltless in creating the problems of the farmer.

The resentment against supposed villains existed alongside a well-developed view of a just and stable society. The Populists argued not only for the destruction of monopolistic power but for a new social morality. Society, they claimed, had an obligation to protect the well-being of its individual citizens. The rights of property ownership were, therefore, secondary to the needs of the community. Populists did not reject the idea of private property; most were themselves landowners or aspirants to land ownership. They did, however, emphatically reject the laissez-faire orthodoxies of their time, the idea that the rights of ownership are absolute. They raised, in short, one of the most overt and powerful challenges of the era to the direction in which American industrial capitalism was moving. Populism was not a challenge to industrialization or to capitalism itself, but to what the Populists considered the brutal and chaotic way in which the economy was developing. Progress and growth should continue, they urged, but it should be strictly defined by the needs of individuals and communities.

The Crisis of the 1890s

The emergence of a powerful movement of agrarian protest was only one of many factors that were combining by the early 1890s to create a national political crisis. There was a severe depression, which began in 1893 and which exacerbated the unhappiness of not

Taking Arms Against the Populists
Kansas was a Populist stronghold in the 1890s, but the new party faced powerful challenges. In 1893 state Republicans disputed an election that the Populists believed had given them control of the legislature. When the Populists occupied the state house, Republicans armed themselves, drove out the Populists, and seized control of the state government. Republican members of the legislature pose here with their weapons in a photograph perhaps intended as a warning to any Populists inclined to challenge them. (Kansas State Historical Society, Topeka)

WHERE HISTORIANS DISAGREE

Populism

American history does not offer many examples of successful popular movements operating outside the two major parties. For that reason Populism, which in its brief, meteoric life became one of the few such phenomena to gain real national influence, has attracted particular attention from historians—and has produced deep disagreements among them. Scholars have differed on many grounds in their interpretations of Populism, but at the heart of many such disagreements have been disparate views of popular, insurgent politics. Some historians have harbored a basic mistrust of such popular uprisings and have, therefore, viewed the Populists with suspicion and hostility. Others have viewed such insurgency approvingly, as evidence of a healthy resistance to oppression and exploitation; and to them, the Populists have appeared as essentially admirable, democratic activists.

This latter view underlay the first, and for many years the only, general history of Populism: John D. Hicks's *The Populist Revolt* (1931). Rejecting the popular view of the Populists as misguided and unruly radicals, Hicks described them as people reacting rationally and progressively to economic misfortune. Hicks was writing in an era in which the ideas of Frederick Jackson Turner were dominating historical studies, and he brought to his analysis of Populism a strong emphasis on regionalism. Populists, he argued, were part of the democratic West, resisting the pressures from the more aristocratic east. (He explained Southern Populism somewhat awkwardly, describing the South as an "economic frontier" region—not newly settled like the West but prey to many of the same pressures and misfortunes.) The Populists, Hicks suggested, were aware of the harsh, even brutal impact of Eastern industrial growth on rural society; and

they were proposing reforms that would limit the oppressive power of the new financial titans and restore a measure of control to the farmers themselves. Populism was, he wrote, "the last phase of a long and perhaps a losing struggle—the struggle to save agricultural America from the devouring jaws of industrial America." A losing struggle, perhaps, but not a vain one; for many of the reforms the Populists advocated, Hicks implied, became the basis of later progressive legislation.

This generally approving view of Populism prevailed among historians for more than two decades. But in the early 1950s—when the memory of European fascism and the uneasiness about contemporary communism combined to create a general hostility among scholars toward mass popular politics—a harsh new attack on the Populist movement appeared in a work by one of the nation's leading historians. Richard Hofstadter, in *The Age of Reform* (1955), admitted in passing that Populism contained some progressive themes. But the bulk of his effort was devoted to exposing both the "soft" and the "dark" sides of the movement. Populism was "soft," he claimed, because it rested on a nostalgic and unrealistic myth, because it romanticized the nation's agrarian past and refused to confront the hard realities of modern life. And it was "dark," he argued, because it was permeated with bigotry and ignorance. Populists, he claimed, revealed anti-Semitic tendencies; and they displayed animosity as well toward intellectuals, Easterners, and urbanites. He stopped short of linking Populism directly with fascism, but other scholars—adopting his approach—made such connections explicitly.

Almost immediately, historians more favorably disposed toward mass politics in general, and Populism in particular, began to challenge what soon

only farmers but other groups as well. There was widespread labor unrest and violence, culminating in the tumultuous strikes of 1894, of which the Pullman strike was only the most prominent example. There was the continuing failure of either major party to respond to the growing distress. And there was the rigid conservatism of Grover Cleveland, who took

office (for the second time) just at the moment that the economy collapsed. Out of this growing sense of crisis came some of the most heated political battles in American history, culminating in the dramatic campaign of 1896, which seemed—in the eyes of many Americans—to threaten the future of the nation.

─────WHERE HISTORIANS DISAGREE─────

became known as the "Hofstadter thesis." Norman Pollack argued in a 1962 study, *The Populist Response to Industrial America,* and in a number of articles, that the agrarian revolt had rested not on nostalgic, romantic concepts but on a sophisticated, farsighted, and possibly radical vision of reform—one which recognized, and even welcomed, the realities of an industrial economy, but one which sought to make that economy more equitable and democratic by challenging many of the premises of capitalism. Walter T. K. Nugent, in *The Tolerant Populists* (1963), argued—as his title implies—that the Populists in Kansas were far from bigoted, that they not only tolerated but welcomed Jews and other minorities into their party, and that they offered a practical, sensible program.

It was not until 1976, however, that a comprehensive study of Populism emerged that could rival Hicks and Hofstadter in its influence. Lawrence Goodwyn, in *Democratic Promise* (1976, and in a briefer version of the same work, *The Populist Moment,* published in 1978), described the Populists as members of a "cooperative crusade," battling against the "coercive potential of the emerging corporate state." Populists were more than the nostalgic bigots Hofstadter described, more even than the progressive reformers portrayed by Hicks. They offered a vision of truly radical change, widely disseminated through what Goodwyn called a "movement culture," and offering an intelligent and, above all, a democratic alternative to the inequities of modern capitalism.

At the same time that historians were debating the question of what Populism meant, they were arguing as well over who the Populists were. Hicks, Hofstadter, and Goodwyn disagreed on many things, but they shared a general view of the Populists as victims of economic distress: usually one-crop farmers in economically marginal agricultural regions victimized by drought and debt. Other scholars, however, have suggested that the problem of identifying the Populists is more complex. Sheldon Hackney, in *Populism to Progressivism in Alabama* (1969), has argued that the Populists were not only economically troubled but socially rootless, "only tenuously connected to society by economic function, by personal relationships, by stable community membership, by political participation, or by psychological identification with the South's distinctive myths." Peter Argersinger, Stanley Parsons, James Turner, and others have similarly suggested that Populists were characterized by a form of social and even geographical isolation. Steven Hahn's 1983 study, *The Roots of Southern Populism,* identifies poor white farmers in the "upcountry" as the core of Populist activity in Georgia; and he argues that they were reacting not simply to the psychic distress of being "left behind" but also to a real economic threat to their way of life—to the pressures of a new commercial order in which they had never been and could never be a part.

There has been continuing debate over the legacy of Populism. Historians and politicians alike have argued repeatedly that a Populist tradition has survived throughout the twentieth century, influencing movements as disparate as those led by Huey Long in the 1930s, George Wallace in the 1960s, and even Ronald Reagan in the 1980s. Others have maintained that the term "Populism" has been used (and misused) so widely as to have become virtually meaningless, that its only real value is in reference to the agrarian insurgents of the 1890s, who first gave meaning to the word.

The Panic of 1893

Benjamin Harrison sent a message to Congress early in 1893, shortly before he left the White House, stating, "There has never been a time in our history when work was so abundant or when wages were so high." Only months later, with the second Cleveland administration hardly settled in office, the Panic of 1893 precipitated the most severe depression the nation had yet experienced.

The panic began in March 1893, when the Philadelphia and Reading Railroad declared bankruptcy. Two months later, the National Cordage Company (a new national corporation that was trying, but failing, to establish itself as the dominant force in the industry) collapsed as well. Together, the two corporate failures precipitated a collapse of the stock market. And since many of the major New York banks were heavy investors in the market, a wave of bank failures soon began. The problems of the banking system caused a contraction of credit, which meant that many of the new, aggressive businesses that had recently begun operations soon went bankrupt because they were unable to secure the loans they needed. There were other, longer-range causes of the financial collapse. Depressed prices in agriculture since 1887 had weakened the purchasing power of farmers, the largest group in the population. Depression conditions that had begun earlier in Europe were resulting in a loss of American markets abroad, a decline in the export trade, and a withdrawal by foreign investors of gold invested in the United States.

Above all, perhaps, the depression was a result of several structural flaws in the American economy. In the frenzied atmosphere of competition and growth of the 1880s, businessmen had made enormous capital investments in enterprises that could not possibly pay for themselves. Railroads, in particular, were expanding far too rapidly, well beyond market demand. The depression reflected, too, the degree to which the American economy was now interconnected, the degree to which failures in one area affected all other areas. And the depression showed how excessively dependent the economy remained on the health of the railroads, which remained the nation's most powerful corporate and financial institutions. When the railroads suffered, as they did beginning in 1893, everything suffered.

Once the panic began, its effects spread with startling speed. In a period of six months, more than 8,000 business concerns failed, 156 railroads went into receivership, and 400 banks suspended operations. Agricultural prices tumbled to new lows. Perhaps as many as 1 million workers, 20 percent of the labor force, lost their jobs—the highest level of unemployment in American history to that point, a level comparable to that of the Great Depression of the 1930s. The leading financial newspaper of the time declared in the summer of 1893: "The month of August will long remain memorable in our industrial history. Never before has there been such a sudden and striking cessation of industrial activity. Nor is any section of the country exempt from the paralysis." There had been serious financial crises before, but the depression of the 1890s was unprecedented both in its severity and its persistence. Although there was slight improvement beginning in 1895, real prosperity did not return until 1901.

The suffering caused by the depression naturally produced widespread economic and political unrest, not least among the enormous numbers of unemployed workers. In 1894, Jacob S. Coxey, an Ohio businessman and Populist, began advocating a massive public works program, through which the government would spend $500 million and hire the unemployed to do the work. He proposed, too, that local governments wishing to undertake public improvements should be authorized to issue non-interest-bearing bonds that could be exchanged at the federal Treasury for legal-tender notes. He was proposing not only the creation of jobs, but the inflation of the currency. But his ideas were derided and dismissed in conservative circles.

When it became clear that his proposals were making no progress in Congress, Coxey announced that he would "send a petition to Washington with boots on"—a march of the unemployed to the capital to present their demands to the government. "Coxey's Army," as it was known, numbered only about 500 when it reached Washington, after having marched on foot from Massillon, Ohio. The marchers were barred from the Capitol by armed police. Coxey was arrested and later convicted of walking on the grass. He and his followers were herded into camps because their presence supposedly endangered public health. Congress took no action on their demands.

Coxey's Army was only one of several industrial protest movements—some of them much larger than Coxey's—to stage conspicuous marches and rallies in the 1890s. And there were many signs of union unrest as well during the decade—the Homestead and Pullman strikes for example. (See above, pp. 517–518.) To many Americans, the worker unrest seemed to augur a dangerous instability, even perhaps a revolution. Labor radicalism—some of it real, much of it imagined by the frightened middle class—was seldom far from the public mind, heightening the general sense of crisis.

The Silver Question

The financial panic weakened the government's monetary system, and in the minds of such people as Cleveland, the instability of the currency was the primary cause of the depression. The "money question," therefore, became the basis for some of the most dramatic political conflicts of the era. It had a long history.

The currency issue is a complicated and confusing one, and it has often been difficult for later generations to understand the enormous passions the controversy aroused. The heart of the debate was over what would form the basis of the dollar, what would lie behind it and give it value. Today, the value of the dollar rests on little more than public confidence in the government. But in the nineteenth century, currency was assumed to be worthless if there was not something concrete behind it—precious metal (specie), which holders of paper money could collect if they presented their currency to the Treasury.

The United States during most of its existence as a nation had recognized two metals—gold and silver—as a basis for the dollar, a situation known as "bimetallism." By the 1870s, however, the system had begun to produce various problems. The official ratio of the value of silver to the value of gold for purposes of creating currency (the "mint ratio") was established at 16 to 1: Sixteen ounces of silver equaled one ounce of gold. But the actual commercial value of silver (the "market ratio") was, in fact, much higher than that. Owners of silver could get more by selling it for manufacture into jewelry and other objects than they could by taking it to the mint for conversion to coins. So they stopped taking it to the mint, and the mint stopped coining silver.

In 1873, Congress passed a law that seemed simply to recognize the long-existing situation by officially discontinuing silver coinage. Few objected at the time; but within a few years the measure began to create controversy. Silver prices in 1873 had already begun to fall, and it soon became clear that Congress had foreclosed a very real potential method of expanding the currency. Before long, many Americans concluded that a conspiracy of big bankers had been responsible for the "demonetization" of silver. Critics of the law referred to it as the "Crime of '73."

That very year, 1873, the silver price fell to a point at which the market ratio between silver and gold was the same as the mint ratio. In subsequent years, the market value of silver continued to fall—to well below the old mint ratio of 16 to 1. The drop was due simply to changes in demand and supply. The world demand for silver decreased as several European countries abandoned bimetallism and adopted the "gold standard"—defining their currencies only in terms of gold and issuing only gold coins. And at the same time that the world supply of silver increased through European governments disposing of their holdings, huge new deposits of ore were being discovered and exploited in Nevada, Colorado, and other Western states.

Two groups of Americans were especially determined to undo the "Crime of '73." One consisted of the silver-mine owners, now understandably eager to have the government take their surplus silver and pay them much more than the market price. The other group consisted of discontented farmers, who wanted an increase in the quantity of money—an inflation of the currency—as a means of raising the prices of farm products and easing payment of the farmers' debts. The inflationists demanded that the government return at once to "free silver"—that is, to the "free and unlimited coinage of silver" at the old ratio of 16 to 1. In 1878, a coalition of Democrats and Republicans from the South, Midwest, and Far West attempted to push a free-silver bill through Congress. They had to settle for a compromise, the Bland-Allison Act, which directed the government to purchase and coin at the old ratio only a limited amount of silver (from $2 million to $4 million worth per month).

Later, in 1890, the Sherman Silver Purchase Act directed the Treasury to buy 4.5 million ounces of silver each month—an amount estimated to be the maximum domestic production—and to pay for the purchased bullion in Treasury notes. But the bill did little to appease the inflationists. Since the purchased silver was not to be coined, the amount of money in circulation did not increase materially, and the price of silver kept on falling.

Ever since the Resumption Act of 1875 (which had retired the Civil War greenbacks), the Treasury had tried to maintain a minimum gold reserve of $100 million to redeem its paper and silver dollars. During the prosperous 1880s, the reserve increased, and it reached the figure of $190 million by 1890. But in the last two years of the Harrison administration it declined sharply—as revenues declined because of the McKinley Tariff (whose prohibitively high duties kept foreign companies from sending their goods to America and hence from paying duties on them) and as government expenses increased to pay for pensions, internal improvements, and the purchase of silver required by the Sherman Silver Purchase Act. Those who continued to hold greenbacks and silver certificates grew nervous at rumors that the government might abandon the gold standard, which would, they feared, devalue the notes they held; thus they turned their currency in for gold at an increasing rate. When Cleveland returned to office in 1893, the reserve had shrunk to a little over $100 million.

"A Down-Hill Movement"

Even many Democrats repudiated William Jennings Bryan in 1896 after he won the party's nomination for president. Conservatives in both parties considered the "free silver" position to which Bryan and other Democrats were committed dangerous and even revolutionary, as this cartoon by C. J. Taylor suggests. Bryan (arms folded), Illinois governor John Peter Altgeld (waving a firebrand and a red banner), and other prominent Silver Democrats careen toward disaster as their cart breaks loose from the Democratic donkey.   (Granger Collection)

The panic of that year intensified the rush for gold, and soon the reserve had sunk below the minimum deemed necessary to sustain the gold standard. Cleveland had always disliked the Sherman Silver Purchase Act, and now he was convinced that it was the chief factor draining gold from the Treasury, that it would, if allowed to stand, force the country off the gold standard and impair the government's financial honor. Early in his second administration, therefore, he summoned Congress into special session and demanded the repeal of the Sherman Act. He got his way, but only after a bitter and divisive battle that helped create a permanent split in the Democratic party. The president's gold policy had aligned the Southern and Western Democrats in a solid phalanx against him and his Eastern followers.

The division over the money question reflected more than a disagreement over currency. It revealed opposing views of the proper nature of society and government. To its supporters, the gold standard was essential to America's ability to engage in world trade. It was also an important emotional symbol. It stood for stability, fiscal soundness, and public morality. An assault on the gold standard, they believed, would be the same as an assault on the sanctity of contracts or the rights of property. It would be a threat to civilization itself.

Opponents of the gold standard, however, took a different view. To them, gold placed artificial restrictions on the currency, allowing far too little money to circulate for the needs of a growing economy. In particular, the gold standard made it difficult for debtors to repay their loans and for investors to find credit for new ventures. More than that, however, "free silver" became a symbol of liberation. Silver would be a "people's money," as opposed to gold, the money of oppression and exploitation. It would be a panacea that would eliminate the indebtedness of farmers and of whole regions of the country. A graphic illustration of the popularity of the silver issue was the enormous success of William H. Harvey's *Coin's Financial School,* published in 1894, which became one of the great best sellers of its age. The fictional Professor Coin ran a school, an imaginary institution specializing in finance, and the book reproduced his lectures and his dialogues with his students. The professor's brilliant discourses left even his most vehement opponents dazzled as he persuaded his listeners, with simple logic, of the almost miraculous restorative qualities of free silver: "It means the reopening of closed factories, the relighting of fires in darkened furnaces; it means hope instead of despair; comfort in place of suffering; life instead of death."

"A Cross of Gold"

The Populists at first did not pay a great deal of attention to the silver issue. But as the party developed strength, the money question developed an increasing importance, if only for tactical reasons. The Populists desperately needed money to finance their campaigns. Silver-mine owners were willing to provide it but insisted on an elevation of the money plank and the subordination of other proposals. And the Populists needed to form alliances with other political groups. The "money question" seemed a way to win the support of many people not engaged in farming but nevertheless starved for currency. The election of 1896 appeared to the Populists to provide an unmatched opportunity to expand their influence and reach for real national power.

As the election approached, Republicans—gloating over the failure of the Democrats to deal effectively with either the economic crisis or the social chaos that seemed to have emerged from it—were confident of success. The only question of importance that appeared to confront them was the identity of the man they would anoint as the next president. Marcus A. Hanna, boss of the Ohio machine and soon to be national boss of the party, was a wealthy industrialist who aspired to be a president maker. He represented a new type in politics, the businessman who held office (he later served in the United States Senate) and actively manipulated parties instead of remaining in the background and paying out money

for services rendered. Hanna had picked out his man—William McKinley, governor of Ohio, who as a congressman had been the author of the tariff act of 1890—and had been grooming him carefully for years. By calling him "Bill McKinley, the agent of prosperity," and the "champion of protection" for American producers, Hanna secured McKinley the Republican nomination. The party platform opposed the free coinage of silver except by international agreement with the leading commercial nations (which everyone realized was highly unlikely). Thirty-four delegates from the mountain and plains states walked out in protest. Their destination was the Democratic party.

The Democrats met amid scenes of drama seldom equaled in American politics. Southern and Western delegates came to the convention determined to seize control of the party from conservative Easterners. Eager to stem challenges from the Populists in their sections, they hoped to incorporate some important Populist demands—among them free silver—into the Democratic platform. And they wanted as well to nominate a prosilver candidate.

The divided platform committee presented two reports to the convention—one expressing the majority opinion, the other a minority dissent. The majority report demanded tariff reduction, endorsed the principle of the income tax, denounced the issuing of currency notes by the national banks, condemned the use of injunctions in industrial disputes, pledged a "stricter control" of trusts and railroads, and—most prominently—supported free silver: "We demand the free and unlimited coinage of both silver and gold at the present legal ratio of 16 to 1, without waiting for the aid or consent of any other nation." The minority report echoed the Republican platform by opposing the free coinage of silver except by international agreement. The debate over the two competing platforms dominated the convention.

A series of speakers on both sides debated the resolutions, and the defenders of the gold standard had the better of the argument—until the final address. Then a handsome young man from the Nebraska delegation walked to the platform to close the debate. He was William Jennings Bryan, thirty-six years old, whose political experience was limited to two terms in the House of Representatives. But Bryan was widely known in the plains country as a magnetic orator, and he eagerly (and not entirely secretly) hoped that his rhetorical talents might win him the presidential nomination. His magnificent, organlike voice echoed through the farthest reaches of the hall,

William Jennings Bryan
Bryan addresses a crowd late in his career, displaying the flamboyant oratorical style that characterized his public life from the beginning. The poster at the lower left of the platform shows him as he appeared in the 1890s, when, as a young congressman from Nebraska, he became known as the "Boy Orator of the Platte" and the leader of the national free-silver movement.   (Library of Congress)

as he delivered what became one of the most famous political speeches in American history. He ended with a peroration that sent his audience into an impassioned frenzy and that was repeated by later generations of schoolboys all over rural America: "If they dare to come out in the open and defend the gold standard as a good thing, we will fight them to the uttermost. Having behind us the producing masses of this nation and the world, supported by the commercial interests, the laboring interests and the toilers everywhere, we will answer their demand for a gold standard by saying to them: 'You shall not press down upon the brow of labor this crown of thorns; you shall not crucify mankind upon a cross of gold.'"

The convention voted to adopt the prosilver platform. The agrarians had found their leader. And the following day, Bryan was nominated for president on the fifth ballot. One Republican, Joseph Foraker, when asked if he thought the epithet Boy Orator of the Platte was an apt one for Bryan, replied that it was, because the Platte River was six inches deep and six miles wide at the mouth. But many of Bryan's admirers applied a more accurate label to their hero: the Great Commoner. Born in Illinois of typical middle-class stock, he had attended a small sectarian

college, had practiced law with only average success, and then, repeating a normal American pattern, had moved to Nebraska, a frontier area, to try his fortune. He served as a potent symbol of rural, Protestant, middle-class America.

The choice of Bryan and the nature of the Democratic platform placed the Populists in a cruel quandary. They had expected both the major parties to adopt conservative programs and nominate conservative candidates, leaving the Populists to represent the growing forces of protest. But now the Democrats had stolen much of their thunder. The Populists faced the choice of naming their own candidate and splitting the protest vote or endorsing Bryan and losing their identity as a party. When the party assembled, the convention (amid considerable acrimony) voted to approve Bryan but nominated its own vice-presidential candidate, Tom Watson, whom they expected the Democrats to embrace but whom the Democrats ignored. Many Populists argued fervently that "fusion" with the Democrats—who had endorsed free silver, but ignored other and more important Populist demands—would destroy their party. But the majority concluded that there was no viable alternative.

McKinley the Protectionist
Although the free-silver issue generated the most heat in the 1896 presidential contest, William McKinley, the Republican candidate, had no strong feelings on the subject. He campaigned instead on the issue on which he had based his political career: the protective tariff. This campaign poster is cluttered with images and promises, but it is principally concerned with illustrating the happy results of protecting American industry and the disastrous consequences of free trade. (Library of Congress)

The Conservative Victory

The campaign of 1896 produced unequaled drama, intense excitement, a clear-cut issue, and a David-and-Goliath theme: the boy orator Bryan contending against the powerful boss Hanna and his hand-picked candidate, McKinley. Hanna had the great advantage of ample funds to spend on organization. The business and financial community, frightened beyond reason at the prospect of Bryan's sitting in the White House and taking advice from John P. Altgeld and Ignatius Donnelly, pressed lavish contributions on the Republicans—perhaps as much as $7 million. The Democrats, in contrast, reported expenditures of only $300,000, a sum only slightly larger than the contribution of a single firm, Standard Oil, to the Republican war chest.

Shrewdly, Hanna kept McKinley largely out of sight, knowing better than to pit his dull and solemn candidate against the matchless Bryan. From his home at Canton, Ohio, McKinley conducted a dignified "front-porch" campaign before pilgrimages of the Republican faithful, organized and paid for by Hanna. They came every day, and McKinley always had a

Election of 1896 (79.3% of electorate voting)

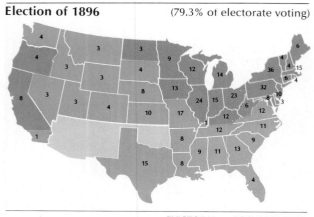

	ELECTORAL VOTE	POPULAR VOTE (%)
William McKinley (Republican)	271	7,104,779 (51.1)
William Jennings Bryan (Democratic)	176	6,502,925 (47.7)

speech ready for them. He stressed one theme: The Republican party was the only agency that could bring prosperity to the country.

No such decorous restraint marked the campaigning of the young and vital Bryan. Previous candidates had addressed audiences in campaigns and had even toured the country to speak at a few selected points. But Bryan was the first to stump every section systematically, to appear in villages and hamlets, indeed the first to say frankly to the voters that he wanted to be president. He traveled 18,000 miles, speaking several times a day, and addressed an estimated 5 million people.

Some businessmen grew almost hysterical at the thought of a possible Bryan victory. Many a company told its employees that if Bryan should win, the company would have to go out of business. Employers threatened to fire workers who voted for him. Bankers said they could not renew the mortgages of farmers who did so. Such threats, however, were less important than Bryan's own character in turning Democratic voters away from him. His revivalistic, camp-meeting style was pleasing enough to most Protestant sectarians of old native stock, but it antagonized many of the immigrant Catholics, who normally voted Democratic. Many of them decided to stay home on election day, if not to go out and vote Republican. Meanwhile, Bryan attracted fewer Republican farmers than he had hoped for—in part be-

cause shortly before the election the price of wheat suddenly rose, and Western farm discontent just as suddenly fell.

On election day, McKinley polled 271 electoral votes to Bryan's 176 and received 51.1 percent of the popular vote to Bryan's 47.7. Bryan won the Confederate South plus Missouri, swept the plains and mountain states except North Dakota, but lost California and Oregon on the Pacific coast. In short, he carried only the mining regions and the areas where staple farming was predominant and agricultural prices were lowest. He went down to defeat in all the Granger states in the Midwest. The Democratic program, like that of the Populists, had been designed to serve the needs of only one segment of one class—the most depressed fraction of agriculture—and this appeal was too narrow to win a national election.

Conservative Americans breathed a collective sigh of relief at the results of the 1896 election. What they had perceived as a radical threat to the nation's future had been averted—but only barely. It would be many years before they would forget that the "spirit of revolution" had seized control of one of the two major parties.

For the Populists and their allies, the election results were nothing short of a disaster. They had gambled everything on their "fusion" with the Democratic party, and they had lost. The Populist movement stood exposed, it seemed, as a phenomenon too weak to influence national politics. And within months of the election, the People's party began to dissolve. Never again would American farmers unite so militantly to demand economic reform. And never again would so large a group of Americans raise so forceful a protest against the nature of the industrial economy.

McKinley and Prosperity

The administration of William McKinley, which began in the aftermath of turmoil, saw the nation return to a relative calm. One reason was simple exhaustion. By 1897, the labor unrest that had so frightened many middle-class Americans and so excited working-class people had subsided, victim of the internal weaknesses of the labor movement and of the strength of the corporate forces opposing it. And with the simultaneous decline of agrarian protest, the greatest destabilizing forces in the nation's politics were—temporarily at least—removed. Another reason was the character of the McKinley administration itself, which was politically shrewd and nothing if not committed to a reassuring stability. Most important, however, was the gradual easing of the economic crisis, a change that undercut many of those who were agitating for change.

William McKinley was the last of the long list of veteran officers of the Union army (beginning with Grant) to sit in the White House. Friendly and generous in nature, he was inclined to defer to stronger characters such as Hanna and to act in harmony with his party's leaders. His administration was passive, cautious, and conservative.

McKinley and his allies were eager to avoid inflaming the divisions they knew lurked beneath the surface of their party. They committed themselves fully to only one issue, one on which they knew virtually all Republicans were agreed: the need for higher tariff rates. Immediately after assuming office, McKinley summoned Congress into special session to consider tariff revision. With record brevity, the Republican majority whipped into shape and passed the Dingley Tariff, raising the duties to an average of 57 percent—the highest in history.

The administration dealt more gingerly with the explosive silver question (an issue that McKinley himself had never considered very important in any case). In accordance with the party's platform pronouncement that bimetallism could not be established except by international action, McKinley sent a commission to Europe to explore the possibility of a silver agreement with Great Britain and France. As he and everyone else anticipated, Britain refused to abandon its gold standard, thus effectively ending any hopes for international bimetallism. The administration could now argue that if the United States embarked on a silver program alone, it would be economically isolated from the rest of the world. Believing that their position was unassailable, the Republicans finally moved to enact currency legislation. The Currency, or Gold Standard, Act of 1900 confirmed the nation's commitment to the gold standard.

And so the "battle of the standards" ended in victory for the forces of conservatism. Economic developments at the time seemed to prove that the conservatives had been right in the struggle. In 1898 prosperity began to return to America. Foreign crop failures enlarged the farmers' market and sent farm prices surging upward. At the same time, business entered another cycle of booming expansion. Prosperity and gold had come hand in hand—the lesson seemed obvious.

But it was not quite that simple. Bryan and the silverites were essentially right in demanding currency inflation. In the quarter century before 1900, the countries of the Western world had experienced a spectacular growth in productive facilities and population. Yet the supply of money had not kept pace with economic progress, because the supply was tied to gold and the amount of gold had remained practically constant. Populist predictions of continuing financial distress might have proved correct had it not been for the fortuitous increase in the gold supply

soon after the Republicans took over the government in 1897. A new technique for extracting gold from low-content ores, the cyanide process, made it possible to work mines previously considered marginal or unprofitable. At the same time, huge new gold deposits were discovered in Alaska, South Africa, and Australia. In 1898, two and a half times as much gold was produced as in 1890, and the currency supply was soon inflated far beyond anything proposed by Bryan.

The McKinley administration brought a tariff increase, the gold standard, and prosperity. It also brought a new departure in foreign policy, as the nation entered upon the path of overseas imperialism and took its place among the "great powers" of the world.

SUGGESTED READINGS

General Studies   Overviews of the political history of the late nineteenth century include Sean Denis Cashman, *America and the Gilded Age* (1984); R. Hal Williams, *Years of Decision: American Politics in the 1890s* (1978); John H. Dobson, *Politics in the Gilded Age* (1972); John A. Garraty, *The New Commonwealth* (1969), for the period 1877–1890; and Harold U. Faulkner, *Politics, Reform, and Expansion* (1959), for the turbulent 1890s. Samuel P. Hays, *The Response to Industrialism, 1885–1914* (1957), and Robert Wiebe, *The Search for Order, 1877–1920* (1967), are important syntheses that include some attention to political events. Morton Keller, *Affairs of State* (1977), is a more interpretive analysis of public life in the late nineteenth century. Matthew Josephson, *The Politicos* (1963), is a hostile study of late-nineteenth-century politicians; David J. Rothman, *Politics and Power: The United States Senate, 1869-1901* (1966), and Robert D. Marcus, *Grand Old Party* (1971), are more temperate in their judgments. H. Wayne Morgan, *From Hayes to McKinley* (1969), is a basic narrative of the political events of the period; and Leonard D. White, *The Republican Era* (1958), examines the administrative developments of the time. Alan Trachtenberg, *The Incorporation of America: Culture and Society in the Gilded Age* (1982), examines popular culture.

Politics and Reform   Several specialized studies examine some of the specific political issues of the Gilded Age. Ari Hoogenboom, *Outlawing the Spoils* (1961), examines civil-service reform. Walter T. K. Nugent, *Money and American Society* (1968), Allen Weinstein, *Prelude to Populism: Origins of the Silver Issue, 1867–1878* (1970), and Irwin Unger, *The Greenback Era* (1964), consider the money issue. John G. Sproat, *The Best Men* (1968), is a fine study of the origins of mugwumpery; Geoffrey Blodgett, *The Gentle Reformers* (1966), examines reform Democrats in Massachusetts. James Bryce, *The American Commonwealth*, 2 vols. (1888), is a classic contemporary study of American politics by a

British observer. The cultural aspects of late-nineteenth-century politics are considered in two books by Paul Kleppner: *The Cross of Culture: A Social Analysis of Midwestern Politics, 1850–1900* (1970) and *The Third Electoral System, 1853–1892* (1979), and in Richard Jensen, *The Winning of the Midwest: Social and Political Conflict, 1888–1896* (1971).

Party Leaders   Important biographies of leading political figures of the era are Harry Barnard, *Rutherford B. Hayes and His America* (1954); Kenneth Davison, *The Presidency of Rutherford B. Hayes* (1972); Allan Peskin, *Garfield* (1978); Margaret Leech and Harry J. Brown, *The Garfield Orbit* (1978); Thomas C. Reeves, *Gentleman Boss* (1975), on Chester A. Arthur; David Jordan, *Roscoe Conkling of New York* (1971); Allan Nevins, *Grover Cleveland: A Study in Courage* (1933); Horace Samuel Merrill, *Bourbon Leader: Grover Cleveland and the Democratic Party* (1957); Harry J. Sievers, *Benjamin Harrison*, 3 vols. (1952–1968); H. Wayne Morgan, *William McKinley and His America* (1963); Lewis L. Gould, *The Presidency of William McKinley* (1981); Margaret Leech, *In the Days of McKinley* (1959); and Herbert Croly, *Marcus Alonzo Hanna* (1912).

The Depression   The economic problems of the 1890s (and some of their political consequences) are the subject of Charles Hoffman, *The Depression of the Nineties: An Economic History* (1970), and Samuel McSeveney, *The Politics of Depression* (1972), which focuses on the Northeast. On labor unrest, see Donald McMurray, *Coxey's Army* (1929); Ray Ginger, *The Bending Cross* (1949), on Eugene Debs, the socialist leader; Almot Lindsey, *The Pullman Strike* (1942); and Ray Ginger, *Altgeld's America* (1958).

Populism   A large literature has emerged on the issue of Populism, of which the standard work was for many years John D. Hicks, *The Populist Revolt* (1931). Superseding

Hicks as the most important single study of Populism is Lawrence Goodwyn, *Democratic Promise* (1976), also published in an abridged paperback version entitled *The Populist Moment* (1978). Norman Pollack, *The Populist Response to Industrial America* (1962), argues that the Populists were forward-looking radicals, thus challenging the view of Richard Hofstadter, *The Age of Reform* (1955), that they were nostalgic and basically reactionary. Differing with both Pollack and Hofstadter is Sheldon Hackney, *Populism to Progressivism in Alabama* (1969). C. Vann Woodward, *Origins of the New South* (1972), includes a classic analysis of Southern Populism. Robert McMath, *Populist Vanguard* (1975), is a good study of the Farmers' Alliances that helped create the People's party. Bruce Palmer, *Man over Money* (1980), is an admiring examination of Populist ideology. Other important studies of Populism include Walter T. K. Nugent, *The Tolerant Populists* (1963), a study of Kansas that challenges Hofstadter's view of the Populists as narrow-minded and often bigoted; Theodore Saloutos, *Farmer Movements in the South, 1865–1933* (1960), which places Populism in a larger chronological context; Fred Shannon, *The Farmer's Last Frontier* (1945); and Peter Argersinger, *Populism and Politics: William Alfred Peffer and the People's Party* (1974). Barton C. Shaw, *The Wool-Hat Boys: Georgia's Populist Party* (1984), is an important local study. C. Vann Woodward, *Tom Watson, Agrarian Rebel* (1938), is a classic biography of the Populist leader. Also valuable are Francis B. Simkins, *Pitchfork Ben Tillman* (1944); Martin Ridge, *Ignatius Donnelly: The Portrait of a Politician* (1962); and Stuart Noblin, *Leonidas Lafayette Polk* (1949).

The Election of 1896   On the important election of 1896, several good studies are available, among them Paul Glad, *McKinley, Bryan, and the People* (1964) and *The Trumpet Soundeth* (1960); Stanley Jones, *The Presidential Election of 1896* (1964); and J. Rogers Hollingsworth, *The Whirligig of Politics: The Democracy of Cleveland and Bryan* (1963). Paolo Coletta, *William Jennings Bryan: Political Evangelist* (1964), is the first of three volumes of the most thorough biography of Bryan and covers the first of Bryan's three campaigns for the presidency.

"Measuring Uncle Sam for a New Suit," by J. S. Pughe, in *Puck* Magazine, 1900   (Culver Pictures)

Chapter 20

The Imperial Republic

The American republic had been an expansionist nation since the earliest days of its existence. Throughout the first half of the nineteenth century, as the population of the United States grew and pressed westward, the government continually acquired new territory for its citizens to occupy: the trans-Appalachian West, the Louisiana Territory, Florida, Texas, Oregon, California, New Mexico, Alaska, and more. It was the nation's "Manifest Destiny," many Americans believed, to expand into new realms.

In the last years of the nineteenth century, the United States was nearing the limits of its capacity to develop new territory on the North American continent. And in those years, expansionism moved into a new phase. In the past, the nation had almost always annexed land contiguous to its existing boundaries, land that could provide new areas of settlement for the American people, land that could be organized as territories and, ultimately, admitted to the Union as states. But the expansionism of the 1890s, the new Manifest Destiny, involved acquiring possessions separate from the continental United States: island territories, many of which were already thickly populated, most of which were not suitable for massive settlement from America, few of which were expected ever to become states of the Union. The United States was acquiring colonies. It was joining England, France, Germany, and other expanding nations in the great imperial drive that was, by the end of the century, to bring much of the underdeveloped world under the control of the industrial powers of the West.

There had been some agitation in America for overseas expansion as early as the 1850s, agitation that continued after the Civil War and, to some extent, during the ensuing decades. Not until the 1890s, however, did the nation seriously embark on the new imperialism. In the wake of a brief, victorious war with Spain, the United States suddenly found itself in possession of a substantial empire and in the position of a widely recognized "world power." Out of the imperial experience of the late nineteenth century emerged many of the basic premises that would dominate American foreign policy for many decades to come. And out of it, too, would emerge many of the problems that would accompany the nation's position as a great power.

Stirrings of Imperialism

For over two decades after the Civil War, the American people seemed to have abandoned the expansionist impulse that had been so powerful in the antebellum years. They were occupied with things closer to home—reconstructing the South, settling the Far West, building a network of railroads, and expanding their great industrial system. By the 1890s, however, some Americans were ready—indeed, eager—to resume the course of Manifest Destiny that had inspired their forebears to wrest an empire from Mexico in the expansionist 1840s.

The New Manifest Destiny

Several developments played a part in shifting the attention of Americans from their own country to

Imperialism at High Tide: The World in 1900

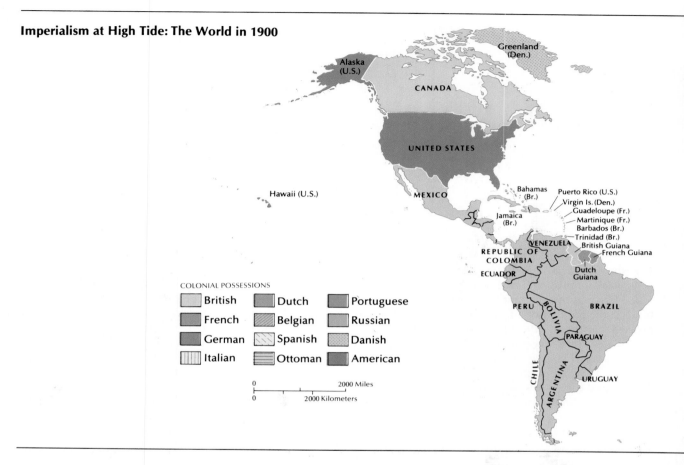

lands across the seas. The "closing of the frontier," widely heralded by Frederick Jackson Turner and many others in the 1890s, produced fears that natural resources would soon dwindle and that alternative sources must be found abroad. The depression that began in 1893 convinced some businessmen that industry had overexpanded and was producing more goods than customers at home could buy. The bitter social protests of the time—the Populist movement, the free-silver crusade, the bloody labor disputes— led many people to believe that the nation was threatened with internal collapse; some politicians advocated a more aggressive foreign policy to provide an outlet for frustrations that would otherwise destabilize domestic life.

Foreign trade was becoming increasingly important to the American economy in the late nineteenth century. The nation had exported about $392 million worth of goods in 1870; by 1890, the figure was $857 million; and by 1900, it had leaped to $1.4 billion. Once convinced of the great advantages of overseas

markets, many Americans began to consider the possibility of acquiring colonies that might expand such markets further. "Today," Senator Albert J. Beveridge of Indiana cried in 1899, "we are raising more than we can consume. Today, we are making more than we can use. Therefore, we must find new markets for our produce, new occupation for our capital, new work for our labor."

Americans could not, moreover, insulate themselves entirely from the imperialist fever that was raging through Europe. In the last years of the century, the major powers of Europe were partitioning most of Africa among themselves and turning eager eyes on the Far East and the feeble Chinese Empire. Some Americans feared that their nation would soon be left out, that no territory would remain to be acquired. Senator Henry Cabot Lodge of Massachusetts, a leading imperialist, warned that the United States "must not fall out of the line of march."

A philosophic justification for expansionism was provided by historians, professors, clergymen, and

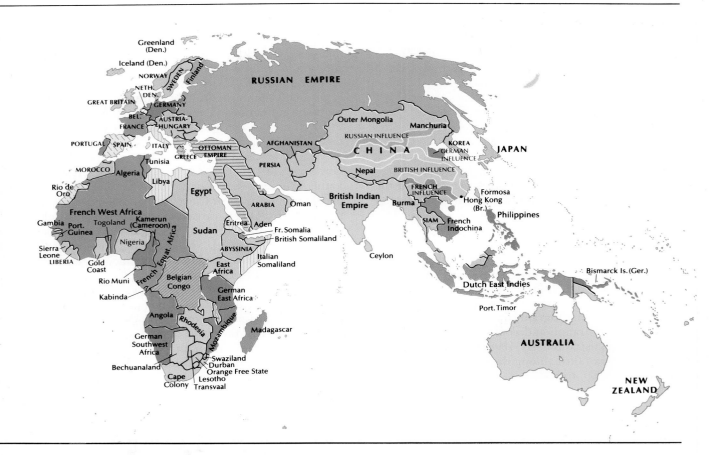

others who found a basis for imperialism in their interpretations of Charles Darwin's theories (interpretations that Darwin himself never intended). These intellectuals contended that nations or "races," like biological species, struggled constantly for existence and that only the fittest could survive. For strong nations to dominate weak ones was, therefore, in accordance with the law of nature. This was an application to world affairs of the same distortion of Darwinism that industrialists and others had long been applying to domestic economic affairs in the form of Social Darwinism.

One of the first to advance this argument was the popular writer John Fiske, who predicted in an 1885 article in *Harper's Magazine* that the English-speaking peoples would eventually control every land that was not already the seat of an established civilization. Support for Fiske's position came the same year from Josiah Strong, a Congregational clergyman and champion of overseas missionary work. In a book entitled *Our Country: Its Possible Future and Its Present*

Crisis, Strong declared that the Anglo-Saxon "race," and especially its American branch, represented the great ideas of civil liberty and pure Christianity and was "divinely commissioned" to spread its institutions over the earth. John W. Burgess, founder of Columbia University's School of Political Science, gave the stamp of scholarly approval to imperialism. In his 1890 study *Political Science and Comparative Law,* he flatly stated that the Anglo-Saxon and Teutonic nations possessed the highest political talents. It was the duty of these nations, he said, to uplift less fortunate peoples, even to force superior institutions on them if necessary: "There is no human right to the status of barbarism."

The ablest and probably the most effective apostle of imperialism was Alfred Thayer Mahan, a captain and later an admiral in the navy. Mahan presented his philosophy in three major works: *The Influence of Sea Power upon History, 1660–1783* (1890), *The Influence of Sea Power upon the French Revolution and Empire, 1793–1812* (1892), and *The Interest of America in Sea*

Power (1897). His thesis was reasonably simple: The sea-power nations were the great nations of history, and the United States, a huge island, had to build its greatness on sea power. The essential links in sea power were a productive domestic economy, foreign commerce, a merchant marine to monopolize national trade, a navy to defend the trade routes and national interests—and colonies, which would provide raw materials and markets and could serve as bases for the navy. Specifically, Mahan advocated that the United States construct a canal across the isthmus of Central America to join the oceans, acquire defensive bases on both sides of the canal in the Caribbean and the Pacific, and take possession of Hawaii and other Pacific islands. "Whether they will or no," he proclaimed, "Americans must now begin to look outward."

Mahan doubted that the United States would achieve its destiny, because its navy was not large enough to play the role he envisioned for it. But Mahan did not accurately gauge the progress of the naval construction program launched in the Garfield-Arthur administration and continued by every succeeding administration. By 1898, the United States had advanced to fifth among the world's naval powers; and by 1900, to third.

Hemispheric Hegemony

The most ardent practitioner of the new, assertive diplomacy was Benjamin Harrison's secretary of state, James G. Blaine. Blaine believed that his country was destined to dominate the Caribbean and the Pacific. And he believed that it needed to do so because it had to find enlarged foreign markets for its surplus goods. The most likely foreign outlet, he thought, was Latin America, with whose countries he wanted advantageous commercial relations.

Blaine had served briefly as secretary of state once before—under James Garfield, in 1881. During his six months in office, he had invited the Latin nations to a Pan-American conference in Washington to discuss trade matters and the arbitration of disputes. Blaine left office after the Garfield assassination, and his successor withdrew the invitations. But sentiment for such a meeting survived, and the first Pan-American Congress finally took place in Washington in October 1889, with delegates from nineteen American nations in attendance. The Latin delegates rejected both of Blaine's principal proposals: the creation of an inter-American customs union and the establishment of arbitration procedures to resolve hemispheric disputes. They preferred to buy in the cheaper European market, and they feared the dominance of the United States in arbitration. But the meeting was not a failure. Out of it arose the Pan-American Union, an agency in Washington that became a clearinghouse for distributing information to the member nations. Other congresses would meet in the future to discuss common hemispheric matters.

The Cleveland administration continued the newly aggressive approach to American interests in Latin America when it assumed office in 1893. Indeed, in 1895 President Cleveland and his secretary of state, Richard Olney, carried the country to the brink of war in a dispute with Great Britain over the boundary of Venezuela. Britain and Venezuela had been arguing for years about the boundary between Venezuela and British Guiana, and the dispute assumed new importance when gold was discovered in the disputed area. Both Cleveland and Olney, as well as the American public, were disposed to sympathize with Venezuela—the little underdog country confronting the great European power. The president and Congress both urged Britain to submit the matter to arbitration, but the British government took no action.

Olney drafted a harsh note to Lord Salisbury at the Foreign Office, charging that Britain was violating the Monroe Doctrine: "Today the United States is practically sovereign on this continent, and its fiat is law upon the subjects to which it confines its interposition." Salisbury waited four months before sending a curt and condescending reply. The Monroe Doctrine, he insisted, did not apply to boundary disputes or the present situation and had no standing as international law in any case. Britain would not submit to arbitration. Cleveland was enraged. In December 1895, he asked Congress for authority to create a special commission to determine the boundary line; if Britain resisted the commission's decision, he insisted, the United States should be willing to go to war to enforce it.

Congress supported Cleveland's plan with enthusiasm, and war talk raged all over the country. Belatedly, the British government realized that it had stumbled into a genuine diplomatic crisis and was on the verge of a war with the United States it did not want and could not afford. The British quickly backed down and agreed to arbitration. And the dusty Monroe Doctrine, to which few Europeans (and not many Americans) had paid much attention in recent decades, suddenly assumed new importance. Equally significant, the peaceful settlement of the dispute began a long era of friendship between America and Britain and made it possible for the United States to consider new imperialist ventures of its own without risking opposition from the British.

Hawaii and Samoa

The islands of Hawaii in the mid-Pacific had been an important stopover station for American ships in the China trade since the early nineteenth century and was the home of a growing number of American settlers. New England missionaries had arrived in Hawaii as early in 1820; and like their fellow missionaries elsewhere, they advertised the economic possibilities of the islands in the religious press. Soon other Americans arrived to become sugar planters and to found a profitable new industry. Eventually, officers of the growing navy looked longingly on the magnificent natural base of Pearl Harbor on the island of Oahu.

Gradually, the American residents of Hawaii came to dominate the economic and political life of the islands, despite the presence of native rulers. Commercial relations were inexorably pushing Hawaii into the American orbit and making it, as Blaine accurately contended, a part of the American economic system. A treaty signed in 1875 permitted Hawaiian sugar to enter the United States duty-free and bound the Hawaiian kingdom to make no territorial or economic concessions to other powers. The trade arrangement tied the islands to the American economy, and the political clauses meant that, in effect, the United States was guaranteeing Hawaii's independence and hence was making the islands a protectorate. In 1887, a new treaty renewed the existing arrangements and granted the United States exclusive use of Pearl Harbor as a naval station. The course of events in the Pacific was rendering outright political union almost inevitable.

Sugar production in Hawaii boomed, and prosperity burgeoned for the American planters. Then the McKinley Tariff of 1890 dealt the planters a harsh blow; by removing the duty on foreign raw sugar and giving domestic producers a bounty, it deprived Hawaii of its privileged position in the American sugar market. Annexation (which would give Hawaiian planters the same bounty that American planters were receiving) seemed the only alternative to economic strangulation.

In the midst of growing sentiment among white Hawaiians for union with the United States, the passive native king, Kalakaua, died, to be succeeded in 1891 by Queen Liliuokalani, a nationalist determined to eliminate American influence in the government. Two years later, the American residents staged a revolution and called on the United States for protection. At a critical moment the American minister, John L. Stevens, an ardent annexationist and a friend of Blaine's, ordered 160 marines from a warship in Honolulu harbor to go ashore to aid the rebels. The queen yielded her authority, and a delegation representing the triumphant provisional government set out for Washington to negotiate a treaty of annexation. President Harrison happily signed an annexation agreement in February 1893, only weeks before leaving office. But the Senate refused to ratify the treaty, and Grover Cleveland, the new president, refused to support it. However disposed Cleveland was to upholding American rights under the Monroe Doctrine, his conservative ideas about the sanctity of property ownership made him wary of the proposed annexation. He withdrew the treaty and sent a special representative to the islands to investigate. When his agent reported that Americans had engineered the revolution, Cleveland endeavored to restore the queen to her throne. But Americans were now firmly in control of the kingdom and refused to budge. Reluctantly, the president had to recognize their government as the new "republic" of Hawaii. Cleveland had only delayed the inevitable. Debate over the annexation of Hawaii continued until 1898, when—with the Republicans again in power and with the United States constructing a colonial empire in both oceans—Hawaii was annexed by joint resolution of both houses of Congress.

Three thousand miles to the south of Hawaii, the Samoan islands dominated the sea lanes of the South Pacific and had long served as a way station for American ships in the Pacific trade. As American commerce with Asia increased after the completion of the first transcontinental railroad in 1869 and the extension of a steamship line from San Francisco to New Zealand, certain business groups regarded Samoa with new interest; and the navy eyed the harbor at Pago Pago on the island of Tutuila. In 1872, a naval officer visited the islands and negotiated a treaty granting the United States the use of Pago Pago; but the Senate rejected the agreement. President Grant nevertheless sent a special representative to Samoa to encourage American trading and business interests. A chain of events leading to greater American in-

Iolani Palace, Hawaii
American flags and American troops are prominent during ceremonies in 1898 marking the annexation of Hawaii by the United States. Iolani Palace had been the home of Queen Liliuokalani, whose unsuccessful efforts to strip American sugar planters of their political power in the islands helped lead to the transformation of her kingdom into an American territory.   (Library of Congress)

volvement was being set in motion. In 1878, the Hayes administration brought a native prince to Washington to sign a treaty, which was approved by the Senate, providing for an American naval station at Pago Pago and binding the United States to use its "good offices" to adjust any differences between a foreign power and Samoa. This treaty indicated that the American government meant to have a voice in Samoan affairs.

The opportunity to use that voice soon came. Great Britain and Germany were also interested in the islands, and they hastened to secure treaty rights from the native princes. For the next ten years the three powers scrambled and intrigued for dominance in Samoa, playing off one ruler against another and coming dangerously close to war. In 1889, warships of the contending nations appeared in one Samoan harbor, and a clash seemed imminent. But a tropical hurricane dispersed the vessels, and the German government, not wishing to antagonize the United States, suggested a conference of the interested powers in Berlin to settle the dispute. Germany and Britain

would have preferred a division of the islands, but Secretary Blaine insisted on preserving native Samoan rule. The result was that the conferees agreed on a tripartite protectorate over Samoa, with the native chiefs exercising only nominal authority.

The three-way arrangement proved unsatisfactory, failing altogether to halt the intrigues and rivalries of the signatory members. It was abandoned in 1899, when the United States and Germany divided the islands between them, compensating Britain with territories elsewhere in the Pacific. Germany obtained the two largest islands, but the United States retained Tutuila with its incomparable harbor at Pago Pago.

War with Spain

Imperial ambitions had thus begun to stir within the United States well before the late 1890s. But it was the war with Spain in 1898 that turned those stirrings into an overt expansionism. The war transformed America's relationship to the rest of the world, and it left the nation with a vast overseas empire.

Controversy over Cuba

The immediate background of the Spanish-American War lay in the Caribbean island of Cuba, which with nearby Puerto Rico represented nearly all that was left of Spain's once extensive Latin American empire. The Cubans had long resented Spanish rule, and they had engaged in a notable but unsuccessful attempt to overthrow it between 1868 and 1878 (the Ten Years' War). During that revolt, the American people were strongly sympathetic to the Cuban cause, but their feelings did not go beyond vague expressions of support. America even resisted strong provocations. In 1873, Spanish authorities had seized a ship carrying arms to the Cuban rebels and had executed fifty-three members of its crew as pirates. The vessel had flown an American flag (although its owners were Cuban), and some of its seamen were Americans. Popular indignation was intense, but Secretary of State Hamilton Fish had avoided a crisis by inducing the Spanish government to return the *Virginius* and pay an indemnity to the families of the executed men.

In 1895, the Cubans rose up again. Not only the continuing Spanish misrule but also the American tariff policy created conditions of misery that prepared the way for revolt. Cuba's principal export was sugar, and the bulk of the crop went to the United States. The Wilson-Gorman Tariff of 1894, with its high duties on raw sugar, shut off the island's chief source of wealth and prostrated its economy.

From the beginning, the struggle took on aspects of ferocity that horrified Americans. The Cubans deliberately devastated the island to force the Spaniards

The Duty of the Hour

This 1892 lithograph was no doubt inspired by the saying "Out of the frying pan and into the fire." A despairing Cuba, struggling to escape from the frying pan of Spanish misrule, contemplates an even more dangerous alternative: "anarchy" (or home rule). Cartoonist Louis Dalrymple here suggests that the only real solution to Cuba's problems is control by the United States, whose "duty" to Cuba is "To Save Her not Only from Spain, but from a Worse Fate." (Granger Collection)

THE DUTY OF THE HOUR:—TO SAVE HER NOT ONLY FROM SPAIN BUT FROM A WORSE FATE.

to leave. To put down the insurrection, the Spanish resorted to methods equally extreme. General Valeriano Weyler—or "Butcher" Weyler, as he soon came to be known in the American press—confined all civilians in certain areas to hastily prepared concentration camps, where they died by the thousands, victims of disease and malnutrition.

Many of the same savage techniques had been employed earlier in the Ten Years' War without shocking American sensibilities. But in the 1890s a wave of anger ran through the American public. The revolt of 1895 was reported more fully and floridly by the American press than the former outbreak—and so reported as to give the impression that all the cruelties were being perpetrated by the Spaniards.

At this time, Joseph Pulitzer with his New York *World* and William Randolph Hearst with his New York *Journal* were revolutionizing American journalism. The new "yellow press" specialized in lurid and sensational news; when such news did not exist, editors were not above creating it. To Hearst and Pulitzer, engaged in a ruthless circulation war, the struggle in Cuba was a journalist's dream. Both sent batteries of reporters and illustrators to Cuba with orders to provide accounts of Spanish atrocities. "You furnish the pictures," Hearst supposedly told an overly scrupulous artist, "and I'll furnish the war."

The mounting storm of indignation against Spain left President Cleveland unmoved. Convinced that both sides in Cuba were guilty of atrocities and that the United States had no interests justifying involvement in the struggle, he issued a proclamation of neutrality and attempted to stop the numerous filibustering expeditions being organized by a "junta" of Cuban refugees in New York City. When Congress, in a state of excitement, passed a resolution favoring recognition of Cuban belligerency, he ignored it. His only concession to the demands for intervention was to offer to mediate the conflict, a proposal that Spain declined.

When McKinley became president in 1897, he renewed the American mediation offer, which the Spanish again refused. Taking a stronger line than his predecessor, he protested to Spain against its "uncivilized and inhuman" conduct. The Spanish government, alarmed that McKinley's course might lead to American intervention in Cuba, recalled Weyler, modified the concentration policy, and took steps to grant the island a qualified autonomy. At the end of 1897, with the insurrection losing ground, it seemed that war might be averted.

But whatever chance might have existed for a peaceful settlement vanished as a result of two dramatic incidents in February 1898. The first occurred when a Cuban agent in Havana stole a private letter written by Dupuy de Lôme, the Spanish minister in Washington, and thoughtfully turned it over to the American press. Published first in Hearst's New York *Journal,* and later in newspapers across the land, the minister's letter described McKinley as a weak man and "a bidder for the admiration of the crowd." This was no more than many Americans, including some Republicans, were saying about their president (Theodore Roosevelt described McKinley as having "no more backbone than a chocolate éclair"), but because a foreigner had made the remark it was considered a national insult. Popular anger was intense, and Dupuy de Lôme resigned before the outraged McKinley could demand his recall.

While the excitement was still at fever pitch, even more sensational news hit the front pages: The American battleship *Maine* had been blown up in Havana harbor with a loss of more than 260 lives. The ship had been ordered to Cuban waters in January on a supposedly "friendly" visit but really to protect American lives and property against possible attacks by Spanish loyalists. Many Americans jumped to the conclusion that the Spanish had sunk the ship—"an act of dirty treachery," Theodore Roosevelt announced—and the imperialists and the jingoists screamed for war. This opinion seemed confirmed when a naval court of inquiry reported that an external explosion by a submarine mine had caused the disaster. In fact, the real cause of the *Maine* disaster was never determined. Later evidence suggested that it was the result of an accidental explosion inside one of the engine rooms. Nevertheless, war hysteria swept the country, and Congress unanimously appropriated $50 million for military preparations. "Remember the *Maine*!" became a national chant for revenge.

After the *Maine* incident, there was little chance that the government could suppress the popular demand for war, although McKinley still preferred to avoid a conflict. In March 1898, he asked Spain to agree to an armistice, with negotiations for a permanent peace to follow, and an immediate ending of the concentration system. After a slight delay, Spain accepted some of the American demands—an end to hostilities, the elimination of the concentration camps—on April 9. But it refused to agree to an armistice or to negotiations with the rebels; and it reserved the right to resume hostilities at its discretion. Two days later, McKinley asked Congress for

The Wreckage of the *Maine*
After the explosion on February 15, 1898, that destroyed the ship and killed 260 Americans, the *Maine* settled into the mud of Havana's harbor so that only its mast and a small part of its superstructure remained visible. Divers examining the hull produced evidence that suggested the ship had hit an underwater mine and that the explosion of the mine had set off other explosions in the ship's powder magazine. A second investigation, in 1911, raised questions about the findings of the first but did not openly challenge its conclusions. After that, the hulk was towed out to sea and sunk in deep water, leaving the questions surrounding the explosion permanently unanswered. (National Archives)

authority to use military force to end the hostilities in Cuba—in short, for a declaration of war, "in the name of humanity, in the name of civilization, in behalf of endangered American interests." His long, dull, cautious message seemed deliberately designed not to evoke enthusiasm. But on April 19, by huge majorities, Congress passed a joint resolution declaring Cuba free and authorizing the president to employ force to expel the Spanish from the island. Spain broke diplomatic relations with the United States two days later, and a day after that McKinley established a naval blockade of the island and summoned volunteers to fight there. Finally, on April 25, Congress passed a formal declaration of war.

There was, as yet, only limited support for annexation of Cuba as a war aim. Some national leaders were calling openly for imperialism, but a powerful anti-imperialist movement more than counterbalanced them for the time. Evidence of the anti-imperialists' strength was the addition to the congressional resolution of the Teller Amendment, which disclaimed any intention on the part of the United States to annex Cuba.

"A Splendid Little War"

The Spanish-American conflict was, in the words of Roosevelt's friend John Hay, "a splendid little war." Indeed, to virtually all Americans—with the exception of many of the enlisted men who fought in it—it seemed almost an ideal conflict. It was the last small, short, individualistic war before the huge, protracted, impersonal struggles of the twentieth century. Declared in April, it was over in August. Newspaper readers easily and eagerly followed the campaigns and the heroic exploits of American soldiers and sailors. Only 460 Americans were killed in battle or died of wounds, but some 5,200 perished of disease: malaria, dysentery, typhoid, among others.

The Spanish-American War in Cuba, 1898

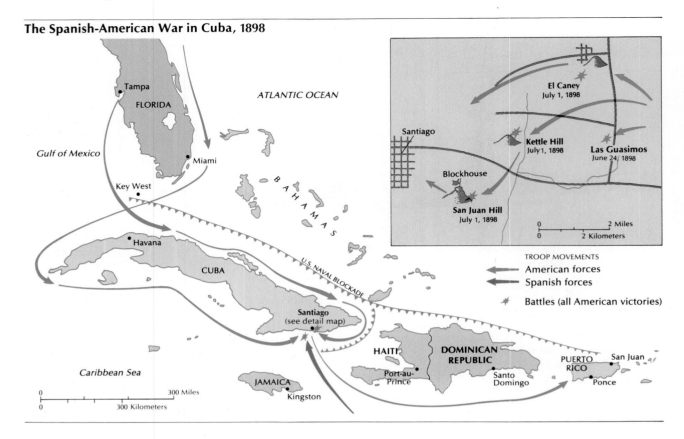

Blithely and confidently, the United States embarked on a war it was not prepared to fight. The agencies responsible for supplying the troops, manned by elderly bureaucratic officers, proved incapable of meeting the modest wants of the armed forces during the war. There were enough Krag-Jorgensen repeating rifles, using smokeless powder, for the regulars; but the volunteers had to make do with the old black-powder, single-shot Springfields of the Civil War. American soldiers fighting in tropical regions were clothed in the traditional heavy blue uniforms and fed canned rations that they called "embalmed beef." Medical supplies and services were inadequate, which contributed to the heavy impact of tropical diseases on the troops.

The regular army—numbering only 28,000 troops and officers scattered around the country at various posts—was a tough little force, skilled at quelling Indian outbreaks, but with no experience in large-scale warfare. Hastily Congress directed the president to increase the army to 62,000 and to call for 125,000 volunteers.

National Guard units, organized by local communities and commanded for the most part by local leaders, did the bulk of the fighting. Each unit considered itself a representative of its own town, and friends and relatives at home took a special pride in the performance of their "boys" and their unit. It was, in fact, the connection between the war and this pride in community that helped make the conflict so popular. More than 1 million young men volunteered for service, nearly ten times the number the president had requested. The invasion army also included several volunteer cavalry units, including the celebrated Rough Riders, nominally commanded by Leonard Wood but actually by Theodore Roosevelt, who was about to make the front pages as a war hero.

The character or the American war effort was determined in part by the nature of the opposition. The Spanish army numbered almost 130,000 men, of whom 80,000 were already in Cuba at the beginning of the war. Despite its size, however, its commanders seemed to be paralyzed by a conviction of certain defeat. The American navy, fifth largest in the world, was far superior to the Spanish in ships, guns, and personnel.

No agency in the American military had clear authority over strategic planning. Only the navy had worked out an objective, and its objective had little to do with freeing Cuba. The assistant secretary of the navy in the McKinley administration was Theodore Roosevelt, ardent imperialist, active proponent of war, and uninhibited by the fact that he was a relatively minor figure in the military hierarchy. In consultations with naval officers, Roosevelt prepared to seize Spain's Philippine Islands in the far Pacific. He strengthened the Asiatic squadron and instructed its commander, Commodore George Dewey, to attack the Philippines in the event of war.

Immediately after war was declared, Dewey left the China coast and headed for Manila, where an aging Spanish fleet was stationed. On May 1 he steamed into Manila Bay, and as his ships prepared to pass down the line of anchored enemy vessels he uttered the first slogan of the war: "You may fire when ready, Gridley." When the firing was finished, the Spanish fleet was completely destroyed, one American sailor lay dead (of a heat stroke) and George Dewey, immediately promoted to admiral, had become the first hero of the war. The Spaniards still held Manila, and Dewey had no troops with which

to attack them. While he waited nervously, the American government assembled an expeditionary force to relieve him and take the city. On August 13, the Americans received the surrender of Manila. In the rejoicing over Dewey's victory, few Americans paused to note that the character of the war was being subtly altered. What had begun as a war to free Cuba was becoming a war to strip Spain of its colonies.

But Cuba was not to be left out of the war picture. Late in April, the American government learned that a Spanish fleet under Admiral Pascual Cervera had sailed for the west, presumably for a Cuban harbor. Cervera's antique armada was no match for the powerful American Atlantic squadron, as the Spanish government well knew. The Atlantic squadron, commanded by Admiral William T. Sampson, was expected to intercept and destroy Cervera before he reached his destination. But the Spaniard eluded his pursuers and slipped into Santiago harbor, on the southern coast of Cuba, where he was not discovered by the Americans until ten days after his arrival. Immediately the Atlantic fleet moved to bottle him up.

While the navy was monopolizing the first phases of the war, the War Department was trying to mobilize and train an army. The volunteer and National Guard units were collected near Chattanooga, Tennessee, while the regulars, plus the Rough Riders,

The Rough Riders
This volunteer cavalry regiment—organized in New York, commanded by Theodore Roosevelt, and christened the "Rough Riders"—was typical of the community-based, amateur military units with which the United States fought its first overseas conflict. (Culver Pictures)

Dewey in Manila, 1898
In this 1898 oil painting by Rufus Zogbaum, Commodore George Dewey stands on the observation platform of an American ship as it enters Manila Bay in the Philippines. Dewey's fleet of four cruisers and two gunboats quickly sank ten Spanish vessels and took control of the harbor, and with it the islands. (Vermont Travel Division)

were assembled at Tampa, Florida, under the command of General William R. Shafter. The entire mobilization process was conducted with remarkable inefficiency.

There were also racial conflicts. A large proportion of the American invasion force consisted of black soldiers. Some were volunteer troops put together by black communities in several states (although some governors refused to allow the formation of such units). Others were members of the four black regiments in the regular army, who had been stationed on the frontier to defend white settlements against Indians and were now transferred east to fight in Cuba. As the black soldiers traveled through the South toward the training camps, they chafed at the

rigid segregation that was imposed and occasionally openly resisted the restrictions. Black soldiers in Georgia deliberately made use of a "whites-only" park; in Florida, they beat a soda-fountain operator for refusing to serve them; in Tampa, white provocations and black retaliation led to a night-long riot that left thirty wounded. Although regiments and even troop ships were strictly segregated, black and white soldiers in the heat of battle often forgot the customary separation and fought together as equals. In some areas, black officers briefly took command of white troops.

The army's commanding general, Nelson A. Miles, veteran of the Civil War, had planned to train the troops until autumn, then to occupy Puerto Rico and, in conjunction with the Cuban rebels, attack Havana. But with a Spanish naval force at Santiago, plans hastily changed. In June, Shafter left Tampa with a force of 17,000 to take Santiago. The departure occurred amid scenes of fantastic incompetence, but it was efficiency itself compared to the landing. Five days were required to put the army ashore, and this with the enemy offering no opposition.

Once landed, Shafter moved his army toward Santiago, planning to surround and capture it. On the way he fought and defeated the Spaniards at the crossroads at Las Guasimas and, a week later, in two simultaneous battles, El Caney and San Juan Hill. In all the engagements the Rough Riders were in the middle of the fighting and on the front pages of the newspapers. Colonel Roosevelt, who had resigned from the Navy Department to get into the war and who had struggled with an almost desperate fury to ensure that his regiment made it to the front before the fighting ended, rapidly emerged as a hero of the conflict. His fame rested in large part on his role in leading a bold, even reckless charge up Kettle Hill (a charge that was a minor part of the larger battle for the adjacent San Juan Hill) directly into the face of Spanish guns. Roosevelt himself emerged unscathed, but nearly a hundred of his soldiers were killed or wounded. To the end of his life, he remembered the battle as "the great day of my life."

Having chased the Spaniards from the hills around Santiago, Shafter was now in position to assault the city. But his army was so weakened by sickness that he feared he might have to abandon his position. When he appealed to Sampson to unite with him in a joint attack on the city, the admiral answered that mines in the harbor made it too dangerous to take his big ships in. At this point, disaster seemingly confronted the Americans. But unknown to them, the

Spanish government had decided that Santiago was lost. On July 3, Cervera, acting under orders from home, broke from the harbor to attempt an escape that he knew was hopeless. The waiting American squadron destroyed his entire fleet. Shafter then pressed the Spanish army commander to surrender, and that official, after bargaining for generous terms, including free transportation back to Spain for his troops, turned over Santiago on July 16. While the Santiago campaign was in its last stages, an American army landed in Puerto Rico and occupied it against virtually no opposition.

Spain was defeated (more as a result of its own weakness and incompetence than because of American strength) and knew it. Through the French ambassador in Washington, the Spanish government asked for peace; and on August 12, an armistice ended the war.

Decision for Imperialism

The terms of the armistice confirmed what the military situation had already established. Spain recognized the independence of Cuba and ceded Puerto Rico (now occupied by American troops) to the

"Smoked Yankees"

Nearly one-fourth of the American invasion force in Cuba consisted of black soldiers, many of whom had already served with distinction in campaigns against Indians in the West. Spanish troops called them "smoked Yankees" and often looked on them with more respect than did their American commanders, who kept black troops in rigidly segregated regiments. In this painting members of the all-black Tenth Cavalry support a charge by the Rough Riders. Members of the Twenty-fourth and Twenty-fifth Negro Infantry Divisions played a crucial role at the battle of San Juan Hill.   (Library of Congress)

The American South Pacific Empire, 1900

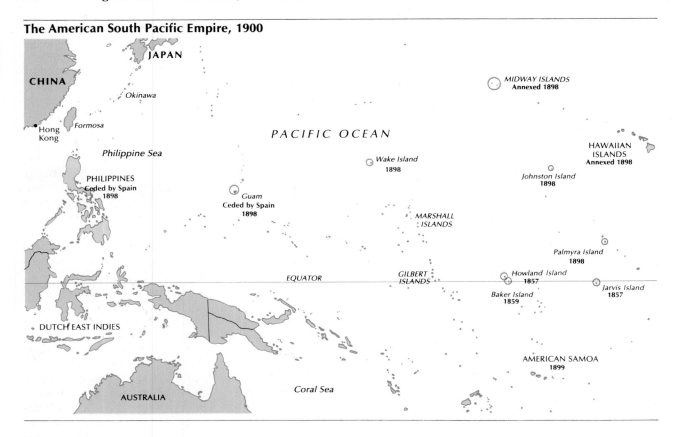

United States. It also ceded to the victor the Pacific island of Guam, midway between Hawaii and the Philippines, and agreed to permit the Americans to hold Manila pending the final disposition of the Philippines.

The uncertainty of the provisions concerning the Philippines did not reflect Spanish resistance. It reflected the confusion in the McKinley administration as to what to do about the islands the United States now occupied. There was little controversy about the annexation of Puerto Rico and Guam. Puerto Rico was close enough to the mainland to seem a tempting acquisition to almost everyone. And Guam seemed too small and insignificant to be worthy of dispute. But the Philippines constituted a large and important territory; and American annexation of it would mean a major change in the nation's position in the world.

McKinley weighed a number of options for dealing with the Philippines. Returning them to Spain was politically impossible. Granting the islands independence appealed to almost no one; Americans believed the Filipinos unfit to rule themselves.

Ultimately, McKinley decided that only actual annexation would do. He later said that he had arrived at his decision as a result of divine guidance, but growing popular sentiment for annexation in the country and the pressure of the imperialist leaders of his party undoubtedly influenced his thinking more.

In October 1898, commissioners from the United States and Spain met in Paris to negotiate a treaty formally ending the war. Spain readily agreed to recognize Cuba's independence, to assume the Cuban debt, and to cede Puerto Rico and Guam to the United States. Then the American commissioners, acting under instruction from McKinley, startled the conference by demanding the cession of all the Philippines. Stubbornly the Spanish resisted the American demand, although they realized they could retain the islands only by resuming the war. They yielded to the inevitable when the United States offered to pay $20 million for the islands. The Treaty of Paris was signed on December 10, 1898, and sent to the United States for ratification by the Senate.

When the treaty was submitted to the Senate, it

encountered immediate and fierce criticism and occasioned in that body and throughout the country one of those "great debates" that frequently precede a departure in American foreign policy. The chief point at issue was the acquisition of the Philippines, denounced by many, including prominent Republicans, as a repudiation of America's high moral position in the war and a shameful occupation of a land that wanted to be free.

The anti-imperialists were a varied and powerful group and included some of the nation's wealthiest and most powerful figures: Andrew Carnegie, John Sherman, Mark Twain, Samuel Gompers, and others. Their opposition to annexation stemmed from various motives. Some feared the "pollution" of the American population by introducing "inferior" Asian races into the national community. Industrial workers feared a flood of cheap laborers from the new colonies who would undercut their wages and take their jobs. Conservatives feared annexation would produce a large standing army and entangling foreign alliances, which would threaten American liberties. Certain economic interests (most notably sugar growers) feared the new territories would provide unwelcome competition. Many Democrats opposed annexation because they considered it a Republican tactic to enhance the party's prestige. Others saw in the annexation a repudiation of basic American principles of independence and self-determination: The United States could not impose colonial rule on other peoples without debasing its own democratic heritage.

The Anti-Imperialist League, established by upper-class Bostonians, New Yorkers, and others late in 1898 to fight against annexation, attracted a widespread following in the Northeast and waged a vigorous campaign against ratification of the Paris treaty. But the League, and the anti-imperialist movement as a whole, had a number of crippling weaknesses. Its appeal was limited for the most part to a few areas; it attracted little support in the West and the South. It suffered from internal divisions; some anti-imperialists opposed annexing any new possessions, while others opposed only the acquisition of the Philippines. Most important, however, the anti-imperialists, for all their strength, represented a distinct minority sentiment—both in the country and, of more immediate importance, in the Senate.

Favoring ratification was an equally varied group. There were the exuberant imperialists such as Theodore Roosevelt, who saw the acquisition of empire as a way to reinvigorate the nation, to keep alive the healthy, restorative influence of the war. "A nation cannot safely absorb itself in its own affairs," wrote one Midwestern annexationist. "It breeds strange and dangerous disorders." Other supporters of annexation included businessmen, who saw economic potential in the Philippines and believed annexation would position the United States to dominate the Oriental trade; shipbuilders and others, who stood to benefit from the creation of a larger navy, which the new empire would certainly require; the Protestant clergy, who saw in a colonial empire enlarged fields for missionary enterprise; and most Republicans, who saw clear partisan advantages in acquiring valuable new territories in the aftermath of a war fought and won by a Republican administration. Perhaps the strongest argument in favor of annexation, however, was the apparent ease with which it could be accomplished. The United States, after all, already possessed the islands as a result of its military triumph.

After weeks of bitter wrangling, the Senate ratified the treaty on February 6, 1899, but only because it received an unexpected assist from William Jennings Bryan, a fervent anti-imperialist, who expected to be his party's candidate again in the election of 1900. Bryan persuaded a number of Democratic senators to vote for ratification. Some charged that he was looking for a campaign issue, but Bryan claimed that he wanted only to end the war. The question of the Philippines could, he believed, be decided by a national referendum. If the Democrats won in 1900, they would free the islands.

If the election of 1900 was such a referendum, it proved beyond doubt that the nation had decided in favor of imperialism. Once again, Bryan ran against McKinley; and once again, Bryan went down to defeat—an even more crushing defeat than he had experienced four years earlier. It was not only the issue of the colonies, however, that ensured McKinley's victory. The Republicans effectively exploited the money and tariff issues; they harped on the continuing prosperity in the country under a Republican administration; and they exploited to the full the colorful personality of their vice-presidential candidate, the hero of San Juan Hill, Colonel Theodore Roosevelt.

The Republic as Empire

The new colonial empire was a small one by the standards of the great imperial powers of Europe.

But it spanned a vast area of the globe. It stretched from the Caribbean to the far reaches of the Pacific. It embraced Puerto Rico, Alaska, Hawaii, a part of Samoa, Guam, the Philippines, and a chain of minor Pacific islands.

But with the empire came new problems. Many of the predictions of the anti-imperialists proved accurate. Ultimately, as a colonial power, the United States had to maintain large stockpiles of armaments, concern itself with the complexities of Far Eastern international politics, and modify its traditional policy of holding aloof from alliances.

Governing the Colonies

A host of perplexing questions arose as the nation tried to decide how to administer its new possessions. Did Congress have to administer the colonies in accordance with the Constitution? Did the inhabitants of the new possessions have the rights of American citizens? Could Congress levy tariff duties on colonial imports? Or, in a phrase that pleased the public fancy, did the Constitution follow the flag? The Supreme Court suggested a solution in the so-called insular cases (*De Lima* v. *Bidwell, Downes* v. *Bidwell,* and others, 1900–1904), by distinguishing between "incorporated" and "unincorporated" territories. In legislating for "unincorporated" territories—the insular possessions—Congress had great latitude and need not be bound by all the provisions of the Constitution. The Constitution followed the flag, the Court implied, only if Congress so decided. The government could administer its colonies in almost any way it saw fit.

Three of the dependencies—Hawaii, Alaska, and Puerto Rico—received territorial status relatively quickly. A 1900 act granted American citizenship to all citizens of Hawaii, authorized an elective two-house legislature there, and vested executive authority in a governor appointed from Washington. Alaska (which had been purchased from Russia in 1869) was being governed by appointed civil officials. The discovery of gold there in 1896 caused the first substantial influx of Americans; and in 1912, Alaska received territorial status and a legislature, and its inhabitants were given the rights of citizenship. In Puerto Rico, the natives seemed readily to accept American rule. Military occupation of the island ended quickly, and a civilian government was established by the Foraker Act in 1900. The governor and upper house of the legislature were to be appointed from Washington,

while only the lower house was to be elected. The 1900 act did not grant Puerto Ricans American citizenship, but a 1917 law did. Smaller possessions in the empire received more arbitrary treatment. Guam and Tutuila came under the control of naval officials; and some of the small Pacific islands, containing only a handful of inhabitants, experienced no form of American government at all.

American military forces, commanded by General Leonard Wood, remained in Cuba until 1902 under orders to prepare the island for the independence promised in the peace treaty of 1898. The occupiers built roads, schools, and hospitals, reorganized the legal, financial, and administrative systems, and introduced far-reaching sanitary reforms. They also laid the basis for years of American domination of the island—a domination that ultimately would become as intolerable to the Cuban people as the Spanish rule against which they had first rebelled.

At Wood's urging, a convention assembled to draft a constitution for independent Cuba. The document contained no provisions concerning relations with the nation responsible for Cuba's freedom. Many Americans considered this a significant oversight, for the United States, with its expanding interests in the Caribbean, expected to exercise some kind of control over the island republic. In 1901, therefore, Congress passed the Platt Amendment, as a rider to an army appropriations bill, and pressured Cuba into incorporating the terms of the amendment into its constitution. The Platt Amendment declared that Cuba could make no treaties with any foreign powers (this was equivalent to giving the United States a veto over Cuba's diplomatic policy); that the United States had the right to intervene in Cuba to preserve Cuba's independence, life, and property; and that Cuba must sell or lease to the United States lands for naval stations. The amendment left Cuba only nominally independent. With American capital taking over the island's economy—investments jumped from $50 million in 1898 to $220 million by 1914— Cuba was in fact, if not in name, an American appendage.

The Philippine War

Americans did not like to think of themselves as imperial rulers in the European mold. Their mission, they believed, was different—to enlighten and reform the societies they had acquired, to improve the lives of their newly subjugated peoples. Yet like other imperial powers, the United States soon discovered that controlling a foreign colony required more than ideals; it required strength as well and often brutality. That, at least, was the lesson of the American experience in the Philippines, where American forces soon became engaged in a long and bloody war with insurgent forces fighting for independence.

The conflict in the Philippines is the least remembered of all American wars. It was also one of the longest (it lasted from 1898 to 1902) and one of the most vicious. It involved 200,000 American troops and resulted in 4,300 American deaths, nearly ten times the number who died in combat in the Spanish-American War. Controversy still rages over the number of Filipinos killed in the conflict, but it seems likely that over 50,000 of the natives died. (Some claim the number is far higher than that.) The American occupiers faced guerrilla tactics in the Philippines very similar to those the Spanish occupiers had faced

prior to 1898 in Cuba. And they soon found themselves drawn into the same pattern of brutality that had outraged so many Americans when employed by Weyler in the Caribbean.

The Filipinos had been rebelling against Spanish rule even before 1898, and they had hailed Admiral Dewey and the expeditionary force he sent to Manila as their deliverers from tyranny. When the hard fact sank in that the Americans had come to stay, the Filipinos resolved to expel the new invaders. Ably led by Emilio Aguinaldo, who claimed to head the legitimate government of the nation, Filipinos harried the American army of occupation from island to island for more than three years. At first, American commanders believed that the rebels represented only a small minority; but by early 1900, they were beginning to recognize otherwise. General Arthur MacArthur (father of Douglas), an American commander in the islands, wrote at the time:"I have been

Filipino Prisoners
American troops guard captured Filipino guerrillas in Manila. The suppression of the Filipino insurrection was a much longer and costlier military undertaking than the Spanish-American War, by which the United States first gained possession of the islands. By mid-1900 there were 70,000 American troops in the Philippines, under the command of General Arthur MacArthur (whose son, Douglas, won fame in the Philippines during World War II). (Library of Congress)

reluctantly compelled to believe that the Filipino masses are loyal to Aguinaldo and the government which he heads."

To MacArthur and others, however, that realization was not a reason to moderate American tactics or conciliate the rebels. It was a reason to adopt far more severe measures. And gradually, the American military effort became systematically vicious and brutal. Captured Filipino guerrillas were treated not as prisoners of war, but as murderers. Most were summarily executed. On some islands, entire communities were evacuated—the residents forced into concentration camps while American troops destroyed their villages, farms, crops, livestock, and everything else that might give sustenance to the "rebels." A spirit of savagery grew among American soldiers, who came to view the Filipinos as almost subhuman and at times seemed to take pleasure in killing almost arbitrarily. One American commander ordered his troops "to kill and burn, the more you kill and burn the better it will please me. . . . Shoot everyone over the age of 10." Over fifteen Filipinos were killed for every one wounded; in the Civil War—the bloodiest conflict in American history to that point—one person had died for every five wounded.

By 1902, reports of the brutality and the American casualties had soured the American public on the war. But by then, the rebellion had largely exhausted itself and the occupiers had established control over most of the islands. The key to their victory was the capture of Aguinaldo in March 1901 by five American soldiers who had used deception to enter the Filipino's remote camp in the mountains. They took Aguinaldo to Manila, where he signed a document urging his followers to stop fighting and declaring his own allegiance to the United States. (He then retired from public life and lived quietly until 1964.) Fighting continued in places for another year, and the war revived intermittently until as late as 1906; but American possession of the Philippines was now secure.

President McKinley had sent a special commission to the islands in 1900, under the direction of William Howard Taft, to establish a civilian government there; and in the summer of 1901, the military transferred final authority over the islands to'Taft, who became the first civilian governor. He announced that the American purpose was to prepare the islands for independence, and he oversaw the creation of a civilian government that gave the Filipinos broad local autonomy. The Americans also built roads, schools, bridges, and sewers; instituted major admin-istrative and financial reforms; and established a public health system. Filipino autonomy gradually increased; and on July 4, 1946, the islands finally won their independence.

The Open Door

The acquisition of the Philippines made the United States an Asian power and greatly increased American interest in the Far East, which had already grown strong as a result of the increasing trade with China. But other nations more experienced in the ways of empire were casting covetous eyes on China, ancient, enfeebled, and seemingly open to exploitation by stronger countries. By the turn of the century, the great European imperialistic powers—England, France, Germany, and Russia—and one Asian power—Japan—were beginning to partition China into "spheres of influence." One nation would force the Chinese government to grant it "concessions" for developing a particular area; another would use pressure to secure a long-term lease to a specific region. In some cases, the outside powers even asserted ownership of territory. The process, if continued, threatened to destroy American hopes for a vast trade with China.

The situation posed a delicate problem for the men directing American foreign policy. Knowing that public opinion would not support any use of force, they had to find a way to protect American interests in China without risking war. McKinley suggested the American answer in a statement in September 1898, when he said that the United States sought trade with China, but no special advantages there. "Asking only the open door for ourselves, we are ready to accord the open door to others." McKinley's secretary of state, John Hay, translated McKinley's words into policy a year later, in September 1899, when he addressed identical messages—what became known as the "Open Door notes"—to England, Germany, and Russia, and later to France, Japan, and Italy. The new policy that he asked them to approve embodied three principles: Each nation with a sphere of influence was to respect the rights and privileges of other nations in its sphere; Chinese officials were to continue to collect tariff duties in all spheres (the existing tariff favored the United States); and nations were not to discriminate against other nations in levying port dues and railroad rates within their own spheres.

The Open Door policy was appealing to the

Suppressing the Chinese Boxers, 1900

The aggressively nationalistic Boxers staged a revolt in the spring of 1900 in an attempt to expel from China the "foreign devils" who had taken control of much of the country's commerce. The Boxers occupied the Chinese capital, Peking, and laid siege to the compound containing the foreign legations. Nearly two months later, an international military expedition—containing American, British, and Japanese troops (and depicted here in a 1900 Japanese print)—expelled the Boxers from Peking and rescued the diplomats. (Library of Congress)

United States for a number of reasons. It would preserve at least the illusion of Chinese sovereignty, thus preventing formal colonial dismemberment of the empire. More important, it allowed the United States to trade freely with the Chinese without fear of interference and without the need for American military occupation.

Hay could hardly have expected an enthusiastic response to his notes, and he got none. Russia rejected the Open Door proposals, and the remaining powers gave evasive replies. Each one stated in effect that it approved Hay's ideas in principle but could make no commitment until the others had acted. Apparently, the United States had met a humiliating rebuff; but Hay boldly announced that since all the powers had accepted the principle of the Open Door, his government considered their assent to be "final and definitive." Although the American public applauded his diplomacy, Hay had won little more than a theoretical victory. Unless the United States was willing to resort to war, it could not prevent any nation that wanted to violate the Open Door from doing so.

No sooner had the diplomatic maneuvering over the Open Door ended than a secret Chinese society known as the Boxers instigated an uprising against foreigners in China. The movement came to a blazing climax when the Boxers and their supporters besieged the entire foreign diplomatic corps in the British embassy in Peking. At this point, the powers with interests in China decided to send an international expeditionary force to rescue the diplomats. The situation seemed to offer a perfect excuse to those nations with ambitions to dismember China.

The United States contributed 2,500 troops to the rescue force, which in August 1900 fought its way into Peking and broke the siege. McKinley and Hay had decided on American participation in order to secure a voice in the settlement of the uprising and to prevent the partition of China. Again Hay sent a note to the world powers. This time he called for the Open Door not only in the spheres of influence but in "all parts of the Chinese Empire." He also called for the maintenance of China's "territorial and administrative integrity," for a return to the situation preceding the rebellion. Hay won support for his approach from England and Germany and then induced the other participating powers to accept compensation from the Chinese for the damages the Boxer Rebellion had caused.

A Modern Military System

The war with Spain had revealed glaring deficiencies in the American military system. The greatest weakness had appeared in the army, but there had been an absence of coordination in the entire military organization that might have resulted in disaster had the United States been fighting a more powerful nation. After the war, McKinley appointed Elihu Root, an

SIGNIFICANT EVENTS

1868–1878 Cubans revolt against Spanish rule in Ten Years' War

1889 First Pan-American Congress meets

1890 Alfred Thayer Mahan publishes *The Influence of Sea Power upon History*

1893 Harrison signs annexation agreement with Hawaii, but Cleveland rejects it

1894 Wilson-Gorman Tariff on sugar ravages Cuban economy

1895 United States and Britain dispute Venezuelan boundary

Insurrection against Spanish begins in Cuba

1896 Alaska gold rush begins

1897 McKinley offers to mediate Cuban conflict; Spain refuses

1898 William Randolph Hearst publishes de Lôme letter

U.S. battleship *Maine* explodes in Havana harbor

Congress declares war on Spain (April 25)

Spanish army in Cuba retreats

Dewey captures Philippines

United States and Spain sign armistice (August 12)

1898 Treaty of Paris cedes Puerto Rico, Philippines, and other Spanish possessions to United States; recognizes Cuban independence

United States formally annexes Hawaii

Anti-Imperialist League formed

1898–1902 Philippines revolt against American rule

1899 Senate ratifies Treaty of Paris

Hay releases "Open Door notes"

1900 Foraker Act establishes civil government in Puerto Rico

Hawaii granted territorial status

Boxer Rebellion breaks out in China

McKinley reelected president

1901 Americans capture Emilio Aguinaldo in Philippines

Congress passes Platt Amendment

U.S. establishes civil government in Philippines

1912 Alaska given territorial status

1917 Puerto Ricans granted U.S. citizenship

1946 United States grants Philippines independence

extremely able administrator, as secretary of war to supervise a major overhaul of the armed forces. Between 1900 and 1903, Root put into effect, by congressional authorization or by executive order, a series of reforms that gave the United States what amounted to a new military system.

The Root reforms included a number of important provisions. They enlarged the regular army from its previous small size of about 25,000 to a maximum of 100,000. They established federal supervision of the National Guard, ensuring that never again would the nation fight a war with volunteer regiments over which the federal government had only limited control. They sparked the creation of a system of officer training schools, crowned by the Army Staff College (later the Command and General Staff School) at Fort Leavenworth, Kansas, and the Army War College at Washington. And they established, in 1903, a general staff headed by a chief of staff, to act as military adviser to the secretary of war.

It was this last reform that Root considered most important: the creation of a central planning agency modeled on the example of European staffs. The general staff was charged with many functions. It was to "supervise" and "coordinate" the entire army establishment, and it was to esablish an office that would plan for possible wars. An Army and Navy Board, on which both services were represented, was to foster interservice cooperation.

As a result of the new reforms, the United States entered the twentieth century with something resembling a modern military system. The country would have need of it, for the coming years would see the American role in the world constantly expanding.

SUGGESTED READINGS

General Studies A useful overview of late-nineteenth-century American foreign policy is Charles S. Campbell, *The Transformation of American Foreign Relations, 1865–1900* (1976). More succinct is Robert L. Beisner, *From the Old Diplomacy to the New, 1865–1900* (1975). Basic works on the expansionism of the 1890s and the early twentieth century include Julius W. Pratt, *Expansionists of 1898* (1936), long the standard work and still a valuable study; Albert K. Weinberg, *Manifest Destiny: A Study in Nationalist Expansionism in American History* (1935); and Walter LaFeber, *The New Empire* (1963). William Appleman Williams, *The Tragedy of American Diplomacy*, rev. ed. (1972), is a provocative interpretation of American foreign policy that begins with late nineteenth-century imperialism and emphasizes the economic motives for expansionism. Ernest May offers a more multidimensional view of the problem in *Imperial Democracy* (1961) and *American Imperialism: A Speculative Essay* (1968). Other general studies are David F. Healy, *U.S. Expansionism: Imperialist Urge in the 1890s* (1970); John Dobson, *America's Ascent: The United States Becomes a Great Power, 1880–1914* (1978); and H. Wayne Morgan, *America's Road to Empire* (1965). A collection of important essays is provided by J. A. S. Grenville and George Berkeley Young, *Politics, Strategy and American Diplomacy: Studies in Foreign Policy, 1873–1917* (1966). Background for this period is available in Milton Plesur, *America's Outward Thrust: Approaches to Foreign Affairs, 1865–1890* (1971), and David M. Pletcher, *The Awkward Years: American Foreign Relations under Garfield and Arthur* (1962).

The Spanish-American War David F. Trask, *The War with Spain in 1898* (1981), is a study of the conflict that precipitated America's imperial expansion. Other studies of the war include Frank Freidel, *The Splendid Little War* (1958), a pictorial work; Walter Millis, *The Martial Spirit* (1931); and Philip S. Foner, *The Spanish-Cuban-American War and the Birth of American Imperialism*, 2 vols. (1972), a revisionist study. Graham A. Cosmas, *An Army for Empire: The United States Army in the Spanish-American War* (1971), examines the performance of the army; Richard S. West, Jr., *Admirals of the American Empire* (1948), discusses the role of the navy. Richard Challener, *Admirals, Generals, and American Foreign Policy, 1889–1914* (1973), discusses the role of the military in policymaking. On race relations in the military, see two books by Willard B. Gatewood, Jr.: *Black Americans and the White Man's Burden, 1898–1903* (1975) and *"Smoked Yankees": Letters from Negro Soldiers, 1898–1902* (1971). Edmund Morris, *The Rise of Theodore Roosevelt* (1979), includes a colorful account of the future president's celebrated role in the Spanish-American War. Some of the domestic implications of the war are examined in Gerald F. Linderman, *The Mirror of War: American Society and the Spanish-American War* (1974).

Imperialism The active anti-imperialist movement is the subject of Robert L. Beisner, *Twelve Against Empire* (1968); E. Berkeley Tompkins, *Anti-Imperialism in the United States, 1890–1920: The Great Debate* (1970); and Thomas J. Osborne, *"Empire Can Wait": American Opposition to Hawaiian Annexation, 1893–1898* (1981). Frederick Merk, *Manifest Destiny and Mission in American History* (1963), is an important study of the forces in American history that produced the imperialist urge. Julius W. Pratt, *America's Colonial Empire* (1950), considers diplomatic activities at the end of the war and subsequent problems of imperial administration. James H. Hitchman, *Leonard Wood and Cuban Independence, 1898–1902* (1971), examines the American experience in Cuba in the aftermath of the war.

The Pacific Empire The experiences of the nation in administering its Pacific conquests are examined in Peter Stanley, *A Nation in the Making: The Philippines and the United States* (1974); Paul M. Kennedy, *The Samoan Tangle* (1974); Glenn May, *Social Engineering in the Philippines* (1980); and Merze Tate, *The United States and the Hawaiian Kingdom* (1965). On the Philippine insurrection, see Richard E. Welch, Jr., *Response to Imperialism: The United States and the Philippine-American War, 1899–1902* (1979); Leon Wolff, *Little Brown Brother* (1961); and Stuart Creighton Miller, *"Benevolent Assimilation": The American Conquest of the Philippines, 1899–1903* (1982). John Morgan Gates, *Schoolbooks and Krags: The United States Army in the Philippines, 1898–1902* (1971), examines the performance of the American military. Daniel B. Schirmer, *Republic or Empire? American Resistance to the Philippine War* (1972), examines domestic responses.

America and Asia America's role in the Far East is considered in several of the general works listed above; a more focused overview is James C. Thomsen, Jr., Peter W. Stanley, and John Curtis Perry, *Sentimental Imperialists: The American Experience in East Asia* (1981). Also valuable are Marilyn B. Young, *The Rhetoric of Empire* (1968); Warren Cohen, *America's Response to China*, rev. ed. (1980); Akira Iriye, *Across the Pacific* (1967) and *Pacific Estrangement: Japanese and American Expansion, 1897–1911* (1972); Robert McClellan, *The Heathen Chinese: A Study of American Attitudes Toward China* (1971); Charles Neu, *The Troubled Encounter* (1975), which examines American relations with Japan; and Paul Varg, *The Making of a Myth: The United States and China, 1897–1912* (1968) and *Missionaries, Chinese, and Diplomats* (1958).

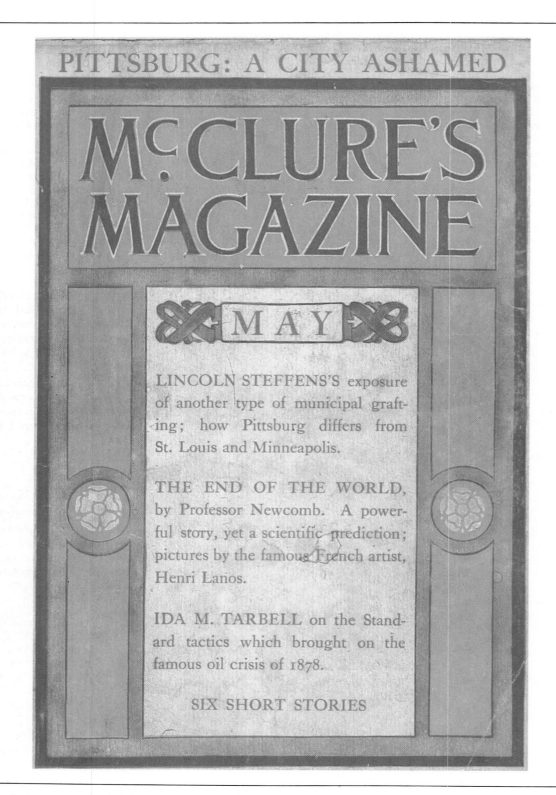

PITTSBURG: A CITY ASHAMED

M^cCLURE'S MAGAZINE

MAY

LINCOLN STEFFENS'S exposure of another type of municipal grafting; how Pittsburg differs from St. Louis and Minneapolis.

THE END OF THE WORLD, by Professor Newcomb. A powerful story, yet a scientific prediction; pictures by the famous French artist, Henri Lanos.

IDA M. TARBELL on the Standard tactics which brought on the famous oil crisis of 1878.

SIX SHORT STORIES

McClure's Magazine, May 1903   (Culver Pictures)

Chapter 21 The Rise of Progressivism

The last decades of the nineteenth century—and the tumultuous 1890s in particular—had a profound effect on the nation's social and political outlook. Well before 1900, a large number of Americans had become convinced that the rapid industrialization and urbanization and the other profound changes their nation was experiencing had created intolerable problems, that new measures would be necessary to impose order on the growing chaos and to curb industrial society's most glaring injustices. In the early years of the new century, that outlook acquired a name: progressivism.

Not even the progressives themselves could always agree on what the word really meant. To some, it suggested simply a broad cultural vision. To others, it meant a cluster of moral and humanitarian goals. To still others, it was a particular set of political reforms (and, later, a particular political party). At times, in fact, it seemed that virtually everyone had become a "progressive": middle-class reformers and machine bosses, big businessmen and small entrepreneurs, white segregationists and black activists, industrial workers and farmers, immigrants and immigration restrictionists. More than one historian has suggested that the word *progressive* ultimately came to mean so many different things to so many different people that it ceased to mean anything at all, that it should be dropped from our vocabulary. (See "Where Historians Disagree," pp. 598–599.)

Yet if progressivism was a phenomenon of remarkable scope and diversity, it was also one that rested on an identifiable set of central assumptions, assumptions that reflected both the hopefulness and the concern that were the legacy of the late nineteenth century. It was, first, an optimistic vision. Progressives believed, as their name implies, in the idea of progress. They believed that society was capable of improvement, even of perfection, that continued growth and advancement were the nation's destiny. There was in progressivism a heady, boisterous enthusiasm, a continuing excitement over possibilities.

But progressives believed, too, that growth and progress could not continue to occur recklessly, as they had in the nineteenth century. Order and stability, they claimed, were essential for social betterment. And direct, purposeful human intervention in social and economic affairs was essential to the creation of that order. The "natural laws" of the marketplace, and the doctrines of laissez faire and Social Darwinism that celebrated those laws, were not sufficient.

Progressives did not always agree on the form their intervention should take; but most believed that government could play an important role in the process. Only government could effectively counter the corrupt special interests that were responsible for social disarray. Only government could provide the services and the regulation that were necessary for future progress. It was essential, therefore, to rescue the nation's political institutions from the influence of corrupt party leaders and selfish interest groups; and it was vital that government expand its role in the society and in the economy. Not all progressive efforts required the assistance of government, but the broad reordering of society that most progressives believed necessary would be impossible without such aid.

────────WHERE HISTORIANS DISAGREE────────

Progressivism

There may be no issue in twentieth-century American historiography that has inspired more disagreement, even confusion, than the nature of progressivism.

Until about 1950, most historians were in general accord about the nature of the progressive "movement." It was, they generally agreed, just what it had said it was: a movement by the "people" to curb the power of the "special interests." In particular, it was a protest by an aroused citizenry against the corruption and excessive power of urban bosses, corporate moguls, and tame elected officials. Progressive reform, scholars argued, was an effort to restore power to the people, to revive political, economic, and social democracy.

In the early 1950s, however, a new interpretation emerged to challenge the traditional view. It retained the earlier view of progressivism as a largely political movement, but it offered a new explanation of who the progressives were and what they were trying to do. George Mowry, in *The California Progressives* (1951), described the reform movement in that state not as a protest by the mass of the people, but as an effort by a relatively small and privileged group of business and professional men to limit the overbearing power of large corporations and labor unions. Viewing themselves as natural social leaders, they resented their loss of political power to these new economic forces and envisioned reform as a way to restore both their economic fortunes and their social importance and self-esteem. Richard Hofstadter expanded on this idea in *The Age of Reform* (1955), in which he described progressives throughout the country as people suffering from "status anxiety"—old, formerly influential, upper-middle-class families seeking to restore their fading prestige by challenging the powerful new institutions that had begun to displace them. Like the Populists, Hofstadter suggested, the progressives were suffering from psychological, not economic, discontent.

The Mowry-Hofstadter thesis was for a time widely influential, but it was not without its critics. In particular, it received strong challenges from historians who disagreed with two of the basic assumptions of the interpretation. First, these scholars maintained, Mowry and Hofstadter were mistaken in examining progressivism purely in terms of its visible political leaders. It was a movement with a far broader social and economic base. Second, they claimed, progressive reformers were not expressing a vague psychological malaise but a clear recognition of their own self-interest. Beyond that, the new historians of progressivism often disagreed with one another as much as they disagreed with Mowry and Hofstadter.

Perhaps the harshest challenge to earlier interpretations came from the New Left historian Gabriel Kolko, whose influential 1963 study, *The Triumph of Conservatism*, dismissed the supposedly "democratic" features of progressivism as meaningless rhetoric and examined instead the impact of progressive economic reforms. Progressivism was, he agreed, an effort to regulate business. But it was not the "people" who were responsible for this regulation. It was the businessmen, who saw in government supervision a way to protect themselves from ruinous competition. Regulation, Kolko claimed, was "invariably controlled by the leaders of the regulated industry and directed towards ends they deemed acceptable or desirable"—ends, he suggested, that generally ran counter to the goals of economic democracy rather than enhancing them.

A somewhat more moderate challenge to the "psychological" interpretation of progressivism came from historians embracing a new "organizational" view of history. Samuel P. Hays was the first to suggest the approach, in *The Response to Industrialism, 1885–1914* (1957) and other writings. Hays argued that progressives were indeed businessmen, as Kolko had suggested. But their impulse was not so much naked self-interest as a broad desire to bring order and efficiency to political and hence economic life. The most important progressives, he claimed, were members of the upper class, who viewed a restoration of stability as essential to the preservation of their privileged position.

Even more influential was a 1967 study by Robert Wiebe, *The Search for Order, 1877–1920*. Wiebe saw progressivism as a response to the dislocations in American life that had resulted from a rapid change in the nature of the economy without a corresponding change in social and political institutions. Economic power was now lodged in large, national organizations, whereas social and

──WHERE HISTORIANS DISAGREE──

political life was centered primarily in local communities. The result was widespread disorder and unrest, culminating in the turbulent 1890s. Progressivism, Wiebe argued, was the effort of a "new middle class"—a class tied to the emerging national economy—to stabilize and enhance its position in society. It was, therefore, an attempt to impose order on the chaos of industrial society by replacing antiquated local institutions with modern, national organizations. Progressivism, in short, went far beyond politics. It was a widespread effort to reshape virtually all of American life.

Yet despite all the challenges to the original view of progressivism as a democratic movement, some historians continued to produce evidence that the reform phenomenon was indeed a movement of the people against vested interests—although some scholars identified the "people" somewhat differently than did earlier such interpretations. J. Joseph Huthmacher argued in 1962 that much of the force behind progressivism came from members of the working class, especially immigrants, who pressed for such reforms as workers' compensation and wage and hour laws. John P. Buenker strengthened this argument in *Urban Liberalism and Progressive Reform* (1973), which argued that political machines and urban "bosses" were important sources of reform energy and helped create twentieth-century liberalism.

David P. Thelen, in a 1972 study of progressivism in Wisconsin, *The New Citizenship*, offered an even broader challenge to both the "status anxiety" and the "conservatism-organizational" views. Thelen found a real clash between the "public interest" and "corporate privilege" in Wisconsin. The depression of the 1890s had mobilized a broad coalition of citizens of highly diverse backgrounds behind efforts to make both business and government responsible to the popular will. It marked the emergence of a new "consumer" consciousness that crossed boundaries of class and community, religion and ethnicity. As consumers, all citizens were affected by the policies of corporations, utilities, and railroads and, therefore, shared in the effort to limit their power. The movement, in short, corresponded quite closely to the progressive rhetoric of the time.

Another group of historians writing in the 1970s and 1980s tackled the question of the nature of progressivism less by looking at particular reformers or particular reforms than by trying to identify some of the broad processes of political change that had created the public battles of the era. Richard L. McCormick's *From Realignment to Reform* (1981), for example, studied political change in New York State and argued that the crucial change in this era was the decline of the political parties as the vital players in public life and the rise of interest groups working for particular social and economic goals. Progressivism, he and others have suggested, was not so much a coherent "movement" as part of a broader process of political adaptation to the realities of modern industrial society.

Given the range of disagreement over the nature of the progressive movement, it is hardly surprising that some historians have despaired of finding any coherent definition for the term at all. Peter Filene, for one, suggested in 1970 that the concept of progressivism as a "movement" had outlived its usefulness. "It is time," he suggested, "to tear off the familiar label and, thus liberated from its prejudice, see the history between 1890 and 1920 for what it was—ambiguous, inconsistent, moved by agents and forces more complex than a [single, uniform] progressive movement." Critics argued that Filene's view was an argument for abandoning the search for any historical meaning in the politics of the early twentieth century. But Daniel Rodgers, in an important 1982 article, "In Search of Progressivism," disagreed. Concluding a review of the new scholarship on the progressive era, he wrote: "Whether historians of the 1980s will call off the search for that great, overarching thing called 'progressivism' is hard to predict. Certainly historians working in the 1970s failed manifestly to find it. In recompense they found out a vast amount about the world in which the progressives lived and the structures of social and political power shifting so rapidly around them. To acknowledge that these are the questions that matter and to abandon the hunt for the *essence* of the noise and tumult of that era may not be, as Filene's first critics feared, to lose the whole enterprise of historical comprehension. It may be to find it."

The Progressive Impulse

Beyond these central premises, progressivism flowed outward in a number of different directions, embodying several different approaches to reform. One powerful impulse shaping many progressive efforts was the spirit of "antimonopoly," the fear of concentrated power and the urge to limit and disperse authority and wealth. That impulse had, of course, a long history in American life and had been central, most recently, to the demands of the Populists. Many progressives absorbed it as well, although they often turned it to more moderate purposes than some earlier antimonopolists had done.

A second progressive impulse was a belief in the importance of social cohesion: the belief that individuals are not autonomous but part of a great web of social relationships, that the welfare of any single person is dependent on the welfare of society as a whole. This impulse suggested both that individuals had responsibilities to their society, and that society had responsibilities to the individual. It marked an open rejection of the laissez-faire orthodoxies of the late nineteenth century.

And a third progressive impulse was a belief in organization and efficiency: a belief that social order was a result of intelligent social organization, a belief in the importance of process, a belief in the need for rational procedures to guide social and economic life. Society was too complex, many progressives believed, to be left in the hands of party bosses, untrained amateurs, old-fashioned institutions. A new breed of leaders and organizations would be necessary to guide America to its future.

These varied reform impulses were not entirely incompatible with one another; and they did not exist in completely separate worlds. Progressives made use, at different times and in different ways, of the whole range of ideas available to them as they tried to restore order and stability to their turbulent society.

The Muckrakers

Historians looking for a starting point for the rise of progressivism have often pointed to the rise of a group of crusading journalists, who in the late nineteenth and early twentieth centuries began to direct public attention at a wide range of social, economic, and political injustices.

They became known as the "muckrakers," after Theodore Roosevelt, in a fit of pique, accused one of them of doing nothing but raking up muck through his writings. And they were committed above all to uncovering scandal, corruption, and injustice and exposing it as widely as possible. The work of the muckrakers achieved an extraordinary impact beginning in the late nineteenth century—in part because of the birth of mass-circulation newspapers and magazines, but also because their work reinforced some of the other reform currents of their time.

At first, their major targets were the trusts and particularly the railroads, whom the muckrakers believed to possess excessive power and to be the source of enormous corruption. Exposés of the great corporate organizations began to appear as early as the 1860s, when Charles Francis Adams, Jr., and others published revelatory magazine articles about nefarious doings among the railroad barons. Such inquiries continued into the twentieth century—the most notable, perhaps, being Ida Tarbell's enormous and influential study of the Standard Oil trust (published as a two-volume book in 1904).

By the turn of the century, many of the muckrakers were turning their attention to government and particularly to the urban political machines. The most influential, perhaps, was Lincoln Steffens, a reporter for *McClure's* magazine, who traveled through much of the country in the first years of the century and produced a series of articles on municipal corruption that aroused a major public outcry. His portraits of "machine government" and "boss rule," his exposures of "boodlers" in cities as diverse as St. Louis, Minneapolis, Cleveland, Cincinnati, Chicago, Philadelphia, and New York, his tone of studied moral outrage (as reflected in the title of his series and of the book that emerged from it, *The Shame of the Cities*)—all combined to persuade urban reformers of the need for a militant response. The alternative to leaving government in the hands of corrupt party leaders, the muckrakers argued, was for the people themselves to take a greater interest in public life. Indeed, some journalists seemed less outraged at the bosses themselves than at the apathetic public that seemed not to care about the corruption occurring in their midst.

The muckrakers reached their peak in the first decade of the twentieth century, when they published startling exposés of a wide range of social and political problems. They investigated governments, labor unions, and corporations. They explored the problems of child labor, immigrant ghettoes, prostitution, and family disorganization. They denounced the waste and destruction of natural resources, the subjugation of women, even occasionally the oppression of blacks. By bringing problems to the attention of the public, and by presenting those problems with indignation and moral fervor, they helped inspire other Americans to take action against their problems. In the process, they themselves expressed some of the most basic progressive impulses: the opposition to monopoly; the belief in the need for social unity in the face of corruption and injustice; even at times the cry for efficiency and organization.

The Social Gospel

The moralistic tone of the muckrakers' exposés reflected one important aspect of the emerging progressive sentiment: the sense of social responsibility and the humanitarian concern for personal injustice. The pursuit of "social justice" became one of the central concerns of many progressive reformers. And perhaps the clearest expression of that concern emerged from an important segment of American religion, through the rise of what became known as the "Social Gospel." A powerful movement within American Protestantism (and, to a lesser extent, within American Catholicism and Judaism), the Social Gospel had emerged by the early twentieth century as a vigorous force in the effort to redeem the nation's cities. The Salvation Army, which had come to the United States from England, boasted a corps of 3,000 officers and 20,000 privates by 1900, offering both material aid and spiritual service to the urban poor. Ministers of many denominations, priests, and rabbis left traditional parish work to serve in the troubled cities, and their efforts soon became part of the folklore of their time. Edward Sheldon's *In His Steps* (1898), the story of a young minister who abandoned a comfortable post to work among the needy, sold more than 15 million copies and established itself as the most successful novel of the era.

Walter Rauschenbusch, a Protestant theologian from Rochester, New York, published a series of influential discourses on the possibilities for human salvation through Christian reform. To him, the message of Darwinism was not that the individual was engaged in a brutal struggle for survival of the fittest, but that all individuals should work for a humanitarian evolution of the social fabric. "Translate the evolutionary themes into religious faith," he wrote, "and you have the doctrine of the Kingdom of God." Some American Catholics seized on the 1893 publication of Pope Leo XIII's encyclical *Rerum Novarum* as justification for their own crusade for social justice. Catholic liberals such as Father John A. Ryan took to heart the pope's warning that "a small number of very rich men have been able to lay upon the masses of the poor a yoke little better than slavery itself. . . . No practical solution of this question will ever be found without the assistance of religion and the church." For decades, he worked to expand the scope of Catholic social welfare organizations.

The Social Gospel was never the dominant element in the movement for urban reform. Some of the most influential progressives dismissed it as irrelevant moralization; others viewed it as little more than a useful complement to their own work. But the engagement of religion with reform helped bring to progressivism a powerful moral component and a commitment to redeem the lives of even the lowliest residents. Walter Rauschenbusch captured some of both the optimism and the spirituality of the Social Gospel with his proud comment, after a visit to a New York slum known as Hell's Kitchen, where Christian reformers were hard at work: "One could hear human virtue cracking and crashing all around."

The Settlement House Movement

Not all efforts to redeem the urban masses were as openly moralistic as those of the advocates of the Social Gospel. The settlement house movement, in particular, combined a humanitarian compassion for the poor with a strong belief in the importance of scientific methods of social organization.

One of the strongest elements of much progressive thought was the belief in the influence of the environment on individual development. Social Darwinists such as William Graham Sumner had argued that people's fortunes reflected their inherent "fitness" for survival; most progressive theorists disagreed. Ignorance, poverty, even criminality, they argued, were not the result of inherent moral or genetic failings or of the workings of divine providence. They were, rather, the effects of an unhealthy environment. To elevate the distressed, therefore, required an improvement of the conditions in which they lived.

Of particular interest to such reformers were the urban immigrant ghettoes, which publicists such as Jacob Riis were exposing through vivid photographs and lurid descriptions. Riis himself adopted a callous approach to the problem; he urged the razing of the

Tenement Cigarmakers
Jacob Riis included this photograph, "Bohemian Cigarmakers at Work in Their Tenement," in his first major exposé of life in the immigrant ghettoes—*How the Other Half Lives* (1890). Riis was himself an immigrant. Born in Denmark, he arrived in New York in 1870 and for several years worked at the usual menial jobs open to newcomers. By the end of the decade, however, he was an established journalist; and after his work as a police reporter exposed him to conditions in the tenements, he developed the commitment that became his life's work: eliminating the slums of New York. (Museum of the City of New York)

most offensive slums without making any provision for the relocation of displaced residents. (Later, he became an advocate of immigration restriction.) Other progressives, however, responded more sensitively. Borrowing ideas from reform movements in Europe, especially England, committed men and women established settlement houses in immigrant neighborhoods.

The most famous American settlement house, and one of the first, was Hull House. It opened in 1889 in Chicago as a result of the efforts of Jane Addams, a college graduate who had studied briefly for a career in medicine; and it became a model for more than 400 similar institutions throughout the nation. Staffed by members of the middle class, these institutions sought to help immigrant families adapt to the language and customs of their new country. Settlement houses offered educational services, staged community events, built libraries, and in general tried to enhance the lives of their neighborhoods without adopting the stance of disapproving moral superiority that had hampered the success of earlier philanthropic efforts. But settlement houses often embodied, too, a belief

that middle-class Americans had a responsibility to impart their own values to immigrants and to teach them to adopt middle-class life styles. The name itself suggests their founders' outlook: The word *settlement* had connotations of the frontier; and settlement house workers saw themselves in many ways as people bringing civilization to the urban frontier.

Central to the settlement houses were the efforts of college women, who found in the movement an outlet for their growing demand for useful, professional work. The settlement houses provided them with an environment that society could view as "appropriate" for women: urban "homes" where workers helped immigrants to become better members of society. Also active in the settlement house movement were some middle-class blacks in Northern cities. They helped recent black arrivals from the rural South, to whom industrial cities were often as alien as they were to European immigrants, to adjust to urban life.

The settlement houses also helped to spawn another important institution of reform: social work—

another profession in which women were to play an important role. Workers at Hull House, for example, maintained a close relationship with the University of Chicago's pioneering work in the field of sociology; and a growing number of programs for the professional training of social workers began to appear in the nation's leading universities, partly in response to the activities of the settlements. The professional social worker combined a compassion for the poor with a commitment to the values of bureaucratic progressivism: scientific study, efficient organization, reliance on experts. The new profession produced elaborate surveys and reports, collected statistics, and published scholarly tracts on the need for urban reform.

The Allure of Expertise

As the emergence of the social work profession suggests, progressives involved in humanitarian efforts often placed high value on knowledge and expertise. Even nonscientific problems, they optimistically believed, could be analyzed and solved scientifically. The allure of expertise, in fact, became one of the most important aspects of many progressive efforts. Many reformers came to believe that only enlight-ened experts and well-designed bureaucracies could create the order that America so badly needed.

This belief found expression in innumerable ways, among them the writings of a new group of scholars and intellectuals. Unlike the Social Darwinists of the nineteenth century, these theorists were no longer content with merely justifying the existing industrial system. They spoke instead of the creation of a new civilization, one in which the expertise of scientists and engineers could be brought to bear on the problems of the economy and society. Among their most influential spokesmen was the social scientist Thorstein Veblen. Harshly critical of the industrial tycoons of the late nineteenth century—the "leisure class" as he satirically described them in his first major work, *A Theory of the Leisure Class* (1899)—Veblen proposed instead a new economic system in which power would reside in the hands of highly trained engineers. Only they, he argued, could fully understand the "machine process" by which modern society must be governed. Only they could provide the efficiency and order necessary for the industrial economy. By the end of his life, Veblen was calling for government by a "soviet of technicians," who would impose on the economy their own instinct for rational process.

In practical terms, the impulse toward expertise

"A Shortcut over the Roofs of Tenements"
This 1908 photograph by Jesse Tarbox Beals shows a nurse in New York's Henry Street Settlement maneuvering across tenement rooftops on her way to bring help to the poor. Residents of the tenements often used this route to avoid the dirty and congested streets below. (Museum of the City of New York)

and organization helped produce the idea of scientific management, or "Taylorism." (See p. 500.) It encouraged the development of modern mass-production techniques and, above all, the assembly line. It inspired a revolution in American education and the creation of a whole new area of inquiry—social science, the use of scientific techniques in the study of society and its institutions. It produced a generation of bureaucratic reformers concerned with the structure of organizations and committed to building new political and economic institutions capable of managing a modern society. It helped as well to create a movement toward organization among the expanding new group of middle-class professionals.

The Professions

The late nineteenth century had seen not only a growth of the industrial work force but also a dramatic expansion in the number of Americans engaged in administrative and professional tasks. Industries needed managers, technicians, and accountants as well as workers. Cities required a growing range of commercial, medical, legal, and educational services. The demand for technology required scientists and engineers who, in turn, required institutions and instructors to train them. The industrial state, in short, had produced an enormous new infrastructure of specialized, professional services. And by the turn of the century, those performing these services had come to constitute a distinct social group—what some have called a new middle class.

Unlike the older middle class, whose position in society often derived from family background and stature within the local community, the new middle class placed a far higher value on education and individual accomplishment. By the early twentieth century, its millions of members were hard at work building organizations and establishing standards to secure and stabilize their position in society.

As their vehicle, they created the modern, organized professions. The idea of professionalism had been a frail one in America even as late as 1880. When every patent-medicine salesman could call himself a doctor, when every frustrated politician could proclaim himself a lawyer, when anyone who could read and write could present himself as a teacher, it was clear that a professional label would by itself carry little weight. There were, of course, skilled and responsible doctors, lawyers, teachers, and others; but they had no way of controlling the charlatans and

other incompetents who presumed to practice their trades. As the demand for services increased, so did the pressures, from both within and without, for reform.

Among the first to respond was the medical profession. Throughout the 1890s, doctors who considered themselves true professionals—who had had formal training in medicine, who understood the new scientific discoveries that were revolutionizing their methods—began forming local associations and societies. In 1901, finally, they reorganized the American Medical Association into a modern, national, professional society. Between 1900 and 1910, membership increased from 8,400 to over 70,000; by 1920, nearly two-thirds of all American doctors were members. The first major effort of the AMA was to insist on strict, scientific standards for admission to the practice of medicine, with doctors themselves serving as protectors of the standards. State and local governments readily complied, passing new laws that required the licensing of all physicians and restricting licenses to those practitioners approved by the profession.

Accompanying the emphasis on strict regulation of the profession came a concern for rigorous scientific training and research. By 1900, medical education at a few medical schools—notably Johns Hopkins in Baltimore (founded in 1893)—compared favorably with that in the leading institutions of Europe. Doctors such as William H. Welch at Hopkins revolutionized the teaching of medicine by moving students out of the classrooms and into laboratories and clinics. Rigorous new standards forced many inadequate medical schools out of existence, and those that remained were obliged to adopt a strict scientific approach.

There was similar movement in other professions. By 1916, lawyers in all forty-eight states had established professional bar associations; and virtually all of them had succeeded in creating central examining boards, composed of lawyers, to regulate admission to the profession. Increasingly, aspiring lawyers found it necessary to enroll in graduate programs, and the nation's law schools accordingly expanded greatly, both in numbers and in the rigor of their curricula. Businessmen supported the creation of schools of business administration and created their own national organizations: the National Association of Manufacturers in 1895 and the United States Chamber of Commerce in 1912. Even farmers, long the symbol of the romantic spirit of individualism, responded to the new order by forming, through the National Farm Bureau Federation, a network of agricultural organizations designed to spread scientific farming methods, teach sound marketing techniques, and lobby for the interests of their members.

Among the most important purposes of the new professionalism was restricting entry into the professions. Professional organizations established rigorous standards for certifying new members and strove to keep control of admission in the hands of the professionals themselves. This was partly an effort to defend the professions from the untrained and incompetent; and the admission procedures served a valuable and important service in keeping out many of the inept doctors, lawyers, and others who had tainted the reputation of their fields in the past. But the admission requirements also served less altruistic purposes: to defend those already in the profession from excessive competition and to lend prestige and status to the professional label. Some professions used their entrance requirements to exclude blacks, women, immigrants, and other "undesirables" from their ranks. Others used them simply to keep the numbers down, to ensure that demand for the services of existing members would remain high.

Women and the Professions

American women found themselves excluded—both by custom and by active barriers of law and prejudice—from most of the emerging professions. But a substantial number of middle-class women—particularly those emerging from the new female colleges and from the coeducational state universities—were beginning to enter professional careers nevertheless.

A few women managed to establish themselves as physicians, lawyers, engineers, scientists, and corporate managers. Most, however, turned by necessity to those professions that society had somehow decided were "suitable" for women. The settlement houses and social work provided two "appropriate" professional outlets for women. The most important, however, was teaching. Indeed, in the late nineteenth century, more than two-thirds of all grammar school teachers were women; and perhaps 90 percent of all professional women were teachers. For educated black women, in particular, teaching was often the only professional opportunity they could hope to find. The existence of a large network of segregated black schools in the South created a substantial market for black teachers.

In many ways, the teaching profession behaved in

Maine School, c. 1900
With the growth of public schools in the late nineteenth century, women came to dominate a new profession: teaching. (Culver Pictures)

these years much like other professions. It established new entrance requirements, policed by teachers' organizations, to restrict entry to those qualified to teach. A growing network of teachers' colleges and schools of education emerged in the late nineteenth century to service the profession. And the National Education Association, founded in 1905, fought for, among other things, a government licensing process for teachers.

Women also came to dominate other activities that were beginning to achieve professional status. Nursing had become primarily a women's field when it was still considered a menial occupation, akin to domestic service. But by the early twentieth century, it too was adopting professional standards. Prospective nurses generally needed certification from schools of nursing and could not simply learn on the job. Women also found opportunities as librarians, another field beginning to define itself in modern, professional terms. And many women entered academia—often receiving advanced degrees at such predominantly male institutions as the University of Chicago, MIT, or Columbia, but usually finding professional opportunities in the new and expanding women's colleges.

The "women's professions" had much in common with other professions: the value they placed on training and expertise, the creation of professional organizations and a professional "identity," the monitoring of admission to professional work. But they also had distinctive qualities that set them apart from the male professional world. They tended to involve activities that society could associate with traditionally female roles. Teaching, nursing, library work, and others were "helping" professions. They involved working primarily with other women or with children. Their activities occurred in places that seemed different from the offices that dominated the predominantly male business and professional worlds; such places as schools, hospitals, and libraries had a vaguely "domestic" image.

The Clubwomen

The great majority of American women did not take up professional careers. But even those who did not found ways to play an active role in the effort to remake society. In the vanguard of many progressive social reforms was a large network of women's associations that proliferated rapidly beginning in the 1880s and 1890s. Large numbers of women gravitated to the growing temperance movement. (See below, pp. 612–613.) Others turned to the new women's clubs.

The women's clubs began largely as cultural organizations to provide middle- and upper-class women with an outlet for their intellectual energies. Gradually, however, they turned their attention to public matters and embraced a substantial reform agenda. In 1892, when women formed the General Federation of Women's Clubs to coordinate the activities of local organizations, there were more than 100,000 members in nearly 500 clubs. Eight years later, there were 160,000 members; and by 1917, over 1 million.

By the early twentieth century, the clubs were becoming less concerned with cultural activities and more concerned with making a contribution to social betterment. Much of what they did was uncontroversial: planting trees; supporting schools,

libraries, and settlement houses; building hospitals and parks. But clubwomen were not afraid to take positions on controversial public issues, and they adopted resolutions supporting such measures as child labor laws, worker compensation, pure food and drug legislation, and—beginning in 1914—woman suffrage. Because club members were so often from wealthy families, the organizations often had ample funds at their disposal and could make their influence felt.

Black women occasionally joined clubs dominated by whites. But blacks formed a network of clubs of their own, which also affiliated with the General Federation. They modeled themselves primarily on their white counterparts, but some black clubs also took positions on issues of particular concern to blacks. Some crusaded against lynching and called for congressional legislation to make lynching a federal crime. Others protested aspects of segregation.

The women's club movement raised few overt challenges to prevailing assumptions about the proper role of women in society. But it did represent an important effort by women to extend their influence beyond their traditional sphere within the home and the family. Few clubwomen were willing to accept the arguments of such committed feminists as Charlotte Perkins Gilman, who in her 1898 book *Women and Economics* argued that the traditional definition of sexual roles was exploitive and obsolete. The club movement, rather, allowed women to define a space for themselves in the public world without openly challenging the existing, male-dominated order.

But the importance of the club movement did not lie simply in what it did for middle-class women. It lay also in what those women did for the working-class people they attempted to help. The women's club movement was an important force in winning passage of state (and ultimately federal) laws that regulated the conditions of woman and child labor, that established government inspection of workplaces, that regulated the food and drug industries, and that applied new standards to urban housing.

In many of these efforts, the clubwomen formed alliances with other women's groups. Among them was the Women's Trade Union League, founded in 1903 by female union members and upper-class reformers and committed to persuading women to join unions. In addition to working on behalf of protective legislation for woman workers, WTUL members held public meetings on behalf of female workers, raised money to support strikes, marched on picket lines, and bailed woman strikers out of jail.

The Assault on the Parties

Sooner or later, most progressive goals required the involvement of government. Social workers wanted laws to protect woman and child workers and to improve conditions in the ghettoes. Professionals advocated legal standards for admission to the practice of law or medicine. Others urged legislative solutions to such problems as the power of trusts or the destructive effects of cutthroat competition. Only government, progressives agreed, could provide the centralized regulation and control necessary to impose order and justice on modern society.

But American government at the dawn of the new century was, progressives believed, peculiarly ill adapted to perform these ambitious tasks. At every level, political institutions were outmoded, inefficient, often corrupt. Before society could be effectively reformed, it would be necessary to reform government itself. In the beginning, at least, many progressives considered one of their principal goals to be an assault on the domination of government and politics by the political parties, which they considered corrupt, undemocratic, and reactionary.

Early Attacks

Attacks on party dominance had emerged repeatedly in the late nineteenth century. Such third-party movements as Greenbackism and Populism had been, at least in part, efforts to break the hammerlock with which the Republicans and Democrats controlled public life. The Independent Republicans (or mugwumps; see p. 551) had attempted to challenge the grip of partisanship; and the mugwumps, in fact, became one of the important cores of progressive political reform activity in the 1890s and later.

The early assaults enjoyed some success. In the 1880s and 1890s, for example, most states adopted the secret ballot. Prior to that, the political parties themselves had printed ballots (or "tickets"), which they distributed to their supporters, who then simply went to the polls to deposit their "tickets" in the ballot box. The old system had made it possible for bosses to monitor the voting behavior of their constituents; it had also made it difficult for voters to "split" their tickets—to vote for candidates of different parties for different offices. The new secret ballot—printed by the government and distributed at the polls to be filled out and deposited in secret—helped chip away at the power of the parties over the voters.

By the late 1890s, critics of the parties had expanded their goals and were beginning to challenge directly some of the structures of government that they believed made possible the existence of bosses. Party rule could be broken, they believed, in one of two ways. It could be broken by increasing the power of the people, by permitting them to circumvent partisan institutions and express their will directly at the polls. Or it could be broken by placing more power in the hands of nonpartisan, nonelective officials, insulated from political life. Reformers promoted measures that moved along both those paths.

Municipal Reform

It was in the cities, many progressives believed, that the impact of party rule was most damaging. And it was municipal government, therefore, that became the first target of those working for political reform. Settlement houses, social workers, and scholars all attempted to focus attention on urban problems and the need for governmental changes to combat them. And muckraking journalists (see above, pp. 600–601) were especially successful in arousing public outrage at the rampant corruption and incompetence in city politics.

The muckrakers struck a responsive chord among a powerful group of urban middle-class progressives. For several decades after the Civil War, "respectable" citizens of the nation's large cities had avoided participation in municipal government. Viewing politics as a debased and demeaning activity, they shrank from contact with the "vulgar" elements who were coming to dominate public life. By the end of the century, however, a new generation of activists—some of them members of old aristocratic families, others a part of the new middle class—were taking a renewed interest in government. The nineteenth-century middle class had abdicated control of politics to the party organizations and the urban masses they manipulated; the twentieth-century middle class, appalled by the abuses and failures that had ensued, would win it back.

They faced a formidable array of opponents. In addition to challenging the powerful city bosses and their entrenched political organizations, they were attacking a large group of special interests: saloon owners, brothel keepers, and perhaps most significantly, those businessmen who had established cozy and lucrative relationships with the urban machines and viewed reform as a threat to their profits. Allied with these interests were many influential newspapers, which ridiculed the reformers as naïve do-gooders or prigs. Finally, there was the great constituency of urban working people, mostly of immigrant origin, to whom the machines were a source of needed services. To them, the progressives often seemed to be middle-class prudes attempting to impose an alien and unappealing life style. Gradually, however, the reformers gained in political strength—in part because of their own growing numbers, in part because of the conspicuous failures of the existing political leadership. And in the first years of the twentieth century, they began to score some important victories.

One of the first major successes came in Galveston, Texas, where the old city government collapsed in ineffectuality in the wake of a destructive tidal wave in 1900. Capitalizing on public dismay, reformers (many of them local businessmen) won approval of a new city charter. The mayor and council were replaced by an elected, nonpartisan commission whose five members would jointly enact ordinances and individually run the main city departments. In 1907, Des Moines, Iowa, adopted its own version of the commission plan, and other cities soon followed. Another approach to reform, similarly motivated by the desire to remove city government from the hands of the parties, was the city-manager plan, by which elected officials hired an outside expert—often a professionally trained business manager or engineer—to take charge of the government. Responsible not to the voters but to the councilors or commissioners who appointed him, the city manager would presumably remain untainted by the corrupting influence of politics. Staunton, Virginia, was one of the first municipalities to hire a city manager, in 1908. Five years later, Dayton, Ohio, attracted wider attention to the device when it adopted the new system after a major flood. By the end of the progressive era, almost 400 cities were operating under commissions, and another 45 employed city managers.

The commission governments and the city-manager systems removed municipal administration from party politics altogether. In most urban areas, and in the larger cities in particular, reformers had to settle for less absolute victories. They attempted to reform municipal elections in various ways. Some cities made the election of mayors nonpartisan (so that the parties could not choose the candidates) or moved them to years when no presidential or congressional races were in progress (to reduce the influence of the large turnouts that party organizations produced on such occasions). Reformers tried to make city councilors run at large, to limit the influence of ward leaders and district bosses. They tried to strengthen the power of the mayor at the expense of the city council, on the assumption that reformers were more likely to succeed in getting a sympathetic mayor elected than to win control of the entire council.

Some of the most successful reformers emerged not from the new commission and city-manager systems but from conventional political structures that progressives came to control. Tom Johnson, the celebrated reform mayor of Cleveland, waged a long and difficult war against the powerful streetcar interests in his city, fighting to raise the ridiculously low assessments on railroad and utilities properties, to lower streetcar fares to 3 cents, and ultimately to impose municipal ownership on certain basic utilities. After Johnson's defeat and death, his talented aide Newton D. Baker won election as mayor and helped maintain Cleveland's reputation as the best-governed city in America. Hazen Pingree of Detroit, Samuel "Golden Rule" Jones of Toledo, and other mayors effectively challenged local party bosses to bring the spirit of progressivism into city government.

Statehouse Progressivism

Often frustrated in their assault on boss rule in the cities, many progressives turned to state government as an agent for reform. Crusading district attorneys such as Hiram Johnson in California and Joseph W. Folk in Missouri left their cities to become reform governors. Elsewhere, progressive leaders arrived in the statehouse by other routes. Whatever their backgrounds, however, such reformers agreed that state government must take a leading role in the task of stabilizing American life.

State-level progressives agreed on the unfitness of existing state governments to provide reform. They looked with particular scorn on state legislatures, whose ill-paid, relatively undistinguished members were, they believed, generally incompetent, often corrupt, and totally controlled by party bosses. In the face of the debasement of the legislatures, they argued, it was necessary to circumvent the parties and return power directly to the people.

The result was a wave of reforms in state after state that attempted to "democratize" state government by limiting the influence of party organizations and the authority of elected officials, and increasing the influence of the electorate. Two of the most important changes were innovations first proposed by leaders of the Populist movement in the 1890s: the initiative and the referendum. The initiative gave reformers the ability to circumvent their legislatures altogether by submitting legislation directly to the voters in general elections. The referendum provided a method by which actions of the legislature could be returned to the electorate for approval. Oregon, in 1902, became the first state to enact such reforms. By 1918, nineteen other states had followed.

Progressives also attempted to improve the quality of elected officials, and for this purpose they created two more devices designed to limit the influence of traditional party politics: the direct primary and the recall. The primary election was an attempt to limit the influence of party machines on the selection of candidates. The recall gave voters the right to remove a public official from office at a special election, which could be called after a sufficient number of citizens had signed a petition. Mississippi adopted the nation's first direct primary in 1902, and by 1915 every state in the nation had instituted primary elections for at least some offices. The recall encountered more strenuous opposition. No progressive measure so horrified conservatives as this effort to subject officeholders to voter censure before the end of their terms, and they blocked the adoption of the recall more effectively than any other reform.

Other reform measures attempted to clean up the legislatures themselves by limiting the influence of corporations on their activities and on the behavior of the parties. Between 1903 and 1908, twelve states passed laws restricting lobbying in state legislatures by business interests. In those same years, twenty-two states banned campaign contributions by corporations, and twenty-four states forbade public officials from accepting free passes from railroads.

Reform efforts proved most effective in states that elevated vigorous and committed politicians to positions of leadership. In New York, Governor Charles Evans Hughes exploited progressive sentiment to create a commission to regulate public utilities. In California, Governor Hiram Johnson used the new reforms to limit the political power of the Southern Pacific Railroad in the state. In New Jersey, Woodrow Wilson, the Princeton University president elected governor in 1910, used executive leadership to win a substantial array of reforms designed to end New Jersey's widely denounced position as the "mother of trusts."

Charles Evans Hughes

Hughes's father, a Welsh immigrant and itinerant Baptist minister in upstate New York, helped instill in his son the evangelistic belief that happiness lay in the performance of duty. So when Hughes received invitations in 1905 to head first an investigation of public utilities in New York and then an inquiry into the scandal-ridden insurance industry, he felt obliged to accept. Hughes was relentless in his exposure of corporate wrongdoing and equally diligent in working for legislative solutions. His activities made him a hero to New York reformers; and in 1906, at the urging of Theodore Roosevelt, he ran for—and won—the governorship. In later years he served as an associate justice of the United States Supreme Court, Republican candidate for president, secretary of state, and—from 1930 to 1941—chief justice of the United States Supreme Court. Hughes's official portrait, seen here, hangs in the Supreme Court building in Washington. (U.S. Supreme Court)

The Laboratory of La Follette

The state that virtually all progressives came to view as the nation's leading center of reform was Wisconsin, the home of the great progressive hero Robert M. La Follette. La Follette had begun his career in Wisconsin as a conservative defender of free enterprise against its "radical" challengers. By the end of the 1890s, however, he had become convinced of the need for major reforms to curb the power of bosses, railroads, trusts, and financiers—the special interests that were, he argued, corrupting American life. Above all, perhaps, he had become convinced of the need for an alternative to the dominance of the traditional party organizations. Elected governor in 1900, he called for a new concept of politics: as the vehicle for enhancing the public interest, rather than as an arena in which special interests contended for favors.

In the years that followed, La Follette and his supporters turned Wisconsin into what reformers across the nation described as a "laboratory of progressivism." The Wisconsin progressives won approval of direct primaries, initiatives, and referendums. They secured the effective regulation of railroads and utilities. They obtained the passage of laws to regulate the workplace and provide compensation for laborers injured on the job. They instituted graduated taxes on inherited fortunes, and they nearly doubled state levies on railroads and other corporate interests.

La Follette brought to progressivism his own fervent, almost evangelical, commitment to reform; and he used his charismatic leadership to widen public awareness of progressive goals and to mobilize the energies of many previously passive groups. Reform was not simply the responsibility of politicians, he argued, but of newspapers, citizens' groups, educational institutions, and business and professional organizations. Progressivism, he suggested, must become a part of the fabric of American life. Ultimately, La Follette would find himself overshadowed by other national progressive leaders. In the early years of the century, however, few men were as effective in publicizing the message of reform. None was as successful in bending state government to that goal.

Parties and Interest Groups

The result of these reforms was not, of course, the elimination of party from American political life. Party organizations and party bosses remained enormously powerful for many years to come. But the many political reforms of the late nineteenth and early twentieth centuries did diminish the centrality of the parties in American life. By removing control of the

Robert La Follette Campaigning in Wisconsin
After three terms as governor of Wisconsin, La Follette began a long career in the United States Senate in 1906 during which he worked uncompromisingly for advanced progressive reforms—so uncompromisingly, in fact, that he was often almost completely isolated. He entitled a chapter of his autobiography "Alone in the Senate." La Follette had a greater impact on his own state, whose politics he and his sons dominated for nearly forty years and where he was able to win passage of many of the reforms that the federal government resisted. (State Historical Society of Wisconsin)

electoral process from the hands of party leaders and placing it more securely with the government, reformers were beginning to wean Americans away from their once fervent party loyalties.

Evidence of that came from, among other things, the decline in voter turnout. In the late nineteenth century, up to 81 percent of eligible voters normally turned out for national elections. In the early twentieth century, while turnout remained very high by today's standards, the figure began to decline markedly. In the presidential election of 1900, 73 percent of the electorate voted. Four years later, the figure had dropped to 65 percent. By 1912, it had declined to about 59 percent. There were fluctuations from year to year, but never again did voter turnout reach as high as 70 percent.

At the same time that the influence of the parties was declining, another force was beginning to establish its power in American politics: what have become known as "interest groups." Indeed, one of the reasons for the assault on the parties had been the conviction of an increasing number of groups that they needed other avenues through which to influence the government. Beginning late in the nineteenth century and accelerating rapidly in the twentieth, a wide range of new organizations emerged, operating outside the party system, designed to pressure government to do the bidding of their members: trade associations, representing particular businesses and industries; labor organizations; farm lobbies; and many others. The new professional organizations saw as one of their central purposes lobbying in Washington and in state capitals for the interests of their members. Social workers, the settlement house movement, the women's clubs, and others learned to operate as interest groups to advance their demands.

Reform by Machine

One result of the assault on the parties was a change in the party organizations themselves, which attempted to adapt to the new realities so as to preserve their influence. Indeed, some of the most powerful party machines emerged from the progressive era almost as powerful as they had entered it. In large part, this was because the bosses themselves, who were usually intelligent men, recognized that they must change in order to survive. Thus they sometimes allowed their machines to become vehicles of social reform. The best example was New York's Tammany Hall, the nation's oldest and most notorious

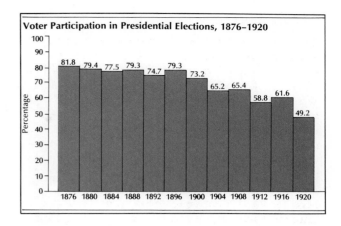

Voter Participation in Presidential Elections, 1876–1920

city machine. Its astute leader, Charles Francis Murphy, began in the early years of the century to fuse the techniques of boss rule with some of the concerns of social reformers. In the process, he ushered his organization into one of the most successful eras in its history.

Murphy did nothing to challenge the fundamental workings of Tammany Hall. The machine continued to mobilize working-class immigrant voters to support its candidates; it continued to offer them favors and services in return; its members continued to use patronage and even graft to strengthen their positions and expand their bank accounts. At the same time, however, Tammany began to take an increased interest in state and national politics, which it had traditionally scorned; and it used its political power on behalf of legislation to improve working conditions, protect child laborers, and eliminate the worst abuses of the industrial economy.

In 1911, a sudden fire swept the factory of the Triangle Shirtwaist Company in New York; 146 workers, most of them women, died. Many of them had been trapped inside the building because management had locked the emergency exits to prevent malingering. It was the worst industrial tragedy in the city's history, and the outrage it produced echoed across the nation. For the next three years, a broad-based state commission studied not only the background of the fire but the general condition of the industrial workplace; and by 1914, it had issued a series of reports calling for major reforms in the conditions of modern labor.

The report itself was a classic progressive document, based on the testimony of experts, replete with statistics and technical data. Yet when its recommendations reached the New York legislature, its most

The Triangle Fire
Policemen and investigators stand amid the coffins of victims of the 1911 fire in the Triangle Shirtwaist Factory in New York, in which 146 workers (almost all of them women) died. Although the proprietors of the factory were acquitted of criminal charges in the deaths, the fire spurred reform groups—most notably the International Ladies Garment Workers Union—to agitate for government action to improve conditions in the sweatshops.   (Culver Pictures)

effective supporters were not middle-class progressives but two Tammany Democrats: Senator Robert F. Wagner and Assemblyman Alfred E. Smith. With the support of Murphy and the backing of other Tammany legislators, they steered through a series of pioneering labor laws that imposed strict regulations on factory owners and established effective mechanisms for enforcement. Tammany Hall, the incarnation of evil in the eyes of many progressives, had itself become a potent agent for reform.

Crusades for Order and Reform

A striking aspect of American political life in the progressive era was the existence of a series of impassioned crusades on behalf of particular reforms that would, their supporters claimed, serve to remake the nation. Progressives crusaded to eliminate alcohol from national life, to stop the flood of immigrants, to win women the vote, to reshape the industrial economy. Proponents of each of those reforms believed that success would mean a regeneration of society as a whole.

The Temperance Crusade

To some progressives, the elimination of alcohol from American life was a necessary step in the task of re-

storing order to society. Workers in settlement houses and social agencies abhorred the effects of drinking on working-class families: Scarce wages vanished as workers spent hours in the saloons. Drunkenness spawned violence, and occasionally murder, within urban families. Women, in particular, saw alcohol as a source of some of the greatest problems of working-class wives and mothers, and hoped through temperance to reform male behavior to improve women's lives. Employers, too, regarded alcohol as an impediment to industrial efficiency; workers often missed time on the job because of drunkenness or, worse, came to the factory intoxicated and performed their tasks sloppily and dangerously. Critics of economic privilege denounced the liquor industry as one of the nation's most sinister trusts. And political reformers, who looked on the saloon (correctly) as one of the central institutions of the machine, saw an attack on drinking as part of an attack on the bosses. Out of such sentiments emerged the temperance movement.

Temperance advocates had been active in some areas since before the Civil War, but the movement began to gather strength in the 1870s. From the beginning, it was a movement led and supported primarily by women. In 1873, temperance advocates met in Chicago to form the Women's Christian Temperance Union (WCTU). And after 1879, when Frances Willard became its leader, the new organization became a militant, national organization. By 1911, it had 245,000 members and had become the largest single women's organization in American history to that point—and a model of administrative efficiency and political skill. The WCTU worked tirelessly to publicize the evils of alcohol and the connection between drunkenness and family violence, unemployment, poverty, and disease. In 1893, the Anti-Saloon League joined the temperance movement and, along with the WCTU, began to press for a specific legislative solution: the legal abolition of saloons. Gradually, that demand grew to include the complete prohibition of the sale and manufacture of alcoholic beverages.

Despite substantial opposition from immigrant and working-class voters, pressure for prohibition grew steadily through the first decades of the new century. By 1900, restrictions on the sale of alcohol were in effect in areas embracing more than a quarter of the population of the nation. By 1916, nineteen states had passed prohibition laws. But since the consumption of alcohol was actually increasing in many unregulated areas, temperance advocates were becoming convinced that what was necessary was a national prohibition law.

America's entry into World War I, and the moral fervor it unleashed, provided the last push to the advocates of prohibition. With the support of rural fundamentalists, who opposed alcohol on moral and religious grounds, progressive advocates of prohibition in 1917 steered through Congress a constitutional amendment embodying their demands. Two years later, after ratification by every state in the nation except Connecticut and Rhode Island (bastions of Catholic immigrants), the Eighteenth Amendment became law, to take effect in January 1920. The federal government, many progressives believed, had taken an important step toward eliminating a major source of social instability and inefficiency. Only later did it become clear that prohibition would create far more disorder than it was able to cure.

Immigration Restriction

A similar concern for order fueled the movement demanding the restriction of immigration, which

Crusading for Temperance

This unflattering painting by Ben Shahn portrays late-nineteenth-century women demonstrating in front of a saloon. It suggests the degree to which temperance and prohibition had fallen out of favor with liberals and progressives by the 1930s, when Shahn was working. In earlier years, however, temperance attracted the support of some of the most advanced American reformers. (Museum of the City of New York)

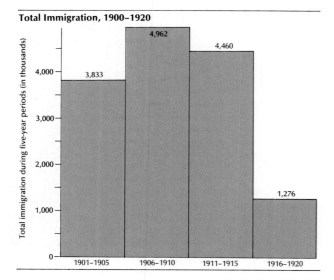

Total Immigration, 1900–1920

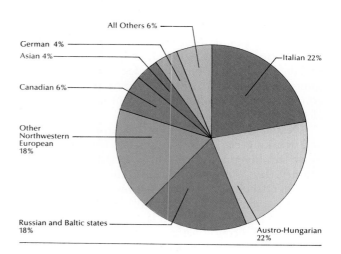

Sources of Immigration, 1900–1920

likewise gained force throughout the progressive era. While virtually all reformers agreed that the burgeoning immigrant population had created social problems, there was wide disagreement on how best to respond. Many progressives, convinced that open immigration was one of the nation's most valued traditions, believed that helping the new residents adapt to American society was the proper approach. Others, however, argued that efforts at assimilation had failed and that the only solution was to limit the flow of new arrivals.

The first decades of the century, therefore, saw a steady growth in pressure on the federal government to close the nation's gates. New scholarly theories, designed to appeal to the progressive respect for expertise, argued that the introduction of immigrants into American society was polluting the nation's racial stock. The spurious "science" of eugenics spread the belief that human inequalities were hereditary and that immigration was contributing to the multiplication of the unfit. Skillful publicists such as Madison Grant, whose *The Passing of the Great Race* (1916) established him as the nation's most effective nativist, warned of the dangers of racial "mongrelization" and of the importance of protecting the purity of Anglo-Saxon and other Nordic stock.

As on other issues, progressives in Washington established a special commission of "experts," chaired by Senator William P. Dillingham of Vermont, to study the problem of immigration. Supported by elaborate statistics and scholarly testimony, the commission's report argued that the newer immigrant groups—largely southern and eastern Europeans—had proven themselves less assimilable than earlier immigrants. Immigration, the report implied, should be restricted by nationality.

Racial arguments helped mobilize impressive support behind the restriction movement, but even many who rejected such arguments supported limiting immigration. The continuing influx of foreigners was, they believed, creating unmanageable urban problems: overcrowding, unemployment, strained social services, social unrest. The combination of these concerns gradually won for the nativists the support of some of the nation's leading progressives: Theodore Roosevelt, Henry Cabot Lodge, and others. Powerful opponents—employers who saw immigration as a source of cheap labor, reformers who valued the ethnic culture of immigrant communities, immigrants themselves and their political representatives—managed to block the restriction movement for a time. But by the beginning of World War I (which itself effectively blocked immigration temporarily), the nativist tide was clearly gaining strength.

Suffrage for Women

Perhaps the largest single reform movement of the progressive era, indeed one of the largest of such movements in American history, was the fight for woman suffrage—a movement that attracted support from both women and men for many reasons. Women, in particular, often supported suffrage as a matter of simple justice or because they believed that the vote would enable them to increase the power and opportunities available to their sex. But many supported suffrage as well because of what they felt it could do to advance other causes. If the agitations for prohibition and immigration restriction were attempts to remove dangerous influences from American life, the suffrage movement was an attempt, its supporters believed, to inject into society a healthy new force. Giving women the right to vote, suffrage advocates claimed, was not only a matter of abstract principle; it was a practical measure to strengthen the forces of reform.

The movement for woman suffrage had already experienced a long and often frustrating history as the twentieth century began. Women had played an important role in the crusade for the abolition of slavery in the 1840s and 1850s, and they had included suffrage among their political demands after the Civil War. Spurred by political leaders of the post–Civil War era, who insisted that this was "the Negro's hour," suffragists continued their efforts through the last decades of the nineteenth century, winning a few victories in some of the new Western states but lacking sufficient power to change national policy.

It is sometimes difficult for today's Americans to understand why the suffrage issue could have become the source of such enormous controversy in the early years of this century. But at the time, suffrage seemed to many of its critics a very radical demand—in part because of the rationale some of its supporters used to advance it. Throughout the late nineteenth century, many suffrage advocates presented their views in terms of "natural rights," arguing that women deserved the same rights as men—including, first and foremost, the right to vote. Elizabeth Cady Stanton, one of the organizers of the 1848 women's rights convention at Seneca Falls (see pp. 354–355) and a suffrage leader for more than forty years, wrote in 1892 of woman as "the arbiter of her own destiny. . . . if we are to consider her as a citizen, as a member of a great nation, she must have the same rights as all other members." A woman's role as "mother, wife, sister, daughter" was "incidental" to her larger role as a part of society.

This was an argument that stood in stark contrast to prevailing views of women among men (and even among many women), who believed that society required a distinctive female "sphere" in which women would serve first and foremost as wives and mothers. To many men, and even to many women, the idea of women's rights seemed frightening and threatening.

And so a powerful antisuffrage movement appeared, which challenged this apparent threat to the existing social order. There were antisuffrage organizations, some with substantial memberships; antisuffrage newspapers; rallies; petitions to legislatures; and widely circulated tracts. Opponents railed against the threat suffrage posed to the "natural order" of civilization. Woman, said one opponent, "was made man's helper, was given a servient place (not necessarily inferior) and man the dominant place (not necessarily superior) in the division of labor." Antisuffragists associated suffrage with divorce (not without at least some reason, since some suffrage advocates also supported revising the laws to make it easier for women to obtain a divorce). They linked suffrage with promiscuity, looseness, and neglect of children.

The suffrage movement began to overcome this opposition and to win some substantial victories in the first years of the twentieth century. That was in part because suffragists were becoming better organized and more politically sophisticated than their opponents. Under the leadership of Anna Howard Shaw, a Boston social worker, and Carrie Chapman Catt, a journalist from Iowa, the National American Woman Suffrage Association grew from a membership of about 13,000 in 1893 to over 2 million in 1917. The involvement of such well-known and widely admired women as Jane Addams gave added respectability to the cause.

But the movement also gained strength because many of its most prominent leaders began to justify suffrage in "safer," less theatening ways. Suffrage, some supporters began to argue, would not challenge the "separate sphere" in which women resided. It would allow women to bring their special and distinct virtues more widely to bear on society's problems. It was, they claimed, precisely because women occupied a distinct sphere—because as mothers and wives and homemakers they had special experiences and special sensitivities to bring to public life—that woman suffrage could make such an important contribution to politics. Jane Addams expressed this more conservative justification for suffrage in a 1909 article: "If women would effectively continue their old avocations, they must take part in the slow upbuilding of that code of legislation which is alone sufficient to protect the home from its dangers incident to modern life." In particular, many suffragists argued that enfranchising women would help the temperance movement, by giving its largest group of supporters a political voice. Some suffrage advocates claimed that once women had the vote, war would become a thing of the past, since women would—by their calming, peaceful influence—help curb the belligerence of men. It was no accident, therefore, that the outbreak of World War I gave the final, decisive push to the movement for suffrage.

Suffrage also attracted support for other, less optimistic reasons. Many middle-class people found persuasive the argument that if blacks, immigrants, and other "base" groups had access to the franchise, then it was not only a matter of justice but of common sense to allow educated, "well-born" women to vote. Some people supported woman suffrage, in fact, because they believed that it would add to the constituency that supported immigration restriction and racial disfranchisement. Florence Kelley, a prominent social reformer who was later to help organize the NAACP, remarked unhappily in 1906 on this aspect of the suffrage movement: "I have rarely heard a ringing suffrage speech which did not refer to the 'ignorant and degraded' men, or the 'ignorant immigrants' as our masters. This is habitually spoken with more or less bitterness."

It was this separation of the suffrage movement from more radical feminist goals, and its association with other reform causes of concern to many Americans, that allowed it in the first years of the new century to become a major national force. And beginning in 1910, it started to win some significant victories. That year, Washington became the first state in fourteen years to extend suffrage to women. California joined it a year later; and in 1912, four other Western states did the same. In 1913, Illinois became the first state east of the Mississippi to accept woman suffrage. And in 1917 and 1918, New York and Michigan—two of the most populous states in the Union—gave women the vote. By 1919, thirty-nine states had granted women the right to vote in at least some elections; fifteen had allowed them full participation. In 1920, finally, suffragists won ratification of the Nineteenth Amendment, which guaranteed political rights to women throughout the nation.

To some feminists, however, the victory seemed less than complete. Alice Paul, the head of the militant National Woman's party (founded in 1916) and a suffragist who had never accepted the relatively conservative "separate sphere" justification for suffrage, argued that the Nineteenth Amendment alone would not be sufficient to protect women's rights. Women needed more: a constitutional amendment that would provide clear, legal protection for their rights and

Suffragists
Suffrage activists hang posters along the boardwalk in the beachfront town of Long Branch, New Jersey. Twenty-nine states had permitted women at least some access to the ballot before ratification of the Nineteenth Amendment in 1920. New Jersey was not one of them. (Culver Pictures)

would prohibit all discrimination on the basis of sex. Such an amendment would do what the suffrage amendment had not. It would provide legal affirmation of women's rights as individuals, of their rights to pursue their interests and abilities on the same terms as men. But Alice Paul's argument found limited favor even among many of the most important leaders of the recently triumphant suffrage crusade. Jane Addams, Florence Kelley, Carrie Chapman Catt, and others showed no interest in the Equal Rights Amendment. Some, such as Addams, denounced it bitterly, fearing it would invalidate the special protective legislation for women that they had fought so hard to have enacted. It would be many years before the divisions between these two wings of American feminism were healed.

As the controversy over the Equal Rights Amendment suggests, the suffrage movement did not, in the end, produce a coherent movement behind any issue other than securing women the vote. On most other issues, in fact, women were generally no more in agreement than men. Once enfranchised, the new voters did little to support the arguments of those suffragists who had claimed that women would operate in politics as a coherent force for reform.

The Dream of Socialism

Prohibition, immigration restriction, woman suffrage—these and other issues attracted large but limited constituencies. Of more general concern to progressives of all backgrounds was the state of the nation's economy. From the beginning, it had been animosity toward the great industrial combinations—the trusts—that had formed the core of progressive sentiment. It was to the task of limiting the power of the giant corporations, therefore, that many reformers devoted their greatest energies.

On how best to deal with the trusts, however, there was wide disagreement. Some reformers believed in the importance of careful government regulation, others in the necessity of destroying the trusts. But others, moving beyond the strictures of progressivism, argued that the problem lay not in the abuses of the economic system but in the system itself—that the solution lay in replacing capitalism with socialism.

At no time in American history to that point, and in few times after it, did radical critiques of the capitalist system attract more support than in the period between 1900 and 1914. Although never a force to

rival, or even seriously threaten, the two major parties, the Socialist party of America grew during the progressive era into a force of considerable strength. In 1900, it had attracted the support of fewer than 100,000 voters; in 1912, its durable leader and perennial presidential candidate, Eugene V. Debs, received nearly 1 million ballots. Strongest in urban immigrant communities (particularly among Germans and Jews in New York, Chicago, Milwaukee, and elsewhere), it won the loyalties, too, of a substantial number of Protestant farmers in the South and Midwest. Socialists won election to over 1,000 state and local offices, and they attracted the admiring attention of some journalists and intellectuals as well as of members of the lower class. Lincoln Steffens, the crusader against municipal corruption, ultimately became a defender of socialism. So for a time did Walter Lippmann, the brilliant young journalist who was to become one of the nation's most important social critics.

Virtually all socialists agreed on the need for basic structural changes in the economy, but they differed widely on how drastic those changes should be. Some endorsed the sweepingly radical goals of European Marxists; others envisioned a more moderate reform that would allow small-scale private enterprise to survive but would nationalize the major industries. Debs spoke for the mainstream of the party in citing economic concentration as the greatest danger to democracy: "If we could but destroy the money monopoly, the land monopoly, all would be different." There was disagreement as well on tactics. Militants within the party favored drastic, even violent, action. Most conspicuous was the radical labor union the Industrial Workers of the World (IWW), known to opponents as the "Wobblies." Under the leadership of William ("Big Bill") Haywood, the IWW advocated a single union for all workers and abolition of the "wage slave" system; it rejected political action and favored strikes and industrial sabotage instead. Although small in numbers, the "Wobblies" struck terror into the hearts of the middle class with their inflammatory rhetoric. They were widely believed to have been responsible for the dynamiting of railroad lines and power stations and other acts of terror.

More moderate socialists advocated peaceful change through political struggle, and it was they who dominated the party. They emphasized a gradual education of the public to the need for change and patient efforts within the system to enact it. It soon became clear, however, that the period before World War I was not the first stage of an effective socialist

Debs for President
Eugene V. Debs was the Socialist party candidate for president five times between 1900 and 1920. In 1904 he received approximately 3 percent of the popular vote. Socialist candidates fared better, however, in many local races—particularly in agrarian areas of the South and West that had once been centers of Populist strength. Debs's own route to socialism was through labor activism. He had been a leader of the Pullman strike in Chicago in 1894 (for which he served six months in prison), and he remained throughout his life an advocate of union organization along industrial, rather than craft, lines.   (Library of Congress)

movement but the last. By the end of the war—in large part because the party had refused to support the war effort, but in part too because of a growing wave of antiradicalism that subjected the socialists to enormous harassment and persecution—socialism was in decline as a significant political force.

Decentralization and Regulation

A more influential debate was raging at the same time between those who believed in the essential premises of capitalism but urged reforms to preserve it. The debate centered on two basic approaches: decentralization and regulation.

To many progressives, the greatest threat to the nation's economy was excessive centralization and consolidation. The trusts had made it impossible for the free market to work as it should; only by restoring the economy to a more human scale could the nation hope for stability and justice. Few such reformers envisioned a return to a society of small, local enterprises; some consolidation, they recognized, was inevitable. They did, however, argue that the federal government should take forceful action to break up the largest combinations, to enforce a bal-

SIGNIFICANT EVENTS

1873 Women's Christian Temperance Union founded

1889 Jane Addams opens Hull House in Chicago

1892 General Federation of Women's Clubs founded

1893 Johns Hopkins Medical School established
Anti-Saloon League founded

1895 National Association of Manufacturers founded

1898 Edward Sheldon publishes *In His Steps*
Charlotte Perkins Gilman publishes *Women and Economics*

1899 Thorstein Veblen publishes *A Theory of the Leisure Class*

1900 Galveston, Texas, establishes commission government
Robert La Follette elected governor of Wisconsin

1901 American Medical Association reorganized

1902 Oregon adopts initiative and referendum
Mississippi adopts direct primary

1903 Women's Trade Union League founded

1904 Ida Tarbell publishes exposé of Standard Oil

1905 National Education Association founded

1909 Herbert Croly publishes *The Promise of American Life*

1911 Fire kills workers at Triangle Company in New York City

1912 United States Chamber of Commerce founded

1913 Dayton, Ohio, establishes city-manager government
Louis D. Brandeis publishes *Other People's Money*

1914 Walter Lippmann publishes *Drift and Mastery*

1916 Madison Grant publishes *The Passing of the Great Race*

1919 Eighteenth Amendment (prohibition) ratified

1920 Nineteenth Amendment (woman suffrage) ratified

ance between the need for bigness and the need for competition. This viewpoint came to be identified with Louis D. Brandeis, the brilliant lawyer and later justice of the Supreme Court, who spoke and wrote widely (most notably in his 1913 book *Other People's Money*) about the "curse of bigness." "If the Lord had intended things to be big," Brandeis once wrote, "he would have made man bigger—in brains and character."

Brandeis and his supporters opposed bigness in part because they considered it inefficient. But their opposition had a moral basis as well. Bigness was a threat not just to efficiency but to freedom. It limited the ability of individuals to control their own destinies. It encouraged abuses of power. Government must, Brandeis insisted, regulate competition in such a way as to ensure that large combinations did not emerge.

To other progressives, competition was an overrated commodity. Far more important was efficiency. And since economic concentration tended to enhance efficiency, the government, they believed, should not discourage it. What government should do, how-

ever, was to ensure that "bigness" did not bring with it abuses of power. It should stand constant guard against irresponsibility and corruption in the great corporations. It should distinguish between "good trusts" and "bad trusts," encouraging the good while disciplining the bad. Such progressives argued that America had entered a new era. Economic consolidation, they foresaw, would remain a permanent feature of society, but continuing oversight by a strong, modernized government would be vital.

The defenders of consolidation looked on the antimonopolists with condescension and some contempt. Brandeis and his allies were outmoded moralists, harking back to the ideals of a vanished age. America needed, instead, to look forward, to a bold new future. One of the most influential spokesmen for this emerging "nationalist" position was Herbert Croly, whose 1909 book *The Promise of American Life* became one of the most influential of all progressive documents. America's greatest need, Croly argued, was for unity—the kind of fervent unity that had made the great civilizations of the past (ancient Greece, the Roman Empire) flourish. And America's economic life, he claimed, needed unity as much as did its social life.

Opinions varied widely, even among nationalists, on how that unity should be achieved. But increasingly, attention focused on some form of coordination of the industrial economy. Society must act, Walter Lippmann wrote in a notable 1914 book, *Drift and Mastery*, "to introduce plan where there has been clash, and purpose into the jungles of disordered growth." To some, the search for "plan" required businesses themselves to learn new ways of cooperation and self-regulation; some of the most energetic "progressive" reformers of the period, in fact, were businessmen searching eagerly for ways to bring order to their own troubled world. To others, the solution was for government to play a far more active role in regulating and planning economic life. One of those who came to endorse that position (although not fully until 1912) was Theodore Roosevelt, who said: "We should enter upon a course of supervision, control, and regulation of those great corporations—a regulation which we should not fear, if necessary, to bring to the point of control of monopoly prices."

SUGGESTED READINGS

Progressivism: Overviews The question of what progressivism is has produced a wide range of answers from historians. Works that reveal some of the contending views include Richard Hofstadter, *The Age of Reform: From Bryan to FDR* (1955), a major interpretive essay; Robert Wiebe, *The Search for Order, 1877–1920* (1967), an overview of the period that advances an important interpretation; Gabriel Kolko, *The Triumph of Conservatism* (1963); and James Weinstein, *The Corporate Ideal in the Liberal States, 1900-1918* (1969). Arthur Link and Richard L. McCormick provide a succinct overview that surveys recent interpretive stances in *Progressivism* (1983). A survey of the period is John Whiteclay Chambers, *The Tyranny of Change* (1980).

The Muckrakers Important studies of progressive journalism, and in particular muckraking, include Harold S. Wilson, *McClure's Magazine and the Muckrakers* (1970); C. C. Regier, *The Era of the Muckrakers* (1932); and David Chambers, *The Social and Political Ideas of the Muckrakers* (1964). Studies of individual reporters include Justin Kaplan, *Lincoln Steffens* (1974), and Leon Harris, *Upton Sinclair* (1975). See also Louis Filler, *The Muckrakers*, rev. ed. (1980).

Progressive Thought Studies of progressive thought include Arthur Ekirch, *Progressivism in America* (1974); Morton White, *Social Thought in America* (1949); D. W. Marcell, *Progress and Pragmatism: James, Dewey, Beard and the American Idea of Progress* (1974); Charles Forcey, *The Crossroads of Liberalism: Croly, Weyl, Lippmann* (1961); and Richard Abrams, *The Burdens of Progress* (1978). Sudhir Kakar, *Frederick Taylor* (1970), examines the father of "scientific management." David W. Noble (ed.), *The Progressive Mind*, rev. ed. (1981), is a useful collection.

Social Work and the Social Gospel The rise of interest in social conditions in the city is examined in Allen F. Davis, *Spearheads of Reform: The Social Settlements and the Progressive Movement, 1890–1914* (1968), and Roy Lubove, *The Progressives and the Slums: Tenement House Reform in New York City* (1962). Allen F. Davis, *American Heroine: The Life and Legend of Jane Addams* (1973), examines the founder of Hull House; Jane Addams was herself the author of an important memoir, *Twenty Years at Hull House* (1910). C. H. Hopkins, *The Rise of the Social Gospel in American Protestantism* (1940), is a general study of Protestant reform impulses. Henry May, *Protestant Churches and Industrial America* (1949), and William R. Hutchinson, *The Modernist Impulse in American Protestantism* (1982), are general examinations of changes in Protestant theology and its approach to social conditions. Robert M. Crunden, *Ministers of Reform: The Progressives' Achievement in American Civilization, 1889–1920* (1982), is a study of the reconciliation of evangelical Protestantism with social realities. Paul Boyer, *Urban Masses and Moral Order, 1820–1920* (1978), argues that nativism and the desire for control lay at the heart of most urban reform efforts.

Education and the Professions Burton Bledstein, *The Culture of Professionalism* (1976), provides a critical view of the rise of the professional ethic. Thomas L. Haskell, *The Emergence of Professional Social Science* (1977), studies the rise of a new academic profession. Paul Starr, *The Social Transformation of American Medicine* (1982), is a major study of the medical profession in the twentieth century; Donald Fleming, *William H. Welch and the Rise of Modern Medicine* (1954), examines one of the central figures in the modernization of medicine. Progressive era education is the subject of David Tyack and Elizabeth Hansot, *Managers of Virtue: Public School Leadership in America, 1820–1980* (1982). See also Lawrence Veysey, *The Emergence of the American University* (1970).

Municipal Reform Urban political reform movements receive attention in Zane Miller, *Boss Cox's Cincinnati* (1968); John D. Buenker, *Urban Liberalism and Progressive Reform* (1973); James B. Crooks, *Politics and Progress: The Rise of Urban Progressivism in Baltimore* (1968); Melvin G. Holli, *Reform in Detroit* (1969); J. Joseph Huthmacher, *Senator Robert F. Wagner and the Rise of Urban Liberalism* (1971); and Oscar Handlin, *Al Smith and His America* (1958).

Women, Reform, and Suffrage Sheila M. Rothman, *Woman's Proper Place* (1978), examines changing ideas about women's roles. Ellen C. Lagemann, *A Generation of Women:*

Education in the Lives of Progressive Reformers (1979), explores the role of schooling in shaping woman reformers. William O'Neill, *Everyone Was Brave: The Rise and Fall of Feminism in America* (1969), is critical of progressive era feminism for the limits of its vision. Rosalind Rosenberg, *Beyond Separate Spheres: Intellectual Roots of Modern Feminism* (1982), is a study of feminist thought. On suffrage, see Aileen S. Kraditor, *Ideas of the Woman Suffrage Movement* (1965); Alan P. Grimes, *The Puritan Ethic and Woman Suffrage* (1967), which examines the acceptance of suffrage in the Western states; and David Morgan, *Suffragists and Democrats: The Politics of Woman Suffrage in America* (1972). The roots of the suffrage movement are examined in Ellen C. Du Bois, *Feminism and Suffrage: The Emergence of an Independent Women's Movement in America, 1848–1869* (1978). Other issues relating to women in this era are the subject of Ruth Rosen, *The Lost Sisterhood: Prostitutes in America, 1900–1918* (1982); William O'Neill, *Divorce in the Progressive Era* (1967); David M. Kennedy, *Birth Control in America: The Career of Margaret Sanger* (1970); and Linda Gordon, *Woman's Body, Woman's Right: A Social History of Birth Control* (1976).

State-Level Reform   George E. Mowry, *California Progressives* (1951), is a pathbreaking work whose conclusions have been challenged by, among others, David P. Thelen, *The New Citizenship: Origins of Progressivism in Wisconsin* (1972), and Sheldon Hackney, *Populism to Progressivism in Alabama* (1969). See also Robert S. Maxwell, *La Follette and the Rise of Progressivism in Wisconsin* (1944); Russel B. Nye, *Midwestern Progressive Politics* (1951); Richard M. Abrams, *Conservatism in a Progressive Era: Massachusetts* (1964); Robert F. Wesser, *Charles Evans Hughes: Politics and Reform in New York State, 1905–1910* (1967); and David Thelen, *Robert La Follette and the Insurgent Spirit* (1976). Richard L. McCormick, *From Realignment to Reform: Political Change in New York State, 1893–1910* (1981), is an important study of the decline of party and the rise of interest-group politics. Dewey Grantham, *Southern Progressivism: The Reconciliation of Progress and Tradition* (1983), is a regional overview. C. Vann Woodward, *Origins of the New South* (1951), includes an examination of Southern progressivism.

National Issues   On temperance, see James T. Timberlake, *Prohibition and the Progressive Movement* (1963), and Joseph Gusfield, *Symbolic Crusade: Status Politics and the Temperance Movement* (1963). John Higham, *Strangers in the Land* (1955), is an indispensable study of American nativism. James Weinstein, *The Decline of Socialism in America* (1967), examines one approach to economic reform. Robert Wiebe, *Businessmen and Reform* (1962), and Sidney Fine, *Laissez Faire and the General Welfare State* (1956), examine other progressive economic beliefs. Melvyn Dubofsky, *We Shall Be All* (1969), is a history of the Industrial Workers of the World (IWW). Michael E. McGerr, *The Decline of Popular Politics: The American North, 1865–1928* (1986), is a study of the changing nature of partisanship.

Theodore Roosevelt, by John Singer Sargent, 1903   (White House Historical Association)

Chapter 22   The Battle for National Reform

The spirit of reform came relatively late to national politics, but come it did. As progressives encountered setbacks and frustrations in their efforts to win social and economic reforms at the state and local level, they began increasingly to look to the federal government as a court of last resort. Efforts to reform the industrial economy, in particular, seemed to require action at the federal level. The great combinations were national in scope; only national action could effectively control their power.

But just as at the state and local levels, the national government seemed at first unable to respond to popular demands, mired as it was in the tired partisan politics of the nineteenth century. Progressives attempted to make it more responsive to their demands in various ways. They tried in Congress to limit the power of conservative party leaders and make the legislative process more responsive to the popular will. Some reformers, for example, urged an end to the system whereby United States senators were elected by the members of their state legislatures; they proposed instead a direct popular election, which they believed would force the Senate to react to public demands. The Seventeenth Amendment provided for that change; after conservatives had delayed action on it for years, it was finally passed by Congress in 1912 and ratified by the states in 1913.

Even a reformed Congress, however, could not be expected to provide the kind of coherent leadership that the progressive agenda required. If the federal government was truly to fulfill its mission, it would, most reformers agreed, have to do so largely through the executive branch. It would require, above

all, strong leadership from the one office capable of providing it: the presidency.

Theodore Roosevelt and the Progressive Presidency

"Presidents in general are not lovable," Walter Lippmann, who had known many, said near the end of his life. "They've had to do too much to get where they are. But there was one President who was lovable—Teddy Roosevelt—and I loved him."

He was not alone. To a generation of progressive reformers, Theodore Roosevelt was more than an admired public figure; he was an idol. No president before and few since could match him in attracting attention and devotion. Yet for all his popularity among reformers, Roosevelt was not the era's most advanced progressive. In many respects he was decidedly conservative. He earned his extraordinary popularity less because of the extent of the reforms he championed than because of the vigor and dynamism with which he approached them. He brought to his office a broad conception of its powers, and he invested the presidency with something of its modern status as the center of national political life.

The Accidental President

Roosevelt was not intended by his party for the presidency. Republican leaders had nominated him to run for vice president with William McKinley in 1900 largely to remove him from the governorship of New York, to which he had been elected in 1898 and where he was proving troublesome to party bosses. When McKinley suddenly died in September 1901, the victim of an assassination, Roosevelt was only forty-two years old, the youngest man ever to assume the presidency. Already, however, he had achieved a notoriety that caused party leaders to feel something close to despair. "I told William McKinley that it was a mistake to nominate that wild man at Philadelphia," Mark Hanna was reported to have exclaimed. "I asked him if he realized what would happen if he should die. Now look, that damned cowboy is President of the United States!"

Roosevelt's reputation as a wild man was, characteristically, a result less of the substance than of the style of his early political career. As a young member of the New York legislature, he had displayed an energy seldom seen in that lethargic body. As a rancher in the Dakota Badlands (where he retired briefly after the sudden death of his first wife), he had helped capture outlaws. As New York City police commissioner, he had been a flamboyant battler against crime and vice. As commander of the Rough Riders, he had led a heroic, if militarily useless, charge in the battle of San Juan Hill in Cuba during the Spanish-American War.

Never, however, had Roosevelt openly rebelled against the leaders of his party; and once in the White House, he continued to balance his personal dynamism against the demands of the political establishment, becoming a champion of cautious, moderate change. Reform was, he believed, less a vehicle for remaking American society than for protecting it against more radical challenges.

Managing the Trusts

For all his cautiousness, however, Roosevelt did bring certain assumptions to the presidency that markedly differentiated him from his predecessors. Imbued with progressive ideas about the importance of the efficient, modern management of society, he envisioned the federal government not as the agent of any particular interest but as a mediator of the public good. The president would be the central figure in that mediation.

Such attitudes found expression in Roosevelt's policies toward the great industrial combinations. Like William McKinley, he was not opposed to the principle of economic concentration. Unlike McKinley, however, he acknowledged that consolidation produced abuses of power that could prove harmful to society. He allied himself, therefore, with those progressives who urged regulation (but not destruction) of the trusts.

At the heart of Roosevelt's policy was his desire to win for government the power to investigate the activities of corporations and to publicize the results. The pressure of educated public opinion, he believed, would alone eliminate most corporate abuses. Government could legislate solutions for those that remained. The new Department of Commerce and Labor, established in 1903 (and later to be divided into two separate departments), was to assist in this task through its investigatory arm, the Bureau of Corporations.

Roosevelt did make occasional flamboyant gestures on behalf of a more drastic approach to reform. Although not a trust buster at heart, he engaged in several highly publicized efforts to break up notorious combinations—actions that strengthened his credentials as a progressive without offering any fundamental challenge to the structure of the economy. In 1902, he ordered the Justice Department to invoke the Sherman Antitrust Act against a great new railroad monopoly in the Northwest, the Northern Securities Company, a $400 million enterprise pieced together by J. P. Morgan, E. H. Harriman, and James J. Hill. To Morgan, accustomed to a warm, supportive relationship with Republican administrations, the action was baffling. Hurrying to the White House with two conservative senators in tow, he told the president, "If we have done anything wrong, send your man to my man and they can fix it up." Roosevelt proceeded with the case nonetheless, and in 1904 the Supreme Court ruled that the Northern Securities Company must be dissolved. At the same time, however, he assured Morgan and others that the suit did not signal a general campaign to dissolve trusts. Other monopolistic corporations, such as United States Steel, he would challenge only if "they have done something we regard as wrong." Although he filed more than forty additional antitrust suits during the remainder of his presidency, and although he succeeded in dissolving several important combinations, Roosevelt made no serious effort to reverse the prevailing trend toward economic concentration. Regulation, with the government serving as mediator between corporate and public interests, remained his central goal.

Government and Labor

A similar commitment to establishing the government as an impartial regulatory mechanism shaped Roosevelt's policy toward labor. In the past, federal intervention in industrial disputes had almost always meant action on behalf of employers, as in the Pullman strike in 1894. Roosevelt, however, was willing to consider labor's position as well.

He displayed this willingness during a bitter strike in 1902 by members of the United Mine Workers employed in the anthracite coal industry. Miners, under the leadership of John Mitchell, were demanding a 20 percent wage increase, an eight-hour day, and

Coal Miners
Powder men (who performed the dangerous task of blasting deeper into the coal veins) emerge from the Perrin coal mine in about 1902. (Theodore Roosevelt Collection, Harvard College Library)

recognition of their union. Management, represented by the combative George F. Baer, was responding with conspicuous arrogance and contempt. When the strike threatened to drag on long enough to endanger coal supplies for the coming winter, Roosevelt decided to step in—not to assist management but to invite both the operators and the miners to the White House, where he asked them to accept impartial federal arbitration. Mitchell readily agreed. Baer balked.

Furious at the obstinacy of the mine owners (who had already alienated public opinion), Roosevelt threatened drastic action. He would, he told them, order 10,000 federal troops to seize the mines and resume coal production if the dispute was not resolved. Under pressure from politicians, the press, and perhaps most significantly, J. P. Morgan, the operators finally relented. Arbitrators awarded the strikers a 10 percent wage increase and a nine-hour day, but no recognition of the union. It was a meager reward for a long and costly strike, but it was more than the miners might have won without the government's intervention.

Despite such episodes, Roosevelt viewed himself as no more the champion of labor than of management. On several occasions, he ordered federal troops to intervene in strikes on behalf of employers—in Arizona in 1903 and in Colorado in 1904. And although he believed in the right of workers to join a union, he believed, too, in the right of employers to refuse to bargain with it.

The Square Deal

Even if Roosevelt had wished to move more quickly on economic reforms (and there was little evidence that he did), he would have been reluctant to do so during his first term as president. Much of his energy in those years he was devoting to the business of winning reelection. Above all, he was working to ensure that the conservative Republican Old Guard, which bristled at even the most modest of reforms, would not block his nomination in 1904. By skillfully dispensing patronage to conservatives and progressives alike, by reshuffling the leadership of unstable Republican organizations in the South, by winning the support of Northern businessmen while making adroit gestures to reformers, he succeeded in all but neutralizing his opposition within the party and won its presidential nomination with ease. And in the general election, where he faced a pallid conservative Democrat, Alton B. Parker, he stormed to one of the largest victories in the nation's history. Roosevelt captured over 57 percent of the popular vote and lost not one state outside the South. Now, relieved of immediate political concerns, he was free to display the full extent (and the real limits) of his commitment to reform.

During the 1904 campaign, Roosevelt boasted that he had worked in the anthracite coal strike to provide everyone with a "square deal." In his second term, he became more aggressive in his efforts to extend the square deal even further. Among his most important targets was the powerful railroad industry. The Interstate Commerce Act of 1887, establishing the Interstate Commerce Commission (ICC), had been an early effort to regulate the industry; but over the years, the courts had virtually nullified its influence. Roosevelt asked Congress for a law that would considerably increase the government's power to set railroad rates. In June 1906, the Hepburn Railroad Regulation Act became law, although not until after the Senate had greatly weakened a much stronger bill passed by the House. It was a classic example of the cautiousness with which Roosevelt, even after his 1904 mandate, approached reform. The bill satisfied even many conservatives; and it infuriated advanced progressives such as La Follette, who never forgave Roosevelt for the concessions he made.

The Hepburn Act was the most conspicuous reform legislation of Roosevelt's second term, but only one of many new regulatory measures. The president won approval of laws providing for compensation by employers to injured workers in the District of Columbia and certain other limited areas. He pressured Congress to enact the Pure Food and Drug Act, which, despite weaknesses in its enforcement mechanisms, did restrict the sale of some dangerous or ineffective medicines. When Upton Sinclair's powerful novel *The Jungle* appeared in 1906, featuring appalling descriptions of the preparation of meats in the nation's stockyards, Roosevelt insisted on passage of the Meat Inspection Act, which ultimately helped eliminate many diseases once transmitted in impure meat.

Starting in 1907, moreover, he seemed to expand his vision of regulation and began to propose even more stringent measures: an eight-hour day for workers, broader compensation for victims of industrial accidents, inheritance and income taxes, regulation of the stock market, and others. In the process, he started openly to criticize conservatives in Congress, who were blocking much of this legislation, and to denounce the judiciary, which was striking down or

weakening many of the measures that did pass. The result was not only a general stalemate in Roosevelt's reform agenda, but a widening gulf between the president and the conservative wing of his party.

Conservation

Nothing contributed more to the creation of that gulf than Roosevelt's aggressive policies on behalf of conservation. An ardent sportsman and naturalist, he had long been concerned about the unregulated exploitation of America's natural resources and the despoiling of what remained of the nation's wilderness. Using executive powers, he began early in his presidency to restrict private development on millions of acres of undeveloped land still controlled by the government, adding them to the hitherto modest system of national forests. When vigorous conservative and Western opposition finally resulted in legislation in 1907 to restrict his authority over public lands, Roosevelt and his chief forester, Gifford Pinchot, worked furiously to seize all the forests and many of the water power sites still in the public domain, before the bill became law.

Roosevelt was the first president to take an active interest in the new and struggling American conservation movement, and his policies had a lasting effect on national environmental policies. More than most public figures, he was sympathetic to the concerns of the naturalists—those within the movement committed to protecting the natural beauty of the land and the health of its wildlife from human intrusion. Early in his presidency, Roosevelt even spent four days camping in the Sierras with John Muir, the nation's leading preservationist and the founder of the Sierra Club. In the end, however, Roosevelt's policy tended to favor less the preservationists than another faction within the conservation movement—those who believed in carefully managed development.

The leading conservation figure in government was Pinchot, who became the first director of the National Forest Service (which he helped to create). The first professionally trained American forester, Pinchot supported rational and efficient human use of the wilderness. The Sierra Club might argue for the "aesthetic" value of the forests; Pinchot insisted, in contrast, that "the whole question is a practical one." He and Roosevelt both believed that trained experts in forestry and resource management, such men as Pinchot himself, should apply to the landscape the

Establishment of National Parks and Forests

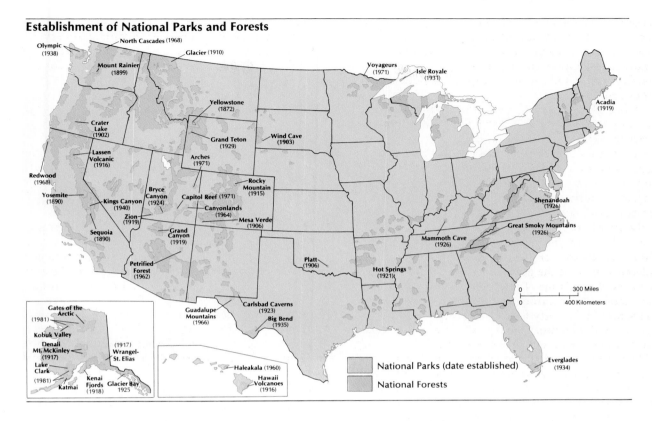

Olympic (1938)
North Cascades (1968)
Glacier (1910)
Mount Rainier (1899)
Voyageurs (1971)
Isle Royale (1931)
Acadia (1919)
Yellowstone (1872)
Crater Lake (1902)
Grand Teton (1929)
Wind Cave (1903)
Lassen Volcanic (1916)
Arches (1971)
Redwood (1968)
Rocky Mountain (1915)
Yosemite (1890)
Kings Canyon (1940)
Bryce Canyon (1924)
Capitol Reef (1971)
Shenandoah (1926)
Zion (1919)
Canyonlands (1964)
Mesa Verde (1906)
Great Smoky Mountains (1926)
Sequoia (1890)
Grand Canyon (1919)
Mammoth Cave (1926)
Petrified Forest (1962)
Platt (1906)
Hot Springs (1921)
Gates of the Arctic (1981)
Kobuk Valley
Denali Mt. McKinley (1917)
Wrangel-St. Elias (1917)
Lake Clark (1981)
Kenai Fjords (1918)
Glacier Bay 1925
Katmai
Guadalupe Mountains (1966)
Carlsbad Caverns (1923)
Big Bend (1935)
Haleakala (1960)
Hawaii Volcanoes (1916)
Everglades (1934)

300 Miles
400 Kilometers

National Parks (date established)
National Forests

---

same scientific standards that others were applying to the management of cities and industries. The president did side with the preservationists on certain issues, but the more important legacy of his conservation policy was to establish the government's role as manager of the continuing development of the wilderness.

To much of the Old Guard, the extension of government control over vast new lands smacked of socialism. Even worse, Roosevelt's use of executive powers to achieve that control smacked of dictatorship. Many of these same interests, however, displayed no such scruples in supporting another important aspect of Roosevelt's natural resource policy: public reclamation and irrigation projects. In 1902, the president supported the Newlands Reclamation Act, which provided federal funds for the construction of huge dams, reservoirs, and canals in the West—projects to open new lands for cultivation and provide cheap electric power. It was the beginning of many years of federal aid for irrigation and power development in the Western states.

The Panic of 1907

The flurry of reforms Roosevelt was able to enact, and the enormous popularity he attracted as a result, made it easy for members of his administration to believe that finally the government had imposed a strong, effective set of regulations on the new industrial economy. But in fact, the Roosevelt record—although substantial when compared with that of his predecessors—was a relatively modest one, and the economy at large remained essentially uncontrolled. That truth was harshly brought home to Roosevelt and his allies in 1907, when a serious panic and recession revealed how flawed the nation's economic structure remained. The scenario was eerily familiar to those who remembered 1893. Once again, American industrial production had outrun the capacity of either domestic or foreign markets to absorb it. Once again, the banking system and the stock market had displayed pathetic inadequacies. Once again, irresponsible speculation and rampant financial mismanagement had helped to shatter a prosperity that many

The Grand Canyon of the Yellowstone
The Philadelphia-born artist Thomas Moran painted this spectacular scene in 1893, twenty years after Yellowstone had become the first national park in the United States. Moran's passion for the West in general and Yellowstone in particular inspired him to make five Western trips in the 1870s, and his dramatic views of Yellowstone from those journeys played an important role in convincing Congress to establish the park system. (National Museum of American Art, Smithsonian Institution)

had come to believe was now permanent. Banks failed; industries cut or ceased production; workers suffered layoffs and wage cuts.

To many conservatives, Roosevelt's "mad" economic policies were the obvious cause of the disaster. The president, naturally (and correctly), disagreed. But the panic was clearly unnerving to him, and he acted quickly to reassure business leaders that he would not interfere with their recovery efforts. J. P. Morgan, in a spectacular display of his financial power, helped construct a pool of the assets of several important New York banks to prop up shaky financial institutions. The key to the arrangement, Morgan told the president, was the purchase by U.S. Steel of the shares of the Tennessee Coal and Iron Company, currently held by a threatened New York bank. He would, he insisted, need assurances that no antitrust action would ensue. Roosevelt tacitly agreed, and the Morgan plan proceeded. Whether or not as a result, the panic soon subsided.

The Roosevelt Retirement

Theodore Roosevelt loved being president. He had made that plain during his first moments in office, when, torn between his excitement at his new position and his distress at McKinley's death, he had written, "It is a dreadful thing to come into the Presidency in this way; but it would be a far worse thing to be morbid about it." As his years in office produced increasing political successes, as his public popularity continued to rise, more and more observers began to doubt that he would happily stand aside in 1908.

Events, however, dictated otherwise. The Panic of 1907, combined with Roosevelt's growing "radicalism" during his second term, had deeply alienated conservatives in his own party. He would, he realized, have considerable difficulty winning the Republican nomination for another term. In 1904, moreover, he had made a public promise to step down four years later, a promise that would surely emerge to haunt him if he decided to run again. And so, after nearly eight energetic years in the White House, during which he had transformed the role of the presidency in American government, Theodore Roosevelt, fifty years old, retired from public life—briefly.

The Troubled Succession

It seemed at first that William Howard Taft, who assumed the presidency in 1909, would be that rare thing among politicians: a leader acceptable to virtually everyone. He had been Theodore Roosevelt's most trusted lieutenant and his hand-picked successor; progressive reformers believed him to be one of their own. But he had also been a restrained and moderate jurist, a man with a punctilious regard for legal process; conservatives expected him to abandon Roosevelt's aggressive use of presidential powers.

It was perhaps unsurprising, then, that in 1908 Taft won election to the White House with almost ridiculous ease. With the support of both Roosevelt and much of the Republican Old Guard, he received his party's nomination virtually uncontested. His victory in the general election in November—over William Jennings Bryan, running forlornly for the Democrats for the third time—was a foregone conclusion. Taft entered the White House on a wave of good feeling.

It was ironic, therefore, that four years later Taft would leave office the most decisively defeated president of the twentieth century, his party deeply, perhaps irrevocably, divided, and the government in the hands of a Democratic administration for the first time in twenty years.

It had been obvious from the start that Taft and Roosevelt were not at all alike, but it was not until Taft took office that the real extent of the differences became clear. Roosevelt had been the most dynamic public figure of his age; Taft was stolid and respectable and little more. Roosevelt was an ardent sportsman and athlete; Taft was sedentary and obese—he weighed over 300 pounds and required a special, oversized bathtub to be installed in the White House. Most of all, Roosevelt had taken an expansive view of the powers of his office; Taft, in contrast, was slow, cautious, even lethargic, insistent that the president must take pains to observe the strict letter of the law.

Yet even had Taft been the most dynamic of political figures, he would still have had difficulties, for he quickly found himself in the middle of a series of political controversies from which no leader could emerge unscathed. Having come into office as the darling of progressives and conservatives alike, he soon found that he could not please them both. Gradually he found himself, without really intending it, pleasing the conservatives and alienating the progressives.

William Howard Taft

Taft could be a jovial companion in small groups, but his public image was of a dull, stolid man who stood in sharp and unfortunate contrast to his dynamic predecessor, Theodore Roosevelt. Taft also suffered public ridicule for his enormous size. He weighed as much as 350 pounds at times, and wide publicity accompanied his installation of a special, oversized bathtub in the White House. (UPI/Bettmann Newsphotos)

Congress and the Tariff

The first fiasco occurred in the opening months of the new administration, when Taft called Congress into special session to enact legislation lowering protective tariff rates. Tariff reduction had been a consistent demand of many progressives for nearly a decade. It had reflected less a belief in free trade than a conviction that foreign competition would weaken the power of the great trusts and thus lower domestic prices. Theodore Roosevelt had made several tentative gestures on behalf of tariff reform but had always pulled away from the issue in the end. Taft was determined to do more.

But the president soon proved completely ineffectual in challenging the power of the congressional Old Guard, which remained committed to protection. At times, he seemed not even to be trying to challenge them. A tariff revision acceptable to most progressives moved relatively easily through the House; but in the Senate, Nelson Aldrich and other conservatives, aided by the relentless efforts of protectionist lobbies, waged a powerful campaign to weaken the bill. Progressives battling for revision needed help from the White House. They never received it. Taft believed it would violate the constitutional doctrine of separation of powers if he were to intervene in legislative matters. On August 5, 1909, the president signed the ineffectual Payne-Aldrich Tariff, which reduced tariff rates scarcely at all and in some areas actually raised them. It had been passed without the support of the Midwestern reformers.

The wedge between Taft and the Republican progressives was driven deeper as a result of the president's role in efforts to reform the House of Representatives. The almost dictatorial power of Speaker Joseph Cannon had been a thorn in the side of progressives for many years; Taft himself harbored a strong dislike for the aging "Uncle Joe." So when reformers began a campaign during the 1909 special session to limit the Speaker's power, Taft at first expressed cautious approval. He soon found, however, that without Cannon's support, his tariff legislation faced almost certain death, and he backed away from the insurgent revolt. Again, congressional progressives watched their reform efforts collapse; again, they blamed Taft for betraying them. The following year, after a fierce debate that raged for nearly thirty hours, progressive Republicans under the leadership of George W. Norris finally succeeded in stripping Cannon of some of his most important powers. Even then, however, they acted without the president's support.

The Pinchot-Ballinger Affair

With Taft's standing among Republican progressives steadily deteriorating and with the party growing more and more deeply divided, a sensational controversy broke out late in 1909 that helped to destroy for good Taft's popularity with admirers of Theodore Roosevelt. Many progressives had been unhappy when Taft replaced Roosevelt's secretary of the interior, James R. Garfield, an aggressive conservationist, with Richard A. Ballinger, a corporate lawyer and a far less fervent environmentalist. Suspicion of Ballinger grew when he attempted to invalidate Roosevelt's actions in removing nearly 1 million acres of forests and mineral reserves from the public lands available for private development.

In the midst of this mounting concern, Louis Glavis, an Interior Department investigator, uncovered information that he believed constituted proof that the new secretary had once connived to turn over valuable coal lands in Alaska to a private syndicate in exchange for personal profit. Glavis took the evidence to Gifford Pinchot, who had remained as head of the Forest Service and had been appalled by Ballinger's retreat from Roosevelt's policies. Pinchot took the charges to the president. Taft listened to Pinchot, heard Ballinger's rebuttal, asked Attorney General George Wickersham to investigate, and finally announced his support for his interior secretary. The charges, he insisted, were groundless.

Pinchot, however, was not satisfied. Unhappy that Ballinger remained in office and angry when Taft fired Glavis for his part in the episode, he leaked the story to the press and appealed directly to Congress to investigate the scandal. The president quickly discharged him for insubordination, and the congressional committee appointed to study the controversy, dominated by the Old Guard, exonerated Ballinger. But Taft's victory had come at a high cost. Progressives throughout the country rallied to the support of Pinchot, whom they considered the defender of the public interest against selfish business interests. Taft, in contrast, appeared to have capitulated to conservatives and to have repudiated the legacy of Theodore Roosevelt. The controversy aroused as much public passion as any dispute of its time; and when it was

Roosevelt at Osawatomie
Roosevelt's famous August 1910 speech at Osawatomie, Kansas, was the most radical of his career and openly marked his break with the Taft administration and the Republican leadership. "The essence of any struggle for liberty," he told his largely conservative audience, "has always been, and must always be to take from some one man or class of men the right to enjoy power, or wealth, or position or immunity, which has not been earned by service to his or their fellows." (Brown Brothers)

over, Taft had alienated the supporters of Roosevelt as completely as his tariff actions had alienated the followers of La Follette.

The Return of Roosevelt

During most of Taft's first year in office, Theodore Roosevelt was far from the political fray. He embarked first on a long hunting safari in the jungles of Africa; from there he traveled to Europe for visits to the major heads of state. To the American public, however, Roosevelt remained a formidable presence. Reports of his triumphant European tour dominated the front pages of newspapers across the country. Rumors that he would return to retake control of his party abounded. His arrival in New York in the spring of 1910 was a major public event; and progressives noted that, although he turned down an invitation from Taft to visit the White House, he met at once with Gifford Pinchot (who had already traveled to England to see him several months before).

Roosevelt insisted that he had no plans to return to active politics, but his resolve lasted less than a week. Politicians began flocking immediately to his home at Oyster Bay, Long Island, for conferences; Roosevelt himself took an active role in several New York political controversies; and within a month, he announced that he would embark on a national speaking tour before the end of the summer. Furious with Taft, who had, he believed, "completely twisted around the policies I advocated and acted upon," he was becoming convinced that he alone was capable of reuniting the Republican party.

The real signal of Roosevelt's return to active leadership of the progressives was a speech on September 1, 1910, in Osawatomie, Kansas, where he outlined a set of principles that he labeled the "New Nationalism." The speech made clear how far Roosevelt had moved from the cautious conservatism that had marked the first years of his presidency. Social justice, he argued, could be attained only through the vigorous efforts of a strong federal government whose executive acted as the "steward of the public welfare." Those who thought primarily of property rights and personal profit "must now give way to the advocate of human welfare, who rightly maintains that every man holds his property subject to the general right of the community to regulate its use to whatever degree the public welfare may require it." Such generalizations were frightening enough by themselves to the Republican Old Guard, but Roosevelt went beyond them with a list of "radical" specific proposals: graduated income and inheritance taxes, workers' compensation for industrial accidents, regulation of the labor of women and children, tariff revision, and firm regulation of corporations through a more powerful Bureau of Corporations and ICC.

Spreading Insurgency

The congressional elections of 1910 provided further evidence of how far the progressive revolt had spread. In primary elections, conservative Republicans suffered defeat after defeat at the hands of progressive insurgents—forty in the House of Representatives alone. Incumbent progressives, moreover, won renomination almost without exception. In the general election, the Democrats, who were increasingly offering progressive candidates of their own, won control of the House of Representatives for the first time in sixteen years and greatly strengthened their position in the Senate. Progressivism appeared to have become a tidal wave. Still, Roosevelt continued to deny any presidential ambitions and to claim that his real purpose was to pressure Taft to return to progressive policies. Two events, however, changed his mind.

The first was a 1911 decision by the Taft admin-istration that became, in Roosevelt's eyes, the final, inexcusable indignity. With his strong respect for the letter of the law, Taft had been far more active than Roosevelt in enforcing the provisions of the Sherman Antitrust Act and had launched dozens of suits against corporate combinations. To Roosevelt, such actions were troubling by themselves, for they reflected what he believed to be a wholly unrealistic attempt to abolish trusts when the proper course was to regulate them. But what truly outraged him was the announcement on October 27, 1911, that the administration was filing an antitrust suit against U. S. Steel, charging, among other things, that the 1907 acquisition of the Tennessee Coal and Iron Company had been illegal. Roosevelt had approved that acquisition in the midst of the 1907 panic, and he was enraged by the implication that he had acted improperly.

There remained, however, a major obstacle to Roosevelt's pursuit of the presidency. Since January 1911, Robert La Follette had been working through the newly formed National Progressive Republican League to secure the presidential nomination for himself. Many reformers believed he had established first claim to the leadership of any insurgent revolt, and Roosevelt was at first reluctant to challenge him. But La Follette's candidacy stumbled in February 1912, when, exhausted and plagued by personal worries (including the illness of his daughter), he appeared to suffer a nervous breakdown during a speech in Philadelphia. With almost indecent haste, many of his supporters abandoned him and turned to Roosevelt, who finally announced his candidacy on February 22.

TR Versus Taft

La Follette never forgave Roosevelt for "using" and then "betraying" him, and some diehard loyalists refused to abandon their allegiance to the Wisconsin senator. But for all practical purposes, the campaign for the Republican nomination had now become a battle between Roosevelt, the champion of the progressives, and Taft, the candidate of the conservatives. Roosevelt scored overwhelming victories in every presidential preference primary (there were thirteen in all) and arrived at the convention convinced that he had proved himself the choice of the party rank and file. Taft, however, remained the choice of most party leaders, and in the end it was their preference that proved decisive.

The battle for the nomination at the Chicago convention revolved around an unusually large number of contested delegates: 254 in all. Roosevelt needed about 100 of the disputed seats to clinch the nomination. But the Republican National Committee, which ruled on credentials, was controlled by members of the Old Guard; and it awarded all but 19 of the disputed seats to Taft. Roosevelt and his followers responded bitterly. The decision to seat the Taft delegates, they claimed, was an example of the same corrupt politics that progressives had been fighting for years; once more the people had been thwarted by the special interests. At a rally the night before the convention opened, Roosevelt addressed 5,000 madly cheering supporters and announced that he would not feel bound by the decision of his party if it refused to seat his delegates, that he would continue to fight for a candidacy that had now, it seemed, become a holy cause. "We stand at Armageddon," he told the roaring crowd, "and we battle for the Lord." As good as his word, Roosevelt the next day led his supporters out of the convention, and out of the party. Taft was then quietly nominated on the first ballot.

With financial support from newspaper magnate Frank Munsey and industrialist George W. Perkins, Roosevelt summoned his supporters back to Chicago in August for another convention, this one to launch the new Progressive party and nominate Roosevelt as its presidential candidate. By now, even Roosevelt was aware that the cause was virtually hopeless, particularly when many of the leading insurgents who had supported him during the primaries refused to follow him out of the Republican party. Nevertheless, he approached the battle feeling, as he put it, "fit as a bull moose" (thus giving his new party an enduring nickname). At the meeting in Chicago, he delivered a resounding "Confession of Faith" in which he castigated both of the traditional parties for representing "government of the needy many by professional politicians in the interests of the rich few"; and he produced a platform that embodied a full array of the most advanced progressive reforms.

Woodrow Wilson and the New Freedom

Yet even while Roosevelt was constructing his New Nationalism as a challenge to conservatives within his own party, another powerful alternative was emerging from the ranks of the Democrats. The con-

test, it soon became clear, was not simply one between conservatives and reformers; it was also one between two brands of progressivism, expressing two apparently different views of America's future.

Woodrow Wilson

For most of the first decade of the century, the Republican party had often seemed the sole home of progressive reform. In fact, however, progressive sentiment had been gaining strength within the Democratic party as well; and by 1912 it was ready to assert its dominance. At the Democratic convention in Baltimore in June, Champ Clark, the conservative Speaker of the House, was the early favorite for the presidential nomination. He controlled a majority of the delegates; but on ballot after ballot he failed to assemble the two-thirds necessary to win. For days the battle dragged on until finally, on the forty-sixth ballot, Woodrow Wilson, the governor of New Jersey, emerged as the party's nominee. His victory was in part a result of the last-minute support of Senator Oscar Underwood of Alabama, who had himself been one of the leading contenders for the nomination, and of William Jennings Bryan, who was to become Wilson's secretary of state. It was also, however, a result of Wilson's position as the only genuinely progressive candidate in the race.

Born in Virginia and raised in Confederate Georgia and Reconstruction South Carolina, Wilson had risen to political prominence by an unusual path. An 1879 graduate of Princeton University, he attended law school and for a time engaged unhappily in practice in Atlanta. He was, however, really more interested in politics and government, and after a few years he enrolled at Johns Hopkins University, where he earned a doctorate in political science. By virtue of his effective teaching and his lucid if unprofound books on the American political system, he rose steadily through the academic ranks until in 1902 he was promoted from the faculty to the presidency of Princeton. There, he displayed both the strengths and the weaknesses that would characterize his later political career. A champion of academic reform, he acted firmly and energetically to place Princeton on the road to becoming a great national university. At the same time, however, he displayed during controversies a self-righteous morality that at times made it nearly impossible for him to compromise.

It was a series of such stalemates that propelled him out of academia and into politics. Elected gov-

Woodrow Wilson and Champ Clark
Woodrow Wilson spent much of the summer of 1912 vacationing in Sea Girt, New Jersey, and preparing for his presidential campaign that fall. Among his visitors was House Speaker Champ Clark (on Wilson's right), who had entered the Democratic convention as the strong favorite for the nomination. Clark at one point received over 60 percent of the delegate votes, but he was never able to accumulate the two-thirds majority necessary for nomination. Wilson finally won the protracted battle on the forty-sixth ballot.   (Culver Pictures)

ernor of New Jersey in 1910, he brought to his new office the same commitment to reform that he had displayed in the past; and during his two years in the statehouse, he compiled an impressive record of progressive legislation—one that earned him a wide national reputation. At the same time, however, he was gradually alienating conservative party leaders with his intransigence and self-righteousness, and greatly hampering his ability to govern. His nomination for president in 1912 rescued him from what might well have become a political disaster in New Jersey.

In later years, Wilson's personal characteristics would help polarize the nation. In 1912, however, he sparked controversy by presenting a brand of progressivism that was both forceful and sharply different from Theodore Roosevelt's New Nationalism. His supporters soon began to describe Wilson's program as the "New Freedom"; and although in later years the two phrases began to seem like meaningless slogans, reflecting few important differences, the opposing philosophies—"nationalism" versus "freedom"—were in fact distinct from each other in important ways.

In its narrowest sense, Wilson's New Freedom differed from Roosevelt's New Nationalism in its approach to economic policy, in particular its approach to the trusts. Roosevelt had always believed in accepting economic concentration and using government to regulate and control it. Wilson, in contrast, appeared to be a disciple of Louis Brandeis's approach to economic reform. He sided with those who believed that bigness was both unjust and inefficient, that the proper response to monopoly was not to regulate it but to destroy it.

The Election of 1912

Despite the philosophical importance of the issues in 1912, the campaign itself was surprisingly uneventful. Voters seemed generally unaware of the ideological differences between Roosevelt and Wilson, and the election in the end reflected traditional party divisions.

It was a three-candidate election but a two-candidate campaign. William Howard Taft, resigned to defeat, delivered a few desultory, conservative speeches and then lapsed into silence. "There are so many people in the country who don't like me," he sadly explained. Roosevelt campaigned energetically (until a gunshot wound from a would-be assassin forced him to the sidelines during the last weeks before the election), and he continued to generate excitement among his Republican followers. He failed, however, to draw any significant numbers of Democratic progressives away from Wilson, who as the campaign wore on was beginning to evoke an enthusiastic national following of his own. The results in November were, therefore, predictable. Roosevelt and Taft split the Republican vote; Wilson held onto the Democratic vote and won. He polled only a plurality of the popular vote: 42 percent, to 27 percent for Roosevelt and a dismal 23 percent for Taft. Eugene Debs, the Socialist candidate, received 6 percent of the vote. But in the electoral college, Wilson won by a landslide: 435 of the 531 votes. Roosevelt had carried only six states, Taft only two.

The Scholar as President

The administration of Woodrow Wilson ended unhappily, both for the president and for the nation. It began, however, in triumph. For nearly five years, until international problems turned his attention elsewhere, Wilson served as the most successful leader of domestic reform of his era.

Wilson brought to the White House a conception of the presidency based on long years of scholarly study. His first published book, *Congressional Government* (1898), expressed what remained a lifelong admiration for the British parliamentary system and a belief in its adaptability to American institutions. In his later writings, however, he began to display more interest in the possibilities of presidential leadership.

"His is the only voice in national affairs," he wrote of the president only four years before he himself assumed the office. His must therefore be the voice of popular aspirations, the hand that guides public demands into legislative realities.

More than William Howard Taft, therefore, more even than Theodore Roosevelt, Wilson concentrated the powers of the executive branch in his own hands. He exerted firm control over his cabinet, and he delegated real authority only to those whose loyalty to him was beyond question. Perhaps the clearest indication of his style of leadership was the identity of the most powerful figure in his administration: Colonel Edward M. House, a man who held no office and whose only claim to authority was his personal intimacy with the president.

In his dealings with Congress, he proved unusually adept at using his position as head of his party to pressure and cajole members of Congress into supporting his positions. He used his appointive powers to weld together a coalition of conservatives and progressives who would, he believed, support his program. His task was eased by the existence of Democratic majorities in both houses of Congress and by the realization of many Democrats that the party must enact a progressive program in order to maintain those majorities.

Tariffs and Taxes

Wilson's first triumph as president was the fulfillment of an old Democratic and progressive promise—a substantial lowering of the protective tariff. Roosevelt had avoided the issue; Taft had failed at it. Wilson moved quickly and forcefully to succeed. On the day he took office, he called a special session of Congress. And when it met, he did what no president since Jefferson had done: He appeared before it in person to ask for genuine tariff reform. The Underwood-Simmons Tariff provided cuts substantial enough, progressives believed, to introduce real competition into American markets and thus to help break the power of trusts. It passed easily in the House; and despite Senate efforts to weaken its provisions, the bill survived more or less intact. Wilson's forceful exercise of party powers mobilized virtually the entire Democratic majority behind it.

To make up for the loss of revenue under the new tariff, Representative Cordell Hull of Tennessee drafted an amendment to the bill that provided for a graduated income tax, which the recently adopted

Election of 1912 (58.8% of electorate voting)

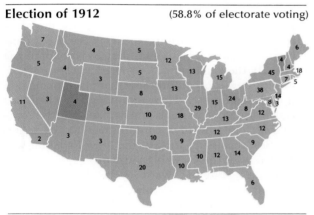

	ELECTORAL VOTE	POPULAR VOTE (%)
Woodrow Wilson (Democratic)	435	6,293,454 (41.9)
Theodore Roosevelt (Progressive/Bull Moose)	88	4,119,538 (27.4)
William H. Taft (Republican)	8	3,484,980 (23.2)
Eugene V. Debs (Socialist)	—	900,672 (6.0)
Other parties (Prohibition; Socialist Labor)	—	235,025

Sixteenth Amendment to the Constitution now permitted. This first modern income tax imposed a 1 percent tax on individuals and corporations earning over $4,000, with rates ranging up to 6 percent on incomes over $500,000. It was the beginning of a fundamental change in the American tax structure.

Banking Reform

President Wilson held Congress in session through the sweltering summer to begin work on a major reform of the American banking system. "The great monopoly in this country," he had declared in 1911, "is the money monopoly. So long as that exists, our old variety and freedom and individual energy of development are out of the question." Few progressives would have disagreed, but there were wide differences of opinion about how best to attack the problem.

Some legislators, of whom Representative Carter Glass of Virginia was one, wanted to decentralize control of the banking system so as to limit the power of the great Wall Street financiers but still leave ultimate authority over it with the bankers themselves. Others, whose hatred of the "money trust" was more intense—for example, William Jennings Bryan and fellow agrarians—wanted firm government control. After consultation with Louis Brandeis, Wilson accepted a plan that divided power in the system. The government would have substantial control at the national level; the bankers would retain control at the local level. With Bryan mediating and Wilson brandishing every presidential weapon in his arsenal, a banking reform bill passed both houses of Congress and was signed by the president on December 23, 1913. It was the most important piece of domestic legislation of Wilson's administration.

The Federal Reserve Act of 1913 created twelve regional banks, each to be owned and controlled by the individual banks of its district. The regional Federal Reserve banks would hold a certain percentage of the assets of their member banks in reserve; they would use those reserves to support loans to private banks at an interest (or "discount") rate that the Federal Reserve system would set; they would issue a new type of paper currency—Federal Reserve notes—which would become the nation's basic medium of trade and be backed by the government. Most important, perhaps, they would serve as central institutions able to shift funds quickly to troubled areas—to meet increased demands for credit or to protect imperiled banks. Supervising and regulating the entire system was a national Federal Reserve Board, whose members were appointed by the president. All "national" banks were required to join the system; smaller banks were encouraged to do the same. Within a year, nearly half the nation's banking resources were represented in the system; by the late 1920s, the proportion had swelled to 80 percent.

For all its limitations, and there were many, the Federal Reserve Act marked a notable advance in American banking practices, historically among the least stable and efficient in the Western world. And it provided the government, through the Federal Reserve Board, with a powerful instrument of economic influence—although it was not until many years later that economists recognized the power that control over the nation's money supply provided. The Great Depression of the 1930s would prove that, despite these changes, the American banking structure remained weak and unstable; but the Federal Reserve Act was an important first step toward the stabler system that ultimately emerged.

The Problem of the Trusts

The cornerstone of Wilson's campaign for the presidency had been his promise to attack economic concentration, most notably to destroy monopolistic trusts. By the beginning of his second year in office, however, it was becoming clear that his thinking had changed significantly. He was moving away from his earlier insistence that government dismantle the combinations and toward a commitment to regulating them. On this issue, at least, the New Freedom was giving way to the New Nationalism.

Wilson's attitude toward several major pieces of economic legislation symbolized the trend. When in 1914 he began to promote a sweeping plan to deal with the problem of monopoly, two elements emerged at its core. There was a proposal to create a federal agency through which the government would help business police itself—in other words, a regulatory commission of the type Roosevelt had advocated in 1912. There were, in addition, proposals to strengthen the government's power to prosecute and dismantle the trusts—a decentralizing approach more characteristic of Wilson's campaign. The two measures took shape, ultimately, as the Federal Trade Commission Act and the Clayton Antitrust Act.

Wilson fought hard for the Federal Trade Commission Act, which created a regulatory agency of the same name, and he signed it happily when it arrived at the White House. The new commission would, he promised, remove "uncertainty" within the corporate community, allowing businesses to determine in advance whether their actions would be acceptable to the government. It would also have authority to launch prosecutions against "unfair trade practices," which the law did not define, and it would have wide power to investigate corporate behavior. The act, in short, increased the government's regulatory authority significantly. But Wilson seemed to lose interest in the Clayton Antitrust bill and showed a notable lack of vigor in fighting to protect it from conservative assaults, which greatly weakened its potential effectiveness. When the emasculated bill finally reached his desk, he lauded it as a major accomplishment.

Nor did Wilson act very forcefully within the executive branch to prosecute the trusts. The relative ineffectiveness of the new Federal Trade Commission—to which Wilson appointed men so inept or so sympathetic to the trusts they were supposed to regulate that Brandeis once dismissed them as useless and "stupid"—was one indication of his attitude. And the Justice Department remained less than aggressive in its pursuit of illegal combinations. The vigorous legal pursuit of monopoly that Wilson had promised in 1912 never materialized. The future, he had apparently decided, lay with government supervision.

Retreat and Advance

By the fall of 1914, Wilson believed that the program of the New Freedom was essentially complete and that the agitation for reform would now subside. As a result, he himself began a conspicuous retreat from political activism. Citing the doctrine of states' rights, he declined to support the movement for woman suffrage. Accepting the inclinations of the many Southerners in his cabinet, he condoned the reimposition of segregation in the agencies of the federal government (a sharp contrast to Theodore Roosevelt, who had ordered the elimination of many such barriers and had even taken the unprecedented step of inviting a black man—Booker T. Washington—to the White House). When congressional reformers attempted to enlist his support for new social legislation, he breezily dismissed their proposals as unconstitutional or unnecessary.

The president's complacency could not, however, long survive the congressional elections of 1914. It

was disturbing enough that Democrats suffered major losses in the House of Representatives. But it was even more alarming that voters who had in 1912 supported the Progressive party were returning in droves to the Republicans. Wilson would not be able to rely on a divided opposition when he ran for reelection in 1916; he would need more than his 1912 total of 42 percent of the vote, and he would need the support of some of Theodore Roosevelt's former constituency to get it.

By the end of 1915, therefore, Wilson had shed his lethargy and begun to support a second flurry of reforms. In January 1916, he appointed Louis Brandeis to the Supreme Court, making him not only the first Jew but the most advanced progressive to be so named; and he weathered a conservative uproar in the Senate to obtain Brandeis's confirmation. Later, he supported a measure to make it easier for farmers to receive credit and one creating a system of workers' compensation for federal employees.

The real significance of this renewed effort at reform was that Wilson seemed now to have capitulated to the New Nationalism almost entirely; indeed, he had moved beyond it. No longer was the president appealing for the restoration of a competitive, decentralized economy. No longer was he warning about excessive federal power. Instead, Wilson was sponsoring measures that expanded the role of the national government in important ways, giving it new instruments by which it could not only regulate the economy but help shape the economic and social structure itself.

In 1916, for example, Wilson supported the Keating-Owen Act, the first federal law regulating child labor. It was important not only for the problem it addressed but for the means it adopted. The measure prohibited the shipment of goods produced by underage children across state lines, thus giving a new and expanded importance to the constitutional clause assigning Congress the task of regulating interstate commerce. (It would be some years before the Supreme Court would uphold this interpretation of the clause; the Court invalidated the Keating-Owen Act in 1918.) The president similarly supported measures that used federal taxing authority as a vehicle for legislating social change. When the Court struck down Keating-Owen, a new bill attempted to achieve the same goal by imposing a heavy tax on the products of child labor. (The Court later struck it down too.) The government's spending authority likewise became an instrument of social control. The Smith-Lever Act, for example, had as early as 1914 offered

Louis Brandeis
Brandeis graduated from Harvard Law School in 1877 with the best academic record of any student in the school's previous or subsequent history. His success in his Boston law practice was such that by the early twentieth century he was able to spend much of his time in unpaid work for public causes. His investigations of monopoly power soon made him a major figure in the emerging progressive movement. Woodrow Wilson nominated him for the United States Supreme Court in January 1916. He was one of only three or four nominees in the Court's history never to have held prior public office, and he was the first Jew ever to have been nominated. The appointment aroused five months of bitter controversy in the Senate before Brandeis was finally confirmed. For the next twenty years, he was one of the Court's most powerful members—all the while lobbying behind the scenes on behalf of the many other political causes (preeminent among them Zionism—the founding of a Jewish state) to which he remained committed.   (UPI/Bettmann Newsphotos)

matching federal grants to states that agreed to support agricultural extension education.

Wilson had, by the end of his first term, made significant strides toward expanding the role of the federal government in American society. He had accepted the importance of orderly bureaucratic procedures and enlightened expertise in governing an industrial society, and he had backed away from his earlier vision of a nation liberated from centralized controls. It was not, as one conservative congressman charged, "the first step away from the democracy of Thomas Jefferson . . . to the socialism of Karl Marx." But it was an important step toward the creation of the modern state.

The "Big Stick": America and the World, 1901–1917

American foreign policy during the progressive years reflected many of the same impulses that were motivating domestic reform. But it reflected far more clearly the nation's new sense of itself as a world power with far-flung economic and political interests. To the general public, foreign affairs remained largely remote. Walter Lippmann once wrote: "I cannot remember taking any interest whatsoever in foreign affairs until after the outbreak of the First World War." But to Theodore Roosevelt and later presidents, that made foreign affairs even more appealing. There the president could act with less regard for the Congress or the courts. There, he could free himself from concerns about public opinion. Overseas, the president could exercise power unfettered and alone.

Sea Power and Civilization

Theodore Roosevelt was well suited, both by temperament and by ideology, for an activist foreign policy. A vigorous athlete and once an enthusiastic college boxer, he spoke often of the virtues of the "strenuous life" and viewed physical combat as an ennobling, manly challenge. His fondness for battle had been greatly enhanced by his famous charge up San Juan Hill, a crucial event in the development of his political career.

Roosevelt believed, moreover, that an important

distinction existed between the "civilized" and "uncivilized" nations of the world. "Civilized" nations, as he defined them, were predominantly white and Anglo-Saxon or Teutonic; "uncivilized" nations were generally nonwhite, Latin, or Slavic. But racism was only partly the basis of the distinction. At least as important was economic development. Thus it was that Japan, a rapidly industrializing society, seemed to Roosevelt to have earned admission to the ranks of the civilized.

There was another important aspect of this global division. Civilized nations were, by Roosevelt's definition, producers of industrial goods; uncivilized nations were suppliers of raw materials and markets. There was, he believed, an economic relationship between the two parts that was vital to both of them; and it was natural, perhaps, that he should come to believe in the right and duty of the civilized societies to intervene in the affairs of "backward" nations to preserve order and stability. The economic health of the globe might depend on the result.

Accordingly, Roosevelt early became an outspoken champion of the development of American sea power. A friend and admirer of Alfred Thayer Mahan, Roosevelt had believed since his days as assistant secretary of the navy in 1897 that the United States must move rapidly to expand the size and power of its fleet. By 1906, Roosevelt's support had enabled the American navy to attain a size and strength surpassed only by that of Great Britain (although Germany was fast gaining ground).

Challenges in Asia

The new strength was not, however, always enough to enable the president to have his way in global developments, as events in the Pacific soon illustrated. Roosevelt believed that the "Open Door" was vital to maintain American trade in the Pacific and to prevent any single nation from establishing dominance there. (See above, pp. 592–593.) He looked with alarm, therefore, at the military rivalries involving Japan, Russia, Germany, and France in the region.

He was particularly concerned by Russian efforts to expand southward into Manchuria, a province of China; and when in 1904 the Japanese attacked the Russian fleet at Port Arthur in southern Manchuria, Roosevelt, like most Americans, was inclined to approve. Yet the president was no more eager for Japan to control Manchuria than for Russia to do so. In

1905, therefore, he eagerly agreed to a Japanese request to mediate an end to the conflict. Russia, faring badly in the war—and, as a result, already experiencing a domestic instability that twelve years later would culminate in revolution—had no choice but to agree.

At a peace conference in Portsmouth, New Hampshire, Roosevelt extracted from the embattled Russians a recognition of Japan's territorial gains—control of Korea, South Manchuria, and part of Sakhalin Island, formerly a Russian outpost. Japan, in return, agreed to cease the fighting and expand no further. At the same time, Roosevelt worked to secure American interests by negotiating a secret agreement with the Japanese to ensure that the United States could continue to trade freely in the region.

Roosevelt was pleased with his work at the Portsmouth Conference, particularly when it helped him to win the Nobel Peace Prize in 1906. But his triumph was, in fact, a hollow one. In the years that followed, relations between the United States and Japan steadily deteriorated, and the careful assurances Roosevelt had won in 1905 proved all but meaningless. Having destroyed the Russian fleet at Port Arthur, Japan now emerged as the preeminent naval power in the Pacific and soon began to exclude American trade from many of the territories it controlled.

It did not help matters that in 1906 the school board of San Francisco voted to segregate Oriental schoolchildren in the city in separate schools; or that a year later, the California legislature attempted to pass legislation limiting the immigration of Japanese laborers into the state. Anti-Oriental riots in California and inflammatory stories in the Hearst papers about the "Yellow Peril" further fanned resentment in Japan. The president did his best to douse the flames. He quietly persuaded the San Francisco school board to rescind its edict in return for a Japanese agreement to stop the flow of agricultural immigrants into California. Then, lest the Japanese government construe his actions as a sign of weakness, he sent sixteen battleships of the new American navy on an unprecedented 45,000-mile voyage around the world that included a call on Japan. Despite fears by some members of Congress that a naval conflict might ensue, the "Great White Fleet," as the flotilla was called, received a warm reception when it arrived in Yokohama. For the moment, Roosevelt's foreign policy—which he once summarized with the African proverb: "Speak softly and carry a big stick"—seemed to have borne important fruit. But the problem of

The Great White Fleet
Theodore Roosevelt agreed with his friend Alfred Thayer Mahan that a great nation needed to be a great sea power, and he transformed the American navy into the second most powerful in the world (after Great Britain). In 1907 he dispatched a fleet of sixteen battleships—painted white to indicate their peaceful intent—on a voyage around the world to demonstrate the nation's new naval might. It is seen here, in a painting by Henry Reuterdahl, steaming through the Straits of Magellan on its way to the Pacific in 1908. (U.S. Naval Academy Museum)

Japanese expansion in the Far East had not been resolved, and Japan continued to look for ways to extend its power in the region.

The Iron-Fisted Neighbor

Roosevelt took a special interest in events in what he (and most other Americans) considered the nation's special sphere of interest: Latin America. And very early in his presidency, he become concerned—some believed almost obsessed—by the possibility of German penetration into the region. Unwilling to share trading rights, let alone military control, with any other nation, Roosevelt embarked on a series of ventures in the Caribbean and South America that established a pattern of American intervention in the region that would long survive his presidency.

Crucial to Roosevelt's thinking was an incident early in his administration. When the government of Venezuela began in 1902 to renege on debts to European bankers, naval forces of Britain, Italy, and Germany erected a blockade along that country's coast. Roosevelt at first expressed little concern. But when German ships began to bombard a Venezuelan port and when rumors spread that Germany planned to establish a permanent base in the region, Roosevelt changed his mind. In 1903, he warned the Germans (according to his own later account) that Admiral Dewey and his fleet were standing by in the Carib-

bean and would act against any German effort to acquire new territory. The German navy finally withdrew.

The incident helped to persuade Roosevelt that European intrusions into Latin America could result not only from aggression but from internal instability or irresponsibility (such as defaulting on debts) within the Latin American nations themselves. As a result, he added a new "corollary" to the Monroe Doctrine. In a 1904 message to Congress, he claimed that the United States had the right not only to oppose European intervention in the Western Hemisphere but to intervene itself in the domestic affairs of its neighbors if those neighbors proved unable to maintain order on their own.

The immediate motivation for the Roosevelt Corollary, and the first opportunity for putting the doctrine into practice, was a crisis in the Dominican Republic. A revolution had toppled the corrupt and bankrupt government of that nation in 1903, but the new regime proved no better able than the old to make good on the country's $22 million of debts to European nations. Both France and Italy were threatening to intervene to recover their losses, and the new Dominican leaders had turned to the United States for help. Using the rationale he had outlined in his address to Congress, Roosevelt established, in effect, an American receivership, assuming control of Dominican customs and distributing 45 percent of the revenues to Santo Domingo and the rest to foreign creditors. This arrangement lasted, in one form or another, for more than three decades.

Two years later, another opportunity for intervention in the Caribbean arose. In 1902, the United States had granted political independence to Cuba, but only after the new government had agreed to the so-called Platt Amendment to its constitution, giving the United States the right to prevent any foreign power from intruding into the new nation. When, in 1906, a series of domestic uprisings seemed to threaten the internal stability of the island, Roosevelt reasoned that America must intervene to "protect" Cuba from disorder. American troops landed in Cuba, quelled the fighting, and remained there for three years.

The Panama Canal

The most celebrated accomplishment of Roosevelt's presidency, and the one that illustrated most clearly his own expansive view of the powers of his office and the role of the United States abroad, was the completion of the Panama Canal. Construction of a channel through Central America linking the Atlantic and the Pacific had been a dream of many nations since the mid-nineteenth century, but somehow the canal had never been built. Roosevelt was determined to do better.

The first step was the removal of an old obstacle. In 1850, the United States and Great Britain had agreed to a treaty under which the two nations would construct, operate, and defend any such canal together. The McKinley administration had already begun negotiations to cancel the agreement; Roosevelt completed the process. In 1901, the Hay-Pauncefote Treaty gave the United States the right to undertake the canal project alone.

The next question was where to locate the canal. At first, the Roosevelt administration (and many congressional leaders) favored a route across Nicaragua, which would permit a sea-level canal requiring no locks. A possible alternative was the Isthmus of Panama in Colombia, the site of an earlier, abortive effort by a French company to construct a channel.

The United States in Latin America, 1895–1941

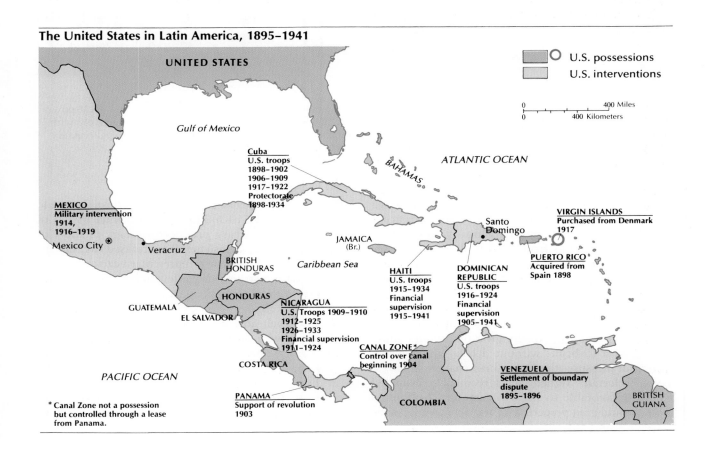

"The New Diplomacy"

This 1904 drawing by the famous *Puck* cartoonist Louis Dalrymple conveys the new image of America as a great power that Theodore Roosevelt was attempting to project to the world. Roosevelt the world policeman deals effectively with "less civilized" peoples (Asians and Latin Americans, seen clamoring at left) by using the "big stick" and deals equally effectively with the "civilized" nations (at right) by offering arbitration. (Culver Pictures)

The Panama route was shorter (although not at sea level), and construction was already about 40 percent complete. When the French company lowered its price for its holdings from $109 million to $40 million, and when it combined this gesture with skillful lobbying efforts in Washington, the president and Congress changed their minds.

Roosevelt quickly dispatched John Hay, his secretary of state, to negotiate an agreement with Colombian diplomats in Washington that would allow construction to begin without delay. Under heavy American pressure, the Colombian chargé d'affaires, Tomas Herrán, signed an agreement considered highly unfavorable to his own nation. The United States would gain perpetual rights to a six-mile-wide

"canal zone" across Colombia; in return, it would pay Colombia $10 million and an annual rental of $250,000. The treaty produced outrage in the Colombian Senate, whose members refused to ratify the agreement and sent a new representative to the United States with instructions to demand at least $20 million from the Americans plus a share of the payment to the French.

Roosevelt now was furious. The Colombians, he charged, were "inefficient bandits" and "blackmailers"; and he began to contemplate ways to circumvent the Bogotá government. He found a ready ally in the person of Philippe Bunau-Varilla, chief engineer of the French canal project. Bunau-Varilla watched with dismay as the government of Colombia appeared ready to destroy his efforts, and in November 1903 he helped organize and finance a revolution in Panama. There had been many previous revolts, all of them failures. But this one had an important additional asset: the support of the United States. Using an 1846 American-Colombian treaty as justification, Roosevelt landed troops from the U.S.S. *Nashville* in Panama to "maintain order." Their presence prevented Colombian forces from suppressing the rebellion, and three days later the United States recognized Panama as an independent nation. The new Panamanian government, under the influence of Bunau-Varilla, quickly agreed to a treaty with the United States. It granted America a canal zone ten miles wide; the United States would pay Panama the $10 million fee and the $250,000 annual rental that the Colombian Senate had rejected. Work on the canal proceeded rapidly, despite the enormous cuts and elaborate locks (which alone cost $375 million) that the construction required. It opened in 1914, three years after Roosevelt had proudly boasted to a university audience, "I took the Canal Zone and let Congress debate!"

Taft and "Dollar Diplomacy"

Many of those who had admired Roosevelt's vigorous command of American foreign policy and his strenuous efforts to maintain a world balance of power were dismayed by William Howard Taft's performance in international affairs. Although the new president made no decisive break with the policies of his predecessor, and while in some areas he actually extended American involvement abroad, he was in general no readier to exert strong leadership internationally than he was domestically. He worked to advance the nation's economic interests overseas, but he seemed to lack Roosevelt's larger vision of world stability. Worst of all, several of his most important foreign policy initiatives were conspicuous failures.

The thrust of Taft's foreign policy was best symbolized by the man he chose to administer it: Secretary of State Philander C. Knox, a corporate lawyer committed to using his position to promote American business interests overseas. Roosevelt, of course, had promoted American economic interests too; but Knox seemed at times to regard the State Department as little more than an agent of the corporate community. He worked aggressively to extend American investments into underdeveloped regions, motivating critics to label his policies "Dollar Diplomacy."

The Taft-Knox foreign policy faced its severest test, and encountered its greatest failure, in the Far East. Ignoring Roosevelt's tacit 1905 agreement with Japan to limit American involvement in Manchuria, the new administration succumbed to the persuasive powers of American bankers and began to move aggressively to increase America's economic influence in the region. When British, French, and German bankers formed a consortium to finance a vast system of railroads in China, Knox insisted that Americans should also participate; and when in 1911 the Europeans finally agreed to include the United States in their venture, Knox proposed that an international syndicate purchase the South Manchurian Railroad to remove it from Japanese control. Japan responded by signing a treaty of friendship with Russia—a warning to the Europeans—and the entire railroad project quickly collapsed. Having attempted to expand its influence in Asia, America now found the door to Manchuria slammed in its face.

In the Caribbean, the new administration continued and even expanded upon Roosevelt's policies of maintaining order and stability in troubled areas, without regard for the national integrity of the nations involved. Limiting European influence in the region meant, Taft and Knox believed, not only preventing disorder but establishing a significant American economic presence there—replacing the investments of European nations with investments from the United States. In 1909, Knox tried (unsuccessfully) to arrange for American bankers to establish a financial receivership in Honduras. Later, he persuaded New York bankers to invest in the National Bank of Haiti.

But Dollar Diplomacy was not always so peaceful. When a revolution broke out in Nicaragua in 1909, the administration quickly sided with the insurgents (who had been inspired to revolt by an American mining company) and sent American troops into the country to seize the customs houses. As soon as peace was restored, Knox encouraged American bankers to move into Nicaragua and offer substantial loans to the new government, thus increasing Washington's financial leverage over the country. Within two years, however, the new pro-American government faced a revolt of its own; and Taft again landed American troops in Nicaragua, this time to protect the existing regime. The troops remained there for more than a decade.

Diplomacy and Morality

"It would be the irony of fate," Woodrow Wilson remarked shortly before assuming the presidency, "if my administration had to deal chiefly with foreign affairs." It would also, as it turned out, be a tragedy. Wilson faced international challenges of a scope and gravity unmatched by any president before him; and he brought to his treatment of them not only remarkable vision but an often inflexible, even self-righteous morality that would ultimately destroy both him and many of the goals for which he fought. Although the true ordeal of Wilsonian diplomacy did not occur until after World War I, many of the qualities that would help produce it were evident in his foreign policy from his first moments in office.

Through much of his administration, Wilson made strenuous but generally unsuccessful efforts to maintain an open door for American trade in China and to resist the expansion of Japanese influence in the Pacific. At the same time, however, the United States was itself working energetically to close the door to all nations but itself in Latin America. Wilson presided over a foreign policy that not only continued but greatly increased American intervention in the Caribbean and in Latin America, justifying his actions by citing both economic necessity and moral imperative.

The list of American incursions was lengthy and impressive. Having already seized control of the finances of the Dominican Republic in 1905, the United States established a military government there in 1916 when the Dominicans refused to accept a treaty that would have made the country a virtual American protectorate. The military occupation lasted eight years. In Haiti, which shares the island of Hispaniola with the Dominican Republic, Wilson landed the marines in 1915 to quell a revolution in the course of which a mob had murdered an unpopular president. American military forces remained in the country until 1934, and American officers drafted the new Haitian constitution adopted in 1918. When Wilson began to fear that the Danish West Indies might be about to fall into the hands of Germany, he bought the colony from Denmark and renamed it the Virgin Islands. Concerned about the possibility of European influence in Nicaragua, he signed a treaty with that country's government ensuring that no other nation would build a canal there and winning for the United States the right to intervene in Nicaragua's internal affairs to protect American interests.

In one case after another, the United States was openly disregarding the national integrity of its neighbors, acting instead in response to what Wilson considered a higher mission: the creation of order and, not coincidentally, the protection of American markets and investments. The president had no doubt that the recipients of his attention would become stabler, more democratic nations as a result. In most cases, he was wrong.

Mission in Mexico

It was in Mexico that Wilson's missionary view of America's role in the Western Hemisphere received its greatest test and suffered its greatest frustrations. For many years, under the friendly auspices of dictator Porfirio Díaz, American businessmen had been establishing an enormous presence in Mexico, with investments totaling more than $1 billion. In 1910, however, the corrupt and tyrannical Díaz had been overthrown by the popular leader Francisco Madero, who excited many of his countrymen by promising democratic reform but alarmed many American businessmen by threatening their investments in his country. With the approval of, among others, the American ambassador in Mexico, Madero was himself deposed early in 1913 by a reactionary general, Victoriano Huerta.

A relieved Taft administration prepared, in its last weeks in office, to recognize the new Huerta regime and welcome back a receptive environment for American investments in Mexico. Before it could do so, however, the new government murdered Madero, producing horror and outrage around the world. Wilson, therefore, inherited a difficult and unresolved dilemma. But he displayed no hesitation in responding. He would never, he insisted, recognize Huerta's "government of butchers."

The problem dragged on for years. At first, Wilson hoped that simply by refusing to recognize Huerta he could help topple the regime and bring to power the opposing Constitutionalists, led by Venustiano Carranza. When Huerta established a full military dictatorship in October 1913, however, the president decided on a more forceful approach. First he pressured the British to stop supporting Huerta. Then he offered to send American troops to assist Carranza. Carranza, aware that such an open alliance with the United States would undermine his popular support in Mexico, declined the offer; but he did

SIGNIFICANT EVENTS

1898 Theodore Roosevelt elected governor of New York

1900 Roosevelt elected vice president

1901 McKinley assassinated; Roosevelt becomes president
Hay-Pauncefote Treaty ratified

1902 Northern Securities antitrust case filed
Roosevelt intervenes in anthracite coal strike
Newlands Reclamation Act passed

1903 Department of Commerce and Labor created

1904 Roosevelt mediates settlement of Russo-Japanese War
"Roosevelt Corollary" announced
United States orchestrates Panamanian independence; new government signs treaty allowing United States to build Panama Canal
Roosevelt elected president

1906 Hepburn Railroad Regulation Act passed
Upton Sinclair publishes *The Jungle*
Meat Inspection Act passed
American troops intervene in Cuba

1907 Financial panic and recession

1908 William Howard Taft elected president

1909 Payne-Aldrich Tariff passed
Pinchot-Ballinger dispute begins
U.S. troops intervene in Nicaragua

1910 Roosevelt's Osawatomie speech outlines "New Nationalism"

1910 Woodrow Wilson elected governor of New Jersey
Porfirio Díaz overthrown by Francisco Madero in Mexico

1911 Taft administration files antitrust suit against U.S. Steel

1912 Roosevelt challenges Taft for Republican nomination; wins all party primaries
Taft receives Republican nomination; Roosevelt and followers walk out
Roosevelt forms Progressive party
Woodrow Wilson elected president

1913 Thirteenth Amendment, establishing direct popular election of U.S. senators, ratified
Federal Reserve Act passed
Victoriano Huerta overthrows Madero in Mexico

1914 Federal Trade Commission Act passed
Clayton Antitrust Act passed
Panama Canal opens
U.S. troops intervene in Haiti
Tampico incident strains U.S. relations with Mexico
Venustiano Carranza deposes Huerta in Mexico

1916 Wilson appoints Louis Brandeis to Supreme Court
United States establishes military government in Dominican Republic
U.S. troops pursue Pancho Villa into Mexico

1917 United States recognizes Carranza government

request and receive from Wilson the right to buy arms in the United States. Still the stalemate continued.

Finally, a minor naval incident provided the president with an excuse for more open intervention. In April 1914, an officer in Huerta's army briefly arrested several American sailors from the U.S.S. *Dolphin* who had gone ashore in Tampico. Although a superior officer immediately released them and apologized to the ship's commander, the American admiral demanded that the Huerta forces fire a twenty-one-gun salute to the American flag as a pub-

lic display of penance. The Mexicans refused. Wilson seized on the silly incident as a pretext for sending all available American naval forces into Mexican waters; and a few days later, eager to prevent a German ship from delivering munitions to the Huerta forces, he ordered the navy to seize the Mexican port of Veracruz.

Wilson had envisioned a bloodless action, but he was not to have his way. In a clash with Mexican troops in the city, the Americans killed 126 of the defenders and suffered 19 casualties of their own. With the two nations at the brink of war, Wilson now drew back and began to look for alternative measures to deal with the crisis. His show of force, however, had in the meantime helped strengthen the position of the Carranza faction, which captured Mexico City in August and forced Huerta to flee the country. At last, it seemed, the crisis might be over.

It was not to be. Wilson reacted angrily when Carranza refused to accept American guidelines for the creation of a new government, and he briefly considered throwing his support to still another aspirant to leadership: Carranza's erstwhile lieutenant Pancho Villa, who was now leading a rebel army of his own. When Villa's military position deteriorated, however, Wilson abandoned the scheme and finally, in October 1915, granted preliminary recognition to the Carranza government. But by now the president had created yet another crisis. Angry at what he considered an American betrayal, Villa retaliated in January 1916 by taking sixteen Americans from a train in northern Mexico and shooting them. Two months later, he led his soldiers (or bandits, as the United States preferred to call them) across the border into New Mexico, where they murdered nineteen more Americans. His goal, apparently, was to destabilize relations between Wilson and Carranza and provoke a war between them, which might provide him with an opportunity to improve his own declining fortunes. He almost succeeded.

With the permission of the Carranza government,

Wilson ordered General John J. Pershing to lead an American expeditionary force across the Mexican border in pursuit of Villa. The American troops, during their 300-mile penetration of Mexico, were never able to manage a clash with Villa. They did, however, engage in two ugly skirmishes with Carranza's army, in which forty Mexicans and twelve Americans died. Again, the United States and Mexico stood at the brink of war. But at the last minute, Wilson agreed to the face-saving expedient of referring the dispute to an international commission, which debated for six months without agreeing on a solution. In the meantime, Wilson was quietly withdrawing American troops from Mexico; and in March 1917, having spent four years of effort and gained nothing but a lasting Mexican hostility toward the United States, he at last granted formal recognition to the Carranza regime.

By now, however, Wilson's attention was turning elsewhere—to the far greater international crisis engulfing the European continent and ultimately much of the world. The American response to the Great War transformed the nation's position in the world. It also provided Woodrow Wilson with his most important, and in the end most disastrous, opportunity to bring his strong sense of moralism to the conduct of international relations.

SUGGESTED READINGS

General Studies   Several of the general studies of the progressive era listed in the readings for Chapter 21 provide overviews of national politics from 1900 to 1917. Also useful are George E. Mowry, *The Era of Theodore Roosevelt* (1958), and Arthur Link, *Woodrow Wilson and the Progressive Era, 1910–1917* (1954), both volumes in the New American Nation series. John Milton Cooper, Jr., *The Warrior and the Priest: Woodrow Wilson and Theodore Roosevelt* (1983), is a comparative biography and argues that the ideological tensions between Wilson and Roosevelt provide the framework for understanding the course of twentieth-century liberalism.

Theodore Roosevelt   An eloquent popular study of Theodore Roosevelt's life before his presidency is Edmund Morris, *The Rise of Theodore Roosevelt* (1979). Important full-scale biographies include Henry F. Pringle, *Theodore Roosevelt* (1931), a critical study, and William H. Harbaugh, *Power and Responsibility* (1961), published in paperback under the title *The Life and Times of Theodore Roosevelt*. John Morton Blum, *The Republican Roosevelt* (1954), provides a succinct, interpretive account of TR's career. Another work on Roosevelt's presidency and the national politics of his

era is G. Wallace Chessman, *Theodore Roosevelt and the Politics of Power* (1969). John A. Garraty, *The Life of George W. Perkins* (1960), chronicles the career of one of Roosevelt's most important political allies. Party politics is the subject of Horace S. Merrill and Marion G. Merrill, *The Republican High Command* (1971).

William Howard Taft   The standard biography of Taft is Henry F. Pringle, *The Life and Times of William Howard Taft,* 2 vols. (1939), which contrasts its subject favorably with Theodore Roosevelt. Studies of Taft's presidency include Paolo E. Coletta, *The Presidency of Taft* (1973), and Donald E. Anderson, *William Howard Taft* (1973), which applies a political science model developed by Richard Neustadt to the Taft administration and finds Taft wanting. The acrimonious Pinchot-Ballinger controversy receives discussion in James L. Penick, *Progressive Politics and Conservation: The Ballinger-Pinchot Affair* (1968), and Harold T. Pinkett, *Gifford Pinchot: Private and Public Forester* (1970). The Republican rift of 1912 is chronicled in George Mowry, *Theodore Roosevelt and the Progressive Movement* (1946). See also Norman Wilensky, *Conservatives in the Progressive Era: The Taft Republicans of 1912* (1965).

Woodrow Wilson   Arthur S. Link, long the nation's pre-eminent Wilson scholar, is the author of the most definitive biography, although it is not yet complete. The five volumes of his *Woodrow Wilson* (1947–1965) follow Wilson's life from birth to the American entrance into World War I. Other standard studies of Wilson include John Morton Blum, *Woodrow Wilson and the Politics of Morality* (1956), and Alexander George and Juliette George, *Woodrow Wilson and Colonel House* (1956), a psychoanalytic study of the careers of and the relationship between the two intimate friends. Edwin A. Weinstein, *Woodrow Wilson: A Medical and Psychological Biography* (1981), is a controversial study which argues that Wilson's erratic public behavior can be explained by a series of strokes he suffered beginning many years before he became president. John Morton Blum, *Joseph Tumulty and the Wilson Era* (1951), explores the events of the Wilson administration through the career of the president's closest White House associate. L. J. Holt, *Congressional Insurgents and the Party System, 1909–1916* (1967), explores the nature of congressional politics during the Taft and Wilson administrations.

National Issues   Samuel P. Hays has provided a penetrating study of progressive conservation policies in *The Gospel of Efficiency: The Progressive Conservation Movement, 1890–1920* (1962). See also Elmo P. Richardson, *The Politics of Conservation* (1962). O. E. Anderson, *The Health of a Nation* (1958), is a study of the fight for regulation of the meat-packing and other food industries. Craig West, *Banking Reform and the Federal Reserve, 1863–1923* (1977), examines the most important financial reform of the era.

Roosevelt's Foreign Policy   Howard K. Beale, *Theodore Roosevelt and the Rise of America to World Power* (1956), is the standard work on TR's foreign policy. Other useful studies include Richard Challener, *Admirals, Generals, and American Foreign Policy, 1898–1914* (1973); David H. Burton, *Theodore Roosevelt: Confident Imperialist* (1969); and Julius W. Pratt, *Challenge and Rejection: The United States and World Leadership, 1900–1921* (1967). Richard Leopold, *Elihu Root and the Conservative Tradition* (1954), examines the man who served Roosevelt first as secretary of war and then as secretary of state. On American policy in Asia, see Akira Iriye, *Pacific Estrangement: Japanese and American Expansion, 1897–1911* (1972); Charles E. Neu, *An Uncertain Friendship: Roosevelt and Japan, 1906–1909* (1967); and Charles Vevier, *United States and China* (1955).

America and the Caribbean   For American policy in the Caribbean, see Dana G. Munro, *Intervention and Dollar Diplomacy in the Caribbean, 1900–1921* (1964); Dwight C. Miner, *Fight for the Panama Route* (1966); Walter LaFeber, *The Panama Canal* (1978); and David McCullough *The Path Between the Seas* (1977), a lucid popular history of the building of the canal. For the foreign policy of the Taft years, consult Walter Scholes and Marie Scholes, *The Foreign Policies of the Taft Administration* (1970).

Wilson's Foreign Policy   Wilson's foreign policy has spawned a particularly large literature. Arthur Link is the author of *Wilson the Diplomatist* (1957), a series of concise essays, and *Woodrow Wilson: Revolution, War, and Peace* (1979), a major revision of the 1957 essays. See also Robert Freeman Smith, *The United States and Revolutionary Nationalism in Mexico, 1916–1932* (1972); Kenneth Grieb, *The United States and Huerta* (1969); Robert Quirk, *An Affair of Honor: Woodrow Wilson and the Occupation of Veracruz* (1962) and *The Mexican Revolution, 1914–1915* (1960); and David Healy, *Gunboat Diplomacy in the Wilson Era: The U.S. Navy in Haiti, 1915–1916* (1976).

World War I Recruiting Poster, 1917   (Culver Pictures)

Chapter 23 America and the Great War

The Great War, as it was known to a generation unaware that another, greater war would soon follow, began modestly in August 1914 when Austria invaded the tiny Balkan nation of Serbia. Within weeks, however, it had grown into a widespread conflagration, engaging the armies of all the major nations of Europe and shattering forever the delicate balance of power that had maintained a general peace on the Continent since the early nineteenth century. Americans looked on with horror but also at first with a conviction that the conflict had little to do with them. They were wrong.

After nearly three years of attempting to affect the outcome of the conflict without becoming embroiled in it, the United States formally entered the war in April 1917. In doing so, it joined the most savage conflict in history. The fighting had already dragged on for two and a half years, inconclusive, almost inconceivably murderous, engaging not only the armies of the contending nations but their civilian populations as well. Although the American Civil War had greatly increased the ferocity and extent of combat, World War I was the first truly "total" war. It pitted entire societies against one another, and it had by 1917 left Europe exhausted and on the brink of utter collapse. By the time it ended late in 1918, Germany had lost nearly 2 million soldiers in battle, Russia 1.7 million, France 1.4 million, Great Britain 900,000. An entire generation of European youth was decimated; centuries of political, social, and economic traditions were eroded and all but destroyed.

For America, however, the war was the source of a very different experience. As a military struggle, it was brief, decisive, and—in relative terms—without great cost. Only 112,000 American soldiers died in the conflict, half of them from disease rather than combat. Economically, it was the source of a great industrial boom, which helped spark the years of prosperity that would follow. And the war propelled the United States into a position of almost unquestioned world supremacy.

In other respects, however, World War I was a painful, even traumatic experience for the American people. At home, the nation became obsessed with not only a search for victory but a search for social unity—a search that continued and even intensified in the troubled years following the armistice, and that helped shatter many of the progressive ideals of the first years of the century. And in the world at large, once the conflict ended, the United States encountered frustration and disillusionment. The "war to end wars," the war "to make the world safe for democracy," became neither. Instead, it led directly to twenty years of international instability that would ultimately generate another great conflict.

The Road to War

Wilson's policy of maintaining American neutrality was based on a false premise. The United States had nothing at stake in this war, he told the nation. In fact, America had a great deal at stake, and as the war continued, that stake grew.

A False Neutrality

Wilson called on his countrymen in 1914 to remain "impartial in thought as well as deed." His own thoughts, however, were far from neutral. Like many Americans of his background, he was a fervent admirer of England—its traditions, its culture, its political system; almost instinctively, therefore, he attributed to the cause of the Allies (Britain, France, Italy, and Russia) a moral quality that he denied to the Central Powers (Germany, the Austro-Hungarian Empire, and the Ottoman—or Turkish—Empire).

More important, however, he soon recognized that economic realities made it essential for him to adopt one policy toward England and quite another toward Germany. The neutral rights that he so ardently sought to uphold included, among other things, the right of an impartial nation such as the United States to trade freely with both sides in the conflict. But the British, whose control of the seas was their most effective weapon, clamped a naval blockade on Germany to prevent munitions and supplies—from neutrals as well as belligerents—from reaching the enemy. Wilson had two choices. He could preserve a genuine American neutrality by denouncing the blockade and imposing an embargo on trade with Great Britain; or he could accept the situation and allow trade with England to continue and trade with Germany to cease.

Economic realities, combined with his own inclination to support the British, caused him to choose the latter. The United States could survive an interruption of trade with the Central Powers. It could not, however, easily weather an embargo on trade with the Allies as well, particularly when war orders from Britain and France jumped from $824 million in 1914 to $3.2 billion two years later. The war had produced the greatest economic boom in the nation's history, and Wilson could ill afford to destroy it.

By 1915, therefore, the United States had gradually transformed itself into the arsenal of the Allies. In the process, it had replaced its stance of genuine neutrality with something quite different. Quietly, or with only feeble protests, Americans acquiesced in violations of their rights by the British, who periodically seized American ships suspected of carrying supplies destined for Germany. When Germany infringed on neutral rights, however, the response of the United States was harsh and unyielding.

The Germans intensified that antagonism by resorting to a new and, in American eyes, barbaric tactic: submarine warfare. Unable to challenge British domination on the ocean's surface, Germany began early in 1915 to use the newly improved submarine to try to stem the flow of supplies to England. Enemy vessels, the Germans announced, would be sunk on sight, prompting Wilson to declare that he would hold Germany to "strict accountability" for unlawful acts.

A test of this pronouncement came only months later, when on May 7, 1915, a German U-boat (short for *Unterseeboot,* "undersea boat") sank the British

Submarine Warfare
A German submarine (or U-boat) stops a Spanish steamer for inspection on the North Sea in 1917. Germany claimed the right to search (and at times, the right to sink) all neutral vessels suspected of carrying war matériel to the Allied powers. (Culver Pictures)

passenger liner *Lusitania* without warning, causing the deaths of 1,198 people, 128 of them Americans. The ship was, it later became clear, carrying not only passengers but munitions; at the time, however, the attack seemed to most Americans to be what Theodore Roosevelt called it: "an act of piracy."

Wilson reacted by initiating an angry exchange of notes with Germany, demanding assurances that such outrages would not recur and that the Central Powers would respect the rights of neutral nations, among which, he insisted, was the right of their citizens to travel on the nonmilitary vessels of belligerents. (After one particularly threatening note, Secretary of State William Jennings Bryan—who argued that equally strenuous protests should be sent to the British in response to their blockade—resigned from office as a matter of principle, one of the few high government officials of the United States ever to do so.) The Germans finally agreed to Wilson's demands, but a pattern of relations had been established that would increasingly bring the two nations into conflict.

Early in 1916, American-German relations soured anew when, in response to an announcement that the Allies were now arming merchant ships to sink submarines, Germany proclaimed that it would fire on such vessels without warning. A few weeks later, it did just that, attacking the unarmed French steamer *Sussex* and injuring several American passengers. Again, Wilson demanded that Germany abandon its "unlawful" tactics; again, the German government relented. Lacking sufficient naval power to enforce an effective blockade against Britain, the Germans decided that the marginal advantages of unrestricted submarine warfare did not yet justify the possibility of drawing America into the war.

Preparedness Versus Pacifism

Despite the president's increasing bellicosity in 1916, he was still far from ready to commit the United States to war. One obstacle was American domestic politics. Facing a difficult battle for reelection, Wilson could not ignore the powerful factions that continued to oppose intervention. His policies, therefore, represented an effort to satisfy the demands both of those who, like Theodore Roosevelt, insisted that the nation defend its "honor" and economic interests and those who, like Bryan, La Follette, and others (including many German-Americans and Irish-Americans hostile to Britain), denounced any action that seemed to increase the chance of war.

The question of whether America should make military and economic preparations for war provided a preliminary issue over which the two coalitions could battle. Wilson at first sided with the anti-preparedness forces, denouncing the idea of an American military build-up as needless and provocative. As tensions between the United States and Germany grew, however, he changed his mind. In the fall of 1915, he endorsed an ambitious proposal by American military leaders for a large and rapid increase in the nation's armed forces, to cost more than half a billion dollars; and amid howls of outrage from pacifists in Congress and elsewhere, he worked hard to win approval of it. He even embarked on a national speaking tour early in 1916 to arouse support for the proposal. By midsummer his efforts had in large part succeeded, and rearmament for a possible conflict was well under way.

Still, the peace faction wielded considerable political strength. How much strength became clear to Wilson at the Democratic Convention that met to renominate him in the summer of 1916. The keynote speaker turned his address into a litany of praise for Wilson's efforts to avoid American intervention. He evoked a remarkable response. As he recited the pres-

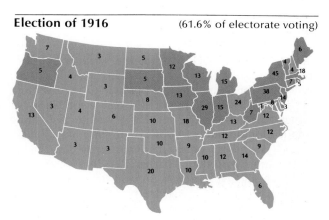

Election of 1916　(61.6% of electorate voting)

	ELECTORAL VOTE	POPULAR VOTE (%)
Woodrow Wilson (Democratic)	277	9,129,606 (49.4)
Charles E. Hughes (Republican)	254	8,538,221 (46.2)
A. L. Benson (Socialist)	—	585,113 (3.2)
Other parties (Prohibition; Socialist Labor)	—	233,909

ident's diplomatic accomplishments, the delegates chanted again and again, "What did we do? What did we do?" And the speaker shouted in response, "We didn't go to war! We didn't go to war!" Out of that almost hysterical exchange came one of the most prominent slogans of Wilson's reelection campaign (although one that he himself never used or approved): "He kept us out of war."

In the face of such pressures, therefore, Wilson remained highly cautious. When prowar rhetoric became particularly heated, Wilson spoke defiantly of the nation being "too proud to fight." And when the Republicans chose as their 1916 presidential candidate Charles Evans Hughes, a progressive who attracted the support of the bellicose Theodore Roosevelt, Wilson did nothing to discourage those who argued that Hughes was more likely than he to lead the nation into war. At times, he issued such warnings himself. Wilson's promises of progressivism and peace ultimately combined to give the Democrats, once again a minority party against the reunited Republicans, a narrow victory in November. Wilson won reelection by one of the smallest margins in American history: fewer than 600,000 popular votes and only 23 electoral votes, with the Democrats retaining a precarious control over Congress.

A War for Democracy

With the election behind him, and with tensions between the United States and Germany unabated, there remained for Wilson a final obstacle to involvement in the world war. He required a lofty justification for American intervention, one that would not only unite public opinion but satisfy his own sense of morality. The Germans had gone far toward providing such a justification with their "barbaric" tactics on the seas and their alleged atrocities on land (including, as the American prowar press ardently reported, the use of poison gas and the senseless butchering of women and children). Wilson himself, however, created the most important rationale. The United States, he insisted, had no material aims of its own in the conflict. The nation was, rather, committed to using the war as a vehicle for constructing a new world order, one based on the same progressive ideals that had motivated reform in America.

In a speech before Congress in January 1917, he presented a plan for a postwar order in which the United States would help maintain peace through a permanent league of nations—a peace that would in-

clude self-determination and equality for all nations, a "peace among equals," a "peace without victory."

In the first months of 1917, when new provocations once again inflamed German-American relations, Wilson was at last ready to fight. In January, after months of inconclusive warfare in the trenches of France, the military leaders of Germany decided on one last dramatic gamble to achieve a quick and decisive victory. They would launch a series of major assaults on the enemy's lines in France. At the same time, they would begin unrestricted submarine warfare in an effort to cut off vital supplies from Britain. The Allies would collapse, they hoped, before the United States had time to intervene. Beginning February 1, the German ambassador informed Wilson, U-boats would sink all ships, enemy and neutral alike, in a broad zone around the British Isles. If America chose to continue supplying the Allies, it would have to risk attack.

With that, the president recognized that war was inevitable; the only question remaining was the appropriate time to declare it. Two additional developments helped clear the way. On February 25, the British turned over to him an intercepted telegram from the German foreign minister, Arthur Zimmermann, to the government of Mexico. It proposed that in the event of war between Germany and the United States, the Mexicans should join the struggle against the Americans. In return, they would regain their "lost provinces" to the north when the war was over. Widely publicized by British propagandists and in the American press, the Zimmermann telegram inflamed public opinion and helped build up popular sentiment for war.

A second event, in March, provided Wilson with additional comfort. A revolution in Russia toppled the reactionary czarist regime, which had been tottering ever since the Russo-Japanese War in 1905. A new, republican government took its place. The United States would now be spared the embarrassment of allying itself with a despotic monarchy. The war for a progressive world order could proceed untainted.

On the rainy evening of April 2, two weeks after German submarines had torpedoed three American ships, Wilson appeared before a joint session of Congress and spoke words that brought to an end the years of uncertain waiting:

> It is a fearful thing to lead this great peaceful people into war, into the most terrible and disastrous of all wars, civilization itself seeming to be in the balance. But the

right is more precious than peace, and we shall fight for the things which we have always carried nearest our hearts—for democracy, for the right of those who submit to authority to have a voice in their own Governments, for the rights and liberties of small nations, for a universal dominion of right by such a concert of free peoples as shall bring peace and safety to all nations and make the world itself at last free.

The audience in the House chamber roared its approval. In Europe, the Allied nations rejoiced at their deliverance. Even some of Wilson's bitterest enemies, men such as Theodore Roosevelt and Henry Cabot Lodge, offered warm words of praise.

The sentiment for war was not, however, unanimous. For four days, amid cries of treason and cowardice, pacifists in Congress carried on their futile struggle. When the declaration of war finally passed on April 6, fifty representatives and six senators had voted against it. America was entering a new era, but it was doing so divided and fearful. And Woodrow Wilson, perhaps aware of the ordeal that lay ahead, returned to the White House after his dramatic war address and, according to one account, broke down and wept.

"War Without Stint"

Armies on both sides in Europe were decimated and exhausted by the time of Woodrow Wilson's declaration of war. The German offensives of early 1917 had failed to produce an end to the struggle, and French and British counteroffensives had accomplished little beyond adding to the appalling number of casualties. The ghastly stalemate continued, and the Allies looked desperately to the United States to provide them with a chance for victory.

The Americans were eager to oblige. Wilson had called on the nation to wage war "without stint or limit." And in that spirit, the American government proceeded to launch massive campaigns against German submarines in the Atlantic and against German armies in France, and to mobilize the nation's economic resources on a grand scale.

The Military Struggle

The conflicts at sea had brought the United States into the war; and it was on the naval struggle that American participation had the most immediate effect. By the spring of 1917, Great Britain was suffering such vast losses from attacks by German submarines—one of every four ships setting sail from British ports never returned—that its ability to continue ferrying vital supplies across the Atlantic was coming into serious question. Within weeks of joining the war, the United States had begun to alter the balance. A fleet of American destroyers aided the British navy in its assault on the U-boats; other American warships escorted merchant vessels across the Atlantic; American assistance was crucial in sowing antisubmarine mines in the North Sea.

The results were dramatic. Sinkings of Allied ships had totaled nearly 900,000 tons in the month of April 1917; by December, the figure had dropped to 350,000; by October 1918, it had declined to 112,000. The flow of weapons and supplies from the United States to England and France continued; without it, the Allied cause would have been lost.

At first, most Americans believed that this naval assistance was all that would be required of them. It soon became clear, however, that a major commitment of American ground forces would be necessary as well. Britain and France by 1917 had few reserves left on which to draw. Russia was in even direr straits; and after the Bolshevik Revolution in November 1917, the new government, led by Nikolai Lenin, negotiated a hasty and costly peace with the Central Powers. Battalions of German troops were now free to fight on the western front. It would be up to American forces to counterbalance them.

In 1917, however, those forces barely existed. The regular army was pathetically small, and little thought had been given to an effective method for expanding it. Theodore Roosevelt, old and ill, swallowed his personal hatred of President Wilson and visited the White House, offering to raise a regiment to fight in Europe. Others, similarly, urged an entirely voluntary recruitment process. The president, however, decided otherwise. Only a national draft, he insisted, could provide the needed men; and despite the protests of those who agreed with House Speaker Champ Clark that "there is precious little difference between a conscript and a convict," he won passage of the Selective Service Act in mid-May. The draft brought nearly 3 million men into the army; another 2 million joined various branches of the armed services voluntarily.

The engagement of these forces in combat was intense but brief. Not until the end of 1917 did the first members of the American Expeditionary Force

America in World War I: The Western Front, 1918

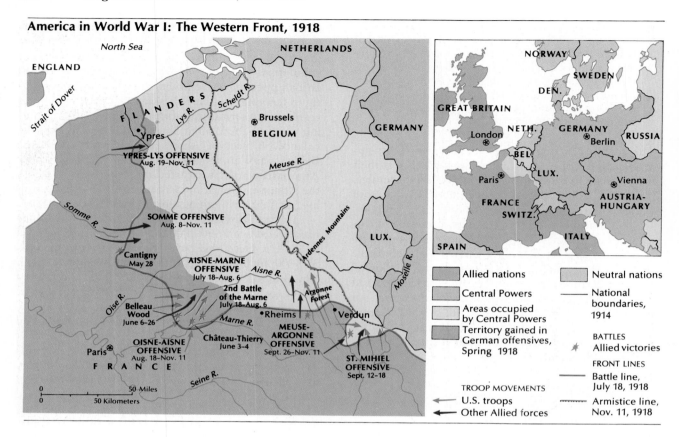

(AEF), as it was called, arrive in Europe. Not until the following spring were American troops there in significant numbers. Eight months later, the war was over.

Under the command of General John J. Pershing, whose unhappy experience in Mexico only a year before had not diminished his military reputation, the fresh American troops first joined the existing Allied forces in turning back a series of new German assaults. In early June, they assisted the French in repelling a bitter German offensive at Château-Thierry, near Paris. Six weeks later, the AEF helped turn away another assault, at Rheims, farther south. By July 18, the German advance had been halted; and for the first time in what seemed years, the Allies began a successful offensive of their own.

On September 26, an enormous American fighting force began to advance against the Germans in the Argonne Forest as part of a grand, 200-mile attack that was to last nearly seven weeks. Over 1 million American soldiers took part in the assault, using more ammunition than the entire Union army had used in four years of the Civil War; and by the end of

October, they had helped push the Germans back to their own border and had cut the enemy's major supply lines to the front.

Faced with an invasion of their own country, German military leaders now began to seek an armistice—an immediate cease-fire that would, they hoped, serve as a prelude to negotiations among the belligerents. Pershing wanted to drive on into Germany itself; but other Allied leaders, after first insisting on terms so stringent as to make the agreement little different in effect from a surrender, accepted the German proposal. On November 11, 1918, the Great War shuddered to a close. And American troops, having fought in it for only about eight months of its four years, boasted proudly that it had been they who had won it. Whether or not the claim was militarily accurate, it was already clear that the United States was the only real victor in the conflict.

Financing the War

At home, in the meantime, the war was having profound economic and social effects. The conflict had

Americans at Meuse-Argonne
This photo shows American troops and equipment moving along crowded country roads and past charred ruins during the Battle of the Meuse-Argonne, part of the great 1918 offensive that finally turned the tide of war in favor of the Allies. The gasoline-driven trucks and horse-drawn carts jostling for space on the crowded roadway suggest the transitional character of the conflict. It was the last major war in which horses would play a significant role and the first to employ motorized vehicles, airplanes, and modern submarines.   (National Archives)

begun to transform the American economy even before the United States joined the struggle. After the declaration of war, the pace of change quickly accelerated.

Americans encountered many surprises in 1917. They were surprised when they learned that substantial American ground troops would be necessary in Europe. They were surprised when they discovered that a draft would be necessary to recruit them. And they were surprised above all when they learned how much the war was going to cost them. Many government officials had scoffed at early predictions that the United States would need to spend $10 billion before the fighting ceased, but it soon became clear that even that figure was preposterously low. Before

it was over, the federal government had appropriated $32 billion for expenses directly related to the war.

This was an enormous sum by the standards of the day; the entire federal budget had seldom exceeded $1 billion before 1915. To raise it, the government relied on two devices. First, it launched a major drive to solicit loans from the American people by selling "Liberty Bonds" to the public. By 1920, the sale of bonds, which was accompanied by a carefully orchestrated appeal to patriotic fervor, had produced $23 billion. At the same time, new taxes were bringing in an additional sum of nearly $10 billion—some of it from levies on the "excess profits" of corporations, much of it from new, steeply graduated income and inheritance taxes that ultimately rose as high as 70 percent in some brackets. The nation financed the war by spreading the burden widely and reasonably efficiently.

The War Boards

An even greater challenge than raising the necessary funds was the task of organizing the nation's economy to ensure that war needs could be met. The administration made use of two very different approaches.

The first approach was in many ways reminiscent of Wilson's early commitment to the New Freedom concept of economic decentralization. In 1916, Wilson established a Council of National Defense, composed of members of his cabinet, to coordinate policy; connected with it was a Civilian Advisory Commission, which set up local defense councils in every state, county, and school district. Economic mobilization, according to this early plan, was to rest on a large-scale dispersal of power to local communities.

But this early administrative structure soon proved completely unworkable. And some members of the Council of National Defense, many of them disciples of the engineering gospel of Thorstein Veblen and the "scientific management" principles of Frederick Winslow Taylor, began to urge a more centralized approach. Instead of dividing the economy geographically, they proposed dividing it functionally by organizing a series of planning bodies, each to supervise a specific sector of the economy. Thus one agency would control transportation, another agriculture, another manufacturing. Associated with each agency would be "consulting boards," to encourage efficiency and standardization within industries.

The administrative structure that slowly emerged reflected many of the technocrats' assumptions, although it seldom worked as smoothly as they had envisioned. It was dominated by a series of "war boards." A Railroad War Board, under the direction of Treasury Secretary William McAdoo, attempted to run the nation's major transportation resource as a single unified system. Using a half-billion-dollar budget for improving equipment and raising wages, McAdoo succeeded in untangling the flow of rail traffic and dramatically increasing the transportation of goods to the East, where they could be shipped on to Europe. A new Fuel Administration was charged with allocating the increasingly scarce supplies of coal among the many contending groups seeking to buy

it. Production increased, but the fuel shortage continued to intensify, forcing the agency to adopt drastic measures. Eastern industries were forced to endure several coal "holidays" early in 1918; some energy consumers were encouraged to forgo using coal altogether and convert to a newer, cheaper, and more plentiful fuel: oil.

Perhaps the most dramatically effective of all the new war agencies was the Food Administration, headed by the brilliant young engineer and business executive Herbert Hoover. Hoover had supervised a spectacularly successful effort earlier in the war to provide food and relief to Belgium, which had been devastated by the German invasion. He brought the same administrative skills to bear on the far greater task of supervising the feeding of the nation, its armies, and its Allies—all of whom were becoming dependent on the products of American agriculture. Hoover attempted to increase supplies by encouraging voluntary conservation. At the same time, he encouraged increased production of basic foodstuffs such as wheat by arranging for the government to purchase crops at high prices to stimulate farmers to plant as much as possible. The nation managed to supply many of the needs of Europe as well as to continue feeding itself; and Hoover emerged from the war as one of the most admired figures in the country.

Government, Industry, and Labor

At the center of the effort to rationalize the economy was the War Industries Board, an agency created in July 1917 to coordinate government purchases of military supplies. Casually organized at first, it stumbled badly until March 1918, when Wilson restructured it and placed it under the control of the Wall Street financier Bernard Baruch. From then on, the board wielded powers greater than any government agency had ever possessed. Baruch became, in popular legend, a virtual czar of American industry. It was Baruch who decided which factories would convert to the production of which war materials; it was he who set prices for the goods that resulted; it was he who imposed standardized production procedures on industries to increase the efficiency of their operations and to promote interchangeability of parts among their products. When materials were scarce, Baruch decided to whom they should go. When corporations were competing for government contracts, he chose among them. He had become, it seemed, the ultimate expression of the progressive ideals of the New Nationalism. He was providing the centralized regulation of the economy that many reformers had long urged.

There was, however, a crucial difference between the image and the reality. For one thing, the WIB never worked as well as Baruch and his admirers liked to claim. It performed better than it had earlier in the war; but confusion and mismanagement continued rampant. Only because American resources and productive capacities were so great was the nation able to meet its war needs. Nor was the WIB in any real sense an example of state control of the economy. Baruch viewed himself, openly and explicitly, as the partner of business; and within the WIB, businessmen themselves—the so-called dollar-a-year men, who took leave from their corporate jobs and worked for the government for a token salary—supervised the affairs of the private economy.

Indeed, the relationship between the public and private sectors during the war was so warm and mutually supportive that to many people it began to seem as though the line between the two had all but dissolved. Baruch ensured that manufacturers coordinating their efforts in accord with his goals would be exempt from antitrust laws. He helped major industries earn enormous profits from their efforts. Steel manufacturers, for example, saw their prices rise 300 percent during a single year of the war. Corporate profits as a whole increased threefold between 1914 and 1919. Rather than working to restrict private power and limit corporate profits, as many progressives had urged, the government was working to enhance the private sector through a mutually beneficial alliance. Business itself, once antagonistic to the idea of any government interference, was beginning to see the advantages of having the state control competition and sanction what were, in essence, collusive arrangements.

This growing link between the public and private sectors extended, although in greatly different form, to labor. The National War Labor Board, established in April 1918, served as a kind of supreme court for labor disputes. It pressured industry to grant important concessions to workers: an eight-hour day, the maintenance of minimal living standards, equal pay for women doing equal work, recognition of the right of unions to organize and bargain collectively. In return, it insisted that workers forgo all strikes and that employers not engage in lockouts. Samuel Gompers, president of the American Federation of Labor, sat on the board and supported its decisions; and he watched

Women War Workers
With much of the male work force fighting overseas, women moved into occupations that in other times would have been considered unsuitable for them. One such occupation, pictured here, was delivering huge blocks of ice daily to households to be used (in this age before refrigeration) in wooden iceboxes. (National Archives)

approvingly as membership in labor unions increased by more than 1.5 million between 1917 and 1919. Many of these organizational gains, however, would not long survive the armistice.

The Results of Organization

Despite the enthusiasm with which government and business alike greeted their new, cooperative relationship, the material results were often disappointing. The proliferation of government agencies at times created more confusion than order. Bureaucracies occasionally contradicted one another in the directives they issued. Lines of authority were never entirely clear. And excessive regulation sometimes slowed, rather than enhanced, production.

There were spectacular accomplishments, of course: Hoover's efficient organization of food supplies, McAdoo's success in untangling the railroads, and others. In some areas, however, progress was so slow that the war was over before many of the supplies ordered for it were ready. The Aircraft Production Board, for example, had promised to deliver 22,000 new planes to the western front by July 1918. By the time the armistice was signed, it had managed to produce only 1,185 of them. The Emergency Fleet Corporation, created to oversee production of a vast armada of merchant vessels, took more than a year to overcome the effects of its own incompetent management. By the end of the war, American shipbuilding facilities were beginning to produce new ships at a remarkable rate; but most were not completed in time to contribute to the war effort. Had the fighting continued another year, it is likely that the productive machinery the Wilson administration had so painstakingly constructed would have begun to accomplish great feats. As it was, the eighteen months of war were not enough time for the war economy to learn to function with real efficiency. Even so, many leaders of both government and industry emerged from the experience convinced of the advantages of a close, cooperative relationship between the public and private sectors. Some hoped to continue and extend the wartime experiments in the peacetime world.

The Search for Social Unity

The idea of unity—not only in the direction of the economy but in the nation's social purpose—had been the dream of many progressives for decades. To them, the war seemed to offer an unmatched opportunity. At last, America was to close ranks behind a great common cause. In the process, they hoped, society could achieve a lasting sense of mutual purpose.

In fact, however, the search for unity that the progressives had so optimistically foreseen became an experience of ugly hysteria and bitter repression. American society remained divided, both in its attitude toward the war and in its larger political and social goals. And the attempt to impose unity on a diverse and contentious people became a painful exercise.

Selling the War

Government leaders were painfully aware of how deeply divided public opinion had been up to the moment of America's declaration of war. They knew, too, that many pacifists and isolationists remained opposed to United States participation even after that participation had begun. It was easy to argue, therefore, that a crucial prerequisite for victory was the uniting of public opinion behind the war effort. The government approached that task in several ways.

Most conspicuous was a propaganda campaign far greater than any the government had ever undertaken. A Committee on Public Information (CPI), under the direction of journalist George Creel, supervised the distribution of innumerable tons of prowar literature (75 million pieces of printed material in all). War posters plastered the walls of offices, shops, theaters, schools, churches, homes. Newspapers dutifully printed official government accounts of the reasons for the war and the prospects for quick victory. Creel encouraged reporters to exercise "self-censorship" when reporting news about the struggle; and although many people in the press resented the suggestion, the veiled threats that accompanied it persuaded most of them to comply.

The CPI attempted at first to distribute only the "facts," believing that the truth would speak for itself. As the war continued, however, their tactics became increasingly crude. Government-promoted films, at first relatively mild in tone, were by 1918 becoming vicious portrayals of the savagery of the Germans, bearing such titles as *The Prussian Cur.* CPI-financed advertisements in magazines appealed to citizens to report to the authorities any evidence among their neighbors of disloyalty, pessimism, or yearning for peace.

Legal Repression

The Wilson administration soon began not only to encourage public approval but to suppress opposition. The Espionage Act of 1917 imposed heavy fines and stiff jail terms on those convicted of spying, sabotage, or obstruction of the war effort. Those crimes were often broadly defined. The law also empowered the postmaster general to ban from the mails any "seditious" material—an authority he exercised enthusiastically and often capriciously. More repressive were two measures of 1918: the Sabotage Act of April 20 and the Sedition Act of May 16. These bills expanded the meaning of the Espionage Act to make illegal any public expression of opposition to the war; in practice, it allowed officials to prosecute anyone who criticized the president or the government.

The most frequent target of the new legislation (and one of the reasons for its enactment in the first place) were such anticapitalist groups as the Socialist party and the Industrial Workers of the World (IWW). Unlike their counterparts in Europe, American socialists had not dropped their opposition to the war after their country had decided to join it; the impact of this decision on them was devastating. Many Americans had favored the repression of socialists and radicals even before the war; now, the new government policies made it possible to move against them with full legal sanction. Eugene V. Debs, the humane leader of the party, an opponent of the war but no friend of Germany, was sentenced to ten years in prison in 1918. Only a presidential pardon ultimately won his release in 1921. Big Bill Haywood and members of the IWW were especially energetically prosecuted. Only by fleeing to the Soviet Union did Haywood avoid long imprisonment. In all, more than 1,500 people were arrested in 1918 for the crime of criticizing the government.

Popular Repression

The federal government was not alone in fueling the hysteria of the war years. State governments, local governments, corporations, universities, and above all the actions of private citizens contributed as well to the climate of repression. Vigilante mobs sprang up to "discipline" those who dared challenge the war. A dissident Protestant clergyman in Cincinnati was pulled from his bed one night by a mob, dragged to a nearby hillside, and whipped "in the name of the women and children of Belgium." An IWW organizer in Montana was seized by a mob and hanged from a railroad bridge.

A cluster of citizens' groups emerged to mobilize "respectable" members of their communities to root out disloyalty. The American Protective League, probably the largest of such groups, enlisted the services of 250,000 people, who served as "agents"—prying into the activities and thoughts of their neighbors, stopping men on the street and demanding to see their draft cards, opening mail, tapping telephones, and in general attempting to impose unity of opinion on their communities. Attorney General Thomas W. Gregory described them approvingly as a "patriotic organization." Other vigilante organiza-

Fanning the Anti-German Hysteria
This government poster, with its lurid depiction of a barbaric and almost subhuman German soldier, suggests the pervasiveness of anti-German propaganda during World War I—propaganda that not only inspired Americans to fight harder against the Germans in Europe but also helped promote harsh measures against people of German ancestry in the United States. (West Point Museum)

tions—the National Security League, the Boy Spies of America, the American Defense Society—performed much the same function.

The most frequent victims of such activities were immigrants, who had throughout the early decades of the century been a source of concern to much of American society. Now they became the targets of special abuse. "Loyal" Americans described immigrant communities as spawning grounds for radicalism. Vigilantes devoted special attention to immigrant groups suspected of sympathizing with the enemy. Irish-Americans faced constant accusations because of their historic animosity toward the British and because they had, before 1917, often expressed hopes for a German victory. Jews aroused suspicion because many had expressed opposition to the anti-Semitic policies of the Russian government, until 1917 one of the Allies. Immigrant ghettoes were strictly policed by the "loyalist" citizens' groups. Even some settlement house workers, many of whom had once championed ethnic diversity, contributed to such efforts.

The German-Americans

The greatest target, perhaps the inevitable target, of abuse was the German-American community. Its members had unwittingly contributed to their plight; in the first years of the war in Europe, some had openly advocated American assistance to the Central Powers, and many had opposed United States intervention on behalf of the Allies. But while most German-Americans loyally supported the American war effort once it began, public opinion turned hostile.

A campaign to purge society of all things German quickly gathered speed, at times assuming ludicrous forms. Sauerkraut was renamed "liberty cabbage." Hamburger became "liberty sausage." Performances of German music were frequently banned; German books were removed from the shelves of libraries; courses in the German language were removed from school curricula. For Americans of German descent, moreover, life became a dangerous ordeal. Germans were routinely fired from jobs in war industries, lest they "sabotage" important tasks. Others were fired from positions entirely unrelated to the war; Karl Muck, the German-born conductor of the Boston Symphony Orchestra, was forced to resign his position and was interned for the last months of the war. Vigilante groups routinely subjected Germans to harassment and beatings; there was even a lynching—in southern Illinois in 1918. Relatively few Americans favored such extremes, but many came to agree with the belief of the eminent psychologist G. Stanley Hall (the man responsible for the first visit of Sigmund Freud to America in 1909) that "there is something fundamentally wrong with the Teutonic soul."

The Search for a New World Order

In the meantime, the United States was articulating a vision of a new international order based on lofty democratic principles. Woodrow Wilson had led the nation into war promising a more just and stable peace at its conclusion. Even before the armistice, therefore, he was beginning preparations to lead the fight for a postwar settlement based on principle, not selfish nationalism.

It was, he realized, a difficult task. America had barely joined the war when the new Bolshevik government in Russia began disclosing terms of secret treaties negotiated earlier among the Allies. Britain, France, and imperial Russia had already agreed, according to these reports, on how to divide the colonies of their enemies among them. To Wilson, such treaties ran counter to the idealistic vision for which he was exhorting Americans to fight. It was all the more important, he decided as a result, to build strong international support for his own war aims.

The Fourteen Points

On January 8, 1918, therefore, Wilson appeared before a joint session of Congress to present the principles for which he claimed the nation was fighting. The war aims fell under fourteen headings, widely known as the Fourteen Points; but their essential elements clustered in three major categories. First, Wilson's proposals contained a series of specific recommendations for adjusting postwar boundaries and for establishing new nations to replace the defunct Austro-Hungarian and Ottoman empires, all reflecting his belief in the right of all peoples to self-determination. Second, it contained a set of general principles to govern international conduct in the future: freedom of the seas, open covenants instead of secret treaties, reductions in armaments, free trade, and impartial mediation of colonial claims. Finally, and most important of all to Wilson, there was a proposal for a league of nations that would help to implement these new principles and territorial adjustments, and serve to resolve future controversies. It would be, Wilson announced, "a general association of nations . . . formed under specific covenants for the purpose of affording mutual guarantees of political independence and territorial integrity to great and small states alike.'' Together, Wilson told Congress, the Fourteen Points would help make the world "fit to live in."

There were serious flaws in Wilson's proposals, a result more of what they omitted than of what they contained. He provided no formula for deciding how to implement the "national self-determination" he promised for subjugated peoples. He made no mention of the new Soviet government in Russia, even though its existence had struck fear in the hearts of all Western governments (and had helped spur Wilson to announce his own war aims in an effort to undercut Lenin's appeal). He said little about economic rivalries and their effect on international relations, even though it had been just such economic rivalries that had been in large part responsible for the war.

Nevertheless, Wilson's picture of the postwar world was the clearest and most eloquent expression of an international vision that would enchant not only much of his own generation but members of generations to come. It reflected his belief, strongly rooted in the ideas of progressivism, that the world was as capable of just and efficient government as were individual nations; that once the international community accepted certain basic principles of conduct, and once it constructed modern institutions to implement them, the human race could at last live in peace. The rule of law, he promised, would replace the rule of national passions and self-interested diplomacy.

The Fourteen Points came at a low moment in the war—before American troops had arrived in Europe in substantial numbers, at a time when many among the Allies believed the struggle might still be lost. It was greeted, therefore, with special yearning both in America and in Europe. The Allied leaders might have been cool toward the proposals, but there was an enthusiastic popular response among liberals, working people, and others throughout the world.

Early Obstacles

Wilson was confident, as the war neared its end, that this popular support would enable him to win Allied approval of his peace plan. He seemed at times to expect virtually to dictate a settlement. There were, however, ominous signs both at home and abroad that his path might be more difficult than he expected. In Europe, leaders of the Allied powers were marshaling their energies to resist him even before the armistice was signed. Most of them had long

resented what they considered Wilson's tone of moral superiority. They had reacted unhappily when Wilson refused to make the United States their "ally" but had kept his distance as an "associate" of his European partners. They had been offended by his insistence on keeping American military forces separate from the Allied armies they were joining. Most of all, however, Britain and France, having suffered incalculable losses in their long years of war, and having stored up an enormous reserve of bitterness toward Germany as a result, were in no mood for a benign and generous peace. They were determined to gain something from the struggle to compensate them for the catastrophe they had suffered.

At the same time, Wilson was encountering signs that he might also face problems at home. In 1918, with the war almost won, Wilson unwisely appealed to the American people to show their support for his peace plans by returning Democrats to Congress in the November elections. A Republican victory, he declared, would be "interpreted on the other side of the water as a repudiation of my leadership." Only days later, the Republicans captured majorities in both houses of Congress. Domestic economic troubles, more than international issues, had been the most important factor in the voting; but because of the president's ill-timed appeal, the results were interpreted both at home and abroad just as he had predicted: as a sign of his own political weakness.

The election fiasco contributed as well to another dangerous development: Wilson's alienation of the leaders of the Republican party. They had been furious when he attempted to make the 1918 balloting a referendum on his war aims, especially since many Republicans had been loyally supporting the Fourteen Points. And Wilson further antagonized the Republican leadership when he refused to appoint any important Republicans to the negotiating team that would represent the United States in Paris, where a treaty was to be drafted. Although such men as Elihu Root and William Howard Taft had supported his war aims, Wilson named only one Republican—a little-known diplomat—to the group.

To the president, who was becoming almost obsessed with his own moral mission, such matters were unimportant. There would be only one member of the American negotiating team with any real authority: Wilson himself. And once he had produced a just and moral treaty, the weight of world and American opinion would compel his enemies to support him. Confident of his ability to create a new world,

Woodrow Wilson stepped aboard the steamer *George Washington* and on December 3, 1918, sailed for Europe.

The Paris Peace Conference

Wilson arrived in Europe to a welcome such as few men in history have experienced. To the war-weary people of the Continent, he was nothing less than a savior, the man who would create a new and better world. And when he arrived in Paris on the afternoon of December 13, 1918, he saw clear evidence of their adulation in the form of the largest crowd in the history of France. It was the kind of demonstration that Wilson believed would make it impossible for other world leaders to oppose his peace plans. The negotiations themselves, however, proved far less satisfying.

The meeting in Paris to draft a peace treaty was almost without precedent, and it entailed a sizable risk. International negotiations had traditionally been the province of diplomats; kings, presidents, and prime ministers had generally avoided direct encounters. In Paris there were four national leaders meeting face to face: David Lloyd George, the prime minister of Great Britain; Georges Clemenceau, the president of France; Vittorio Orlando, the prime minister of Italy; and Wilson, who hoped to dominate them all. Some of Wilson's advisers had warned him that if agreement could not be reached at the "summit," there would be nowhere else to go and that it would therefore be better to begin negotiations at a lower level. Wilson, however, was adamant; he alone would represent the United States.

Wilson's commitment to personal diplomacy encountered difficulties from the start. Heads of state in the glare of world publicity were, he soon found, reluctant to modify their nations' demands. The atmosphere of idealism he had sought to create was, therefore, competing with a spirit of national aggrandizement. There was, moreover, a pervasive sense of unease about the situation in eastern Europe, where starvation seemed imminent and the threat of communism menacing. Russia, whose new Bolshevik government was still fighting "White" counterrevolutionaries, was unrepresented in Paris; but the radical threat it seemed to pose to Western governments was never far from the minds of the delegates.

In this tense and often vindictive atmosphere, the Fourteen Points did not fare well. Wilson was unable to win approval of many of the broad principles he

The Big Four in Paris
Surface amiability during the Paris Peace Conference hid serious tensions among the so-called Big Four, particularly the growing resentment among European leaders of Woodrow Wilson's high (and some thought sanctimonious) moral posture in the negotiations. Shown here, from left to right, are David Lloyd George of Great Britain, Vittorio E. Orlando of Italy, Georges Clemenceau of France, and Wilson. (Library of Congress)

had espoused: freedom of the seas, which the British refused even to discuss; free trade; "open covenants openly arrived at" (the Paris negotiations themselves were often conducted in secret). Despite his support for "impartial mediation" of colonial claims, he was forced to accept a transfer of German colonies in the Pacific to Japan, to whom the British had promised them in exchange for Japanese assistance in the war. His pledge of "national self-determination" for all peoples suffered numerous assaults. Italy, for example, obtained new territory in which 200,000 Austrians lived, and then expressed outrage at not also receiving the port of Fiume, which became part of the new nation of Yugoslavia. Poland received a corridor to the sea which ran through territory that was ethnically German. Economic and strategic demands were constantly coming into conflict with the principle of cultural nationalism.

Where the treaty departed most conspicuously from Wilson's ideals was on the question of reparations. As the conference began, the president was staunchly opposed to exacting punitive damages from the defeated Central Powers. The other Allied leaders, however, were intransigent, and slowly Wilson gave way. Although he resisted the demand of the French government that Germany be required to pay $200 billion to the Allies, he ultimately bowed to pressure and accepted the principle of reparations, the specific sum to be set later by a commission. The final figure, established in 1921, was $56 billion, supposedly to pay for civilian damages and military pensions. Although lower than some earlier demands, it was still far more than the crippled German economy could absorb. The reparations, combined with other territorial and economic penalties, constituted an effort to keep Germany not only weak but prostrate for the indefinite future. Never again, the Allied leaders believed, should the Germans be allowed to become powerful enough to threaten the peace of Europe.

Wilson did manage to win some important victories in Paris. He secured approval of a plan to place many former colonies in "trusteeship" to be supervised by the League of Nations—the so-called mandate system. He blocked a French proposal to break up western Germany into a group of smaller states, although in return he had to concede to France the disputed territory of Alsace-Lorraine and agree to a demilitarization and Allied occupation of the Rhineland. He oversaw the creation of the new nations of Yugoslavia and Czechoslovakia and the strengthening of Poland.

Such accomplishments were of secondary impor-

tance to Wilson, however, when compared with his most visible triumph: the creation of a permanent international organization to oversee world affairs and prevent future wars. On January 25, 1919, the Allies voted to accept the "covenant" of the League of Nations; and with that, Wilson believed, the peace treaty was transformed from a disappointment into a success. Whatever mistakes and inequities had emerged from the peace conference, he was convinced, could be corrected later by the League.

The covenant provided for an assembly of nations that would meet regularly to debate means of resolving disputes and protecting the peace. Authority to implement League decisions would rest with a nine-member Executive Council; the United States would be one of five permanent members of the council, along with Britain, France, Italy, and Japan. The covenant, like the larger treaty of which it was a part, left many questions unanswered, most notably how the League would enforce its decisions. Wilson, however, was confident that once established, the new organization would find suitable answers. The League of Nations, he believed, would become not only the centerpiece of the treaty, but the cornerstone of a new world order. Like other progressives considering other issues, the president was placing his hopes for the future in the process, rather than the substance, of international relations. If rational institutions could be established, then the actual conduct of world affairs would become rationalized as well.

The Ratification Battle

Wilson was well aware of the political obstacles awaiting him at home. Many Americans, accustomed to their nation's isolation from Europe, questioned the wisdom of this major new commitment to internationalism. Others had serious reservations about the specific features of the treaty and the covenant. On a brief trip to Washington in February 1919, during a recess in the peace conference, the president listened to harsh objections from members of the Senate and others; and although he reacted angrily and haughtily to his critics, he returned to Europe and insisted on certain modifications in the covenant to satisfy them. The amendments provided that a nation need not accept a mandate (responsibility for overseeing a League territory) against its will, that a member could withdraw from the organization with two years' notice, and that the League would not infringe on the Monroe Doctrine. Beyond that, however, Wilson refused to go. When Colonel House, his close friend and trusted adviser, told him he must be prepared to compromise further, the president retorted sharply: "I have found that you get nothing in this world that is worth-while without fighting for it."

How bitter that fight would be soon became clear, for there was ample inflexibility and self-righteousness on both sides of the conflict. Wilson presented the Treaty of Versailles (which took its name from the palace outside Paris where the final negotiating sessions had taken place) to the Senate on July 10, 1919, asking: "Dare we reject it and break the heart of the world?" In the weeks that followed, he consistently refused to consider even the most innocuous compromise. (His deteriorating physical condition—he was suffering from hardening of the arteries and had apparently experienced something close to a stroke in Paris—may have contributed to his intransigence.)

The Senate, in the meantime, was raising a host of objections to the treaty. For the fourteen so-called "irreconcilables"—Western progressives who included Hiram Johnson, William Borah, and Robert La Follette—the Versailles agreement was totally unacceptable. The United States should never become embroiled in the sordid politics of Europe, they argued; not even the most generous compromise could have won their support for the League. Other opponents, with less fervent convictions, were more concerned with constructing a winning issue for the Republicans in 1920 and with embarrassing a president whom they had not yet forgiven for his political tactics in 1918. Most notable of these was Senator Henry Cabot Lodge of Massachusetts, the powerful chairman of the Foreign Relations Committee. A man of stunning arrogance and a close friend of Theodore Roosevelt (who had died early in 1919, spouting hatred of Wilson to the end), Lodge loathed the president with genuine, unrestrained passion. "I never thought I could hate a man as I hate Wilson," he once admitted. He used every possible tactic to obstruct, delay, and amend the treaty.

Public sentiment clearly favored ratification, so Lodge at first could do little more than play for time. When the document reached his committee, he spent two weeks slowly reading aloud each word of its 300 pages; then he held six weeks of public hearings to air the complaints of every disgruntled minority (Irish-Americans, for example, angry that the settlement made no provision for an independent Ireland). Gradually, Lodge's general opposition to the treaty crys-

tallized into a series of "reservations"—amendments to the League covenant limiting American obligations to the organization.

Wilson might still have won approval at this point if he had agreed to some relatively minor changes in the language of the treaty. But the president refused to yield. The United States had a moral obligation, he claimed, to respect the terms of the agreement precisely as they stood. When one senator warned him that his position was becoming hopeless, that he would have to accept some of the Lodge reservations to have any hope of victory, Wilson retorted: "Never! Never! . . . I'll appeal to the country!"

Wilson's Ordeal

What followed was a political disaster and a personal tragedy. Against the stern warnings of his physician, Wilson decided to embark on a grueling, cross-country speaking tour to arouse public support for the treaty. For more than three weeks, he traveled by train from city to city, covering more than 8,000 miles, writing his own speeches as he went along, delivering them as often as four times a day, an hour at a time. He received little rest. In the beginning, the crowds were small and the speeches clumsy. As the tour progressed, however, both the size and the enthusiasm of the audiences grew; and Wilson's own eloquence and fervor increased. Had it been possible to sway the Senate through public opinion, the tour might have been a success. But it had long ago become plain that the opposition in Washington had little to do with popular sentiment. So the tour was not only an exhausting ordeal for Wilson but a futile one as well.

Finally, the president reached the end of his strength. After speaking at Pueblo, Colorado, on September 25, he collapsed with severe headaches. Canceling the rest of his itinerary, he rushed back to Washington, where, a few days later, he suffered a major stroke. For two weeks, he was close to death; for six weeks more, he was so seriously ill that he could conduct virtually no public business. His wife and his doctor formed an almost impenetrable barrier around him, shielding the president from any official pressures that might impede his recovery, preventing the public from receiving any accurate information about the gravity of his condition.

Wilson ultimately recovered fully enough to resume a limited official schedule, but he was essentially an invalid for the eighteen remaining months of

Campaigning for the League
Wilson so exhausted himself during his 1919 cross-country journey to arouse public support for the Treaty of Versailles
that he helped precipitate a serious stroke that left him debilitated for the rest of his life. Here, he greets an enthusiastic
crowd in California.   (Bancroft Library, University of California, Berkeley)

his presidency. His left side was partially paralyzed; more important, his mental and emotional state was precarious and unstable. Like many stroke victims, he found it difficult to control his feelings, often weeping at the slightest provocation. And his condition only intensified what had already been his strong tendency to view public issues in moral terms and to resist any attempts at compromise. When the Senate Foreign Relations Committee finally reported the treaty, recommending nearly fifty amendments and reservations, Wilson refused to consider any of them. When the full Senate voted in November to accept fourteen of the reservations, Wilson gave stern directions to his Democratic allies: they must vote only for a treaty with no changes whatsoever; any other version must be defeated. On November 19, 1919, forty-two Democrats, following the president's instructions, joined with the thirteen Republican "irreconcilables" to reject the amended treaty. When the

Senate voted on the original version without any reservations, thirty-eight senators, all but one a Democrat, voted to approve it; fifty-five voted no.

It did not seem so at the time, but the battle was now for all intents and purposes over; Wilson's long and painful struggle for a new world order was lost. There were sporadic efforts to revive the treaty over the next few months; on March 19, 1920, the day of the final vote, the amended version came as close as seven votes short of the necessary two-thirds majority. But Wilson's opposition to anything but the precise settlement he had negotiated in Paris remained too formidable an obstacle to surmount. He was, moreover, becoming convinced that the 1920 national election would serve as a "solemn referendum" on the League, that the force of public opinion could still compel ratification of the treaty. He even spoke, somewhat pathetically, of running for reelection himself. By now, however, public interest in the peace process had begun to fade—partly as a reaction against the tragic bitterness of the ratification fight, but more in response to a series of other crises.

A Society in Turmoil

Even during the Paris Peace Conference, the attention of many Americans was directed less toward international matters than toward events at home. There were increasing economic problems; there was widespread social unrest and violence; there was a growing fear of revolution. Some of this unease was a legacy of the almost hysterical social atmosphere of the war years; some of it was a response to issues that surfaced after the armistice. Whatever the reasons, however, America was, in the immediate postwar years, a turbulent and often unhappy place.

The Troubled Economy

Citizens of Washington, on the day after the armistice, found it impossible to place long-distance telephone calls. The lines were jammed with officials of the war agencies canceling government contracts. The fighting had ended sooner than anyone had anticipated; and without warning, without planning, the nation was launched into the difficult task of economic reconversion.

At first, to the surprise of almost everyone, the wartime boom continued. But it was a troubled and precarious prosperity, based largely on the lingering effects of the war (government deficit spending continued for some months after the armistice) and on sudden, temporary demands (a booming market for scarce consumer goods at home, a strong European market in the war-ravaged nations). It was accompanied, moreover, by raging inflation, a result in part of the precipitous abandonment of wartime price controls. Through most of 1919 and 1920, prices rose at an average of more than 15 percent a year.

Finally, late in 1920, the economic bubble burst, as many of the temporary forces that had created it disappeared and as inflation began killing the market for consumer goods. Between 1920 and 1921, the gross national product (GNP) declined nearly 10 percent; the index of wholesale prices fell from 227.9 to 150.6; 100,000 businesses went bankrupt; 453,000 farmers lost their land; nearly 5 million Americans lost their jobs.

Labor Unrest

Perhaps the most visible result of the postwar economic problems was a dramatic increase in labor unrest. American workers had generally refrained from strikes during the war. But with the fighting over, they were willing to be patient no longer. Many factors combined to produce labor discontent: the raging inflation, which wiped out what had been at best modest gains in wages during the war; concern about job security, heightened by the return to the labor force of hundreds of thousands of veterans; arduous working conditions—such as the perpetuation of the twelve-hour day in the steel industry. Employers aggravated the discontent by using the end of the war (and the end of government controls) as an excuse for taking back some of the benefits they had been forced to concede to workers in 1917 and 1918—most notably recognition of unions. Mine owners reneged on promised wage increases. In such a climate, conflict was virtually inevitable.

The year 1919, therefore, saw an unprecedented wave of strikes—more than 3,600 in all, involving over 4 million workers. Several of the strikes received wide national attention and raised particular alarm. In January, a walkout by shipyard workers in Seattle, Washington, evolved into a general strike that

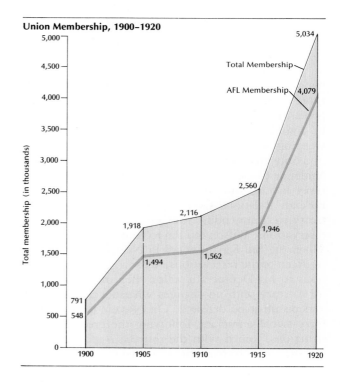

Union Membership, 1900–1920

The Great Steel Strike

Mounted police charge a group of striking steelworkers in Philadelphia during the steel strike of 1919. The strike lasted three and a half months and was the greatest single labor action in American history to that point. The strike centered around five demands: recognition of the steelworkers' union, the right of workers to bargain collectively with management through the union, abolition of the twelve-hour day, abolition of company unions, and wage increases. It finally dissolved in failure in early January 1920. (Culver Pictures)

brought the entire city to a virtual standstill. The mayor requested and received the assistance of U.S. Marines to keep the city running, and eventually the strike failed. But the incident was widely cited as evidence of the vulnerability of any community to disruption from labor agitation. In September, there was an even more alarming strike by the Boston police force, which was demanding recognition of its union. Seattle had remained generally calm; but with its police off the job, Boston erupted in violence and looting. Efforts by local businessmen, veterans, and college students to patrol the streets proved ineffective; and finally Governor Calvin Coolidge called in the National Guard to restore order. (His public statement at the time that "there is no right to strike against the public safety by anybody, anywhere, any time" attracted national acclaim.) Eventually, Boston officials dismissed the entire police force and hired a new one.

Of all the strikes of 1919, the greatest was the one, also in September, by 350,000 steelworkers in several Midwestern cities. They were demanding an eight-hour day and recognition of their union; but Elbert Gary, president of U.S. Steel, led the industry management in standing firm. The strike was long and bitter, marked by frequent violent conflicts, and climaxed by a riot in Gary, Indiana, in which eighteen strikers were killed. With the assistance of their own armed guards, steel executives managed to keep most plants running with nonunion labor; and by

January, the strike had collapsed. Public opinion had turned so decisively against the strikers that Samuel Gompers and the AFL had finally and timidly repudiated them. It was a setback from which organized labor would not recover for more than a decade.

The Red Scare

The great wave of strikes seems notable in retrospect chiefly for its failure, for how it demonstrated the weakness of the American labor movement and the strength of the corporate establishment. To much of the public at the time, however, the industrial warfare appeared to be a frightening omen of social instability. More than that, it was a sign of a dangerous increase in domestic radicalism. The mayor of Seattle claimed that the general strike was an attempt by revolutionaries "to establish a Soviet government." The leaders of the steel industry insisted that "radical agitators" had stirred up trouble among their employees, who were, they claimed, content with things as they were.

This was in part because other evidence emerging at the same time seemed likewise to suggest the existence of a radical menace. The Russian Revolution of November 1917 had been disturbing enough by itself—so disturbing to Woodrow Wilson, in fact, that in 1918 he permitted the landing of American troops in the Soviet Union. They were there, he claimed, to help a group of 60,000 Czech soldiers trapped in Russia escape. But the Americans soon became involved, both directly and indirectly, in assisting the White Russians (the anti-Bolsheviks) in their fight against the new regime. Some American troops remained as late as April 1920. Wilson's actions failed to undermine Lenin's communist regime; they did, however, become a source of lasting Russian-American hostility and mistrust. American concerns about the communist threat grew even more intense in 1919 when the Soviet government announced the formation of the Communist International (or Comintern), whose purpose was to export revolution around the world.

In America, meanwhile, there was, in addition to the great number of imagined radicals, a modest number of real ones. And when they heard the frightened warnings that a revolution was imminent, they tended to believe them. Some engaged in sporadic acts of terrorism to speed the supposed crisis on its way. It was these small bands of radicals, presumably, who were responsible for a series of bombings

in the spring of 1919 that produced great national alarm. In April, the post office intercepted several dozen parcels addressed to leading businessmen and politicians that were triggered to explode when opened; several reached their destinations, one of them severely injuring the servant of a Georgia public official. Two months later, eight bombs exploded in eight cities within minutes of one another, suggesting a nationwide conspiracy. One of them damaged the façade of Attorney General A. Mitchell Palmer's home in Washington.

In response to these and other provocations, the nation embarked on a crusade against radicalism that resembled in many ways its wartime crusade against disloyalty and dissent. Nearly thirty states enacted new peacetime sedition laws imposing harsh penalties on those who promoted revolution; some 300 people went to jail as a result. Citizens in many communities removed "subversive" books from the shelves of libraries; administrators in some universities dismissed "radical" members from their faculties. A mob of off-duty soldiers in New York City ransacked the offices of a socialist newspaper and beat up its staff. Another mob, in Centralia, Washington, dragged an IWW agitator from jail and castrated him before hanging him from a bridge.

Perhaps the greatest contribution to the Red Scare, as it later became known, came from the federal government. Attorney General Palmer, angered by the bombing of his home and ambitious for his party's 1920 presidential nomination, ordered the Justice Department to take steps to quell what he later called the "blaze of revolution . . . sweeping over every American institution of law and order." On New Year's Day, 1920, he orchestrated a series of raids on alleged radical centers throughout the country and arrested more than 6,000 people. The Palmer Raids had been intended to uncover huge caches of weapons and explosives; they netted a total of three pistols and no dynamite. Nevertheless, many of those arrested spent days and weeks in jail with no formal charges filed against them. Most were ultimately released, but about 500 who were not American citizens were summarily deported. For these violations of civil liberties, A. Mitchell Palmer, who harbored thinly concealed ambitions for the presidency, received a barrage of favorable publicity and enjoyed a period of intense (if brief) national popularity.

The ferocity of the Red Scare soon abated, but its effects lingered well into the 1920s, most notably in the celebrated case of Sacco and Vanzetti. In May of 1920, two Italian immigrants, Nicola Sacco and

Bartolomeo Vanzetti, were charged with the murder of a paymaster in Braintree, Massachusetts. The evidence against them was at best questionable; but because both men were confessed anarchists, they faced a widespread public presumption of guilt. The judge in their trial, Webster Thayer, was openly prejudiced; and it was perhaps unsurprising under the circumstances that they were convicted and sentenced to death. Over the next several years, however, public support for Sacco and Vanzetti grew to formidable proportions. But all requests for a new trial or a pardon were denied. On August 23, 1927, amid widespread protests around the world, Sacco and Vanzetti, still proclaiming their innocence, died in the electric chair. It was a cause that a generation of Americans never forgot, an episode that kept the bitter legacy of the Red Scare alive for many years.

Racial Unrest

No group suffered more from the inflamed climate of the postwar years than American blacks. To them more than to most, the war seemed to offer a major opportunity for social and economic advancement. Over 400,000 blacks served in the army, half of them in Europe, over 40,000 of them in combat. They had endured numerous indignities during the conflict. They had been placed in segregated units, under the command of white officers who often held them in contempt. They had put up with these humiliations, however, in the belief that their service would earn them the gratitude of the nation when they returned.

For many other American blacks, the war raised expectations in other ways. Nearly half a million migrated from the rural South to industrial cities (often enticed by Northern "labor agents," who offered them free transportation) in search of the factory jobs that the war was rapidly generating. Almost overnight, the nation's racial demographics were transformed; suddenly there were enormous black communities crowding into the urban North, most of which had received only a relatively few blacks in the past. Just as black soldiers expected their military service to enhance their social status, so black factory workers regarded their move north as an escape from racial prejudice and an opportunity for economic gain.

Even before the war ended, however, the racial climate had begun to sour; and in 1919, it turned savage and murderous. In the South, there was a sudden increase in lynchings: More than seventy

A Black Veteran
Residents of Harlem watch the 309th Colored Infantry parading through New York on the occasion of their return from Europe in March 1919. One little girl stares intently at a disabled veteran, still in uniform, who is standing somberly among the crowd—perhaps already aware of the deep disappointments awaiting other black veterans as they reenter civilian life. (UPI/Bettmann Newsphotos)

blacks, some of them war veterans, died at the hands of white mobs in 1919 alone. In the North, conditions were in many respects even worse. When the war ended, black factory workers faced widespread layoffs as returning white veterans displaced them from their jobs. Black veterans were cruelly disillusioned when they returned to find a society still unwilling to grant them any significant social or economic gains. These immediate economic problems helped inflame an already tense racial climate.

The Great Migration, which had begun in 1915, had thrown thousands of blacks into close proximity with Northern whites who were unfamiliar with and generally hostile to them. The new black migrants were often unskilled and uneducated rural men and women, whose country ways often made them seem

Black Migration, 1910–1950

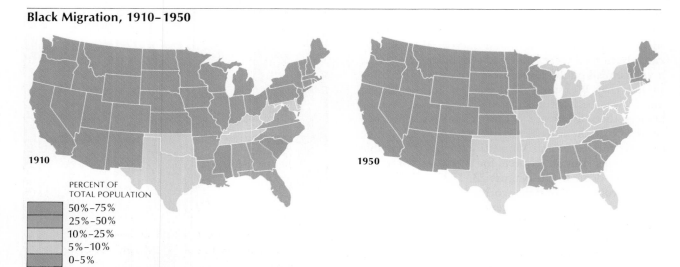

1910

1950

PERCENT OF
TOTAL POPULATION

50%–75%
25%–50%
10%–25%
5%–10%
0–5%

even more alien to their new urban neighbors. As they jostled together on the streets, trolleys, and subways of the overcrowded cities, tensions escalated; and as whites became convinced that black workers with their lower wage demands were hurting them economically, the animosity grew further. The result was a rash of disorder and violence. As early as 1917, serious race riots had flared in cities as diverse as Houston, Philadelphia, and East St. Louis (where forty-nine people, thirty-nine of them blacks, were killed). In 1919, things grew worse. In Chicago, a black teen-ager swimming in Lake Michigan on a hot July day happened to drift toward a white beach. Whites on shore allegedly stoned him unconscious; he sank and drowned. The incident became the match that ignited already severe racial tensions in the city; and for more than a week, Chicago was virtually at war. White mobs roamed into black neighborhoods, shooting, stabbing, and beating passers-by, destroying homes and properties. Blacks fought back and inflicted violence and destruction of their own. In the end, 38 people died—15 whites and 23 blacks—and 537 were injured; over 1,000 people were left homeless. The Chicago riot was the worst but not the only racial violence during the so-called red summer of 1919; in all, 120 people died in such racial outbreaks in the space of little more than three months.

Blacks responded to the turmoil in various ways. Some were simply bewildered, deeply disillusioned at the shattering of their hopes, frightened by the savagery to which they were now exposed. Others were defiant. The NAACP urged blacks to fight back,

to defend themselves and demand government protection. At the same time, a black Jamaican, Marcus Garvey, began to attract a wide American following with an ideology of black nationalism. Black culture was superior to that of white society, he told supporters; blacks should leave America and return to Africa, where they could create a new society of their own. At the peak of his popularity, Garvey claimed a following of 4 million. In the end, however, most blacks had little choice but to acquiesce in the social and economic subjugation being forced on them. Although they continued to make certain limited gains, it would be more than thirty years before they made any substantial progress toward social or economic equality.

Retreat from Idealism

The economic problems, the labor unrest, the fear of radicalism, the racial tensions—all combined in the years immediately following the war to produce a general sense of disillusionment. By 1920, the American people seemed to have grown tired of idealism, reform, controversy, and instability. For decades, they had been living in turbulent times. They yearned now for tranquillity.

How deeply they yearned for it became apparent in the election of 1920. Woodrow Wilson wanted the campaign to be a referendum on the League of Nations. The Democratic candidates, Ohio Governor James M. Cox and Assistant Secretary of the Navy Franklin D. Roosevelt, worked hard to keep Wilson's

---

SIGNIFICANT EVENTS

1914 Austria invades Serbia; World War I begins

Wilson declares American neutrality

1915 Wartime economic boom begins

Great Migration of blacks to the North begins

Germany begins submarine warfare

Lusitania torpedoed

Wilson launches preparedness program

1916 *Sussex* attacked

Wilson reelected president

1917 Germany announces unrestricted submarine warfare

Germans launch major offensive in France

Zimmerman telegram

Russian czar overthrown

United States declares war on Central Powers

Selective Service Act passed

War Industries Board created

Espionage Act passed

1918 Russia signs a separate peace with Central Powers

Sedition Act passed

U.S. troops repel Germans at Château Thierry and Rheims

U.S. troops launch offensive in Argonne Forest

1918 Armistice ends war (November 11)

Bernard Baruch takes over War Industries Board

Wilson announces Fourteen Points

American troops land in Soviet Union

Republicans gain control of Congress

Paris Peace Conference convenes

1919 Treaty of Versailles signed

Senate proposes modifications to treaty

Wilson suffers stroke

Senate rejects treaty

Economy experiences postwar inflation

Race riots break out in Chicago and other cities

Workers engage in steel strike and other unrest

Soviet Union creates Comintern

Theodore Roosevelt dies

1920 Economic recession disrupts economy

United States reacts to "radicalism" with Palmer Raids and Red Scare

Sacco and Vanzetti charged with murder

Warren G. Harding elected president

1924 Woodrow Wilson dies

1927 Sacco and Vanzetti executed

---

ideals alive. The Republican presidential nominee, however, offered a different vision. He was Warren Gamaliel Harding, an obscure Ohio senator whose only real asset seemed to be his pliability; party leaders had settled on him late one night in a "smoke-filled room" in a Chicago hotel, confident that he would do their bidding once in office. In the course of his brief and spiritless campaign, Harding offered no soaring ideals, only a vague and comfortable reassurance of stability, the promise of a return, as he later phrased it, to "normalcy." He won in a landslide. The Republican ticket received 61 percent of the popular vote and carried every state outside the South. The party made major gains in Congress as well.

Woodrow Wilson, for so long a symbol of many of the nation's ideals, stood repudiated. Early in 1921, he retired to a house on S Street in Washington, where for the next three years he lived quietly and generally inconspicuously. In February 1924, he died.

SUGGESTED READINGS

The Road to War Ernest R. May, *The World War and American Isolation* (1959), is an important account of domestic American attitudes toward the war. Also useful are Patrick Devlin, *Too Proud to Fight: Woodrow Wilson's Neutrality* (1974); Jeffrey J. Sanford, *Wilsonian Maritime Diplomacy* (1978); Manfred Jonas, *The United States and Germany* (1984); and John Milton Cooper, Jr., *The Vanity of Power: American Isolation and the First World War* (1969). Ross Gregory, *The Origins of American Intervention in the First World War* (1971), and Daniel Smith, *Robert Lansing and American Neutrality* (1958), examine the diplomatic events leading to intervention. C. Roland Marchand, *The Ameri-*

can *Peace Movement and Social Reform* (1973), is a study of antiwar activities in America. Thomas A. Bailey and Paul B. Ryan, *The Lusitania Disaster* (1975), examines one of the first major challenges to American neutrality; and Barbara Tuchman, *The Zimmerman Telegram* (1958), examines one of the last.

Military Histories   For the American military experience in World War I, see Edward M. Coffman, *The War to End All Wars* (1969); Harvey A. De Weerd, *President Wilson Fights His War* (1968); A. E. Barbeau and Florette Henri, *The Unknown Soldiers: Black American Troops in World War I* (1974); J. Garry Clifford, *The Citizen Soldiers* (1972); and Russell Weigley, *The American Way of War* (1973). Frank Freidel, *Over There* (1964), is a pictorial history. David Trask, *The United States in the Supreme War Council* (1961), examines America's military relationship with its allies.

Wartime Diplomacy   Several works examine the diplomatic posture of the United States during the war itself. See Arno Mayer, *Political Origins of the New Diplomacy* (1959); George F. Kennan, *Russia Leaves the War* (1956) and *Russia and the West Under Lenin and Stalin* (1961); W. B. Fowler, *British-American Relations, 1917–1918* (1969); and Carl Parrini, *Heir to Empire: United States Economic Diplomacy, 1916–1923* (1969).

Domestic Impact   David M. Kennedy, *Over Here* (1980), offers the best overview of the impact of the war on American society. It should be supplemented with Jordan Schwarz, *The Speculator* (1981), a study of Bernard Baruch; Robert D. Cuff, *The War Industries Board: Business Government Relations During World War I* (1973), an excellent study of wartime industrial mobilization; Valerie Jean Conner, *The National War Labor Board* (1983); and Daniel Beaver, *Newton D. Baker and the American War Effort, 1917–1919* (1966). Seward Livermore, *Politics Is Adjourned* (1966), examines relations between Wilson and Congress during the war. See also Charles Gilbert, *American Financing of World War I* (1970). On wartime propaganda and public opinion, see George T. Blakey, *Historians on the Homefront* (1970); J. R. Mock and Cedric Larson, *Words That Won the War* (1939); Stephen Vaughn, *Holding Fast the Inner Lines: Democracy, Nationalism, and the Committee on Public Information* (1979); and Zechariah Chaffee, Jr., *Free Speech in the United States* (1941). Studies of dissent and civil liberties include William Preston, Jr., *Aliens and Dissenters: Federal Suppression of Radicals, 1903–1933* (1963); H. C. Peterson and Gilbert Fite, *Opponents of War, 1917–1918* (1957); Harry N. Scheiber, *The Wilson Administration and Civil Liberties, 1917–1921* (1960); and Donald Johnson, *The Challenge to America's Freedoms* (1963). Chapters in John Higham, *Strangers in the Land* (1955), discuss the effects of the war on immigrant communities; Frederick C. Luebke, *Bonds of Loyalty* (1974), examines the plight of German-Americans. On the experience of women during the war, see Maurine W. Greenwald, *Women, War, and Work* (1980), and Barbara J. Steinson, *American Women's Activism in World War I* (1982). Carol S. Gruber, *Mars and Minerva* (1975), is a study of higher education during the war. Charles Chatfield, *For Peace and Justice: Pacifism in America,*

1914–1941 (1971), Sondra Herman, *Eleven Against War* (1969), and Charles DeBenedettis, *Origins of the Modern Peace Movement* (1978), examine resistance to the war. Otis L. Graham, Jr., *The Great Campaigns* (1971), and Ellis W. Hawley, *The Great War and the Search for a Modern Order* (1979), provide overviews.

Wilson and the Peace   As an introduction to the vast literature on postwar diplomacy, consult Arthur S. Link, *Wilson the Diplomatist* (1957); N. Gordon Levin, Jr., *Woodrow Wilson and World Politics* (1968); Robert H. Ferrell, *Woodrow Wilson and World War I* (1985); and two works by Thomas A. Bailey: *Woodrow Wilson and the Lost Peace* (1944) and *Woodrow Wilson and the Great Betrayal* (1945). A controversial analysis of the Versailles Conference, emphasizing the influence of anticommunist sentiment on the negotiations, can be found in Arno Mayer, *Wilson vs. Lenin* (1959) and *Politics and Diplomacy of Peacemaking* (1965). See also Peter Filene, *Americans and the Soviet Experiment* (1967); Christopher Lasch, *The American Liberals and the Russian Revolution* (1962); and Lloyd C. Gardner, *Safe for Democracy: The Anglo-American Response to Revolution, 1913–1923* (1984). Inga Floto, *Colonel House at Paris* (1980), studies the Versailles negotiations through the activities of Wilson's closest adviser. For the battle over ratification, see, in addition to the above, John A. Garraty, *Henry Cabot Lodge* (1953); Ralph Stone, *The Irreconcilables* (1970); Warren F. Kuehl, *Seeking World Order* (1969); Denna Fleming, *The United States and the League of Nations* (1932); and Arthur Link, *Woodrow Wilson: War, Revolution, and Peace* (1979). Gene Smith, *When the Cheering Stopped* (1964), is a moving popular account of Wilson's last years. George Kennan, *Decision to Intervene* (1958), and sections of John L. Gaddis, *Russia, the Soviet Union, and the United States* (1978), examine American intervention in the Soviet Union during the Revolution. William C. Widenor, *Henry Cabot Lodge and the Search for an American Foreign Policy* (1980), is an important study of Wilson's chief antagonist and his international vision. Robert E. Osgood, *Ideals and Self-Interest in American Foreign Relations* (1953), is an important interpretive study.

Postwar America   Postwar economic turmoil is summarized in Burl Noggle, *Into the Twenties* (1974). Stanley Coben, *A. Mitchell Palmer* (1963), and Robert K. Murray, *The Red Scare* (1955), examine the antiradicalism of the postwar years. Roberta Strauss Feuerlicht, *Justice Crucified* (1977), is one of many studies of the Sacco-Vanzetti case. David Brody, *Labor in Crisis* (1965), examines the steel strike of 1919; Francis Russell, *A City in Terror* (1975), considers the Boston police strike; and Robert L. Friedheim, *The Seattle General Strike* (1965), examines another labor uprising. William M. Tuttle, Jr., *Race Riot* (1970), analyzes the Chicago riot of the same year; Elliott Rudwick, *Race Riot at East St. Louis* (1964), and Robert V. Haynes, *A Night of Violence: The Houston Riot of 1917* (1976), examine earlier disturbances. On Marcus Garvey and Garveyism, see David Cronon, *Black Moses* (1955), and Amy J. Garvey, *Garvey and Garveyism* (1963). Wesley M. Bagby, Jr., *The Road to Normalcy* (1962), examines the campaign of 1920.

P·A·R·T S·I·X

Prosperity, Depression, and War, 1920–1945

In many respects the period between the end of World War I and the end of World War II was one of sharp discontinuities. Few eras in American history present such vivid contrasts compressed into so short a time.

Politically, the nation experienced what many considered a fundamental change after the election of 1920. For a full decade, the government remained in the hands of the Republican party and—for eight of those years at least—in the hands of two conservative presidents who rejected most of the liberal assumptions of the progressive era. An age of reform seemed to have given way to an era of reaction. Then, beginning in 1933 with the inauguration of Franklin Delano Roosevelt, the Democratic party—the minority organization for most of the previous seventy-five years—established a dominance that it was not to relinquish for decades. And with it came a new administration and a new Congress that would together produce major reforms and a drastic expansion of the role of government in American life. Finally, after the outbreak of World War II, the nation witnessed a rapid strengthening of conservative forces that brought the march toward liberal reform once again to a virtual halt.

Economically, the nation experienced equally profound shifts.

P·A·R·T S·I·X

Beginning in 1921 the American economy embarked on a period of growth without precedent in the history of the world. The nation's industrial capacity grew rapidly; the income of its citizens soared; America's position in world trade became one of unrivaled supremacy. And the American corporate world, after having been on the defensive for many years, basked in a widespread public popularity that turned once-despised captains of industry into national heroes. Then, starting with a dramatic stock market crash in 1929, the imposing economic edifice collapsed, and the country entered the worst economic crisis in its history. Industrial production declined; new investment virtually ceased; unemployment reached epic proportions. Although the magnitude of the crisis varied from one year to the next, the Great Depression, as it soon became known, continued for nearly a full decade. Only the outbreak of World War II and the stimulus that the conflict gave to the economy brought the misery to an end. By 1942 the United States had once again embarked on a period of economic growth—one that soon put even the prosperous 1920s to shame.

Culturally, there seemed to be equally sharp contrasts. In the 1920s a bitter conflict emerged between the forces of modernism associated with the new urban-industrial society and the forces of traditionalism associated with more provincial, often rural communities. On issues such as prohibition, religion, and race, the tensions between the new society and the old were vividly displayed. In the 1930s, by contrast, the nation's outlook appeared to shift dramatically. Cultural divisions now seemed less important than economic ones, and the controversies of the 1930s centered less on questions of values than on questions of wealth and power. The outbreak of World War II, however, dampened the economic conflicts and helped to produce a new search for national unity.

Yet for all the very real differences between the 1920s and the 1930s, and between both periods and World War II, there were also important continuities. For the United States during these years remained involved in a struggle that transcended the changing fortunes of the moment: a struggle between the forces promoting national consolidation and the forces sustaining social disunity.

Through prosperity, depression, and war, the nation experienced a steady increase in government influence on the lives of its people, a continuing movement toward centralization of economic power in great national institutions, and the emergence of a social and cultural outlook that helped to overcome local and regional differences and to draw the entire country together. At the same time, America in those years encountered strong resistance to all these developments—resistance that could not reverse the trend toward consolidation but that could and did limit and reshape it. The story of American life in these years, therefore, is both the story of how the United States became a more modern, united nation and the story of how it remained at the same time in many ways a fragmented, localized, individualistic society.

Magazine Cover, 1925   (Culver Pictures)

Chapter 24 The New Era

" America's present need is not heroics, but healing; not nostrums, but normalcy," Warren G. Harding, soon to become president of the United States, told the nation in 1920. "The world needs to be reminded that all human ills are not curable by legislation."

The 1920s have often been portrayed as an era fully in accord with Harding's conservative words—an era of affluence, conservatism, and cultural frivolity; the Roaring Twenties; the age of "normalcy." In reality, however, the decade was a time of significant, even dramatic social, economic, and political change. It was an era in which the American economy not only enjoyed spectacular growth but began to assume its modern forms of organization. It was a time in which American popular culture reshaped itself to reflect the realities of urban, industrial society. And it was a decade in which American government, for all its conservatism, experimented with new approaches to public policy that helped pave the way for the important period of reform that was to follow. Contemporaries liked to refer to the 1920s as the "New Era"—an age in which America was becoming a modern nation. In many ways, it was an appropriate label.

At the same time, however, the decade saw the rise of a series of spirited and at times effective rebellions against the modern developments that were transforming American life. The intense cultural conflicts that characterized the 1920s were evidence of how much of American society remained unreconciled to the modernizing currents of the New Era.

The New Economy

Growth and affluence were the most striking and visible characteristics of American life in the 1920s; and the remarkable performance of the economy in those years lay at the heart of the many other social and cultural changes of the era. After the recession of 1921–1922, the United States began a period of almost uninterrupted prosperity and economic expansion; indeed, American industry came to seem one of the wonders of the world. Less visible at the time, but equally significant, was the survival (and even extension) of serious inequalities and imbalances, in which lay the seeds of future economic troubles.

Economic Performance

No one could deny the remarkable, some believed miraculous, feats that the American economy was performing in the 1920s. The nation's manufacturing output rose by more than 60 percent during the decade; the gross national product increased at an average of 5 percent a year; output per worker rose by more than 33 percent. Per capita income grew by a third. Inflation was negligible. A mild recession in 1923 momentarily interrupted the pattern of growth; but when it subsided early in 1924, the economy expanded with even greater vigor than before.

The economic boom was a result of many things. The most obvious immediate cause was the debilitation of Europe after World War I, leaving the United States for a time the only truly vigorous industrial power in the world. More important, however, was technology, and the great industrial expansion it made possible. The automobile industry, as a result of the invention of the assembly line and other technological innovations, grew from a relatively modest size in the years before the war to become one of the most important forces in the nation's economy. Americans bought 1.5 million cars in 1921; in 1929 they purchased more than 5 million. Expansion in one industry meant, of course, expansion in others. Auto manufacturers purchased the products of steel, rubber, glass, and tool companies. Auto owners bought gasoline from the oil corporations. Road construction in response to the proliferation of motor vehicles became itself an important industry. The increased mobility that the automobile afforded increased the demand for suburban housing, fueling a boom in the construction industry.

Other new industries benefiting from technological innovations contributed as well to the economic growth. The new radio industry became a booming concern within a few years of its commercial debut in 1920. The motion picture industry expanded dramatically, especially after the introduction of sound in 1927. Aviation, electronics, and home appliances all helped sustain American economic growth. The invention of new plastics and synthetic fibers helped the chemical industry to become an important force. Improved methods of extraction and transportation, as well as new production techniques, helped the aluminum and magnesium industries to develop.

Cheap, readily available energy—from newly discovered oil reserves, from the expanded network of electric power, and from the nation's abundant coal fields—further enhanced the ability of industry to produce. Improvements in management techniques also played a role in increasing productivity. More and more industries were subscribing to the "scientific management" theories of Frederick Winslow Taylor, making deliberate efforts to improve the efficiency of their operations.

Economic Organization

This quest for improved efficiency in the factory was only part of a larger trend. Large sectors of American business in the 1920s were making rapid strides toward national organization and consolidation. The process had begun, of course, decades before; but the New Era witnessed an acceleration of such trends. By the end of the decade, 8,000 small mining and manufacturing companies had been swallowed up into larger combinations; 5,000 utilities had disappeared, most of them into great holding companies. Local merchants foundered and vanished as national chain stores cornered more than a quarter of the nation's food, apparel, and general merchandise markets. In some industries, power resided in so few firms that competition had all but vanished. U.S. Steel, the nation's largest corporation, controlled its industry almost alone; its dominance was suggested by the widely accepted use of the term "Little Steel" to refer to all of its competitors combined.

This consolidation did not occur in all segments of the economy. Some industries—notably those dependent on large-scale mass production—seemed naturally to move toward concentrating production in a few large firms. Others—industries less dependent on technology, less susceptible to great economies of scale—proved resistant to consolidation, despite the efforts of many businessmen to promote it. By the end of the decade, it was becoming clear that the American economy would not be dominated by any single form of organization; that in some industries there would be a high degree of consolidation, while in others power would remain widely dispersed.

In those areas where industry did consolidate, new forms of corporate organization emerged to advance the trend. General Motors, which was by 1920 not only the largest automobile manufacturer but the fifth largest American corporation, was a classic example. Under the leadership of Alfred P. Sloan, GM developed a modern administrative system with an efficient divisional organization, which replaced a chaotic management structure. With the new system, not only was it easier for GM to control its many subsidiaries; it was also a simpler matter for it—and for the many other corporations that adopted similar administrative systems—to expand further.

Some industries less susceptible to domination by a few great corporations attempted to stabilize themselves not through consolidation but through cooperation. An important vehicle was the trade association—a national organization created by various members of an industry to encourage coordination in production and marketing techniques. Trade associations often succeeded in limiting competition and stabilizing the market in industries dominated by a few large firms. But in industries such as cotton textiles, where power remained widely dispersed, their effectiveness was limited.

The strenuous efforts by industrialists throughout the economy to find ways to curb competition through consolidation or cooperation reflected the survival of a basic corporate fear: the fear of overcapacity. Even in the booming 1920s, industrialists remembered how too rapid expansion and overproduction had helped produce disastrous recessions in 1893, 1907, and 1920. The great dream of the New Era—a dream that remained unfulfilled—was to find a way to stabilize the economy so that such collapses would never occur again.

Labor's Dilemma

The remarkable economic growth was only one side of the American economy in the 1920s. Another was the maldistribution of wealth and purchasing power that persisted during the decade. New Era prosperity was real enough, but it was restricted to a minority of the population. More than two-thirds of the American people in 1929 lived at no better than what one study described as the "minimum comfort level." Half of those languished at or below the level of "subsistence and poverty." Large segments of the society remained unable to organize, and they found themselves without sufficient power to protect their economic interests.

American labor experienced both the benefits and the deficiencies of the 1920s as much as any other group. On the one hand, most workers saw their standard of living rise during the decade; many enjoyed greatly improved working conditions and other benefits. Employers in the 1920s, eager to avoid disruptive labor unrest and forestall the growth of unions, adopted paternalistic techniques that came to be known as "welfare capitalism." Industrialists such as Henry Ford shortened the work week for employees and instituted paid vacations. Manufacturers such as U.S. Steel spent millions of dollars installing safety devices and improving sanitation in the workplace. Most important, perhaps, many employers offered their workers substantial raises in pay and other financial benefits. By 1926, nearly 3 million industrial workers were eligible for pensions on retirement. In some companies, employees were permitted to buy stock at below-market value. When labor grievances surfaced despite these efforts, workers could voice them through the so-called company unions that were emerging in many industries—workers' councils and shop committees, organized by the corporations themselves. Welfare capitalism brought workers important economic benefits. It did not, however, offer employees any real control over their own fates.

The Steamfitter
Lewis Hine was among the first American photographers to turn his craft into an art. In this photograph from the mid-1920s, Hine made a point that many other artists were making in other media: The rise of the machine could not only serve human beings but also bend them to its own needs. The steamfitter here is forced to shape his body to the contours of his machine in order to complete his task. (International Museum of Photography at George Eastman House)

Company unions may have been psychologically comforting, but they were for the most part feeble vehicles for demanding benefits. In most companies, the workers' councils were forbidden to deal with questions of wages and hours. And welfare capitalism survived only as long as industry prospered. After 1929, with the economy in crisis, the entire system quickly collapsed.

Welfare capitalism affected only a relatively small number of workers, in any case. Most laborers worked for employers interested only in keeping their labor costs to a minimum, and workers as a whole, therefore, received wage increases that were proportionately far below the increases in corporate profits. Unskilled workers, in particular, saw their wages increase very slowly—by only a little over 2 percent between 1920 and 1926. Many workers, moreover, enjoyed no real security in their jobs. Unemployment in the 1920s was lower than during most of the previous decades. But while historians and economists disagree about the levels of joblessness in these years, the most recent evidence suggests that an average of between 5 and 7 percent of nonfarm workers were unemployed between 1923 and 1929.

In the end, American workers remained in the 1920s a relatively impoverished and powerless group. Their wages rose; but the average annual income of a worker remained below $1,500 a year at a time when $1,800 was considered necessary to maintain a minimally decent standard of living. In some industries, such as coal mining and textiles, hours remained long and wages rose scarcely at all. Nor could workers do very much to counter the effects of technological unemployment. Total factory employment increased hardly at all during the 1920s, even while manufacturing output was soaring.

Some laborers continued to regard an effective union movement as the best hope for improving their position. But the New Era was a bleak time for labor organization. Part of the blame lay with the workers themselves, many of whom were seduced by the benefits of welfare capitalism and displayed no interest in organizing. Even more of the blame rested with the unions, which failed to adapt to the realities of the modern economy. The conservative American Federation of Labor remained wedded to the concept of the craft union, in which workers were organized on the basis of particular skills. In the meantime, a huge new segment of the work force was emerging: unskilled industrial workers, many of them immigrants from southern or eastern Europe. They received little sympathy or attention from the craft unions and found themselves, as a result, with no organizations to join. The AFL, moreover, remained throughout the 1920s painfully timid about supporting strikes—partly in reaction to the disastrous setbacks it had suffered in 1919. William Green, who became president of the organization in 1924, was committed to peaceful cooperation with employers and strident opposition to communism and socialism.

A growing proportion of the work force consisted of women, who were concentrated in what have since become known as "pink-collar" jobs—low-paying service occupations with many of the

same problems as manufacturing employment. Large numbers of women worked as secretaries, salesclerks, and telephone operators, and in similar capacities. Because such positions were not technically industrial jobs, the AFL and other labor organizations were uninterested in organizing these workers.

Black workers were another group that could hope for little help from the unions. The half-million blacks who had migrated from the rural South into the cities during the Great Migration after 1914 constituted a small but significant proportion of the unskilled work force in industry; but as unskilled workers, they had few opportunities for union representation. The skilled crafts represented in the AFL often worked actively to exclude blacks from their trades and from their organizations. Most blacks worked in jobs in which the AFL took no interest at all—as janitors, dishwashers, and garbage collectors, and in other menial service jobs.

But however much the workers and unions themselves contributed to the weakness of the labor movement, corporate and government policies contributed more. If welfare capitalism was the carrot for inducing workers to accept the status quo, the antiunion policies of most industrialists constituted the stick. Corporate leaders worked hard after the turmoil of 1919 to spread the doctrine that unionism was somehow subversive and un-American, that a crucial element of democratic capitalism was the protection of the open shop (a shop in which no worker could be required to join a union). The crusade for the open shop, euphemistically titled the "American Plan," received the endorsement of the National Association of Manufacturers in 1920 and became a pretext for a harsh campaign of union busting across the country.

When such tactics proved insufficient to counter union power, government assistance often made the difference. In 1921, the Supreme Court upheld a ruling that declared picketing illegal and supported the right of lower courts to issue injunctions against strikers. In 1922, the Justice Department intervened to quell a strike by 400,000 railroad workers. In 1924, the courts refused protection to members of the United Mine Workers Union when mine owners launched a violent campaign in western Pennsylvania to drive the union from the coal fields.

The result of all these factors was that union membership suffered a serious decline in the 1920s. Union membership as a whole fell from more than 5 million in 1920 to under 3 million in 1929. Not until the mid-1930s, when a combination of increased labor militancy and active government assistance added strength to the labor movement, would the antiunion syndrome be broken.

The Plight of the Farmer

Despite their other problems, many American workers gained at least an increase in income during the 1920s. In contrast, most American farmers of the New Era experienced only decline. Agriculture, like industry, was discovering the advantages of new technology for increasing production. The number of tractors at work on American farms, for example, quadrupled during the 1920s, helping to open 35 million new acres to cultivation. But while the increases in industrial production were matched by increases in consumer demand, the expansion of agricultural production was not. The European market for American foodstuffs contracted rapidly after the war, as European agriculture began to resume production. At the same time, domestic demand for food rose only slightly.

The result was a disastrous decline in food prices and a severe drop in income for farmers. The per capita annual income for Americans not engaged in agriculture in 1929 was $870. For farmers, it was $223. In 1920, farm income had been 15 percent of the national total; by 1929, it was 9 percent. More than 3 million people left agriculture altogether in the course of the decade. Of those who remained, an alarming number were forced into tenancy—losing ownership of their lands and having to rent instead from banks or other landlords.

In response, farmers began to demand government relief. A few gravitated to such vaguely radical organizations as the Nonpartisan League of North Dakota or its successor, the Farmer-Labor party, which established a foothold as well in Minnesota and other Midwestern states. Most farmers, however, adopted a more moderate approach, agitating for some form of government price supports.

Farm Tenancy, 1910 and 1930

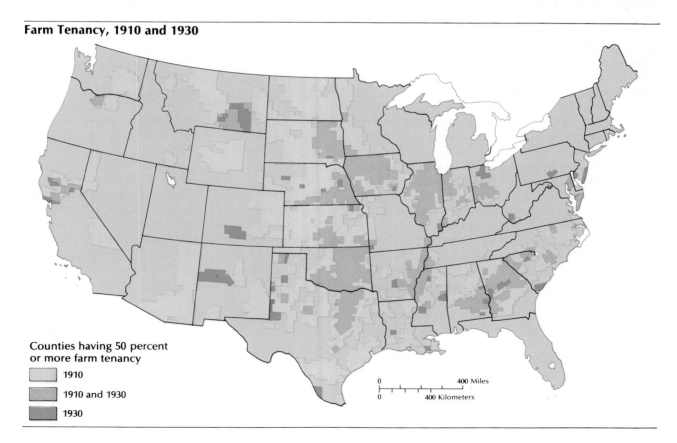

Counties having 50 percent or more farm tenancy

1910

1910 and 1930

1930

0   400 Miles

0   400 Kilometers

Through such organizations as the Farm Bureau Federation, they put increasing pressure on Congress (where farmers continued to enjoy disproportionately high representation); and while reform sentiment in most other areas made little headway in the 1920s, the movement for agrarian reform rapidly gathered strength.

One price-raising scheme in particular came to dominate agrarian demands: the idea of parity. "Parity" referred to a price for crops determined by a complicated formula. The parity price of agricultural goods was to reflect what farmers called a "fair exchange formula," which was based on the average price of the crop during the decade preceding the war (a good time for farmers) as compared with the general average of all prices during the same period. Its purpose was to ensure that farmers would earn back at least their production costs no matter how the national or world agricultural market might fluctuate. The government would guarantee parity to farmers in two ways: first, by maintaining a high tariff barrier against foreign competition, thus enabling American agriculture to sustain high prices at home; second, by buying up any surplus crops at parity and selling them abroad at whatever the world market would bring. An "equalization fee"—that is, a general tax on all crops—would compensate the government for any loss while spreading the burden evenly among all farmers.

The legislative expression of the demand for parity was the McNary-Haugen bill, named after its two principal sponsors in Congress and introduced repeatedly between 1924 and 1928. In 1924, a bill requiring parity only for grain failed in the House. Two years later, with cotton, tobacco, and rice added to win Southern support, the measure passed, only to fall victim to a veto by President Coolidge. In 1928, it won congressional approval again, only to succumb to another presidential veto. Although farmers had impressive political strength, as long as agrarian problems did not seem to affect the general prosperity there was little hope for reform.

Despite the inequities, and despite structural flaws that would ultimately contribute to the coming of a great crisis, the American economy in the 1920s did experience real and important growth. It helped spur the development of a host of new industries that would be of long-range importance to American economic health. It increased the size of the affluent middle class and thus helped create the mass consumer market that would be so crucial to future economic growth. It changed the American landscape by pro-

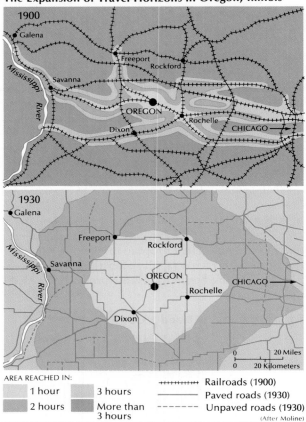

Breaking Down Rural Isolation:
The Expansion of Travel Horizons in Oregon, Illinois

AREA REACHED IN:

1 hour	3 hours
2 hours	More than 3 hours

++++++++ Railroads (1900)
———— Paved roads (1930)
‑‑‑‑‑‑‑ Unpaved roads (1930)

(After Moline)

ducing new residential and travel patterns and, in the process, breaking down the isolation of rural areas. And it helped create the outlines of a new national culture, which reflected both the fruits of American industry and the growing importance of urban life.

The New Culture

Americans in the 1920s experienced a series of profound changes in the way they lived and thought. A new urban culture emerged that helped people in all regions to live their lives and perceive their world in increasingly similar ways; and it exposed them to a new set of values that reflected the prosperity and complexity of the modern economy.

Consumerism

The United States of the 1920s was for the first time becoming a true consumer society—a society in which not only the affluent but many ordinary men and women bought items not just because of need but for the sheer pleasure of buying. What they bought, moreover, helped change the way they lived. Middle-class families rushed to purchase such new appliances as electric refrigerators, washing machines, and vacuum cleaners. Men and women wore wristwatches and smoked cigarettes. Women purchased cosmetics and mass-produced fashions. Americans in every part of the country ate commercially processed foods distributed nationally through chain stores and super-markets. The clearest illustration of the new consumerism was the frenzied excitement with which Americans greeted the automobile, which was in the 1920s becoming more widely available and affordable than ever before. By the end of the decade, there were more than 30 million cars on American roads. Automobiles had, in the process, become not just a

means of transportation but the first great national consumer obsession.

No group was more aware of the emergence of consumerism (or more responsible for creating it) than a new and growing sector of the economy: the advertising industry. The first advertising and public relations firms (N. W. Ayer and J. Walter Thompson) had appeared well before World War I; but it was in the 1920s, partly as a result of techniques pioneered by wartime propaganda, that advertising truly came of age. Publicists began to see themselves as more than purveyors of information. They viewed themselves, rather, as agents of the growing American economy; and they advertised products by attempting to invest them with glamour and prestige.

They also encouraged the public to absorb the values of promotion and salesmanship and to admire those who were effective "boosters" and publicists. One of the most successful books of the 1920s was the work of an advertising executive, Bruce Barton. In *The Man Nobody Knows,* Barton drew a portrait of Jesus Christ as less a religious prophet than a "super

Urbanization in 1920

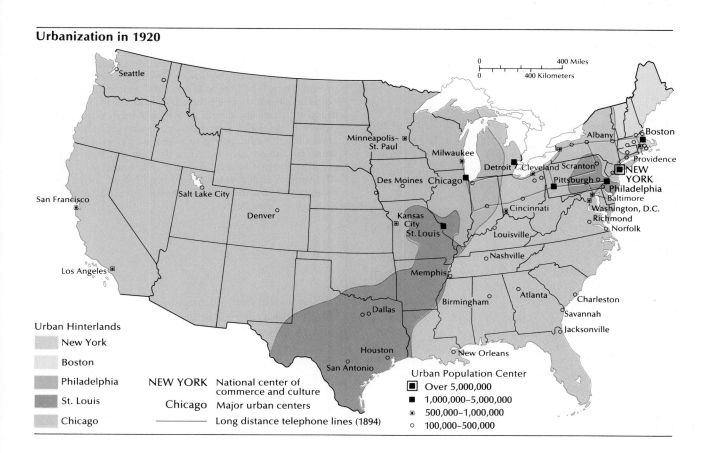

Urban Hinterlands

New York
Boston
Philadelphia
St. Louis
Chicago

NEW YORK National center of commerce and culture
Chicago Major urban centers
——— Long distance telephone lines (1894)

Urban Population Center
◼ Over 5,000,000
■ 1,000,000–5,000,000
▣ 500,000–1,000,000
○ 100,000–500,000

salesman" who "picked up twelve men from the bottom ranks of business and forged them into an organization that conquered the world." The parables, Barton argued, were "the most powerful advertisements of all time." Barton's message, a message apparently in tune with the new spirit of the consumer culture, was that Jesus had been a man concerned with living a full and rewarding life in this world; twentieth-century men and women should do the same. "Life," Barton wrote on another occasion, "is meant to live and enjoy as you go along."

National Communications

The advertising industry could never have had the impact it did but for the emergence of new vehicles of communication that made it possible to reach large audiences quickly and easily. Some of these vehicles were traditional media in changing guises. The number of local newspapers was shrinking rapidly; and those that survived often became members of great national chains—which meant that readers in widely scattered cities were reading the same material in their various newspapers. There was, as well, a growing number of national, mass-circulation magazines—*Time, Reader's Digest, The Saturday Evening Post,* and others—aimed at the widest possible audience. Fewer and fewer sources of information were servicing larger and larger groups of people.

Even more influential in shaping the popular culture of the 1920s was the growing popularity of the movies. Over 100 million people saw films in 1930, as compared to only 40 million in 1922. The addition of sound to motion pictures, beginning with the first "talkie" in 1927—*The Jazz Singer* with Al Jolson—created nationwide excitement. All across the nation, Americans were watching the same films, idolizing the same screen stars, and absorbing the same set of messages and values.

The most important communications vehicle of all, however, was the only one that was truly new to the 1920s: radio. The first commercial radio station in America, KDKA in Pittsburgh, began broadcasting on election night in 1920; and the first national radio network, the National Broadcasting Company, took form in 1927. By 1923, there were more than 500 radio stations, covering virtually every area of the country; by 1929, more than 12 million families owned radio sets. Broadcasting became the ultimate vehicle for linking the nation together, providing Americans everywhere with instant access to a common source of information and entertainment.

The Jazz Singer, 1927
This poster advertises the first feature film with sound, *The Jazz Singer,* starring Al Jolson. Sound came to motion pictures when the American film industry was for the first time facing stiff competition from abroad (and especially from the Soviet Union) for international preeminence. The "talkie revolution" restored Hollywood to primacy. The poster here and the film it promotes illustrate the degree to which American popular culture in the 1920s seized on demeaning images of blacks for the amusement of white audiences. Jolson, a white entertainer, re-created in the film a role he had often performed in real life—that of a vaudeville "minstrel singer" in blackface, who sang "Negro" songs of exaggerated sentimentality.   (Museum of Modern Art, New York. Gift of Celeste Bartos)

One result of the communications revolution was that America became in the 1920s a society in which fads and obsessions could emerge suddenly and powerfully. Radio helped elevate professional sports, and in particular professional baseball, from the level of limited local activities to that of a national craze. Men and women across the country shared a pleasure in popular stunts—flagpole sitting, marathon dancing, goldfish swallowing. They shared an interest in national sensations, such as the famous murder trial of

Leopold and Loeb or the tortuous progress of the Sacco-Vanzetti case. It is not surprising that Frederick Lewis Allen, the celebrated chronicler of the 1920s, referred to the decade as the "ballyhoo years."

Modern Religion

It was not only fads that were engaging the attention of the nation. Americans in the 1920s were being exposed as well to a wide range of new standards of thought and behavior. Such changes affected some of the nation's most basic institutions, among them religion.

The scientific advances of the late nineteenth and early twentieth centuries had by the 1920s already produced profound changes in American theology. Liberal Protestant clergymen in particular had revised religious doctrine in an effort to reconcile traditional faith with the theories of Charles Darwin. Ministers in the progressive era had played an important role in promoting social issues; churches had become not only centers of worship but agents of reform. After World War I, the increasing secularism of American society worked even further changes on both religious faith and religious behavior. Theological modernists—among them Harry Emerson Fosdick and A. C. McGiffert—taught their followers to abandon many of the traditional trappings of religion (literal interpretation of the Bible, belief in the Trinity, attribution of human traits to the deity) and to accept a faith that would help individuals to live more fulfilling lives in the modern world. Critics considered the most advanced forms of this new, more secular Protestantism only one step removed from agnosticism.

The extremes of religious modernism found acceptance among only a relatively few people; Americans remained, by the standards of a later time, highly religious. Even so, changes in popular religious assumptions and patterns were widespread. The sociologists Robert and Helen Merrell Lynd discovered during a study of community life in Muncie, Indiana, for example, that while most people continued to attend church and express a belief in God, their faith was also experiencing important changes. Fewer people seemed to believe in hell; many admitted that they "think of Heaven less than they used to." "One infers," the Lynds reported in their famous study *Middletown* (1929), "that doubts and uneasiness among individuals may be greater than a generation ago."

The New Woman

The decade of the 1920s was particularly important in redefining the role of women, both within the family and within American society as a whole. The new economy and culture affected women in a number of ways. For many, it meant a turning away from the social activism of the progressive era and into a more personal, private search for satisfaction. For others, it meant new kinds of professional careers. And for still others, it meant political activism, an effort to keep feminism alive as a vital force after the victory of the suffrage crusade.

College-educated women were no longer pioneers in the 1920s. They were forming the second and third generations of graduates of women's or coeducational colleges and universities; and they were occasionally making their presence felt in professional areas that in the past they had rarely penetrated. A substantial group of women now attempted to combine marriage and careers; 25 percent of all woman workers were married in the 1920s. In the progressive era, middle-class women had generally had to choose between work and family. Still, professional opportunities remained limited by society's assumptions about what were suitable occupations for women. Although there were notable success stories about woman business executives, journalists, doctors, and lawyers, most professional women remained confined to such fields as fashion, education, social work, nursing, and the lower levels of business management.

The "new professional woman" was a vivid and widely publicized image in the 1920s. In reality, however, most employed women were nonprofessional, lower-class workers. Middle-class women, in the meantime, remained largely in the home. The number of employed women rose by several million in the 1920s, but the percentage of women employed rose scarcely at all. Society as a whole still had little tolerance for the idea of combining marriage and a career, and women who might otherwise have been inclined to try to do so found little support for their ambitions.

Yet the 1920s nevertheless constituted a new era for non-professional middle-class women. In particular, the decade saw a redefinition of motherhood. In the first years of the twentieth century, most Americans had believed that a woman's principal mission was to bear and raise children. They had assumed that women were uniquely and instinctively qualified for parenthood. After World War I, however, an influential group of psychologists—the "behaviorists," led by John B. Watson—began to challenge such assumptions. Maternal affection was not, they claimed, sufficient preparation for child rearing. Instead, mothers should rely on the advice and assistance of experts and professionals: doctors, nurses, and trained educators in nursery schools and kindergartens.

For many middle-class women, these changes devalued what had been an important and consuming activity. Motherhood and housekeeping continued to occupy a large proportion of most women's time (except for the affluent few able to afford servants). But it did not provide satisfaction commensurate with its costs. Some middle-class women turned to professional careers to find fulfillment. Many more, however, attempted to enrich their lives by devoting new attention to their roles as wives and companions. A woman's relationship with her husband assumed a greatly enhanced importance. She increasingly shared in her husband's social life; she devoted attention to cosmetics and seductive clothing in an effort to please her husband; she tried to prevent her children from interfering with the development of the marital relationship. Most of all, perhaps, a woman was encouraged to think of her sexual relationship with her husband not simply as a means of procreation, as earlier generations had been taught, but as an important and pleasurable experience in its own right, as the culmination of romantic love.

Thus it was that the 1920s saw important new advances in the creation of a national birth control movement. The pioneer of American birth-control was Margaret Sanger, who had spent most of her adult life promoting and publicizing new birth-control techniques (especially the diaphragm). At first, she had been principally concerned with birth control for working-class women, believing that large families were among the major causes of poverty and distress in poor communities. By the 1920s (partly because she had limited success in persuading working-class women to accept her teachings), she was becoming more concerned with persuading middle-class women of the benefits of birth control. Women should, Sanger argued, be free to enjoy the pleasures of sexual activity without relation to the bearing of children. Birth-control devices began to find a large market among middle-class women, even though some techniques remained illegal in many states (and abortion remained illegal nearly everywhere).

In some senses, these changes offered women a form of liberation. The declining birth rate meant that many women had to spend fewer years caring for children. The introduction of labor-saving appliances (washing machines, refrigerators, vacuum cleaners) in the home reduced some of the burdens of housework (although not always the amount of time devoted to housework, since standards of cleanliness rose simultaneously). Many middle-class women experienced a significant increase in their leisure time. And the new secular view of womanhood, the new emphasis on woman as part of her husband's social world, meant that no longer did women have to maintain a rigid, Victorian "respectability." They were free to adopt far less inhibited life styles. They could smoke, drink, dance, wear seductive clothes and make-up, and attend lively parties. The popular image of the "flapper"—the modern woman whose liberated life style found expression in dress, hair style, speech, and behavior—became one of the most widely discussed features of the era.

But the changes were not always as liberating as they might appear. For one thing, they generally affected only a relatively small group of middle-class women, leaving the lives of vast numbers of rural and working-class women unchanged. And even among the middle class, the transformation was not without cost. By placing more and more emphasis on their relationships with men, women were increasing their vulnerability to frustration and unhappiness when those relationships proved unsatisfactory. It was not surprising, perhaps, that the national divorce rate climbed dramatically in the 1920s; nor that many women who remained married experienced boredom and restlessness.

The realization that the "new woman" was more myth than reality inspired some American feminists to continue their crusade for reform. The National Woman's party, under the leadership of Alice Paul, pressed onward with its campaign for the Equal Rights Amendment, although members found little support in Congress (and met continued resistance from other feminist groups such as the League of Women Voters). The campaign for the ERA made little headway in the 1920s.

Feminists of another sort won an apparent triumph in 1921 when they helped secure passage of a measure more in keeping with the traditional goal of securing "protective" legislation for women: the Sheppard-Towner Act. It provided federal funds to states to establish prenatal and child health-care programs. From the start, however, it produced controversy both inside and outside women's ranks. Alice Paul and her supporters opposed the measure, com-

The New Kitchen and the New Woman

Manufacturers attempted to associate their new consumer appliances with the elegant lifestyle of the affluent middle class. Advertisers tried to suggest that modern conveniences could liberate the "new woman" from the drudgery of housework and enable her to enter the glamorous world of society. (Culver Pictures)

It hasn't a single belt, fan or drain pipe....

It always works perfectly and never needs oiling ....

ONE of the first things that made me favor this General Electric Refrigerator was the fact that it was so unusually quiet. And I liked the idea of never having to oil it. All you have to do is plug it into an electric outlet . . . and then you can forget it. It hasn't any belts, drains, fans, or stuffing boxes.

But, of course, the thing that appeals to me most is the way it has cut my housekeeping job. I only market twice a week now, because I have plenty of space and just the right temperature to keep all sorts of foods in perfect condition.

We go away for week-ends without having to worry about ice. Everything is ready for use when we get back.

Cooking has become easier, too. Desserts, which used to be the most difficult part of the dinner to prepare, now are beautifully simple —and ever so much more attractive.

Expensive to run? Not a bit. It uses very little current to make all the ice we need and give us perfect refrigeration. And, do you know, it's quite remarkable the way the top

of this box never gets dusty. The circulation of air through those coils seems to drive the dust away.

For fifteen years the vast laboratories of General Electric have been busy developing a simplified refrigerator that would be about

as easy to operate as an electric fan . . . and almost as portable. Four thousand models of nineteen different types were built, field-tested and improved before this new-day refrigerator was brought to its present simplicity and efficiency.

You will want to see the models. Let us send you the address of the dealer who has them on display and booklet 11-J, which is interesting and completely descriptive.

Electric Refrigeration Department *of* General Electric Company

Hanna Building   Cleveland, Ohio

GE Refrigerator

GENERAL ELECTRIC

---

plaining that it classified all women as mothers. Margaret Sanger complained that the new programs would discourage birth-control efforts. More important, the American Medical Association fought Sheppard-Towner, warning that it would introduce untrained outsiders into the health-care field, which should remain solely the province of doctors. In 1929, Congress terminated the program. On the whole, feminists willing to challenge the belief that women occupied a separate sphere and had special needs were relatively few in the 1920s. Most feminists continued to accept the idea of a distinct place for women in society; and with suffrage now achieved, many re-

treated from controversial political efforts and, like many other groups in American life, concentrated instead on working for personal fulfillment.

Education and Youth

The growing secularism of American culture and its expanding emphasis on training and expertise found reflection in the changing role of education, which was beginning to occupy an increasingly important role in the lives of American youth. The changes were evident in numerous ways. First, more people were going to school in the 1920s than ever before. High-school attendance more than doubled during the decade: from 2.2 million to over 5 million. Enrollment in colleges and universities increased three-fold between 1900 and 1930, with much of that increase occurring after World War I. In 1918, there had been 600,000 college students; in 1930, there were 1.2 million, nearly 20 percent of the college-age population. Attendance was increasing as well at trade and vocational schools and in other institutions providing the specialized training that the modern economy demanded. Schools were, in addition, beginning to perform new and more varied functions. Instead of offering simply the traditional disciplines, they were providing training in modern technical skills: engineering, management, economics.

The growing importance of education was contributing as well to the emergence of a separate youth culture. The idea of adolescence as a distinct period in the life of an individual was for the most part new to the twentieth century. It was a result in some measure of the influence of Freudian psychology. But it was a result, too, of society's recognition that a more extended period of training and preparation was necessary before a young person was ready to move into the workplace. Schools and colleges provided adolescents with a setting in which they could develop their own social patterns, their own hobbies, their own interests and activities. An increasing number of students saw school as a place not just for academic training but for organized athletics, other extracurricular activities, clubs, and fraternities and sororities—that is, as an institution that allowed them to define themselves less in terms of their families and more in terms of their peer group.

The Decline of the "Self-Made Man"

The increasing importance of education and the changing nature of adolescence underscored one of the most important changes in American society: the gradual disappearance of the reality, and to some degree even of the ideal, of the "self-made man." The belief that any person could, simply through hard work and innate talent, achieve wealth and renown had always been largely a myth; but it had had enough basis in reality to remain a convincing myth for generations. By the 1920s, however, it was becoming difficult to believe any longer that success was possible without education and training. "The self-made manager in business," wrote *Century Magazine* in

1925, "is nearing the end of his road. He cannot escape the relentless pursuit of the same forces that have eliminated self-made lawyers and doctors and admirals."

The "Doom of the Self-Made Man," as *Century* described it, was a difficult development for Americans to accept. It suggested that individuals were no longer entirely in control of their own destinies, that a person's future depended in large part on factors over which he or she had only limited control. And like many of the other changes of the decade, many Americans greeted this one with marked ambivalence. These mixed feelings were reflected in the identity of three men who became the most widely admired heroes of the New Era: Thomas Edison, the inventor of the electric light bulb and many other technological marvels; Henry Ford, the creator of the assembly line and one of the founders of the automobile industry; and Charles Lindbergh, the first aviator to make a solo flight across the Atlantic Ocean. All received the adulation of much of the American public. Lindbergh, in particular, became a national hero the like of which the country had never seen before.

The reasons for their popularity indicated much about how Americans viewed the new epoch in which they were living. On the one hand, all three men represented the triumphs of the modern technological and industrial society. On the other hand, all three had risen to success without the benefit of formal education and largely through their own private efforts. They were, it seemed, genuinely self-made men. Even many Americans who were happily embracing a new society and a new culture were doing so without entirely diverting their gaze from a simpler past.

The Disenchanted

To a generation of artists and intellectuals coming of age in the 1920s, the new society in which they lived was even more disturbing. Many were experiencing a disenchantment with modern America so fundamental that they were often able to view it only with contempt. As a result, they adopted a role sharply different from that of most intellectuals of earlier eras. Rather than involving themselves with their society's popular or political culture and attempting to influence and reform the mass of their countrymen, they isolated themselves and embarked on a restless search for personal fulfillment. Gertrude Stein once referred to the young Americans emerging from World War I as a "Lost Generation." For many writers and intellectuals, at least, it was an apt description.

At the heart of the Lost Generation's critique of modern society was a sense of personal alienation, a belief that contemporary America no longer provided the individual with avenues by which he or she could achieve personal fulfillment. Modern life, they argued, was cold, impersonal, materialistic, and thus meaningless. The sensitive individual could find no happiness in the mainstream of American society.

This disillusionment had its roots in many things, but in nothing so deeply as the experience of World War I. To those who had fought in France and experienced the horror and savagery of modern warfare—and even to those who had not fought but who nevertheless had been aware of the appalling costs of the struggle—the aftermath of the conflict was shattering. Nothing, it seemed, had been gained. The war had been a fraud; the suffering and the dying had been in vain. Ernest Hemingway, one of the most celebrated (and most commercially successful) of the new breed of writers, expressed the generation's contempt for the war in his novel *A Farewell to Arms* (1929). Its hero, an American officer fighting in Europe, decides that there is no justification for his participation in the conflict and deserts the army with a nurse with whom he has fallen in love. Hemingway made it clear that he was to be admired for doing so.

At least equally dispiriting was the character of the nation these young intellectuals found on their return home at war's end. It was, they believed, a society utterly lacking in vision or idealism, obsessed with materialism, steeped in outmoded, priggish morality. Worst of all, it was one in which the individual had lost the ability to control his or her own fate. It was a sleek, new, industrialized and professionalized world that was organized in a dehumanizing way.

One result of this alienation was a series of savage critiques of modern society by a wide range of writers, some of whom were often described as the "debunkers." Particularly influential was the Baltimore journalist H. L. Mencken. In the pages of his magazines, first the *Smart Set* and later the *American Mercury,* he delighted in ridiculing everything Americans held dear: religion, politics, the arts, even democracy itself. He found it impossible to believe, he claimed, that "civilized life was possible under a democracy," because it was a form of government that placed power in the hands of the common people, whom he ridiculed as the "booboisie." When someone asked

Mr. Lewis and the American Eagle
The novels of Sinclair Lewis were notable for their harsh, satiric tone. This 1931 caricature by William Cotton suggests the writer's dour view of his society. Lewis looks quizzically and somewhat sourly at an American eagle, just as he had looked with disdain on many aspects of national life in his writing. (Conde Nast Publications/American Heritage)

Mencken why he continued to live in a society he found so loathsome, he replied: "Why do people go to the zoo?"

Echoing Mencken's contempt was the novelist Sinclair Lewis, the first American to win a Nobel Prize in literature. In a series of savage novels, he lashed out at one aspect of modern society after another. In *Main Street* (1920), he satirized life in a small Midwestern town (much like the one in which he himself had grown up). In *Babbitt* (1922), he ridiculed life in the modern city. *Arrowsmith* (1925) attacked the medical profession (and by implication professionalism in general). *Elmer Gantry* (1927) satirized popular religion.

To those who held the values of their society in such contempt, the standard avenues for advancement held little appeal. Intellectuals of the 1920s turned their backs on the traditional goals of their parents. They claimed to reject the "success ethic" that they believed dominated American life (even though many of them hoped for—and a few achieved—commercial and critical success on their own terms). F. Scott Fitzgerald, whose first novel, *This Side of Paradise* (1920), established him as a spokesman for his generation, ridiculed the American obsession with material success in *The Great Gatsby* (1925). The novel's hero, Jay Gatsby, spends his life accumulating wealth and social prestige in order to win the woman he loves. The world to which he has aspired, however, turns out to be one of pretension, fraud, and cruelty, and Gatsby is ultimately destroyed by it. Fitzgerald and his intellectual contemporaries claimed to want nothing to do with conventional American society (although Fitzgerald himself seemed at the same time desperately to crave acceptance by it). They chose, instead, to search elsewhere for fulfillment.

A Refuge in Art

Their quest took them in several different directions, often at the same time. Many Lost Generation intellectuals left America to live in France, making Paris for a time a center of American artistic life. Some adopted hedonistic life styles, indulging in conspicuous debauchery: drinking, drugs, casual sex, wild parties, and a generally flamboyant way of life. (The publicity they received helped set the tone for other less alienated members of their generation, who began to imitate this uninhibited pursuit of pleasure.) Many intellectuals resorted to an outspoken self-absorption, openly repudiating any responsibility for anyone but themselves. For most of these young men and women, however, the only real refuge from the travails of modern society was art—not art for any social purpose, but art for its own sake. Only art, they argued, could allow them full individual expression; only the act of creation could offer them fulfillment.

The result of this quest for fulfillment through art was not, for the most part, personal satisfaction for the writers and artists involved. They remained throughout the 1920s a restless, usually unhappy generation, searching in vain for contentment. They did, however, produce a body of work that made the decade one of the great eras of American art. Most notable were the writers: Hemingway, Fitzgerald, Lewis, as well as others such as Thomas Wolfe, John

Dos Passos, Ezra Pound, Gertrude Stein, and Eugene O'Neill—the first great American playwright and the only one ever to win a Nobel Prize. T. S. Eliot, a native of Boston who spent most of his adult life in England, led a generation of poets in breaking with the romanticism of the nineteenth century. His epic work *The Waste Land* (1922) brought to poetry much of the harsh tone of despair that was invading other areas of literature.

The writers of the 1920s were notable not only for the effectiveness of their critiques but for their success in pioneering new literary styles and techniques. Some incorporated Freudian psychology into their work, using literature to explore the workings of the psyche as well as the external actions of characters. Others produced innovations in form, structure, and dialogue: Ernest Hemingway, with his spare, clean prose; Sinclair Lewis, with his biting satire; John Dos Passos, with his use of the techniques of journalism as well as of literature. The literature of the 1920s was escapist; but it was also intensely creative, even revolutionary.

Other Visions

Not all intellectuals of the 1920s, however, expressed such total alienation and despair. Some expressed reservations about their society not by withdrawing from it but by advocating reform. Older progressive theorists continued to expound the values they had celebrated in the years before the war. Thorstein Veblen, for example, continued to attract a wide audience with his argument that modern society should adopt the "discipline of the machine" and assign control to engineers and technocratic experts. John Dewey remained influential with his appeals for "practical" education and experimentation in social policy. Charles and Mary Beard, perhaps the most influential historians of their day, also promoted progressive principles. In their book *The Rise of American Civilization* (1927), they stressed economic factors in tracing the development of modern society and suggested the need for social and economic planning.

These progressive intellectuals were often harshly critical of the society of the 1920s; yet they were, indirectly, legitimizing some of its most important features. Society was not, they were saying, excessively routinized and disciplined, as members of the Lost Generation were complaining. If anything, it was not disciplined and organized enough.

To another group of intellectuals, the solution to

contemporary problems lay neither in escapism nor in progressivism, but in an exploration of their own regional or cultural origins. In New York City, a new generation of black intellectuals created a flourishing Afro-American culture widely described as the "Harlem Renaissance." The Harlem poets, novelists, and artists drew heavily from their African roots in an effort to prove the richness of their own racial heritage (and not incidentally to prove to the white race that the black was worthy of respect). The poet Langston Hughes captured much of the spirit of the movement in a single sentence: "I am a Negro—and beautiful." Other black writers in Harlem and elsewhere—James Weldon Johnson, Countee Cullen, Zora Neale Hurston, Claude McKay, Alain Locke—as well as emerging black artists and musicians helped to establish a thriving culture rooted in the historical legacy of their race.

A similar effort was under way among an influential group of Southern intellectuals. Known first as the "Fugitives" and later as the "Agrarians," these young poets, novelists, and critics sought to counter the depersonalization of industrial society by evoking the strong rural traditions of their own region. In their controversial manifesto *I'll Take My Stand* (1930), a collection of twelve essays by twelve Southern intellectuals, they issued a simultaneously radical and conservative appeal for a rejection of the doctrine of "economic progress" and the spiritual debilitation that had accompanied it. The supposedly "backward" South, they argued, could serve as a model for a nation drunk with visions of limitless growth and modernization.

One of the greatest of all American writers of this era also expressed the Southerner's strong sense of place and of cultural heritage. William Faulkner, in a remarkable series of novels set in the fictional Mississippi county of Yoknapatawpha—*The Sound and the Fury* (1929), *Absalom, Absalom* (1936), and others—was, like many of his contemporaries, concerned with the problems of the individual seeking fulfillment in the modern world. But unlike others, he painstakingly re-created the bonds of region, family, and community, rather than expressing a detachment from society.

A Conflict of Cultures

The modern, secular culture of the 1920s was not unchallenged. It grew up alongside an older, more traditional culture, with which it continually and often bitterly competed. The new culture reflected the values and aspirations of an affluent, largely urban middle class, committed to a new, increasingly uninhibited life style, linked to a national cultural outlook. The older culture expressed the outlook of generally less affluent, less urban, more provincial Americans—men and women who continued to revere traditional values and customs and who feared and resented the modernist threats to their way of life. Beneath the apparent stability of the New Era and its celebrated business civilization, therefore, raged a series of harsh cultural controversies.

Prohibition

When the prohibition of the sale and manufacture of alcohol went into effect in January 1920, it had the support of most members of the middle class and most of those who considered themselves progressives. Within a year, however, it had become clear that the "noble experiment," as its defenders called it, was not working well. For a time, at least, prohibition did seem substantially to reduce drinking, at least in many regions of the country. But it also produced conspicuous and growing violations that made the law an almost immediate source of disillusionment and controversy.

The first prohibition commissioner promised rigorous enforcement of the new law. But violations were soon so rampant that the resources available to him proved ludicrously insufficient. The government hired only 1,500 agents to do the job. Before long, it was almost as easy to acquire illegal alcohol in much of the country as it had once been to acquire legal alcohol. More disturbing than the laughable ineffectiveness of the law, however, was the role prohibition played in stimulating organized crime. An enormous, lucrative industry was now barred to legitimate businessmen; underworld figures quickly and decisively took it over. In Chicago, Al Capone built a vast criminal empire based largely on illegal alcohol. He guarded it against interlopers with an army of as many as 1,000 gunmen, whose zealousness contributed to the violent deaths of more than 250 people in the city between 1920 and 1927. Other regions produced gangsters and gang wars of their own. Prohibition, in short, became not only a national joke but a national scandal.

Nevertheless, it survived. The middle-class progressives who had originally supported prohibition may have lost interest; but an enormous constituency of provincial, largely rural, overwhelmingly Protestant Americans continued vehemently to defend it. To them, drinking and the general sinfulness with which they associated it were an assault on their conservative code of morality. Prohibition had taken on implications far beyond the issue of drinking itself. It had come to represent the effort of an older America to maintain its dominance in a society that was moving forward in spite of it.

As the decade proceeded, opponents of prohibition (or "wets," as they came to be known) gained steadily in influence. Not until 1933, however, when the Great Depression added weight to their appeals, were they finally able effectively to challenge the "drys" and win repeal of the Eighteenth Amendment.

Nativism and the Klan

Hostility to immigrants was not new to the 1920s. Nor was it restricted to the defenders of traditional, provincial society. Like prohibition, agitation for a curb on immigration had begun in the nineteenth century; and like prohibition, it had gathered strength in the years before the war largely because of the support of middle-class progressives. Such concerns had not been sufficient in the first years of the century to win passage of curbs on immigration; but when in the years immediately following the war immigration began to be associated with radicalism, popular sentiment on behalf of restriction grew rapidly.

In 1921, therefore, Congress passed an emergency immigration act, establishing a quota system by which annual immigration from any country could not exceed 3 percent of the number of persons of that nationality who had been in the United States in 1910. The new law cut immigration from 800,000 to 300,000 in a single year, but the nativists remained unsatisfied. In 1924, Congress enacted an even harsher law: the National Origins Act, which banned immigration from east Asia entirely (deeply angering Japan) and reduced the quota for Europeans from 3 to 2 percent. The quota would be based, moreover, not on the 1910 census, but on the census of 1890, a year in which there had been far fewer southern and eastern Europeans in the country. What immigration there was, in other words, would heavily favor northwestern Europeans—people of "Nordic" or "Teutonic" stock. The 1924 act cut the yearly flow almost in half, to 164,000. Five years later, a further restriction set a rigid limit of 150,000 immigrants a year. In the years that followed, immigration officials seldom permitted even half that number actually to enter the country.

The legislative expression of nativism reflected largely the doctrines of progressivism, even if a harsh and narrow progressivism. Restricting immigration, its proponents believed, would contribute to the efficient and productive operation of society. There were, however, other expressions of nativism that reflected very different sentiments. To defenders of an older, more provincial America, the growth of large communities of foreign peoples, alien in their speech, their habits, and their values, came to seem a

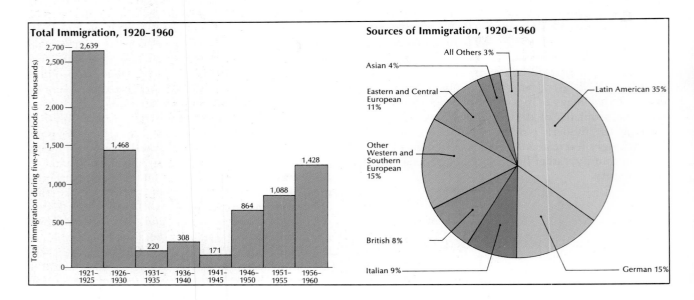

Total Immigration, 1920–1960

Total immigration during five-year periods (in thousands)

Period	Thousands
1921–1925	2,639
1926–1930	1,468
1931–1935	220
1936–1940	308
1941–1945	171
1946–1950	864
1951–1955	1,088
1956–1960	1,428

Sources of Immigration, 1920–1960

All Others 3%
Asian 4%
Eastern and Central European 11%
Other Western and Southern European 15%
British 8%
Italian 9%
Latin American 35%
German 15%

direct threat to their own embattled way of life. This provincial nativism took a number of forms. But the most prominent was the resurgence of the Ku Klux Klan as a major force in American life.

The Klan was originally the product of the first years after the Civil War. That early organization had died in the 1870s. But in 1915, shortly after the premiere of the film *The Birth of a Nation,* which celebrated the early Klan, a new group of Southerners gathered on Stone Mountain outside Atlanta, Georgia, to establish a modern version of the society. At first the new Klan, like the old, was largely concerned with intimidating blacks, who were, Klan leader William J. Simmons claimed, becoming dangerously insubordinate. After World War I, however, concern about blacks gradually became secondary to concern about Catholics, Jews, and foreigners. The Klan would devote itself, its leaders proclaimed, to purging American life of impure, alien influences.

It was then that the modern Klan experienced its greatest growth. Membership in the small towns and rural areas of the South soon expanded dramatically;

more significantly, the Klan was now spreading northward, establishing a strong foothold particularly in the industrial cities of the Midwest. By 1923, there were reportedly 3 million members; by 1924, 4 million.

In some communities, where Klan leaders came from the most "respectable" segments of society, the organization operated much like a fraternal society, engaging in nothing more dangerous than occasional political pronouncements. Often, however, the Klan also operated as a brutal, even violent, opponent of "alien" groups and as a defender of traditional, fundamentalist morality. Klansmen systematically terrorized blacks, Jews, Catholics, and foreigners: boycotting their businesses, threatening their families, and attempting to drive them out of their communities. Occasionally, they resorted to violence: public whipping, tarring and feathering, arson, and lynching.

What the Klan most deeply feared, it soon became clear, was not simply "foreign" or "racially impure" groups; it was anyone who posed a challenge to traditional values. Klansmen persecuted not

The Ku Klux Klan in Washington, 1926

So powerful was the Ku Klux Klan in the mid-1920s that its members felt emboldened to march openly and defiantly down the streets of major cities—even down Pennsylvania Avenue in Washington, in the shadow of the Capitol of the United States.   (Culver Pictures)

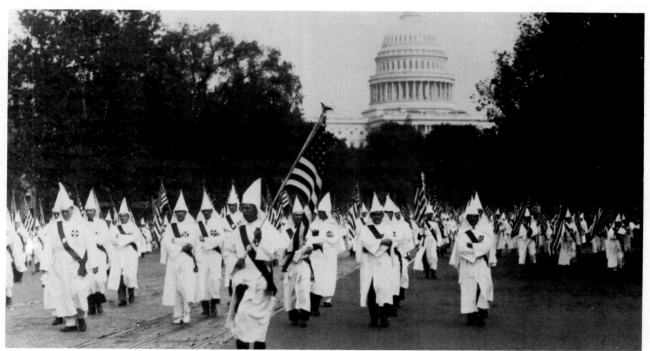

only immigrants and blacks but those white Protestants they considered guilty of irreligion, sexual promiscuity, or drunkenness. The Klan worked to enforce prohibition; it attempted to institute compulsory Bible reading in schools; it worked to punish divorce. The Ku Klux Klan, in short, was fighting not just to preserve racial homogeneity but to defend a traditional culture against the values and morals of modernity. The organization itself began to decline in influence after 1925, when a series of internal power struggles and several sordid scandals discredited some of its most important leaders. The issues it had raised, however, retained strength among some Americans for many years.

Religious Fundamentalism

Another great cultural controversy of the 1920s revealed even more starkly the growing gulf between the new culture and the old. It was a bitter conflict over questions of religious doctrine and, even more, over the place of religion in contemporary society. By 1921, American Protestantism was already divided into two warring camps. On one side stood the modernists: mostly urban, middle-class people who had attempted to adapt religion to the teachings of modern science and to the realities of their modern, secular society. On the other side stood the fundamentalists: provincial, largely (although not exclusively) rural men and women, fighting to preserve traditional faith and to maintain the centrality of religion in American life. The fundamentalists looked with horror at the new morality of the modern city. (They formed a substantial part of the constituency defending prohibition in the 1920s.) They expressed outrage at the abandonment of traditional beliefs in the face of scientific discoveries, insisting that the Bible was to be interpreted literally. Above all, they opposed the teachings of Charles Darwin, who had openly challenged the biblical story of the Creation. Human beings had not evolved from lower orders of animals, the fundamentalists insisted. They had been created by God, as described in Genesis.

Fundamentalism had been growing in strength in American Protestantism since the 1870s, but for many years it had found expression chiefly within the denominations. But it was as well an evangelical movement, interested in spreading the doctrine to new groups. Evangelists, among them the celebrated Billy Sunday, traveled from state to state (particularly in the South and parts of the West) attracting huge crowds to their revival meetings.

Protestant modernists looked on much of this activity with condescension and amusement. But by the mid-1920s evangelical fundamentalism was beginning to take a form that many regarded with real alarm. In a number of states, fundamentalists were gaining political strength with their demands for legislation to forbid the teaching of evolution in the public schools. To the modernists, such laws were almost unthinkable. Darwinism had to them become indisputable scientific fact; to forbid the teaching of evolution, they believed, would be like forbidding teachers to tell their students that the world was round. Yet they watched with incredulity as one state after another seriously considered the fundamentalist demands. In Tennessee in March 1925, the legislature actually adopted a measure making it illegal for any public school teacher "to teach any theory that denies the story of the divine creation of man as taught in the Bible."

The result was one of the most celebrated events of the decade. When the American Civil Liberties Union offered free counsel to any Tennessee educator willing to defy the law and become the defendant in a test case, a twenty-four-year-old biology teacher in the town of Dayton, John T. Scopes, arranged to have himself arrested. And when the ACLU decided to send the famous attorney Clarence Darrow to defend Scopes, the aging William Jennings Bryan (now an important fundamentalist spokesman) announced that he would travel to Dayton to assist the prosecution. Journalists from across the country, among them H. L. Mencken, flocked to Tennessee to cover the trial, which opened in an almost circus atmosphere. Scopes had, of course, clearly violated the law; and a verdict of guilty was a foregone conclusion, especially when the judge refused to permit "expert" testimony by evolution scholars. Scopes was fined $100, and the case was ultimately dismissed in a higher court because of a technicality. Nevertheless, Darrow scored an important victory for the modernists by calling Bryan himself to the stand to testify as an "expert on the Bible." In the course of the cross-examination, Darrow made Bryan's churlish defense of biblical truths appear increasingly foolish and finally tricked him into admitting the possibility that not all religious dogma was subject to only one interpretation.

The Scopes trial did not resolve the conflict between fundamentalists and modernists. Indeed, four other states soon proceeded to pass antievolution laws of their own. The issue continued to smolder for decades until it emerged in full force once again in the form of the creationist movement of the early 1980s.

**Bryan and Darrow
in Dayton**
Clarence Darrow (left) and William
Jennings Bryan pose for photographers
during the 1925 Scopes trial in Dayton,
Tennessee. Both men are in shirt
sleeves; Bryan is tieless and holding a
fan—testimony to the intense heat that
plagued the large crowd throughout
the trial.   (Brown Brothers)

The Democrats' Ordeal

The anguish of provincial Americans attempting to
defend an embattled way of life proved particularly
troubling to the Democratic party, which suffered a
serious debilitation during the 1920s as a result of
tensions between its urban and rural factions. Far
more than the Republicans, the Democrats consisted
of a diverse coalition of interest groups, linked more
by local tradition than common commitment. Among
those interest groups were prohibitionists, Klansmen,
and fundamentalists on one side and Catholics, urban
workers, and immigrants on the other.

In 1924, the tensions between them proved devastating. At the Democratic National Convention in
New York that summer, bitter conflict broke out
over the platform when the party's urban wing attempted to win approval of planks calling for the
repeal of prohibition and a denunciation of the Klan.
Both planks narrowly failed. More serious was a
deadlock in the balloting for a presidential candidate.
Urban Democrats supported Alfred E. Smith, the
Irish Catholic Tammanyite who had risen to become
a progressive governor of New York; rural Democrats backed William McAdoo, Woodrow Wilson's
Treasury secretary (and son-in-law), later to become
a senator from California, who had skillfully posi-
tioned himself to win the support of Southern and

Western delegates suspicious of Tammany Hall and
modern urban life. For 103 ballots, the convention
dragged on, until finally both Smith and McAdoo
withdrew and the party settled on a compromise: the
corporate lawyer John W. Davis.

In the years that followed, the schism between the
two wings of the party continued to plague the Democrats. In 1928, Al Smith finally did manage to secure
his party's nomination for president after another acrimonious but less prolonged battle. He was not,
however, able to unite his divided party. As a result,
he became the first Democrat since the Civil War to
fail to carry the South. (He won only six of the eleven
states of the former Confederacy.) Elsewhere, although he did well in the large cities, he carried no
states at all except Massachusetts and Rhode Island.

Smith's opponent, and the victor in the presidential election, was a man who perhaps more than any
other personified the modern, prosperous, middle-
class society of the New Era: Herbert Hoover. The
business civilization of the 1920s, with its new institutions, fashions, and values, continued to arouse the
animosity of large portions of the population; but the
majority of the American people appeared to have
accepted and approved it. In 1928, at least, the New
Era seemed to be permanently enshrined—as the success of the Republican party, its political embodiment, suggested.

Election of 1928 (56.9% of electorate voting)

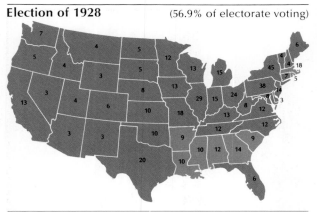

	ELECTORAL VOTE	POPULAR VOTE (%)
Herbert Hoover (Republican)	444	21,391,381 (58.2)
Alfred E. Smith (Democratic)	87	15,016,443 (40.9)
Norman Thomas (Socialist)	—	267,835 (0.7)
Other parties (Socialist Workers, Prohibition)	—	62,890

Republican Government

For twelve years, beginning in 1921, both the presidency and the Congress rested securely in the hands of the Republican party—a party in which the power of reformers had greatly dwindled since the heyday of progressivism before the war. For most of those years, the federal government expressed a profound conservatism and enjoyed a warm and supportive relationship with the American business community. Yet the government of the New Era was more than the passive, pliant instrument that critics often described. It attempted to serve in many respects as an active and powerful agent of economic change.

Warren G. Harding

Nothing seemed more clearly to illustrate the death of crusading idealism in the 1920s than the characters of the two men who served as president during most of the decade: Warren G. Harding and Calvin Coolidge.

Harding was elected to the presidency in 1920, having spent many years in public life doing little of note. He had advanced from the editorship of a newspaper in his hometown of Marion, Ohio, to the state legislature by virtue of his good looks, polished speaking style, and geniality. He had moved from there to the United States Senate as a result of his party regularity. And he had moved from there to the White House as a result of a political agreement among leaders of his party who considered him, as one noted, a "good second-rater."

The new president had few illusions about his own qualifications for office. Awed by his new responsibilities, he made sincere efforts to perform them with distinction. He appointed capable men to the most important cabinet offices; he attempted to stabilize the nation's troubled foreign policy; and he displayed on occasion a vigorous humanity, as when he pardoned socialist Eugene V. Debs in 1921. Even as he attempted to rise to his office, however, he exhibited a sense of bafflement about his situation, as if he recognized his own unfitness. "I am a man of limited talents from a small town," he reportedly told friends on one occasion. "I don't seem to grasp that I am President." Unsurprisingly, perhaps, Harding soon found himself delegating much of his authority to others: to members of his cabinet, to political cronies, to Congress, to party leaders. In the meantime, the nation's press, overwhelmingly Republican, was portraying him as a wise and effective leader.

Harding's personal weaknesses as much as his political naïveté finally resulted in his demise. He realized the importance of capable subordinates in an administration in which the president himself was reluctant to act. At the same time, however, he lacked the strength to abandon the party hacks who had helped create his political success. One of them, Harry Daugherty, the Ohio party boss principally responsible for his meteoric political ascent, he appointed attorney general. Another, Albert B. Fall, he made secretary of the interior. Members of the so-called Ohio Gang filled important offices throughout the administration. It was widely known within the government that the president's cronies led active, illicit social lives; that they gathered nightly at the famous "House on K Street" to drink illegal alcohol, play poker, and entertain attractive women; and that the president himself often joined in all these activities.

The Harding Scandals

What remained for a time generally unknown was that Daugherty, Fall, and others were engaged in a

Teapot Dome
Democrats may have been gleeful when the Teapot Dome scandal first broke. But the death of Warren Harding and the ascension of Calvin Coolidge to the presidency helped derail the scandal and restore the strength of the Republican party. The Democrats themselves contributed to the Republican revival by engaging in prolonged and destructive internal battles—the most notable of which created a deadlock at the 1924 Democratic convention for 103 ballots between supporters of William McAdoo (seen in this cartoon) and Alfred Smith. (Brown Brothers)

widespread pattern of fraud and corruption. They sold government offices and favors, bribed congressmen and senators to support legislation favorable to their interests, and plundered the agencies and departments in which they worked.

The most spectacular scandal involved the rich naval oil reserves at Teapot Dome, Wyoming, and Elk Hills, California. At the urging of Albert Fall, Harding transferred control of those reserves from the Navy Department to the Interior Department. Fall then secretly leased them to two wealthy businessmen—Harry F. Sinclair and Edward L. Donehny—and received in return nearly half a million dollars

in "loans" to ease his private financial troubles. Fall was ultimately convicted of bribery and sentenced to a year in prison; Harry Daugherty barely avoided a similar fate for his part in another scandal.

For several years, apparently, Harding himself remained generally unaware of the corruption infecting his administration. But by the summer of 1923, only months before Senate investigations and press revelations brought the scandals to light, he began to realize how desperate his situation had become. Tired and depressed, the president left Washington for a speaking tour in the West and a visit to Alaska. In Seattle late in July, he suffered severe pain, which his doctors wrongly diagnosed as food poisoning. A few days later, he seemed to rally and traveled on to San Francisco. There, on August 2, he died. He had suffered two major heart attacks.

Calvin Coolidge

In many ways, Calvin Coolidge, who succeeded to the presidency on the death of Harding, was utterly different from his predecessor. Where Harding was genial and garrulous, Coolidge was dour and silent. Where Harding adopted a loose, even debauched life style, Coolidge lived soberly and puritanically. And while Harding was if not personally corrupt then at least tolerant of corruption in others, Coolidge was honest beyond reproach. The image of stolid respectability that he projected was so unassailable that the Republican party managed to avoid any lasting damage from Teapot Dome and related scandals. In other ways, however, Harding and Coolidge were similar figures. Both represented no soaring ideals but an unadventurous conservatism. Both took a passive approach to their office.

Like Harding, Coolidge rose to the presidency on the basis of few substantive accomplishments. During his years in Massachusetts politics, he had won a reputation as a safe, trustworthy figure; and largely as a result of that, he had become governor in 1919. His response to the Boston police strike won him national attention and, in 1920, his party's vice-presidential nomination. Three years later, news of Harding's death reached him in Vermont; and there, by the light of a kerosene lamp on a kitchen table, he took the oath of office from his father, a justice of the peace.

If anything, Coolidge was an even less active president than Harding, partly as a result of his conviction that government should interfere as little as possible in the life of the nation and partly as a result of his own personal lassitude. He took long naps every afternoon. He kept official appointments to a minimum and engaged in little conversation with those who did manage to see him. He proposed no significant legislation and took little part in the running of the nation's foreign policy. "He aspired," wrote one of his contemporaries, "to become the least President the country ever had. He attained his desire."

In 1924, he received his party's presidential nomination virtually unopposed. Running against Democrat John W. Davis, a wealthy corporate lawyer who had served in the Wilson administration, he won a comfortable victory: 54 percent of the popular vote and 382 of the 531 electoral votes. Robert La Follette, the candidate of the reincarnated Progressive party,

Calvin Coolidge at Leisure
Coolidge was a silent man of simple tastes. He was not, however, a man of the soil, despite his efforts to appear so. He is shown here on his family's farm in Vermont, looking awkward and uncomfortable while posing with a milk pail. (Culver Pictures)

received 16 percent of the popular vote but carried only his home state of Wisconsin. Coolidge's negative, custodial view of the presidency clearly had the approval of the great majority of the American people. Four years later, it still did. The president could probably have won renomination and reelection easily in 1928. Instead, in characteristically laconic fashion, he walked into a press room one day and handed each reporter a slip of paper containing a single sentence: "I do not choose to run for president in 1928."

Government and Business

The story of Harding and Coolidge themselves, however, is only a part—and by no means the most important part—of the story of their administrations. However inert the New Era presidents may have been, much of the federal government was working effectively and efficiently during the 1920s to adapt public policy to the widely accepted goal of the time: helping business and industry to operate with maximum efficiency and productivity. The close relationship between the private sector and the federal government that had been forged during World War I continued.

In the executive branch, the most active efforts came from members of the cabinet. Secretary of the Treasury Andrew Mellon, the wealthy steel and aluminum tycoon who became one of the most influential and respected figures in government, devoted himself to working for substantial reductions in taxes on corporate profits and personal incomes and inheritances. Largely because of his efforts, Congress cut them all by more than half. The result, Mellon claimed, would be to stimulate investment and ensure general prosperity. Mellon also worked closely with President Coolidge after 1924 on a series of measures to trim dramatically the already modest federal budget. The administration even managed to retire half the nation's World War I debt.

The most prominent member of the cabinet was Commerce Secretary Herbert Hoover, who considered himself, and was considered by others, a notable progressive. Hoover was active in so many areas that he often seemed to be running the entire federal government single-handedly. He used his position to promote a better organized, more efficient national economy. Only thus, he claimed, could the nation hope to fulfill its most important task: the elimination of poverty.

During his eight years in the Commerce Department, Hoover constantly encouraged voluntary cooperation in the private sector as the best avenue to stability. But the idea of voluntarism did not require the government to remain passive; on the contrary, public institutions, Hoover believed, had a duty to play an active role in creating the new, cooperative order. Above all, he became the champion of the concept of business associationalism—a concept that envisioned the creation of national organizations of businessmen in particular industries. Through such trade associations, private entrepreneurs could, Hoover believed, stabilize their industries and promote efficiency in production and marketing. Hoover strongly resisted those who urged that the government sanction collusion among manufacturers to fix prices, arguing that competition was essential to a prosperous economy. He did, however, believe that shared information and limited cooperation would keep that competition from becoming destructive and thus improve the strength of the economy as a whole.

The Supreme Court in the 1920s further confirmed the business orientation of the federal government, particularly after the appointment of William Howard Taft as chief justice in 1921. The Court struck down federal legislation regulating child labor (*Bailey* v. *Drexel Furniture Company*, 1922); it nullified a minimum wage law for women in the District of Columbia (*Adkins* v. *Children's Hospital*, 1923); and it sanctioned the creation of trade associations, ruling in *United States* v. *Maple Flooring Association* (1925) that such organizations did not violate antitrust statutes as long as some competition survived within an industry. Five years earlier, in *United States* v. *U.S. Steel*, the Court had applied the same doctrine to the monopolistic United States Steel Corporation; there was no illegal "restraint of trade," it ruled, as long as U.S. Steel continued to face any competition, no matter how slight.

The probusiness policies of the Republican administrations were not without their critics. There survived in Congress throughout the 1920s a large and influential group of progressive reformers of the old school, whose vision of public power as an antidote to private privilege remained very much alive. They continued to criticize the monopolistic practices of big business, to attack government's alliance with the corporate community, to decry social injustices, and to call for economic reform. Occasionally, they were able to mobilize enough support to win congressional approval of progressive legislation,

SIGNIFICANT EVENTS

1920   First commercial radio station, KDKA in Pittsburgh, begins broadcasting
Prohibition begins
Warren G. Harding elected president

1921   Sheppard-Towner Act funds maternity assistance

1922   Sinclair Lewis publishes *Babbitt*

1921–1922   Nation experiences economic recession

1923   Nation experiences mild recession
Harding dies; Calvin Coolidge becomes president
Teapot Dome and other scandals revealed
Ku Klux Klan reaches peak membership

1924   National Origins Act passed
Coolidge elected president

1925   Congress passes McNary-Haugen bill; Coolidge vetoes it
F. Scott Fitzgerald publishes *The Great Gatsby*
Scopes trial in Dayton, Tennessee

1927   First sound motion picture, *The Jazz Singer*, released
Charles Lindbergh makes solo transatlantic flight
Babe Ruth establishes single-season home run record (60)

1928   Congress passes, and Coolidge vetoes, McNary-Haugen bill again
Herbert Hoover elected president
Stock market boom begins

1929   Sheppard-Towner program terminated
William Faulkner publishes *The Sound and the Fury*

most notably the McNary-Haugen plan for farmers and an ambitious proposal to use federal funds to develop public electric power projects on the Tennessee River at Muscle Shoals. But the progressive reformers were clearly no longer the dominant force in American political life. When the president vetoed the legislation they had promoted, as he almost always did, they lacked the strength to override him.

Some progressives derived encouragement from the results of the 1928 election, which elevated Herbert Hoover—widely regarded as the most progressive member of the Harding and Coolidge administrations—to the presidency. Hoover easily defeated Alfred Smith, the Democratic candidate. And he entered office promising bold new efforts to solve the nation's remaining economic problems. But Hoover had scant opportunity to demonstrate his commitment to extending American prosperity to those who had not shared in it. Because less than a year after his inauguration, the nation plunged into the severest and most prolonged economic crisis in its history—a crisis that brought many of the optimistic assumptions of the New Era crashing to the ground and launched the nation into a period of unprecedented social innovation and reform.

SUGGESTED READINGS

General Studies   General surveys of politics and society in the 1920s include William Leuchtenburg, *The Perils of Prosperity* (1958); John D. Hicks, *Republican Ascendancy* (1960); Arthur M. Schlesinger, Jr., *The Crisis of the Old Order* (1957); Ellis Hawley, *The Great War and the Search for a Modern Order* (1979); Donald R. McCoy, *Coming of Age* (1973); Geoffrey Perrett, *America in the Twenties* (1982); and John Braeman (ed.), *Change and Continuity in Twentieth Century America: The 1920s* (1968). Frederick Lewis Allen, *Only Yesterday* (1931), remains a classic popular account of the decade; and Isabel Leighton (ed.), *The Aspirin Age* (1949), contains a series of entertaining essays on the period.

The Economy   On the 1920s economy, see George Soule, *Prosperity Decade* (1947). Alfred Chandler, *Strategy and Structure* (1962), examines the development of several modern corporations; Louis Galambos, *Competition and Cooperation* (1966), explores the growth of a trade association (the Cotton Textile Institute). A full account of the labor movement in the 1920s is available in Irving Bernstein, *The Lean Years: A History of the American Worker, 1920–1933* (1960). See also David Brody, *Steelworkers in America* (1960) and *Workers in Industrial America* (1980), Chapter 2; Robert Zieger, *Republicans and Labor* (1969); and Leslie Woodcock, *Wage-Earning Women* (1979). On American agriculture during the decade, consult Gilbert Fite, *George Peek and the*

Fight for Farm Parity (1954), and Theodore Saloutos and John D. Hicks, *Twentieth Century Populism* (1951).

The New Culture   Daniel Boorstin, *The Americans: The Democratic Experience* (1973), offers an overview of American culture in the 1920s. Ed Cray, *Chrome Colossus* (1980), Bernard A. Weisberger, *The Dream Maker* (1979), and James Flink, *The Car Culture* (1975), provide observations on the growing importance of the automobile; while Stuart Ewen, *Captains of Consciousness* (1976), examines the advertising industry. See Larry May, *Screening Out the Past* (1980), and Robert Sklar, *Movie-Made America* (1975), for discussion of the growth of the film industry and its effects on American culture. There is surprisingly little literature on the impact of radio in the 1920s; see, however, Erik Barnouw, *A Tower of Babel,* vol. 1 (1966), and Philip T. Rosen, *The Modern Stentors: Radio Broadcasting and the Federal Government, 1920–1933* (1980). Robert Creamer, *Babe* (1974), Kenneth S. Davis, *The Hero: Charles A. Lindbergh* (1959), and Randy Roberts, *Jack Dempsey, The Manassa Mauler* (1979), are studies of some popular heroes of the era. Robert Lynd and Helen Merrell Lynd, *Middletown* (1929), a sociological portrait of Muncie, Indiana, in the mid-1920s, is invaluable for understanding community life in the decade and particularly useful for examining middle-class religion. Paul Carter, *Another Part of the Twenties* (1977), discusses a range of popular social attitudes.

Women and Family   Sheila Rothman, *Woman's Proper Place* (1978), is an important study of the changing roles of women. See also William Chafe, *The American Woman* (1972), a general study. Linda Gordon, *Woman's Body, Woman's Right* (1976), considers birth control. J. Stanley Lemons, *The Woman Citizen: Social Feminism in the 1920s* (1973), discusses female social activism. Winifred Wandersee, *Women's Work and Family Values, 1920–1940* (1981), is a useful study of the relationship between women's private and public roles. See also Lois Scharf, *To Work and to Wed* (1980). Paula Fass, *The Damned and Beautiful* (1977), examines American youth.

Intellectuals   General studies of American intellectual life in the 1920s include Roderick Nash, *The Nervous Generation: American Thought, 1917–1930* (1969), and Robert Crunden, *From Self to Society: Transition in American Thought, 1919–1941* (1972). Malcolm Cowley, *Exiles Return* (1934), is an eloquent memoir of the Lost Generation. See also Edmund Wilson, *The Twenties* (1975), and Frederick J. Hoffman, *The Twenties* (1949). Nathan Huggins, *Harlem Renaissance* (1971), and David L. Lewis, *When Harlem Was in Vogue* (1981), examine the outstanding black cultural movement of the decade. John Stewart, *The Burden of Time* (1965), is a study of the Southern Fugitives and Agrarians. The best critical study of William Faulkner is Cleanth Brooks, *William Faulkner: The Yoknapatawpha County* (1963).

Cultural Conflict   Norman Clark, *Deliver Us from Evil* (1976), examines the prohibition movement, tracing it back to its progressive roots. See also Joseph Gusfeld, *Symbolic Crusade* (1963); Andrew Sinclair, *The Era of Excess* (1962); and Herbert Asbury, *The Great Illusion* (1950). The best study of American nativism is John Higham, *Strangers in the Land* (1963). David Chalmers, *Hooded Americanism* (1965), and Kenneth Jackson, *The Ku Klux Klan in the City* (1965), examine the impact of the Klan. An account of the Scopes trial is available in Ray Ginger, *Six Days or Forever?* (1958), while Norman Furniss, *The Fundamentalist Controversy* (1954), William G. McLoughlin, *Modern Revivalism* (1959), and George M. Marsden, *Fundamentalism and American Culture* (1980), offer broader views of the fundamentalist movement. See also Lawrence Levine, *Defender of the Faith, William Jennings Bryan: The Last Decade, 1915–1925* (1965).

Politics and Government   The Harding presidency is examined in Robert K. Murray, *The Politics of Normalcy* (1973) and *The Harding Era* (1969), and in Eugene Trani and David Wilson, *The Presidency of Warren G. Harding* (1977). Burl Noggle, *Teapot Dome* (1962), examines the major scandal of the Harding years. James N. Giglio, *H. M. Daugherty and the Politics of Expediency* (1978), considers one of the leading figures of the Harding scandals. Francis Russell, *The Shadow of Blooming Grove* (1968), and Andrew Sinclair, *The Available Man* (1965), are popular biographies of the twenty-ninth president. A scholarly overview of the Coolidge presidency is available in Donald McCoy, *Calvin Coolidge* (1967); while journalist William Allen White has provided an engaging biography in *A Puritan in Babylon* (1940). The relationships between government and business are explored in James Gilbert, *Designing the Industrial State* (1972); John Hoff Wilson, *Herbert Hoover: Forgotten Progressive* (1975); and David Burner, *Herbert Hoover* (1979). Robert F. Himmelberg, *The Origins of the National Recovery Administration: Business, Government, and the Trade Association Issue, 1921–1933* (1976), examines one of the major experiments in business-government relations of the decade; Ellis Hawley, *Herbert Hoover as Secretary of Commerce: Studies in New Era Thought and Practice* (1974), is a valuable collection of essays. The difficulties of progressive opponents of the administration receive attention in LeRoy Ashby, *Spearless Leader* (1972), which focuses on William Borah; Richard Lowitt, *George W. Norris*, vol. 2 (1971); and David P. Thelen, *Robert M. La Follette and the Insurgent Spirit* (1978). On Southern politics, see George B. Tindall, *The Emergence of the New South* (1967). The troubled history of the Democratic party in the 1920s can be examined in William Harbaugh, *Lawyer's Lawyer* (1973), a biography of John W. Davis; David Burner, *The Politics of Provincialism* (1967), a particularly useful study; Alan Lichtman, *Prejudice and the Old Politics* (1979), a pathbreaking quantitative study of the 1928 election; and Kristi Andersen, *The Creation of a Democratic Majority, 1928–1936* (1979), which offers an alternative view. Oscar Handlin, *Al Smith and His America* (1958), and Paula Elder, *Governor Alfred E. Smith: The Politician as Reformer* (1983), examine the New York governor and 1928 Democratic presidential candidate. Frank Freidel, *The Ordeal* (1954) and *The Triumph* (1956), part of a multivolume biography of Franklin Roosevelt, examine the future president's career up to 1932.

Detail of *Private Car*, Leconte Stewart, c. 1932   (Museum of Church History & Art, Salt Lake City, Utah)

Chapter 25 The Great Depression

Few Americans in the first months of 1929 saw any reason to question the strength and stability of the nation's economy. Most agreed with their new president that the booming prosperity of the years just past would not only continue but increase, and that dramatic social progress would follow in its wake. "We in America today," Herbert Hoover had proclaimed in August 1928, "are nearer to the final triumph over poverty than ever before in the history of any land. The poorhouse is vanishing from among us."

Only fifteen months later, those words would return to haunt him, as the nation plunged into the severest and most prolonged economic depression in its history. It began with a stock market crash in October 1929; it slowly but steadily deepened over the next three years until the nation's economy (and, many believed, its social and political systems) approached a total collapse; and it continued in one form or another for a full decade, not only in the United States but throughout much of the rest of the world, until war finally restored American prosperity.

America had experienced economic crises before. The Panic of 1893 had ushered in a prolonged era of economic stagnation, and there had been more recent recessions, in 1907 and in 1920. The Great Depression of the 1930s, however, affected the nation more profoundly than any economic crisis that had come before—not only because it lasted longer, but because its impact was far more widely felt. The American economy by 1929 had become so interconnected, so dependent on the health of large national corporate institutions, that a collapse in one sector of the economy now reached out to affect virtually everyone. Even in the 1890s, large groups of Americans had lived sufficiently independent of the national economy to avoid the effects of economic crisis. By the 1930s, few such people remained.

The misery of the Great Depression was, then, without precedent in the nation's history. There was prolonged massive unemployment; over a quarter of the work force is estimated to have been without work in 1932, the worst year of the crisis. Even those who retained their jobs often had to accept drastic pay cuts, reduced hours, and continued uncertainty. On the nation's farms, the economic problems that had been growing in severity through the 1920s became far worse; great numbers of farmers lost their land, and many of them left the countryside altogether in search of work in other regions—work that generally did not exist. The Depression was not only a traumatic experience for individual Americans. It also placed great strains on the political and social fabric of the nation. And out of those strains emerged a series of fundamental reforms—most notably in the role of government in American life. Private institutions and local governments were completely unprepared to deal with a crisis of this magnitude; and despite occasionally strenuous attempts, their efforts gradually collapsed under the burden. Slowly, Americans began to look to the federal government for some solution to their problems.

Herbert Hoover was the first to expand the federal presence in the economy in response to the crisis. His innovative programs in the early 1930s made his the most activist peacetime administration in American history to that point. But Hoover's efforts, inhibited by conservative assumptions about the proper functions of government, were in the end painfully insufficient. And so, in 1932, the American people turned to the Democratic party and to its presidential candidate Franklin Delano Roosevelt to show them the way out of the Depression.

The Coming of the Depression

The sudden financial collapse in 1929 came as an especially severe shock because it followed so closely a period in which the New Era seemed to be performing another series of economic miracles. In particular, the nation was experiencing in 1929 a spectacular boom in the stock market.

The Great Crash

In February 1928, stock prices began a steady ascent that continued, with only a few temporary lapses, for a year and a half. By the autumn of that year, the market had become a national obsession, attracting the attention not only of the wealthy but of millions of people of modest means. Many brokerage firms gave added encouragement to the speculative mania by offering absurdly easy credit to purchasers of stocks.

It was not hard to understand why so many Americans flocked to invest in the market. Stocks seemed to provide a certain avenue to quick and easy wealth. Between May 1928 and September 1929, the average price of stocks rose over 40 percent. The stocks of the major industrials—the stocks that are used to determine the Dow Jones Industrial Average—doubled in value in that same period. Trading mushroomed from 2 or 3 million shares a day to over 5 million, and at times to as many as 10 or 12 million. There was, in short, a widespread speculative fever that grew more intense with every passing day. A few economists warned that the boom could not continue, that the prices of stocks had ceased to bear any relation to the earning power of the corporations that were issuing them. But most Americans refused to listen.

In the autumn of 1929, the market began to fall apart. On October 21, stock prices dipped sharply, alarming those who had become accustomed to an uninterrupted upward progression. Two days later,

after a brief recovery, an even more alarming decline began. J. P. Morgan and Company and other big bankers managed to stave off disaster for a while by conspicuously buying up stocks to restore public confidence. But on October 29, all the efforts to save the market failed. That day—"Black Tuesday," as it became known—saw a devastating panic. Sixteen million shares of stock were traded; the industrial index dropped 43 points; stocks in many companies became virtually worthless. In the weeks that followed, the market continued to decline, with losses in October totaling $16 billion. And despite occasional hopeful signs of a turnaround, the market remained deeply depressed for more than four years and did not fully recover for more than a decade.

Popular folklore has established the stock market crash as the beginning, and even the cause, of the Great Depression. But although October 1929 might have been the first visible sign of the crisis, the Depression had earlier beginnings and more important causes.

Causes of the Depression

The nation's economy had been showing some signs of distress for months before October 1929. Business inventories of all kinds were three times as large as they had been a year before (an indication that the public was not buying products as rapidly as in the past); and other signposts of economic health—freight carloads, industrial production, wholesale prices—were slipping downward. The extraordinary performance of the stock market kept many Americans from noticing these alarming signs. But the bull market was, in fact, an artificial phenomenon, flourishing at a time when the nation was already sliding into a recession.

Economists and other observers have argued for decades about what was principally responsible for this economic decline. Most agree, however, that many factors were involved. There was, first, a serious lack of diversification in the American economy in the 1920s. Prosperity had been excessively dependent on a few basic industries, notably construction and automobiles; in the late 1920s, those industries began to decline. Between 1926 and 1929, expenditures on construction fell from $11 billion to under $9 billion. Automobile sales began to decline somewhat later, but in the first nine months of 1929 they declined by more than a third. Once these two crucial industries began to weaken, there was not

Wall Street, 1929
Anxious crowds gather on the steps of the Federal Reserve building across the street from the New York Stock Exchange during the dramatic collapse of the stock market in October 1929.   (AP/Wide World Photos)

enough strength in other sectors of the economy to take up the slack.

Another important factor was a fundamental maldistribution of purchasing power in the New Era. As industrial and agricultural production increased, the proportion of the profits going to farmers, factory workers, and other potential consumers was too small to create a market for the goods they were producing. Even in 1929, after nearly a decade of economic growth, more than half the families in America lived on the edge of or below the minimum subsistence level—too poor to share in the great consumer boom of the 1920s, too poor to buy the cars and houses and other goods the industrial economy was producing, too poor in many cases to buy even adequate food and shelter for themselves. As long as corporations had continued to expand their capital facilities (their factories, warehouses, heavy equipment, and other investments), the economy had

flourished. By the end of the 1920s, however, capital investments had created more plant space than could profitably be used, and factories were pouring out more goods than consumers could purchase.

A third major problem was the credit structure of the economy. Farmers were deeply in debt—their land mortgaged, and crop prices too low to allow them to pay off what they owed. Small banks, especially those tied to the agricultural economy, were in constant trouble in the 1920s as their customers defaulted on loans; there was a steady stream of failures among these smaller banks throughout the decade. The banking system as a whole, moreover, was only very loosely regulated by the Federal Reserve System. Although most American bankers in this era were intensely conservative, some of the nation's largest banks were failing to maintain adequate reserves and were investing recklessly in the stock market or making unwise loans. In other words, the banking system was not well prepared to absorb the shock of a major recession.

A fourth factor contributing to the coming of the Depression was America's position in international trade. The United States was far less dependent on overseas trade than it would later become, but exports formed a significant part of the economy in the 1920s. Beginning late in the decade, European demand for American goods began to decline. That was partly because European industry and agriculture were becoming more productive, and partly because some European nations (most notably Germany, under the government of the Weimar Republic) were suffering serious financial crises and could not afford to buy goods overseas. But it was also because the European economy was being destabilized by the international debt structure that had emerged in the aftermath of World War I.

The international debt structure, therefore, was a fifth factor contributing to the Depression. When the war came to an end in 1918, all the European nations that had been allied with the United States owed large sums of money to American banks, sums much too large to be repaid out of their shattered economies. That was one reason why the Allies had insisted (over Woodrow Wilson's objections) on demanding reparation payments from Germany and Austria. Reparations, they believed, would provide them with a way to pay off their own debts. But Germany and Austria were themselves in deep economic trouble after the war; they were no more able to pay the reparations than the Allies were able to pay their debts.

The debtor nations put strong pressure on the United States in the 1920s to forgive the debts, or at least to reduce them. The American government refused. Instead, American banks began making large loans to the nations of Europe. Thus debts (and reparations) were being paid only by piling up new and greater debts. In the late 1920s, and particularly after the American economy began to weaken in 1929, the European nations found it much more difficult to borrow money from the United States. At the same time, high American protective tariffs were making it more difficult for them to sell their goods in American markets. Without any source of foreign exchange with which to repay their loans, they began to default. The collapse of the international credit structure was one of the reasons why the Depression spread to Europe (and grew much worse in America) after 1931. (See below, pp. 719–720.)

Progress of the Depression

The stock market crash of 1929 did not so much cause the Depression, then, as help trigger a chain of events that exposed a large number of weaknesses that had long existed in the American economy. And over the next three years, the crisis grew steadily worse.

The collapse of the stock market meant, of course, that companies now found it far more difficult to raise money to expand their enterprises. That was one reason for the rapid decline in investment after 1929. More important, perhaps, was the collapse of the American banking system. Over 9,000 American banks either went bankrupt or closed their doors to avoid bankruptcy between 1930 and 1933. Depositors lost over $2.5 billion in deposits. Partly as a result of these banking closures, the nation's money supply greatly decreased. As banks stopped making loans, farmers, businessmen, and others found it more and more difficult to get money with which to invest. The total money supply, according to some measurements, fell by more than a third between 1930 and 1933. And the declining money supply meant a decline in purchasing power, and thus deflation. With fewer and fewer Americans able to buy, manufacturers and merchants began reducing prices, cutting back on production, and laying off workers. A cycle of economic contraction began early in 1930 that would not be reversed until 1933. Full recovery would not arrive until the 1940s.

Historians and economists disagree over why things got so bad so quickly. Some leading economists argue that while a recession of some sort was probably inevitable by the late 1920s, the Depression itself could have been avoided if the Federal Reserve system had acted more responsibly. Instead of acting to increase the money supply so as to keep things from getting worse in the early 1930s, the Federal Reserve first did nothing and then did the wrong thing: Late in 1931 it raised interest rates, which contracted the money supply even further. Others argue that the maldistribution of purchasing power that had been building throughout the 1920s, and the decline in spending that it had caused, was much more important. Whatever the causes, however, the economy grew steadily worse until by 1932 it appeared to have reached rock bottom.

The collapse had been so rapid and so devastating that at the time it created only bewilderment among many of those who attempted to explain it. The

American gross national product plummeted from over $104 billion in 1929 to $76.4 billion in 1932—a 25 percent decline in three years. By 1933, Americans had virtually ceased making investments in productive enterprises. In 1929, they had spent $16.2 billion to promote capital growth; in 1933, they invested only a third of a billion. The consumer price index declined 25 percent between 1929 and 1933, the wholesale price index 32 percent. Farm prices, already depressed in the 1920s, fell even more dramatically. Gross farm income dropped from $12 billion to $5 billion in four years. With economic activity contracting so sharply, it was inevitable that industrial unemployment would greatly increase. By 1932, according to the relatively crude estimates of the time, 25 percent of the American work force was unemployed. (Some believe the figure was even higher.)

For the rest of the decade, unemployment averaged nearly 20 percent, never dropping below 15 percent.

The American People in Hard Times

Someone asked the British economist John Maynard Keynes in the 1930s whether he was aware of any historical era comparable to the Great Depression. "Yes," Keynes replied. "It was called the Dark Ages, and it lasted 400 years." The Depression did not last 400 years. It did, however, bring unprecedented despair to the economies of the United States and much of the Western world. And it had far-reaching effects on American society and American culture.

Selling Apples, New York City
In the fall of 1931 and again in the fall of 1932, large numbers of the unemployed took to selling apples on the streets of major cities and became in the process a popular symbol of the economic despair of those years. Herbert Hoover later wrote bitterly of the phenomenon: "One incident of these times has persisted as the eternal damnation of Hoover. Some Oregon or Washington growers' association shrewdly appraised the sympathy of the public for the unemployed. They set up a system of selling apples on the street corners in many cities, thus selling their crop and raising their prices. Many persons left their jobs for the more profitable one of selling apples. When any leftwinger wishes to indulge in scathing oratory, he demands, 'Do you want to return to selling apples?' " (Culver Pictures)

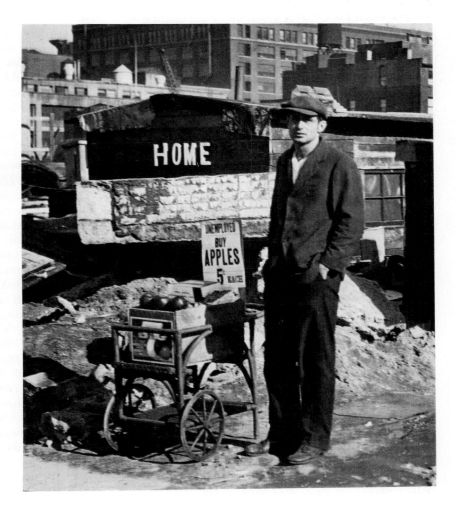

Unemployment and Relief

It is hard to know whether the suffering was worse in the cities or on the farms. In the industrial Northeast and Midwest, cities were becoming virtually paralyzed by the burden of unemployment. Cleveland, Ohio, for example, had an unemployment rate of 50 percent in 1932; Akron, 60 percent; Toledo, 80 percent. To the men and women suddenly without incomes, the situation was frightening and bewildering. Most had grown up believing that every individual was responsible for his or her own fate, that unemployment and poverty were signs of personal failure; and even in the face of national distress, many continued to believe it. Unemployed workers walked through the streets day after day looking for jobs that did not exist. When finally they gave up, they often just sat at home, hiding their shame.

An increasing number of families were turning in humiliation to local public relief systems, just to be able to eat. But that system, which had in the 1920s served only a small number of indigents, was totally unequipped to handle the new demands being placed on it. In many cities, therefore, relief simply collapsed. New York, which offered among the highest relief benefits in the nation, was able to provide families an average of only $2.39 per week. Private charities attempted to supplement the public relief efforts, but the problem was far beyond their capabilities as well.

With local efforts rapidly collapsing, state governments began to feel new pressures to expand their own assistance to the unemployed. Most resisted the pressure. Tax revenues were declining, along with everything else, and state leaders balked at placing additional strains on already tight budgets. Many public figures, moreover, feared that any permanent welfare system would undermine the moral fiber of its clients.

As a result of all this, American cities were experiencing scenes that a few years earlier would have seemed almost inconceivable. Bread lines stretched for blocks outside Red Cross and Salvation Army kitchens. Thousands of people sifted through garbage cans for scraps of food or waited outside restaurant kitchens in hopes of receiving plate scrapings. Nearly 2 million young men simply took to the roads, riding freight trains from city to city, living as virtual nomads.

In rural areas conditions were in many ways even worse, especially in a large area of the South and Midwest known as the Dust Bowl. Between 1929 and 1932, not only did farm income decline by more than 60 percent; not only did an estimated one-third of all American farmers lose their land through mortgage foreclosures or eviction. Much of the farm belt was suffering as well from a catastrophic natural disaster: one of the worst droughts in the history of the nation. Beginning in 1930, a large area of the nation—and particularly a group of states stretching north from Texas into the Dakotas—began to experience a steady decline in rainfall and an accompanying increase in heat. The drought continued for a full decade, turning what had once been fertile farm regions into virtual deserts. In Kansas, the soil in some places was completely without moisture as far as three feet below the surface. In Nebraska, Iowa, and other states, summer temperatures were averaging over 100 degrees. Swarms of grasshoppers were moving from region to region, devouring what meager crops farmers were able to raise, often even devouring fenceposts or clothes hanging out to dry. Great dust storms—"black blizzards," as they were called—swept across the plains, blotting out the sun and suffocating livestock as well as any people unfortunate or foolish enough to stay outside.

It is a measure of how productive American farmers were and how depressed the market for agricultural goods had become that even with these disastrous conditions, the farm economy continued through the 1930s to produce far more than American consumers could afford to buy. With the domestic market dwindling and the international market having almost vanished, farmers were able to sell their goods only at prices so low as to make continued operations unprofitable. Thus many farmers, like many urban unemployed, left their homes and traveled to what they hoped would be better areas. In the South, in particular, many dispossessed farmers—black and white—simply wandered from town to town, hoping to find jobs or handouts. Hundreds of thousands of families from the Dust Bowl (often known as "Okies," since many came from Oklahoma) packed their belongings in rickety cars or trucks and traveled to California and other states, where they found conditions little better than those they had left. Owning no land of their own, many worked as agricultural migrants, traveling from farm to farm picking fruit and other crops at starvation wages.

For urban and rural Americans alike, malnutrition and homelessness became a growing problem.

City hospitals reported an alarming increase in deaths by starvation. Although such deaths in rural areas often went unreported, they too were increasing. People who had lost their farms or their homes were often unable to afford any permanent shelter. Large shantytowns began to spring up on the outskirts of major cities, where homeless families lived in makeshift shacks constructed of flattened tin cans, scraps of wood, abandoned crates, and other debris. Many homeless Americans simply kept moving—sleeping in freight cars, in city parks, in subways, or in unused sewer ducts.

Black Americans and the Depression

Those Americans whose access to opportunities had been limited even in prosperity found the Depression especially devastating. Thus black Americans encountered special hardships in the 1930s. They had not generally shared in the prosperity of the previous decade; they now experienced the problems of unemployment, homelessness, malnutrition, and disease to a far greater degree than in the past, and to a far greater degree than most whites.

As the Depression began, over half of all American blacks still lived in the South, most of them farmers. The collapse of prices for cotton and other staple crops left many with no income at all. Those who stayed on their farms had to grow their own food or scavenge or beg for it. Many left the land altogether—either by choice or because forced to by landlords who no longer found the sharecropping system profitable. Some migrated to Southern cities, where it was now difficult to secure even the menial jobs traditionally considered suitable for blacks. Unemployed whites believed they had first claim to all work, and some now began to take positions as janitors, street cleaners, and domestic servants, displacing the blacks who formerly occupied them.

As the Depression deepened, whites in many Southern cities began to demand that all blacks be dismissed from their jobs. In Atlanta in 1930, an or-

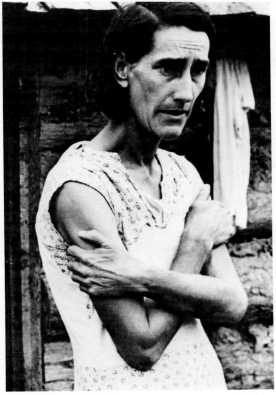

White Migrants
The plight of uprooted agricultural families from the South and Southwest captured the attention of many Americans in the 1930s. In particular, it captured the attention of some of the country's most talented photographers, many of whom worked for a time in the late 1930s for the Farm Security Administration recording the lives of migrant farmworkers. Russell Lee photographed a Texas family (above) moving west in search of work; and Ben Shahn recorded this portrait of a weary rural woman (right) and entitled it "Destitute." (Library of Congress)

Black Migrants

The Great Migration of blacks from the rural South into the cities had begun before World War I. But in the 1930s and 1940s the movement accelerated. Jacob Lawrence, a black artist, created a series of paintings entitled, collectively, *The Migration of the Negro* to illustrate this major event in the history of American blacks. (Phillips Collection, Washington, D.C.)

ganization calling itself the Black Shirts organized a campaign with the slogan "No Jobs for Niggers Until Every White Man Has a Job!" In other areas, whites used intimidation and violence to drive blacks from jobs. By 1932, over half the blacks in the South were without employment. Even unemployed, blacks continued to encounter discrimination. What limited relief there was went almost invariably first to whites; benefits for blacks were consistently lower than those for whites. Some private organizations, and some local governments, refused to provide any assistance at all to blacks.

Unsurprisingly, therefore, many Southern blacks—perhaps 400,000 in all—left the South in the 1930s and journeyed to the cities of the North. There they found less direct discrimination, perhaps, but

conditions that were in most respects little better than those in the South. In Harlem, the median income of skilled workers dropped by nearly half between 1929 and 1932. But most blacks, there and elsewhere, were unskilled workers; and as always, they tended to be the first fired when layoffs began. In New York, black unemployment was nearly 50 percent. In other cities, it was even higher. A black sociologist reported in 1932 that a third of all black Americans were unemployed and another third underemployed. Two million blacks—half the total black population of the country—were on some form of relief by 1932. But relief provided most of them with far less support than was necessary to sustain health.

Relatively few white Americans showed any sensitivity to the special plight of blacks during the 1930s.

Traditional patterns of segregation and disfranchisement in the South survived largely unchallenged. The horrible problem of lynching continued, with all efforts to win passage of a law making the practice a federal crime frustrated by the opposition of national leaders afraid of antagonizing powerful white Southern politicians. But several particularly notorious examples of racism did attract the attention of the nation.

The most celebrated, perhaps, was the Scottsboro case. In March 1931, nine black teen-agers were taken off a freight train in Alabama (in a small town near Scottsboro) and arrested for vagrancy and disorder. Later, two white women who had also been riding the train accused them of rape. In fact, there was overwhelming evidence, medical and otherwise, that the women (both of them prostitutes) had not been raped at all; they probably made their accusations out of fear of being arrested themselves. Nevertheless, an all-white jury in Alabama quickly convicted all nine of the Scottsboro boys and sentenced eight of them to death.

After the Supreme Court overturned the convictions in 1932, a series of new trials began that gradually attracted national attention. This was in part because the International Labor Defense, an organization associated with the Communist party, came to the aid of the accused youths and began to publicize the case. The trials continued throughout the 1930s. Although the white Southern juries who sat on the case never acquitted any of the defendants, all of them eventually gained their freedom— four because the charges were dropped, four because of early paroles, and one because he escaped. The last of the Scottsboro boys did not leave prison until 1950.

Although the Depression generally did little to alter white racial attitudes, it was a time of important changes in the role and behavior of the leading black organizations. The NAACP, for example, began to work diligently to win a position for blacks within the emerging labor movement, supporting the formation of the Congress of Industrial Organizations and helping to break down racial barriers within labor unions. Walter White, secretary of the NAACP, once even made a personal appearance at an auto plant to implore blacks not to work as strikebreakers. Partly as a result of such efforts, more than half a million blacks were able to join the labor movement. In the Steelworkers Union, for example, blacks constituted about 20 percent of the membership.

At the same time, many black leaders were beginning to question their traditional belief that patient lobbying in Congress and through the courts would ultimately produce racial equality. The economic distress of American blacks, combined with adverse judicial decisions and the continuing disinterest of Congress and state legislatures in their problems, caused many to contemplate more direct forms of protest.

Hispanics and Indians

Similar patterns of discrimination confronted many Mexicans and Mexican-Americans. The Hispanic population in the United States had been growing steadily since early in the century, largely in California and other areas of the Southwest through massive immigration from Mexico (which was specifically excluded from the immigration restriction laws of the 1920s). Some Chicanos filled many of the same menial jobs there that blacks had traditionally filled in other regions. Others began to farm on small, marginal tracts. Still others became agricultural migrants, traveling from region to region harvesting fruit, lettuce, and other crops. Even during the prosperous 1920s, it had been a precarious existence. The Depression made things significantly worse. As in the South, so in the Southwest: Unemployed whites began to demand jobs held by Hispanics, jobs that whites had previously considered beneath them. Thus Mexicans and Mexican-Americans found themselves, like blacks in the South, the last to be hired and the first to be fired; and Mexican unemployment rose quickly to levels far higher than those for whites. Some Mexicans—those willing to move across the border into Mexico—were provided free transportation. Others were, in effect, forced to leave by officials who arbitrarily removed them from relief rolls or simply rounded them up and transported them across the border. Perhaps half a million Chicanos left the United States for Mexico in the first years of the Depression.

For those who remained, there were both economic hardships and increasing social discrimination. Most relief programs excluded Mexicans from their rolls or offered them benefits far below those available to whites. Hispanics generally had no access to American schools. Many hospitals refused them admission. Unlike American blacks, who had established certain educational and social facilities of their own in response to discrimination, Hispanics generally had nowhere to turn. Even those who possessed American citizenship found themselves treated like foreigners.

There were, occasionally, signs of organized resistance by Mexican-Americans themselves, most notably in California, where they attempted to form a union of migrant farm workers. But harsh repression by local growers and the public authorities allied with them prevented such organizations from making significant progress. Like black farm workers, many Hispanics began as a result to migrate to the cities. In Los Angeles and other Western cities, they lived in a poverty comparable to that of urban blacks in the South and Northeast.

For the most tragically exploited of all American minorities—the Indians—the 1930s were years of several important changes. The Indian Reorganization Act of 1934 reversed the longstanding government policy of encouraging the assimilation of Native Americans into the mainstream of the nation's culture, a policy that had generally served as an excuse for robbing Indians of their tribal lands and reducing them to indigence. The act returned significant authority to the tribes to govern themselves, provided government funds to support education and cultural activities, and perhaps most important, restored the right of tribes to own land as collective entities. Previously, the government had required all Indian land to be owned by individuals. Several other government policies also assisted Indians. The Soil Conservation Service of the New Deal, for example, helped the Navajos improve their range lands and offered needed employment to many Indians on soil conservation and erosion prevention projects.

Nevertheless, American Indians through the 1930s remained what they had been for many years: an impoverished and isolated minority. Even with the redistribution of lands under the 1934 act, Indians continued to possess, for the most part, only territory that whites did not want—much of it arid, some of it desert. They continued to lack real authority to govern their own economic and social relationships, even inside their reservations. And they continued to lose property to white encroachment. Most of all, they continued to live in desperate poverty. In 1934, the average income of an American Indian was $48 a year.

Women in the Work Force

The Depression had conflicting effects on the ability and willingness of women to obtain paid employment. The economic crisis served in many ways to strengthen the widespread belief that a woman's

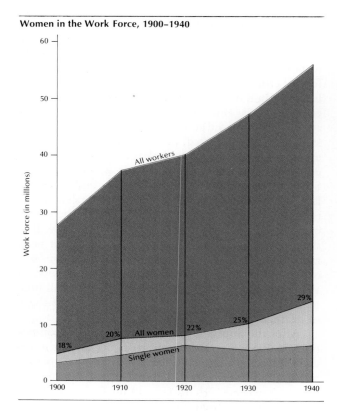

Women in the Work Force, 1900–1940

proper place was in the home. Most men and also many women believed that with employment so scarce, what work there was should go to men—that female workers were taking jobs away from male breadwinners. There was a particularly strong belief that no woman whose husband was employed should accept a job, that to do so would take income away from other, needier families. That belief, in fact, was for a time enshrined in law. From 1932 until 1937, it was illegal for more than one member of a family to hold a federal civil-service job. State and local governments often introduced similar restrictions. And in over twenty states, the legislatures considered (but never passed) laws prohibiting women from working in any paid jobs.

But the widespread assumption that married women, at least, should not work outside the home did not stop them from doing so. Both single and married women worked in the 1930s, despite public condemnation of the practice, because they or their families needed the money. In fact, the largest new group of female workers consisted of precisely those people who, according to popular attitudes, were supposed to be leaving the labor market: wives and mothers. Such women worked to supplement reduced family incomes or, often, because their husbands had lost their jobs. By the end of the Depression, 25 percent more women were working than had been doing so at the beginning.

Few of the new woman workers were entering professional work. In fact, the Depression saw an erosion of the already limited professional opportunities for women. That was partly because unemployed men now began moving into professions such as teaching and social work that had previously been considered women's fields. It was also because the general prejudice against women taking jobs away from men operated particularly strongly in the professions. Female industrial workers suffered similar discrimination. They were far more likely to be laid off or to experience wage reductions than their male counterparts. But women also had certain advantages in the workplace in the 1930s. The nonprofessional jobs that women traditionally held—as salesclerks and stenographers, and in other service positions—were less likely to disappear than the predominantly male jobs in heavy industry. Nor were many men, even unemployed men, likely to search for such jobs.

Black women, however, enjoyed few such advantages. In the South, in particular, they suffered massive unemployment because of a great reduction of domestic service jobs. Doing without paid servants was often one of the first economies that troubled white families imposed on themselves. Thus, over half of all black working women lost their jobs in the 1930s. Even so, at the end of the 1930s, 38 percent of black women were employed, as compared to 24 percent of white women. Married black women were twice as likely to be employed as married white women. That was because black women—both married and unmarried—had always been more likely to work than white women, less out of preference than out of economic necessity. And that pattern continued despite the setbacks of the Depression.

For American feminists, the Depression years were, on the whole, a time of frustration. Although economic pressures pushed more women into the work force, those same pressures helped to erode the frail support that feminists had won in the 1920s for the idea of women becoming economically and professionally independent. Most Americans could accept the idea of women working as a way to meet pressing family needs, but few could accept the idea of women working as an assertion of independence and individualism. In the difficult years of the 1930s, such aspirations seemed to many to be less important than dealing with economic hardship.

The Depression saw the virtual extinction of the National Woman's party, which had fought throughout the 1920s for the Equal Rights Amendment and for other egalitarian goals. Even more moderate feminists, committed to "protective" legislation for women, found their gains in decline by the end of the decade—although they did achieve some significant gains in the early years of the New Deal. (See below, pp. 752–753.) By the end of the New Deal, American feminism had reached its lowest ebb in nearly a century.

Depression Families

The economic hardships of the Depression years placed great strains on American families, particularly on the families of middle-class people who had become accustomed in the 1920s to a steadily rising standard of living and now found themselves plunged suddenly into uncertainty. It was not only unemployment that shook the confidence of middle-class families, although that was of course the worst blow. It was also the reduction of incomes among those who remained employed.

Economic circumstances forced many families, therefore, to retreat from the consumer patterns they had developed in the 1920s. Women often returned to making their own clothes (and those of their families) and to preserving their own food rather than buying such products in stores. Others engaged in home businesses—taking in laundry, selling baked goods, accepting boarders. Many households expanded to include more distant relatives. Parents often moved in with their children and grandparents with their grandchildren, or vice versa.

The Depression made family life in many ways more important economically. It also worked to erode the strength of many family units. There was a decline in the divorce rate, but that was largely because divorce was now too expensive for some. More common was the informal breakup of families, particularly the desertion of families by unemployed men bent on escaping the humiliation of being unable to earn a living. The marriage rate and the birth rate both declined.

The families whose structure and behavior were perhaps least affected by the onset of the Depression were those that had not shared in the affluence of the 1920s. Rural families, black families, and migrant families continued to survive in traditional ways. But in middle-class families the sudden deterioration of conditions often caused significant changes. Men, who had been accustomed to the role of breadwinner and central authority figure within the family and who now found themselves unemployed or underemployed, tended to experience strong feelings of failure and inadequacy. Married women who had not worked before the Depression might find the changes less jarring. Sociologists examining family structure in these years noted the frequent phenomenon of husbands becoming secondary to their wives as the center of family life. In some cases, it was the children who assumed leadership when their parents lost the ability to support the family. Young men and women sometimes managed to obtain paid employment when their parents could not, and their authority within the family rose as a result—often with disorienting results for everyone.

Social Values

Much of American culture in the 1920s had been a response to prosperity and industrial growth. It had celebrated affluence and consumerism and had stressed the importance of personal gratification through both. The economic crisis of the 1930s thus came as a special shock to those men and women who had come to expect continued and increasing prosperity. Many Americans assumed, therefore, that the experience of hard times would have profound effects on the nation's social values, on the way the society defined its goals.

In general, however, American social values seemed to change very little in response to the Depression. On the contrary, many people responded to hard times by redoubling their commitment to familiar ideas and goals. The sociologists Robert and Helen Merrell Lynd, who had published a celebrated study of Muncie, Indiana, in 1929 (*Middletown*), returned there in the mid-1930s to see how the city had changed. They described their findings in their 1937 book, *Middletown in Transition;* and they concluded that in most respects "the texture of Middletown's culture has not changed. . . . Middletown is overwhelmingly living by the values by which it lived in 1925." Above all, the men and women of "Middletown"—and by implication the people of the nation at large—remained committed to the traditional American emphasis on the individual.

No assumption would seem to have been more vulnerable to erosion during the Depression than the belief that the individual was in control of his or her own fate, that anyone displaying sufficient talent and industry could become a success. And in some respects, the economic crisis did work to undermine the traditional "success ethic" in America. People became during the 1930s more accustomed to looking to their government for assistance; they learned to blame corporate moguls, international bankers, economic royalists, and others for their distress. Yet the Depression fell far short of destroying the success ethic.

The survival of the ideals of work and individual advancement was evident in many ways, not least in the reactions of those most traumatized by the Depression: responsible, conscientious working people of all economic levels who suddenly, bewilderingly found themselves without employment. Some expressed anger and struck out at the economic system. More, however, blamed themselves—if not openly, at least subconsciously. Nothing so surprised foreign observers of America in the 1930s than the apparent passivity of the unemployed, many of whom were so ashamed of their joblessness that they refused to leave their homes. Perhaps that was why people who continued in the 1930s to work and to live more or less as they always had sometimes found it easy to forget that there was an economic crisis. The Depression was sometimes hard to see, because the unemployed tended to hide themselves, unwilling to display to the world what many of them considered their own personal failure.

At the same time, millions responded eagerly to reassurances that they could, through their own efforts, restore themselves to prosperity and success. Dale Carnegie's *How to Win Friends and Influence People* (1936), a self-help manual preaching individual initiative, was one of the best-selling books of the decade. Harry Emerson Fosdick, a Protestant theologian who similarly preached the virtues of positive thinking and individual initiative, attracted large audiences with his radio addresses. And although many of the great financial moguls fell into wide disrepute after 1929, the public continued to revere such "self-made men" as Thomas Edison and even, to some extent, Henry Ford.

The Depression also seemed to reinforce the belief of many Americans in the importance of conforming to the predominant standards of their society. If failure was, as many people believed, a result of personal inadequacies, then the best way to compensate for those inadequacies was to conform more and more tightly to the values of the community, to try harder to be like other, more successful people. Dale Carnegie's message was not only that personal initiative was the route to success; it was also that the best way for people to make something of themselves was to adapt to the world in which they lived, to understand the values and expectations of others and mold themselves accordingly. The way to get ahead, Carnegie taught, was to make other people feel important, to fit in.

Depression Culture

Not all Americans, of course, responded to the crisis of the Depression so passively. Large groups of men and women did come to believe that the economic problems of their time were the fault of society, not of individuals, and that some collective social response was necessary. Such beliefs found expression in, among other places, American artistic and intellectual life.

Just as many progressives had become alarmed when, early in the twentieth century, they "discovered" the existence of widespread poverty in the cities, so many Americans were shocked during the 1930s at their discovery of debilitating rural poverty. The plight of the farmer—and particularly of the Southern tenant farmer and sharecropper—became one of the leading themes of Depression intellectual life.

Perhaps most effective in conveying the dimensions of rural poverty was a group of documentary photographers, many of them employed by the Farm Security Administration in the late 1930s, who traveled through the South recording the nature of agricultural life. Men such as Roy Stryker, Walker Evans, Arthur Rothstein, and Ben Shahn and women such as Margaret Bourke-White and Dorothea Lange produced memorable studies of farm families and their surroundings, studies designed to show the savage impact of a hostile environment on its victims. Through their work, not only did the problems of poverty receive wider public attention but the art of photography earned new stature.

Many writers, similarly, turned away from the personal concerns of the 1920s and devoted themselves to exposés of social injustice. Erskine Caldwell exposed many of the same injustices that the documentary photographers had studied, in *Tobacco Road* (1932)—a novel about life in the rural South, which later became a long-running play. James Agee pro-

duced one of the most powerful portraits of the lives of sharecroppers, in *Let Us Now Praise Famous Men* (1941)—a careful, nonjudgmental description of the lives of three Southern families, illustrated with photographs by Walker Evans. Other writers and artists turned their gaze on social injustice in other settings. Richard Wright, a major black novelist, exposed the plight of residents of the urban ghetto, in *Native Son* (1940). James T. Farrell, in his Studs Lonigan trilogy (1932–1935), depicted the savage world of urban, lower-class white youth.

Other artists and intellectuals moved beyond social realism and combined an effort to expose social problems with a commitment to political solutions. Some were successful novelists of the 1920s who now turned to new themes. Ernest Hemingway, in *To Have and Have Not* (1937), displayed for the first time a concern with social issues by portraying a bitter labor struggle and advocating a collective solution; in *For Whom the Bell Tolls* (1940), he used the Spanish Civil War as a setting through which to illustrate the importance of solidarity in the face of oppression. Other, newer writers were discussing similar themes. John Steinbeck's *The Grapes of Wrath* (1939) portrayed the trials of a migrant family in California, concluding with an open call for collective social action against injustice (although in an earlier novel, *In Dubious Battle,* in 1936, Steinbeck had expressed grave reservations about the most collective political effort of the 1930s: the Communist party). John Dos Passos's *U.S.A.* trilogy (1930) explicitly attacked modern capitalism. Playwright Clifford Odets provided a particularly explicit demonstration of the appeal of political radicalism in *Waiting for Lefty* (1935).

For the most part, however, the cultural products of the 1930s that attracted wide popular audiences were those that diverted attention away from the Depression rather than illuminate its problems. The two most powerful instruments of popular culture in the 1930s—radio and the movies—were particularly careful to provide mostly light and diverting entertainment. The radio industry, still fearful of the possibility of nationalization (which was occurring in many other countries just establishing broadcasting systems), made every effort to avoid controversy. Although stations occasionally carried inflammatory programs, the staple of broadcasting was escapism: comedies such as *Amos 'n Andy,* adventures such as *Superman* or *Dick Tracy,* and other programs of pure entertainment. Hollywood continued to exercise tight control over its products through its resilient censor Will Hays, who in response to growing pressure from the

Twenty Cent Movie, 1936
Although moviegoing declined in the 1930s from its peak levels of the previous decade, it remained the most popular (and affordable) form of entertainment for Depression-era Americans. This painting by Reginald Marsh captures the riotous lights and colors at the Lyric Theater on Forty-second Street in New York. The stylish young women and cocky young men in front of the theater are juxtaposed against pictures of similarly flashy movie stars.   (Whitney Museum of American Art)

Catholic church's Legion of Decency, founded in 1934, redoubled his efforts to ensure that movies carried only safe, conventional messages. There were some films that did explore provocative political themes. The film version of *The Grapes of Wrath* (1940) faithfully evoked Steinbeck's social criticism. Director Frank Capra provided a muted social message in several of his comedies—*Mr. Deeds Goes to Town* (1936), *Mr. Smith Goes to Washington* (1939), and *Meet John Doe* (1941)—which celebrated the vir-

tues of the small town and the decency of the common people in contrast to the selfish, corrupt values of the city and the urban rich. More often, however, the commercial films of the 1930s were deliberately and explicitly escapist: lavish musicals and "wacky" comedies designed to divert audiences from their troubles and, very often, satisfy their fantasies about quick and easy wealth.

Popular literature, similarly, offered Americans an escape from the Depression rather than an investigation of it. Two of the best-selling novels of the decade were romantic sagas set in bygone eras: Margaret Mitchell's *Gone with the Wind* (1936), which became the source of one of the most celebrated films of all time; and Hervey Allen's *Anthony Adverse* (1933). Leading magazines, and particularly such popular new photographic journals as *Life*, did offer occasional glimpses of the ravages of the Depression. But for the most part they concentrated on fashions, stunts, and eye-catching scenery. Even the newsreels distributed to movie theaters across the country tended to give more attention to beauty contests and ship launchings than to the Depression itself. The American people lived through the 1930s without experiencing a radical change in their values in part because they managed so frequently and effectively to divert themselves from their problems.

The Allure of the Left

For a small but important group of Americans—intellectuals, artists, workers, blacks, and others who became disenchanted for various reasons with the prevailing values of American life—the Depression meant a commitment, for a time at least, to radical politics. Some became members of the American Communist party, which achieved a size and visibility in the 1930s it had never attained before and would never attain again. Others expressed sympathy for the party and its ideas without actually becoming members. The United States has always been distinctive for the weakness of radicalism in its political tradition; and even during the Depression, the left remained, by the standards of other nations, very weak. But the 1930s marked one of the high-water marks of radical activism in American life.

For intellectuals, in particular, the left offered an escape from the lonely and difficult stance of detachment and alienation that many had embraced in the 1920s. It combined a harsh critique of mainstream American society with an intense commitment to a political movement that seemed to give meaning and purpose to their lives. The particular importance of the Spanish Civil War (see below, p. 766) to many American intellectuals was a good example of how the left's sense of commitment proved appealing. The battle against the Spanish fascists of Francisco Franco (who was receiving support from Hitler and Mussolini) attracted a substantial group of young Americans, about 450 in all, who formed the Abraham Lincoln brigade and traveled to Spain to join in the fight. About a third of its members died in combat; but for those who survived, the experience was profoundly rewarding. Ernest Hemingway, who spent time in Spain as a correspondent, wrote in *For Whom the Bell Tolls* of how the war provided those Americans who fought in it with "a part in something which you could believe in wholly and completely and in which you felt an absolute brotherhood with others who were engaged in it."

Instrumental in creating the Lincoln brigade, and directing many of its activities throughout its existence, was the American Communist party. The Communist party of the 1930s remains the subject of considerable controversy among historians and many others. Its membership peaked at perhaps 100,000 during its heyday in the mid-1930s; and for a time it made efforts to present itself as a genuinely American organization, no more threatening or alien than any other political organization. For several years beginning in 1935, the party dropped its insistence on working completely apart from other organizations and began to advocate a great democratic alliance of all antifascist groups in the United States, a "Popular Front." It began to praise Franklin Roosevelt and John L. Lewis, a powerful (and strongly anticommunist) labor leader. It adopted the slogan "Communism is twentieth-century Americanism."

The party did perform functions in the 1930s that even many Americans unsympathetic to its long-range goals found appealing. It was active in organizing the unemployed in the early 1930s and staged a hunger march in Washington, D.C. in 1931. Party members were active in the labor movement, were in fact often among the most effective union organizers in some industries. And the party was one of the few political organizations to take a firm, unequivocal stand in favor of racial justice; its active defense of the Scottsboro boys was but one example of its efforts to ally itself with the aspirations of blacks. It also helped organize a union of black sharecroppers in Alabama, which resisted—in several instances violently—efforts of white landowners and authorities to displace them from their farms.

But it is also clear that despite its efforts to appear to be a humane, patriotic organization, the American Communist party was always under the close and rigid supervision of the Soviet Union. Its leaders took their orders from the Comintern in Moscow. Its members followed the "party line" or found themselves expelled from its ranks. The subordination of the party leadership to the Soviet Union was most

American Communists Rally the Unemployed
Unemployed men and women in San Francisco demonstrate on behalf of the Communist party in the early 1930s. Although the American Communist party achieved a size and influence during the Depression it had never enjoyed before and would never attain again, most of those who attended its meetings and listened to its speakers had no real commitment to the party's goals. Actual membership never rose much above 100,000. (Bettmann Archive)

clearly demonstrated in 1939, when Stalin signed a nonaggression pact with Nazi Germany. Moscow then sent orders to the American Communist party to abandon the Popular Front idea and return to its old stance of harsh criticism of American liberals; and the leaders in the United States immediately obeyed—although thousands of disillusioned members left the party as a result.

The Socialist party of America, now under the leadership of Norman Thomas, also cited the economic crisis as evidence of the failure of capitalism and sought vigorously to win public support for its own political program. In particular, it attempted to mobilize support among the most desperate elements of society—especially the rural poor. The Southern Tenant Farmers Union, supported by the party and organized by a young socialist, attempted to create a biracial coalition of sharecroppers, tenant farmers, and others to demand economic reform. Neither the Farmers Union nor the party itself, however, made any real progress toward establishing socialism as a major force in American politics. By 1936, in fact, membership in the Socialist party had fallen below 20,000.

In the end, what is most striking about American radicalism in the 1930s is less its unprecedented strength than its continuing limits. Neither the Communist party nor any other radical organization ever achieved dimensions during the Depression sufficient to make it a truly important political force. Even the most distressed Americans seemed to find the subordination of the Communists to Moscow unappealing. But the more moderate Socialist party, whose independence from foreign control was not in question, fared no better in increasing its membership in these years. However strong radical sentiment may have become, the strength of antiradicalism remained far stronger.

The Ordeal of Herbert Hoover

Herbert Hoover entered the presidency in March 1929 believing, like most Americans, that the nation faced a bright and prosperous future. For the first six months of his administration, he attempted to expand the policies he had advocated during his eight years as secretary of commerce, policies that would, he believed, complete the stable system of cooperative individualism that he thought key to a successful economy. The economic crisis that began before the year was out forced the president to deal with a new set of problems; but for most of the rest of his term, he continued to rely on the principles that had always governed his public life.

The Hoover Program

Hoover's first response to the Depression was to attempt to restore public confidence in the economy. "The fundamental business of this country, that is, production and distribution of commodities," he said in 1930, "is on a sound and prosperous basis." Consequently, he held a series of highly publicized meetings, summoning leaders of business, labor, and agriculture to the White House and urging upon them a program of voluntary cooperation for recovery. He persuaded businessmen not to cut production or lay off workers; he talked labor leaders into forgoing demands for higher wages or better hours. For a few brief months, the president's efforts seemed to be having some effect; but by mid-1931, economic conditions had deteriorated so much that the structure of voluntary cooperation he had erected quickly collapsed. Frightened industrialists soon began cutting production, laying off workers, and slashing wages. Hoover was powerless to stop them.

Hoover also attempted to use government spending as a tool for fighting the Depression. Rejecting the demands of some fiscal conservatives that the government cut back its own programs to ensure a balanced budget, the president proposed to Congress an increase of $423 million—a substantial sum by the standards of the time—in federal public works programs; and he exhorted state and local governments to engage in the "energetic yet prudent pursuit" of public construction. Nevertheless, Hoover's spending programs were in the end no more effective than his efforts at persuasion; for he was not willing to spend enough money, or to spend it for a long enough time, to do any good. He viewed his public works program as a temporary expedient, something to promote a rapid recovery. When economic conditions worsened, he became far less willing to increase government spending, worrying instead about maintaining federal solvency. In 1932, at the depth of the Depression, he proposed a tax increase to help the government avoid a deficit.

Even before the stock market crash, Hoover had begun to construct a program to assist the troubled agricultural economy. It embodied two major initiatives, which the president proposed to a special session of Congress in April 1929. The Agricultural Marketing Act established for the first time a major government bureaucracy to help farmers maintain prices. A federally sponsored Farm Board of eight members would administer a budget of $500 million, from which it could make loans to national marketing cooperatives or establish "corporations" to buy surpluses and thus raise prices. At the same time, Hoover attempted to protect American farmers from international competition by raising agricultural tariffs. The Hawley-Smoot Tariff of 1930 contained protective increases on seventy-five farm products and raised rates from the average of 26 percent established by the 1922 Fordney-McCumber Tariff to a new high of 50 percent.

Neither the Agricultural Marketing Act nor the Hawley-Smoot Tariff ultimately helped American farmers in any significant way. The Marketing Act relied on voluntary cooperation among farmers and gave the government no authority to do what the agricultural economy most badly needed: limit production. Hoover's call for a reduction of the wheat crop, for example, resulted in a drop in acreage of only 1 percent in Kansas. The Farm Board lacked sufficient funds to deal effectively with the crisis. Prices continued to fall despite its efforts. The Hawley-Smoot tariff was an unqualified disaster—as 1,000 members of the American Economic Association had warned the president even before he signed it into law. It provoked foreign governments to enact trade restrictions of their own in reprisal, further diminishing the market for American agricultural goods. And it raised rates not only on farm products but on 925 manufactured goods as well, making industrial products more expensive for farmers.

A Change of Direction

By the spring of 1931, Herbert Hoover's political position had deteriorated considerably. Democrats had made major gains in the 1930 congressional elections, winning control of the House and making substantial inroads in the Senate. Large portions of the public were beginning to hold the president personally to blame for the crisis, and Hoover's name soon became synonymous with economic distress. Shantytowns established on the outskirts of cities were known as "Hoovervilles." Progressive reformers both inside and outside the government urged the president to support more vigorous programs of relief and public spending. Hoover ignored the recommendation. Instead, he seized on a slight improvement in economic conditions early in 1931 as proof that his policies were working.

The international financial panic of the spring of 1931 destroyed the illusion that the economic crisis was coming to an end. The ability of European nations to secure loans from American banks, which had been so crucial to their solvency throughout the 1920s, largely disappeared after 1929; and shortly thereafter, the financial fabric of many European nations began to unravel. In May 1931, the largest bank in Austria collapsed. Over the next several months, panic gripped the financial institutions of neighboring countries. European governments, desperate for sound assets, withdrew their gold reserves from American banks. European investors, in need of dollars to pay off their loans and protect their solvency, dumped their shares of American stocks onto the market, further depressing prices. More and more European nations were abandoning the gold standard and devaluing their currencies, leaving the United States, which remained tied to gold, at a disadvantage in international trade. American economic conditions rapidly declined to new lows, and Herbert Hoover quickly adopted a new approach to the Depression.

It was not the domestic American economy that was to blame for the Depression, he now argued, but the structure of international finance. The proper response to the crisis, therefore, was not to adopt active social and economic programs at home but to work to restore international stability. Hoover's solution was to propose a moratorium—first on the payment of all war debts and reparations, then on the payment of international private debts as well. It was a sound proposal, but it came too late to halt the panic.

By the time Congress convened in December 1931, conditions had grown so desperate that Hoover finally decided to support an expanded federal role in the economy. He persuaded Congress to increase funding for federal land banks and to create a system of government home loan banks. Through them, financial institutions holding mortgages on farms, homes, and other properties could receive cash from the government for the mortgages instead of foreclosing on them—thus keeping the banks afloat and, incidentally, preventing many Americans from losing their homes and properties. Hoover also supported the Glass-Steagall Banking Act of 1932, designed to make it easier for American banks to meet the demands of overseas depositors who were withdrawing their gold from the United States. And he encouraged New York financiers to establish a $500 million fund to help troubled banks stay afloat.

The most important piece of legislation of his presidency, however, was a bill passed in January 1932 establishing the Reconstruction Finance Corporation (RFC), a government agency whose purpose was to provide federal loans to troubled banks, railroads, and other businesses. It even made funds available to local governments to support public works projects and assist relief efforts. It was an unprecedented use of federal power; and unlike many earlier Hoover programs, it operated on a large scale. In 1932, the RFC had a budget of $1.5 billion for public works alone.

Nevertheless, the new agency failed to deal directly or forcefully enough with the real problems of the economy to produce any significant recovery. Because the RFC was permitted to lend funds only to those financial institutions with sufficient collateral, much of its money went to large banks and corporations, prompting some critics to dub it a "bread line for big business." The RFC could only provide loans; it could not purchase stock or otherwise provide capital to troubled institutions, even though that was what they most desperately needed. And at Hoover's insistence, it helped finance only those public works projects that promised ultimately to pay for themselves (toll bridges, public housing, and others), thus severely limiting the scope of its efforts. Its chairman, the conservative Texas banker Jesse Jones, prided himself on the solvency of his agency and followed sound, prudent banking practices. This meant that the RFC itself remained healthy by refusing to make loans to those institutions that most desperately needed them. Above all, the RFC did not have enough money to make any real impact on the Depression; and it did not even spend all the money it had. Of the $300 million available to support local relief efforts, the RFC lent out only $30 million in 1932. Of the $1.5 billion public works budget, it released only about 20 percent. Even Hoover's most vigorous and expansive program had been crippled by the cautiousness and fiscal conservatism of his administration.

Agrarian Unrest

For the first several years of the Depression, most Americans were either too stunned or too confused to raise any effective protest. By the middle of 1932, however, the crisis had continued so long and had grown so severe that dissident voices began to be heard.

In the Midwest, farmers sensing themselves near economic extinction raised new and louder demands for government assistance. In particular, they called for legislation similar to the McNary-Haugen bill of

The Rout of the Bonus Army, July 1932
Soldiers of the United States army, wearing gas masks and carrying rifles with fixed bayonets, drove members of the Bonus Army from the abandoned buildings on lower Pennsylvania Avenue in which they had been living. In this picture, troops move through clouds of tear gas toward the fleeing, terrified veterans. (Bettmann Archive)

the 1920s by which the government would guarantee them a return on their crops at least equal to the cost of production. Lobbyists from the larger farm organizations converged on Washington to pressure members of Congress to act. Some disgruntled farmers staged public protests in the capital. But when neither the president nor Congress showed any signs of movement, they adopted a more drastic approach. In the summer of 1932, a group of unhappy farm owners gathered in Des Moines, Iowa, to establish a new organization: the Farm Holiday Association. Under the leadership of Milo Reno, the association endorsed the withholding of farm products from the market—in effect a farmers' strike. The strike began in August in western Iowa, spread briefly to a few neighboring areas, and succeeded in blockading several markets; but in the end it dissolved in failure. The scope of the effort was too modest to affect farm prices, and many farmers in the region refused to cooperate in any case. When clashes between strikers and local authorities resulted in several episodes of violence, Reno called off the strike. Nevertheless, the uprising created considerable consternation in state governments in the farm belt and even more in Washington, where the president and much of Congress were facing a national election.

The Bonus March

A more celebrated protest movement emerged from a less likely quarter: American veterans. In 1924,

Congress had approved the payment of a bonus to all those who had served in World War I, the money to be distributed in 1945. By 1932, however, economic distress had mobilized a widespread demand among veterans that the bonus be paid immediately. Hoover would not consider the request, fearing that acquiescence would ruin his hopes for a balanced budget; but the veterans refused to be denied. In June, more than 20,000 veterans, members of the self-proclaimed "Bonus Army," marched into Washington, built crude camps in the city and its environs, and promised to stay until Congress approved legislation to pay the bonus. A few of the veterans departed in July, after Congress had voted down their proposal. Most, however, remained where they were.

Their continued presence in Washington was an irritant and an embarrassment to Herbert Hoover, who had problems enough already and who gradually became defensive and even paranoid about the protesters. Finally, in mid-July, he ordered police to clear the marchers out of several abandoned federal buildings in which they had been staying. The police arrived; a few marchers threw rocks at them; someone opened fire; and two veterans fell dead. To Hoover, the incident seemed proof of dangerous radicalism, and he ordered the U. S. Army to assist the police in clearing out the buildings.

General Douglas MacArthur, the army chief of staff, chose to carry out the order himself. In full battle dress, he led the Third Cavalry (under the command of George S. Patton), two infantry regiments, a machine-gun detachment, and six tanks down Pennsylvania Avenue in pursuit of the motley Bonus Army. The veterans fled in terror as the troops hurled tear gas canisters and flailed at them with their bayonets. MacArthur followed them across the Anacostia River, where he ordered the soldiers to burn their camp to the ground. More than 100 marchers were injured. One baby died.

The incident served as perhaps the final blow to Hoover's already battered political standing. To much of the public, he now stood confirmed as an aloof and insensitive figure, locked in the White House, uncomprehending of the distress around him. Hoover's own cold and gloomy personality did nothing to change the public image, and some of his embattled public statements at the time made his plight even worse. "Nobody is actually starving," he assured reporters (inaccurately) in 1932. "The hoboes, for example, are better fed than they have ever been." The Great Engineer, the personification of the optimistic days of the 1920s, had become a symbol of the nation's failure to deal effectively with its startling reversal of fortune.

The Election of 1932

Most of the American people looked to the 1932 presidential election as their most effective vehicle of protest. Almost no one had any doubts about the outcome. The Republican party dutifully renominated Herbert Hoover for a second term in office, but the lugubrious atmosphere of their convention made it clear that few delegates believed he could carry the November election. The Democrats, in the meantime, gathered jubilantly in Chicago to nominate a candidate who, they were certain, would be the next president of the United States. Their choice was the governor of New York, Franklin Delano Roosevelt.

Roosevelt had been a well-known figure in the party for many years already. The son of a wealthy Hudson Valley railroad tycoon, schooled at Harvard and at Columbia Law School, Roosevelt had begun his political career in 1910 in the New York State legislature. Because he was handsome, charming, and articulate, and because he was a distant cousin of Theodore Roosevelt (a connection strengthened by his marriage in 1904 to the president's niece, Eleanor), he attracted increasing attention. He served as assistant secretary of the navy under Woodrow Wilson during World War I; and in 1920, he received his party's nomination for vice president on the ill-fated ticket with James M. Cox.

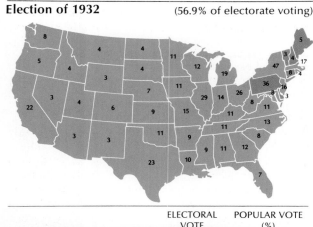

Election of 1932 (56.9% of electorate voting)

	ELECTORAL VOTE	POPULAR VOTE (%)
Franklin D. Roosevelt (Democratic)	472	22,821,857 (57.4)
Herbert Hoover (Republican)	59	15,761,841 (39.7)
Norman Thomas (Socialist)	—	881,951 (1.2)
Other candidates (Communist, Prohibition, Socialist Labor, Liberty)	—	271,355

Less than a year later, however, his public career appeared to come to an end when he was stricken with polio and lost the use of his legs. For seven years, Roosevelt worked hard at his recovery, but he was never again able to walk without the use of crutches and braces. Nevertheless, he built up sufficient physical strength to make a courageous appearance at the 1924 Democratic Convention to nominate Al Smith for president. In 1928, when Smith finally received the Democratic nomination and left Albany to run for president, Roosevelt succeeded him as governor; and in 1930, he easily won reelection.

Roosevelt worked no miracles in New York as the state suffered through the first years of the Depression. He did, however, initiate enough positive programs of government assistance to be able to present himself as a more energetic and imaginative leader than Herbert Hoover. At least as important to his political future, however, was his astute effort to win support from both the urban and rural wings of his party. By avoiding such divisive cultural issues as religion and prohibition, and by emphasizing the economic grievances that most Democrats shared, he assembled a coalition within the party that enabled him to win his party's nomination. And the next day, in a dramatic break with tradition, he flew to Chicago to address the convention in person and accept the nomination.

In the course of his acceptance speech, Roosevelt aroused the delegates with his ringing promise: "I pledge you, I pledge myself, to a new deal for the American people," giving his program a name that would long endure. Neither then nor in the subsequent campaign, however, did Roosevelt give much indication of what that program would be. In part, of course, it was because there was no need to be specific. Herbert Hoover's unpopularity virtually ensured Roosevelt's election; his only real concern was to avoid offending any voters unnecessarily. In part, however, it was because Roosevelt had no firm or coherent program to describe. Surrounded by advisers holding widely disparate views, the candidate seemed at times to be little more than a genial mediator—listening to everyone, disagreeing with no one.

There was, however, evidence of important differences between Roosevelt and Hoover. Drawing from the ideas of a talented team of university professors (whom the press quickly dubbed the "Brains Trust"), Roosevelt espoused an amalgam of ideas that combined old progressive reform principles with some of the newer ideas of associationalism that had gained currency in the 1920s. Hoover liked to insist that the Depression was international in origin and that any attempt to combat it must be international as well. Roosevelt, in contrast, portrayed the crisis as a domestic (and Republican) problem and argued that the most important solutions could be found at home. Above all, perhaps, Roosevelt's style—his dazzling smile, his floppy broad-brimmed hat, his cigarette holder held at a jaunty angle between his teeth, his skillful oratory, his unfailing wit—all combined to win him a wide personal popularity only vaguely related to the specifics of his programs.

In November, to the surprise of no one, Roosevelt won by a landslide. He received 57.4 percent of the popular vote to Hoover's 39.7. The Socialist party, in this year of despair, garnered only 1.2 percent of the ballots. The Communist party polled a meager 103,000 votes. In the electoral college, the result was even more overwhelming. Hoover carried Pennsylvania, Connecticut, Vermont, New Hampshire, and Maine. Roosevelt won everything else. And Democrats won majorities in both houses of Congress. It was a broad and convincing mandate, but it was not yet clear what Roosevelt intended to do with it.

The Changing of the Guard
Long before the event actually occurred, Peter Arno of the *New Yorker* magazine drew this image of Franklin D. Roosevelt and Herbert Hoover traveling together to the Capitol for Roosevelt's inauguration. It predicted with remarkable accuracy the mood of the uncomfortable ride—Hoover glum and uncommunicative, Roosevelt buoyant and smiling. This was to have been the magazine's cover for the week of the inauguration; but after an attempted assassination of the president-elect several weeks earlier in Florida (in which the mayor of Chicago was killed), the editors decided to substitute a more subdued drawing. (© 1933, 1961 Peter Arno/Franklin D. Roosevelt Library)

The Interregnum

The period between the election and the inauguration (which in the early 1930s still lasted more than four months) was traditionally a time of quiet planning and federal inaction. The winter of 1932–1933, however, was a season of growing economic crisis; and traditional patterns seemed to many Americans to be

SIGNIFICANT EVENTS

1929 Stock market crash signals onset of Great Depression

Agricultural Marketing Act passed

1930 Hawley-Smoot Tariff enacted

1931 Federal Reserve raises interest rates

Depression spreads to Europe and deepens in United States

Scottsboro boys arrested

1932 Erskine Caldwell publishes *Tobacco Road*

Glass-Steagall Banking Act passed

Reconstruction Finance Corporation established

Farm Holiday Association formed in Iowa

Bonus Marchers come to Washington, D.C.

Banking crisis

Franklin D. Roosevelt elected president

1934 Indian Reorganization Act passed

1935 American Communist party proclaims Popular Front

1936 Dale Carnegie publishes *How to Win Friends and Influence People*

Margaret Mitchell publishes *Gone with the Wind*

1939 John Steinbeck publishes *The Grapes of Wrath*

Nazi-Soviet pact weakens American Communist party

1940 Richard Wright publishes *Native Son*

Ernest Hemingway publishes *For Whom the Bell Tolls*

1941 James Agee and Walker Evans publish *Let Us Now Praise Famous Men*

---

irrelevant. Among those who believed that the president-elect should act forcefully even before taking office was Herbert Hoover, who argued that international economic stability depended on a clear affirmation by the United States of the sanctity of the gold standard. He argued as well that fear of "radical" economic measures by the new administration was unsettling the domestic financial climate. In a series of brittle exchanges with Roosevelt in the months following the election, Hoover tried to exact from the president-elect a pledge to maintain policies of economic orthodoxy. Roosevelt genially refused.

In February, only a month before the inauguration, a new crisis developed. The American banking system had been in desperate trouble since the middle of 1930. By 1932, it was beginning to collapse. Public confidence in the banks was ebbing; depositors were withdrawing their money in panic; and one bank after another was closing its doors and declaring bankruptcy. In mid-February, the governor of Michigan, one of the states hardest hit by the panic, ordered all banks temporarily closed. Other states soon followed,

and by the end of the month banking activity was restricted drastically in every state but one. Once again, Hoover wrote to Roosevelt insisting that the problem was a result of "steadily degenerating confidence" in the incoming administration. The only way to restore calm, he insisted, was for Roosevelt to give prompt public assurances that there would be no tinkering with the currency, no heavy borrowing, no unbalancing of the budget. "I realize," he wrote a Republican senator at the time, "that if these declarations be made by the president-elect, he will have ratified the whole major program of the Republican Administration." Roosevelt realized the same thing and refused to comply.

March 4, 1933, was, therefore, a day not only of economic crisis but of considerable personal bitterness. The nation waited anxiously as Herbert Hoover, convinced that the United States was headed for disaster, rode glumly down Pennsylvania Avenue with a beaming, buoyant Franklin Roosevelt, who would shortly be sworn in as the thirty-second president of the United States.

SUGGESTED READINGS

The Coming of the Depression   Robert Sobel, *The Great Bull Market* (1968), chronicles the Wall Street boom of the 1920s; John Kenneth Galbraith, *The Great Crash* (1954), examines the bust. Conflicting interpretations of the causes

of the Depression are available in Milton Friedman and Anna Schwartz, *The Great Contraction* (1965), a reprint of Chapter 7 of their classic *Monetary History of the United States* (1963), and in Peter Temin, *Did Monetary Forces Cause the Great Depression?* (1976). Friedman and Schwartz's answer to Temin's question is yes; Temin's is no. Overviews of the Depression economy include Broadus Mitchell, *Depression Decade* (1947); Lester V. Chandler, *America's Greatest Depression* (1970); and Charles Kindelberger, *The World in Depression* (1973). Susan E. Kennedy, *The Banking Crisis of 1933* (1973), examines one of the Depression's low moments.

The Impact of the Depression   Irving Bernstein, *The Lean Years* (1960), provides a compelling picture of the impact of the Depression on workers in the first years after the crash; Arthur M. Schlesinger, Jr., *The Crisis of the Old Order* (1957), offers a picture of the broader impact of the crisis. Valuable oral histories of the impact of the Depression are available in Studs Terkel, *Hard Times* (1970), a series of interviews conducted years after the 1930s. Drawing from interviews conducted in the 1930s are Federal Writers Project, *These Are Our Lives* (1939); Tom Terrill and Jerrold Hirsch, *Such as Us* (1978); and Ann Banks, *First-Person America* (1980). Donald Worster, *Dust Bowl* (1979), and Walter Stein, *California and the Dust Bowl Migration* (1973), offer differing views of the agricultural crisis in the Southern plains.

Depression Culture and Society   Warren Susman, *Culture as History* (1984), includes several influential essays on 1930s popular culture. Robert Lynd and Helen Merrell Lynd, *Middletown in Transition* (1935), examines the impact of the Depression on Muncie, Indiana, the town they had earlier studied in *Middletown* (1929). Frederick Lewis Allen, *Since Yesterday* (1940), is a contemporary view of social mores. William Stott, *Documentary Expression and Thirties America* (1973), offers a powerful examination of Depression photography and other forms of documentary expression. Richard Pells, *Radical Visions and American Dreams* (1973), is the most thorough study of artistic responses to the Depression. Robert Sklar, *Movie-Made America* (1975), and Andrew Bergman, *We're in the Money* (1971), explore the films of the era. Daniel Aaron, *Writers on the Left* (1961), is an important study of the interaction between literature and politics. The ways in which the Depression affected women's lives are analyzed in Susan Ware, *Holding Their Own: American Women in the 1930s* (1982); William Chafe, *The American Woman* (1972); Lois Scharf, *To Work and to Wed: Female Employment, Feminism, and the Great Depression* (1980); and Jeane Westin, *Making Do: How Women Survived the '30s* (1976). For changing views of ethnicity, consult Richard Krickus, *Pursuing the American Dream* (1976), and Gilman Ostrander, *American Civilization in the First Machine Age* (1970). Racial issues in the 1930s are examined in

Raymond Wolters, *Negroes and the Great Depression* (1970); Nancy Weiss, *The National Urban League* (1974); and Ralph Bunche, *The Political Status of the Negro in the Age of FDR* (1973), a reissue of a study originally published during World War II. John Dollard, *Caste and Class in a Southern Town,* 3rd ed. (1957), is a classic study, originally published in 1937, of racial relationships in a Southern town. Dan T. Carter, *Scottsboro* (1969), is a compelling account of one of the most celebrated racial issues of the decade. The Hispanic experience during the Depression is considered in Abraham Hoffman, *Unwanted Mexican Americans in the Great Depression* (1974), and in the appropriate chapters of Rodolfo Acuña, *Occupied America* (rev. 1981). Carey McWilliams, *Factories in the Field* (1939), studies the plight of migrant farm workers in California.

The Hoover Presidency   Important studies of the Hoover presidency include Albert Romasco, *The Poverty of Abundance* (1965); Joan Hoff Wilson, *Herbert Hoover* (1975); David Burner, *Herbert Hoover* (1978); Harris Warren, *Herbert Hoover and the Great Depression* (1959); Jordan Schwarz, *The Interregnum of Despair* (1970); and Hoover's own *Memoirs: The Great Depression* (1952). James Olson, *Herbert Hoover and the Reconstruction Finance Corporation* (1977), considers the administration's major economic innovation. Martin Fausold and George Mazuzun (eds.), *The Hoover Presidency* (1974), examines the Hoover years in a series of essays. Martin Fausold, *The Presidency of Herbert C. Hoover* (1985), is a recent overview.

Politics and Protest   John Shover, *Cornbelt Rebellion* (1965), studies the Farm Holiday movement; and Roger Daniels, *The Bonus March* (1971), and Donald Lisio, *The President and Protest* (1974), examine the veterans' efforts in Washington, D.C., in 1932. Harvey Klehr, *The Heyday of American Communism: The Depression Decade* (1984), offers a critical view of the American Communist party. Mark Naison, *Communists in Harlem During the Depression* (1983), is more sympathetic. Irving Howe and Lewis Coser, *The American Communist Party* (1957), is an earlier study. David Shannon, *The Socialist Party of America* (1955), chronicles another challenge to the New Deal from the left. The emergence of Franklin Roosevelt and the election of 1932 receive extensive treatment in Arthur M. Schlesinger, Jr., *The Crisis of the Old Order* (1957); David Burner, *The Politics of Provincialism* (1967); and Frank Freidel, *The Triumph* (1956). The interregnum of 1932–1933 is examined in Frank Freidel, *Launching the New Deal* (1973); Eliot Rosen, *Hoover, Roosevelt, and the Brains Trust* (1977); and Rexford G. Tugwell, *The Brains Trust* (1968).

WPA Poster, 1930s (Library of Congress)

Chapter 26

The New Deal

Franklin Roosevelt not only served longer as president than any man in American history. He became during his years in office more central to the life of the nation than any chief executive before him. More important, perhaps, his administration constructed a series of programs that permanently altered the role and structure of the federal government. The accomplishments of the New Deal, and their impact on all subsequent discussions of the role of government in American society, have helped to shape the nation's political life ever since.

And yet the Roosevelt administration itself was never firmly committed to any particular philosophy of government. Pragmatic, experimental, unwedded to any single set of social or economic beliefs, the New Deal defied easy classification or neat description. Roosevelt himself gave perhaps the clearest statement of the New Deal's political philosophy. "Try something," he once exhorted the nation. "If it works, keep doing it. If it doesn't, try something else."

By the end of the 1930s, when the outbreak of war in Europe finally brought the crusade for domestic reform temporarily to a close, the Roosevelt administration had created many of the broad outlines of the political world we know today. It had constructed the beginnings of a modern welfare system. It had extended federal regulation over new areas of the economy. It had presided over the birth of the modern labor movement. It had made the government a major force in the agricultural economy. It had created a powerful coalition within the Democratic party that would dominate American politics for most of the next thirty years. And it had pro-

duced the beginnings of a new liberal ideology that would govern reform efforts for several decades after the war.

One thing the New Deal had not done, however, was end the Great Depression. It had, to be sure, helped stabilize the economy in the desperate early months of 1933 and had kept things from getting worse. And there had been a limited, if erratic, recovery in many areas of economic life. But by the end of 1939, many of the basic problems of the Depression remained unsolved. An estimated 15 percent of the work force remained unemployed. And the gross national product was no larger than it had been ten years before.

Inevitably, these long years of economic stagnation took their toll on the nation's political and social life. And the Roosevelt administration faced repeated challenges throughout the 1930s from groups impatient with its programs. The political fortunes of the New Deal ebbed and flowed throughout the 1930s, and at times a major political upheaval seemed to be at hand. But in the end, Franklin Roosevelt managed, despite the challenges, to retain a firm grip on the loyalties of a majority of the public.

Launching the New Deal

Roosevelt's first task, he knew, was to alleviate the crisis that was threatening in early 1933 to bring the financial system and the economy as a whole to its knees. In particular, he had to stop the panic that was

The Roosevelt Smile
The battered hat, the uptilted cigarette holder, the jaunty smile—all were hallmarks of Franklin Roosevelt's ebullient public personality. In part, at least, the president's hearty optimism was a deliberate pose, adopted to distract attention from the paralysis that had denied him the use of his legs since 1921. Roosevelt took elaborate precautions to hide signs of his affliction from the public. He learned to "walk" short distances with the aid of metal braces, a cane, and the support of an aide (or, often, one of his sons). He appeared often in public (as seen in this 1939 photograph) driving a specially designed automobile with hand controls. In private, however, Roosevelt remained largely confined to his wheelchair; he had to be lifted in and out of cars, even in and out of bed; and as the years passed and his strength ebbed, he seldom ventured from the White House. (AP/Wide World Photos)

rapidly gripping the nation. He did so remarkably quickly—in part by sheer force of personality and in part by constructing, in a few months, an ambitious and diverse program of legislation. This "First New Deal," as many historians have called it, embraced many different approaches to reform (as well as some intensely conservative measures).

Restoring Confidence

Much of Roosevelt's success was a result of his ebullient personality. Beginning with his inaugural address—in which he assured the American people that "the only thing we have to fear is fear itself"—he projected an infectious optimism that helped dispel the growing despair. He was the first president to make regular use of the radio, and his friendly "fireside chats," during which he explained his programs and plans to the people, helped to build public confidence in the administration. Roosevelt was also a master at handling his relations with the press. He

held frequent informal press conferences, and he won both the respect and the friendship of most reporters. Their regard for him was such that by unwritten agreement, no newsman ever photographed the president getting into or out of his car or being wheeled in his wheelchair. Much of the American public remained unaware throughout the Roosevelt years that their president's legs remained completely paralyzed.

Image alone, however, could not solve the serious economic problems of March 1933; and within twenty-four hours of his inauguration, Roosevelt was moving forcefully to construct a positive program that would restore at least momentary stability to the nation. With the banking crisis at a fever pitch and with Congress apparently in a mood to do virtually anything the new president suggested, Roosevelt might well have taken drastic steps, such as nationalizing the banking system. Instead, he worked to shore up existing financial institutions and to revive business faith in the economy. On March 6, two days after taking office, he issued a proclamation closing all American banks for four days until Congress could meet in special session. Under other circumstances, shutting down the nation's banks would have created wide alarm. But since many states had already closed their banks before Roosevelt's proclamation, the "bank holiday," as the president euphemistically described it, created a general sense of relief. Finally, the federal government was stepping in to stop the alarming pattern of bank failures.

Three days later, Roosevelt sent to Congress the Emergency Banking Act, a generally conservative bill (much of it drafted by holdovers from the Hoover administration) designed primarily to protect the larger banks from being dragged down by the weakness of smaller ones. The bill provided for Treasury Department inspection of all banks before they would be allowed to reopen, for federal assistance to some troubled institutions, and for a thorough reorganization of those in the greatest difficulty. A confused and frightened Congress passed the bill within four hours of its introduction. "I can assure you," Roosevelt told the public on March 12, in his first fireside chat, "that it is safer to keep your money in a reopened bank than under the mattress." The public apparently believed him. Three-quarters of the banks in the Federal Reserve system reopened within the next three days, and $1 billion in hoarded currency and gold flowed back into them within a month. The immediate banking crisis was over.

On the morning after passage of the Emergency Banking Act, Roosevelt sent to Congress another measure—the Economy Act—designed to convince the public (and especially the business community) that the federal government was in safe, responsible hands. The act proposed to balance the federal budget by cutting the salaries of government employees and reducing pensions to veterans by as much as 15 percent. Otherwise, the president warned, the nation faced a $1 billion deficit. The bill revealed clearly what Roosevelt had always maintained: that he was at heart as much a fiscal conservative as his predecessor. And like the banking bill, it passed through Congress almost instantly—despite heated protests from some congressional progressives.

Roosevelt also moved in his first days in office to put to rest one of the divisive issues of the 1920s. He supported and then signed a bill to legalize the manufacture and sale of beer with a 3.2 percent alcohol content—an interim measure pending the repeal of prohibition, for which a constitutional amendment (the Twenty-first) was already in process. The amendment was ratified later in 1933.

Agricultural Adjustment

Roosevelt realized that these initial actions were nothing but stopgaps, that more comprehensive government programs would be necessary. The first such program was on behalf of the troubled agricultural economy, and it established an important and long-lasting federal role in the planning of the entire agricultural sector of the economy.

The Agricultural Adjustment Act, which Congress passed in May 1933, reflected the desires of leaders of various farm organizations and the ideas of Roosevelt's secretary of agriculture, Henry A. Wallace. It included scraps and reworkings of many long-cherished agricultural schemes, but its most important feature was its provision for crop reductions.

Under the "domestic allotment" system of the act, producers of seven basic commodities (wheat, cotton, corn, hogs, rice, tobacco, and dairy products) would decide on production limits for their crops. The government would then, through the Agricultural Adjustment Administration (AAA), tell individual farmers how much they should plant and would pay them subsidies for leaving some of their land idle. A tax on food processing (for example, the milling of wheat) would provide the funds for the new payments. Farm prices were to be subsidized up to the point of parity.

Because the 1933 agricultural season was already under way by the time the AAA began operations, the agency oversaw a large-scale destruction of existing crops and livestock to reduce surpluses. Six million pigs and 220,000 sows were slaughtered. Cotton farmers plowed under a quarter of their crop. In a society plagued by want, in which many families were suffering from malnutrition and starvation, it was difficult for the government to explain the need for destroying surpluses, and the crop and livestock destruction remained controversial for many years. Beginning in 1934, however, crop and livestock limitations were accomplished in less provocative ways.

The results of the AAA efforts were in many ways heartening. Prices for farm commodities did indeed rise in the years after 1933, and gross farm income increased by half in the first three years of the New Deal. The relative position of farmers in the nation, therefore, improved significantly for the first time in twenty years; and the agricultural economy as a whole emerged from the 1930s much more stable and prosperous than it had been in the past. The AAA did, however, tend to favor larger farmers over smaller ones, particularly since local administration of its programs often fell into the hands of the most powerful producers in a community. At times, even if unintentionally, the New Deal farm program actually dispossessed some struggling farmers. In the cotton belt, for example, planters who were reducing their acreage evicted their tenants and sharecroppers and fired many field hands.

In January 1936, the Supreme Court struck down the crucial provisions of the Agricultural Adjustment Act, arguing that the government had no constitutional authority to require farmers to limit production. But the essence of the AAA programs survived, because within a few weeks the administration had secured passage of new legislation (the Soil Conservation and Domestic Allotment Act), which permitted the government to pay farmers to reduce production so as allegedly to "conserve soil," prevent erosion, and accomplish other secondary goals. The new law apparently met the Court's objections.

It also attempted to correct one of the most glaring injustices of the original act: its failure to protect sharecroppers and tenant farmers. Now landlords were required to share the payments they received for cutting back production with those who worked their land. (The new requirements were, however, largely evaded.) The administration launched other efforts to assist poor farmers as well. The Resettlement Administration, established in 1935, and its successor, the Farm Security Administration, created in 1937, attempted through short- and long-term loans to help farmers cultivating submarginal soil to relocate on better lands. But the programs never moved more than a few thousand farmers. Of more importance was the Rural Electrification Administration, created in 1935, which worked to make electric power available to farmers through utility cooperatives.

Industrial Recovery

The industrial economy in 1933 was, as it had been for nearly three years, suffering from a vicious cycle of deflation. Ever since 1931, leaders of the U.S. Chamber of Commerce and many others had been urging the government to adopt an antideflation scheme that would permit trade associations to cooperate in stabilizing prices within their industries. Existing antitrust laws clearly forbade such practices, but businesspeople argued that the economic emergency justified a suspension of the restrictions.

Herbert Hoover had long been a supporter of the trade association movement, but he had refused to lend his assistance to the scheme.

The Roosevelt administration was far more receptive to the idea of cooperation among producers, and even to the demands of some businesspeople that the government enforce trade association agreements on pricing and production. But New Dealers insisted on additional provisions that would deal with other economic problems as well. Businesspeople would have to make important concessions to labor to ensure that the incomes of workers would rise along with prices. And lest consumer buying power lag behind and defeat the scheme, the administration added another ingredient: a major program of public works spending designed to pump needed funds into the economy. The result of these many impulses was the National Industrial Recovery Act, which Congress passed in June 1933. Roosevelt, signing the bill, called it "the most important and far-reaching legislation ever enacted by the American Congress." Businesspeople hailed it as the beginning of a new era of cooperation between government and industry. Labor leaders praised it as a "Magna Carta" for trade unions. There was, it seemed, something in the bill for everyone.

At first, moreover, the new program appeared to work miracles. At its center was a new federal agency, the National Recovery Administration (NRA); and to head it, Roosevelt chose the flamboyant and energetic Hugh S. Johnson, a retired general and successful businessman. Johnson envisioned himself as a kind of evangelist, whose major mission was to generate public enthusiasm for the NRA. He did so in two ways. First, he called on every business establishment in the nation to accept a temporary "blanket code": a minimum wage of between 30 and 40 cents an hour, a maximum workweek of 35 to 40 hours, and the abolition of child labor. The result, he claimed, would be to raise consumer purchasing power, increase employment, and eliminate the infamous sweatshop. To generate enthusiasm for the blanket code, Johnson devised a symbol—the famous NRA Blue Eagle—which employers who accepted the provisions could display in their windows. Soon Blue Eagle flags, posters, and stickers, carrying the NRA slogan "We Do Our Part," were decorating commercial establishments in every part of the country.

At the same time, Johnson was busy negotiating another, more specific set of codes with leaders of the nation's major industries. These industrial codes set floors below which no company would lower

Saluting the Blue Eagle, 1933
Eight thousand schoolchildren gathered on a San Francisco baseball field in 1933 as part of a demonstration in support of the NRA. The children formed the NRA's symbol: an eagle clutching a cogwheel (to symbolize industry) and a lightning bolt (to symbolize energy). NRA administrators drew from their memories of the World War I Liberty Loan drives and attempted to establish the Blue Eagle as a symbol of patriotic commitment to recovery. Merchants and householders displayed the emblem (accompanied by the NRA slogan "We Do Our Part") on posters and stickers in their windows; and many communities staged rallies and parades to promote compliance.   (UPI/Bettmann Newsphotos)

prices or wages in its search for a competitive advantage, and they included agreements on maintaining employment and production. The extraordinary public support Johnson had managed to generate for the blanket code gave him substantial bargaining strength; in a remarkably short time, he won agreements from almost every major industry in the country. A nation eager for positive action was giving the NRA its fervent support.

From the beginning, however, the New Deal's bold experiment in economic cooperation encountered serious difficulties, and the entire effort ultimately dissolved in failure. The codes themselves were hastily and often poorly written. Administra-

tion of them proved to be a bureaucratic nightmare, far beyond the capacities of federal officials with no prior experience in administering so vast a program. Large producers consistently dominated the code-writing process and ensured that the new regulations would work to their advantage and to the disadvantage of smaller firms. And the codes often did more than simply set floors under prices; they actively and artificially raised them—at times to levels higher than was necessary to ensure a profit and far higher than market forces would normally have dictated.

A closely related problem was that attempts to increase consumer purchasing power did not progress as quickly as the efforts to raise prices. Section 7(a) of the National Industrial Recovery Act—the NRA's charter—gave legal protection to the right of workers to form unions and engage in collective bargaining. Partly as a result, many new workers joined unions in the ensuing months; but actual recognition of unions by employers (and thus the significant wage increases the unions were committed to winning) did not follow. The Public Works Administration (PWA) established by the bill to administer spending programs was placed in the hands of Interior Secretary Harold Ickes, a self-described "curmudgeon" who only gradually allowed the $3.3 billion in public works funds to trickle out. Not until 1938 was the PWA budget pumping an appreciable amount of money into the economy.

For a while, most Americans enthusiastically supported the NRA experiment, expecting a major industrial revival to result. But the revival did not come. Indeed, industrial production actually declined in the months after the establishment of the NRA—from an index of 101 in July 1933 to 71 in November—despite the rise in prices that the codes had helped to create. By the spring of 1934, therefore, the NRA was besieged by criticism. Businesses were beginning once again to cut wages and prices or to violate agreements on levels of production—claiming as they did so that the wage requirements of the codes were making it impossible to earn adequate profits. They were also openly flaunting the provisions requiring them to bargain with unions, which attracted increasing labor hostility to the NRA. Economists were charging that the price fixing encouraged by the codes was undermining efforts to raise purchasing power. Reformers were complaining that the NRA was encouraging economic concentration and monopoly. A national Recovery Review Board, chaired by the famous criminal lawyer Clarence Darrow, reported in the spring of 1934 that the NRA was excessively dominated by big business and unduly encouraging monopoly; and Hugh Johnson's vituperative response served only to undermine the agency's prestige even further.

Finally, in the fall of 1934, Roosevelt pressured Johnson to resign and established a new board of directors to oversee the NRA. Then in 1935, the Supreme Court intervened to bring an end to the troubled experiment. The constitutional basis for the NRA had been Congress's power to regulate commerce among the states, a power the administration had interpreted very broadly. The case before the Court involved alleged code violations by the Schechter brothers, who operated a wholesale poultry business confined to one locality: Brooklyn, New York. The Court ruled unanimously that the Schechters were not engaged in interstate commerce and, further, that Congress had unconstitutionally delegated legislative power to the president to draft the NRA codes. The legislation establishing the agency, therefore, was declared void; the NRA was forced to cease its operations.

Roosevelt expressed outrage at what became known as the "sick chicken" decision and denounced the justices for their "horse-and-buggy" interpretation of the interstate commerce clause. He was rightly concerned, for the reasoning in the *Schechter* case threatened many other New Deal programs as well. But the destruction of the NRA itself was probably more of a blessing than a catastrophe for the New Deal, providing it with a face-saving way to abolish the failed experiment.

Regional Planning

The AAA and the NRA largely reflected the beliefs of New Dealers who favored economic planning but wanted private interests (farmers or business leaders) to dominate the planning process. In some areas, however, other reformers—those who believed that the government itself should be the chief planning agent in the economy—managed to establish dominance. Their most conspicuous success, and one of the most celebrated accomplishments of the New Deal as a whole, was an unprecedented experiment in regional planning: the Tennessee Valley Authority (TVA).

The TVA had its roots in a political controversy that had surfaced repeatedly in the 1920s. Throughout that decade, one of the cherished goals of progressive reformers had been public development of the nation's water resources as a source of cheap electric power. In particular, they had urged completion of a great dam at Muscle Shoals on the Tennessee River in Alabama—a dam begun during World War I but left unfinished when the hostilities concluded. The nation's utility companies, predictably opposed to the concept of public power in any form, had fought desperately and successfully against completion of the project.

In 1932, however, one of the great utility empires—that of the electricity magnate Samuel Insull—had collapsed spectacularly, amid widely publicized exposés of corruption. That and other scandals had combined by 1933 to create indignation against the

The Tennessee Valley Authority

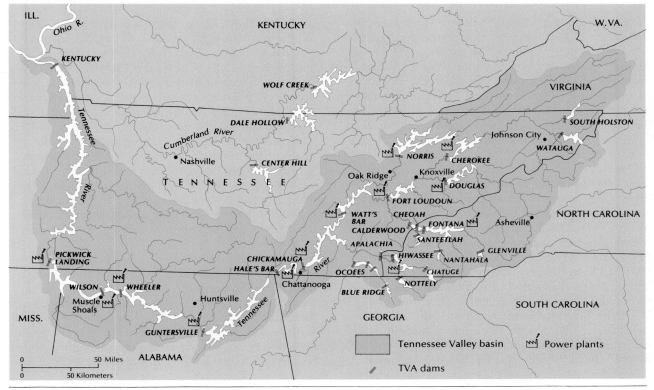

private power interests so intense that they were no longer able to block the public power movement. The result was legislation supported by the president and enacted by Congress in May 1933 creating the Tennessee Valley Authority, a public corporation whose mandate was "national planning for a complete river watershed." The TVA was intended not only to complete the dam at Muscle Shoals and build others in the region, and not only to generate and sell electricity from them to the public at reasonable rates. It was also to be the agent for a comprehensive redevelopment of the entire region: for stopping the disastrous flooding that had plagued the Tennessee Valley for centuries, for encouraging the development of local industries, for supervising a substantial program of reforestation, and for helping farmers to improve productivity.

On the whole, it succeeded quite well. Although opposition by conservatives within the administration ultimately blocked some of the most ambitious social planning projects proposed by David Lilienthal

and other TVA administrators, the project did revitalize the region in numerous ways. It improved five existing dams, built twenty new ones, and constructed an extensive (and heavily trafficked) system of inland waterways. It managed as a result virtually to eliminate flooding in the region and to provide electricity to thousands who had never before had it. Indeed, the TVA soon became the greatest producer of electric power in the United States, as well as one of the cheapest suppliers. Throughout the country, largely because of the yardstick provided by the TVA, private power rates soon declined as well. The TVA also produced inexpensive phosphate fertilizers, helped farmers to prevent soil erosion, and generally raised agricultural productivity—and through it the standard of living—for the entire region. But the Authority worked no miracles. The Tennessee Valley remained a generally impoverished region despite its efforts. And like many other New Deal programs, it made no serious effort to challenge local customs and prejudices.

Financial Reforms

For more than half a century, many Americans concerned about the health of their economy had believed that the nation's monetary system—its currency—was the key to solving most economic problems. In the early days of the New Deal, this preoccupation with the currency continued to affect policy and helped produce a number of important initiatives. In particular, the administration made a controversial decision: to take the country off the gold standard.

Roosevelt was not an inflationist at heart, but he soon came to recognize the gold standard as a major obstacle to the restoration of adequate prices. "I have always favored sound money," he told one critical congressman, "and do now, but it is 'too darned sound' when it takes so much of farm products to buy a dollar." The Emergency Banking Act of March 1933 had been the first step toward taking the country off the gold standard; it had included provisions forbidding the exporting of gold. Then on April 18, 1933, the president made the shift official with an executive order (over the warnings of his budget director, Lew Douglas, who had predicted the action would lead to "the end of Western civilization"). A few weeks later, Congress passed legislation confirming his decision. By itself, the repudiation of the gold standard meant relatively little. But both before and after the April decision, the administration experimented in various ways with manipulating the value of the dollar—by making substantial purchases of gold and silver and later by establishing a new, fixed standard for the dollar (reducing its gold content substantially from the 1932 amount). The resort to government-managed currency—that is, to a dollar whose value could be raised or lowered by government policy according to economic circumstances—created an important precedent for future federal policies and permanently altered the relationship between the public and private sectors. It did not, however, have any immediate impact on the depressed American economy.

Through other legislation, the early New Deal increased federal authority over previously unregulated or weakly regulated areas of the economy. The Glass-Steagall Act of June 1933 gave the government authority to curb irresponsible speculation by banks. More important, in the public mind at least, it established the Federal Deposit Insurance Corporation, which guaranteed all bank deposits up to $2,500. In other words, even should a bank fail, small deposi-

tors would be able to recover their money. Roosevelt opposed the FDIC during congressional debate over the bill, but once in operation it proved so successful that he later approved a gradual raising of the limit on guaranteed deposits, which by the end of the decade had reached $15,000. (It is now $100,000.)

It was a more difficult task to work out a comprehensive overhaul of the Federal Reserve system so as to remedy the serious financial defects that had appeared during the Depression. Finally, in 1935, Congress passed a major banking act that transferred much of the authority once wielded by the regional Federal Reserve banks to the Federal Reserve Board in Washington, whose seven members now exercised direct control over interest rates. By lowering the rates, the board could make it easier to borrow money from banks and thus, in most cases, encourage prices to rise.

To protect investors in the once popular and now mistrusted stock market, Congress passed the so-called Truth in Securities Act of 1933, requiring corporations issuing new securities to register them with the Federal Trade Commission and provide full and accurate information about them to the public. In June 1934, Congress went further and established the Securities and Exchange Commission (SEC) to police the stock market. Among other things, the establishment of the SEC was an indication of how far the financial establishment had fallen in the estimation of the public. In earlier years, J. P. Morgan and other important financiers could have wielded enough influence to stop such government interference in the financial world. Now Morgan could not even get a respectful hearing on Capitol Hill. The criminal trials of a number of once respected Wall Street figures for grand larceny and fraud (including the conviction and imprisonment of Richard Whitney, one-time head of the New York Stock Exchange and a close Morgan associate) eroded the public stature of the financial community still further.

The Growth of Federal Relief

The most important purpose of the New Deal, Franklin Roosevelt and his colleagues believed, was to reform and revive the economy—to restore stability and enhance productivity so that prosperity would return. In the meantime, however, millions of Americans were in desperate need of assistance, and the administration quickly recognized the necessity of providing them with relief.

Like his predecessor, Roosevelt believed that aid to the indigent was primarily a local responsibility and should remain so. But he also recognized that under the circumstances of the Depression, localities were unable to fulfill that responsibility. Among his first acts as president, therefore, was the establishment of the Federal Emergency Relief Administration (FERA), which provided cash grants to states (rather than loans, as the Hoover administration had favored) to prop up bankrupt relief agencies. To administer the program, he chose the director of the New York State relief agency, Harry Hopkins, who was ultimately to become one of the most important members of his administration. Hopkins, unlike Harold Ickes, realized the importance of speed in distributing government funds, and he disbursed the FERA grants widely and rapidly. Even he, however, shared Roosevelt's basic misgivings about establishing a government dole. "It is probably going to undermine the independence of hundreds of thousands of families," he once lamented.

Both Roosevelt and Hopkins felt somewhat more comfortable with another form of government assistance: work relief. Unlike the dole, Hopkins believed, work relief "preserves a man's morale. It saves his skill. It gives him a chance to do something socially useful." Thus when it became clear that the FERA grants would not be sufficient to pull the country through the winter, the administration established a second program: the Civil Works Administration. Between November and April, it put more than 4 million people to work on temporary projects: some of them of real value, such as the construction of roads, schools, and parks; others little more than make-work, such as raking leaves or supervising playgrounds. The important thing, however, was that the 400,000 CWA projects (with a budget of $1 billion) were pumping money into an economy badly in need of it and were providing assistance to people with nowhere else to turn. This use of government spending to stimulate the economy—later to be known as "pump priming" and an important element of Keynesian economics (see below, p. 746)—was one of the New Deal's most important contributions to public policy. But in 1933, at least, members of the administration were only vaguely aware of the broad effects of this spending on the economy as a whole; most thought of it more as a way to help particular people than as a way to stimulate a broader recovery.

Evidence of this limited view of the value of government spending was that most of these early relief programs had short lives. Like the FERA, the CWA was intended to be only a temporary expedient. As the winter continued, not only congressional critics but Roosevelt himself became increasingly uncomfortable with the program. In the spring of 1934, the president began to dismantle the agency, and he ultimately disbanded it altogether. Most economists now agree that massive and sustained government spending would have been the most effective way to end the Depression. Few policymakers in the 1930s shared that belief.

Of all the New Deal relief projects, the one closest to Roosevelt's own heart, and the one he had the least difficulty reconciling with his conservative beliefs, was the Civilian Conservation Corps. Established in the first weeks of the new administration, the CCC was designed to provide employment to the millions of urban youths who could find no jobs in the cities and who, in many cases, were moving restlessly from one region of the country to another in search of work. At the same time, it was intended to advance the work of conservation and reforestation—goals Roosevelt had long cherished. The CCC created a series of camps in national parks and forests and in other rural and wilderness settings. There young men worked in a semimilitary environment on such projects as planting trees, building reservoirs, developing parks, and improving agricultural irrigation. As with the CWA, many of the CCC projects were of only marginal value. But the president took great pride in the success of the corps in providing jobs to over 500,000 young men, offering them not only incomes but an opportunity to work in a "healthy and wholesome" atmosphere.

Mortgage relief was a pressing need of millions of farm owners and homeowners. Roosevelt had provided some assistance to farmers in danger of losing their land, through the AAA and particularly through the Farm Credit Administration, which within two years refinanced one-fifth of all farm mortgages in the United States. The Frazier-Lemke Farm Bankruptcy Act of 1933 went further, enabling some farmers to regain their land even after the foreclosure of their mortgages. Despite such efforts, however, small farmers continued to lose their property in many regions; by 1934, 25 percent of all American farm owners had lost their land.

Homeowners were similarly troubled, and in June 1933 the administration established the Home Owners' Loan Corporation, which in a three-year period loaned out more than $3 billion to refinance the mortgages of more than 1 million householders. Al-

FDR and the CCC
President Roosevelt lunches with workers at a Civilian Conservation Corps camp in Virginia in August 1933. Shown with him are, from left to right, Louis Howe, a longtime political adviser; Secretary of the Interior Harold Ickes; CCC director Robert Fechner; Secretary of Agriculture Henry A. Wallace; and Rexford G. Tugwell, one of the original members of the Roosevelt "Brains Trust."
(Franklin D. Roosevelt Library)

together, it carried about one-sixth of the nation's urban mortgage burden. A year later, Congress established the Federal Housing Administration to insure mortgages for new construction and home repairs—a measure that combined an effort to provide relief with a program to stimulate lasting recovery of the construction industry.

The Reconstruction Finance Corporation continued under the New Deal to provide loans to troubled businesses. Democrats in Congress, unhappy with the RFC's tendency during the Hoover administration to make most of its loans to large banks and corporations, broadened the agency's authority so as to allow it to lend funds to smaller enterprises. The effort was only partially successful. Some small businesses did benefit from the reforms; but under the conservative management of Jesse Jones (originally appointed by Hoover but retained by Roosevelt), the RFC continued to make loans only to those enterprises it believed likely to repay them. In the eyes of the agency, that meant for the most part large organizations.

The relief efforts of the first two years of the New Deal were intended to be limited and temporary, so few of these early programs survived as a permanent part of the federal government. But they helped stimulate interest in other forms of social protection. Ultimately, the creation of a permanent welfare sys-

tem would be one of the New Deal's most important and lasting accomplishments.

The New Deal in Transition

Seldom has an American president enjoyed such remarkable popularity as Franklin Roosevelt during his first two years in office. By early 1935, however, the New Deal was faced with serious problems. The Depression continued—softened, perhaps, by government programs, but generally unabated. And as a result, the New Deal was beginning to find itself the target of fierce public criticism. For a time, the president's political future seemed in doubt. Roosevelt himself, however, appeared unperturbed by the problems; and in the spring of 1935, he launched a forceful campaign of new legislation designed to preempt his critics and move the government more forcefully into the fight against the Depression.

Attacks from Right and Left

In the first heady days of 1933, critics of the New Deal (of whom there were, even then, considerable numbers) had difficulty finding any substantial public support for their position. But by the time two years had passed and the economy still had not revived, the situation had changed. Attacks on the New Deal were now generating a large response.

Some of the most strident attacks came from critics on the right. Roosevelt had for a time tried to conciliate conservatives and had allowed corporate leaders to play a major role in shaping some of his early policy initiatives—most notably by allowing business executives themselves to control most aspects of the NRA. By the end of 1934, however, it was clear that the American right in general, and much of the corporate world in particular, had become irreconcilably hostile to the New Deal. Indeed, so intense was conservative animosity toward the New Deal's "reckless spending," "economic crackpots," and "socialist" reforms that some of Roosevelt's critics could not even bear to say the president's name. They called him, simply and bitterly, "that man in the White House."

In August 1934, a group of the most fervent (and wealthiest) Roosevelt opponents formed the American Liberty League, designed specifically to arouse public opposition to the New Deal's "dictatorial" policies and its supposed attacks on free enterprise. The new organization generated wide publicity and caused some concern within the administration. In fact, however, it was never able to expand its constituency much beyond the Northern industrialists (most of them Republicans) who had founded it. At its peak, membership in the organization numbered only about 125,000.

The real impact of the Liberty League and other conservative attacks on Roosevelt was not to undermine the president's political strength. It was, rather, to convince Roosevelt that his efforts to conciliate the business community had failed. By 1936, he no longer harbored any illusions about cooperation with conservatives. The forces of "organized money," he said near the end of his campaign for reelection, "are unanimous in their hate for me—and I welcome their hatred."

Roosevelt's critics on the far left also managed to produce alarm among some supporters of the administration; but like the conservatives, they proved to have only limited strength. The Communist party, the Socialist party, and other radical and semiradical organizations were at times harshly critical of the New Deal. But not only did they fail ever to attract genuinely widespread support; they proved at times uncertain about how best to combine their commitment to radical change with their fervent opposition to the growth of fascism elsewhere in the world. The Communist party, in particular, spent much of the 1930s tacitly and at times explicitly supporting the Roosevelt programs.

Popular Protest

More menacing to the New Deal than either the far right or the far left was a group of dissident political movements that defied easy ideological classification. Some were marginal "crackpot" organizations with little popular following, but others gained substantial public support within particular states and regions. And three men, in particular, succeeded in mobilizing genuinely national followings.

Dr. Francis E. Townsend, an elderly California physician, rose from obscurity to lead a movement of more than 5 million members with his plan for federal pensions for the elderly. According to the Townsend plan, all Americans over the age of sixty would receive monthly government pensions of $200, providing they retired from their current employment (thus freeing jobs for younger, unemployed Americans) and spent the money in full each month (which would pump needed funds into the economy). The movement expanded quickly from its founding in 1933, and within two years it had attracted the support of a formidable block of voters, most of them older men and women. The Townsend plan made little progress in Congress when it was introduced by sympathetic representatives. But the public sentiment behind the plan helped build support for the Social Security system, which Congress did approve in 1935.

Father Charles E. Coughlin, a Catholic priest in the small Detroit suburb of Royal Oak, Michigan, achieved even greater renown by means of his weekly sermons broadcast nationally over the radio. Drawing on Populism and other earlier political movements, as well as on what he claimed were the teachings of his church, he proposed a series of monetary reforms—remonetization of silver, issuing of greenbacks, and nationalization of the banking system—that he insisted would restore prosperity and provide economic justice. At first a warm supporter of Franklin Roosevelt, he had by 1934 become disheartened by what he claimed was the president's failure to deal harshly enough with the "money powers." In the spring of 1935, he established his own political organization, the National Union for Social

Justice, which many people believed was the first step toward the formation of a third party. He was also displaying an apparently remarkable influence in Congress. (An avalanche of telegrams inspired by a Coughlin radio sermon was generally believed to have been responsible for the defeat in the Senate of a treaty admitting the United States to the World Court.) And he was attracting public support throughout much of the nation—primarily from Catholics, but from others as well. He was widely believed to have one of the largest regular radio audiences of anyone in America.

Most alarming of all to the administration was the growing national popularity of Senator Huey P. Long of Louisiana. Long had risen to power in his home state through his strident attacks on the banks, oil companies, and utilities, and on the conservative political oligarchy allied with them that had for decades dominated the Louisiana government. Elected governor in 1928, he launched an assault on his opposition so thorough and forceful that they were soon left with virtually no political power whatever. Long dominated the legislature, the courts, and the executive departments; and he brooked no interference. When opponents accused him of violating the Louisiana constitution, he brazenly replied, "I'm the Constitution here now." Many claimed that he had, in effect, become a dictator.

If so, he was a dictator who maintained the overwhelming support of the Louisiana electorate, in part because of his flamboyant personality and in part because of his record of accomplishment: building roads, schools, and hospitals; revising the tax codes; distributing free textbooks; lowering utility rates; and more. Barred by law from succeeding himself as governor, he ran in 1930 for a seat in the U.S. Senate, won easily, and left the state government in the hands of loyal, docile allies.

Once in Washington, Long, like Coughlin, soon became harshly critical of Herbert Hoover's ineffectual policies for dealing with the Depression. And also like Coughlin, he supported Franklin Roosevelt for president in 1932. Far more rapidly than the priest, however, Long broke with the New Deal—a break that was all but complete within six months of the inauguration. As an alternative, he advocated a drastic program of wealth redistribution, a program he ultimately named the Share-Our-Wealth Plan. According to Long, the government could end the Depression easily and quickly simply by confiscating through taxation the surplus riches of the wealthiest men and women in America, whose fortunes were,

Huey Long
Few public speakers could arouse a crowd more effectively than Huey Long of Louisiana, known to many as the "Kingfish" (a nickname borrowed from the popular radio show "Amos 'n Andy"). It was Long's effective use of radio, however, that contributed most directly to his spreading popularity in the early 1930s.   (Culver Pictures)

he claimed, so bloated that not enough wealth remained to satisfy the needs of the great mass of citizens. By limiting incomes to $1 million annually and by limiting capital accumulation and inheritances to $5 million, the government would soon acquire enough assets to guarantee every family a minimum "homestead" of $5,000 and an annual wage of $2,500.

Long made little effort to disguise his interest in running for president. In 1934, he established his own national organization: the Share-Our-Wealth Society, which soon attracted a large following—not only in

Long's native South but in New York, Pennsylvania, parts of the Midwest, and above all California. There were no accurate figures to indicate the movement's precise size, but even Long's critics admitted it might have as many as 4 million members. A poll by the Democratic National Committee in the spring of 1935 disclosed that Long might attract more than 10 percent of the electorate running as a third-party candidate, enough to tip a close election to the Republicans.

Observers in the 1930s hotly debated the significance of these dissident movements. Some believed they represented the rise of fascism in America; others claimed they were dangerously close to socialism or communism. In fact, they were neither. They represented, rather, two competing popular sentiments: the urgent desire of many Americans for government assistance in this time of need, and their equally strong desire to protect their ability to control their own lives from the encroachments of large and powerful organizations. Long, Coughlin, Townsend, and others spoke harshly of the "plutocrats," "international bankers," and other remote financial powers who were, they claimed, not only impoverishing the nation but exercising tyrannical power over individuals and communities. They spoke equally harshly, however, of the dangers of excessive government bureaucracy, attacking the New Deal for establishing a menacing, "dictatorial" state. They envisioned a society in which government would, through a series of simple economic reforms, guarantee prosperity to every American without exercising intrusive control over private and community activities.

However much their critics may have disagreed about the merits of these programs, most agreed on one thing: the specter of dissident politics seemed in 1935 to have become a genuine threat to the established political parties. An increasing number of advisers were warning the president that he would have to do something dramatic to counter their strength.

The Second New Deal

In response both to the growing political pressures and to the continuing economic crisis, Roosevelt embarked in 1935 on a set of new initiatives that together became known as the "Second New Deal." In some respects, the new proposals were simply an attempt to steal the thunder of the administration's critics. But they also represented, if not a new direction at least a change in the emphasis of New Deal policy. "We have not weeded out the over-privileged," the president told Congress in January 1935, "and we have not effectively lifted up the underprivileged." His new programs, he claimed, were designed to do both.

Perhaps the most conspicuous change in New Deal policy in 1935 was its new attitude toward big business. Rhetorically at least, the president was now openly attacking the great corporate interests. In March, for example, he proposed to Congress an act to combat the concentration of power in the great utility holding companies. In 1935, thirteen such companies controlled three-quarters of the nation's electric power; and Roosevelt spoke harshly of the injustices inherent in their monopolistic position. The companies fought desperately against the "death-sentence" bill; one of them spent $700,000 to lobby against the measure. In the end, neither side emerged entirely victorious. Congress did indeed pass the Holding Company Act of 1935, but the bill contained amendments favored by the companies that sharply limited its effects.

Equally alarming to affluent Americans was a series of tax reforms proposed by the president in 1935, a program conservatives quickly labeled a "soak the rich" scheme. Apparently designed to undercut the appeal of Huey Long's Share-Our-Wealth Plan, the Roosevelt proposals called for establishing the highest and most progressive peacetime tax rates in history. Rates in the upper brackets reached 75 percent on income, 70 percent on inheritances, and 15 percent on corporate incomes. In fact, the actual impact of these taxes was far less radical than the president liked to claim (as Huey Long quickly pointed out). Like the Holding Company Act, the New Deal's tax legislation served progressive political purposes; but in terms of its actual impact on the economy, it had only modest results.

The Supreme Court decision in 1935 to invalidate the National Industrial Recovery Act solved some problems for the administration, but it also created others. The now defunct act had contained, among other things, the important clause—Section 7(a)—guaranteeing to workers the right to organize and bargain collectively. Supporters of labor, both in the administration and in Congress, advocated quick action to restore that protection. With the president himself slow to respond, the initiative fell to a group of progressives in Congress led by Senator Robert F. Wagner of New York, who in 1935 introduced what was to become the National Labor Relations Act. The new bill, ultimately known as the Wagner Act, provided workers with far more federal protection than Section 7(a) of the National Industrial Recovery Act had offered. It specifically outlawed a group of "unfair practices" by which employers had been fighting unionization. And it created a National Labor Relations Board (NLRB) to police employers, with power to compel them to recognize and bargain with legitimate unions. The president was not happy with the bill as it moved through Congress. But when the measure reached his desk, he signed it. That was in large part because American workers themselves had by 1935 become so important and vigorous a force that Roosevelt realized his own political future would depend in part on responding to their demands.

Labor Militancy

The emergence of a powerful American trade union movement in the 1930s was perhaps the most important social development of the decade, and one of the most significant political developments as well. It occurred in part in response to government efforts to enhance the power of unions; but it was primarily a result of the increased militancy of American workers and their leaders.

During the 1920s, workers had displayed little militancy in challenging employers or demanding recognition of their unions. They had faced a powerful and highly popular business establishment. They were often coopted by the system of welfare capitalism, which provided them with increased wages and benefits. And they had been saddled with conservative labor organizations, unwilling to risk the modest gains already won.

In the 1930s, these inhibiting factors began to vanish. Business leaders and industrialists lost (if only temporarily) the high public standing they had enjoyed in the New Era; and on matters of labor policy at least, they lost the support of the government. Both Section 7(a) of the National Industrial Recovery Act of 1933 and the Wagner Act of 1935 were passed over the strong objections of corporate leaders. The "welfare capitalism" of the 1920s had vanished almost overnight; with the economy in sharp decline, employers had quickly rescinded most of the gains offered to labor in the preceding years. Those workers who kept their jobs often did so only by accepting reduced wages and fewer benefits. Finally, as the decade progressed, new labor organizations emerged to challenge the established, conservative unions. The result was, among other things, an important change in the outlook of many workers: a growing resentment of conditions as they were, and an increasing commitment to the idea of organizing to rectify them.

The new militancy first became obvious in 1934, when newly organized workers (many of them inspired by the collective bargaining provisions of the National Industrial Recovery Act) staged a series of strikes to demand recognition of their unions. In Minneapolis, Toledo, and San Francisco, in particular, striking workers demonstrated a militancy and radicalism seldom seen in recent years and became involved at times in violent confrontations with employers and local authorities. Both the strength and the failure of these labor uprisings were important in promoting passage of the Wagner Act of 1935. Industrial workers were, it was clear, becoming too militant to ignore any longer. But it was equally clear that without stronger legal protection, their organizing drives would end in frustration. Once the Wagner Act became law, the search for more effective forms of organization rapidly gained strength in labor ranks.

Even though the American Federation of Labor, under the leadership now of William Green, increased its activities in response to the Depression, it proved in most cases painfully inadequate to the task at hand. The AFL remained committed to the idea of the craft union: the idea of organizing workers on the basis of their skills. As a result, the Federation offered little hope to unskilled laborers, even though it was the unskilled who now constituted the bulk of the industrial work force.

During the 1930s, therefore, another concept of labor organization emerged to challenge the traditional craft union ideal: industrial unionism. Advocates of this approach argued that all the workers in a particular industry should be organized in a single union, regardless of what functions the workers performed. All auto workers should be in a single automobile union; all steel workers should be in a single steel union. Workers divided into many small unions would lack the strength to deal successfully with the great corporations. United into a single great union, however, they would wield considerable power.

Leaders of the AFL craft unions for the most part opposed the new concept. But industrial unionism found a number of important advocates, most prominent among them John L. Lewis. Lewis was the talented, flamboyant, and eloquent leader of the United Mine Workers—the oldest major union in the country organized along industrial rather than craft lines. He was also a charismatic public figure, whose personal magnetism alone helped win thousands of recruits to his cause.

At first, Lewis and his allies attempted to work within the AFL, but friction between the new industrial organizations and the older craft unions grew rapidly as a result. At the 1935 AFL convention, Lewis became embroiled in a series of angry confrontations (and one celebrated fistfight) with craft union leaders before finally walking out. A few weeks later, he created the Committee on Industrial Organization—a body officially within the AFL but unsanctioned by its leadership. After a series of bitter jurisdictional conflicts, the AFL finally expelled the new committee from its ranks, and along with it all the industrial unions it represented. In response, Lewis renamed the committee the Congress of Industrial Organizations (CIO), established it in 1936 as an organization directly rivaling the AFL, and became its first president. The schism clearly weakened the labor movement as a whole in many ways. But by freeing the advocates of industrial unionism from the restrictive rules of the Federation, it gave important impetus to the creation of powerful new organizations.

Organizing Battles

Those new organizations had been struggling for recognition even before the schism of 1936. Major battles were under way, in particular, in the automobile and steel industries. Out of a myriad of competing auto unions, the United Auto Workers (UAW) was, during the early and mid-1930s, gradually emerging preeminent. But through 1936, although steadily gaining recruits, it was making little progress in winning recognition from the corporations.

In December 1936, however, auto workers employed a controversial and dramatically effective technique for challenging corporate opposition: the sit-down strike. Employees in several General Motors plants in Detroit simply sat down inside the plants, refusing either to work or to leave, thus preventing the company from making use of strikebreakers. The tactic quickly spread to other locations, so that by February 1937 strikers had occupied seventeen GM plants. The strikers ignored court orders to vacate the buildings, and they successfully resisted sporadic efforts by local police to remove them. When Michigan's governor, Frank Murphy, a liberal Democrat, refused to call out the National Guard to clear out the strikers, and when the federal government refused as well to intervene on behalf of employers, the company had little choice but to relent. General Motors became in February 1937 the first major

manufacturer to recognize the UAW; other automobile companies soon did the same. The sit-down strike proved effective for rubber workers (who, in fact, were the first to use the technique in 1936) and workers in other industries as well; but it survived only briefly as a labor technique. Its apparent illegality aroused widespread public outrage and alarm; so labor leaders ultimately abandoned it.

In the steel industry, the battle for unionization was less easily won. In 1936, the CIO had appropriated $500,000 to support the Steel Workers' Organizing Committee (later United Steelworkers of America) in a major campaign. Over the next few months, the onslaught began, with the SWOC quickly recruiting tens of thousands of workers and staging a series of prolonged and often bitter strikes. In March 1937, to the amazement of almost everyone, U.S. Steel, the giant of the industry, relented. Rather than risk a costly strike at a time when it sensed itself on the verge of recovery from the Depression, the company signed a contract with the SWOC, the new organization's first important victory.

The lesser companies (known collectively as "Little Steel") were, however, far less ready to surrender. On Memorial Day 1937, a group of striking workers from Republic Steel gathered with their families for a picnic and demonstration in South Chicago; and when they attempted to march peacefully (and legally) toward the steel plant, police opened fire on them. Ten demonstrators were killed; another ninety were wounded. Despite a public outcry against the "Memorial Day Massacre," the harsh tactics of "Little Steel" ultimately proved successful. The 1937 strike failed.

But the victory of Little Steel was the exception rather than the rule; it was, in fact, one of the last gasps of the kind of brutal, naked strikebreaking that had proved so effective in the past. In the course of 1937, one of the most turbulent years in the history of American labor, there were 4,720 strikes—over 80 percent of them settled in favor of the unions. By the end of the year, more than 8 million workers were members of unions recognized as official bargaining units by employers (as compared with 3 million in 1932). By 1941, that number had expanded to 10 million and included the workers of Little Steel, which had finally relented. Workers were slower to win major new wage increases and benefits than they were to achieve union recognition. But the organizing battles of the 1930s had established the labor movement as a powerful force in the American economy.

The "Memorial Day Massacre"
A newsreel photographer filmed the melee on May 30, 1937, during which police wielding guns and billy clubs savagely attacked strikers outside the Republic Steel Plant in South Chicago. Ten picketers died and many others were seriously wounded in the battle, which workers quickly dubbed the "Memorial Day Massacre." Hollywood studios suppressed newsreel footage of the event for a time.
(AP/Wide World Photos)

Social Security

From the first moments of the New Deal, important members of the administration, most notably Secretary of Labor Frances Perkins, had been lobbying patiently for a system of federally sponsored social insurance for the elderly and the unemployed. The popularity of the Townsend movement added strength to their cause, and in 1935, finally, Roosevelt gave public support to what became the Social Security Act. It established a variety of programs. For the elderly, there were two types of assistance. Those who were presently destitute could receive up to $15 a month in federal assistance (depending on what matching sums the state might provide). More important for the future, Americans presently working were incorporated into a pension system, to which they and their employers would contribute by paying a payroll tax and which would provide them with an income on retirement. There were severe limits on the program. Pension payments would not begin until 1942 and even then would provide only $10 to $85 a month to recipients. And wide categories of workers (including domestic servants and agricultural laborers, many of whom were black) were excluded from the program. But it was a crucial first step in creating the nation's most important social program for the elderly.

In addition, the Social Security Act expanded the government's activities on behalf of the unemployed and dispossessed. It provided for a system of unemployment insurance, to which employers alone would contribute and which made it possible for workers laid off from their jobs to receive government assistance for a limited period of time. It also established a system of federal aid to disabled people and to dependent children.

New Dealers did not like to think of Social Security as a "welfare" system; even the strongest supporters of the new program continued to oppose the idea of a "dole." They insisted, rather, that Social Security was an "insurance" system, most of whose recipients would earn their benefits. Those assumptions were reflected in the structure of the programs the act created. The pensions to the elderly were to be based not on need but on contributions to the system. Even the wealthiest retired Americans would be entitled to their Social Security payments. Unemployment insurance, similarly, was not to be "welfare," with benefits based on economic need. Any unemployed person would be eligible to receive assistance, no matter what his or her financial situation. Where the Social Security Act did provide direct assistance based on need—to the elderly poor, to the disabled, to dependent children—it was servicing groups widely perceived to be small and genuinely unable to support themselves.

In the years to come, however, Social Security was to evolve in ways its planners neither foresaw nor desired. The old-age pension program would ultimately become far more expensive (and far more generous) than the founders of the system had expected. Aid to Dependent Children, envisioned as a relatively modest program to aid a small number of needy people, would in the 1950s expand to become one of the cornerstones of the modern welfare system. However one evaluates the long-range effects of Social Security, however, it is clear that the 1935 act was the most important single piece of social welfare legislation in American history.

New Directions in Relief

Social Security was designed primarily to fulfill long-range goals. Of more immediate concern were the millions of Americans who remained unemployed and who had not yet found relief through existing government programs. To meet their needs (and not incidentally to replace such early New Deal programs of direct relief as the FERA, with which the president had always felt uncomfortable), the administration established in 1935 the Works Progress Administration (WPA). Like the Civil Works Administration and other earlier efforts, the WPA established a system of work relief for the unemployed. It far surpassed all earlier agencies, however, both in the size of its budget ($5 billion at first) and in the energy and imagination of its operations.

Under the direction of Harry Hopkins, who had by now emerged as the New Deal's "minister of relief," the WPA employed an average of 2.1 million workers at any given moment between 1935 and 1941. The agency was responsible ultimately for the erection or renovation of 110,000 public buildings (schools, post offices, office buildings) and for the construction of almost 600 airports, more than 500,000 miles of roads, and over 100,000 bridges. More important, however, the WPA provided incomes to those it employed and helped stimulate the economy in general by increasing the flow of money into it.

The WPA also displayed remarkable flexibility and imagination in offering assistance to those whose occupations did not fit into any traditional category of relief. The Federal Writers Project of the WPA, for example, offered unemployed writers support to pursue their own creative endeavors and to work on projects initiated by the agency itself. The Federal Art Project, similarly, provided aid to painters, sculptors, and others to continue their careers. The Federal Music Project and the Federal Theater Project oversaw the production of concerts and of plays, skits, and even a controversial review of public affairs

WPA Mural Art
The Federal Arts Project of the Works Progress Administration commissioned an impressive series of public murals from the artists it employed. Many of them adorned post offices, libraries, and other public buildings constructed by the WPA. William Gropper's *Construction of a Dam,* a detail of which is seen here, is typical of much of the mural art of the 1930s in its celebration of the workingman. Workers are depicted in heroic poses, laboring in unison to complete a great public project. (Department of the Interior)

known as the "Living Newspaper," thus creating work for unemployed musicians, actors, directors, and others.

Other relief agencies emerged alongside the WPA. The National Youth Administration provided assistance to those between the ages of sixteen and twenty-five, largely in the form of scholarship assistance to high-school and college students. The Emergency Housing Division of the Public Works Administration (the agency that had been established in 1933 along with the NRA, but whose benefits were slow to be felt) began federal sponsorship of public housing. It cleared some of the nation's most notorious slums and built instead some fifty new housing developments, containing nearly 22,000 units—but most of them priced too high for those who had been displaced by slum clearance. Not until 1937, when Congress approved Senator Wagner's bill creating the United States Housing Authority, did the government begin to provide a substantial amount of housing for low-income families.

The 1936 "Referendum"

The presidential election of 1936, it was clear from the start, was to be a national referendum on Franklin Roosevelt and the New Deal. And whereas in 1935 there had been reason to question the president's political prospects, by the middle of 1936 there could be little doubt that he would win a second term.

The conservative opposition to Roosevelt had always been intense but never large. In 1936, it was not even strong enough to win control of the Republican party. Ignoring the anguished pleas of Herbert Hoover and others who detested all aspects of the New Deal, the party nominated the moderate governor of Kansas, Alf M. Landon, who had supported Theodore Roosevelt's 1912 crusade (see pp. 631–633) and who had never abandoned his progressive commitments. The Republican platform promised, in effect, to continue the programs of the New Deal—but constitutionally, and without running a deficit.

As for the dissidents, their strength seemed to evaporate as quickly as it had emerged. One reason was the violent death of their most effective leader, Huey Long, who was assassinated in a corridor of the Louisiana state capitol in September 1935 by a young Baton Rouge doctor. (No one ever had a chance to discover the motives of the assailant; he was gunned down on the spot by Long's bodyguards.) Another reason was the ill-fated alliance among several of the remaining dissident leaders in 1936. Father Coughlin, Dr. Townsend, and Gerald L. K. Smith (a sycophantic henchman of Huey Long trying unsuccessfully to establish himself as Long's political heir) joined forces that summer to establish a new political movement—the Union party. But the incessant squabbling among them combined with the colorlessness of their presidential candidate—a mediocre North Dakota congressman, William Lemke—made the new party a sorry spectacle. It polled only 890,000 votes. The most important reason for the dissidents' collapse, however, was their failure ever to turn their supporters fully against Franklin Roosevelt, who had skillfully undercut the appeal of his critics by espousing many of their ideas.

The campaign was a lopsided contest. Roosevelt drew huge crowds and evoked widespread enthusiasm with his impassioned attacks on the "economic royalists." Landon's pallid rhetoric and moderate platform could not effectively compete. The result was the greatest landslide in American history to that point. Roosevelt polled just under 61 percent of the vote to Landon's 36 percent. The Republican candidate carried only Maine and Vermont. The Democrats increased their already large majorities in both houses of Congress.

In addition to ensuring Roosevelt a second term, the election displayed the fundamental party realignment that the New Deal had managed to effect. The Democrats now controlled a broad coalition of Western and Southern farmers, the urban working classes, the poor and unemployed, and the black communities of the Northern cities, as well as traditional progressives and committed new liberals—a coalition that constituted a substantial majority of the electorate. It would be many years before the Republican party could again muster anything approaching a true majority coalition of its own.

The New Deal in Disarray

Roosevelt emerged from the 1936 election at the zenith of his popularity. Within months, however, the New Deal was mired in serious new difficulties—a result of continuing opposition, of the president's own political errors, and of serious economic setbacks. His administration would never fully recover. Throughout Roosevelt's second term, recovery from the Depression remained elusive; and the New Deal, stumbling from one policy to another, appeared unable to regain the initiative it had once held.

The Court Fight and the "Purge"

If the 1936 election had been a mandate for anything, Franklin Roosevelt believed, it was a mandate to do something about the Supreme Court. No program of reform, he had become convinced, could long survive the ravages of the obstructionist justices, who had already struck down the NRA and the AAA and threatened to invalidate even more legislation. Foes of such New Deal measures as the National Labor Relations Act, the Social Security Act, and the Holding Company Act were openly flouting the new laws, confident that the Supreme Court would soon disallow them. Through its narrow interpretation of the federal power over interstate commerce and taxation, and through its broad interpretation of freedom of contract, the Court seemed to have created an economic no man's land within which neither the federal government nor the state governments could act. Early in 1937, Roosevelt proposed a solution: expanding the Supreme Court through the addition of new justices—justices he would appoint and whose liberal views would presumably counterbalance the conservatism of the existing justices.

It was a bold measure, but it was not as radical as many of its critics charged. The Constitution called for no specific number of Supreme Court justices, and Congress had from time to time changed the size of the Court in the past (although not since the early nineteenth century). Nevertheless, the plan aroused a great public furor, largely because Roosevelt displayed what was, for him at least, an astounding political ineptitude in proposing and promoting it. Without informing congressional leaders in advance, he sent a surprise message to Capitol Hill in February proposing a general overhaul of the federal court system and including, among many provisions, one to add up to six new justices to the Supreme Court. The courts were "overworked," he claimed, and needed additional manpower and younger blood to enable them to cope with their increasing burdens. The explanation fooled almost no one.

Conservatives throughout the country expressed outrage at the "court-packing plan," warning that such constitutional shortcuts were the common route by which dictators seized power. And while in the past few Americans had been disposed to heed such warnings, now, as a result of Roosevelt's heavy-

Fallout from the Court Fight
No proposal in Franklin Roosevelt's twelve years as president aroused such bitter opposition as his 1937 plan to add six justices to the Supreme Court so as to remove the judicial obstacles to his domestic programs. The "court-packing plan" not only failed to win passage; it reinvigorated the president's opponents and caused him political problems throughout his second term. This 1937 cartoon shows the Democratic donkey jumping for cover in the face of attacks on Roosevelt's proposal. (Library of Congress)

handed tactics, much of the public seemed to agree. Still the president had considerable political clout at his disposal; and he might well have forced Congress to approve at least a compromise measure had not the Supreme Court itself intervened in the controversy.

Even before the court-packing fight began, the ideological balance of the Court had been a precarious one. Four conservative justices could be relied on to oppose the New Deal on almost all occasions; three were generally inclined to support it. The remaining two tended to waver, with Chief Justice Hughes often siding with the progressives and Associate Justice Owen J. Roberts more often voting with the conservatives. Were Hughes and Roberts both to side with the liberals, there would be a 5-to-4 majority in support of the New Deal without the appointment of additional justices. That is precisely what happened. On March 29, 1937, Roberts, Hughes, and the three progressive justices voted together to uphold a state minimum wage law—in the case of *West Coast Hotel v. Parrish*—thus reversing a 5-to-4 decision of the previous year invalidating a similar law. Two weeks later, again by a 5- to 4-margin, the Court upheld the

Wagner Act; and in May, it validated the Social Security Act. The necessity for Roosevelt's judicial reform bill had vanished. The Supreme Court had prudently moderated its position in order to avert what it considered a disastrous precedent. "You may have saved the country," Hughes jubilantly told Owen Roberts after the first decision favorable to the New Deal in March.

On one level, the affair was a significant victory for Franklin Roosevelt. No longer would the Court serve as an obstruction to New Deal reforms, particularly after a group of older justices began retiring in the following months, to be replaced by Roosevelt appointees. On another level, however, the court-packing episode was a serious defeat for the president, and one that did lasting damage to his administration. By generating public suspicion of his motives, he had reinvigorated the conservative opposition, which only months before had been in disarray. By giving members of his own party an excuse to oppose him, he had helped destroy his congressional coalition. From 1937 on, Southern Democrats and other conservatives voted against his measures with alarming consistency; never again would the president enjoy the freedom of legislative action he had had during his first years in office. Roosevelt was not even spared the embarrassment of having his Court plan publicly voted down by Congress.

A year later, the president's political situation deteriorated further. Determined to regain the initiative in his legislative battles, Roosevelt launched an ill-considered effort to "purge" Congress of some of its most conservative members. In Democratic primaries that spring, he openly campaigned against members of his own party who had opposed his programs. The effort was a humiliating failure. Not only was Roosevelt unable to unseat any of the five Democratic senators against whom he campaigned, but his "purge" efforts drove an even deeper wedge between the administration and its conservative opponents, ensuring that Roosevelt would suffer more legislative frustrations in the future.

Retrenchment and Recession

Hard on the heels of the court-packing fiasco came another economic crisis: a severe recession that began in the fall of 1937, continued for more than nine months, and plunged the nation into its worst suffering since 1932. It was a bitter pill for a society that was just beginning to believe that true recovery was under way; and it was a particularly bitter pill for

Franklin Roosevelt, whose policies seemed to have contributed to the new collapse.

By the summer of 1937, it no longer seemed fanciful to believe that prosperity was about to return. The national income, which had dropped from $82 billion in 1929 to $40 billion in 1932, had risen to nearly $72 billion. Other economic indices showed similar improvements. To the president, the time seemed ripe for a retrenchment in government spending, for allowing the business community, as Roosevelt put it, to stand once again on its own two feet. Not incidentally, it also seemed to be a good time to balance the federal budget, whose mounting deficits had never ceased to trouble the president. And there were even arguments that the real danger now was no longer depression but inflation.

As a result, the administration moved on several fronts to cut back its recovery programs. Roosevelt persuaded the Federal Reserve Board to tighten credit by raising interest rates. At the same time, he reduced government spending by slashing the budget for one relief program after another. Between January and August 1937, for example, he cut the WPA in half, sending 1.5 million relief workers on unpaid "vacations." A few weeks later, the fragile boom collapsed. The index of industrial production dropped from 117 in August 1937 to 76 in May 1938. Four million additional workers lost their jobs.

The recession of 1937 was a result of many factors. But to many observers at the time (including, apparently, Franklin Roosevelt), it seemed to be a direct result of the administration's unwise decision to reduce spending. And so the new crisis forced yet another reevaluation of policies by the president and his advisers and produced yet another shift of emphasis within the New Deal. The advocates of government spending as an antidote to the Depression had always had to struggle for the president's favor against those who believed in more conservative fiscal policies. Now, it seemed, they stood vindicated; and the notion of using government deficits to stimulate the economy—an idea associated with the great British economist John Maynard Keynes—had established its first, timid foothold in American public policy. In April 1938, the president asked Congress for an emergency appropriation of $5 billion for public works and relief programs, and government funds soon began pouring into the economy once again. Within a few months, another tentative recovery seemed to be under way, and the advocates of spending pointed to it as proof of the validity of their approach.

At the same time, advocates of another approach to the economic crisis began to win Franklin Roosevelt's ear: a group of younger liberals who saw the recession as the result of excessively concentrated corporate power and who wanted the government to move forcefully to curb that power and restore competition. It was time, they said, to launch a genuine assault on monopoly. There had been antimonopoly advocates in New Deal circles from the beginning, but until now their position had been weak. By 1937, however, the president was sufficiently disillusioned with the American business community (a disillusionment only strengthened by the 1937 recession, which he too tried to blame on "selfish interests") that he was willing to experiment with their approach. In April 1938, Roosevelt sent a stinging message to Congress, vehemently denouncing what he called an unjustifiable concentration of economic power and asking for the creation of a commission to examine that concentration with an eye to major reforms in the antitrust laws. In response, Congress established the Temporary National Economic Committee (TNEC), including representatives of both houses of Congress and of several executive agencies. At about the same time, Roosevelt appointed a new head of the antitrust division of the Justice Department: Thurman Arnold, a Yale Law School professor who soon proved to be the most vigorous director ever to serve in that office. Making new and sophisticated use of the Sherman and Clayton acts, Arnold filed (and won) more antitrust cases in the next three years than the Justice Department had filed in its entire previous history.

Despite the apparent triumph of antimonopoly advocates, the policies of the late New Deal did not really represent a frontal assault on economic concentration. For one thing, neither the TNEC nor, in the end, Thurman Arnold's crusades had very much lasting impact. The TNEC investigation ran on for nearly three years and produced volumes of testimony, but in the end it made no important recommendations for action. And Arnold's vigorous tenure in the Justice Department came to an end when wartime pressures convinced the president and others that the time for antitrust activity was over. But even at its peak, these antimonopoly efforts were not in any real sense attempts to restore a small-scale, decentralized economy. Arnold himself admitted that such efforts would be nostalgic nonsense and explained that he was using the antitrust laws not to break up combinations but to regulate their behavior. That, in fact, was the principal ideological commitment of many New

Dealers in the late 1930s: not destroying monopoly, but increasing the regulatory functions of the federal government. Roosevelt's much vaunted (and only partially successful) effort to reorganize the executive branch of the federal government was motivated in part by the idea that a streamlined state would be able to exert its influence more effectively in the economy.

By the end of 1938, however, it was becoming clear that these ambitious new goals faced an uncertain future. For the New Deal had by then essentially come to an end. Congressional opposition now made it difficult for the president to enact any major new programs. But more important, perhaps, the threat of world crisis hung heavy in the political atmosphere, and Roosevelt was gradually growing more concerned with persuading a reluctant nation to prepare for war than with pursuing new avenues of reform.

The New Deal: Limits and Legacies

To some of Roosevelt's embittered conservative contemporaries, the New Deal was a dangerous, radical break with the past, a time in which constitutional safeguards were abandoned, in which the president sought to establish a dictatorship, in which the American economy fell under the control of a meddlesome and intrusive federal bureaucracy. To critics on the left, both in the 1930s and since, the New Deal was little more than a painfully timid defense of traditional capitalism, a bulwark of conservatism against demands for more fundamental change. (See "Where Historians Disagree," pp. 748–749.) There are elements of truth in both those views, although neither captures the essence of the New Deal experiment in reform. Any evaluation of this crucial episode in the history of American government must take into consideration both the extent and the limits of its legacy.

The Idea of the "Broker State"

In 1933, many New Dealers dreamed of using their new popularity and authority somehow to remake American capitalism—to produce new forms of cooperation and control that would create a genuinely harmonious, ordered economic world. By 1939, it was clear that what they had created was in fact

─────WHERE HISTORIANS DISAGREE─────

The New Deal

For many years, the debate among historians over the nature of the New Deal seemed to mirror the debate among Americans in the 1930s over the achievements of the Roosevelt administration. Historians tended to debate the question of whether the New Deal was a good thing or a bad thing. Did it go too far in expanding the size and power of the government? Did it go far enough in helping the dispossessed and reforming capitalism? Was it a valuable progressive moment in the development of modern government or an example of squandered opportunities and conservative retrenchment?

The conservative critique of the New Deal has received relatively little scholarly expression. Edgar Robinson, in *The Roosevelt Leadership* (1955), and John T. Flynn, in *The Roosevelt Myth* (1956), attacked Roosevelt as both a radical and a despot; but few historians have ever taken such charges seriously. By far the dominant view of the New Deal among scholars has been an approving, liberal interpretation—one that has appeared in various forms but rests on certain basic common assumptions. First, liberals maintain, the New Deal was not a radical, socialistic, or communistic program. It was firmly within the mainstream of the American political tradition. Second, they argue, the New Deal represented a powerful response by the government to glaring social needs that had long gone unmet. And third, it marked a decisive repudiation of old orthodoxies about the proper role of government, business, labor, and other groups in society.

The leading voice in the liberal chorus has long been Arthur M. Schlesinger, Jr., who argued in the three volumes of *The Age of Roosevelt* (1957–1960)—a work still to be completed—that the New Deal marked a continuation of the long struggle between public power and private interests but that Roosevelt had moved that struggle to a new level. The unrestrained power of the business community was finally confronted with an effective challenge, and what emerged was a system of reformed capitalism, with far more protection for workers, farmers, consumers, and others than in the past.

Other liberals have gone further. Carl Degler, in *Out of Our Past* (1959), called the Roosevelt years a "Third American Revolution" (the first two being the Revolution of 1776 and the Civil War). It marked, he claimed, "the crossing of a divide from which, it would seem, there could be no turning back." Eric Goldman, in *Rendezvous with Destiny* (1952) and later works, called the New Deal the culmination of a "half-century of revolution." Although Roosevelt drew heavily on the traditions of the progressive past, "there was something more to New Deal liberalism" because it included unprecedented new departures such as Social Security.

Richard Hofstadter offered a more skeptical assessment of the New Deal in the 1950s but one that fell largely within the liberal framework. In *The Age of Reform* (1955), he emphasized the New Deal's discontinuities with the past. It was, he said, a "drastic new departure . . . different from anything that had yet happened in the United States"— a program that even many old progressives found alarming and opposed. The crucial change, Hofstadter argued, was in the New Deal's conception of the purpose of liberal reform. The New Deal had largely abandoned the old progressive concern about reshaping the corporate world— what Hofstadter called "entrepreneurial" reform. Instead, New Deal liberalism took on a "social-democratic tinge that had never before been present in American reform movements" and raised a new set of issues to prominence: "social security, unemployment insurance, wages and hours, and housing. "

Hofstadter not only echoed the view of other liberals that the New Deal marked an important break with the past; he also gave early expression to some of the criticisms that historians in the 1960s would begin to offer. In *The American Political Tradition* (1948), and again in *The Age of Reform,* he complained that the New Deal's fragmented, "pragmatic" approach had lacked a central, guiding philosophy. James MacGregor Burns, in *Roosevelt: The Lion and the Fox* (1956), raised other objections: that Roosevelt's wily political methods had often led him away from the proper goals of reform; that he had failed to make full use of his potential as a leader and had accommodated himself unnecessarily to existing patterns of political power. The first systematic "revisionist" interpre-

───────WHERE HISTORIANS DISAGREE───────

tation of the New Deal came in 1963, in William Leuchtenburg's *Franklin D. Roosevelt and the New Deal*. Leuchtenburg was a generally sympathetic critic, arguing that most of the limitations of the New Deal were a result of the restrictions imposed on Roosevelt by the political and ideological realities of his time—that the New Deal probably could not have done much more than it did. Nevertheless, Leuchtenburg openly challenged earlier views of the New Deal as a revolution in social policy. He was able to muster only enough enthusiasm to call it a "halfway revolution," one that enhanced the positions of some previously disadvantaged groups (notably farmers and workers) but did little or nothing for many others (including blacks, sharecroppers, and the urban poor). Ellis Hawley augmented these moderate criticisms of the Roosevelt record in *The New Deal and the Problem of Monopoly* (1966). In examining 1930s economic policies, Hawley challenged liberal assumptions that the New Deal acted as the foe of private business interests. On the contrary, he argued, New Deal efforts were in many cases designed to enhance the position of private entrepreneurs—even, at times, at the expense of some of the liberal, reform goals that administration officials espoused.

Other historians in the 1960s, writing from the perspective of the New Left, expressed much harsher criticisms of the New Deal. Barton Bernstein, in a 1968 essay, compiled a dreary chronicle of missed opportunities, inadequate responses to problems, and damaging New Deal initiatives. The Roosevelt administration may have saved capitalism, Bernstein charged, but it failed to help—and in many ways actually harmed—those groups most in need of assistance. Paul Conkin, in *The New Deal* (1967), similarly chastised the government of the 1930s for its policies toward marginal farmers, its failure to institute meaningful tax reform, and its excessive generosity toward certain business interests. Even the most important progressive measures of the New Deal—the Social Security Act, for example—were marked by inadequate and regressive funding. And Howard Zinn, in an essay in 1966, harshly criticized the New Deal for working actively to preserve the worst evils of capitalism.

The New Left attack on the New Deal never developed very far beyond these preliminary statements. Instead, by the 1970s and 1980s, scholars seemed largely to have accepted the revised liberal view: that the New Deal was a significant (and most agree valuable) chapter in the history of reform but one that worked within rigid, occasionally crippling limits. Much of the recent work on the New Deal, therefore, has been less interested in the question of whether it was a "conservative" or "revolutionary" phenomenon than in the question of the constraints within which it was operating. The sociologist Theda Skocpol, in an important series of articles, has emphasized the issue of "state capacity" as an important New Deal constraint; ambitious reform ideas often foundered, she argued because of the absence of a government bureaucracy with sufficient strength and expertise to administer them. James T. Patterson, Barry Karl, and others have emphasized the political constraints the New Deal encountered. Both in Congress and among the public at large, conservative inhibitions about government remained strong; and the New Deal was as much a product of the pressures of its conservative opponents as of its liberal supporters. Frank Freidel, Ellis Hawley, Herbert Stein, and many others point as well to the ideological constraints affecting Franklin Roosevelt and his supporters. Even the most advanced New Dealers harbored great suspicions about excessive federal power, expansive welfare systems, and large-scale government spending.

The phrase "New Deal liberalism" has come, in the postwar era to seem synonymous with modern ideas of aggressive federal management of the economy, elaborate welfare systems, a powerful bureaucracy, and large-scale government spending. The "Reagan revolution" of the 1980s often portrayed itself as a reaction to the "legacy of the New Deal." Many historians of the New Deal, however, would argue that the modern idea of "New Deal liberalism" bears only a limited relationship to the ideas that New Dealers themselves embraced. The liberal accomplishments of the 1930s can be understood only in the context of their own time; later liberal efforts drew from that legacy but also altered it to fit the needs and the assumptions of a very different era.

MAJOR ACHIEVEMENTS OF THE NEW DEAL

1933 Emergency Banking Act	**1935** Works Progress Administration
Economy Act	National Youth Administration
Civilian Conservation Corps	Social Security Act
Agricultural Adjustment Act	National Labor Relations Act
Tennessee Valley Authority	Public Utilities Holding Company Act
National Industrial Recovery Act	Resettlement Administration
Banking Act	Rural Electrification Administration
Federal Emergency Relief Act	Revenue Act ("wealth tax")
Home Owners' Refinancing Act	**1936** Soil Conservation and Domestic Allotment Act
Civil Works Administration	
Federal Securities Act	**1937** Farm Security Administration
	National Housing Act
1934 National Housing Act	
National Labor Relations Board	**1938** Second Agricultural Adjustment Act
Securities and Exchange Act	Fair Labor Standards Act
Home Owners' Loan Act	**1939** Executive Reorganization Act

something quite different. But rather than bemoan the gap between their original intentions and their ultimate achievements, New Deal liberals, both in 1939 and in later years, chose to accept what they had produced and to celebrate it—to use it as a model for future reform efforts.

What they had created was something that in later years would become known as the "broker state." Instead of forging all elements of society into a single, harmonious unit, as some reformers had once hoped to do, the effect of the New Deal was to elevate and strengthen new interest groups so as to allow them to compete more effectively in the national marketplace. And it was to make the federal government a mediator in that constant competition—a force that could intercede when necessary to help some groups and limit the power of others.

In 1933, there had been only one great interest group with genuine power in the national economy (albeit a varied and divided one): the corporate world. By the end of the 1930s, American business found itself competing for influence with an increasingly powerful labor movement, with an organized agricultural economy, and with aroused consumers. In later years, the "broker state" idea would expand to embrace other groups as well: racial and ethnic minorities, women, and many others. One of the enduring legacies of the New Deal, in other words, was to make the federal government a protector of interest groups and a supervisor of the competition among them, rather than an instrument attempting to create a universal harmony of interests.

What determines which interest groups receive government assistance in a "broker state"? The experience of the New Deal suggests that such assistance goes largely to those groups able to exercise enough political or economic power to demand it. Thus in the 1930s, farmers—after decades of organization and agitation—and workers—as the result of militant action and mass mobilization—won from the government new and important protections. Other groups, less well organized perhaps but politically important because so numerous and visible, won more limited assistance as well: imperiled homeowners, the unemployed, the elderly.

By the same token, the interest-group democracy that the New Deal came to represent offered much less to those groups either too weak to demand assistance or not visible enough to arouse widespread public support. And yet those same groups were often the ones most in need of help from their government. One of the important limits of the New Deal, therefore, was its very modest record on behalf of several important social groups.

Black America and the New Deal

One such group was black Americans, whose economic problems were accompanied by widespread political disfranchisement and who were subjected throughout the nation to forms of discrimination that prevented them from making any significant advances. The New Deal did relatively little to improve their lot.

It was not that the administration was hostile to blacks. On the contrary, the New Deal was probably more sympathetic to the cause of racial justice than any previous government of the twentieth century. Indeed, the cause of racial equality had one of its greatest champions in the White House itself. It was not the president, however, but the first lady. Eleanor Roosevelt spoke throughout the 1930s on behalf of racial justice. She put continuing pressure on her husband and others in the federal government to ease discrimination against blacks. She was also in part responsibile for what was, symbolically at least, one of the most important events of the decade for American blacks. When the black opera singer Marian Anderson was refused permission in the

spring of 1939 to give a concert in the auditorium of the Daughters of the American Revolution (Washington's only concert hall), Eleanor Roosevelt resigned from the organization and then (along with Interior Secretary Harold Ickes, another champion of racial equality) helped secure government permission for her to sing on the steps of the Lincoln Memorial. Anderson's Easter Sunday concert attracted 75,000 people and became, in effect, the first modern civil-rights demonstration.

The president himself made some important gestures to blacks as well. Unlike his Democratic predecessor, Woodrow Wilson, he did not move to increase government discrimination against blacks; on the contrary, he worked to repeal certain partic-

Eleanor Roosevelt and Mary McLeod Bethune

Mrs. Roosevelt was the leading champion of racial equality within the administration of her husband, and her commitment had an important impact on the behavior of the government even though she held no official post. She is seen here meeting in 1937 with Aubrey Williams, executive director of the National Youth Administration, and Mary McLeod Bethune, the agency's director of black affairs. Founder and president of Bethune-Cookman College in Florida, Mrs. Bethune became a member of the New Deal's informal "Black Cabinet" and, with the encouragement of the First Lady and others, attempted to ensure that blacks participated equally in the NYA and other government relief programs. (UPI/Bettmann Newsphotos)

ularly glaring racial restrictions within the federal government. He appointed a number of blacks to significant second-level positions in his administration, creating a network of officeholders that became known as the "Black Cabinet." Roosevelt appointees such as Robert Weaver, William Hastie, and Mary McLeod Bethune consulted with one another frequently and served as an active lobby for the interests of their race. Blacks also benefited in significant though limited ways from New Deal relief programs. Eleanor Roosevelt, Harold Ickes, and Harry Hopkins all made efforts to ensure that such programs did not exclude blacks. By 1935, an estimated 30 percent of all blacks were receiving some form of government assistance. One result of all this was a historic change in black electoral behavior. As late as 1932, the great majority of American blacks were voting Republican, as they had since the Civil War. By 1936, more than 90 percent of them were voting Democratic—the beginnings of a political alliance that would endure for many decades.

Blacks supported Franklin Roosevelt because they knew he was not their enemy. And they supported him because the New Deal created relief agencies and other programs of public assistance that were of great economic importance to this particularly impoverished group. But they had few illusions that the New Deal represented a millennium in American race relations. The president was generally sympathetic to the plight of blacks, but he believed that other problems were far more pressing; he was never willing, therefore, to risk losing the support of Southern Democrats by becoming too much identified with the issue of race. Typical of his equivocal attitude was his harsh denunciation of lynching combined with his refusal to support legislation making lynching a federal crime. He declined as well to support efforts to enact legislation banning the poll tax, one of the most potent tools by which white Southerners kept blacks from voting.

Similarly, Roosevelt refused to use the relief agencies he was creating to challenge local patterns of discrimination. On the contrary, he permitted them to reinforce such patterns. The Civilian Conservation Corps established separate black camps. The NRA codes tolerated the widespread practice of paying blacks less than whites doing the same jobs. The FERA, the CWA, and other relief agencies permitted discriminatory practices in hiring and paying their workers. Blacks were largely excluded from employment in the TVA. The Federal Housing Administra-

tion refused to provide mortgages to blacks moving into white neighborhoods, and the first public housing projects financed by the federal government were racially segregated. The AAA and its successor agencies were almost entirely ineffectual in protecting the interests of black sharecroppers and tenant farmers, thousands of whom were evicted from their land.

The New Deal was not often actively hostile to black Americans, and it did much—both directly and indirectly—to help them advance. But the Roosevelt years did not see American blacks emerge as a potent interest group capable of seriously challenging the discriminatory forces arrayed against them. That emergence would await the development of a powerful movement among blacks themselves during and after World War II.

Women and the New Deal

Nor were the 1930s years in which American women emerged as an interest group powerful enough to challenge the obstacles to female advancement. This was not because the New Deal was hostile to feminist aspirations; it was because those aspirations did not yet attract widespread enough support to make it politically necessary for the administration to back them.

There were, to be sure, important symbolic gestures on behalf of women. Roosevelt appointed the first female member of the cabinet in the nation's history: Secretary of Labor Frances Perkins. He also named more than 100 other women to positions at lower levels of the federal bureaucracy; they created an active female network within the government and cooperated with one another in advancing causes of interest to women. Such appointments were in part a response to pressure from Eleanor Roosevelt, who was a committed advocate of women's rights and a champion of humanitarian causes. Mary Dewson, head of the Women's Division of the Democratic National Committee, was also influential in securing federal appointments for women as well as in increasing their role within the Democratic party. Several women received appointments to the federal judiciary. And one, Hattie Caraway of Arkansas, became the first woman ever elected to a full term in the U.S. Senate. (She was running to succeed her husband, who had died in office.)

But New Deal support for women operated within strict limits, partly because New Deal women themselves often had limited views of what was appropriate for their sex. Frances Perkins and many others in the administration emerged out of the old feminist tradition of the progressive era, which emphasized not so much sexual equality as special protections for women. Perkins herself had been instrumental in fighting for passage of various state laws safeguarding female workers. She opposed the National Woman's party and its goal of securing the Equal Rights Amendment because she feared the amendment would threaten the protective mechanisms she had helped secure.

The New Deal also supported the prevailing belief that in hard times women should withdraw from the workplace to open up more jobs for men. Frances Perkins herself spoke out against what she called the "pin-money worker"—the married woman working to earn extra money for the household. Such women, the secretary of labor said, were a "menace to society." New Deal relief agencies offered relatively little employment for women. The NRA sanctioned sexually discriminatory wage practices. The Social Security program excluded domestic servants, waitresses, and other predominantly female occupations.

As with blacks, so also with women: The New Deal was not actively hostile; in many ways, it was unprecedentedly supportive. It did, however, accept prevailing cultural norms. There was not yet sufficient political pressure from women themselves to persuade the administration to do otherwise.

The "broker state" approach to reform, therefore, provided important opportunities for some groups to advance their interests. But for other, less powerful but at least equally imperiled interests—not only blacks and women, but Hispanics, Native Americans, small farmers, small entrepreneurs, and many others—the New Deal offered relatively little. It did, however, help establish a pattern in American politics—individual interest groups mobilizing themselves to demand assistance from the government—that would govern the nation's public life for many decades.

The New Deal and the Economy

The most frequent criticisms of the New Deal involve its failure genuinely to revive or reform the American economy. New Dealers never fully recognized the value of government spending as a vehicle for recovery, and their efforts along other lines never succeeded in ending the Depression. Unemployment remained high throughout the New Deal years; consumption, investment, and economic growth remained low. It was World War II, not the New Deal, that finally ended the crisis. Nor did the New Deal substantially alter the distribution of power within American capitalism; and it had only a small impact on the distribution of wealth among the American people. Large economic organizations continued to

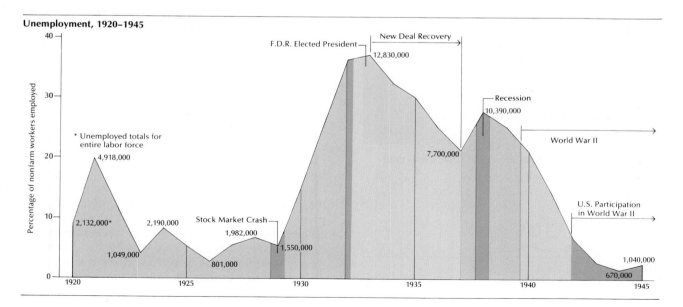

Unemployment, 1920–1945

Percentage of nonfarm workers employed

* Unemployed totals for entire labor force

4,918,000

2,132,000*

1,049,000

2,190,000

Stock Market Crash
1,982,000

801,000

1,550,000

F.D.R. Elected President

12,830,000

New Deal Recovery

7,700,000

Recession
10,390,000

World War II

U.S. Participation in World War II

1,040,000

670,000

dominate the American economy at the end of the New Deal; in many respects, in fact, their power was greater than it had been a decade before.

Nevertheless, the New Deal did have a number of important and lasting effects on both the behavior and the structure of the American economy. It may not have ended the Depression, but it created a large array of protections for various groups of citizens who suffered from the crisis, and it helped prevent the economy from decaying further. It may not have altered the face of capitalism, but it helped elevate new groups—workers, farmers, and others—to positions from which they could on occasion effectively challenge the power of the corporations. It increased the regulatory functions of the federal government in ways that helped stabilize previously troubled areas of the economy: the stock market, the banking system, among others. And although the New Dealers themselves did not fully realize it at the time, the

administration helped establish the basis for new forms of federal fiscal policy, which would in the postwar years give the government a series of important tools for promoting and regulating economic growth.

The New Deal also created the rudiments of the American welfare state, through its many relief programs and above all through the Social Security system. The conservative inhibitions New Dealers brought to this task ensured that the welfare system that ultimately emerged would be limited in its impact (at least in comparison with those of other industrial nations) and expensive and cumbersome to administer. But for all its limits, the new system marked a historic break with the nation's traditional reluctance to offer any public assistance whatever to indigent citizens.

The New Deal and American Politics

Perhaps the most dramatic effect of the New Deal was on the structure and behavior of American government and politics. Franklin Roosevelt helped enhance the power of the federal government as a whole. By the end of the 1930s, state and local governments were clearly of secondary importance to the government in Washington; in the past, that had not always been clear. Roosevelt also established the presidency as the preeminent center of authority within the federal government. Never again would Congress be able to wield as much independent power as it had in the years before the New Deal. And never again would it have the same control over presidential authority. The expansion of presidential authority would lead, in later eras, to several major political crises as well as to important social and diplomatic accomplishments.

Finally, the New Deal had a profound impact on how the American people defined themselves politically. It took a weak, divided Democratic party, which had been a minority force in American politics for many decades, and turned it into a mighty coalition that would dominate national party competition for more than forty years. It turned the attention of many voters away from the cultural issues that had preoccupied them in the 1920s and awakened in them an interest in economic matters of direct importance to their lives. And it created among the American people at large greatly increased expectations of government—expectations that the New Deal itself did not always fulfill but that survived to become the basis of new liberal crusades in the postwar era.

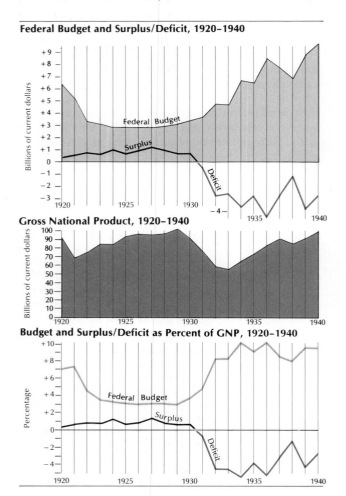

SIGNIFICANT EVENTS

1933   Franklin Roosevelt inaugurated

"Hundred Days" New Deal legislation enacted

United States officially abandons gold standard

Prohibition ends with repeal of Twenty-first Amendment

Dr. Francis Townsend begins campaign for old-age pensions

1934   Conservatives create American Liberty League

Huey Long establishes Share Our Wealth Society

Labor militancy increases

1935   Supreme Court invalidates NRA

"Second New Deal" legislation passed

Father Charles Coughlin establishes National Union for Social Justice

John L. Lewis and allies break with AFL

1936   Supreme Court invalidates Agricultural Adjustment Act

CIO established

Sit-down strikes begin

Huey Long assassinated

1936   Roosevelt wins reelection by record margin

1937   U.S. Steel recognizes Steel Workers' Organizing Committee

Roosevelt proposes "court-packing" plan

Supreme Court validates Wagner Act

"Memorial Day Massacre" in Chicago

New Deal spending reduced

Severe recession begins

1938   Roosevelt proposes new spending measures

Temporary National Economic Committee established

Executive Reorganization plan proposed

1939   Marian Anderson sings at Lincoln Memorial

SUGGESTED READINGS

General Studies   The best one-volume overview of the New Deal is William E. Leuchtenburg, *Franklin D. Roosevelt and the New Deal* (1963). Robert S. McElvaine, *The Great Depression* (1984), is a more recent general study. Barry Karl, *The Uneasy State* (1983), is an overview of the period between the wars but one that pays special attention to the New Deal era. A more thorough account of the first years of the Roosevelt administration, and one more favorable to FDR, is Arthur M. Schlesinger, Jr., *The Age of Roosevelt*, 3 vols, (1957–1960). Paul Conkin, *The New Deal* (1967), is a brief revisionist view that is more skeptical of the New Deal's achievements. Edgar Robinson, *The Roosevelt Leadership* (1955), is a conservative criticism. An important study of the early Roosevelt years is James MacGregor Burns, *Roosevelt: The Lion and the Fox* (1956). Gerald Nash, *The Great Depression and World War II* (1979), is a general account. The most comprehensive study of Roosevelt himself is Frank Freidel's biography in progress, *Franklin D. Roosevelt,* 4 vols. to date (1952–1973), the fourth volume of which follows Roosevelt through his first hundred days in the White House. Joseph P. Lash, *Eleanor and Franklin* (1971), studies the most celebrated of all first ladies and sheds light on her relationship with her husband. Harvard Sitkoff (ed.), *Fifty Years Later: The New Deal Evaluated* (1985), is a collection of essays evaluating various aspects of the New Deal. John Braeman et al. (eds.), *The New Deal,* 2 vols. (1975), is an earlier collection of essays. Katie Louchheim, *The Making of the New Deal* (1983), offers a series of reminiscences by surviving New Dealers.

New Deal Reforms   The first months of the New Deal receive intensive scrutiny in Frank Freidel, *Launching the New Deal* (1973); Raymond Moley and Eliot Rosen, *The First New Deal* (1966); and Herbert Feis, *Characters in Crisis* (1966). Otis Graham, *Encore for Reform* (1967), examines the old progressives' role in the New Deal. An invaluable study of New Deal economic policy is Ellis Hawley, *The New Deal and the Problem of Monopoly* (1966). Bernard Bellush, *The Failure of the NRA* (1975), examines the cornerstone of the early New Deal economic program; and Sidney Fine, *The Automobile Under the Blue Eagle* (1963), examines the impact of the NRA on one industry. Peter H.

Irons, *The New Deal Lawyers* (1982), looks at the activities of young New Deal litigators in three agencies. Thomas McCraw, *Prophets of Regulation* (1984), examines the careers of four major figures in government regulation, one of them the SEC's James Landis. Susan Ware, *Beyond Suffrage* (1981), examines the experiences of women in the federal government during the Roosevelt administration. Thomas K. McCraw, *TVA and the Power Fight* (1970), is a valuable study of the most conspicuous social project of the New Deal. Michael Parrish, *Securities Regulation and the New Deal* (1970), and Ralph F. De Bedts, *The New Deal's SEC* (1964), analyze the most prominent of the administration's financial reforms. Mark Leff, *The Limits of Symbolic Reform: The New Deal and Taxation, 1933–1939* (1984), is an important study of changing tax policies in the 1930s. Albert U. Romasco, *The Politics of Recovery: Roosevelt's New Deal* (1983), is an overview of New Deal recovery efforts.

Relief Programs   Searle Charles, *Minister of Relief* (1963), examines the origins of welfare policies through the career of Harry Hopkins. John Salmond, *The Civilian Conservation Corps* (1967), studies the most popular of the relief agencies; and Bonnie Fox Schwartz, *The Civil Works Administration, 1933–1934* (1984), examines the short-lived relief effort of the first New Deal winter. James T. Patterson, *America's Struggle Against Poverty, 1900–1980* (1981), is an examination of the growth of social welfare policies, including the New Deal.

Agriculture   New Deal agricultural policy receives attention in Van L. Perkins, *Crisis in Agriculture* (1969); Richard S. Kirkendall, *Social Scientists and Farm Politics in the Age of Roosevelt* (1966); Christina Campbell, *The Farm Bureaus* (1962); and Gilbert Fite, *George M. Peek and the Fight for Farm Parity* (1954). David Conrad, *The Forgotten Farmers* (1965), examines those who did not share in the benefits of the AAA, as does Paul Mertz, *The New Deal and Southern Rural Poverty* (1978).

Depression Dissidents   A sweeping account of dissident opposition to the New Deal and of the administration's response is Arthur M. Schlesinger, Jr., *The Politics of Upheaval* (1960). George Wolfskill, *Revolt of the Conservatives* (1962), examines the challenge from the Liberty League. Donald Grubbs, *Cry from the Cotton* (1971), is an important study of the Southern Tenant Farmers Union. Opposition to the New Deal from less radical groups is examined in Donald McCoy, *Angry Voices* (1958); R. Alan Lawson, *The Failure of Independent Liberalism* (1971), which deals with the political efforts of disaffected intellectuals; Alan Brinkley, *Voices of Protest: Huey Long, Father Coughlin, and the Great Depression* (1982), which examines the rise of the leading dissident movements; and David H. Bennett, *Demagogues in the Depression* (1969), which chronicles their decline. Leo Ribuffo, *The Old Christian Right: The Protestant Far Right from the Great Depression to the Cold War* (1983), is an important study of three "extremists" of the era. Individual studies of the most prominent insurgents include Abraham

Holzman, *The Townsend Movement* (1963); Charles J. Tull, *Father Coughlin and the New Deal* (1965); and T. Harry Williams, *Huey Long* (1969), a highly praised definitive biography. Robert Penn Warren's extraordinary novel *All the King's Men* (1946) is the story of a Southern leader reminiscent of Huey Long.

The Second New Deal   J. Joseph Huthmacher, *Senator Robert Wagner and the Rise of Urban Liberalism* (1968), is useful for examining New Deal labor and housing legislation. W. D. Rowley, *M. L. Wilson and the Campaign for Domestic Allotment* (1970), and Sidney Baldwin, *Poverty and Politics: The Farm Security Administration* (1968), explore changes in agricultural policy. Roy Lubove, *The Struggle for Social Security* (1968), examines the major welfare innovation of the later New Deal; and Paul Conkin, *Tomorrow a New World* (1971), explores the government's experimental community program. The WPA has spawned a large literature of its own, much of it focusing on the innovative art and literature programs. See, especially, Jane deHart Matthews, *The Federal Theater* (1967); Jerre Mangione, *The Dream and the Deal* (1972), on the Federal Writers Project; and William F. McDonald, *Federal Relief Administration and the Arts* (1968).

The Late New Deal   The troubled years after 1936 have received less attention from historians, but several important works are available. On the rise of conservative opposition, see James T. Patterson, *Congressional Conservatism and the New Deal* (1967); Frank Freidel, *FDR and the South* (1965); and George Wolfskill and John Hudson, *All But the People* (1969). On the court-packing fight, consult Leonard Baker, *Back to Back* (1967), and William Leuchtenburg, "The Origins of Franklin D. Roosevelt's 'Court-Packing' Plan," in Philip B. Kurland (ed.), *The Supreme Court Review* (1966). Richard Polenberg, *Reorganizing Roosevelt's Government* (1966), and Barry Karl, *Executive Reorganization and Reform in the New Deal* (1963), examine the bureaucratic reform efforts of the second term. James T. Patterson, *The New Deal and the States* (1969), explores the relationship between federal and local governments; and Charles Trout, *Boston: The Great Depression and the New Deal* (1977), examines that relationship in a single city. Herbert Stein, *The Fiscal Revolution in America* (1969), is an important study of changing ideas about federal fiscal policy and the emergence of Keynesianism. Theodore Rosenof, *Patterns of Political Economy in America* (1983), is a study of the evolution of liberal and left political ideology in the late 1930s and the war years.

Nonwhites and the New Deal   The most comprehensive study of the experience of blacks during the Depression is Harvard Sitkoff, *A New Deal for Blacks* (1978). Nancy Weiss, *Farewell to the Party of Lincoln: Black Politics in the Age of FDR* (1983), examines the changing political allegiance of American blacks in the 1930s. Also useful is John B. Kirby, *Black Americans in the Roosevelt Era* (1980). Robert L. Zangrando, *The NAACP Crusade Against Lynching*

(1980), examines one of the principal concerns of black Americans in the 1930s. Laurence C. Kelly, *The Assault on Assimilation: John Collier and the Origins of Indian Policy Reform* (1983), is a study of new approaches to Indian policy in the 1930s. See also Donald L. Parman, *The Navajos and the New Deal* (1975), and Kenneth Philp, *John Collier's Crusade for Indian Reform, 1920-1954* (1977).

Labor The most thorough account of the labor movement during the Depression is Irving Bernstein, *Turbulent Years* (1970). See also Melvyn Dubofsky and Warren Van Tine, *John L. Lewis* (1977); David Brody, *Workers in Industrial America* (1980); Jerold Auerbach, *Labor and Liberty* (1966); Sidney Fine, *Sit-Down* (1969), on the 1936–1937 GM strike; Bert Cochran, *Labor and Communism* (1977); and Peter Friedlander, *The Emergence of a UAW Local* (1975). John Barnard, *Walter Reuther and the Rise of the Auto Workers* (1983), looks at one of the major labor leaders of the era. Ronald W. Schatz, *The Electrical Workers* (1983), examines labor organizing at Westinghouse. David Milton, *The Politics of U.S. Labor: From the Great Depression to the New Deal* (1980), is an overview. August Meier and Elliott Rudwick, *Black Detroit and the Rise of the UAW* (1979), considers some of the racial aspects of labor organization.

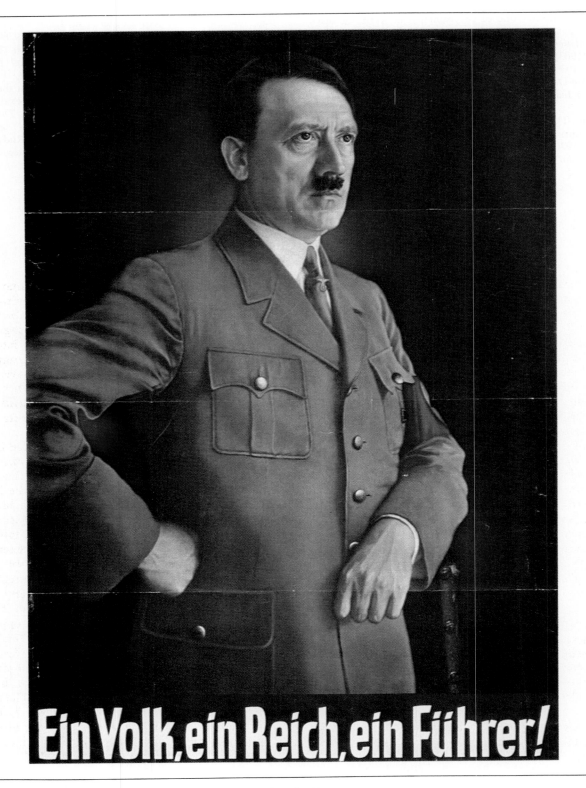

Nazi Poster, "One People, One Empire, One Leader" (Library of Congress)

Chapter 27 # The Global Crisis, 1921–1945

Henry Cabot Lodge of Massachusetts, chairman of the Senate Foreign Relations Committee and one of the most powerful figures in the Republican party, led the fight against ratification of the Treaty of Versailles in 1918 and 1919. In part because of his efforts, the treaty was defeated; the United States failed to join the League of Nations; and American foreign policy embarked on an independent course that for the next two decades would attempt, but ultimately fail, to expand American influence and maintain international stability without committing the United States to any lasting relationships with other nations.

Lodge was not an isolationist. He recognized that America had emerged from World War I the most powerful nation in the world. He believed the United States should use that power and should exert its influence internationally. But he believed, too, that America's expanded role in the world should reflect the nation's own interests and its own special virtues; it should leave the nation unfettered with obligations to anyone else. He said in 1919:

> We are a great moral asset of Christian civilization. . . . How did we get there? By our own efforts. Nobody led us, nobody guided us, nobody controlled us. . . . I would keep America as she has been—not isolated, not prevent her from joining other nations for . . . great purposes—but I wish her to be master of her own fate.

Lodge was not alone in voicing such sentiments. Throughout the 1920s, those controlling American foreign policy attempted continually to increase America's role in the world while at the same time keeping the nation free of burdensome commitments that might limit its own freedom of action. In 1933, Franklin Roosevelt became president, bringing with him his own legacy as a leading Wilsonian internationalist and an erstwhile supporter of the League of Nations. But for more than six years, Roosevelt too attempted to keep America the "master of her own fate," to avoid important global commitments that might reduce the nation's ability to pursue its own ends.

In the end, the cautious, limited American internationalism of the interwar years proved insufficient either to protect the interests of the United States or to encourage global stability. Throughout the 1920s and 1930s, the fragile international order established in the aftermath of World War I suffered a series of devastating blows—economic, political, and military. By the late 1930s, a new world crisis had emerged, which threatened to create a new world war. The United States moved slowly to respond to the emerging dangers—partly because the government itself was not certain how to act, partly because it was aware of how strongly much of the public opposed any involvement in international conflicts. But after war broke out in Europe in 1939, the nation found it increasingly difficult to maintain a detached stance. By the fall of 1941, the United States was deeply involved in the conflict in countless ways. The Japanese attack on Pearl Harbor on December 7, 1941, only made official what had been growing obvious for some time: that America would play a critical role in the greatest war in human history.

The Diplomacy of the New Era

Critics of American foreign policy in the 1920s often used a single word to describe the cause of their disenchantment: *isolationism.* Having rejected the Wilsonian vision of a new world order, the nation had, many charged, turned its back on the rest of the globe and repudiated its international responsibilities. But in reality, the United States played a more active role in world affairs in the 1920s than it had at almost any previous time in its history.

Replacing the League

It was clear when the Harding administration took office in 1921 that American membership in the League of Nations was no longer a realistic possibility. As if finally to bury the issue, Secretary of State Charles Evans Hughes secured legislation from Congress in 1921 declaring the war with Germany at an end and then proceeded to negotiate separate peace treaties with the former Central Powers. Through these treaties, American policymakers believed, the United States would receive all the advantages of the Versailles Treaty with none of the burdensome responsibilities. Hughes was, however, committed to finding something to replace the League as a guarantor of world peace and stability. He embarked, therefore, on a series of efforts to build safeguards against future wars—but safeguards that would not hamper American freedom of action in the world.

The most important of such efforts was the Washington Conference of 1921—an attempt to prevent what was threatening to become a costly and destabilizing naval armaments race among America, Britain, and Japan. Hughes startled the delegates by proposing in his opening speech a plan for dramatic reductions in the fleets of all three nations and a ten-year moratorium on the construction of large warships. He envisioned the actual scrapping of nearly 2 million tons of existing shipping. Far more surprising than the proposal was that the conference ultimately agreed to accept most of its terms, something that Hughes himself apparently had not anticipated. The Five-Power Pact of February 1922 established both the limits for total naval tonnage and a ratio of armaments among the signatories. For every 5 tons of American and British warships, Japan would maintain 3 and France and Italy 1.75 each. (Although the treaty seemed to confirm the military inferiority

of Japan, in fact it sanctioned Japanese dominance in East Asia. America and Britain had to spread their fleets across the globe; Japan was concerned only with the Pacific.) The Washington Conference also produced two other, related treaties: the Nine-Power Pact, pledging a continuation of the Open Door policy in China, and the Four-Power Pact, by which the United States, Britain, France, and Japan promised to respect one another's Pacific territories and cooperate to prevent aggression.

The Washington Conference began the New Era effort to protect the peace (and to protect the international economic interests of the United States) without accepting active international duties. The Kellogg-Briand Pact of 1928 concluded it. When the French foreign minister, Aristide Briand, asked the United States in 1927 to join an alliance against a resurgent Germany, Secretary of State Frank Kellogg (who had replaced Hughes in 1925) proposed instead a multilateral treaty outlawing war as an instrument of national policy. Fourteen nations signed the agreement in Paris on August 27, 1928, amid great solemnity and wide international acclaim. Forty-eight other nations later joined the pact. It contained no instruments of enforcement but rested, as Kellogg put it, on the "moral force" of world opinion.

Debts and Diplomacy

The first responsibility of diplomacy, Hughes, Kellogg, and others agreed, was to ensure that American overseas trade faced no obstacles to expansion and that, once established, it would remain free of interference. Preventing a dangerous armaments race and reducing the possibility of war were two steps to that end. So were the new financial arrangements that emerged at the same time. Most important to the United States was Europe, on whose economic health American prosperity in large part depended. Not only were the major industrial powers there suffering from the devastation of war; they were also staggering under a heavy burden of debt. The Allied powers were struggling to repay $11 billion in loans they had contracted with the United States during and shortly after the war, loans that the Republican administrations were unwilling to reduce or forgive. "They hired the money, didn't they?" Calvin Coolidge replied when queried about the debts. At the same time, an even more debilitated Germany was attempting to pay the enormous reparations levied against it by the Allies. With the financial structure of Europe on the brink of collapse as a result, the United States stepped in with a solution.

Charles B. Dawes, an American banker, negotiated an agreement in 1924 among France, Britain, Germany, and the United States under which American banks would provide enormous loans to the Germans, enabling them to meet their reparations payments; in return, Britain and France would agree to reduce the amount of those payments. The Dawes Plan became the centerpiece of a growing American economic presence in Germany. It also became the source of a troubling circular pattern in international finance. America would lend money to Germany, which would use that money to pay reparations to France and England, which would in turn use those funds (as well as large loans they themselves were receiving from American banks) to repay war debts to the United States. The flow was able to continue only by virtue of the enormous debts Germany and the other European nations were acquiring to American banks and corporations.

Those banks and corporations were doing more than providing loans. They were becoming a daily presence in the economic life of Europe. American automobile manufacturers were opening European factories, capturing a large share of the overseas market. Other industries in the 1920s were establishing subsidiaries worth more than $10 billion throughout the Continent, taking advantage of the devastation of European industry and the inability of domestic corporations to recover. Some groups within the American government warned that the reckless expansion of overseas loans and investments, many in enterprises of dubious value, threatened disaster; that the United States was becoming too dependent on unstable European economies. The high tariff barriers that the Republican Congress had erected (through the Fordney-McCumber Act of 1922) were creating additional problems, such skeptics warned. European nations unable to export their goods to the United States were finding it difficult to earn the money necessary to repay their loans. Such warnings fell, for the most part, on deaf ears; and American economic expansion in Europe continued until disaster struck in 1931.

The government felt even fewer reservations about assisting American economic expansion in Latin America. The United States had, after all, long considered that region its exclusive sphere of influence; and its investments there had become large even before World War I. During the 1920s, American military forces maintained a presence in numerous countries in the region, despite Hughes's withdrawal of troops from the Dominican Republic and Nicaragua. United States investments in Latin America more than doubled between 1924 and 1929; American corporations built roads and other facilities in many areas—partly, they argued, to weaken the appeal of revolutionary forces in the region, but at least equally to increase their own access to Latin America's rich natural resources. American banks were offering large loans to Latin American governments, just as they were in Europe; and just as in Europe, the Latin Americans were having great difficulty earning the money to repay them, in the face of the formidable United States tariff barrier. By the end of the 1920s, resentment of "Yankee imperialism" was already reaching alarming proportions; the economic troubles after 1929 would only accentuate such problems.

Hoover and the World Crisis

After the relatively placid international climate of the 1920s, the diplomatic challenges facing the Hoover administration must have seemed ominous and bewildering. The world financial crisis that had begun in 1929 and greatly intensified after 1931 was not only creating economic distress; it was producing a heightened nationalism that threatened the weak international agreements established during the previous decade. Above all, the Depression was toppling many existing political leaders and replacing them with powerful, belligerent governments bent on expansion as a solution to their economic problems. Hoover was confronted, therefore, with the beginning of a process that would ultimately lead to war, and he was finding himself without sufficient tools to deal with it.

In Latin America, Hoover worked studiously to repair some of the damage created by earlier American actions. He made a ten-week good-will tour through the region before his inauguration. Once in office, he attempted to abstain from intervening in the internal affairs of neighboring nations and moved to withdraw American troops from Nicaragua and Haiti. When economic distress led to the collapse of one Latin American regime after another, Hoover announced a new policy: America would grant diplomatic recognition to any sitting government in the region without questioning the means it had used to obtain power. He even repudiated the Roosevelt Corollary to the Monroe Doctrine by refusing to permit American intervention when several Latin American countries defaulted on debt obligations to the United States in October 1931.

In Europe, the administration enjoyed few successes in its efforts to promote economic stability. When Hoover's proposed moratorium on debts in 1931 failed to attract broad support or produce financial stability (see above, pp. 719–720), many economists and political leaders appealed to the president to cancel all war debts to the United States. Like his predecessors, Hoover refused; and several European nations promptly went into default, severely damaging an already tense international climate. American efforts to extend the disarmament agreements of the 1920s met with similar frustration. At a conference in London in January 1930, American negotiators reached agreement with European and Japanese delegates on extending the limits on naval construction established at the Washington Conference of 1921. But France and England, fearful of a resurgent Germany and an expanding Japan, insisted on so many loopholes as to make the treaty virtually meaningless. The increasing irrelevance of the New Era approach to diplomacy became even clearer at the World Disarmament Conference that opened in Geneva in January 1932. France rejected the idea of disarmament entirely and called for the creation of an international army to counter the growing power of Germany. Hoover continued to urge major reductions in armaments, including an immediate abolition of all "offensive" weapons (tanks, bombers) and a 30 percent reduction in all land and naval forces. The conference ultimately dissolved in failure.

The ineffectiveness of diplomacy in Europe was particularly troubling in view of the character of some of the new governments coming to power on the Continent. Benito Mussolini's Fascist party had been in control of Italy since the early 1920s; by the 1930s, the regime was growing highly nationalistic and militaristic, and fascist leaders were loudly threatening an active campaign of imperial expansion. Even more ominous was the growing power of the National Socialist (or Nazi) party in Germany. The Weimar Republic, which had emerged as the nation's government at the end of World War I, had by the late 1920s lost virtually all popular support; it was discredited by, among other things, a ruinous inflation. And Adolf Hitler, the stridently nationalistic leader of the Nazis, was rapidly growing in popular favor. Although he lost a 1932 election for chancellor, Hitler would sweep into power less than a year later. His belief in the racial superiority of the Aryan (German)

people, his commitment to providing *Lebensraum* (living space) for his "master race," his blatant anti-Semitism, and his passionate militarism—all posed a threat to European peace.

More immediately alarming was a major crisis in Asia—one that proved to be an early step toward World War II. The Japanese, reeling from an economic depression of their own, had developed an intense concern about the increasing power of the Soviet Union and of Chiang Kai-shek's nationalist China. In particular, they were alarmed at Chiang's insistence on expanding his government's power in Manchuria, which remained officially a part of China but over which the Japanese had since 1905 maintained effective economic control. When the moderate government of Japan failed to take forceful steps to counter Chiang's ambitions, Japan's military leaders staged what was, in effect, a coup in the autumn of 1931—seizing control of foreign policy from the weakened liberals. Only weeks later, they launched a major invasion of northern Manchuria.

The American government had few options. For a while, Secretary of State Henry Stimson (who had served as secretary of war under Taft) continued to hope that Japanese moderates would regain control of the Tokyo government and halt the invasion. The militarists, however, remained in command; and by the beginning of 1932, the conquest of Manchuria was complete. Hoover permitted Stimson to issue warnings to Japan and attempt to use moral suasion to end the crisis. He forbade him, however, to cooperate with the League of Nations in imposing economic sanctions against the Japanese. Stimson's only real tool in dealing with the Manchurian invasion was a refusal to grant diplomatic recognition to the new Japanese territories. Japan was unconcerned and early in 1932 expanded its aggression farther into China, attacking the city of Shanghai and killing thousands of civilians.

By the time Hoover left office early in 1933, therefore, it was clear that the international system the United States had attempted to create in the 1920s—a system based on voluntary cooperation among nations and on an American refusal to commit itself to the interests of other countries—had collapsed. The United States faced a choice. It could adopt a more energetic form of internationalism and enter into firmer and more meaningful associations with other nations. Or it could resort to nationalism and rely on its own devices for dealing with its problems. For the next six years, it experimented with elements of both approaches.

Isolationism and Internationalism

The administration of Franklin Roosevelt faced, therefore, a dual challenge as it entered office in 1933. It had to deal with the worst economic crisis in the nation's history; and it had to deal as well with the effects of a decaying international structure. The two problems were not unrelated. It was the worldwide Depression itself that was producing much of the political chaos throughout the globe; and it was partly in response to the economic problems of the 1930s that the highly nationalistic, dangerously belligerent new governments were emerging.

Through most of the 1930s, however, the United States was unwilling to make more than the faintest of gestures toward restoring stability to the world. Like many other peoples suffering economic hardship, Americans were turning inward. Yet the realities of world affairs were not to allow the nation to remain isolated for very long—as Franklin Roosevelt realized earlier than many other Americans.

Depression Diplomacy

From Herbert Hoover, Roosevelt inherited a foreign policy less concerned with issues of war and peace than with matters of economic policy. And although the New Deal rejected some of the initiatives the Republicans had begun, it continued for several years to base its foreign policy almost entirely on the nation's immediate economic needs.

Perhaps Roosevelt's sharpest break with the policies of his predecessor was on the question of American economic relations with Europe. Hoover had argued that only by resolving the question of war debts and reinforcing the gold standard could the American economy hope to recover. He had, therefore, agreed to participate in the World Economic Conference, to be held in London in June 1933, to attempt to resolve these issues. By the time the conference assembled, however, Roosevelt had already become convinced that the gold value of the dollar had to be allowed to fall in order for American goods to be able to compete in world markets. Shortly after the conference convened, Roosevelt released a famous "bombshell" message repudiating the orthodox views of most of the delegates and rejecting any agreement on currency stabilization. The conference quickly dissolved without reaching agreement, and

not until 1936 did the administration finally agree to new negotiations to stabilize Western currencies.

At the same time, Roosevelt was moving to abandon the commitments of the Hoover administration to settle the issue of war debts through international agreement. In effect, he simply let the issue die. Not only did he decline to negotiate a solution at the London Conference, but in April 1934 he signed a bill to forbid American banks from making loans to any nation in default on its debts. The result was to stop the old, circular system by which debt payments continued only by virtue of increasing American loans; within months, war-debt payments from every nation except Finland stopped for good.

If the new administration had no interest in international currency stabilization or settlement of war debts, it did have an active interest in improving America's position in world trade. Roosevelt approved the Reciprocal Trade Agreement Act of 1934, authorizing the administration to negotiate treaties lowering tariffs by as much as 50 percent in return for reciprocal reductions by other nations. The immediate effects of the reciprocal trade agreements negotiated as a result of the act were not impressive. Most agreements in the 1930s were carefully drafted to admit only products not competitive with American industry and agriculture. By 1939, Secretary of State Cordell Hull, a devoted advocate of free trade, had succeeded in negotiating new treaties with twenty-one countries. The result was an increase in American exports to them of nearly 40 percent, but imports into the United States continued to lag. Thus other nations were not obtaining the American currency needed to buy American products, and foreign debts to the United States increased considerably.

America and the Soviet Union

America's hopes of expanding its foreign trade produced particular efforts by the administration to improve its diplomatic posture in two areas: the Soviet Union and Latin America. The United States and Russia had viewed each other with mistrust and even hostility since the Bolshevik Revolution of 1917, and the American government still had not officially recognized the Soviet regime by 1933. But powerful voices within the United States were urging a change in policy—less because the revulsion with which most Americans viewed communism had diminished than because the Soviet Union appeared to be a possible source of important trade. The Russians, too, were eager for a new relationship. They were hoping for American cooperation in containing the power of Japan on Russia's southeastern flank. In November 1933, therefore, Soviet Foreign Minister Maxim Litvinov reached an agreement with the president in Washington. The Soviets would cease their propaganda efforts in the United States and protect American citizens in Russia; in return, the United States would recognize the communist regime.

Despite this promising beginning, however, relations with the Soviet Union soon soured once again. American trade failed to establish a foothold in Russia, disappointing hopes in the United States; and the American government did little to reassure the Soviets that it was interested in stopping Japanese expansion in Asia, dousing expectations in Russia. By the end of 1934, the Soviet Union and the United States were once again viewing each other with considerable mistrust. And Stalin, having abandoned whatever hopes he might once have had of cooperation with America, was beginning to consider making agreements of his own with the fascist governments of Japan and Germany.

The Good Neighbor Policy

Somewhat more successful were American efforts to enhance both diplomatic and economic relations with Latin America through what became known as the "Good Neighbor Policy." Latin America was one of the most important targets of the new policy of trade reciprocity, and the United States succeeded during the 1930s in increasing both exports to and imports from the other nations of the Western Hemisphere by over 100 percent. Closely tied to these new economic relationships was a new American attitude toward intervention in Latin America. The Hoover administration had unofficially abandoned the earlier American practice of using military force to compel Latin American governments to repay debts, respect foreign investments, or otherwise behave "responsibly." The Roosevelt administration went further. At the Inter-American Conference in Montevideo in December 1933, Secretary of State Hull signed a formal convention declaring: "No state has the right to intervene in the internal or external affairs of another." Roosevelt respected that pledge throughout his years in office, refusing to use force against Latin American governments even in the face of occasionally strong domestic pressure.

The Good Neighbor Policy did not mean, how-

American Tractors and Soviet Agriculture
Soviet farm workers drive International Harvester tractors, purchased from the United States, as they cultivate an enormous collective farm (nearly as large as the state of Rhode Island) near Rostov. The Roosevelt administration had high hopes for encouraging trade with the Soviet Union when it established diplomatic relations with Stalin's government in 1933; but Soviet purchases of American goods remained limited. (Bettmann Archive)

ever, that the United States had abandoned its influence in Latin America. On the contrary, it had simply replaced one form of leverage with another. Instead of military force, Americans would now use economic influence. The new reliance on economic pressures eased tensions between the United States and its neighbors considerably, eliminating the most abrasive and conspicuous irritants in the relationship. It did little, however, to stem the growing American domination of the Latin American economy.

The Rise of Isolationism

The first years of the Roosevelt administration marked not only the death of Hoover's hopes for international economic agreements. They marked, too, the end of any hopes for world peace through treaties and disarmament. That the international arrangements of the 1920s were no longer suitable for the world of the 1930s became obvious in the first months of the Roosevelt presidency, when the new administration attempted to stimulate movement toward world disarmament. The arms control conference in Geneva had been meeting, without result, since 1932; and in May 1933, Roosevelt attempted to spur it to action by submitting a new American proposal for arms reductions. Negotiations stalled and then broke down on the Roosevelt proposal; and only a few months later, first Hitler and then Mussolini withdrew from the talks altogether. The Geneva Conference, it was clear, was a failure. Two years later, Japan withdrew from the London Naval Conference, which was attempting to draw up an agreement to continue the limitations on naval armaments negotiated at the Washington Conference of 1921.

Faced with a choice between more active efforts to stabilize the world or more energetic attempts to isolate the nation from it, most Americans unhesitatingly chose the latter. Support for isolationism emerged from many quarters. Old Wilsonian internationalists had grown disillusioned with the League of Nations and its inability to stop Japanese aggression in Asia; internationalism, they were beginning to argue, had failed. Other Americans were listening to the argument that powerful business interests—Wall Street, munitions makers, and others—had tricked the United States into participating in World War I. An investigation by a Senate committee chaired by Senator Gerald Nye of Colorado revealed exorbitant profiteering and blatant tax evasion by many corporations during the war, and it suggested that bankers had pressured Wilson to intervene so as to protect their loans abroad.

Roosevelt himself shared some of the suspicions voiced by the isolationists and claimed to be impressed by the findings of the Nye investigation. Nevertheless, he continued to hope for at least a modest Amer-

ican role in maintaining world peace. In 1935, he proposed to the Senate a treaty to make the United States a member of the World Court—a treaty that would have expanded America's symbolic commitment to internationalism without increasing its actual responsibilities in any important way. Nevertheless, isolationist opposition (spurred by a passionate broadcast by Father Coughlin on the eve of the Senate vote) resulted in the defeat of the treaty. It was a devastating political blow to the president, and he would not soon again attempt to challenge the isolationist tide.

That tide seemed to grow stronger with every passing month. Through the summer of 1935, it became clear to the world that Mussolini's Italy was preparing to invade Ethiopia in an effort to expand its colonial holdings in Africa. Fearing that a general European war would ensue, American legislators began to design legal safeguards to prevent the United States from being dragged into the conflict. The result was the Neutrality Act of 1935.

The 1935 act, and the Neutrality Acts of 1936 and 1937 that followed, were designed to prevent a recurrence of the events that many Americans now believed had pressured the United States into World War I. The 1935 law established a mandatory arms embargo against both victim and aggressor in any military conflict and empowered the president to warn American citizens that they might travel on the ships of warring nations only at their own risk. Thus, isolationists believed, the "protection of neutral rights" could not again become an excuse for American intervention in war. The 1936 Neutrality Act renewed these provisions. And in 1937, with world conditions growing even more precarious, Congress passed a yet more stringent measure. The new Neutrality Act established the so-called cash-and-carry policy, by which belligerents could purchase only nonmilitary goods from the United States and had to pay cash and ship their purchases themselves.

The American stance of militant neutrality was reinforced in October 1935 when Mussolini finally launched his long-anticipated attack on Ethiopia. When the League of Nations protested, Italy simply resigned from the organization, completed its conquest of Ethiopia, and formed an alliance (the "Axis") with Nazi Germany. Americans responded to the news with renewed determination to isolate themselves from European instability. Two-thirds of those responding to public-opinion polls at the time opposed any American action to deter aggression.

Isolationist sentiment showed its strength once

again in 1936–1937 in response to the civil war in Spain. The Falangists of General Francisco Franco, a group much like the Italian fascists, revolted in July 1936 against the existing government, a moderate constitutional monarchy. Hitler and Mussolini supported Franco, both vocally and with weapons and supplies. Some individual Americans traveled to Spain to assist the republican cause (see above, p. 717); but the United States government joined with Britain and France in an agreement to offer no assistance to either side—although all three governments were sympathetic to the loyalists. In effect, then, the agreement denied what might otherwise have been crucial aid to the anti-Franco forces.

Growing Dangers

Franklin Roosevelt, in the meantime, was viewing the events of 1935 and 1936 with alarm. Slowly, cautiously, he attempted to challenge the grip of the isolationists on the nation's foreign policy; yet for a time, it seemed to be a hopeless cause. The United States appeared unable to do more than watch as a series of new dangers emerged that brought the world closer to war.

Particularly disturbing was the deteriorating situation in Asia, where the growth of Japanese power was becoming a direct threat to international stability. Japan's aggressive designs against China had been clear since the invasion of Manchuria in 1931. In the summer of 1937, Tokyo launched an even broader assault, attacking China's five northern provinces. The United States could not, Roosevelt believed, allow the Japanese aggression to go unremarked or unpunished. In a speech in Chicago in October 1937, therefore, the president warned forcefully of the dangers that Japanese aggression posed to world peace. Aggressors, he proclaimed, should be "quarantined" by the international community to prevent the contagion of war from spreading.

The president was deliberately vague about what such a "quarantine" would mean; and there is evidence that he was contemplating nothing more drastic than a break in diplomatic relations with Japan, that he was not considering economic or military sanctions. Nevertheless, public response to the speech was disturbingly hostile. As a result, Roosevelt drew back. Although his strong words encouraged the British government to call a conference in Brussels to discuss the crisis in Asia, the United States refused to make any commitments to collective action; and the conference produced no agreement.

Only months later, another episode gave renewed evidence of how formidable the obstacles to Roosevelt's efforts remained. On December 12, 1937, Japanese aviators bombed and sank the U.S. gunboat *Panay* as it sailed the Yangtze River in China. The attack was almost undoubtedly deliberate. It occurred in broad daylight, with clear visibility; and a large American flag had been painted conspicuously on the *Panay*'s deck. Even so, the American public seized eagerly on Japanese protestations that the bombing had been an accident and pressured the administration to accept Japan's apologies and overlook the attack.

The Failure of Munich

In the meantime, Roosevelt was unable to find any politically acceptable way to increase American influence in Europe. It was not yet clear, moreover, that he believed the United States should become involved there in any case, even though the forces of war were rapidly gathering momentum. In 1936, Hitler had moved the now powerful German army into the Rhineland, rearming an area that France had, in effect, controlled since World War I. In March 1938, German forces marched into Austria; and Hitler proclaimed a union (or *Anschluss*) between Austria, his native land, and Germany, his adopted one. Neither in America nor in most of Europe was there much more than a murmur of opposition.

The Austrian invasion, however, soon created another crisis; for Hitler had by now occupied territory surrounding three sides of western Czechoslovakia, a region he dreamed of annexing to provide Germany with the *Lebensraum* (living space) he believed it needed. In September 1938, he demanded that Czechoslovakia cede to him part of that region, the Sudetenland, an area on the Austro-German border in which many ethnic Germans lived. Czechoslovakia, which possessed substantial military power of its own, was prepared to fight rather than submit. But it realized it could not hope for success without assistance from other European nations. That assistance it did not receive. Most Western nations, including the United States, were appalled at the prospect of another war and were willing to pay almost any price to settle the crisis peacefully. On September 29, Hitler met with the leaders of France and Great Britain at Munich in an effort to resolve the crisis. The French and British agreed to accept the German demands in Czechoslovakia in return for Hitler's promise to expand no farther. "This is the last territorial claim I have to make in Europe," the Führer solemnly declared. And Prime Minister Neville Chamberlain returned to England to a hero's welcome, assuring his people that the agreement ensured "peace in our time." Among those who had cabled him with encouragement at Munich was Franklin Roosevelt.

The Munich accords were the most prominent element of a policy that came to be known as "appeasement" and that came to be identified (not altogether fairly) almost exclusively with Chamberlain. Whoever was to blame, however, it became clear almost immediately that the policy was a failure. In March 1939, Hitler occupied the remaining areas of Czechoslovakia, violating the Munich agreement unashamedly. And in April, he began issuing threats against Poland. At that point, both Britain and France gave assurances to the Polish government that they would come to its assistance in case of an invasion; they even flirted, too late, with the Stalinist regime in Russia, attempting to draw it into a mutual defense agreement. Stalin, however, had already decided that he could expect no protection from the West; he had, after all, not even been invited to attend the Munich Conference. Accordingly, he signed a nonaggression pact with Hitler in August 1939, freeing the Germans for the moment from the danger of a two-front war.

For a few months, Hitler continued to try to frighten the Poles into submitting to German rule. When that failed, he staged an incident on the border to allow him to claim that Germany had been attacked; and on September 1, 1939, he launched a full-scale invasion of Poland. Britain and France, true to their pledges, declared war on Germany two days later. World War II had begun.

Neutrality Tested

"This nation will remain a neutral nation," the president declared shortly after the hostilities began in Europe, "but I cannot ask that every American remain neutral in thought as well." It was a statement that stood in stark and deliberate contrast to Woodrow Wilson's 1914 plea that the nation remain neutral in both deed and thought; and it was clear from the start that among those whose opinions were decidedly unneutral in 1939 was the president himself. There was never any question that both he and the majority of the American people favored Britain, France, and the other Allied nations in the contest. The question was how much the United States was prepared to do to assist them.

At the very least, Roosevelt believed, the United States should make armaments available to the Allied armies to help them counteract the remarkably productive German munitions industry. As a result, in September 1939, he asked Congress for a revision of the Neutrality Acts. The original measures had forbidden the sale of American weapons to any nation engaged in war; Roosevelt wanted the arms embargo lifted. Powerful isolationist opposition forced him to accept a weaker revision than he would have liked; as passed by Congress, the 1939 measure maintained the prohibition on American ships entering war zones. It did, however, permit belligerents to purchase arms on the same cash-and-carry basis that the earlier Neutrality Acts had established for the sale of nonmilitary materials.

For a time, it was possible to believe that little more would be necessary. After the German armies had quickly subdued Poland, the war in Europe settled into a long, quiet lull that lasted through the winter and spring—a "phony war," as it was beginning to be termed. The only real fighting during this period occurred not between the Allies and the Axis, but between Russia and its neighbors. Taking advantage of the situation in the West, the Soviet Union overran first the small Baltic republics of Latvia, Estonia, and Lithuania and then, in late November, Finland. Americans were, for the most part, outraged; but neither Congress nor the president was willing to do more than impose a "moral embargo" on the shipment of armaments to Russia. By March 1940, the Soviet advance was complete. The American sanctions had had no effect.

Whatever illusions Americans had harbored about the war in Western Europe were shattered in the spring of 1940 when Germany launched an invasion to the west—first attacking Denmark and Norway, sweeping next across the Netherlands and Belgium, and driving finally deep into the heart of France. Allied efforts proved futile against the Nazi *blitzkrieg,* and Americans watched in horror as one stronghold after another fell into German hands. On June 10, Mussolini brought Italy into the war, invading France from the south as Hitler was attacking from the north, and prompting Roosevelt to declare angrily: "The hand that held the dagger has struck it into the back of its neighbor." On June 22, finally, France fell to the German onslaught. Nazi troops marched into Paris; a new collaborationist regime began to assemble in Vichy; and in all Europe, only the shattered remnants of the British army, which had been miraculously rescued from the beaches of Dunkirk, remained to oppose the Axis forces.

The Blitz, London
The German Luftwaffe terrorized London and other British cities in 1940–1941 and again late in the war by bombing civilian areas indiscriminately in an effort to break the spirit of the English. The effort failed, and the fortitude of the British in the face of the attack did much to arouse support for their cause in the United States. St. Paul's Cathedral, miraculously undamaged throughout the raids, looms in the background of this photograph, as buildings crumble under the force of German bombs.   (Brown Brothers.)

Roosevelt had already begun to expand not only American aid to the Allies but preparations to resist a possible Nazi invasion of the United States. On May 16, he asked Congress for an additional $1 billion for defense (much of it for the construction of an enormous new fleet of warplanes) and received it quickly. With France tottering a few weeks later, he proclaimed that the United States would "extend to the opponents of force the material resources of this nation." And on May 15, Winston Churchill, the new British prime minister, sent Roosevelt the first of many long lists of requests for ships, armaments, and other assistance without which, he insisted, England could not long survive. Many Americans (including the United States ambassador to London, Joseph P.

Kennedy) argued that the British plight was already hopeless, that any aid to the English was a wasted effort. The president, however, disagreed and made the bold and dangerous decision to "scrape the bottom of the barrel" to make war materials available to Churchill. He even circumvented the cash-and-carry provisions of the Neutrality Act by trading fifty American destroyers (most of them left over from World War I) to England in return for the right to build American bases on British territory in the Western Hemisphere; and he returned to the factories a number of new airplanes purchased by the American government so that the British could buy them instead.

Roosevelt was able to take such steps in part because of a major shift in American public opinion. Before the invasion of France, most Americans had believed that a German victory in the war would not be a threat to the United States. By July, with France defeated and Britain threatened, more than 66 percent of the public (according to opinion polls) believed that Germany posed a direct threat to the United States. Congress was aware of the change and was becoming more willing to permit expanded American assistance to the Allies. It was also becoming more concerned about the need for internal preparations for war, and in September it approved the Burke-Wadsworth Act, inaugurating the first peacetime military draft in American history.

But while the forces of isolation may have weakened, they were far from dead. On the contrary, there began in the summer of 1940 a spirited and often vicious debate between those who advocated expanded American involvement in the war (who were termed, often inaccurately, "interventionists") and those who continued to insist on neutrality. The celebrated journalist William Allen White served as chairman of a new Committee to Defend America, whose members lobbied actively for increased American assistance to the Allies but opposed actual intervention. Others went so far as to urge an immediate declaration of war (a position that as yet had little public support) and in April created an organization of their own, the Fight for Freedom Committee. Opposing them was a powerful new lobby entitled the America First Committee, which attracted some of America's most prominent leaders. Its chairman was General Robert E. Wood, until recently the president of Sears Roebuck; and its membership included Charles Lindbergh, General Hugh Johnson, Senator Gerald Nye, and Senator Burton Wheeler. It won the editorial support of the Hearst chain and other influential newspapers; and it had at least the indirect support of a large proportion of the Republican party. (It also, inevitably, attracted a small fringe of Nazi sympathizers and anti-Semites.) The debate between the two sides was loud and bitter. Through the summer and fall of 1940, moreover, it was complicated by a presidential campaign.

The Third-Term Campaign

Much of the political drama of 1940 revolved around the question of Franklin Roosevelt's intentions. Would he break with tradition and run for an unprecedented third term? The president himself was deliberately coy and never publicly revealed his own wishes. But by refusing to withdraw from the contest, he made it impossible for any rival Democrat to establish a foothold within the party. And when, just before the Democratic Convention in July, he let it be known that he would accept a "draft" from his party, the issue was virtually settled. The Democrats quickly renominated him and even reluctantly swallowed his choice for vice president: Agriculture Secretary Henry A. Wallace, a man too liberal for the taste of many party leaders.

The Republicans, again, faced a far more difficult task. With Roosevelt effectively straddling the center of the defense debate, favoring neither the extreme isolationists nor the extreme interventionists, the Republicans had few viable alternatives. Their solution was to compete with the president on his own ground. Succumbing to the carefully orchestrated pressure of a remarkable grass-roots movement, they nominated for president a politically inexperienced businessman, Wendell Willkie. Both the candidate and the party platform took positions little different from Roosevelt's: They would keep the country out of war but would extend generous assistance to the Allies. Willkie was left, therefore, with the unenviable task of defeating Roosevelt by outmatching him in personal magnetism and by trying to arouse public fears of the dangers of an unprecedented third term. An appealing figure and a vigorous campaigner, he managed to evoke more public enthusiasm than any Republican candidate in decades. In the end, however, he was no match for Franklin Roosevelt. The election was closer than in either 1932 or 1936, but Roosevelt nevertheless won decisively. He received 55 percent of the popular vote to Willkie's 45 percent, and he won 449 electoral votes to Willkie's 82.

Neutrality Abandoned

With the election behind him and with the situation in Europe deteriorating, Roosevelt began in the last months of 1940 to make subtle but profound changes in the American role in the war. To the public, he claimed that he was simply continuing the now established policy of providing aid to the embattled Allies. In fact, that aid was taking new and far more decisive forms.

In December 1940, Great Britain was virtually bankrupt. No longer could the British meet the cash-and-carry requirements imposed by the Neutrality Acts; yet England's needs, Churchill insisted, were greater than ever. The president, therefore, suggested a method that would "eliminate the dollar sign" from all arms transactions while still, he hoped, pacifying those who opposed blatant American intervention in the war. The new system was labeled "lend-lease." It would allow the president not only to sell but to lend or lease armaments to any nation deemed "vital to the defense of the United States." In other words, America could funnel weapons to England on the basis of no more than Britain's promise to return them when the war was over. Isolationists attacked the measure bitterly, arguing (correctly) that it was simply a device to tie the United States more closely to the Allies; but Congress enacted the bill by wide margins.

With lend-lease established, Roosevelt soon faced another serious problem: ensuring that the American supplies would actually reach Great Britain. Shipping lanes in the Atlantic had become extremely dangerous, as German submarines destroyed as much as a half-million tons of shipping each month. The British navy was losing ships more rapidly than it could replace them and was finding it difficult to transport materials across the Atlantic from America. Secretary of War Henry Stimson (who had been Hoover's secretary of state and who returned to the cabinet at Roosevelt's request in 1940) argued that the United States should itself convoy vessels to England; but Roosevelt decided to rely instead on the concept of "hemispheric defense." He argued that the western Atlantic was a neutral zone and the responsibility of the American nations. By July 1941, therefore, American ships were patrolling the ocean as far east as Iceland, escorting convoys of merchant ships, and radioing information to British vessels about the location of Nazi submarines.

At first, Germany did little to challenge these obviously hostile American actions. By September 1941, however, the situation had changed. Nazi forces had invaded the Soviet Union in June of that year, driving quickly and forcefully deep into Russian territory. When the Soviets did not surrender, as many had predicted, Roosevelt persuaded Congress to extend lend-lease privileges to them—the first step toward creating a new relationship with Stalin that would ultimately lead to a formal Soviet-American alliance. Now American industry was providing the lifeblood to Hitler's foes on two fronts, and the navy was playing a more active role than ever in protecting the flow of goods to Europe. In September, Nazi submarines began a concerted campaign against American vessels. Early that month, a German U-

boat fired on the American destroyer *Greer* (which was radioing the U-boat's position to the British at the time). Roosevelt responded by ordering American ships to fire on German submarines "on sight." In October, Nazi submarines actually hit two destroyers and sank one of them, the *Reuben James,* killing many American sailors in the process. An enraged Congress now voted approval of a measure allowing the United States to arm its merchant vessels and to sail all the way into belligerent ports. The United States had, in effect, launched a naval war against Germany.

At the same time, a series of meetings, some private and one public, were tying the United States and Great Britain ever more closely together. In April 1941, senior military officers of the two nations had met in secret and agreed on a joint strategy to be followed were the United States to enter the war. In August, Roosevelt met with Winston Churchill aboard a British vessel anchored off the coast of Newfoundland. The president made no military commitments, but he did join with Churchill in releasing a document that became known as the Atlantic Charter, in which the two nations set out "certain common principles" on which to base "a better future for the world." It was, in only vaguely disguised form, a statement of war aims that called openly for, among other things, "the final destruction of the Nazi tyranny."

By the fall of 1941, therefore, it seemed only a matter of time before the United States became an official belligerent. Roosevelt remained convinced that public opinion would support a declaration of war only in the event of an actual enemy attack. But an attack seemed certain to come, if not in the Atlantic, then in the Pacific.

The Road to Pearl Harbor

The Japanese had not sat idle during the crisis in Europe. With Great Britain preoccupied with Germany, and with Soviet attention diverted to the west, Japan sensed an unparalleled opportunity to extend its empire in the Pacific. And in September 1940, Japan signed the Tripartite Pact, a loose defensive alliance with Germany and Italy that seemed to extend the Axis into Asia. (In reality, the European Axis powers never developed a very strong relationship with Japan.)

Roosevelt had already displayed his animosity toward the Japanese by harshly denouncing their continuing assault on China and by terminating a longstanding American commercial treaty with the Tokyo government. Still the Japanese drive continued. In July 1941, imperial troops moved into Indochina and seized the capital of Vietnam. The United States, having broken Japanese codes, knew that their next target would be the Dutch East Indies; and when Tokyo failed to respond to Roosevelt's stern warnings, the president froze all Japanese assets in the United States, severely limiting Japan's ability to purchase needed American supplies.

Tokyo now faced a choice. It would either have to repair relations with the United States to restore the flow of supplies, or it would have to find those supplies elsewhere, most notably by seizing British and Dutch possessions in the Pacific. At first, the Tokyo government seemed willing to compromise. The Japanese prime minister, Prince Konoye, had begun negotiations with the United States even before the freezing of his country's assets; and in August he increased the pace by requesting a personal meeting with President Roosevelt. On the advice of Secretary Hull, who feared that Konoye lacked sufficient power within his own government to be able to enforce any agreement, Roosevelt replied that he would meet with the prime minister only if Japan would give guarantees in advance that it would respect the territorial integrity of China. Konoye could give no such assurances, and the negotiations collapsed. In October, the militants in Tokyo forced Konoye out of office and replaced him with the leader of the war party, General Hideki Tojo. There seemed little alternative now to war.

The Tojo government maintained for several weeks a pretense of wanting to continue negotiations. On November 20, 1941, Tokyo proposed a *modus vivendi* highly favorable to itself and sent its diplomats in Washington to the State Department to discuss it. But Tokyo had already decided that it would not yield on the question of China, and Washington had made clear that it would accept nothing less than a reversal of that policy. Hull rejected the Japanese

Pearl Harbor
The destroyer U.S.S. *Shaw,* immobilized in a floating drydock in Pearl Harbor in December 1941, survived the first wave of Japanese bombers unscathed. But in the second attack, the Japanese scored a direct hit and produced this spectacular explosion, which blew off the ship's bow. Damage to the rest of the ship, however, was slight. Only months later the *Shaw* was fitted with a new bow; later it rejoined the fleet. (US Navy Photo)

WHERE HISTORIANS DISAGREE

The Question of Pearl Harbor

"Remember Pearl Harbor!" became a rallying cry during World War II—reminding Americans of the treachery and savagery of the surprise Japanese attack on the American naval base in Hawaii, arousing the nation to even greater efforts to exact revenge. But within a few years of the close of hostilities, some Americans remembered Pearl Harbor for different reasons and began to challenge the official version of the attack on December 7, 1941. Their charges sparked a debate that has never fully subsided. Was the Japanese attack on Pearl Harbor unprovoked, and did it come without warning, as the Roosevelt administration claimed at the time? Or was it part of a deliberate plan by the president to have the Japanese force a reluctant United States into the war? And most controversial of all, did the administration know of the attack in advance? Did Roosevelt deliberately refrain from warning the commanders in Hawaii so that the air raid's effect on the American public would be more profound?

Among the first to challenge the official version of Pearl Harbor was the historian Charles A. Beard, who maintained in *President Roosevelt and the Coming of the War, 1941* (1948) that the United States had deliberately forced the Japanese into a position where they had no choice but to attack. By cutting off Japan's access to the raw materials it needed for its military adventure in China, by refusing stubbornly to compromise, the United States ensured that the Japanese would strike out into the southwestern Pacific to take the needed supplies by force—even at the risk of war with the United States. Not only was American policy provocative in effect, Beard suggested. It was also *deliberately* provocative. More than that, the administration, which had some time before cracked the Japanese code, must have known weeks in advance of Japan's plans to attack. Beard supported his argument by citing Secretary of War Henry Stimson's comment in his diary: "The question was how we should maneuver them into the position of firing the first shot."

A partial refutation of the Beard argument appeared in 1950 in Basil Rauch's *Roosevelt from Munich to Pearl Harbor.* The administration did not know in advance of the planned attack on Pearl Harbor, Rauch argued. It did, however, expect an attack somewhere; and it had made subtle efforts to "maneuver" Japan into firing the first shot in the conflict. But Richard N. Current, in *Secretary Stimson: A Study in Statecraft* (1954), offered an even stronger challenge to Beard. Stimson did indeed anticipate an attack, Current argued, but not an attack on American territory; he anticipated, rather, an assault on British or Dutch possessions in the Pacific. The problem confronting the administration was not how to maneuver the Japanese into attacking the United States but how to find a way to make a Japanese attack on British or Dutch territory *appear* to be an attack on America. Only thus, he believed, could Congress be per-

---

overtures out of hand; on November 27, he told Secretary of War Henry Stimson, "I have washed my hands of the Japanese situation, and it is now in the hands of you and [Secretary of the Navy Frank] Knox, the Army and Navy." He was not merely speculating. American intelligence had already decoded Japanese messages which made clear that war was imminent, that after November 29 an attack would be only a matter of days.

What Washington did not know was where the attack would take place. Most officials were convinced that the Japanese would move first not against American territory but against British or Dutch pos-sessions to the south. American intelligence took note of a Japanese naval task force that began sailing east from the Kurile Islands in the general direction of Hawaii on November 25; and a routine warning was sent to the United States naval facility at Pearl Harbor, near Honolulu. Officials were paying far more attention, however, to a large Japanese convoy moving southward through the China Sea. A combination of confusion and miscalculation caused the government to overlook clear indications that Japan intended a direct attack on American forces.

At 7:55 A.M. on Sunday, December 7, 1941, a wave of Japanese bombers attacked the United States

WHERE HISTORIANS DISAGREE

suaded to approve a declaration of war.

Roberta Wohlstetter took a different approach to the question, in *Pearl Harbor: Warning and Decision* (1962), the most thorough scholarly study to appear to that point. De-emphasizing the question of whether the American government *wanted* a Japanese attack, she undertook to answer the question of whether the administration *knew* of the attack in advance. Wohlstetter concluded that the United States had ample warning of Japanese intentions and should have realized that the Pearl Harbor raid was imminent. But government officials failed to interpret the evidence correctly—largely because their preconceptions about Japanese intentions were at odds with the evidence they confronted. Admiral Edwin T. Layton, who had been a staff officer at Pearl Harbor in 1941, also blames political and bureaucratic failures for the absence of advance warning of the attack. In a 1985 memoir, *And I Was There,* he argues that the Japanese attack was not only a result of "audacious planning and skillful execution" by the Japanese, but of "a dramatic breakdown in our intelligence process . . . related directly to feuding among high-level naval officers in Washington."

Probably the most thorough study of Pearl Harbor appeared in 1981, in Gordon W. Prange's *At Dawn We Slept.* Like Wohlstetter, Prange concluded that the Roosevelt administration was guilty of a series of disastrous blunders in interpreting Japanese strategy; the American government had possession of enough information to predict the attack but failed to do so. Prange, however, dismissed the arguments of the "revisionists" (Beard and his successors) that the president had deliberately maneuvered the nation into the war by permitting the Japanese to attack. Instead, he emphasized the great daring and skill with which the Japanese orchestrated an ambitious operation that few Americans believed possible.

But the revisionist claims have not been laid to rest. John Toland revived the charge of a Roosevelt betrayal in 1982, in *Infamy: Pearl Harbor and Its Aftermath,* claiming to have discovered new evidence (the testimony of an unidentified seaman) that proves the navy knew at least five days in advance that Japanese aircraft carriers were heading toward Hawaii. From that, Toland concluded that Roosevelt must have known that an attack was forthcoming and that he allowed it to occur in the belief that a surprise attack would arouse the nation. Warning the commanders in Hawaii in advance, Roosevelt feared, might cause the Japanese to cancel their plans. The president was gambling that American defenses would be sufficient to repel the attack, but his gamble failed—and resulted in the deaths of over 2,000 people and the crippling of the American Pacific fleet. But like the many previous writers who have proferred the same argument, Toland was unable to produce any direct evidence of Roosevelt's knowledge of the planned attack.

---

naval base at Pearl Harbor. A second wave came an hour later. Because the military commanders in Hawaii had taken no precautions against such an attack, allowing ships to remain bunched up defenselessly in the harbor and airplanes to remain parked in rows on airstrips, the results of the raid were catastrophic. Within two hours, the United States lost 8 battleships, 3 cruisers, 4 other vessels, 188 airplanes, and several vital shore installations. More than 2,000 soldiers and sailors died, and another 1,000 were injured. The Japanese suffered only light losses.

American forces were now greatly diminished in the Pacific (although by sheer accident, none of the four American aircraft carriers—the heart of the Pacific fleet—had been at Pearl Harbor on December 7). Nevertheless, the raid on Pearl Harbor did overnight what more than two years of effort by Franklin Roosevelt had been unable to do: It unified the American people in a fervent commitment to war. On December 8, the president traveled to Capitol Hill, where he grimly addressed a joint session of Congress: "Yesterday, December 7, 1941—a date which will live in infamy—the United States of America was suddenly and deliberately attacked by the naval and air forces of the Empire of Japan." Within four hours, the Senate unanimously and the

House 388 to 1 approved a declaration of war against Japan. Three days later, Germany and Italy, Japan's European allies, declared war on the United States; and on the same day, December 11, Congress reciprocated without a dissenting vote. For the second time in less than twenty-five years, the United States had joined in a terrible international conflagration.

War on Two Fronts

Whatever political disagreements and social tensions the war may have produced among the American people, there was from the beginning a remarkable unity of opinion about the conflict itself—"a unity," as one member of Congress proclaimed shortly after Pearl Harbor, "never before witnessed in this country." But that unity and confidence were severely tested in the first, troubled months of 1942. For despite the impressive display of patriotism and the dramatic flurry of activity, the war was going very badly. Britain appeared ready to collapse. The Soviet Union was staggering. One after another, Allied strongholds in the Pacific were falling to the forces of Japan. The first task facing the United States, therefore, was less to achieve victory than to stave off defeat.

Containing the Japanese

Ten hours after the strike at Pearl Harbor, Japanese airplanes attacked the American airfields at Manila in the Philippines, destroying much of America's remaining air power in the Pacific. Three days later Guam, an American possession, fell to Japan; then Wake Island and Hong Kong. The great British fortress of Singapore in Malaya surrendered in February 1942, the Dutch East Indies in March, Burma in April. In the Philippines, exhausted Filipino and American troops, under the command of General Douglas MacArthur, finally abandoned the islands on May 6. MacArthur's defiant promise, "I shall return," seemed at the time a forlorn hope.

Alone among the warring nations, the United States was committed to major military endeavors in both Europe and the Pacific. But despite the setbacks in the struggle with Japan, American policymakers remained committed to a decision they had made in 1940. The defeat of Germany would be the nation's first priority. This meant that American forces in the Pacific would at first concentrate not so much on driving the Japanese from the areas it possessed as on defending scattered island territories not yet overcome by the Japanese onslaught. It would attempt not to defeat but to contain the Japanese.

After the Japanese conquest of the Philippines, American strategists planned two broad offensives. One, under the command of General MacArthur, would move north from Australia, through New Guinea, and eventually back to the Philippines. The other, under Admiral Chester Nimitz, would move west from Hawaii toward major Japanese island outposts in the central Pacific. Eventually, the two offensives would come together to invade Japan itself.

The first test of this strategy came just northwest of Australia, which in mid-1942 stood almost undefended. (Only weak outposts in southern New Guinea stood between the Australian mainland and the Japanese forces.) There the Allies at last achieved their first important victory. In the Battle of Coral Sea on May 7–8, 1942, American aircraft carriers and ground troops turned back the hitherto unstoppable Japanese forces.

A month later, there was an even more important turning point northwest of Hawaii. The American navy had broken the Japanese codes and knew that an enormous enemy offensive was taking shape there; it rushed every available airplane and vessel into the area. An enormous battle raged for four days, June 3–6, 1942, near the small American outpost at Midway Island. Both sides suffered great losses, but the encounter was, in the end, a significant American victory. Nimitz's forces had not only prevented the Japanese from securing their original objectives—the capture of Midway and the destruction of what was left of American naval power in the Pacific. They had also destroyed four Japanese aircraft carriers (the United States lost only one) and regained control of the central Pacific for the United States.

The Americans took the offensive for the first time several months later in the southern Solomon Islands, to the east of New Guinea, where the Japanese were establishing a base for air raids against American communications with Australia. In August 1942, American forces assaulted three of the islands: Gavutu, Tulagi, and Guadalcanal. A struggle of unprecedented ferocity developed at Guadalcanal and continued for six months, inflicting heavy losses on both sides. In the end, however, the Japanese were forced to abandon the island—and with it their last chance of launching an effective offensive to the south.

World War II in the Pacific

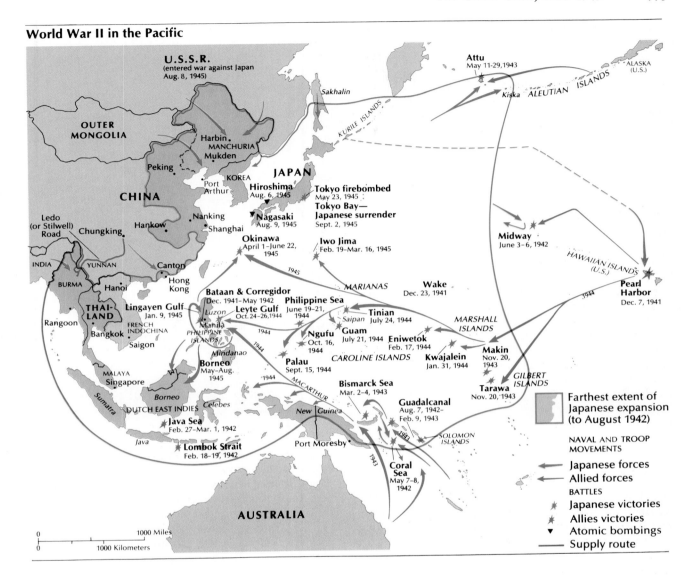

Farthest extent of Japanese expansion (to August 1942)

NAVAL AND TROOP MOVEMENTS
→ Japanese forces
→ Allied forces
BATTLES
✳ Japanese victories
✳ Allies victories
▼ Atomic bombings
— Supply route

In both the southern and central Pacific, therefore, the initiative had by mid-1943 shifted to the United States. The Japanese advance had been halted. The Americans, with aid from the Australians and the New Zealanders, now began the slow, arduous process of moving toward the Philippines and, ultimately, Japan itself.

Holding Off the Germans

In the European war, the United States was less able to shape military operations to its liking. It had to cooperate with Britain and with the exiled "Free French" forces in the west; and it had to conciliate its new ally, the Soviet Union, which was engaged in a savage conflict with Hitler in the east. The army chief of staff, George C. Marshall, supported a plan for a major Allied invasion of France across the English Channel in the spring of 1943; and he placed a hitherto little known general, Dwight D. Eisenhower, in charge of planning the operation. But Marshall and Eisenhower faced strong and conflicting pressures from their allies. The Soviet Union, which was absorbing (as it would throughout the war) the brunt of the German war effort, was desperate for

World War II in North Africa and Italy: The Allied Counteroffensive, 1942–1943

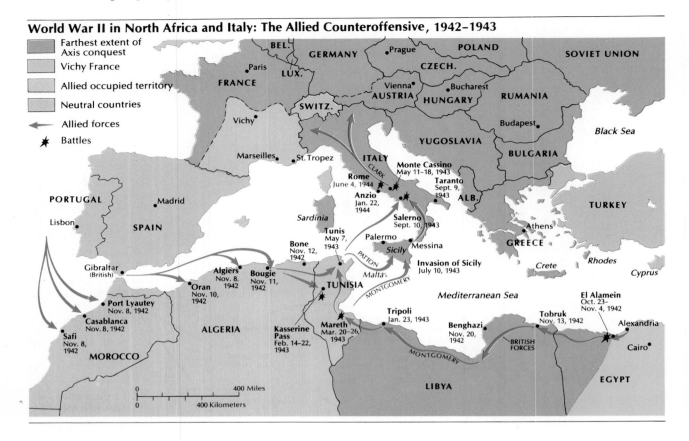

relief and wanted the Allied invasion to proceed at the earliest possible moment. The British, however, wanted to wait. Winston Churchill, in particular, argued strenuously for a series of Allied offensives around the edges of the Nazi empire—in northern Africa and southern Europe—before undertaking the major invasion in France itself.

The conflicting pressures came to a head in the spring of 1942. By then, the German Afrika Korps under the command of General Erwin Rommel had advanced to El Alamein, only seventy-five miles west of Alexandria, Egypt, threatening the Suez Canal and the Middle East, still under British control. At the same time, German armies in Russia were plunging toward the Caucasus. In May the Russian foreign minister, Vyacheslav Molotov, visited Washington to demand an immediate second front that would divert at least forty German divisions from Russia; otherwise, he warned, the Soviet effort might collapse. A month later, however, Churchill arrived in Washington to urge an invasion of North Africa instead. Roosevelt knew that a Mediterranean offensive would be of less value than an invasion of the Con-

tinent, but he also knew that such an invasion would require many months of preparation. Eager to engage American forces in combat as soon as possible, he supported Churchill and ordered American forces to join the British in the defense of northern Africa.

At the end of October 1942, the British opened a counteroffensive against Rommel at El Alamein and sent the Afrika Korps reeling back from Egypt. On November 8, Anglo-American forces landed at Oran and Algiers in Algeria and at Casablanca in Morocco—areas under the Nazi-controlled French government at Vichy. A controversial deal with French admiral Jean Darlan (a notorious collaborator with the Nazis) halted what was for a time fierce fighting between Vichy forces and the Americans at Casablanca and enabled Eisenhower to begin moving his forces east toward Rommel. The Germans, having moved west from Egypt across Libya, now threw the full weight of their forces in Africa against the inexperienced Americans and inflicted a serious defeat on them at the Kasserine Pass in Tunisia. General George S. Patton, however, regrouped the American troops and began an effective counteroffensive. With the help of Allied air and naval power and of British forces attacking from the east under Field Marshall Bernard Montgomery (the hero of El Alamein), the American offensive finally drove the last Germans from Africa in May 1943.

The North African campaign, combined with continuing shipping losses from German submarine attacks in the Atlantic, had tied up so large a proportion of the Allied resources that the planned May 1943 cross-channel invasion of France had to be postponed, despite angry complaints from the Soviet Union. By now, however, the threat of a Soviet collapse seemed much diminished; for during the winter of 1942–1943, the Red Army had successfully held off a major German assault at Stalingrad in southern Russia. Hitler had committed such enormous forces to the battle, and had suffered such appalling losses, that his ability to continue his eastern offensive was now shattered.

The Soviet victory made it possible, then, for Roosevelt to agree to Churchill's plan for an Allied invasion of Sicily, a plan the two men worked out together in January 1943 at a meeting in Casablanca. General Marshall opposed the plan, fearing that it would further delay the vital invasion of France. But Churchill prevailed with his argument that the operation in Sicily might knock Italy out of the war and force the Germans to tie up many divisions in defense of Italy and the Balkans. On the night of July 9, 1943, American and British armies landed in the extreme southeast of Sicily; thirty-eight days later, they had conquered the island and begun moving onto the Italian mainland. In the face of these setbacks, Mussolini's government collapsed and the dictator himself fled north to Germany. But although Mussolini's successor, Marshal Pietro Badoglio, moved quickly to commit Italy to the Allies, Germany moved eight divisions into the country and established a powerful defensive line south of Rome. The Allied offensive on the Italian peninsula, which began on September 3, 1943, soon bogged down against the powerful, entrenched Nazi forces, particularly after a serious Allied setback at Monte Cassino early in 1944. Not until May 1944 did the Allies finally capture Cassino and resume their northward advance. On June 4, 1944, they captured Rome.

The invasion of Italy contributed to the Allied war effort in several important ways, but on the whole it was probably a strategic mistake. It delayed the invasion of France by as much as a year. It deeply embittered the Soviet Union, which was convinced that America and Britain were deliberately delaying in order to force the Russians to absorb the bulk of the German offensive. And it gave the Soviets time to reverse the course of battle and begin moving toward the countries of Eastern Europe.

America and the Holocaust

In the midst of this intensive fighting, the leaders of the American government found themselves confronted with one of history's great tragedies: the Nazi campaign to exterminate the Jews of Europe—the Holocaust. As early as 1942, high officials in Washington had incontrovertible evidence that Hitler's forces were rounding up Jews and others from all over Europe, transporting them to concentration camps in eastern Germany and Poland, and systematically murdering them. (The death toll would ultimately reach 6 million Jews and approximately 4 million others.) News of the atrocities was reaching the public as well, and pressure began to build for some Allied response, some effort to end the killing or at least to rescue some of the surviving Jews.

The American government consistently resisted almost all such entreaties. Although Allied bombers were flying missions within a few miles of the most notorious death camp at Auschwitz in Poland, pleas that the planes try to destroy the crematoria at the camp were rejected as militarily unfeasible. So were similar requests that the Allies try to destroy railroad lines leading to the camp.

The United States also resisted entreaties that it admit large numbers of the Jewish refugees attempting to escape the horrors of Europe. One ship, the *St. Louis,* arrived in Miami carrying nearly 1,000 escaped German Jews, only to be refused entry and forced to return to Europe. Throughout the war, the State Department did not even use up the number of visas permitted by law; almost 90 percent of the quota remained untouched. One opportunity after another to assist the imperiled Jews was either ignored or rejected.

In fairness to American leaders, there was probably little they could have done to save the majority of Hitler's victims. But more forceful action by the United States (and Britain, which was even less amenable to Jewish requests for assistance) might well have saved at least some lives. The failure to take such action is difficult to understand; but in the midst of a terrible conflict, policymakers found it possible to justify abandoning the Jews to their fate by concentrating their attention solely on the larger goal of winning the war. Any diversion of energy and attention to other purposes, they apparently believed, would distract them from the overriding goal of victory.

The American People in Wartime

"War is no longer simply a battle between armed forces in the field," an American government report of 1939 concluded. "It is a struggle in which each side strives to bring to bear against the enemy the coordinated power of every individual and of every material resource at its command. The conflict extends from the soldier in the front line to the citizen in the remotest hamlet in the rear."

The United States had experienced the demands of "total war" before. But never had the nation experienced so consuming a military experience as World War II. American armed forces engaged in combat around the globe—and not just for a few months, as during World War I, but for nearly four years. American society, in the meantime, experienced changes and distortions that reached into virtually every corner of the nation.

The War Economy

World War II had its most profound impact on American domestic life by ending at last the Great Depression. By the middle of 1941, the economic problems of the 1930s—unemployment, deflation, industrial sluggishness—had virtually vanished before the great wave of wartime industrial expansion.

The most important agent of the new prosperity was federal spending, which within months was pumping far more money into the economy than all the New Deal relief agencies combined had done. In 1939, the federal budget had been $9 billion; by 1945, it had risen to $100 billion. Largely as a result, the gross national product soared: from $91 billion in 1939 to $166 billion in 1945. The index of industrial production doubled. Seventeen million new jobs were created.

Perhaps most striking was the increase in personal income. In New York, the average family income in 1938 had been $2,760; by 1942, it had risen to $4,044. In Boston, the increase was from $2,455 to $3,618; in

Washington, D.C., from $2,227 to $5,316. There were, of course, limits on what the recipients of these expanded incomes could do with their money. Many consumer goods—automobiles, radios, and appliances, even many types of food and clothing—were in short supply. Wage earners diverted much of their new affluence, therefore, into savings, which would later help keep the economic boom alive in the postwar years.

The war years not only increased the total wealth of the nation; it produced the only significant change of the century in the distribution of wealth among the population. Almost everyone's income grew during the war; but the incomes of the poorest 20 percent rose by nearly 70 percent—substantially more than those of the wealthiest 20 percent, which rose by only 20 percent. Farmers, whose earnings had risen very slightly if at all during the previous two decades, saw their incomes rise by 400 percent. Industrial workers enjoyed somewhat less substantial gains; union leaders agreed to limit wage increases to 15 percent during the war. But workers who had been unemployed or underemployed in the 1930s were now fully employed, often working substantial overtime.

Labor and the War

Instead of the prolonged and debilitating unemployment that had been the most troubling feature of the Depression economy, the war created a serious labor shortage. The armed forces diverted over 15 million men and women from the civilian work force at the same time that the demand for labor was rising rapidly. Nevertheless, the civilian work force jumped from 46.5 million at the beginning of the war to over 53 million at the end. The 7 million who had previously been unemployed accounted for some of the increase; the employment of many people previously considered inappropriate to be part of the work force—the very young, the elderly, and perhaps most important, several million women—accounted for the rest of it.

The war gave an enormous boost to union membership, which rose from about 10.5 million in 1941 to over 13 million in 1945. But it also created important new restrictions on the ability of unions to win increased wages for their members. The government was determined to prevent strikes, which would disrupt war production, and to forestall large wage increases, which might contribute to inflation. It

Women at War

Late in the war, during a meeting with Roosevelt and Winston Churchill, Josef Stalin offered a toast: "To American production, without which the war would have been lost." The American military was well aware of how important production was to the war effort, and it gave evidence of its concern in official posters, such as this one exhorting American women to perform vital tasks in the civilian economy.   (Library of Congress)

managed to win from union leaders important concessions on both issues. One was the "no-strike" pledge, by which unions agreed not to stop production in wartime. Another was the so-called Little Steel formula, which set a 15 percent limit on wage increases. That limit was the result of negotiations conducted by the National War Labor Board, which included representatives of labor, management, and government and which was charged with settling all labor disputes. In return for these agreements, the government provided labor with a "maintenance-of-membership" agreement, which promised that the

thousands of new workers pouring into defense plants would be automatically enrolled in unions that had previously established bargaining rights there. The agreement ensured the continued health of the union organizations, but in return workers had to give up the right to demand major economic gains during the war.

Many rank-and-file union members, and some union leaders, resented the restrictions imposed on them by the government and the labor hierarchy. Despite the no-strike pledge, there were nearly 15,000 work stoppages during the war. When the United

Mine Workers defied the government by striking in May 1943, Congress reacted by passing a month later, over Roosevelt's veto, the Smith-Connally Act (War Labor Disputes Act), which required unions to wait thirty days before striking and empowered the president to seize a struck war plant. A far more drastic proposal, a bill to conscript workers into government service, made considerable progress in Congress before the administration managed to block it. In the meantime, public animosity toward labor rose rapidly, and many states passed laws to limit union power. By the end of the war, pressure was growing for federal action to limit the influence of the unions.

Stabilizing the Boom

The fear of deflation, which had been the central concern of most American economists in the 1930s, gave way during the war to an at times equally serious fear of inflation. Fueling that fear was a rapid and destabilizing 25 percent increase in prices in the two years before Pearl Harbor.

In response to growing public concern, the Office of Price Administration (the war agency charged with stabilizing prices) began freezing prices and rents in certain areas of particularly rapid economic growth. But with farm prices still rising rapidly, the OPA's policies failed to reduce pressure from workers for further wage increases. In October 1942, therefore, Congress grudgingly responded to the president's request and passed the Anti-Inflation Act, which gave the administration authority to freeze agricultural prices, wages, salaries, and rents throughout the country.

The first director of the OPA, the vigorous New Dealer Leon Henderson, resigned exhausted and frustrated in mid-1943. To replace him, Roosevelt appointed Chester Bowles, a former advertising executive with remarkable administrative talents, who managed to hold the increase in living costs during the next two years to 1.4 percent. In part because of his success, inflation was a much less serious problem during World War II than it had been during World War I.

The OPA was never popular. There was widespread resentment of its "meddlesome" controls over wages and prices. And there was only grudging acquiescence in its complicated system of rationing scarce consumer goods: coffee, sugar, meat, butter, canned goods, shoes, tires, gasoline, and fuel oil. Black-marketing and overcharging grew in proportions far beyond OPA policing capacity.

Among the most important methods of controlling inflation were the government's revenue-raising programs: borrowing and taxation. About half the revenues it needed the government borrowed from the American people, by selling $100 billion worth of bonds. Most of the rest it raised by radically increasing taxes on incomes. The Revenue Act of 1942, which Roosevelt hailed as "the greatest tax bill in American history," levied a 94 percent tax on the highest incomes; and for the first time, the income tax fell as well on those in lower income brackets. To simplify payment for these new millions, Congress enacted a withholding system of payroll deductions in 1943.

From 1941 to 1945, the federal government spent a total of $321 billion—twice as much as it had spent in the entire 150 years of its existence to that point, and ten times as much as the cost of World War I. The national debt rose from $49 billion in 1941 to $259 billion in 1945, yet the black warnings of national bankruptcy that had punctuated the New Deal years were almost entirely muted.

Mobilizing Production

It was production of the armaments, equipment, and supplies necessary for fighting the war that was responsible for the government spending, the industrial growth, and the economic problems of the war years. America's great productive capacity was its most important weapon in the fight against the Axis; it was, in the end, probably the decisive factor in the Allied victory. But that capacity, and its importance, also created difficult challenges, which the government was never entirely successful in meeting.

The search for an effective mechanism to mobilize the economy for war began as early as 1939 and continued for nearly four years. One failed agency after another attempted to bring order to the mobilization effort: the National Defense Advisory Commission, the Office of Production Management, the Supply Priorities and Allocation Board. Finally, in January 1942, the president responded to widespread criticism by creating the War Production Board (WPB), under the direction of former Sears Roebuck executive Donald Nelson. In theory, the WPB was to be a "superagency," controlling government purchases of war matériel and supervising the allocation of materials and manpower. In fact, it never had as much authority as its World War I equivalent, the War Industries Board. And the genial Donald Nelson never displayed the administrative or political strength of his 1918 counterpart, Bernard Baruch.

Throughout its troubled history, therefore, the WPB found itself constantly outmaneuvered and frustrated. It was never able to win complete control over military purchases; the army and navy often circumvented the board entirely in negotiating contracts with producers. It was never able to satisfy the complaints of small business, which charged (correctly) that most contracts were going to large corporations. Gradually, the president transferred much of the authority he had originally delegated to Nelson to a new office located within the White House: the Office of War Mobilization, directed by a former South Carolina senator, James F. Byrnes. But the OWM was only modestly more successful than the WPB.

Despite the administrative problems, however, the war economy managed to meet almost all of the nation's critical war needs. Enormous new factory complexes were constructed in the space of a few months, many of them funded by the federal government's Defense Plants Corporation. An entire new industry producing synthetic rubber was created to make up for the loss of access to natural rubber in the Pacific. By the beginning of 1944, American factories were, in fact, producing more than the government needed. Their output was twice that of all the Axis countries combined. There were even complaints late in the war that military production was becoming excessive, that a limited resumption of civilian production should now begin. (The military staunchly and successfully opposed such demands.)

Blacks and the War

During World War I, many American blacks had eagerly seized the chance to serve in the armed forces, believing that their patriotic efforts would win them an enhanced position in postwar society. They had been cruelly disappointed. As World War II approached, blacks were again determined to use the conflict to improve the position of their race—this time, however, not by currying favor but by making demands.

In the summer of 1941, with preparedness efforts at their height, A. Philip Randolph, president of the Brotherhood of Sleeping Car Porters, an important black union, began to insist that the government require those companies receiving defense contracts to integrate their work forces. To mobilize support for the demand, Randolph planned a massive march on Washington, which threatened to bring more than

100,000 protesting blacks into the capital. Roosevelt, fearful of both the possibility of violence and the certainty of political embarrassment, finally persuaded Randolph to cancel the march in return for a promise to establish a Fair Employment Practices Commission. Its purpose was to investigate discrimination against blacks in war industries; and although its enforcement powers, and thus its effectiveness, were limited, it did mark an important step toward a government commitment to racial equality.

The economic realities of the war years greatly increased the migration of blacks from the rural areas of the South into the industrial cities, where there were suddenly factory jobs available in war plants. In the South, the migration produced white resentment and suspicion, including the false rumor among white homeowners that blacks were engaged in a conspiracy to deprive the region of domestic servants. In the North, the migration produced much more severe tensions. In Detroit in 1943, a violent race riot erupted when black families began moving into a new housing project near a Polish neighborhood. Thirty-four people died in the rioting, twenty-five of them blacks.

Despite such tensions, the leading black organizations redoubled their efforts during the war to challenge the system of segregation. The Congress of Racial Equality (CORE), organized in 1943 by Randolph, mobilized mass popular resistance to discrimination in a way that the older, more conservative organizations had never done. Randolph, Bayard Rustin, James Farmer, and other, younger black leaders helped organize sit-ins and demonstrations in segregated theaters and restaurants. In 1944, they won a much publicized victory by forcing a Washington, D.C., restaurant to agree to serve blacks. In other areas, their victories were few. Nevertheless, the war years aroused a defiant public spirit among many blacks that would survive into the 1950s and help produce the civil-rights movement.

Racial agitation was most pronounced in civilian institutions, but the winds of change were blowing within the military as well. At first, the armed forces maintained their traditional practice of limiting blacks to the most menial assignments, keeping them in segregated training camps and units, and barring them entirely from the Marine Corps and the Army Air forces. Gradually, however, military leaders were forced to make adjustments—in part because of public and political pressures, but also because they recognized that these forms of segregation were wasting manpower. By the end of the war, the number of black servicemen had increased sevenfold, to 700,000; some training camps were being integrated; blacks were being allowed to serve on ships with white sailors; and more black units were being sent into combat. But tensions remained. In some of the integrated army bases—Fort Dix, New Jersey, for example—riots occasionally broke out when blacks protested having to serve in segregated divisions. Substantial discrimination survived in all the services until well after the war. But within the military, as within the society at large, the traditional pattern of race relations was slowly but substantially eroding.

"Rosie the Riveter"

The war was also an important event in the modern history of American women, who found themselves—because of social and economic necessity—suddenly thrust into roles long considered inappropriate for them. With so many men serving in the military, women became crucial to the successful operation of industry. And so the number of women in the work force increased by over 6 million, or by nearly 60 percent, in the course of the war. The new working women were far more likely to be married and were on the whole considerably older than those who had entered the work force in the past. They were also more likely to work in heavy industrial jobs that had previously been reserved for men. The famous wartime image of "Rosie the Riveter" symbolized the new importance of the female industrial work force.

Working women encountered far less popular hostility than they had in previous decades. But the new opportunities produced new problems of their own. Many mothers whose husbands were in the military tried to combine jobs with caring for their children and found the task extraordinarily difficult. The absence of child-care facilities or other community services meant that some women had no choice but to leave young children—often known as "latchkey children" or "eight-hour orphans"—at home alone (or sometimes locked in cars) while they worked. The search for wartime employment also required many women to move to new communities. This geographical mobility often had beneficial economic results, but it also took its toll on family stability.

Perhaps in part because of the family dislocations the war produced, juvenile crime rose markedly in the war years. Young boys were arrested at rapidly increasing rates for car theft and other burglary, vandalism, and vagrancy. The arrest rate for prostitutes, many of whom were teen-age girls, rose too, as did the incidence of venereal disease. For many children, however, the distinctive experience of the war years was not crime but work. More than a third of all teen-agers between the ages of fourteen and eighteen were employed late in the war, causing some reduction in high-school enrollments.

The return of prosperity helped increase the rate and lower the age of marriage, but many of these young marriages were unable to survive the pressures of wartime separation. The divorce rate rose rapidly as well. The rise in the birth rate that accompanied the increase in marriages was the first sign of what would become the great postwar "baby boom."

The Internment of the Japanese-Americans

World War I had produced in America a virtual orgy of hatred, vindictiveness, and hysteria, as well as widespread and flagrant violations of civil liberties. World War II did not. A few papers, among them Father Coughlin's *Social Justice,* were barred from the mails as seditious; but there was no general censorship of dissident publications. A few Nazi agents and American fascists were jailed; but there was no major assault on those suspected of sympathizing with the Axis. Indeed, the most ambitious effort to punish domestic fascists, a sedition trial of twenty-eight people, ended in a mistrial, and the defendants went free. Unlike during World War I, socialists and communists (most of whom strongly supported the war effort) were left unpunished and unpersecuted.

Nor was there much of the ethnic or cultural animosity that had characterized World War I. Americans continued to eat sauerkraut without calling it "liberty cabbage." They displayed little hostility toward German- and Italian-Americans. Instead, they seemed to share the view of government propaganda that the enemy was less the German and Italian people than the vicious political systems to which they had been subjected.

But there was a glaring exception to the general rule of tolerance: the treatment of the small, politically powerless group of Japanese-Americans. From the beginning, Americans adopted a different attitude toward their Asian enemy than they did toward their European foes. They attributed to the Japanese people certain racial and cultural characteristics that made it easier to hold them in contempt. The Japanese, both government and private propaganda encouraged Americans to believe, were a devious, malign, and

Allied Unity

Many Americans hoped to sustain the wartime unity among the Allies in the postwar world and saw in the alliance the key to a stable peace. This poster, celebrating the cooperative efforts of the United States, Britain, the Soviet Union, China, and others, was as much an expression of hope for the future as it was a tribute to the accomplishments of the war years themselves. (West Point Museums Collection, United States Military Academy)

cruel people. The infamous attack on Pearl Harbor seemed to many to confirm that assessment.

It was perhaps unsurprising, therefore, that this growing racial animosity soon extended to Americans of Japanese descent. There were not many Japanese-Americans in the United States—only about 127,000, most of them concentrated in a few areas in California. About a third of them were unnaturalized, first-generation immigrants (Issei); two-thirds were naturalized or native-born citizens of the United States (Nisei). Because they generally kept to themselves and preserved traditional Japanese cultural pat-

terns, it was easy for others to imagine that the Japanese-Americans were engaged in conspiracies on behalf of their ancestral homeland. Wild stories circulated about sabotage at Pearl Harbor and plots to aid a Japanese landing on the coast of California—all later shown to be entirely without foundation. Public pressure to remove the "threat" grew steadily.

Finally, in February 1942, in response to pressure from military officials and political leaders on the West Coast and recommendations from the War Department, the president authorized the army to "intern" the Japanese-Americans. More than 100,000 people (Issei and Nisei alike) were rounded up, told to dispose of their property however they could (which often meant simply abandoning it), and taken to what the government euphemistically termed "relocation centers" in the "interior." In fact, they were facilities little different from prisons, many of them located in the desert. Conditions in the internment camps were not, for the most part, inhumane. Neither, however, were they especially comfortable. More important, a large group of loyal, hard-working Americans were forced to spend up to three years in grim, debilitating isolation, barred from lucrative employment, provided with only minimal medical care, and deprived of decent schools for their children. (Some young men, however, were encouraged to join a Nisei army unit, which fought in Europe.) The Supreme Court upheld the evacuation in a 1944 decision; and although most of the Japanese-Americans were released later that year (after the reelection of the president), they were largely unable to win any compensation for their losses.

The Retreat from Reform

Late in 1943, Franklin Roosevelt publicly suggested that "Dr. New Deal," as he called it, had served its purpose and should now give way to "Dr. Win-the-War." The statement reflected the president's own genuine shift in concern: that victory was now more important than reform. But it reflected, too, the political reality that had emerged during the first two years of war. Liberals in government were finding themselves unable to enact new programs. They were even finding it difficult to protect existing ones from conservative assault.

Within the administration itself, many of the liberals who had in the late 1930s established positions of influence found themselves displaced by the new managers of the wartime agencies, who were drawn overwhelmingly from large corporations and conservative Wall Street law firms. The greatest assault on liberal reform, however, came from Congress. The war provided conservatives there with the excuse they had been waiting for to dismantle many of the achievements of the New Deal, which they had always mistrusted. By the end of 1943, Congress had eliminated the Civilian Conservation Corps, the National Youth Administration, and the Works Progress Administration; and the Farm Security Administration was left virtually impotent. With budget deficits mounting because of war costs, liberals made no headway in their efforts to increase Social Security benefits and otherwise extend social welfare programs.

Even had Roosevelt had the inclination to resist this conservative trend, his awareness of political realities would have been enough to stop him from trying very hard. In the congressional elections of 1942, Republicans gained 47 seats in the House and 10 in the Senate. Increasingly, the president quietly accepted the defeat or erosion of New Deal measures in order to win support for his war policies and peace plans. He also accepted the changes, however, because he realized that his chances for reelection in 1944 depended on his ability to identify himself less with domestic issues than with world peace.

Republicans approached the 1944 election determined to exploit what they believed was a smoldering national resentment of wartime regimentation and privation and a general unhappiness with the pattern of Democratic reform. Also hoping to play on concerns about the deteriorating health of the president, they nominated as their candidate the young and vigorous governor of New York, Thomas E. Dewey. Roosevelt faced no opposition for the Democratic nomination for president; but because he was so visibly in poor health, there was great pressure on him to abandon Vice President Henry Wallace, an advanced New Dealer and hero of the CIO, and replace him with a more moderate figure, acceptable to conservative party bosses and Southern Democrats. Roosevelt reluctantly succumbed to the pressure and selected Senator Harry S. Truman of Missouri, who had won national acclaim as chairman of the Senate War Investigating Committee (known as the Truman Committee), which had compiled an impressive record uncovering waste and corruption in wartime production.

Republican and Democratic leaders agreed in advance that the conduct of the war and the plans for the peace would not be an issue in the campaign. Instead, the campaign revolved around domestic economic issues and, indirectly, the president's health. In reality, the president was suffering from a range of very serious physical maladies (including arteriosclerosis) and also, apparently, from intermittent depression. It may not be too much to say that he was dying. But the campaign seemed momentarily to revive him. At the end of September, he addressed a raucously appreciative audience of members of the Teamsters Union and was at his sardonic best. He followed this triumph with strenuous campaign appearances in Chicago and a day-long drive in an open car through New York City in a soaking rain.

Roosevelt's apparent capacity to serve four more

years, his stature as an international leader, and his promise to workers to revive the New Deal after the war combined to ensure him a substantial victory. He captured 53.5 percent of the popular vote to Dewey's 46 percent; and he won 432 electoral votes to Dewey's 99. Democrats lost 1 seat in the Senate, gained 20 in the House, and maintained control of both.

The Defeat of the Axis

By the middle of 1943, America and its allies had succeeded in stopping the Axis advance both in Europe and in the Pacific. In the next two years, the Allies themselves seized the offensive and launched a series of powerful drives that rapidly led the way to victory.

The Liberation of France

In the fall of 1943, Germany was already reeling under incessant blows from Allied air power. By early 1944, American and British bombers were attacking German industrial installations and other targets almost around the clock, drastically cutting production and impeding transportation. By the winter of 1944, the bombing had seriously demoralized the German people. Especially devastating was the massive bombing of such German cities as Leipzig, Dresden, and Berlin. A February 1944 incendiary raid on Dresden created a great firestorm that destroyed three-fourths of the previously undamaged city and killed tens of thousands of civilians.

The morality of such attacks has been much debated in the years since the war, but the bombing did much to clear the way for the great Allied invasion of France in the late spring. An enormous invasion force had been gathering in England for two years: almost 3 million troops, and perhaps the greatest array of naval vessels and armaments ever assembled in one place in the history of warfare. On the morning of June 6, 1944, after several delays, this vast invasion force moved into action. The landing came not at the narrowest part of the English Channel, where the Germans had expected and prepared for it, but along sixty miles of the Cotentin peninsula on the coast of Normandy. While airplanes and battleships offshore bombarded the Nazi defenses, 4,000 vessels, stretching as far as the eye could see, landed troops and

supplies on the beaches. (Three divisions of paratroopers had been dropped behind the German lines the night before.) Fighting was intense along the beach, but the superior manpower and equipment of the Allied forces gradually prevailed. Within a week, the German forces had been dislodged from virtually the entire Normandy coast; but for more than a month further progress remained slow.

The Battle of Saint-Lô, late in July, was an important turning point. General Omar Bradley's First Army smashed the German lines after a heavy bombardment. George S. Patton's Third Army, spearheaded by heavy tank attacks, then broke through the hole Bradley had created and began a steady drive into the heart of France. On August 25, amid scenes of delirious joy, Free French forces arrived in Paris and liberated the city from four years of German occupation. By mid-September the Allied armies had driven the Germans almost entirely out of France and Belgium. But then they came to a halt at the Rhine River against a firm line of German defenses.

Cold weather, rain, and floods provided the Germans with a temporary respite from the Allied advance in late 1944. Then, in mid-December, the German forces struck in desperation along fifty miles of front in the Ardennes Forest. In the ensuing Battle of the Bulge (named for a large bulge that appeared in the American lines as the Germans pressed forward), they drove fifty-five miles toward Antwerp before they were finally stopped at Bastogne. The battle marked the end of serious German resistance in the west.

While the Allies were fighting their way through France, Soviet forces were sweeping westward into Central Europe and the Balkans. In late January 1945, the Russians launched an offensive of more than 150 divisions toward the Oder River, far inside Germany. By early spring, they were ready to launch a final offensive against Berlin. Omar Bradley pushed on in the meantime toward the Rhine and early in March captured the city of Cologne, on the river's west bank. The next day, through a remarkable stroke of luck, he discovered and seized an undamaged bridge across the river at Remagen; and Allied troops were soon pouring across the Rhine. In the following weeks the British commander, Montgomery, with a million troops, pushed into Germany in the north while Bradley's army, sweeping through central Germany, completed the encirclement of 300,000 German soldiers in the Ruhr.

The German resistance was finally broken on both fronts, and the only real questions remaining involved how the Allies would divide the final tasks of con-

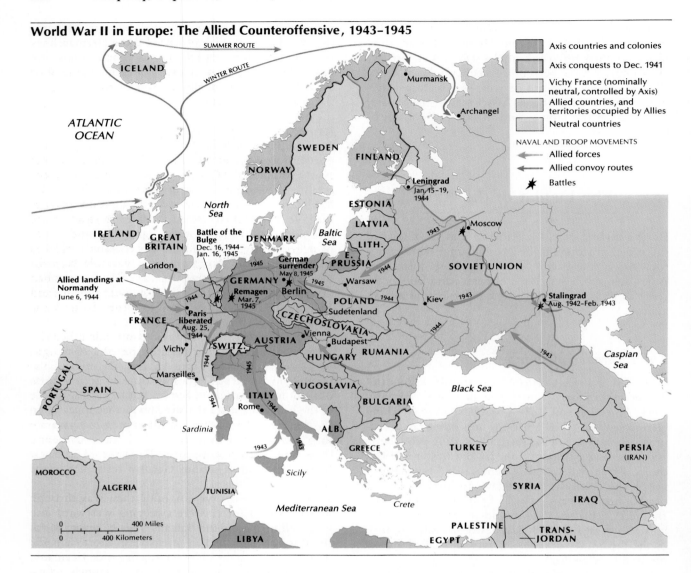

World War II in Europe: The Allied Counteroffensive, 1943–1945

Legend:
- Axis countries and colonies
- Axis conquests to Dec. 1941
- Vichy France (nominally neutral, controlled by Axis)
- Allied countries, and territories occupied by Allies
- Neutral countries

NAVAL AND TROOP MOVEMENTS
- Allied forces
- Allied convoy routes
- ✴ Battles

quest. American forces were moving eastward much faster than they had anticipated and could have beaten the Russians to Berlin and Prague. General Eisenhower decided, instead, to halt his advance along the Elbe River in central Germany to await the Russians. That decision enabled the Soviets to occupy eastern Germany and Czechoslovakia, with major consequences for the future of both countries and the world.

On April 30, with Soviet forces on the outskirts of Berlin, Adolf Hitler killed himself in his bunker in the capital. And on May 8, 1945, the remaining German forces surrendered unconditionally. V-E (Victory in Europe) Day prompted great celebrations in Western Europe and in the United States, tempered only by the knowledge of the continuing war against Japan.

The Pacific Offensive

The victory in Europe had come more quickly than most military leaders had expected; less than a year after the Normandy landing, the war against Germany was over. The victory in the Pacific was expected to take far longer, but events there proceeded with unexpected speed as well.

In February 1944, American naval forces under

Admiral Nimitz won a series of victories in the Marshall Islands and cracked the outer perimeter of the Japanese Empire. Before the month was out, the navy had plunged far within it to destroy other Japanese bastions. American submarines, in the meantime, were wreaking havoc on Japanese shipping and crippling the nation's domestic economy. By the summer of 1944, the already skimpy food rations for the Japanese people had been reduced by nearly a quarter; there was also a crucial gasoline shortage.

A more frustrating struggle was in progress in the meantime on the Asian mainland. In 1942, the Japanese had forced General Joseph H. Stilwell out of Burma and had moved their own troops as far west as the mountains bordering on India. Stilwell organized an aerial ferry over the Himalayas to supply the isolated Chinese forces continuing to resist Japan and to bring Chinese troops out for Stilwell to train and arm. In 1943, Stilwell led Chinese, Indian, and a few American troops back through northern Burma, constructing a road and a parallel pipeline across the rugged mountains into Yunnan province of China. The Burma Road (also known as the Ledo Road or Stilwell Road) finally opened in the fall of 1944. By then, however, the Japanese had launched a major counteroffensive, capturing some of the bases from which American air strikes against the Japanese mainland had been launched and driving so deep into the Chinese interior that they threatened the terminus of the Ledo Road and the center of government at Chungking.

The great Japanese offensive precipitated a long-simmering crisis in Chinese-American affairs, centering on the relations between General Stilwell and Premier Chiang Kai-shek. Stilwell was contemptuous of Chiang and indignant because the Chinese leader was using many of his troops to maintain an armed frontier against the Chinese communists and would not deploy those troops against the Japanese.

The decisive battles of the Pacific War, however, occurred not on the mainland but in the central and western Pacific. In mid-June 1944, an enormous American armada struck the heavily fortified Mariana Islands and, after some of the bloodiest operations of the war, captured Tinian, Guam, and Saipan, 1,350 miles from Tokyo. In September, American forces landed on the western Carolines. And on October 20, General MacArthur's troops landed on Leyte Island in the Philippines. The Japanese now mobilized their remaining strength for a last defense of their empire and employed virtually their entire fleet against the Allied invaders in three major encoun-

ters—which together constituted the decisive Battle of Leyte Gulf, the largest naval engagement in history. American forces held off the Japanese onslaught and sank four Japanese carriers, all but destroying Japan's capacity to continue a serious naval war.

Toward Final Victory

The defeat of Japan now seemed inevitable, but the war was not yet over. As American forces advanced steadily closer to the Japanese mainland early in 1945, the imperial forces seemed only to increase their resistance. Fighting continued in the Philippines. In the meantime, American marines moved in February to seize the tiny volcanic island of Iwo Jima, only 750 miles from Tokyo, a potentially valuable base for future air strikes against Japan. The Japanese defended the island so ferociously that the marines suffered over 20,000 casualties. It was the costliest battle in the history of the Marine Corps.

The battle for Okinawa, an island only 370 miles south of Japan, was further evidence of the strength of the Japanese resistance in these last desperate days. Week after week, the Japanese sent Kamikaze suicide planes against American and British ships, sacrificing 3,500 of them while inflicting great damage. Japanese troops on shore launched equally desperate nighttime attacks on the American lines. The United States and its allies suffered nearly 50,000 casualties on land and sea before finally capturing Okinawa in late June 1945. Over 100,000 Japanese died in that encounter.

The same kind of bitter fighting seemed to await the Americans when they invaded Japan. But there were signs early in 1945 that such an invasion might not be necessary. The Japanese had almost no ships or planes left with which to fight and seemed unable to mount even token resistance to American challenges at sea. In July 1945, for example, American warships stood off the shore of Japan and shelled industrial targets (many already in ruins from aerial bombings) with impunity. The brutal firebombing of Tokyo in May, in which American bombers dropped napalm on the city and created a firestorm in which over 80,000 died, had further weakened the will to resist.

Moderate Japanese leaders, who had long since decided that the war was lost, were in the meantime increasing their power within the government. After the invasion of Okinawa, Emperor Hirohito appointed a new premier and gave him instructions to sue for peace. Although the new leader could not persuade military leaders to give up the fight, he did try, along with the emperor himself, to obtain mediation through the Soviet Union. The Russians showed little interest in playing the role of arbitrator, but other developments made their participation superfluous in any case. For at a meeting of Allied leaders in Potsdam, Germany, in mid-July 1945, President Harry S. Truman (who had succeeded to the office on the death of Franklin Roosevelt three months earlier) received news of the first successful test of an atomic weapon.

The Manhattan Project

Reports had reached the United States in 1939, through the Italian physicist Enrico Fermi and the German mathematician Albert Einstein (then living in exile in America), that Nazi scientists had learned how to produce atomic fission in uranium. That knowledge, they warned, could be the first step toward the creation of a bomb more powerful than any weapon ever devised. The United States and Britain immediately began a race to develop the weapon before the Germans did.

In December 1942, American physicists produced a controlled chain reaction in an atomic pile at the University of Chicago, solving the first great problem in producing an atomic weapon. There remained the enormous technical problems of achieving the release of this power in a bomb. Over the next three years, the government secretly poured nearly $2 billion into the so-called Manhattan Project—a massive scientific effort conducted at hidden laboratories in Oak Ridge, Tennessee, Los Alamos, New Mexico, and other sites. (Its name had emerged earlier, when many of the atomic physicists had been working at Columbia University in New York.) Hundreds of scientists, many of them not fully aware of what they were working on, labored feverishly to complete two complementary projects. One (at Oak Ridge) was the production of fissionable plutonium, the fuel for an atomic explosion; the other (at Los Alamos, under the supervision of J. Robert Oppenheimer) was the construction of a bomb that could employ the fuel. The scientists pushed ahead far faster than anyone had predicted. Even so, the war in Europe had ended by the time they were ready to test the first bomb. (Only later did they discover that the Germans had never come close to constructing a usable atomic device.)

On July 16, 1945, the Manhattan Project scientists stood on a hill near Los Alamos, New Mexico,

Kamikazes in the Pacific
In the last months of the war, as the fighting moved closer to the Japanese mainland, desperate military leaders dispatched waves of suicide bombers ("kamikazes"), whose pilots attempted to crash their planes into American ships. Here a burning kamikaze, already damaged by antiaircraft fire, takes aim at one of the ships escorting an American carrier.   (UPI/Bettmann Newsphotos)

watching a tower several miles away on which was suspended the fruits of their labor. And just before dawn, they witnessed the first atomic explosion in history: a blinding flash of light brighter than any ever seen on earth, and a huge, billowing mushroom cloud. Some were exhilarated by their success. Others, among them J. Robert Oppenheimer, were already troubled by the implications of what they had done. Standing on the New Mexico desert watching the terrible explosion, Oppenheimer thought grimly of the words from Hindu Scripture: "Now I am become death, the destroyer of worlds."

Atomic Warfare

As soon as news of the explosion reached Truman in Potsdam, he issued an ultimatum to the Japanese (signed jointly by the British) demanding that they surrender immediately or face utter devastation. He set a deadline of August 3. The Japanese premier wanted to accept the Allied demand, but by the time the deadline arrived he had not yet been able to persuade the military leaders to agree. There was reason to believe that the government might be willing to surrender, in return for a promise that the Japanese could retain their emperor (who was, even then, a largely symbolic ruler). The American government apparently disregarded those overtures; and when the August 3 deadline came and went without a settlement, Truman ordered the air force to use the new atomic weapons against Japan.

Controversy has raged for decades over whether Truman's decision to use the bomb was justified and what his motives were. Some have argued that the atomic attack was unnecessary, that had the United States agreed to the survival of the emperor (which it ultimately did agree to in any case), or had it waited only a few more weeks, the Japanese would have surrendered anyway. Others argue that nothing less than the atomic bombs could have persuaded the Japanese to surrender without an American invasion.

Some critics of the decision, including some of the scientists involved in the Manhattan Project, have argued that whatever Japanese intentions, the United States, as a matter of moral conviction, should not have used the terrible new weapon. One horrified physicist wrote the president shortly before the attack: "This thing must not be permitted to exist on this earth. We must not be the most hated and feared people in the world." The nation's military and political leaders, however, showed little concern about such matters. Truman, through no fault of his own, had not even been aware of the bomb's existence until a few weeks before he was called on to decide whether to use it. And knowing so little about it, he could hardly have been expected to recognize the full implications of its power. He was, apparently, making what he believed to be a simple military decision. A weapon was available that would end the war quickly; he could see no reason not to use it.

Still more controversy has existed over whether there were other motives at work in Truman's decision as well. With the Soviet Union poised to enter the war in the Pacific, did the United States want to end the conflict quickly to forestall an expanded communist presence in Asia? Did Truman use the bomb as a weapon to intimidate Stalin, with whom he was engaged in difficult negotiations, so the Soviet leader would accept American demands? Little direct evidence is available to support either of these accusations, but historians continue to disagree on the issue.

Whatever the reasons, the decision was made. On August 6, 1945, an American B-29, the *Enola Gay,* dropped an atomic weapon on the Japanese industrial center at Hiroshima. With a single bomb, the United States completely incinerated a four-square-mile area at the center of the previously undamaged city. More than 80,000 civilians died, according to later American estimates. Many more survived to suffer the painful and crippling effects of radioactive fallout or to pass those effects on to their children in the form of serious birth defects.

The Japanese government, stunned by the attack, was at first unable to agree on a response. Two days later, on August 8, the Soviet Union declared war on Japan. And the following day, another American plane dropped another atomic weapon—this time on the city of Nagasaki—inflicting horrible damage on yet another unfortunate community. Finally, the emperor intervened to break the stalemate in the cabinet; and on August 14, the government announced that it was ready to give up. On September 2, 1945, on board the American battleship *Missouri,* anchored in Tokyo Bay, Japanese officials signed the articles of surrender.

The greatest war in the history of mankind had come to an end, and the United States had emerged from it not only victorious, but in a position of unprecedented power, influence, and prestige. It was a victory, however, that few could greet with unambiguous joy. Fourteen million men under arms had died in the struggle. Many more civilians had perished. The United States had suffered only light casualties in comparison with some other nations, but the totals were frightful nevertheless: 322,000 dead, another 800,000 injured. And in spite of having paid so high a price for peace, the world continued to face an uncertain future. The menace of nuclear warfare hung like a black cloud on the horizon. And already the world's two strongest nations—the United States and the Soviet Union—were developing antagonisms toward one other that would darken the peace for many decades to come.

SIGNIFICANT EVENTS

1921   Washington Conference leads to reductions in naval armaments

1922   Fordney-McCumber Tariff passed

1924   Dawes Plan renegotiates European debts, reparations

1928   Kellogg-Briand Pact signed

1930   Hawley-Smoot Tariff passed

1931   Economic crisis spreads worldwide
Japan invades Manchuria

1932   World Disarmament Conference held in Geneva

1933   Adolf Hitler becomes chancellor of Germany
United States scuttles London Economic Conference
United States establishes diplomatic relations with Soviet Union
Roosevelt proclaims Good Neighbor Policy

1935   Senate defeats World Court treaty
Neutrality Act passed
Italy invades Ethiopia

1936   Spanish Civil War begins
Germany reoccupies Rhineland
A second Neutrality Act passed

1937   Japan launches new invasion of China
Roosevelt gives "quarantine" speech
Japan attacks U.S. gunboat *Panay*
A third Neutrality Act passed

1938   Germany annexes Austria (*Anschluss*)

1939   Munich Conference
Nazi-Soviet nonaggression pact signed
Germany invades Czechoslovakia
Germany invades Poland
World War II begins

1940   Soviet Union invades Baltic nations, Finland
German *blitzkrieg* conquers most of Western Europe
Germany, Italy, Japan sign Tripartite Pact
Fight for Freedom Committee founded

1940   America First Committee founded
Roosevelt reelected president
United States makes destroyers-for-bases deal with Britain
Selective Service Act passed

1941   A. Philip Randolph proposes march on Washington
Roosevelt establishes Fair Employment Practices Commission
Lend-lease plan provides aid to Britain
American ships confront German submarines in North Atlantic
Germany invades Soviet Union
Atlantic Charter signed
Japan attacks Pearl Harbor
United States enters war

1942   Japanese capture Philippines
Battle of Midway
North Africa campaign begins
News of Holocaust reaches United States
War Production Board created
Japanese-Americans interned
Manhattan Project begins

1943   Americans capture Guadalcanal
Soviets defeat Germans at Stalingrad
Allies launch invasion of Italy
Smith-Connally Act passed
Race riot breaks out in Detroit

1944   Allies invade Normandy
Roosevelt reelected president
Americans recapture Philippines

1945   Roosevelt dies; Truman becomes president
Hitler kills himself
Allies capture Berlin
Germany surrenders
Americans capture Okinawa
Atomic bomb tested in New Mexico
United States drops atomic bombs on Hiroshima and Nagasaki
Japan surrenders

SUGGESTED READINGS

The 1920s   For the foreign policy of the 1920s, see L. Ethan Ellis, *Republican Foreign Policy, 1921–1933* (1968); Selig Adler, *The Uncertain Giant* (1965); and Merlo J. Pusey, *Charles Evans Hughes,* 2 vols. (1963). Joan Hoff Wilson, *American Business and Foreign Policy, 1920–1933* (1968) and *Ideology and Economics* (1974), discuss corporate influence on diplomacy and the relationship with the Soviet Union, respectively. William Appleman Williams, *The Tragedy of American Diplomacy* (1962), is a revisionist critique of economic influences on foreign policy. American policy toward Europe is the subject of Frank Costigliola, *Awkward Dominion: American Political, Economic, and Cultural Relations with Europe, 1919–1933* (1984). For American policy in the Pacific, see Akira Iriye, *After Imperialism* (1965), and Warren Cohen, *America's Response to China* (1971). Roger Dingman, *Power in the Pacific* (1976), and Thomas Buckley, *The United States and the Washington Conference* (1970), examine the 1921–1922 naval conference; while Robert H. Ferrell, *Peace in Their Time* (1952), looks at the Kellogg-Briand Pact. For the United States and Latin America, see Joseph Tulchin, *The Aftermath of War* (1971), and William Kamman, *A Search for Stability* (1968). Michael J. Hogan, *Informal Entente: The Private Structure of Cooperation in Anglo-American Economic Diplomacy, 1918–1928* (1977), examines America's relationship to the world economy.

The Hoover Years   See Robert H. Ferrell, *American Diplomacy in the Great Depression* (1970); Elting Morison, *Turmoil and Tradition* (1960), a biography of Henry Stimson; Alexander DeConde, *Hoover's Latin American Policy* (1951); Raymond O'Connor, *Perilous Equilibrium* (1962), a study of the 1930 London Naval Conference; and Armin Rappaport, *Stimson and Japan* (1963).

New Deal Diplomacy   The best and most thorough account of the foreign policy of the Roosevelt administration is Robert Dallek, *Franklin D. Roosevelt and American Foreign Policy, 1932–1945* (1979). New Deal international economic policy is considered in Lloyd Gardner, *Economic Aspects of New Deal Diplomacy* (1964). Frank Freidel, *Launching the New Deal* (1973), examines the London Economic Conference. Two areas that received special diplomatic attention during the first years of the New Deal are dealt with in Beatrice Farnsworth, *William C. Bullitt and the Soviet Union* (1967); Robert Browder, *The Origins of Soviet-American Diplomacy* (1953); Edward E. Bennett, *Recognition of Russia* (1970); Bryce Wood, *The Making of the Good Neighbor Policy* (1961); Irwin F. Gellman, *Good Neighbor Diplomacy: United States Policies in Latin America, 1933–1945* (1979); and David Green, *The Containment of Latin America* (1971). Dorothy Borg, *The United States and the Far Eastern Crisis of 1933–1938* (1964), examines New Deal diplomacy in Asia.

The Coming of World War II   Overviews of the origins of American involvement in World War II include Selig Adler, *The Uncertain Giant* (1966); Robert Divine, *The Reluctant Belligerent* (1965); and Arnold Offner, *The Origins of the Second World War* (1975). William Langer and S. Everett

Gleason, *The Challenge to Isolation* (1952) and *The Undeclared War* (1953), are thorough, standard accounts. The rise of isolationist sentiment is chronicled in Selig Adler, *The Isolationist Impulse* (1957), and in Manfred Jonas, *Isolationism in America* (1966). Wayne S. Cole, *Charles A. Lindbergh and the Battle Against American Intervention in World War II* (1974), is a valuable specialized study; while his *Roosevelt and the Isolationists, 1932–1945* (1983) is a major overview. See also John K. Nelson, *The Peace Prophets* (1967), and Wayne S. Cole, *Senator Gerald P. Nye and American Foreign Relations* (1962). The 1940 campaign receives attention in Bernard F. Donahoe, *Private Plans and Public Dangers* (1965). The final steps toward war are recounted in James Leutze, *Bargaining for Supremacy* (1977), a valuable study of Anglo-American cooperation; Joseph Lash, *Roosevelt and Churchill* (1976); Warren Kimball, *The Most Unsordid Act* (1970), a study of lend-lease; Herbert Feis, *The Road to Pearl Harbor* (1950); and James MacGregor Burns, *Roosevelt: The Soldier of Freedom* (1970). Roberta Wohlstetter, *Pearl Harbor: Warning and Decision* (1962), is an invaluable study of the American handling of the 1941 fiasco. Gordon W. Prange, *At Dawn We Slept* (1981), is an important study of Pearl Harbor, much of it from the Japanese perspective.

War and American Society   General studies of the effects of the war on American society include John Morton Blum, *V Was for Victory* (1976), and Richard Polenberg, *War and Society* (1972). For the story of the war production effort specifically, see Donald Nelson, *Arsenal of Democracy* (1946), the WPB director's personal memoirs; Bruce Catton, *War Lords of Washington* (1946); and Eliot Janeway, *Struggle for Survival* (1951). Joel Seidman, *American Labor from Defense to Reconversion* (1953), and Nelson Lichtenstein, *Labor's War at Home* (1982), examine the experience of workers. Howell John Harris, *The Right to Manage* (1982), is a study of the efforts of business executives to regain power over their workers during the war. Leslie R. Groves, *Now It Can Be Told* (1962), is an account of the development of the atomic bomb by the general who commanded the Manhattan Project; Oscar E. Anderson, Jr., *The New World* (1962), is another valuable study of the subject. Chester Bowles, *Promises to Keep* (1971), and Lester V. Chandler, *Inflation in the United States, 1940–1948* (1951), are studies of price controls. Alan Winkler, *The Politics of Propaganda* (1978), and Philip Knightley, *The First Casualty* (1975), examine the effects of war on the press and vice versa. James MacGregor Burns, *Roosevelt: The Soldier of Freedom* (1970), includes information about domestic politics and the 1944 election. Ellsworth Barnard, *Wendell Willkie* (1966), sheds light on the activities of the Republicans during the war. For wartime civil-rights activities, see Louis Ruchames, *Race, Jobs, and Politics* (1953), a study of the establishment of the Fair Employment Practices Commission; Neil Wynn, *The Afro-American and the Second World War* (1976); and Herbert Garfinkel, *When Negroes March* (1959). Richard M. Dalfiume, *Desegregation of the U.S. Armed Forces* (1969), examines the racial situation within the military; and August Meier and Elliott Rudwick, *CORE* (1973), studies the emergence of an important civil-rights organization. Roger Daniels, *The Politics of Prejudice* (1962) and *Concentration Camps, USA* (1971), Audrie Girdner and Anne Loftis, *The Great Betrayal* (1969), and Bill Hosokawa, *Nisei* (1969), study the internment of Japanese-Americans; but the most comprehensive study is Peter Irons, *Justice at War* (1983).

Wartime Military and Diplomatic Experiences   James MacGregor Burns, *Roosevelt: The Soldier of Freedom* (1970), recounts the military struggle through the experiences of the president. See also Robert Divine, *Roosevelt and World War II* (1969) and *Second Chance* (1967). Albert Russell Buchanan, *The United States and World War II,* 2 vols. (1962), is an extensive survey of both the domestic and the military experience. Briefer accounts include Fletcher Pratt, *War for the World* (1951); Margaret Hoyle, *A World in Flames* (1970); and Kenneth Greenfield, *American Strategy in World War II* (1963). See also Samuel Eliot Morison, *Strategy and Compromise* (1958), an analysis of strategic decision making, and *History of United States Naval Operations in World War II,* 14 vols. (1947–1960). A summary of the latter work is *The Two Ocean War* (1963). Winston S. Churchill, *The Second World War,* 6 vols. (1948–1953), is an invaluable account, written from a British perspective. Chester Wilmot, *The Struggle for Europe* (1952), and Charles B. McDonald, *The Mighty Endeavor* (1969), consider the American effort in Europe. See also Stephen Ambrose, *The Supreme Commander* (1970), an examination of Eisenhower's wartime command; Michael Howard, *The Mediterranean Strategy in World War II* (1968); and Dwight D. Eisenhower, *Crusade in Europe* (1948). Forrest Pogue, *George C. Marshall,* 2 vols. (1963–1966), examines the chief American strategist. Cornelius Ryan, *The Last Battle* (1966), and John Toland, *The Last Hundred Days* (1966), recount the end of the war in Europe. David S. Wyman, *The Abandonment of the Jews: America and the Holocaust, 1941–1945* (1984), is sharply critical of American failures to do more to help the Jews of Europe. Gaddis Smith, *American Diplomacy During the Second World War* (1965), examines the relationships among the wartime Allies. For the war in the Pacific, see E. J. Kind and W. M. Whitehill, *Fleet Admiral King* (1952); Barbara Tuchman, *Stilwell and the American Experience in China* (1971); John Toland, *The Rising Sun* (1970); Ronald Spector, *Eagle Against the Sun: The American War with Japan* (1985); and William Manchester, *American Caesar* (1979), a biography of Douglas MacArthur. On the use of the atomic bomb in Japan (and the diplomatic implications of the weapon), see Martin Sherwin, *A World Destroyed* (1975); Gar Alperovitz, *Atomic Diplomacy: Hiroshima and Potsdam,* rev. ed. (1985); Robert Jungk, *Brighter Than a Thousand Suns* (1958); Nuel Davis, *Lawrence and Oppenheimer* (1969); Gregg Herken, *The Winning Weapon* (1980); and W. S. Schoenberger, *Decision of Destiny* (1969). Robert Donovan, *Conflict and Crisis* (1977), an account of the first years of Truman's presidency, examines the new president's decision to use the nuclear weapon. John Hersey, *Hiroshima* (1946), describes the horrible effects of the first atomic attack.

The American Century, Since 1945

"What can we say and foresee about an American Century?" the publisher Henry Luce asked in 1941. "How shall it be created?" It was a question that many Americans were asking in the aftermath of World War II. Having emerged from the conflict not only victorious but the most admired and powerful nation in the world, the United States in 1945 viewed its future with high and fervent hopes. To predict that the coming years would constitute an "American Century" did not seem presumptuous.

To Henry Luce and to many others, America's destiny seemed clear. "It must be a sharing with all peoples of our Bill of Rights, our Declaration of Independence, our Constitution, our magnificent industrial products, our technological skills." The United States must serve as "the dynamic center of ever-widening spheres of enterprise . . . as the training center of the skilled servants of mankind—as the Good Samaritan, really believing again that it is more blessed to give than to receive." Out of these elements, Luce predicted, "surely can be fashioned a vision of the 20th Century to which we can and will devote ourselves in joy and gladness and vigor and enthusiasm."

It was a heady vision—a vision of a peaceful world united by bonds of mutual cooperation. But it was more than that. It was a vision of a world molded in the American image, a world in which the

United States would reign unchallenged as the preeminent military, economic, and moral force. And it was a vision that would enchant the American people for more than two decades.

This sense of America's special virtues was in some respects a defensive reaction to a pervasive unease in the postwar years. For shortly after the end of World War II, the United States found itself embroiled in a new world struggle—a long, grim, and dangerous competition with the Soviet Union for international supremacy. The world had moved from the horrors of "total war" to the tensions of another type of conflict: what the columnist Walter Lippmann christened the "Cold War." And although only intermittently did the Cold War produce actual military conflict, it maintained an unbroken, icy grip on the world, and on American society, for decades.

But the enduring appeal of the American Century idea was a result, too, of the remarkable growth and prosperity of American society in the postwar years. The nation's economy, having revived from the Great Depression during the war, continued in the following decades to perform remarkable feats. Indeed, never in the history of the world had a nation enjoyed such astounding economic progress as did the United States in the twenty years after 1945. For a time, it was possible to believe that America had found the secret of permanent, uninterrupted prosperity.

In both foreign and domestic affairs, therefore, the United States behaved in the postwar years with remarkable assertiveness. Having abandoned most of the vestiges of isolationism, the nation now used its influence in the world in ways that earlier generations had never contemplated. The struggle against communism seemed to require constant vigilance and constant activism. No area of the globe was outside the range of American concerns; and in large ways and small, the United States found itself involved—economically, politically, and at times militarily—throughout the world in an apparently ceaseless effort to protect its own vision of the future.

At home, Americans were similarly expansive in their vision of their obligations and capabilities. By the late 1950s, in particular, a vigorous, crusading liberalism was emerging as the dominant force in

P·A·R·T S·E·V·E·N

American politics. And in response to that spirit, the nation embarked on a series of ambitious efforts to solve its remaining social problems. Because the economy was creating such enormous wealth, it did not seem unreasonable to assume that society could be purged at last of poverty and injustice. And it was the federal government, most liberals believed, that would be the essential agent of change.

For a time, it all seemed to work. The Cold War was not won, certainly; but America's aggressive foreign policy appeared to be an effective response to the communist challenge. Social problems were not eliminated, but there was impressive progress. In the mid–1960s, however, the dream of an American Century began to encounter powerful obstacles. The commitment to combating communism throughout the world led the United States into a disastrous military venture in Vietnam—a war that dragged on inconclusively for more than seven years, eroding America's stature in the world and poisoning the political and social atmosphere at home. And the commitment to solving domestic social problems propelled Americans into an ambitious assault on the deepest national injustice of all: the oppression of the nation's black citizens. That assault produced important and long-overdue improvements in the status of blacks in America. But like the war in Vietnam, it proved to be a far more difficult and costly commitment than most Americans had at first envisioned. And it helped to produce widespread social conflict and bitterness.

Together, these twin crises—war and race—led the United States into a period of wrenching national turbulence in the late 1960s, a crisis that for a time appeared to threaten the very foundations of American society. The turmoil ultimately subsided; but in its aftermath nothing was quite the same. For a time, at least, Americans appeared to have lost confidence in their ability to shape the destiny of the world and to solve their problems at home. Confronted with evidence of the limits of its capacities, the nation seemed to be seized with self-doubt—until a new, conservative political spirit emerged in the early 1980s and attempted to revive at least some of the expansive visions of earlier years.

American Cold War Poster Aimed at the Philippines, late 1940s . (Library of Congress)

Chapter 28 America and the Cold War

The immediate aftermath of World War II was a trying time for the United States. Having emerged from the struggle indisputably the greatest power in the world, America assumed that the peace would take a form to its liking. It did not. Almost immediately, it became clear that another great power—a nation not yet as strong as the United States, but strong enough to make its influence felt—had a very different vision of the postwar order. Even before the war ended, there were signs of tension between the United States and the Soviet Union, who had fought together so effectively as allies. Once the hostilities were over, those tensions quickly grew to create an enduring "Cold War" between the two nations that would cast its shadow over the entire course of international affairs for decades.

At the same time, the American people were experiencing the predictable upheavals of readjustment to civilian life. The economy was undergoing a difficult transformation in preparation for the remarkable growth that was soon to follow. Politics was in some confusion, partly as a result of the death of Franklin Roosevelt in April 1945. And the specter of the Cold War was having profound effects on American domestic life, ultimately producing the most corrosive outbreak of antiradical hysteria of the century. America in the postwar years was both powerful and prosperous; but it was also for a time troubled and uncertain about its future.

Origins of the Cold War

No issue in twentieth-century American history has aroused more debate than the question of the origins of the Cold War. Two questions, in particular, have provoked controversy: When did it begin? Who was to blame? Some have argued that the Cold War could have been avoided as late as 1947 or 1948, others that it was virtually inevitable long before the end of World War II. Some have claimed that Soviet duplicity and expansionism created the international tensions, others that American provocations and imperial ambitions were at least equally to blame. On virtually every aspect of the history of the Cold War, disagreement remains rampant. (See "Where Historians Disagree," pp. 798–799.)

But if historians have reached no general accord on these questions, they have gradually arrived at something approaching a consensus on some of the outlines of the debate. Most would agree that the origins of the Cold War can be understood only by looking at both the historic background of Soviet-American relations and the specific events of 1945 through 1948. And most would also agree that, wherever the preponderance of blame may lie, both the United States and the Soviet Union contributed to the atmosphere of hostility and suspicion that quickly clouded the peace.

A Legacy of Mistrust

The wartime alliance between the United States and the Soviet Union was an aberration from the normal tenor of Soviet-American relations. Ever since the Bolshevik Revolution of 1917, the two nations had viewed each other with deep mutual mistrust.

The reasons for American hostility toward the Soviet Union were both obvious and many. There was, of course, the fundamental American animosity

─────────── WHERE HISTORIANS DISAGREE ───────────

Origins of the Cold War

No issue in recent American history has produced more controversy than that of the origins of the Cold War between the United States and the Soviet Union. In particular, historians have disagreed as to who was responsible for the breakdown of American-Soviet relations and whether the conflict between the two superpowers was inevitable or could have been avoided.

For more than a decade after the end of World War II, few historians saw any reason to challenge the official American interpretation of the beginnings of the Cold War. Thomas A. Bailey spoke for most students of the conflict when he argued, in *America Faces Russia* (1950), that the breakdown of relations was a direct result of aggressive Soviet policies of expansion in the immediate postwar years. Stalin's government violated solemn promises he had made in the Yalta accords, imposed Soviet-dominated governments on the unwilling nations of Eastern Europe, and schemed to spread communism throughout the world. American policy was the logical and necessary response: a firm commitment to oppose Soviet expansionism and to retain its armed forces in a continual state of preparedness.

The American involvement in Vietnam in the 1960s disillusioned many historians with the premises of the containment policy and thus with the traditional view of the origins of the Cold War. But even before the conflict in Asia had reached major proportions, the first works in what would become known as the "revisionist" interpretation began to appear. William Appleman Williams began to challenge the accepted wisdom as early as 1952; and in 1959 he published *The Tragedy of American Diplomacy*, which studied the Cold War in the context of American foreign policy throughout the twentieth century. The United States had operated in world affairs, Williams argued, in response to one overriding concern: its commitment

to maintaining an "open door" for American trade in world markets. The confrontation with the Soviet Union, therefore, was less a response to Russian aggressive designs than an expression of the American belief in the necessity of capitalist expansion.

Later revisionists modified many of Williams's claims. But most accepted some of the basic outlines of his thesis: that the United States had been primarily to blame for the Cold War; that the Soviet Union had displayed no aggressive designs toward the West (and was so weak and exhausted at the end of World War II as to be unable to pose any serious threat to America in any case); that the United States had used its nuclear monopoly to attempt to threaten and intimidate Stalin; that Harry Truman had recklessly abandoned the conciliatory policies of Franklin Roosevelt and taken a provocative hard line against the Russians; and that the Soviet response had reflected a legitimate fear of capitalist encirclement. Walter LaFeber, in *America, Russia, and the Cold War, 1945-1967* (1967), maintained that America's supposedly idealistic internationalism at the close of the war—its vision of "One World," with every nation in control of its own destiny—was in reality an effort to ensure a world shaped in the American image, with every nation open to American influence (and to American trade).

Crucial to many revisionist arguments has been the American decision to use atomic weapons against Japan in the closing days of World War II. As early as 1948, a British physicist, P. M. S. Blackett, wrote in *Fear, War, and the Bomb* that the destruction of Hiroshima and Nagasaki was "not so much the last military act of the second World War as the first major operation of the cold diplomatic war with Russia." Gar Alperovitz expanded that idea in *Atomic Diplomacy* (1965), in which he claimed that American decision makers

toward communism, which had strong roots in the nation's past and had been a powerful force in society since well before the Russian Revolution. But there were more specific reasons as well. Americans never forgot the separate peace that the Soviet government had negotiated with Germany in 1917, leaving the West to fight the Central Powers alone. They had

chafed at the strident attacks on the American capitalist system emanating from Moscow—attacks that proved particularly grating during the 1930s, when that system was under duress. They had long been concerned about the Soviet regime's open avowal of the need for world revolution. They had felt a deep and understandable revulsion at the bloody Stalinist

WHERE HISTORIANS DISAGREE

used the bombs on an already defeated Japan not to win the war (for the war was already won) but to impress and intimidate the Soviets, to make them more "manageable." In fact, Alperovitz argued, this atomic diplomacy had the opposite effect: It convinced the Soviet Union of America's hostile intentions and helped bring about the Cold War.

Ultimately, the revisionist interpretation began to produce a reaction of its own, what some have called the "counterrevisionist" view of the conflict. Some manifestations of this reaction have consisted of little more than a reaffirmation of the traditional view of the Cold War. Herbert Feis, for example, argued in *The Atomic Bomb and the End of World War II* (1966) that the revisionist claim that the use of nuclear weapons on Japan was a tactic to intimidate the Soviets was unfounded, that Truman had made his decision on purely military grounds—to ensure a speedy American victory and eliminate the need for what was expected to be a long and costly invasion of Japan. Others challenged the revisionists by accepting some of their findings but rejecting their most important claims. Arthur M. Schlesinger, Jr., admitted in a 1967 article that the Soviets may not have been committed to world conquest, as most earlier accounts had claimed. Nevertheless, the Soviets (and Stalin in particular) were motivated by a deep-seated paranoia about the West, which made them insistent on dominating Eastern Europe and rendered any amicable relationship between them and the United States impossible.

But the dominant works of counterrevisionist scholarship have attempted to strike a balance between the two camps, to identify areas of blame and misconception on both sides of the conflict. Thomas G. Paterson, in *Soviet-American Confrontation* (1973), viewed Russian hostility and American efforts to dominate the postwar world as equally responsible for the Cold War. John Lewis Gaddis, in *The United States and the Origins of the Cold War, 1941–1947* (1972), similarly maintained that "neither side can bear sole responsibility for the onset of the Cold War." American policymakers, he argued, had only limited options because of the pressures of domestic politics. And Stalin was immobilized by his obsessive concern with maintaining his own power and ensuring absolute security for the Soviet Union. But if neither side is entirely to blame, Gaddis concluded, the Soviets must be held at least slightly more accountable for the problems; for Stalin was in a much better position to compromise, given his broader power within his own government, than the politically hamstrung Truman.

Out of the postrevisionist literature has begun to emerge a new and more complex view of the Cold War, one that de-emphasizes the question of who was to blame and adopts a more detached view of the conflict. The Cold War, recent historians suggest, was not so much the fault of one side or the other as it was the natural result, perhaps the inevitable result, of predictable tensions between the world's two most powerful nations—two nations that had been suspicious of, if not hostile toward, one another for nearly a century. As Ernest May has written, in a 1984 essay:

> After the Second World War, the United States and the Soviet Union were doomed to be antagonists. . . . There probably was never any real possibility that the post-1945 relationship could be anything but hostility verging on conflict. . . . Traditions, belief systems, propinquity, and convenience . . . all combined to stimulate antagonism, and almost no factor operated in either country to hold it back.

purges of the 1930s. And they had been deeply embittered in 1939 when Stalin and Hitler agreed to the short-lived Nazi-Soviet Pact.

But Soviet hostility toward the United States had deep roots as well. Russian leaders were well aware of the American opposition to their revolution in 1917, and they never forgot that the United States had sent troops into the Soviet Union at the end of World War I to work, they believed, to overthrow their new government. They resented their exclusion from the international community throughout the two decades following World War I; Russia had been invited to participate in neither the Versailles Conference in 1919 nor the Munich Conference in 1938.

The Stalin regime remembered, too, the long delay by the United States in recognizing the Soviet government; the two nations did not exchange ambassadors until 1933, sixteen years after the Revolution. And just as most Americans viewed communism with foreboding and contempt, so did most Russian communists harbor deep suspicions of and a genuine distaste for industrial capitalism. There was, in short, a powerful legacy of mistrust on both sides.

In some respects, the wartime experience helped to abate that mistrust. Both the United States and the Soviet Union tended to focus during the war less on the traditional image of a dangerous potential foe and more on the image of a brave and dauntless ally. Americans expressed open admiration for the courage of Soviet forces in withstanding the Nazi onslaught and began to depict Stalin less as the bloody ogre of the purges than as the wise and persevering "Uncle Joe." The Soviet government, similarly, praised both the American fighting forces and the wisdom and courage of Franklin Roosevelt.

In other respects, however, the war deepened the gulf between the two nations. Americans did not forget the Soviet invasion of Finland and the Baltic states late in 1939, once the war with Germany had begun in the west. Nor were they unaware, as the war continued, of Soviet brutality—not only toward the fascist enemies but toward supposedly friendly forces: for example, the Polish resistance fighters. Stalin harbored even greater resentments toward the American approach to the war. Despite repeated assurances from Roosevelt that the United States and Britain would soon open a second front on the European continent, thus drawing German strength away from the assault on Russia, the Allied invasion did not finally occur until June 1944, more than two years after Stalin had first demanded it. In the meantime, the Russians had suffered appalling casualties—some estimates put them as high as 20 million; and it was easy for Stalin to believe that the West had deliberately delayed the invasion to force the Soviets to absorb the brunt of the German strength. So although in most respects the wartime alliance worked well, with both sides making serious efforts to play down their differences, an undercurrent of tension and hostility remained.

Two Visions of the World

At least as important as these deep-seated suspicions was a fundamental difference in the ways the great powers envisioned the postwar world—a difference that was not at first immediately obvious, but one that ultimately shattered any hope for international amity. The first vision was that of many people in the United States, one perhaps best expressed by the title of a famous book by Wendell Willkie, *One World* (1943), and first openly outlined in the Atlantic Charter, drafted by Roosevelt and Churchill in 1941. It was a vision of a world in which nations abandoned their traditional belief in military alliances and spheres of influence. Instead, the world would govern itself through democratic processes, with an international organization serving as the arbiter of disputes and the protector of the peace. No nation would control any other. Every people would have the right "to choose the form of government under which they will live."

The other vision was that of the Soviet Union and to some extent, it gradually became clear, of Great Britain. Both Stalin and Churchill had agreed to sign the Atlantic Charter espousing the "One World" principles. But neither man truly shared them. Britain had always been uneasy about the implications of the self-determination ideal for its own empire, which remained at the close of World War II the largest in the world. The Soviet Union was determined to create a secure sphere for itself in Eastern Europe as protection against future aggression from the West. Both Churchill and Stalin, therefore, tended to envision a postwar structure in which the great powers would control areas of strategic interest to them, in which something vaguely similar to the traditional European balance of power would reemerge.

This difference of opinion was particularly serious because the internationalist vision of Roosevelt had, by the end of the war, become a fervent commitment among many Americans. It was a vision composed equally of expansive idealism and national self-interest. Roosevelt had never forgotten the excitement with which he had greeted the principles of Wilsonian idealism during World War I, and he saw his mission in the 1940s as one of bringing lasting peace and genuine democracy to the world. But it was clear, too, that the "One World" vision would enhance the position of the United States in particular. As the world's greatest industrial power, and as one of the few nations unravaged by the war, America stood to gain more than any other country from opening the entire world to unfettered trade. The United States would have a global market for its exports, and it would have unrestricted access to vital raw materials. Determined to avoid another economic catastrophe like that of the 1930s, Roosevelt saw the creation of the postwar order as a way to ensure continuing American prosperity.

Thus when Britain and the Soviet Union began to

balk at some of the provisions the United States was advocating, the debate seemed to become more than a simple difference of opinion. It became an ideological struggle for the future of the world. And on that rock the hope for a genuine peace would ultimately founder. Roosevelt was by the end of the war able to win at least the partial consent of Winston Churchill to his principles; but although he believed at times that Stalin would similarly relent, he never managed to steer the Soviets from their determination to control Eastern Europe, from their vision of a postwar order in which each of the great powers would dominate its own sphere. Gradually, the irreconcilable differences between these two positions would turn the peacemaking process into a form of warfare.

Wartime Diplomacy

Almost from the moment of Pearl Harbor, the Roosevelt administration devoted nearly as much attention to planning the peace as it did to winning the war. Indeed, the president himself realized that the conduct of the war—the relationships among the Allies in coordinating their efforts—would go far toward determining the shape of the postwar world.

Throughout 1942, Roosevelt had engaged in inconclusive discussions with the Soviet Union, and particularly with Foreign Minister Vyacheslav Molotov, about how best to implement the principles of the Atlantic Charter, to which all the Allies had in theory subscribed. Until 1943, however, neither nation was ready for any specific commitments. In the meantime, serious strains in the alliance were beginning to appear as a result of Stalin's irritation at delays in opening the second front and his resentment of the Anglo-American decision to invade North Africa before Europe.

It was in this deteriorating atmosphere that the president called for a meeting of the "Big Three"—Roosevelt, Churchill, and Stalin—in Casablanca, Morocco, in January 1943. Stalin declined the invitation, but Churchill and Roosevelt met nevertheless. Because the two leaders agreed that they could not accept Stalin's most important demand—the immediate opening of a second front—they reached another decision designed to reassure the Soviet Union. The Allies, Roosevelt announced, would accept nothing less than the unconditional surrender of the Axis powers. The announcement was a signal to Stalin that the Americans and British would not negotiate a separate peace with Hitler and leave the Soviets to fight on alone.

In November 1943, Roosevelt and Churchill traveled to Teheran, Iran, for their first meeting with Stalin. By now, however, Roosevelt's most effective bargaining tool—Stalin's need for American assistance in his struggle against Germany—had been removed. The German advance against Russia had been halted; Soviet forces were now launching their own westward offensive. New tensions had emerged in the alliance, moreover, as a result of the refusal by the British and Americans to allow any Soviet participation in the creation of a new Italian government following the fall of Mussolini. To Stalin, at least, the "One World" doctrine was already embodying a double standard: America and Britain expected to have a voice in the future of Eastern Europe, but the Soviet Union was to have no voice in the future of the West.

Nevertheless, the Teheran Conference seemed in most respects a success. Roosevelt and Stalin established a cordial relationship, one that the president hoped would eventually produce the same personal intimacy he enjoyed with Churchill. Stalin agreed to an American request that the Soviet Union enter the war in the Pacific soon after the end of hostilities in Europe. Roosevelt, in turn, promised that an Anglo-American second front would be established within six months. More important to Roosevelt, all three leaders agreed in principle to a postwar international organization and to efforts to prevent a resurgence of German expansionism.

On other matters, however, the origins of future disagreements could already be discerned. Most important was the question of the future of Poland. Roosevelt and Churchill were willing to agree to a movement of the Soviet border westward, thus allowing Stalin to annex some historically Polish territory. But on the nature of the postwar government in the portion of Poland that would remain independent, there were sharp differences. Roosevelt and Churchill supported the claims of the Polish government-in-exile that had been functioning in London since 1940; Stalin wished to install another, procommunist exiled government that had spent the war in Lublin, in the Soviet Union. The three leaders avoided a bitter conclusion to the Teheran Conference only by leaving the issue unresolved. There had, however, been little evidence to support hopes that an amicable settlement of the Polish question would be possible.

Yalta

For more than a year, during which the Soviet Union began finally to destroy German resistance and the

British and Americans launched their successful invasion of France, the Grand Alliance among the United States, Britain, and the Soviet Union alternated between high tension and warm amicability. In the fall of 1944, Churchill flew by himself to Moscow for a meeting with Stalin to resolve issues arising from a civil war in Greece. In return for a Soviet agreement to cease assisting Greek communists, who were challenging the British-supported monarchical government, Churchill consented to a proposal whereby control of Eastern Europe would be divided between Britain and the Soviet Union. "This memorable meeting," Churchill wrote Stalin after its close, "has shown that there are no matters that cannot be adjusted between us when we meet together in frank and intimate discussion." To Roosevelt, however, the Moscow agreement was evidence of how little the Atlantic Charter principles seemed to mean to his two most important allies.

It was in an atmosphere of some gloom, therefore, that Roosevelt joined Churchill and Stalin for a great peace conference in the Soviet city of Yalta in February 1945. The American president sensed resistance to his internationalist dreams. The British prime minister was already becoming disillusioned about Stalin's willingness to make concessions and compromises, warning even before the conference met that "I think the end of this war may well prove to be more disappointing than was the last." Stalin, whose armies were now only miles from Berlin and who was well aware of how much the United States still wanted his assistance in the Pacific, was confident and determined.

On a number of issues, the Big Three reached amicable and mutually satisfactory agreements. In return for Stalin's promise to enter the war against Japan, Roosevelt agreed that the Soviet Union should receive the Kurile Islands north of Japan; should regain southern Sakhalin Island and Port Arthur, both of which Russia had lost in the 1904 Russo-Japanese War; and could exercise some influence (along with the government of China) in Manchuria.

The negotiators agreed as well on a plan for a new international organization: the United Nations. Tentative plans for the UN had been hammered out the previous summer at a conference in Washington, D.C., at the Dumbarton Oaks estate. At Yalta, the leaders ratified the Dumbarton plan to create (1) a General Assembly, in which every member would be represented, and (2) a Security Council, on which would sit permanent representatives of the five major powers (the United States, Britain, France, the Soviet Union, and China), along with temporary dele-

gates from several other nations. They accepted, too, the provision giving each of the major powers a veto over all Security Council decisions. These agreements became the basis for the drafting of the United Nations charter at a conference of fifty nations beginning April 25, 1945, in San Francisco. The United States Senate ratified the charter in July by a vote of 80 to 2 (a striking contrast to the slow and painful defeat it had administered to the charter of the League of Nations twenty-five years before).

On other issues, however, the Yalta Conference produced no real agreement, either leaving fundamental differences unresolved or papering them over with weak and unstable compromises. As at Teheran, the most important stumbling block remained Poland. Fundamental disagreement remained about the postwar Polish government, with each side continuing to insist on the rights of its own government-in-exile. Stalin, whose armies had by now occupied Poland, had already installed a government composed of the procommunist "Lublin" Poles, to the chagrin of the British and Americans.

Roosevelt and Churchill protested strongly at Yalta against Stalin's unilateral establishment of a new Polish government, insisting that the pro-Western "London" Poles must be allowed a place in the Warsaw regime. Roosevelt envisioned a complete restructuring of the Soviet-controlled government, based on free, democratic elections—which both he and Stalin recognized the pro-Western forces would win. Stalin agreed only to a vague compromise by which an unspecified number of pro-Western Poles would be granted a place in the government. Although he reluctantly consented to hold "free and unfettered elections" in Poland, he made no firm commitment to a date for them. They never took place.

Nor was there agreement about one of the touchiest issues facing the three leaders: the future of Germany. All three leaders were determined to ensure that Germany could not soon again become a major military power, but there were wide differences in their views of how to accomplish that goal. Stalin wanted to impose $20 billion in reparations on the Germans, of which Russia would receive half. Churchill protested, arguing that the result would be that Britain and America would have to feed the German people. Roosevelt finally accepted the $20 billion figure as a "basis for discussion" but left final settlement to a future reparations commission. To Stalin, whose hopes for the reconstruction of Russia rested in part on tribute from Germany, it was an unsatisfactory compromise.

The Big Three at Yalta

Churchill, Roosevelt, and Stalin meet in the Soviet Crimea at Yalta to discuss the shape of the postwar order. Churchill and Stalin were alarmed by Roosevelt's gaunt appearance and his apparent weariness during the meeting—evidence of a physical deterioration that would lead to the president's death only months later. By the time the Allied leaders next met—at Potsdam, Germany, in July—only Stalin would remain in power. By then, Truman had succeeded Roosevelt, and Clement Atlee had succeeded Churchill as prime minister of Great Britain after Atlee's Labour party won a postwar election. (Franklin D. Roosevelt Library)

Roosevelt was uncertain at first about how he wished to resolve the German question. In 1944, he and Churchill had met in Quebec and agreed on what became known as the Morgenthau Plan—a plan for dismantling much of Germany's industrial capacity and turning that country into a largely agricultural society. But by accepting the principle of reparations at Yalta, he was clearly abandoning the idea of destroying German industry; without it, the Germans would have no means by which to pay. Instead, he seemed to be hoping for a reconstructed and reunited Germany—one that would be permitted to develop a prosperous, modern economy, but one that would remain under the careful supervision of the Allies. Stalin, in contrast, wanted a permanent dismemberment of Germany, a proposal the British and Americans firmly rejected. The final agreement was, like the Polish agreement, a vague and unstable one. The United States, Great Britain, France, and the Soviet Union would each control its own "zone of occupation" in Germany—the zones to be determined by the position of troops at the time when the war would end. (Berlin, the German capital, was already well inside the Soviet zone, but because of its symbolic importance it would itself be divided into four sectors, one for each nation to occupy.) At an unspecified date, the nation would be reunited; but no specific agreement was reached on how the reunification would occur.

As for the rest of Europe, the conference produced a murky accord on the establishment of interim governments "broadly representative of all democratic elements." They would be replaced ultimately by permanent governments "responsible to the will of the people" and created through free elections. Once again, no specific provisions or timetables accompanied the agreements.

The Yalta accords, in other words, were less a settlement of postwar issues than a general set of loose principles that side-stepped the most divisive issues. Roosevelt, Churchill, and Stalin returned home from the conference each apparently convinced that he had signed an important agreement. But the Soviet interpretation of the accords differed so sharply from the Anglo-American interpretation that the illusion endured only briefly. Stalin continued to believe that Soviet control of Eastern Europe was essential and considered the Yalta accords little more than a set of small concessions to Western punctiliousness. Roosevelt, in contrast, thought the agreements represented a mutual acceptance of the idea of an "open" Europe, under the direct control of no single nation. In the weeks following the Yalta Conference, therefore, he watched with horror as the Soviet Union moved systematically to establish procommunist governments in one Eastern European nation after another and as Stalin refused to make the changes in Poland that the president believed he had promised.

Still, Roosevelt refused to abandon hope. His personal relationship with Stalin was such, he believed, that a settlement of these issues remained possible. Continuing to work to secure his vision of the future, he left Washington early in the spring for a vacation at his private retreat in Warm Springs, Georgia. There, on April 12, 1945, he suffered a sudden, massive stroke and died.

The Collapse of the Peace

Harry S. Truman, who succeeded Roosevelt in the presidency, inherited an international predicament that would have taxed the most experienced and patient statesman. He did not, however, inherit Roosevelt's familiarity with the world situation. (He had served in the administration only three months

and had received few substantive briefings on foreign policy.) Nor did he share Roosevelt's belief in the flexibility of the Soviet Union. Roosevelt had insisted until the end that the Russians could be bargained with, that Stalin was, essentially, a reasonable man with whom an ultimate accord could be reached. Truman, in contrast, sided with those in the government (and there were many) who considered the Soviet Union fundamentally untrustworthy and viewed Stalin himself with deep suspicion and basic dislike.

There was also a significant contrast between the personalities of the two men. Roosevelt had always been a wily, even devious public figure, using his surface geniality to disguise his intentions. He had, as a result, been an unusually effective negotiator. Truman, on the other hand, was a sharp, direct, and impatient leader, a man who said what he thought and seldom wavered from decisions once he had made them. They were qualities that would win him the admiration of many of his contemporaries and of an even larger proportion of later generations of Americans. They were not, however, qualities well suited to patient negotiation.

The Failure of Potsdam

Truman had been in office only a few days before he decided on his approach to the Soviet Union. He would "get tough." Stalin had made what the new president considered solemn agreements with the United States at Yalta. The United States, therefore, would insist that he honor them. Dismissing the advice of Secretary of War Stimson that the Polish question was a lost cause and not worth a world crisis, Truman met on April 23 with Soviet Foreign Minister Molotov and sharply chastised him for violations of the Yalta accords. "I have never been talked to like that in my life," a shocked Molotov reportedly replied. "Carry out your agreements and you won't get talked to like that," said the president.

In fact, however, Truman had only limited leverage by which to compel the Soviet Union to carry out its agreements. Russian forces already occupied Poland and much of the rest of Eastern Europe. Germany was already divided among the conquering nations. The United States was still engaged in a war in the Pacific and was neither able nor willing to engage in a second conflict in Europe. Despite Truman's professed belief that the United States should be able to get "85 percent" of what it wanted, he was ultimately forced to settle for much less.

He conceded first on Poland. When Stalin made a few minor concessions to the pro-Western exiles, Truman recognized the Warsaw government, hoping that noncommunist forces might gradually expand their influence there. (They never did.) Other questions remained, and to settle them Truman met in July with Churchill (who was replaced in the midst of the negotiations by Clement Atlee, who had ousted him as prime minister) and Stalin at Potsdam, near Berlin, in Russian-occupied Germany. The British and Americans hoped to use the Potsdam Conference to resolve the question of Germany, and in one sense they succeeded. But the resolution was not, ultimately, to the liking of the Western leaders. Truman reluctantly accepted the adjustments of the Polish-German border that Stalin had long demanded; he refused, however, to permit the Russians to claim any reparations from the American, French, and British zones of Germany. The result, in effect, was to confirm that Germany would remain divided, with the western zones united into one nation, friendly to the United States, and the Russian zone surviving as another nation, with a pro-Soviet, communist government. Stalin had failed to receive the reparations he wanted, and he had been unable to secure other forms of financial assistance from the West (a failure symbolized by the abrupt termination by the Truman administration in May of all lend-lease assistance). He would, therefore, use eastern Germany to help rebuild the shattered Russian economy. Soon, the Soviet Union was siphoning between $1.5 and $3 billion a year out of its zone of occupation.

A Dilemma in Asia

Throughout the frustrating course of its negotiations over the future of Europe, the United States was facing an equally troubling dilemma in Asia. Central to American hopes for an open, peaceful world "policed" by the great powers was a strong, independent China. But even before the war ended, the American government was aware that those hopes faced a major, perhaps insurmountable obstacle: the Chinese government of Chiang Kai-shek. Chiang was generally friendly to the United States, but he had few other virtues. His government was hopelessly corrupt and incompetent. His popular legitimacy was feeble. And Chiang himself lived in a world of surreal isolation, unable or unwilling to face the problems that were threatening to engulf him. Ever since 1927, the nationalist government he headed had been engaged in a prolonged and bitter rivalry with the communist armies of Mao Zedong. So successful had the communist challenge grown that Mao was in control of one-fourth of the population by 1945.

Truman had managed at Potsdam to win Stalin's agreement that Chiang would be recognized as the legitimate ruler of China; but Chiang himself was rapidly losing his grip on his country. Some Americans urged the government to try to find a third faction to support as an alternative to either Chiang or Mao. A few argued that America should try to reach some accommodation with Mao. Truman, however, decided reluctantly that he had no choice but to continue supporting Chiang, despite the weakness of Chiang's position. American forces in the last months of the war diverted their attention from the Japanese long enough to assist Chiang against the communists in Manchuria. For the next several years, as the long struggle between the nationalists and the communists erupted into a full-scale civil war, the United States continued to pump money and weapons to Chiang. By late 1947, however, it was clear to the president that the cause was lost. Although he did not abandon China entirely or immediately, he was not prepared to intervene to save the nationalist regime.

Instead, the American government was beginning to consider an alternative to China as the strong, pro-Western force in Asia: a revived Japan. During the first years of American occupation of Japan after the war, the United States commander, Douglas MacArthur, provided a firm and restrictive administration of the island. A series of purges removed what remained of the warlord government of the Japanese Empire. Americans insisted, too, on dismantling the nation's munitions industry. But after two years of occupation, American policy toward Japan shifted. All limitations on industrial development were lifted, and rapid economic growth was encouraged. The vision of an open, united Asia had been replaced, as in Europe, with an acceptance of the necessity of developing a strong, pro-American sphere of influence.

The Containment Doctrine

By the end of 1945, the Grand Alliance was in shambles, and with it any realistic hope of a postwar world constructed along the lines Americans had urged. Although few policymakers were willing to admit openly that the United States must abandon its "One

The Chinese Revolution
Jubilant demonstrators in Shanghai show their support for the new communist regime in 1949, the year in which Mao and his followers consolidated control over China and expelled the Nationalist regime of Chiang Kai-shek.
(Henri Cartier-Bresson/Magnum)

World" ideals, a new American policy was slowly emerging to replace them. Rather than attempting to create a unified, "open" world, the West would work to "contain" the threat of further Soviet expansion. The United States would be the leading force in that effort.

The new doctrine received one test before it was even fully formulated. When Stalin refused in March 1946 to follow the British and American lead in pulling his occupation forces out of Iran, the Truman administration issued a strong and threatening ultimatum. Stalin relented and withdrew. But new crises were emerging—in Turkey, where Stalin was exerting heavy pressure to win some control over the vital straits to the Mediterranean, and in Greece, where once again communist forces were threatening the

pro-Western government and where the British had announced they could no longer provide assistance. Faced with these challenges, the president finally decided to enunciate a firm new policy.

For some time, Truman had been convinced that the Soviet Union, like Nazi Germany before it, was an aggressor nation bent on world conquest. He had accepted the arguments of the influential American diplomat George F. Kennan, who warned that the United States faced "a political force committed fanatically to the belief that with the U.S. there can be no permanent *modus vivendi*," and that the only answer was "a long-term, patient but firm and vigilant containment of Russian expansive tendencies." On March 12, 1947, Truman appeared before Congress and used Kennan's warnings as the basis of what became known as the Truman Doctrine. "I believe," he argued, "that it must be the policy of the United States to support free peoples who are resisting attempted subjugation by armed minorities or by outside pressures." In the same speech he requested $400 million—part of it to bolster the armed forces of Greece and Turkey, another part to provide economic assistance to Greece. Congress quickly approved the measure.

The American commitment ultimately eased Soviet pressure on Turkey and helped the Greek government to defeat the communist insurgents. More important, it established a fundamental new doctrine that would become the basis of American foreign policy for more than two decades. Communism, Truman seemed to claim, was an ideological threat; it was indivisible; its expansion anywhere was a threat to democracy because, as Secretary of State Dean Acheson had argued, the fall of one nation to communism would have a "domino effect" on surrounding nations. It was, therefore, the policy of the United States to assist pro-Western forces in any struggle against communism anywhere in the world, whether that struggle directly involved the Soviet Union or not. The Truman Doctrine marked the final American abandonment of the "One World" vision of a generation of idealists. But it replaced it with another, equally powerful vision—a vision of two worlds, one enslaved and one free, in which every rivalry and every conflict could be defined as a struggle between the United States and the Soviet Union. In the years to come, the ideology of the Truman Doctrine would at times blind Americans to local or regional particularities, with the result that the United States would on more than one occasion interpret an internal revolution as an expression of Soviet expansionism.

The Marshall Plan

The Truman Doctrine was only one half—the military half—of the new containment doctrine. The second part of the new American policy was a proposal to aid in the economic reconstruction of Western Europe. There were a number of motives for the assistance. One was a simple humanitarian concern for the European peoples, whose economies lay in ruins and whose future appeared bleak. Another was practical necessity: Until Europe could support itself economically, it would remain a drain on the United States, which was endeavoring in the meantime to

feed it. But there was powerful self-interest at work as well. Without a strong European market for American goods, most policymakers believed, the United States economy would be unable to sustain the prosperity it had achieved during the war. Above all, unless something could be done to strengthen the perilous position of the pro-American governments in Western Europe, they might well fall under the control of domestic communist movements, which were gaining strength as a result of the economic misery.

In June 1947, therefore, Secretary of State George C. Marshall spoke before a commencement gathering at Harvard University and announced a plan to provide economic assistance to all European nations (including the Soviet Union) that would join in drafting a program for recovery. Although Russia and its Eastern satellites quickly rejected the plan, claiming that it represented an American attempt to reshape Europe in its own image, sixteen Western European nations eagerly participated. There was substantial opposition at first to Truman's request for an enormous appropriation to fund the effort; but congressional opponents lost power quickly, embarrassed by the unwelcome support of the American Communist party and shocked by a sudden seizure of power by communists in Czechoslovakia, which had hitherto remained at least nominally free of Soviet control. In April 1948, the president signed a bill establishing the Economic Cooperation Administration and providing an initial budget of $4 billion. Over the next three years, the Marshall Plan, as it soon became known, channeled over $12 billion of American aid into Europe, sparking what many viewed as a miraculous economic revival. By the end of 1950, European industrial production had risen 64 percent, communist strength in the member nations was declining, and the opportunities for American trade had revived.

Mobilization at Home

That the United States had fully accepted a continuing commitment to the containment policy became clear in 1947 and 1948 through a series of measures designed to maintain American military power at near wartime levels. Although the government had moved rapidly in 1945 to release almost 7 million men from the armed forces in the space of a few months, it was not long before the president began to demand a renewal of universal military training through a continuing draft. Congress finally restored the Selective

Service System in 1948. The United States had announced, shortly after the surrender of Japan, that it was prepared to accept an international agreement banning nuclear weapons (through a proposal known as the Baruch Plan). The Soviet Union, arguing that since only America had developed a bomb, America alone should abandon it, resisted any system of international inspection and controls. In response, the United States simply redoubled its own efforts in atomic research, elevating nuclear weaponry to a central place in its military arsenal. The Atomic Energy Commission, established in 1946, became the supervisory body charged with overseeing all nuclear research, civilian and military alike.

Perhaps the clearest indication of America's continuing concern with military power, however, came through the National Security Act of 1947. It created a new Department of Defense, whose secretary would combine the traditional functions of the secretary of war and the secretary of the navy and preside over all branches of the armed services. The National Security Council (NSC), operating out of the White House and including the president, several members of his cabinet, and others, would govern foreign and military policy. The Central Intelligence Agency (CIA) would be responsible for collecting information through both open and covert methods and, as the Cold War continued, for engaging secretly in active political and military operations on behalf of American goals.

Despite some problems of administration, the National Security Act effected important changes in the nation's ability to conduct a cold war. It transferred to the president expanded powers over all defense activities, centralizing in the White House control that had once been widely dispersed; it enabled the administration to take warlike actions without an open declaration of war; and it created vehicles by which the government could at times act politically and militarily overseas behind a veil of secrecy.

The Road to NATO

At about the same time, the United States was moving to strengthen the military capabilities of Western Europe. Convinced that only a reconstructed Germany could serve as the necessary bulwark against communist expansion, Truman abandoned earlier policies designed to restrain German power and forged an agreement with England and France to merge the three western zones of occupation into a new West German republic (which would include the American, British, and French sectors of Berlin, even though that city lay well within the Soviet zone).

Stalin interpreted the move (correctly) as a direct challenge to his hopes for a subdued Germany and a docile Europe. At almost the same moment, he was facing a challenge from inside what he considered his own sphere. The government of Yugoslavia, under the leadership of Marshall Josip Broz Tito, broke openly with the Soviet Union and declared the nation an unaligned communist state. The United States offered Tito assistance.

Stalin's response came quickly. On June 24, 1948, taking advantage of the lack of a written guarantee of Western transit through eastern Germany, he imposed a tight blockade around the western sectors of Berlin. If Germany was to be officially divided, he was implying, then the country's Western government would have to abandon its outpost in the heart of the Soviet-controlled eastern zone. The United States was being given a choice between dropping its plan for a united West Germany or surrendering Berlin. Truman refused to do either. He was unwilling to risk war by responding militarily to the blockade; but he ordered a massive airlift to supply the city with food, fuel, and supplies. The airlift continued for more than ten months, transporting nearly 2.5 million tons of material, keeping alive a city of 2 million people, and transforming West Berlin into a symbol of the West's resolve to resist communist expansion. Finally, late in the spring of 1949, Stalin lifted the now ineffective blockade. And in October, the division of Germany into two nations—the Federal Republic in the west and the Democratic Republic in the East—became official.

The crisis in Berlin accelerated the consolidation of what was already in effect an alliance of the United States and the countries of Western Europe. On April 4, 1949, twelve nations signed an agreement establishing the North Atlantic Treaty Organization (NATO) and declaring that an armed attack against one member would be considered an attack against all. The NATO countries would, moreover, maintain a standing military force in Europe to defend against what many believed was the threat of a Soviet invasion. The American Senate quickly ratified this first peacetime alliance between the United States and Europe since the eighteenth century—an agreement that fused European nations that had been fighting one another for centuries into a strong and enduring

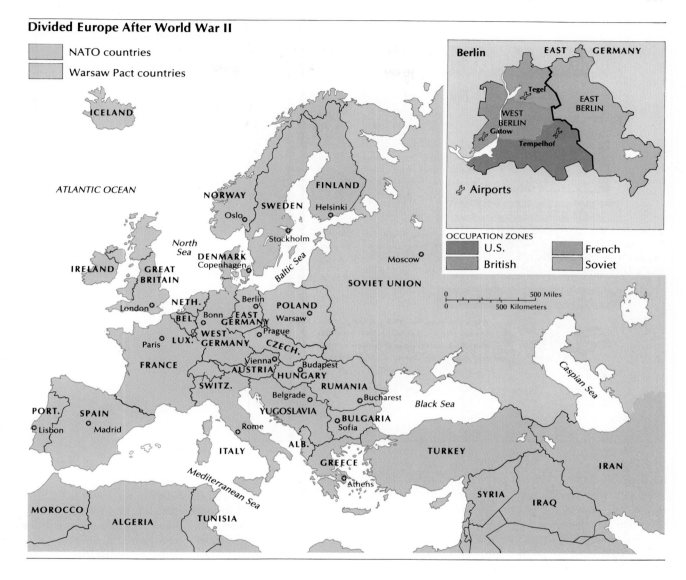

Divided Europe After World War II

NATO countries

Warsaw Pact countries

OCCUPATION ZONES

U.S.

British

French

Soviet

Berlin

Airports

alliance. Whatever effects NATO may have had on the global balance of power, it created a stable peace in Western Europe. (It also spurred the Soviet Union to create an alliance of its own with the communist governments in Eastern Europe—an alliance formalized in 1955 by the Warsaw Pact.)

The NATO alliance also greatly increased American influence in Europe. The United States quickly became the most important supplier of the NATO military forces; and an American officer, General Dwight D. Eisenhower, assumed the powerful posi-

tion of supreme commander of Allied forces in Europe.

The Enduring Crisis

The Berlin blockade, the offer of aid to Yugoslavia, the creation of NATO—all had in most respects been expressions of American confidence. Truman had believed, along with most other policymakers, that the United States was easily the more powerful of the

Survival Secrets for Atomic Attacks

ALWAYS PUT FIRST THINGS FIRST

Try to Get Shielded

If you have time, get down in a basement or subway. Should you unexpectedly be caught out-of-doors, seek shelter alongside a building, or jump in any handy ditch or gutter.

Drop Flat on Ground or Floor

To keep from being tossed about and to lessen the chances of being struck by falling and flying objects, flatten out at the base of a wall, or at the bottom of a bank.

Bury Your Face in Your Arms

When you drop flat, hide your eyes in the crook of your elbow. That will protect your face from flash burns, prevent temporary blindness and keep flying objects out of your eyes.

NEVER LOSE YOUR HEAD

Surviving Nuclear War
Preoccupation with the possibility of a nuclear war reached a fever pitch in the first years of the atomic era. The Federal Civil Defense Agency, which in 1950 issued these simple rules for dealing with an atomic attack, was one of many organizations attempting to convince the American public that a nuclear war was survivable. (Federal Civil Defense Agency)

two great rivals, that the Soviet Union would not dare provoke war because of the certainty of defeat. For a time, it had seemed that the battle against communism was being won.

But a series of events in 1949 began seriously to erode that confidence and launched the Cold War into a new and more enduring phase. An announcement in September that the Soviet Union had successfully exploded its first atomic weapon, years before most Americans had considered it possible, came as a severe shock to the nation. So did the collapse of Chiang Kai-shek's nationalist government in China, which occurred with startling speed in the last months of 1949. Chiang fled with his political allies and the remnants of his army to the offshore island of Formosa (Taiwan), and the entire Chinese mainland came under the control of a communist government that many Americans believed to be a mere extension of the Soviet Union. The United States, powerless to stop the communists without a major military commitment that virtually no one wanted, had no choice

but to watch the collapse of its ill-chosen ally. Few policymakers shared the belief of the so-called China lobby that the United States should now commit itself to the rearming of Chiang Kai-shek. But neither would the administration recognize the new communist regime, particularly after the Maoist government began expropriating American property, expelling American businesspeople, and strengthening its ties to the Soviet Union. The Chinese mainland would remain almost entirely closed to the West for a full generation. The United States, in the meantime, would devote increased attention to the revitalization of Japan as a buffer against Asian communism, ending the American occupation of the island, finally, in 1952.

With the containment policy in apparent disarray, and with political opposition mounting at home, Truman called for a thorough review of American foreign policy. The result was a National Security Council report, commonly known as NSC-68, which outlined a shift in the American position. The April

1950 document argued that the United States could no longer rely on other nations to take the initiative in resisting communism. It must itself establish firm and active leadership of the noncommunist world. Among other things, the report called for a major expansion of American military power, with a defense budget almost four times the previously projected figure. It also reinforced what was already a strong sense of mission in the formulation of American foreign policy. Upon the United States, the report maintained, lay the sole responsibility of defending freedom in the world.

America After the War

The increasing dangers overseas were only a part of the frustrations facing the United States after the war. The nation also encountered serious difficulties in adapting its complex economy to the new demands of peace; the instability that resulted contributed to the creation of a heated political climate.

The Problems of Reconversion

The bombs that destroyed Hiroshima and Nagasaki ended the war months earlier than almost anyone had predicted and propelled the nation precipitously into a process of reconversion. The lack of planning was soon compounded by a growing popular impatience for a return to normal. Under intense public pressure, the Truman administration attempted to hasten that return, despite dire warnings by some planners and economists. The result was a period of economic problems.

They were not, however, the problems that most Americans had feared. There had been many predictions that peace would bring a return of Depression unemployment, as war production ceased and returning soldiers flooded the labor market. But there was no general economic collapse in 1946—for several reasons. Government spending dropped sharply and abruptly, to be sure; $35 billion of war contracts were canceled at a stroke within weeks of the Japanese surrender. But increased consumer demand soon compensated. Consumer goods had been generally unavailable during the war, so many workers had saved a substantial portion of their wages and were now ready to spend. A $6 billion tax cut pumped additional money into general circulation. The Servicemen's Readjustment Act of 1944, better known as the GI Bill of Rights, provided economic and educational assistance to veterans, increasing spending even further.

But while the sudden flood of consumer demand ensured that there would be no new depression, it also created rampant, debilitating inflation. For more than two years inflation continued, with prices rising at rates of 14 or 15 percent annually. In the summer of 1946, the president vetoed an extension of the authority of the wartime Office of Price Administration because Congress had weakened the agency's authority. In so doing, he permitted government price controls, which were already having difficulty holding down price increases, to be removed altogether. A month later, he relented and signed a bill little different from the one he had rejected. But in the meantime inflation had soared briefly to 25 percent.

Compounding the economic difficulties was a sharp rise in labor unrest. Most unions had grudgingly accepted government-imposed restraints on their demands during the war, but now they were willing to wait no longer, particularly as inflation cut into the existing wage scales with painful force. By the end of 1945, there had already been major strikes in the automobile, electrical, and steel industries. Government intervention had helped settle the strikes relatively quickly, but the agreements fueled inflation even further.

In April 1946, a fresh crisis emerged when John L. Lewis led the United Mine Workers out on strike, shutting down the coal fields for forty days. The economic impact was devastating. Freight and shipping activity declined by 75 percent; the steel industry made plans to shut down operations; fears grew that without vital coal supplies, the entire nation might virtually grind to a halt. Truman finally forced coal production to resume by ordering government seizure of the mines. But in the process, he induced mine owners to concede to the union most of its demands, which he had earlier denounced as inflationary. Almost simultaneously, the nation's railroads suffered a total shutdown—the first in the nation's history—as two major unions walked out on strike. By threatening to use the army to run the trains, Truman pressured the workers back to work after only a few days.

The Fair Deal Rejected

On September 16, 1945, only four days after the formal Japanese surrender, Truman submitted to Congress a twenty-one point domestic program outlining what he later termed the "Fair Deal." It called for expansion of Social Security benefits, the raising of the legal minimum wage from 40 to 65 cents an hour, a program to ensure full employment, a permanent Fair Employment Practices Act, public housing and slum clearance, long-range environmental and public works planning, and government promotion of scientific research. Weeks later he added other proposals: federal aid to education, government health insurance, prepaid medical care, funding for the St. Lawrence Seaway, and nationalization of atomic energy. The president was, it was clear, declaring an end to the wartime moratorium on reform and creating an impressive new liberal agenda. The announcement of the Fair Deal, he later wrote, symbolized "for me my assumption of the office of President in my own right."

Truman's proposals greatly heartened Democratic liberals, who had continued to wonder whether the new president would prove a satisfactory successor to Franklin Roosevelt. But the Fair Deal made little progress in Congress. Truman's programs fell victim to the same general public and congressional conservatism that had crippled the last years of the New Deal and had increased during the war. The economic problems and labor unrest of 1946 only intensified congressional resistance to further spending and reform. And what little hope there had been for legislative progress died in November 1946, when the Republican party—making use of the simple but devastating slogan "Had Enough?"—won control of both houses of Congress.

With the new Congress in place, the retreat from reform rapidly became a stampede. The president bowed to what he claimed was the popular mandate to lift most remaining wage and price controls, and Congress moved further to deregulate the economy. Inflation rapidly increased. When a public outcry arose over the soaring prices for meat, Senator Robert Taft, perhaps the most influential Republican conservative in Congress, advised consumers to "Eat less," and added, "We have got to break with the corrupting idea that we can legislate prosperity, legislate equality, legislate opportunity." True to the spirit of Taft's words, the Republican Congress quickly applied what one congressman described as a "meat-axe to government frills." It refused to appropriate funds to aid education, increase Social Security, or support reclamation and power projects in the West. It defeated a proposal to raise the minimum wage. It passed tax measures that cut rates dramatically for high-income families and moderately for those with lower incomes. Only vetoes by the president finally forced a more progressive bill.

The most notable action of the Eightieth Congress was an open assault on one of the cornerstones of Depression reform: the Wagner Act of 1935. Conservatives had always resented the enormous powers the legislation had granted unions; and in the light of the labor difficulties during and after the war, such resentments intensified sharply. The result was the Labor-Management Relations Act of 1947, better known as the Taft-Hartley Act, which loosened several of the earlier restrictions on employers and added some important new prohibitions against the unions. The act made illegal the so-called closed shop (a

Labor's Plea, 1947

Truman did veto the bill, but to no avail. Despite the desperate efforts of American workers to thwart the antiunion legislation, Congress easily overrode the president's veto and made the 1947 Taft-Hartley Act law. This giant banner hung in Madison Square Garden in New York during a rally by members of the International Ladies Garment Workers Union. (I.L.G.W.U.)

workplace in which no one could be hired without first being a member of a union). And although it continued to permit the creation of so-called union shops (in which workers must join a union after being hired), it permitted states to pass "right-to-work" laws prohibiting even that. This provision, the controversial Section 14(b), remained a particular target of the labor movement for decades. The act also empowered the president to call for a "cooling-off" period before a strike by issuing an injunction against any work stoppage that endangered national safety or health.

These and other provisions delighted conservatives, who viewed union power as one of the nation's greatest social evils. But they outraged workers and union leaders, who denounced the measure as a "slave labor bill" and called on the president to veto it. Truman needed little persuading. He had opposed the Taft-Hartley Act from the beginning and on June 20, 1947, returned it to Congress with a stinging veto message. Both houses easily overruled him the same day.

The Taft-Hartley Act did not destroy the labor movement, as many union leaders had predicted. But it did seriously damage the position of weaker unions in relatively lightly organized industries such as chemicals and textiles; and it made far more difficult the organizing of workers who had never been union members at all, especially in the South. Powerful unions remained powerful, for the most part; but unorganized or loosely organized workers now faced serious obstacles. Equally important in the short run, the passage of Taft-Hartley served as a symbol of the repudiation of New Deal reform by the Republican party and its Congress, a warning that government innovations that many had come to take for granted were now in jeopardy. "Victories fought and won years ago were suddenly in doubt," a columnist for the *New Republic* wrote at the time. "Everything was debatable again."

The Election of 1948

Truman and his advisers were convinced that the American public was not ready to abandon the achievements of the New Deal, that the 1946 election had not been a mandate for a surrender to conservatism. As they planned strategy for the 1948 campaign, therefore, they placed their hopes in an appeal to enduring Democratic liberalism. Throughout 1948, Truman proposed one reform measure after

The Man from Independence
Ben Shahn painted this whimsical portrait of Harry Truman in 1948 and entitled it "Hot Piano." Truman lived most of his adult life in Independence, Missouri; and he retained as president the aura of a small-town Midwesterner—an image that won him both affection and derision. He enjoyed playing the piano for friends and admirers, and his renditions of "The Missouri Waltz" became a campaign trademark. (Harry S. Truman Library and Museum, Independence, Missouri)

another (including, on February 2, the first major civil-rights bill of the century). Congress ignored or defeated them all; but the president was effectively building a campaign issue for the fall.

There remained, however, the serious problem of Truman's personal unpopularity—the assumption among a vast segment of the electorate that he lacked stature, that his administration was weak and inept. Many of the qualities that made him such an admired figure in later years—his outspokenness, his impatience, his common-man demeanor—seemed at the time to be evidence of his unfitness to fill the shoes of Franklin Roosevelt. Liberals within his own party were actively looking for an alternative candidate. Conservatives were regarding the president with disgust.

All of these tensions came to a head at the Democratic Convention that summer. Two factions abandoned the party altogether. Southern conservatives were angered by Truman's proposed civil-rights bill and outraged by the approval at the convention of a civil-rights plank in the platform (engineered by Hubert Humphrey, the mayor of Minneapolis). They walked out and formed the States' Rights (or "Dixiecrat") party, with Governor Strom Thurmond of South Carolina as its nominee. At the same time, the party's left wing formed a new Progressive party, with Henry A. Wallace as its candidate. Wallace supporters objected to what they considered the slow and ineffective domestic policies of the Truman administration, but they resented even more the president's confrontational stance toward the Soviet Union.

In addition, many Democrats unwilling to leave the party attempted to dump the president in 1948. The Americans for Democratic Action (ADA), a coalition of liberals, tried to entice Dwight D. Eisenhower, the popular war hero, to contest the nomination, certain that he could win the November election while Truman could not. Only after Eisenhower had refused did the party bow to the inevitable and, in near despair, give the nomination to Truman. The Republicans, in the meantime, had once again nominated Governor Thomas E. Dewey of New York, whose substantial reelection victory in 1946 had made him one of the nation's leading political figures. Austere, dignified, and competent, he seemed to offer an unbeatable alternative to the president. That his views on most issues were only marginally different from Truman's appeared further to strengthen his chances of victory.

Nothing, it seemed, could save the president from certain defeat. His party was seriously splintered. Polls showed him trailing so far behind Dewey that late in September public-opinion analysts stopped taking surveys. Dewey was conducting a quiet, statesmanlike campaign, behaving much as if he were already president. Only Truman, it seemed, believed he could win. As the campaign gathered momentum, he became ever more aggressive, turning his fire away from himself and toward Dewey the "do-nothing, good-for-nothing" Republican Congress, which was, he told the voters, responsible for fueling inflation

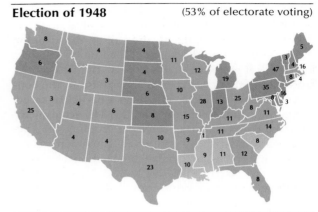

	ELECTORAL VOTE	POPULAR VOTE (%)
Harry S. Truman (Democratic)	303	24,105,695 (49.5)
Thomas E. Dewey (Republican)	189	21,969,170 (45.1)
Strom Thurmond (States' Rights)	39	1,169,021 (2.4)
Henry A. Wallace (Progressive)	—	1,156,103 (2.4)
Other candidates (Socialist, Prohibition, Socialist Labor, Socialist Workers)	—	272,713

and abandoning the workers and the common people. To dramatize his point, he called Congress into special session in July to give it a chance, he said, to enact the liberal measures the Republicans had recently written into their platform. Congress met for two weeks and, predictably, did almost nothing. Truman was delighted.

Before the campaign was over, the president had traveled nearly 32,000 miles and made 356 speeches, delivering blunt, extemporaneous attacks. He had told Alben Barkley, his running mate, "I'm going to fight hard. I'm going to give them hell." He called for repeal of the Taft-Hartley Act, increased price supports for farmers, and strong civil-rights protection for blacks. (He was the first president to campaign in Harlem.) He sought, in short, to re-create much of Franklin Roosevelt's New Deal coalition. And to the surprise of virtually everyone, he suceeded. When the returns came in, the nation was stunned to learn that Truman had won a narrow but decisive victory: 49.5 percent of the popular vote to

Dewey's 45.1 percent (with the two splinter parties dividing the small remainder between them), and an electoral margin of 303 to 189. Democrats, in the meantime, had regained both houses of Congress by substantial margins. It was the most dramatic upset in the history of presidential elections.

The Fair Deal Revived

Truman interpreted the 1948 election as a mandate for the revival of liberal reform. But despite the Democratic victories, it often seemed that the Eighty-first Congress was no more hospitable to reform than its Republican predecessor. Truman failed once again to win approval of such major new reforms as aid to education and national health insurance. Nevertheless, his administration managed in the first two years of its second term to consolidate and extend a number of already established New Deal reforms that before the election had seemed to be in jeopardy.

On three issues, in particular, Truman won important victories. Congress raised the legal minimum wage from 40 cents to 75 cents an hour. It approved an expansion of the Social Security system, increasing benefits by 75 percent and extending them to 10 million additional people. And it strengthened the federal commitment to public housing. The National Housing Act of 1949 called for the construction of 810,000 units of low-income housing over six years, to be accompanied by long-term rent subsidies. (Inadequate funding plagued the program for years, and the initial goal was reached only in 1972.)

While many of the other initiatives Truman had sponsored before 1948 gradually faded from view, he continued to press strenuously on what was perhaps the most controversial domestic issue of all: civil rights. The president had little luck persuading Congress to accept the civil-rights legislation he proposed in 1949, legislation that would have made lynching a federal crime, provided federal protection of black voting rights, abolished the poll tax, and established a Fair Employment Practices Commission to curb discrimination in hiring. Although a majority of the Senate appeared ready to support at least some aspects of this package, a vigorous filibuster by Southern Democrats (who also controlled crucial committees) managed to block the legislation. Nevertheless, Truman proceeded on his own to battle several forms of racial discrimination. He had appointed a federal Civil Rights Commission in 1946, whose 1947 report became the first important gov-

ernment call for the total elimination of segregation. Truman publicly approved its recommendations, although he was as yet unable to implement them. He ordered an end to discrimination in the hiring of government employees. He began to dismantle segregation within the armed forces. And he allowed the Justice Department to become actively involved in court battles against discriminatory statutes. The Supreme Court, in the meantime, signaled its own growing awareness of the issue by ruling, in *Shelley v. Kraemer* (1948), that the courts could not be used to enforce private "covenants" meant to bar blacks from residential neighborhoods. The Truman record, and the judicial decisions that accompanied it, made only minor dents in the structure of segregation. They did, however, signal the beginning of a commitment by liberal Democrats—and by the federal government as a whole—finally to confront the problem of race.

The Korean War

Truman's domestic policies had had a difficult time from the beginning in competing against the nation's obsession with the Soviet threat in Europe. In 1950, a new and more dangerous element of the Cold War emerged and all but killed hopes for further Fair Deal reform. On June 24, 1950, the armies of communist North Korea swept across their southern border and began a major invasion of the pro-Western half of the Korean peninsula to the south. Suddenly, the United States found itself embroiled in a new kind of conflict. The nation was neither fully at war nor fully at peace. It was, rather, discovering the peculiar demands of "limited war."

The Divided Peninsula

Korea had long been a source of international controversy. A peninsula of great strategic importance in Asia, it was easily accessible to the Soviet Union, Japan, and China. At the end of World War II, therefore, neither the United States nor the Soviet Union—both of which had sent troops into Korea against the Japanese—was willing to leave. As a result, the nation had been divided, supposedly temporarily, along the 38th parallel. The Russians departed in 1949, leaving behind a communist government in the north with a strong, Soviet-equipped army. The Americans left only months later, handing control to the pro-Western government of Syngman Rhee, a ruthless and only nominally democratic leader. He possessed a far less imposing army than his northern counterparts, and he used it primarily to strengthen his own position against internal political opposition.

The situation proved a strong temptation to the nationalists in the North Korean government and, apparently, to the Soviet leadership. The communist government of the north, recognizing its military superiority, was eager to invade the south and reunite the nation—particularly after the American govern-

ment had implied that it did not consider South Korea within its own "defense perimeter." The evidence remains murky as to how much the Soviet Union was involved in initiating the invasion; there is some reason to believe that the North Koreans acted without Stalin's approval. But the Soviets supported the offensive once it began.

The Truman administration was quick to respond. On June 27, 1950, the president ordered American air and naval forces to assist the South Korean army against the invaders; and on the same day he appealed to the United Nations to intervene. Because the Soviet Union was boycotting the Security Council at the time (to protest the council's refusal to recognize

The Korean War, 1950–1953

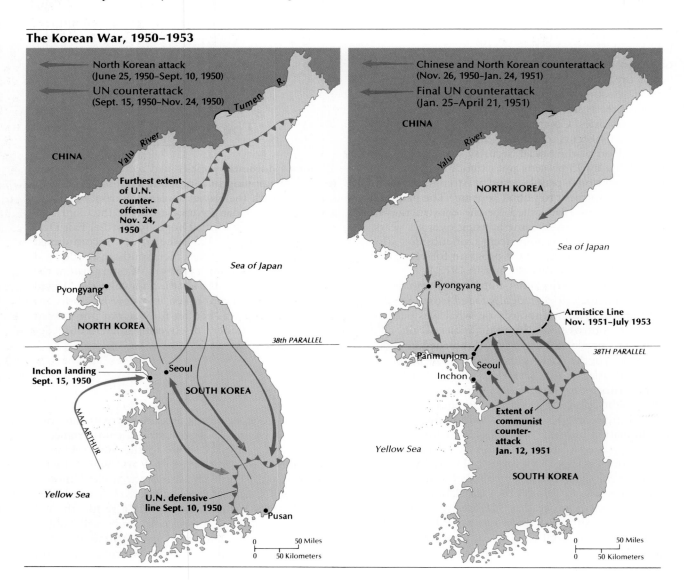

the new communist government of China), American delegates were able to win UN agreement to a resolution calling for international assistance to the embattled Rhee government. On June 30, the United States ordered its own ground forces into Korea, and Truman appointed General Douglas MacArthur to command the UN operations there. (Several other nations offered minor assistance to the effort, but the "UN" armies were, in fact, overwhelmingly American.)

The intervention in Korea was the first expression of the newly militant American foreign policy outlined in NSC-68. Very quickly, the administration decided that the war would be an effort not simply at containment but also at "liberation." After a surprise American invasion at Inchon in September had routed the North Korean forces from the south and sent them fleeing back across the 38th parallel, Truman gave MacArthur permission to pursue the communists into their own territory. His aim, as an American-sponsored UN resolution proclaimed in October, was to create "a unified, independent and democratic Korea." (Paralleling this decision came new American initiatives in other areas: efforts to strengthen the Chiang regime in Taiwan for a possible future assault on the Chinese mainland; and assistance to the French, who were attempting to rout communist forces from Vietnam and Laos.)

From Invasion to Stalemate

For several weeks, MacArthur's invasion of North Korea proceeded smoothly. On October 19, the capital, Pyongyang, fell to the UN forces. At the same time, parachutists managed to trap and immobilize much of the rest of the North Korean army. Victory seemed near. Slowly, however, the United States was becoming aware of the growing presence of forces from communist China; and by November 4, it was clear that eight Chinese divisions had entered the war. Suddenly, the UN offensive stalled and then collapsed. Through December 1950, American forces fought a bitter, losing battle against far more numerous Chinese divisions, retreating at almost every juncture. Within weeks, communist forces had pushed the Americans back below the 38th parallel once again and had captured the South Korean capital of Seoul. By mid-January 1951 the rout had ceased; and by March the UN armies had managed to regain much of the territory they had so recently lost, taking back Seoul and pushing the communists north of the

MacArthur at Inchon
Surrounded by members of his staff, General Douglas MacArthur sits on the bridge of the *U.S.S. Mt. McKinley* as American troops land at Inchon Harbor in South Korea in September 1950. MacArthur was seventy years old at the beginning of the Korean War and had been a legendary figure for decades already. He had been army chief of staff in the 1930s, Allied supreme commander in the Pacific during World War II, and the virtually omnipotent ruler of Japan during the postwar occupation. His service in Korea, which ended unhappily in 1951, marked the end of his public career.   (Bettmann Archive)

38th parallel for the second time. But with that, the war degenerated into a protracted, brutal stalemate.

It was then that the nation first began to experience the true dilemmas of limited war. Truman had been determined from the beginning to avoid embroiling the nation in a direct conflict with China, a conflict that would, he believed, lead to a world conflagration. As early as December 1950, he had begun seeking a negotiated solution to the struggle; and he continued through the next two years to insist that there would be no wider war. He faced, however, a formidable opponent in General MacArthur, a soldier of the old school who could not accept the idea of any limits on a military endeavor. The United States was fighting the Chinese, he argued. It should, therefore, attack China itself, if not through an actual invasion, then at least by bombing communist forces massing north of the Chinese border. In March 1951 he gave a public indication of his unhappiness with the administration's policy, sending to House Republican leader Joseph W. Martin a message that concluded: "There is no substitute for victory." His position quickly won wide popular support from a nation frustrated by the long, inconclusive war.

For nine months, Truman had chafed at MacArthur's resistance to his decisions about the conduct of the war. More than once, he had warned him to keep his objections to himself. The release of the Martin letter, therefore, struck the president as intolerable insubordination. On April 11, 1951, he relieved MacArthur of his command.

The result was a virtual firestorm of public outrage. Sixty-nine percent of the American people supported MacArthur in the controversy, a Gallup poll reported. When the general returned to the United States in 1951, the first time he had set foot in the country since 1935, he was greeted with hysterical enthusiasm. His televised farewell appearance before a joint session of Congress attracted an audience of millions. Public criticism abated somewhat when a number of prominent military figures, including General Omar Bradley, publicly supported the president's decision. But the controversy had cast in sharp relief the dilemmas of limited war.

In the meantime, the Korean stalemate continued for what seemed interminable months. In July 1951, negotiations began between the opposing forces at Panmunjom, near the 38th parallel; but they produced no swift resolution. Instead, the talks—and the war—dragged on until 1953.

Limited Mobilization

Just as the war in Korea produced only a limited American military commitment abroad, so it created only a limited economic mobilization at home. Although the Truman administration drew heavily on the experiences of World War II in meeting the demands for armaments and supplies, never was it necessary to create the enormous bureaucracy and pervasive controls that had been required a decade earlier.

Nevertheless, the Korean War did place pressure on the government to control the economy in several important ways. First, Truman attempted to halt a new wave of inflation by setting up the Office of Defense Mobilization to hold down prices and discourage high union wage demands. Then, confronted with the failure of these cautious regulatory efforts, the president took more drastic action. When railroad workers walked off the job in 1951, Truman ordered the government to seize control of the railroads. But while the dramatic gesture helped keep the trains running, it was of no effect in restraining union demands. Workers ultimately got most of what they had demanded before the railroads were returned to their owners. In 1952, a nationwide steel strike threatened to interrupt vital war production; and again Truman moved to seize the steel mills, citing his powers as commander in chief. This time, however, the courts intervened. In a 6-to-3 decision, the Supreme Court ruled that the president had exceeded his authority, and Truman was forced to relent. A lengthy and costly strike followed.

The effects of the war on American society at large were mixed. The conflict gave a significant boost to national prosperity. Just at the point when some economists believed the postwar consumer demand was about to decline, a new surge of funds was being pumped into the economy by the federal government, which increased military expenditures more than fourfold, to $60 billion in 1953. Unemployment declined. Industry embarked on a new wave of capital expansion. But the war had other, less healthy effects on American life. Coming at a time of rising insecurity about the position of the United States in the world, it intensified anxiety about communism. As the long stalemate continued, producing 140,000 American casualties (and more than 1 million South Korean dead and wounded), frustration increasingly turned to anger. The United States, which had recently won the greatest war in history, seemed unable to conclude what many Americans considered a minor border skirmish in an unimportant country. Many began to believe that something must be deeply wrong—not only in Korea but within the United States as well. Such fears became one of many factors contributing to the rise of the second major campaign of the century against domestic communism.

The Crusade Against Subversion

There has never been a single, satisfactory explanation of why, in the years following World War II, the

American people developed a growing fear of internal communist subversion that by the early 1950s had reached the point of near hysteria. Only by looking at the convergence of many factors at once is it possible to understand the era of the "great fear."

One factor was obvious. Communism was not an imagined enemy in the 1950s. It had tangible shape, in the person of Joseph Stalin and the Soviet Union. It was a dark and menacing threat to America's hopes for the world. The continuing setbacks overseas, the frustrations in Korea, the "loss" of China, the shocking realization that Russia had developed an atomic bomb—all created a sense of unease and a need to find someone to blame. The idea of a communist conspiracy within American borders was a natural outlet. But there were other factors as well, rooted in events in American domestic politics.

HUAC and Alger Hiss

Much of the anticommunist furor emerged out of the search by the Republican party for an issue with which to attack the Democrats, and out of the efforts of the Democrats to take that issue away. Beginning in 1947, the House Un-American Activities Committee (HUAC), established by the Democrats in 1938 to uncover malign foreign influences in the United States and now under the control of conservative Republicans, launched a series of widely publicized and inflammatory investigations to prove that, under Democratic rule, the nation had allowed communist subversion to reach alarming levels. The committee turned first to the movie industry, arguing that communists had so infiltrated Hollywood that American films were being tainted with Soviet propaganda. A parade of writers and producers was summoned to testify; and when some of them ("the Hollywood Ten") refused to answer questions about their political beliefs, they were sent to jail for contempt. Others were barred from employment in the industry when Hollywood, attempting to protect its public image, adopted a blacklist of those of "suspicious loyalty."

Far more frightening to much of the public, how-

Hollywood on Trial
Many of Hollywood's greatest stars attended the hearings of the House Un-American Activities Committee in the late 1940s, as the committee investigated charges of communist influence in the film industry. Danny Kaye, June Havoc, and Humphrey Bogart stand in the HUAC meeting room in Washington during one such hearing; Lauren Bacall is seated at right. (Martha Holmes, Life Magazine © 1947 Time, Inc.)

ever, was HUAC's investigation into charges of disloyalty leveled against a former high-ranking member of the State Department: Alger Hiss. Whittaker Chambers, a self-avowed former communist agent, now an editor at *Time* magazine, told the committee in 1948 that Hiss had passed classified documents to him in 1937 and 1938. When Hiss sued him for slander, Chambers produced microfilms of the documents (called the "pumpkin papers," because Chambers had kept them hidden in a pumpkin in his garden). Hiss could not be tried for espionage because of the statute of limitations (a law that protects individuals from prosecution for most crimes after seven years have passed). But as a result of the committee's efforts (and particularly because of the relentless pursuit of the case by Richard M. Nixon, a freshman Republican congressman from California), Hiss was charged with lying to the HUAC inquisitors. After a sensational trial, in which a number of leading Democratic liberals—including Adlai Stevenson, Felix Frankfurter, and Dean Acheson—testified as character witnesses for Hiss, the jury was unable to reach a verdict. A second trial produced a conviction for perjury, and Hiss served several years in prison, still proclaiming his innocence. The Hiss case not only discredited a talented young diplomat; it cast suspicion on an entire generation of liberal Democrats and made it possible for the public to believe that communists had actually infiltrated the government.

The Federal Loyalty Program

The Truman administration, in the meantime, was making its own contribution to increasing the popular fear. Partly to protect itself against Republican attacks, partly to encourage support for the president's foreign policy initiatives, the executive branch in 1947 initiated a widely publicized program to review the "loyalty" of federal employees. A series of "loyalty boards" undertook a sweeping investigation of the government; and in August 1950, the president authorized the dismissal in sensitive departments of even those deemed no more than "bad security risks." The faintest suspicion of disloyalty could cause a federal employee to lose his or her job. By 1951, more than 2,000 government employees had resigned and 212 had been dismissed.

Not only was the employee loyalty program itself being abused; the program also served as a signal throughout the executive branch to launch a major assault on subversion. The attorney general estab-

lished a list of dissident organizations and, in 1948, obtained indictments of eleven American communists for "conspiring to teach the violent overthrow of the government." The Federal Bureau of Investigation (FBI), whose director, J. Edgar Hoover, had been obsessed with the issue of communism for years, launched major crusades to investigate and harass alleged radicals. Federal information and education programs began to become tinged with strident anticommunist propaganda.

By now, the anticommunist frenzy was growing so intense that even a Democratic Congress was becoming obsessed with it. In 1950, over the objections of the Department of Defense, the Department of Justice, and the CIA, it enacted the McCarran Internal Security Act. The bill required all communist organizations to register with the government and to publish their records. Americans were now to be liable for prosecution on grounds as vague as "fomenting revolution." Communists were barred from working in defense plants and denied passports. Members of overseas "subversive organizations" were denied visas to enter the country. Truman vetoed the bill. Congress easily overrode his veto.

Of particular importance in fanning public fears were the efforts of the FBI and the Justice Department to prove a communist conspiracy to steal America's atomic secrets for the Soviet Union. The early explosion of a Russian nuclear weapon made such charges credible. And the testimony in 1950 of Klaus Fuchs, a young British scientist, that he had delivered to the Russians full details of the manufacture of the bomb gave the charges substance. Through an arcane series of connections, the case ultimately settled on an obscure New York couple, Julius and Ethel Rosenberg, members of the Communist party, whom the government claimed had been the masterminds of the conspiracy. The Rosenbergs had allegedly received the information from Ethel's brother, a machinist who had worked on the Manhattan Project, and passed it on to the Soviet Union. Several witnesses corroborated the story; although the Rosenbergs vehemently denied any guilt, they were found guilty and, on April 5, 1951, sentenced to death. A rising chorus of public protests and a long string of appeals failed to save them. On June 19, 1953, they died in the electric chair.

All these factors—the HUAC investigations, the Hiss trial, the loyalty investigations, the McCarran Act, the Rosenberg case, and more—combined, by the early 1950s, to create a paranoia about communist subversion that seemed to grip the entire country. State and local governments launched loyalty programs of their own, dismissing thousands of employees. Local courts began handing down extraordinarily harsh sentences to defendants convicted of anything resembling subversion. Schools and universities rooted out teachers suspected of teaching "un-American" ideas. Unions found themselves under continuing assault for suspected (and sometimes real) communist leanings. And a pervasive fear settled on the country—not only the fear of communist infiltration but the fear of being suspected of communism. It was a climate that made possible the rise of an extraordinary public figure, whose behavior at any other time would have been dismissed as preposterous.

McCarthyism

Joseph McCarthy was an undistinguished, first-term, Republican senator from Wisconsin when, in February 1950, he suddenly burst into national prominence. In the midst of a speech in Wheeling, West Virginia, he raised a sheet of paper into the air and claimed to "hold in my hand" a list of 205 known communists currently working in the American State Department. No person of comparable stature had ever made so bold a charge against the federal government; and in the weeks to come, as McCarthy repeated and expanded on his accusations, he emerged as the nation's preeminent leader of the crusade against communism.

He had seized on the issue less out of a deep concern about domestic subversion than because he needed something with which to run for reelection in 1952. And he continued to exploit the issue for the next four years because, to his surprise, it won him fame and notoriety beyond his wildest dreams. His rise was meteoric. Within weeks of his charges against the State Department he was expanding his accusations to other agencies. After 1952, with the Republicans in control of the Senate and McCarthy the chairman of a special subcommittee, he conducted highly publicized investigations of subversion—investigations that probed virtually every area of the government. His unprincipled assistants, Roy Cohn and David Schine, sauntered arrogantly through federal offices and American embassies overseas looking for evidence of communist influence. One hapless government official after another found himself summoned before McCarthy's subcommittee, where the senator belligerently and often cruelly badgered witnesses and destroyed public careers.

In the course of this extraordinary crusade, not once did McCarthy produce conclusive evidence that any federal employee had communist ties. But much of the public seemed not to care. A growing constituency adored him for his coarse, "fearless" assaults on a government establishment that many considered arrogant, effete, even effeminate. They admired his efforts to expose the "traitors" who had, he claimed, riddled the Truman administration. They even tolerated his attacks on public figures who earlier would have been considered unassailable, men such as General George C. Marshall and Governor Adlai Stevenson. Republicans, in particular, rallied to his claims that the Democrats had been responsible for "twenty years of treason," that only a change of parties could rid the country of subversion. McCarthy, in short, provided his followers with an issue into which they could channel a wide range of resentments: fear of communism, animosity toward the country's "Eastern establishment," and frustrated partisan ambitions.

For several years, McCarthy terrorized American public life, intimidating all but a very few from speaking out in opposition to him. In 1952, when some Democratic senators dared to denounce him, McCarthy openly campaigned against their reelection, and several went down to defeat. Journalists and intellectuals, with some notable exceptions, drew back from challenging him for fear of being themselves discredited by his attack. Even the highly popular Dwight D. Eisenhower, running for president in 1952, did not dare to oppose him. Outraged at McCarthy's attacks on General Marshall, Eisenhower briefly considered issuing a public protest. In the end, however, he remained silent.

The Republican Revival

Public frustration over the stalemate in Korea and popular fears of internal subversion combined to make 1952 an inhospitable year for the Democratic party. Truman, whose own popularity had diminished almost to the vanishing point, wisely withdrew from that year's presidential contest, creating the first open battle for the nomination since 1932. Senator Estes Kefauver of Tennessee launched a spirited campaign, performing well in the primaries. But party leaders ultimately settled on Governor Adlai E. Stevenson of Illinois, whose early reluctance to run seemed only to enhance his attractiveness.

Stevenson's dignity, wit, and eloquence quickly made him a beloved figure to many liberals and intellectuals, who developed a devotion to him that they had never offered Harry Truman. But those same

Nominating Ike

A song from an Irving Berlin musical provided the slogan for Dwight D. Eisenhower's 1952 campaign: "I Like Ike." Enthusiasm for the former general had less to do with his positions on public issues than with his distinguished military record and his image of stability and geniality. In this photograph, delegates at the 1952 Republican convention demonstrate on behalf of Eisenhower's nomination.   (AP/Wide World Photos)

qualities seemed only to fuel Republican charges that Stevenson lacked the strength or the will to combat communism sufficiently. McCarthy described him as "soft" and took delight in deliberately confusing him with Alger Hiss.

Stevenson's greatest problem, however, was the candidate the Republicans chose to oppose him. Rejecting the efforts of conservatives to nominate either Robert Taft or Douglas MacArthur, the Republicans turned to a man who had had so little previous identification with the party that liberal Democrats had

tried to draft him four years earlier. Their choice was General Dwight D. Eisenhower, military hero, former commander of NATO, now president of Columbia University in New York. Despite a vigorous struggle by the Taft forces, Eisenhower won nomination on the first ballot. He chose as his running mate the young California senator who had won national prominence through his crusade against Alger Hiss: Richard M. Nixon.

Eisenhower and Nixon proved to be a powerful combination in the autumn campaign. While Eisen-

SIGNIFICANT EVENTS

1941 Roosevelt and Churchill draft
Atlantic Charter

1943 Wendell Willkie publishes *One World*
Roosevelt, Churchill, Stalin meet at Teheran

1944 G.I. Bill of Rights enacted

1945 Yalta Conference
Roosevelt dies; Harry S. Truman becomes
president
Potsdam Conference
United Nations founded

1946 Atomic Energy Commission established
Postwar inflation
Coal and railroad strikes
Republicans win control of Congress
Crisis in Iran

1947 Communists take control in Hungary
Truman Doctrine announced
Marshall Plan proposed
National Security Act passed
Taft-Hartley Act passed
HUAC begins investigating Hollywood
Federal employee loyalty program
launched

1948 Communists stage coup in Czechoslovakia
Economic Cooperation Administration
established

1948 Selective Service System restored
Berlin blockade prompts U.S. airlift
Truman elected president
Hiss case begins
State of Israel established

1949 NATO established
Soviet Union explodes atomic bomb
Communists seize power in China

1950 NSC-68 outlines new U.S. policy toward
communism
Korean War begins
American troops enter North Korea
Chinese troops enter war
McCarran Act passed
Fuchs-Rosenberg case begins
Joseph McCarthy begins campaign against
communists in government
United States begins development of
hydrogen bomb

1951 Truman removes MacArthur from command
in Korea
Railroad workers strike
Negotiations begin in Korea

1952 American occupation of Japan ends
Steelworkers strike
Dwight D. Eisenhower elected president

hower attracted support by virtue of his geniality and his statesmanlike pledges to settle the Korean conflict (at one point dramatically promising to "go to Korea" himself), Nixon effectively exploited the issue of domestic anticommunism. After surviving early accusations of financial improprieties (which he effectively neutralized in a famous television address, the "Checkers speech"), Nixon went on to launch harsh attacks on Democratic "cowardice," "appeasement," and "treason." He spoke derisively of "Adlai the appeaser" and ridiculed Secretary of State Dean Acheson for running a "cowardly college of communist containment." And he missed no opportunity to publicize Stevenson's early support for Alger Hiss as opposed to Nixon's own role in exposing Hiss's misdeeds. Eisenhower and Nixon both made effective use of allegations of corruption in the Truman ad-

ministration and pledged repeatedly to "clean up the mess in Washington."

The response at the polls was overwhelming. Eisenhower won both a popular and an electoral landslide: 55 percent of the popular vote to Stevenson's 44 percent, 442 electoral votes to Stevenson's 89. Republicans gained marginal control of both houses of Congress; but it was clear that their presidential candidate was far more popular than the party as a whole. Nevertheless, the election of 1952 ended twenty years of largely uninterrupted Democratic control of the federal government. And while it might not have seemed so at the time, it also signaled the end of the turbulent postwar era and the beginning of a period marked by a search for cohesion and stability.

SUGGESTED READINGS

Origins of the Cold War   A good introduction to the vast literature on the Cold War is Walter LaFeber, *America, Russia, and the Cold War*, rev. ed. (1985), which carries the story to 1985. Stephen Ambrose, *Rise to Globalism* (1980), is another good overview of postwar foreign policy. Bernard Weisberger, *Cold War, Cold Peace* (1984), examines American-Soviet relations since 1945, as does an important earlier study by Adam Ulam, *The Rivals: America & Russia Since World War II* (1971). George C. Herring, Jr., *Aid to Russia* (1973), discusses one of the early controversies of the Cold War. John Lewis Gaddis, *Strategies of Containment* (1982), is a fine overview of the evolution of American security policies since 1945. Wartime relations between the United States and the Soviet Union are analyzed in John L. Snell, *Illusion and Necessity* (1967); Gaddis Smith, *American Diplomacy During the Second World War* (1965); Herbert Feis, *Churchill, Roosevelt, and Stalin* (1957); and William McNeill, *America, Britain and Russia* (1953). On the wartime accords, see Diane Clemens, *Yalta* (1970); Herbert Feis, *Between War and Peace: The Potsdam Conference* (1960); Athan G. Theoharis, *The Yalta Myths* (1970); and W. L. Neumann, *After Victory* (1969). Broader studies of the origins of the Cold War include John L. Gaddis, *The United States and the Origins of the Cold War* (1972); Daniel Yergin, *Shattered Peace* (1977); and Thomas Paterson, *Soviet-American Confrontation* (1974). Gregg Herken, *The Winning Weapon* (1980), and Martin Sherwin, *A World Destroyed* (1975), examine some of the policy implications of atomic weapons. Gar Alperovitz, *Atomic Diplomacy: Hiroshima and Potsdam*, rev. ed. (1985), is a controversial study linking the decision to use atomic weapons on Japan to America's hopes for curbing Soviet power.

Truman's Foreign Policy   Robert Donovan, *Conflict and Crisis* (1977), gives particular attention to the foreign policies of the Truman administration. Lloyd Gardner, *Architects of Illusion* (1970), and Joyce Kolko and Gabriel Kolko, *The Limits of Power* (1970), are critical studies. George F. Kennan, *American Diplomacy, 1900–1950* (1952) and *Memoirs, 1925–1950* (1967), are invaluable works by one of the architects of the containment doctrine. Dean Acheson's *Present at the Creation* (1970) is an important memoir by one of Truman's secretaries of state. Hadley Arkes, *Bureaucracy, the Marshall Plan and National Interest* (1973), examines the European Recovery Plan. A number of works examine American foreign policy in particular countries or regions. Akira Iriye, *The Cold War in Asia* (1974), and Robert M. Blum, *Drawing the Line: The Origin of the American Containment Policy in East Asia* (1982), are important overviews of American policies in Asia. John King Fairbank, *The United States and China*, rev. ed. (1971), and Edwin O. Reischauer, *The United States and Japan*, rev. ed. (1965), are classic works, which include chapters on the postwar era. See also Warren I. Cohen, *America's Response to China*, rev. ed. (1980). For background to the events of 1949, see Michael Schaller, *The U.S. Crusade in China* (1979) and *Communists* (1971). Lisle Rose, *Roots of Tragedy* (1976), is an overview of American policy in Asia in the postwar years.

Gary May, *China Scapegoat* (1979), examines the ordeal of John Carter Vincent, a China expert in the State Department victimized by countersubversion crusades. Christopher Thorne, *Allies of a Kind* (1978), is an important study of postwar American relations with its Asian allies. Bruce R. Koniholm, *The Origins of the Cold War in the Middle East* (1980), looks at the region whose troubles initially inspired the Truman Doctrine.

Truman's Domestic Policies   Alonzo Hamby, *Beyond the New Deal* (1973), is a useful study of liberal ideas in the Truman era. Robert Donovan, *Conflict and Crisis* (1977) and *Tumultuous Years* (1982), is a two-volume study of the Truman presidency. A useful collection of essays can be found in Barton J. Bernstein (ed.), *Politics and Policies of the Truman Administration* (1970). Andrew J. Dunar; *The Truman Scandals and the Politics of Morality* (1984), Robert H. Ferrell, *Harry S. Truman and the Modern American Presidency* (1983), and Donald R. McCoy, *The Presidency of Harry S. Truman* (1984), provide overviews. Susan Hartmann, *Truman and the 80th Congress* (1971), examines some of the legislative controversies of the Truman years. Stephen K. Bailey, *Congress Makes a Law* (1950), tells the story of the Employment Act of 1946. Particular political issues of the Truman years are examined in Richard O. Davies, *Housing Reform During the Truman Administration* (1966); R. Alton Lee, *Truman and the Steel Seizure Case* (1977); Allen J. Matusow, *Farm Policies and Politics in the Truman Years* (1967); Arthur F. McClure, *The Truman Administration and the Problems of Postwar Labor* (1969); and R. Alton Lee, *Truman and Taft-Hartley* (1967). William Berman, *The Politics of Civil Rights in the Truman Administration* (1970), Donald McCoy and Richard Ruetten, *Quest and Response* (1973), and Richard M. Dalfiume, *Desegregation of the U.S. Armed Forces* (1969), scrutinize the record on race. Maeva Marcus, *Truman and the Steel Seizure* (1977), is a study of one of the administration's flamboyant but unsuccessful attempts to quell instability.

Party Politics   James T. Patterson, *Mr. Republican* (1972), is a good biography of the Republican leader Senator Robert A. Taft. On the dramatic election of 1948, see Irwin Ross, *The Loneliest Campaign* (1968); Norman Markowitz, *The Rise and Fall of the People's Century* (1973), a study of the campaign of Henry Wallace; and Allen Yarnell, *Democrats and Progressives* (1974). Richard Norton Smith, *Thomas E. Dewey and His Times* (1982), is a biography of Truman's opponent in the contest.

The Korean War   An important study of Korean politics and society and how the war emerged out of them is Bruce Cumings, *The Origins of the Korean War* (1980). Glenn D. Paige, *The Korean Decision* (1968), explains American intervention. Joseph C. Goulden, *Korea: The Untold Story of the War* (1982), is a narrative history. John Spanier, *The Truman-MacArthur Controversy* (1959), examines one of the celebrated events of the war. Allen Whiting, *China Crosses the Yalu* (1960), discusses a turning point. Other works examining the conflict include Carl Berger, *The Korean Knot* (1957); Ronald Caridi, *The Korean War and American Politics* (1969), an examination of the domestic impact; Robert Leckie, *Conflict* (1962), a narrative overview; and Robert R. Simmons, *The Strained Alliance* (1975), which examines Korean–American relations. See also Charles W. Dobbs, *The Unwanted Symbol* (1981).

Countersubversion   A survey of the anticommunist frenzy of the postwar years is David Caute, *The Great Fear* (1978). Edward Shils, *The Torment of Secrecy* (1956), is an effort to explain the origins of the anticommunist crusade. Allen Weinstein, *Perjury* (1978), examines the Alger Hiss case and finds Hiss guilty. Ronald Radosh and Joyce Milton, *The Rosenberg File* (1983), argues similarly that the Rosenbergs were guilty; whereas Walter Schneer and Miriam Schneer, *Invitation to an Inquest*, rev. ed. (1983), make the case for the Rosenbergs' innocence. Richard Freeland, *The Truman Doctrine and the Origins of McCarthyism* (1971), studies the relations between the administration's foreign policy goals and its stance toward domestic subversion. Athan Theoharis, *Seeds of Repression* (1971), and Alan Harper, *The Politics of Loyalty* (1969), look similarly at the roots of McCarthyism in the policies of the Truman administration. Michael R. Belknap, *Cold War Political Justice: The Smith Act, the Communist Party, and American Civil Liberties* (1977), discusses some of the early anticommunist efforts within the federal government. Stanley Kutler, *The American Inquisition* (1982), examines several celebrated legal cases arising out of the anticommunist crusade. Larry Ceplair and Steven Englund, *The Inquisition in Hollywood* (1983), is a study of the ordeal of Hollywood screenwriters. Mary Sperling McAuliffe, *Crisis on the Left* (1978), is a good discussion of the deepening schism between liberals and leftists. Harvey Levenstein, *Communism, Anticommunism, and the CIO* (1981), discusses the subversion controversy in the labor movement. On McCarthy himself, two important biographies have recently appeared: Thomas C. Reeves, *The Life and Times of Joe McCarthy* (1982), and Michael Oshinsky, *A Conspiracy So Immense* (1983). See also Michael Paul Rogin, *The Intellectuals and McCarthy* (1967); Robert Griffith, *The Politics of Fear* (1970); and Richard Fried, *Men Against McCarthy* (1976). Richard Rovere, *Senator Joe McCarthy* (1959), is a lively contemporary study. Victor Navasky, *Naming Names* (1980), and William O'Neill, *A Better World* (1983), take starkly different positions on the actions of left-wing intellectuals in the postwar years. Joseph Starobin, *American Communism in Crisis* (1972), examines the plight of the embattled party.

After the Prom, **by Norman Rockwell, 1957** (Norman Rockwell Museum at Stockbridge)

Chapter 29 — The Affluent Society

The Affluent Society

I n later decades, Americans have tended to look back on the 1950s and early 1960s as something of a golden age: an era of boundless prosperity, of social stability, of national optimism and confidence. To some extent, that image has simply been the result of the nostalgia with which most generations view earlier, apparently happier times. But to a remarkable degree, it was also the image that many Americans of the 1950s held of their own society. Seldom before had the United States experienced an era of such pride and self-satisfaction.

Two fundamental realities shaped the mood of the decade. One was a booming national prosperity, which profoundly altered the social, economic, and even physical landscape of the United States as well as the way many Americans thought about their lives and their world. The other was the continuing struggle against communism, a struggle that created an undercurrent of anxiety but that also encouraged Americans to look even more approvingly at their own society.

These two compelling realities blinded many Americans to other aspects of their society—to serious problems that continued to plague large groups of the population. Prosperity, real as it was, did not extend to everyone. More than 30 million Americans, according to some estimates, continued to live in poverty in the 1950s. And despite the smug belief in the essential virtuousness of American life, large minorities within the population—most prominently the 10 percent of the American people who were black—continued to suffer from a vicious system of social, political, and economic discrimination. Gunnar Myrdal, a Swedish sociologist well acquainted

with life in the United States, wrote at the time: "American affluence is heavily mortgaged. America carries a tremendous burden of debt to its poor people." The efforts to pay that debt would ultimately help move the nation out of the complacency of the 1950s and into a far more turbulent era in the 1960s.

For a time, however, such problems seemed far away to most members of the rapidly growing American middle class, who were enjoying an era of rising living standards without precedent in history. And to some degree, they seemed far away to America's political leaders as well, who attempted in the 1950s to limit the role of the federal government in American life and even, in some respects, to limit the role of the United States in the world.

The Economic "Miracle"

Perhaps the most striking feature of American life in the 1950s and early 1960s, one that virtually no observer could ignore, was prosperity—a booming, almost miraculous economic growth that made even the heady 1920s seem pale by comparison. It was a prosperity far better balanced and far more widely distributed than that of thirty years earlier. It was not, however, as universal as some Americans liked to believe.

Economic Growth

By 1949, despite the continuing problems of postwar reconversion, what some called the "miracle" of

American economic expansion had begun. It would continue with only minor interruptions for almost twenty years. The gross national product, the most basic indicator of economic growth, alone provides ample evidence of the prosperity of the era. The GNP had doubled in the five years of World War II. Between 1945 and 1960, it grew by 250 percent, from $200 billion to over $500 billion. That growth appears even more remarkable in view of widespread public expectations in 1945 that the GNP would soon decline once the extraordinary demands of war production subsided. Unemployment, which during the Depression had averaged between 15 and 25 percent, remained throughout the 1950s and early 1960s at about 5 percent or lower. Inflation, in the meantime, hovered at about 3 percent a year or less.

There was no single cause. Government spending, which had ended the Depression in the 1940s, continued to stimulate growth. There was increasing public funding of schools, housing, veterans' benefits, welfare, and interstate highways (for which the government spent over $100 billion in the two decades following passage of the Interstate Highway Act of 1956)—all helping to sustain prosperity. Above all, there was military spending, which continued at almost wartime levels. The Korean War, in particular, helped to spark the economic boom. During the first half of the 1950s, when military spending was at its peak, the annual growth rate was 4.7 percent. For the second half of the decade, with the Korean War concluded and spending on armaments in decline, the rate of growth was only 2.25 percent.

Technological progress also contributed to the boom. Because of advances in production techniques and mechanical efficiency, worker productivity increased more than 35 percent in the first decade after the war, a rate far higher than that of any previous era. The development of electronic computers, which first became commercially available in the mid-1950s, began to improve the performance of some American corporations. And technological research and development itself became an important new sector of the economy, expanding the demand for scientists, engineers, and other highly trained experts.

The national birth rate reversed a long pattern of decline. The so-called baby boom, which had begun during the war, peaked in 1957. The nation's population rose almost 20 percent in the decade, from 150 million in 1950 to 179 million in 1960. This growth mirrored a worldwide demographic explosion that would ultimately place great strains on the resources of the planet. In the United States of the 1950s, how-

ever, the baby boom meant increased consumer demand and expanding economic growth.

The rapid expansion of suburbs—whose population grew 47 percent in the 1950s, more than twice as fast as the population of the nation as a whole—helped stimulate growth in several important sectors of the economy. The automobile industry experienced the greatest boom in its history, as the number of privately owned cars more than doubled in a decade. The demand for new homes helped sustain a vigorous housing industry. The construction of roads, which was both a cause and a result of the growth of suburbs, stimulated the economy even further.

Perhaps the most striking result of this long period of sustained economic growth was the rising standard of living for the majority of the population. In the thirty years after the war, the economy grew nearly ten times as fast as the population. And while that growth was far from equally distributed, it was great enough to affect most of society. The average American in 1960 had over 20 percent more purchasing power than in 1945, and more than twice as much as during the prosperous 1920s. By 1960, per capita income (the average income for every individual man, woman, and child) was over $1,800—$500 more than it had been fifteen years before. Family incomes had risen even more. The American people had created for themselves the highest standard of living in the history of the world.

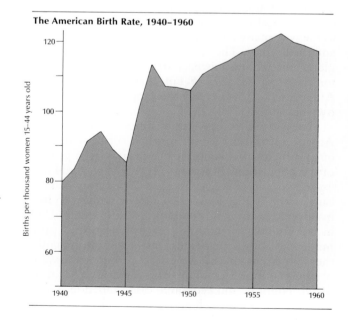

The American Birth Rate, 1940–1960

The Suburban Consumer
This early 1950s advertisement for a Whirlpool washing machine shows one of the many consumer appliances that were then becoming within reach of the average American consumer. Women were a particularly important target of advertisers, as this picture suggests; and manufacturers tried to associate their products with the comfortable, middle-class suburban life styles to which women in the 1950s were encouraged to aspire.

(Whirlpool Corporation)

The New Economics

The exciting (and to some surprising) discovery of the power of the American economic system was a central element in the emergence of the confident tone of American political life in the 1950s. During the Depression, some had questioned the viability of capitalism. In the 1950s, such doubts all but disappeared. Two features in particular made the postwar economy a source of national confidence.

First was the belief that Keynesian economics made it possible for government to regulate and sta-

bilize the economy without intruding directly into the private sector. The British economist John Maynard Keynes had argued as early as the 1920s that by varying the flow of government spending and managing the supply of currency, the state could stimulate the economy to cure recession, and dampen growth to prevent inflation. The experience of the last years of the Depression and the first years of the war had seemed to confirm this argument. And by the mid-1950s, Keynesian theory was rapidly becoming a fundamental article of faith—not only among professional economists but among much of the public at large. The most popular economics textbook of the 1950s and 1960s, Paul Samuelson's *Economics,* imbued generations of college students with Keynesian ideas. Armed with these fiscal and monetary tools, economists now believed, it was possible for the government to maintain a permanent prosperity. The dispiriting boom-and-bust cycle that many had long believed to be a permanent feature of industrial capitalism could now be banished forever. Never again would it be necessary for the nation to experience another Depression.

If any doubters remained, they found ample evidence to dispel their misgivings during the brief recessions the economy experienced during the era. When the economy slackened in late 1953, Secretary of the Treasury George M. Humphrey and the Federal Reserve Board worked to ease credit and make money more readily available. The economy quickly recovered, helping to confirm the value of Keynesian tactics. A far more serious recession began late in 1957 and continued for more than a year. This time, the Eisenhower administration ignored the Keynesians and adopted such deflationary tactics as cutting the budget. The slow, halting nature of the recovery, in contrast with the rapid revival in 1954, seemed further to support the Keynesian philosophy. The new economics finally won full acceptance in 1963, when John Kennedy proposed a tax cut to stimulate economic growth. Although it took Kennedy's death and the political skills of Lyndon Johnson to win passage of the measure in 1964, the result was all that the Keynesians had predicted: an increase in private demand, which stimulated economic growth and reduced unemployment.

In addition to the belief in the possibility of permanent economic stability was the equally exhilarating belief in permanent economic growth. As the economy continued to expand far beyond what any observer had predicted was possible only a few years before, more and more Americans assumed that such growth was now without bounds—that there were few effective limits on the abundance available to the nation. This was not only a comforting thought in itself; it also provided a new outlook on social and economic problems. In the 1930s, many Americans had argued that the elimination of poverty and injustice would require a redistribution of wealth—a limitation on the fortunes of the rich and a distribution of this wealth to the poor. By the mid-1950s, reformers concerned about economic deprivation were arguing that the solution lay in increased production. The affluent would not have to sacrifice in order to eliminate poverty. The nation would simply have to

produce more abundance, thus raising the quality of life of even the poorest citizens to a level of comfort and decency.

Capital and Labor

The prosperity of the 1920s had been accompanied by a rapid increase in economic centralization and concentration. The prosperity of the 1950s brought with it a similar consolidation. There were more than 4,000 corporate mergers in the course of the 1950s; and more than ever, a few large corporations controlled an enormous proportion of the nation's economic activity. This was particularly true in industries benefiting from government defense spending. As during World War II, the federal government tended to award military contracts to large corporations. In 1959, for example, half of all defense contracts went to only twenty firms. But the same pattern repeated itself in many other areas of the economy, as corporations moved from being single-industry firms to becoming diversified conglomerates. By the end of the decade, half of the net corporate income in the nation was going to only slightly more than 500 firms, or one-tenth of 1 percent of the total number of corporations.

A similar consolidation was in process in the agricultural economy. Increasing mechanization reduced the need for farm labor, and the agricultural work force declined by more than half in the two decades after the war. Mechanization rewarded economies of scale, as did the higher productivity that new fertilizers and improved irrigation techniques made possible. As a result, many farms began to come under the control of corporations or very large landowners. The rise of what became known as "agribusiness" challenged the survival of one of the most cherished American institutions: the family farm. By the 1960s, relatively few individuals could any longer afford to buy and equip a modern farm; and much of the nation's most productive land had been purchased by financial institutions and corporations.

Unlike the 1920s, the increase in corporate consolidation was accompanied by a rise in the power of labor organizations. Corporations enjoying such remarkable growth were reluctant to allow strikes to interfere with their operations; and since the most important unions were now so large and entrenched that they could not easily be suppressed or intimidated, business leaders made important concessions to them. As early as 1948, Walter Reuther, president of the United Automobile Workers, obtained from General Motors a contract that included a built-in "escalator clause"—an automatic cost-of-living increase pegged to the consumer price index. The provision set a crucial precedent—not only for the rest of the automobile industry but for the economy at large. In 1955, Reuther received a guarantee from Ford Motor Company of continuing wages to auto workers even during layoffs (although not the guaranteed annual wage he had demanded). A few months later, steelworkers in several corporations did receive guarantees of an annual salary. By the mid-1950s, factory wages in all industries had risen substantially, to an average of $80 per week.

Not all laborers shared in such gains. The labor movement enjoyed great success in winning new benefits for workers already organized in strong unions. For the majority of laborers who were as yet unorganized, there were fewer advances. Total union membership remained relatively stable, at about 16 million, throughout the 1950s; and while this was in part a result of a shift in the work force from blue-collar to white-collar jobs, it was at least as much a result of new obstacles to organization. The Taft-Hartley Act and the state right-to-work laws that it spawned made more difficult the creation of new unions that would be powerful enough to demand recognition from employers.

The economic successes of the entrenched unions in the 1950s helped pave the way for the reunification of the labor movement. In December 1955, the American Federation of Labor and the Congress of Industrial Organizations ended their twenty-year rivalry and merged to create a giant new federation, the AFL-CIO, under the leadership of George Meany. But the climate of the era produced other, less welcome changes in the nature of the labor movement. Some large unions, no longer required to engage in the militant crusades against corporate resistance that had dominated the 1930s, were themselves becoming wealthy, powerful bureaucracies. Most continued to operate responsibly and effectively; but some of the most important unions began to face accusations of corruption and indifference.

The powerful Teamsters Union became in 1957 the focal point of a congressional investigation in which its president, David Beck, was charged with the misappropriation of over $320,000 in union funds. Beck ultimately stepped down from his office to be replaced by Jimmy Hoffa, who was widely believed to have close ties to organized crime. Government investigators pursued Hoffa for nearly a decade before finally winning a conviction against him (for tax

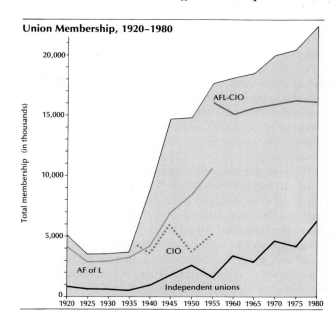

Union Membership, 1920–1980

evasion) in 1967. After his release from prison in 1971 (on a pardon from President Richard Nixon), he attempted to regain his position in the union. But before he could succeed, he disappeared and was generally presumed to have been murdered. The United Mine Workers, the union that had spearheaded the industrial movement in the 1930s, similarly became tainted by suspicions of corruption and by violence. John L. Lewis's last years as head of the union were plagued with scandals and dissent within the organization. His successor, Tony Boyle, was ultimately convicted of complicity in the 1969 murder of Joseph Yablonski, the leader of a dissident faction within the union.

Even more troubling, perhaps, was the growing belief among union members that the leaders of these and other labor organizations had lost touch with the rank and file, that they had become more concerned with the internal bureaucratic and political struggles of the union organization itself than with the welfare of the members.

A People of Plenty

The most striking social development of the immediate postwar era was the rapid extension of a middle-class life style and outlook to large groups of the population previously insulated from it. The new prosperity of social groups that had previously lived on the margins; the growing availability of consumer products at affordable prices and the rising public fascination with such products; and perhaps above all, the massive population movement from the cities to the suburbs: All helped make the American middle class a much larger, more powerful, more homogeneous, and more dominant force than it had ever been before.

The new prosperity, in fact, inspired some Americans to see abundance as the key to understanding the American past and the American character. Leading intellectuals argued that American history had been characterized by a broad "consensus" of agreement about the value and necessity of competitive, capitalist growth. "However much at odds on specific issues," the historian Richard Hofstadter wrote in *The American Political Tradition* (1948), Americans have "shared a belief in the rights of property, the philosophy of economic individualism, the value of competition; they have accepted the economic virtues of capitalist culture as necessary qualities of man." David Potter, another leading American historian of the era, published an influential examination of "economic abundance and American character" in 1954. He called it *People of Plenty*. For the American middle class in the 1950s, at least, it seemed an appropriate label.

The Consumer Culture

At the center of middle-class culture in the 1950s was a growing absorption with consumer goods. It was a result not just of the new prosperity and the increasing variety and availability of products but also of the adeptness of advertisers in creating a demand for those products. It was also a result of the growth of consumer credit, which increased by 800 percent between 1945 and 1957. Easily available credit cards, revolving charge accounts, and easy-payment plans made immediate gratification of consumer yearnings not only desirable but possible. Affluent Americans in the 1950s and 1960s showed renewed interest in such longtime consumer crazes as the automobile, and Detroit responded to the boom with ever-flashier styling and accessories. Consumers also responded eagerly to the development of such new products as dishwashers, garbage disposals, televisions, and "hifis" and stereos. To a striking degree, the prosperity of the 1950s and 1960s was consumer-driven (as opposed to investment-driven).

The Mickey Mouse Club
One of the most popular children's television programs of the 1950s, Walt Disney's "Mickey Mouse Club," was also one of the most successful marketing tools of the era. It helped generate enthusiasm for other products of the Disney organization—films, consumer goods, and the Disneyland amusement park in southern California.
(© Walt Disney Company)

Because consumer goods were so often marketed (and advertised) nationally, the 1950s were notable for the rapid spread of great national consumer crazes. Children, adolescents, and even some adults became entranced in the late 1950s with the "hula-hoop"—a large plastic ring kept spinning around the waist. The popularity of the Walt Disney–produced children's television show, *The Mickey Mouse Club*, created a national demand for related products such as Mickey Mouse watches and hats. (It also helped produce the stunning success of Disneyland, an amusement park near Los Angeles that re-created many of the characters and events of Disney entertainment programs.)

The Disney technique of turning an entertainment success into an effective tool for marketing consumer goods was not an isolated event. Many other entertainers and producers did the same.

The Suburban Nation

A third of the nation's population lived in suburbs by 1960. The growth of suburbs was a result not only of increased affluence, but of important innovations in homebuilding, which made single-family houses affordable to millions of new people. The most famous of the suburban developers, Arthur Levitt, began what became a national trend with his use of mass-production techniques to construct a large housing development on Long Island, near New York City. This first "Levittown" (there would later be others in New Jersey and Pennsylvania) consisted of several thousand two-bedroom Cape Cod style houses, with identical interiors and only slightly varied facades, each perched on its own concrete slab (to eliminate excavation costs), facing curving, treeless streets. Levittown houses sold for under $10,000, and they helped meet an enormous demand for housing that had been developing for more than a decade. Young couples—often newly married war veterans eager to start a family—rushed to purchase the inexpensive homes, not only in the Levittowns but in similar developments that soon began appearing throughout the country.

Why did so many Americans want to move to the suburbs? One reason was the enormous importance postwar Americans placed on family life after five years of war in which families had often been separated or otherwise disrupted. Suburbs provided new families with larger homes than they could find (or afford) in the cities, and thus made it easier to bring up larger numbers of children. They provided privacy. They provided security from the noise and dangers of urban living. They offered space for the new consumer goods—the appliances, cars, boats, outdoor furniture, and other products—that most Americans craved.

For many Americans, suburban life helped provide a sense of community that was sometimes difficult to develop in large, crowded, impersonal urban areas. In later years, the "conformity" and "homogeneity" of the suburbs would be blamed for a wide range of social ills. But in the 1950s, many people were attracted by the idea of living in a community populated largely by people of similar age and background. Not all suburbs were as homogeneous as

they sometimes appeared; a famous study of one of the Levittowns, for example, revealed a striking variety of occupations, ethnic backgrounds, and incomes within a single neighborhood. Nevertheless, suburban societies tended to attract people looking for a similar life style. Women in particular often valued the presence of other nonworking mothers living nearby to share the tasks of child raising.

Another factor motivating white Americans to move to the suburbs was race. Most suburbs were restricted to white inhabitants—both because relatively few blacks could afford to live in them and

Chicago's Annexations and the Suburban Noose

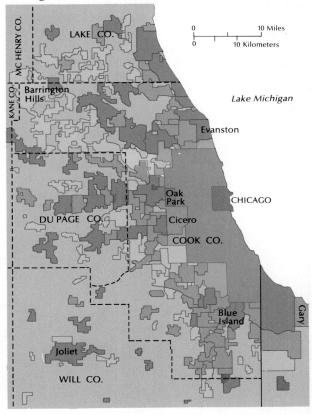

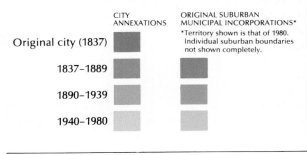

	CITY ANNEXATIONS	ORIGINAL SUBURBAN MUNICIPAL INCORPORATIONS*
		*Territory shown is that of 1980. Individual suburban boundaries not shown completely.
Original city (1837)		
1837–1889		
1890–1939		
1940–1980		

because of formal and informal barriers to keep even affluent blacks out. As the black population of the nation's cities grew rapidly in the postwar years, and as urban school systems began to include increasing numbers of blacks (especially after the Supreme Court desegregation decisions of the mid-1950s), many white families fled to the suburbs to escape the integration of urban neighbhorhoods and schools.

One of the striking aspects of suburban life was how similar it often was from one area of the country to another. Because so many suburbs were built at about the same time, using similar construction techniques, the physical similarities alone were often striking. And because many middle-class profession als were in the 1950s and 1960s living increasingly mobile lives—moving from one city to another as the national corporations for which they worked demanded—suburban populations often did not consist of people with strong local roots. On the other hand, suburban neighborhoods, just like urban neighborhoods, were not uniform. The Levittowns ultimately became the homes of mainly lower-middle-class people, one step removed from the inner city. Other, more affluent suburbs became enclaves of far wealthier families. Around virtually every city, a clear hierarchy emerged of "good" suburban neighbhorhoods and more modest ones, just as such gradations had emerged years earlier within the cities themselves.

The Suburban Family

The growth of suburbs was not only a response to the growing demand for stable family life among the American middle class. It also helped to shape the nature of that life. The suburban family was isolated from the activities of the city. To a large degree, it was even isolated from other suburban families. Homes were designed to maximize privacy; a distinctive feature of many new suburbs was that the back yard of each house, not the front yard, was the center of family activity. Moreover, since commercial and social facilities were generally distant enough from residential areas that they could be reached only by automobile, many suburban neighborhoods did not even include sidewalks; developers assumed that residents would seldom walk anywhere. The nature of the suburbs, in other words, encouraged families to turn inward, to focus their attention on the nuclear family unit.

For professional men (who tended to work at some distance from their homes, in the city), suburban life generally meant a rigid division between their working and personal worlds. For many middle-class women, it means an increased isolation from the workplace. The enormous emphasis on family life of the 1950s created a particularly strong prejudice against women entering the professions, or occupy-

Suburban Life
Stevan Dohanos, an artist who specialized in scenes of life in suburbia, produced this whimsical painting in 1956 for the cover of *The Saturday Evening Post*. Its condescending view of the competence of women, commonplace at the time, was one of the stereotypes that feminists would later challenge.
(*Saturday Evening Post,* © 1956 Curtis Publishing Company)

ing any paid job at all. Husbands often considered it demeaning for their wives to be employed; they feared it would be seen as a sign of their own inability to provide for their families. And women themselves often shied away from the workplace when they could afford to, in part because of new ideas about motherhood that seemed to require them to stay at home with their children.

One of the single most influential books in postwar American life was a famous guide to child rearing: Dr. Benjamin Spock's *Baby and Child Care,* first published in 1946 and reissued repeatedly for years thereafter. Dr. Spock's approach to raising babies was child-centered, as opposed to the parent-centered theories of many previous child-care experts. The purpose of motherhood was to help children learn and grow and realize their own potential. All other considerations, including the mother's own physical and emotional requirements, must be subordinated to the needs of the child. Dr. Spock envisioned only a very modest role for fathers in the process of child rearing.

Affluent women, then, faced heavy pressures—both externally and internally imposed—to remain in the home and concentrate on raising their children. Many women, however, had to balance these pressures against other, contradictory ones. In a society that was increasingly coming to prize the accumulation of consumer goods as a badge of success, many middle-class families found that a second income was essential for the maintenance of the standard of living they desired. As a result, the number of married women working outside the home increased greatly in the postwar years—even as the social pressure for them to stay out of the workplace grew. By 1960, nearly a third of all married women were part of the paid work force. Many of those, of course, were women from working-class families, whose incomes were often essential to family survival. But many were also middle-class women, working to supplement the family income to permit a more comfortable life style.

The experiences of the 1950s worked in some ways to diminish the power of feminism, which for a time ebbed to its lowest point in nearly a century. But they also helped create conditions that would only a decade later create the most powerful feminist movement in American history. The increasing numbers of women in the workplace laid the groundwork for demands for equal treatment that became an important part of the feminist crusades of the 1960s and 1970s. And the growing frustrations of women who remained in the home created a heightened demand for female professional opportunities, a demand that would also soon help to fuel the women's liberation movement.

The Birth of Television

The postwar era witnessed the birth of perhaps the most powerful medium of mass communication in history: television. Experiments in broadcasting pictures (along with sound) over the airwaves had begun as early as the 1920s, but commercial television did not come into existence until shortly after World War II. It experienced a phenomenally rapid growth. In 1946, there were only 17,000 sets in the entire country; by 1953, two-thirds of all American homes had televisions; and by 1957, there were 40 million television sets in use—almost as many sets as there were families. More people had television sets, according to one report, than had refrigerators.

The television industry emerged directly out of the radio industry, and all three of the major networks—the National Broadcasting Company, the Columbia Broadcasting System, and the American Broadcasting Company—had begun their lives as radio companies. The television business, like radio, was driven by advertising. Programming decisions were made largely on the basis of how best to attract advertisers; and in the early days of television, sponsors often played a direct, powerful, and continuing role in determining the content of the programs they chose to sponsor. Many early television shows came to bear the names of the corporations that were paying for them: the "GE Television Theater," the "Chrysler Playhouse," the "Camel News Caravan," and others.

The impact of television on American life was rapid, pervasive, and profound. Television news had by the end of the 1950s replaced newspapers, magazines, and radios as the nation's most important vehicle of information. Television advertising exposed the entire nation to new fashions and products. Television entertainment programming, almost all of it controlled by the three national networks (and their corporate sponsors), created a common image of American life—an image that was predominantly white, middle-class, and suburban. Televised sports events gradually made professional sports one of the important sources of entertainment (and one of the biggest businesses) in America.

Even those unable to share in the affluence of the era could, through television, acquire a vivid picture of how the rest of their society lived. Thus television ultimately became not only a force encouraging increased homogeneity among members of the white middle class. It also became a force that contributed to the sense of alienation and powerlessness of groups excluded from the world it portrayed.

Science and Space

In 1961, *Time* magazine chose as its "man of the year" not a specific person but "the American Scientist." It was an indication of the widespread fascination with which Americans in the age of atomic weapons viewed science and technology. Major medical advances accounted for much of that fascination. In 1955, Jonas Salk's vaccine to prevent polio was made available to the public, free, by the federal government, and within a few years it had virtually eliminated polio from American life. Other dread diseases such as diphtheria and tuberculosis also all but vanished from society as new drugs and treatments were discovered. Infant mortality declined by nearly 50 percent in the first twenty-five years after the war; the death rate among young children declined significantly as well. Average life expectancy in those same years rose by five years, to seventy-one.

The centrality of science in American life owed at least as much to other technological innovations—such as the jet plane, the computer, synthetics, and new types of commercially prepared foods. But nothing better illustrated the nation's veneration of scientific expertise than the popular enthusiasm for the American space program.

The program began in large part because of the Cold War. When the Soviet Union announced in 1957 that it had launched a satellite—*Sputnik*—into outer space, the United States reacted with shock and alarm. Strenuous efforts began—to improve scientific education in the schools, to develop more research laboratories, and above all, to speed the development of America's own exploration of outer space. The centerpiece of that exploration was the manned space program, established in 1958 with the selection of the first American space pilots. For several years, the original seven "astronauts" were the nation's most widely revered heroes. The entire country sat by their televisions on May 5, 1961, as Alan Shepard became the first American launched into space (several months after a Soviet "cosmonaut," Yuri Gagarin, had made a similar flight). John Glenn, who on February 2, 1962, became the first American to orbit the globe (again, only after Gagarin had already done so), was soon an even more celebrated national idol. Yet for all the hero worship, Americans marveling at space exploration were reacting less to the individual men involved than to the enormous scientific effort that lay behind their exploits.

Ultimately, some Americans began to tire of the space program, which never managed to convince everyone that it offered any practical benefits. But interest remained high as late as the summer of 1969, when Neil Armstrong and Edwin Aldrin became the first men to walk on the surface of the moon. Not long after that, the government began to cut the funding for future missions. But even in leaner times, the space program continued to exercise a unique grip on the popular imagination. In the late 1970s and 1980s, the National Aeronautics and Space Administration (NASA) managed to revive some of the earlier enthusiasm for space exploration with the development of a reusable "space shuttle," which performed various commercial functions (such as launching communications satellites) as well as research and military ones. Early in 1986, a terrible explosion destroyed one of the shuttles shortly after it took off. Seven astronauts died. The incident sparked a wave of national grief and anguish that made clear the degree to which the space program continued to embody some of the nation's most romantic hopes.

Organized Society and Its Detractors

Even more than in the 1920s, Americans in the 1950s and 1960s were aware of the importance of organizations and bureaucracies in their lives. White-collar workers, who in the 1950s came to outnumber blue-collar laborers for the first time, found employment predominantly in corporate settings with rigid hierarchical structures. Industrial workers confronted ponderous bureaucracies in their own unions. Consumers discovered the frustrations of bureaucracy in dealing with the large national companies from whom they bought goods and services. More and more Americans were becoming convinced that the key to a successful future lay in acquiring the specialized training and skills necessary for work in large organizations, where every worker performed a particular, well-defined function.

The American educational system, in particular, began to respond to the demands of this increasingly organized society by experimenting with changes in

Moon Landing, 1971

After the successful landing of Neil Armstrong, the first man to set foot on the moon, NASA sent five other manned missions to the lunar surface. Here, astronaut James B. Irwin is shown saluting the American flag he had just planted. Behind him is the Lunar Rover, a battery-operated vehicle that the astronauts used to explore the terrain and collect scientific data. (NASA)

curriculum and philosophy. Elementary and secondary schools gave increased attention to the teaching of science, mathematics, and foreign languages—all of which were believed to be important for the development of skilled, specialized professionals. The National Defense Education Act of 1958 (passed in response to the Soviet Union's *Sputnik* success) provided federal funding for development of programs in those areas. Universities in the meantime were expanding their curricula to provide more opportunities for students to develop specialized skills. The idea of the "multiversity"—a phrase first coined by the chancellor of the University of California at Berkeley to describe his institution's diversity—represented a commitment to making higher education a vehicle for training specialists in a wide variety of fields.

As in earlier eras, Americans reacted to these developments with ambivalence, often hostility. The debilitating impact of bureaucratic life on the individual slowly became one of the central themes of popular and scholarly debate. William H. Whyte, Jr., produced one of the most widely discussed books of the decade: *The Organization Man* (1956), which attempted to describe the special mentality of the worker in a large, bureaucratic setting. Self-reliance, Whyte claimed, was losing place to the ability to "get along" and "work as a team" as the most valuable trait in modern character. Sociologist David Riesman made similar observations in *The Lonely Crowd* (1950), in which he argued that the traditional "inner-directed" man, who judged himself on the basis of his own values and the esteem of his family, was giving way to a new "other-directed" man, more concerned with winning the approval of the larger organization or community. Even those who lived and worked outside bureaucratic settings, some critics argued, were subjected to the homogenizing pressures of a "mass culture," dominated by television and designed to appeal to the "lowest common denominator."

The most decisive critics of the culture of the affluent society were a number of young poets and writers generally known as the "beats" (or, by derisive critics, as "beatniks"). To them, the conventional society of the American middle class was an object of contempt, a world to be avoided and despised. They wrote harsh critiques of the sterility and conformity of American life, the meaningless of American politics, and the banality of popular culture. Allen Ginsberg, one of the most celebrated of the beats, attracted wide acclaim with his dark, bitter poem *Howl* (1955), decrying the "Robot apartments! invincible suburbs! skeleton treasuries! blind capitals! demonic industries!" of modern life. Jack Kerouac, a talented novelist whose severe alcoholism and early death sharply limited his creative output, nevertheless produced what may have been the leading document of the Beat Generation: *On the Road* (1957)—an account of a cross-country automobile trip that depicted the rootless, iconoclastic life style of Kerouac and his friends.

Other, less starkly alienated writers also used their work to express misgivings about the enormity and impersonality of modern society. Saul Bellow produced a series of novels—*The Adventures of Augie March* (1953), *Seize the Day* (1956), *Herzog* (1964), and others—that chronicled the difficulties of modern, urban Jews in finding fulfillment in the dehumanizing environment in which they lived. J. D. Salinger, one of the most popular writers of the era, wrote in *The Catcher in the Rye* (1951) of the crushing impact of modern life on vulnerable, sensitive individuals. The novel described the dilemma of prep-school student Holden Caulfield, unable to find any area of society—school, family, friends, city—in which he could feel secure or committed. In the 1950s and early 1960s, such warnings remained relatively muted, as in the writings of Bellow and Salinger, or had only a limited impact on the culture at large, as with the work of Ginsberg and Kerouac. By the late 1960s, however, these concerns were becoming crucial to the creation of a widespread and at least briefly influential "counterculture."

The Other America

Middle-class Americans in the 1950s liked to believe that their growing prosperity was reaching virtually every area of society. It was not. Important groups continued to struggle on the fringes of the economic boom, unable to share in the abundance.

Between 1948 and 1956, while national income

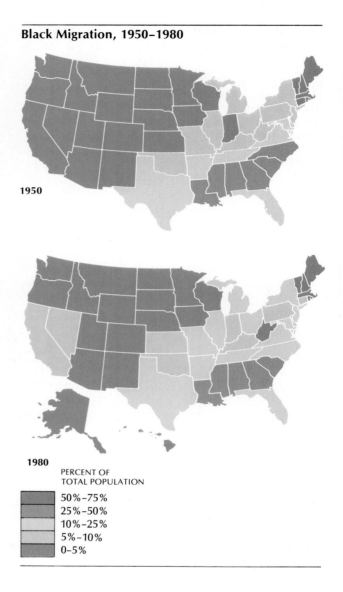

Black Migration, 1950–1980

1950

1980

PERCENT OF
TOTAL POPULATION

50%–75%
25%–50%
10%–25%
5%–10%
0–5%

increased 50 percent, farm prices dropped 33 percent—the victim of enormous surpluses in basic staples. In 1948, farmers had received 8.9 percent of the national income; in 1956, they received only 4.1 percent. In part, this decline reflected the steadily shrinking farm population; in 1956 alone, one out of every eleven rural residents moved into or was absorbed by a city. But it also reflected the deteriorating economic condition of those farmers who remained in agriculture. They experienced not only a decline in their own income but a steady increase in the prices they paid for consumer goods.

Farmers, at least, were able to attract some public

attention to their plight. Other, poorer groups languished in virtual obscurity. As middle-class Americans left the cities for the suburbs, it became easier for them to ignore the existence of severe poverty in the heart of the major industrial metropolises. Black ghettoes were expanding rapidly in the 1950s, as black farmers joined the general exodus from country to city and as the black population as a whole expanded rapidly. Continuing racial discrimination helped doom large proportions of these communities to ever-increasing poverty. In New York City, Los Angeles, and elsewhere, growing Puerto Rican, Mexican, and other Hispanic communities were also earning less than what the government considered the minimum necessary for "adequate" living.

Urban ghettoes were becoming so isolated from the economic mainstream that many of their residents were finding it almost impossible to obtain employment. Thus some "inner cities" were turning into virtual prisons for poor people, who had neither the resources to move to areas where jobs were more plentiful nor the political power to force development of their own communities. A similar predicament faced residents of several particularly destitute rural regions—most notably the Appalachian areas of the Southern and border states, which were experiencing an almost total economic collapse. Lacking adequate schools, health care, and services, the residents of Appalachia, like the residents of the urban ghettoes, were almost entirely shut off from the mainstream of American economic life. Not until the 1960s, when such exposés as Michael Harrington's *The Other America* (1962) began drawing attention to the continuing existence of poverty in the nation, did the middle class begin to recognize the seriousness of the problem.

The Rise of the Civil-Rights Movement

The prosperous 1950s helped produce a mood of cautious moderation among many Americans. On one issue, however, these years were a time in which a major social revolution finally commenced. After decades of skirmishes, there began in the 1950s an open battle against racial segregation and discrimination, a battle that would prove to be one of the longest and most difficult of the century.

The emergence of civil rights as a national issue was a slow and painful process, but it was speeded along its way by several important developments. The Cold War—and the pressures it created at home to remove social blights that might serve communist propaganda purposes—helped force many white Americans to confront racial injustice with special urgency. The federal government—slowly, at times reluctantly—began moving into position to play a crucial role in fighting for civil rights, beginning in 1954 with one of the most important Supreme Court decisions in American history. The increasingly urban character of the black population sped the growth of black protest by creating large communities in which ideas and organizational efforts could expand. It was pressure from blacks themselves that was the crucial element in raising civil rights to prominence.

The Brown *Decision and* *"Massive Resistance"*

In 1954, years of patient legal efforts by the NAACP and other black reformers finally bore fruit when, on May 17, the Supreme Court announced its decision in the case of *Brown* v. *Board of Education of Topeka*. In considering the legal segregation of a Kansas public school system, the Court finally rejected the doctrine of the 1896 *Plessy* v. *Ferguson* decision, which had established that communities could provide blacks with separate facilities as long as the facilities were equal to those of whites.

The *Brown* decision was the culmination of many decades of effort by black opponents of segregation. Above all, perhaps, it was the result of efforts by a group of talented black lawyers, many of them trained at Howard University in Washington by the great legal educator Charles Houston. Thurgood Marshall, William Hastie, James Nabrit, and others (working under the aegis of the NAACP) spent years filing legal challenges to segregation in one state after another, nibbling at the edges of the system, exposing its weaknesses and contradictions, and accumulating precedents to support their assault on the "separate but equal" doctrine itself. It was these NAACP lawyers who filed the suit against the school board of Topeka, Kansas, that became the basis for the *Brown* decision.

The suit involved the case of a black girl in Topeka who had to travel several miles to a black public school every day even though she lived virtually next door to a white elementary school. When the case finally arrived before the Supeme Court, the justices examined it not simply in terms of legal precedent but in terms of history, sociology, and psychology. And they concluded, finally, that school segregation inflicted unacceptable damage on those it affected, regardless of the relative quality of the separate schools. Chief Justice Earl Warren explained the unanimous opinion of his colleagues: "We conclude that in the field of public education the doctrine of "separate but equal' has no place. Separate educational facilities are inherently unequal."

The original decision offered no guidance as to how desegregation was to be accomplished, and the justices apparently believed that any such change would have to be accomplished gradually. The following year, they issued another decision (known as "*Brown* II") to provide guidance for the implementation of the 1954 order. They ruled that communities must work to desegregate their schools "with all deliberate speed," but they set no timetable and left specific decisions up to lower courts.

It was not to be an easy process. In some communities, compliance came relatively quickly and relatively painlessly, as in Washington, D.C. Far more often, however, strong local opposition (what came to be known in the South as "massive resistance") produced long delays and bitter conflicts. Some school districts ignored the ruling altogether. Others attempted to circumvent it with purely token efforts to integrate. The "pupil placement laws" that many school districts enacted allowed school officials to place students in schools according to their scholastic abilities and social behavior. Such laws were transparent devices for maintaining segregation; but in 1958, the Supreme Court (in *Shuttlesworth* v. *Birmingham Board of Education*) refused to declare them unconstitutional.

Southern politicians encouraged the growth of massive resistance. More than 100 Southern members of Congress signed a "manifesto" in 1956 denouncing the *Brown* decision and urging their constituents to defy it. Southern governors sometimes blocked sincere efforts by local officials to implement desegregation. Local school boards themselves occasionally took drastic action; in one country in Virginia, the school board simply closed public schools for several years rather than accede to court-ordered desegregation. White citizens' councils grew up in many Southern communities to place pressure on local officials (and parents) to resist the courts.

By the fall of 1957, only 684 of 3,000 affected school districts in the South had even begun to desegregate their schools. In those that had complied, white resistance often produced angry mob actions and other violence. An increasing number of white parents simply withdrew their children from the public schools and enrolled them in all-white "segregation academies," many of them poorly staffed and equipped. The *Brown* decision, far from ending segregation, launched a prolonged battle between federal authority and state and local governments. In the years to come, federal courts would have to play an ever-increasing role in public education to ensure compliance with the desegregation rulings. And the executive branch, whose responsibility it was to enforce the decisions of the courts, found itself frequently pitted against local authorities attempting to defy the law.

The first such confrontation occurred in September 1957 in Little Rock, Arkansas. The courts had ordered the desegregation of that city's Central High School. Governor Orval Faubus, a rabid and ambitious segregationist, ordered the National Guard to intervene to stop it. Faubus finally called off the Guard in response to the orders of a federal judge; but an angry mob quickly took its place in blocking integration of the school. Faced with this open defiance of federal authority (and with real danger to the safety of the black students involved), President Eisenhower finally responded by sending federal troops to Little Rock to restore order and ensure that the court orders would be obeyed. Central High School admitted its first black students; but controversy continued to plague the Little Rock school system for several years.

Eisenhower was a reluctant convert to the civil-rights cause. He had greeted the 1954 *Brown* decision with open skepticism (and once said it had set back progress on race relations by "at least fifteen years"). He had hoped not to have to intervene on behalf of such a controversial issue. But events in Little Rock forced his hand. Faubus's use of the state National Guard to resist enforcement of a federal court order, and his subsequent refusal to protect the safety of citizens exercising their rights, was too direct a threat to constitutional law for the president to ignore.

The Expanding Movement

The legal assault on school segregation was only one part of the war against racial discrimination in the 1950s. The *Brown* decision seemed also to spark a growing number of popular challenges to segregation in one community after another. The first and most celebrated occurred in Montgomery, Alabama. On December 1, 1955, Rosa Parks, a black woman, was arrested when she refused to give up her seat on a Montgomery bus to a white passenger (as required by the Jim Crow laws that regulated race relations in the city and throughout most of the South). Parks, who had been active for years within the black community as an advocate of civil rights, had apparently decided completely spontaneously to resist the order to move. Her feet were tired, she later explained. The arrest of this admired woman produced outrage in the city's black community, which organized a successful boycott of the bus system to demand an end to segregated seating.

The bus boycott was one of the first examples of a black community mobilizing itself en masse to resist segregation. Committees were formed; leaders were chosen; the boycott was almost completely effective. Blacks formed car pools to ride back and forth to work, or simply walked to their jobs—at times over long distances. The boycott put economic

Jackie Robinson

As the first black to play in the major leagues, Robinson had to face harassment from fans and fellow players. He responded by compiling a lifetime .311 batting average, leading the Brooklyn Dodgers into six World Series, and winning election to the Baseball Hall of Fame. Robinson's aggressive base-running style, which made him the National League's leading base stealer in his rookie year, is evident in this photograph. (Hy Peskin, *Life Magazine* © 1947 Time, Inc.)

pressure not only on the bus company (a private concern) but on many Montgomery merchants. The bus boycotters found it difficult to get to downtown stores and tended to shop instead in their own neighborhoods. Even so, the boycott might well have failed had it not been for a Supreme Court decision in 1955, inspired in part by the protest, that declared segregation in public transportation to be illegal. The buses in Montgomery abandoned their discriminatory seating policies, and the boycott came to a close.

The most important accomplishments of the Montgomery boycott were probably less its immediate victories than its success in establishing a new form of racial protest and, perhaps above all, in elevating to prominence a new figure in the movement for civil rights. The leader of the boycott was a local Baptist pastor, Martin Luther King, Jr., son of a prominent Atlanta minister and the possessor of a charismatic leadership ability that even he had not previously suspected. King was reluctant at first to accept the leadership of the movement. He was new in Montgomery and feared that he would be seen as an outsider. But once he accepted the role, he became consumed by it. His life would never again be the same.

King's approach to black protest was based on the doctrine of nonviolence—that is, of passive resistance even in the face of direct assaults by white segregationists. He drew from the teachings of Mahatma Gandhi, the legendary Indian nationalist leader, whose life he had studied while a student in Boston; from Henry David Thoreau, and his doctrine of civil disobedience; and from Christian dogma. And he produced an approach to racial struggle that captured the moral high ground for the members of his race in a way that made it increasingly difficult for most white Americans to support his opponents. He urged blacks to engage in peaceful demonstrations; to allow themselves to be arrested, even beaten, if necessary; and to respond to hate with love. King's unparalleled oratorical talents ensured that his message would be widely heard. And for the next thirteen years—as leader of the Southern Christian Leadership Conference, an interracial group he founded shortly after the bus boycott—he would serve as the most influential and most widely admired black leader of the century.

Pressure from the courts, from Northern liberals, and from blacks themselves also speeded the pace of racial change in other areas. As early as 1947, one important color line had been breached when the Brooklyn Dodgers signed the great Jackie Robinson as the first black to play major-league baseball. By the mid-1950s, blacks had established themselves as a powerful force in almost all professional sports. Within the government, President Eisenhower completed the integration of the armed forces, attempted to desegregate the federal work force, and in 1957 signed a civil-rights act providing federal protection for blacks who wished to register to vote. It was a weak bill, with few mechanisms for enforcement; but it was a signal that the executive and legislative branches were beginning to join the judiciary in the federal commitment to the "Second Reconstruction."

Eisenhower Republicanism

It was appropriate, perhaps, that Dwight D. Eisenhower, a man who had risen to prominence as a great military leader, should preside over an era in which the American people were preoccupied with international tensions. And it was fitting, too, that this essentially conservative man, who enjoyed the company of wealthy business executives, should serve as president in a period when most Americans wanted nothing so much as a lasting stabilization of their newly prosperous economy. It should not have been surprising, therefore, that Eisenhower, the least experienced politician to serve in the White House in the twentieth century, was nevertheless among the most politically successful presidents of the postwar era. At home, he pursued essentially moderate policies, avoiding most new initiatives but accepting the work of earlier reformers. Abroad, he continued and even intensified American commitments to oppose communism but brought to some of those commitments a measure of restraint that his successors could not always match.

A Business Government

The first Republican administration in twenty years staffed itself with men drawn from the same quarter as those who had staffed Republican administrations in the 1920s: the business community. To his cabinet the president appointed a leading corporation lawyer (Secretary of State John Foster Dulles), the president of General Motors (Defense Secretary Charles E. Wilson), the head of a major financial firm (Treasury Secretary George Humphrey), a New England man-

ufacturer, two automobile distributors, a farm marketing executive, and other wealthy corporate figures. Only Secretary of Labor Martin P. Durkin, president of the plumbers' union, stood apart. "Eight millionaires and a plumber," the *New Republic* caustically remarked. Members of the new administration were not apologetic about their backgrounds. Charles Wilson assured senators considering his confirmation that he foresaw no conflict of interest, because he was certain that "what was good for our country was good for General Motors, and vice versa."

Eisenhower's leadership style, which stressed delegation of authority to subordinates, helped enhance the power of his cabinet officers and others. Secretary of State John Foster Dulles was widely believed to be running American foreign policy almost single-handedly (although subsequently released evidence made it clear that the president was far more deeply involved in international decisions than was often apparent at the time). Treasury Secretary Humphrey and Defense Secretary Wilson enjoyed wide latitude in imposing their own standards of stringency on federal fiscal policy and defense spending. The president's White House chief of staff, former New Hampshire governor Sherman Adams, exercised broad authority over relations with Congress and strictly controlled access to the president. (Late in the Eisenhower presidency, he left office in disgrace after he was discovered to have accepted gifts from a wealthy businessman, presumably in exchange for official favors.)

The inclination of the Eisenhower government to limit federal activities and encourage private enterprise received clear illustration in its policies toward government power development. The president, who referred to the Tennessee Valley Authority in 1953 as an example of "creeping socialism" and once talked wistfully of selling "the whole thing," supported the private rather than public development of natural resources. Throughout his administration, he opposed federal public works projects in favor of private ventures.

Eisenhower moved in other areas as well to limit government involvement in the economy. To the chagrin of farmers, he lowered federal support for farm prices. He also removed the last limited wage and price controls maintained by the Truman administration. He opposed the creation of new social service programs such as national health insurance (although he did support a bill to underwrite private insurance programs, a bill that never passed). He strove constantly to reduce federal expenditures (even during the recession of 1958) and balance the budget. He ended 1960, his last full year in office, with a $1 billion surplus.

The Survival of Social Welfare

Eisenhower's philosophy of "dynamic conservatism," as he termed it, may not have been hospitable to new social programs. But it did permit the survival, and even on occasion the expansion, of some existing ones. The president resisted pressure from the right wing of his party to dismantle those welfare policies of the New Deal that had survived the conservative assaults of the war years and after. During his term, a Republican Congress agreed to extend the Social Security system to an additional 10 million people and unemployment compensation to an additional 4 million people. The minimum hourly wage increased from 75 cents to $1. And the president supported the combination of existing federal education and social welfare programs in the new Department of Health, Education, and Welfare, which began its life in 1953.

In economic terms, the most significant legislative accomplishment of the Eisenhower administration was the Federal Highway Act of 1956, which launched a government program of vast dimensions. It authorized $25 billion for a ten-year building effort to construct over 40,000 miles of interstate highways; the program was to be funded through a highway "trust fund," which would raise revenues through a new tax on the purchase of fuel, automobiles, trucks, and tires. The cost of the program would ultimately expand far beyond that figure and would have a major impact—both directly and indirectly—in spurring economic growth.

That Eisenhower did not launch a stronger assault on existing social programs and that he actually supported some liberal reforms and spending programs resulted partly from political realities. During his first two years in office, although Congress was nominally under Republican control, a coalition of Democrats and liberal Republicans limited the freedom of conservatives to act. And from 1954 to the end of Eisenhower's years in office (indeed, until 1980), both houses of Congress remained securely in Democratic hands.

Not even Eisenhower's personal popularity was sufficient to bring his party back to power in Con-

gress. In 1956, Eisenhower ran for a second term, even though he had suffered a serious heart attack the previous year. With Adlai Stevenson opposing him once again, he won by another, even greater landslide, receiving nearly 57 percent of the popular vote and 442 electoral votes to Stevenson's 89. Still, Democrats retained control of both houses of Congress. And in 1958—on the heels of a serious recession—they increased that control by substantial margins. The American people had endorsed Eisenhower's inclination to moderate the reforming zeal of earlier years, to "hold the line." But they were not ready, apparently, to accept the belief of others in his party that the nation should adopt an even more militantly conservative policy.

The Decline of McCarthyism

The Eisenhower administration did little in its first years in office to discourage the anticommunist furor that had gripped the nation. Indeed, it helped to sustain it. The president actually intensified the already much abused hunt for subversives in the government, which Truman had begun several years earlier. More than 2,220 federal employees resigned or were dismissed as a result of security investigations. Among them were most of the leading Asian experts in the State Department, many of whom were harried from office because they had shown inadequate enthusiasm for the now exiled regime of Chiang Kai-shek. Their absence was later to prove costly, as the government expanded its commitments in Asia without sufficient knowledge of the political realities within the region.

Among the most celebrated episodes of the first year of the new administration was the case of J. Robert Oppenheimer, director of the Manhattan Project during the war and one of the nation's most distinguished and admired physicists. Although Oppenheimer was now out of government service, he continued as a consultant to the Atomic Energy Commission. But he had angered some officials by his public opposition to development of the new, more powerful hydrogen bomb. In 1953, the FBI distributed a dossier within the administration detailing Oppenheimer's prewar association with various left-wing groups. And the president responded by ordering a "blank wall" to be placed between Oppenheimer and government secrets. A federal investigation, requested by Oppenheimer himself and conducted in an inflamed and confused atmosphere,

The Army-McCarthy Hearings
Senator Joseph McCarthy uses a map to show the supposed distribution of communists throughout the United States during the televised 1954 Senate hearings to mediate the dispute between McCarthy and the U.S. Army. Joseph Welch, chief counsel for the army, remains conspicuously unimpressed.   (UPI/Bettmann Newsphotos)

confirmed the decision to deny him a security clearance. The episode deeply embittered much of the scientific community and caused a major public outcry.

The strong opposition to the persecution of Oppenheimer was one indication that the anticommunist hysteria of the early 1950s was beginning to abate. A more important signal of the change was the political demise of Senator Joseph McCarthy. McCarthy continued during the first year of the Eisenhower administration to operate with almost total impunity. The president, who privately loathed him, nevertheless refused to speak out in public. "I will not get into the gutter with that guy," he reportedly explained. But McCarthy finally overreached himself in January 1954 when he began launching oblique attacks against the president and a direct assault on Secretary of the Army Robert Stevens and the armed services in general. In the face of McCarthy's outrageous accusations, the administration and influential members of Congress

decided together that no choice remained but to stage a special investigation of the charges. They became known as the Army-McCarthy hearings, and they were among the first such hearings to be nationally televised. The result was devastating to McCarthy. Day after day, the public watched McCarthy in action—bullying witnesses, hurling groundless (and often cruel) accusations, evading issues, and offering churlish objections at every point. He began to appear less a hero than a villain, and ultimately less that than a mere buffoon. In December 1954, the Senate voted 67 to 22 to condemn him for "conduct unbecoming a senator." And three years later, with little public support left, he died—a victim, apparently, of complications arising from his serious alcoholism.

The Supreme Court, in the meantime, was also beginning to restrict the official harassment of suspected "subversives." Many people had expected the Court to become more conservative once the new president began to appoint new members. In fact, quite the opposite occurred. In 1953, Eisenhower nominated the former Republican governor of California, Earl Warren, to be the new chief justice. And to the surprise of many, including Eisenhower, Warren became the moving force behind the most strenuous judicial effort to protect and expand civil liberties in the nation's history. (See below, pp. 908–909.) In 1957, the Warren Court limited the FBI's latitude in using secret evidence against an opponent. More important, that same year it struck down the Smith Act, ruling that it was not a crime to urge the overthrow of the government unless a person was directly inciting illegal actions. The following year, the Court forbade the State Department to deny passports to members of the Communist party.

Eisenhower, Dulles, and the Cold War

A strong undercurrent of anxiety tinged the domestic events of the Eisenhower years, for Americans were well aware throughout the affluent 1950s how dangerous was the world in which they lived. Above all, they were aware of the horrors of a possible nuclear war, as both the United States and the Soviet Union began to make atomic weapons more and more central to their foreign policies. Yet the nuclear threat had another effect as well. With the costs of war now so enormous, both of the superpowers began to edge away from direct confrontations. And increasingly, the attention of the United States began to turn to the rapidly escalating instability in the nations of the Third World.

Dulles and "Massive Retaliation"

Eisenhower's secretary of state, and (except for the president himself) the dominant figure in the nation's foreign policy in the 1950s, was John Foster Dulles, an aristocratic corporate lawyer with a stern moral revulsion to communism. A deeply religious man, Dulles detested the atheistic dogmas of Marxism; a man closely tied to the nation's financial establishment, he feared the communist challenge to world free enterprise. He entered office denouncing the containment policies of the Truman years as excessively passive, arguing that the United States should pursue an active program of "liberation," which would lead to a "rollback" of communist expansion.

Once in power, however, he had to defer to the far more moderate views of the president himself. Dulles began, instead, to develop a new set of doctrines that reflected the impact of nuclear weapons on the world.

The most prominent of those doctrines was the policy of "massive retaliation," which Dulles announced early in 1954. The United States would, he explained, respond to communist threats to its allies not by using conventional forces in local conflicts (a policy that had led to so much frustration in Korea) but by relying on "the deterrent of massive retaliatory power . . . a great capacity to retaliate instantly, by means and at times of our choosing." He left no doubt that the retaliation he was envisioning was a nuclear one. The new doctrine reflected in part Dulles's inclination for tense confrontations, an approach he once defined as "brinksmanship"—pushing the Soviet Union to the brink of war in order to exact concessions. But the real force behind the massive retaliation policy was an economic one. With pressure growing both in and out of government for a reduction in American military expenditures, an increasing reliance on atomic weapons seemed to promise, as some advocates put it, "more bang for the buck." Many argued further that smaller, so-called tactical nuclear weapons could replace conventional forces even in limited wars. The new look in American defense policy seemed at first to please almost everyone. It maintained the national commitment (and, its advocates argued, the national ability) to counter communist expansion throughout the world. Yet it did so at greatly reduced cost, satisfying those who were demanding new efforts to balance the budget.

At the same time, Dulles intensified the efforts of Truman and Acheson to "integrate" the entire noncommunist world into a system of mutual defense pacts. During his years in office, he logged almost 500,000 miles in foreign travels to cement new alliances that were modeled on NATO—but that were, without exception, far weaker than the European pact. By the end of the decade, the United States had become a party to almost a dozen such treaties in all areas of the world. In Southeast Asia, there was the SEATO alliance, which included Thailand and the Philippines but few other Asian nations. In the Middle East, there was the Baghdad Pact, soon renamed the CENTO alliance (for Central Treaty Organization), which tied the United States to Turkey, Pakistan, Iraq, and Iran. Other, smaller agreements pledged American aid to additional areas.

Eisenhower and Dulles
Although President Eisenhower himself was a somewhat colorless television personality, his was the first administration to make extensive use of the new medium to promote its policies and dramatize its actions. The president's press conferences were frequently televised, and on several occasions Secretary of State John Foster Dulles reported to the president in front of the cameras. Dulles is shown here in the Oval Office on May 17, 1955, reporting on the occasion of his return from Europe, where he had signed the treaty restoring sovereignty to Austria.   (AP/Wide World Photos)

Challenges in Asia

What had been the most troubling foreign policy concern of the Truman years—the war in Korea—plagued the Eisenhower administration only briefly. The new president did indeed "go to Korea" as he had promised in his campaign—visiting briefly in the months between the election and his inauguration. But peace came as a result of other things, primarily a softening of both the American and communist positions. On July 27, 1953, negotiators at Panmunjom finally signed an agreement ending the hostilities. Each antagonist was to withdraw its troops a mile and a half from the existing battle line, which ran roughly along the 38th parallel, the prewar bor-

der between North and South Korea. A conference in Geneva was to consider means by which to reunite the nation peacefully—although in fact the 1954 meeting produced no agreement and left the cease-fire line as the apparently permanent border between the two countries.

In the meantime, however, American attention was being drawn to problems in other parts of Asia. There was, first, continuing pressure on the administration from the so-called China lobby, or "Asia firsters," who insisted on active American efforts to restore Chiang Kai-shek to the Chinese mainland. Such demands were wholly unrealistic. Chiang had nothing approaching sufficient military strength to launch an effective invasion. Even had he been able to muster the forces, he would have found virtually no popular following within China itself. Nevertheless, the administration continued to supply him with weapons and other assistance.

Almost simultaneously, the United States was becoming drawn into a long, bitter struggle in Southeast Asia. Ever since the end of World War II, France had been attempting to restore its authority over Vietnam, its one-time colony, which it had had to abandon to the Japanese during World War II. Opposing the French, however, were the powerful nationalist forces of Ho Chi Minh, determined to win independence for their nation.

Much of the later controversy over American involvement in Vietnam centered on the question of Ho Chi Minh's intentions and commitments. At the end of World War II, Ho had appealed on several occasions to the United States for support but had received no reply. Some Americans have argued that

Ho was eager at that point to develop a close relationship with the United States and that the Truman administration squandered the opportunity. But whatever Ho's views of the United States in 1945, he was then, as he had been for many years, a communist; he had been trained in Moscow, and his commitment to Marxism appears to have been genuine and important to him. At least equally important, however, was Ho's nationalism. He believed in an independent and united Vietnam, and that goal, at least, he was never willing to compromise.

By 1954, Ho was receiving substantial aid from communist China and the Soviet Union. America, in the meantime, had been paying more than 70 percent of French war costs since 1950 (largely because of fears of Ho's communist connections). A crisis emerged in early 1954 when 12,000 French troops became surrounded in a disastrous siege at the city of Dienbienphu, which they were incapable of defend-

The French in Indochina
The famed war photographer Robert Capa captured in 1954 a scene that would later become familiar to Americans: a convoy of Western troops (in this case, French) moving in modern vehicles past a Vietnamese peasant working with traditional tools in the rice paddies. (Robert Capa/Magnum)

ing. Only American intervention, it was clear, could prevent the total collapse of the French military effort.

Eisenhower spoke out strongly about the importance of preserving a "free" Vietnam, using the analogy once employed by Acheson of a row of dominoes. If Vietnam fell to communism, he implied, the rest of Asia would soon follow. Yet despite the urgings of Secretary of State Dulles, Vice President Nixon, and others, Eisenhower refused to permit direct American military intervention in Vietnam, claiming that neither Congress nor America's other allies would support such action. In fact, Eisenhower seemed to sense how difficult and costly such intervention would be.

Without American aid, the French defense of Dienbienphu finally collapsed on May 7, 1954; and France quickly agreed to a settlement of the conflict at a conference in Geneva that summer. The Geneva accords of July 1954, to which the United States was not a party, established a temporary division of Vietnam along the 17th parallel. The north would be governed by Ho Chi Minh, the south by a pro-Western regime. Democratic elections would serve as the basis for uniting the nation in 1956. The agreement marked the effective end of the French commitment to Vietnam, but it became the basis for an expanded American presence. Realizing that Ho Chi Minh would win any election in Vietnam, Eisenhower and Dulles decided almost immediately that they could not accept the agreement. Instead, they helped establish a pro-American government in the south, headed by Ngo Dinh Diem, a wealthy, corrupt member of his country's Roman Catholic minority. Diem, it was clear from the start, would not permit elections. He felt secure in his refusal because the United States had promised to provide him with ample military assistance against any attack from the north. (There is some evidence that the Soviet Union, eager to avoid a confrontation with the United States at this point, was at the same time pressuring Ho and his regime not to press for an election.)

Crises in the Middle East

The redirection of American's international attention toward the problems of the Third World and its growing preoccupation with threats of communism there (threats both real and imagined) were nowhere more clearly illustrated than in the Middle East. The region was a volatile and important one for two reasons: Israel and oil.

The establishment of a Jewish state in Palestine had been the dream of a powerful Zionist movement that gained strength in many parts of the world for more than half a century before World War II. The plight of the hundreds of thousands of homeless Jews uprooted by the war, and the international outrage that followed revelations of the Holocaust, gave new strength to Zionist demands in the late 1940s. Palestine had been a British protectorate since the end of World War I; and in deference to local Arab opposition, the British after 1945 had attempted to limit Jewish immigration there. But despite the British efforts to stop them, Jews had come to Palestine in such enormous numbers that they could not be ignored.

Finally, Britain brought the problem to the United Nations, which responded by recommending the partition of Palestine into a Jewish and an Arab state. On May 14, 1948, the British mandate ended, and Jews proclaimed the existence of the nation of Israel. President Truman recognized the new government the following day, thus effectively blocking a UN proposal to keep the area under a temporary trusteeship. But the creation of Israel was only the beginning of the battle for a Jewish homeland. Palestinian Arabs, unwilling to accept being displaced from what they considered their own country, fought determinedly against the new state in 1948—the first of many Arab-Israeli wars. And the United States found itself with a new ally whose survival would require years of extensive American aid.

The interest of the United States in the Middle East involved much more than its strong support of Israel. America was also concerned about the stability and friendliness of the Arab regimes in the area. The reason was simple: The region contained the richest oil reserves in the world, reserves in which American companies had already invested heavily, reserves on which the health of the American (and world) economy would ultimately come to depend. Thus the United States reacted with alarm as it watched Mohammed Mossadegh, the nationalist prime minister of Iran, begin to resist the presence of Western corporations in his nation. In 1951, he ordered the seizure of Iran's oil wells from the British companies that had been developing them. During the next two years, American observers grew convinced that Mossadegh was becoming friendly with the Soviet Union. In 1953, as a result, the American Central Intelligence Agency (CIA) joined forces with conservative Iranian military leaders to engineer a coup that drove Mossadegh from office. To replace him, the United

States favored elevating the young shah of Iran, Mohammed Reza Pahlevi, from his position as a token constitutional monarch to that of a virtual absolute ruler. In return, the shah allowed American companies to share in the development of Iranian oil reserves; and he remained closely tied to the United States for the next twenty-five years, even as his regime was becoming increasingly despotic and unpopular.

American policy was less effective in dealing with the nationalist government of Egypt, under the leadership of General Gamal Abdel Nasser. Nasser pressured the British in 1954 to remove their remaining troops from his country, an effort the United States accepted and even assisted. But Dulles and other policymakers were less willing to tolerate Nasser's flirtations with the Soviet Union, which took the form of Soviet shipments of armaments in return for Egyptian cotton. To punish Nasser for his transgressions, Dulles suddenly withdrew American offers of assistance in building the great Aswan Dam across the Nile. A week later, Nasser retaliated by seizing control of the Suez Canal from the British, saying that he would use the income from it to build the dam himself.

On October 29, 1956, Israeli forces struck a preemptive blow against Egypt, and the British and French followed the next day by landing troops to drive the Egyptians from the canal. Dulles and Eisenhower reacted with horror, fearing that the Suez crisis would drive the Arab states toward the Soviet Union and precipitate a new world war. By refusing to support the invasion, and by joining in a UN denunciation of it, the United States helped pressure the French and British to withdraw. Egypt and Israel agreed to a cease-fire, and a precarious truce was in place. In the following years, just as Dulles had feared, the government of Egypt turned to the Soviet Union for assistance, accepting Russian financing of the Aswan Dam and giving the Soviets an important (if temporary) foothold in the Middle East.

In Washington, the president responded in 1957 by enunciating the so-called Eisenhower Doctrine, which proclaimed that the United States would offer economic and military aid "to secure and protect the territorial independence" of Middle Eastern nations "against overt armed aggression from any nation controlled by international communism." In practice, that meant more than simply opposing Soviet aggression. It meant working to prevent the spread of pan-Arab nationalism: Nasser's efforts to unite all the Arab states into a single nation, in which he would

be the dominant force. Egypt and Syria merged to form the United Arab Republic in February 1958, causing modest concern in Washington. But that concern soon turned to alarm as pan-Arab forces began to challenge the pro-Western governments of Lebanon, Jordan, and Iraq. The United States could do little about Iraq, which fell under the control of a pro-Nasser military government in July (although only temporarily). But in Lebanon and Jordan, the situation was different. At the request of the embattled Beirut government, Eisenhower ordered 5,000 American marines to land on the beaches of Lebanon in mid-July; British troops entered Jordan at about the same time. The effect of the interventions was negligible. The governments of both countries managed to stabilize their positions on their own, and within months both the American and the British forces withdrew.

Latin America and "Yankee Imperialism"

Similar difficulties were arising in an area important to, but generally neglected by, American foreign policy: Latin America. American economic interests in the region were vast; in some countries, U.S. corporations were the dominant force in the economy. The American government, in the meantime, had all but abandoned even the limited initiatives of Franklin Roosevelt's Good Neighbor Policy and was sending most of its foreign aid to Europe and Asia rather than to Latin America.

Animosity toward the United States, therefore, grew steadily during the 1950s, as many Latin Americans began to regard the influence of U.S. business in their countries as an insidious form of imperialism. Some nationalists in the region had once believed that the United States would support popular efforts to overthrow undemocratic governments. But in 1954, the Eisenhower administration suggested otherwise when it helped topple the new leftist government of Jacobo Arbenz Guzman in Guatemala, a regime that Dulles (responding to the entreaties of the United Fruit Company, a major investor in Guatemala fearful of Arbenz) argued was potentially communist. Four years later, the depths of anti-American sentiment became clear when Vice President Richard Nixon visited the region, to be greeted in city after city by angry, hostile, occasionally dangerous mobs.

Americans were shocked by the outburst of animosity, and the administration began hasty, belated efforts to improve relations with its neighbors. But the legacy of more than fifty years of casual exploitation of Latin America was too strong to prevent the rise of other nationalist movements hostile to the United States. No nation in the region had been more closely tied to America than Cuba. Its leader, Fulgencio Batista, had ruled as a military dictator since 1952, when with American assistance, he had toppled a more moderate government. Cuba's economy (generally a relatively prosperous one) had become a virtual fiefdom of American corporations, which controlled almost all the island's natural resources and had cornered over half of the vital sugar crop. Beginning in 1957, a popular movement of resistance to the Batista regime began to gather power under the leadership of Fidel Castro. By late 1958, the Batista forces were in almost total disarray. And on January 1, 1959, with Batista now in exile in Spain (having taken millions of dollars in government funds along with him), Castro marched into Havana and established a new government.

Despite its long support of the Batista government, the United States had long been vaguely embarrassed by its ties to that corrupt regime. At first, therefore, Americans reacted warmly to Castro, particularly since there was little evidence that he was tied to any communist elements. But once Castro began implementing drastic policies of land reform and expropriating foreign-owned businesses and resources, Cuban-American relations rapidly deteriorated.

The new government was causing particular concern to Eisenhower and Dulles by its growing interest in communist ideas and tactics. When Castro began accepting assistance from the Soviet Union in 1960, the United States cut back the "quota" by which Cuba could export sugar to America at a favored price. Early in 1961, as one of its last acts, the Eisenhower administration severed diplomatic relations with Castro. The American CIA had already begun secretly training Cuban expatriates for an invasion of the island to topple the new regime. Totally isolated by the United States, Castro soon cemented a close and lasting alliance with the Soviet Union.

Europe and the Soviet Union

The problems of the Third World would soon become the central focus of American foreign policy. Through most of the 1950s, however, the United States remained chiefly concerned with its direct relationship with the Soviet Union and with the possibility of communist expansion in Europe. The massive retaliation doctrine was the first American effort to deter such expansion. The rearming of West Germany was another. Beginning in 1954, the West German government began to develop its first armed forces since the end of World War II; and in 1957, the first German forces joined NATO, making the nation a full military ally of the United States.

In the meantime, however, many Americans continued to hope that the United States and the Soviet Union would be able to negotiate solutions to some of their remaining problems. Such hopes were buoyed when, after the death of Stalin in 1953, signs began to emerge of a new Russian attitude of conciliation. The Soviet Union extended a peace overture to the rebellious Tito government in Yugoslavia; it returned a military base to Finland; it signed a peace treaty with Japan; and it agreed at last to terminate its long military occupation of Austria, allowing that nation to become an independent, neutral state. Pressure for negotiation intensified when, in 1953–1954, both the United States and the Soviet Union successfully tested the new hydrogen bomb, a nuclear device of vastly greater power than those developed during the war. These factors seemed briefly to bear fruit in 1955, when Eisenhower and other NATO leaders met with the Soviet premier, Nicolai Bulganin, at a cordial summit conference in Geneva. But when a subsequent conference of foreign ministers met to try to resolve specific issues, the "spirit of Geneva" quickly dissolved, as neither side could agree to the terms of the other.

The failure of conciliation brought renewed vigor to the Cold War, not only helping to produce tensions between the superpowers in the Third World but spurring a vastly increased Soviet-American arms race. Both nations engaged in extensive nuclear testing in the atmosphere, causing deep concern among many scientists and environmentalists. Both nations redoubled efforts to develop effective intercontinental ballistic missiles, which could deliver atomic warheads directly from one continent to another. The apparent Russian lead in such development caused wide alarm in the United States. The American military, in the meantime, developed a new breed of atomic-powered submarines, capable of launching missiles from underwater anywhere in the world.

The arms race not only increased tensions between the United States and Russia; it increased tensions within each nation as well. In America, public concern about nuclear war was becoming an obsessive national nightmare, a preoccupation never far from popular thought. Movies, television programs,

SIGNIFICANT EVENTS

1946	Dr. Benjamin Spock publishes *Baby and Child Care*
1947	Jackie Robinson becomes first black to play in major leagues
	Construction begins on Levittown, New York
1948	UAW and General Motors agree to automatic cost-of-living increases for auto workers
	United Nations votes to partition Palestine and create state of Israel
1950	David Riesman publishes *The Lonely Crowd*
1951	J.D. Salinger publishes *Catcher in the Rye*
1952	Eisenhower elected president
	Republicans win control of Congress
1953	Economic recession sets in
	Saul Bellow publishes *The Adventures of Augie March*
	Department of Health, Education, and Welfare established
	Earl Warren becomes chief justice
	Truce ends Korean War
	CIA helps engineer coup in Iran
	Oppenheimer denied security clearance
	Stalin dies
1954	Supreme Court rules on *Brown* v. *Board of Education*
	Democrats regain control of Congress
	Army-McCarthy hearings
	Senate censures McCarthy
	France surrenders at Dienbienphu
	Geneva agreement partitions Vietnam
	United States helps topple Arbenz regime in Guatemala
1955	Labor organizations reconcile and form AFL-CIO
	Supreme Court announces "*Brown* II" decision

1955	Montgomery bus boycott begins
	Ngo Dinh Diem becomes president of South Vietnam
	Eisenhower and Bulganin meet in Geneva
1956	Federal Highway Act passed
	Eisenhower reelected president
	Suez crisis
1957	Postwar baby boom peaks
	Economic recession begins
	Labor racketeering investigations focus on Teamsters
	Soviet Union launches *Sputnik*
	Jack Kerouac publishes *On the Road*
	Little Rock school desegregation crisis
	Civil rights act passed
	Germany joins NATO
1958	American manned space program founded
	National Defense Education Act passed
	American marines land in Lebanon
1959	Castro seizes power in Cuba
	Nikita Khrushchev visits United States
1960	U-2 incident precedes collapse of Paris summit
1961	Yuri Gagarin of Soviet Union becomes first man in space
	Alan Shepard becomes first American in space
	United States breaks diplomatic relations with Cuba
	Eisenhower gives farewell address
1962	Michael Harrington publishes *The Other America*
1969	Americans land on moon

books, popular songs—all expressed the pervasive fear. Government studies began to appear outlining the hideous casualties that a nuclear war would inflict on the nation. Schools, local governments, and individual families built a huge network of bomb shelters for protection against atomic blasts and radioactive fallout. Fear of communism, therefore, combined with fear of atomic war to create a widespread national unease.

Khrushchev and Berlin

In this tense and fearful atmosphere, new Soviet challenges in Berlin in 1958 created a particularly troubling crisis. The linking of West Germany first to NATO and then to the new European Common Market, establishing that nation as a full partner of the West, made the continuing existence of an anticommunist West Berlin a galling irritation to the

Soviets. In November 1958, therefore, Nikita Khrushchev, who had succeeded Bulganin as Soviet premier and Communist party chief earlier that year, renewed the demands of his predecessors that the NATO powers abandon the city, threatening vaguely to cut its ties to the West if they did not. The United States and its allies refused, and America and Russia were locked in another tense confrontation.

Khrushchev declined to force the issue when it became apparent that the West was unwilling to budge. Instead, he suggested that he and Eisenhower engage in personal discussions, both by visiting each other's countries and by conferring at a summit meeting in Paris in 1960. The United States eagerly agreed. Khrushchev's 1959 visit to America produced a cool but polite response, and plans proceeded for the summit conference and for Eisenhower's visit to Moscow shortly thereafter. Only days before the scheduled beginning of the Paris meeting, however, the Soviet Union announced that it had shot down an American U-2, a high-altitude spy plane, over Russian territory. Its pilot, Francis Gary Powers, was in captivity. The Eisenhower administration responded clumsily, at first denying the allegations and then, when confronted with incontrovertible proof, awkwardly admitting the circumstances of Powers's mission and attempting to explain them. Khrushchev lashed back in anger, breaking up the Paris summit almost before it could begin and withdrawing his invitation to Eisenhower to visit the Soviet Union. But the U-2 incident was really only a pretext. By the spring of 1960, both Khrushchev and Eisenhower were aware that no agreement was possible on the Berlin issue; and Khrushchev, therefore, was eager for an excuse to avoid what he believed would be fruitless negotiations.

The events of 1960 provided a somber backdrop for the end of the Eisenhower administration. After eight years in office, Eisenhower had failed to eliminate the tensions between the United States and the Soviet Union. He had failed to end the costly and dangerous armaments race. And he had presided over a transformation of the Cold War from a relatively limited confrontation with the Soviet Union in Europe to a global effort to resist communist subversion.

Yet Eisenhower had brought to these matters his own sense of the limits of American power. He had refused to commit American troops to anticommunist crusades except in carefully limited and generally low-risk situations, such as Guatemala and Lebanon. He had resisted pressures from the British, from the French, and from hard-liners in his own government to place American force behind efforts to maintain colonial power in Vietnam and in the Suez. He had placed a certain measure of restraint on those who urged the creation of an enormous American military establishment, warning in his farewell address in January 1961 of the "unwarranted influence" of a vast "military-industrial complex." His caution, both in domestic and in international affairs, stood in marked contrast to the attitudes of his successors, who argued that the United States must act far more boldly and aggressively on behalf of its goals at home and abroad.

SUGGESTED READINGS

General Studies   Broad studies of the society of the 1950s include William Leuchtenburg, *A Troubled Feast* (1979); Carl Degler, *Affluence and Anxiety* (1968); John Brooks, *The Great Leap* (1966); Godfrey Hodgson, *America in Our Time* (1976), which examines the 1960s and part of the 1970s as well; and Eric Goldman, *The Crucial Decade and After* (1960), a breezy account of the era from 1945 to 1960.

The Postwar Economy   John K. Galbraith, in *The Affluent Society* (1958) and *The New Industrial State* (1967), views the economy from the perspective of a liberal iconoclast. C. Wright Mills, *The Power Elite* (1956), is a critique from the left. Harold G. Vatter, *The U.S. Economy in the 1950s* (1963), and Robert Heilbroner, *The Limits of American Capitalism* (1965), offer contrasting views. Joel Seidman, *American Labor from Defense to Reconversion* (1953), and John Hutchinson, *The Imperfect Union* (1970), examine changes in the labor movement.

Culture and Society   Paul Carter, *Another Part of the Fifties* (1983), is an impressionistic portrait of society and culture. Marty Jezer, *The Dark Ages: Life in the U.S. 1945–1960* (1982), George Lipsitz, *Class and Culture in Cold War America* (1981), and Douglas T. Miller and Marion Novak, *The Fifties* (1977), also survey postwar society. Herbert Gans, *The Levittowners* (1967), is a sociological study of a lower-middle-class suburb. Kenneth Jackson, *The Crabgrass Frontier* (1985), is an important examination of the phenomenon of suburbanization. The rise of the mass media receives attention in Edward J. Epstein, *News from Nowhere* (1973), and David Halberstam, *The Powers That Be* (1979). Tom Wolfe, *The Right Stuff* (1979), is an engaging and perceptive discussion of the origins of the space program; while Walter A. McDougall, *. . . the Heavens and the Earth: A Political History of the Space Age* (1985), is an important if controversial scholarly study. Other, more conventional studies include R. L. Rosholt, *An Administrative History of*

NASA (1966), and Walter Sullivan (ed.), *America's Race for the Moon* (1962). Of the many books examining the effects of modern, organized society on the individual, see in particular David Riesman, *The Lonely Crowd* (1950); William Whyte, *The Organization Man* (1956); and C. Wright Mills, *White Collar* (1956). On the beats, see Bruce Cook, *The Beat Generation* (1971), and John Tytell, *Naked Angels* (1976). For Jack Kerouac, see Ann Charters, *Kerouac* (1973), and Dennis McNally, *Desolate Angel* (1979). Good examples of the political and intellectual climate of the era include Arthur M. Schlesinger, Jr., *The Vital Center* (1949); Daniel Bell, *The End of Ideology* (1960); David Potter, *People of Plenty* (1954); and Richard Hofstadter, *The Age of Reform* (1954). Mary Sperling McAuliffe, *Crisis on the Left* (1978), is a fine account of the split among liberals and the origins of the "consensus." Daniel Bell (ed.), *The Radical Right* (1963), is a collection of hostile studies of the survival of extreme conservatism.

The Eisenhower Presidency   The most important account of the Eisenhower presidency is Stephen Ambrose, *Eisenhower the President* (1984), the second volume of the first full-scale biography. Fred Greenstein, *The Hidden-Hand Presidency* (1982), is a sympathetic reassessment of Eisenhower's leadership style. General studies include Charles C. Alexander, *Holding the Line* (1975); Herbert S. Parmet, *Eisenhower and the American Crusade* (1972); Peter Lyon, *Eisenhower: Portrait of a Hero* (1974); and Eisenhower's own memoirs, *The White House Years*, 2 vols. (1963–1965). Other memoirs by important figures in the administration include Emmet John Hughes, *The Ordeal of Power* (1963); Sherman Adams, *Firsthand Report* (1961); and Richard Nixon, *Six Crises* (1962).

Foreign Policy   Robert Divine, *Eisenhower and the Cold War* (1981), is a good overview. On Dulles, see Townsend Hoopes, *The Devil and John Foster Dulles* (1973), a generally critical study; and Louis Gerson, *John Foster Dulles* (1967), a more favorable view. On the early stages of American involvement in Vietnam, see Chester Cooper, *Lost Crusade* (1970); Frances Fitzgerald, *Fire in the Lake* (1972); John T. McAlister, Jr., *Vietnam: The Origins of Revolution* (1969); and George Herring, *America's Longest War* (1979). Chester

Cooper, *The Lion's Last Roar* (1978), and Hugh Thomas, *Suez* (1967), examine the most important Middle Eastern crisis of the era. Mira Wilkins, *The Maturing of Multinational Enterprise* (1974), examines a major source of change in American foreign policy. Kermit Roosevelt, *Counter-coup* (1980), is a firsthand account by the CIA operative who organized the 1954 coup in Iran; and Burton Kaufman, *The Oil Cartel Case* (1978), provides additional insights into United States involvement in Iranian affairs. Robert A. Divine, *Foreign Policy and U.S. Presidential Elections*, 2 vols. (1974) and *Blowing in the Wind: The Nuclear Test Ban Debate, 1954-1960* (1978), is also useful.

Legal and Constitutional Issues   Philip Stern, *The Oppenheimer Case* (1969), examines one of the outstanding internal security controversies of the era. Michael Straight, *Trial by Television* (1954), discusses the decline of McCarthy, as do many of the books on McCarthy cited in the readings for Chapter 28. On the Warren Court, see Paul Murphy, *The Constitution in Crisis Times* (1972); Alexander Bickel, *Politics and the Warren Court* (1965) and *The Supreme Court and the Idea of Progress* (1970); Philip Kurland, *Politics, the Constitution, and the Warren Court* (1970); and John Weaver, *Earl Warren* (1967).

Civil Rights   A thorough and rewarding study of the *Brown* decision is Richard Kluger, *Simple Justice* (1975). On the emergence of the civil-rights movement, see Anthony Lewis, *Portrait of a Decade* (1964); Martin Luther King, Jr., *Stride Toward Freedom* (1958), a personal account of the Montgomery bus boycott; and William Chafe, *Civilities and Civil Rights* (1980), a fine study of the origins of the movement in Greensboro, North Carolina. Harvard Sitkoff, *The Struggle for Black Equality, 1954–1980* (1981), is an elegant general study of the civil-rights movement. John W. Anderson, *Eisenhower, Brownell, and the Congress* (1964), discusses the civil-rights bill of 1956-1957. Robert F. Burk, *The Eisenhower Administration and Black Civil Rights* (1984), is an overview of the administration's record on race. Numan V. Bartley, *The Rise of Massive Resistance* (1969), is a study of white Southern reactions to the civil-rights movement in the 1950s. Elizabeth Huckaby, *Crisis at Central High* (1980), is a memoir of the events in Little Rock.

American Soldier at Khe Sanh, Vietnam, 1968. (Robert Ellison/Black Star)

Chapter 30 # The Ordeal of Liberalism

The calm, reassuring presence of Dwight D. Eisenhower seemed perfectly to match the political mood of the 1950s—a mood that combined a desire for domestic stability with a concern for international security. By the end of the decade, however, many Americans were beginning to clamor for a more active and assertive approach to public policy. The United States had, liberals complained, been allowed to "drift." It was time for an energetic assault on both domestic and world problems. Such sentiments helped produce two presidents whose activism transformed the nature of their office and the thrust of American politics.

Those same sentiments helped make the 1960s one of the most turbulent eras of the twentieth century. For several years after the inauguration of John F. Kennedy as president, the nation seemed to move firmly and confidently to combat the expansion of communism; and it seemed to act decisively to confront its most serious social problems at home: racial inequality, economic deprivation, and others. By 1968, however, the United States was embroiled in a major social, cultural, and political crisis. In extending the historic containment doctrine to dictate a deepening American involvement in the civil war in Vietnam, the United States was embroiling itself in a conflict it did not fully understand and was ultimately unable to resolve. And in assaulting the problems of racial injustice and poverty, the nation was undertaking a far more difficult and wrenching task than most reformers at first realized. These and other pressures produced social and political turmoil so profound that those who described them as a "revolution" exaggerated only slightly.

Expanding the Liberal State

The presidency had been growing steadily more important in American public life throughout the twentieth century. The development of atomic weapons—the means of ultimate destruction, which remained (at least in theory) under the personal and exclusive control of the president—added a new dimension to the powers of the office in the 1950s. By 1960, more and more Americans were looking to the presidency as the source of all initiatives and were calling for more assertive leadership. The political scientist Richard Neustadt, for example, published an influential book that year entitled *Presidential Power,* which stressed the importance of presidential action in confronting national problems. Presidents faced many constraints, he argued, but effective presidents must learn to break free of them. Such exhortations found a receptive audience in the two men who served in the White House from 1961 until 1969: John F. Kennedy and Lyndon B. Johnson.

John Kennedy

The campaign of 1960 produced two young candidates who claimed to offer the nation active leadership. The Republican nomination went almost uncontested to Vice President Richard Nixon, who for the occasion abandoned the strident anticommunism that had characterized his earlier career and adopted a centrist position in favor of moderate reform. The Democrats, in the meantime, emerged from a spirited primary campaign united, somewhat uneasily, behind John Fitzgerald Kennedy, an attractive and articulate senator from Massachusetts who had narrowly missed being the party's vice-presidential candidate in 1956.

Kennedy's road to national leadership was an unusual one. He was the son of one of the most powerful and controversial public figures of the 1930s: Joseph P. Kennedy, who had made a large personal fortune in the stock market, who had served as the first chairman of the Securities and Exchange Commission, who had been the American ambassador to Great Britain in the first years of World War II, and who had transferred his own frustrated ambitions for the presidency to his children. John Kennedy grew up in a world of ease and privilege, although he himself suffered from a series of physical ailments throughout his life. He attended Harvard and then served in the navy during World War II. He came to prominence during the war when the PT boat he commanded was sunk at sea; he was decorated for heroism for his efforts to save members of the crew.

Kennedy returned to Massachusetts after the war and, making liberal use of both his own war record and his family's money, won a seat in Congress in 1946. Six years later, he was elected to the United States Senate, and in 1958 reelected by a record margin. Within days of his triumph, he was planning his campaign for the White House. He had by then attracted considerable national attention for his eloquence, his poise, and what was later widely described as his "charisma." In 1956, he had published a successful book, *Profiles in Courage,* which won the Pulitzer Prize for history and which celebrated American leaders who had displayed notable political bravery. But Kennedy himself had compiled a very cautious and modest political record up to that point and had inspired enthusiasm among relatively few liberals.

His presidential campaign, however, was notable for its strong endorsement of the idea of dynamic governmental activism. Kennedy had read and admired Richard Neustadt's book on the presidency, and he seemed committed to energetic use of the office. He had premised his campaign, he said, "on the single assumption that the American people are uneasy at the present drift in our national course." He was, wrote *New Republic* columnist TRB, "a young man offering positive leadership and presidential power to the uttermost."

He was also a Catholic, a political liability that had almost cost him the nomination and that continued to dog him throughout the campaign. Kennedy

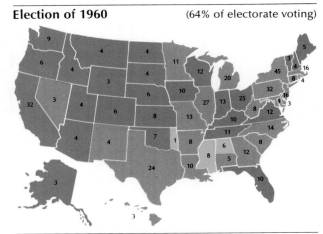

Election of 1960   (64% of electorate voting)

	ELECTORAL VOTE	POPULAR VOTE (%)
John F. Kennedy (Democratic)	303	34,227,096 (49.9)
Richard M. Nixon (Republican)	219	34,108,546 (49.6)
Harry F. Byrd (Dixiecrat)	15	501,643 (0.7)
Other candidates (Socialist Labor; Prohibition; National States Rights, Socialist Workers, Constitution)	—	197,029

compensated for that with his remarkably appealing public image—one that seemed perfectly suited for television—and with an unusually sophisticated and capable campaign. The crucial moment, perhaps, came when he met Vice President Nixon in a series of televised debates. Cool, poised, and relaxed, Kennedy stood in marked contrast to the haggard and somewhat nervous Nixon, who was, during the first debate at least, recovering from an illness. The favorable response Kennedy received from the debates helped propel him to victory.

It was, however, one of the narrowest victories in the history of presidential elections. A vigorous effort on behalf of Nixon by President Eisenhower in the closing days of the campaign, combined with continuing doubts about Kennedy's youth (he turned forty-three in 1960) and religion, almost enabled the Republicans to close what had at one time been a substantial Democratic lead. But in the end, Kennedy held on to win a tiny plurality of the popular vote—

49.9 percent to Nixon's 49.6 percent—and only a slightly more comfortable electoral majority—303 to 219. If a few thousand voters in Illinois and Texas had voted differently, Nixon would have won the election.

The narrowness of Kennedy's victory placed a serious constraint on his ability to accomplish his goals. He had campaigned promising a program of domestic legislation more ambitious than any since the New Deal, a program he described as the "New Frontier." He was able to steer little of it to completion during his presidency.

Kennedy's most serious problem from the beginning was Congress. Although Democrats remained in control of both houses, they owed little to the new president, whose coattails in 1960 had been exceedingly short. Nor did the presence of Democratic majorities ensure a sympathetic reception for reform proposals; those majorities consisted in large part of conservative Southerners, who were far more likely to vote with the Republicans than with Kennedy. Moreover, many of those same Southerners maintained control, by virtue of their seniority, of the most important congressional committees. One after another of Kennedy's legislative proposals, therefore, found themselves hopelessly stalled long before they reached the floor of the House or Senate.

As a result, the president had to look elsewhere for opportunities to display forceful, positive leadership. One such area was the economy, which from the beginning of his administration had been among his primary concerns. Economic growth was sluggish in 1961 when Kennedy entered the White House. Unemployment was hovering at about 6 percent of the work force. In addition to such legislative initiatives as requesting tax credits for businesses investing in capital growth, Kennedy attempted to use his executive powers unilaterally to improve the economy. With congressional approval, he initiated a series of tariff negotiations with foreign governments—the "Kennedy Round"—to reduce barriers to international trade, in an effort to stimulate American exports. He began to consider the use of Keynesian fiscal and monetary tools in more direct and positive ways than those used by any previous administrations—culminating in his 1962 proposal for a substantial federal tax cut to stimulate the economy.

He even put his personal prestige on the line in a battle to curb inflation. In 1962, several steel companies, led by U.S. Steel, announced that they were raising their prices by $6 a ton, a move certain to trigger similar action by the rest of the steel industry.

John Kennedy
The new president and his wife, Jacqueline, attend one of the five balls in Washington marking Kennedy's inauguration in 1961. (Paul Schutzer, *Life* Magazine © 1961 Time, Inc.)

Angrily denouncing the steel companies both publicly and privately, the president exerted enormous pressure on U.S. Steel to rescind its decision—threatening the company with lawsuits and the cancellation of government contracts. He even called the president of U.S. Steel, Roger Blough, to the White House for an impassioned tongue-lashing. Finally, the steel companies relented and abandoned the price rise. But the president had won only a fleeting victory. His relationship with the business community was a strained one from that moment on, and a few months later the steel companies quietly raised prices again. The president did not protest.

Kennedy found the greatest opportunities to display his vision of presidential leadership in two areas: foreign policy and personal style. In his capacity as a world leader, he discovered—like other presidents both before and after him—that he could act without the constraints that hampered his domestic initiatives. And in adopting a new presidential style, he was able to employ his own most effective political skills. More than any other president of the century (excepting perhaps the two Roosevelts and, later, Ronald Reagan), Kennedy made his own personality an integral part of his presidency and a central focus of national attention.

Nothing more clearly illustrates how important Kennedy and the presidency had become to the American people than the tragedy of November 22, 1963, and the popular reaction to it. Already, the president was beginning to campaign for reelection the following year; and in November, he traveled to Texas with his wife and Vice President Lyndon Johnson for a series of political appearances. While the presidential motorcade rode slowly through the streets of Dallas, shots rang out. Two bullets struck the president—one in the throat, the other in the head. He was sped to a nearby hospital, where minutes later he was pronounced dead.

The circumstances of the assassination seemed clearer at the time than they did from the vantage point of later years. Lee Harvey Oswald, who appeared to be a confused and embittered Marxist, was arrested for the crime later that day, on the basis of strong circumstantial evidence. (Among other things, Oswald had shot and killed a police officer who had tried to apprehend him.) Two days later, as Oswald was being moved from one jail to another, Jack Ruby, a Dallas nightclub owner, stepped from a crowd of reporters and fired a pistol into Oswald's abdomen, an event that was broadcast graphically around the world on television. Oswald died only hours later. The popular assumption at the time was that Oswald had acted alone, expressing through the murder his personal frustration and anger, and that Ruby had acted out of grief and out of a desire to make himself a popular hero. These assumptions received what seemed to be conclusive confirmation by a federal commission, chaired by Chief Justice Earl Warren, that was appointed to review the events surrounding the assassination. In later years, however, more and more questions and doubts arose about the circum-

stances of the shooting; and an increasing number of Americans became convinced that the Warren Commission report had not revealed the full story.

The death of President Kennedy was one of those traumatic episodes in national history that have left a permanent mark on all who experienced it. The entire nation seemed to suspend its normal activities for four days to watch the televised activities surrounding the presidential funeral. Images of Kennedy's widow, his small children, his funeral procession, his dramatic grave site at Arlington Cemetery with its symbolic eternal flame—all became deeply embedded in the public mind. For months thereafter, the American people displayed an almost obsessive interest in the martyred president and his family. For years, they continued to venerate him in a way reserved in the past for only a very few public figures. When in later times Americans would look back at the optimistic days of the 1950s and early 1960s and wonder how everything had subsequently seemed to unravel, many would think of November 22, 1963, as the beginning of the change.

Lyndon Johnson

At the time, however, the American public seemed to take comfort in the personality and performance of Kennedy's successor in the White House, Lyndon Baines Johnson. Johnson was a native of the poor "hill country" of west Texas, the son of a once-prominent state politician who ended his days in poverty and obscurity. Johnson himself had risen to eminence by dint of extraordinary, even obsessive effort. He entered public life in the 1930s, first as an aide to a Texas congressman, then as the director of the New Deal's National Youth Administration in Texas, then as a young congressman with close personal ties to Franklin Roosevelt. After twelve years in the House, he won election in 1948 to the United States Senate. And there, by carefully cultivating the favor of party leaders, he rose steadily in influence to become the Senate majority leader. He brought to that post, as he would bring to the presidency, a remarkable level of energy and a legendary ability to persuade and cajole his colleagues into following his lead. He had failed in 1960 to win the Democratic nomination for president; but he had surprised many who knew him by agreeing to accept the second position on the ticket with Kennedy. The events in Dallas thrust him into the White House.

Johnson's personality could hardly have been

Retroactive I, 1964
Within months of his death, John Kennedy had become transformed in the American imagination to a figure far larger than life, a symbol of the nation's thwarted aspirations. The artist, Robert Rauschenberg, gave evidence of Kennedy's new mythological importance by making him the centerpiece of this evocation of contemporary American society.
(Wadsworth Atheneum, Hartford)

more different from Kennedy's. Tall, gawky, inelegant in his public speech, he was the antithesis of the modern media politician. Where Kennedy had been smooth and urbane, Johnson was coarse, even crude. Where Kennedy had been personally reticent and almost unfailingly polite, Johnson was effusive, garrulous, and at times viciously cruel. But like Kennedy, Johnson was a man who believed in the active use of power. And he proved, in the end, far more effective than his predecessor in translating his goals into reality.

Johnson's ability to manage the Congress provided perhaps the most vivid contrast with Kennedy. Between 1963 and 1966, he compiled the most impressive legislative record of any president since Franklin Roosevelt. He was aided by the tidal wave of emotion that followed the death of President Kennedy, which helped win passage of many New Frontier proposals as a memorial to the slain leader. But Johnson also constructed a remarkable reform program of his own, one that he ultimately labeled the "Great Society." And he won approval of much

Johnson the Candidate
Johnson never evoked the sort of
personal adulation that John Kennedy
had attracted. But in the course of the
1964 campaign, at least, his ebullient
style generated considerable popular
enthusiasm. (Popperfoto)

of it through the same sort of skillful lobbying that
had made him an effective majority leader.

Johnson envisioned himself, as well, as a great
"coalition builder," drawing into the Democratic fold
as many different constituencies as possible. Even
more than Kennedy, he tried to avoid the politics of
conflict—that is, of winning the support of one group
by attacking another. Johnson wanted the support of
everyone, and for a time he very nearly got it. His
first year in office was, by necessity, dominated by
the campaign for reelection. And from the beginning, there seemed to be very little doubt that he
would win. As a Democrat in an era of wide support
for liberal reform, as the successor of a beloved and
martyred president, and as a personification of the
same energetic activism that had helped make
Kennedy so popular, he was an almost unbeatable
candidate. He received unexpected assistance from
the Republican party, which in 1964 fell under the
sway of its right wing and nominated the conservative Senator Barry Goldwater of Arizona. Liberal Republicans abandoned Goldwater and openly supported Johnson.

In the fall campaign, Johnson avoided specific,
detailed promises, concentrating instead on attracting
support from as wide a range of voters as possible
and letting Goldwater's stubborn conservatism drive
even more Americans into the Democratic fold. The
strategy worked. Johnson received more votes, over
43 million, than any candidate before him, and a larger
plurality, over 61 percent, than any candidate before

or since. Goldwater managed to carry only his home
state of Arizona and five states in the Deep South.
Record Democratic majorities in both houses of
Congress, many of whose members had been swept
into office only because of the margin of Johnson's
victory, ensured that the president would be able to
fulfill many of his goals. On election night, Johnson
told the nation that he regarded his victory as a
"mandate for unity." For a time, that unity seemed
to survive; and Johnson seemed well on his way to
achieving his own most cherished aim: becoming the
most successful reform president of the century.

The Assault on Poverty

The domestic programs of Kennedy and Johnson
shared two fundamental goals: maintaining the
strength of the American economy and expanding
the responsibilities of the federal government for the
general social welfare. In the first, the two presidents
were simply continuing a commitment that had been
central to virtually every administration since early in
the century. In the second, however, they were responding to a marked change in public assumptions.
In particular, they were responding to what some
described as the "discovery of poverty" in the late
1950s and early 1960s—the rather sudden realization
by Americans who had been glorying in prosperity
that there were substantial portions of the population
that remained destitute.

For the first time since the 1930's, therefore, the federal government took steps in the 1960s not only to strengthen and expand existing social welfare programs but to create a host of important new ones. The effort had begun in the Kennedy administration, although at first without great result. Kennedy did manage to win approval of important changes in existing welfare programs. A revision of the minimum wage law extended coverage to an additional 3.6 million workers and raised the minimum hourly wage from $1.00 to $1.25. Another measure increased Social Security benefits. Kennedy's most ambitious proposals, however, remained unfulfilled until after his death.

The most important of these, perhaps, was Medicare: a program to provide federal aid to the elderly for medical expenses. Its enactment in 1965 came at the end of a bitter, twenty-year debate between those who believed in the concept of national health assistance and those who denounced it as "socialized medicine." But the program as it went into effect removed many objections. For one thing, it avoided the stigma of "welfare" in much the same way the Social Security system had done: by making Medicare benefits available to all elderly Americans, regardless of need. That created a large middle-class constituency for the program. More important, perhaps, it defused the opposition of the medical community. Doctors serving Medicare patients continued to practice privately and to charge their normal fees; Medicare simply shifted responsibility for paying a large proportion of those fees from the patient to the government.

With that barrier now hurdled, advocates of national health insurance pushed for even more extensive coverage; and in 1966, President Johnson steered to passage the Medicaid program, which extended federal medical assistance to welfare recipients of all ages. Criticism of both programs continued. National health insurance advocates continued to insist that coverage be extended to all Americans, young and old, rich and poor. Others spoke harshly of the bureaucratic problems Medicare and Medicaid created, and of the corruption these programs seemed to encourage.

Still more complained bitterly of the tremendous costs the reforms were imposing on the government and the taxpayer. Beginning in 1969, as a result, the government began attempting to limit eligibility for assistance in order to reduce expenses. But public support for the programs was by now too powerful to allow very much limitation, especially on the benefits to the middle class. Medicare costs, in particular, continued to spiral. In 1970, expenditures for the program totaled $6.2 billion. By 1984, they had risen to over $60 billion. The average annual Medicare expenditure per person in that same period rose from $64 to $259, reflecting the dramatic increase in health costs in general.

Medicare and Medicaid were the first steps in a comprehensive assault on poverty—one that Kennedy had been contemplating in the last months of his life and one that Johnson brought to fruition. Determined to eradicate the "pockets of poverty" that were receiving wide public attention, Johnson announced to Congress only weeks after taking office the declaration of an "unconditional war on poverty." The Economic Opportunity Act he then steered to passage provided for, among other things, the establishment of an Office of Economic Opportunity—the centerpiece in Johnson's vision of the Great Society. From the OEO stemmed a vast array of educational programs: vocational training, remedial education, college work-study grants, and others. The office funneled government money as well into programs to provide employment for unemployed youths—through the Job Corps, the Neighborhood Youth Corps, and other agencies. And it established VISTA (Volunteers in Service to America), a program reminiscent of the paternal reform efforts of the progressive era. VISTA volunteers moved out across the country into troubled communities to provide educational and social services. Other OEO programs financed housing assistance, health care, neighborhood improvements, and many more antipoverty efforts.

The war on poverty was designed to encourage communities themselves to take the initiative in planning reforms, and almost half its funds were disbursed to various Community Action programs. But the reality was often far from the ideal. The nearly $3 billion that the OEO spent during its first two years of existence did much to assist those who managed to qualify for funds. It helped significantly to reduce poverty in certain areas. It fell far short, however, of its goal of eliminating poverty altogether. The job-training programs that formed so important a part of the war on poverty produced generally disappointing results, particularly among the urban black unemployed; blacks continued, once trained, to be barred from many jobs because of racial discrimination or because the jobs simply did not exist in their communities. Community Action programs often fell victim either to local mismanagement or to cumbersome federal supervision, and in either case frequently resulted in a substantial waste of funds. Above all, however, the war on poverty never really approached the dimensions necessary to achieve its goals. From the beginning, funds were inadequate. And as the years passed and a costly war in Southeast Asia became the nation's first priority, even those limited funds began to dwindle.

Cities and Schools

Closely tied to the antipoverty program were federal efforts to promote the revitalization of decaying cities and to strengthen the nation's schools. Again, many such programs had received support from the Kennedy administration but won passage under Johnson. President Kennedy himself had managed to steer through Congress the Housing Act of 1961, which offered $4.9 billion in federal grants to cities for the preservation of open spaces, the development of mass-transit systems, and the subsidization of middle-income housing. Johnson went further. He established the Department of Housing and Urban Development to symbolize the government's commitment to the cities. (The first secretary of this department, Robert Weaver, was the first black ever to serve in the cabinet.) And Johnson also inaugurated the Model Cities program, which offered federal subsidies for urban redevelopment.

Kennedy had fought long and in vain to win congressional passage of a program to provide federal aid to public education. Like the idea of federal health insurance, the concept of aid to education aroused deep suspicion in many Americans, who saw it as the first step in a federal effort to take control of the schools from localities. Conservatives argued forcefully that once the government began paying for education, it would begin telling the schools how and what they must teach. Opposition arose from another quarter as well: Catholics insisted that aid to education must extend to parochial as well as public schools, something that President Kennedy had refused to consider and that many Americans believed was unconstitutional. Johnson managed to circumvent both objections with the Elementary and Secondary Education Act of 1965 and a series of subsequent measures. Such bills extended aid to both private and parochial schools—aid that was based on the economic conditions of their students, not the needs of the schools themselves. The formula met criteria established earlier by the Supreme Court, and it satisfied some, although not all, conservatives. Total federal expenditures for education and technical training rose from $5 billion to $12 billion between 1964 and 1967.

Legacies of the Great Society

The great surge of reform of the Kennedy-Johnson years reflected not only a new awareness of the nation's social problems but the boundless confidence of a society that believed its resources and abilities were limitless. By the time Johnson left office, legislation had been either enacted or initiated to deal with almost every imaginable social problem: poverty, health, education, cities, transportation, the environment, the consumer, agriculture, science, the arts. So powerful was the impetus behind many of these reforms that major initiatives continued into the early 1970s, even though the administration was by then in the hands of a conservative Republican, Richard Nixon, who professed to oppose the extension of federal power.

The reforms meant, of course, a radical increase in federal spending. For a time, rising tax revenues from the growing economy nearly compensated for the new expenditures. In 1964, Lyndon Johnson managed to win passage of the $11.5 billion tax cut that Kennedy had first proposed in 1962. Although the cut increased an already sizable federal deficit, it produced substantial economic growth over the next several years that made up for much of the revenue initially lost. But as the Great Society programs began to multiply, and particularly as they began to compete with the escalating costs of America's military ventures, the federal budget rapidly began to outpace increases in revenues. In 1961, the federal government had spent $94.4 billion. By 1970, that sum had more than doubled, to $196.6 billon. And except for 1969, when there was a modest surplus, the budget throughout the decade showed a deficit, which in 1968 rose to $25.1 billion—the highest in history to that point.

The vast costs of the programs of the Great Society, and the apparent inability of American society to raise the government revenues to pay for them, contributed to a growing disillusionment in later years with the idea of federal efforts to solve social problems. By the 1980s, an increasing number of experts were arguing that the Great Society social programs had not worked; that the federal government lacked the expertise or the administrative capacity to make them work; that what progress there had been toward eliminating poverty in the 1960s and 1970s had been a result of economic growth, not government assistance. Others, however, argued equally fervently

MAJOR ACHIEVEMENTS OF THE GREAT SOCIETY

1964 Civil Rights Act
Twenty-fourth Amendment (abolishing poll tax)
Tax Reduction Act
Urban Mass Transportation Act (subsidizing urban mass transit)
Economic Opportunity Act (creating OEO, Job Corps, VISTA)
Wilderness Preservation Act

1965 Elementary and Secondary Education Act (providing aid to schools)
Medicare
Civil Rights Act (protecting voting rights)
Omnibus Housing Act (providing rent supplements to poor)
Department of Housing and Urban Development

1965 National Endowments of the Arts and Humanities
Water Quality Act
Immigration law reform
Air Quality Act
Higher Education Act (offering federally financed scholarships)

1966 National Traffic and Motor Vehicle Safety Act
Highway Safety Act
Minimum wage increase
Department of Transportation
Model Cities

1967 Food Stamps
Corporation for Public Broadcasting

---

that social programs had made important contributions both to the welfare of the specific groups they were designed to help and to the health of the economy as a whole. They pointed, in particular, to the reduction of hunger in America, the inclusion of poor people in health-care programs, and the increased services available to young children.

Whatever the reason, the decade of the 1960s—a decade marked both by stunning economic growth and ambitious government antipoverty efforts—saw the most substantial decrease in poverty in the United States of any period in the nation's history. In 1959, according to the most widely accepted estimates, 21 percent remained below that line. The improvements officially established poverty line. By 1969, only 12 percent remained below that line. The improvements affected blacks and whites in about the same proportion: 56 percent of the black population had lived in poverty in 1959, only 32 percent did so ten years later—a 42 percent reduction; 18 percent of all whites had been poor in 1959, but only 10 percent were poor a decade later—a 44 percent reduction.

The Battle for Racial Equality

The nation's most important domestic initiative in the 1960s was the new national commitment to provide justice and equality to American blacks. It was also the most difficult commitment, the one that produced the severest strains on American society. Yet despite the initial reluctance of many whites, including even many liberals, to confront the problem, it was an issue that could no longer be ignored. Black Americans were themselves ensuring that the nation would have to deal with the problem of race.

Expanding Protests

John Kennedy had long been sympathetic to the cause of racial justice, but he was hardly a committed crusader. His intervention during the 1960 campaign to help win the release of Martin Luther King, Jr., from a Georgia prison won him a large plurality of the black vote. Once in office, however, he was—like many presidents before him—reluctant to jeopardize his legislative program by openly committing himself to racial reform, fearing that he would alienate key Democratic senators. Resisting the arguments of those who urged new civil-rights legislation, the Kennedy administration worked instead to expand the enforcement of existing laws and to support litigation to overturn existing segregation statutes. Both efforts produced only limited results. Still, the administration hoped to contain the issue of race and resisted pressure to do more.

But that pressure was rapidly growing too powerful to ignore. In February 1960, black college students in Greensboro, North Carolina, staged a sit-in at a segregated Woolworth's lunch counter—an event

Sitting In
Black students stage a sit-in at a Woolworth's lunch counter in Charlotte, North Carolina, in 1960, after being refused service by the waitresses there. A similar demonstration at a Woolworth's in Greensboro several weeks earlier sparked a wave of sit-ins across the South.   (BruceRoberts/Rapho-Photo Researchers)

that received wide national attention. In the following months, such demonstrations spread throughout the South, forcing many merchants to integrate their facilities. The sit-in movement had two important consequences: It mobilized large groups of blacks throughout the country to take direct action to protest discrimination; and it aroused the support of a substantial number of Northern whites, particularly on college campuses.

In 1961, students of both races began what they called "freedom rides." Traveling by bus throughout the South, they went from city to city attempting to force the desegregation of bus stations. They were met in some places with such savage violence on the part of whites that the president finally dispatched

federal marshals to help keep the peace and ordered the integration of all bus and train stations.

Continuing judicial efforts to enforce the integration of public education produced an even greater test of the president's resolve. In October 1962, a federal court ordered the University of Mississippi to enroll its first black student, James Meredith; and Governor Ross Barnett, a rabid segregationist, refused to enforce the order. When angry whites in Oxford, Mississippi, began rioting to protest the court decree, Kennedy sent federal troops to the city to restore order and protect Meredith's right to attend the university.

Events in Alabama the following year proved even more influential. In April 1963, Martin Luther King,

Jr., launched a series of extensive nonviolent demonstrations in Birmingham, Alabama, a city unsurpassed in the strength of its commitment to segregation. Local officials responded brutally. Police Commissioner Eugene "Bull" Connor personally supervised measures to prevent King's peaceful marches, using attack dogs, tear gas, electric cattle prods, and fire hoses—at times even against small children. Hundreds of demonstrators were arrested, as much of the nation watched televised reports of the conflicts in horror. Two months later, Governor George Wallace stood in the doorway of a building at the University of Alabama to prevent the court-ordered enrollment of several black students. Only after the arrival of federal marshals did he give way. The same night, NAACP official Medgar Evers was murdered in Mississippi.

A National Commitment

The events in Alabama and Mississippi were both a personal shock and a political warning to the president. He could not, he realized, any longer avoid the issue of race. In a historic television address the night of the University of Alabama confrontation, Kennedy spoke eloquently of the "moral issue" facing the nation. "If an American," he asked, "because his skin is dark, . . . cannot enjoy the full and free life which all of us want, then who among us would be content to have the color of his skin changed and stand in his place? Who among us would then be content with the counsels of patience and delay?" Days later, he introduced a series of new legislative proposals prohibiting segregation in "public accommodations" (stores, restaurants, theaters, hotels), barring discrimination in employment, and increasing the power of the government to file suit on behalf of school integration.

Congressional opposition to the new proposals was strong, and it was clear from the start that only a long and arduous battle would win passage of the legislation. But once again, it was black Americans themselves who made clear that there would be no retreat from the effort. In August 1963, more than 200,000 demonstrators marched down the Mall in Washington, D.C., and gathered before the Lincoln Memorial for the greatest civil-rights demonstration in the nation's history. President Kennedy, who had at first opposed the idea of the march, in the end gave it his open support. And the peaceful gathering, therefore, seemed at the time to denote less the ex-

istence of a bitter racial struggle than the birth of a new national commitment to civil rights. Martin Luther King, Jr., in one of the greatest speeches of his distinguished oratorical career—indeed one of the most memorable speeches of any public figure of the century—aroused the crowd with a litany of images prefaced again and again by the phrase "I have a dream." The march was the high-water mark of the peaceful, interracial civil-rights movement—and one of the high points of liberal optimism as well. Darker days were soon to come.

The assassination of President Kennedy gave new impetus to the battle for civil-rights legislation. The ambitious measure that Kennedy had proposed in June 1963 had passed through the House of Representatives with relative ease; but it seemed hopelessly stalled in the Senate, where a determined filibuster by Southern conservatives continued to prevent a vote. Early in 1964, after Johnson had applied both public and private pressure, supporters of the measure finally mustered the two-thirds majority necessary to close debate; and the Senate passed the most comprehensive civil-rights bill in the history of the nation.

The Battle for Voting Rights

At the very moment of passage of the Civil Rights Act of 1964, however, new efforts were under way in the South to win even greater gains for blacks. And during the "freedom summer" of that year, thousands of civil-rights workers, black and white, Northern and Southern, spread out through the South, establishing "freedom schools," staging demonstrations, and demanding not only an end to segregation but the inclusion of blacks in the political process. Like earlier civil-rights activists, they met a hostile response—in some cases, a murderous response. Three of the first freedom workers to arrive in the South disappeared; several weeks later, the FBI found their bodies buried under an earthen dam.

Black demands continued to escalate during 1965, and government efforts to satisfy them continued to intensify. In Selma, Alabama, in March, Martin Luther King, Jr., helped organize a major demonstration by blacks demanding the right to register to vote. Confronted with official resistance, the demonstrators attempted a peaceful protest march; but Selma sheriff Jim Clark led local police in a brutal attack on the demonstrators—graphically televised to a horrified nation. Two Northern whites participating in the Selma march were murdered in the course of the

Selma
Martin Luther King, Jr., and his wife, Coretta, lead demonstrators on a march through Selma, Alabama, during his turbulent campaign for black voting rights in 1965. Selma was one of the last of the great interracial crusades on behalf of civil rights. Subsequent campaigns, such as King's frustrated effort in Chicago in 1966, attracted much less support from Northern whites and far less attention in the media. (Bruce Davidson/Magnum)

effort there—one, a minister, beaten to death in the streets of the town; the other, a Detroit housewife, shot as she drove along a highway at night. The national outrage that followed the events in Alabama helped Lyndon Johnson win passage of the Civil Rights Act of 1965, which guaranteed federal protection to blacks attempting to exercise their right to vote. The traditional criteria for limiting the fran-

chise to whites—literacy tests, knowledge of the Constitution, "good character," and others—were now illegal. (Another, similar device—the poll tax—had been abolished by constitutional amendment in 1964.)

But the civil-rights acts, the Supreme Court decisions, the new social welfare programs designed to help poor blacks, and other government efforts—all were insufficient. Important as such gains were, they failed to satisfy the rapidly rising expectations of American blacks, whose vision of equality included not only an end to segregation but access to economic prosperity. What had once seemed to many liberals a simple moral commitment was becoming a far more complex and demanding issue. Gradually, the generally peaceful, largely optimistic civil-rights movement of the early 1960s was evolving into what would become a major racial crisis.

The Changing Movement

It was inevitable, perhaps, that the focus of the racial struggle would shift away from the issue of segregation to the far broader and more complex demands of poor urban blacks. For decades, the nation's black population had been undergoing a major demographic shift; and by the 1960s, the problem of race was no longer a primarily Southern or rural one, as it had been earlier in the century. In 1910, only 25 percent of all blacks had lived in cities and only 10 percent outside the South. By 1966, 69 percent were living in metropolitan areas and 45 percent outside the South. In several of the largest cities, the proportion of blacks at least doubled between 1950 and 1968. Blacks constituted 30 percent or more of the population of seven major cities and nearly 70 percent of the population of Washington, D.C.

Conditions in the black ghettoes of most cities were abysmal. And although the economic condition of much of American society was improving, in many poor urban communities—which were experiencing both a rapidly growing population and the flight of white businesses—things were getting worse. More than half of all American nonwhites lived in poverty at the beginning of the 1960s; black unemployment was twice that of whites. And although conditions improved for many blacks during the decade, the residents of the inner cities were usually the last to benefit. Black ghetto residents were far more likely than whites to be victimized by crime, to be enticed into drug addiction, and to be subjected to substandard housing at exploitive prices. They were far less likely than whites to receive an adequate education or to have access to skilled employment.

As the battle against legal segregation progressed in the early 1960s with the passage of the landmark Civil Rights Acts of 1964 and 1965, even such relatively moderate black leaders as Martin Luther King, Jr., began to turn their attention to the deeper, less immediately visible problems of their race. By the mid-1960s, the legal battle against school desegregation had moved beyond the initial assault on de jure segregation (segregation by law) to an attack on de facto segregation (segregation by practice, as through residential patterns), thus carrying the fight into Northern cities. Such attacks would lead (beginning in 1970) to the busing of students from one area of a community to another to achieve integration—an issue that would prove as deeply divisive as any social question of its time.

Many black leaders (and their white supporters) were demanding, similarly, that the battle against job discrimination move beyond the prohibition of overtly racist practices. Employers should not only abandon negative measures to deny jobs to blacks; they should adopt positive measures to recruit minorities, thus compensating for past injustices. Lyndon Johnson gave his support to the concept of "affirmative action" in 1965. Three years later, the Department of Labor ruled that all contractors doing business with the federal government must submit "a written affirmative action compliance program" to the government. Affirmative action guidelines gradually extended to all institutions doing business with or receiving funds from the federal government (including schools and universities). Yet another issue had arisen that would soon anger and alienate many whites.

And civil-rights activists were now, increasingly, directing their attention toward racism in the North. Martin Luther King, Jr. organized a major campaign in the summer of 1966 (a year after Selma) in Chicago. He hoped to direct national attention to housing and employment discrimination in Northern industrial cities in much the same way he had exposed legal racism in the South. But the Chicago campaign not only evoked vicious and at times violent opposition from white residents of that city; it failed to arouse the national conscience to anything approaching the degree the events in the South had done.

Urban Violence

As the Chicago campaign suggested, the most important black problem by the mid-1960s was less legalized segregation than urban poverty. Beginning in 1964, moreover, the problem thrust itself into public prominence when residents of black ghettoes in major cities participated in a series of riots that shocked

Watts, 1965
Watts seemed an unlikely site for the most serious racial violence America had experienced in twenty years. Its neat single-family homes conveyed none of the sense of despair of the crowded tenements of Eastern black ghettoes. But black frustration in the mid-1960s had grown to the point that it could no longer be contained, and virtually no community was now immune from racial tensions.   (UPI/Bettmann Newsphotos)

and terrified much of the nation's white population. There were a few scattered disturbances in the summer of 1964, most notably in New York City's Harlem. But the first major race riot occurred the following summer in the Watts section of Los Angeles. In the midst of a more or less routine traffic arrest, a white police officer struck a protesting black bystander with his club; and the apparently minor incident unleashed a storm of pent-up anger and bitterness that resulted in a full week of mounting violence. As many as 10,000 rioters were estimated to have participated—attacking white motorists, burning buildings, looting stores, and sniping at policemen. As in most race riots, it was the blacks themselves who suffered most; of the thirty-four people who died during the Watts uprising, which was eventually quelled by the National Guard, twenty-eight were black. In the summer of 1966, there

were forty-three additional outbreaks, the most serious of them in Chicago and Cleveland. And in the summer of 1967, there were eight major riots, including the most serious of them all—a racial clash in Detroit in which forty-three people (thirty-three of them black) died.

Televised reports of the violence alarmed millions of Americans and created both a new sense of urgency and a growing sense of doubt among those whites who had embraced the cause of racial justice only a few years before. After the Detroit uprising, President Johnson expressed the ambivalence of many white liberals about the riots, calling sternly on the one hand for a restoration of law and order, and appealing simultaneously for an attack on the social problems that were causing despair and violence. A special Commission on Civil Disorders echoed the latter impulse. Its celebrated report, issued in the spring of 1968, recommended massive spending to eliminate the abysmal conditions of the ghettoes. "Only a commitment to national action on an unprecedented scale," the commission concluded, "can shape a future compatible with the historic ideals of American society." To much of the nation, however, the lesson of the riots was that racial change was moving too quickly and that stern, coercive measures were necessary to stop violence and lawlessness.

Black Power

Disillusioned with the ideal of peaceful change in cooperation with whites, an increasing number of blacks were turning to a new approach to the racial issue: the philosophy of "black power." Black power could mean many different things. In its most moderate form, it was simply a belief in the importance of black self-reliance. In its more extreme guises, black power could mean complete separatism and even violent revolution. In all its forms, however, black power suggested a move away from interracial cooperation and toward increased black racial awareness.

The most important and lasting impact of the black-power ideology was a social and psychological one: the instilling of racial pride in black Americans who had long been under pressure from their nation's dominant culture to think of themselves as somehow inferior to whites. It encouraged the growth of "black studies" in schools and universities. It helped stimulate important black literary and artistic movements. It produced a new interest among many blacks in their African roots. It led to a rejection by some blacks of certain cultural practices borrowed from white society: "Afro" hair styles began to replace artificially straightened hair; some blacks began to adopt African styles of dress, even to change their names.

But black power had political manifestations as well, most notably in creating a deep schism within the civil-rights movement. Traditional black organizations that had emphasized cooperation with sympathetic whites—groups such as the NAACP, the Urban League, and King's Southern Christian Leadership Conference (SCLC)—now faced competition from younger, more radical groups. The Student Nonviolent Coordinating Committee (SNCC) and the Congress of Racial Equality (CORE) had both begun as relatively moderate, interracial organizations. SNCC, in fact, had been a student branch of the SCLC. By the mid-1960s, however, these and other groups were calling for more radical and occasionally even violent action against the "racism" of white society and were openly rejecting the approaches of older, more established black leaders.

Other groups were emerging entirely outside the civil-rights movement as well. Particularly alarming to whites were such overtly revolutionary organizations as the Black Panthers, based in Oakland, California, and the separatist group, the Nation of Islam, which denounced all whites as "devils" and appealed to blacks to embrace the Islamic faith and work for complete racial separation. The most celebrated of the Black Muslims, as whites often termed them, was Malcolm Little, who adopted the name Malcolm X ("X" to denote his lost African surname). His *Autobiography* (1965)—written in collaboration with Alex Haley—became one of the most influential documents of the 1960s. Malcolm X himself died shortly before publication of his book when black gunmen, presumably under orders from rivals within the Nation of Islam, burst into a meeting he was addressing and assassinated him.

From "Flexible Response" to Vietnam

In international affairs as much as in domestic reform, the optimistic liberalism of the Kennedy and Johnson administrations dictated a more positive, more active approach to dealing with the nation's problems than in the past. Just as social difficulties at home required a search for new solutions, so the threat of communism overseas seemed to call for new methods and strategies. And just as the new activism in domestic reform ultimately produced frustration and disorder, so did the new activism overseas gradually pull the nation toward disaster.

Diversifying Foreign Policy

John Kennedy's stirring inaugural address was a clear indication of how central to his and to the nation's thinking was opposition to communism. "In the long history of the world," he proclaimed, "only a few generations have been granted the role of defending freedom in its hour of maximum danger. I do not shrink from this responsibility; I welcome it." Yet the speech—which significantly made no mention whatever of domestic affairs—was also an indication of Kennedy's belief that the United States had not done enough to counter Soviet expansion. The defense policies of the new administration, therefore, emphasized not only strengthening existing implements of warfare but developing new ones—a strategy that came to be known as "flexible response."

Kennedy had charged repeatedly during his campaign that the United States was suffering from a "missile gap," that the Soviet Union had moved ahead of America in the number of missiles and warheads it could deploy. Even before the election, Kennedy received information indicating that whatever missile gap there was favored the United States. Nevertheless, once in office, he insisted on substantial increases in the nation's nuclear armaments. The Soviet Union, which had several years earlier decided to slow the growth of its atomic arsenal, responded with a new missile-building program of its own.

At the same time, Kennedy expressed dissatisfaction with the nation's ability to meet communist threats in "emerging areas" of the Third World—the areas in which, Kennedy believed, the real struggle against communism would be waged in the future. A nuclear deterrent might prevent a Soviet invasion of Western Europe; but in the Middle East, in Africa, in Latin America, in Asia, where insurgent forces had learned to employ methods of jungle and guerrilla warfare, different methods would be necessary. Kennedy gave enthusiastic support to the development of new counterinsurgency forces—a million soldiers trained specifically to fight modern, limited wars. He even chose their uniforms, which included the distinctive green beret from which the Special Forces derived their nickname.

Along with military diversification, Kennedy favored the development of methods for expanding American influence through peaceful means. To repair the badly deteriorating relationship with Latin America, he proposed an "Alliance for Progress": a series of projects undertaken cooperatively by the United States and Latin American governments for peaceful development and stabilization of the nations of that region. Its purpose was both to spur social and economic development and to inhibit the rise of Castro-like movements in other Central or South American countries. Poor coordination and inadequate funding sharply limited the impact of the program, but relations between the United States and some Latin American countries did improve.

Kennedy also inaugurated the Agency for International Development (AID) to coordinate foreign aid. And he established what became one of his most popular innovations: the Peace Corps, which trained and sent abroad young volunteers to work in developing areas.

Fiasco in Cuba

Kennedy's efforts to improve relations with developing countries were not aided by a hopelessly bungled assault on the Castro government in Cuba. Convinced that "communist domination in this hemisphere can never be negotiated" and that Castro represented a threat to the stability of other Latin American nations, Kennedy agreed in the first weeks of his presidency to continue a project the Eisenhower administration had begun. For months, the CIA had been helping secretly to train a small army of anti-Castro Cuban exiles in Central America. On April 17, 1961, with the approval of the president, 2,000 of the armed exiles landed at the Bay of Pigs in Cuba, expecting first American air support and then a spontaneous uprising by the Cuban people on their behalf. They received neither. At the last minute, Kennedy withdrew the air support, fearful of involving the United States too directly in the invasion. And the expected uprising did not occur. Instead, well-armed Castro forces easily crushed the invaders, and within two days the entire mission had collapsed.

A somber President Kennedy took full responsibility for the fiasco. Governments around the world—not only communist but neutral and pro-Western as well—joined in condemning the United States. But despite the humiliation, Kennedy refused to abandon the principle of overthrowing Castro by force. "We do not intend to abandon Cuba to the Communists," he said only three days after the Bay of Pigs.

Confrontations with the Soviet Union

In the grim aftermath of the Bay of Pigs, Kennedy traveled to Vienna in June 1961 for his first meeting with Soviet Premier Nikita Khrushchev. Their frosty exchange of views did little to reduce tensions between the two nations. Nor did Khrushchev's continuing irritation over the existence of a noncommunist West Berlin in the heart of East Germany.

Particularly embarrassing to the communists was the mass exodus of residents of East Germany to the West through the easily traversed border in the center of Berlin. Before dawn on August 13, 1961, the Soviet Union stopped the exodus by directing East Germany to construct a wall between East and West Berlin. Guards fired on those who continued to try to escape.

The rising tensions culminated the following October in the most dangerous and dramatic crisis of the Cold War. During the summer of 1962, American intelligence agencies had become aware of the arrival of Soviet technicians and equipment in Cuba and of military construction in progress. At first, the administration assumed that the new weapons system was, as the Soviets claimed, purely defensive. On October 14, however, aerial reconaissance photos produced clear evidence that in fact the Soviets were constructing missile sites on the island. The reasons for the Russian effort were not difficult to discern. The existence of offensive nuclear missiles in Cuba would go far toward compensating for the American lead in deployable atomic weapons, giving the Soviet Union the same easy access to enemy territory that the United States had long possessed by virtue of its missile sites in Europe and the Middle East. The weapons would, moreover, serve as an effective deterrent against any future American invasion of Cuba—a possibility that seemed very real both to Castro and to the Soviet leadership.

To Kennedy, and to most other Americans, the missile sites represented an unconscionable act of aggression by the Soviets toward the United States. Almost immediately, he decided that the weapons could not be allowed to remain. On October 22, after nearly a week of tense deliberations by a special task force in the White House, the president announced on television that he was establishing a naval and air blockade around Cuba, a "quarantine" against all offensive weapons. Soviet ships bound for the island slowed course or stopped before reaching the point of confrontation. But work on the missile sites continued at full speed. Preparations were under way for an American air attack on the missile sites when, late in the evening of October 26, Kennedy received a message from Khrushchev implying that the Soviet Union would remove the missile bases in exchange for an American pledge not to invade Cuba. Ignoring other, tougher Soviet messages, the president agreed; privately, moreover, he gave assurances that the United States would remove its missiles from Turkey (a decision he had already reached months before but had not yet implemented). On October 27, the agreement became public. The crisis was over.

The Cuban missile crisis brought the world closer to nuclear war than at any time since World War II. It exposed in dangerous fashion the perils that both the Soviet Union and the United States were creating by allowing their own rivalry to extend into Third World countries. But it also, ironically, helped produce a significant alleviation of Cold War tensions. Both the United States and the Soviet Union had been forced to confront the momentous consequences of war, and both seemed ready in the following months to move toward a new accommodation. In June 1963, President Kennedy addressed a commencement audience at American University in Washington, D.C., with a message starkly different from those of his earlier speeches. The United States did not, he claimed, seek a "Pax Americana enforced on the world by American weapons of war." And he seemed for the first time to offer hope for a peaceful rapprochement with the Soviet Union. "If we cannot now end our differences," he said, "at least we can help make the world safe for diversity." That same summer, the United States and the Soviet Union concluded years of negotiation by agreeing to a treaty to ban the testing of nuclear weapons in the atmosphere. It was the first step toward mutual arms reduction since the beginning of the Cold War—a small step, but one that seemed to augur a new era of international relations.

Johnson and the World

Lyndon Johnson entered the presidency lacking even John Kennedy's limited prior experience with international affairs. He had never been much involved with foreign relations during his years in the Senate. He had traveled widely while vice president, but he had been included in few important decisions. He was eager, therefore, not only to continue the policies of his predecessor but to prove quickly that he too was a strong and forceful leader. As a result, he quickly came to depend on those members of the Kennedy administration with the most assertive view of the proper uses of American power.

Johnson was even less adept than his predecessor—who had displayed little sensitivity on the subject—at distinguishing between nationalist insurgency and communist expansion. His response to an internal rebellion in the Dominican Republic was a clear illustration. A 1961 assassination had toppled the repressive dictatorship of General Rafael Trujillo, and for the next four years various factions in the country had struggled for dominance. In the spring of 1965, a conservative military regime began to col-

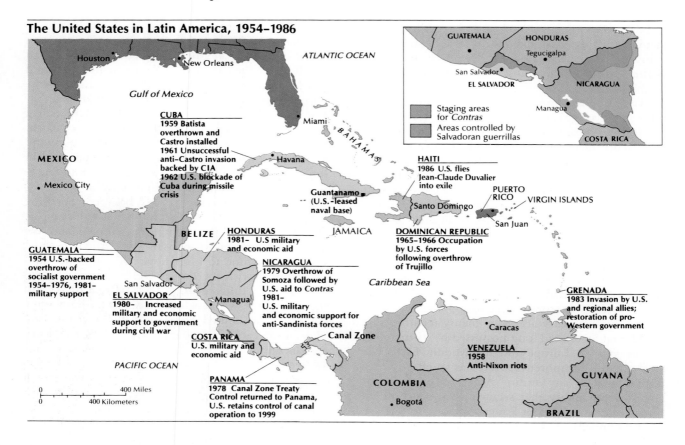

The United States in Latin America, 1954–1986

ATLANTIC OCEAN

Houston
New Orleans

Gulf of Mexico

CUBA
1959 Batista
overthrown and
Castro installed
1961 Unsuccessful
anti-Castro invasion
backed by CIA
1962 U.S. blockade of
Cuba during missile
crisis

Miami

Havana

BAHAMAS

MEXICO

Mexico City

Guantanamo
(U.S.-leased
naval base)

HAITI
1986 U.S. flies
Jean-Claude Duvalier
into exile

PUERTO
RICO   VIRGIN ISLANDS

Santo Domingo

San Juan

BELIZE

HONDURAS
1981– U.S military
and economic aid

JAMAICA

DOMINICAN REPUBLIC
1965–1966 Occupation
by U.S. forces
following overthrow
of Trujillo

GUATEMALA
1954 U.S.-backed
overthrow of
socialist government
1954–1976, 1981–
military support

San Salvador

NICARAGUA
1979 Overthrow of
Somoza followed by
U.S. aid to *Contras*
1981–
U.S. military
and economic support for
anti-Sandinista forces

Caribbean Sea

GRENADA
1983 Invasion by U.S.
and regional allies;
restoration of pro-
Western government

EL SALVADOR
1980– Increased
military and economic
support to government
during civil war

Managua

Canal Zone

Caracas

COSTA RICA
U.S. military and
economic aid

VENEZUELA
1958
Anti-Nixon riots

GUYANA

PACIFIC OCEAN

PANAMA
1978 Canal Zone Treaty
Control returned to Panama,
U.S. retains control of canal
operation to 1999

COLOMBIA

Bogotá

BRAZIL

0 — 400 Miles
0 — 400 Kilometers

GUATEMALA   HONDURAS
Tegucigalpa
San Salvador
EL SALVADOR   NICARAGUA
Managua
Staging areas
for *Contras*
Areas controlled by
Salvadoran guerrillas
COSTA RICA

---

lapse in the face of a revolt by a broad range of groups (including some younger military leaders) on behalf of the left-wing nationalist Juan Bosch. For Johnson, the situation seemed an ideal opportunity to display the effectiveness of American force. Arguing that Bosch planned to establish a pro-Castro, communist regime, he dispatched 30,000 American troops to quell the disorder. The troops remained—although later they came under the auspices of the Organization of American States—until the Johnson administration had assurances that the Dominican Republic would establish a pro-American, anticommunist regime. Only after a conservative candidate defeated Bosch in a 1966 election were the forces withdrawn.

From Johnson's first moments in office, however, his foreign policy was almost totally dominated by the bitter civil war in Vietnam and by the expanding involvement of the United States there. That involvement had been growing slowly for more than a decade by the time Johnson assumed the presidency. In many respects, therefore, he was simply the unfortunate legatee of commitments initiated by his pre-

decessors. But the determination of the new president, and of others within his administration, to prove their worthiness in the battle against communism led to the final, decisive steps toward a full-scale and catastrophic commitment.

Guns and Advisers

The American involvement in Vietnam had developed so slowly and imperceptibly that when it began spectacularly to expand, in 1964 and 1965, few could remember how it had originated. The first steps toward intervention, certainly, had seemed at the time to be little more than minor events on the periphery of the larger Cold War. American aid to French forces in Indochina before 1954 had been limited and indirect; the nation's involvement with the Diem regime thereafter, while more substantial, seemed for several years no greater than its involvement with many other Third World governments. But as Diem began to face growing internal opposition, and as the threat from the communists to the north appeared to grow, the United States found itself drawn ever deeper into what would ultimately become widely known as the "quagmire."

Ngo Dinh Diem had been an unfortunate choice as the basis of American hopes for a noncommunist South Vietnam. Autocratic, aristocratic, and corrupt, he staunchly resisted any economic reforms that would weaken the position of the Vietnamese upper class and the power of his own family. A belligerent Roman Catholic in a nation with many Buddhists, he invited dissent through his efforts to limit the influence of the Buddhist religion.

Diem's own limitations intensified problems that would have faced any South Vietnamese ruler, for the partition of the country in 1954 had never satisfied Ho Chi Minh and his government. By the late 1950s, therefore, a powerful insurgency was growing in strength in South Vietnam—an insurgency encouraged and supplied in large part by the government of the north. By 1958, a fierce civil war was in progress. And two years later, that war intensified, as communist guerrillas (or Viet Cong, as they were derisively known to their opponents) organized the National Front for the Liberation of South Vietnam (NLF). The NLF had close ties to the government of Ho Chi Minh and, as the war expanded in the ensuing years, received increasing assistance from the north.

Faced with a steadily deteriorating political and military position, Diem appealed to the United States for assistance. The Eisenhower administration increased the flow of weapons and ammunition to South Vietnam during its last years in office and introduced the first few American military advisers to the area— about 650 in all. But it was the Kennedy administration, with its fervent belief in the importance of fighting communism in emerging areas, that expanded that assistance into a major commitment. Despite misgivings about the reliability of Diem, Kennedy substantially increased the flow of munitions into South Vietnam. More important, he raised the number of American military personnel to 15,500.

But the real depth of the American commitment to the war became clear in 1963, when the Diem regime stood on the brink of collapse. The military struggle against the Viet Cong was going badly. And Diem's brutal tactics in dispersing Buddhist demonstrators in Saigon had produced a religious crisis as well. Several Buddhist monks burned themselves to death in the streets of the capital, arousing further popular resistance to the government and horrifying the American public, which witnessed the immola-

The Buddhist Crisis, 1963
It was not communists but Buddhist monks who ultimately led to the downfall of South Vietnamese President Ngo Dinh Diem in 1963. The Buddhists fought back against the repressive measures directed against them by the Roman Catholic Diem regime, and they attracted the attention of the world when several monks set themselves afire in the streets of Saigon to protest government policies. (UPI/Bettmann Newsphotos)

tions on television. Early in November, after receiving tacit assurances of support from the United States, South Vietnamese military leaders seized control of the government from Diem, executing the deposed president, his brother, and other associates. The Americans had not sanctioned the killings, but they had been instrumental in instigating the coup. Faced

─────── WHERE HISTORIANS DISAGREE ───────

The Vietnam Commitment

In 1965 the Department of Defense released a film, intended for American soldiers about to embark for service in Vietnam and designed to explain why the United States had found it necessary to commit so many lives and resources to the defense of a small and distant land. The film was entitled *Why Vietnam?* The question it asked is one many Americans have pondered, and debated, in the two decades since. The debate has proceeded on two levels. At one level, it is an effort to assess the broad objectives that Americans believed they were pursuing in Vietnam. At another, it is an effort to explain how and why policymakers made the specific decisions that led to the American commitment.

The Defense Department film itself offered one answer to the question of America's broad objectives, an answer that for a time most Americans tended to accept: The United States was fighting in Vietnam to defend freedom and stop aggression; and it was fighting in Vietnam to prevent the spread of communism into a new area of the world, to protect not only Vietnam but also the other nations of the Pacific that would soon be threatened if Vietnam itself were to fall. That explanation—that America intervened in Vietnam to defend its ideals and its legitimate interests—continues to attract support. Journalist Norman Podhoretz's 1982 book *Why We Were in Vietnam* argues that America was in Vietnam "to save the Southern half of that country from the evils of communism" and that the tragic events in Indochina since 1975 prove the essential morality of the American cause. Political scientist Guenter

Lewy contends, in *America in Vietnam* (1978), that the United States entered Vietnam to help an ally combat "foreign aggression." And historian Ernest R. May has stated: "The paradox is that the Vietnam War, so often condemned by its opponents as hideously immoral, may well have been the most moral or at least the most selfless war in all of American history. For the impulse guiding it was not to defeat an enemy or to serve a national interest; it was simply not to abandon friends."

Others have argued that America's broad objectives in Vietnam were less altruistic, that the intervention was a form of imperialism—part of a larger effort by the United States after World War II to impose a particular political and economic order on the world. "The Vietnam War," historian Gabriel Kolko wrote in *Anatomy of a War* (1985), "was for the United States the culmination of its frustrating postwar effort to merge its arms and politics to halt and reverse the emergence of states and social systems opposed to the international order Washington sought to establish." Economist Robert Heilbroner, writing in 1967, saw the American intent as somewhat more defensive; the intervention in Vietnam was a response to "a fear of losing our place in the sun," to a fear that a communist victory "would signal the end of capitalism as the dominant world order and would force the acknowledgement that America no longer constituted the model on which the future of world civilization would be mainly based."

Those who have looked less at the nation's broad objectives than at the internal workings of the policymaking process have likewise produced

─────────────────────────────

with what he considered a choice between allowing South Vietnam to fall or expanding the American involvement, John Kennedy had chosen the latter. Before he could indicate what further steps he was prepared to take, he himself fell victim to an assassin on November 22.

From Aid to Intervention

Lyndon Johnson, therefore, inherited what was already a substantial American commitment to the sur-

vival of an anticommunist South Vietnam. During his first two years in office, he expanded that commitment into a full-scale American war. Why he did so has long been a subject of debate. (See "Where Historians Disagree," above.)

Many factors played a role in Johnson's fateful decision. But the most obvious explanation is that the new president faced many pressures to expand the American involvement and only a very few to limit it. As the untested successor to a revered and martyred president, he felt obliged to prove his worthiness for the office by continuing the policies of his

WHERE HISTORIANS DISAGREE

competing explanations. Journalist David Halberstam's *The Best and the Brightest* (1972) argues that policymakers deluded themselves into thinking they could achieve their goals in Vietnam by ignoring, suppressing, or dismissing the information that might have suggested otherwise. The foreign policy leaders of the Kennedy and Johnson administrations were so committed to the idea of American activism and success that they refused to consider the possibility of failure; the Vietnam disaster was thus, at least in part, a result of the arrogance of the nation's leaders.

Larry Berman, a political scientist, offers a somewhat different view in *Planning a Tragedy* (1982). Lyndon Johnson never believed that American prospects in Vietnam were bright or that a real victory was within sight, Berman argues. Johnson was not misled by his advisers. He committed American troops to the war in Vietnam in 1965 not because he expected to win but because he feared that allowing Vietnam to fall would destroy him politically. To do otherwise, Johnson believed, would destroy his hopes for winning approval of his Great Society legislation at home.

Leslie H. Gelb (who as an official in the Defense Department in the 1960s directed the writing of the official study of the war that became known as the Pentagon Papers) has produced another, related explanation for American intervention, which sees the roots of the involvement in the larger imperatives of the American foreign policy system. In *The Irony of Vietnam: The System Worked*, published in 1979 and written in collaboration with political scientist Richard K. Betts,

Gelb argues that intervention in Vietnam was the logical, perhaps even inevitable result of a political and bureaucratic order shaped by certain ideological assumptions. The American foreign policy system was wedded to the doctrine of containment and operated, therefore, in response to a single, overriding imperative: the need to prevent the expansion of communism.

The United States, Gelb maintains, stumbled into a commitment to a shaky government in South Vietnam in the 1950s, and the unvarying policy of every subsequent administration until 1975 was to do what was necessary to prevent the collapse of that government. And they were doing so not because they anticipated victory but because they saw no alternative. However high the costs of intervention, they believed, the costs of not intervening, of allowing South Vietnam to fall, would be higher. At every step, American presidents did the minimum they thought necessary to stave off the collapse of South Vietnam. In the 1950s and early 1960s, that meant modest economic and military assistance. In the mid-1960s, as the military situation worsened, the same commitment required the introduction of American troops in large numbers. Only when the national and international political situation had shifted to the point where it was possible for American policymakers to reassess the costs of the commitment—to conclude that the costs of allowing Vietnam to fall were less than the costs of continuing the commitment (a shift that began to occur in the early 1970s)—was it possible for the United States to begin disengaging.

---

predecessor. Aid to South Vietnam had been one of the most prominent of those policies. Johnson also felt it necessary to retain in his administration many of the important figures of the Kennedy years. In doing so, he surrounded himself with a group of foreign policy advisers—Secretary of State Dean Rusk, Secretary of Defense Robert McNamara, National Security Adviser McGeorge Bundy—who believed not only that the United States had an obligation to resist communism in Vietnam but that it possessed the ability and resources to make that resistance successful. As a result, Johnson seldom had

access to information making clear how difficult the new commitment might become. A compliant Congress raised little protest to, and indeed at one point openly endorsed, Johnson's use of executive powers to lead the nation into war. And for several years at least, public opinion remained firmly behind him—in part because Barry Goldwater's bellicose remarks about the war during the 1964 campaign made Johnson seem by comparison to be a moderate on the issue. Above all, intervention in South Vietnam was fully consistent with nearly twenty years of American foreign policy. An anticommunist ally was appealing to the United States for assistance; all the assumptions of the containment doctrine seemed to require the nation to oblige. Johnson seemed unconcerned that the government of South Vietnam existed largely because the United States had put it there and that the regime had never succeeded in acquiring the loyalty of its people. Vietnam, he believed, provided a test of American willingness to fight communist aggression, a test he was determined not to fail.

During his first months in office, Johnson expanded the American involvement in Vietnam only slightly, introducing an additional 5,000 military advisers there and preparing to send 5,000 more. Then, early in August 1964, the president announced that American destroyers on patrol in international waters in the Gulf of Tonkin had been attacked by North Vietnamese torpedo boats. Later information raised serious doubts as to whether one of the attacks had actually occurred and, if it had, whether it had been, as the president insisted, "unprovoked." At the time, however, virtually no one questioned Johnson's portrayal of the incident as a serious act of aggression or his insistence that the United States must respond. By a vote of 416 to 0 in the House and 88 to 2 in the Senate (with only Wayne Morse of Oregon and Ernest Gruening of Alaska dissenting), Congress hurriedly passed the Gulf of Tonkin Resolution, which authorized the president to "take all necessary measures" to protect American forces and "prevent further aggression" in Southeast Asia. The resolution became, in Johnson's view at least, an open-ended legal authorization for escalation of the conflict.

Publicly committed now to the defense of what the United States claimed was an independent, democratic government in the south, the administration had to confront the failure of any faction to establish a stable regime there to replace Diem. With the South Vietnamese leadership in disarray, more and more of the burden of opposition to the Viet Cong fell on the United States. In February 1965, seven marines died when communist forces attacked an American military base at Pleiku. Johnson retaliated by ordering the first United States bombings of the north, attempting to destroy the depots and transportation lines that were responsible for the flow of North Vietnamese soldiers and supplies into South Vietnam. The bombing continued until 1972, even though there was little evidence that it was effective in limiting North Vietnamese assistance to the NLF.

A month later, in March 1965, two battalions of American marines landed at Da Nang in South Viet-

nam. Although Johnson continued to insist that he was not leading the United States into a ground war in Southeast Asia, there were now more than 100,000 American troops in Vietnam. The following July, finally, the president publicly admitted that the character of the war had changed. American soldiers would now, he admitted, begin playing an active role in the conduct of the war. By the end of the year, there were more than 180,000 American combat troops in Vietnam; in 1966, that number doubled; and by the end of 1967, there were nearly 500,000 American soldiers fighting on the ground, while the air war had intensified until the tonnage of bombs dropped ultimately exceeded that in Europe during World War II. Meanwhile, American casualties were mounting. In 1961, 14 Americans had died in Vietnam; in 1963, the toll was 489. By the spring of 1966, more than 4,000 Americans had been killed; and they were continuing to die at a faster rate than soldiers in the ineffective South Vietnamese army. Yet the gains resulting from the carnage had been negligible. The United States had finally succeeded in 1965 in creating a reasonably stable government in the south under General Nguyen Van Thieu. But the new regime was hardly less corrupt or brutal than its predecessors, and no more able than they to maintain control over a vast proportion of its own countryside. The Viet Cong, not the Thieu regime, controlled the majority of South Vietnam's villages and hamlets.

The Quagmire

For more than seven years, therefore, American combat forces remained bogged down in a war that the United States was never able either to win or fully to understand. Combating a foe whose strength lay not in weaponry but in a pervasive infiltration of the population, the United States responded with the kind of heavy-handed technological warfare designed for conventional battles against conventional armies. American forces succeeded in winning most of the major battles in which they became engaged, routing the Viet Cong and their North Vietnamese allies from such strongholds as Dak To, Con Thien, and later, Khe Sanh. There were astounding (if not always reliable) casualty figures showing that far more communists than Americans were dying in combat—statistics that the United States military referred to as a "favorable kill ratio." There was a continuing stream of optimistic reports, from American military commanders, civilian officials, and others, that the

The War in Vietnam and Indochina, 1964–1975

CHINA

Lao Cai

Than Uyen

Red River

Yen Bay

BURMA

Dienbienphu

NORTH VIETNAM

Hanoi

Red River Delta

Haiphong

Gulf of Tonkin

Hainan

Pak Seng

Luang Prabang

Ban Ban

Plain of Jars

Vang Vieng

L A O S

Vinh

Vientiane

Mekong River

Udon Thani

Phanom

Dong Hoi
Partition Line 1954
Vinh Linh
DMZ (Demilitarized Zone)
QUANG TRI PROVINCE
Khesanh
Hue
Phu Bai
Da Nang
Hoi An
Tamky
Chulai
My Lai
Quang Ngai

FRIENDSHIP HIGHWAY

THAILAND

Takhli

Udon Ratchathani

Don Muang

Dak To

Lop Buri

Ratchasima

Kontum

South China Sea

Plateau of Kontum

Pleiku
Ankhe

Quinhon

Bangkok

Angkor Wat

Tonle Sap

CAMBODIA

Mekong River

Plateau of Darlac

Ban Me Thout

Battambang

Sattahip

Nhatrang

Da Lat

Camranh Bay

Kompong Cham

Bo Duc

Phanrang

Phnom Penh

Prey Veng

1970: U.S. and South Vietnam troops entered Viet Cong strongholds inside Cambodia

Tay Ninh

Ben Cat

SOUTH VIETNAM

Gulf of Thailand

Bienhua

Tan Son Nhut Airbase

Saigon

Sihanoukville

Vung Tau

Rach Gia

Cantho

Mekong Delta

Quan Long

Ca Mau Peninsula

Con Son

| 0 | | 150 Miles |
| 0 | | 150 Kilometers |

■ U.S. bases

⬅ U.S. and South Vietnam invasion of Cambodia

← Ho Chi Minh Trail (communist supply route)

war was progressing—including the famous words of Secretary of Defense McNamara that he could "see the light at the end of the tunnel." But if the war was not actually being lost, neither was it being won. It was, moreover, becoming clear to some observers that it was a war that perhaps could not be won.

At the heart of the problem was the fact that the United States was not fighting an army as much as a popular movement. The Viet Cong derived their strength in part from the aid they received from North Vietnam and, indirectly, from the Soviet Union and China. At least as important, however, was their success in mobilizing members of the native population—men, women, and even children—who were indistinguishable from their neighbors and who fought not only openly in major battles but covertly through sabotage, ambush, and terror. American troops might drive Viet Cong forces from a particular village or city; but as soon as the Americans left, the NLF forces would return. The frustrations of this kind of warfare mounted steadily, until the United States found itself involved in a series of desperate strategies.

Central to the American war effort was the heralded "pacification" program, designed in part by General William Westmoreland, whose purpose was to rout the Viet Cong from particular regions and then "pacify" those regions by winning the "hearts and minds" of the people. Routing the Viet Cong was often possible, but the subsequent pacification was not. American forces were incapable of establishing the same kind of rapport with provincial Vietnamese that the highly nationalistic Viet Cong forces were able to achieve.

Gradually, therefore, the pacification program gave way to the more desperate "relocation" strategy. Instead of attempting to win the loyalty of the peasants in areas in which the Viet Cong were operating, American troops would uproot the villagers from their homes, send them fleeing to refugee camps or into the cities (producing by 1967 more than 3 million refugees), and then destroy the vacated villages and surrounding countryside. Saturation bombing, bulldozing of settlements, chemical defoliation of fields and jungles—all were designed to eliminate possible Viet Cong sanctuaries. But the Viet Cong responded simply by moving to new sanctuaries elsewhere. The futility of the United States effort was suggested by the statement of an American officer after flattening one such hamlet that it had been "necessary to destroy the town in order to save it."

As the war dragged on and victory remained elusive, some American officers and officials began to urge the president to expand military efforts in Indochina. Some argued for heavier bombing and increased troop strength; others insisted that the United States attack communist enclaves in surrounding countries; a few began to urge the use of nuclear weapons. The Johnson administration, however, resisted. Unwilling to abandon its commitment to South Vietnam for fear of destroying American "credibility" in the world, the government was also

Casualties of War
A young woman carries an infant as she and others flee from a burning town in South Vietnam. The destruction of settlements by both Viet Cong and American troops created a huge refugee population in South Vietnam and greatly increased the instability that constantly plagued the succession of governments there. (Dick Swanson/ Black Star)

unwilling to expand the war too far, for fear of provoking direct intervention by the Chinese, the Soviets, or both. Caught in a trap largely of his own making, the president began to encounter additional obstacles and frustrations at home.

The War at Home

Few Americans, and even fewer influential ones, had protested the American involvement in Vietnam as late as the end of 1965. But as the war dragged on and its futility began to become apparent, political support for it began to erode. At first, the attack emerged from the perimeters of politics: from intellectuals, from students, and from the press. By the end of 1967, the debate over the war had moved fully into the mainstream of national public life.

Many of the earliest objections to the war emerged on college and university campuses. Political scientists, historians, Asian experts, and others began in 1965 to raise questions about both the wisdom and the morality of the Vietnam adventure, arguing that it reflected, among other things, a fundamental American misunderstanding of politics and society in Southeast Asia. A series of "teach-ins" on university campuses, beginning at the University of Michigan in 1965, sparked a national debate over the war, before such debate developed inside the government. By the end of 1967, American students opposed to the war had grown so numerous and so vocal as to form a major political force. Enormous peace marches in New York, Washington, D.C., and other cities drew increasing public attention to the antiwar movement. Campus demonstrations occurred almost daily. A growing number of journalists, particularly reporters who had spent time in Vietnam, helped sustain the movement with their frank revelations about the brutality and futility of the war.

The chorus of popular protest soon began to stimulate opposition to the war from within the government itself. Senator J. William Fulbright of Arkansas, chairman of the powerful Senate Foreign Relations Committee, became one of the earliest influential public figures to turn against the war. Beginning in January 1966, he began to stage highly publicized and occasionally televised congressional hearings to air criticisms of the war, summoning as witnesses such distinguished public figures as George F. Kennan and General James Gavin. Other prominent members of Congress joined Fulbright in opposing Johnson's policies—including, in 1967, Robert F. Kennedy, brother of the slain president, then a senator from New York. Even within the administration, the consensus seemed to be crumbling. Secretary of State Rusk remained a true believer until the end; but McGeorge Bundy and Robert McNamara, both of whom had used their political and intellectual talents to extend the American involvement in Vietnam, quietly left the government in 1967 and 1968. Bundy's successor, Walt W. Rostow, was if anything even more committed to the war than his predecessor and one-time mentor. But the new secretary of defense, Clark Clifford, became a powerful voice within the administration on behalf of a cautious scaling down of the commitment.

Other factors weakened the position of supporters of the war as well. America's most important allies—Great Britain, France, West Germany, and Japan—all began to criticize the Vietnam involvement. Of more immediate concern, the American economy was beginning to suffer. Johnson's commitment to fighting the war while continuing his Great Society reforms—his promise of "guns and butter"—proved impossible to maintain. The inflation rate, which had remained at 2 percent through most of the early 1960s, rose to 3 percent in 1967, 4 percent in 1968, and 6 percent in 1969. In August 1967, Johnson asked Congress for a tax increase—a 10 percent surcharge that was widely labeled a "war tax"—which he knew was necessary if the nation was to avoid even more ruinous inflation. In return, congressional conservatives demanded and received a $6 billion reduction in the funding for Great Society programs. The war in Vietnam, in other words, was now not only a source of concern for its own sake. It had also become a direct threat to liberal efforts to redress social injustices at home.

The Traumas of 1968

By the end of 1967, the twin crises of the war in Vietnam and the deteriorating racial situation at home, crises that fed upon and exacerbated each other, had helped to create deep social and political tension. In the course of 1968, those tensions seemed suddenly to burst to the surface and threaten national chaos. Not since World War II had the United States experienced so profound a sense of crisis. Perhaps never before in its history had the nation suffered as many traumatic shocks in such short order.

The Tet Offensive

On January 31, 1968, the first day of the Vietnamese New Year (Tet), Viet Cong forces launched an enormous, concerted attack on American strongholds throughout South Vietnam. The attack displayed a strength that American commanders had long insisted the Viet Cong did not possess. Some major cities, most notably Hue, fell to the communists. Others suffered major disruptions. But what made the Tet offensive genuinely shocking to the American people, who saw vivid reports of it on television, was what happened in Saigon. If any place in South Vietnam had seemed secure from enemy attack, it was the capital city. Now, suddenly, Viet Cong forces were in the heart of Saigon, setting off bombs, shooting down South Vietnamese officials and troops, and holding down fortified areas.

Even more chilling was the evidence the Tet offensive gave of the brutality of the fighting in Vietnam, of the savagery it seemed to have aroused in those who became involved in it. In the midst of the Tet offensive, television cameras recorded the sight of a captured Viet Cong guerrilla being led up to a South Vietnamese officer in the streets of Saigon. Without a word, the officer pulled out his pistol and shot the young guerrilla through the head, leaving him lying dead with his blood pouring onto the street. No single event did more to undermine support in the United States for the war. American forces soon dislodged the Viet Cong from most of the positions they had seized, and the Tet offensive in the end cost the communists such appalling casualties that they were significantly weakened for months to come. But that had little impact on American opinion. Tet may have been a military victory for the United States; but it was a political defeat for the administration, a defeat from which it would never fully recover.

In the weeks that followed, many of the pillars of American public opinion finally began to move into opposition to the war. Leading newspapers began taking editorial stands in favor of deescalation of the conflict. *Time, Newsweek,* and other national magazines began running searing exposés and urging American withdrawal. Network commentators began voicing open doubts about the wisdom of American policies. Within weeks of the Tet offensive, public opposition to the war had almost doubled. And Johnson's personal popularity rating had slid to 35 percent, the lowest of any president since the darkest days of the Truman administration.

The Political Challenge

As early as the summer of 1967, dissident Democrats had been attempting to mobilize support behind an antiwar candidate who would challenge Lyndon Johnson in the 1968 primaries. For many months, they tried to enlist Senator Robert Kennedy, the most widely known critic of the war. But mindful of the difficulties in challenging an incumbent president, Kennedy declined. In his stead, the dissidents recruited Senator Eugene McCarthy of Minnesota, a subdued, cerebral candidate who avoided heated rhetoric in favor of carefully reasoned argument and attracted a particularly devoted following among college students. A brilliantly orchestrated campaign by young volunteers in the New Hampshire primary produced a startling triumph for McCarthy in March; he came within 1 percentage point of outpolling the president.

A few days later, Robert Kennedy finally entered the campaign, deeply embittering many of those who had dedicated themselves to the cause of McCarthy, but bringing his own substantial strength among blacks, poor people, and workers to the antiwar cause. Polls showed the president trailing badly in the next scheduled primary, in Wisconsin. Public animosity toward Johnson was such that he did not dare venture from the White House to campaign. On March 31, Johnson went on television to announce a limited halt in the bombing of North Vietnam—his first major concession to the antiwar forces—and, far more surprising, his withdrawal from the presidential contest.

For a moment, it seemed as though the antiwar forces had won—that nothing could stop them from seizing the Democratic presidential nomination and even the presidency itself. Robert Kennedy quickly established himself as the champion of the Democratic primaries, winning one election after another. In the meantime, however, Vice President Hubert Humphrey, with the support of President Johnson, entered the contest and began to attract the support of party leaders and of the many delegations that were selected not by popular primaries but by state party organizations. He soon appeared to be the front runner in the race.

The King Assassination

In the midst of this bitter political battle, in which the war had been the dominant issue, the attention of the nation suddenly turned again to the matter of race in response to a shocking tragedy. On April 4, Martin Luther King, Jr., who had traveled to Memphis, Tennessee, to lend his support to a strike by black sanitation workers in the city, was shot and killed while standing on the balcony of his motel. The assassin, James Earl Ray, who was captured days later in London, had no apparent motive. Later evidence suggested that he had been hired by others to do the killing, but he himself never revealed the identity of his employers.

The tragic death of King, who had remained the most widely admired black leader among both blacks and whites, deeply affected Americans of all races, producing an outpouring of grief matched in recent memory only by the reaction to the death of John Kennedy. Among blacks, however, it also produced widespread anger. In the days after the assassination, major riots broke out in more than sixty American cities. Forty-three people died; more than 3,000 suffered injuries; as many as 27,000 people were arrested. None of these riots was as intense as some earlier disturbances, but together the disorders were the greatest manifestation of racial unrest in the nation's history.

The Kennedy Assassination and Chicago

Robert Kennedy continued his campaign for the presidential nomination. Late in the night of June 6, he appeared in the ballroom of a Los Angeles hotel to acknowledge the cheers of his supporters for his victory in that day's California primary. Waiting for him in a nearby corridor, in the meantime, was Sirhan Sirhan, a young Palestinian who had become enraged, apparently, by pro-Israeli remarks Kennedy had made several days earlier in a televised debate with Eugene McCarthy. As Kennedy was leaving the ballroom after his victory statement, Sirhan emerged from a crowd and shot him in the head. Early the next morning, Kennedy died.

By the time of his death, Robert Kennedy—who earlier in his career had been widely considered a cold, ruthless agent of his more appealing brother—had emerged as a figure of enormous popular appeal. Far more than John Kennedy, Robert identified his hopes with the American "underclass"—with blacks, Hispanics, Indians, the poor—and with the many American liberals who were coming to believe that the problems of such groups demanded attention.

Robert Kennedy, 1968
During the few months of his 1968 presidential campaign, Robert Kennedy evoked an extraordinary public reaction. Crowds grew almost hysterical at his appearance, and admirers fought to touch his hair and his clothes or to grab cufflinks or buttons as souvenirs. (Burt Glinn/Magnum)

Indeed, it was Robert Kennedy, far more than John, who shaped what some would later call the "Kennedy legacy" and what would for a time become central to American liberalism: the fervent commitment to using government to help the powerless. In addition, Robert had an impassioned following among many people who saw in him (and his family) the kind of glamour and hopefulness they had come, at least in retrospect, to identify with the martyred president. His campaign appearances inspired outbursts of public enthusiasm rarely seen in political life.

The passions Kennedy aroused made his violent death a particularly shattering experience for the American people. In reality, he had been the victim of a single, apparently crazed individual. But to much of the nation, stunned and bewildered by yet another public tragedy, Kennedy seemed to have been a victim of national social chaos.

The presidential campaign continued desultorily during the last weeks before the convention. Hubert Humphrey, who had seemed likely to win the nomination even before Robert Kennedy's death, now faced only minor opposition. Despite the embittered claims of many Democrats that Humphrey would simply continue the bankrupt policies of the Johnson administration, there seemed no possibility of stopping him. The approaching Democratic Convention, therefore, began to take on the appearance of an exercise in futility; and antiwar activists, despairing of winning any victories within the convention, began to plan major demonstrations outside it.

When the Democrats finally gathered in Chicago in August, even the most optimistic observers were predicting a turbulent convention. Inside the hall, carefully sealed off from all demonstrators by Mayor Richard Daley, delegates engaged in a long, bitter debate over an antiwar plank that both Kennedy and McCarthy supporters wanted to insert in the platform. Miles away, in a downtown park, thousands of students and other antiwar protesters had set up camps and were staging demonstrations. On the third night of the convention, as the delegates were beginning their balloting on the now virtually inevitable nomination of Hubert Humphrey, demonstrators and police clashed in a bloody riot in the streets of Chicago. Miraculously, no one was killed; but hundreds of protesters were injured as police attempted to disperse them with tear gas and billy clubs. Aware that the violence was being televised to the nation, the demonstrators taunted the authorities with the chant, "The whole world is watching!" And Hubert Humphrey, who had spent years dreaming of becoming his party's candidate for president, received a nomination that night which appeared at the time to be almost worthless.

The Conservative Response

The turbulent events of 1968 persuaded many observers that American society was on the verge of a fundamental social upheaval. Newspapers, magazines, the press—all helped create the impression of a

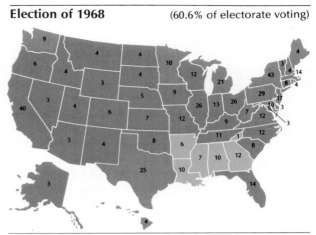

Election of 1968   (60.6% of electorate voting)

	ELECTORAL VOTE	POPULAR VOTE (%)
Richard M. Nixon (Republican)	301	31,770,237 (43.4)
Hubert H. Humphrey (Democratic)	191	31,270,533 (42.7)
George C. Wallace (American Independence)	46	9,906,141 (13.5)
Other candidates (Socialist Labor; D. Gregory; Socialist Workers; Peace and Freedom; McCarthy; Prohibition)	—	218,347

nation in the throes of revolutionary change. In fact, however, the prevailing response of the American people to the turmoil was a conservative one.

The most visible sign of the conservative backlash was the surprising success of the campaign of George Wallace for the presidency. Wallace had established himself in 1963 as one of the leading spokesmen for the defense of segregation when, as governor of Alabama, he had attempted to block the admission of black students to the University of Alabama. In 1968, he became a third-party candidate for president, basing his campaign on a host of conservative grievances. Although he tempered some of his earlier positions on the race issue, he continued to appeal to those who resented the intrusion of the federal government into local affairs. He denounced the forced busing of students, the proliferation of government regulations and social programs, and the permissiveness of authorities toward race riots and antiwar demonstrations. He chose as his running mate a re-

SIGNIFICANT EVENTS

1960 John F. Kennedy elected president
Greensboro sit-ins

1961 Freedom rides
United States supports invasion of Bay of Pigs
Kennedy meets Khrushchev in Vienna
Berlin Wall erected
Peace Corps established
Alliance for Progress established

1962 Steel price increase provokes controversy
Kennedy proposes tax cut to stimulate economy
Desegregation crisis at University of Mississippi
Cuban missile crisis

1963 Martin Luther King, Jr., begins Birmingham campaign
Desegregation crisis at University of Alabama
Kennedy proposes civil-rights bill
March on Washington
Test ban treaty signed
Diem toppled by coup in Vietnam
Kennedy assassinated; Lyndon B. Johnson becomes president

1964 Johnson launches war on poverty
Congress passes tax cut
"Freedom summer" campaign in Mississippi
Congress passes Civil Rights Act
Gulf of Tonkin Resolution passed
United States begins bombing of North Vietnam

1964 Johnson elected president by record margin

1965 Medicare enacted
Elementary and Secondary Education Act passed
Selma campaign for voting rights
Race riot breaks out in Watts, Los Angeles
Malcolm X publishes *Autobiography*
Malcolm X assassinated
Congress passes Voting Rights Act
United States intervenes in Dominican Republic
American combat troops sent to Vietnam

1966 Medicaid enacted
King leads Chicago campaign
Senate Foreign Relations Committee holds hearings on Vietnam

1967 Johnson requests tax increase

1968 Department of Labor issues affirmative action rules
Race riots break out in Detroit and Newark
Viet Cong launch Tet offensive
Johnson withdraws from presidential contest
Martin Luther King, Jr., assassinated
Racial violence breaks out in American cities
Robert Kennedy assassinated
Demonstrators clash with police at Democratic National Convention
George Wallace launches third-party presidential campaign
Richard M. Nixon elected president

tired air force general, Curtis LeMay, who was a bellicose advocate of expanding the war in Vietnam. There was never any serious chance that Wallace would win the election; but his remarkable standing in the polls over many months—rising at times to over 20 percent of those interviewed—was a clear indication that he had struck a responsive chord.

A far more skillful effort to mobilize the "silent majority" in favor of order and stability was under way within the Republican party. Richard Nixon, whose political career had seemed at an end after his losses in the presidential race of 1960 and a California gubernatorial campaign two years later, re-emerged as the preeminent spokesman for "Middle America." Although he avoided the crudeness and stridency of the Wallace campaign, he skillfully exploited many of the same concerns that were sustaining the Alabama governor. Nixon was far more perceptive than other leaders of public opinion in realizing that many Americans were now tired of hearing about their obligations to the poor, tired of hearing about the sacrifices necessary to achieve racial justice, tired of judicial reforms that seemed designed to help criminals. By offering a vision of stability, law and order, government retrenchment, and "peace with honor" in Vietnam, he easily captured the nomination of his party for the presidency. And after the spectacle of the Democratic Convention, he and his running mate, Governor Spiro Agnew of Maryland, enjoyed a commanding lead in the polls as the November election approached.

That lead diminished greatly in the last weeks before the voting. Old doubts about Nixon's character—doubts based in part on the sometimes vicious anticommunism of his earlier career—continued to haunt the Republican candidate. A skillful last-minute surge by Hubert Humphrey, who somehow managed to restore at least a tenuous unity to the Democratic party, narrowed the gap further. And the continuing appeal of George Wallace appeared to be

hurting the Republicans more than the Democrats. In the end, however, Nixon eked out a victory almost as narrow as his defeat in 1960. He received 43.4 percent of the popular vote to Humphrey's 42.7 percent (a margin of only about 500,000 votes), and 301 electoral votes to Humphrey's 191. George Wallace, who like most third-party candidates faded in the last weeks of the campaign, still managed to poll 13.5 percent of the popular vote and to carry five Southern states with a total of 46 electoral ballots. Nixon had hardly won a decisive mandate. But the election had made one thing clear. The majority of the American people were more interested in the restoration of stability than in fundamental social change.

SUGGESTED READINGS

Kennedy and Johnson On the election of 1960, see Theodore H. White, *The Making of the President, 1960* (1961), a now classic study. On Kennedy himself, Arthur M. Schlesinger, Jr., *A Thousand Days* (1965), and Theodore Sorensen, *Kennedy* (1965), are admiring portraits by administration insiders. See also Herbert Parmet, *Jack* (1980) and *JFK—The Presidency of John F. Kennedy* (1983); Henry Fairlie, *The Kennedy Promise* (1973); Lewis Paper, *The Promise and the Performance* (1975); and Bruce Miroff, *Pragmatic Illusions* (1976). Garry Wills, *The Kennedy Imprisonment* (1982), is a devastatingly critical reassessment, which examines the entire Kennedy family. On the Kennedy assassination, see *The Report of the Warren Commission* (1964), for the official investigation; William Manchester, *The Death of a President* (1967), for an emotional portrait of the days following the slaying; and Anthony Summers, *Conspiracy* (1980), and E. J. Epstein, *Inquest* (1966), for a discussion of the continuing controversy surrounding the event. Studies of Lyndon Johnson include Doris Kearns, *Lyndon Johnson and the American Dream* (1976), and Eric Goldman, *The Tragedy of Lyndon Johnson* (1968). Ronnie Dugger, *The Politician* (1982), and Robert Caro, *The Years of Lyndon Johnson: The Path to Power* (1982), examine Johnson's prepresidential career. Johnson's memoirs, *Vantage Point* (1971), offer a defense of his record. George Reedy, *The Twilight of the Presidency* (1970), provides valuable reflections by Johnson's press secretary. Jim Heath, *Decade of Disillusionment* (1975), is an overview of the Kennedy-Johnson years.

Domestic Policies On the domestic policies of the Kennedy-Johnson era, see Tom Wicker, *JFK and LBJ* (1968), for a study of congressional politics and the presidency; Jim Heath, *John F. Kennedy and the Business Community* (1969); Victor Navasky, *Kennedy Justice* (1971), a critique of the Justice Department under Robert Kennedy; and four books on the era's social programs: James Sundquist, *Politics and Policy* (1968); Sar Levitan, *The Great Society's Poor Law* (1969); Sar Levitan and Robert Taggart, *The Promise of Greatness* (1976); and Daniel Knapp and Kenneth Polk, *Scouting the War*

on Poverty (1971). Robert H. Haveman (ed.), *A Decade of Federal Antipoverty Programs* (1977), is a collection of essays analyzing the results of the 1960s initiatives. Greg J. Duncan, *Years of Poverty, Years of Plenty* (1984), is a provocative reassessment of the nature of American poverty. Charles Murray, *Losing Ground* (1984), is a controversial attack on postwar social policy. Frances Fox Piven and Richard Cloward, *Regulating the Poor* (1971), is an attack on antipoverty programs from the left. Hugh Davis Graham, *Uncertain Trumpet* (1984), is a study of federal education policy under Kennedy and Johnson. Allen J. Matusow, *The Unraveling of America: A History of Liberalism in the 1960s* (1984), is an important, and skeptical, overview of the domestic events of the decade. James T. Patterson, *America's Struggle Against Poverty, 1900–1980* (1981), is a sweeping study of twentieth-century attitudes and policies, which gives particular attention to the 1960s. Henry J. Aaron, *Politics and the Professors* (1978), discusses the role of the academic world in shaping Great Society programs.

Race Relations For the maturing of the civil-rights movement, see David Lewis, *King* (1970); Carl Brauer, *John F. Kennedy and the Second Reconstruction* (1977); Martin Luther King, Jr., *Why We Can't Wait* (1964); David Garrow, *Protest at Selma* (1978); William Chafe, *Civilities and Civil Rights* (1980), a study of the civil-rights movement in Greensboro, North Carolina; and Harris Wofford, *Of Kennedy and Kings* (1980). Stephen Oates, *Let the Trumpet Sound* (1982), is a biography of King. David Garrow, *The FBI and Martin Luther King* (1981), reveals how government officials investigated the civil-rights leader. On the rise of black power, see Stokely Carmichael and Charles Hamilton, *Black Power* (1967), the book that gave the phenomenon its name; *The Autobiography of Malcolm X* (1966), which was ghostwritten by Alex Haley; Benjamin Muse, *The American Negro Revolution* (1969); Archie Epps, *Malcolm X and the American Negro Revolution* (1969); and Eugene Wolfenstein, *The Victims of Democracy: Malcolm X and the Black Revolution* (1981). On the urban riots, consult Robert Fogelson, *Violence as Protest* (1971); Joe R. Feagin and Harlan Hahn, *Ghetto Re-*

volts (1973); and the *Report of the National Advisory Commission on Civil Disorders* (1968).

Foreign Policy   On the foreign policy of the Kennedy-Johnson years, see Richard Walton, *Cold War and Counterrevolution* (1972); Louise Fitzsimmons, *The Kennedy Doctrine* (1972); Godfrey Hodgson, *America in Our Time* (1976), which is also valuable for its study of the domestic climate of the era; Roger Hilsman, *To Move a Nation* (1965); Philip Geyelin, *Lyndon B. Johnson and the World* (1966); and Richard Barnet, *Intervention and Revolution* (1968), which examines American policies toward the Third World. On the disastrous 1961 invasion of Cuba, consult Haynes Johnson, *The Bay of Pigs* (1964), and Peter Wyden, *Bay of Pigs* (1969). On the Cuban missile crisis, see Elie Abel, *The Missile Crisis* (1966); Graham Allison, *Essence of Decision* (1971), an innovative examination of decision making; Robert Kennedy, *Thirteen Days* (1969), a personal memoir; and Herbert Dinerstein, *The Making of a Missile Crisis* (1976), which considers the Soviet position. Dan Kurzman, *Santo Domingo* (1966), and Jerome Slater, *Intervention and Negotiation* (1970), discuss the American intervention in the Dominican Republic in 1964. Richard D. Mahoney, *JFK: Ordeal in Africa* (1983), considers Democratic foreign policy in another region. Warren Cohen, *Dean Rusk* (1980), examines the secretary of state.

Vietnam   Two important general accounts of the war are George C. Herring, *America's Longest War*, rev. ed. (1986), and Stanley Karnow, *Vietnam* (1983). An indispensable source on American involvement in the Vietnam War through the late 1960s is the Defense Department studies published as *The Pentagon Papers,* of which several editions are available. One of the most complete is the four-volume Senator Gravel edition (1975). Other books on Vietnam, in addition to those cited in the readings for Chapter 29, include David Halberstam, *The Best and the Brightest* (1972), a study of the decision makers who engineered the commitment; Guenter Lewy, *America in Vietnam* (1978), a controversial defense of the commitment; John Galloway, *The Gulf of Tonkin Resolution* (1970); and Alexander Kendrick, *The Wound Within* (1974). Norman Podhoretz, *Why We Were in Vietnam* (1982), makes a case for the American commitment. Leslie Gelb and Richard Betts, *The Irony of Vietnam: The System Worked* (1979), is a fatalistic view. Larry Berman, *Planning a Tragedy* (1982), examines events leading up to the decision to send American ground troops into Vietnam in 1965. Wallace J. Thies, *When Governments Collide* (1980), assesses American efforts to influence the behavior of North Vietnam in the mid-1960s. Michael Herr, *Dispatches* (1977), is a collection of essays by a war correspondent expressing the agony of the military experience. Lawrence Baskir and William Strauss, *Chance and Circumstance* (1978), examines the draft during the Vietnam War. Gloria Emerson, *Winners and Losers* (1976), assesses the wide-reaching impact of the war. Among the many memoirs and oral histories of the experience of soldiers in Vietnam, Mark Baker, *Nam* (1982), Al Santoli, *Everything We Had* (1981), and Wallace Terry, *Bloods* (1984), are particularly useful examples. Thomas Powers, *Vietnam: The War at Home* (1973), and Irwin Unger, *The Movement* (1974), discuss domestic opposition. Peter Braestrup, *Big Story* (1977; abridged ed., 1978), assesses media coverage of the Tet offensive. Don Oberdorfer, *Tet* (1971), is a study of the offensive itself. Bruce C. Palmer, Jr., *The 25-Year War* (1984), is a study of American military strategy and tactics by a former army chief of staff who served as Westmoreland's deputy in Vietnam. Another military man, Harry Summers, in *On Strategy* (1981), offers a slightly different view of American military policy. Ronald Spector, *Advice and Support* (1983), studies the early years of American military involvement.

1968   The traumas of 1968 are examined in Lewis Chester, Godfrey Hodgson, and Lewis Page, *American Melodrama* (1969), as well as in Godfrey Hodgson's important general study of modern America, *America in Our Time* (1976). Arthur M. Schlesinger, Jr., *Robert Kennedy and His Times* (1978), is a thorough and sympathetic biography. Norman Mailer, *Miami and the Siege of Chicago* (1968), is a personalized examination of the political conventions. Ben Stavis, *We Were the Campaign* (1969), is a study of the McCarthy crusade. Marshall Frady, *Wallace,* rev. ed. (1976), is a portrait of the conservative challenger. Theodore White, *The Making of the President, 1968* (1969), is a sober view of the Nixon election.

Richard Nixon After Resigning the Presidency, August 9, 1974 (UPI/Bettmann Newsphotos)

Chapter 31 # The Crisis of Authority

The election of Richard Nixon in 1968 was the result of more than the unpopularity of Lyndon Johnson's policies and the divisions within the Democratic party. It was the result, too, of a widespread public reaction against what many believed was a frontal assault on the basis of American culture. Throughout American life in the late 1960s and early 1970s, new interest groups were mobilizing to demand protections and benefits. New values and assumptions were emerging to challenge traditional patterns of thought and behavior. The United States was in the throes, some believed, of a genuine cultural revolution.

But many Americans—a clear majority, it seemed, on the basis of the 1968 election returns—were tired of and frightened by the social turmoil. They were coming to resent the attention directed toward minorities and the poor, the federal social programs that were funneling billions of dollars into the inner cities to help the poor and unemployed, the increasing tax burden on the middle class, the "hippies" and radicals who were dominating public discourse with their bitter critiques of everything middle-class Americans held dear. It was time, such men and women believed, for a restoration of stability.

In Richard Nixon they found a man who seemed perfectly to match their mood. Himself a product of a hard-working, middle-class family, he had risen to prominence on the basis of his own unrelenting efforts. His public demeanor displayed nothing of the flashiness of the Kennedys or the stridency of the Democratic left. He projected instead an image of stern dedication to traditional values. The extraordinary narrowness of his margin of victory in 1968 suggested that many Americans continued to consider him sanctimonious, "tricky," and unappealing. To much of the nation, however, he was the embodiment of the search for a new, more placid social order.

Yet the presidency of Richard Nixon, far from returning calm and stability to American politics, produced an unparalleled national crisis. The new president inherited many problems from his predecessor that would have plagued any leader. The war in Vietnam, the social conflicts of the 1960s, the failure of major institutions to perform as the public had come to expect—all had combined by 1969 to make Americans suspicious of their leaders and mistrustful of their government. Yet it was the performance of Nixon's own administration that caused the most rapid erosion of that public respect for authority. By the early 1970s, the once vigorous American economy had begun a long descent into crisis; and the failure of government to reverse its course raised serious questions about the ability of elected officials to govern. Of more immediate importance, beginning in 1972, the administration found itself embroiled in a series of scandals that not only resulted in Nixon's untimely departure from office but further increased public cynicism about the nation's leadership.

The Turbulent Society

What was perhaps most alarming to conservative Americans in the 1960s and 1970s was a pattern of social and cultural protest that seemed to produce constant turmoil and uncertainty. Younger Americans, in particular, were raising a direct and wide-ranging challenge to the conventions of national life; and they were doing so by giving vent to two distinct impulses.

One was the impulse, emerging from the political left, to create a great new community of "the people," which would rise up to break the power of corrupt elites and would force the nation to end the war, pursue racial and economic justice, and transform its political life. The other, at least equally powerful impulse was the vision of individual "liberation." It found expression in part through the efforts of particular groups—blacks, Indians, Hispanics, women, and others—to define and assert themselves as coherent interests and to make demands on the larger society. It also found expression through the efforts of individuals to create a new culture—one that would allow them to escape from what many considered the dehumanizing pressures of the modern "technocracy."

The New Left

Among the products of the racial crisis and the war in Vietnam was a radicalization of many American students, who in the course of the 1960s formed what became known as the New Left. The New Left emerged from many sources, but from nothing so much as the civil-rights movement, in which many idealistic young Americans had become involved in the early 1960s. Exposed as a result to evidence of social injustice, enraged by the violence and racism they encountered at the hands of segregationists and others, some civil-rights activists were by the mid-1960s beginning to consider far more radical political commitments than they once had embraced. As early as 1962, a group of students gathered in Michigan to form an organization to give voice to their political demands: Students for a Democratic Society (SDS). Their declaration of beliefs, the Port Huron Statement, signaled much of what was to come. "Many of us began maturing in complacency," the statement (most of it the work of student activist Tom Hayden) declared. "As we grew, however, our comfort was penetrated by events too troubling to dismiss." In the following years, as the racial crisis grew more intense and the war in Vietnam expanded, members of SDS became even more troubled, extending the scope of their demands and the range of their activities until

they had become the cutting edge of student radicalism.

For a time, that radicalism centered on issues related to modern universities, with which most members of the New Left were associated. A 1964 dispute at the University of California at Berkeley over the rights of students to engage in political activities on campus was the first outburst of what was to be nearly a decade of campus turmoil. The tumultuous Berkeley Free Speech Movement soon moved beyond the immediate issue of pamphlet distribution and produced far more fundamental protests against the depersonalized nature of the modern "multiversity" and against the role of educational institutions in sustaining corrupt or immoral public policies. The antiwar movement greatly inflamed and expanded the challenge to the universities; and beginning in 1968, campus demonstrations, riots, and building seizures became almost commonplace. At Columbia University in New York, students seized the offices of the president and other members of the administration, occupying them for days until local police forcibly ejected them. At Harvard University a year later, the seizure of administrative offices resulted in an even more violent confrontation with police. Over the next several years, hardly any major university was immune to some level of disruption from radicals and activists among its own student body. Occasionally, there were more serious episodes. Small groups of particularly fervent radicals—most notably the "Weathermen," an offshoot of SDS—were responsible for instances of arson and bombing that destroyed some campus buildings and claimed several lives.

The New Left never succeeded in attracting the support of more than a few students to its most radical tactics and demands. It succeeded brilliantly, however, in elevating the antiwar movement to a major national crusade. Among other things, student activists were instrumental in organizing some of the largest political demonstrations in American history to protest the war in Vietnam. The march on the Pentagon of October 1967, where demonstrators were met by a solid line of armed troops; the "spring mobilization" of April 1968, which attracted hundreds of thousands of demonstrators in cities around the country; the Vietnam "moratorium" of the fall of 1969, during which millions of opponents of the war gathered in major rallies across the nation; and countless other demonstrations, large and small—all helped thrust the issue of the war into the center of American politics.

Closely related to opposition to the war—and another issue that helped to fuel the New Left—was opposition to military conscription. Since the early 1950s, the government had relied on the draft to staff its peacetime army, generally without controversy. But when in the 1960s draftees began to be called on to fight in a stalemated, unpopular war, dissent grew quickly. The gradual abolition of many traditional deferments—for students, teachers, husbands, fathers, and others—swelled the ranks of those faced with conscription (and thus likely to oppose it). And the high-handed manner in which the draft was being administered by General Lewis Hershey spawned even greater bitterness. The shadow of the draft—the possibility of being compelled to join a despised military and fight in a hated war—loomed large over an entire generation of American youth. Draft card burnings became common features of antiwar rallies on college campuses. Many draft-age Americans simply refused induction, accepting what were occasionally long terms in jail as a result. Thousands of others fled to Canada, Sweden, and elsewhere (where they were joined by many deserters from the armed forces) to escape conscription, even though they realized it might be years before they could return home without facing prosecution. Not until 1977, when President Jimmy Carter issued a general pardon to draft resisters and a far more limited amnesty for deserters, did the Vietnam exiles begin to return to the country in substantial numbers.

The Counterculture

Closely allied to the emergence of the New Left, although very different in its basic impulses, was the growth of a new youth culture openly scornful of the values and conventions of middle-class society. The most visible characteristic of the counterculture, as it became known, and the one that seemed to have the widest influence, was a change in life style. As if to display their contempt for conventional standards, young Americans flaunted long hair, shabby or flamboyant clothing, and a rebellious disdain for traditional speech and decorum. Central to the counterculture were drugs: marijuana smoking—which from 1966 began to become as common a youthful diversion as beer drinking had once been—and the use of other, more potent hallucinogens, such as LSD. There was as well among members of the counterculture a new, more permissive view of sex.

It was these open challenges to traditional life styles that parents and others found most disturbing about the counterculture, and there was a temptation among many in the older generation to dismiss such youths simply as iconoclasts and hedonists. That was no doubt true of many. But the counterculture also encompassed a clear philosophy, one that offered a far more fundamental challenge to the American mainstream than the changes in appearance and social behavior. Like the New Left, with which it in many ways overlapped, the counterculture challenged the very structure of modern American society, attacking its banality, its hollowness, its artificiality, its isolation from nature. Among the heroes of the counterculture were some of the beat poets and writers of the 1950s—Allen Ginsberg and others—who had been making similar criticisms years before, when few would listen.

The most committed adherents of the counterculture—the hippies, who came to dominate the Haight-Ashbury neighborhood of San Francisco and whose influence spread to many other areas, and the "dropouts," who retreated to rural communes in Colorado, New Hampshire, and elsewhere—rejected modern society altogether and attempted to find refuge in a simpler, more natural existence. But even those whose commitment to the counterculture was less dramatic shared a pervasive commitment to the idea of personal fulfillment. Such popular phrases as "Do your own thing" and "If it feels good, do it" seemed to capture much of the spirit of the counterculture. In a corrupt and alienating society, the new creed seemed to suggest, the first responsibility of the individual is cultivation of the self, the unleashing of one's own full potential for pleasure and fulfillment.

Theodore Roszak, whose book *The Making of a Counter Culture* (1969) became a central document of the era, captured much of the spirit of the movement in his frank admission that "the primary project of our counter culture is to proclaim a new heaven and a new earth so vast, so marvelous that the inordinate claims of technical expertise must of necessity withdraw to a subordinate and marginal status in the lives of men." Charles Reich, in *The Greening of America* (1970), was even more explicit, arguing that the individual should strive for a new form of consciousness—"Consciousness III," as he called it—in which the self would be the only reality.

The effects of the counterculture were not restricted to rebellious youths. They reached out as well to the society at large and provided a set of social norms that many young people (and some adults)

MILTON GLASER

DYLAN

**An Icon of
the Counterculture**
Milton Glaser, a commercial artist who
became a major figure in the transformation of American magazine design
in the 1960s, produced this poster
in 1966 of folk singer Bob Dylan. It
suggests not only how important
Dylan and other musicians had become
to the emerging youth culture of the
1960s, but also the flamboyance that
would soon become a hallmark of the
counterculture.   (Museum of Modern Art)

chose to imitate. Long hair and freakish clothing became the badge not only of hippies and radicals but of
an entire generation. The use of marijuana, the freer
attitudes toward sex, the iconoclastic (and often obscene) language—all spread far beyond the realm of
the true devotees of the counterculture. And perhaps
the most pervasive element of the new youth society
was one that even the least radical members of the
generation embraced: rock music.

Rock-'n'-roll had first achieved wide popularity
in the 1950s, on the strength of such early performers
as Buddy Holly and, above all, Elvis Presley. Early
in the 1960s, its influence began to spread, a result in
large part of the phenomenal popularity of the Beatles,
whose music was first heard in the United States in
1964. For a time, most rock musicians—like most
popular musicians before them—concentrated largely
on uncontroversial romantic themes. But rock's driv-

ing rhythms, its undisguised sensuality, its often harsh and angry tone—all made it an appropriate vehicle for expressing the themes of the social and political unrest of the late 1960s. By the end of the decade, therefore, rock had begun to reflect many of the new iconoclastic values of its time. The Beatles helped lead the way by abandoning their once simple and seemingly innocent style for a new, experimental, even mystical approach that reflected the growing popular fascination with drugs and Eastern religions. Others, such as the Rolling Stones, turned even more openly to themes of anger, frustration, and rebelliousness. Many popular musicians used their music to express explicit political radicalism as well—especially some of the leading folk singers of the era, such as Bob Dylan and Joan Baez.

Even those Americans who had no interest in rock music or other aspects of the counterculture could not avoid the evidence of how rapidly the norms of their society were changing. Those who attended movies saw a gradual disappearance of the banal, conventional messages that had dominated films since the 1920s. Instead, they saw explorations of political issues, of new sexual mores, of violence, of social conflict. And the most influential source of entertainment of all, television, began similarly to turn away (even if more slowly than the other media) from its evocation of the stable, middle-class, suburban family. Beginning in the early 1970s, it started to offer programming imbued with social conflict—as exemplified by the enormously popular *All in the Family*, whose protagonist, Archie Bunker, was a lower-middle-class bigot.

Indian Militancy

The 1960s saw the emergence as well of powerful "liberation" movements among racial, ethnic, and other minority groups. The emergence of black self-awareness and black political power was, of course, the most obvious manifestation of the new spirit. But other groups, too, became engaged in the search for liberation.

Few minorities had deeper or more justifiable grievances against the prevailing culture than American Indians—or Native Americans, as they began to call themselves in the 1960s. Ever since the 1890s, Indians had lived in unalleviated poverty as wards of the federal government, which subjected them to a series of fluctuating and often brutal policies. By the 1960s, not only had the Indian population grown

much faster than that of the rest of the nation (nearly doubling between 1950 and 1970 to a total of about 800,000), but Indians had established themselves as the least prosperous, least healthy, and least stable group in the society. Annual family income for Indians was $1,000 less than that for blacks. The Native American unemployment rate was ten times the national rate. Joblessness was particularly high on the reservations, where nearly half the Indians lived and where few industries or other sources of employment existed. But even the many Indians who left the reservations for the cities found only limited opportunities. Many had received inadequate education and training and were qualified only for menial jobs. Life expectancy among Indians was more than twenty years lower than the national average. Suicides among Indian youths were 100 times more frequent than among white youths. And while black Americans attracted the attention (for good or for ill) of many whites, Indians remained all but totally ignored.

Although the Kennedy administration attempted to restore government support for tribal autonomy—a policy maintained by succeeding administrations as well—Indian grievances were, like the grievances of other minorities, soon receiving open expression. In 1961, more than 400 members of sixty-seven tribes gathered in Chicago to discuss ways of bringing all Indians together in an effort to redress common wrongs. The manifesto they issued, the Declaration of Indian Purpose, reflected the same impulse toward cultural liberation that other segments of the population would soon adopt. It stressed the "right to choose our own way of life" and the "responsibility of preserving our precious heritage." In succeeding years, younger and more militant Indians formed their own organizations—modeled on the new black-power groups—of which the most prominent was the American Indian Movement (AIM), established in 1968 and drawing its greatest support from those Indians who lived in urban areas. The new activism succeeded in winning some attention from the government to the plight of the tribes. Congress included Indians in the benefits of the Economic Opportunity Act; and Lyndon Johnson promised in 1968 a "new goal" for Indian programs that "stresses self-determination" and "erases old attitudes of paternalism." The results, however, were negligible.

Leaders of AIM and other insurgent groups soon turned instead to direct action. In 1968, Indian fishermen, seeking to exercise old treaty rights on the Columbia River and in Puget Sound, clashed with officials of the state of Washington. The following

Wounded Knee

Wounded Knee, South Dakota, had been the site of an 1890 conflict between American soldiers and Teton Sioux. The soldiers had attempted to suppress Indian religious rites ("Ghost Dances"), which whites considered threatening. The result had been a substantial massacre of the tribespeople. In 1973 armed members of the new American Indian Movement seized the village of Wounded Knee (now part of a Sioux reservation) and occupied it for over two months to demonstrate their demands for reforms in federal Indian policy and tribal government.   (Michael Abramson/Black Star)

year, members of several tribes occupied the abandoned federal prison on Alcatraz Island in San Francisco Bay, claiming the site "by right of discovery." In response to the growing pressure, the new Nixon administration appointed a Mohawk-Sioux to the position of Commissioner of Indian Affairs in 1969; and in 1970, the president promised both increased tribal self-determination and an increase in federal aid. The promises were not fulfilled.

Indian frustration finally produced the most forceful protests in decades in the winter of 1972-1973. In November 1972, nearly 1,000 protesters forcibly occupied the building of the Bureau of Indian Affairs in

Washington, D.C., for six days. A more celebrated protest occurred later that winter at Wounded Knee, South Dakota, the site of the 1890 massacre of Sioux Indians by federal troops.

In the early 1970s, Wounded Knee was part of a large Sioux reservation, two-thirds of which was under the control of white ranchers. Conditions for the Indian residents were desperate and alone might have been sufficient to spark resistance. Passions among younger and more militant tribal members were aroused further after the 1972 murder of a Sioux by a group of whites, who were not, many Indians believed, adequately punished. In February 1973, members of AIM seized and occupied for two months the town of Wounded Knee, demanding radical changes in the administration of the reservation and insisting that the government honor its long-forgotten treaty obligations. A brief clash between the occupiers and federal forces left one Indian dead and another wounded. Shortly thereafter the siege came to an end.

Generally more effective than these militant protests were the victories that various tribes were achieving in the 1970s in a wave of lawsuits in the federal courts. Citing violations by the federal government of ancient treaty obligations, Native Americans began winning judicial approval of their demands for restitution. Beginning with a case in Alaska in 1969, the legal actions spread quickly across the country, establishing a possible basis for a major change in the economic status of many tribes.

Hispanic Americans

More numerous and more visible than the Indians were Hispanic Americans, the fastest-growing minority group in the nation. In 1960, Hispanics had numbered only slightly over 3 million; in 1970, they had increased to more than 9 million; in 1980, the U.S. census (which many believed had failed to count many Hispanics) listed 14.6 million, making them the second largest minority (after blacks) in the country. They were also among the poorest.

Hispanics were not, of course, a single, undifferentiated group. There were large numbers of people of Puerto Rican background, concentrated in New York City. A substantial Cuban population was settled in Florida: at first largely the result of a wave of middle-class refugees who had fled the Castro regime in the early 1960s, then enlarged by a flood of poorer immigrants in 1980, when Castro temporarily lifted exit restrictions. The most numerous group—Mexican-Americans—lived in California, Texas, and other states of the Southwest. An uncounted number of them—as many as 7 million according to some estimates—were illegal immigrants (*mojados,* or "wetbacks"). Others were temporary migrant workers (*braceros*). Many, however, were descendants of families who had been living in Mexican territory when it was incorporated into the United States in the nineteenth century.

Like blacks and Indians, Hispanic Americans responded to the highly charged climate of the 1960s by developing their own sense of ethnic identification and by organizing for political and economic power.

Their successes were impressive. Affluent Hispanics became an important force in Miami, where they operated major businesses and filled influential positions in the professions; in Los Angeles, where they organized as an influential political group; and in the Southwest, where they elected Mexican-Americans to seats in Congress and to several governorships.

For the majority of Hispanics, however, the path to economic and political power was more arduous. In New York, Puerto Rican immigrants were crammed into the city's worst slums, including the notorious South Bronx, which became in the 1970s a national symbol of urban decay. In other cities, Hispanics suffered economic deprivation and overt discrimination; in many areas, they became involved in bitter and violent rivalries with blacks.

One Hispanic group, at least, brought the power of organization and political action strongly to bear against problems of poverty and oppression. In California, an Arizona-born Mexican-American farm worker, César Chávez, succeeded where generations of migrants before him had tried and failed: He created an effective union of itinerant farm workers. His United Farm Workers (UFW), a largely Hispanic organization, launched a prolonged strike in 1965 against growers to demand, first, recognition of their union and, second, increased wages and benefits. When employers resisted, Chávez enlisted the cooperation of college students, churches, and civil-rights groups (including CORE and SNCC) and organized a nationwide boycott, first of table grapes and then of lettuce. In 1968, he campaigned openly for Robert Kennedy, bringing his farm workers into the coalition of the dispossessed that the senator was attempting to establish and, more important, winning national recognition of the UFW's cause. Two years later, Chávez won a substantial victory when the growers of half of California's table grapes signed contracts with his union. In the ensuing years, his union suffered less from the opposition of growers than from competition with the powerful Teamsters Union, which attempted to entice farm workers into its own vast labor network.

Hispanic Americans also became the focus of another dispute that was to prove divisive into the 1980s: the issue of bilingualism. It was a question that aroused the opposition not only of many whites but of some Hispanics as well. Supporters of bilingualism in education argued that Spanish-speaking Americans were entitled to schooling in their own language, that only thus could they achieve an equal footing with English-speaking students. Opponents cited not only the cost and difficulty of bilingualism but the dangers it posed to the ability of Spanish-speaking students to become assimilated into the mainstream of American culture. Even many Hispanics feared that bilingualism would isolate their communities further from the rest of America and increase resentments toward them.

The efforts of blacks, Hispanics, Indians, and others to forge a clearer group identity ran counter to a longstanding premise of American political thought—the idea of the "melting pot." Older immigrant groups liked to believe that they had advanced in American society by assimilating, by adopting the values and accepting the rules of the world to which they had moved and advancing within it on its terms. The newly militant ethnic groups of the 1960s seemed less willing to accept the standards of the larger society and were demanding instead recognition of their own ethnic identity.

To a large degree, they succeeded. Recognition of the special character of particular groups was embedded in federal law through a wide range of affirmative action programs, which extended not only to blacks but to Indians, Hispanics, and others as well. The rise of "black studies" programs in schools and universities helped pave the way for new attention to Hispanic and Indian culture and heritage in many institutions as well. The Ethnic Heritage Act of 1972 appropriated federal funds to set up such ethnic studies programs and in the process gave federal recognition to the idea that the preservation of ethnicity was a "positive constructive force in our society," rather than an obstacle to be overcome by the workings of the melting pot.

The New Feminism

American women in the 1960s were hardly a minority. They constituted 51 percent of the population. In the course of the decade, however, many women began to identify with members of other, smaller oppressed groups and to demand a liberation of their own. Sexual discrimination was so deeply embedded in the fabric of society that when feminists first began to denounce it, many Americans responded with bafflement and anger. By the 1970s, however, public awareness of the issue had increased dramatically, and the role of women in American life had changed more radically than that of any other group in the nation.

Early Stirrings

Feminism was a weak and often embattled force in American life for more than forty years after the adoption of the woman suffrage amendment in 1920. A few determined women kept feminist political demands alive in the National Woman's Party and other organizations. Many more women expanded the acceptable bounds of female activity by entering the workplace or engaging in political activities. Nevertheless, through the 1950s and early 1960s, it seemed at times as if feminism was virtually extinct. Yet within a very few years, it evolved from an almost invisible remnant to one of the most powerful social movements in American history.

The 1963 publication of Betty Friedan's *The Feminine Mystique* is often cited as the first event of contemporary women's liberation. Friedan had graduated from Smith College in 1947. Fifteen years later she traveled around the country to interview her classmates—the great majority of whom were suburban housewives and mothers—and to ask them about the state of their lives. These women were living out the dream that postwar American society had created for them, what Friedan called the "mystique of feminine fulfillment." And yet many of them were deeply frustrated and unhappy. The suburbs, Friedan claimed, had become a "comfortable concentration camp," providing the women who inhabited them with no outlets for their intelligence, talent, and education. The "feminine mystique" was responsible for "burying millions of women alive." The only escape was for them to begin to fulfill "their unique possibilities as separate human beings."

Friedan's book did not so much cause the revival of feminism as give voice to a movement that was already stirring. By the time the book appeared, John Kennedy had already established the President's Commission on the Status of Women; and although the president's motives in creating it probably had more to do with deflecting more substantive feminist demands than with real commitment to women's goals, the commission brought widespread attention to sexual discrimination and helped create important networks of feminist activists who would lobby for legislative redress. Also in 1963, the Kennedy administration secured passage of the Equal Pay Act, which barred the pervasive practice of paying women less than men for equal work.

A year later, Congress incorporated into the Civil Rights Act of 1964 an amendment—Title VII—that extended to women many of the same legal protections against discrimination that were being extended to blacks. It had been introduced as a joke by Southern Democrats attempting to discredit the entire civil-rights package; but it survived the legislative debate and became the basis for a major federal assault on sexual discrimination in later years.

The events of the early 1960s helped expose a contradiction that had been developing for decades between the image and the reality of women's roles in America. The image was what Friedan had called the "feminine mystique"—the ideal of women living happy, fulfilled lives in purely domestic roles. The reality was that increasing numbers of women (including, by 1963, over a third of all married women) had already entered the workplace and were encountering widespread discrimination there; and the reality was, too, that many other women were finding their domestic lives suffocating and frustrating. The conflict between the ideal and the reality was crucial to the rebirth of feminism.

The Rebirth

In 1966, three years after publishing her book, Friedan joined with other feminists to create the National Organization for Women (NOW), which was to become the nation's largest and most influential feminist organization. "The time has come," the founders of NOW maintained, "to confront with concrete action the conditions which now prevent women from enjoying the equality of opportunity and freedom of choice which is their right as individual Americans and as human beings." Like other movements for liberation, feminism drew much of its inspiration from the black struggle for freedom. "There is no civil rights movement to speak for women," the NOW organizers claimed, "as there has been for Negroes and other victims of discrimination."

The new organization reflected the varying constituencies of the emerging feminist movement. It responded to the complaints of the women Friedan's book had examined—affluent suburbanites with no outlet for their interests—by demanding greater educational opportunities for women and denouncing the domestic ideal and the traditional concept of marriage. But the heart of the movement, at least in the beginning, was directed toward the needs of women in the workplace. NOW denounced the exclusion of women from professions, from politics, and from countless other areas of American life because of an-

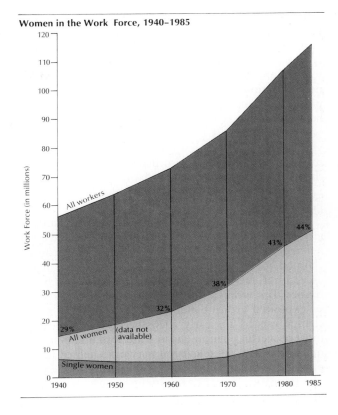

Women in the Work Force, 1940–1985

cient male prejudices about the proper role of women. It decried legal and economic discrimination, including the practice of paying women less than men for equal work (a practice the Equal Pay Act had not eliminated). The organization called for "a fully equal partnership of the sexes, as part of the worldwide revolution of human rights."

By the late 1960s, such demands had attracted a large following among affluent, white, educated women—although generally not among the older women whose lives Friedan had studied. The new feminists were younger, the vanguard of the "baby-boom" generation; many of them drew inspiration from the New Left and the counterculture. Some were involved in the civil-rights movement, others in the antiwar crusade. Many had found that even within those movements, they faced discrimination and exclusion, that they were constantly subordinated to male leaders. Moving from those experiences, some embraced a more radical feminism than the founders of NOW had envisioned.

By 1971, the membership of NOW had expanded to 15,000; and with that expansion had come a significant change in the tone and direction of the organization and of the women's movement as a whole. New books by younger feminists expressed a harsher critique of American society than Friedan had offered. Kate Millett's *Sexual Politics* (1969) signaled the new direction by complaining that "every avenue of power within the society is entirely within male hands." The answer to women's problems, in other words, was not, as Friedan had suggested, for individual women to search for greater personal fulfillment; it was for women to band together to assault the male power structure. Shulamith Firestone's *The Dialectic of Sex* (1970) was subtitled "The Case for Feminist Revolution."

In its most radical form, the new feminism rejected the whole notion of marriage, family, and even heterosexual intercourse (a vehicle, some women claimed, of male domination). Not many women, indeed not even many feminists, embraced such extremes. But women's growing sense of themselves as an exploited group banding together to force social change was by the early 1970s becoming one of the most powerful phenomena in American life. National magazines and the television networks helped legitimize the women's movement by giving it extensive and increasingly respectful attention. *Ms.* magazine, founded by Gloria Steinem and others, had attracted 200,000 subscribers by 1973.

Expanding Achievements

By the early 1970s, the achievements of the women's movement were already substantial. In 1971, the government extended its affirmative action guidelines to include women—linking sexism with racism as an officially acknowledged social problem. Women were making rapid progress, in the meantime, in their efforts to move into the economic and political mainstream. The nation's major educational institutions began in the late 1960s to open their doors to women for the first time. Princeton and Yale, two of the most prestigious all-male colleges, accepted female undergraduates in 1969. Within a few years, all but a few previously all-male academic institutions had done the same. (Some women's colleges, in the meantime, began accepting male students.)

Women were becoming an important force in business and in the professions. Nearly half of all married women held jobs by the mid-1970s, and almost nine-tenths of all women with college degrees worked. The two-career family, in which both the husband and the wife maintained active professional lives, was becoming a widely accepted norm; many women were postponing marriage or motherhood for the sake of their careers. There were also important symbolic changes, such as the refusal of many women to adopt their husbands' names when they married and the use of the term "Ms." in place of "Mrs." or "Miss"—the latter change intended to denote the irrelevance of a woman's marital status in the professional world.

Women were also advancing in some of the most visible areas of American life. In politics, they were by the early 1970s beginning to compete effectively with men for both elected and appointive positions. In 1980, two women won seats in the United States Senate—both elected in their own right rather than, like all woman senators before them, to succeed their husbands. A substantial number of women served in the United States House of Representatives throughout the 1970s, and two won election to state governorships. The number of female appointments in the executive branch rose steadily; two women held cabinet positions in the Carter administration, and one in the Reagan administration. The first female justice of the Supreme Court—Sandra Day O'Connor—took her seat in 1981. And in 1984, the Democratic party chose a woman, Representative Geraldine Ferraro of New York, as its vice-presidential candidate.

In professional athletics, in the meantime, women were beginning to compete with men both for attention and for an equal share of prize money. Billie Jean King spearheaded the most effective female challenge to male domination of sports. Under her leadership, professional woman tennis players established their own successful tours and demanded equal financial incentives when they played in the same tournaments as men. By the late 1970s, the federal government was pressuring colleges and universities to provide women with athletic programs equal to those available to men. In academia, women were expanding their presence in traditional scholarly fields; they were also creating a wholly new field of their own—women's studies, which by the early 1980s was the fastest-growing area of American scholarship. Women even joined what had previously been the most celebrated all-male fraternity in American culture: the space program. Sally Ride became the first woman astronaut to fly in space in 1983.

Of all the feminist crusades of the 1960s and 1970s, none united more women from more different backgrounds than the campaign for passage of the Equal Rights Amendment (ERA). Congress approved the

Feminist Politics
This poster was issued by the National Organization for Women in the 1970s. After the 1984 election, nearly two dozen women were members of Congress, there were two women governors, and women were serving as mayors in San Francisco, Houston, and several other cities. (Courtesy of NOW)

woman's place is in the House... and in the Senate

NOW

amendment in 1972 and sent it to the states; and for a while it seemed that eventual ratification was only a matter of time. By the end of the 1970s, however, the momentum behind the amendment had died. Approval of the ERA remained several states short of the three quarters necessary for enactment; and some state legislatures that had earlier voted in favor were trying to rescind their approval. In 1979, Congress granted a three-year extension of the time permitted for ratification.

The ERA was in trouble not because of indifference but because of a rising chorus of objections to it from those who feared it would create a major dis-ruption of traditional social patterns. In 1980, the Republican party—after forty years of support for the idea of the ERA—wrote into its platform a new plank opposing the amendment. And two years later, the amendment finally died when the time allotted for ratification expired.

The Abortion Controversy

A vital element of American feminism since the 1920s had been the effort by women to win greater control of their own physical and sexual lives. In its least controversial form, this impulse helped produce an increasing awareness in the 1960s and 1970s of the problems of rape, sexual abuse, and wife beating. Far more divisive, however, was the desire of many women to control their reproductive function in new ways. There continued to be some controversy over the dissemination of contraceptives and birth-control information; but that issue, at least, seemed to have lost much of the explosive character it had possessed in the 1920s, when Margaret Sanger had become a figure of public scorn for her efforts on its behalf. A related issue, however, stimulated as much popular passion as any question of its time: abortion.

Abortion had once been legal in much of the United States, but by the beginning of the twentieth century it was banned by statute in most of the country and remained so into the 1960s (although abortions continued to be performed quietly, and at times dangerously, out of sight of the law). But the growing strength of the women's movement increased pressure on behalf of the legalization of abortion. Several states had abandoned restrictions on abortion by the end of the 1960s. And in 1973, the Supreme Court's decision in *Roe* v. *Wade* invalidated all laws prohibiting abortion during the "first trimester"—the first three months of pregnancy. The issue, it seemed, had been settled.

In the following years, however, opposition to abortion revived, growing by the 1980s into one of the nation's most powerful political forces. The right-to-life movement, as it called itself, managed first to persuade Congress to ban all federal Medicaid funding for abortions; many state legislatures imposed similar bans. At the same time, pressure was growing for a "human life" amendment to the Constitution, prohibiting abortion even for those women who could afford it. The moral and religious fervor that the antiabortion movement had aroused, among American Catholics and fundamentalist Protestants in particular, and the growing numbers of followers it had attracted, won it support from many politicians (including President Ronald Reagan), even though public-opinion polls showed that a majority of the public continued to support the right to an abortion.

The women's movement was at once the most potent symbol and the most glaring exception to the general impulse toward political and cultural "liberation" of the late 1960s. Feminism expressed both a desire to win social justice through collective political action—a desire that characterized the New Left— and a concern for individual fulfillment and personal freedom—a concern that typified much of the coun-

terculture. But it differed from both in one fundamental respect: its success. The women's movement may not have fulfilled all its goals. But it achieved fundamental and permanent changes in the position of women in American life, and it had itself become a lasting political and social force.

Nixon, Kissinger, and the War

Richard Nixon assumed office in 1969 committed not only to restoring stability at home but to creating a new and more stable order in the world. Few presidents have entered the White House with such well-developed ideas about foreign policy; few have moved as decisively to translate those ideas into practice.

Central to Nixon's hopes for international stability was a resolution of the stalemate in Vietnam. Yet the new president felt no freer than his predecessor to abandon the American commitment in Indochina. He realized that the endless war was undermining both the nation's domestic stability and its position in the world. But he feared that a precipitous retreat would destroy American honor and "credibility."

During the 1968 campaign, Nixon claimed to have formulated a plan to bring "peace with honor" in Vietnam. He had refused to disclose its details. Once in office, however, he soon made clear that the plan consisted of little more than a vague set of general principles, not of any concrete measures to extricate the United States from the quagmire. American involvement in Indochina continued for four more years, during which the war expanded both in its geographic scope and in its bloodiness. And when a settlement finally emerged early in 1973, it produced neither peace nor honor. It succeeded only in removing the United States from the wreckage.

Vietnamization

Nixon had long considered himself an expert in foreign affairs, and he was as president far more drawn to international matters than to domestic ones. But despite his own passionate interest in diplomacy, he brought with him into government a public figure who ultimately seemed to overshadow the president himself in the conduct of international affairs: Henry Kissinger.

Kissinger was a respected and prolific professor of international politics at Harvard when Nixon tapped him to serve as his special assistant for national security affairs. Both Secretary of State William Rogers, who had served as Eisenhower's attorney general, and Secretary of Defense Melvin Laird, who had been an influential member of Congress, were far more experienced in public life. But Kissinger quickly out-shone them both. Nixon's passion for concentrating decision making in the White House was in large measure responsible, but Kissinger's keen intelligence and his remarkable adeptness both in fighting for bu-reaucratic influence and in currying favor with the press were at least equally important. Together, Nixon and Kissinger set out to find an acceptable solution to the stalemate in Vietnam.

The new Vietnam policy moved along several fronts. One was an effort to limit domestic opposi-tion to the war so as to permit the administration more political space in which to maneuver. Aware that the military draft was one of the most visible targets of dissent, the administration devised a new "lottery" system, through which only a limited group of nineteen-year-olds—those with low lottery num-bers—would be eligible for the draft. The new sys-tem would continue to supply the military with its manpower needs while removing millions of poten-tial critics from the danger of conscription. Later, the president urged the creation of an all-volunteer army that would permit the abolition of the draft altogether. By 1973, the Selective Service System was on its way to at least temporary extinction.

More important in stifling dissent, however, was the new policy of "Vietnamization" of the war—that is, the training and equipping of the South Vietnam-ese military to assume the burden of combat in place of American forces. In the fall of 1969, Nixon an-nounced the withdrawal of 60,000 American ground troops from Vietnam, the first reduction in U.S. troop strength since the beginning of the war. The withdrawals continued steadily for more than three years, so that by the fall of 1972 relatively few Amer-ican soldiers remained in Indochina. From a peak of more than 540,000 in 1969, the number had dwindled to about 60,000.

Vietnamization did help undermine domestic op-position to the war. It did nothing, however, to break the stalemate in the negotiations with the North Vietnamese in Paris. The new administration quickly decided that new military pressures would be neces-sary to do that.

Escalation

By the end of their first year in office, Nixon and Kissinger had decided that the most effective way to tip the military balance in America's favor was to destroy the "staging areas" in Cambodia from which the North Vietnamese had been launching many of their attacks. Very early in his presidency, Nixon ordered the air force to begin a series of secret bomb-ings of Cambodian territory to destroy the enemy sanctuaries. He withheld information about the raids from Congress and the public. In the spring of 1970, with what some have claimed was American encour-agement and support, conservative military leaders overthrew the neutral government of Prince Norodom Sihanouk, Cambodia's leader for two de-cades, and established a new, pro-American regime under General Lon Nol. Lon Nol quickly gave his approval to American incursions into his territory; and on April 30, Nixon went on television to an-nounce that he was ordering American troops across the border into Cambodia to "clean out" the bases that the enemy had been using for its "increased mil-itary aggression."

So successful had Nixon been in seeming to deescalate the war that the once-powerful peace movement had by mid-1970 begun to lose much of its strength. The Cambodian invasion, however, re-stored it to life. The first days of May saw the most widespread and vocal antiwar demonstrations ever. Hundreds of thousands of protesters gathered in Washington to denounce the president's policies. Millions, perhaps, participated in countless smaller demonstrations on campuses nationwide. Antiwar frenzy was reaching so high a level that it became possible briefly to believe that a genuine revolution was imminent.

The mood of crisis intensified on May 4, when four college students were killed and nine others in-jured after members of the National Guard opened fire on an antiwar rally at Kent State University in Ohio. The incident seemed to many young Ameri-cans to confirm their worst suspicions of their gov-ernment and their society. Ten days later, police killed two black students at Jackson State University in Mississippi during a demonstration there.

The clamor against the war quickly spread be-yond the campuses and into the government and the press. Congress angrily repealed the Gulf of Tonkin Resolution in December, stripping the president of what had long served as the legal basis for the war. Nixon ignored the action, claiming that he had the authority to continue military efforts in Vietnam to protect American troops already there. Then, in June 1971, first the *New York Times* and later other news-papers began publishing excerpts from a secret study of the war prepared by the Defense Department dur-ing the Johnson administration. The so-called Penta-

Kent State
In the spring of 1970, the fatal shooting by National Guardsmen of four student demonstrators at Kent State University in Ohio (and the deaths of two students at the hands of state police at Jackson State University in Mississippi several days later) seemed to many young Americans to mark the beginning of a long and bloody battle between authorities and protesters. In fact, the uprisings were among the last of the major campus disturbances of the era.   (John Filo/Valley News Dispatch)

gon Papers, leaked to the press by former Defense official Daniel Ellsberg, provided apparent confirmation of what many had long believed: that the government had been frequently dishonest, both in reporting the military progress of the war and in explaining its own motives for American involvement. The administration went to court to suppress the documents, but to no avail. The Supreme Court ruled that the press had the right to publish them.

Particularly troubling, both to the public and to the government itself, were signs of decay within the American military. Morale and discipline among U.S. troops in Vietnam, who had been fighting a savage and inconclusive war for more than five years, were rapidly deteriorating. The trial and conviction in 1971 of Lieutenant William Calley, who was charged with overseeing a massacre of more than 100 unarmed South Vietnamese civilians, attracted wide public attention to the dehumanizing impact of the war on those who fought it. Less publicized were other, more widespread problems among American troops in Vietnam: desertion, drug addiction, refusal to obey orders, even the occasional killing of unpopular officers by enlisted men. Among the disenchanted—deserters, draft resisters, and others—were

not simply the radical college students so unpopular with most Americans but many otherwise conventional sons of middle- and lower-class families. The continuing carnage, the increasing savagery, and the social distress at home were drawing an ever-larger proportion of the population into opposition to the war. By 1971, nearly two-thirds of those interviewed in public-opinion polls were urging American withdrawal from Vietnam.

From Richard Nixon, however, there came no sign of retreat. On the contrary, the events of the spring of 1970 left him more convinced than ever of the importance of resisting what he once called the "bums" who opposed his military policies. With the approval of the White House, both the FBI and the CIA intensified their surveillance and infiltration of antiwar and radical groups, often resorting to blatant illegalities in the process. Administration officials sought to discredit prominent critics of the war by leaking damaging personal information about them. At one point, White House agents broke into the office of a psychiatrist in an unsuccessful effort to steal files on Daniel Ellsberg. During the congressional campaign of 1970, Vice President Spiro Agnew, using the acid rhetoric that had already made him the hero of many conservatives, stepped up his attack on the "effete" and "impudent" critics of the administration. The president himself once climbed on top of an automobile to taunt a crowd of angry demonstrators.

In Indochina, meanwhile, the fighting raged on. In February 1971, the president ordered the air force to assist the South Vietnamese army in an invasion of Laos—a test, as he saw it, of his Vietnamization program. Within weeks, the badly mauled South Vietnamese scrambled back across the border in defeat. American bombing in Vietnam and Cambodia continued to increase, despite its apparent ineffectiveness, so that by the end of 1971 the Nixon administration had dropped more explosives on the region than the Johnson administration had done in five years. When in March 1972 the North Vietnamese mounted their biggest offensive since 1968, Nixon responded by escalating the bombing once again, ordering attacks on targets near Hanoi, the capital of North Vietnam, and Haiphong, its principal port. He called as well for the mining of seven North Vietnamese harbors (including Haiphong) to stop the flow of supplies from China and the Soviet Union.

"Peace with Honor"

The approach of the 1972 presidential election, in which the war promised to be the leading issue, seemed finally to do what years of military frustration and escalating public protests had failed to do: convince the administration that it must alter its terms for the withdrawal of American forces. In April 1972, the president dropped his longtime insistence on a removal of North Vietnamese troops from the south before any American withdrawal. In July, word leaked out that Henry Kissinger had been meeting privately in Paris with the North Vietnamese foreign secretary, Le Duc Tho, and rumors abounded that a cease-fire was near. On October 26, only days before the presidential election, Kissinger announced that "peace is at hand."

Several weeks later (after the election), negotiations broke down once again. Although both the American and the North Vietnamese governments were ready to accept the Kissinger-Tho plan for a cease-fire, the Thieu regime balked, still insisting that the full withdrawal of North Vietnamese forces from the south be a prerequisite to any agreement. Kissinger tried to win additional concessions from the communists to meet Thieu's objections, but on December 16—despite the American insistence that the agreement was "99 percent complete"—talks broke off.

The next day, December 17, American B-52s began twelve days of bombing of North Vietnamese cities, the heaviest and most destructive raids of the entire war. The Pentagon announced that the bombers were attacking docks, airfields, railyards, power plants, and the like; but many of those targets were located in the middle of heavily populated urban areas, and civilian casualties were high. So were American losses. Fifteen of the giant bombers were shot down by the North Vietnamese; in the entire war to that point, the United States had lost only one B-52. Then, on December 30, Nixon terminated the "Christmas bombing" as quickly as he had begun it. The United States and the North Vietnamese returned to the conference table. And on January 27, 1973, representatives of the four interested parties (the governments of the United States, North Vietnam, and South Vietnam, together with the "Provisional Republican Government" of the south—the Viet Cong) signed an "agreement on ending the war and restoring peace in Vietnam." Nixon liked to claim that the Christmas bombing had forced the North Vietnamese to relent. But a more important factor was the increasing American pressure on Thieu to accept the cease-fire and Nixon's promise to him that the United States would respond "with full force" to any violation of the agreement. Some have suggested that the Christmas bombing was designed more to convince Thieu of American resolve than to break the will of the North.

The terms of the Paris accords were little different from those that Kissinger and Tho had accepted in principle the previous fall. There would be an immediate cease-fire, and the North Vietnamese would release several hundred American prisoners of war, whose fate had become an emotional issue of great importance within the United States. After that, the agreement descended quickly into murky and plainly unworkable political arrangements. The Thieu regime would survive for the moment—perhaps the only major concession Kissinger was able to wrest from Tho. But there would be no withdrawal of North Vietnamese forces from the south and no abandonment of the communist commitment to a reunified Vietnam. What Nixon described as a "peace with honor" turned out to be little more than a formula for allowing the United States to extricate itself from the quagmire before the South Vietnamese regime collapsed, a recipe for providing what some officials caustically described as a "decent interval." Few knowledgeable military observers believed that the South Vietnamese military could hold off the communists without continuing American support.

Defeat in Indochina

The American forces were hardly out of Indochina and the prisoners of war barely reunited with their families before the Paris accords collapsed. During the first year after the cease-fire, the contending Vietnamese armies suffered greater battle losses than the Americans had endured during ten years of fighting. In Laos, fighting came to an end only after communist forces had established control of more than half the country. In Cambodia, the war raged on, and American planes continued to bomb communist installations in that country until Congress compelled the president to desist in August 1973. In March 1975, finally, the North Vietnamese launched a full-scale offensive against the now hopelessly weakened forces of the south. Thieu appealed to Washington for assistance; the president (by now, Gerald Ford)

appealed to Congress for additional funding; Congress refused. Late in April 1975, communist forces marched into Saigon, shortly after officials of the Thieu regime and the American embassy had fled the country in humiliating disarray. Communist forces quickly occupied the capital, renamed it Ho Chi Minh City, and began the process of reuniting Vietnam under the harsh and often brutal rule of Hanoi. At about the same time, the Lon Nol regime in Cambodia fell to the Khmer Rouge, the Cambodian equivalent of the Viet Cong.

Still the war in Indochina did not end. Although Vietnam was soon reunited after more than thirty years of civil war, conflict continued in the surrounding nations. In Cambodia, the Khmer Rouge government of Pol Pot (who renamed the country Kampuchea) launched a reign of terror perhaps unparalleled in modern history. His vision of an agrarian society, unpolluted by urban or Western influences, caused him literally to empty the nation's cities and towns and force virtually the entire population to move to the countryside. The result was the death—by murder, exhaustion, or starvation—of more than a third of the country's residents. In 1978, the communist government of the now united Vietnam launched an invasion of Cambodia and

The Fall of Saigon
The chaotic evacuation of Americans from Saigon in the spring of 1975, only hours before victorious North Vietnamese troops entered the city, was a humiliating spectacle. Desperate South Vietnamese soldiers and officials fought with American soldiers and diplomats for space on the few airplanes and helicopters available. (UPI/Bettmann Newsphotos)

drove Pol Pot and the Khmer Rouge from power. The war, however, only added to the problems of that unhappy country.

Vietnam, in the meantime, faced an invasion of its territory by the forces of communist China, which supported Pol Pot and feared the extension of Russian influence in the region. The two sides established an uneasy truce after several weeks of fighting, but there remained no stable peace between the ancient adversaries. American officials had claimed for years that the collapse of South Vietnam would lead quickly to coordinated communist domination of all of Southeast Asia. In fact, the new regimes were soon fighting each other as bitterly as they had once fought against the West.

Such were the dismal results of more than a decade of direct American military involvement in Vietnam. More than 1.2 million Vietnamese soldiers had died in combat, along with countless civilians throughout the region. A beautiful land had been ravaged; an ancient culture had been all but destroyed. The agrarian economy of much of Indochina lay in ruins. Even in the mid-1980s, Vietnam remained one of the poorest nations in the world. And a country the United States had attempted in vain to make into a viable democratic nation was now under the control of a repressive, authoritarian regime closely tied to the Soviet Union.

The United States had paid a heavy price as well. The war had cost the nation almost $150 billion in direct costs and incalculably more indirectly. It had resulted in the deaths of over 55,000 young men and the injury of 300,000 more, some of whom were permanently maimed or crippled. An entire generation had been scarred by the experience, many of them cruelly disillusioned, some of them deeply and permanently embittered toward their government and their political system. And the nation at large had suffered a blow to its confidence and self-esteem from which it would not soon recover. A decade before, Americans had believed that they could create a great society at home and maintain peace and freedom in the world. Now many harbored serious doubts about their ability to do either.

Nixon, Kissinger, and the World

The continuing war in Vietnam provided a dismal backdrop to what Nixon considered his larger mis-

sion in world affairs: the construction of a new international order. The president had become convinced that old assumptions of a "bipolar" world—in which the United States and the Soviet Union were the only truly great powers—were now obsolete. The rise of China, Japan, and Western Europe, the increasing nationalism of the Third World, the growing disunity within the communist alliance—all augured a new, "multipolar" international structure. To deal with this changing world, Nixon drew on the theories of Henry Kissinger, a longtime student of the nineteenth-century European balance of power. The United States must, Nixon and Kissinger believed, work for a new equilibrium. "It will be a safer world and a better world," the president proclaimed in 1971, "if we have a strong, healthy United States, Europe, Soviet Union, China, Japan—each balancing the other, not playing one against the other, an even balance."

Nixon and Kissinger believed it was possible to construct something like the "balance of power" that had permitted nineteenth-century Europe to enjoy nearly a century of relative stability. To do that, America would need to do several things. It would need to encourage what became known as "trilateralism," recognizing that the noncommunist world was not a single bloc dominated by the United States, but three major power centers (America, Europe, and Japan), each with its own role to play in the world. America would also have to bring China out of its isolation so that it too could play its proper role as one of the major elements in the international balance. And the United States would have to find some means of reaching accommodation with the Soviet Union, by recognizing that country's legitimate interests in the world and by trying to induce the Soviets to defend those interests with restraint and responsibility in a multipolar world.

The China Initiative

For more than twenty years, ever since the fall of Chiang Kai-shek in 1949, the United States had treated China, the second largest nation on earth, as if it did not exist. One of the world's greatest powers, a nation now in possession of nuclear weapons, was living in almost total isolation from the West, while the United States continued to recognize the decaying regime-in-exile on Taiwan as the legitimate government of China.

Nixon and Kissinger were determined to forge

a new relationship with the Chinese communists. A rapprochement would, among other things, strengthen China's position as a counterbalance to the Soviet Union, thus inducing the Russians to adopt a more conciliatory attitude toward the United States. The Chinese, for their part, were at least equally eager for a new relationship with the United States. Their own dispute with the Soviet Union had grown far more bitter than any rivalry with the West. By 1970, Soviet and Chinese forces were massed along both sides of the border, poised, it seemed, for a war between the two communist powers. The Beijing government was eager, therefore, both to forestall the possibility of a Soviet-American alliance against China and to end China's own isolation from the international arena.

In July 1971, Nixon sent Henry Kissinger on a secret mission to Beijing. When Kissinger returned, the president made the startling announcement that he would visit China himself within the next few months. That fall, the United States dropped its long opposition to the admission of communist China to the United Nations; and in October that body admitted the communist delegation and expelled the representatives of the Taiwan regime. Finally, in February 1972, Nixon arrived in China for a week-long visit. American television broadcast vivid pictures of presidential tours of famous Chinese landmarks, which had been invisible to much of the West for more than two decades, of meetings with Zhou Enlai and Mao Zedong, and of gracious and friendly exchanges of toasts during elaborate state dinners. At a single stroke, Nixon managed to erase much of the deep animosity toward China that the American people had developed over the course of a generation.

The summit meeting did not produce any agreement on establishing formal diplomatic relations between the United States and China. Nixon was not yet prepared openly to repudiate the Chiang regime, which the United States had supported for so long. But a year after the Nixon visit, the two countries set up "liaison offices" in Washington and Beijing that served as embassies in all but name.

The Birth of Détente

The initiatives in China helped pave the way as well for a new relationship with the Soviet Union, which was as eager to prevent a Chinese-American alliance as Beijing was to prevent a Soviet-American one.

The road to what soon became known as détente had actually begun in 1968, the last year of the Johnson administration, when the United States and the Soviet Union signed a treaty agreeing to discourage the further proliferation of nuclear weapons in the world. More important, however, was the beginning of talks between American and Russian diplomats in Helsinki in 1969 on a strategic arms limitation treaty (SALT). The negotiations continued for two and a half years, and the result was the conclusion in 1972 of the first phase of a new arms control accord: the so-called SALT I. In May of that year, the president traveled to Moscow for a cordial meeting with the Soviet leadership and a glittering ceremony to sign the agreement. The Moscow summit produced as well a series of accords establishing new trade and other exchanges between the two nations—including the soon to be infamous Soviet-American wheat deal, by which the United States would sell nearly one quarter of the total American grain supply to the Russians at a cost far below the world market price. The federal government would make up the price difference through subsidies to American farmers.

Nixon returned from Moscow in triumph, boasting of dramatic progress toward bringing the arms race to an end. In fact, SALT I did less to end the arms race (or even slow it) than to move it in a different direction. The two nations agreed to limit themselves to their existing number of intercontinental ballistic missiles (ICBMs), thus institutionalizing Soviet superiority in total missile strength. But the United States continued to possess a substantial lead in the total number of its warheads; it had almost twice as many submarines equipped with nuclear missiles as the Soviets. Each country would, in addition, sharply limit its construction of antiballistic missile systems (ABMs). The treaty thus limited the quantity of certain weapons on both sides. It said nothing, however, about limiting quality or about forestalling the creation of entirely new weapons systems.

SALT I had always been intended as the first step toward a far more comprehensive arms control agreement. In June 1973, during a visit by the Soviet premier, Leonid Brezhnev, to Washington, the Russian and American governments pledged renewed efforts to speed the completion of the next phase of the negotiations. Nixon and Brezhnev agreed in principle to abstain from nuclear war, to work for a permanent freeze on offensive nuclear weapons, and to extend Soviet-American cooperation in other areas as well.

Détente at High Tide
The visit of Soviet Premier Leonid Brezhnev to Washington in 1973 was a high-water mark in the search for détente between the two nations, a search that had begun as early as 1962, that continued through parts of five presidential administrations, and that collapsed in disarray in the late 1970s. Here, Brezhnev and Nixon share friendly words while standing on the White House balcony.   (J. P. Laffont/Sygma)

The Problems of Multipolarity

The policies of rapprochement with communist China and détente with the Soviet Union reflected several basic assumptions of the Nixon-Kissinger foreign policy. The communist world was no longer a monolithic bloc, the administration now believed, and the situation required a far more flexible and var-

ied diplomatic approach than had been the case in the 1950s. The Soviet threat to Western Europe, American officials were convinced, was much abated, removing the most serious source of tension from the Cold War. Above all, the new policies reflected a belief that world stability depended primarily on the relationships among the great powers, that the pervasive concern of previous administrations with "emerging areas" had diverted American policy from pursuit of its most important goals. By the last years of the Nixon administration, however, it had become clear that it was the Third World that remained the most volatile and dangerous source of world instability; that tensions in developing countries had the capacity not only to produce local turmoil but to erode the new relationships among the superpowers.

Central to the Nixon-Kissinger policy toward the Third World was the effort to maintain a stable status quo without involving the United States too deeply in local disputes. In 1969 and 1970, the president laid out the elements of what became known as the Nixon Doctrine, by which the United States would "participate in the defense and development of allies and friends" but would leave the "basic responsibility" for the future of those "friends" to the nations themselves. In practice, the Nixon Doctrine meant a declining American interest in contributing to Third World development; a growing contempt for the United Nations, where underdeveloped nations were gaining influence through their sheer numbers; and increasing support to authoritarian regimes attempting to withstand radical challenges from within. In 1970, for example, the CIA poured substantial funds into Chile to help support the established government against a communist challenge. When the Marxist candidate for president, Salvador Allende, came to power through an honest election, the United States began funneling more money to opposition forces in Chile to help "destabilize" the new government. In 1973, a military junta seized power from Allende, who was subsequently murdered under mysterious circumstances. The new regime of General Augusto Pinochet, which was as brutally repressive as any in the Western Hemisphere, received warm approval and increased military and economic assistance from the United States.

More troubling than Latin America was the Middle East. Long an area of interest to the United States because of its strategic position between the Soviet Union and the Mediterranean, the region was now also of vital economic importance to the West, which

Crises in the Middle East

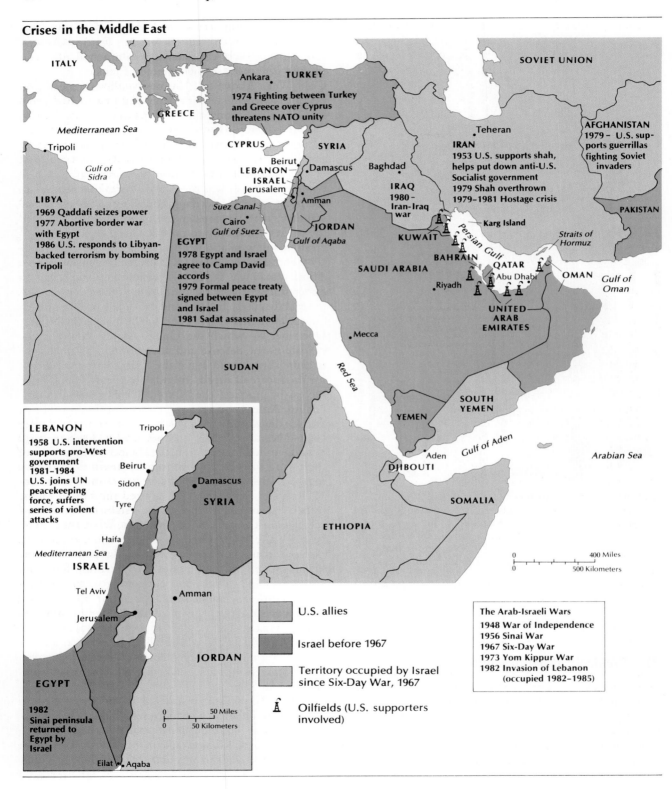

ITALY

Mediterranean Sea

Tripoli

Gulf of Sidra

GREECE

Ankara   **TURKEY**

1974 Fighting between Turkey and Greece over Cyprus threatens NATO unity

CYPRUS

SYRIA

Beirut
LEBANON
ISRAEL
Jerusalem

Damascus

Suez Canal

Cairo
Gulf of Suez

JORDAN
Gulf of Aqaba

Amman

Baghdad

IRAQ
1980 – Iran-Iraq war

KUWAIT

Teheran

IRAN
1953 U.S. supports shah, helps put down anti-U.S. Socialist government
1979 Shah overthrown
1979–1981 Hostage crisis

AFGHANISTAN
1979 – U.S. supports guerrillas fighting Soviet invaders

SOVIET UNION

PAKISTAN

Karg Island

Straits of Hormuz

Persian Gulf

BAHRAIN

QATAR
Abu Dhabi

OMAN

Gulf of Oman

LIBYA
1969 Qaddafi seizes power
1977 Abortive border war with Egypt
1986 U.S. responds to Libyan-backed terrorism by bombing Tripoli

EGYPT
1978 Egypt and Israel agree to Camp David accords
1979 Formal peace treaty signed between Egypt and Israel
1981 Sadat assassinated

SAUDI ARABIA

Riyadh

UNITED ARAB EMIRATES

Mecca

SUDAN

Red Sea

YEMEN

SOUTH YEMEN

Aden   *Gulf of Aden*

DJIBOUTI

SOMALIA

ETHIOPIA

Arabian Sea

| 0 | | 400 Miles |
| 0 | | 500 Kilometers |

LEBANON
1958 U.S. intervention supports pro-West government
1981–1984 U.S. joins UN peacekeeping force, suffers series of violent attacks

Tripoli

Beirut

Sidon

Tyre

Damascus

SYRIA

Haifa

Mediterranean Sea

ISRAEL

Tel Aviv

Amman

Jerusalem

JORDAN

EGYPT

1982 Sinai peninsula returned to Egypt by Israel

Eilat   Aqaba

| 0 | | 50 Miles |
| 0 | | 50 Kilometers |

U.S. allies

Israel before 1967

Territory occupied by Israel since Six-Day War, 1967

Oilfields (U.S. supporters involved)

The Arab-Israeli Wars
1948 War of Independence
1956 Sinai War
1967 Six-Day War
1973 Yom Kippur War
1982 Invasion of Lebanon
     (occupied 1982–1985)

beginning in the 1960s had become highly dependent on the purchase of oil from the Arab states. For the United States, this energy dependence presented special problems. As the most important ally and defender of Israel, America was standing squarely in opposition to the Islamic states, which were unanimous in their condemnation of Zionism.

Hostility toward Israel had grown particularly intense after the humiliating Arab defeat in the Six-Day War of 1967, in which Israeli forces had routed the attacking armies of Egypt, Jordan, and Syria and had seized territory from all three nations. For many years thereafter, Israel refused to relinquish the newly occupied territories.

Conditions in the region grew more volatile as a result of the desperate plight of hundreds of thousands of Palestinian Arab refugees, some of whom had been virtually homeless since 1948 and whose numbers had increased drastically after the 1967 war. Many of them lived in Jordan, whose ruler, King Hussein, was eager to maintain stable relations with the United States. Disturbed by the activities of the new Palestinian Liberation Organization (PLO) and other radical or terrorist groups, Hussein used his own armies to attack the Palestinians and expel them from Jordan after a series of uprisings in 1970, almost precipitating another general war in the region. Many of the exiled Palestinians moved to Lebanon, helping to precipitate many years of instability and civil war there.

In October 1973, on the Jewish high holy day of Yom Kippur, Egyptian and Syrian forces suddenly attacked Israel. The ensuing conflict was very different from the 1967 war, during which Israel had quickly and decisively overwhelmed its opponents. For ten days, the Israelis struggled to recover from the surprise attack; finally, they launched an effective counteroffensive against Egyptian forces in the Sinai. Only then did the United States intervene to bring an end to the fighting in the region. Under heavy American pressure, the government of Israel agreed not to press its advantage and accepted a cease-fire.

The imposed settlement of the Yom Kippur War reflected a significant change in the American position in the Middle East. Above all, perhaps, it served as evidence of the growing dependence of the United States and its allies on Arab oil. Permitting Israel to continue its drive into Egypt might have jeopardized the ability of the United States to purchase needed petroleum from the Arab states. A brief but painful embargo by the Islamic governments on the sale of oil to America in 1973 provided an ominous warning. (See pp. 911–912.) The lesson of the Yom Kippur War, therefore, was that the United States could no longer ignore the interests of the Arab nations in its efforts on behalf of Israel.

A larger lesson of 1973 was even more disturbing. The Yom Kippur War and the oil embargo had given clear evidence of the new limits facing the United States in its effort to construct a stable world order. The nations of the Third World could no longer be depended on to act as passive, cooperative "client states." The easy access to raw materials on which the American economy had come to depend was becoming a thing of the past. The United States could not even rely any longer on the automatic support of its NATO allies. None of the principal nations of Western Europe had joined the United States in providing military support for Israel in the 1973 war, and most had complained bitterly when American policies had resulted in their own temporary loss of access to vital Middle Eastern oil.

Politics and Economics Under Nixon

For a time in the 1960s, it had seemed to many Americans that the forces of chaos and radicalism were taking control of the nation. The domestic policy of the Nixon administration was an attempt to restore balance: between the needs of the poor and the desires of the middle class, between the power of the federal government and the interests of local communities. The president himself described the effort as the "New Federalism"—a series of programs to "reverse the flow of power and resources from the states and communities to Washington and start power and resources flowing back . . . to the people." In the end, however, economic and political crises sharply limited the administration's ability to fulfill its domestic goals.

Domestic Initiatives

Many of Nixon's domestic policies were a response to what he believed to be the demands of his constituency—conservative Middle America, or what he liked to call the "silent majority"—for retreat from federal interference with local affairs. He tried, unsuccessfully, to persuade Congress to pass legislation prohibiting school desegregation through the use of forced busing. He forbade the Department of Health, Education, and Welfare to cut off federal funds from school districts that had failed to comply with court orders to integrate (precipitating the resignation of Secretary Robert Finch and other HEW officials). At the same time, he began to reduce or dismantle many of the social programs of the Great Society and the New Frontier. He cut off hundreds of federal grants for urban renewal, social welfare, job training, and educational assistance. He attempted to reduce funding for dozens of other social programs, only to be blocked by the Democratic Congress; on occasion, he attempted to defy congressional opposition by simply impounding funds for programs he considered unnecessary. In 1973, he abolished the Office of Economic Opportunity, the centerpiece of the antipoverty program of the Johnson years.

Yet Nixon's effort to satisfy the demands of Middle Americans were not entirely negative. One of the administration's boldest efforts was an attempt to overhaul the nation's enormous welfare system. The cumbersome, expensive, and inefficient welfare bureaucracy was the most glaring symbol of what Nixon and his supporters considered the excessive intrusiveness of the federal government. The primary vehicle for federal relief—Aid to Families with Dependent Children—was not only costly; it required a large, awkward infrastructure of caseworkers, administrators, and others, and it extended the authority of the federal government directly into the daily lives of families and communities. As an alternative, Nixon proposed what he called the Family Assistance Plan. Designed in large part by the president's urban adviser, Daniel Patrick Moynihan, the FAP proposed what would in effect have been a guaranteed annual income for all Americans: $1,600 in federal grants, which could be supplemented by outside earnings up to $4,000. Even many liberals applauded the proposal as an important step toward expanding federal responsibility for the poor. To Nixon, however, the appeal of the plan was its simplicity. It would reduce the supervisory functions of the federal government and transfer to welfare recipients themselves daily responsibility for their own lives. Although the FAP won approval in the House in 1970, concerted attacks by welfare recipients (who considered the benefits inadequate) and members of the welfare bureaucracy (whose own influence stood to be sharply diminished by the bill) helped kill it in the Senate.

Nixon appealed to conservative and provincial sentiments in other ways as well. He issued strident denunciations of protesters and radicals, ordered the Justice Department to arrest demonstrators and dissidents, and unleashed Vice President Agnew to attack not only youthful critics of the administration but the liberal news media and the "biased" television networks. He rejected as "morally bankrupt" the recommendations of a special commission on pornography, which saw no reason for the government to suppress the distribution of obscene materials. He expressed sympathy for those who opposed abortion. He refused to consider extending amnesty to draft resisters. He was, in short, establishing a new stance for the federal government: one that balanced its commitments to the poor and minorities against a larger concern for preserving traditional values and protecting the status of the middle class.

From the Warren Court to the Nixon Court

One of the loudest cheers during Richard Nixon's acceptance speech at the 1968 Republican Convention greeted his pledge to change the composition of the Supreme Court. The reaction was unsurprising. Of all the liberal institutions that had aroused the enmity of the "silent majority" in the 1950s and 1960s, none had evoked more anger and bitterness than the Warren Court. Not only had its rulings on racial matters disrupted traditional social patterns in both the North and the South, but its staunch defense of civil liberties had, in the eyes of many Americans, contributed directly to the increase in crime, disorder, and moral decay. One after another landmark decision seemed to tread on the sensibilities of provincial and conservative Americans. In *Engel* v. *Vitale* (1962), the Court had ruled that prayers in public schools were unconstitutional, sparking outrage among religious fundamentalists and others, who began a long battle against the edict. In *Roth* v. *United States* (1957), the Court had sharply limited the authority of local governments to curb pornography. In a series of decisions, the Court had greatly strengthened the civil rights of criminal defendants and had, in the eyes of many Americans, greatly weakened the power of law-enforcement officials to do their jobs. For example, in *Gideon* v. *Wainwright* (1963), the Court had ruled that every felony defendant was entitled to a lawyer regardless of his or her ability to pay. In *Escobedo* v. *Illinois* (1964), it had ruled that a defendant must be allowed access to a lawyer before questioning by police. Above all, in *Miranda* v. *Ari-*

zona (1966), the Court had confirmed the obligation of authorities to inform a criminal suspect of his or her rights.

Other examples of "judicial activism" had antagonized both local and national political leaders. In *Baker* v. *Carr* (1962), the Warren Court, in its most influential decision since *Brown* v. *Board of Education,* had ordered state legislatures to apportion representation so that the votes of all citizens would carry equal weight. In dozens of states, systems of legislative districting that had given disproportionate representation to rural areas were thus rendered invalid. The reapportionment that resulted greatly increased the political voice of blacks, Hispanics, and other poor urban residents. By 1968, in short, the Warren Court had become the target of Americans of all kinds who felt that the balance of power in the United States had shifted too far toward the poor and dispossessed at the expense of the middle class.

Richard Nixon shared such sentiments, and he was determined to use his judicial appointments to give the Court a more conservative cast. His first opportunity came almost as soon as he entered office. Chief Justice Earl Warren, who had tried to resign during the last months of the Johnson administration only to be stymied by the refusal of Congress to approve the appointment of liberal Associate Justice Abe Fortas as his successor, announced his resignation early in 1969. Nixon replaced him with a federal appeals court judge of known conservative leanings, Warren Burger.

The president had less success in filling the next Court opening to become available. In May 1969, Abe Fortas resigned his seat after the disclosure of a series of alleged financial improprieties. To replace him, Nixon named Clement F. Haynsworth, a respected federal circuit court judge from South Carolina. Haynsworth received the endorsement of the American Bar Association, but he came under fire from Senate liberals, black organizations, and labor unions for his conservative record on civil rights. The revelation that he had sat on cases involving corporations in which he himself had a financial interest finally doomed his nomination; the Senate rejected him. Nixon's next choice was a particularly unfortunate one. G. Harold Carswell, a judge of the Florida federal appeals court, was almost entirely lacking in distinction and widely considered unfit for the Supreme Court. After weeks of damaging revelations about Carswell's record, the Senate rejected his nomination too.

An enraged President Nixon announced that the votes had been a result of prejudice against the South. But he was careful thereafter to choose men of standing within the legal community to fill vacancies on the Supreme Court. Harry Blackmun, a moderate jurist from Minnesota; Lewis F. Powell, Jr., a respected judge from Virginia; and William Rehnquist, a member of the Nixon Justice Department—all met with little opposition from the Senate. And the Warren Court gradually gave way to what many observers came to describe as the "Burger Court" but which others termed the "Nixon Court."

The new Court, however, fell short of what the president and many conservatives had hoped. Far from retreating from its commitment to social reform, the Court in many areas actually extended its reach. In *Swann* v. *Charlotte-Mecklenburg Board of Education* (1971), it ruled in favor of the use of forced busing to achieve racial balance in schools. Not even the intense and occasionally violent opposition of local communities as diverse as Boston and Louisville, Kentucky, was able to weaken the judicial commitment to integration. In *Furman* v. *Georgia* (1972), the Court overturned existing capital punishment statutes and established strict new guidelines for such laws in the future. In *Roe* v. *Wade* (1972), it struck down laws forbidding women to have abortions.

In other decisions, however, the Burger Court did signal a marked withdrawal from the crusading commitment to civil liberties and reform. It attempted instead to follow a moderate path. Although the justices approved busing as a tool for achieving integration, they rejected, in *Milliken* v. *Bradley* (1974), a plan to transfer students across district lines (in this case, between Detroit and its suburbs) to achieve racial balance. While the Court upheld the principle of affirmative action in its celebrated 1978 decision *Bakke* v. *Board of Regents of California,* it established restrictive new guidelines for such programs in the future. In *Stone* v. *Powell* (1976), the Court agreed to certain limits on the right of a defendant to appeal a state conviction to the federal judiciary.

The Election of 1972

However unsuccessful the Nixon administration may have been in achieving some of its specific goals, it had by 1972 scored a series of triumphs in enlisting the loyalties of the electorate. The "real majority"—what a 1970 book of that name by Richard Scammon and Ben Wattenberg called the "unyoung, unblack, and unpoor"—responded enthusiastically to the president's attacks on liberals and radicals as well as to his apparent diplomatic successes in China and the Soviet Union.

Nixon entered the presidential race in 1972, therefore, with a substantial reserve of strength. The events of that year improved his position immeasurably. His energetic reelection committee collected enormous sums of money to support the campaign. The president himself made full use of the powers of incumbency, refraining from campaigning in the primaries (in which he faced, in any case, only token opposition) and concentrating on highly publicized international decisions and state visits. Agencies of the federal government dispensed funds and favors to communities around the country in a concerted effort to strengthen Nixon's political standing in questionable areas.

Nixon was most fortunate in 1972, however, in his opposition. The return of George Wallace to the presidential fray caused some early concern, for Nixon's own reelection strategy rested on the same appeals to the troubled middle class that Wallace was so skillfully expressing. But although Wallace showed remarkable strength in the early Democratic primaries, the possibility of another third-party campaign vanished in May, when a would-be assassin shot the Alabama governor during a rally at a Maryland shopping center. Paralyzed from the waist down, Wallace was unable to continue campaigning.

The Democrats, in the meantime, were making the greatest contribution to the Nixon cause by nominating for president a representative of their most liberal faction: Senator George S. McGovern of South Dakota. An outspoken critic of the war, a forceful advocate of advanced liberal positions on virtually every social and economic issue, McGovern seemed to embody those aspects of the turbulent 1960s that middle-class Americans were most eager to reject. McGovern profited greatly from party reforms (which he himself had helped to draft) that gave increased influence to women, blacks, and young people in the selection of the Democratic ticket. But those same reforms helped make the Democratic Convention of 1972 an unappealing spectacle to much of the public. The candidate then disillusioned even some of his own supporters by his confused response to revelations that his running mate, Senator Thomas Eagleton of Missouri, had undergone treatment for an emotional disturbance. McGovern first announced that he supported Eagleton "1,000 percent," then suddenly dropped him from the ticket. The remainder of the Democratic presidential campaign was an exercise in futility.

For Nixon, in contrast, the fall campaign was an uninterrupted triumphal procession. After a Republican Convention utterly devoid of controversy, the president made a few carefully planned appearances in strategic areas of the country. Most of his time, however, he devoted to highly publicized work on behalf of "world peace." And in October, although by then it was clearly unnecessary politically, he sealed the victory with a skillfully orchestrated demonstration that a settlement of the war in Vietnam was near. On election day, Nixon won reelection by one of the largest margins in history: 60.7 percent of the popular vote compared with 37.5 percent for the forlorn McGovern, an electoral margin of 520 to 17. The Democratic candidate had carried only Massachusetts and the District of Columbia. The new commitments that Nixon had so effectively expressed—to restraint in social reform, to decentralization of political power, to the defense of traditional values, and to a new balance in international relations—had clearly won the approval of the American people. But other problems, some beyond the president's control and some of his own making, were already lurking in the wings.

The Troubled Economy

Although it was political scandal that would ultimately destroy the Nixon presidency, an even more serious national crisis was emerging in the early 1970s: the decline of the American economy. For more than twenty years, the American economy had been the envy of the world. The United States had been responsible for as much as a third of the world's industrial production and had dominated international trade. The American dollar had been the strongest currency in the world, the yardstick by which other nations measured their own monetary health. The American standard of living, already high at the end of World War II, had improved dramatically in the years since. Most Americans had begun to assume that this remarkable prosperity was the normal condition of their society. In fact, however, it had rested in part on several artificial conditions that were by the late 1960s rapidly disappearing.

The most disturbing economic problem, one that was symptomatic of all the others, was inflation, which had been creeping upward for several years when Richard Nixon took office and which shortly thereafter began to soar. Its most visible cause was the performance of the federal government in the mid-1960s. At the same time that President Johnson

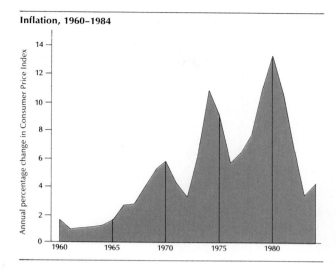

Inflation, 1960–1984

had persuaded Congress to accept a tax cut in 1964, he was rapidly increasing spending both for domestic social programs and for the war in Vietnam. The result was a major expansion of the money supply, resting largely on government deficits, that pushed prices rapidly upward.

But there were other, equally important causes of the inflation and of the economic problems that lay behind it. Much of America's economic strength in the 1950s and 1960s had rested on the nation's unquestioned supremacy in international trade. This meant that the United States enjoyed easy access to raw materials and a substantial market for its goods abroad. More important, it meant that American industrial goods faced little competition at home. The United States had its vast domestic market to itself.

By the late 1960s, however, the world economic picture had changed. No more did the United States have exclusive access to cheap raw materials around the globe; not only were other industrial nations now competing for increasingly scarce raw materials, but Third World suppliers of those materials were beginning to realize their value and demand higher prices for them. And American manufacturers of automobiles, steel, and other industrial products were facing more intense competition—in the world market and in the domestic market—from Japanese and Western European producers.

But the greatest immediate blow to the American economy was the interruption of its access to sources of energy. More than any nation on earth, the United States had based its economy on the easy availability of cheap and plentiful fuels. No society was more dependent on the automobile; none was more prof-

ligate in its use of oil and gas in its homes, schools, and factories. As the economy expanded in the 1960s, an already high demand for energy soared much higher. And with domestic petroleum reserves beginning to dwindle, the nation increased its dependence on imports from the Middle East and Africa.

For many years, the Organization of Petroleum Exporting Countries (OPEC) had operated as an informal bargaining unit for the sale of oil by Third World nations. Not until the early 1970s, however, did it begin to display its strength. Aware of the growing dependence of Western economies on the resources of its member nations, OPEC was no longer willing to follow the direction of American and European oil companies. Instead, it began to use its oil both as an economic tool and as a political weapon. In 1973, in the midst of the Yom Kippur War, Arab members of OPEC announced that they would no longer ship petroleum to nations supporting Israel—that is, to the United States and its allies in Western Europe. At about the same time, the OPEC nations agreed to raise their prices 400 percent.

These twin shocks produced momentary chaos in the West. The United States suffered its first fuel shortage since World War II, and the disruptive effects were a painful reminder to the American people of their dependence on plentiful energy. Motorists faced long lines at gas stations; schools and offices closed down to save on heating oil; factories cut production and laid off workers for lack of sufficient

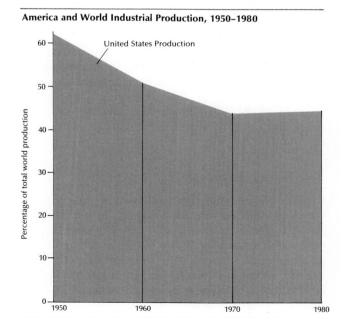

America and World Industrial Production, 1950–1980

The Energy Crisis
Draper Hill, a cartoonist for the Memphis *Commercial Appeal,* captures the dilemma Americans
faced in the energy crisis of the early 1970s. Long accustomed to cheap and plentiful energy
supplies, the United States reluctantly confronted the necessity of changing many of its economic habits in the face of spiraling prices and reduced supplies. In this 1975 drawing, Henry
Kissinger "thinks it over" in the style of comedian Jack Benny.   (Draper Hill, Commercial Appeal)

fuel. A few months later, the crisis eased. But the
price of energy continued to skyrocket in the following years, both because of OPEC's new militant policies and because of the weakening competitive
position of the dollar in world markets. No single
factor did more to produce the soaring inflation of
the 1970s.

The Nixon Response

Richard Nixon, therefore, inherited an economy in
which growth was already sluggish, in which inflation was already troubling, and in which even greater
new problems lurked. Within weeks of taking office,
he announced a "game plan" for dealing with these
various woes. He would, he promised, spend less
and tax more. But such policies were easier announced

than implemented, evoking as they did both congressional and popular protest. As a result, Nixon turned
increasingly to an economic tool more readily available to him: control of the currency. Placing conservative economists at the head of the Federal Reserve
Board, he ensured sharply higher interest rates and a
contraction of the money supply. But the tight money
policy did little to curb inflation. The cost of living
rose a cumulative 15 percent during Nixon's first two
and a half years in office. In 1971, moreover, the
United States recorded its first balance-of-trade deficit (an excess of imports over exports) in nearly
eighty years. With inflation unabated and economic
growth in decline, the United States was encountering a new and puzzling dilemma: "stagflation," a
combination of rising prices and general economic
stagnation.

By the summer of 1971, therefore, the president was under strong public pressure to act decisively to reverse the economic tide. First, he released the dollar from the fluctuating gold standard that had controlled its worth since the end of World War II, allowing its value to fall in world markets. The devaluation helped stimulate exports, but it also made more expensive the American purchase of vital raw materials abroad. At the same time, the president announced an even bolder and more startling new policy. For years, he had denounced the idea of using government controls to curb inflation. On August 15, 1971, however, he reversed himself. Under the provisions of the Economic Stabilization Act of 1970, the president imposed a ninety-day freeze on all wages and prices at their existing levels. Then, in November, he launched Phase II of his economic plan: mandatory guidelines for wage and price increases, to be administered by a federal agency. Inflation subsided temporarily, but the recession continued. The unemployment rate for 1971 was 6 percent, compared with 4 percent two years earlier.

Fearful that the recession would be more damaging than inflation in an election year, the administration reversed itself once again late in 1971: Interest rates were allowed to drop sharply, and government spending was increased—producing the largest budget deficit since World War II. The new tactics served their purpose. By election day, personal incomes were up and unemployment was down. But there were disastrous side effects. Even though wage and price controls managed to hold down inflation in some areas, consumers were soon paying drastically higher prices for food and other basic goods. At this critical moment, with both domestic and world inflation on the verge of skyrocketing, Nixon abandoned the strict Phase II controls and replaced them with a set of flexible, largely voluntary, and almost entirely ineffective guidelines—Phase III of the administration's economic program. With the end of wage and price controls, inflation quickly resumed its upward course. In 1973, it rose to 9 percent; in 1974, after the Arab oil embargo and the OPEC price increases, it soared to 12 percent—the highest rate since shortly after the end of World War II. The value of the dollar continued to slide, and the nation's international trade continued to decline.

Nixon now turned his attention to solving the new "energy crisis," which had become America's most pressing preoccupation. But the administration seemed to have no clearer idea of how to deal with that problem than it had of how to deal with the inflation. The president spoke vaguely of conservation, of increasing production, of restoring "energy independence." But there were few concrete proposals for accomplishing them. And Nixon, in the meantime, was becoming so embroiled in his own political problems that he would have had great difficulty winning approval of a major new program in any case.

The stumbling and erratic economic programs of the Nixon administration were indicative of a broader national confusion about the future prospects for American prosperity. With little understanding of the international forces creating the economic problems, both the government and the people focused on immediate issues and short-range solutions. The Nixon pattern—of lurching from a tight money policy to curb inflation at one moment to a spending policy to cure recession at the next—repeated itself during the two administrations that followed. Such policies had little effect, ultimately, either on inflation or on the general economic stagnation.

The Watergate Crisis

Although economic problems greatly concerned the American people in the 1970s, another stunning development almost entirely preoccupied the nation beginning early in 1973: the fall of Richard Nixon. The president's demise was a result in part of his own personality. Defensive, secretive, resentful of his critics, he brought to his office an element of meanspiritedness that helped undermine even his most important accomplishments. But the larger explanation lay in Nixon's view of American society and the world, and of his own role in both. Far more than most of his compatriots, the president was convinced that the United States faced grave dangers from the radicals and dissidents who were challenging his policies. Obsessed with his mission to create a new "structure of peace" in the world, he came increasingly to consider any challenge to his policies a threat to "national security." By identifying his own political fortunes with those of the nation, in other words, Nixon was creating a climate in which he and those who served him could justify extraordinary measures to stifle dissent and undermine opposition.

The White House Autocracy

Nixon's outlook was in part a culmination of decades of changes in the nature of the presidency. Public expectations of the president had increased dramatically in the years since World War II; yet the constraints on the authority of the office had grown as well. Congress had become more difficult to control; the bureaucracy had become cumbersome and unmanageable; the press, particularly in light of the war in Vietnam, had become suspicious and increasingly hostile. In response, a succession of presidents had sought out new methods for the exercise of power, often stretching the law, occasionally breaking it.

Nixon not only continued but greatly accelerated these trends. Facing a Democratic Congress hostile to his goals, he attempted to find ways to circumvent the legislature whenever possible. Saddled with a federal bureaucracy unresponsive to his wishes, he constructed a hierarchy of command in which virtually all executive power became concentrated in the White House. A few cabinet members retained direct access to the president—among them Attorney General John Mitchell, a longtime personal friend, and Henry Kissinger, who became secretary of state in 1973. For the most part, however, Nixon isolated himself almost completely, relying on a few trusted advisers through whom he exercised his power. At the head of what critics sometimes called the "palace guard" stood two particularly influential aides: H. R. Haldeman, the president's chief of staff, and John Ehrlichman, his chief domestic adviser.

Operating within this rigid, even autocratic structure, the president became a solitary, brooding figure, whose contempt for his opponents and impatience with obstacles to his policies festered and grew. Insulated from criticism, surrounded by flatterers, he became increasingly blatant in his defiance of the normal constraints on his office. Unknown to all but a few intimates, he also became mired in a pattern of illegalities and abuses of power that late in 1972 began to break through to the surface.

The Scandals

Early on the morning of June 17, 1972, police arrested five men who had broken into the offices of the Democratic National Committee, located in the Watergate office building in Washington, D.C. Two others were seized a short time later and charged with supervising the break-in. And when reporters for the *Washington Post* began researching the backgrounds of the culprits, they discovered a series of startling facts. Among those involved in the burglary were former employees of the Committee for the Re-Election of the President (CRP). One of them had worked in the White House itself. They had, moreover, been paid for the break-in from a secret fund of the reelection committee, a fund controlled by members of the White House staff. The further the reporters looked, the more evidence they found that the burglary had been part of a larger pattern of illegalities, planned and financed by the president's closest associates.

Public interest in the disclosures grew only slowly in the last months of 1972. Few Americans, apparently, chose to question the president's assurances that neither he nor his staff had any connection with what he called "this very bizarre incident." Early in 1973, however, the Watergate burglars went on trial; and under relentless prodding from federal judge John J. Sirica, one of the defendants, James W. McCord, agreed to cooperate both with the grand jury and with a special Senate investigating committee recently established under Senator Sam J. Ervin of North Carolina. McCord's testimony opened a floodgate of confessions, and for months a parade of White House and campaign officials exposed one illegality after another. Foremost among them was a member of the inner circle of the White House, Counsel to the President John Dean, who leveled allegations against Nixon himself.

Two different sets of scandals were emerging from the investigations. One was a general pattern of abuses of power involving both the White House and the Nixon campaign committee. Every week, it seemed, there was a new, even more damaging revelation. White House "plumbers"—under the direction of John Ehrlichman—had established illegal wiretaps, intercepted mail, and engaged in burglaries (including the attempt to steal files from Daniel Ellsberg's psychiatrist) in an effort to prevent leaks of sensitive or politically embarrassing information or, as in Ellsberg's case, to discredit critics of the administration. Members of the reelection committee had solicited illegal contributions, "laundered" the money through accounts in Mexico, and used the funds to support a variety of "dirty tricks" against Democratic presidential candidates and to pay for other maneuvers to sabotage the campaigns of Nixon's oppo-

Haldeman Testifies

White House Chief of Staff H. R. Haldeman, who had been an advertising executive in California before joining Richard Nixon's administration, was one of the most powerful (and feared) figures in Washington in the early 1970s. He and other White House officials became known to their critics as the "Prussians," a label derived from their reputation for toughness bordering on ruthlessness. Here Haldeman testifies before the special Senate committee investigating the Watergate scandals in 1973. He would later resign from the White House, stand trial for his part in the scandals, and serve time in federal prison.   (J. P. Laffont/Sygma)

nents. In addition, associates of the president had created devious opportunities for Nixon to increase his personal wealth, including several real-estate transactions and income-tax dodges of dubious legality.

The other scandal, and the one that became the major focus of public attention for nearly two years, was the Watergate break-in itself and the events that it had set in motion. There was never any conclusive evidence that the president had planned or approved

the burglary in advance. John Dean and others testified that then Attorney General Mitchell had ordered the break-in, hoping to plant electronic bugs in and steal copies of files from the Democratic offices. (Mitchell had resigned from the Justice Department shortly after the burglary to head the president's re-election committee; then, after the scandals began to break, he resigned from CRP as well, citing "personal problems.")

But if there was no proof that Nixon had planned the break-in, there was mounting suspicion that he had been involved in what became known as the "cover-up"—illegal efforts to obstruct investigations of and withhold information about the episode. Testimony before the Ervin committee provided evidence of the complicity not only of Dean and Mitchell but of Haldeman, Ehrlichman, and other key White House figures. As interest in the case grew to something approaching a national obsession, only one question remained: In the words of Senator Howard Baker of Tennessee, a member of the Ervin committee, "What did the President know and when did he know it?"

Nixon, in the meantime, steadfastly denied knowing anything. One by one, he accepted the departure of those members of his administration implicated in the scandals: first a string of lower-level aides; then, with great reluctance, Haldeman and Ehrlichman, who resigned on the same day that Nixon dismissed John Dean. But the president himself continued to insist on his own innocence. At one news conference he declared, "I am not a crook."

There the matter might have rested had it not been for the disclosure during the Senate hearings of a White House taping system that had recorded virtually every conversation in the president's office during the period in question. All the various groups investigating the scandals sought access to the tapes; Nixon, pleading "executive privilege," refused to release them. A special prosecutor appointed by the president to handle the Watergate cases, Harvard law professor Archibald Cox, took Nixon to court in October 1973 in an effort to force him to relinquish the recordings. Nixon, now clearly growing desperate, fired Cox and suffered the humiliation of watching both Attorney General Elliot Richardson (who had succeeded Mitchell) and his deputy resign in protest. This "Saturday night massacre" made the president's predicament infinitely worse. Not only did public pressure force him to appoint a new special prosecutor, Texas attorney Leon Jaworski, who proved just as determined as Cox to subpoena the tapes; but the episode precipitated an investigation by the House of Representatives into the possibility of impeachment.

The Fall of Richard Nixon

Nixon's situation deteriorated further in the following months. Late in 1973, Vice President Agnew be-

came embroiled in a scandal of his own, when evidence surfaced that he had accepted bribes and kickbacks while serving as governor of Maryland. In return for a Justice Department agreement not to press the case, Agnew pleaded *nolo contendere* (no contest) to a lesser charge—of income-tax evasion—and resigned from the government. With the controversial Agnew no longer in line to succeed to the presidency, the prospect of removing Nixon from the White House suddenly became far less worrisome to his opponents. The new vice president (the first appointed under the terms of the Twenty-fifth Amendment, which had been adopted in 1967) was House Minority Leader Gerald Ford, an amiable and popular Michigan congressman whom most Nixon critics considered more acceptable. The impeachment investigation quickly gathered pace. In April 1974, in an effort to head off further subpoenas of the tapes, the president released transcripts of a number of relevant conversations, claiming that they proved his innocence. Investigators and much of the public felt otherwise. Even these edited tapes seemed to suggest not only appalling ill will on Nixon's part but also his complicity in the cover-up.

In July, finally, the crisis came to a boil. First the Supreme Court ruled unanimously, in *United States* v. *Richard M. Nixon,* that the president must relinquish the tapes to Special Prosecutor Jaworski. Days later, the House Judiciary Committee voted to recommend three articles of impeachment, charging that Nixon had, first, obstructed justice in the Watergate cover-up; second, misused federal agencies to violate the rights of citizens; and third, defied the authority of Congress by refusing to deliver tapes and other materials subpoenaed by the committee. Even without additional evidence, Nixon might well have been impeached by the full House and convicted by the Senate. Early in August, however, he provided at last the "smoking gun"—the concrete proof of his guilt that his defenders had long contended was missing from the case against him. Among the tapes that the Supreme Court compelled Nixon to relinquish were several that offered incontrovertible evidence of his involvement in the Watergate cover-up. Only days after the burglary, the recordings disclosed, the president had ordered the FBI to stop investigating the break-in. Impeachment and conviction now loomed inevitable.

For several days, Nixon brooded in the White House, on the verge, some claimed, of a mental breakdown. Many of the normal operations of the government ground to a virtual halt as the nation

SIGNIFICANT EVENTS

1962	Students for a Democratic Society formed at Port Huron, Michigan
	Supreme Court decides *Baker* v. *Carr*
1963	Betty Friedan publishes *The Feminine Mystique*
1964	Free Speech Movement begins at UC Berkeley
	Beatles come to America
1965	United Farm Workers strike
1966	National Organization for Women (NOW) formed
	Miranda v. *Arizona* expands rights of criminal suspects
1967	Antiwar protestors march on Pentagon
	Israel and Arabs clash in Six-Day War
1968	Campus riots break out at Columbia and elsewhere
	Antiwar "mobilization" day
	American Indian Movement (AIM) launched
	Nuclear nonproliferation treaty signed
1969	Antiwar movement stages Vietnam "moratorium"
	Theodore Roszak publishes *The Making of a Counter Culture*
	Nixon orders secret bombing of Cambodia
	Nixon begins withdrawing American troops from Vietnam
1970	American troops enter Cambodia
	Antiwar protests increase; students killed at Kent State and Jackson State universities
	Palestinians expelled from Jordan
1971	Pentagon Papers published

1971	Supreme Court decides *Swann* v. *Charlotte-Mecklenburg Board of Education*
	Nixon imposes wage-price freeze and controls
1972	Congress approves Equal Rights Amendment
	Nixon visits China
	SALT I treaty signed
	United States mines Haiphong harbor in North Vietnam
	Nixon orders "Christmas bombing" of North Vietnam
	Supreme Court decides *Furman* v. *Georgia*
	Burglary interrupted in Watergate office building
	Nixon reelected president
1973	Indians demonstrate at Wounded Knee
	Supreme Court decides *Roe* v. *Wade*
	Paris accords produce cease-fire, American withdrawal from Vietnam
	Israel and Arabs clash in Yom Kippur War
	Arab oil embargo produces first American energy crisis
	Watergate scandal expands
1974	Impeachment proceedings begin against Nixon
	Vice President Spiro Agnew resigns; Gerald Ford appointed to replace him
	Nixon resigns; Ford becomes president
1975	South Vietnam falls
	Khmer Rouge seize control of Cambodia
1978	Vietnam invades Cambodia
	Supreme Court hands down *Bakke* decision
1982	Equal Rights Amendment fails

waited tensely for a resolution of the greatest constitutional crisis since Reconstruction. Finally, on August 8, 1974, Nixon addressed the nation and announced his resignation—the first president in American history ever to do so. At noon the next day, while Nixon and his family were flying west to their home in California, Gerald Ford took the oath of office as president.

Americans expressed both relief and exhilaration that, as the new president put it, "Our long national nightmare is over." They were relieved to be rid of Richard Nixon, who had lost virtually all of the wide popularity that had won him his landslide reelection victory only two years before. And they were exhil-

arated that, as some boasted, "the system had worked." A president had been held accountable to the law, and the transfer of power had been smooth and orderly. But the wave of good feeling could not obscure the deeper and more lasting damage of the Watergate crisis. In a society in which distrust of leaders and of institutions of authority was already widespread, the fall of Richard Nixon seemed to confirm the most cynical assumptions about the character of American public life. The depths of that cynicism were evident in the widespread belief, documented in public-opinion polls, that what Nixon had done, bad as it was, was little worse than what other presidents had done undetected before him.

SUGGESTED READINGS

Culture and Society   For an overview of social and cultural developments of the late 1960s and early 1970s, see William O'Neill, *Coming Apart* (1971); Ronald Berman, *America in the Sixties* (1968); Milton Viorst, *Fire in the Streets* (1979); and Morris Dickstein, *Gates of Eden* (1977). Allan J. Matusow, *The Unraveling of America* (1984), offers a particularly useful picture of the social turbulence of the era. For an examination of the New Left, see Todd Gitlin, *The Whole World Is Watching* (1981); Irwin Unger, *The Movement* (1974); Lawrence Lader, *Power on the Left* (1979); Kirkpatrick Sale, *SDS* (1973); and Peter Clecak, *Radical Paradoxes* (1973). Kenneth Keniston, *Young Radicals* (1968), and Lewis Feuer, *The Conflict of Generations* (1969), are also useful. Sources for examining the counterculture include Paul Goodman, *Growing Up Absurd* (1960), one of the early statements of its philosophy; Theodore Roszak, *The Making of a Counter Culture* (1969), a ringing defense; Charles Reich, *The Greening of America* (1970), an influential contemporary work; and Ronald Berman, *America in the Sixties* (1968), a hostile view. For provocative reflections on the mood of the counterculture, see Joan Didion, *Slouching Towards Bethlehem* (1967) and *The White Album* (1979). Other important works on the political and cultural climate of the era include John Diggins, *The American Left in the Twentieth Century* (1973), and Richard Flacks, *Youth and Social Change* (1971).

Indians and Hispanics   On the issue of American Indians, see Wilcomb Washburn, *Red Man's Land/White Man's Land* (1971); Vine Deloria, Jr., *Behind the Trail of Broken Treaties* (1974) and *Custer Died for Your Sins* (1969); D'Arcy McNickle, *Native American Tribalism* (1973); Stan Steiner, *The New Indians* (1968); and Peter Iverson, *The Navajo Nation* (1981). A survey of the history of Hispanic Americans is Rodolfo Acuña, *Occupied America,* 2nd ed. (1981). See also Julian Samora, *Los Mojados* (1971); Oscar Lewis, *La Vida* (1969); and Matt Meier and Feliciano Rivera, *The Chicanos* (1972). Ronald Taylor, *Chavez and the Farm Workers* (1975), considers the labor struggles of Mexican-Americans.

Feminism   Literature on the contemporary women's movement includes William Chafe, *The American Woman* (1972), which traces feminism back to the 1920s; Sheila Rothman, *Woman's Proper Place* (1978), which examines women's roles since the turn of the century; Jo Freeman, *The Politics of Women's Liberation* (1975); Sara Evans, *Personal Politics* (1979); and Gayle Yates, *What Women Want* (1975). The book that helped launch the movement is Betty Friedan, *The Feminine Mystique* (1963). Carol Gilligan, *In a Different Voice* (1982), is an influential theoretical work that has suggested new directions for feminism. Alice Kessler-Harris, *Out to Work: A History of Wage-Earning Women in the United States* (1982), includes attention to postwar employment patterns. Robin Morgan (ed.), *Sisterhood Is Powerful* (1970), is a useful collection of feminist writings and statements. Ethel Klein, *Gender Politics* (1984), explains how women's concerns created a political movement. Kristin

Luker, *Abortion and the Politics of Motherhood* (1984), is a sensitive discussion of one of the most important contemporary controversies.

Nixon and the World   Robert S. Litwak, *Détente and the Nixon Doctrine: American Foreign Policy and the Pursuit of Stability* (1984), is an interpretive overview. On the Nixon-Kissinger policies in Southeast Asia, see (in addition to the general works on the war cited in the readings for Chapter 30) Kissinger's memoirs, *White House Years* (1979), for a defense. More hostile are Gareth Porter, *A Peace Denied* (1975), and William Shawcross, *Sideshow: Nixon, Kissinger, and the Destruction of Cambodia* (1978), a controversial attack. General studies of the Nixon-Kissinger foreign policy, in addition to Kissinger's memoirs, include Roger Morris, *Uncertain Greatness* (1977), and Seyom Brown, *The Crises of Power* (1979). On Kissinger himself, see David Landau, *Kissinger: The Uses of Power* (1972); Marvin Kalb and Bernard Kalb, *Kissinger* (1974); and Seymour Hersh, *The Price of Power* (1983), a harsh attack. Kissinger's second volume of memoirs, *Years of Upheaval* (1982), discusses the period 1973–1975. Other relevant works include Tad Szulc, *The Illusion of Peace* (1978), and Roger Hilsman, *The Crouching Future* (1975). On arms control and détente, see Harland Moulton, *From Superiority to Parity* (1973), and John Newhouse, *Cold Dawn* (1973), on SALT I. John Stockwell, *In Search of Enemies* (1977), and Thomas Powers, *The Man Who Kept the Secrets* (1979), examine the CIA. The changing Sino-American relationship is the subject of Michel Oksenberg and Robert Oxnam (eds.), *Dragon and Eagle* (1978). William Quandt, *Decade of Decision* (1977), and Robert Stookey, *America and the Arab States* (1975), discuss the United States and the Middle East.

Nixon's Domestic Policies   William Safire, *Before the Fall* (1975), is an insider's view of the White House before Watergate. See Daniel P. Moynihan, *The Politics of a Guaranteed Income* (1973), and Vincent Burke and Vee Burke, *Nixon's Good Deed* (1974), on welfare reform. R. L. Miller, *The New Economics of Richard Nixon* (1972), and R. P. Nathan et al., *Monitoring Revenue Sharing* (1975), examine economic policy and the New Federalism. John Ehrlichman, *Witness to Power* (1982), is a memoir by Nixon's chief domestic adviser. In *The Brethren* (1980) Bob Woodward and Scott Armstrong offer a gossipy but revealing picture of the Nixon Court. Theodore H. White, *The Making of the President, 1972* (1973), is an admiring account of Nixon's triumphant reelection. The changing economic climate is examined in Richard Barnet, *The Lean Years* (1980), a controversial study of scarcity. Barry Bluestone and Bennett Harrison, The *Deindustrialization of America* (1982); and Joan Edelman Spero, *The Politics of International Economic Relations* (1977). J. C. Hurewitz (ed.), *Oil, the Arab-Israeli Dispute, and the Industrial World* (1976), examines the energy crisis.

Nixon and Watergate   Richard Nixon's personality and character attracted intensive attention even before Watergate. A particularly interesting study is Garry Wills, *Nixon Agonistes* (1970). Fawn Brodie, *Richard Nixon* (1981), and Bruce Mazlish, *In Search of Nixon* (1972), are psychological portraits. Jonathan Schell, *The Time of Illusion* (1975), is a provocative interpretation placing Watergate in the context of the larger history of the Nixon administration and the Vietnam War. Nixon's own account, *RN: The Memoirs of Richard Nixon* (1978), covers many aspects of his presidency and offers a defense of his actions in the Watergate crisis. Theodore H. White, *Breach of Faith* (1975), and Anthony Lukas, *Nightmare* (1976), are general studies of the Watergate scandals. For a personal account by the reporters who first broke the Watergate story, see Bob Woodward and Carl Bernstein, *All the President's Men* (1974). *The Final Days* (1976), by the same authors, chronicles Nixon's last days in the White House. John Dean, *Blind Ambition* (1976), is the most revealing of the many Watergate memoirs by members of the Nixon administration, although its veracity is challenged in the Ehrlichman memoir cited above. Richard Cohen and Jules Witcover, *A Heartbeat Away* (1974), chronicles the fall of Spiro T. Agnew. A broad study of the expanding powers of the presidency, culminating in a review of Watergate, is Arthur M. Schlesinger, Jr., *The Imperial Presidency* (1973).

Fireworks at the Statue of Liberty Centennial, July 4, 1986 (Wesley Frank/Woodfin Camp & Associates)

Chapter 32 # Confusion and Conservatism

The years after 1974 inflicted still more damaging blows to the confident, optimistic nationalism of the early 1960s. The war in Vietnam and the Watergate crisis had already brought disrepute to the institution Americans had earlier made central to their hopes: the presidency. The problems of the economy, which grew steadily more serious in the second half of the 1970s, cast doubt on the assumption that abundance was a natural and permanent feature of American life. Growing international frustrations—the fall of Vietnam in 1975, the traumatic hostage crisis in Iran beginning late in 1979, the Russian invasion of Afghanistan a few weeks later, the spread of international terrorism, the acceleration of the arms race—and the apparent inability of the United States to do anything about them raised questions about the nation's capacity to control, or even significantly influence, the course of world affairs. For a time in the late 1970s, many feared that American society was losing faith in its future. Others celebrated the arrival of an "age of limits," in which a more "mature" America would learn to live within increasingly constricted boundaries—reining in both its economic expectations and its projection of power in the world.

By the end of the decade, however, the contours of another response to these challenges was beginning to become visible in both American culture and American politics. It was a response that combined a conservative retreat from some of the heady visions of the 1960s with a reinforced commitment to the idea of economic growth, international power, and American exceptionalism. The same fervent belief in the nation's special virtues that had fueled the liberal crusades of the New Frontier and the Great Society became the basis for the Reagan administration's commitment to a reduced federal presence in national life and a more forceful American role in the world. At the same time, many Americans seemed to be embracing a new cultural outlook that focused less on the direction of society than on the hopes of the individual. The United States was attempting, in short, to reconcile its continuing anxieties about the future with a reaffirmation of its traditional faith in its virtues and capacities.

Whether such efforts were suitable to the realities of American society in the 1970s and 1980s was a more difficult question to answer. For the complexity and diversity that had always characterized the United States were in these years reaching new dimensions. The new celebratory public spirit of the 1980s was, it seemed, not just a rejection of the criticisms and doubts of earlier years; it was a defense against the troubling realities of a society in the midst of bewildering change.

Politics and Diplomacy After Watergate

The Watergate crisis—and the war in Vietnam, which had helped produce that crisis—shook the nation's confidence in its elected leaders; and in the aftermath of Richard Nixon's ignominious departure from office, many wondered whether faith in the presidency, and in the government as a whole, could be easily restored. The administrations of the two presidents

921

who succeeded Nixon did little to answer those questions.

The Ford Custodianship

Gerald Ford inherited the presidency under unenviable circumstances. He had to try to rebuild confidence in the presidency in the face of the widespread cynicism the Watergate scandals had unleashed. And he had to try to revive a stable prosperity in the face of increasing domestic and international challenges to the American economy. He enjoyed modest success in the first of these efforts but very little in the second.

Few Americans considered Ford a brilliant or exceptionally skillful leader. But for a time, his candor and unpretentiousness—and the apparent contrast those qualities provided to his predecessor—won him wide popularity. Polls showed that nearly three quarters of the nation approved his performance during his first weeks in office. But the new president's effort to establish himself as a symbol of political integrity suffered a severe setback only a month after his inauguration when he suddenly granted Richard Nixon "a full, free, and absolute pardon . . . for all offenses against the United States" during his presidency. Ford explained that he was attempting to spare the nation the ordeal of years of litigation and to spare Nixon himself any further suffering. It was, he insisted, an act of "compassion," an effort "to firmly shut and seal this book." To much of the public, however, it seemed evidence of bad judgment at best and a secret deal with the former president at worst. Ford defended the pardon decision vigorously, even appearing before a congressional committee to explain it. But his action caused a decline in his popularity from which he never fully recovered.

Nevertheless, relatively few Americans actively disliked Gerald Ford in the way so many had come to dislike Lyndon Johnson and Richard Nixon. Most believed him to be a decent man, even if many considered him a weak leader. He liked to make his own breakfast, to take skiing vacations with his family, and to mingle with his former congressional colleagues. His attractive and outspoken wife, Betty, became one of the most active and popular first ladies in recent history. Ford's honesty and amiability did much to reduce the bitterness and acrimony of the Watergate years.

The Ford administration enjoyed less success in its effort to deal with the other challenge it inherited:

Ford Addresses Congress
Gerald Ford assumed office amid a wave of good feeling, and he moved quickly to calm the tensions of the Watergate crisis. His own popularity, however, suffered a series of rapid blows as he antagonized groups on both the left and the right. His pardon of Richard Nixon enraged many Democrats. His appointment to the vice presidency of former New York Governor Nelson Rockefeller (shown here during a presidential address to Congress seated behind the president, and next to House Speaker Thomas P. O'Neill) outraged the Republican right, which had long resented Rockefeller for his refusal to support Barry Goldwater in 1964. (Dennis Brack/Black Star)

reversing the decline in the American economy. In particular, the president was unable to devise an effective strategy to deal with the related problems of inflation and energy.

In his efforts to curb inflation, the president rejected the idea of wage and price controls and called instead for voluntary efforts. He appeared at one press conference wearing a large button with the word "WIN" emblazoned across it—a symbol, he said, of his new campaign to "Whip Inflation Now." The

WIN campaign had no discernible effect on the economy and invited wide public ridicule. Of somewhat greater impact was the administration's pursuit of the familiar path of tightening the money supply to curb inflation and then struggling to deal with the recession that resulted. By supporting high interest rates, opposing increased federal spending (largely by use of presidential vetoes), and resisting pressures for a tax reduction, Ford helped produce in 1974 and 1975 the severest recession since the 1930s. Production declined more than 10 percent in the first months of 1975, and unemployment rose to nearly 9 percent of the labor force. There was a temporary abatement of inflation, which dropped briefly below 5 percent in 1976; but by then, the administration was already beginning to reverse its course and support new measures to stimulate the economy.

Complicating these problems was the expanding energy crisis. In the aftermath of the Arab oil embargo of 1973, the OPEC cartel began dramatically and suddenly to raise the price of oil—a 400 percent increase in 1974 alone. At the same time, American dependence on OPEC supplies continued to grow. By 1976, the United States was importing almost a third of its energy supply from OPEC. That was one of the principal reasons why inflation in that year reached 11 percent. The Ford administration responded as tentatively to the energy crisis as it did to the problem of inflation. It imposed a few new regulations to force energy conservation, but to little effect. More important to its strategy was the proposed deregulation of the petroleum industry, which would have allowed American oil companies to charge more for their energy so as to encourage increased domestic production. The Democratic Congress resisted such proposals.

Seeking International Stability

At first it seemed that the foreign policy of the new administration would differ little from that of its predecessor. The new president retained Henry Kissinger as secretary of state and continued the general policies of seeking rapprochement with China, détente with the Soviet Union, and stability in the Middle East. For a time, there were signs of progress in all these areas.

In particular, there appeared to be major progress in the effort to produce another arms control agreement with the Soviet Union. Ford met with Leonid Brezhnev late in 1974 at Vladivostok in Siberia and signed a new arms control accord that was to serve as the basis for SALT II. The following summer, a European security conference in Helsinki, Finland, produced an agreement that seemed to advance détente even further. The Soviet Union and Western nations agreed, at last, to ratify the borders that had divided Europe since the end of World War II; and, particularly important in American eyes, the Russians accepted the so-called Basket Three clause, which pledged increased respect for human rights. In the Middle East, in the meantime, the tireless efforts of Henry Kissinger produced important results. After months of shuttling back and forth between Cairo and Tel Aviv, Kissinger announced a major new accord by which Israel agreed to return large portions of the occupied Sinai to Egypt, and the two nations pledged not to resolve future differences by force. In China, finally, the death of Mao Zedong in 1976 brought to power a new, more moderate government, eager to expand its ties with the United States.

But these successes came in the midst of mounting frustrations. The new relationship with the Soviet Union was already showing signs of wear by 1975. And at least equally disturbing was a pattern of defeats and embarrassments in other areas of the world. South Vietnam and Cambodia fell to the communists in 1975, underscoring the futility of years of American effort. (See above, pp. 902–903.) Arab nations that had once treated the United States with deference were now defying Western oil companies, raising petroleum prices, and threatening to reduce production. And other Third World countries were becoming increasingly vocal in attacking the United States; the United Nations became a particularly visible (and to many Americans, particularly galling) forum for those who wished to denounce American policies. Humiliation seemed to pile on humiliation, until the government felt obliged to respond.

When members of the Cambodian Khmer Rouge (the brutal communist organization that had seized control of the nation in 1975) captured an unarmed American merchant ship, the *Mayaguez,* in the spring of 1975, the administration's patience seemed finally to snap. Ford sent in marines to rescue the crew, even though the captors had by then already agreed to release them. This display of American force appealed to the nation's wounded sense of pride, but critics insisted that it also caused the death of several dozen American servicemen unnecessarily. At about the same time, the new American ambassador to the United Nations, Daniel Patrick Moynihan, launched his own campaign to restore American pride. His harsh counterattack against Third World delegates and his open denunciations of the United Nations itself won him great popularity (and, in 1976, a United States Senate seat from New York).

The Election of 1976

As the 1976 presidential election approached, Ford's policies were coming under attack from both the right and the left. In the Republican primary campaign, Ford faced a powerful challenge from Ronald Reagan, former governor of California and leader of the party's conservative wing. Ford only barely survived the assault, in part because he agreed to abandon Nelson Rockefeller, former governor of New York, whom he had appointed vice president in 1974, and choose a running mate less troubling to the right: Senator Robert Dole of Kansas.

The Democrats, in the meantime, were experiencing problems of their own. The McGovern fiasco of 1972 had left the party numb and confused, and there was little agreement in 1976 about who could best appeal to the troubled electorate. From this disarray emerged a new candidate almost entirely unknown to the nation at large: Jimmy Carter, a former governor of Georgia, who organized a brilliant primary campaign and appealed to the general unhappiness with government by offering honesty, piety, and an outsider's skepticism of the federal government. Capitalizing on the momentum of his early primary victories, Carter secured the Democratic nomination before most Americans had developed any very distinct impression of him. His campaign continued after the convention to emphasize "themes"—integrity, compassion, morality—rather than issues. And although the tentativeness of Carter's support became clear when his early, mammoth lead dwindled to almost nothing by election day, unhappiness with the economy and a general disenchantment with Ford enabled the Democrat to hold on for a narrow victory. Despite an unusually low voter turnout, which most observers believed was helpful to the Republicans, Carter emerged with 50 percent of the popular vote to Ford's 47.9 percent and 297 electoral votes to Ford's 241.

The Trials of Jimmy Carter

It was Jimmy Carter's misfortune to assume the presidency at a moment when the nation faced problems

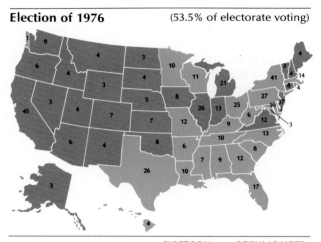

Election of 1976　　(53.5% of electorate voting)

	ELECTORAL VOTE	POPULAR VOTE (%)
Jimmy Carter (Democratic)	297	40,828,587 (50.0)
Gerald R. Ford (Republican)	240	39,147,613 (47.9)
Ronald Reagan (Independent Republican)	1	—
Other candidates McCarthy (Ind.), Libertarian	—	1,575,459 (2.1)

of staggering complexity and difficulty. No leader could have avoided antagonizing much of the public under such inhospitable circumstances. But Carter seemed at times to make his predicament worse by a style of leadership that evoked little popular enthusiasm and, as time went on, increasing derision. He left office in 1981 as one of the least popular presidents of the century.

Carter had campaigned for the presidency as an "outsider," a representative of ordinary Americans who were deeply suspicious of the entrenched bureaucracies and complacent officials who had dominated American government for decades. He carried much of that suspiciousness with him to Washington. He surrounded himself in the White House with a group of close-knit associates from Georgia; and in the beginning, at least, he seemed deliberately to spurn assistance from more experienced political figures. Carter was among the most intelligent, quick-witted, and hard-working men ever to serve in the White House; but his critics charged that he provided no overall vision or direction to his administration. Although he took firm and often courageous stands on individual issues, he often seemed not to recognize how such issues were linked together. His was, as a disenchanted member of his own White House staff later described it, a peculiarly "passionless presidency."

In the absence of any clear set of guiding principles (beyond a strong and openly expressed Christian piety), Carter seemed at times to rely almost exclusively on the use of symbols. On inauguration day,

Jimmy and Rosalynn Carter, January 20, 1977

Jimmy Carter startled the crowds (and alarmed the Secret Service) on his Inauguration Day by walking down Pennsylvania Avenue from the Capitol to the White House after taking the oath of office. Not since Jefferson, whose effort to identify with the "common man" Carter hoped to emulate, had a president walked in his inaugural parade.   (Owen Franken/Sygma)

he spurned the traditional limousine and walked with his family down Pennsylvania Avenue from the Capitol to the White House; and he continued these populist gestures in the following months. To explain a new policy, he arranged a televised "fireside chat"; dressed informally in a cardigan sweater, the president spoke to the nation while seated in a wing chair beside a blazing fire. On several occasions, he visited small communities, attended town meetings, and spent the night in the homes of ordinary citizens. From time to time, he participated in radio programs during which members of the public could telephone the White House and speak directly with the president.

Carter's perceived lack of purpose gradually helped make him the target of criticism from almost every quarter. No political faction could be certain that the new president was its ally. Liberals began to complain that he was more conservative than his Republican predecessors. Conservatives, who had taken heart at Carter's antigovernment campaign rhetoric, expressed scorn for his failure adequately to "tame" the federal bureaucracy. Even when Carter adopted a policy to the liking of a particular group, there was always an uneasy sense that the policy might soon be abandoned if political pressures dictated a different approach. Ultimately the president, who had won election by a narrow margin to begin with, lost almost all leverage in his dealings with Congress. So low was his popularity with the public through most of his term that few legislators feared the political costs of opposing him.

In spite of these problems, Carter did achieve a measure of success in his effort to reform and reorganize the federal government. He instituted a series of important reforms in the civil service, in an effort to make permanent government employees more responsive to the needs of the public and to give administrators more control over their staffs. He reshuffled many of the offices and agencies that had been springing up, often chaotically, for nearly two decades. And he created two new executive departments: the Department of Energy and the Department of Education. He also sponsored a reform of the Social Security system that provided it with at least a temporary reprieve from bankruptcy.

In other areas, Carter made genuine efforts to pursue reform, only to fall victim to congressional opposition. He proposed a major restructuring of the federal welfare system during his first year in office, only to see it die quietly in Congress. He introduced measures to reform the tax system, one of his most conspicuous campaign promises, but proved powerless to keep them from being gutted by special-interest groups. Carter's own political errors contributed to these failures. But there is room for doubt as to whether any leader, working in the confused political climate in which Carter was operating, would have fared much better in confronting these controversial issues.

Energy and the Economy

Like his two immediate predecessors, Carter devoted the bulk of his domestic efforts to the problems of the economy, which remained linked to the problems of energy. Entering office in the midst of a severe recession, Carter moved first to reduce unemployment through an increase in public spending for public works and public services and a substantial cut in federal taxes. Unemployment soon began to decline—from nearly 8 percent late in 1976 to slightly above 5 percent by the end of 1978. But inflation in the meantime soared. The Ford administration had left behind an inflation rate of slightly under 5 percent per year. In 1977, it rose to 7 percent, and in 1978 to nearly 10 percent. During Carter's last two years in office, things grew even worse, with inflation averaging well over 10 percent ("double-digit inflation," it began to be called) and at one point in 1980 reaching as high as 18 percent.

Like Nixon and Ford before him, Carter responded with a combination of tight money and calls for voluntary restraint. He appointed first G. William Miller and then Paul Volcker, conservative economists both, to head the Federal Reserve Board, thus ensuring a policy of high interest rates and reduced currency supplies. By 1980, interest rates had risen to the highest levels in American history; at times, they exceeded 20 percent. And although he introduced nothing as easily ridiculed as Gerald Ford's WIN program, he too created a voluntary and generally ineffective system of wage and price "restraint," to be administered through the Council on Wage and Price Stability. Its director, Alfred Kahn, became an energetic and articulate spokesman for fiscal caution, helping to elevate public awareness of the inflation problem. But neither Kahn's efforts nor any other aspects of the administration's policy succeeded in stopping the inflationary spiral.

The president also attempted to bring the federal budget into balance. Some economists claimed that a balanced budget was a prerequisite to price stability; others argued that it would only marginally reduce inflation. But the argument was never resolved because the president never managed to eliminate the deficits. He cut back on some areas of government spending and vetoed some of the same public works and welfare proposals he had supported during his first year in office. He reduced and delayed the tax cuts he had earlier proposed. But most of the growth in federal spending was a result of factors over which the president had relatively little control—particularly the rising cost of welfare and entitlement programs that had been created by earlier administrations. The federal deficit in the Carter years ranged from a low of just under $28 billion in 1979 to a high of just under $60 billion in 1980.

Closely tied to the problem of inflation was the problem of energy, which grew steadily more troublesome in the course of the Carter years. One of the president's first acts was to present to the public what he called a "comprehensive energy program," whose success, he insisted, was vital to the nation's future. Solving the energy problem, he claimed (in words borrowed from the philosopher William James), was "the moral equivalent of war." But the specific features of the Carter plan—which relied largely on energy conservation—were less dramatic than the rhetoric; and Congress took this already modest program and gutted it. The energy bill it passed in 1978 was almost entirely without substance or effect.

In the summer of 1979, the energy battle moved into a new and more desperate phase. Increasing instability in the Middle East produced a second major fuel shortage, forcing American motorists to wait in long gasoline lines once again and creating problems for businesses, industries, and homeowners. In the midst of the crisis, OPEC announced another major price increase, clouding the economic picture still further. Faced with increasing pressure to act (and with public-opinion polls showing his approval rating at a dismal 26 percent—lower than that of Richard Nixon in his worst moments), Carter canceled a planned television address, went to the presidential retreat Camp David in the Maryland mountains, and invited a string of visitors to advise him—not only on a new energy program but on the revitalization of his administration as a whole.

Ten days later, he emerged to deliver a remarkable television address. It included a series of proposals for resolving the energy crisis (including the creation of a vast new synthetic fuels industry to reduce American reliance on imported oil). But the speech was most notable for Carter's broad assess ment of the national condition. Speaking with unusual fervor, he complained of a "crisis of confidence" that had reduced the nation to confusion and despair and had struck "at the very heart and soul of our national will." The address became known as the "malaise" speech (although Carter himself had never used that word), and it helped fuel later charges that the president was trying to blame his own problems on the American people.

Human Rights and National Interests

Among Jimmy Carter's most frequent campaign promises was a pledge to build a new basis for American foreign policy, one in which the defense of "human rights" would replace the pursuit of "selfish interests" as the cornerstone of America's role in the world. Rhetorically, at least, Carter maintained that commitment during his first months in office, speaking out sharply and often about violations of human rights in many countries (including, most prominently, the Soviet Union) and establishing an Office of Human Rights in the State Department.

Beyond the general commitment to establishing a new "tone" for American foreign policy, the Carter administration focused on several areas of particular concern—the same areas, essentially, that had been the focus of the Kissinger era. (As efforts on behalf of these specific goals began to conflict at numerous points with the emphasis on human rights, the president often retreated from his concern with the rights issue.) Carter's first major diplomatic accomplishment was the completion of negotiations on a pair of treaties that would turn over control of the Panama Canal to the government of Panama. In exchange for Panamanian agreement to maintain the neutrality of the canal, the United States would gradually hand over the Canal Zone, which it had administered since Theodore Roosevelt's bold maneuvers at the beginning of the century, to Panama. Domestic opposition to the treaties was intense, especially among conservatives, who viewed the new arrangements as part of a general American retreat from international power. Supporters argued that control of the canal by the United States had become the source of deep resentment in Central America. Relinquishing it was the best way to improve relations with the region and avoid the possibility of years of violence. After an acrimonious debate, the Senate ratified the treaties by a vote of 68 to 32, only one vote more than the necessary two-thirds.

Less controversial, within the United States at least, was Carter's dramatic success in arranging a peace treaty between Egypt and Israel—the crowning diplomatic accomplishment of his presidency. Inheriting from Henry Kissinger a negotiating process that seemed hopelessly stalled, Carter tried at first to arouse support for a "comprehensive" settlement of the Middle Eastern crisis through an international conference in Geneva. The response from the nations involved was not heartening. It fell to the Egyptian president, Anwar Sadat, and the Israeli prime minister, Menachem Begin, therefore, to initiate the first great breakthrough. In November 1977, accepting a formal invitation from Begin, Sadat flew to Tel Aviv for a dramatic state visit, declaring in the course of it that Egypt was now willing to accept the state of Israel as a legitimate political entity. With that, the greatest single obstacle to peace between the two nations—the obstacle that had frustrated nearly thirty years of diplomatic efforts—was removed.

There remained, however, the tortuous task of translating these good feelings into a concrete treaty of peace. When talks between Israeli and Egyptian negotiators stalled, Carter invited Sadat and Begin to a summit conference at Camp David in September 1978, holding them there for two weeks while he, Secretary of State Cyrus Vance, and others mediated the disputes between them. On September 17, Carter escorted the two leaders into the White House to announce agreement on a "framework" for an Egyptian-Israeli peace treaty. Final agreement, the two sides promised, would be completed within three months.

In the months that followed, the euphoria of the Camp David summit faded as new obstacles to the treaty seemed to emerge almost daily, a result in part of the insistence of the Begin government that Israel continue to establish new settlements in the disputed territory of the West Bank of the Jordan River (which Israel had seized during the 1967 war and which some displaced Palestinian Arabs hoped might become a new homeland for them). Only after Carter himself had intervened again, persuading Sadat to agree to a postponement of resolution of the sensitive Palestinian refugee issue, did the negotiations finally bear fruit. On March 26, 1979, Begin and Sadat returned together to the White House to sign a formal peace treaty between their two nations in the presence of Jimmy Carter, whose personal diplomacy had been largely responsible for the moment.

Carter's efforts to produce a settlement were an expression, in some respects, of American strength.

But they were also a sign of American weakness, for peace in the Middle East was as important to the United States as it was to the nations of the region. Another Arab-Israeli war, accompanied by another oil embargo, would pose grave dangers to the American economy. Nor was the treaty a final solution to the problems of the area. Other Arab nations reacted with hostility—not only toward Egypt and Israel but toward the United States as well.

In the first years after the signing of the treaty, tensions in the region escalated further. The assassination of Anwar Sadat by dissident Egyptian fundamentalists in 1981 complicated the peace process; Sadat's successor, Hosni Mubarak, almost immediately gave signs of renewed interest in restoring Egypt's ties to the rest of the Arab world. The unyielding stance of the Israeli government—which officially annexed several disputed territories in 1981 and continued to refuse to make any important concessions to the Palestinians—further fueled antagonisms in the region. Although Israel lived up to its treaty agreement and in April 1982 returned to Egypt the territories of the Sinai, which Israel had captured in 1967, the exchange seemed at the time less the culmination of a successful peace process than its dying gasp.

Great-Power Diplomacy

In the meantime, Carter attempted to continue progress toward improving relations with China and the Soviet Union and toward completing a new arms control agreement. The new relationship with China progressed rapidly during 1978, as Chinese leader Deng Xiaoping began concerted efforts to change the rigid policies of the late Mao Zedong and open his nation to the outside world. In particular, Deng wanted at least indirect support from the West for China's increasingly tense cold war with the Soviet Union. Carter responded eagerly to Deng's overtures; and on December 15, 1978, Washington and Beijing issued a joint communiqué announcing the restoration of formal diplomatic relations between the two nations as of January 1, 1979. In March 1979, America and China exchanged ambassadors.

Only a few months later, Carter traveled to Vienna to meet with Brezhnev, who was visibly ailing, to complete the final steps in the drafting of SALT II. Lower-level negotiators had been working for months to resolve remaining differences; and in Vienna, the Soviet and American leaders took the final step—settling the last details, signing the documents, and clasping each other in a warm embrace. The treaty set limits on the number of long-range missiles, bombers, and nuclear warheads on each side—limits that some critics denounced as far too high to constitute meaningful disarmament but that supporters claimed marked an important first step in limiting the construction of new weapons. Future negotiations, the two sides agreed, would work toward actually reducing the existing arsenals.

Almost immediately, however, SALT II met with fierce conservative opposition. A powerful group of Senate Republicans denounced the treaty as excessively favorable to the Soviet Union, citing in particular provisions that restricted development of the American cruise missile while leaving the Soviets free to proceed with their new backfire bomber. Others denounced concessions permitting increases in certain Soviet missile systems that would, they charged, increase an already large Russian advantage in that area. Central to the arguments of the opposition, however, was a larger issue: a fundamental distrust of the Soviet Union that nearly a decade of détente had failed to destroy. Pointing to Soviet activities in Africa, to increasing Russian influence among radical governments in the Middle East, and to allegations of Soviet support of international terrorism, conservatives argued for the "linkage" of arms control agreements with agreements about Soviet behavior in other areas. By the fall of 1979, with the Senate scheduled to begin debate on the treaty shortly, ratification was already in jeopardy. Events in the ensuing months would provide the final blow—both to the treaty and to the larger framework of détente.

The Year of the Hostages

The accumulated frustrations of more than a decade seemed to culminate in the events of the last months of 1979 and the full year that followed. Not since 1968 had the United States experienced such a sense of cascading crisis.

For more than thirty years, the United States had provided political support and, more recently, massive military assistance to the government of the shah of Iran and relied on his regime to provide a bulwark against Soviet expansion in the Middle East. By 1979, however, the shah was in deep trouble with his own people, reaping the harvest of years of brutal and unpopular policies. Iranians resented the repressive, authoritarian tactics through which the

Parading for Khomeini

Iranians staged massive demonstrations on behalf of the Ayatollah Khomeini in Teheran, their capital, in 1979. The ayatollah's militant religiosity and hatred of the West (and of the United States) appealed to fundamentalist Muslims and helped sustain the Iranian revolution. (C. Spengler/Sygma)

shah had maintained his autocratic rule. The SAVAK, the monarch's secret police, which had long made use of torture and arbitrary imprisonment to stifle dissent, aroused particular hatred. At the same time, the shah was earning the animosity of the Islamic clergy (and much of the fiercely religious populace) through his rapid efforts to modernize and Westernize his fundamentalist society. The combination of resentments produced a powerful revolutionary movement; and in January 1979, finally, the shah fled the country for an uncertain exile.

The United States, which had supported the shah unswervingly until very near the end, was caught unawares by his fall from power. The Carter administration was even less aware, apparently, of the deep resentments that the Iranian people continued to harbor toward America, which had become a hated symbol of Western intrusion into their society. The

president made cautious efforts in the first months after the shah's abdication to establish cordial relations with the succession of increasingly militant regimes that followed. By late 1979, however, such efforts were beginning to appear futile. Not only did revolutionary chaos in the nation make any normal relationships impossible, but what formal power there was in Iran resided with a zealous religious leader, the Ayatollah Ruhollah Khomeini, whose hatred of the West in general and the United States in particular seemed deep, abiding, and intense.

The shah spent most of his first months of exile living in Mexico, having been quietly informed that the American government would not welcome his presence in the United States. Late in October, however, the president succumbed to the urgings of several friends of the shah and admitted the monarch to New York, where he entered a hospital for treatment of cancer. Days later, on November 4, 1979, an armed mob invaded the American embassy in Teheran, seized the diplomats and military personnel inside, and held them as hostages—demanding the return of the shah to Iran in exchange for their freedom. Although the militants released a few of the hostages within days, fifty-three Americans remained prisoners in the embassy.

American citizens had been held hostage by foreign governments before. In 1968, eighty-two members of the crew of the *Pueblo,* a navy intelligence-gathering ship, were captured and held prisoner by the government of North Korea. It took eleven months for the Johnson administration to win their release, during which time the American public all but forgot about the problem. But the reaction of the nation to the events in Teheran was radically different. Coming after years of what Americans considered international humiliations and defeats, the hostage seizure released a surprising well of anger and emotion. President Carter, facing a difficult re-election battle, did much to sustain the sense of crisis. But even without his efforts, it was clear, the American people would have reacted strongly. Television newscasts relayed daily pictures of angry anti-American mobs outside the embassy, the faces of many demonstrators contorted with hatred as they chanted such slogans as "Death to America" and "Death to Carter." Contemptuous statements by the militants guarding the hostages that "the U.S. can do nothing" further aroused American passions. The nation responded not only with anger but with remarkable displays of emotional patriotism.

Then, on December 27, 1979, only weeks after the hostage seizure, troops of the Soviet Union invaded Afghanistan, the mountainous country lying between Russia and Iran. The Soviet Union had, in fact, been a power in Afghanistan for years, and the dominant force since April 1978, when a coup had established a Marxist government there with close ties to the Kremlin. The invasion, some Soviet experts argued, was Moscow's response to the failure of that new Afghan government to restore stability to the nation. The Soviets were particularly concerned about the activities of Islamic insurgents, whose presence raised the possibility of a fundamentalist revolution in Afghanistan (and perhaps even in Islamic areas of the Soviet Union itself) similar to the one in progress in Iran.

But while some observers claimed that the Soviet invasion was a Russian attempt to secure the status quo, others—most notably the president—viewed the situation differently. The invasion of Afghanistan, Carter claimed, was a Russian "stepping stone to their possible control over much of the world's oil supplies." It was also the "gravest threat to world peace since World War II." Dire warnings began issuing from the White House about the possibility of a Soviet attack on Iran or other Middle Eastern nations.

Whatever the reasons for the Soviet invasion, the situation in Afghanistan dealt the final blow to the already badly weakened structure of détente. Carter angrily imposed a series of economic sanctions on the Russians, called for an American boycott of the 1980 summer Olympic Games in Moscow, and announced the withdrawal of SALT II from Senate consideration. He also announced a new American policy—what came to be known as the "Carter Doctrine"—by which the United States pledged to oppose, by force if necessary, any further aggression in the Persian Gulf.

The Campaign of 1980

By the time of the crises in Iran and Afghanistan, Jimmy Carter was in desperate political trouble. His standing in popularity polls was lower than that of any president in history. His economic policies were in shambles. Senator Edward Kennedy, one of the most magnetic figures in the Democratic party, was preparing to challenge him in the primaries. The president's position seemed hopeless. But the seizure of the hostages and the stern American response to the Soviet invasion did wonders for Carter's candidacy. His standing in the polls improved dramatically, and his moribund campaign suddenly revived and produced for the president a series of impressive victories in the early primaries.

Carter's troubles, however, were far from over. As month followed month without any discernible progress in efforts to secure the release of the hostages in Iran, public clamor began to build. In April, after the collapse of one round of negotiations, the president ordered a rescue attempt by American commandos. It ended in abject failure when several military helicopters broke down in the desert. Eight commandos died when two aircraft collided during the hasty retreat. Secretary of State Cyrus Vance, who had opposed both the rescue mission and much of the new belligerence in the nation's foreign policy, resigned in protest. Kennedy, in the meantime, managed to revive his flagging campaign and win a series of victories over the president in the later primaries.

Election of 1980   (52.6% of electorate voting)

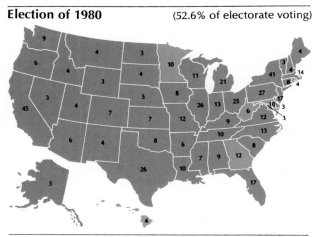

	ELECTORAL VOTE	POPULAR VOTE (%)
Ronald Reagan (Republican)	489	43,901,812 (50.7)
Jimmy Carter (Democratic)	49	35,483,820 (41.0)
John B. Anderson (Independent)	—	5,719,722 (6.6)
Other candidates (Libertarian)	—	921,299 (1.1)

Carter continued to benefit greatly from the many personal controversies surrounding Edward Kennedy (most notably a 1969 automobile accident at Chappaquiddick Island in Massachusetts that had left a young woman dead), and he managed in the end to stave off the challenge and win his party's nomination. But it was an unhappy convention that listened to the president's listless call to arms, and Carter's campaign aroused little enthusiasm from the public at large as he prepared to face a powerful challenge.

The Republican party had, in the meantime, rallied enthusiastically behind a man whom, not many years before, many Americans had considered a dangerous reactionary. But Ronald Reagan, a one-time film actor, a former California governor, and a poised and articulate campaigner, seemed in 1980 to be a man fully in tune with his times. Like Carter before him, he was a strident critic of the excesses of the federal government. More important, he championed a restoration of American "strength," "pride," and international prestige. Although he refrained from

discussing the issue of the hostages, Reagan clearly benefited from the continuing popular unhappiness with Carter's inability to resolve the crisis. In a larger sense, he benefited as well from the accumulated frustrations of more than a decade of domestic and international disappointments.

Election day was the anniversary of the seizure of the hostages in Iran, a fact that was not lost on much of the press and the public. It was also the day on which the conservative forces that had been gathering strength in the nation for more than a decade finally moved to the center of the nation's political life and swept Ronald Reagan to victory in the presidential election. His popular margin was decisive: 50.7 percent of the ballots cast, to 41 percent for Jimmy Carter and 6.6 percent for John Anderson—a moderate Republican congressman who had mounted an independent campaign. Reagan's electoral margin was overwhelming. He swept not only the Western half of the nation, which had been Republican territory for years, but virtually all of the traditional bastions of Democratic strength: the South, the industrial states of the Midwest and Northeast, even such traditionally liberal strongholds as Massachusetts and New York. Carter carried only six states and the District of Columbia, for a total of 49 electoral votes to Reagan's 489. At least as startling was the wave of Republican victories in the congressional races. The party won control of the Senate for the first time since 1952; and although the Democrats retained a diminished majority in the House, the lower chamber too seemed firmly in the hands of conservatives.

At almost the very moment of Reagan's inauguration, the American hostages remaining in Iran were boarding a plane en route to freedom after their 444-day ordeal. Jimmy Carter, in the last hours of his presidency, had concluded months of negotiations by agreeing to release several billion dollars in Iranian assets that he had frozen in American banks shortly after the seizure of the embassy. The government of Iran, desperate for funds to support a floundering war effort against neighboring Iraq, had ordered the hostages freed in return. The next few days produced a virtual orgy of national emotion, as Americans welcomed the hostages home with mingled relief, joy, and anger. Not since the end of World War II had there been such demonstrations of patriotism and celebration. But while the joy in 1945 had marked a great American triumph, the euphoria in 1981 marked something quite different—a troubled nation grasping for reassurance. Ronald Reagan set out to provide it.

The "Reagan Revolution"

Ronald Reagan assumed the presidency in January 1981 promising a change in government more fundamental than any since the New Deal of fifty years before. But while his first six years in office produced a significant shift in public policy, they brought nothing so radical as many of his supporters had hoped or his opponents had feared. The president himself found it prudent at times to moderate his more extreme demands; Congress and the public strongly resisted other conservative initiatives. The Reagan administration won some important legislative victories, but it rarely enjoyed very much freedom of action in either domestic or international affairs.

If the record of the new administration on matters of policy was a mixed one, however, there was no ambiguity about its purely political achievements. Ronald Reagan succeeded brilliantly in making his own engaging personality the central fact of American politics in the 1980s. Few presidents in American history have so effectively captured the imagination of the American public.

Ronald Reagan

Even many people who disagreed with the president's policies found themselves drawn to his attractive and carefully honed public image. Reagan was a master of television, a warm and appealing raconteur, a gifted public speaker, and—in public at least—rugged, fearless, and seemingly impervious to misfortune. He spent vacations on a California ranch, where he chopped wood and rode horses. When he was wounded in an assassination attempt in 1981, he joked

Reagan at the Ranch
Ronald Reagan relaxes at his ranch in the mountains near Santa Barbara, California, demonstrating the informal geniality that accounted for much of his remarkable popularity. (Michael Evans/Sygma)

with doctors on his way into surgery and bounced back from the ordeal with remarkable speed. Four years later, he rebounded from cancer surgery with similar zest. He had few visible insecurities. He seldom displayed the anger or vindictiveness or humorlessness that had plagued his predecessors. Even when things went wrong, as they often did, the blame seemed seldom to attach to Reagan himself (inspiring some journalists to begin referring to the "Teflon presidency"). Reagan managed to stand above the fray, a symbol of America's search to regain confidence in itself.

He had reached the presidency by an unusual route. The product of small-town Illinois and a struggling middle-class family, he spent most of his career in the entertainment business—first as a radio sportscaster, then as a successful film actor, and later as a television show host and corporate spokesman for General Electric. In that last capacity, he began to speak widely on political issues. Although he had once been a New Deal liberal, he had by the early 1950s embraced strong conservative beliefs, absorbed in part through his marriage to Nancy Davis, a powerful and intelligent woman of deep right-wing convictions. Toward the end of the 1964 presidential campaign, Reagan appeared on national television to deliver an eloquent endorsement of Barry Goldwater; his speech established him almost overnight as the new leader of American conservatives.

Two years later, Reagan won a decisive victory over the Democratic incumbent in a race for the governorship of California, and he served two four-year terms. But as early as 1968, he was already eyeing the presidency. He launched a last-minute campaign for the Republican nomination that year—too late to raise an effective challenge to Richard Nixon. In 1976, now out of office, he mounted a strong challenge to Gerald Ford. And in 1980, he captured both the Republican party nomination and the presidency itself. A few weeks after entering office, he celebrated his seventieth birthday. He was the oldest man ever to assume the presidency.

From his first moments in office, Reagan made his personal poise and charisma a central element of his administration's political strategy. He was not, apparently, much involved in the day-to-day affairs of running the government; he surrounded himself with tough, energetic administrators, who insulated him from many of the pressures of the office and apparently relied on him largely for general guidance, not specific decisions. At times, in fact, the president revealed a startling ignorance about the na-

ture of his own policies; aides often had to step in to "clarify" or correct presidential misstatements.

But Reagan did make active use of his office to generate support for his administration's programs—by appealing repeatedly to the public over television, in weekly radio addresses, and through public appearances. He liked to fuse his proposals to a nationalistic rhetoric that seemed perfectly to match the public mood. Nothing so characterized his administration as his increasing appeals to the nation's sense of its own greatness.

The Contours of Reaganism

The Reagan administration was from the beginnning one of the most conservative of the twentieth century. But its conservatism took many different forms, reflecting the range of political ideologies competing for that label in the 1980s.

In some senses, Reagan was a traditional Republican "business" conservative, sympathetic to the desires of the corporate world, eager to ease the burdens and restrictions that he believed previous governments had placed on the wealthy. Reagan and his wife numbered among their closest friends some of the richest men and women in the country. The president's cabinet and other high administration offices were peopled with affluent corporate executives and corporate lawyers. The president's tax policies were designed to give particular benefits to the upper brackets and to reduce drastically the levies on corporations. Conservative Republicans had long argued that people of wealth, people with capital to invest in the economy, were essential to prosperity. The economic policies of the Reagan administration reflected that belief.

Reagan's policies also reflected the ideas of another group of conservatives—many of whom in previous years had considered themselves liberals—who were concerned above all with restoring American resolve to resist radicalism at home and abroad. Often described as "neo-conservatives," they consisted of journalists, academics, intellectuals, and others distraught at what they considered the debasement of American culture by a radical left and the flagging will of the United States (and the West in general) to resist communism. The Reagan administration's foreign policies did not always satisfy their demands, but the president supported their desire for an enormous defense build-up and a much harder public line toward the Soviet Union. The administration also often seemed to embrace their belief in the need for renewed efforts to combat communism in the Third World—efforts that Americans had for a time resisted in the aftermath of Vietnam.

Reagan gave voice as well to the demands of a third group of conservatives, drawn from a wide range of social groups, whose concerns were primarily social. Much of the impetus behind these demands came from fundamentalist Christian groups, whose new political activism had become an important fact of American public life. Other groups, similarly concerned with protecting "basic values" against encroachments from the increasingly secular and—many believed—amoral mainstream culture, also became active on behalf of social issues. (See below, pp. 947–948.) The president supported the campaigns to make abortion illegal, to restore prayer to public schools, to retreat from affirmative action and court-ordered busing, and to defeat the Equal Rights Amendment. Except for the last, the administration witnessed the fulfillment of few of its social goals in its first six years; but the president's rhetorical support for them was important in keeping together the uneasy conservative coalition on which he depended.

Supply-Side Economics

Reagan's 1980 campaign for the presidency had centered on several goals. It had promised to end the drift in American foreign policy and restore the nation's military strength. It had promised to reduce the intrusive influence of government on American life. And it had promised to restore the economy to health by a bold experiment in what became known as "supply-side" economics. It was this last pledge that the new administration attempted to fulfill first and that, initially at least, became the source of its most conspicuous triumphs.

Supply-side economics operated on the assumption that the woes of the American economy were in large part a result of excessive taxation, which siphoned money away from potential investors and thus stifled economic growth. The solution, therefore, was to reduce taxes and to offer particularly generous benefits to corporations and wealthy individuals, in order to encourage new investments. The result would be a general economic revival that would affect all levels of the population. But cutting taxes was only one part of the supply-side program. Because a tax cut would reduce government revenues, it would be necessary also to reduce government expenses. Otherwise, large

federal deficits might negate the effects of the tax cut by requiring the government to borrow in the marketplace, thus raising interest rates and drying up capital for investment once again. A cornerstone of the Reagan economic program, therefore, was a drastic cut in the federal budget, one intended to produce—within four years—a balance between government revenues and expenditures for the first time since 1969.

In his first months in office, Reagan hastily assembled a legislative program that would enact the basic features of the supply-side program. His energetic budget director, David Stockman, proposed cutting some $40 billion in expenditures; and despite grumbling by special interest groups and liberals, and impassioned pleas by constituencies threatened by the loss of social services, the new budget cuts passed through Congress with relative ease, almost in the form the administration had proposed. In addition, the president proposed a bold three-year rate reduction on both individual and corporate taxes. The tax cut encountered more serious opposition in Congress and was subjected to numerous amendments. But in the summer of 1981, it too was passed, generally in the form the administration had proposed. No president since Lyndon Johnson had compiled so impressive a legislative record in his first months in office.

But by early 1982, the Reagan economic program was beset with difficulties. The nation had entered the most severe recession since the Great Depression of the 1930s, with national unemployment approaching 10 percent of the work force. Some regions of the country, most notably the industrial Midwest, had descended into virtual depression conditions. It was not at all clear that the Reagan economic program was to blame for the problems; the causes of the recession stretched well back into the Carter years and before. But a growing number of critics claimed in 1982 that the administration's policies had done nothing to improve the situation and promised ultimately to make things worse.

In fact, however, the economy recovered more rapidly and impressively than almost anyone had expected. By the middle of 1983, unemployment (which had reached nearly 11 percent in 1982, the highest level since the 1930s) had fallen to 8.2 percent. The gross national product was growing at 3.3 percent annually, the highest rate since the mid-1970s. Inflation was below 5 percent. And despite the predictions of many economists that the recovery was weak, erratic, and artificial, the economy continued to flourish through 1984 and 1985. By the beginning of

1986, unemployment had declined to below 7 percent; the stock market had reached record levels; inflation remained under 4 percent; economic growth continued—although there were signs later in 1986 of a significant weakening of economic performance.

The recovery came in part because the administration altered its course and began pressing for a reduction in interest rates and an expansion of the money supply—in effect subordinating concern about inflation (which now seemed under control) to concern about unemployment and declining investment. The recovery was also a result of a radical drop in oil prices, the result of a worldwide "energy glut" that led to the virtual collapse of the OPEC cartel and at least a temporary end to the inflationary pressures of spiraling fuel costs. And the recovery was a result, too, of staggering budget deficits, which pumped billions of dollars into the flagging economy. Those deficits, many believed, also threatened ultimately to destroy the very recovery it was helping to create.

The Fiscal Crisis

By 1986, this growing fiscal crisis had become one of the central issues in American domestic politics. Having entered office promising a balanced budget within four years, Reagan presided over record budget deficits and accumulated more debt in his first four years in office than the American government had accrued in its entire previous history. Prior to the 1980s, the highest single-year budget deficit in American history had been $66 billion (in 1976). In 1982, the federal budget deficit was over $110 billion; in 1983, $195 billion; in 1984, $175 billion; and in 1985, $200 billion. The national debt rose from $907 billion in 1980 to just under $2 trillion in 1986.

Economists and policymakers disagreed over the effect of budget deficits. But even those who had always believed in the value of deficit spending as an economic stimulus found the dimensions of the budget shortfalls of the 1980s alarming. The deficits, economists argued, were keeping interest rates high and threatening to push them higher; the government was forced to borrow so much money itself to pay its bills that it was leaving too little for investors and thus driving up the price of borrowing. Should that continue, new private investment would dry up and the economy would once again sag.

For much the same reason, the deficits were also keeping the American dollar overvalued. With such a high demand for dollars (a result in large part of gov-

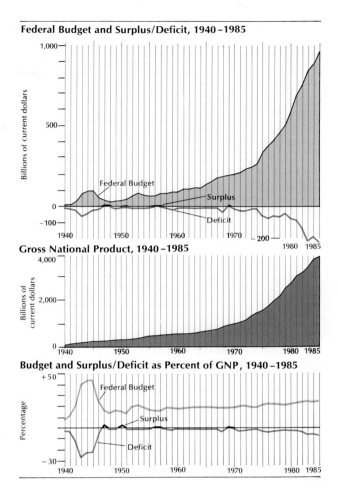

Federal Budget and Surplus/Deficit, 1940–1985

Gross National Product, 1940–1985

Budget and Surplus/Deficit as Percent of GNP, 1940–1985

ernment borrowing), the nation's currency achieved a new and in many ways dangerous strength against the other currencies of the world. The high value of the dollar made it more difficult for foreigners to buy American goods and more tempting for Americans to buy products from overseas. One result was that the American balance of trade grew increasingly unfavorable; between 1980 and 1986, the trade deficit grew from $20 billion to well over $100 billion. A related result was the increasing problems of such fundamental American industries as automobiles and steel, which not only found it difficult to export their goods abroad but faced growing competition within the American market as well.

The enormous deficits had many causes, some of them stretching back over decades of American public policy decisions. But some of the most important causes lay in the policies of the Reagan administration. The 1981 tax cuts, the largest in American history, sharply eroded the revenue base of the federal government and accounted for a large percentage of the deficit. The massive increase in military spending (a proposed $1.6 trillion over five years) on which Reagan and his defense secretary, Caspar Weinberger, fervently insisted added far more to the federal budget than the administration's sharp cuts in domestic spending removed.

In his efforts to reduce the deficit, the president steadfastly refused to consider raising taxes (or even reducing the 25 percent reduction in tax rates he had himself initiated). When he proposed a major tax reform package in 1985, he insisted that it remain "revenue neutral"—that it do nothing to increase the overall tax revenues. He refused to reduce military expenditures (despite rising demands from leaders of both major parties to do so). He resisted any substantial revision of the major "entitlement" programs (Social Security, Medicare, federal and military pensions, and others), whose spiraling costs accounted for a large part of the budget. He could not, by law, reduce the growing proportion of the budget devoted to interest payments on the enormous national debt. Instead, he concentrated largely on reducing the relatively small portion of the budget devoted to "discretionary" domestic spending. By the end of 1985, however, funding for domestic programs had been cut nearly as far as the Congress (and, apparently, the public) were willing to tolerate. The budget process had reached an impasse, and Congress was struggling to find new solutions.

The so-called Gramm-Rudman bill, passed late in 1985, mandated major deficit reductions over five years and provided for automatic budget cuts in all areas of government spending should the president and Congress fail to agree on an alternative solution. It was a drastic plan, of questionable constitutionality; and in the summer of 1986, the Supreme Court struck down one crucial provision of the new law, leaving its future in doubt. But the concept of Gramm-Rudman continued to attract support from leaders of both parties and even, somewhat uneasily, from the president. It was an indication of how deep concerns about the American fiscal crisis had become.

Reagan and the World

Reagan encountered a similar combination of triumphs and difficulties in international affairs. Determined to restore American pride and prestige in the world, he attacked what he claimed was the weakness and "defeatism" of previous administrations, which had allowed Vietnam, Watergate, and other crises to paralyze their will to act. The United States, he argued, should once again become active and assertive in opposing communism throughout the world and in supporting friendly governments whatever their internal policies.

Relations with the Soviet Union, which had been steadily deteriorating in the last years of the Carter administration, grew still more chilly after Reagan took office. Both the president and his first secretary of state, Alexander Haig, spoke harshly of the Soviet regime, accusing it of sponsoring world terrorism and declaring that any armaments negotiations must be linked to negotiations about Soviet behavior in other areas. Relations with the Russians deteriorated further after the government of Poland (under strong pressure from Moscow) imposed martial law on the country in the winter of 1981 to crush a growing challenge from an independent labor organization, Solidarity.

Perhaps the most conspicuous evidence of the new tone of American foreign policy was the president's often strident anti-Soviet rhetoric. The Soviet Union, he once claimed, was the "focus of evil in the world." It was the principal source of international terrorism. Its leaders were willing to "commit any crime, to lie, to cheat" to advance their aims. In 1983, Soviet forces shot down a Korean passenger liner that had strayed into their air space, killing 269 people. The public outrage the attack produced helped reinforce the administration's anti-Sovietism. It also helped produce support for the president's enormous military buildup, which he claimed was necessary to counter a Soviet arms program that had given the communists an advantage over the United States in crucial areas.

Although the president had long denounced SALT-II as unfavorable to the United States, he continued for a time to honor provisions of the agreement. But the Reagan administration made little progress toward arms control in other areas, despite the growing political power of a popular antinuclear movement in both Europe and the United States. In fact, the president proposed the most ambitious new military program in many years: the so-called Strategic Defense Initiative (SDI), widely known as "Star Wars" (after a popular movie of that name). Reagan claimed that SDI, through the use of lasers and satellites, could provide an impenetrable shield against incoming missiles and thus make nuclear war obsolete—a claim that produced considerable skepticism in the scientific community. The Soviet Union reacted with anger and alarm and insisted that the new program would elevate the arms race to new and more dangerous levels. For nearly four years, Soviet leaders insisted that any arms control agreement begin with an American abandonment of SDI; the president refused even to consider it.

Late in 1985, the president traveled to Geneva for a meeting with the new Soviet leader, Mikhail Gorbachev. This first summit in more than six years was a cordial (and widely publicized) affair. But it produced no agreements of significance, and it resulted in only a brief lull in the rhetorical war between the two superpowers. Indeed, the months after the summit witnessed new strains in the relationship. The administration abruptly rebuffed several Soviet proposals for arms accords; and in the spring of 1986, it announced that it would comply no longer with the provisions of the SALT-II treaty. Reagan and Gorbachev met again in October 1986, this time in Reykjavik, Iceland. But the two leaders could reach no agreement on arms reduction because of basic differences over SDI.

In many respects American foreign policy in the mid-1980s seemed to embrace once again many of the assumptions that had fueled the nation's international activities in the 1950s and early 1960s. In particular, the Reagan administration began, rhetorically at least, to commit itself to opposing the spread of communism anywhere in the world, whether or not the radicalism it was resisting was directly allied to the Soviet Union. That meant, above all, a new American activism in the Third World.

The most conspicuous examples of the new activism came in Latin America. In El Salvador, where first a repressive military regime and later a moderate civilian one were engaged in murderous struggles with communist revolutionaries (who were supported, according to the Reagan administration, by Cuba and the Soviet Union), the president committed himself to increased military and economic assistance—although he insisted that this assistance would not extend to the introduction of American forces into the region. In neighboring Nicaragua, a pro-American dictatorship had fallen to the revolutionary "Sandinistas" in 1970; the new government had grown increasingly anti-American (and increasingly Marxist) throughout the early 1980s. Despite substantial domestic opposition, the administration gave more and more support, both rhetorical and material, to the "contras"—a guerrilla movement recruited and trained largely by the

American CIA, drawn from several antigovernment groups, and fighting (without great success) to topple the Sandinista regime.

The administration's greatest foreign policy success, Reagan believed, came in October 1983, when American soldiers and marines invaded the tiny Caribbean island of Grenada to oust an anti-American Marxist regime that showed signs of forging a relationship with the Soviet Union. The invasion was brief, successful, and not particularly costly. It was highly popular with the American public (and, apparently, with many of the residents of Grenada).

In other parts of the world, the administration's bellicose rhetoric seemed for a while little more than an effort to disguise its restraint. In June 1982, the Israeli army launched an invasion of Lebanon in an effort to drive guerrillas of the Palestinian Liberation Organization from the country. The United States supported the Israelis rhetorically, but it also worked to reduce the violence and to permit the PLO forces to depart Lebanon peacefully. An American peacekeeping force entered Beirut to supervise the evacuation. Later, American marines remained in the city, apparently to protect the fragile Lebanese government, which was embroiled in a vicious civil war. Once identified with one faction in the struggle, the Americans became the targets of increasing violence—including a terrorist bombing of a marine barracks in Beirut that left over 200 Americans dead. In the face of this difficult situation, Reagan chose to withdraw American forces rather than become more deeply involved in the Lebanese struggle.

For a time the administration showed similar restraint in response to a series of terrorist incidents directed against American citizens in Europe and the Middle East. The president made bellicose remarks about several Arab leaders but took no visible action against them. By the spring of 1986, however, the pressures to act—both from the American public and from within the administration itself—apparently became too strong to resist. The administration ordered American naval forces to stage exercises in the Mediterranean, off the cost of Libya (whose radical leader, Muammar Qaddafi, was generally believed to be a principal sponsor of terrorism). Qaddafi claimed the American ships were operating in his territorial waters, a claim the United States denied. In the course of the exercises, Libyan forces apparently harassed the Americans; U.S. bombers then launched a series of retaliatory attacks on Libyan military positions.

Victims of Terrorism
President and Mrs. Reagan pay tribute to some of the over 200 U.S. Marines killed in Beirut, Lebanon, when Palestinian terrorists drove a truck loaded with explosives into an American barracks. The tragedy was one of a number of somber reminders to Americans of the degree to which terrorism had become an integral part of international life in the 1980s.   (UPI/Bettmann Newsphotos)

Several weeks later, after additional terrorist attacks on Americans and others in which Qaddafi had evidently been involved, American planes staged a far more extensive bombing raid on the Libyan capital. Several important military targets were destroyed. But the raid also damaged some nonmilitary sites and killed a number of civilians (including one of Qaddafi's children). The bombing was highly popular with the American people, but it evoked strong denunciations throughout the Arab Middle East and from many of America's allies in Europe.

In its first years, the Reagan administration's preoccupation with communism had seemed to dictate firm American support for pro-Western regimes, regardless of their characters. Jeanne Kirkpatrick, outspoken American ambassador to the United Nations, expressed the belief of many government officials when she denounced those who were willing to allow despotic pro-American regimes to topple even at the risk of permitting communist regimes (which would, she claimed, be far more despotic) to succeed them. The failure of the United States to thwart the revolutions in Iran and Nicaragua were, Kirkpatrick and others argued, evidence of the need to back friendly allies however dictatorial their methods.

At times, however, events made it impossible for the administration to adhere to this course. In early 1986, a popular revolution drove the tyrannical Jean-Claude Duvalier (whom the United States had long tacitly supported) from power in the Caribbean na-

tion of Haiti; American officials worked quietly to persuade Duvalier to leave the country and provided him with transportation to France. At about the same time, a far more important drama was in progress in the Philippines—the former American colony that was now one of America's most important allies in the Pacific. The United States had close ties with the twenty-year regime of President Ferdinand Marcos, and the Reagan administration continued to support him in the early 1980s despite growing evidence of his increasingly despotic methods and of growing popular resistance to them. But in 1985, Marcos precipitated a popular revolution when he announced plans for a national election, apparently certain that he could control the campaign and win an easy victory. The violence, intimidation, and corruption with which the Marcos regime supervised the campaign and election aroused such widespread popular anger that the Philippine president gradually lost the support even of many of his own longtime allies. The Reagan administration, fearing chaos in the Philippines, gradually shifted its support to Corazon Aquino, widow of a prominent Marcos opponent who had been murdered in 1983 under circumstances that seemed to implicate Marcos himself. Aquino proclaimed herself the victor in the controversial 1986 election, and the American government quietly persuaded Marcos to leave the country and settle in Hawaii.

Similar pressures began to make themselves felt in Washington in 1985 and 1986 as political instability rocked the government of South Africa. The United

States, along with most of the rest of the world, had long deplored the system of apartheid by which the white regime of South Africa denied basic social and political rights to the country's black majority. In the mid-1980s, however, rapidly increasing opposition to apartheid within South Africa itself produced new pressures on the United States and its allies to take more active measures against the existing regime. Above all, South African blacks and their supporters elsewhere called on the West to impose economic sanctions on and disinvest from the country.

The Reagan administration had long opposed the idea of economic sanctions and continued to fear that the collapse of the existing South African regime might produce a communist government. So the president stood firm against critics of his policies and defended what he described as "constructive engagement": working to influence the existing regime to change its policies. By mid-1986, however, the political pressure to do more was growing in both political parties; and members of Congress overrode the president's veto and imposed mild sanctions against the apartheid regime.

The Election of 1984

Reagan approached the campaign of 1984 at the head of a united Republican party firmly committed to his candidacy. The Democrats, as had become their custom, followed a more fractious course. Walter Mondale, who had been a senator from Minnesota and later Jimmy Carter's vice president, established an early and commanding lead in the race by soliciting support from a wide range of traditional Democratic interest groups, including the politically powerful AFL-CIO and National Education Association. But while many Democrats liked Mondale, few found him exciting. And for a time, he seemed to lose the initiative to a younger and apparently more dynamic candidate: Senator Gary Hart of Colorado, who presented himself as the leader of a "new generation" and the spokesman for vaguely defined "new ideas." Hart scored a series of stunning upsets in the early primaries and left the Mondale campaign reeling. In addition, the controversial black leader Jesse Jackson staged an impressive primary campaign, which drew substantial black support away from Mondale and weakened him further against Hart. But with the help of the AFL-CIO and other established groups, and as a result of a series of blunders by the Hart campaign, Mondale revived and managed to capture the nomination. At the Democratic Conven-

tion in San Francisco that summer, he brought momentary excitement to the campaign by selecting a woman, Representative Geraldine Ferraro of New York, to be his running mate—the first time in American history a woman was chosen for the national ticket of a major party.

The Democratic Convention displayed to the public a parade of diverse constituencies asking for greater representation in the political process: blacks, Hispanics, women, the handicapped, gays, the poor, and others. The Republican Convention, by contrast, presented an image of a united, homogeneous society rallying comfortably behind a revered leader. The meeting in Dallas was, in fact, a tribute to the "new spirit" the Reagan administration was attempting to create: a celebration of American strength and pride. Few Republicans gave more than passing attention there to the nation's social problems.

The spectacle of the two major parties in 1984 suggested how profoundly the political stance of both had shifted in the course of twenty years. In 1964, it had been the Republicans who had seemed doubting, querulous, and divided and the Democrats who had embodied confident, optimistic nationalism. Now the Republicans boasted of their faith in the future and portrayed the Democrats as the party of defeatism and despair. Both implicitly and openly, Ronald Reagan invoked the image of John Kennedy and identified himself with the activism and confidence that Kennedy had once embodied. The Democrats tried their best to evoke a similarly optimistic nationalism, but with little success.

Reagan's victory in 1984 was one of the most decisive in American political history. His popular majority was impressive; he won approximately 59 percent of the vote. His electoral majority was overwhelming; he carried every state but Mondale's native Minnesota and the District of Columbia. But only 53.3 percent of the electorate had voted for president—the lowest figure in over fifty years.

Republicans liked to claim that the 1984 election confirmed that a historic realignment of partisan loyalties had taken place, that the Republican party was now the dominant voice in American politics. The results of the presidential election, taken alone, seemed to confirm that claim. But the wider pattern of voter behavior in the 1980s suggested less a fundamental realignment than a weakening of party loyalties on both sides. While Reagan was carrying forty-nine states, Democrats gained a seat in the Senate and maintained only slightly reduced control of the House of Representatives. Thirty-five of fifty state

Election of 1984 (53.3% of electorate voting)

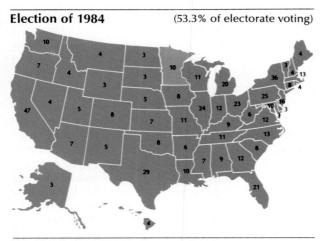

	ELECTORAL VOTE	POPULAR VOTE (%)
Ronald Reagan (Republican)	525	54,455,075 (59)
Walter Mondale (Democratic)	13	37,577,185 (41)

governors were Democratic, as were most state legislatures. Not only were fewer Americans voting, but fewer of the voters who remained seemed to be basing their decisions on party label alone. Reagan's 1984 victory was an enormous personal triumph. Its implications for the future of party alignments were less clear.

Modern Times

Much of the anxiety that beset American life in the 1970s, and much of the conservative sentiment that emerged to dominate American politics in the 1980s, was a result of jarring public events that left many men and women shaken and uncertain. But much of it was a result as well of significant changes in the nature and behavior of American society. Old assumptions were being called into question. New strains and new challenges were forcing significant adjustments in belief.

The New Demography

One of the most fundamental changes in American life in the postliberal era was the new profile of the

American population. After decades of steady growth, the nation's birth rate began to decline in the 1970s. In 1970, there were 18.4 births for every 1,000 people in the population. By 1975, the rate had declined to 14.6, the lowest in the twentieth century. And despite a modest increase in the early 1980s, the rate remained below 16 in 1984.

The declining birth rate had several causes. Many men and women were marrying later, were postponing having children because of professional pressures, and were having fewer children because of financial stringencies. (The dramatic increase in housing costs across the country in the 1970s undoubtedly played a role in discouraging large families.) The greater availability of contraceptives and sterilization procedures also reduced births, as did the legalization of abortion. There is no way to know how many abortions were performed illegally before the Supreme Court's 1973 decision invalidating most restrictions on them; but an increase in the number of abortions almost certainly occurred once the process became legal in all states: Nearly 1.6 million legal abortions were reported in the United States in 1983, more than twice the number reported a decade earlier.

One result of the declining birth rate was a marked increase in the proportion of elderly citizens. Nearly 12 percent of the population in 1983 was more than sixty-five years old, as compared with 8 percent in 1970; and the figure was projected to rise to over 20 percent by the end of the century. The median age in

The American Birth Rate, 1960–1985

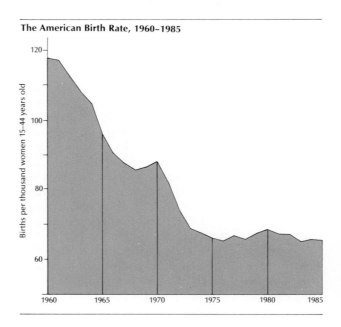

1983 was 30.9 years, as compared with 28.0 in 1970. The "graying" of America, as some described it, was a result not only of the declining birth rate but of higher life expectancy. The American death rate declined from 9.5 per thousand in 1970 to 8.6 in 1983; the average life expectancy at birth rose in the same period from 67.1 years to 71 for males and from 74.7 to 78.3 for females. The aging of the population had important, if still not fully understood, implications. It was, for example, a major cause of the increasing costliness of the Social Security program; the ratio of people paying into the system versus people drawing out of it was shifting rapidly to favor the latter. It meant increased health costs, both for the federal Medicare system and for private hospitals and insurance companies. And it meant a declining school enrollment, as the number of young Americans fell: Over 60 million people were enrolled in American schools in 1970; fewer than 58 million were enrolled by 1983.

The population as a whole was growing at a reduced rate, but it was nevertheless continuing to grow—from 204 million in 1970 to over 237 million at the beginning of 1985. A striking feature of that general growth was the changing racial and ethnic profile of the American people, as some groups grew far more rapidly than others. The Hispanic population grew at a faster rate than any other group, partly through continued immigration from Mexico (the largest single source of immigrants—both legal and illegal—in the 1970s and 1980s), Puerto Rico, and other Latin American nations and partly through a high birth rate among Hispanics already living in the United States. The 1980 census disclosed that 6 percent of the population was of Spanish origin in that year, as compared to slightly more than 4 percent a decade earlier. Because so many Hispanics in the Southwest were illegal immigrants, it seemed likely that many of them had not been counted in the census and that the real percentage was considerably higher. There was also a significant increase in the nation's Asian population, largely through immigration. Asians composed over 40 percent of the new arrivals in 1980, with particularly large influxes from Vietnam, the Philippines, and Korea.

The rising number of immigrants (who accounted for 40 percent of the nation's population increase in the 1970s) created varying reactions among the American people. There was rising sentiment among non-Hispanics in the Southwest for stronger restrictions on the immigration of Mexicans and others, who were forming a growing proportion of the popula-

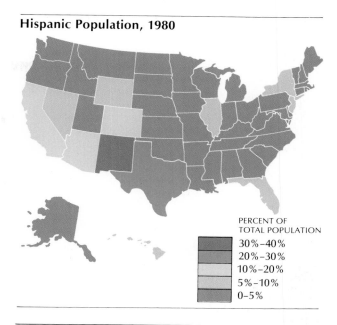

Hispanic Population, 1980

PERCENT OF TOTAL POPULATION

- 30%–40%
- 20%–30%
- 10%–20%
- 5%–10%
- 0–5%

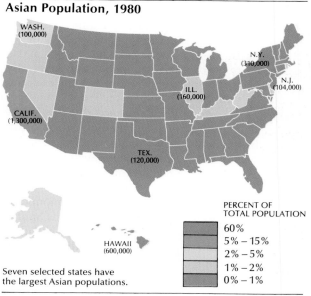

Asian Population, 1980

WASH. (100,000)
N.Y. (310,000)
N.J. (104,000)
ILL. (160,000)
CALIF. (1,300,000)
TEX. (120,000)
HAWAII (600,000)

Seven selected states have the largest Asian populations.

PERCENT OF TOTAL POPULATION

- 60%
- 5%–15%
- 2%–5%
- 1%–2%
- 0%–1%

tion in some areas; for example, over 20 percent of the population of Texas was of Spanish origin in 1980. In 1986, after years of debate, Congress passed a law strongly opposed by Hispanic groups prohibiting employers from hiring illegal aliens. Those in the country prior to 1982 would be permitted to stay, however.

Total Immigration, 1960–1980

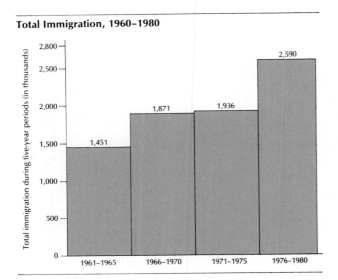

Sources of Immigration, 1960–1980

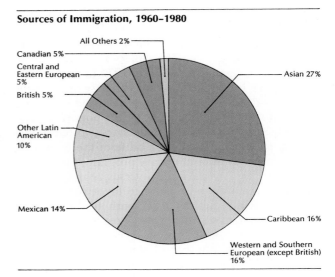

The Sunbelt and the Cities

Equally striking was the change in the geographic distribution of the American population. The most widely discussed demographic phenomenon of the 1970s was the rise of what became known as the "Sunbelt" or "Southern rim"—the Southeast, the Southwest, and above all, California, which became the nation's most populous state (surpassing New York) in 1964 and which continued to grow in the years that followed. By 1980, the population of the Sunbelt had risen to exceed that of the industrial regions of the North and East, which were experiencing not only a relative but in some cases an absolute decline in their numbers.

In addition to shifting the nation's economic focus from one region to another, the rise of the Sunbelt was, for the moment at least, producing a change in the political climate. The South and the West had always been more conservative than many other regions of the country. The changes in these areas during the 1960s and 1970s seemed, if anything, to strengthen that conservatism. In particular, the boom mentality of this growing region conflicted sharply with the concerns of the Northeast, which—saddled with a declining economic base, highly congested, and home to large, impoverished minority groups—remained far more committed to social programs and far more interested in regulated growth than the more wide-open areas of the Sunbelt.

Acutely affected by the changing distribution of population were the major industrial cities, particularly some of those in the Northeast and Midwest,

which continued to confront the specter of social and financial decay. As more and more industries moved their plants and corporate headquarters from the older urban centers to the suburbs or to the beckoning Sunbelt (or to foreign countries in search of cheap labor), many cities experienced a major contraction of their economic bases. Unemployment increased. Tax bases declined, as municipalities lost the revenues from the enterprises that had departed. And the demand for social services increased, as members of minorities found it ever more difficult to find even menial employment. Under the twin burdens of shrinking economic bases and expanding demands for social services, one city after another encountered fiscal crises. New York City barely averted bankruptcy in 1975—and then only after federal assistance and an unprecedented arrangement to finance municipal loans. Cleveland, Ohio, became, in late 1978, the first major metropolis in the nation to go into receivership since the Great Depression.

The crusading liberal urban leaders of the 1960s—such as New York's Mayor John Lindsay, who served from 1966 to 1974—had no place in the cities of the late 1970s and 1980s. Successful urban politicians were now far more likely to be people such as Edward I. Koch, who became mayor of New York in 1978 and who was overwhelmingly reelected (almost without opposition) in both 1981 and 1985. Koch openly subordinated concern for the poor to a commitment to fiscal stability and to the welfare of the middle class.

By the late 1970s, many observers were pointing to signs of an urban renaissance. In older cities such as Boston, Washington, New York, and San Fran-

Growth of the Sunbelt: Population and Urban Center Shifts

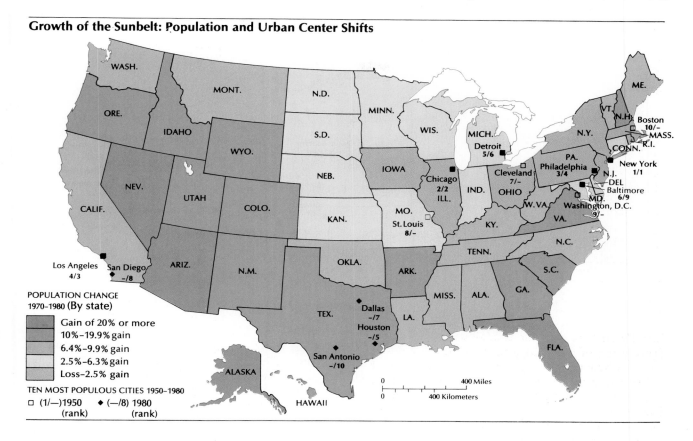

POPULATION CHANGE
1970–1980 (By state)

- Gain of 20% or more
- 10%–19.9% gain
- 6.4%–9.9% gain
- 2.5%–6.3% gain
- Loss–2.5% gain

TEN MOST POPULOUS CITIES 1950–1980
- □ (1/—)1950
- ◆ (—/8) 1980
  - (rank)
  - (rank)

cisco and in newer metropolises such as Houston and Dallas, downtown commercial districts experienced a remarkable boom. Great new office and retail complexes changed the skylines of one urban area after another. And along with the downtown commercial revival came a change in residential patterns: a return of the middle class to the cities. Affluent men and women began to abandon the suburbs (which were developing problems of their own) and return to downtown areas, where they often bought up declining real estate, refurbished it, and created prosperous new communities—a process that became known as gentrification. The phenomenon had many obvious benefits for cities: It helped restore a viable tax base; it attracted new businesses; and it meant that the community's most affluent members would now have a direct stake in the well-being of the city. But the urban revival did not eliminate the woes of the cities. Increased commercial growth meant increased congestion. And the return of affluent, middle-class people to urban neighborhoods drove housing prices up and displaced poorer residents, who found it more difficult and expensive than ever to find decent shel-

ter. The gentrification process thus increased the social stratification within many urban areas. The economic profile of some cities became that of a large group of the least affluent members of society, a growing group of the most affluent, and little in between.

Despite the positive effects of gentrification on some neighborhoods, moreover, urban dwellers continued to struggle with a gradual decay of services and a rise in social disorder. Urban public schools suffered an increase in violence, drug addiction, and truancy; and the white middle class looked on the school system as a virtually hopeless morass and showed little inclination to improve it. Graduates of public high schools in some major cities were found to be virtually illiterate. City streets became zones of increasing danger. The rate of violent crime nearly quadrupled between 1960 and 1980. The trend was not confined to the declining cities of the North; the boom towns of the Sunbelt were similarly affected. Houston, by the early 1980s, had the highest murder rate in the country.

The increasing scarcity of housing for low-income

America in 1986

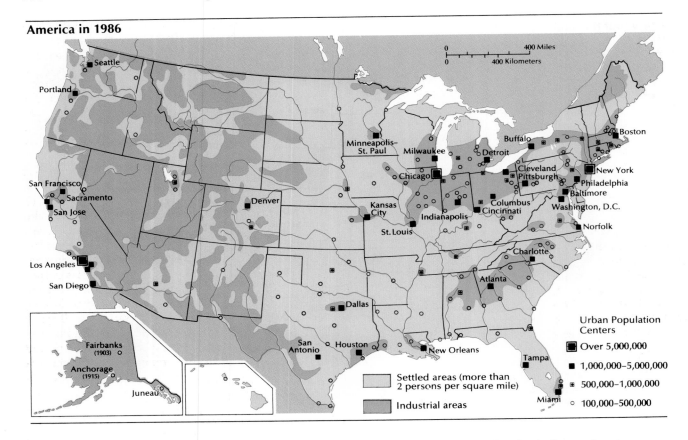

Urban Population Centers

■ Over 5,000,000
■ 1,000,000–5,000,000
⊞ 500,000–1,000,000
○ 100,000–500,000

Settled areas (more than 2 persons per square mile)

Industrial areas

people contributed to one of the most widely discussed phenomena of the mid-1980s: homelessness. There were no reliable figures to show how many men and women were now living without homes, sleeping on streets, depending on handouts or public shelters for food and protection from the cold. There had always been some homeless men and women in most major cities, but their numbers were clearly increasing at an alarming rate. Homelessness was in part a product of new policies for care of the mentally ill—the trend toward deinstitutionalization, which released into society many men and women apparently unable to care for themselves. But many of the homeless seemed to be people who had previously managed to support themselves but who—in the face of rising housing costs, reduced welfare assistance, and the declining availability of unskilled jobs—had somehow "fallen through the cracks" and found themselves helplessly on the streets. The phenomenon of tens of thousands of homeless people at large in the cities confronted municipal governments with a vexing problem. There were strong public pressures to provide

shelter and assistance for the indigent; but in an age of fiscal stringency and greatly reduced federal aid, city government often found it difficult to produce responses adequate to the dimensions of the problem.

The plight of the homeless was only the most visible sign of a new and troubling phenomenon: an increase in American poverty after nearly forty years of decline. Even after the economy recovered from the severe recession of the early 1980s, unemployment remained significantly higher than it had been a decade earlier. In 1979, just before the recession began, the unemployment rate had been 5.9 percent. In the aftermath of the recession, it remained consistently above 7 percent (except for a brief drop to 6.6 percent in early 1986). The percentage of Americans living below the poverty level declined steadily through the 1960s and 1970s: from slightly over 22 percent in 1960 to 12.6 percent in 1970 to a low of 11.4 percent in 1978. By 1984, the percentage had increased to 14.4 percent (11.5 percent for whites, 33.8 percent for blacks, and 28.4 percent for Hispanics).

Nonwhites in the Postliberal Era

In the aftermath of the civil-rights movement and the other liberal efforts of the 1960s, America's non-whites encountered two very different experiences. On the one hand, there were unprecedented opportunities for advancement for those who were in a position to take advantage of them. On the other hand, there was a significant deterioration in the condition of those nonwhites who remained unable to advance.

The story of the black middle class is an inspiring example of social success. At least a third, and perhaps as many as half, of all American blacks had achieved middle-class status by the mid 1980s. Forty-one percent of black workers were employed in white-collar jobs in 1985, as opposed to under 20 percent in 1965. Forty-five percent of black adults owned their own homes in 1983, as opposed to 38 percent in 1960. The percentage of blacks attending college nearly tripled in the two decades following passage of the civil-rights acts; and by 1980 the percentage of black high-school graduates going to college was virtually the same as that of white high-school graduates (although a far smaller proportion of blacks than whites managed to complete high school). Income disparities between black and white workers did not disappear, but they diminished substantially. And perhaps most striking, the proportion of blacks living in poverty dramatically declined—from above 56 percent in the early 1960s to approximately 33 percent in the mid-1980s (a figure

that remained far higher than the 12 percent for whites and even than the approximately 20 percent for Hispanics, but that nevertheless marked a substantial improvement over past conditions). It was clear, in short, that substantial numbers of American blacks, perhaps a majority, had realized significant benefits from the legislation of the 1960s, from changing national attitudes toward race, from the creation of controversial affirmative action programs, and from their own efforts.

But in these years the black middle class had also begun to inhabit a world increasingly detached from that of other nonwhites—people who had not much benefited from the liberal programs of the 1960s, who remained in the decaying ghettoes of the inner cities, and whose condition was growing steadily worse even as that of the black middle class was improving. Indeed, the very success of that middle class helped produce the deteriorating conditions in the ghettoes. As late as the mid-1960s, virtually all urban blacks, however educated, however successful, had lived in segregated neighborhoods. The black middle class had in those years provided a certain stability and leadership in the ghetto communities and had made it possible for many of its residents to advance and ultimately to escape—in much the same way other, white immigrant groups had done in earlier times. By the late 1970s, however, the black middle class had almost entirely departed from the ghettoes, which became neighborhoods where only the poorest nonwhites lived.

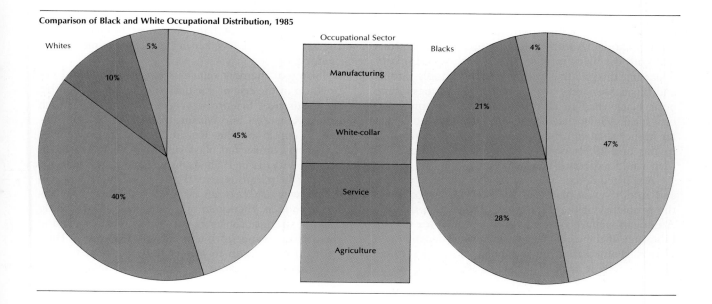

Comparison of Black and White Occupational Distribution, 1985

Whites — 5%, 10%, 45%, 40%

Occupational Sector: Manufacturing, White-collar, Service, Agriculture

Blacks — 4%, 21%, 47%, 28%

Perhaps the most distinctive aspect of life in the new ghettoes was the stunning increase in female-headed households—families headed by unwed and often very young mothers. In 1986, according to official government statistics, 51 percent of all black children were born into single-parent, female-headed households (as opposed to only 15 percent of white children). In 1960, only 20 percent of all black children had lived in single-parent homes. A quarter of all black babies were born to teen-age mothers, perhaps one reason why black teen-age unemployment remained at around 50 percent even as nationwide unemployment declined to 7 percent.

Most studies of urban poverty suggested that people living in female-headed households were those most likely to be poor and to stay poor. Black two-parent families continued to make rapid economic progress; in the mid-1980s their income had risen to approximately 80 percent of that of white families. At the same time, however, the economic status of female-headed black families was declining. Fifty-two percent of such families lived below the poverty line; most unwed mothers subsisted on welfare and only occasional employment; few completed high school, and even fewer received any college education. Their prospects for economic advancement were slim.

Despite the achievements of the civil-rights movement, therefore, inner-city blacks in the 1980s were far more isolated from the mainstream of American life than their counterparts of two decades before. They had virtually no contact with the white world; despite two decades of school desegregation, most inner-city school systems remained largely segregated—in part because so many white families had fled the cities or withdrawn their children from the public schools. And they had increasingly little contact with the black middle class, which was similarly departing the ghettoes and inner-city schools. Stores and businesses were abandoning the ghettoes; some poor blacks had to travel long distances simply to buy food. Violent crime in such neighborhoods was far higher than in other urban areas, and increasing. In the mid-1980s nearly 5 percent of young black men could expect to be murdered.

A spirited debate arose in the 1980s among whites and middle-class blacks about how best to address the problems of the ghettoes. Some argued that the American welfare system was responsible for the debilitation of the underclass by fostering dependency. Others claimed that the reduction of social services and the retreat from aggressive affirmative action

programs had reduced prospects for advancement. Most agreed, however, that the growth of this impoverished underclass, living almost totally apart from the rest of American society, was one of the nation's most difficult problems. In the mid-1960s, the Kerner Commission, appointed by President Johnson to study the causes of urban race riots, had warned that "our nation is moving toward two societies, one black, one white—separate and unequal." By the mid-1980s, many blacks were living in conditions that were much less separate and much more equal than they had experienced in the 1960s. But the gap between the American middle class (black and white) and the underclass was even wider than it had been twenty years before.

The New Religion and the New Right

A constant feature of rapidly changing societies is the search for stability, the quest for a haven from uncertainty and confusion. So it was in the United States in the 1970s and 1980s as its people faced the new realities of a troubled world. Americans flocked in growing numbers to movements and creeds that seemed to offer refuge from the perils of modern life.

Above all, it seemed, they flocked to religion. Many social critics had in the 1960s predicted the virtual extinction of religious influence in American life. *Time* magazine had reflected such assumptions in 1966 with a celebrated cover emblazoned with the question "Is God Dead?" Only a few years later, in the mid-1970s, America began to experience a major religious revival, perhaps the most powerful since the Second Great Awakening of the early nineteenth century.

Some of the new religious enthusiasm found expression in the rise of various cults and pseudofaiths: the Church of Scientology; the Unification Church of the Reverend Sun Myung Moon; the tragic People's Temple of the Reverend Jim Jones, whose members committed mass suicide in their jungle retreat in Guyana in 1978. But the most important impulse of the religious revival was the growing activism and power of Christian evangelicals. Their rise was not a sudden phenomenon. They had been quietly gaining strength for more than half a century. And in the 1950s, evangelicals such as the Reverend Billy Graham had begun to attract huge national followings for their energetic revivalism. For many years, however, the new religion had gone unnoted by much of the media, which had dismissed it as a limited, provincial phenomenon. By the early 1980s, they could no longer do so. More than 70 million Americans now described themselves as "born-again" Christians—those who had established a "direct personal relationship with Jesus." Christian evangelicals owned their own newspapers, magazines, radio stations, and television networks. They operated their own schools and universities. They occupied positions of eminence in the worlds of entertainment and professional sports. And one of their number ultimately occupied the White House itself—Jimmy Carter, who during the 1976 campaign had talked proudly of his own "conversion experience" and who continued openly to proclaim his born-again Christian faith during his years in office.

The Christian revivalism took many different forms. For some (Jimmy Carter, for example), evangelical Christianity served as a route to liberal social action and public service; it had formed the basis for Carter's professed commitment to racial and economic justice and world peace. For many others, however, it became a bulwark against the modern world and—increasingly—a prod to social and political activism to defend conservative values and institutions.

Important theological differences divided the Christian right. Fundamentalists believed that the Bible, literally interpreted, was the only reliable guide to God's intentions for the world. Except for the experience of conversion, the individual could hope for no direct communication with the Lord until the second coming of the Messiah as predicted in the Old Testament. Pentecostals (the fastest-growing group among evangelical Christians) also believed in the infallibility of the Bible and the second coming of Jesus; but they argued that God could and did communicate directly with individual men and women in the meantime. Pentecostals such as Oral Roberts, William Branham, and Pat Robertson insisted that they received detailed instructions directly from the Holy Spirit. Robertson claimed to be following God's directions in 1986 when he began campaigning for the Republican nomination for president.

Fundamentalists, Pentecostals, and other evangelicals, however, shared an interest in expanding their reach; and in the 1970s they began to enjoy enormous success. A growing number of Christian activists began developing "television ministries" (following the lead of Oral Roberts and Billy Gra-

ham, who had pioneered in the use of the airwaves in the 1950s and early 1960s). By the mid-1980s dozens of evangelical ministers were broadcasting regularly—some via their own cable channels, others through the Christian Broadcast Network, which owned a string of stations in cities across the country. Conservative Christians were forming political organizations (among them the Reverend Jerry Falwell's Moral Majority) to advance their social agenda, which included opposition to federal interference in local affairs, opposition to legalized abortion, defense of unrestricted free enterprise, and a strong American posture in the world, even a substantial military buildup. Some reopened issues that had long seemed closed. Some evangelical Christians questioned the scientific doctrine of evolution and urged the teaching of the biblical story of the creation instead. Others drew criticism from defenders of civil liberties by urging stricter supervision (and even censorship) of the contents of television programs, movies, books, magazines, and the lyrics of popular music.

Closely tied to the new religion was a new political right, many of whose members were themselves evangelical Christians. The New Right drew heavily from the conservative dogmas of earlier eras; but in addition to doctrinal enthusiasm, it displayed a remarkable organizing zeal. While earlier right-wing political groups, such as the John Birch Society, had stumbled along in administrative chaos, the new organizations marshaled their influence with skill and effectiveness. Mass mailing campaigns of staggering size, such as those orchestrated by Richard Viguerie, raised great sums of money to support conservative efforts. The National Conservative Political Action Committee, for example, spent millions of dollars in support of its chosen political candidates in 1980 and claimed credit for the defeat of many liberal senators and congressmen.

The power of the New Right in the early 1980s represented the culmination of many decades of steadily growing conservative sentiment. Such sentiment had surfaced occasionally in the 1950s in the form of militantly anticommunist political organizations. It had shown itself in 1964, when it helped to engineer the Republican nomination of Barry Goldwater for president. And it had triumphed, finally, in 1980, when it became a central force in propelling Ronald Reagan into the White House. But the phenomenon was, despite its conspicuous strength, difficult to define with any precision. The most active groups within the New Right were not conservatives of traditional stripe—

people associated with and supportive of the business community, defending the position of established economic and social elites. They were, rather, middle-class and lower-middle-class people, whose political demands centered more around social and cultural issues than economic ones, who seemed to exhibit not so much a staid conservatism as a right-wing populism.

Most expressive of this cultural thrust within the New Right was its emphasis on what became known as "family" issues. In effect, the new conservative groups were waging a frontal attack on feminism. Leaders of the New Right campaigned fervently (and successfully) against the proposed Equal Rights Amendment. Even more powerful was the movement to prevent women from aborting unwanted pregnancies. (See pp. 897–898.) Other issues dear to the New Right were similarly cultural in focus: the restoration of prayer in the public schools; opposition to gun-control legislation; an end to busing as a tool for achieving school desegregation. And running throughout the ideology of the New Right was a broader theme: the effort of men and women with traditional values to defend their communities and their life styles from the incursions of a new, secular, and—as they saw it—immoral culture. Animosity toward the federal government, a basic element of the New Right, rested on the belief that the nation's leadership had become the agent of these new, radical forces in American life.

The Changing Left

The New Left of the 1960s did not disappear after the end of the war in Vietnam, but it faded rapidly as an important influence in American political life. Students who had fought in its battles grew up, left school, and entered conventional careers. Radical leaders, disillusioned by the unresponsiveness of American society to their demands, resignedly gave up the struggle and chose instead to work "within the system." Marxist critiques continued to flourish in academic circles, but to much of the public they came to appear dated and irrelevant. Yet a left of sorts did survive through the 1970s, giving evidence in the process of how greatly the nation's political climate had changed. Instead of promoting radical change, activists more often fought for preservation and restraint.

Nothing better symbolized the concerns of the

changing left than its commitment to protection of the environment. Where 1960s activists had rallied to protest racism, poverty, and war, their 1970s and 1980s counterparts often fought to save the wilderness, protect endangered species, and limit reckless economic development. Above all, they mobilized themselves to confront the danger of nuclear power and, ultimately, nuclear war. The spread of atomic power plants in the 1950s and 1960s had aroused little controversy at the time; but by the mid-1970s, a well-organized and often militant antinuclear movement had emerged in almost every region of the country to oppose new plant construction and to warn of the dangers of existing facilities. A frightening accident in 1979 at a nuclear power plant at Three Mile Island in Pennsylvania seemed to expose serious deficiencies in the safety mechanisms that both government and private industry had assured the public were in place; and the result was an intensification of antinuclear activity.

Of even greater potential significance was a related movement that seemed to surface almost overnight in 1981 and 1982: a movement to stop the spread of nuclear weapons and to promote world disarmament. Opposition to atomic weapons had never entirely vanished in America. No rational person, of course, had ever hoped for a nuclear war, and small groups of scientists and others had attempted for years to produce public pressure for an end to the arms race; but for most of the first thirty-five years after the detonation of atomic bombs in New Mexico and Japan in 1945, such protests had remained muted and isolated. Then, beginning in the late 1970s, a powerful antinuclear movement emerged in Europe, gaining so rapidly in numbers and intensity that by 1980 it had become a formidable political force. And in 1981, partly in response to the European movement, partly in response to the deteriorating international climate, and partly, it seemed, in response to bellicose statements by officials of the federal government, the antinuclear movement gained force in the United States as well.

It took many forms. Some advocated a return to the disarmament negotiations that had produced SALT II—which the Senate had never ratified. Others called for an American commitment to "no-first-use" of atomic weapons. Still others agitated for a "nuclear freeze"—halting production of any new weapons or weapons systems (a position that the Reagan administration opposed because it would, they claimed, leave the United States in a position of military inferiority vis-à-vis the Soviet Union). By 1982, the nuclear freeze movement, in particular, had attracted wide support. State and local governments in widely scattered areas of the country (including parts of the supposedly conservative South) were going on record in support of the idea. Influential members of Congress (among them Senator Edward M. Kennedy) were publicly endorsing the idea. Referendum questions on the issue were being placed on ballots in several states.

Within three years, however, the power of the new movement seemed to be fading. The 1984 campaign saw the nuclear question relegated largely to the sidelines. The nuclear freeze proposal, which attracted the support of many Democratic candidates in 1983, was scarcely mentioned. The great public demonstrations on behalf of disarmament that activists had mobilized in the early 1980s had no counterparts in 1984 and 1985.

The concern for the environment, the opposition to nuclear power, the fear of nuclear war—all were reflections of a fundamental assumption of the post-Vietnam left. In a sharp break from the nation's long commitment to growth and progress, the new dissidents argued that only by limiting growth and curbing traditional forms of progress could society hope to survive. Industrial society had, they claimed, created a desperate threat to the planet's ecological balance. Continued growth would place intolerable strains on the world's finite resources. Some of these critics of the "idea of progress" expressed a gloomy resignation, urging a lowering of social expectations and foreseeing an inevitable deterioration in the quality of life. Other advocates of restraint believed that change did not require decline; human beings could live more comfortably and more happily if they simply learned to respect the limits imposed on them by their environment. But in either case, such arguments evoked strong opposition from conservatives and others, who ridiculed the no-growth ideology as an expression of defeatism and despair. Ronald Reagan, in particular, made an attack on the "limits" idea central to his political success.

Turning Inward

For many Americans the answer to the dilemmas of living in uncertain times lay not in religion or in politics but in the cultivation of the self. No aspect of the era aroused more comment than this tendency of individuals to "turn inward"—that is, to replace social concerns with personal ones.

Among affluent Americans, at least, there emerged a pervasive concern with personal life style. Newspapers introduced special sections devoted to such newly popular pursuits as gourmet cooking, physical fitness, and home decorating. Magazines specialized in helping Americans achieve personal fulfillment through a satisfying way of life; among the new periodicals was one with the frank and revealing title *Self.* Along with the interest in life style came a growing concern for self-expression—for "getting in touch with one's feelings." Such pseudoscientific theories as EST, Esalen, and Lifespring encouraged their followers to drop traditional social inhibitions against displaying anger, hatred, or jealousy. The key to emotional stability, they claimed, was the open expression of personal emotions. Nor did economic life remain immune from the new spirit. Books such as Robert Ringer's *Looking Out for Number One* (1978) became national best sellers by urging individuals to behave selfishly in the marketplace.

The commitment to self-cultivation and individual fulfillment was not new in American life, of course. It had roots in the self-made man ethos of the turn of the century, in the creed of Lost Generation intellectuals of the 1920s, in the philosophy of the beats of the 1950s, and in the counterculture of the 1960s. But by the 1970s, the impulse seemed to be taking a new and, in the eyes of some observers. disturbing form: emphasizing less the idea of personal liberation than the drive for a bland, elitist conformity; placing less value on creative accomplishment than on material comfort.

The American people had suffered many trials and disappointments since the heady days at the end of World War II when an American Century seemed about to dawn, when the United States had appeared poised for a prolonged era of domestic tranquillity and international preeminence. By the mid-1980s, America—like much of the rest of the world—was faced with the problems of a faltering international economy, an increasing world population, a domestic social fabric showing signs of strain, and a nuclear threat to the survival of the human race that showed few signs of abating.

For a time in the 1970s, these "new realities" (as they were often called) had seemed to produce a fundamental shift in the nation's social outlook: a lowering of expectations, a growing sense of doubt about the nation's capacities, a reassessment of America's

Doonesbury

Garry Trudeau created his celebrated comic strip in the 1960s, when he was an undergraduate at Yale University. Since then, he has used it both to offer political commentary and to chronicle the changing values and life styles of his own generation and those that have followed it. Here he lampoons the retreat from political activism and the rampant preprofessionalism that, according to many observers, characterized college students in the 1980s. (Universal Press Syndicate)

traditional image of itself as a special nation with a special mission. In the 1980s, however, the idea of an "age of limits" met a strong social and political challenge. Much of the public seemed determined in those years to repudiate what they called the "defeatism" of the 1970s, to rebuild national confidence, to restore a belief in American exceptionalism, to revive faith in the ideas of growth and progress.

The political victories of Ronald Reagan, whose successful presidential campaigns rested in large part on unembarrassed nationalism, were among the signs of this willed shift in the nation's image of itself, what *Time* magazine once called "America's new upbeat mood." So were the patriotic fervor with which Americans greeted the successes of their athletes in the 1984 Olympics and the orgy of celebration that accompanied the rededication of the Statue of Liberty in July 1986.

The idea of the United States as a special place with a special mission has enchanted the American people through most of their history. It is an idea that helped sustain the American Revolution, that motivated Northerners and Southerners alike in the Civil War, and that inspired American soldiers fighting in two world wars. It is an idea that fueled the international crusades of the Cold War and the great liberal efforts of the 1960s. And it is an idea that in the 1980s served as the basis of a conservative nationalism determined to restore American greatness.

"Tonight, freedom is on the march," Ronald Reagan said in his 1986 State of the Union address:

> The United States is the economic miracle, the model to which the world once again turns. We stand for an idea whose time is now. . . . We have done well, but we cannot stop at the foothills when Everest beckons. It is time for America to be all that we can be.

Despite the frustrations of the previous twenty years, despite troubling dilemmas at home and in the world for which few solutions were readily apparent, the belief in America as a "chosen place," as the "last best hope of man on earth," as a "city on a hill"—a belief first expressed by European settlers as they planted their tiny colonies on the shores of North America 350 years ago—survived.

SIGNIFICANT EVENTS

1974   OPEC raises oil prices
Recession begins
Inflation increases
Ford pardons Nixon
Ford meets Brezhnev at Vladivostok

1975   Cambodian forces seize *Mayaguez*; U.S. Marines sent to rescue crew

1976   Jimmy Carter elected president
Mao Zedong dies

1977   Panama Canal treaties ratified

1978   Camp David accords signed

1979   United States experiences major energy crisis
United States and China establish diplomatic relations
Iranians overthrow shah
American diplomats taken hostage in Teheran
Soviet Union invades Afghanistan
Sandinista revolution triumphs in Nicaragua
Nuclear accident at Three Mile Island
SALT-II treaty signed

1980   United States boycotts Moscow Olympics
Attempt to rescue hostages in Iran fails
Edward Kennedy challenges Carter in primaries
Ronald Reagan elected president

1981   Hostages in Iran released

1981   Reagan imposes tax and budget cuts
Major U.S. military build-up begins
Martial law imposed in Poland
Inflation and interest rates peak

1982   Severe recession
Inflation and interest rates decline
United States invades Grenada
Israel invades Lebanon
Nuclear freeze movement expands

1983   Unemployment reaches 10.2 percent
Economic recovery begins
Soviet Union shoots down Korean passenger plane
U.S. Marines killed in terrorist attack in Beirut

1984   Jesse Jackson campaigns for Democratic presidential nomination
Democrats nominate Geraldine Ferraro for vice president
Reagan reelected president

1985   Reagan meets Gorbachev in Geneva
Congress passes Gramm-Rudman bill

1986   United States confronts Libya in Gulf of Sidra and bombs Libyan targets
Duvalier in Haiti and Marcos in Philippines overthrown with U.S. approval
Reagan meets Gorbachev in Reykjavik, Iceland

SUGGESTED READINGS

The Ford Presidency   The Ford administration has not spawned a large literature; but see Gerald Ter Horst, *Gerald Ford* (1975); Robert T. Hartmann, *Palace Politics* (1980); Richard Reeves, *A Ford Not a Lincoln* (1976); and Ford's own memoirs, *A Time to Heal* (1979). James L. Sundquist, *The Decline and Resurgence of Congress* (1981), examines the post-Watergate legislature. A. James Reichley, *Conservatives in an Age of Change: The Nixon and Ford Administrations* (1981), is an overview.

The Carter Presidency   Several useful studies of the Carter presidency have already appeared. A contemporary appraisal is a series of articles—"The Passionless Presidency"—by James Fallows, a former Carter speech writer, in the *Atlantic Monthly* (1979). Fallows has also published an analysis of the state of the American military, *National Defense* (1981). Jimmy Carter's campaign autobiography, *Why*

Not the Best (1975), is an unusually revealing example of the genre. His presidential memoirs, *Keeping Faith* (1982), are less interesting. Jules Witcover, *Marathon* (1977), and James Wooten, *Dasher* (1978), examine the remarkable Carter campaign of 1976. Clark Mollenhoff, *The President Who Failed* (1980), is a hostile account. For an examination of the changing South, whose politics spawned Carter, see Jack Bass and Walter Devries, *The Transformation of Southern Politics* (1976). Rosalynn Carter, *First Lady from Plains* (1984), is a revealing memoir. Hamilton Jordan, *Crisis* (1982), is an account of the Carter presidency by the White House chief of staff. Haynes Johnson, *In the Absence of Power* (1980), is a sober overview. Zbigniew Brzezinski, *Power and Principle* (1983), is a memoir by Carter's national security adviser; Cyrus Vance, *Hard Choices* (1983), gives the secretary of state's perspective. Gaddis Smith, *Morality, Reason, and Power* (1986), is a historian's early evaluation of the Carter foreign policy.

The Reagan Presidency   Theodore H. White, *America in Search of Itself* (1982), includes an account of the 1980 campaign within a somber discussion of the nation's social and political plight. William Boyarsky, *The Rise of Ronald Reagan* (1968), is an early view of the fortieth president; Hedrick Smith et al., *Reagan: The Man, the President* (1980), is a more recent study. Lou Cannon, *Reagan* (1982), is an analysis by a journalist who has covered the president since his days as governor of California. Robert Dallek, *Ronald Reagan: The Politics of Symbolism* (1984), is a historian's assessment. Ronnie Dugger, *On Reagan* (1983), is a hostile account. Richard Reeves, *The Reagan Detour* (1985), and Laurence I. Barrett, *Gambling with History* (1984), offer other journalistic perspectives. For an admiring analysis, see Rowland Evans and Robert Novack, *The Reagan Revolution* (1981), which discusses the first months of the new administration. Fred I. Greenstein (ed.), *The Reagan Presidency* (1983), is a collection of essays. George Gilder, *Wealth and Poverty* (1981), is a statement of the controversial economic ideology of the Republican administration; while Frank Ackerman, *Reaganomics* (1982), Thomas Byrne Edsall, *The New Politics of Inequality* (1984), and Sidney Weintraub and Marvin Goodstein (eds.), *Reaganomics in the Stagflation Economy* (1983), discuss Reagan's economic policies. Burton Yale Pines, *Back to Basics* (1982), is an admiring description of the "traditionalist" revival. David W. Reinhard, *The Republican Right Since 1945* (1983), discusses the preconditions to the emergence of Reagan. Alexander Haig, *Caveat: Realism, Reagan, and Foreign Policy* (1984), is a memoir by Reagan's first secretary of state. Strobe Talbott, *Deadly Gambits* (1984), is an examination of nu-clear arms control efforts in the Reagan years. Walter LaFeber, *Inevitable Revolutions*, rev. ed. (1984), discusses American policies in Latin America. Raymond Bonner, *Weakness and Deceit: U.S. Policy and El Salvador* (1984), deals with one of the particular Latin American controversies of the Reagan years.

Society and Culture   Peter N. Carroll, *It Seemed Like Nothing Happened* (1982), is an overview of the 1970s. Peter Clecak, *America's Quest for the Ideal Self* (1983), and Jim Hougan, *Decadence: Radical Nostalgia, Narcissism, and Decline in the Seventies* (1975), are cultural studies of the 1960s and 1970s. The new demographic patterns that had emerged in American society by the 1970s are examined in Kirkpatrick Sale, *Power Shift* (1975), which considers the rise of the Sunbelt. Douglas Glasgow, *The Black Underclass* (1980), studies the plight of inner-city ghetto residents. On recent immigration patterns, see John Crewden, *The Tarnished Door* (1983). On the new evangelicism, see John Woodridge, *The Evangelicals* (1975), and Marshall Frady, *Billy Graham* (1979). Peter Steinfels, *The Neo-conservatives* (1979), discusses an increasingly important element of the New Right. Jonathan Schell, *The Fate of the Earth* (1982), is a passionate document of the antinuclear movement. Christopher Lasch, *The Culture of Narcissism* (1978), is a gloomy view of America in the 1970s. Andrea Dworkin, *Right-Wing Women* (1983), discusses antifeminism. Barbara Ehrenreich, *The Hearts of Men: American Dreams and the Flight from Commitment* (1983), is a provocative study of men in the era of feminism.

Appendices

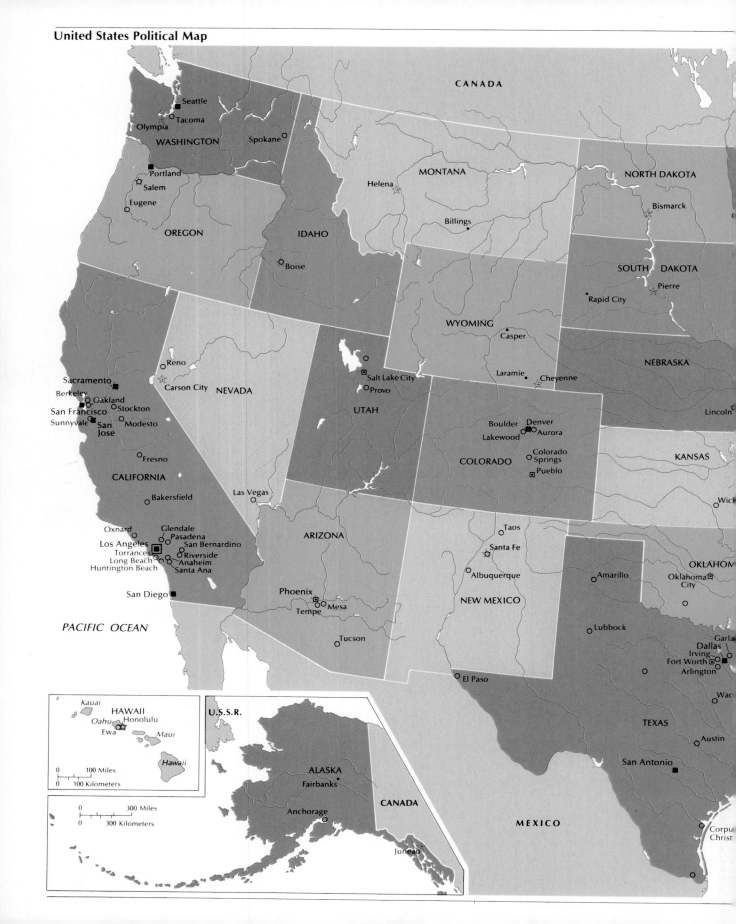

United States Political Map

CANADA

Lake Superior

MINNESOTA

MICHIGAN

Lake Huron

St. Paul

nneapolis

WISCONSIN

Milwaukee

Madison

Lake Michigan

Grand
Rapids

Flint

Warren
Lansing

Sterling Heights
Detroit
Livonia

Rockford

Lake Erie

Buffalo

Lake Ontario

Rochester

Syracuse

NEW YORK

Albany

MAINE

Augusta

Portland

VERMONT

Burlington
Montpelier

NEW
HAMPSHIRE
Concord

Manchester

Worcester
Springfield
Hartford

Boston
MASSACHUSETTS
Providence

RHODE ISLAND

CONNECTICUT

New Haven
Bridgeport
Stamford

IOWA

Moines

na

Cedar
Rapids

Iowa
City

Chicago

Davenport

Peoria

South
Bend

Gary

Fort Wayne

Ann Arbor

Cleveland

Toledo

Akron

OHIO

Columbus

PENNSYLVANIA

Youngstown

Pittsburgh

Harrisburg

Allentown

Newark

Trenton

New York

Jersey City

Philadelphia

NEW JERSEY

Baltimore

Dover

DELAWARE

Urbana

Springfield

ILLINOIS

Indianapolis

Bloomington

INDIANA

Dayton

Cincinnati

Louisville

Evansville

WEST
VIRGINIA

Charleston

WASHINGTON
D.C.
Alexandria

Annapolis

MARYLAND

MISSOURI

ansas
City

Independence

Kansas City

Jefferson City

St. Louis

Columbia

Frankfort

Lexington

KENTUCKY

VIRGINIA

Richmond

Hampton

Newport News

Portsmouth

Norfolk

Virginia Beach

Chesapeake

ce

Roanoke

Springfield

Fayetteville

ARKANSAS

Nashville

Chattanooga

TENNESSEE

Knoxville

Asheville

Greensboro

Winston-
Salem

Durham

Raleigh

NORTH CAROLINA

Charlotte

Greenville

Columbia

Little Rock

Memphis

Huntsville

Oxford

Birmingham

University

Columbia

SOUTH CAROLINA

Charleston

ATLANTIC OCEAN

MISSISSIPPI

Shreveport

Jackson

ALABAMA

Montgomery

Columbus

Atlanta

Athens

GEORGIA

Macon

Savannah

eaumont
ton

Galveston

LOUISIANA

Baton
Rouge

Biloxi

Mobile

Pensacola

New Orleans

Gulf of Mexico

Tallahassee

Jacksonville

Gainesville

Orlando

Tampa

St. Petersburg

FLORIDA

Hialeah

Hollywood

Miami

Fort Lauderdale

URBAN POPULATION CENTERS

◼ Over 5,000,000

■ 1,000,000–5,000,000

▣ 500,000–1,000,000

○ 100,000–500,000

☆ State capitals

△ Major university
centers

0   300 Miles

0   300 Kilometers

A3

United States Physical Map

Puget Sound

Coast Ranges

Cascade Range

Columbia R.

Columbia R.

Willamette R.

Snake R.

Columbia Plateau

Owyhee R.

Snake R.

Kootenai R.

Marias R.

Milk R.

Missouri R.

Assiniboine R.

Red River of the

ROCKY MOUNTAINS

Yellowstone R.

Bighorn R.

Tongue R.

Powder R.

Belle Fourche R.

Black Hills

Cheyenne R.

Little Missouri R.

James R.

Missouri R.

G R E A T

Sacramento R.

Humboldt R.

Great Salt Lake

GREAT BASIN

Niobrara R.

Loup R.

Platte R.

Sierra Nevada

San Joaquin R.

Central Valley

Death Valley

Green R.

Yampa R.

White R.

N. Platte R.

Laramie R.

N. Platte R.

Lodgepole Cr.

Republican R.

P L A I N S

Coast Ranges

Mohave Desert

Virgin R.

Sevier R.

Colorado R.

Colorado Plateau

Gunnison R.

ROCKY MOUNTAINS

Rio Grande

S. Platte R.

Smoky Hill R.

Kansa

Arkansas R.

Cimarron R.

N. Canadian R.

Colorado R.

Verde R.

Gila R.

Canadian R.

Pecos R.

Red R.

Trinity R.

PACIFIC OCEAN

Rio Grande

Pecos R.

Colorado R.

Brazos R.

Nueces R.

Rio Grande

G

125°

120°

115°

110°

105°

100°

Inset: Hawaii

PACIFIC OCEAN

PACIFIC OCEAN

20°

160°

Inset: Alaska

ARCTIC OCEAN

Brooks Range

Arctic Circle

Yukon R.

70°

Alaska Range

Mt. McKinley

60°

BERING SEA

PACIFIC OCEAN

180°

170°

160°

150°

140°

Lake Superior

Lake Huron

Lake Michigan

Lake Ontario

Lake Erie

Adirondack Mts.

Mohawk R.

St. Lawrence R.

Kennebeck R.

Connecticut R.

Hudson R.

Delaware R.

Susquehanna R.

APPALACHIAN MOUNTAINS

Allegheny R.

Ohio R.

Scioto R.

Potomac R.

Shenandoah Valley

James R.

Roanoke R.

Chesapeake Bay

Kanawha R.

Mts.

APPALACHIAN MOUNTAINS

Allegheny

Blue Ridge Mountains

Cumberland R.

Tennessee R.

Saluda R.

Savannah R.

Altamaha R.

CENTRAL PLAINS

Missouri R.

Osage R.

Ozark Plateau

White R.

Mississippi R.

St. Croix R.

Minnesota R.

Des Moines R.

Iowa R.

Cedar R.

Rock R.

Fox R.

Kankakee R.

Illinois R.

Wabash R.

Ohio R.

S. Francis R.

Arkansas R.

Ouachita R.

Yazoo R.

Tombigbee R.

Alabama R.

Chattahoochee R.

Pearl R.

Mississippi R.

Red R.

Sabine R.

Galveston Bay

COASTAL PLAIN

ATLANTIC COASTAL PLAIN

ATLANTIC OCEAN

Gulf of Mexico

50°

45°

40°

35°

30°

25°

65°

70°

75°

80°

85°

90°

95°

A5

World Political Map

United States and
its possessions

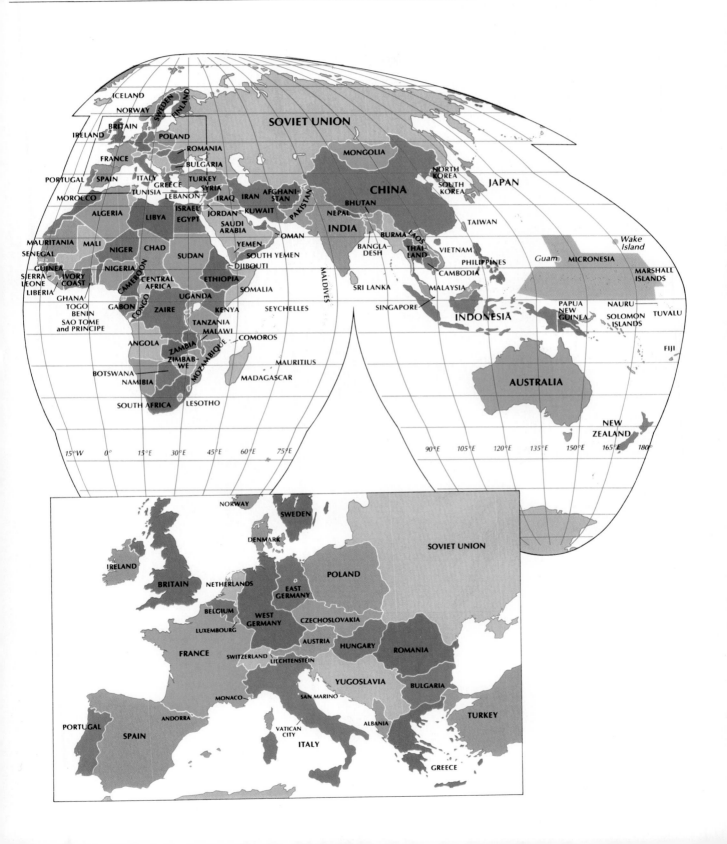

United States Territorial Expansion, 1783–1898

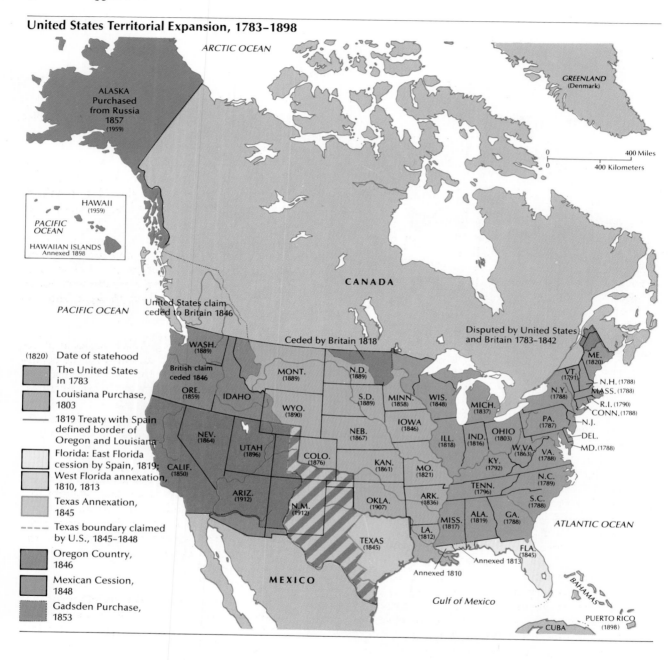

ARCTIC OCEAN

ALASKA
Purchased
from Russia
1857
(1959)

GREENLAND
(Denmark)

HAWAII
(1959)

PACIFIC
OCEAN

HAWAIIAN ISLANDS
Annexed 1898

0   400 Miles
0   400 Kilometers

PACIFIC OCEAN

CANADA

United States claim
ceded to Britain 1846

Ceded by Britain 1818

Disputed by United States
and Britain 1783–1842

(1820)   Date of statehood

The United States
in 1783

Louisiana Purchase,
1803

1819 Treaty with Spain
defined border of
Oregon and Louisiana

Florida: East Florida
cession by Spain, 1819;
West Florida annexation,
1810, 1813

Texas Annexation,
1845

Texas boundary claimed
by U.S., 1845–1848

Oregon Country,
1846

Mexican Cession,
1848

Gadsden Purchase,
1853

WASH.
(1889)

British claim
ceded 1846

ORE.
(1859)

IDAHO

MONT.
(1889)

WYO.
(1890)

N.D.
(1889)

S.D.
(1889)

NEB.
(1867)

MINN.
(1858)

WIS.
(1848)

IOWA
(1846)

MICH.
(1837)

ME.
(1820)

VT.
(1791)

N.H. (1788)

MASS. (1788)

N.Y.
(1788)

R.I. (1790)

CONN. (1788)

N.J.

PA.
(1787)

NEV.
(1864)

UTAH
(1896)

CALIF.
(1850)

COLO.
(1876)

KAN.
(1861)

MO.
(1821)

ILL.
(1818)

IND.
(1816)

OHIO
(1803)

W.VA.
(1863)

VA.
(1788)

DEL.

MD. (1788)

KY.
(1792)

ARIZ.
(1912)

N.M.
(1912)

OKLA.
(1907)

ARK.
(1836)

TENN.
(1796)

N.C.
(1789)

S.C.
(1788)

ATLANTIC OCEAN

TEXAS
(1845)

MISS.
(1817)

ALA.
(1819)

GA.
(1788)

LA.
(1812)

Annexed 1810

Annexed 1813

FLA.
(1845)

MEXICO

Gulf of Mexico

BAHAMAS

CUBA

PUERTO RICO
(1898)

The Declaration of Independence

In Congress, July 4, 1776,

THE UNANIMOUS DECLARATION OF THE THIRTEEN UNITED STATES OF AMERICA

When, in the course of human events, it becomes necessary for one people to dissolve the political bands which have connected them with another, and to assume, among the powers of the earth, the separate and equal station to which the laws of nature and of nature's God entitle them, a decent respect to the opinions of mankind requires that they should declare the causes which impel them to the separation.

We hold these truths to be self-evident, that all men are created equal; that they are endowed by their Creator with certain unalienable rights; that among these, are life, liberty, and the pursuit of happiness. That, to secure these rights, governments are instituted among men, deriving their just powers from the consent of the governed; that, whenever any form of government becomes destructive of these ends, it is the right of the people to alter or to abolish it, and to institute a new government, laying its foundation on such principles, and organizing its powers in such form, as to them shall seem most likely to effect their safety and happiness. Prudence, indeed, will dictate that governments long established, should not be changed for light and transient causes; and, accordingly, all experience hath shown, that mankind are more disposed to suffer, while evils are sufferable, than to right themselves by abolishing the forms to which they are accustomed. But, when a long train of abuses and usurpations, pursuing invariably the same object, evinces a design to reduce them under absolute despotism, it is their right, it is their duty, to throw off such government and to provide new guards for their future security. Such has been the patient sufferance of these colonies, and such is now the necessity which constrains them to alter their former systems of government. The history of the present King of Great Britain is a history of repeated injuries and usurpations, all having, in direct object, the establishment of an absolute tyranny over these States. To prove this, let facts be submitted to a candid world:

He has refused his assent to laws the most wholesome and necessary for the public good.

He has forbidden his governors to pass laws of immediate and pressing importance, unless suspended in their operation till his assent should be obtained; and, when so suspended, he has utterly neglected to attend to them.

He has refused to pass other laws for the accommodation of large districts of people, unless those people would relinquish the right of representation in the legislature; a right inestimable to them, and formidable to tyrants only.

He has called together legislative bodies at places unusual, uncomfortable, and distant from the depository of their public records, for the sole purpose of fatiguing them into compliance with his measures.

He has dissolved representative houses repeatedly for opposing, with manly firmness, his invasions on the rights of the people.

He has refused, for a long time after such dissolutions, to cause others to be elected; whereby the legislative powers, incapable of annihilation, have returned to the people at large for their exercise; the state remaining, in the meantime, exposed to all the danger of invasion from without, and convulsions within.

He has endeavored to prevent the population of these States; for that purpose, obstructing the laws for naturalization of foreigners, refusing to pass others to encourage their migration hither, and raising the conditions of new appropriations of lands.

He had obstructed the administration of justice, by refusing his assent to laws for establishing judiciary powers.

He has made judges dependent on his will alone, for the tenure of their officers, and the amount and payment of their salaries.

He has erected a multitude of new offices, and sent hither swarms of officers to harass our people, and eat out their substance.

He has kept among us, in time of peace, standing armies, without the consent of our legislatures.

He has affected to render the military independent of, and superior to, the civil power.

He has combined, with others, to subject us to a jurisdiction foreign to our Constitution, and unacknowledged by our laws; giving his assent to their acts of pretended legislation:

For quartering large bodies of armed troops among us:

For protecting them by a mock trial, from punishment, for any murders which they should commit on the inhabitants of these States:

For cutting off our trade with all parts of the world:

For imposing taxes on us without our consent:

For depriving us, in many cases, of the benefit of trial by jury:

For transporting us beyond seas to be tried for pretended offences:

For abolishing the free system of English laws in a neighboring province, establishing therein an arbitrary government, and enlarging its boundaries, so as to render it at once an example and fit instrument for introducing the same absolute rule into these colonies:

For taking away our charters, abolishing our most valuable laws, and altering, fundamentally, the powers of our governments:

For suspending our own legislatures, and declaring themselves invested with power to legislate for us in all cases whatsoever.

He had abdicated government here, by declaring us out of his protection, and waging war against us.

He has plundered our seas, ravaged our coasts, burnt our towns, and destroyed the lives of our people.

He is, at this time, transporting large armies of foreign mercenaries to complete the works of death, desolation, and tyranny, already begun, with circumstances of cruelty and perfidy scarcely paralleled in the most barbarous ages, and totally unworthy the head of a civilized nation.

He has constrained our fellow citizens, taken captive on the high seas, to bear arms against their country, to become the executioners of their friends, and brethren, or to fall themselves by their hands.

He has excited domestic insurrections amongst us, and has endeavored to bring on the inhabitants of our frontiers, the merciless Indian savages, whose known rule of warfare is an undistinguished destruction of all ages, sexes, and conditions.

In every stage of these oppressions, we have petitioned for redress, in the most humble terms; our repeated petitions have been answered only by repeated injury. A prince, whose character is thus marked by every act which may define a tyrant, is unfit to be the ruler of a free people.

Nor have we been wanting in attention to our British brethren. We have warned them, from time to time, of attempts made by their legislature to extend an unwarrantable jurisdiction over us. We have reminded them of the circumstances of our emigration and settlement here. We have appealed to their native justice and magnanimity, and we have conjured them, by the ties of our common kindred, to disavow these usurpations, which would inevitably interrupt our connections and correspondence. They, too, have been deaf to the voice of justice and consanguinity. We must, therefore, acquiesce in the necessity which denounces our separation, and hold them as we hold the rest of mankind, enemies in war, in peace, friends.

We, therefore, the representatives of the United States of America, in general Congress assembled, appealing to the Supreme Judge of the world for the rectitude of our intentions, do, in the name, and by the authority of the good people of these colonies, solemnly publish and declare, that these united colonies are, and of right ought to be, free and independent states: that they are absolved from all allegiance to the British Crown, and that all political connection between them and the state of Great Britain is, and ought to be, totally dissolved; and that, as free and independent states, they have full power to levy war, conclude peace, contract alliances, establish commerce, and to do all other acts and things which independent states may of right do. And, for the support of this declaration, with a firm reliance on the protection of Divine Providence, we mutually pledge to each other our lives, our fortunes, and our sacred honor.

The foregoing Declaration was, by order of Congress, engrossed, and signed by the following members:

JOHN HANCOCK

New Hampshire
Josiah Bartlett
William Whipple
Matthew Thornton

Massachusetts Bay
Samuel Adams
John Adams
Robert Treat Paine
Elbridge Gerry

Rhode Island
Stephen Hopkins
William Ellery

Connecticut
Roger Sherman
Samuel Huntington
William Williams
Oliver Wolcott

New York
William Floyd
Philip Livingston
Francis Lewis
Lewis Morris

New Jersey
Richard Stockton
John Witherspoon
Francis Hopkinson
John Hart
Abraham Clark

Pennsylvania
Robert Morris
Benjamin Rush
Benjamin Franklin
John Morton
George Clymer
James Smith
George Taylor
James Wilson
George Ross

Delaware
Caesar Rodney
George Reed
Thomas M'Kean

Maryland
Samuel Chase
William Paca
Thomas Stone
Charles Carroll,
   of Carrollton

Virginia
George Wythe
Richard Henry Lee
Thomas Jefferson
Benjamin Harrison
Thomas Nelson, Jr.
Francis Lightfoot Lee
Carter Braxton

North Carolina
William Hooper
Joseph Hewes
John Penn

South Carolina
Edward Rutledge
Thomas Heyward, Jr.
Thomas Lynch, Jr.
Arthur Middleton

Georgia
Button Gwinnett
Lyman Hall
George Walton

Resolved, That copies of the Declaration be sent to the several assemblies, conventions, and committees, or councils of safety, and to the several commanding officers of the continental troops; that it be proclaimed in each of the United States, at the head of the army.

The Constitution of the United States of America[1]

We the People of the United States, in Order to form a more perfect Union, establish Justice, insure domestic Tranquility, provide for the common defence, promote the general Welfare, and secure the Blessings of Liberty to ourselves and our Posterity, do ordain and establish this CONSTITUTION for the United States of America.

Article 1

Section 1.

All legislative Powers herein granted shall be vested in a Congress of the United States, which shall consist of a Senate and House of Representatives.

Section 2.

The House of Representatives shall be composed of Members chosen every second Year by the People of the several States, and the Electors in each State shall have the Qualifications requisite for Electors of the most numerous Branch of the State Legislature.

No Person shall be a Representative who shall not have attained to the Age of twenty-five Years, and been seven Years a Citizen of the United States, and who shall not, when elected, be an Inhabitant of that State in which he shall be chosen.

[Representatives and direct Taxes[2] shall be apportioned among the several States which may be included within this Union, according to their respective Numbers, which shall be determined by adding to the whole Number of free Persons, including those bound to Service for a Term of Years, and excluding Indians not taxed, three fifths of all other Persons.][3] The actual Enumeration shall be made within three Years after the first Meeting of the Congress of the United States, and within every subsequent Term of ten Years, in such Manner as they shall by Law direct. The Number of Representatives shall not exceed one for every thirty Thousand, but each State shall have at Least one Representative; and until such enumeration shall be made, the State of New Hampshire shall be entitled to chuse three, Massachusetts eight, Rhode-Island and Providence Plantations one, Connecticut five, New York six, New Jersey four, Pennsylvania eight, Delaware one, Maryland six, Virginia ten, North Carolina five, South Carolina five, and Georgia three.

When vacancies happen in the Representation from any State, the Executive Authority thereof shall issue Writs of Election to fill such Vacancies.

The House of Representatives shall chuse their Speaker and other Officers; and shall have the sole Power of Impeachment.

Section 3.

The Senate of the United States shall be composed of two Senators from each State, chosen by the Legislature thereof, for six Years; and each Senator shall have one Vote.

Immediately after they shall be assembled in Consequence of the first Election, they shall be divided as equally as may be into three Classes. The Seats of the Senators of the first Class shall be vacated at the Expiration of the second Year, of the second Class at the Expiration of the fourth Year, and of the third Class at the Expiration of the sixth Year, so that one-third may be chosen every second Year; and if Vacancies happen by Resignation, or otherwise, during the Recess of the Legislature of any State, the Executive thereof may make temporary Appointments until the next Meeting of the Legislature, which shall then fill such Vacancies.

No Person shall be a Senator who shall not have attained to the Age of thirty Years, and been nine Years a Citizen of the United States, and who shall not, when elected, be an Inhabitant of that State for which he shall be chosen.

The Vice President of the United States shall be President of the Senate, but shall have no vote, unless they be equally divided.

The Senate shall chuse their other Officers, and also a President pro tempore, in the absence of the Vice President, or when he shall exercise the Office of President of the United States.

---

[1] This version, which follows the original Constitution in capitalization and spelling, was published by the United States Department of the Interior, Office of Education, in 1935.

[2] Altered by the Sixteenth Amendment.

[3] Negated by the Fourteenth Amendment.

The Senate shall have the sole Power to try all Impeachments. When sitting for that purpose they shall be on Oath or Affirmation. When the President of the United States is tried, the Chief Justice shall preside: And no person shall be convicted without the Concurrence of two thirds of the Members present.

Judgment in Cases of Impeachment shall not extend further than to removal from Office, and disqualification to hold and enjoy any Office of honor, Trust, or Profit under the United States: but the Party convicted shall nevertheless be liable and subject to Indictment, Trial, Judgment, and Punishment, according to Law.

Section 4.

The Times, Places and Manner of holding Elections for Senators and Representatives, shall be prescribed in each State by the Legislature thereof; but the Congress may at any time by Law make or alter such Regulations, except as to the Places of Chusing Senators.

The Congress shall assemble at least once in every Year, and such Meeting shall be on the first Monday in December, unless they shall by Law appoint a different Day.

Section 5.

Each House shall be the Judge of the Elections, Returns and Qualifications of its own Members, and a Majority of each shall constitute a Quorum to do Business; but a smaller number may adjourn from day to day, and may be authorized to compel the Attendance of absent Members, in such Manner, and under such Penalties, as each House may provide.

Each House may determine the Rules of its Proceedings, punish its Members for disorderly Behaviour, and, with the Concurrence of two thirds, expel a Member.

Each House shall keep a Journal of its Proceedings, and from time to time publish the same, excepting such Parts as may in their Judgment require Secrecy; and the Yeas and Nays of the Members of either House on any question shall, at the Desire of one fifth of those Present, be entered on the Journal.

Neither House, during the Session of Congress, shall, without the Consent of the other, adjourn for more than three days, nor to any other Place than that in which the two Houses shall be sitting.

Section 6.

The Senators and Representatives shall receive a Compensation for their Services, to be ascertained by Law, and paid out of the Treasury of the United States. They shall in all Cases, except Treason, Felony, and Breach of the Peace, be privileged from Arrest during their Attendance at the Session of their respective Houses, and in going to and returning from the same; and for any Speech or Debate in either House, they shall not be questioned in any other Place.

No Senator or Representative shall, during the Time for which he was elected, be appointed to any civil Office under the Authority of the United States, which shall have been created, or the Emoluments whereof shall have been increased, during such time; and no Person holding any Office under the United States shall be a Member of either House during his continuance in Office.

Section 7.

All Bills for raising Revenue shall originate in the House of Representatives; but the Senate may propose or concur with Amendments as on other bills.

Every Bill which shall have passed the House of Representatives and the Senate, shall, before it become a Law, be presented to the President of the United States; If he approve he shall sign it, but if not he shall return it, with his Objections, to that House in which it shall have originated, who shall enter the Objections at large on their Journal, and proceed to reconsider it. If after such Reconsideration two thirds of that House shall agree to pass the bill, it shall be sent, together with the objections, to the other House, by which it shall likewise be reconsidered, and if approved by two thirds of that House, it shall become a Law. But in all such Cases the Votes of both Houses shall be determined by Yeas and Nays, and the Names of the Persons voting for and against the Bill shall be entered on the Journal of each House respectively. If any Bill shall not be returned by the President within ten Days (Sundays excepted) after it shall have been presented to him, the Same shall be a Law, in like Manner as if he had signed it, unless the Congress by their Adjournment prevent its Return, in which Case it shall not be a Law.

Every Order, Resolution, or Vote to which the Concurrence of the Senate and House of Representatives may be necessary (except on a question of Adjournment) shall be presented to the President of the United States; and before the Same shall take

Effect, shall be approved by him, or being disapproved by him, shall be repassed by two thirds of the Senate and House of Representatives, according to the Rules and Limitations prescribed in the Case of a Bill.

Section 8.

The Congress shall have Power To lay and collect Taxes, Duties, Imposts and Excises, to pay the Debts and provide for the common Defence and general Welfare of the United States; but all Duties, Imposts and Excises shall be uniform throughout the United States;

To borrow money on the credit of the United States;

To regulate Commerce with foreign Nations, and among the several States, and with the Indian Tribes;

To establish an uniform rule of Naturalization, and uniform Laws on the subject of Bankruptcies throughout the United States;

To coin Money, regulate the Value thereof, and of foreign Coin, and fix the Standard of Weights and Measures;

To provide for the Punishment of counterfeiting the Securities and current Coin of the United States;

To establish Post Offices and post Roads;

To promote the Progress of Science and useful Arts, by securing for limited Times to Authors and Inventors the exclusive Right to their respective Writings and Discoveries;

To constitute Tribunals inferior to the Supreme Court;

To define and punish Piracies and Felonies committed on the high Seas, and Offenses against the Law of Nations;

To declare War, grant Letters of Marque and Reprisal, and make Rules concerning Captures on Land and Water;

To raise and support Armies, but no Appropriation of Money to that Use shall be for a longer Term than two Years;

To provide and maintain a Navy;

To make Rules for the Government and Regulation of the land and naval forces;

To provide for calling forth the Militia to execute the Laws of the Union, suppress Insurrections and repel Invasions;

To provide for organizing, arming, and disciplining the Militia, and for governing such Part of them as may be employed in the Service of the United States, reserving to the States respectively, the Appointment of the Officers, and the Authority of training the Militia according to the discipline prescribed by Congress;

To exercise exclusive Legislation in all Cases whatsoever, over such District (not exceeding ten Miles square) as may, by Cession of particular States, and the acceptance of Congress, become the Seat of the Government of the United States, and to exercise like Authority over all Places purchased by the Consent of the Legislature of the State in which the Same shall be, for the Erection of Forts, Magazines, Arsenals, Dock-yards, and other needful Buildings;—And

To make all Laws which shall be necessary and proper for carrying into Execution the foregoing Powers, and all other Powers vested by this Constitution in the Government of the United States, or in any Department or Officer thereof.

Section 9.

The Migration or Importation of such Persons as any of the States now existing shall think proper to admit, shall not be prohibited by the Congress prior to the Year one thousand eight hundred and eight, but a tax or duty may be imposed on such Importation, not exceeding ten dollars for each Person.

The privilege of the Writ of Habeas Corpus shall not be suspended, unless when in Cases of Rebellion or Invasion the public Safety may require it.

No bill of Attainder or ex post facto Law shall be passed.

No capitation, or other direct, Tax shall be laid unless in Proportion to the Census or Enumeration herein before directed to be taken.

No Tax or Duty shall be laid on Articles exported from any State.

No Preference shall be given by any Regulation of Commerce or Revenue to the Ports of one State over those of another: nor shall Vessels bound to, or from, one State, be obliged to enter, clear, or pay Duties in another.

No Money shall be drawn from the Treasury, but in Consequence of Appropriations made by Law; and a regular Statement and Account of the Receipts and Expenditures of all public Money shall be published from time to time.

No Title of Nobility shall be granted by the United States: And no Person holding any Office of Profit or Trust under them, shall, without the Consent of the Congress, accept of any present, Emolument, Office, or Title, of any kind whatever, from any King, Prince, or foreign State.

Section 10.

No State shall enter into any Treaty, Alliance, or Confederation; grant Letters of Marque and Reprisal; coin Money; emit Bills of Credit; make any Thing but gold and silver Coin a Tender in Payment of Debts; pass any Bill of Attainder, ex post facto Law, or Law impairing the Obligation of Contracts, or grant any Title of Nobility.

No State shall, without the Consent of the Congress, lay any Imposts or Duties on Imports or Exports, except what may be absolutely necessary for executing its inspection Laws; and the net Produce of all Duties and Imposts, laid by any State on Imports or Exports, shall be for the use of the Treasury of the United States; and all such Laws shall be subject to the Revision and Control of the Congress.

No state shall, without the Consent of Congress, lay any duty of Tonnage, keep Troops, or Ships of War in time of Peace, enter into any Agreement or Compact with another State, or with a foreign Power, or engage in War, unless actually invaded, or in such imminent Danger as will not admit of delay.

Article II

Section 1.

The executive Power shall be vested in a President of the United States of America. He shall hold his Office during the Term of four years, and, together with the Vice President, chosen for the same Term, be elected, as follows:

Each State shall appoint, in such Manner as the Legislature thereof may direct, a Number of Electors, equal to the whole Number of Senators and Representatives to which the State may be entitled in the Congress: but no Senator or Representative, or Person holding an Office of Trust or Profit under the United States, shall be appointed an Elector.

[The Electors shall meet in their respective States, and vote by Ballot for two persons, of whom one at least shall not be an Inhabitant of the same State with themselves. And they shall make a List of all the Persons voted for, and of the Number of Votes for each; which List they shall sign and certify, and transmit sealed to the Seat of the Government of the United States, directed to the President of the Senate. The President of the Senate shall, in the Presence of the Senate and House of Representatives, open all the Certificates, and the Votes shall then be counted. The Person having the greatest Number of Votes shall be the President, if such Number be a Majority of the whole Number of Electors appointed; and if there be more than one who have such Majority, and have an equal Number of Votes, then the House of Representatives shall immediately chuse by Ballot one of them for President; and if no Person have a Majority, then from the five highest on the List the said House shall in like Manner chuse the President. But in chusing the President, the Votes shall be taken by States, the Representation from each State having one Vote; a quorum for this Purpose shall consist of a Member or Members from two-thirds of the States, and a Majority of all the States shall be necessary to a Choice. In every Case, after the Choice of the President, the Person having the greatest Number of Votes of the Electors shall be the Vice President. But if there should remain two or more who have equal votes, the Senate shall chuse from them by Ballot the Vice President.][4]

The Congress may determine the Time of chusing the Electors, and the Day on which they shall give their Votes; which Day shall be the same throughout the United States.

No person except a natural-born Citizen, or a Citizen of the United States, at the time of the Adoption of this Constitution, shall be eligible to the Office of President; neither shall any Person be eligible to that Office who shall not have attained to the Age of thirty-five years, and been fourteen Years a Resident within the United States.

In Case of the Removal of the President from Office, or of his Death, Resignation, or Inability to discharge the Powers and Duties of the said Office, the same shall devolve on the Vice President, and the Congress may by Law provide for the Case of Removal, Death, Resignation, or Inability, both of the President and Vice President, declaring what Officer shall then act as President, and such Officer shall act accordingly, until the disability be removed, or a President shall be elected.

The President shall, at stated Times, receive for his Services a Compensation, which shall neither be increased nor diminished during the Period for which he shall have been elected, and he shall not receive within that Period any other Emolument from the United States, or any of them.

Before he enter on the execution of his Office, he shall take the following Oath or Affirmation:—"I do solemnly swear (or affirm) that I will faithfully execute the Office of President of the United States, and

---

[4] Revised by the Twelfth Amendment.

will, to the best of my Ability, preserve, protect, and defend the Constitution of the United States."

Section 2.

The President shall be Commander in Chief of the Army and Navy of the United States, and of the Militia of the several States, when called into the actual Service of the United States; he may require the Opinion, in writing, of the principal Officer in each of the executive Departments, upon any subject relating to the Duties of their respective Offices, and he shall have Power to Grant Reprieves and Pardons for Offenses against the United States, except in Cases of Impeachment.

He shall have Power, by and with the Advice and Consent of the Senate, to make Treaties, provided two-thirds of the Senators present concur; and he shall nominate, and by and with the Advice and Consent of the Senate, shall appoint Ambassadors, other public Ministers and Consuls, Judges of the supreme Court, and all other Officers of the United States, whose Appointments are not herein otherwise provided for, and which shall be established by Law: but the Congress may by Law vest the Appointment of such inferior Officers, as they think proper, in the President alone, in the Courts of Law, or in the Heads of Departments.

The President shall have Power to fill up all Vacancies that may happen during the Recess of the Senate, by granting Commissions which shall expire at the End of their next Session.

Section 3.

He shall from time to time give to the Congress Information of the State of the Union, and recommend to their Consideration such Measures as he shall judge necessary and expedient; he may, on extraordinary occasions, convene both Houses, or either of them, and in Case of Disagreement between them, with respect to the Time of Adjournment, he may adjourn them to such Time as he shall think proper; he shall receive Ambassadors and other public Ministers; he shall take care that the Laws be faithfully executed, and shall Commission all the Officers of the United States.

Section 4.

The President, Vice President and all civil Officers of the United States, shall be removed from Office on Impeachment for, and Conviction of, Treason, Bribery, or other high Crimes and Misdemeanors.

Article III

Section 1.

The judicial Power of the United States, shall be vested in one supreme Court, and in such inferior Courts as the Congress may from time to time ordain and establish. The Judges, both of the supreme and inferior Courts, shall hold their Offices during good Behaviour, and shall, at stated Times, receive for their Services, a Compensation, which shall not be diminished during their Continuance in Office.

Section 2.

The judicial Power shall extend to all Cases, in Law and Equity, arising under this Constitution, the Laws of the United States, and Treaties made, or which shall be made, under their Authority;—to all Cases affecting ambassadors, other public ministers and consuls;—to all cases of admiralty and maritime Jurisdiction;—to Controversies to which the United States shall be a Party;—to Controversies between two or more States;—between a State and Citizens of another State;[5]—between Citizens of different States—between Citizens of the same State claiming Lands under Grants of different States, and between a State, or the Citizens thereof, and foreign States, Citizens, or Subjects.

In all Cases affecting Ambassadors, other public Ministers and Consuls, and those in which a State shall be Party, the supreme Court shall have original Jurisdiction. In all the other Cases before mentioned, the supreme Court shall have appellate Jurisdiction, both as to Law and Fact, with such Exceptions, and under such Regulations as the Congress shall make.

The trial of all Crimes, except in Cases of Impeachment, shall be by Jury; and such Trial shall be held in the State where the said Crimes shall have been committed; but when not committed within any State, the Trial shall be at such Place or Places as the Congress may by Law have directed.

Section 3.

Treason against the United States, shall consist only in levying War against them, or in adhering to their

---

[5] Qualified by the Eleventh Amendment.

Enemies, giving them Aid and Comfort. No Person shall be convicted of Treason unless on the Testimony of two Witnesses to the same overt Act, or on Confession in open Court.

The Congress shall have power to declare the Punishment of Treason, but no Attainder of Treason shall work Corruption of Blood, or Forfeiture except during the Life of the Person attainted.

Article IV

Section 1.

Full Faith and Credit shall be given in each State to the public Acts, Records, and judicial Proceedings of every other State. And the Congress may by general Laws prescribe the Manner in which such Acts, Records and Proceedings shall be proved, and the Effect thereof.

Section 2.

The Citizens of each State shall be entitled to all Privileges and Immunities of Citizens in the several States.

A Person charged in any State with Treason, Felony, or other Crime, who shall flee from Justice, and be found in another State, shall on demand of the executive Authority of the State from which he fled, be delivered up, to be removed to the State having Jurisdiction of the crime.

No Person held to Service or Labour in one State, under the Laws thereof, escaping into another, shall, in Consequence of any Law or Regulation therein, be discharged from such Service or Labour, but shall be delivered up on Claim of the Party to whom such Service or Labour may be due.

Section 3.

New States may be admitted by the Congress into this Union; but no new State shall be formed or erected within the Jurisdiction of any other State; nor any State be formed by the Junction of two or more States, or parts of States, without the Consent of the Legislatures of the States concerned as well as of the Congress.

The Congress shall have Power to dispose of and make all needful Rules and Regulations respecting the Territory or other Property belonging to the United States; and nothing in this Constitution shall be so construed as to Prejudice any Claims of the United States, or of any particular State.

Section 4.

The United States shall guarantee to every State in this Union a Republican Form of Government, and shall protect each of them against Invasion; and on Application of the Legislature, or of the Executive (when the Legislature cannot be convened) against domestic Violence.

Article V

The Congress, whenever two-thirds of both Houses shall deem it necessary, shall propose Amendments to this Constitution, or, on the Application of the Legislatures of two-thirds of the several States, shall call a Convention for proposing Amendments, which, in either Case, shall be valid to all Intents and Purposes, as part of this Constitution, when ratified by the Legislatures of three-fourths of the several States, or by Conventions in three-fourths thereof, as the one or the other Mode of Ratification may be proposed by the Congress; Provided that no Amendment which may be made prior to the Year One thousand eight hundred and eight shall in any Manner affect the first and fourth Clauses in the Ninth Section of the first Article; and that no State, without its Consent, shall be deprived of its equal Suffrage in the Senate.

Article VI

All Debts contracted and Engagements entered into, before the Adoption of this Constitution, shall be as valid against the United States under this Constitution, as under the Confederation.

This Constitution, and the Laws of the United States which shall be made in Pursuance thereof; and all Treaties made, or which shall be made, under the Authority of the United States, shall be the supreme Law of the Land; and the Judges in every State shall be bound thereby, any Thing in the Constitution or Laws of any State to the Contrary notwithstanding.

The Senators and Representatives before mentioned, and the Members of the several State Legislatures, and all executive and judicial Officers, both of the United States and of the several States, shall be bound by Oath or Affirmation to support this Constitution; but no religious Tests shall ever be required as a qualification to any Office or public Trust under the United States.

Article VII

The Ratification of the Conventions of nine States shall be sufficient for the Establishment of this Constitution between the States so ratifying the same.

George Washington
President and deputy and deputy from Virginia

New Hampshire
John Langdon
Nicholas Gilman

Massachusetts
Nathaniel Gorham
Rufus King

Connecticut
William Samuel
  Johnson
Roger Sherman

New York
Alexander Hamilton

New Jersey
William Livingston
David Brearley
William Paterson
Jonathan Dayton

Pennsylvania
Benjamin Franklin
Thomas Mifflin
Robert Morris
George Clymer
Thomas FitzSimons
Jared Ingersoll
James Wilson
Gouverneur Morris

Done in Convention by the Unanimous Consent of the States present the Seventeenth Day of September in the Year of our Lord one thousand seven hundred and Eighty seven, and of the Independence of the United States of America the Twelfth. In Witness whereof We have hereunto subscribed our Names.[6]

Delaware
George Read
Gunning Bedford, Jr.
John Dickinson
Richard Bassett
Jacob Broom

Maryland
James McHenry
Daniel of
  St. Thomas Jenifer
Daniel Carroll

Virginia
John Blair
James Madison, Jr.

North Carolina
William Blount
Richard Dobbs
  Spaight
Hugh Williamson

South Carolina
John Rutledge
Charles Cotesworth
  Pinckney
Charles Pinckney
Pierce Butler

Georgia
William Few
Abraham Baldwin

Articles in Addition to, and Amendment of, the Constitution of the United States of America, Proposed by Congress, and Ratified by the Legislatures of the Several States, Pursuant to the Fifth Article of the Original Constitution[7]

[Article I]

Congress shall make no law respecting an establishment of religion, or prohibiting the free exercise thereof; or abridging the freedom of speech, or of the press; or the right of the people peaceably to assemble, and to petition the Government for a redress of grievances.

[Article II]

A well regulated Militia, being necessary to the security of a free State, the right of the people to keep and bear Arms shall not be infringed.

[Article III]

No Soldier shall, in time of peace, be quartered in any house, without the consent of the Owner, nor in time of war, but in a manner to be prescribed by law.

[Article IV]

The right of the people to be secure in their persons, houses, papers, and effects, against unreasonable searches and seizures, shall not be violated, and no

[6] These are the full names of the signers, which in some cases are not the signatures on the document.

[7] This heading appears only in the joint resolution submitting the first ten amendments.

Warrants shall issue, but upon probable cause, supported by Oath or affirmation, and particularly describing the place to be searched, and the persons or things to be seized.

[Article V]

No person shall be held to answer for a capital or otherwise infamous crime, unless on a presentment or indictment of a Grand Jury, except in cases arising in the land or naval forces, or in the Militia, when in actual service in time of War or public danger; nor shall any person be subject for the same offence to be twice put in jeopardy of life or limb; nor shall be compelled in any criminal case to be a witness against himself, nor be deprived of life, liberty, or property, without due process of law; nor shall private property be taken for public use, without just compensation.

[Article VI]

In all criminal prosecutions, the accused shall enjoy the right to a speedy and public trial, by an impartial jury of the State and district wherein the crime shall have been committed, which district shall have been previously ascertained by law, and to be informed of the nature and cause of the accusation; to be confronted with the witnesses against him; to have compulsory process for obtaining witnesses in his favour, and to have the Assistance of Counsel for his defence.

[Article VII]

In suits at common law, where the value in controversy shall exceed twenty dollars, the right of trial by jury shall be preserved, and no fact tried by a jury, shall be otherwise reexamined in any Court of the United States, than according to the rules of the common law.

[Article VIII]

Excessive bail shall not be required, nor excessive fines imposed, nor cruel and unusual punishments inflicted.

[Article IX]

The enumeration of the Constitution, of certain rights, shall not be construed to deny or disparage others retained by the people.

[Article X]

The powers not delegated to the United States by the Constitution, nor prohibited by it to the States, are reserved to the States respectively, or to the people.
  [Amendments I-X, in force 1791.]

[Article XI][8]

The Judicial power of the United States shall not be construed to extend to any suit in law or equity, commenced or prosecuted against one of the United States by Citizens of another State, or by Citizens or Subjects of any Foreign State.

[Article XII][9]

The Electors shall meet in their respective States and vote by ballot for President and Vice-President, one of whom, at least, shall not be an inhabitant of the same State with themselves; they shall name in their ballots the person voted for as President, and in distinct ballots the person voted for as Vice-President, and they shall make distinct lists of all persons voted for as President, and of all persons voted for as Vice-President, and of the number of votes for each, which lists they shall sign and certify, and transmit sealed to the seal of the government of the United States, directed to the President of the Senate;—The President of the Senate shall, in the presence of the Senate and House of Representatives, open all the certificates and the votes shall then be counted;—The person having the greatest number of votes for President, shall be the President, if such number be a majority of the whole number of Electors appointed; and if no person have such majority, then from the persons having the highest numbers not exceeding three on the list of those voted for as President, the House of Representatives shall choose immediately, by ballot, the President. But in choosing the President, the votes

---

[8] Adopted in 1798.

[9] Adopted in 1804.

shall be taken by states, the representation from each state having one vote; a quorum for this purpose shall consist of a member or members from two-thirds of the states, and a majority of all the states shall be necessary to a choice. And if the House of Representatives shall not choose a President whenever the right of choice shall devolve upon them, before the fourth day of March next following, then the Vice-President shall act as President, as in the case of the death or other constitutional disability of the President.—The person having the greatest number of votes as Vice-President, shall be the Vice-President, if such number be a majority of the whole number of Electors appointed, and if no person have a majority, then from the two highest numbers on the list, the Senate shall choose the Vice-President; a quorum for the purpose shall consist of two-thirds of the whole number of Senators, and a majority of the whole number shall be necessary to a choice. But no person constitutionally ineligible to the office of President shall be eligible to that of Vice-President of the United States.

[Article XIII][10]

Section 1.

Neither slavery nor involuntary servitude, except as a punishment for crime whereof the party shall have been duly convicted, shall exist within the United States, or any place subject to their jurisdiction.

Section 2.

Congress shall have power to enforce this article by appropriate legislation.

[Article XIV][11]

Section 1.

All persons born or naturalized in the United States, and subject to the jurisdiction thereof, are citizens of the United States and of the State wherein they reside. No State shall abridge the privileges or immunities of citizens of the United States; nor shall any State deprive any person of life, liberty, or property, without due process of law; nor deny to any person within its jurisdiction the equal protection of the laws.

Section 2.

Representatives shall be apportioned among the several States according to their respective numbers, counting the whole number of persons in each State, excluding Indians not taxed. But when the right to vote at any election for the choice of electors for President and Vice-President of the United States, Representatives in Congress, the Executive and Judicial officers of a State, or the members of the Legislature thereof, is denied to any of the male inhabitants of such State, being twenty-one years of age, and citizens of the United States, or in any way abridged, except for participation in rebellion, or other crime, the basis of representation therein shall be reduced in the proportion which the number of such male citizens shall bear to the whole number of male citizens twenty-one years of age in such State.

Section 3.

No person shall be a Senator or Representative in Congress, or elector of President and Vice-President, or hold any office, civil or military, under the United States, or under any State, who, having previously taken an oath, as a member of Congress, or as an officer of the United States, or as a member of any State legislature, or as an executive or judicial officer of any State, to support the Constitution of the United States, shall have engaged in insurrection or rebellion against the same, or given aid or comfort to the enemies thereof. But Congress may by a vote of two-thirds of each House, remove such disability.

Section 4.

The validity of the public debt of the United States, authorized by law, including debts incurred for payment of pensions and bounties for services in suppressing insurrection or rebellion, shall not be questioned. But neither the United States nor any State shall assume or pay any debts or obligation incurred in aid of insurrection or rebellion against the United States, or any claim for the loss or emancipation of any slave; but all such debts, obligations, and claims shall be held illegal and void.

Section 5.

The Congress shall have the power to enforce, by appropriate legislation, the provisions of this article.

---

[10] Adopted in 1865.

[11] Adoped in 1868.

[Article XV]¹²

Section 1.

The right of citizens of the United States to vote shall not be denied or abridged by the United States or by any State on account of race, color, or previous condition of servitude—

Section 2.

The Congress shall have power to enforce this article by appropriate legislation.

[Article XVI]¹³

The Congress shall have power to lay and collect taxes on incomes, from whatever source derived, without apportionment among the several States, and without regard to any census or enumeration.

[Article XVII]¹⁴

The Senate of the United States shall be composed of two Senators from each State, elected by the people thereof, for six years; and each Senator shall have one vote. The electors in each State shall have the qualifications requisite for electors of the most numerous branch of the State legislatures.

When vacancies happen in the representation of any State in the Senate, the executive authority of such State shall issue writs of election to fill such vacancies: *Provided,* That the legislature of any State may empower the executive thereof to make temporary appointments until the people fill the vacancies by election as the legislature may direct.

This amendment shall not be so construed as to affect the election or term of any Senator chosen before it becomes valid as part of the Constitution.

[Article XVIII]¹⁵

Section 1.

After one year from the ratification of this article the manufacture, sale, or transportation of intoxicating liquors within, the importation thereof into, or the exportation thereof from the United States and all territory subject to the jurisdiction thereof for beverage purposes is hereby prohibited.

Section 2.

The Congress and the several States shall have concurrent power to enforce this article by appropriate legislation.

Section 3.

This article shall be inoperative unless it shall have been ratified as an amendment to the Constitution by the legislatures of the several States, as provided in the Constitution, within seven years from the date of the submission hereof to the States by the Congress.

[Article XIX]¹⁶

The right of citizens of the United States to vote shall not be denied or abridged by the United States or by any State on account of sex.

Congress shall have power to enforce this article by appropriate legislation.

[Article XX]¹⁷

Section 1.

The terms of the President and Vice-President shall end at noon on the 20th day of January, and the terms of Senators and Representatives at noon on the 3d day of January, of the years in which such terms would have ended if this article had not been ratified; and the terms of their successors shall then begin.

Section 2.

The Congress shall assemble at least once in every year, and such meeting shall begin at noon on the 3d day of January, unless they shall by law appoint a different day.

Section 3.

If, at the time fixed for the beginning of the term of the President, the President elect shall have died, the

---

¹² Adopted in 1870.
¹³ Adopted in 1913.
¹⁴ Adopted in 1913.
¹⁵ Adopted in 1918.

---

¹⁶ Adopted in 1920.
¹⁷ Adopted in 1933.

Vice-President elect shall become President. If a President shall not have been chosen before the time fixed for the beginning of his term or if the President elect shall have failed to qualify, then the Vice-President elect shall act as President until a President shall have qualified; and the Congress may by law provide for the case wherein neither a President elect nor a Vice-President elect shall have qualified, declaring who shall then act as President, or the manner in which one who is to act shall be selected, and such person shall act accordingly until a President or Vice-President shall have qualified.

Section 4.

The Congress may by law provide for the case of the death of any of the persons from whom the House of Representatives may choose a President whenever the right of choice shall have devolved upon them, and for the case of the death of any of the persons from whom the Senate may choose a Vice-President whenever the right of choice shall have devolved upon them.

Section 5.

Sections 1 and 2 shall take effect on the 15th day of October following the ratification of this article.

Section 6.

This article shall be inoperative unless it shall have been ratified as an amendment to the Constitution by the legislatures of three-fourths of the several States within seven years from the date of its submission.

[Article XXI][18]

Section 1.

The eighteenth article of amendment to the Constitution of the United States is hereby repealed.

Section 2.

The transportation or importation into any State, Territory, or possession of the United States for delivery or use therein of intoxicating liquors, in violation of the laws thereof, is hereby prohibited.

---

[18] Adopted in 1933.

Section 3.

This article shall be inoperative unless it shall have been ratified as an amendment to the Constitution by conventions in the several States, as provided in the Constitution, within seven years from the date of the submission hereof to the States by the Congress.

[Article XXII][19]

No person shall be elected to the office of the President more than twice, and no person who has held the office of President, or acted as President, for more than two years of a term to which some other person was elected President shall be elected to the office of the President more than once.

But this Article shall not apply to any person holding the office of President when this Article was proposed by the Congress, and shall not prevent any person who may be holding the office of President, or acting as President, during the term within which this Article becomes operative from holding the office of President or acting as President during the remainder of such term.

This article shall be inoperative unless it shall have been ratified as an amendment to the Constitution by the legislatures of three-fourths of the several states within seven years from the date of its submission to the states by the Congress.

[Article XXIII][20]

Section 1.

The District constituting the seat of Government of the United States shall appoint in such manner as the Congress may direct:

A number of electors of President and Vice-President equal to the whole number of Senators and Representatives in Congress to which the District would be entitled if it were a State, but in no event more than the least populous State; they shall be in addition to those appointed by the States, but they shall be considered, for the purposes of the election of President and Vice-President, to be electors appointed by a State; and they shall meet in the District and perform such duties as provided by the twelfth article of amendment.

---

[19] Adopted in 1961.

[20] Adopted in 1961.

Section 2.

The Congress shall have power to enforce this article by appropriate legislation.

[Article XXIV][21]

Section 1.

The right of citizens of the United States to vote in any primary or other election for President or Vice President, for electors for President or Vice President, or for Senator or Representative in Congress, shall not be denied or abridged by the United States or any state by reason of failure to pay any poll tax or other tax.

Section 2.

The Congress shall have the power to enforce this article by appropriate legislation.

[Article XXV][22]

Section 1.

In case of the removal of the President from office or of his death or resignation, the Vice President shall become President.

Section 2.

Whenever there is a vacancy in the office of the Vice President, the President shall nominate a Vice President who shall take office upon confirmation by a majority vote of both Houses of Congress.

Section 3.

Whenever the President transmits to the President Pro Tempore of the Senate and the Speaker of the House of Representatives his written declaration that he is unable to discharge the powers and duties of his office, and until he transmits to them a written declaration to the contrary, such powers and duties shall be discharged by the Vice President as Acting President.

Section 4.

Whenever the Vice President and a majority of either the principal officers of the executive departments or of such other body as Congress may by law provide, transmit to the President Pro Tempore of the Senate and the Speaker of the House of Representatives their written declaration that the President is unable to discharge the powers and duties of his office, the Vice President shall immediately assume the powers and duties of the office as Acting President.

Thereafter, when the President transmits to the President Pro Tempore of the Senate and the Speaker of the House of Representatives his written declaration that no inability exists, he shall resume the powers and duties of his office unless the Vice President and a majority of either the principal officers of the executive departments or of such other body as Congress may by law provide, transmit within four days to the President Pro Tempore of the Senate and the Speaker of the House of Representatives their written declaration that the President is unable to discharge the powers and duties of his office. Thereupon Congress shall decide the issue, assembling within forty-eight hours for that purpose if not in session. If the Congress, within twenty-one days after receipt of the latter written declaration, or, if Congress is not in session, within twenty-one days after Congress is required to assemble, determines by two-thirds vote of both Houses that the President is unable to discharge the powers and duties of his office, the Vice President shall continue to discharge the same as Acting President; otherwise, the President shall resume the powers and duties of his office.

[Article XXVI][23]

Section 1.

The right of citizens of the United States, who are eighteen years of age or older, to vote shall not be denied or abridged by the United States or by any State on account of age.

Section 2.

The Congress shall have power to enforce this article by appropriate legislation.

---

[21] Adopted in 1964.
[22] Adopted in 1967.

---

[23] Adopted in 1971.

Presidential Elections

Year	Candidates	Parties	Popular Vote	Percentage of Popular Vote	Electoral Vote	Percentage of Voter Participation
1789	**GEORGE WASHINGTON (Va.)★**				69	
	John Adams				34	
	Others				35	
1792	**GEORGE WASHINGTON (Va.)**				132	
	John Adams				77	
	George Clinton				50	
	Others				5	
1796	**JOHN ADAMS (Mass.)**	Federalist			71	
	Thomas Jefferson	Democratic-Republican			68	
	Thomas Pinckney	Federalist			59	
	Aaron Burr	Dem.-Rep.			30	
	Others				48	
1800	**THOMAS JEFFERSON (Va.)**	Dem.-Rep.			73	
	Aaron Burr	Dem.-Rep.			73	
	John Adams	Federalist			65	
	C. C. Pinckney	Federalist			64	
	John Jay	Federalist			1	
1804	**THOMAS JEFFERSON (Va.)**	Dem.-Rep.			162	
	C. C. Pinckney	Federalist			14	
1808	**JAMES MADISON (Va.)**	Dem.-Rep.			122	
	C. C. Pinckney	Federalist			47	
	George Clinton	Dem.-Rep.			6	
1812	**JAMES MADISON (Va.)**	Dem.-Rep.			128	
	De Witt Clinton	Federalist			89	
1816	**JAMES MONROE (Va.)**	Dem.-Rep.			183	
	Rufus King	Federalist			34	
1820	**JAMES MONROE (Va.)**	Dem.-Rep.			231	
	John Quincy Adams	Dem.-Rep.			1	
1824	**JOHN Q. ADAMS (Mass.)**	Dem.-Rep.	108,740	30.5	84	26.9
	Andrew Jackson	Dem.-Rep.	153,544	43.1	99	
	William H. Crawford	Dem.-Rep.	46,618	13.1	41	
	Henry Clay	Dem.-Rep.	47,136	13.2	37	
1828	**ANDREW JACKSON (Tenn.)**	Democratic	647,286	56.0	178	57.6
	John Quincy Adams	National Republican	508,064	44.0	83	
1832	**ANDREW JACKSON (Tenn.)**	Democratic	687,502	55.0	219	55.4
	Henry Clay	National Republican	530,189	42.4	49	
	John Floyd	Independent			11	
	William Wirt	Anti-Mason	33, 108	2.6	7	

★ State of residence at time of election.

Year	Candidates	Parties	Popular Vote	Percentage of Popular Vote	Electoral Vote	Percentage of Voter Participation
1836	**MARTIN VAN BUREN (N.Y.)**	Democratic	765,483	50.9	170	57.8
	W. H. Harrison	Whig			73	
	Hugh L. White	Whig	739,795	49.1	26	
	Daniel Webster	Whig			14	
	W. P. Magnum	Independent			11	
1840	**WILLIAM H. HARRISON (Ohio)**	Whig	1,274,624	53.1	234	80.2
	Martin Van Buren	Democratic	1,127,781	46.9	60	
	J. G. Birney	Liberty	7,069		—	
1844	**JAMES K. POLK (Tenn.)**	Democratic	1,338,464	49.6	170	78.9
	Henry Clay	Whig	1,300,097	48.1	105	
	J. G. Birney	Liberty	62,300	2.3	—	
1848	**ZACHARY TAYLOR (La.)**	Whig	1,360,967	47.4	163	72.7
	Lewis Cass	Democratic	1,222,342	42.5	127	
	Martin Van Buren	Free-Soil	291,263	10.1	—	
1852	**FRANKLIN PIERCE (N.H.)**	Democratic	1,601,117	50.9	254	69.6
	Winfield Scott	Whig	1,385,453	44.1	42	
	John P. Hale	Free-Soil	155,825	5.0	—	
1856	**JAMES BUCHANAN (Pa.)**	Democratic	1,832,955	45.3	174	78.9
	John C. Frémont	Republican	1,339,932	33.1	114	
	Millard Fillmore	American	871,731	21.6	8	
1860	**ABRAHAM LINCOLN (Ill.)**	Republican	1,865,593	39.8	180	81.2
	Stephen A. Douglas	Democratic	1,382,713	29.5	12	
	John C. Breckinridge	Democratic	848,356	18.1	72	
	John Bell	Union	592,906	12.6	39	
1864	**ABRAHAM LINCOLN (Ill.)**	Republican	2,213,655	55.0	212	73.8
	George B. McClellan	Democratic	1,805,237	45.0	21	
1868	**ULYSSES S. GRANT (Ill.)**	Republican	3,012,833	52.7	214	78.1
	Horatio Seymour	Democratic	2,703,249	47.3	80	
1872	**ULYSSES S. GRANT (Ill.)**	Republican	3,597,132	55.6	286	71.3
	Horace Greeley	Democratic; Liberal Republican	2,834,125	43.9	66	
1876	**RUTHERFORD B. HAYES (Ohio)**	Republican	4,036,298	48.0	185	81.8
	Samuel J. Tilden	Democratic	4,300,590	51.0	184	
1880	**JAMES A. GARFIELD (Ohio)**	Republican	4,454,416	48.5	214	79.4
	Winfield S. Hancock	Democratic	4,444,952	48.1	155	
1884	**GROVER CLEVELAND (N.Y.)**	Democratic	4,874,986	48.5	219	77.5
	James G. Blaine	Republican	4,851,981	48.2	182	
1888	**BENJAMIN HARRISON (Ind.)**	Republican	5,439,853	47.9	233	79.3
	Grover Cleveland	Democratic	5,540,309	48.6	168	
1892	**GROVER CLEVELAND (N.Y.)**	Democratic	5,556,918	46.1	277	74.7
	Benjamin Harrison	Republican	5,176,108	43.0	145	
	James B. Weaver	People's	1,041,028	8.5	22	
1896	**WILLIAM McKINLEY (Ohio)**	Republican	7,104,779	51.1	271	79.3
	William J. Bryan	Democratic-People's	6,502,925	47.7	176	
1900	**WILLIAM McKINLEY (Ohio)**	Republican	7,207,923	51.7	292	73.2
	William J. Bryan	Dem.-Populist	6,358,133	45.5	155	
1904	**THEODORE ROOSEVELT (N.Y.)**	Republican	7,623,486	57.9	336	65.2
	Alton B. Parker	Democratic	5,077,911	37.6	140	
	Eugene V. Debs	Socialist	402,283	3.0	—	

Year	Candidates	Parties	Popular Vote	Percentage of Popular Vote	Electoral Vote	Percentage of Voter Participation
1908	**WILLIAM H. TAFT (Ohio)**	Republican	7,678,908	51.6	321	65.4
	William J. Bryan	Democratic	6,409,104	43.1	162	
	Eugene V. Debs	Socialist	420,793	2.8	—	
1912	**WOODROW WILSON (N.J.)**	Democratic	6,293,454	41.9	435	58.8
	Theodore Roosevelt	Progressive	4,119,538	27.4	88	
	William H. Taft	Republican	3,484,980	23.2	8	
	Eugene V. Debs	Socialist	900,672	6.0	—	
1916	**WOODROW WILSON (N.J.)**	Democratic	9,129,606	49.4	277	61.6
	Charles E. Hughes	Republican	8,538,221	46.2	254	
	A. L. Benson	Socialist	585,113	3.2	—	
1920	**WARREN G. HARDING (Ohio)**	Republican	16,152,200	60.4	404	49.2
	James M. Cox	Democratic	9,147,353	34.2	127	
	Eugene V. Debs	Socialist	919,799	3.4	—	
1924	**CALVIN COOLIDGE (Mass.)**	Republican	15,725,016	54.0	382	48.9
	John W. Davis	Democratic	8,386,503	28.8	136	
	Robert M. LaFollette	Progressive	4,822,856	16.6	13	
1928	**HERBERT HOOVER (Calif.)**	Republican	21,391,381	58.2	444	56.9
	Alfred E. Smith	Democratic	15,016,443	40.9	87	
	Norman Thomas	Socialist	267,835	0.7	—	
1932	**FRANKLIN D. ROOSEVELT (N.Y.)**	Democratic	22,821,857	57.4	472	56.9
	Herbert Hoover	Republican	15,761,841	39.7	59	
	Norman Thomas	Socialist	881,951	2.2	—	
1936	**FRANKLIN D. ROOSEVELT (N.Y.)**	Democratic	27,751,597	60.8	523	61.0
	Alfred M. Landon	Republican	16,679,583	36.5	8	
	William Lemke	Union	882,479	1.9	—	
1940	**FRANKLIN D. ROOSEVELT (N.Y.)**	Democratic	27,244,160	54.8	449	62.5
	Wendell L. Willkie	Republican	22,305,198	44.8	82	
1944	**FRANKLIN D. ROOSEVELT (N.Y.)**	Democratic	25,602,504	53.5	432	55.9
	Thomas E. Dewey	Republican	22,006,285	46.0	99	
1948	**HARRY S TRUMAN (Mo.)**	Democratic	24,105,695	49.5	304	53.0
	Thomas E. Dewey	Republican	21,969,170	45.1	189	
	J. Strom Thurmond	State-Rights Democratic	1,169,021	2.4	38	
	Henry A. Wallace	Progressive	1,156,103	2.4	—	
1952	**DWIGHT D. EISENHOWER (N.Y.)**	Republican	33,936,252	55.1	442	63.3
	Adlai E. Stevenson	Democratic	27,314,992	44.4	89	
1956	**DWIGHT D. EISENHOWER (N.Y.)**	Republican	35,575,420	57.6	457	60.6
	Adlai E. Stevenson	Democratic	26,033,066	42.1	73	
	Other	—	—		1	
1960	**JOHN F. KENNEDY (Mass.)**	Democratic	34,227,096	49.9	303	62.8
	Richard M. Nixon	Republican	34,108,546	49.6	219	
	Other	—	—		15	
1964	**LYNDON B. JOHNSON (Tex.)**	Democratic	43,126,506	61.1	486	61.7
	Barry M. Goldwater	Republican	27,176,799	38.5	52	

Year	Candidates	Parties	Popular Vote	Percentage of Popular Vote	Electoral Vote	Percentage of Voter Participation
1968	**RICHARD M. NIXON (N.Y.)**	Republican	31,770,237	43.4	301	60.6
	Hubert H. Humphrey	Democratic	31,270,533	42.7	191	
	George Wallace	American Indep.	9,906,141	13.5	46	
1972	**RICHARD M. NIXON (N.Y.)**	Republican	47,169,911	60.7	520	55.2
	George S. McGovern	Democratic	29,170,383	37.5	17	
	Other	—	—		1	
1976	**JIMMY CARTER (Ga.)**	Democratic	40,828,587	50.0	297	53.5
	Gerald R. Ford	Republican	39,147,613	47.9	241	
	Other	—	1,575,459	2.1	—	
1980	**RONALD REAGAN (Calif.)**	Republican	43,901,812	50.7	489	52.6
	Jimmy Carter	Democratic	35,483,820	41.0	49	
	John B. Anderson	Independent	5,719,722	6.6	—	
	Ed Clark	Libertarian	921,188	1.1	—	
1984	**RONALD REAGAN (Calif.)**	Republican	54,455,075	59.0	525	53.3
	Walter Mondale	Democratic	37,577,185	41.0	13	

Vice Presidents and Cabinet Members

The Washington Administration (1789–1797)

Vice President	John Adams	1789–1797
Secretary of State	Thomas Jefferson	1789–1793
	Edmund Randolph	1794–1795
	Timothy Pickering	1795–1797
Secretary of Treasury	Alexander Hamilton	1789–1795
	Oliver Wolcott	1795–1797
Secretary of War	Henry Knox	1789–1794
	Timothy Pickering	1795–1796
	James McHenry	1796–1797
Attorney General	Edmund Randolph	1789–1793
	William Bradford	1794–1795
	Charles Lee	1795–1797
Postmaster General	Samuel Osgood	1789–1791
	Timothy Pickering	1791–1794
	Joseph Habersham	1795–1797

The John Adams Administration (1797–1801)

Vice President	Thomas Jefferson	1797–1801
Secretary of State	Timothy Pickering	1797–1800
	John Marshall	1800–1801
Secretary of Treasury	Oliver Wolcott	1797–1800
	Samuel Dexter	1800–1801
Secretary of War	James McHenry	1797–1800
	Samuel Dexter	1800–1801
Attorney General	Charles Lee	1797–1801
Postmaster General	Joseph Habersham	1797–1801
Secretary of Navy	Benjamin Stoddert	1798–1801

The Jefferson Administration (1801–1809)

Vice President	Aaron Burr	1801–1805
	George Clinton	1805–1809
Secretary of State	James Madison	1801–1809
Secretary of Treasury	Samuel Dexter	1801
	Albert Gallatin	1801–1809
Secretary of War	Henry Dearborn	1801–1809
Attorney General	Levi Lincoln	1801–1805
	Robert Smith	1805
	John Breckinridge	1805–1806
	Caesar Rodney	1807–1809
Postmaster General	Joseph Habersham	1801
	Gideon Granger	1801–1809
Secretary of Navy	Robert Smith	1801–1809

The Madison Administration (1809–1817)

Vice President	George Clinton	1809–1813
	Elbridge Gerry	1813–1817
Secretary of State	Robert Smith	1809–1811
	James Monroe	1811–1817
Secretary of Treasury	Albert Gallatin	1809–1813
	George Campbell	1814
	Alexander Dallas	1814–1816
	William Crawford	1816–1817
Secretary of War	William Eustis	1809–1812
	John Armstrong	1813–1814
	James Monroe	1814–1815
	William Crawford	1815–1817
Attorney General	Caesar Rodney	1809–1811
	William Pinkney	1811–1814
	Richard Rush	1814–1817
Postmaster General	Gideon Granger	1809–1814
	Return Meigs	1814–1817
Secretary of Navy	Paul Hamilton	1809–1813
	William Jones	1813–1814
	Benjamin Crowninshield	1814–1817

The Monroe Administration (1817–1825)

Vice President	Daniel Tompkins	1817–1825
Secretary of State	John Quincy Adams	1817–1825
Secretary of Treasury	William Crawford	1817–1825
Secretary of War	George Graham	1817
	John C. Calhoun	1817–1825
Attorney General	Richard Rush	1817
	William Wirt	1817–1825
Postmaster General	Return Meigs	1817–1823
	John McLean	1823–1825
Secretary of Navy	Benjamin Crowninshield	1817–1818
	Smith Thompson	1818–1823
	Samuel Southard	1823–1825

The John Quincy Adams Administration (1825–1829)

Vice President	John C. Calhoun	1825–1829
Secretary of State	Henry Clay	1825–1829
Secretary of Treasury	Richard Rush	1825–1829
Secretary of War	James Barbour	1825–1828
	Peter Porter	1828–1829
Attorney General	William Wirt	1825–1829
Postmaster General	John McLean	1825–1829
Secretary of Navy	Samuel Southard	1825–1829

The Jackson Administration (1829–1837)

Vice President	John C. Calhoun	1829–1833
	Martin Van Buren	1833–1837
Secretary of State	Martin Van Buren	1829–1831
	Edward Livingston	1831–1833
	Louis McLane	1833–1834
	John Forsyth	1834–1837
Secretary of Treasury	Samuel Ingham	1829–1831
	Louis McLane	1831–1833
	William Duane	1833
	Roger B. Taney	1833–1834
	Levi Woodbury	1834–1837
Secretary of War	John H. Eaton	1829–1831
	Lewis Cass	1831–1837
	Benjamin Butler	1837
Attorney General	John M. Berrien	1829–1831
	Roger B. Taney	1831–1833
	Benjamin Butler	1833–1837
Postmaster General	William Barry	1829–1835
	Amos Kendall	1835–1837
Secretary of Navy	John Branch	1829–1831
	Levi Woodbury	1831–1834
	Mahlon Dickerson	1834–1837

The Van Buren Administration (1837–1841)

Vice President	Richard M. Johnson	1837–1841
Secretary of State	John Forsyth	1837–1841
Secretary of Treasury	Levi Woodbury	1837–1841
Secretary of War	Joel Poinsett	1837–1841
Attorney General	Benjamin Butler	1837–1838
	Felix Grundy	1838–1840
	Henry D. Gilpin	1840–1841
Postmaster General	Amos Kendall	1837–1840
	John M. Niles	1840–1841
Secretary of Navy	Mahlon Dickerson	1837–1838
	James Paulding	1838–1841

The William Harrison Administration (1841)

Vice President	John Tyler	1841
Secretary of State	Daniel Webster	1841
Secretary of Treasury	Thomas Ewing	1841
Secretary of War	John Bell	1841
Attorney General	John J. Crittenden	1841
Postmaster General	Francis Granger	1841
Secretary of Navy	George Badger	1841

The Tyler Administration (1841–1845)

Vice President	None	
Secretary of State	Daniel Webster	1841–1843
	Hugh S. Legaré	1843
	Abel P. Upshur	1843–1844
	John C. Calhoun	1844–1845
Secretary of Treasury	Thomas Ewing	1841
	Walter Forward	1841–1843
	John C. Spencer	1843–1844
	George Bibb	1844–1845
Secretary of War	John Bell	1841
	John C. Spencer	1841–1843
	James M. Porter	1843–1844
	William Wilkins	1844–1845
Attorney General	John J. Crittenden	1841
	Hugh S. Legaré	1841–1843
	John Nelson	1843–1845
Postmaster General	Francis Granger	1841
	Charles Wickliffe	1841
Secretary of Navy	George Badger	1841
	Abel P. Upshur	1841
	David Henshaw	1843–1844
	Thomas Gilmer	1844
	John Y. Mason	1844–1845

The Polk Administration (1845–1849)

Vice President	George M. Dallas	1845–1849
Secretary of State	James Buchanan	1845–1849
Secretary of Treasury	Robert J. Walker	1845–1849
Secretary of War	William L. Marcy	1845–1849
Attorney General	John Y. Mason	1845–1846
	Nathan Clifford	1846–1848
	Isaac Toucey	1848–1849
Postmaster General	Cave Johnson	1845–1849
Secretary of Navy	George Bancroft	1845–1846
	John Y. Mason	1846–1849

The Taylor Administration (1849–1850)

Vice President	Millard Fillmore	1849–1850
Secretary of State	John M. Clayton	1849–1850
Secretary of Treasury	William Meredith	1849–1850
Secretary of War	George Crawford	1849–1850
Attorney General	Reverdy Johnson	1849–1850
Postmaster General	Jacob Collamer	1849–1850
Secretary of Navy	William Preston	1849–1850
Secretary of Interior	Thomas Ewing	1849–1850

The Fillmore Administration (1850–1853)

Vice President	None	
Secretary of State	Daniel Webster	1850–1852
	Edward Everett	1852–1853
Secretary of Treasury	Thomas Corwin	1850–1853

The Fillmore Administration (1850–1853) *continued*

Secretary of War	Charles Conrad	1850–1853
Attorney General	John J. Crittenden	1850–1853
Postmaster General	Nathan Hall	1850–1852
	Sam D. Hubbard	1852–1853
Secretary of Navy	William A. Graham	1850–1852
	John P. Kennedy	1852–1853
Secretary of Interior	Thomas McKennan	1850
	Alexander Stuart	1850–1853

The Pierce Administration (1853–1857)

Vice President	William R. King	1853–1857
Secretary of State	William L. Marcy	1853–1857
Secretary of Treasury	James Guthrie	1853–1857
Secretary of War	Jefferson Davis	1853–1857
Attorney General	Caleb Cushing	1853–1857
Postmaster General	James Campbell	1853–1857
Secretary of Navy	James C. Dobbin	1853–1857
Secretary of Interior	Robert McClelland	1853–1857

The Buchanan Administration (1857–1861)

Vice President	John C. Breckinridge	1857–1861
Secretary of State	Lewis Cass	1857–1860
	Jeremiah S. Black	1860–1861
Secretary of Treasury	Howell Cobb	1857–1860
	Philip Thomas	1860–1861
	John A. Dix	1861
Secretary of War	John B. Floyd	1857–1861
	Joseph Holt	1861
Attorney General	Jeremiah S. Black	1857–1860
	Edwin M. Stanton	1860–1861
Postmaster General	Aaron V. Brown	1857–1859
	Joseph Holt	1859–1861
	Horatio King	1861
Secretary of Navy	Isaac Toucey	1857–1861
Secretary of Interior	Jacob Thompson	1857–1861

The Lincoln Administration (1861–1865)

Vice President	Hannibal Hamlin	1861–1865
	Andrew Johnson	1865
Secretary of State	William H. Seward	1861–1865
Secretary of Treasury	Samuel P. Chase	1861–1864
	William P. Fessenden	1864–1865
	Hugh McCulloch	1865
Secretary of War	Simon Cameron	1861–1862
	Edwin M. Stanton	1862–1865
Attorney General	Edward Bates	1861–1864
	James Speed	1864–1865

Postmaster General	Horatio King	1861
	Montgomery Blair	1861–1864
	William Dennison	1864–1865
Secretary of Navy	Gideon Welles	1861–1865
Secretary of Interior	Caleb B. Smith	1861–1863
	John P. Usher	1863–1865

The Andrew Johnson Administration (1865–1869)

Vice President	None	
Secretary of State	William H. Seward	1865–1869
Secretary of Treasury	Hugh McCulloch	1865–1869
Secretary of War	Edwin M. Stanton	1865–1867
	Ulysses S. Grant	1867–1868
	Lorenzo Thomas	1868
	John M. Schofield	1868–1869
Attorney General	James Speed	1865–1866
	Henry Stanbery	1866–1868
	William M. Evarts	1868–1869
Postmaster General	William Dennison	1865–1866
	Alexander Randall	1866–1869
Secretary of Navy	Gideon Welles	1865–1869
Secretary of Interior	John P. Usher	1865
	James Harlan	1865–1866
	Orville H. Browning	1866–1869

The Grant Administration (1869–1877)

Vice President	Schuyler Colfax	1869–1873
	Henry Wilson	1873–1877
Secretary of State	Elihu B. Washburne	1869
	Hamilton Fish	1869–1877
Secretary of Treasury	George S. Boutwell	1869–1873
	William Richardson	1873–1874
	Benjamin Bristow	1874–1876
	Lot M. Morrill	1876–1877
Secretary of War	John A. Rawlins	1869
	William T. Sherman	1869
	William W. Belknap	1869–1876
	Alphonso Taft	1876
	James D. Cameron	1876–1877
Attorney General	Ebenezer Hoar	1869–1870
	Amos T. Ackerman	1870–1871
	G. H. Williams	1871–1875
	Edwards Pierrepont	1875–1876
	Alphonso Taft	1876–1877
Postmaster General	John A. J. Creswell	1869–1874
	James W. Marshall	1874
	Marshall Jewell	1874–1876
	James N. Tyner	1876–1877
Secretary of Navy	Adolph E. Borie	1869
	George M. Robeson	1869–1877
Secretary of Interior	Jacob D. Cox	1969–1870
	Columbus Delano	1870–1875
	Zachariah Chandler	1875–1877

The Hayes Administration (1877–1881)

Vice President	William A. Wheeler	1877–1881
Secretary of State	William M. Evarts	1877–1881
Secretary of Treasury	John Sherman	1877–1881
Secretary of War	George W. McCrary	1877–1879
	Alex Ramsey	1879–1881
Attorney General	Charles Devens	1877–1881
Postmaster General	David M. Key	1877–1880
	Horace Maynard	1880–1881
Secretary of Navy	Richard W. Thompson	1877–1880
	Nathan Goff, Jr.	1881
Secretary of Interior	Carl Schurz	1877–1881

The Garfield Administration (1881)

Vice President	Chester A. Arthur	1881
Secretary of State	James G. Blaine	1881
Secretary of Treasury	William Windom	1881
Secretary of War	Robert T. Lincoln	1881
Attorney General	Wayne MacVeagh	1881
Postmaster General	Thomas L. James	1881
Secretary of Navy	William H. Hunt	1881
Secretary of Interior	Samuel J. Kirkwood	1881

The Arthur Administration (1881–1885)

Vice President	None	
Secretary of State	F. T. Frelinghuysen	1881–1885
Secretary of Treasury	Charles J. Folger	1881–1884
	Walter Q. Gresham	1884
	Hugh McCulloch	1884–1885
Secretary of War	Robert T. Lincoln	1881–1885
Attorney General	Benjamin H. Brewster	1881–1885
Postmaster General	Timothy O. Howe	1881–1883
	Walter Q. Gresham	1883–1884
	Frank Hatton	1884–1885
Secretary of Navy	William H. Hunt	1881–1882
	William E. Chandler	1882–1885
Secretary of Interior	Samuel J. Kirkwood	1881–1882
	Henry M. Teller	1882–1885

The Cleveland Administration (1885–1889)

Vice President	Thomas A. Hendricks	1885–1889
Secretary of State	Thomas F. Bayard	1885–1889
Secretary of Treasury	Daniel Manning	1885–1887
	Charles S. Fairchild	1887–1889
Secretary of War	William C. Endicott	1885–1889
Attorney General	Augustus H. Garland	1885–1889
Postmaster General	William F. Vilas	1885–1888
	Don M. Dickinson	1888–1889
Secretary of Navy	William C. Whitney	1885–1889
Secretary of Interior	Lucius Q. C. Lamar	1885–1888
	William F. Vilas	1888–1889
Secretary of Agriculture	Norman J. Colman	1889

The Benjamin Harrison Administration (1889–1893)

Vice President	Levi P. Morton	1889–1893
Secretary of State	James G. Blaine	1889–1892
	John W. Foster	1892–1893
Secretary of Treasury	William Windom	1889–1891
	Charles Foster	1891–1893
Secretary of War	Redfield Proctor	1889–1891
	Stephen B. Elkins	1891–1893
Attorney General	William H. H. Miller	1889–1891
Postmaster General	John Wanamaker	1889–1893
Secretary of Navy	Benjamin F. Tracy	1889–1893
Secretary of Interior	John W. Noble	1889–1893
Secretary of Agriculture	Jeremiah M. Rusk	1889–1893

The Cleveland Administration (1893–1897)

Vice President	Adlai E. Stevenson	1893–1897
Secretary of State	Walter Q. Gresham	1893–1895
	Richard Olney	1895–1897
Secretary of Treasury	John G. Carlisle	1893–1897
Secretary of War	Daniel S. Lamont	1893–1897
Attorney General	Richard Olney	1893–1895
	James Harmon	1895–1897
Postmaster General	Wilson S. Bissell	1893–1895
	William L. Wilson	1895–1897
Secretary of Navy	Hilary A. Herbert	1893–1897
Secretary of Interior	Hoke Smith	1893–1896
	David R. Francis	1896–1897
Secretary of Agriculture	Julius S. Morton	1893–1897

The McKinley Administration (1897–1901)

Vice President	Garret A. Hobart	1897–1901
	Theodore Roosevelt	1901
Secretary of State	John Sherman	1897–1898
	William R. Day	1898
	John Hay	1898–1901
Secretary of Treasury	Lyman J. Gage	1897–1901
Secretary of War	Russell A. Alger	1897–1899
	Elihu Root	1899–1901
Attorney General	Joseph McKenna	1897–1898
	John W. Griggs	1898–1901
	Philander C. Knox	1901

The McKinley Administration (1897–1901) *continued*

Postmaster General	James A. Gary	1897–1898
	Charles E. Smith	1898–1901
Secretary of Navy	John D. Long	1897–1901
Secretary of Interior	Cornelius N. Bliss	1897–1899
	Ethan A. Hitchcock	1899–1901
Secretary of Agriculture	James Wilson	1897–1901

The Theodore Roosevelt Administration (1901–1909)

Vice President	Charles Fairbanks	1905–1909
Secretary of State	John Hay	1901–1905
	Elihu Root	1905–1909
	Robert Bacon	1909
Secretary of Treasury	Lyman J. Gage	1901–1902
	Leslie M. Shaw	1902–1907
	George B. Cortelyou	1907–1909
Secretary of War	Elihu Root	1901–1904
	William H. Taft	1904–1908
	Luke E. Wright	1908–1909
Attorney General	Philander C. Knox	1901–1904
	William H. Moody	1904–1906
	Charles J. Bonaparte	1906–1909
Postmaster General	Charles E. Smith	1901–1902
	Henry C. Payne	1902–1904
	Robert J. Wynne	1904–1905
	George B. Cortelyou	1905–1907
	George von L. Meyer	1907–1909
Secretary of Navy	John D. Long	1901–1902
	William H. Moody	1902–1904
	Paul Morton	1904–1905
	Charles J. Bonaparte	1905–1906
	Victor H. Metcalf	1906–1908
	Truman H. Newberry	1908–1909
Secretary of Interior	Ethan A. Hitchcock	1901–1907
	James R. Garfield	1907–1909
Secretary of Agriculture	James Wilson	1901–1909
Secretary of Labor and Commerce	George B. Cortelyou	1903–1904
	Victor H. Metcalf	1904–1906
	Oscar S. Straus	1906–1909
	Charles Nagel	1909

The Taft Administration (1909–1913)

Vice President	James S. Sherman	1909–1913
Secretary of State	Philander C. Knox	1909–1913
Secretary of Treasury	Franklin MacVeagh	1909–1913
Secretary of War	Jacob M. Dickinson	1909–1911
	Henry L. Stimson	1911–1913
Attorney General	George W. Wickersham	1909–1913
Postmaster General	Frank H. Hitchcock	1909–1913
Secretary of Navy	George von L. Meyer	1909–1913
Secretary of Interior	Richard A. Ballinger	1909–1911
	Walter L. Fisher	1911–1913
Secretary of Agriculture	James Wilson	1909–1913
Secretary of Labor and Commerce	Charles Nagel	1909–1913

The Wilson Administration (1913–1921)

Vice President	Thomas R. Marshall	1913–1921
Secretary of State	William J. Bryan	1913–1915
	Robert Lansing	1915–1920
	Bainbridge Colby	1920–1921
Secretary of Treasury	William G. McAdoo	1913–1918
	Carter Glass	1918–1920
	David F. Houston	1920–1921
Secretary of War	Lindley M. Garrison	1913–1916
	Newton D. Baker	1916–1921
Attorney General	James C. McReyolds	1913–1914
	Thomas W. Gregory	1914–1919
	A. Mitchell Palmer	1919–1921
Postmaster General	Albert S. Burleson	1913–1921
Secretary of Navy	Josephus Daniels	1913–1921
Secretary of Interior	Franklin K. Lane	1913–1920
	John B. Payne	1920–1921
Secretary of Agriculture	David F. Houston	1913–1920
	Edwin T. Meredith	1920–1921
Secretary of Commerce	William C. Redfield	1913–1919
	Joshua W. Alexander	1919–1921
Secretary of Labor	William B. Wilson	1913–1921

The Harding Administration (1921–1923)

Vice President	Calvin Coolidge	1921–1923
Secretary of State	Charles E. Hughes	1921–1923
Secretary of Treasury	Andrew Mellon	1921–1923
Secretary of War	John W. Weeks	1921–1923
Attorney General	Harry M. Daugherty	1921–1923
Postmaster General	Will H. Hays	1921–1922
	Hubert Work	1922–1923
	Harry S. New	1923
Secretary of Navy	Edwin Denby	1921–1923
Secretary of Interior	Albert B. Fall	1921–1923
	Hubert Work	1923
Secretary of Agriculture	Henry C. Wallace	1921–1923
Secretary of Commerce	Herbert C. Hoover	1921–1923
Secretary of Labor	James J. Davis	1921–1923

The Coolidge Administration (1923–1929)

Vice President	Charles G. Dawes	1925–1929
Secretary of State	Charles E. Hughes	1923–1925
	Frank B. Kellogg	1925–1929

Secretary of Treasury	Andrew Mellon	1923–1929
Secretary of War	John W. Weeks	1923–1925
	Dwight F. Davis	1925–1929
Attorney General	Henry M. Daugherty	1923–1924
	Harlan F. Stone	1924–1925
	John G. Sargent	1925–1929
Postmaster General	Harry S. New	1923–1929
Secretary of Navy	Edwin Derby	1923–1924
	Curtis D. Wilbur	1924–1929
Secretary of Interior	Hubert Work	1923–1928
	Roy O. West	1928–1929
Secretary of Agriculture	Henry C. Wallace	1923–1924
	Howard M. Gore	1924–1925
	William M. Jardine	1925–1929
Secretary of Commerce	Herbert C. Hoover	1923–1928
	William F. Whiting	1928–1929
Secretary of Labor	James J. Davis	1923–1929

The Hoover Administration (1929–1933)

Vice President	Charles Curtis	1929–1933
Secretary of State	Henry L. Stimson	1929–1933
Secretary of Treasury	Andrew Mellon	1929–1932
	Ogden L. Mills	1932–1933
Secretary of War	James W. Good	1929
	Patrick J. Hurley	1929–1933
Attorney General	William D. Mitchell	1929–1933
Postmaster General	Walter F. Brown	1929–1933
Secretary of Navy	Charles F. Adams	1929–1933
Secretary of Interior	Ray L. Wilbur	1929–1933
Secretary of Agriculture	Arthur M. Hyde	1929–1933
Secretary of Commerce	Robert P. Lamont	1929–1932
	Roy D. Chapin	1932–1933
Secretary of Labor	James J. Davis	1929–1930
	William N. Doak	1930–1933

The Franklin D. Roosevelt Administration (1933–1945)

Vice President	John Nance Garner	1933–1941
	Henry A. Wallace	1941–1945
	Harry S. Truman	1945
Secretary of State	Cordell Hull	1933–1944
	Edward R. Stettinius, Jr.	1944–1945
Secretary of Treasury	William H. Woodin	1933–1934
	Henry Morgenthau, Jr.	1934–1945
Secretary of War	George H. Dern	1933–1936
	Henry A. Woodring	1936–1940
	Henry L. Stimson	1940–1945
Attorney General	Homer S. Cummings	1933–1939
	Frank Murphy	1939–1940
	Robert H. Jackson	1940–1941

Attorney General	Francis Biddle	1941–1945
Postmaster General	James A. Farley	1933–1940
	Frank C. Walker	1940–1945
Secretary of Navy	Claude A. Swanson	1933–1940
	Charles Edison	1940
	Frank Knox	1940–1944
	James V. Forrestal	1944–1945
Secretary Interior	Harold L. Ickes	1933–1945
Secretary of Agriculture	Henry A. Wallace	1933–1940
	Claude R. Wickard	1940–1945
Secretary of Commerce	Daniel C. Roper	1933–1939
	Harry L. Hopkins	1939–1940
	Jesse Jones	1940–1945
	Henry A. Wallace	1945
Secretary of Labor	Frances Perkins	1933–1945

The Truman Administration (1945–1953)

Vice President	Alben W. Barkley	1949–1953
Secretary of State	Edward R. Stettinius, Jr.	1945
	James F. Byrnes	1945–1947
	George C. Marshall	1947–1949
	Dean G. Acheson	1949–1953
Secretary of Treasury	Fred M. Vinson	1945–1946
	John W. Snyder	1946–1953
Secretary of War	Robert P. Patterson	1945–1947
	Kenneth C. Royall	1947
Attorney General	Tom C. Clark	1945–1949
	J. Howard McGrath	1949–1952
	James P. McGranery	1952–1953
Postmaster General	Frank C. Walker	1945
	Robert E. Hannegan	1945–1947
	Jesse M. Donaldson	1947–1953
Secretary of Navy	James V. Forrestal	1945–1947
Secretary of Interior	Harold L. Ickes	1945–1946
	Julius A. Krug	1946–1949
	Oscar L. Chapman	1949–1953
Secretary of Agriculture	Clinton P. Anderson	1945–1948
	Charles F. Brannan	1948–1953
Secretary of Commerce	Henry A. Wallace	1945–1946
	W. Averell Harriman	1946–1948
	Charles W. Sawyer	1948–1953
Secretary of Labor	Lewis B. Schwellenbach	1945–1948
	Maurice J. Tobin	1948–1953
Secretary of Defense	James V. Forrestal	1947–1949
	Louis A. Johnson	1949–1950
	George C. Marshall	1950–1951
	Robert A. Lovett	1951–1953

The Eisenhower Administration (1953–1961)

Vice President	Richard M. Nixon	1953–1961
Secretary of State	John Foster Dulles	1953–1959
	Christian A. Herter	1959–1961
Secretary of Treasury	George M. Humphrey	1953–1957
	Robert B. Anderson	1957–1961

The Eisenhower Administration (1953–1961)
continued

Attorney General	Herbert Brownell, Jr.	1953–1958
	William P. Rogers	1958–1961
Postmaster General	Arthur E. Summerfield	1953–1961
Secretary of Interior	Douglas McKay	1953–1956
	Fred A. Seaton	1956–1961
Secretary of Agriculture	Ezra T. Benson	1953–1961
Secretary of Commerce	Sinclair Weeks	1953–1958
	Lewis L. Strauss	1958–1959
	Frederick H. Mueller	1959–1961
Secretary of Labor	Martin P. Durkin	1953
	James P. Mitchell	1953–1961
Secretary of Defense	Charles E. Wilson	1953–1957
	Neil H. McElroy	1957–1959
	Thomas S. Gates Jr.	1959–1961
Secretary of Health, Education, and Welfare	Oveta Culp Hobby	1953–1955
	Marion B. Folsom	1955–1958
	Arthur S. Flemming	1958–1961

The Kennedy Administration (1961–1963)

Vice President	Lyndon B. Johnson	1961–1963
Secretary of State	Dean Rusk	1961–1963
Secretary of Treasury	C. Douglas Dillon	1961–1963
Attorney General	Robert F. Kennedy	1961–1963
Postmaster General	J. Edward Day	1961–1963
	John A. Gronouski	1963
Secretary of Interior	Stewart L. Udall	1961–1963
Secretary of Agriculture	Orville L. Freeman	1961–1963
Secretary of Commerce	Luther H. Hodges	1961–1963
Secretary of Labor	Arthur J. Goldberg	1961–1962
	W. Willard Wirtz	1962–1963
Secretary of Defense	Robert S. McNamara	1961–1963
Secretary of Health, Education, and Welfare	Abraham A. Ribicoff	1961–1962
	Anthony J. Celebrezze	1962–1963

The Lyndon Johnson Administration (1963–1969)

Vice President	Hubert H. Humphrey	1965–1969
Secretary of State	Dean Rusk	1963–1969
Secretary of Treasury	C. Douglas Dillon	1963–1965
	Henry H. Fowler	1965–1969
Attorney General	Robert F. Kennedy	1963–1964
	Nicholas Katzenbach	1965–1966
	Ramsey Clark	1967–1969
Postmaster General	John A. Gronouski	1963–1965
	Lawrence F. O'Brien	1965–1968
	Marvin Watson	1968–1969
Secretary of Interior	Stewart L. Udall	1963–1969
Secretary of Agriculture	Orville L. Freeman	1963–1969
Secretary of Commerce	Luther H. Hodges	1963–1964
	John T. Connor	1964–1967
	Alexander B. Trowbridge	1967–1968
	Cyrus R. Smith	1968–1969
Secretary of Labor	W. Willard Wirtz	1963–1969
Secretray of Defense	Robert F. McNamara	1963–1968
	Clark Clifford	1968–1969
Secretary of Health, Education, and Welfare	Anthony J. Celebrezze	1963–1965
	John W. Gardner	1965–1968
	Wilbur J. Cohen	1968–1969
Secretary of Housing and Urban Development	Robert C. Weaver	1966–1969
	Robert C. Wood	1969
Secretary of Transportation	Alan S. Boyd	1967–1969

The Nixon Administration (1969–1974)

Vice President	Spiro T. Agnew	1969–1973
	Gerald R. Ford	1973–1974
Secretary of State	William P. Rogers	1969–1973
	Henry A. Kissinger	1973–1974
Secretary of Treasury	David M. Kennedy	1969–1970
	John B. Connally	1971–1972
	George P. Shultz	1972–1974
	William E. Simon	1974
Attorney General	John N. Mitchell	1969–1972
	Richard G. Kleindienst	1972–1973
	Elliot L. Richardson	1973
	William B. Saxbe	1973–1974
Postmaster General	Winton M. Blount	1969–1971
Secretary of Interior	Walter J. Hickel	1969–1970
	Rogers Morton	1971–1974
Secretary of Agriculture	Clifford M. Hardin	1969–1971
	Earl L. Butz	1971–1974
Secretary of Commerce	Maurice H. Stans	1969–1972
	Peter G. Peterson	1972–1973
	Frederick B. Dent	1973–1974
Secretary of Labor	George P. Shultz	1969–1970
	James D. Hodgson	1970–1973
	Peter J. Brennan	1973–1974
Secretary of Defense	Melvin R. Laird	1969–1973
	Elliot L. Richardson	1973
	James R. Schlesinger	1973–1974
Secretary of Health, Education, and Welfare	Robert H. Finch	1969–1970
	Elliot L. Richardson	1970–1973
	Caspar W. Weinberger	1973–1974

Secretary of Housing and Urban Development	George Romney James T. Lynn	1969–1973 1973–1974
Secretary of Transportation	John A. Volpe Claude S. Brinegar	1969–1973 1973–1974

The Ford Administration (1974–1977)

Vice President	Nelson A. Rockefeller	1974–1977
Secretary of State	Henry A. Kissinger	1974–1977
Secretary of Treasury	William E. Simon	1974–1977
Attorney General	William Saxbe Edward Levi	1974–1975 1975–1977
Secretary of Interior	Rogers Morton Stanley K. Hathaway Thomas Kleppe	1974–1975 1975 1975–1977
Secretary of Agriculture	Earl L. Butz John A. Knebel	1974–1976 1976–1977
Secretary of Commerce	Frederick B. Dent Rogers Morton Elliot L. Richardson	1974–1975 1975–1976 1976–1977
Secretary of Labor	Peter J. Brennan John T. Dunlop W. J. Usery	1974–1975 1975–1976 1976–1977
Secretary of Defense	James R. Schlesinger Donald Rumsfeld	1974–1975 1975–1977
Secretary of Health, Education, and Welfare	Caspar Weinberger Forrest D. Mathews	1974–1975 1975–1977
Secretary of Housing and Urban Development	James T. Lynn Carla A. Hills	1974–1975 1975–1977
Secretary of Transportation	Claude Brinegar William T. Coleman	1974–1975 1975–1977

The Carter Administration (1977–1981)

Vice President	Walter F. Mondale	1977–1981
Secretary of State	Cyrus R. Vance Edmund Muskie	1977–1980 1980–1981
Secretary of Treasury	W. Michael Blumenthal G. William Miller	1977–1979 1979–1981
Attorney General	Griffin Bell Benjamin R. Civiletti	1977–1979 1979–1981
Secretary of Interior	Cecil D. Andrus	1977–1981
Secretary of Agriculture	Robert Bergland	1977–1981
Secretary of Commerce	Juanita M. Kreps Philip M. Klutznick	1977–1979 1979–1981
Secretary of Labor	F. Ray Marshall	1977–1981
Secretary of Defense	Harold Brown	1977–1981
Secretary of Health, Education, and Welfare	Joseph A. Califano Patricia R. Harris	1977–1979 1979
Secretary of Health and Human Services	Patricia R. Harris	1979–1981
Secretary of Education	Shirley M. Hufstedler	1979–1981
Secretary of Housing and Urban Development	Patricia R. Harris Moon Landrieu	1977–1979 1979–1981
Secretary of Transportation	Brock Adams Neil E. Goldschmidt	1977–1979 1979–1981
Secretary of Energy	James R. Schlesinger Charles W. Duncan	1977–1979 1979–1981

The Reagan Administration (1981–   )

Vice President	George Bush	1981–
Secretary of State	Alexander M. Haig George P. Shultz	1981–1982 1982–
Secretary of Treasury	Donald Regan James A. Baker, III	1981–1985 1985–
Attorney General	William F. Smith Edwin A. Meese, III	1981–1985 1985–
Secretary of Interior	James Watt William P. Clark, Jr. Donald P. Hodel	1981–1983 1983–1985 1985–
Secretary of Agriculture	John Block Richard E. Lyng	1981–1986 1986–
Secretary of Commerce	Malcolm Baldrige	1981–
Secretary of Labor	Raymond Donovan William E. Brock	1981–1985 1985–
Secretary of Defense	Caspar Weinberger	1981–
Secretary of Health and Human Services	Richard Schweiker Margaret Heckler Otis R. Bowen	1981–1983 1983–1985 1985–
Secretary of Education	Terrel H. Bell William J. Bennett	1981–1985 1985–
Secretary of Housing and Urban Development	Samuel Pierce	1981–
Secretary of Transportation	Drew Lewis Elizabeth Dole	1981–1983 1983–
Secretary of Energy	James Edwards Donald P. Hodel John S. Herrington	1981–1982 1982–1985 1985–

Population of the United States, 1790–1985

Year	Population	Percent Increase	Population Per Square Mile	Percent Urban/ Rural	Percent White/ Nonwhite	Median Age
1790	3,929,214		4.5	5.1/94.9	80.7/19.3	NA
1800	5,308,483	35.1	6.1	6.1/93.9	81.1/18.9	NA
1810	7,239,881	36.4	4.3	7.3/92.7	81.0/19.0	NA
1820	9,638,453	33.1	5.5	7.2/92.8	81.6/18.4	16.7
1830	12,866,020	33.5	7.4	8.8/91.2	81.9/18.1	17.2
1840	17,069,453	32.7	9.8	10.8/89.2	83.2/16.8	17.8
1850	23,191,876	35.9	7.9	15.3/84.7	84.3/15.7	18.9
1860	31,443,321	35.6	10.6	19.8/80.2	85.6/14.4	19.4
1870	39,818,449	26.6	13.4	25.7/74.3	86.2/13.8	20.2
1880	50,155,783	26.0	16.9	28.2/71.8	86.5/13.5	20.9
1890	62,947,714	25.5	21.2	35.1/64.9	87.5/12.5	22.0
1900	75,994,575	20.7	25.6	39.6/60.4	87.9/12.1	22.9
1910	91,972,266	21.0	31.0	45.6/54.4	88.9/11.1	24.1
1920	105,710,620	14.9	35.6	51.2/48.8	89.7/10.3	25.3
1930	122,775,046	16.1	41.2	56.1/43.9	89.8/10.2	26.4
1940	131,669,275	7.2	44.2	56.5/43.5	89.8/10.2	29.0
1950	150,697,361	14.5	50.7	64.0/36.0	89.5/10.5	30.2
1960	179,323,175	18.5	50.6	69.9/30.1	88.6/11.4	29.5
1970	203,302,031	13.4	57.4	73.5/26.5	87.6/12.4	28.0
1980	226,545,805	11.4	64.0	73.7/26.3	86.0/14.0	30.0
1985	237,839,000	5.0	64.0	NA/NA	85.0/15.0	31.3

NA = Not available.

Employment, 1870–1985

Year	Number of Workers (in Millions)	Male/Female Employment Ratio	Percentage of Workers in Unions
1870	12.5	85/15	—
1880	17.4	85/15	—
1890	23.3	83/17	—
1900	29.1	82/18	3
1910	38.2	79/21	6
1920	41.6	79/21	12
1930	48.8	78/22	7
1940	53.0	76/24	27
1950	59.6	72/28	25
1960	69.9	68/32	26
1970	82.1	63/37	25
1980	108.5	58/42	23
1985	108.9	57/43	19

Production, Trade, and Federal Spending / Debt, 1790–1985

Year	Gross National Product (GNP) (in billions $)	Balance of Trade (in millions $)	Federal Budget (in billions $)	Federal Surplus/Deficit (in billions $)	Federal Debt (in billions $)
1790	—	− 3	.004	+ 0.00015	.076
1800	—	− 20	.011	+ 0.0006	.083
1810	—	− 18	.008	+ 0.0012	.053
1820	—	− 4	.018	− 0.0004	.091
1830	—	+ 3	.015	+ 0.100	.049
1840	—	+ 25	.024	− 0.005	.004
1850	—	− 26	.040	+ 0.004	.064
1860	—	− 38	.063	− 0.01	.065
1870	7.4	− 11	.310	+ 0.10	2.4
1880	11.2	+ 92	.268	+ 0.07	2.1
1890	13.1	+ 87	.318	+ 0.09	1.2
1900	18.7	+ 569	.521	+ 0.05	1.2
1910	35.3	+ 273	.694	− 0.02	1.1
1920	91.5	+ 2,880	6.357	+ 0.3	24.3
1930	90.7	+ 513	3.320	+ 0.7	16.3
1940	100.0	− 3,403	9.6	− 2.7	43.0
1950	286.5	+ 1,691	43.1	− 2.2	257.4
1960	506.5	+ 4,556	92.2	+ 0.3	286.3
1970	992.7	+ 2,511	196.6	+ 2.8	371.0
1980	2,631.7	+ 24,088	579.6	− 59.5	914.3
1985	4,087.7	− 148,480	946.3	− 212.3	1,827.5

Index

Note: Some page numbers are in *italics* and are preceded by letters. They refer to *(i)* illustrations, *(m)* maps, and *(c)* charts.

About the Authors

Richard N. Current is University Distinguished Professor of History Emeritus at the University of North Carolina at Greensboro. He is coauthor of the Bancroft Prize-winning *Lincoln the President*. His books include: *Three Carpetbag Governors; The Lincoln Nobody Knows; Daniel Webster and the Rise of National Conservatism;* and *Secretary Stimson.* Professor Current has lectured on United States history in Europe, Asia, South America, Australia, and Antarctica. He has been a Fulbright Lecturer at the University of Munich and the University of Chile at Santiago and has served as Harmsworth Professor of American History at Oxford. He is past president of the Southern Historical Association.

T. Harry Williams was Boyd Professor of History at Louisiana State University. He was awarded both the 1969 Pulitzer Prize and National Book Award for his biography of *Huey Long*. His books include: *Lincoln and His Generals; Lincoln and the Radicals; P. G. T. Beauregard; Americans at War; Romance and Realism in Southern Politics; Hayes of the Twenty-Third; McClellan, Sherman, and Grant; The Union Sundered;* and *The Union Restored.* Professor Williams was a Harmsworth Professor of American History at Oxford and President of both the Southern Historical Association and the Organization of American Historians.

Frank Freidel is Charles Warren Professor Emeritus of History at Harvard University and most recently was Bullitt Professor of American History at the University of Washington. He is writing an eight-volume biography of Franklin D. Roosevelt, four volumes of which have been published. Among his other books are: *Our Country's Presidents; F.D.R. and the South;* and *America in the Twentieth Century.* He is co-editor of the 1974 edition of the *Harvard Guide to American History* and past president of the Organization of American Historians. He is also a former president of the New England Historical Society.

Alan Brinkley is Dunwalke Associate Professor of American History at Harvard University. He has also taught at the Massachusetts Institute of Technology. He is a graduate of Princeton University, received his Ph.D. from Harvard, and has been awarded fellowships by the John Simon Guggenheim Foundation, the Woodrow Wilson Center for International Scholars, the American Council of Learned Societies, and the National Endowment for the Humanities. He is the author of *Voices of Protest: Huey Long, Father Coughlin, and the Great Depression,* for which he won the American Book Award in 1983. He is coauthor of *America in the Twentieth Century* and has published many articles, essays, and reviews.

A Note on the Type

The text of this book was set in a digitized version of Bembo, a well-known Monotype face. Named for Pietro Bembo, the celebrated Renaissance writer and humanist scholar who was made a cardinal and served as secretary to Pope Leo X, the original cutting of Bembo was made by Francesco Griffo of Bologna only a few years after Columbus discovered America.

Sturdy, well-balanced, and finely proportioned, Bembo is a face of rare beauty, extremely legible in all of its sizes.